BRITISH IMPERIAL

A milestone in the understanding of British history and imperialism, this groundbreaking book radically reinterprets the course of modern economic development and the causes of overseas expansion during the past three centuries. Employing their concept of 'gentlemanly capitalism', the authors draw imperial and domestic British history together to show how the shape of the nation and its economy depended on international and imperial ties, and how these ties were undone to produce the post-colonial world of today.

Containing a significantly expanded and updated Foreword and Afterword, this third edition assesses the development of the debate since the book's original publication, discusses the imperial era in the context of the controversy over globalisation, and shows how the study of the age of empires remains relevant to understanding the post-colonial world. Covering Britain's formal empire and informal influence and taking a broad chronological view from the seventeenth century to post-imperial Britain today, *British Imperialism: 1688–2015* is an essential text for all students of imperial and global history.

P. J. Cain is Emeritus Research Professor of History, Sheffield Hallam University.

A. G. Hopkins is Emeritus Smuts Professor of Commonwealth History, University of Cambridge and an Emeritus Fellow of Pembroke College, Cambridge.

BRITISH IMPERIALISM

1688–2015

P. J. Cain and A. G. Hopkins

LONDON AND NEW YORK

First published 2016
by Routledge
2 Park Square, Milton Park, Abingdon, Oxon OX14 4RN

and by Routledge
711 Third Avenue, New York, NY 10017

Routledge is an imprint of the Taylor & Francis Group, an informa business

First edition published by Pearson in 1993

Second edition published by Pearson in 2002

British Library Cataloguing in Publication Data
A catalogue record for this book is available from the British Library

Library of Congress Cataloging-in-Publication Data
Cain, P. J., 1941- author.
British imperialism : 1688–2015 / P.J. Cain and A.G. Hopkins. — Third edition.
pages cm
Includes bibliographical references and index.
ISBN 978-1-138-81772-2 (hardback : alk. paper) — ISBN 978-1-138-81773-9 (pbk. : alk. paper) — ISBN 978-1-315-67779-8 (ebook) 1. Great Britain—Colonies—History. I. Hopkins, A. G. (Antony G.), author. II. Title.
JV1011.C17 2001
325′.341—dc23
2015034345

ISBN: 978-1-138-81772-2 (hbk)
ISBN: 978-1-138-81773-9 (pbk)
ISBN: 978-1-315-67779-8 (ebk)

Typeset in Bembo
by Apex CoVantage, LLC

Printed and bound in Great Britain by
TJ International Ltd, Padstow, Cornwall

CONTENTS

TABLES AND MAPS

Tables

Maps

EXTRACTS FROM REVIEWS

'This study presents a major theory that makes a great deal of sense and explains much about how the imperial system operated. It is sure to stimulate a great amount of thought while scholars ponder its lessons. This is a tremendous work of scholarship, synthesising an enormous body of research, and presenting an original thesis with possibly huge implications. It is the standard work on British imperialism and may remain so for the foreseeable future.' (R.D. Long, *Choice*, Nov. 1993).

'This two-volume study offers the most significant and sweeping reassessment of the history of modern British imperialism since the publication of *Africa and the Victorians* more than three decades ago.' (Charles Ambler, *International Journal of African Historical Studies*, 28, 1995).

'. . . the most important reworking of economic history since Hobson and Tawney. It is a stunning mixture of narrative, analysis and brilliant historiographical deconstruction.' (Denis MacShane, *New Statesman*, 11 March 94).

'Once every few years a new interpretative synthesis of an entire historical field appears, makes us think again about long-held assumptions and continues to be mined for quotations for examination fodder for years to come. Ronald Robinson and John Gallagher's *Africa and the Victorians* (1961, 1981) was one such and this two-volume work may well become another. It is a brilliantly written and challenging tour de force that attempts to provide a unified explanation for British imperial expansion, and the changes which it underwent, by locating the decisive agents in the class defined as "gentlemanly capitalists".' (John Flint, *International History Review*, 16, 1994).

'. . . a magisterial account of 300 years of British history, properly putting the empire right at the centre of British commercial and political considerations. . . .' (Will Hutton, *The Guardian*, 7 June 93).

'It is thus a total revision, not only of the history of colonisation but also of the history of Great Britain in general, which offers us a picture of empire that is as erudite as it is stimulating.' (Catherine Coquery-Vidrovitch, *Le Monde Diplomatique*, Oct. 1993: translated from French).

'The authors have worked through an immense secondary literature in an extraordinarily impressive way. Known facts are newly illuminated and placed in new contexts. The differences with other historians are differentiated and fair, even "gentlemanly". The study is skilful, the reading a pleasure. In my opinion, the two volumes by Cain and Hopkins can be counted among the most important achievements of modern historical scholarship.' (Rudolf von Albertini, *Neue Zurcher Zeitung*, 4 March 1995: translated from German).

'Nothing can however detract from the epic scale of Cain and Hopkins's achievement. Students of empire or its legacy may debate or disagree with *British Imperialism* but none now can avoid it.' (Richard Drayton, *Journal of Southern African Studies*, 20, 4).

'Dr Cain and Professor Hopkins cannot be praised sufficiently for their work, the product of extraordinary research, a wide historical imagination, high ability at synthesis, and most of all, accurate analysis.' (W. D. Rubinstein, *Business History*, 36, 1994).

'Cain and Hopkins' arguments are unlikely to be accepted in their entirety by other scholars, any more than those of Robinson and Gallagher were 30 years ago, but they represent the most important new thinking for a decade and will undoubtedly spark off a debate every bit as lively as that of the sixties and seventies.' (Muriel Chamberlain, *The Historian*, Autumn 1993).

'Written with rare elegance and matchless erudition, this brilliant study will be the benchmark against which other contributions will be measured well into the next century.' (Ian Phimister, *Journal of African History*, 35, 1994).

'. . . one of the most important developments in the study of British history and is essential reading for anyone working in the City' (Bill Jamieson, *Sunday Telegraph*, 20 March 1994).

'To force so many specialists to re-examine and probably to adjust their long-accepted ideas is in itself a very remarkable achievement' . . . 'a most powerful element in the complex fabric of British imperial expansion has emerged from their books. All historians of empire are deeply in their debt.' (P. J. Marshall, *Times Literary Supplement*, 20 August 1993).

'*British Imperialism* is a work of impressive scholarship that draws upon a multiplicity of published sources. Its authors' achievement is the more remarkable when it is considered that a companion volume, outside the scope of this review, takes their analysis forward to 1990.' (David Nicholls, *Victorian Studies*, 37, 1994).

'The authors of these two books make modest claims for what is nothing less than a major reinterpretation of British imperalism that is certain to arouse controversy and insure debate for many years.' (Thomas C. Howard, *Albion*, 1994).

'. . . two volumes of brilliant analysis of the real driving force that had made the empire what it was . . .' (B.A. Santamaria, *Weekend Australian*, 8 January 1994).

'The growth of European empires, and most of all the British one, is a topic so vast and controversial (if indeed it is really a single topic at all) that no one work will ever say the last word on it. But for the foreseeable future this remarkable book is certain to play a central role in any discussion of it.' (M.S. Anderson, *Archives*, April 94).

'. . . this work is tremendously stimulating and useful, and its ideas should be hotly contested.' (Laurence Kitzan, of Vol. I, *The Historian*, 1995).

'Cain and Hopkins provide a critique of imperialism that will oblige all interested in the topic to argue that positions anew. Its scope is impressive, both in the period of time covered and in the area considered.' (Peter Harnetty, *American Historical Review*, 99, 1994).

'The general reader will find many of his or her assumptions about British history challenged by this splendid book, and even those specialists who disagree with parts of the interpretation on offer will have to acknowledge that Cain and Hopkins have constructed a new framework of explanation that future generations of imperial historians will be unable to ignore.' (Huw Bowen, of Vol. I, *History*, 79, 1994).

'Cain and Hopkins have written the definitive history of "home counties" imperialism.' (A.J.H. Latham, *Economic History Review*, 47, 1994).

'The debate over the origins and dynamic of imperialism has preoccupied historians and economists for as long as the phenomenon has existed, and it is quite an achievement to produce an original, provocative interpretation. Cain and Hopkins have succeeded; their two volumes manage the difficult task of combining massive detail on the extension of the British empire, which makes a huge volume of scholarship readily accessible to non-specialists, with a clearly stated and subversive general argument.' (Martin Daunton, *Twentieth Century History*, 5, 1995).

'Cain and Hopkins are standing on the shoulders of giants but look out towards a further horizon. The theoretical debate will from now on have to be based upon this new, integrated framework.' (Jurgen Osterhammel, *Neue Politische Literatur*, 39, 1994: translated from German).

'Cain and Hopkins have produced two self-contained books on British imperialism that constitute an authoritative and stimulating contribution to the history of international relations. More imporantly, however, they have succeeded in establishing one coherent interpretation of the rationale of Britain's imperial connection, explaining impulses of expansion as well as the British presence overseas from the late seventeenth century to the end of the twentieth centuries. In doing so, they suggest nothing less than a novel way of viewing Britain's history in the modern period.' (Gerold Krozewski, *Journal of European Economic History*, 23, 1994).

'Such is Cain and Hopkins's account of the rise and fall of the British Empire, and no praise can be too high for the skill with which it is unfolded and sustained across more than eight hundred pages of text. This prodigious labour of scholarship and learning, synthesis and argument, is a landmark in its breadth of vision, and its boldness of spirit. It will be essential reading for anyone interested in the history of Britain, of the British Empire, or of any of the separate nations which were once part of it. We may live in a post-colonial world, but thanks to Cain and Hopkins, the British Empire has struck back with a vengeance . . . it is difficult to believe that a more comprehensive and compelling study of the economic dynamics to Empire will ever be produced.' (David Cannadine, 'The Empire Strikes Back', *Past & Present*, 147, 1995).

'These are stimulating and challenging volumes that represent a major contribution to the subject and whose conclusions will have to be addressed by all imperial historians.' (Martin Lynn, *English Historical Review*, April 1996).

PREFACE TO THE FIRST EDITION

The origins, scope and argument of this study are set out in some detail in Chapter 1. We have also acknowledged specific debts to enlisted scholars at appropriate points throughout the text. It remains for us to express here our appreciation of those who have done so much, in different ways, to keep the whole enterprise afloat. We should like to record our gratitude to the Social Science Research Council for Personal Research Grants in 1980–81 and 1983, to colleagues in the University of Birmingham and the Graduate Institute of International Studies for their advice and tolerance of our various impositions, to our students, whose exposure to several versions of our interpretation helped to educate their teachers, and to libraries and librarians, especially in the University of Birmingham and the University of California, Los Angeles, for their resourcefulness in supplying the wide range of materials needed for this study. We also owe a special debt to Sue Kennedy and Diane Martin whose secretarial help has been invaluable. Finally, and most important of all, we must pay tribute to our families, who have borne the deprivations imposed by slow-moving authors with unwavering fortitude and whose limitless support has finally been rewarded by an event that is as surprising as it has been long-promised: this time, the book really is finished.

P.J.C.
University of Birmingham

A.G.H.
The Graduate Institute of International Studies, Geneva.
May 1992

PREFACE TO THE SECOND EDITION

The opportunity to produce a second edition of *British Imperialism* has allowed us to make a number of alterations, which we hope are also improvements. The most visible change is that two volumes have become one. The long Introduction, which appeared in Volume I, and the substantial Conclusion, which was located at the end of Volume II, were intended to apply to both books and not just one. Placing them between the same covers should enable readers to access and evaluate our points of departure and arrival far more easily than was possible in the first edition. We have also provided a combined and much larger index, which dispenses with the need to manipulate two indexes and two sets of pagination and should enable readers to find their way through one large volume more easily.

The amalgamation should make the text as a whole more coherent by uniting an interpretation that was designed to span several centuries and cover the greater part of the world. The gain can be illustrated by the presentation of the continuities that, in our view, characterise the two periods conventionally divided by World War I. In the first edition they were severed by being assigned to different volumes; in the new edition they are brought together and made more accessible. One result of this closer association might be to create more interest in the period after 1914, which has attracted less attention, as far as our argument is concerned, than has the nineteenth century. Admittedly, the period covered by Volume I has more immediate appeal to historians of imperialism because the weight of the existing historiography leans in that direction. From our perspective however, the period after 1914 offered a greater challenge because far less thought had been given to the idea that British imperialism was an on-going and even a developing force than to the more familiar notion that it was concerned primarily with managing a long retreat from empire.

The union of the two volumes should also enable regional comparisons and contrasts to be made more readily. One case that should now stand out more clearly is the importance, and hence the space, we allocated to the empire of settlement. The white dominions, as they used to be called, have been demoted in recent decades, even by historians of empire, and greater prominence has been given instead to the history of non-Western parts of the world. The latter trend has our full support. However, there is a case for saying that, within the imperial and international context, the emphasis needs adjusting to reflect the objective weight of the white dominions as measured by conventional economic indices. A striking, if not entirely surprising, feature of the extensive discussion of the first edition was how much of it bypassed Canada, Australia and New Zealand, which have now nationalised the study of their own histories so successfully that they are scarcely thought about outside their own borders. We hope that our attempt to relocate the history of the old dominions in the new empire story we tried to tell will stand out more clearly and attract greater interest in the future than it has in the recent past.

In joining the two volumes we have consolidated the title and also moved the terminal date from 1990 to 2000. This adjustment is not meant to imply that British imperialism remains a significant and effective force in the world today; it is intended rather to enable us to reflect, albeit briefly, on some of the main changes that have affected Britain in the post-colonial era. These developments are dealt with in Chapter 26, which now incorporates amendments to the final section, and in the Afterword, a wholly new chapter that assesses the relationship between empire and contemporary processes of globalisation. Although corrections have been made to the body of the text, we decided against attempting to rewrite it. The evidence has been augmented and elaborated, but it has not been dramatically transformed since the publication of the first edition. However, in recognition of the fact that the central argument has been widely discussed, we have added a substantial new chapter, the Foreword, which sets out and comments on the main lines of debate as they have emerged since 1993. This chapter refers to other recent contributions to the debate on imperialism, including our own. Additional guidance can be found in two helpful sets of essays that discuss British Imperialism. One of these, *Gentlemanly Capitalism and British Imperialism: The New Debate on Empire* (1999), edited by Raymond Dumett, includes a bibliography; the other, *Gentlemanly Capitalism, Imperialism and Global History* (forthcoming), edited by Shigeru Akita, makes use of the new edition of the present book.

At the beginning of the new century, the supra-national processes represented by globalisation and by the infra-national forces symbolised by provincialism and ethnicity have raised new questions about the future of seemingly well-entrenched institutions, not least the nation state. These questions provide historians with opportunities to assess, in the post-colonial era, the origins of the world order (and disorder) that is now emerging. In doing so, they are bound to revisit the history of the great empires that projected their own form of globalisation and destroyed, diverted and sometimes developed the myriad ethnic groups that fell under their sway. Out of these and allied considerations a new kind of imperial history is beginning to appear – one that tries to see the past 'as it was' but with the freshness that comes from revisionist thinking. We hope that the changes we have made to this edition will enable our study to retain its value and thus to contribute to the history of nationality and inter-nationality as seen from the highest vantage point, that provided by the age of great empires.

P.J.C., Sheffield Hallam University
A.G.H., Cambridge University
March 2001

PREFACE TO THE THIRD EDITION

For the new edition we have retained the practice, adopted in the second edition, of providing a Foreword and an Afterword. Both have been significantly expanded. The Foreword discusses criticisms of our book and the use made of it by other scholars over the more than 20 years since it was first published. As such, it provides a guide to a great deal of the literature on the economics and politics of British imperialism since 1688. Where appropriate, it also covers cultural history and, at the end, suggests where the debate may now be heading. As in the second edition, the Afterword looks at the British imperial past in the context of recent work on the history of globalisation, which has been extended and refined for this edition. We have also taken the opportunity to consider the legacy of British imperialism, by examining the remnants of the gentlemanly class who are the major subject of our book, its relation to the ongoing debate over 'Britishness', and the threat of a break-up of the United Kingdom now that the imperial glue that held it together has dissolved.

We have not attempted to revise the text because we recognise that if we changed one part, we would be obliged to change all the others, and since we cannot do the latter, we have avoided the former. We have, however, discussed in the Foreword specific issues, such as Britain's role in South Africa between the late 1890s and 1910, which have been particularly contentious; and our present views on the status of our central concept, gentlemanly capitalism, are laid out in some detail in the revised Afterword. We have also taken the opportunity to root out as many misprints as possible and make a few minor changes to the notes. The maps have been refreshed: and the index has also been updated to take in the new material in the Foreword and the Afterword.

This may very well be the last edition of *British Imperialism* and is almost certainly the last we can supervise ourselves. So we would like to end by thanking all those, critics and supporters alike, who have contributed to keeping the book alive and who have forced us over the years to reconsider our own views up to the point where, as we suggest at the end of the Foreword, we can no longer claim ownership of what Michael Oakeshott would have called the 'conversation' that began over 30 years ago.

Peter Cain and Tony Hopkins,
3 March 2015

NOTE ON SOURCES

Since our book makes judgements that rest upon a wide range of detailed research, we have provided copious notes to acknowledge the many scholars whose contributions have made our own work possible. The economics of publishing, however, have determined that, for this edition, citations have been converted from footnotes to endnotes and placed at the end of each chapter. Books and articles are cited in full on first mention in each chapter, are referred to subsequently by short titles, and should therefore be readily identifiable and easily traced. The place of publication of books is London unless another location is given. Had we added a consolidated list of references we would have required another volume – a prospect that neither the authors nor even their accommodating publishers could have faced.

ACKNOWLEDGEMENTS

The publishers would like to thank the following for permission to reproduce copyright material: Cambridge University Press for table 3.2 from *British Regional Employment Statistics*, 1841–1971, C.H. Lee (1979), table 5.6 from *Abstract of British Historical Statistics*, B.R. Mitchell and P. Deane (1962), tables 6.1 and 6.2 from *Mammon and the Pursuit of Empire: The Political Economy of British Imperialism, 1860–1912*, Lance E. Davis and Robert A. Huttenback (1987), table 18.2 from *National Income, Expenditure and Output of the United Kingdom*, 1856–1965, C.H. Feinstein (1972), and table 21.3 from *Abstract of British Historical Statistics*, B.R. Mitchell and P. Deane (1962); Harvard University Press for table 5.7 from *Economic Elements in the Pax Britannica*, A.H. Imlah (1958); Oxford University Press for table 5.8 from *British Economic Growth, 1856–1973*, R.C.O. Matthews, C.H. Feinstein and J.C. Odling-Smee (1983), table 18.6 from *British Economic Growth 1856–1973*, R.C.O. Matthews, C.H. Feinstein and J.C. Odling-Smee (1983); Gage Educational Publishing Company for table 8.2 from *Canada: An Economic History*, W.L. Marr and D.G. Paterson (1980); the Editor of the *Australian Economic Papers* for table 21.2 from 'The Australian Balance of Payments on Current Account, 1901 to 1964–5', I.W. McLean (Vol. 7, 1968); Croom Helm for tables 3.3, 3.4, 17.3 and 17.4 from *Men of Property: The Very Wealthy in Great Britain Since the Industrial Revolution*, W.D. Rubinstein (1981).

Whilst every effort has been made to trace the owners of copyright material in one case this has proved impossible, and we take this opportunity to offer our apologies to any copyright holders whose rights we may have unwittingly infringed.

ABBREVIATIONS

African Aff.	*African Affairs*
African Econ. Hist.	*African Economic History*
African Stud. Rev.	*African Studies Review*
Am. Hist. Rev.	*American Historical Review*
Am. Pol. Sci. Rev.	*American Political Science Review*
Austral. Econ. Hist. Rev.	*Australian Economic History Review*
Austral. Jour. Pol. and Hist.	*Australian Journal of Politics and History*
Brit. Jour. Internat. Stud.	*British Journal of International Studies*
Brit. Jour. Middle Eastern Stud.	*British Journal of Middle Eastern Studies*
Brit. Jour. Pol. Sci.	*British Journal of Political Science*
Brit. Jour. Soc.	*British Journal of Sociology*
Bull. Asia-Pac. Stud.	*Bulletin of Asia-Pacific Studies*
Bull. Bus. Hist. Soc.	*Bulletin of the Business History Society*
Bull. Inst. Hist. Research	*Bulletin of the Institute of Historical Research*
Bull. Inst. Mod. Hist.	*Bulletin of the Institute of Modern History*
Bull. Jap. Stud.	*Bulletin of Japanese Studies*
Bus. Hist.	*Business History*
Bus. Hist. Rev.	*Business History Review*
Canadian Hist. Rev	*Canadian Historical Review*
Canadian Jour. Econ.	*Canadian Journal of Economics*
Canadian Jour. Econ. and Pol. Sci.	*Canadian Journal of Economics and Political Science*
Canadian Jour. Hist.	*Canadian Journal of History*
Canadian Jour. Pol.	*Canadian Journal of Politics*
Comp. Stud. in Soc. and Hist.	*Comparative Studies in Society and History*
Contemp. Brit. Hist.	*Contemporary British History*
Dip. Hist.	*Diplomatic History*
Econ. Hist. Rev.	*Economic History Review*
Econ. Jour.	*Economic Journal*

Eng. Hist. Rev.	*English Historical Review*
Expl. Econ. Hist.	*Explorations in Economic History*
Geog. Jour.	*Geographical Journal*
Hisp. Am. Hist. Rev.	*Hispanic American Historical Review*
Hist. Jour	*Historical Journal*
Hist. Pol. Econ.	*History of Political Economy*
Hist. Research	*Historical Research*
Hist. Stud.	*Historical Studies*
Indian Econ. and Soc. Hist. Rev.	*Indian Economic and Social History Review*
Indian Hist. Rev.	*Indian Historical Review*
Internat. Hist. Rev.	*International History Review*
Int. Jour. African Hist. Stud.	*International Journal of African Historical Studies*
Int. Jour. Middle East Stud.	*International Journal of Middle East Studies*
Jour. African Hist.	*Journal of African History*
Jour. Asian Stud.	*Journal of Asian Studies*
Jour Brit. Stud.	*Journal of British Studies*
Jour. Comm. and Comp. Pol.	*Journal of Commonwealth and Comparative Politics*
Jour. Contemp. Hist.	*Journal of Contemporary History*
Jour. Econ. Hist.	*Journal of Economic History*
Jour. Eur. Econ. Hist.	*Journal of European Economic History*
Jour. Hist. Geog.	*Journal of Historical Geography*
Jour. Hist. Soc. Nigeria	*Journal of the Historical Society of Nigeria*
Jour. Imp. and Comm. Hist.	*Journal of Imperial and Commonwealth History*
Jour. Indian Hist.	*Journal of Indian History*
Jour. Interdisc. Hist.	*Journal of Interdisciplinary History*
Jour. Latin Am. Stud.	*Journal of Latin American Studies*
Jour. Mod. Hist.	*Journal of Modern History*
Jour. South-East Asian Stud.	*Journal of South-East Asian Studies*
Jour. Southern African Stud.	*Journal of Southern African Studies*
Jour. Transport Hist.	*Journal of Transport History, 3rd Series*
Latin Am. Research Rev.	*Latin American Research Review*
Midd. East. Stud.	*Middle Eastern Studies*
Mod. Asian Stud.	*Modern Asian Studies*
PP	*Parliamentary Papers*
Pac. Aff.	*Pacific Affairs*
Pacific Hist. Rev.	*Pacific Historical Review*
Rev. Internat. Stud.	*Review of International Studies*
Scottish Econ. and Soc. Hist.	*Scottish Economic and Social History*
Soc. and Econ. Stud.	*Social and Economic Studies*
Soc. Hist.	*Social History*
Soc. Rev.	*Sociological Review*
South Afr. Hist. Jour.	*South African Historical Journal*
Trans. Royal Hist. Soc.	*Transactions of the Royal Historical Society*
Wom. Hist. Rev.	*Women's History Review*

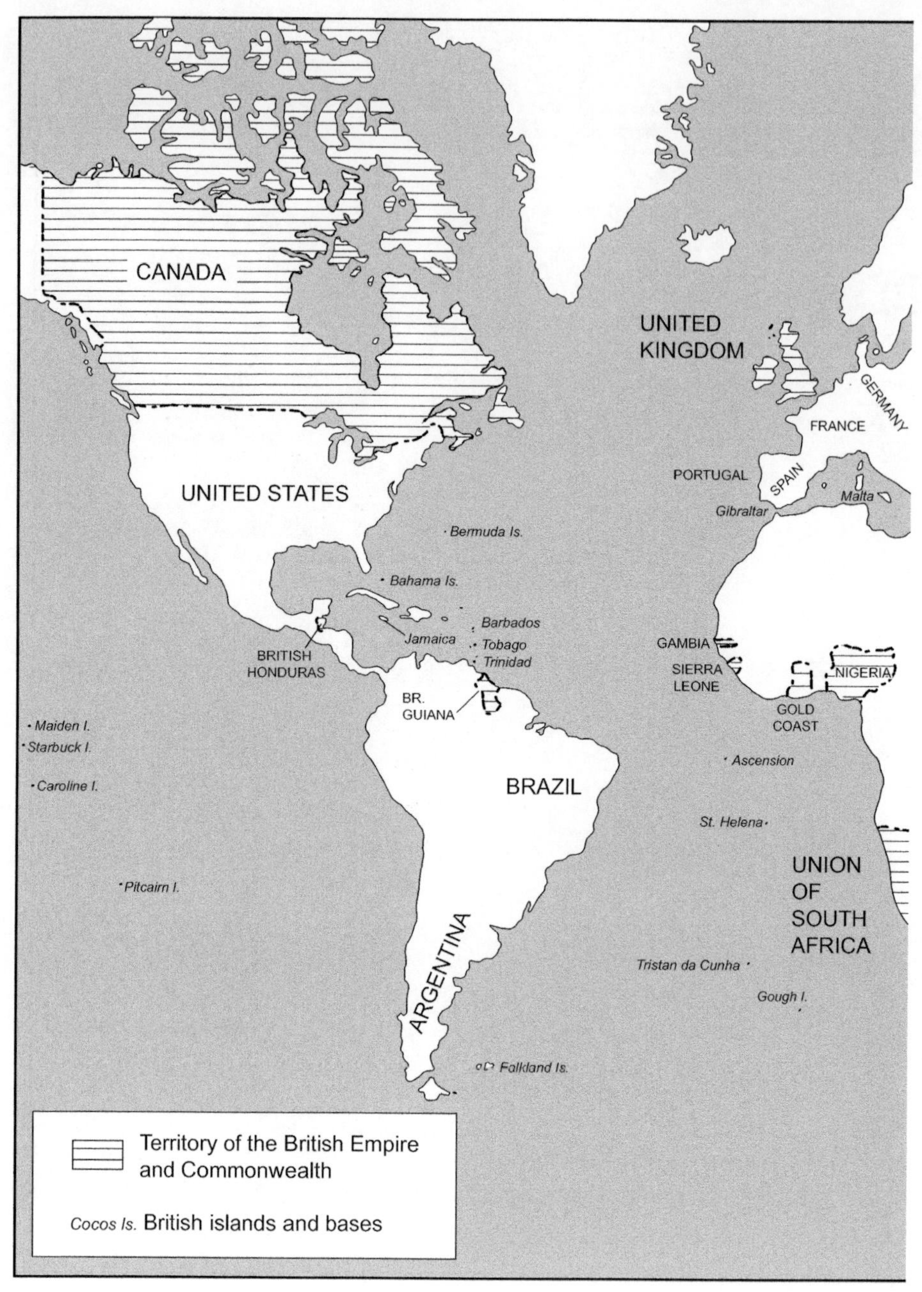

MAP 1 The British Empire in 1920

After: T.O. Lloyd, *The British Empire, 1558–1983* (Oxford, 1984)

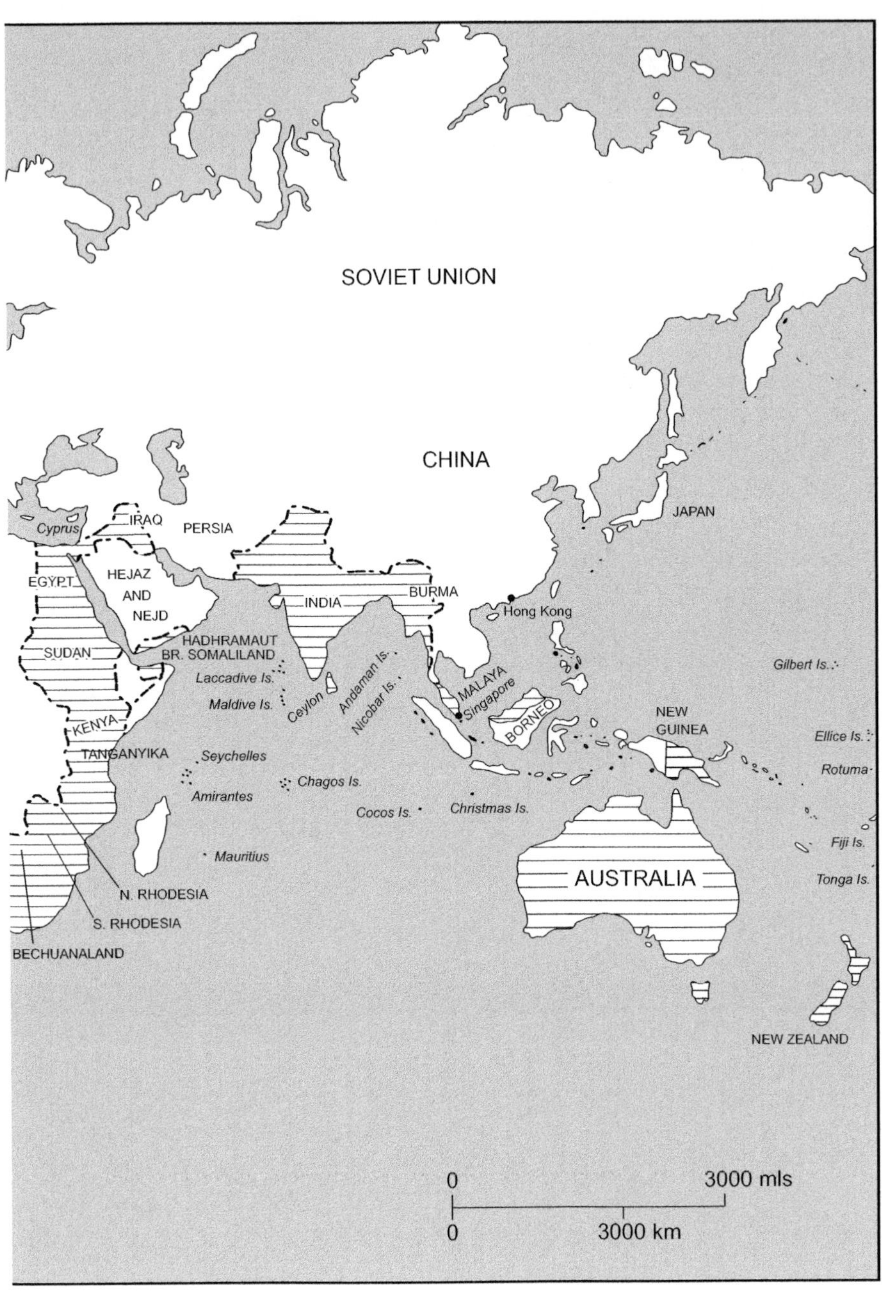
SOVIET UNION
CHINA
JAPAN
Cyprus
IRAQ
PERSIA
EGYPT
HEJAZ
AND
NEJD
INDIA
BURMA
Hong Kong
HADHRAMAUT
BR. SOMALILAND
SUDAN
Laccadive Is.
Maldive Is.
Ceylon
Andaman Is.
Nicobar Is.
MALAYA
Singapore
BORNEO
Gilbert Is.
NEW
GUINEA
KENYA
TANGANYIKA
Seychelles
Amirantes
Chagos Is.
Cocos Is.
Christmas Is.
Ellice Is.
Rotuma
Fiji Is.
Tonga Is.
Mauritius
AUSTRALIA
N. RHODESIA
S. RHODESIA
BECHUANALAND
NEW ZEALAND
0
3000 mls
0
3000 km

FOREWORD

THE CONTINUING DEBATE ON EMPIRE

'The life so short, the craft so long to learn'[1]

It is now 35 years since we began to reappraise the causes of British imperialism. Our first jointly written essay on this subject appeared in 1980; two further articles were published in 1986 and 1987; *British Imperialism* emerged from the press in 1993.[2] Since then, our thinking has developed in the various ways referred to in this Foreword and in the Afterword. Scholars who attack large historical issues must reconcile themselves to spending far more time on the problem than they originally intended, and to giving up other, seemingly more manageable, opportunities. At some point, too, they have to face the dark prospect that, like Mr Casaubon, they might gather dust as well as material and fail to find the key to the mythologies of the world.[3] They certainly come to realise that the problem is greater than any solution they can offer. It appears to recede as it is approached; once in the foothills, the peak seems higher than ever. As they labour, they acquire a growing respect for those who have 'climbed the north face' before them, irrespective of differences of interpretation.[4] At the end, they are relieved to have survived, unlike Casaubon, to complete their work, even if the result falls short of their original ambitions.

One consequence of the passage of time is that scholarship moves on. Authors who begin with one set of assumptions, priorities and starting points may well find, a generation later, that these are judged to have lost freshness, visibility and significance. Casaubon, had he survived and published his work, might have met a scholarly death at the hands of reviewers who regarded him as being trapped, irretrievably, in an outdated problematic. One response to this intractable difficulty is to adjust to the historiography of the subject as it changes shape, or at least to catch the tide by publishing at a moment when there is still a high level of responsiveness to the standpoint originally adopted. This strategy, however, is akin to herding cats.

There are too many uncontrollable elements: if one is captured, others are sure to escape. Had we given full weight to the influences of the day, we would have had to shift the basis of our work from economic to social and then to cultural history, and to assimilate in turn Marxists, *Annalistes* and postmodernists. A counsel of perfection might point in that direction; reality dictates otherwise. It is impossible, at least for us, to see how these acts of incorporation could have been executed intelligibly: linguistic bedlam alone would have given the text a manic incomprehensibility as articulating modes of production ran into discursive discourses of The Other.

Our own, imperfect solution was to approach the problem primarily from the perspective of economic history, but also to suggest how material forces were linked to political, social and cultural developments.[5] We also attempted, deliberately, to present our argument in a way that was free from the transient linguistic fashions that can easily disfigure and date historical studies, especially in fields that attract commitment and place a premium on novelty – which may or may not prove to have lasting value. This decision had a price: by the time our books appeared in 1993, economic history had fallen out of favour, and interest had shifted to the other end of the spectrum, where post-colonial studies, strongly influenced by trends in literary criticism, had directed the attention of a new generation of researchers to cultural issues centred on imagined empires and representations of subject peoples. In some scholarly circles 'productive forces', as they were once termed, had been taken off the agenda, and 'totalising projects' that attempted to generalise about long-term structural change were regarded as being theoretically flawed and ideologically suspect.

Had we planned or even hoped to catch the historiographical tide, we undoubtedly failed. In the event, however, this disadvantage was counterbalanced by other considerations, some of which were wholly unforeseen, that helped our work to attract the interest of journalists as well as scholars. *British Imperialism* received extensive publicity in the serious daily and weekly press when it appeared, notwithstanding the length of the text and the density of the footnotes. Beyond academic circles, the general argument was taken up because it chimed with the 'condition of England' question that was being discussed in its new guise in 1993, when our books were first published. At that time, the painful restructuring of the 1980s had resulted in economic crisis and high unemployment, the Thatcher era had come formally to an end, and there was an intensive debate about the future of economic policy, including Britain's role in the world in the aftermath of the Cold War. The Conservatives had lost faith in monetarism and economic miracles, and were toying with new nostrums, such as 'back to basics', that lacked substance and turned out to have only limited appeal. Old Labour, meanwhile, had yet to become New Labour and was still uncertain about how much of its interventionist and pro-manufacturing traditions to carry forward. In these shifting circumstances, our books were seen to provide a timely historical perspective on current dilemmas and prospects. Some commentators used our emphasis on the power and priorities of the City to argue that the deindustrialisation of the 1980s was the culmination of a long-standing bias in British economic policy.[6] Others fastened upon the same evidence to show that the City and the service sector generally were where Britain's true international comparative advantage lay.[7] The notion of gentlemanly capitalism entered public debate: it made an appearance in Will Hutton's best-selling paperback,[8] and was even adopted, albeit briefly, by television pundits.

Despite the shift to cultural history, our study caught the attention of a wide range of scholars principally because it dealt with a large subject and advanced a revisionist thesis on two extensive and (so we suggested) connected issues: the process of modern economic development and the causes of imperial expansion.[9] In doing so, it brought together new research on the evolution of the British economy, advanced a fresh interpretation of causation, and suggested a different chronology for the rise and fall of the empire. The book also emphasised the importance of the interactions between British and imperial history. From an economic perspective, the empire could be seen as a transnational organisation that reduced transaction costs by extending abroad the institutions associated with the metropolitan economy.[10] Britain exported the settlers, political ideology and cultural values that were needed to animate the imperial system, to endow it with a degree of coherence, and to impose compliance. Reciprocally, the empire contributed significantly to the enduring international bias of the British economy, to the formation of the British state, and to the very definition of what it was to be British.[11] In seeking to reunite the study of British and imperial history, we hoped to engage the attention of two sizeable but separate sets of specialists: those concerned with the process of industrialisation in Britain, and those in Area Studies who were less interested in Britain than in specific territories within the empire.

The continuing scholarly debate on gentlemanly capitalism and empire suggests that economic history has an important contribution to make to an understanding of the key issues of economic development and state-building.[12] Postmodernism, for all the stimulus it gave to the study of cultural influences, contributed little to these questions. Writing in 2001, we suggested that the next historiographical shift would return to some of the classic themes of historical enquiry, given that poverty remained one of the world's great unsolved problems and that the future of the nation state in an era of globalisation had become a subject of intense discussion. The change has now taken place. Recent interest in the history of globalisation has authorised a return to studies of long-run developments and of their material component in particular.[13] Naturally, there are approaches to writing economic history other than the one we adopted. The interpretation advanced in *British Imperialism* offers just one view of an immensely complex subject, and the discussion it has generated includes a good deal of criticism.[14] Nevertheless, the scholarly reception of our work has been very generous, even among those who have disagreed with some or all of our interpretation.[15] Those who attack large problems should not baulk at the adverse comments that inevitably come their way: dissent has the merit of forestalling the worst of all fates, neglect, and the major attribute of advancing understanding.

The main purpose of the revised Foreword is to reflect on the scholarly response to *British Imperialism*. The most important areas of discussion can be grouped under three headings: analytical issues, especially those relating to the key concept of gentlemanly capitalism; developments within Britain itself; and the link between events at home and imperial expansion abroad. We conclude by suggesting some of the ways in which the subject can be carried forward. The relationship between our interpretation and the changes that have occurred in Britain and in her position in the world since the early 1990s will be considered in the Afterword.

Several commentators have raised methodological objections to the undertaking as a whole. General interpretations of major historical events inevitably prompt difficult questions about the nature of historical explanation, as we ourselves noted.[16] One critic, for example, has claimed that generalisation on this scale is invalid because it cannot possibly provide an adequate explanation of particular episodes and events.[17] This is an interesting, if also an extreme, reaction because it points to a very different conception of what historians mean when they speak of causation. Most commentators have accepted that the explanatory chain we constructed has validity in principle, even though they may also have questioned the fit between hypothesis and evidence in particular cases.[18] A rather different objection has been made to the 'Popperian approach' implied by our discussion of aims.[19] What we sought to do in setting out our argument was to state our assumptions as explicitly as possible and to avoid investing our hypotheses with an undeclared ideology or simplistic verificatory procedures.[20] The assumptions themselves are unverifiable; the hypotheses derived from them are subject to the normal tests of historical enquiry. Our interpretation, like other interpretations, can be improved in two ways: by advancing a more plausible set of assumptions and by providing a better fit between hypothesis and evidence. These are deep waters,[21] and readers should be alerted to the need to navigate them with care – whichever direction they decide to take.

A methodological concern that is frequently raised against selective interpretations of complex historical events centres on the charge that the argument 'comes dangerously near to monocausality'.[22] Readers have been warned. But they have also been forewarned by our own statement of our aims and procedures.[23] In essence, what we tried to do was to identify a theme that would provide a route, like Ariadne's thread, through the labyrinth. The theme we chose had not been explored by previous work;[24] it was founded on recent research, and it seemed to us to offer a powerful means of explaining developments and connections that had eluded previous interpretations. We did not claim that our interpretation eliminated all other explanations of imperialism; rather that it added to them. This implied that the existing historiography would need to be revised, but the extent of the revision could only be determined by future research.[25] In the light of the discussion generated by *British Imperialism*, it is hard now to see the debate reverting to a position that either ignores the themes we identified or rejects them on the grounds that they constitute a monocausal explanation. The significant question, in our judgement, is not whether we are right or wrong, but how much weight should be attached to our interpretation. As we see it, the answer to that question has already carried the subject forward and will continue to do so.

Most of the discussion of the British basis of our argument has focussed on the concept of gentlemanly capitalism. Our main purpose in formulating this organising principle was to direct attention to the non-industrial forms of capitalism that, in our view, had been greatly underestimated by historians of modern Britain. In this aim, we can fairly claim to have succeeded – though at the cost of provoking some marked disagreement. Predictably, it has been said that, in elevating the role of finance and services, we have relegated the part played by the forces of industrialisation.[26] To the extent that we were trying to insert non-industrial forms of capitalism into the story of modern economic development, some shift in the relative importance attached to the two sectors was, in our view, both desirable and consistent with new research. Surveys of British economic history have now adjusted their treatment to reflect this change.[27] However, we also made it clear that 'the process of industrialisation is undoubtedly central to modern British history',[28] and we saw no purpose, and much perversity, in trying to eliminate it.[29] The interesting problem now, in our view, is to unravel the relations between finance and industry over the centuries in more detail and with greater subtlety than was possible in our study, which of course had to keep other matters in view. Precisely where the balance lies has still to be decided and is a matter primarily for specialists in economic history rather than in the history of imperialism. What can be said, however, is that the story can no longer be told as if all routes led into or out of industrialisation and that the assumption that services derived from or were parasitic on manufacturing has to be demonstrated and not simply taken as given.

It has also been pointed out that we failed to identify the group of gentlemanly capitalists with sufficient precision. One critic felt that the concept was too undertheorised to be useful and was in any case redundant;[30] another felt that it claimed too much but was still insufficiently developed to provide a theory of the state.[31] As these comments suggest, a taxonomy of criticisms would show that a good number of them cancel each other out. Nevertheless, the merit of these objections, irrespective of the view taken of them, is that they direct attention to another key area where, surprising though it may seem, a large amount of detailed research remains to be done. When we began thinking about this subject, it was still common for historians of international relations to refer to 'British policy', as if it were an unproblematic representation of the national interest mediated by short-term considerations of faction, party and personality. Robinson and Gallagher went even further than this: in their view the 'official mind', though not entirely closed to outside influences, was for the most part above party and economic processes.[32] The most persistent attempt to establish an alternative approach was by applying class analysis, but this ambition foundered on the insuperable difficulty of showing that the bourgeoisie (which in most readings meant the industrial middle class) had ever taken firm hold of the levers of power. In default of the required series of case studies demonstrating how industrial pressure groups imposed their will on imperial policy, radical explanations of empire-building too often fell back on reification: it was capitalism, not its representatives, that imposed and disposed. This device short-circuited the need to provide an account of agency, but it also drained the analysis of its essential empirical content.

Our aim in looking behind the composite notion of British policy was to identify a gentlemanly elite who promoted and served capitalist interests of the kind we described. If our analysis lacked precision, it was partly because the number of case studies available to us, especially on the period after 1914, was very limited. Thirty years ago, little detailed work on the City had been completed, and the service sector was scarcely recognised as being a separate and significant element in modern British history.[33] Imprecision also derived from the fact that fluidity reflected historical reality: the gentlemanly order was continually redefining and renewing itself with the result that at any single moment there were status and other differences between new recruits and full members of the establishment.[34] To acknowledge these difficulties, however, is a long way from accepting that the exercise itself was misplaced. Had we inferred political action from economic imperatives without systematic reference to human agency,[35] we would have been heavily criticised for adopting the crudest possible form of economic determinism. Accordingly, it was essential for us to identify and describe the sources of social recruitment and the value system of the gentlemanly elite, even if we could not explore them fully, and to indicate how the qualities represented by gentility were linked to political power.

Most commentators have accepted the proposition that there were gentlemen who were capitalists and gentlemen who aligned themselves in a supportive role with gentlemanly capitalism. We, in turn, accept that the gentlemanly elite needs closer definition than we were able to give it originally. A fuller characterisation would establish more clearly than we did that gentlemanly capitalists were one element among a larger cohort of gentlemen who occupied high-ranking positions in the military, the professions and the Anglican Church. These men were removed from the business of money-making but were related to it through a shared code of conduct, dependence on income streams that flowed from the City and landed rents, and social connections, often extending to inter-marriage. Most gentlemen, even if not active in the market, were aware of the economic world through land or finance, and it was natural for them to imagine that these activities, rather than the distant mills of industry, were central to Britain's power and progress.

As prominent members of the cohort, missionaries, humanitarians and the military deserve a larger place in the story.[36] To the extent that their upper reaches were staffed by gentlemen, these groups were important adjuncts to the money-makers in the City. The American Revolution, to take one prominent example, created a crisis of legitimacy for Britain's vaunted 'empire of liberty' and stimulated new thinking about its existence and purpose.[37] Evangelicals provided the means of regaining the moral high ground. The loss of the mainland colonies was God's judgment on the sin of slavery; abolition became the means of atonement. Humanitarians added Enlightenment principles in an appeal to universal rights, which, with the considerable help of John Stuart Mill, they transformed into a mission to civilise the non-Western world.[38] Once started, the abolitionist movement acquired popular momentum that quickly extended below the elite leadership, attracted women as well as men, and reached far beyond the capital.[39] This revised version of 'freedom', devised from on high, contributed to the creation of a more inclusive political community, which in turn helped to shape Britain's national identity.[40]

The military component stands as an exceptional example of continuity from the eighteenth century to today and is currently one of the few remaining unqualified examples of the gentlemanly values of honour, duty and public service. The French Wars gave the military an unprecedented degree of public prominence. Horatio Nelson and Arthur Wellesley, representing the navy and the army respectively, both came from gentlemanly stock: Nelson, the son of a cleric, was related to the Walpole dynasty; Wellesley was a member of the Irish aristocracy.[41] Both were super-celebrities who became canonised as heroes of their age. The values they embodied, or were imputed to them, had an immense and enduring influence in elevating and inculcating the gentlemanly ethos and welding it to a sense of nationality that was at once English and British.[42] By the time that Wellesley, the 1st Duke of Wellington, died in 1852, the military-fiscal state had also been laid to rest. Thereafter, the heroic image and its attendant values lived on through the medium of the public schools and the reformed civil and armed services. The death of Major-General Charles Gordon in Khartoum in 1885, after a career spent in imperial service, gave new impetus to the ideal of the Christian warrior 'marching as to war'. Gordon, himself the son of a Major-General and also an evangelical Christian, exerted more influence after his death than during his life.[43] His example, propagated by popular novelists such as G. A. Henty, inspired a new generation to embrace the ideals of manliness, chivalry, duty and patriotism. War was portrayed as a means of shaping character at least down to 1914, when even Kipling and Newbolt, the two most eminent enthusiasts, had second thoughts.

The City itself was a complex entity that contained a dark side of shysters and fraudsters, observed by Dickens and Trollope among others, whose code of behaviour fell far short of standards of chivalry and honour.[44] It is evident, too, that 'the contingent and unforeseen' played an important part in the evolution of the gentlemanly capitalist order. Its representatives were not always 'on the right side of history'. They were not in the forefront of the move towards free trade, and they did not present a wholly united front with regard to the controversial issues of bimetallism and tariff reform. It is also the case that our account of the evolution of gentlemanly capitalism could have been more nuanced. For example, there were important shifts in the structure of the aristocracy and of aristocratic capitalism around 1800 that need to be incorporated into a fuller evaluation of the trajectory of gentlemanly capitalism than we were able to give.[45]

Despite the need for elaborations and refinements, the concept of gentlemanly capitalism has now embedded itself in the literature and helped to stimulate new thinking on the issues we raised.[46] By the time the second edition of *British Imperialism* was published in 2002, a wide span of detailed research had already appeared, some confirming our research findings and some stimulated by our work, but independent of it. Deslandes unravelled the process by which undergraduates at Oxford and Cambridge defined themselves as Britons, Protestant Christians, imperial rulers and gentlemen during the period 1850–1920.[47] Torrance showed how Lord Selborne, a gentleman by birth as well by training, united material and moral values in his thinking about South Africa and the empire in general.[48] Complementary work in business history revealed how a cosmopolitan mercantile elite with aspirations to acquire gentlemanly status arose in London in the eighteenth century,[49] how bankers became gentlemen in the nineteenth century,[50] and how imperfect boundaries were drawn between gentlemen and fringe financial elements in the City.[51] David Kynaston's masterful study of the City of London between 1890 and 1914 emphasised the key part gentlemanly capitalists played in its success;[52] Jonathan Schneer's account of the metropolis confirmed the judgment;[53] John Wilson's survey of the history of British business applied the concept to an even longer period.[54] Other studies underlined the extent to which recruitment criteria continued to adhere to the gentlemanly ideal in the different circumstances of the nineteenth and twentieth centuries down to the period of decolonisation.[55] Rubinstein's work on British elites is particularly valuable in this connection both in carrying research beyond 1914 and in emphasising the resilience and continuing strength of the pre-war order.[56]

Research completed since 2002 has further extended the notion of gentlemanly capitalism – often far beyond our own reach, as the following examples, selected for their chronological range, make clear. Søren Mentz has unravelled the close ties between private traders in India and the City of London in the eighteenth century; James Fichter's study of American colonial trade with Asia has explored the rise of merchant-capitalists with gentlemanly pretensions.[57] Albert Schrauwers has revealed how, in the 1830s, a local elite of gentlemanly capitalists in Upper Canada used chartered companies to promote a market in land and labour and entrench their own political control.[58] Andrew Smith has pursued this theme by showing how a coalition of City interests and 'Fathers of the Confederation' worked together to produce the unification of Canada.[59] Edward Beasley has seen the turbulent 1840s as a moment when observers began to inspect the composition and attitudes of the gentlemanly elite and criticise its warlike disposition.[60] Stuart Sweeney's detailed study has confirmed the 'mutual dependence' of the City and Whitehall in arranging finance for Indian railways, which were the largest single British investment project in the late nineteenth century;[61] and David Sunderland has shown how the India Office helped British investors by channelling money to the City while simultaneously ensuring that India did not default on its debts.[62] Gregory Barton and Brett Bennett have traced the connection between City investors and the exploitation of teak forests in Burma and Siam.[63] David Blaazer has underlined the importance of the financial element in understanding the policy of appeasement in the 1930s.[64] Geographers have used the concept of gentlemanly capitalism to analyse the development of 'power networks' among directors of 12 transnational corporations between 1899–1900 and 1929–1930.[65] Finally, David Chambers has shown how the Accepting Houses Committee 'exemplified the power and influence of the gentlemanly capitalists' in the 40 years after World War II.[66]

Our discussion of gentlemen and gentility was cast, by definition, in a masculine mould. Our interest in the causes of imperialism led us to a consideration of the exercise of power, and this in turn directed the analysis to the male world formed by the City, London clubs, public schools and the military. This focus is now being widened in two ways. In the first place, on the assumption that expressions of masculinity are expressions of gender and that these are constructed rather than given, it would now be possible to give a fuller account of the processes that brought these developments into being.[67] Recent work suggests that gentlemanly capitalists were a significant part of a male elite who believed that the development of 'character', honed in the public schools and embodying notions of an energetic pursuit of duty and public service, were the key to Britain's moral and material success over many centuries, and the foundation of the civilising mission that imperialists took to the dependent empire.[68] Further studies of the empire will undoubtedly enlarge our knowledge of how concepts of masculinity came to be formed and endorsed through the creation of boundaries of gender, class and race.[69]

Second, the role of women, and specifically of the 'ladies' who complemented gentlemen, is now being brought into the story of a masculine power elite.[70] Despite the rapid expansion of interest in the history of women and empire in recent years, an authoritative study of the emergence of the new, urban lady in the nineteenth century has still to be written, and a good deal of the work that has appeared has taken the form of colonial case studies that lie at the edge of our remit.[71] Research on 'gentlewomanly capitalists', however, has produced an impressive advance in understanding the role of women as investors.[72] Interest in the subject has now spread not only to former constituents of the empire, but also to Greece and Italy, among other countries.[73] Women's opposition to imperialism has also been well documented.[74] At the same time, there is now a considerable body of research that shows how elite women acted as influential adjuncts to the masculine empire, whether as missionaries, doctors, managers of emigration societies, founders of the Girl Guides, or as propagandists.[75] The gentlemanly elite was to this extent strengthened by its lady-like complement; both also had their roles shaped by the empire they were trying to civilise.

It is still possible, nevertheless, to argue that we exaggerated the influence of the gentlemanly elite on the direction of City firms and the formulation of government policy.[76] While accepting that a gentlemanly elite was both present and highly visible, some commentators have claimed that the real dynamism of City businesses sprang from the continuous infusion of new talent, especially from the continent of Europe.[77] It is incontestable that the City fraternity formed, in principle at least, an open elite that could be joined after appropriate tests of social acceptability had been passed. However, it does not follow that gentlemanly status, once acquired, became a drag on enterprise. Gentlemanly qualities, and the social bonding that went with them, were well suited to the requirements of merchant banking,[78] and they served the City well right down to the 1980s.[79] With regard to the shaping of government policy, it has been claimed that 'the striking feature of the British state was its stance of neutrality, its desire to preserve balance'.[80] On this view, the state, as represented by the official mind, maintained its independence and was unwilling and indeed unable to favour one interest above another. No student of British history would deny the importance of compromise and balance in the calculations of policy-makers.[81] But applying these principles in this way drains the official mind of much of its content and reduces policy-making to a series of unending compromises in which the only discernible value is compromise itself. This outcome is incapable of explaining how government policy and official decisions generally helped to shape the distinctive features of British society: the persistence of marked inequalities of wealth, status and class; the inculcation of a value system that endorsed privilege and encouraged deference; the creation of an empire that benefited some groups much more than others. It is hard to see how these enduring constituents of 'Britishness' can be understood without according due weight to the international bias of economic policy and to the influence of the City and Treasury in holding it in place.[82]

The best way of resolving this problem is by analysing the role of the gentlemanly elite and other competing interest groups in important policy-making decisions. One of the fullest and most sustained assessments made so far relates to the eighteenth century, which we were obliged to compress as our study expanded. The Glorious Revolution, our starting point, has been subjected recently to different forms of revisionism: one has drawn attention to the antecedents of the revolution in finance;[83] another has suggested that the events of 1688 represented a contest between two different modernising policies.[84] Antecedents, however, do not reduce the importance of the events they anticipate, and policies of development can be identified without joining them to the difficult concept of modernity. The Revolution of 1688 deserves to retain its title as a label for innovations that had a decisive influence on the course of British history. It made the monarch accountable to parliament and compelled parliament to find permanent means of financing the needs of state. It defended the Protestant succession and gave Britain an extensive commitment to Hanover and continental Europe.[85] The Bank of England and the national debt were founded after the Revolution and not before; the development of the stock market, improved means of payment through currency reform and bills of exchange, and the rise of private institutions, such as insurance companies, all followed.[86] These innovations underpinned the Revolution settlement, funded an assertive foreign policy, facilitated domestic transactions, and made the City of London a world financial centre. Changes of this order were not the product of an *ancien régime*, despite the presence of antecedents and continuities.[87] Whether or not they pointed towards modernity, they undoubtedly laid the foundations of a powerful military-fiscal state that Britain expanded to include Scotland and Ireland, and later the overseas empire.

Bowen's thorough and thoughtful synthesis of emerging gentlemanly interests after 1688 both extends and modifies our account but is, in general, consistent with it.[88] The most recent work on the period has provided answers to some of the questions we raised by confirming the centrality of the government and its allies in London in formulating imperial policy.[89] The need to defend the Revolution of 1688 led to a political struggle between two competing views of the role of the empire in this task. One position, held by Tories and conservative Whigs, regarded the empire as an extractive resource to be tapped to meet metropolitan financial needs; the other position, adopted by reforming Whigs and progressive Tories, aimed for a co-operative empire in which expanding trade would calm dissenting voices and generate the wealth needed to service the national debt. The struggle between the proponents of these positions, which included powerful figures in the City of London, did much to shape policy towards the mainland colonies and India in the second half of the century. The extractive view prevailed; the reactions to it within North America and India turned one set of colonies out of the empire and brought another into it.

When we prepared our second edition, research on the nineteenth century had unpicked the composition of the malleable coalitions engaged in the campaigns over bimetallism and tariff reform, and confirmed the City's bias towards orthodoxy.[90] Recent work has produced complementary results with respect to the enduring subject of free trade.[91] The research now available strengthens our original judgment that the City of London was far from united on all of these issues, but it enables internal differences to be weighed with greater precision. As a result, we would now place greater emphasis on uncertainty within the Square Mile about the wisdom of breaking out of the mercantilist system, and its initial hesitancy about embracing the gold standard, even though the City was the ultimate major beneficiary of these reforms. Our original analysis could now be strengthened at this point by locating the advent of free trade more firmly in the context of the final demise of the military-fiscal state. The defeat of a conservative Christian political economy inspired by Malthus and the evangelical revival during the first half of the century led to the installation of a new moral order based on minimal government at home, paternalism abroad, indirect taxes, and the sanctification of approved forms of consumption.[92]

Probably the most important revision to our depiction of nineteenth-century Britain is the suggestion that we exaggerated the position of London and, as a corollary, downplayed the role of the provinces.[93] We would accept that the balance needs adjusting and also that there was greater interplay between London and major centres, such as Edinburgh, Manchester, Liverpool and Birmingham, than we allowed. It may be, too, that the gap in wealth between the Home Counties and the great English provincial cities and centres in Scotland was narrower than our sources indicated, though this remains a disputed issue.[94] However, revisions of this kind need themselves to be placed in context. The importance of the large provincial towns relative to London appears to have reached its peak during the first half of the nineteenth century, when the City was still heavily invested in the military-fiscal state and the national debt.[95] Thereafter, with the opening of huge investment opportunities abroad, London pulled ahead again.[96] After 1850, there was a trend among large provincial firms to move their headquarters to the capital.[97] Wealth remained disproportionately concentrated in London, which was the main focus of share-dealing and share-holding.[98] Within London itself, the wealthiest investors increased their shareholdings from 50 per cent of the total in the 1870s to 70 per cent in the 1920s. The City became admired as the creator of national wealth, even though its image was dented from time to time by speculative scandals.[99] David Kynaston's full and authoritative history of the Square Mile leaves no ambiguity about its supremacy.[100]

Few, if any, case studies of 'new imperialism' at the close of the century rank higher or have attracted more attention than South Africa, which accordingly merits an additional comment here. In discussing the run-up to the Boer War of 1899–1902, we should have distinguished more clearly between the priorities of two of the principal figures, Joseph Chamberlain and Alfred Milner, and those of the gentlemen of the City. Chamberlain and Milner saw the problem of South Africa as part of their wider concern with the economic unity of the white empire and Britain's industrial future within 'Greater Britain'.[101] There is no doubt that Chamberlain thought that a united South Africa under British control was vital to the success of his broader plan. Although Chamberlain's view prevailed in 1899, and the war was eventually won, his imperial dream was not realised: in 1906, the electorate decisively rejected his bid to promote imperial economic union through tariff reform. Milner's attempt to flood South Africa with British immigrants failed too, and British governments had to reconcile themselves to an Afrikaner-dominated polity. In 1910, the Liberal government agreed to accept a union rather than a federation, an outcome which made Afrikaner dominance more emphatic. Nonetheless, South Africa was still heavily dependent on British trade and its economy was beholden to London finance. Indeed, Selborne, as High Commissioner in South Africa between 1906 and 1910, encouraged union as a means of ending uncertainty about the future and of improving South Africa's credit in the City in the hope that increased investment would bring Briton and Afrikaner together in a strong, fast-growing state.[102] Despite Chamberlain's efforts, the economic component of the South African settlement bore the stamp of London rather than Birmingham.[103]

Scholars specialising in twentieth-century history have paid particular attention to the link between finance and decolonisation after World War II.[104] Reassessments of the decision to withdraw from empire in the 1950s have confirmed the importance of financial priorities in the formulation of international policy while drawing attention to their shifting basis. Successive British governments did not cling to sterling for reasons of nostalgia but because the currency remained highly important in international trade. Policy arose from contending views of the future: government anxiety over the sterling balances after the war, when cheap oil from the Middle East did much to sustain sterling's role as a reserve currency; Whitehall's gathering concern from the mid-1950s with the burdens that sterling's status imposed; and the City's changing priorities. Initially, the City hoped to recreate a golden era, when sterling was the dominant international currency. By the early 1960s, however, when it was clear that that this ambition was beyond reach, the City began to transfer its interest to the developing Eurodollar market, and thereafter reshaped itself as a centre specialising in international financial instruments.[105] With remarkable speed and aplomb, the City shed its imperial past and became the global financial hub we know today.

Our decision to locate the fundamental causes of imperial expansion in developments within the imperial power itself had important implications for established approaches to the chronology and the geography of the subject. The argument advanced by many historians that Britain was falling behind her competitors, both technologically and organisationally, in the late nineteenth century was based solely on assessments of industrial performance. A different set of indices had to be deployed if, as we claimed, the main dynamic behind overseas expansion, within and beyond the empire, was the continuing growth of the financial and service sector. These indices revealed that anaemia had not set in: the vitality of the patient continued to carry British influence and the British presence into the remaining corners of the world in the late nineteenth century, when international rivalry for colonies was at its peak. On this interpretation, the forces promoting imperial expansion were changing but not weakening; an informal empire was being assembled not dismantled; the causes of British imperialism did not need to be attributed either to foreign rivals or to turbulent frontiers, though of course these had performing parts in the drama. It followed from this line of reasoning that the chronology of the rise and fall of the empire needed to be rethought.

We further argued that this revision should be carried forward into the twentieth century. Despite the disruption it caused, World War I did not bring forward a ruling elite of a different stamp; nor did it promote a new set of economic policies. The aim was rather to recreate the pre-war world, which policy-makers treated as having been suspended rather than liquidated. Britain's influence in Europe and her status as a colonial power were enhanced by the defeat of Germany and the withdrawal of both Russia and the United States after 1918. The balance did not shift against Britain until the late 1930s, when Germany rearmed and Japan asserted her power in the Far East.[106] The vision of an international order shaped by British power was not lost, even after World War II. To the victors, it was hoped, went the spoils and these included a reconstituted empire at the centre of Britain's continuing global influence. The end, when it came, was abrupt rather than lingering.[107]

With regard to external policy, we advanced a revisionist interpretation that reasserted the importance of metropolitan interests in shaping Britain's presence abroad. A generation of historians had shifted the emphasis away from the centre and towards what was called the periphery – a term that now seems to be an uncomfortable fit for parts of the world that were often centres in their own right. This trend was propelled by two important influences: the rise of Area Studies, which were committed to restoring historical independence to former constituents of the empire, and the complementary stimulus given by the 'ex-centric' theory of imperialism, which sought to export the causes of empire from the metropolis to the frontier.[108]

The geographical emphasis shifted, too, because the weight of financial and commercial flows redirected attention to parts of the empire, such as Canada, Australia and New Zealand, which had been moved to the edge of the picture following the decolonisation of what was to become the new Commonwealth after World War II. Their demotion was understandable: in the post-colonial era the old 'white empire' had become an unfashionable subject of study in Britain, and the constituents themselves were keen to develop their own national histories without drawing an intellectual subsidy from what used to be called the 'mother country'. Asia and Africa, on the other hand, had received far less attention from historians and were in greater need of outside academic support. While recognising and sympathising with these trends, the evidence we assembled required us, nevertheless, to give the white dominions greater visibility in the continuing story of British overseas expansion and imperialism. At the time of publication, the chapters on the 'white' empire received little attention. By the time the second edition appeared in 2002, interest had quickened. Today, discussion of the Anglo-world, its networks, exchanges and frontier values, is one of the most vibrant themes in the history of empire and globalisation.[109] The new literature, though independent of our own work, has taken up, enlarged and improved our understanding of many of the topics we began to explore in 1993.[110]

Our central concern with imperial financial relations has been greatly advanced by research that reflects the revival of interest in the 'white' dominions, a new enthusiasm for the history of globalisation and the re-emergence of economic history.[111] Historians and economists have pursued business networks across the Anglo-world and explored the financial and social bonds that held them together.[112] New global histories have drawn economic, and specifically financial, elements into their interpretations. Financial history has developed, quite independently, in ways that have contributed significantly to the understanding of international and imperial history. Philip Cottrell, one of the pioneers of the subject, provided an admirable example of the connection in his account of the Ionian Bank, which used the concept of gentlemanly capitalism to recount the history of a City venture in the Ionian Isles when they were a British protectorate.[113] Other studies in this vein have extended beyond Britain to Europe and even further afield.[114] The revival of the history of the 'old dominions' has also prompted the suggestion that their effective independence was not fully achieved until after World War II.[115] If this idea finds support from further research, it would integrate studies of the 'white empire' with the current literature on decolonisation and further enhance the importance of the period as one of global transformation.

The repositioning our argument entailed has provoked considerable comment, though our fear that we would be accused of turning the clock back rather than trying to move it forward has in general been unfounded. Most scholars have refrained from charging us with trying to restore an outmoded historiography or, worse still, of being imperialists ourselves. Needless to say, this does not mean that the case we put has passed unchallenged. Our emphasis on the metropolitan roots of imperialism has prompted some specialists to reassert the importance of the frontier in the making of empire; our stress on the continuing strength of Britain's influence overseas has led others to respond by reaffirming the extent to which parts of the empire, notably the white dominions, were able to act independently from the 'mother country'.[116] To some extent, the debate about the relative importance of metropolitan and peripheral influences is one about perspective, which is hard to resolve. The view from London and the view from Ottawa may vary but may nevertheless be accurate descriptions of the world from different vantage points. The debate is also about evidence, which rarely meets all the tests of adequacy.

Accordingly, our treatment of case studies was not uniform: where sufficient detail existed and space allowed, we were able to offer an account that provided what we felt to be a close fit between cause and agency; where insufficient research had been completed, we were confined to describing the context within which actions took place. Opinions about whether our case studies demonstrate the soundness of our argument or are merely indicative of its possible plausibility will vary. As yet, no one has suggested that we failed to make use of evidence that would have made a material difference, one way or the other, to the case we presented. On the other hand, the availability of new evidence has begun to improve our understanding of the issues. In some cases, we have modified our original judgment;[117] in others we have found it strengthened.[118] What matters, in our view, is that the consideration of spacious and important issues, such as the role of the dominions and the nature of informal empire, is being reinvigorated.[119] In an age of globalisation, it is hard to think of a more pressing priority for historians than the need to recognise the importance of stepping outside the conventional boundaries of the nation state.

One area of dissent, however, arises from a misunderstanding of the concept of gentlemanly capitalism. Some authors have criticised our argument on the grounds that businessmen operating in various parts of the empire either did not fit our definition of the term or were capable of taking initiatives that were independent of London. These actors may have been gentlemen or capitalists, but were rarely both and sometimes neither. Jim McAloon, for example, has put an interesting case along these lines with reference to New Zealand in the late nineteenth century.[120] Sandip Hazareesingh has suggested that the concept of 'interconnected synchronicity' captures the relationship between London and the outer empire better than an account that treats causation as flowing from the metropolitan centre.[121] Nicholas White's discussion of business interests shows that opinion in Malaya at the time of decolonisation differed from the views expressed in the City of London.[122]

The range of these contributions suggests that we carry a measure of responsibility for underspecifying our key concept in the first edition, though we have tried to remedy some of the defects subsequently. Further thought on the nature of power in international relations, prompted by Susan Strange's analysis, led us to draw a distinction between structural and relational power.[123] The former sets the 'rules of the game', such as free trade and the gold standard; the latter describes negotiations among participants within the set structure. The distinction is both simple and effective. The City was active in establishing the rules and urging governments to uphold them; business interests in the empire did their utmost to achieve a favourable outcome in regional and individual bargains, and often did so. Success at this level, however, did not change the structure within which bargaining took place.

Andrew Dilley has deployed the distinction effectively in his study of the power exercised by the City in Australia and Canada, as has Bernard Attard in his work on New Zealand.[124] With regard to the location of gentlemanly capitalists, we never claimed that colonial business formed part of the City's elite, or that the interests of businessmen in the empire were identical to those in the Square Mile, even where the two were closely connected. It is unsurprising to find, especially at moments of crisis, such as imminent decolonisation, that relations between the two parties were severely strained. The City's interest lay in seeing that the rules of the game were followed. Success depended on cultivating common values and installing appropriate institutional supports, but these were consistent with the development of degrees of diversity arising from local conditions.

Notwithstanding the vast amount of work published since our first edition appeared, a number of important areas of research relating to the issues we have raised need more attention than they have received so far. For example, we felt that the influence of organisations representing manufacturing, which conventionally had been accorded considerable importance in the formulation of economic policy, had been exaggerated.[125] Although work published since the appearance of our first edition has tended to support this view, it is worth noting that the subject has not been in the forefront of research in recent years and needs to be revisited.[126] Whether this research will produce a better understanding of the workings of the British state remains to be seen, but it will surely provide a more systematic account of the formulation of policy by building a bridge between the detail of diplomatic history, which rarely reaches down to the grass roots of society, and the broader swell of domestic developments, which are only exceptionally connected to questions of international and imperial policy.

The scope for comparative research, which we noted at the close of *British Imperialism*, remains an inviting prospect for scholars who are prepared to range beyond national borders.[127] Our own work was confined to the British world, which in an era of globalisation is now too limited. Admittedly, there are some formidable hurdles: language requirements constitute one barrier; the need to study more than one imperial power in depth is another. Consequently, the supply of serious comparative research is limited and is likely to remain so. Nevertheless, some impressive work has been completed since our study was first published; it deserves advertisement both in its own right and to encourage others to follow suit.

Studies of continental Europe merit particular attention in this connection. Martin Thomas has now drawn some much needed comparisons between Britain and France in his studies of colonial rule.[128] Detailed research by Youssef Cassis has traced the emergence of financial elites in Paris, Berlin and London between the 1880s and the 1930s. His conclusions drew attention to similarities arising from the development of financial and banking services in all three countries, but also underlined the distinctiveness as well as the eminence of the gentlemen of the City of London.[129] His subsequent work has compared the size, competitiveness and relations with manufacturing of financial centres, not only in Europe, but also in the wider world.[130]

A parallel study by Maarten Kuitenbrouwer has outlined a revisionist account of Dutch imperialism.[131] What began as a lively but insular dispute among scholars in the Netherlands has developed into a novel approach that adapts our own work to the Dutch case. Kuitenbrouwer draws a parallel between London's gentlemanly capitalists and the *regenten* (regents') capitalism that had long flourished in Amsterdam, Rotterdam and The Hague. As the financial and service sector in the Netherlands grew rapidly in the late nineteenth century, it elevated a small but powerful elite of bankers, insurers and overseas merchants who became influential in promoting Dutch imperialism in Indonesia. In the light of Kuitenbrouwer's interpretation, Dutch expansion overseas in the nineteenth century can no longer be explained as a passive reaction to events on the periphery or to initiatives taken by greater powers. Just as an understanding of British overseas expansion has to be founded, so we argued, on an analysis of developments at home, so the study of Dutch imperialism has now to incorporate developments in the Netherlands itself. Albert Schrauwers has made a fascinating start on this problem by showing how in the mid-nineteenth century a small group of gentlemanly financiers diversified the economy by promoting manufacturing, while transforming the government from an autocracy to an oligarchy that perpetuated its own dominance.[132]

A third line of enquiry has come from a reconsideration of the causes of Japanese expansion and imperialism.[133] Our own study first joined this growing stream of research by prompting a discussion of our argument that British influence in the Far East remained much stronger than standard interpretations allowed, at least down to Japan's invasion of China in 1937.[134] The debate then widened to include a reconsideration of the role of the City in helping to promote Japanese industrialisation and the economic penetration of China from the 1890s, and of the effect of the world slump on the Far East during the 1930s.[135] Shigeru Akita has added to his publications on this period by showing how the complementarity between British finance and Japanese and Chinese industries also upheld Britain's geopolitical position at a time when Indian troops could no longer be deployed at will and the Royal Navy was overstretched.[136] Akita's essay carries forward Kaoru Sugihara's far-reaching contribution on the growth of inter-regional trade.[137] Sugihara suggests that Japan's economic development capitalised on long-standing commercial ties within Asia that were independent of Western influences. But he goes on to emphasise that this process was greatly assisted by the complementarity that existed between Japan and the City of London: Japan's 'national purpose . . . was to become an internationally competitive industrial power'; the City 'came to depend on the global diffusion of industrialisation'.[138] As important centres of manufacturing developed outside the empire, the City's commitment to what might be termed national imperialism steadily weakened. How far this interpretation modifies or extends our own is a matter that is open to discussion.[139] Irrespective of the outcome, however, Sugihara's analysis illuminates the international ramifications of national expansion and suggests how the unravelling of empire helped to produce the globalised world of today.[140]

Our attempt to point the subject in new directions also obliged us to commit errors of omission. Our concern to re-incorporate the white dominions and to allow space for an examination of the leading examples of informal influence led us to exclude parts of the formal empire and some additional examples of what Gallagher and Robinson termed 'moral suasion', such as Thailand.[141] The most serious omission within the empire was Singapore and the Malay Peninsula. The early stages of this story and the finale have now been re-examined,[142] and a strong case has been made for the role of mercantile and specifically City interests in prompting the move inland from the 1870s.[143] However, other developments, such as those in the inter-war period, need to be looked at afresh in the light of the current debate on the causes and timing of the decline of empire.[144] Burma, another piece missing from the puzzle, was left aside partly because we followed custom in concentrating on India and partly because of the difficulty of fitting together the limited evidence then available. Fortunately, with the completion of significant new research on the period of British expansion in the nineteenth century, important parts of the story have now been told.[145] Anthony Webster has described the role of the City and allied commercial interests in the acquisition of Burma in 1885; Ian Brown has shown how independence in 1948 followed from the demise of Britain's strategic economic interests there.[146] When the empire was revived and repositioned after 1945, Burma had ceased to figure in the calculations.

The West Indies was ruled out almost entirely on historiographical grounds. The literature on the islands exhibits an exceptional degree of imbalance: historians of the Caribbean remain glued to the great age of slave-trading in the eighteenth century, which we referred to briefly. With the abolition of slavery in 1833, the region virtually disappears from general histories of the empire and does not feature again until the West Indian riots of 1938, which are conventionally seen as marking the rise of modern nationalism. The declining plantation economy may not have been the most promising venue for either gentlemen or capitalists, but the Caribbean's missing century is still well worth investigating from an imperial perspective, not least because there are few comparable opportunities in a field of study that has itself now colonised most of the countries of the former empire.[147] The troubled years shortly before independence are an exception because they have attracted important new work linked particularly to the Cold War and the civil rights movement in the United States.[148]

The comparative dimension of our work also opens interesting possibilities for extending our chosen chronology. We began with the Glorious Revolution of 1688, by which date overseas explorations, migrations and settlement had already taken place, if only on a relatively small scale. The question arises as to whether the causes of these earlier manifestations of imperialism were anticipations of those we identified operating in the eighteenth century or were significantly different. An adequate answer needs to take a view of the nature of European capitalism and the empire-building activities of Britain's continental predecessors in the sixteenth and seventeenth centuries. The seminal work of Steensgaard drew a distinction between the Portuguese and Spanish, who had navigational skills and the ability to extract wealth from other parts of the world, and the Dutch and English, whose East India Companies, both founded at the start of the seventeenth century, were able to co-ordinate, distribute and finance long-distance trade with far greater efficiency.[149] If Steensgaard is correct, then the institutional basis of Britain's eighteenth-century mercantile success can be traced formally to the foundation of the English East India Company in 1600. Brenner's work is suggestive here in drawing attention to the colonial ambitions of London's merchants in the middle of the seventeenth century;[150] Chaudhuri's authoritative study underlines the strongly capitalist qualities of the Company down to the mid-eighteenth century.[151] On the other hand, Steensgaard has been criticised for distinguishing too sharply between the capacities of the southern and northern European states, and the Portuguese in particular have found advocates who have made a case for the capitalist qualities of their enterprise.[152] The resolution of these issues would make a considerable contribution both to our understanding of the origins of Britain's international success as a commercial power, to our appreciation of the 'peculiarities' of the English, and to the larger debate on the so-called great divergence.[153]

Finally, we note an emerging view of the imperial past that applies cultural perspectives to imperial economic development. Keynes's later thoughts about the role of uncertainty and 'animal spirits' in determining investment have stimulated the recent claim that the continual re-imagining of the imperial economy is the key to understanding its economic development.[154] So, for example, many investments in infrastructure in the white Dominions in the late nineteenth century may seem to us to be either irrational or perverse. However, they can be explained if the widely held, though erroneous, belief of the time that the population of Greater Britain would equal that of the United States by the mid-twentieth century is taken into account.[155] Similar attempts to recover the original visions on which development was based in other parts of the empire might yield equally interesting results.

Closer to home, and with *British Imperialism* in mind, the sociologist and cultural historian Pardo-Guerra has attacked the idea of gentlemanly capitalism as 'a stable cultural reference that spanned centuries'.[156] Instead, he suggests that 'narratives of finance as a gentleman's affair were artefacts, instruments constructed for generating groupness . . . Gentlemanly capitalism, we could argue, was a fiction fashioned and materialised in magazines and galleries, though evoked in the speech and practice of the marketplace'. Nonetheless, it was, he insists, 'a fiction that mattered' both to the participants and those with whom they interacted. Pardo-Guerra's evidence is confined to the twentieth century and to the London Stock Exchange, which was not the central feature of our own investigations. Besides that, we would argue that the adoption of gentlemanly narratives on the Exchange was something that arose naturally out of the 'stable cultural reference' he dismisses. However, whatever our own views on the issues, Pardo-Guerra's work is path-breaking and may help to stimulate more comprehensive cultural assessments of our work and of traditional approaches to imperial economic history.

Enough has been said, we hope, for readers to be aware of the main areas of debate as far as our own book is concerned, and of some of the ways in which the argument and the subject generally might be developed in future. We had already decided, before publication in 1993, not to reply immediately to the comments we anticipated our thesis would provoke. Having spent so long on our own work, we felt there was a danger that we might find ourselves committed to a series of responses that, in the aftermath of publication, might amount to little more than automatic and unreflective defensive reactions. By the time we had produced our second edition, it had become possible to view the debate with a measure of detachment. Accordingly, we took the opportunity to deal with some of the numerous comments, both general and detailed, that required attention. Although we have followed this procedure in the present edition, we are conscious that we face mounting difficulties in doing so. The subject has not only become voluminous, but has also taken on a life of its own. It has escaped our control and, in some cases, our vision too.[157] In some respects, we are now just readers of *British Imperialism* with no privileged insight into the meaning and the use of the ideas it contains. Indeed, we may be less able to appreciate its merits, its deficiencies, and its inevitable silences than others who are free of our parental prejudices. This is as it should be, given that our aim was to open the subject up rather than to close it down.

The empire has now gone, but its legacy lives on at home and abroad. The dilemmas of the post-colonial era arise at least partly from the weakening of the institutions that helped to shape the nation state and its imperial international order. The history of those institutions therefore has considerable contemporary relevance; conversely the large issues facing nation states in a globalised world can provide fresh inspiration for the study of imperialism and empires.[158] From either standpoint, imperial history, however it is named or re-branded, is a subject that is full of vitality and therefore has a future and not just a past.

Notes

1 Geoffrey Chaucer, *The Parliament of Fowls*, 1, i. Chaucer was writing of a rather different craft (courtly love), but since he was borrowing from the *Aphorisms* of Hippocrates, it may be assumed that he was well aware of the maxim's wider applications.

2 P. J. Cain and A.G. Hopkins, 'The Political Economy of British Expansion Overseas, 1750–1914', *Economic History Review*, 2nd ser. 33 (1980); 'Gentlemanly Capitalism and British Expansion Overseas, I : The Old Colonial System, 1688–1850', *Econ. Hist. Rev.*, 2nd ser. 39 (1986); 'Gentlemanly Capitalism and British Expansion Overseas, II: New Imperialism, 1850–1945', *Econ. Hist. Rev.*, 2nd ser. 40 (1987).

3 Casaubon died before completing his doomed project. Long before then, however, 'the difficulty of making his work unimpeachable weighed like lead upon his mind'. George Eliot, *Middlemarch* (1872; Oxford, 1986), p. 230.

4 The phrase was used by the late Prof. Ronald Robinson in a personal communication to one of the authors following the publication of *British Imperialism*.

5 Kelly Boyd and Rohan McWilliam recognised our wider purpose in reprinting part of our original articles in *The Victorian Studies Reader* (2007), Ch. 3.

6 For example, Will Hutton in *The Guardian*, 6 June 1993.

7 For example, Bill Jamieson in *The Sunday Telegraph*, 20 March 1994.

8 *The State We're In* (1994).

9 Anthony Webster provides an accessible survey in *The Debate on the Rise of British Imperialism* (2006).

10 The standard statement of the 'new institutional economics' is Douglass C. North, *Institutions, Institutional Change and Economic Performance* (1990).

11 These interactions are considered further in A. G. Hopkins, 'Back to the Future: From National History to Imperial History', *Past & Present*, 164 (1999).

12 David Cannadine had already noted in his perceptive review essay that the tide was beginning to change: 'The Empire Strikes Back', *Past & Present*, 147 (1995). Richard Price makes a similar observation in his valuable review essay, 'One Big Thing: Britain, Its Empire, and Their Imperial Culture', *Journal of British Studies*, 45 (2006).

13 As the striking impact of Thomas Piketty's assessment of inequality bears witness: *Capital in the Twenty-First Century* (2014). Other examples include: John Darwin, *The Empire Project: The Rise and Fall of the British World-System* (Cambridge, 2009) that, citing *British Imperialism*, argues strongly for a renewed emphasis on the economic history of empire to an understanding the whole; Niall Ferguson, *Empire: How Britain Made the Modern World* (2003) stresses the importance of economic considerations, which are also illustrated in his *The World's Banker: The History of the House of Rothschild* (1998). Gary B. Magee and Andrew S. Thompson, *Empire and Globalisation: Networks of People, Goods and Capital in the British World, c. 1850–1914* (Cambridge, 2010), generously recognises the importance of our own contribution. Given the links between economic and technological history, we should note too Daniel R. Headrick, *Power over Peoples: Technology, Environments, and Western Imperialism, 1400 to the Present* (Princeton, NJ, 2010).

14 Two substantial guides are Raymond E. Dumett, ed. *Gentlemanly Capitalism and British Imperialism: The New Debate on Empire* (1999); Shigeru Akita, ed. *Gentlemanly Capitalism and Global History* (2002). Additional constructive criticism includes: J. Forbes Munro, *Maritime Enterprise and Empire: Sir William McKinnon and His Business Networks, 1823–1893* (Woodbridge, 2003); David Sunderland, *Managing the British Empire: The Crown Agents, 1833–1914* (Woodbridge, 2004); idem, *Managing British Colonial and Post-Colonial Development: The Crown Agents, 1914–1974* (Woodbridge, 2007).

15 Our most valued comments have come from the master of the subject, the late Prof. Ronald Robinson, who offered a characteristically warm commendation for a work that took issue with his own, and a generous judgement in what turned out to be his last publication: 'Wm. Roger Louis and the Official Mind of Decolonization', *Journal of Imperial and Commonwealth History*, 27 (1999), p. 11. As far as we are aware, only two critics, Prof. Andrew Porter and Dr. Ronald Hyam, have been unable to find any merit in our two volumes: 'Birmingham, Westminster and the City of London: Visions of Empire Compared', *Journal of Historical Geography*, 21 (1995), repeated in 'Gentlemanly Capitalism and the British Empire-Commonwealth in the Nineteenth and Twentieth Centuries', *Bulletin of Asia-Pacific Studies*, 9 (1999); Ronald Hyam, *Understanding the British Empire* (2010), Ch. 4. See our 'Afterword: The Theory and Practice of British Imperialism', in Dumett, *Gentlemanly Capitalism and British Imperialism*; and Akita, *Gentlemanly Capitalism and Global History*, Ch. 11; also P. J. Cain, 'Gentlemanly Capitalism and British Imperialism: A Critical Survey', *Pauwlonia*, 12 (1997).

16 See above, Ch. 1.

17 Andrew Porter, 'Gentlemanly Capitalism and Empire: The British Experience Since 1750?' *Journal of Imperial and Commonwealth History*, 18 (1990).

18 See above, pp. 61–5.

19 Geoffrey Ingham, 'British Capitalism: Empire, Merchants and Decline', *Social History*, 3 (1995), p. 346.

20 The approach adopted by R. G. Collingwood in his *Idea of History* (1984 ed.) might have been a better starting point for us, though that would probably have made very little difference to how we handled and interpreted our evidence in practice.

21 Ingham, 'British Capitalism', p. 346.

22 See, for example, the observations made in the very generous review essays by David Fieldhouse, 'Gentlemen, Capitalists, and the British Empire', *Journal of Imperial and*

Commonwealth History, 22 (1994); and David Cannadine, 'The Empire Strikes Back', *Past and Present*, 147 (1995).

23 See above, pp. 61–5.

24 See above, pp. 40–42.

25 See above, pp. 63, 701–2.

26 See the commentary in Maxine Berg and Pat Hudson, 'Rehabilitating the Industrial Revolution', *Economic History Review*, 2nd ser. 45 (1992), and the important restatement by J. R. Ward, 'The Industrial Revolution and British Imperialism, 1750–1850, *Econ. Hist. Rev.*, 47 (1994). Ward's contribution is a model of constructive criticism. It restates the case for giving greater prominence to the forces represented by industrialisation, while nevertheless acknowledging that 'for the most of the period under review, British imperial policy remained in the hands of elements which fit the description "gentlemanly capitalist"' (p. 46). Michael Barratt Brown's attempt to rehabilitate a Marxist interpretation of imperialism also emphasises the importance of industrialisation, but relies on dated sources and fails to incorporate recent work that has underlined the significance of landed wealth, the service sector and the non-industrial middle class. His commentary on *British Imperialism* makes some interesting observations but misrepresents our interpretation in a number of significant ways: 'Imperialism Revisited', in Ronald M. Chilcote, ed. *The Political Economy of Imperialism: Critical Appraisals* (Boston, 1999).

27 The transformation that has occurred since the 1980s is neatly symbolised by the difference between the 1st ed. of Roderick Floud and Donald McCloskey, eds. *The Economic History of Britain Since 1700*, 3 Vols. (Cambridge, 1981), which made no mention of the service sector, and the 2nd ed. (1994), which devoted a chapter (Vol. 2, Ch. 5) to the subject (written, appropriately, by Clive Lee, one of the pioneers of the subject). The 3rd ed. (2004), edited by Roderick Floud and Paul Johnson, confirms and extends the trend. The shift of emphasis is also perceptible in Peter Clarke and Clive Trebilock, eds. *Understanding Decline: Perceptions and Realities of British Economic Performance* (1997).

28 See above, p. 44.

29 It is unfortunate that K. Theodore Hoppen's comprehensive survey should merge our argument with one that claims that Britain 'was never at heart an industrial nation at all': *The Mid-Victorian Generation, 1846–1886* (Oxford, 1998), p. 314, n. 110. Our position on this matter is rather different from that put by W. D. Rubinstein, *Capitalism, Culture and Decline in Britain, 1750–1990* (1993), as most reviewers have noted.

30 Geoffrey Ingham, 'British Capitalism: Empire, Merchants and Decline', *Social History*, 20 (1995), pp. 341–4.

31 Martin Daunton, 'Gentlemanly Capitalism and British Industry, 1820–1914', *Past & Present*, 132 (1991); also 'Home and Colonial', *Twentieth-Century British History*, 6 (1995), p. 353; and 'The Entrepreneurial State, 1700–1914', *History Today*, June 1994, p. 16.

32 Ronald Robinson and Jack Gallagher with Alice Denny, *Africa and the Victorians: The Official Mind of Imperialism* (1961; 2nd ed. 1981).

33 We are greatly indebted to the pioneers of this subject, especially W. D. Rubinstein and Clive Lee. See, for example, *Rubinstein's Men of Property: The Very Wealthy in Britain since the Industrial Revolution* (1981); and *Elites and the Wealthy in Modern British History: Essays in Social and Economic History* (1987); and Lee's *The British Economy since 1700: A Macroeconomic Perspective* (1986).

34 Penny Corfield, 'The Democratic History of the English Gentleman', *History Today*, 42 (1992); idem, 'Class by Name and Number in Eighteenth-Century Britain', *History*, 72 (1987).

35 As Ingham suggests: 'British Capitalism'.

36 See for example, Jonathan Parry, *The Politics of Patriotism: English Liberalism, National Identity and Europe, 1830–1886* (2006); Andrew Porter, *Religion Versus Empire? British Protestant Missionaries and Overseas Expansion, 1700–1914* (2004); Norman Etherington, ed. *Missions and Empire* (2005), Ch. 19. Catherine Hall, et al., *Legacies of British*

Slave-Ownership: Colonial Slavery and the Formation of Victorian Britain (2014) appeared too late for us to do more than note its importance.

37 Christopher L. Brown, *Moral Capital: Foundations of British Abolitionism* (2006); Young Hwi Yoon, 'The Rise of Abolitionism during the Revolutionary Period, 1770–1800', *East Asian Journal of British History* (2013) provides a valuable supplement.

38 Seymour Drescher, *Abolition: A History of Slavery and Anti-Slavery* (Cambridge, 2009); idem, 'Capitalism and Abolitionism', *History & Theory*, 32 (1993). The relationship was often fraught: Simon Morgan, 'The Anti-Corn Law League and British Anti-Slavery in Trans-Atlantic Perspective, 1838–1846', *Historical Journal*, 52 (2009).

39 J. R. Oldfield, *Popular Politics and British Anti-Slavery: The Mobilisation of Public Opinion against the Slave Trade, 1787–1807* (1998); Clare Midgley, *Women Against Slavery: The British Campaigns, 1780–1870* (1992).

40 Christer Petly, '"Devoted Islands" and "That Madman Wilberforce": British Proslavery Patriotism during the Age of Abolition', *Journal of Imperial & Commonwealth History*, 39 (2011).

41 See, amidst a plethora of studies, Terry Coleman, *The Nelson Touch: The Life and Legend of Horatio Nelson* (Oxford, 2002); John Severn, *Architects of Empire: The Duke of Wellington and His Brothers* (Norman, Oklahoma, 2007).

42 Peter W. Sinnema, *The Wake of Wellington: Englishness in 1852* (Athens, Ohio, 2006), gives details of the statues, street names, publications, and other memorabilia that followed the Duke's death in 1852.

43 Denis Judd, 'Gordon of Khartoum: The Making of an Imperial Martyr', *History Today*, 35 (1985), pp. 19–25.

44 See especially Ian Phimister, 'The Chrome Trust: The Creation of an International Cartel, 1908–38', *Business History*, 38 (1996); idem, 'Making Markets: Base Minerals and the City of London before World War II', in Toyin Falola and Emily Brownell, eds. *Africa, Empire, and Globalization: Essays in Honor of A. G. Hopkins* (Durham, NC, 2011), Ch. 18.

45 See David Cannadine, *Aspects of Aristocracy: Grandeur and Decline in Modern Britain* (1994), Ch. 1.

46 Some of our further thoughts on the subject are contained in Cain and Hopkins, 'Afterword', in Dumett, *Gentlemanly Capitalism*, pp. 199–201; and Peter Cain, 'The City of London, 1880–1914: Tradition and Innovation', in Jean-Pierre Dormais and Michael Dintenfass, eds. *The British Industrial Decline* (1999).

47 Paul R. Deslandes, '"The Foreign Element": Newcomers and the Rhetoric of Race, Nation, and Empire in "Oxbridge" Undergraduate Culture, 1850–1920', *Journal of British Studies*, 37 (1998).

48 David E. Torrance, *The Strange Death of Liberal England: Lord Selborne in South Africa* (Liverpool, 1996).

49 David Hancock, *Citizens of the World: London Merchants and the Integration of the British Atlantic Community, 1735–1785* (Cambridge, 1995).

50 Youssef Cassis, *City Bankers, 1890–1914* (Cambridge, 1994).

51 Ian Phimister, 'Corners and Company-Mongering: Nigerian Tin and the City of London, 1909–12', *Jour. of Imp. & Comm. Hist.*, 28 (2000); idem, 'Foreign Devils, Finance and Informal Empire: Britain and China, 1900–1912', *Modern Asian Studies*, 40 (2006); idem, 'Making Markets: Base Minerals and the City of London before World War II', in Falola and Brownell. *Africa, Empire and Globalization*. Ch. 18.

52 *The City of London: The Golden Years, 1890–1914* (1995).

53 *London, 1900: The Imperial Metropolis* (1999).

54 *British Business History, 1720–1994* (1995).

55 We are glad to have an opportunity to pay tribute to the work of Youssef Cassis, *City Bankers, 1880–1914* (Cambridge, 1994); Geoffrey Jones, *British Multinational Banking, 1830–1990* (Oxford, 1993); idem, *Merchants to Multinationals: British Trading Companies in the Nineteenth and Twentieth Centuries* (Oxford, 2000); and Charles Jones, *International*

Business in the Nineteenth Century: The Rise and Fall of a Cosmopolitan Bourgeoisie (1987). Between them, these studies have put the historical importance of the City and allied services overseas beyond dispute.

56 W. D. Rubinstein, 'Britain's Elites in the Inter-War Period, 1918–39', *Contemporary British History*, 12 (1998). The continuity of elites and policies after 1914 is one of the main themes of *British Imperialism*.

57 *The English Gentleman Merchant at Work: Madras and the City of London, 1660–1740* (Copenhagen, 2005); James R. Fichter, *So Great a Proffit: How the East Indies Trade Transformed Anglo-American Capitalism* (2010), pp. 279–83.

58 'Revolutions without a Revolutionary Movement: Joint Stock Democracy and the Transition in Capitalism in Upper Canada', *Canadian Historical Review*, 89 (2008); idem, 'The Gentlemanly Order and the Politics of Production in the Transition to Capitalism in the Home District, Upper Canada', *Labour/LeTravail*, 65 (2010).

59 *British Businessmen and Canadian Confederation: Constitution-Making in an Era of Anglo-Globalization* (2008).

60 'Views of Gentlemanly Capitalism, 1837–1842: The Colonial Society and the Chartists', in Falola and Brownell, *Africa, Empire and Globalisation*, Ch. 14.

61 'Indian Railroading: Floating Railway Companies in the Late Nineteenth Century', *Economic History Review*, 62 (2009).

62 *Financing the Raj: The City of London and Colonial India, 1858–1914* (2013).

63 'A Case Study in the Environmental History of Gentlemanly Capitalism: The Battle between Gentlemen Teak Merchants and State Foresters in Burma and Siam, 1827–1901', in Falola and Brownell, *Africa, Empire and Globalization*, Ch. 15.

64 'Finance and the End of Appeasement: The Bank of England, the National Government and the Czech Gold', *Journal of Contemporary History*, 40 (2005).

65 Mark Brayshaw, Mark Cleary and John Selwood, 'Social Networks and the Transnational Reach of the Corporate Class in the Early Twentieth Century', *Journal of Historical Geography*, 33 (2007).

66 'Gentlemanly Capitalism Revisited: A Case Study of the Underpricing of Initial Public Offerings on the London Stock Market', *Economic History Review*, 62 (2009), p. 31.

67 It is now recognised, as perhaps it was not a decade ago, that these processes defy simplicity. Penelope J. Corfield provided an excellent starting point in, 'History and the Challenge of Gender History', *Rethinking History*, 1 (1997). Ronald Hyam, *Empire and Sexuality: the British Experience* (Manchester, 1990), Ch. 3, offered a controversial discussion of the institutional bases of Victorian masculinity. Philippa Levine, ed. *Gender and Empire* (2004), provides a recent survey of the field.

68 P. J. Cain, 'Empire and the Languages of Character and Virtue in Later Victorian and Edwardian Britain', *Modern Intellectual History*, 2 (2007); idem. 'Character, "Ordered Liberty" and the Mission to Civilise: British Moral Justification of Empire, 1870–1914', *Journal of Imperial & Commonwealth History,* 40 (2012).

69 These elements came together dramatically in the crisis in Bechuanaland in 1948, when Seretse Khama married Ruth Williams. See Ronald Hyam, 'The Political Consequences of Seretse Khama: Britain, the Bangwato and South Africa, 1948–52', *Historical Journal*, 29 (1986).

70 K. D. Reynolds, *Aristocratic Women and Political Society in Victorian Britain* (Oxford, 1998) shows, through her valuable study of the wives of Tory cabinet ministers, just how difficult it is to secure a wide range of documentation on this subject.

71 See, for example, the otherwise valuable studies by Nupur Chaudhuri and Margaret Strobel, eds. *Western Women and Imperialism* (Bloomington, 1992); Ruth R. Pierson and Nupur Chaudhuri, eds. *Nation, Empire, Colony: Historicising Gender and Race* (Bloomington, 1998); Antoinette Burton, ed. *Gender, Sexuality, and Colonial Modernities* (1999); The influential view that women were a coherent cohort, though less prominent now than it was, has not advanced our interest in the class divisions implied by the concept of a lady.

72 David R. Green and Alastair Owens, 'Gentlewomanly Capitalism? Spinsters, Widows and Wealth-Holding in England and Wales, c.1870–1860', *Economic History Review*,

56 (2006); Donna Loftus, 'Entrepreneurialism or Gentlemanly Capitalism', in Martin Hewitt, ed. *The Victorian World* (2012), Ch. 10.

73 Anne Laurence, Josephine Maltby and Janette Rutterford, eds. *Women and their Money. 1700–1950* (2009); David R. Green, Alastair Owens, Josephine Maltby and Janette Rutterford, eds. *Men, Women and Money: Perspectives on Gender, Wealth and Investment, 1850–1920* (2011).

74 Examples can be found in a number of the studies referred to in n. 71.

75 Reynolds, *Aristocratic Women*; Julia Bush, *Edwardian Ladies and Imperial Power* (Leicester, 2000); Dominic Allessio, 'Domesticating the "Heart of the Wild": Female Personification of the Colonies, 1886–1940', *Women's History Review*, 6 (1997); Anne Summers, 'Pride and Prejudice: Ladies and Nurses in the Crimean War', *History Workshop Journal*, 16 (1983); Jane Haggis, '"A Heart that Has Felt the Love of God and Longs for Others to Know it": Conventions of Gender, Tensions of Self and Constructions of Difference in Offering to Be a Lady Missionary', *Women's History Review*, 7 (1998); Carroll Pursell, '"Am I a Lady or an Engineer?": The Origins of the Women's Engineering Society in Britain, 1918–1940', *Technology and Culture*, 34 (1994); Richard A. Voeltz, 'The Antidote to "Khaki Fever": The Expansion of the British Girl Guides during the First World War', *Journal of Contemporary History*, 27 (1992).

76 A. C. Howe, 'Free Trade and the City of London, c.1820–1870', *History*, 77 (1992), and *Free Trade and Liberal England, 1846–1946* (Oxford, 1997) offers some pertinent criticisms of the view of the City's influence summarised in our compressed articles, published in 1986 and 1987. However, we had already expressed caution on these issues in *British Imperialism: Innovation and Expansion*, p. 83.

77 Stanley Chapman, *Merchant Enterprise in Britain: From the Industrial Revolution to World War I* (Cambridge, 1992); David Kynaston, *The City of London: Golden Years, 1890–1914* (1995).

78 Peter Cain, 'The City of London, 1880–1914: Tradition and Innovation', in Jean-Pierre Dormois and Michael Dintenfass, eds. *The British Industrial Decline* (1999).

79 Philip Augar, *The Death of Gentlemanly Capitalism: The Collapse of British Banking* (2000), esp. Chs. 3–4, which emphasise the continuing importance and efficiency, right down to Big Bang, of paternal family structures, personal relationships, and a code of honour that stressed probity and loyalty.

80 Daunton, 'The Entrepreneurial State', p. 16. Prof. Daunton has also attacked the view that a gentlemanly capitalist elite retained a special position of influence in policy-making. In reprinting his original criticism in *State and Market in Victorian Britain: War, Welfare and Capitalism* (Woodbridge, 2008), however, he did not take account of our comments either in the 'Foreword' of the second edition of *British Imperialism*, or in the volumes edited by Dumett and Akita cited in n. 14 above.

81 See above, pp. 84–5.

82 As cogently argued by E. H. H. Green, 'The Influence of the City over British Economic Policy, c.1880–1960', in Youssef Cassis, ed. *Finance and Financiers in European History, 1880–1960* (Cambridge, 1992).

83 Anne L. Murphy, *The Origins of English Financial Markets: Investment and Speculation before the South Sea Bubble* (Cambridge, 2009), building on Henry Roseveare, *The Financial Revolution, 1660–1760* (London, 1991).

84 Steve Pincus, *1688: The First Modern Revolution* (New Haven, 2009); *British Scholar*, 2 (2010), pp. 295–338, provides a representative example of the discussion this book has provoked.

85 Jeremy Black, *The Continental Commitment: Britain, Hanover and Interventionism, 1714–1793* (Abingdon, 2005), provides an accessible survey; Stephen Conway, *Britain, Ireland, and Continental Europe in the Eighteenth Century: Similarities, Connections, Identities* (Oxford, 2011), moves beyond high politics to emphasise the strength of the European connection.

86 The fundamental work remains P. G. M. Dickson, *The Financial Revolution in England: A Study in the Development of Public Credit, 1688–1756* (London, 1967).

87 As argued by J. C. D. Clark, *English Society, 1660–1832: Religion, Politics and Society During the Ancien Régime* (2nd ed. Cambridge, 2000); and the commentary by Joanna Innes, 'Social History and England's "Ancien Régime"', *Past & Present*, 115 (1987).

88 H. V. Bowen, *Elites, Enterprise and the Making of the British Overseas Empire, 1688–1775* (1996), which he has now extended to cover the previously 'lost' period of the East India Company's history: *The Business of Empire: The East India Company and Imperial Britain, 1756–1833* (2005).

89 We are indebted here to two important, complementary pieces of research: James M. Vaughn, *Empire and Revolution from Cromwell to Clive: The East India Company and the Rise and Fall of the First British Empire, 1650–1776* (2015); Justin DuRivage, 'Taxing Empire: Political Economy and the Ideological Origins of the American Revolution, 1747–1776' (Ph.D. thesis, Yale University, 2013).

90 E. E. H. Green, 'Gentlemanly Capitalism and British Economic Policy, 1880–1914: The Debate over Bimetallism and Protection', in Dumett, *Gentlemanly Capitalism*; Cain and Hopkins, 'Afterword', in ibid., pp. 198–202; Cain, 'The City of London', and the further references given in these sources, including J. Peters, 'The British Government and the City-Industry Divide: The Case of the 1914 Financial Crisis', *Contemporary British History*, 4 (1993).

91 Paul A. Pickering and Alex Tyrrell, *The People's Bread: A History of the Anti-Corn Law League* (Leicester, 2000); For a valuable guide to 'Cobden Studies', see Anthony Howe and Simon Morgan, eds. *Rethinking Nineteenth-Century Liberalism: Richard Cobden Bicentenary Essays* (Aldershot, 2006); Cheryl Schonhardt-Bailey, *From the Corn Laws to Free Trade: Interests, Ideas and Institutions in Historical Perspective* (Cambridge, Mass., 2006); Paul Sharp, '1846 and All That: The Rise and Fall of British Wheat Protection in the Nineteenth Century', *Agricultural History Review*, 58 (2010); Henry Miller, 'Popular Petitioning and the Corn Laws, 1823–46', *English Historical Review*, 127 (2012).

92 Boyd Hilton, *A Mad, Bad, and Dangerous People? England, 1783–1846* (Oxford, 2006), which builds on his *The Age of Atonement: The Influence of Evangelicals on Social and Economic Thought, 1785–1865* (Oxford, 1986); Frank Trentman, *Commerce, Consumption, and Civil Society in Modern Britain* (2008).

93 See for example, Anthony Webster, *Twilight of the East India Company: The Evolution of Anglo-Asian Commerce and Politics, 1790–1860* (2009).

94 Tom Nicholas, 'Wealth Making in Nineteenth- and Early Twentieth-Century Britain: Industry v. Commerce and Finance', *Business History*, 41 (1999); W. D. Rubinstein, 'Wealth Making in the Late Nineteenth and Early Twentieth Centuries: A Response', *Business History*, 42 (2000). Nicholas White, 'Ferry off the Mersey: The Business and Impact of Decolonisation on Liverpool', *History*, 96 (2009), pp. 194–5, shows that Liverpool had produced a sprinkling of gentlemanly capitalists by the end of the colonial era.

95 Yukihisa Kamagai, *Breaking into the Monopoly: Provincial Merchants and Manufacturers Campaigns for Access to the Asian Market, 1790–1833* (2012).

96 We believe that this chronological revision is consistent with Anthony Webster's position and indeed has been encouraged by it: 'Reassessing Gentlemanly Capitalism: British Economic Interests and Colonial Policy in Asia, 1790–1860', in Falola and Brownell, *Africa, Empire and Globalization*, Ch. 13.

97 The essays in Sheryllyne Hagerty, Anthony Webster and Nicholas White, eds. *The Empire in One City? Liverpool's Inconvenient Imperial Past* (2008) represent both viewpoints.

98 David R. Green and Alastair Owens, 'Geographies of Wealth: Real Estate and Personal Property-Ownership in England and Wales, 1870–1902', *Economic History Review*, 66 (2013).

99 R. C. Michie, *The City of London in Victorian and Edwardian Culture, 1815–1914* (2009).

100 David Kynaston, *The City of London*, 4 Vols. (1995–2002).

101 This point is emphasised in the best biography: P. T. Marsh, *Joseph Chamberlain: Entrepreneur in Politics* (1994).

102 'The New Britannia', *Daily Express*, 24 April, 1900. The editor of the paper was an enthusiastic supporter of Chamberlain. For Milner's adherence to Chamberlain's approach to politics see P. J. Cain, 'The Economic Philosophy of Constructive Imperialism', in C. Navari ed. *British Politics and the Spirit of the Age: Political Concepts in Action* (Keele, 1996).

103 On Selborne the key reference is David E. Torrance, *The Strange Death of Liberal Empire: Lord Selborne in South Africa* (Liverpool. 1996). See also Peter Cain, *Hobson and Imperialism: Radicalism, New Liberalism and Finance, 1887–1938* (Oxford, 2002), pp. 267–71.

104 See especially Catherine R. Schenk, *The Decline of Sterling: Managing the Retreat of an International Currency, 1945–1992* (2010), which follows from idem, *Britain and the Sterling Area: From Devaluation to Convertibility in the 1950s* (1994); Ranald Michie and Philip Williamson, eds. *The British Government and the City of London in the Twentieth Century: The New City and the State in the 1960s* (2004); Steven G. Galpern, *Money, Oil and Empire in the Middle East: Sterling and Postwar Imperialism* (2009). Also Gerold Krozewski, *Money and the End of Empire: British Economic Policy and the Colonies, 1947–58* (2001); idem, 'Finance and Empire: The Dilemma Facing Great Britain in the 1950s', *International History Review*, 18 (1996); S. E. Stockwell, 'Instilling the "Sterling Tradition": Decolonization and the Creation of a Central Bank in Ghana', *Jour. Imp. and Comm. Stud.*, 26 (1988); A. G. Hopkins, 'Macmillan's Audit of Empire, 1957', in Peter Clarke and Clive Trebilcock, eds. *Understanding Decline: Perceptions and Realities of British Economic Performance* (Cambridge, 1997).

105 Paul Thompson, 'The Pyrrhic Victory of Gentlemanly Capitalism: The Financial Elite of the City of London, 1945–90', *Journal of Contemporary History*, 32 (1997).

106 See John R. Ferris, '"The Greatest Power on Earth": Great Britain in the 1920s', *International History Review* 13 (1991); and B. J. McKercher '"Our Most Dangerous Enemy": Great Britain Pre-Eminent in the 1930s', ibid.

107 L. J. Butler, *Britain and Empire: Adjusting to a Post-Imperial World* (2002); Martin Lynn, ed. *The British Empire in the 1950s: Retreat or Revival?* (2006), confirms the emphasis we placed on the mid-1950s as being the turning point between advance and retreat. See also Darwin, *Empire Project.*

108 Ronald Robinson, 'Non-European Foundations of European Imperialism: Sketch for a Theory of Collaboration', in Roger Owen and Bob Sutcliffe, eds. *Studies in the Theory of Imperialism* (1972).

109 See, for example, James Belich, *Replenishing the Earth: The Settler Revolution and the Rise of the Anglo-World, 1783–1939* (2009); Deryck M. Schreuder and Stuart Ward, eds. *Australia's Empire* (2008); Phillip Buckner, ed. *Canada and the British Empire* (2008).

110 The Companion Series attached to the Oxford History of the British Empire provides a good guide to the shift of emphasis.

111 See, for example, the essays edited by Bernard Attard and Andrew Dilley, 'Finance, Empire and the British World', *Journal of Imperial & Commonwealth History*, 41 (2013).

112 See especially, Gary B. Magee and Andrew S. Thompson, *Empire and Globalisation: Networks of People, Goods and Capital in the British World, 1850–1914* (2010).

113 P. L. Cottrell, *The Ionian Bank: An Imperial Institution, 1839–1864* (2007).

114 Laurence, Maltby, and Rutterford, *Women and Their Money;* Green, Owens, Maltby and Rutterford, *Men, Women and Money.*

115 A. G. Hopkins, 'Rethinking Decolonisation', *Past & Present*, 200 (2008).

116 See, for example, Robert Kubicek, 'Economic Power at the Periphery: Canada, Australia and South Africa, 1850–1914' in Dumett, *Gentlemanly Capitalism and British Imperialism;* Lance Davis, 'The Late Nineteenth-Century Imperialist: Specification, Quantification and Controlled Conjectures', ibid.; Angela Redish, 'British Financial Imperialism after the First World War', ibid.; Luke Trainor, *British Imperialism and Australian Nationalism: Manipulation, Conflict and Compromise in the Late Nineteenth Century* (Cambridge, 1994).

117 See, for example, Angela Redish, 'British Financial Imperialism after the First World War', in Dumett, *Gentlemanly Capitalism and British Imperialism*; and P. J. Cain, 'Gentlemanly

Capitalism at Work: The Bank of England, Canada, and the Sterling Area, 1932–1936', *Economic History Review,* 49 (1996).

118 To cite just three very varied examples: John Singleton, 'New Zealand, Britain and the Survival of the Ottawa Agreement, 1945–77', *Australian Journal of Politics and History,* 43 (1997); I. R. Phimister, 'The Chrome Trust: The Creation of an International Cartel, 1908–38', *Business History,* 38 (1996); Paul Auchterlonie, 'A Turk of the West: Sir Edgar Vincent's Career in Egypt and the Ottoman Empire', *British Journal of Middle Eastern Studies,* 27 (2000).

119 Lance Davis, 'The Late Nineteenth-Century British Imperialist: Specification, Quantification and Controlled Conjectures', in Dumett, *Gentlemanly Capitalism and British Imperialism,* Ch. 3; P. J. Cain and A. G. Hopkins, 'Afterword', in ibid., pp. 202–10; A. G. Hopkins, 'Informal Empire in Argentina: An Alternative View', *Journal of Latin American Studies,* 26 (1994); John Darwin, 'Imperialism and the Victorians: The Dynamics of Territorial Expansion', *English Historical Review,* CXII (1997).

120 Jim McAloon, 'Gentlemanly Capitalism and Settler Capitalists: Imperialism, Dependent Development and Colonial Wealth in the South Island of New Zealand', *Australian Economic History Review,* 42 (2002); A. G. Hopkins, 'Gentlemanly Capitalism in New Zealand', ibid. 43 (2003); Jim McAloon, 'Gentlemen, Capitalists, and Settlers: A Reply to Hopkins', ibid.

121 Sandip Hazareesingh, 'Interconnected Synchronicities: The Production of Bombay and Glasgow as Modern Global Ports, c.1850–1880', *Journal of Global History,* 4 (2009).

122 Nicholas White, 'The Business and Politics of Decolonization: The British Experience in the Twentieth Century', *Econ. Hist. Rev.,* 53 (2000).

123 Susan Strange, *States and Markets* (1988), Ch. 2.

124 Andrew Dilley, *Finance, Politics and Imperialism: Australia, Canada and the City of London, c.1896–1914* (2012). Bernard Attard, 'From Free Trade Imperialism to Structural Power: New Zealand and the Capital Market, 1856–68', *Journal of Imperial and Commonwealth History* 35 (2007); and his complementary essay, 'Making the New Zealand State: Development, Debt, and Warfare in New Zealand, 1853–76', *Australian Economic History Review,* 52 (2012).

125 See above, pp. 56–8, 82–3.

126 The limited influence of the manufacturing lobby, even at the height of the industrial revolution, is emphasised by Geoffrey Searle, *Entrepreneurial Politics in Mid-Victorian Britain* (Oxford, 1993), and A. Marrison, *British Business and Protection 1903–1932* (Oxford, 1996).

127 See above, pp. 701–2.

128 See especially, *Violence and Colonial Order: Police, Workers and Protest in the European Colonial Empires, 1918–40* (2012); and *Fight or Flight: Britain, France and their Roads from Empire* (2014).

129 'Financial Elites in Three European Centres: London, Paris, Berlin, 1880s–1930s', *Business History,* 33 (1991), which should be read in conjunction with an important set of essays edited by Cassis: *Finance and Financiers in European History, 1880–1960* (Cambridge, 1992). Neither contribution was available to us when our study first went to press. It is worth noting in this connection that the latest instalment of W. D. Rubinstein's path-breaking work on wealth in nineteenth-century England confirms the special significance of London and the City, while also drawing attention to the growing affluence of provincial towns: 'The Role of London in Britain's Wealth Structure, 1809–99: Further Evidence', in Jon Stobart and Alastair Owens, eds. *Property and Inheritance in the Town, 1700–1900* (1999).

130 *Capitals of Capital: A History of Financial Centres 1780–2005* (2006); Laure Quennouelle-Core and Youssef Cassis, eds. *Financial Centres and International Capital Flows in the Nineteenth and Twentieth Centuries* (2011).

131 In *The Netherlands and the Rise of Modern Capitalism: Colonies and Foreign Policy, 1870–1902* (Oxford 1991; first published in Dutch in 1985), Kuitenbrouwer took issue in particular with the position adopted by Henk Wesseling, the doyen of Dutch historians

of imperialism. Further references and a summary of Kuitenbrouwer's views are given in his essay, 'Capitalism and Imperialism: Britain and the Netherlands', *Itinerario*, 18 (1994).

132 '"Regenten" (Gentlemanly) Capitalism: Saint-Simonian Technology and the Emergence of the "Industrialist Great Club" in the Mid-Nineteenth Century Netherlands', *Enterprise & Society*, 11 (2010).

133 This is an appropriate point to draw attention to the remarkable interest Japanese scholars have shown in our work, and to acknowledge the independence of their own perspective on the problem of modern imperialism, as the following citations indicate.

134 Shigeru Akita, 'British Informal Empire in East Asia, 1880–1939: A Japanese Perspective', in Dumett, *Gentlemanly Capitalism and British Imperialism*; Cain and Hopkins, 'Afterword', ibid, pp. 211–13; P. J. Cain, 'British Economic Imperialism in China in the 1930s: The Leith-Ross Mission', *Bulletin of Asia-Pacific Studies*, 7 (1997).

135 Shigeru Akita, '"Gentlemanly Capitalism", Intra-Asian Trade and Japanese Industrialisation at the Turn of the Last Century', *Japan Forum*, 8 (1996); Shigeru Akita and Naoto Kagotani, 'The International Order of Asia in the 1930s', Osaka University of Foreign Studies Discussion Paper, March 2000; Shizuya Nishimura, Toshio Suzuki and Ranald Michie, *The Origins of International Banking in the Nineteenth and Twentieth Centuries* (2012), underlines the importance of the City's influence on Asian banking.

136 Shigeru Akita, 'The British Empire as "Imperial Structural Power" within an Asian International Order', in Falola and Brownell, *Africa, Empire and Globalization*, Ch. 22.

137 'Japan as an Engine of the Asian International Economy, c.1880–1936', *Japan Forum*, 2 (1990).

138 Kaoru Sugihara, 'British Imperialism, the City of London and Global Industrialisation: Some Comments on Cain and Hopkins, *British Imperialism*', *Economic Review* (Japan), 49 (1998), p. 279; Sugihara has developed this theme in Shigeru Akita and Nicholas J. White, eds. *The International Order of Asia in the 1930s and 1950s* (2010), Ch. 3.

139 Akita and Kagotani, 'The International Order of Asia in the 1930s', consider ways of fitting these views together.

140 Our own position is also that the City assisted the growth of manufacturing within and beyond the empire in ways that in the long run contributed to the process of decolonisation: above, pp. 550–51, 573–4, 593–5, 637–40, 648–9, 697–9, emphasises the importance of the 1930s as a turning point in this regard.

141 Ronald Robinson and John Gallagher with Alice Denny, *Africa and the Victorians: The Official Mind of Imperialism* (1961; 2nd ed. 1981), Ch. 2. On Thailand see Ira Klein, 'Salisbury, Rosebery and the Survival of Siam', *Journal of British Studies*, (1968); Ian G. Brown, 'British Financial Advisors in Siam in the Reign of King Chulalongkorn', *Modern Asian Studies*, 12 (1978); idem, 'Siam and the Gold Standard', *Journal of South-East Asian Studies*, 10 (1979). We also followed tradition in omitting the Pacific islands, within and beyond the empire. The best introduction is now Donald Denoon, ed. *The Cambridge History of the Pacific Islands* (Cambridge, 1997). See also Colin Newbury, 'Mammon in Paradise: Economic Enterprise in Pacific Historiography', *Jour. Imp. and Comm. Hist.*, 26 (1998).

142 Anthony J. Webster, *Gentlemen Capitalists: British Imperialism in South-East Asia, 1770–1890* (1998); Nicholas J. White, *Business and Government in the Era of Decolonisation: Malaya, 1942–57* (Oxford, 1997); idem, 'Gentlemanly Capitalism and the Empire in the Twentieth Century: The Forgotten Case of Malaya, 1914–1965', Ch. 8, in Dumett, *Gentlemanly Capitalism*; idem, 'The Business and Politics of Decolonization: The British Experience in the Twentieth Century', *Econ. Hist Rev.*, 53 (2000), and the comments by Cain and Hopkins, 'Afterword', in Dumett, *Gentlemanly Capitalism*, pp. 214–19.

143 Webster, *Gentlemen Capitalists*, Chs. 7 and 9.

144 A succinct guide to the state of the literature is Nicholas Tarling, 'The British Empire in South-East Asia', in Robin W. Winks, ed. *The Oxford History of the British Empire*, Vol. 5 (Oxford, 1999), Ch. 26.

145 Thant Myint U, *The Making of Modern Burma* (Cambridge, 2001) tells the story from the inside but in a way that enables the expanding foreign presence to be slotted into

place. His work is complemented by Webster, *Gentlemen Capitalists*, Chs. 6 and 8, and idem, 'Business and Empire: A Reassessment of the British Conquest of Burma in 1885', *Historical Journal*, 43 (2000).

146 Anthony Webster, *Gentlemen Capitalists*, Chs. 6 and 8; idem, 'Business and Empire: A Reassessment of the British Conquest of Burma in 1885', *Historical Journal*, 43 (2000); Ian Brown, The Economics of Decolonisation in Burma', in Falola and Brownell, *Africa, Empire, and Globalization*, Ch. 21.

147 See B. W. Higman, *Writing West Indian Histories* (Basingstoke, 1999); idem, 'The British West Indies', in Winks, *Oxford History*, Vol. 5, Ch. 7. The evolution of the labour force from slavery to wage-earning is one of the few themes to have engaged the attention of historians in the period after abolition.

148 Peter Clegg, 'Independence Movements in the Caribbean: Withering on the Vine?' *Commonwealth & Comparative Politics*, 50 (2012); Cary Fraser, 'Decolonization and the Cold War', in Richard Immerman and Petra Goedde, eds. *Oxford Handbook of the Cold War* (Oxford, 2013), Ch. 27; and the relevant chapters in Melvyn Leffler and Odd Arne Westad, eds. *Cambridge History of the Cold War*, I and II (2010).

149 Niels Steensgaard, *The Asian Trade Revolution of the Seventeenth Century* (Chicago, 1974).

150 Robert Brenner, *Merchants and Revolution: Commercial Change, Political Conflict and London's Mercantile Community, 1550–1653* (Princeton, 1992). See also D. W. Jones, *War and Economy in the Age of William III and Marlborourgh* (Oxford, 1988).

151 K. N. Chaudhuri, *The Trading World of Asia and the English East India Company, 1660–1760* (Cambridge, 1978).

152 Lakshi Subramaniam, *Indigenous Capital and Imperial Expansion: Bombay, Surat and the West Coast* (Oxford, 1996); Om Prakesh, *New Cambridge History of India, Vol. 5: European Commercial Enterprise in Pre-Colonial India* (Cambridge, 1998). Historians have also revised the stereotype of 'backward Spain'. See Regina Grafe, *Distant Tyranny: Markets, Power, and Backwardness in Spain, 1650–1800* (Princeton, 2012). Nevertheless, David Goodman has shown that the navy was poorly funded and badly managed: *Spanish Naval Power, 1589–1665* (Cambridge, 1996); and José Jurado Sánchez, 'Military Expenditure, Spending Capacity and Budget Constraints in Eighteenth-Century Spain and Britain', *Revista de Historia Económica*, 27 (2009), contrasts Spain's inferior financial institutions with those of Britain.

153 Kenneth Pomeranz, *The Great Divergence: China, Europe and the Making of the Modern World Economy* (Princeton, 2000); the riposte by Ricardo Duchesne, *The Uniqueness of Western Civilisation* (Leiden, 2011); and the full assessment by Peer Vries, *State, Economy and the Great Divergence: Great Britain and China, 1680s to 1860s* (2014).

154 John Maynard Keynes, *General Theory of Employment, Interest and Money* (1936), Ch. 12.

155 Peter Cain, 'Afterword: the Economics of the "British World"', *Journal of Imperial and Commonwealth History*, 40 (2013).

156 Juan Pablo Pardo-Guerra, 'Imagined Worlds: Gentlemanly Capitalism, Narrative and the Reinvention of Culture in British Finance'. (unpublished paper, 2014). We are very grateful to Dr Pardo-Guerra of the London School of Economics for allowing us to reference his work before publication.

157 Two examples of historians who have boldly gone with the idea of gentlemanly capitalism where we never expected it to go, are: M. S. J. Hodge, 'Capitalist Contexts for Darwin's Theory: Land, Finance, Industry and Empire', *Journal of the History of Biology* 42 (2009); and Cannon Schmitt, 'Rumour, Shares and Novelistic Form: Joseph Conrad's *Nostromo*', in Nancy Henry and Cannon Schmitt, eds. *Victorian Investment: New Perspectives on Finance and Culture* (Bloomington, 2009).

158 These possibilities are explored further in the Afterword.

PART ONE

Introduction, 1688–1914

1

THE PROBLEM AND THE CONTEXT

In a decolonised world the empire no longer strikes back, but there is a sense in which it lives on after its demise. The present generation, the first in Britain for some 300 years to survey a world without prominent imperial landmarks, has seen a remarkable increase of interest in the empire, as witness the formidably impressive volume of historical research published since the 1950s and the growth of public nostalgia for a world we have lost and, in some respects, may never have had. Given that the explosion of research can intimidate as well as aid further scholarship and that the imperial content of novels and television programmes may be approaching saturation level, the appearance of yet another book on British imperialism needs an explicit justification beyond that provided by the enduring importance of the subject itself. In the case of a general work, such as this one, good cause can be shown either by updating previous surveys or by venturing a new interpretation. It is difficult to say which is the more hazardous enterprise: the former threatens to bury the surveyor alive under an avalanche of specialised research which descends faster than it can be moved; the latter offers the prospect of ordeal by public exposure, a fate reserved for those who suppose that they have something new to say on a topic which, being so vast, has absorbed novelties from more ingenious minds in the course of the past century.

Well might prospective authors pause before setting course for a journey which harbours such irreducible risks. Our own route follows the high road in search of novelty but also scans the alternatives by synthesising a good deal of detailed research. Whether this decision provides insurance against disaster, or compounds the risk by inviting two fates instead of one, is for readers to judge. Our aspiration developed, not out of a sense of superior vision, but from a need to address some basic anomalies in existing explanations of the impulse towards imperial expansion; our commitment took shape when our lectures on this subject, having reached the high point of exegesis so readily inspired by criticism of others, were eventually brought down to earth by the formidable and protracted task of constructing an alternative. This sobering experience has enhanced our appreciation of the contribution made by our predecessors, even where we disagree with them. Indeed, the fact that there have been so few attempts to offer a fundamental reappraisal of the causes of British imperialism during the century which has passed since Sir John Seeley published *The Expansion of England* suggests just how extraordinarily difficult it is to devise an interpretation which combines an awareness of the detailed literature with a measure of independence from existing approaches, whether marked out by apologists or by enemies of empire.[1]

The discussion which follows seeks to place our own contribution in its wider analytical framework. We begin by setting the issue we have chosen to address, that of the causes of imperialism, in its historiographical context and by outlining the evolution of our own views on the subject. Any interpretation of a problem as vast as this one necessarily involves the use of correspondingly large terms which, if left undefined, may confuse the reader and which, if improperly defined, may also prejudice the argument. The rest of the chapter is therefore devoted to laying out for inspection the assumptions and concepts which underpin our interpretation. We continue by defining our use of the term 'capitalism' and by drawing attention to its hitherto underemphasised non-industrial forms. This discussion leads to a consideration of the social agents of capitalist enterprise, and here we lay stress on the concept of gentility and its relationship to economic activity and political authority. The implication of this approach, that manufacturing interests had less influence on the formulation of economic and international policy than has usually been assumed, is then made explicit, though this conclusion is not to be read as an attempt to minimise the importance of the process of industrialisation. We next examine the overseas manifestations of what we term 'gentlemanly capitalism' by looking specifically at the concept of imperialism and at its various guises. Finally, since the whole of this discussion rests upon a view of what constitutes historical explanation, we conclude with a brief statement of our methodology, not to promote the claims we make but to enable readers to evaluate them.

The historiographical setting

The difficulty of making an effective case for looking at the causes of British imperialism afresh may suggest that the answers are already known, or at least that one interpretation has come to dominate the subject to the extent of threatening to make its rivals redundant. There have certainly been times when a particularly illuminating thesis has gained majority support among liberals or radicals (though never among both). But no solution has proved to be permanent, and if there is one judgement that scholars of different persuasions can agree on today it is that no such certainties exist at present. Specialists will have their own explanations of why the growth of knowledge should have brought less, and not more, coherence to historical understanding. Our own argument will be that the central weakness in existing accounts of overseas expansion and imperialism is that they underplay or misjudge the relationship between the British economy and Britain's presence abroad. Putting the metropolitan economy back at the centre of the analysis, we suggest, makes it possible to establish a new framework for interpreting Britain's historic role as a world power.

Writers in the Marxist tradition cannot, of course, be accused of underplaying this relationship, but in our view they often misjudge both the development of the British economy and its links with overseas expansion. The classical theories of Marxist imperialism will be considered later, but it is clear that their modern successors have allotted a crucial role to industrialisation in precipitating imperialism[2] and that this position, as we shall try to demonstrate, is ill-founded. Neo-Marxist analyses of imperialism suffer from other serious weaknesses. Key terms such as 'capitalism' are insufficiently defined and are applied with too much generality to retain their explanatory power;[3] the use made of historical evidence is at times quixotic;[4] and a primary concern with the underdevelopment of regions outside Europe has led to a stereotyped view of the 'exploiting metropole'.[5] Although these interpretations have achieved considerable popularity in recent years, it is perhaps worth noting that their greatest influence has been on social scientists other than historians.

The large number of scholars who deny the existence of a close relationship between the development of the home economy and imperialist forms of expansion draw on two influential traditions. The first, which prevailed down to the 1950s, confined the study of imperialist impulses to the creation and evolution of colonies which made up the constitutional empire.[6] This definition gave the presentation of imperial history a political and legal bias, and this was reinforced by the fact that economic history was still in its infancy. In a world of shifting concepts the formal empire, the area painted red on the map, had a reassuringly solid physical presence. On inspection, however, its limitations readily became apparent. In the first place, the constitutional standing of the member-countries was neither identical nor fixed. Some parts of the empire rose to dominion status and acquired considerable formal control over their own affairs; others remained crown colonies, governed from London and subordinated in all significant matters of policy to decisions made in Westminster; in between were various intermediate categories, such as protectorates, mandates and condominiums.[7] Historians usually deal with this problem by sorting the empire into different constitutional groups. This strategy serves for narrative purposes, but it leaves untouched the central issue of the degree of control exercised by the centre, for this is not necessarily measured by an index of constitutional standing.

The second important influence stems from the work of Robinson and Gallagher, which has set the agenda for the study of imperial history during the last forty years. Robinson and Gallagher were the first historians to give prominence to the distinction between the formal empire of legal control and the 'informal' empire of influence and were also the progenitors of the 'peripheral' or 'excentric' theory of imperialism.[8] The concept of informality has helped to define imperial history in terms of the various frontiers and peripheries which were created or touched by the foreign presence. In doing so, it has greatly enlarged the earlier orthodoxy, with its narrow focus on political formalities. According to Robinson and Gallagher, the formal empire was the tip of an iceberg: submerged below the waterline lurked the invisible or informal empire, which at times was larger than the area under sovereign control. Members of the informal empire saw neither colonial governors nor colonial tax-gatherers, but they remained, nevertheless, under London's economic, cultural or diplomatic dominion. The notion of informal empire has prompted a long-running debate between its advocates, for whom the invisible has indeed materialised, and the sceptics, who question the validity of elevating an informal presence to imperial status. The controversy has flagged in recent years, not least because of the admitted difficulty of giving precision to such a broad concept;[9] but the debate has been invaluable in underlining the importance of considering shades of influence, degrees of effective control and measures of diminished sovereignty. In theory at least, it is now hard, though not impossible, to write a naive history of British imperialism.

The coverage offered by the present study examines the central issue of the exercise of power in international relations by considering both regions which were brought into the formal empire and those which remained outside it. We accept, of course, the need to give prominence to the constitutional empire because of its collective importance, whatever measure is chosen, in the history of British imperial expansion. Accordingly, we have examined the leading constituents, Canada, Australia, New Zealand, India and Africa, in some detail, though our survey of the empire is not fully comprehensive.[10] Outside the formal empire, we have chosen as case studies South America, China and the Ottoman Empire, regions where Britain's presence was both prominent and subject to keen rivalry from other foreign powers. Following our previous discussion, we do not assume that effective influence within the empire can be easily inferred from the constitutional status of the territory concerned; nor do we begin by supposing that Britain's informal influence automatically gave her an informal empire. Our procedure, in both cases, is to consider what Britain's interests were, how they were represented, and with what results in terms of limiting the independence of other countries. This involves an assessment, where the evidence permits, of different levels of influence – from the 'rules of the game' governing international relations to business pressures and domestic political decisions.

According to Robinson and Gallagher, the extension of informal empire was the outstanding feature of Britain's expansion overseas after 1815. They linked the spread of informal control to Britain's growing need for new markets and sources of supply as industrialisation proceeded, though without specifying the precise relation between the changing economy and the informally dominated frontier. On this view, informal empire was preferred to formal rule largely because it was cheap; but informal control could be exercised only if the frontier territory was both willing and able to cope with the impact of Britain's invading influence by throwing up local collaborators. However, despite linking the expansion of both formal and informal empire before 1870 to the process of economic development, and especially to industrialisation, Robinson and Gallagher claimed that economic or social change in Britain was of insufficient importance thereafter to account for the rapid expansion of formal empire in Africa and Asia at the close of the century. Instead, they directed attention to the periphery and, in particular, to the collapse of the collaborative regimes which had sustained Britain's informal presence, to the activities of independent (or at least semi-independent) sub-imperialists on the frontiers, and to Britain's need to counter the expansive tendencies of other industrialising nations which established themselves as world powers for the first time after 1870. One clear implication of this analysis was that the growth of the formal empire was a product of Britain's relative decline as a great power: the extension of sovereignty in Africa was only a poor recompense for the shrinkage of the informal economic empire elsewhere. This 'peripheral' theory of imperialism has informed many of the major recent studies of both European and British expansion overseas in the late nineteenth and early twentieth centuries.[11]

The peripheral interpretation was an understandable and appropriate response to two powerful contemporary influences. The first, the intellectual climate created by the Cold War, produced an awareness of Britain's own subordination to the United States and provoked a reaction to Marxist theories, and especially to their metropolitan-based determinism and often cavalier treatment of evidence. The second influence sprang from decolonisation, which encouraged a shift away from traditional imperial history and created a new interest in the history of former colonial territories. By combining opposition to the intellectual dirigisme of Marxism with the fruits of fresh research on and beyond the frontiers of empire, the peripheral thesis offered an appealing way of updating liberal interpretations of imperialism. Any analysis of imperialism advanced today undoubtedly needs to demonstrate an awareness of the now considerable literature connecting European interests and indigenous societies.

To accept this point, however, is not necessarily to accept the peripheral thesis, any more than to establish a metropolitan economic basis for imperialism is to embrace Marxism. Precise judgement on this issue depends on the exact weight attributed to the periphery as a cause of imperialism, and on this matter proponents of the thesis speak with different inflections. Dilute versions amount to a plea for incorporating new evidence on the turbulent frontier by making space for the part played by sub-imperialists and by indigenous societies themselves in resisting imperialist forces or negotiating with them. This is a welcome and, in principle, an uncontroversial corrective to older approaches.

The strong version of the thesis, however, makes the far larger claim that the fundamental cause of imperialism is to be found on the periphery itself. This claim runs into serious objections stemming from a degree of analytical imprecision underlying the thesis. One problem is that the peripheral approach cannot account for the fact that local crises occurred in identifiable chronological clusters in parts of the world often far removed from each other, except by appealing to a law of coincidence which itself is an admission of weakness. A further problem arises from the failure to distinguish symptoms from causes. To identify crises on the periphery is not necessarily to prove that they had their origins there. The strongest version of the thesis ought to be able to demonstrate not only that there was friction on the frontier (in itself a commonplace finding), but also that its origins lay in independent developments within the local society concerned. In theory, this is perfectly possible: the ideal case would hold the European presence constant and show that the local crisis which drew foreign interests (reluctantly) inland emerged from deep-seated demographic, religious or other causes which had not been provoked or significantly altered by previous external influences.

As it happens, however, the leading advocates of the peripheral thesis have yet to make this case. They focus on local crises at points where European and indigenous interests intersect, and attribute the cause to the locality and personalities involved. But, as we have just suggested, this perspective may focus on the symptoms rather than the cause, and it certainly mistakes part of the cause for the totality. It seems reasonable to conclude that, from the perspective adopted here, the peripheral thesis is as valuable but also as modest as its name implies: it examines aspects of causation which are restricted to the periphery. It is not, in principle, in conflict with a view from the metropolis which aims to show how the frontier came into being and to identify the underlying causes of turbulence which expressed themselves in local crises.

The attempt to downplay the role of economic change in the metropole and to shift causation to the periphery has not passed unchallenged. Inspired initially by the work of D.C.M. Platt,[12] some imperial historians have emphasised the importance of the 'Great Depression' in the late nineteenth century in rousing British business pressure groups to agitate for safe markets in an expanded empire and to demand government backing in their search for new openings for commodity exports and capital investment in hitherto marginal areas, like China.[13] The pressure exerted by Chambers of Commerce and other influential groups representing business to extend the boundaries of formal empire in tropical Africa when trade was depressed has also been thoroughly documented;[14] a host of monographs and articles on the background to specific imperialist episodes has suggested that the crises on the periphery which led to extensions of British control were often triggered by economic changes originating in the metropolitan economy. In 1980, our own dissatisfaction with the peripheral thesis led us to try to synthesise this growing body of research and to relate its findings more closely to the evolution of the British economy as revealed by the recent work of economic historians.[15]

The resulting essay indicated that there was a correlation between changes in economic structure and in the nature and pace of growth of Britain's overseas trade on the one hand, and the extension of informal and formal control abroad on the other. But the argument suffered from two important defects. In the first place, although the article gave some prominence to the importance of invisible income and foreign investment after 1850, and endeavoured to connect this with imperialism, it gave industry, and provincial manufacturers and merchants, too much space in the story and did not pay the service sector enough attention. Secondly, it proved impossible, except in one or two exceptional cases, to establish that the business agitation which was so clearly apparent in times of crisis, both in Britain and on the frontier, actually influenced the decisions of the policy-makers. Robinson and Gallagher assumed that what they called the 'official mind' was separate from business, free of its influence and capable of acting in the national interest rather than merely responding to the narrow prejudices of the market-place. Subsequent research, pointing to the social gulf between gentlemanly governing elites and 'trade', seemed to magnify this particular problem.[16] In the circumstances, it was quite reasonable for the supporters of the peripheral thesis to claim that, even when British interests on the frontier were purely economic, governments would act to extend British authority only when some political problem on that frontier, arising from the local situation – for example a breakdown in law and order – appeared to affect the national interest.[17]

In 1986 we tried to remedy these defects by developing a clearer line of argument based on the evolution of what we called 'gentlemanly capitalism'.[18] This advance was greatly helped by the publication of new research on the service sector and the City of London. The evidence now available makes it possible to argue that the rapid growth of services after 1850 is the key to a better understanding of the peculiar nature of British overseas expansion and imperialism. If commerce and finance were the most dynamic element in the nation's economic thrust overseas, then concentrating on the rise of services rather than upon the decline of industry inevitably changes perspectives on imperialism, down-grading to some extent the importance of formal acquisitions, including the Scramble for Africa, while bringing into better focus a vigorous and expanding informal presence, notably in areas of white settlement.

Furthermore, our reading of the literature on services and finance led us to conclude that the periodisation of British imperialism needed to be recast. It became clear that our analysis ought to be pushed back to cover the financial revolution and the rise of the 'moneyed interest' at the close of the eighteenth century, and extended well beyond 1914, which is the conventional halting point for studies of Britain's imperial expansion, and, accordingly, for the debate over the existence of informal empire too. However, in 1986 we were concerned principally to suggest a way of looking at British history afresh, and our treatment of the imperial dimension was necessarily and deliberately abbreviated. In the present study, and with more space at our disposal, we hope to substantiate claims on both fronts. Even so, it has proved impossible to analyse all three centuries of British and world history with the degree of detail needed to engage fully with the specialised literature. We have dealt with the resulting problem of emphasis by outlining our argument for the period as a whole in this chapter and in the Conclusion (Chapter 27), by treating the eighteenth century and the period after 1939 in more schematic fashion in Chapter 2 and in the penultimate chapter of the book, and by concentrating on the sizeable period in between. This has enabled us to focus on the principal debates about British imperialism at the time when the empire was at its greatest extent, and to reappraise the period after World War I, when discussion of colonial nationalism and imperial decline gathers pace. The alternative would have been to have begun in 1815 or 1850 and to have ended in 1914 or 1939 without incorporating previous or subsequent events, except perhaps as part of a brief sketch of the general historical context. Our compromise, imperfect though it is, ought to make it possible for readers to see how our interpretation applies to the whole period and should enable specialists to enlarge the argument should they wish to do so.

Examining service-sector capitalism also provides the crucial link between the economy and the process of decision-making, since senior officials were recruited from the service sector and were inevitably infected by its perspectives and its values. In other words, we would now argue with some confidence that it is impossible to separate the world of 'acceptable' business from that of elite politicians and from their perceptions of the national interest. If leading politicians were invariably gentlemen, they were also products of the most successful part of British capitalism; some of them were major participants in non-industrial enterprise at home and abroad. Hence our conviction that a fuller understanding of the connections between British economy and society and British imperialism requires a close acquaintance with gentlemanly capitalism.

In reaching this position we must acknowledge our indebtedness to some of the classic contributions to the understanding of the emergence of modem imperialism. In emphasising finance, services and other non-industrial sources of wealth and power in our own inquiries we are returning, to some extent, to the preoccupations of the classical theorists of imperialism whose ideas were formulated in the first 30 years of the century. Most of the early theories, including the Marxist variants associated with writers such as Hilferding and Lenin, were attempts to understand continental economies whose history and structures were different in crucial respects from those of Britain. Moreover, the most popular version of the original thesis of finance or monopoly capitalism, that put forward by Lenin in *Imperialism: The Highest Stage of Capitalism* (1916), suffers from serious analytical flaws, as even sympathetic critics now acknowledge.[19] Nonetheless, these theories have proved useful in helping us to put British imperialism in a global context.

We must also recognise how much we have learned from those early theorists who claimed that imperialism could be understood only by attending, not to modern capitalism itself, but to the fact that capitalism was under the social and political direction of older elites. Joseph Schumpeter, writing in 1919 with the recent industrialisation of the European continent in mind, felt that there was still a marked distinction between the aristocracy and the bourgeoisie: 'the social pyramid of the present age has been formed, not by the substance and laws of capitalism alone, but by two different social substances and the laws of two different epochs'.[20] The bourgeoisie were the main creators of wealth and the great driving force behind economic and social change; but ideologically and politically they were dependent upon the prestige of the landed and military classes who could use the power of capitalism to further their own, profoundly anti-capitalist, ends. Heirs to an age-old tradition of warfare and conquest, the dominant elites of Europe had bent capitalism to their will, and the rampant imperialism of the recent past, like World War I itself, was the outcome. Had the capitalists managed to sweep away feudal power or had the traditional force 'changed its profession and function and become the ruling class of the capitalist world',[21] then, Schumpeter believed, the cultural life of modem Europe would have been profoundly different. In this case, imperialism (which he seems to have equated with the extension of formal empires) might never have existed because capitalism, if left to develop freely, would have laid the foundations for international peace by bringing about economic interdependence among nations. As the European country which had industrialised first and moved furthest from feudalism, Britain seemed to Schumpeter less prone to imperialist aggression than her neighbours and nearer the ultimate (and historically inevitable) goal of pacific internationalism.

Schumpeter's pure and pacific capitalism has yet to make an appearance and is not now expected. On the other hand, his insight that the capitalist system's development was significantly affected by the non-capitalist environment from which it sprang and that imperialism cannot be understood simply as a manifestation of modern economic forces, is a profound one. But, whereas Schumpeter stressed the gulf between traditional elites and the modern economy, our own emphasis is placed on the extent to which capitalism and tradition came to terms with each other to create a unique domestic 'substance' and, as a result, to produce a unique form of overseas expansion and imperialism. We argue that the rulers of Britain in the seventeenth and eighteenth centuries changed their 'profession and function' to a considerable degree, and that out of the union between land and the market emerged what we have called gentlemanly capitalism. As we have already suggested (and will demonstrate in detail later), gentlemanly capitalism then developed in ways which emphasised the distance between land, high finance and the upper reaches of the service sector on the one side, and mechanical industry on the other. There was no sharp, Schumpeterian antithesis between aristocracy and capitalism in Britain after 1850, but there was a distinction to be drawn between gentlemanly and industrial capital. The former set the cultural tone, was closer to the centre of power and was the dominant influence upon the expression of that power overseas. In this connection, we should also point out that Schumpeter's concern was to show how ruling elites distorted and used an alien force, capitalism, which would eventually destroy them. In our own account, capitalism is actually absorbed by the elites and adapted to suit their needs; from this perspective, imperialism becomes one of the methods by which that elite can prosper and continually renew itself.

In this particular context, we should mention also the work of Thorstein Veblen, the most neglected of the classical writers on the subject of modern imperialism. Like Schumpeter, Veblen saw imperialism as being driven mainly by the needs of old-fashioned, dynastic power structures which harnessed capitalist wealth to their own purposes. At the same time, he recognised the inevitability of the development of big business and worked out a theory of 'business enterprise' which had strong similarities to Hilferding's finance capitalism. Most of Veblen's reasoning was based upon a close study of American capitalism and of the evolving relationship between new forms of business enterprise and traditional landed hierarchies in Wilhelmine Germany. Nonetheless, Veblen was well aware that British capitalism had followed a different historical course and that traditional elites in Britain had come to terms with the market to an unusual degree. Hence his description of British policy-makers as 'gentlemanly investors' and his recognition of the fact that they were the key actors in the drama of British imperialism.[22]

J.A. Hobson's writings have been a further valuable source of inspiration. Hobson's claim that 'finance is . . . the governor of the imperial engine'[23] led him far too frequently to assume that politicians were in the pockets of the most powerful men in the City, and his tendency to resort to conspiracy theories, perhaps exacerbated by his occasional employment as a journalist on sensitive imperial frontiers, has often discredited him in the eyes of modern historians. Moreover, unlike his Marxist contemporaries, Hobson tended, as did Schumpeter, to identify imperialism with the subjugation of 'backward nations' in Africa and Asia, and he never offered an analysis of imperialism that accounted for the vast flows of capital to the emerging Dominions and to South America. He also shared with Schumpeter the naive idea that it was possible to find a form of capitalism that would bring peace and prosperity to all.

Despite these flaws, Hobson sometimes showed a better understanding of the unique nature of the British economy and its international ramifications than his contemporaries or many of his later critics. He drew a distinction between the industrial north and the service-sector south which, though crude by modern standards and somewhat disfigured by his own political prejudices, we can now see to have been basically valid and important. Hobson was sure that this division was vital to a true understanding of imperialism, since the foreign investment which lay behind it emanated largely from the south of England. And he was aware, too, of the extent to which the prestige accompanying Britain's particular brand of imperialism derived from the links between modern finance and traditional sources of power. Hobson was too astute to believe that export manufacturers were free of the taint of imperialism or that they did not benefit from it materially, but he always felt that industrialists were contained within a power system they neither directed nor controlled. The most interesting of Hobson's ideas from our vantage point do not figure prominently in his most famous work, *Imperialism: A Study,* first published in 1902, and his other writings on imperialism have only recently received some of the scholarly attention they deserve.[24] But his British version of the theory of finance capital has been important in helping us to put together our own picture of the domestic origins of imperialism, to which we now turn.

The argument

The detailed argument we wish to advance begins with the observation that modern British history is bound up with the evolution of several separate but interacting forms of capitalist enterprise – agricultural, commercial and financial, as well as industrial. This initial statement is not designed to point towards a naive, multicausal interpretation of imperialism which includes everything and explains very little; nor is it intended to promote a new, albeit broadly-based form of economic determinism. But it does involve some reconsideration of capitalism both as a concept and in its historical application; it also requires a reappraisal of the social agents of capitalist enterprise, particularly, as we shall see, the role of that elusive creature, the English gentleman.

Historians approach the definition of large terms with a degree of caution which suggests their keen awareness of the prospect of failure. Short definitions are inadequate and long definitions are rarely practicable, while the absence of definitions lays a trap for others to spring. In the case of the much-discussed concept of capitalism, our main purpose is to clarify the usage adopted here rather than to tilt at the impossible by trying to establish a universal and eternal meaning. Evidently, if the definition is too broad it will explain everything and therefore nothing; if it is drawn too narrowly it will fail by excluding phenomena that need to be explained.

Some attributes of capitalism are uncontroversial: profit-seeking, individualism, specialisation, a market economy, rational calculation and the postponement of present consumption for the sake of future returns are characteristics that enter most definitions, if in varying proportions and combinations. Other features, however, are sometimes implied or even omitted. To take just one example, Braudel and Wallerstein, in their different ways, use the term to refer to exchange relationships generally without linking them to productivity gains or to the commercialisation of factors of production.[25] This definition is adequate for the purpose of contrasting exchange with subsistence, but it misses the cumulative element in capitalist enterprise, which in turn provides the key to its ability to transform as well as to expand economic structures. Marx and Weber both distinguished between mercantile or trading capitalism and other forms, especially those which held out the prospect of continuous accumulation by the application of capital (and, for Weber, capital accounting) to the production of manufactures.

Considering capitalism as an abstract construction opens the way to further, virtually boundless, theoretical discussion. Our aim at this point, however, is simply to list the ingredients of an uncontentious definition in order to avoid prefabricating its historical forms and stages. In fact, nearly all historical discussion has followed the classic evolutionary route, beginning with hunting and gathering and moving on to agriculture, commerce and industry, and has focused on the transition from pre-capitalist structures to industrial capitalism – with an optional extension to post-industrial society. Economists have traditionally endorsed this progression, which they have seen as a transition in three stages: from primary to secondary and finally to tertiary activity.[26] As a generalisation at the highest level, this conception of history has considerable merit. When tailored to specific events and periods, however, it can misconstrue the history of capitalism by minimising or misplacing activities which, though meeting the criteria listed above, do not fit into accepted categories or phases. Established approaches to modern British economic history, for example, concentrate on explaining one central problem, the cause and course of the Industrial Revolution. One consequence of this focus is to rank developments in the eighteenth century according to their function in promoting or retarding future industrialisation; another is to underplay the role of important non-industrial activities in the nineteenth century; and a third is to treat events in the twentieth century as the outcome of Britain's decline as an industrial power.

This focus has an evident and powerful justification: Britain did create the world's first Industrial Revolution, and the process of industrialisation is undoubtedly central to modern British history. To accept these propositions, however, is not necessarily to agree that the emphasis has been correctly placed or that the connections with antecedent and subsequent events have been well joined. We shall argue here that non-industrial forms of capitalist enterprise, particularly those in finance and commercial services, have not received the historical recognition they deserve, and that they were in fact much more important in terms of output and employment before, during, and after the Industrial Revolution than standard interpretations of British economic history allow. They also had a greater degree of independence than has been acknowledged: their role in history was not merely to serve as minor contributors to the industrial revolution before being subsumed by it; nor were they simply offshoots of one of its subsequent development stages. The prosperity of the financial and service sector was derived from land and from trade in goods other than British manufactured exports, as well as from the products of the Industrial Revolution. Productivity gains in the transactions sector played a part in keeping staple exports competitive in overseas markets after manufacturing had entered a less innovative phase.[27]

This interpretation runs against both an older, heroic conception of the Industrial Revolution and a newer, growth-oriented historiography which tends to equate development with industrialisation. As we shall try to show, however, our argument is consistent with specialised, if still fragmented, research on British history which has begun to appear in recent years. It draws support, too, from the work of economists whose interest in the service sector has been stimulated by the problem of deindustrialisation, by the emergence of post-industrial societies, and by development prospects in the Third World.[28]

No satisfactory definition of services has yet been devised.[29] At the most general level, and often for purposes of national accounting, services are treated as a vast residual, the sum of all activities which are neither primary nor secondary. This approach has the minor merit of tidiness, but its inherently negative quality and its presumption that the definition of primary and secondary activities is unproblematic severely limit its value. More positively, efforts have been made to classify services from the perspectives of production and consumption. This approach yields two slightly different lists, the former being the larger because it includes intermediate services, whereas the latter is restricted to services intended for final demand. Both have their uses, but they obviously carry different implications for the analysis and measurement of the service sector as a whole. Attempts to identify characteristics which are common to all services have concentrated on the fact that they supply a demand but are not physical commodities. In Adam Smith's phrase, they 'perish in the very instant of their performance'; that is to say, a service is acquired as it is produced and cannot be stocked. Moving and selling goods are services because they connect points of supply and demand by acts of transport and exchange which are not, in themselves, storable commodities. This definition produces a substantial list of activities, notably in banking, insurance, the professions, communications, distribution, transport, public service and a multiplicity of personal services. It is in this sense and with these occupations in mind that we refer, in general terms, to the service sector.

It is apparent from this list of occupations that the service sector is closely linked with other sectors, and that part of the problem of definition (and measurement) stems from the intimacy of the connection. As we have noted, the conventional assumption, though one which has attracted little historical research, is that services were the junior, dependent partner of manufacturing during the classic phase of industrialisation and achieved a sizeable degree of importance and independence only at a late stage, uncertainly dated but clearly identified as post-industrialism; it is easy to see how this belief, together with the somewhat intangible quality of service activities, has led to the view that services are essentially derivative from and even parasitic on the anterior and superior process of producing goods, and do not themselves create 'real' value.[30]

A full consideration of these complex issues would involve a lengthy detour from our intended course; but some brief comments on the role of the service sector are required to underpin the historical discussion which follows. Our argument treats services as being dynamic rather than passive: it sees the service sector as being characterised by a process, referred to by Bhagwati as splintering, which allows services to be derived from goods but also enables goods to be derived from services.[31] This process involves specialisation, productivity gains, and the transformation of production. Specialisation, as we shall see, took place through the more or less continuous creation of new employments in the service sector, beginning, as far as this study is concerned, with the rise of the new moneyed interest in the eighteenth century. Productivity gains arose from innovations such as bills of exchange, actuarial tables, transport improvements, company law, the financial press, and the submarine cable – to cite just a few varied examples from an extensive list. The transformation of production occurred most obviously through the creation of export economies in many parts of the world beyond Europe, where British finance, transport and allied commercial services were much in evidence. The relationship between finance and domestic production, especially manufacturing, is a complex matter which will be referred to later in this study. For the present, it can be said that the City of London (and to a large extent the banking system in general) played a much greater part in financing the distribution of manufactured goods than it did in their production. Whether or not the City's separation from manufacturing retarded Britain's industrial progress is an important and controversial subject in its own right. It is not, however, one that we propose to explore fully here because the outcome does not affect the substance of our argument, which is to relate the City and associated activities to an understanding of Britain's presence abroad rather than to the debate over the timing and causes of Britain's decline as an industrial power.

One crucial characteristic of the service sector needs special emphasis in the context of the present argument: in its higher reaches it provided suitable occupations for gentlemen. However, before taking our argument further, we must first define what we mean by gentility and explain the nature of the relationship between the gentleman and the market.

Gentility and the market

The English gentleman was made as well as born.[32] Gentle birth conferred an unmatched advantage, the lustre of time; but gentle status could also be acquired by initiation. The history of the English gentleman is therefore one of continuous evolution accompanied by social tension, as established gentlemen, whose rank was burnished by age, were confronted by aspirants whose time had not quite come. The fact that definitions of gentlemanly status were constantly shifting, albeit subtly and slowly, undoubtedly presents problems for historical generalisation; equally, however, changes in the meaning of the term provide a way of plotting the moving contours of English social history over a long period of time.

In their ideal form, however, the main qualities of gentility remained fixed points of reference from Chaucer to Waugh.[33] The perfect gentleman adhered to a code of honour which placed duty before self-advancement. His rules of conduct were Christian as well as feudal in inspiration, and his rank entitled him to a place in the vanguard of Christ's army, though with the knights and officers rather than among the infantry. Young gentlemen passed through a long process of education designed to meld these social and religious values; subsequently, they commanded positions in society which provided them with sufficient leisure to practise the gentlemanly arts, namely leadership, light administration and competitive sports. A gentleman required income, and preferably sizeable wealth, but he was not to be sullied by the acquisitive process any more than he was to be corrupted by the power which leadership entailed.

In an order dominated by gentlemanly norms, production was held in low repute. Working directly for money, as opposed to making it from a distance, was associated with dependence and cultural inferiority. Writing well after machine industry had become an accepted feature of life in Europe and America, Veblen observed that

> there are few of the better class who are not possessed of an instinctive repugnance for the vulgar forms of labour. . . . Vulgar surroundings . . . and vulgarly productive occupations are unhesitatingly condemned and avoided. . . . From the days of the Greek philosophers to the present, a degree of leisure and of exemption from contact with such industrial processes as serve the immediate everyday purposes of human life has ever been recognised by thoughtful men as a pre-requisite to a worthy or beautiful, or even a blameless, human life.[34]

The problem of living in the world while also rising above its sordid realities was negotiated by a process of delicate social diplomacy. Gentlemen bridged the gap between their need for income and their disdain for work by participating in approved activities, the most favoured of which interposed an appropriately wide distance between the mundane world of producing commodities and the higher calling of directing others, and enabled wealth to be accumulated in ways that were consistent with a gentlemanly life-style.

In this particular, as in most others, the tone of gentlemanly life was set by the ambivalent attitude to capitalism expressed by the landed aristocracy, the dominant social force in Britain until the late nineteenth century. It is easily forgotten that, initially, the most important form of capitalist wealth in Britain was the rentier capitalism which arose from the ownership of land by a numerically small elite. By the close of the seventeenth century the landed magnates had ceased to be a feudal aristocracy and were ready to embrace a market philosophy. Nonetheless, they were still the heirs of a feudal tradition: the landed capitalism which evolved in Britain after the Stuarts was heavily influenced by pre-capitalist notions of order, authority and status. Hence the emphasis which continued to be placed on land as an inalienable asset to be passed on intact, as far as possible, through the generations; the assumed primacy of relations, even economic ones, based upon personal loyalties and family connections; the 'studied opposition to the matter-of-fact attitude and business routine';[35] the contempt for the everyday world of wealth creation and of the profit motive as the chief goal of activity; and the stress laid on the link between heredity and leadership. Since the prestige of birth, together with independent means, allowed an unusual degree of freedom of action, the landed elite also had an authority 'beyond any precise professional or functional limits'. The 'cult of the amateur', so familiar until recent times in every sphere of life from sport to politics, had its origins in this 'distinctive – because innate, hereditary and hence general – character of aristocratic power'.[36]

The peculiar character of the modern British aristocracy was shaped by merging its pre-capitalist heritage with incomes derived from commercial agriculture. The landed class not only controlled the traditional levers of authority but also was the most successful element within emergent capitalism. The more a career or a source of income allowed for a life-style similar to that of the landed class, the higher the prestige it carried and the greater the power it conferred. Because of their remoteness from the world of daily work, some traditional service occupations proved compatible with the gentlemanly ideal. Indeed, gentlemen could use the weapon of social exclusion, reinforced by their political influence, to colonise and monopolise acceptable occupations, such as the higher reaches of the law, the upper echelons of the established church, and the officer class of the armed services, ensuring, as a result, that they afforded suitably high incomes.[37] Intermediate levels were filled by semi-gentlemen in the same manner; among the lower ranks were included gentlemen's gentlemen whose status – and income – reflected the prestige of those they served.

This division between gentlemanly and ungentlemanly occupations and forms of wealth is similar to Weber's distinction between 'propertied' wealth on the one hand and 'acquisitive' or 'entrepreneurial' wealth on the other.[38] The first implies a rentier interest, not just in land but in other forms of property, while the second involves active participation in the market and in the creation of goods and services. Weber recognised the generally higher status accorded to propertied wealth and the greater power and authority which it commanded.[39] In the present context, however, Weber's categories need modifying to allow for the fact that some forms of 'entrepreneurial' wealth were closer to the gentlemanly ideal than others. A line has to be drawn not just between rentiers and businessmen but also, among the latter, between those whose relationship with the productive process was direct and those whose involvement was only indirect. Manufacturing was less eligible than the service sector: even at the highest levels, captains of industry did not command as much prestige as bankers in the City.[40]

In view of the prominent position occupied by the financial and commercial activities of the City of London in the ensuing argument, it is important for us to stress that, although the City was a centre of 'entrepreneurial' activity in Weber's sense, it eventually became, in its higher reaches, a branch of gentlemanly capitalism and, as such, exercised a disproportionate influence on British economic life and economic policy. Bankers and financiers often rose to prominence in societies dominated by aristocrats because the aristocracy's propensity for 'generosity' promoted indebtedness.[41] And, as will become clear in the next chapter, the fate of the City was entwined with that of the aristocracy in Britain after 1688 – with all the expected consequences in terms of wealth, prestige and incorporation into the body politic. Before the twentieth century, the great businesses of the City generated fortunes that were much larger than those acquired in industry and they were conducted upon principles that were much closer to the ideals of gentlemanly capitalism fostered by the landed class and their supporters than to the mores of manufacturing, even before mechanisation. Merchant bankers and merchant princes, for example, could possess great wealth without at the same time having a means of support that was wholly visible. More positively, gentlemanly ideals were vital to the success of the activities discussed here because they provided a shared code, based on honour and obligation, which acted as a blueprint for conduct in occupations whose primary function was to manage men rather than machines. The greatest bankers and merchants were located in the City, close to the centres of political power, and the nature of their occupation gave them sufficient leisure to enjoy a gentlemanly life-style while enabling them to cultivate the social connections which were, at the same time, a vital source of their success in business.[42] Their activities fitted the definition of capitalism offered earlier, and they were also capitalists in the direct sense of owning, mobilising and controlling capital.

In addition, capitalists at the top of the gentlemanly hierarchy created or commanded an invaluable scarce resource which was a form of capital in itself: information. The most eminent figures in the Square Mile were those who had access to information which was either denied to others, including fellow members of the City fraternity, or which reached them at a later date. Privileged information, from which large fortunes and high standing flowed, came principally from contact with those who controlled the machinery of state. Once in the charmed circles of power, bankers gained both immediate profit and entry to a network of contacts and information that opened up additional prospects; as their connections multiplied, so too did their prestige and authority. As confidence in selected bankers grew, they were entrusted with the savings of the elite, and this advantage gave them a position in financial markets which less favoured competitors could not match. The greatest bankers were able to amass huge fortunes without having to mobilise vast stocks of their own resources because they were able to channel the capital of others. A banker's chief asset was not his immediate reserve of capital but his prestige, which depended in turn on his standing as a key agent of elite groups whose leadership was universally acknowledged. For these reasons, the relations formed between the upper reaches of the financial world on the one hand and high society and high politics on the other were rooted more in face-to-face contact and personal understandings than in perfect market competition or in the cold rationality which Weber associated with modern bureaucracy and with modernisation itself.[43]

This is not to say that all capitalists were in the service sector or that all gentlemen were capitalists. Landed wealth was the product of capitalist enterprise, even if it also produced rentier incomes, but it clearly lay outside the service sector. As our argument suggests, however, landed wealth steadily gave way to wealth generated in the service sector in the course of the nineteenth century, which is when our subject and our study begin to expand. Some other occupations, however, present more complex problems of classification. Senior military officers, clerics and civil servants were unquestionably gentlemen and their occupations can be allocated firmly to the service sector, but they scarcely qualified as capitalists. The resolution of this conundrum lies in recognising that capitalist activities in the service sector were accompanied by services which were not in themselves capitalistic. In fact, all forms of capitalism attach services and servants to themselves and may also be subject to rulers who are not capitalists either. However, it is worth remarking here that, like the landed class, gentlemen in both the private and public parts of the non-business sector became increasingly infected with the capitalist ethic. The move to meritocratic recruitment in the professions in the nineteenth century was intended both as a device to maintain and enhance gentlemanly status and as a method of rigging the market effectively once patronage had ceased to be a socially acceptable means of rationing. In this manner, the burgeoning market system in the service sector was captured and used by the forces of tradition, providing one further instance of the axiom that capitalism 'is less active than acted upon by existing forms of social stratification'.[44] Moreover, insofar as the elites in the professions and in government had any direct contact with the world of business, it was much more likely that they would meet and take advice from City financiers than from men of industry, of whom they were often both ignorant and suspicious.

Nonetheless, there is a valid distinction to be drawn between capitalism as a broadly encompassing structure and the capitalists whose activities give the structure its particular cast and colour. This distinction raises a further set of analytical issues, the most important of which, in the present context, concerns the relationship between economics and politics. It would be naive, though scarcely novel, to assume that economic wealth automatically confers political power or that government is simply the executive arm of particular class interests. On the other hand, in rejecting this view we do not feel obliged to join the esoteric (and inconclusive) discussion over the 'relative autonomy' of the state or to try to define the precise degree of 'semi-independence' enjoyed by the agents of government.[45] For our purposes, it is sufficient to accept that non-capitalist elements can and often do play an important part in a capitalist system and to outline the nature of the relationship which pertained in the historical case under review.[46]

In essence, we shall argue that the gentlemanly ethic formed a tight bond between capitalist and non-capitalist elements within service capitalism with the result that the gentlemanly elite had a common view of the world and how it should be ordered. This degree of coherence or like-mindedness explains why, at the top of the gentlemanly order, the barriers between business and government were no more than mobile Chinese walls. This is not of course to suggest that unity meant unanimity: disagreements of priority and perspective were not only possible but also common, both between the City and Whitehall and among banking houses and government departments. The point to emphasise, however, is that disputes occurred within the family. Disagreements were expressed freely because the values underlying them were not in question and because both sides were aware that they were arguing about the precise route to be taken rather than about the general direction of policy.

Given the importance of this common world view in understanding the link between economic and political dimensions of international policy, it is worth stressing at this point that the most senior British officials, at home and abroad, were drawn largely from the ranks of those whose ties were with landed, rentier or service-sector wealth rather than with industry. In the post-imperial era, members of the home civil service still exhibit an extraordinarily high degree of cohesion, which continues to flow from shared social and educational experience and is focused on London.[47] Even today, in a world increasingly characterised by impersonal relations, it is possible to speak of 'family life in the Treasury or village life in Whitehall', where 'mutual trust is a pervasive bond' and where business is transacted 'in the market place exchange of an agreed culture' – albeit a culture distanced from industrial capitalism and often hostile to it.[48]

The evolution of the gentlemanly order

While the sociology of the gentleman, and more generally of what Veblen called the leisure class, merit further exploration, our interest lies in the historical shape taken by the gentlemanly ideal.[49] The original heraldic definition of a gentleman was one who had been granted the right to possess a coat of arms. The symbolic power of this usage outlived its practical application: a gentleman continued to be identified by his bearing even though he carried a furled umbrella instead of a sword; he remained closely associated with military and civil authority; and he subscribed to the values of the landed interest long after land had ceased to be the main source of national wealth. What changed, amidst these continuities, was the social form assumed by gentlemanly rank.

The Glorious Revolution of 1688 was an important moment in this transformation because it entrenched the landed interest in the countryside and consolidated its hold on the polity. As the gentry celebrated their deliverance from the tyrannies imposed or threatened during the seventeenth century in conspicuous consumption and the revitalised pleasures of the chase,[50] so too they were reminded by commentators such as Richardson, Addison and Steele that the moral basis of privilege lay in meeting the social obligations of rank.[51] If this contest proved somewhat one-sided, it was also enlivened by claims for gentlemanly status from those whose origins lay outside the land. At the close of the seventeenth century, Locke noted that trade was 'wholly inconsistent with a gentleman's calling',[52] and early in the eighteenth century Bolingbroke campaigned to keep the new 'moneyed interest' at bay.[53] By the end of the century, however, leading financiers and merchants in the City had been accorded gentlemanly status.[54] Their promotion rewarded their support of the landed order and reflected subtle changes in the concept of property which further defined and improved the status of financial instruments and moveable goods.[55] Lower down the commercial hierarchy, Locke's dictum still applied, and newcomers who made wealth in unacceptable ways or with unacceptable speed remained beyond the pale. Nabobs could buy property and favours, but they had difficulty purchasing social status and they remained, in Burke's view, 'animated with all the avarice of the age'.[56]

The process of redefinition gathered pace from the late eighteenth century, and was decisively altered during the Victorian era, when gentlemen were produced on an unprecedented scale.[57] The public schools, reformed and greatly expanded, were the crucial agents of this transformation, creating gentlemen out of those who lacked property by educating them in country houses set in broad acres, emphasising individual effort within a context of communal endeavour, and instilling the values of order, duty and loyalty. If the content of education still emphasised the heritage from Greece and Rome, it was partly because the classical model provided a blueprint for training an elite cadre dedicated to the service of the state. The higher reaches of education were similarly infused: in the course of the century Oxford and Cambridge turned seriously to the task of equipping the new guardians with the principles of good government, while developments in political economy fashioned a new vision of progress, a complex fusion of Benthamite utilities and Tory virtues which offered a programme of moral and material advancement set within a cautious evolutionary context.[58] These developments were accompanied by a renewed reverence for royalty.[59] The panoply of state occasions was reinvented and much elaborated, the honours system was enlarged and refined by the introduction of arcane gradations, and the upper echelons of the social hierarchy were swollen by the entry of new nobles and knights.

A spirit of chivalrous medievalism left its imprint on virtually every facet of Victorian high culture – from the artistic influence of the pre-Raphaelites and the enthusiastic construction of medieval castles and gothic churches to the elaboration of a complex etiquette of deportment and manners devised to separate gentlemen from players and calculated to subdue, by the ordeal of social humiliation, those who attempted to rise above their station without first completing a long and costly *rite de passage*. In these and many other ways, Victorian England was looking back, not merely in nostalgia but with creative intent, at the same time as its technological inventiveness was opening up new economic and geographical frontiers. As the Industrial Revolution gathered pace, so too the demand for ramparts and armour rose.

A full explanation of this phenomenon falls beyond the scope of these pages, and in any case does not yet lie readily to hand. The interpretation offered here will focus on two particularly important developments. The first was the creation in the late eighteenth century of a form of new conservatism as the propertied order closed ranks against the threat of radical criticism at home and republican invasion from abroad.[60] While this conservatism carried a strong die-hard element into and through the nineteenth century, it also contained a growing and ultimately preponderant reformist strand.[61] Liberal Tories were never quite the same as progressive Whigs, but their differences were contained within a common framework of understanding. As Edward Collins's marquis explained to his attentive listener, a Manchester manufacturer: 'A Tory is a man who believes England should be governed by gentlemen. A Liberal is a man who believes any Englishman may become a gentleman if he likes'.[62] During the French Wars, political opposition at home was muted by checks on civil liberties and by a spirit of solidarity produced by the needs of national defence, and the economy was placed on a war footing funded by the continued expansion of the national debt. After 1815, however, it was clear that fundamental changes were needed to restore the health of the economy, to meet criticism of Old Corruption, and ultimately to keep civil order. The first step in meeting this challenge was to redefine the role and purpose of the ruling class; the price of survival was the introduction of far-reaching, if gradual, reforms of the constitution, of the patronage system, of social legislation and of economic policy – culminating in the shift to free trade in the middle of the century.

The second development centred on claims for gentlemanly status from a new set of aspirants in the burgeoning service sector in London and the Home Counties. From the 1820s Whigs and reforming Tories recognised the need for allies if the landed interest was to survive the reforms it had set in train. At the point where this realisation met the social and political ambitions of service interests, an alliance was struck which strengthened and greatly enlarged established ties between the land and the merchant princes and bankers of the City, and added representatives from the professions and from newer branches of tertiary employment. These claimants coveted gentility but lacked the acres and rural background needed to gain access to it. The problem was overcome in the course of the century by allowing gentlemen to be fashioned by the public schools. This compromise caused much heart-searching and moralising among social commentators, especially novelists, over the definition of gentility and the consequences of allowing the true aristocracy of birth to mingle with the pseudo-aristocracy of wealth.[63] By the late nineteenth century, however, the amalgamation had taken place and the landed interest, once the senior partner, had come to lean heavily on money made in the service sector, especially in the City of London.

The nineteenth-century gentleman was therefore a compromise between the needs of the landed interest whose power was in decline and the aspirations of the expanding service sector. In return for social recognition, the middle-class urban gentleman was co-opted into the struggle against radicalism and its looming consequence, democracy, and assigned a leading role in introducing an alternative programme of improvement. He was also seen as a counterpoise to the claims of provincial manufacturing industry, which threatened to elevate the provinces over the centre by means of money made in unacceptable ways. Finance and the service sector were vital in this regard in that they provided capitalism with an acceptable face by generating income streams that were invisible or indirect. Moreover, the gentleman's code of government purported to rise above class and rank, and to serve the interests of the nation as a whole. By exercising authority in a manner that exemplified selfless dedication to duty, the gentleman was able to justify his continued right to rule, while also defending property and privilege. It is easy to dismiss gentlemanly claims of service to the community as being rhetorical devices which were useful chiefly in protecting a privileged position in society. If this had been the case, it is hard to see how the gentleman could have survived the upheavals of nineteenth-century British society. In practice, gentlemen were often active in the community and offered leadership on terms which were generally acceptable. Hippolyte Taine, who visited Britain in the 1860s, was sure that gentlemen of 'independent fortune' were not simply 'privileged persons, ornamental parasites' or even a 'tolerated memorial', but 'an effective moving power'. Taine was equally convinced that they were 'the most enlightened, the most independent, the most useful citizens in the country' and that, at his very best, 'a real gentleman is a real noble . . . capable . . . of sacrificing himself for those whom he leads'.[64]

The imperial mission was the export version of the gentlemanly order. In some respects, indeed, the gentlemanly code appeared in bolder format abroad in order to counter the lure of an alien environment. Roman discipline had not prevented Mark Antony from 'going native'; lesser mortals needed uncompromising values and unwavering control, injections of Spartan spirit which the costly deprivations of the public school environment readily supplied.[65] When confronted with the challenge of new frontiers, gentlemen assumed proportions that were larger than life and at times became heroic figures. The empire was a superb arena for gentlemanly endeavour, the ultimate testing ground for the idea of responsible progress, for the battle against evil, for the performance of duty, and for the achievement of honour.[66]

Individual endeavour, however, has to be placed in its social context: the refurbished gentlemen who played the game overseas both expressed and reinforced the new forces emerging at home during a period of profound transformation. Not surprisingly, Britain's representatives abroad shared the social origins and values of their counterparts in the metropole. They took to paternalism as squires to the manner born, and they tried to recreate abroad the hierarchy which they were familiar with at home. British diplomacy sought to identify gentlemen abroad, to create them where they did not exist, and to decide, in the case of societies which resisted acculturation, whether to invoke the 'forbearing use of power' which Samuel Smiles regarded as being 'one of the surest attributes of the true gentleman'.[67] At the same time, the reforming principles of political economy were eagerly applied to distant lands: approved property rights, individualism, free markets, sound money and public frugality provided discipline and purpose for both moral and material life, underpinned good government and produced congenial allies. The Anglican version of the Christian message, closely entwined with economic orthodoxy, was transmitted by like-minded missionaries: the Bible accompanied the plough; spiritual rectitude marched with fiscal prudence. Utilitarians treated the empire as a vast laboratory for experimenting with scientific principles of human betterment; missionaries came to see it as a crusading vehicle for collective salvation. Together, they created a new international order in the nineteenth century by devising and implementing the world's first comprehensive development programme.

World War I decimated the gentlemanly ranks and knocked more than the edges off notions of chivalry and honour. Thereafter, commentators were more inclined to see the weaknesses in the gentlemanly ideal, to parody gentlemanly amateurs and privileged drones, and to explore, whether with regret or approval, the decline of the gentlemanly order.[68] There seems little doubt that the gentlemanly code was diluted by becoming generalised and secularised, and that democracy cost the gentleman some of his exclusiveness and respect. As W.S. Gilbert observed: 'when everybody's someone then no one's anybody'. Yet the gentlemanly ideal was not replaced by an alternative, and the widening use of the term was a measure of the spread of gentlemanly values, even if, at the fringes of rank, there was often more form than substance. At the centre, however, the upper reaches of the gentlemanly order were untroubled and to some extent reinforced by their unplanned democratic success, which increased the number of those who recognised their betters and were still willing to defer to them. The established educational routes to gentility lost none of their vitality, and the extension of gentlemanly status to top industrialists (principally those who directed large firms with headquarters in London) was less of a take-over by industry than its final absorption. Overseas, the gentlemanly code, like the gentlemanly spirit, was kept alive by the challenges of Bolshevism, nationalism and war, and was applied, after 1945, to new problems: managing the Labour Party at home, and development and decolonisation abroad.

The genius of the English, in Burke's judgement, was to infuse tradition with modernity, thereby preserving it. Gentlemanly capitalism was a formidable mix of the venerable and the new: it combined inherited and invented traditions with profitable enterprise in occupations which were compatible with gentility. The gentlemanly capitalist had a clear understanding of the market economy and how to benefit from it: at the same time he kept his distance from the ordinary and demeaning world of work. In his own sphere he was also highly efficient. Tom Paine's jibe that the nobility were men of no ability is not lacking in illustrious examples;[69] but the feudal remnants, and the tendency for aristocrats and gentlemen to behave in an 'economically irrational' manner,[70] could be useful assets in occupations which placed a premium on organising men and information rather than on processing raw materials. High finance, like high farming, called for leadership from 'opinion-makers' and trust from associates and dependants. A gentleman possessed the qualities needed to inspire confidence; and because his word was his bond transactions were both informal and efficient. Shared values, nurtured by a common education and religion, provided a blueprint for social and business behaviour. The country house led to the counting house; the public school fed the service sector; the London club supported the City. Gentlemanly enterprise was strongly personal, and was sustained by a social network which, in turn, was held together by the leisure needed to cultivate it. The predominance of in-group marriage, like the elaboration of techniques of heirship to entail property, was not a gesture to traditionalism, but a strategy to reinforce group solidarity, to create economic efficiency and political stability, and to take out an option on the future by ensuring dynastic continuity. Social proximity was aided by geographical concentration; both came together in London, the focal point of the gentleman and his activities. In this world conspicuous consumption was not merely wasteful; it was a public manifestation of substance, a refined advertisement which used hospitality to sustain goodwill, to generate new connections and to exclude those of low income or low repute.[71]

In describing how ethics fit actions, our aim has been to establish the characteristics of gentlemanly capitalism, not to pass judgement on it. We have deliberately avoided adopting the radical distinction between productive and unproductive labour, for instance, not only because it is hedged with difficulties of definition but also because it fails to recognise the capitalist qualities of the activities we have identified.[72] What can be said, however, is that the bias of incomes and status favoured gentlemanly occupations to a much greater extent than standard accounts of British economic history allow, and that the attributes of the leisured amateur, though highly effective in his own sphere of enterprise, were less well suited to the needs of industry in an age of 'scientific rationalism'.[73]

The manufacturing interest

Cobdenite entrepreneurial ideologies which stressed the need for a social revolution to place the industrial bourgeoisie at the centre of the social and political stage faced formidable barriers, even at the high point of the Industrial Revolution. The impressive success of gentlemanly capitalism in its landed form until 1850 and the growing wealth and power of service capitalism after that date meant that manufacturers who sought prestige and authority often had to adapt to gentlemanly ideals. And players could become gentlemen only by abandoning the attitudes or even the occupations which had brought them their original success.[74] The Industrial Revolution emerged from an already highly successful capitalist system, and it took place without any fundamental transformation in the nature of property ownership or in the disposition of social or political power. The benefits of the dynamic growth of manufacturing, whether via the division of labour or through the advent of machinery, were bound to lead, in these circumstances, to a large proportion of the gains accruing to non-industrial forms of property. One result of this development was that, in a society which was only slowly becoming democratic, even in the early twentieth century,[75] and where power was concentrated in the hands of wealthy elites, manufacturers neither owned enough 'top wealth' nor made it in a sufficiently acceptable way to be able to impose their will on the political system. In the nineteenth century the industrial bourgeoisie in Britain was forced to come to terms with gentlemanly capitalism: it modified rather than superseded it, and in turn felt the weight of its compelling influence. Marx's assumption that industrial capitalism was the dominant force after 1850 and that the 'moneyed interests' were subservient to it is overdrawn, as we shall see.[76]

Industrialists who traced their descent from yeomen and small gentry might refer to themselves as 'gentleman manufacturers',[77] but the claim, however authentic, was also contradictory because full-time involvement in the 'vile and mechanical' world of industry,[78] with its long hours and need for unremitting attention to detail, was incompatible with the freedom necessary to gentlemanly status.[79] Some prominent manufacturers were only too eager to use their wealth to lift their families into the landed and gentlemanly sphere, and the prestige of the gentlemanly life continued to exert a powerful influence: even Samuel Smiles, the leading ideologist of the provincial business class, held the status of an independent Christian gentleman to be the desired end of the pursuit of self-help, and it must have been difficult for his readers to dissociate this position from the life-style of the more benevolent and public-spirited of the existing gentlemanly class.[80] Radicals like Richard Cobden, who dedicated their lives to the abolition of aristocratic power and wealth in Britain, failed badly, partly because the gentlemanly ideal was so attractive; but even when industrialists were profoundly antagonistic to the landed interest and their associates, they were often forced by the pressures of working-class discontent to come to terms with the existing social order. Industrialists were the shock troops of capitalism; the hostility that they generated, especially after 1815, undermined some of the authority which growing wealth might otherwise have offered them. Given their indirect relationship to the productive process and the more fragmented and less class-conscious work-force they employed, gentlemanly capitalists could present themselves more easily as natural leaders capable of offering disinterested advice, whilst also deriving substantial benefits from developments in which industrialists were the most visible agents of change.[81] British industrialists were thus trapped between a gentlemanly culture which flourished on capitalist wealth but derided technology, and trades unionists and socialists who exalted production but were deeply suspicious of the profit motive.

From this perspective, the Industrial Revolution can be seen as a new phase in what was already a highly successful and broad-based process of economic development. Britain was the most advanced economic power in Europe long before the onset of mechanisation or the beginning of the factory system. Given aristocratic adaptation to capitalism and Britain's early achievements as a commercial and financial nation, it is hardly surprising that, in 1850, power remained largely in traditional hands or that the elite proved capable of adapting its policies to suit changing times. The re-adoption of the gold standard, the rigorous discipline exercised over government expenditure and even the initial moves towards free trade had more to do with the elite's recognition of Britain's status as an international service centre than with her position as the world's workshop. The growth of provincial manufacturing appears also to have been accompanied by a progressive withdrawal of the landed classes from contact with industry and by a reemphasis on class and status differences, including, as we have seen, a revamping of the idea and ideal of the gentleman. It is noticeable, too, that few recruits to industry came from well-connected merchants in London and the outports, and that on the occasions when industrialisation forced merchants 'to take a new look at their prospects' they went into shipping, banking and financial services in preference to industry.[82]

Despite the growth of organisations such as the Anti-Corn Law League in the 1840s, provincial manufacturing interests were not in the political mainstream in the nineteenth century. In a fiercely competitive business world, few manufacturers felt wealthy enough or secure enough to turn their attention from work to politics or to the social activities which were indispensable to political success at national level. From the standpoint of policy-makers in London, provincial manufacturers were regarded as outsiders who might become a dangerous and destabilising radical force if squeezed too hard by economic crises. In these circumstances they would have to be bought off. But there was a difference between accommodation and assimilation. Palmerston's aggressive imperialism during the severe depression of the late 1830s and early 1840s provides a perfect example of a policy designed to keep industry content but also at arm's length.

If provincial manufacturers had not found their way to the centres of power by 1850, they were unlikely to do so thereafter, despite the steady decline in the importance of agriculture and of the landed interest. Before 1850 the great staple industries were the single most important driving force in economic development; after this date the epicentre of dynamic economic change began to shift back from north to south, from export industries in the provinces to the combination of services and industries characteristic of the south-east, where the newly evolving forms of gentlemanly capitalism were most in evidence. Despite a considerable growth in the numbers of rich manufacturers, wealth derived from heavy industry did not become of overmastering importance in Britain nor did the prestige of manufacturing improve markedly, given the impressive success of non-industrial forms of capitalism, especially finance. The wealth of most manufacturing capitalists remained limited and their interests local. Before the appearance of the large firm in the twentieth century, manufacturers inhabited a world in which atomistic competition prevailed, and this had the further consequence of making political cohesion more difficult.[83] Moreover, the minority who amassed fortunes on a par with those made from land or in the City often adopted gentlemanly life-styles and attitudes, becoming incorporated into a system created by others rather than devising a distinctive and prestigious social presence of their own. As a result, economic policy continued to be the preserve of the gentlemanly elites who controlled the machinery of central government. Manchester, Leeds and Birmingham were heard of only at times when a particular event or crisis compelled them to present their case in London, where finance and commerce achieved overwhelming dominance.

The distance which separated the gentlemen of power from the bulk of the manufacturing class was graphically illustrated in the late nineteenth century, when the former grappled with the agonising problem of how and when to introduce the latter to the benefits of the honours system, the great status-conferring machine of the gentlemanly order, a system which many industrialists were only too ready to accept on terms set by the traditional holders of power and prestige.[84] It is, of course, true that heavy industry and services were interdependent and that the City and provincial exporters co-operated to their mutual benefit.[85] But, as we shall try to show, both the domestic and the international economies evolved in ways which advanced the cause of services more than the cause of export industries. This was the case after 1850, and it applied even more forcefully after 1914: when free trade cosmopolitanism came under threat, policy-makers almost automatically assumed that their chief priority was to retain Britain's status as an international financial power.

In suggesting that the influence of the manufacturing sector was relatively limited, even in the early twentieth century, it needs to be emphasised that we are attacking a presumption and a prejudice that the opposite must, somehow, have been the case, rather than adopting a paradoxical stance in the face of a substantial body of research supporting an interpretation that conflicts with our own. Historians who recognise the fact that the political elite rarely contained an industrial element often fall back on the argument that these elites maintained their position only because they were willing to carry out the wishes of their supposed masters; but, in the nature of things, this is almost impossible to prove. Direct evidence of successful industrial pressure is even harder to come by, and the number of empirical studies of the influence of manufacturers on imperial policy is very limited. Indeed, few scholars take care to differentiate between manufacturers and businessmen in general; but what little information there is tends to suggest that, although provincial industry could often make an immense amount of noise, its substantive achievements in influencing imperial policy were small.

The terms of the trade: expansion and imperialism

Specialists in imperial history well understand the frustration which prompted Sir Keith Hancock's much-quoted remark that 'imperialism is no word for scholars', and they may even sympathise with his plan for consigning it to the dustbin.[86] Disposing of the term, however, does not dispose of the problem, and any substitute is likely to come with the ideological accoutrements which Hancock rightly wished to jettison. The fact is that historians need holistic terms, even if they also need to be wary of them.[87] Their principal obligation in this regard is to declare the contents of their baggage and to avoid smuggling bias under the cover of objectivity.

The term 'imperialism' is used here to refer to a species of the genus expansion. States commonly sponsor or permit pacific expansion beyond their own borders, typically through trade, cultural exchange and the movement of peoples. International relations arise from these contacts, and diplomatic ties follow where they are not already present. Such forms of expansion are not necessarily imperialist: they may be too slight to impinge significantly on the host country or, if weighty, they may be counterbalanced by inflows of comparable magnitude, in which case the result is a set of more or less mutually agreed arrangements between approximately equal partners. These characteristics of external expansion are noted here in schematic fashion simply to make the point that imperialism is a branch of international relations and not its totality. The distinguishing feature of imperialism is not that it takes a specific economic, cultural or political form, but that it involves an incursion, or an attempted incursion, into the sovereignty of another state. Whether this impulse is resisted or welcomed and whether it produces costs or benefits are important but, separate questions. What matters for purposes of definition is that one power has the will, and, if it is to succeed, the capacity to shape the affairs of another by imposing upon it. The relations established by imperialism are therefore based upon inequality and not upon mutual compromises of the kind which characterise states of interdependence.

Since most attention is usually paid to cases which illustrate the success of imperialist ambitions, it is worth recording that there were also failures. The difference between knocking on the door and opening it can be regarded, conceptually, as marking a distinction between an imperialism of intent and an imperialism of result. Britain's relations with the world beyond Europe before the mid-nineteenth century can easily be misread unless this difference is borne in mind. The notion of an imperialism of intent also underlines the fact that imperialist impulses express a conscious act of will: the agents of imperialism normally believe that they represent a superior power, ideologically as well as materially, and their actions are driven on by a sense of mission which embraces, legitimises and uplifts their private ambitions.

Emphasising the conscious intentions of the actors concerned makes appropriate allowance for the role of individual agency in imperialism; but it lends little support to the view that the events and episodes normally included in the history of imperialism were no more than idiosyncratic or random occurrences. The fact that the individuals concerned had a sense of wider purpose, which they shared with like-minded compatriots beached on other shores, itself casts doubt on the thesis that imperialism was a big accident caused by a 'fit of absence of mind'.[88] Such judgements represent understandable reactions to brands of history which claim to foretell the future by offering a partial reading of the past, but the suggestion that an essentially chaotic view of history is preferable to an excessively regimented one simply substitutes one doubtful view of the past for another. Accidents of course happen, but when they occur in clusters and on a global scale some thought needs to be given to the possibility that they had underlying causes which, while still being man-made, were not, in themselves, accidental.

Consequently, we need also to think of imperialism as a process transmitting impulses from a particular source of energy. The definition needs to be kept open at this point to encompass types of domination which are not confined to a single brand of assertiveness or to a specific historical stage. One of the major problems of assigning imperialism to a particular phase in the evolution of capitalism, for instance, is the presumption that the 'normal' course of capitalism is known and that its future can therefore be predicted. If imperialism is indeed the highest stage of capitalism, as Lenin thought, it becomes difficult to see how to relate it to subsequent episodes which ought not to exist. Historians with an inventive turn of mind may reach for terms such as late capitalism, but if the terminus continues to recede even sympathetic observers may come to suspect that the truth lies less in the prediction than in supposed deviations from it. This cautionary example shows how interpretations which begin as spacious and illuminating insights can easily make historians hostages in cells of their own choosing. Imperialism can be linked to a distinctive form of capitalism, but this can be done without excluding causes which may carry more weight in explaining forms of imperialism other than those dealt with here, and without presuming that the historic path of capitalism is known and predictable.

Gentlemanly capitalism undoubtedly helped to promote expansionist forces of investment, commerce and migration throughout the world, including Europe and the United States. Its main dynamic was the drive to create an international trading system centred on London and mediated by sterling. World trade was to be financed by short-term credits (principally bills on London); world development was to be promoted initially by long-term loans to foreign governments and subsequently through direct overseas investments. The whole package was to be tied together by a regime of international free trade, which would encourage specialisation, cut transaction costs and create an interlocking system of multilateral payments. The resulting expansion of global commerce was to be handled, transported and insured by British firms. British manufactured exports were a very visible part of this panorama, but the design was not drawn by industrialists and, as we have already noted, their interests were not paramount.

This vision was not inevitably imperialistic; nor were its imperialist forms invariably militaristic.[89] Nevertheless, there was a tendency for expansionist impulses to become imperialist, especially where they came up against societies which needed reforming or restructuring before expansionist ambitions could be realised, and which also seemed to be either amenable to change or incapable of resisting it. If industrialists were the shock troops who took the brunt of the class struggle at home, representatives of the service sector formed the advance guard of capitalism abroad. In promoting their interests, they necessarily came into direct contact with potential clients, customers and producers in distant parts of the world in ways that British manufacturers (and consumers) did not.[90] Not surprisingly, officers in the front line gathered much of the reconnaissance reaching London, passed on judgements about the suitability of foreign countries for the role assigned to them, and made recommendations about how they might be aligned to fit Britain's international purpose.

The marriage of private and public interests was readily arranged, partly because of the increasing importance of invisible earnings and income from foreign investment in settling Britain's balance of payments, and partly because the gentlemen at the top of the banking and service hierarchy shared the values and spoke the language of the political decision-makers. But the resulting alliance was much more than a narrow sectional deal between segments of the elite. Put simply, overseas expansion and the imperialism which accompanied it played a vital role in maintaining property and privilege at home in an age of social upheaval and revolution. The alliance was equally involved in promoting abroad sets of like-minded rulers and congenial states which were designed to be dependable allies in a global campaign to subdue republicanism and democracy by demonstrating the superiority of the liberal ideal of improvement. The link between the domestic and overseas parts of this strategy was forged by the gentlemanly diaspora, which was also perfectly placed to ease the transition from expansion to imperialism by extending the ideology of mission and rendering it patriotic. It is no coincidence that the most pervasive images of imperialism and empire were those which projected gentility rather than industry. The public portrait of the imperial world was framed by civic virtues and depicted manly exploits, country life on estates and plantations, and social gatherings under tropical verandahs.[91] By stretching a point, it was possible to speak of the 'romance of the steamship'; but the chivalry of empire never embraced Birmingham or Manchester.

Imperialism, then, was neither an adjunct to British history nor an expression of a particular phase of its industrial development but an integral part of the configuration of British society, which it both reinforced and expressed. It is a telling comment on the power of scholarly specialisation that the principal debates on the evolution of British history during the past three centuries have managed, nevertheless, to marginalise the study of imperialism and empire.[92] At the same time, imperialist enterprise was enfolded in a grand development strategy designed by Britain to reshape the world in her own image. It was spearheaded, not by manufacturing interests, but by gentlemanly elites who saw in empire a means of generating income flows in ways that were compatible with the high ideals of honour and duty, and it remained a dynamic, expanding force long after decline, as measured by British comparative industrial performance, is conventionally thought to have set in.

Ideology and methodology

As is now abundantly clear, the subject of this study requires the use of terms which have powerful ideological connotations. Accordingly, we ought not to venture further into the history of imperialism without offering an explicit statement of our own perspective and its attendant methodology.[93] Our principal aim here is to understand the causes of British imperialism, not to pass judgement on them. Some readers may seek to connect our account of causation to their own views of the costs or benefits of imperialism, at home and abroad; but of course the merits of this exercise cannot be evaluated in advance of its execution. To avoid misunderstanding, however, we ought to note that our neutrality on this important subject is prompted by pragmatic considerations rather than by a concern to steer clear of controversy or to claim a special immunity for our own argument.[94] Quite simply, the problem of causation is itself so vast and so fiercely contested that to attempt an account of equal substance on its wide-ranging consequences would have led to congestion and to a loss of focus.

This reasoning suggests that the consequences of imperialism are not simply entailed by its causes; had they been similar in time and place, it might have been feasible to have squeezed extra answers from the evidence we had already consulted. But, even when the moral aspects of imperialism have been separated from its material impact (an operation which itself requires micro-surgery), it is still not possible to 'read off' results from axioms of causation. This does not diminish the relevance of the history presented here to the study of the present day; it is still possible to make a case for treating history as a practical art needed, as Ibn Khaldun put it, 'for the acquisition of excellence in ruling'. But it does mean that the appeal of simple theories of a complex world is likely to exceed their accuracy, and that the first step for those who seek to change or conserve the present is to understand how it came to be fashioned.

We do not suppose that the results of our inquiry are value-free in the naive sense of standing apart from assumptions and priorities which all authors necessarily carry with them. But we have tried to distinguish between our presuppositions and the testable propositions derived from them. Our interpretation therefore has no privileged status: it stands or falls by normal tests of evidence and inference. We do not invoke iron laws or appeal to an 'inner logic' of history; nor do we suppose that the terms we use or the forces we identify have lives of their own which are independent of the human beings who create them.[95] But, since there is no fruitful empiricism without hypotheses, we have constructed a central proposition, based on gentlemanly capitalism and its impulses, and tested it against various case studies. In doing so, we have attempted to steer a course between excessively broad arguments, which subsume the world under the most generalised conceptions of capitalism, nationalism or racism, and readily become tautological, and an excessively narrow preoccupation with the particularities of place and time, which either rules out the possibility of generalisation or tries to infer too much from too little. Our examples have not been pre-selected to serve our particular line of inquiry, but have been chosen because they are generally agreed to be the most important cases which any theory of British imperialism has to encompass. At the same time – to borrow an analogy from statistics – our analysis has tried to find a measure of central tendency which provides the best fit for the evidence rather than to explain every single observation. Contrary facts inevitably arise, and it is open to others to decide whether these are qualifications and exceptions which do not disturb our main hypothesis or whether they are fatal to it. If the possibility of refutation is disquieting for the authors concerned, they can take comfort from the fact that the principle of falsification can be applied to science but not to necromancy.

The chief aim of our interpretation is to establish the context within which actions took place; that is, to understand why actors of a certain kind were where they were when they were, and why their views of the world inclined them to act in the way they did. Translated into historical practice, this task involves the description of two contexts, one at home and one abroad, and of the links between them. We address this problem primarily by organising the evidence to identify the processes of which individuals were a part.[96] This procedure involves the selection and emphasis of some facts rather than others and the use of hindsight to bring out aspects of causation which may not have been stated or perceived clearly by participants at the time. To this extent, we accept that we are seeking to explain trends and events in terms of causes rather than trying to understand individual actions in terms of motives. Thus, we are concerned less with anatomising the biographical entrails of a Dilke or a Rhodes than with explaining why Dilke-like and Rhodes-like figures arose in the first place.

This approach to historical method does not imply a preference for types of causal explanations which infer individual actions from general 'covering laws', still less that our argument has been suborned by the tempting simplicities of determinism. On the contrary, our account of historical context is based on the interplay between process and agency; and if we focus on the former rather than on the latter it is because it is more appropriate to the purpose and scale of our particular inquiry, and not because of a belief in its inherent superiority. In this matter we follow Weber, who distinguished between causal explanation and empathy without suggesting that the two were incompatible, and also more recent philosophical opinion, which has moved away from earlier overstatements of the opposition between naturalistic and other forms of historical explanation.[97] Accordingly, we have attempted to read out of the evidence rather than to read into it, and to use contemporary opinion to check that our retrospective vantage point has not imposed unacceptable anachronisms on the past – even though much illustrative detail has had to be compressed and some of it has had to be omitted.

At the same time, reconstructing the historical context provides a measure for explanations which assign priority to individual motivation, and it helps, too, to distinguish between reasons for action and causes of action, which may or may not be the same. Historians who feel that explanations of imperialism fail if they do not trace the hand with the smoking gun may be disappointed with an account that concentrates on locating the stance of the combatants at the point of the draw; but they should also bear in mind that identifying the finger on the trigger provides an incomplete reconstruction of the causes of conflict.[98] The appropriate test of our interpretation, we suggest, is not whether it puts the case beyond all doubt but whether it offers an account which is both plausible and illuminating. In some respects, this is the more difficult examination, for being right about small issues is easier than shedding light on large ones.

The fact that our interpretation emphasises economic considerations and also traces the direction of causation from centre to periphery may give rise to doubts over the claims made so far about its neutral and non-deterministic character. While there is a great deal to be said on the problems of monocausality and bias in historical explanation, we shall confine ourselves here to two observations which have particular relevance to our analysis. In the first place, the stress laid on economic aspects of imperialism does not imply a commitment to the belief that economic forces are, *a priori,* more important than other considerations. It means only that the extent of their significance is to be determined by empirical investigation. In principle, there is no reason why the emphasis of causation should not be found elsewhere: the fact that we could not see how to do this does not mean that it cannot be done. At the same time, it will become clear that our own interpretation draws on political and ideological considerations without treating them as superstructures built on an economic base, and that we have attempted to point to interconnections without also losing the main thread of the argument. Secondly, and similarly, drawing a line of causation from the centre to the periphery is not to be seen as the product of a Euro-centric bias complemented by a dated disregard for the internal history of countries outside Europe. If we have restricted ourselves in this regard, it is because our concern is with the causes of imperialism and not with its consequences or with the domestic history of colonialism. Aspects of causation are of course to be found on the periphery, and these will be dealt with. Within these limits, we hope that our case studies show some understanding of the spirit as well as of the empirical findings of recent research on the various frontiers we have covered. But the generic causes, in our view, have their origins at the centre. This judgement accounts for the focus of our work; once again, however, it owes its status to empirical evidence and not to assumptions about the immanence of the European destiny.

This defence, even if extended, will not reassure historians who invoke the principle of multicausality. Nevertheless, it is worth noting that this position contains its own, often unacknowledged, difficulties. We can all agree that complex events are likely to have complex causes. By drawing up an impressive list of candidates, historians can readily display their scholarship, and by including everything they can protect themselves from hungry critics on the prowl for omissions. The trouble with this procedure is that it can easily redefine the problem instead of solving it. To accept the infinite complexity of historical events is not to acquire immunity from the obligation to select some segments of evidence rather than others and to judge their relative importance. The appeal to multicausality can easily degenerate into an attempt to duck this challenge by referring to the need to avoid the errors of monocausality and determinism. This is a sleight of hand that succeeds more often than it deserves: the exercise of selectivity and judgement may produce monocausal and determinist arguments, but this is just one of several more desirable possible outcomes.

Multicausal accounts of historical problems frequently culminate in the verdict that the truth lies somewhere between two extremes. The claim sounds judicious; but it may also reflect the predicament of those who wish to reach a conclusion while also expressing their determination, in Burke's phrase, 'to die in the last dyke of prevarication'. The truth may indeed lie somewhere between two extremes, but, then again, it may not. Clio has not laid down a law to this effect, and even if she had we might reasonably appeal for directions as to where, even approximately, the somewhere in question might be found.

Conclusion

Judgement on the originality of the thesis advanced here must be left to others. Our obligation at this point is simply to summarise the nature of the claims we wish to make in this regard. These can be placed under two headings. The first centres on our account of the origins of imperial impulses, and is based on a reinterpretation of the character and course of modem British history. Our argument draws particularly on research into economic history, but it has implications for social and political history and is therefore not confined solely to one specialised branch of historical studies. The second claim follows the first and takes the form of a historiographical revision of standard approaches to the study of British imperialism in order to reunite the history of the centre and of its diverse peripheries and to suggest adjustments to the accepted chronology of the subject.

Although these are substantial claims, they have also to be related to a modest definition of historical originality. Historical knowledge and understanding advance incrementally rather than seismically, and even the most original interpretations shift the emphasis rather than rewrite the script. This is why Thucydides remains highly relevant to the study of international relations, whereas Ptolemy has no part to play in contemporary astronomy.[99] Put another way, it can be said that most of the cards of historical interpretation have long been dealt; professional scholars can hope, at best, to reshuffle the pack. The point is clearly illustrated by the study of British imperialism, which has been the subject of serious and detailed scrutiny for over a century, and it is underlined by the present work, which rests on the backs of other scholars, as our copious references readily acknowledge. Once found, moreover, originality can turn out to be a qualified merit. One scholar, for example, might be original in his discovery of evidence but unoriginal in his use of it; another might have an original idea but a limited mastery of historical sources. The former contributes knowledge but not understanding; the latter offers understanding without knowledge. Our attempt to move some of the accepted boundary stones of the vast subject we have chosen to address has to be placed in this cautionary context. We have ourselves kept in mind the fact that Sisyphus laboured in vain.

Notes

1 Seeley's book, first published in 1883, is generally taken to mark the beginning of the modern, professional study of the subject. See J.G. Greenlee, 'A "Succession of Seeleys": the "Old School" Re-examined', *Jour. Imp. and Comm. Hist.*, 4 (1976).

2 See, for example, Immanuel Wallerstein, *The Modern World System, II, Mercantilism and the Consolidation of the European World Economy, 1600–1750* (New York, 1980), p. 258.

3 This is particularly the case in the work of Andre Gunder Frank, *Latin America: Underdevelopment or Revolution* (1969), but there are also difficulties of usage in Immanuel Wallerstein, *The Capitalist World-Economy* (1979).

4 Andre Gunder Frank argues that the Industrial Revolution 'began with the year 1760' and was based on 'Bengal Plunder'. See his *Dependent Accumulation and Underdevelopment* (1978), pp. 72–3.

5 Ibid. Ch. 4; Wallerstein, *Capitalist World-Economy,* p. viii. An excellent recent study of neo-Marxist theories of imperialism can be found in Anthony Brewer, *Marxist Theories of Imperialism: A Critical Survey* (2nd edn 1990), Chs. 7–11.

6 In its original meaning a colony was a place of settlement and on this definition a number of British possessions would not be classified as colonies. However, we follow here conventional usage whereby the term refers to parts of the formal empire. For a discussion of neglected nineteenth-century terminology, from which so much present-day debate springs see M.I. Finley, 'Colonies: an Attempt at a Typology', *Trans. Royal Hist. Soc.,* 26 (1976).

7 And others: see Martin Wight, *British Colonial Constitutions, 1947* (Oxford, 1952), pp. 1–5.

8 J. Gallagher and R.E. Robinson, 'The Imperialism of Free Trade', *Econ. Hist. Rev.,* 2nd ser. VI (1953). Although Gallagher and Robinson were the first to employ the concept of informality in an analytically important way, they did not invent it. They borrowed the term 'informal empire' from C.R. Fay, *Imperial Economy and its Place in the Foundation of Economic Doctrine, 1600–1932* (Oxford, 1934). The phrase was also employed by H.S. Ferns in his pioneering article, 'Britain's Informal Empire in Argentina, 1806–1914', *Past and Present,* 4 (1953). The idea, if not the precise terminology, has a long history. Lenin, for example, referred to Persia, China and Turkey as 'semi-colonial countries' as early as 1916. See V.I. Lenin, *Collected Works,* XXII (Moscow, 1964), p. 257. Leland H. Jenks used the term 'invisible empire' in his famous study *The Migration of British Capital to 1875* (1927), and it is echoed in W.K. Hancock, *Survey of British Commonwealth Affairs,* II, Pt. I (Oxford, 1940), p. 27. Hancock also used Fay's phrase, 'informal empire', though without acknowledgement.

9 The most determined recent attempt to define informal empire can be found in Jürgen Osterhammel, 'Semi-Colonialism and Informal Empire in Twentieth-Century China: Towards a Framework of Analysis', in Wolfgang J. Mommsen and Jürgen Osterhammel, eds. *Imperialism and After: Continuities and Discontinuities* (1986).

10 The principal omissions are the West Indies, Burma and south-east Asia (Singapore and Malaya). In an ideal world these areas would be included: they have been omitted purely for pragmatic reasons of space and time, as has a study of Siam (Thailand), which is a fascinating example of informal empire. We have also left aside the problem of Ireland. Anglo-Irish relations, besides being of daunting complexity, raise the wider question of Britain's ties with the so-called 'Celtic Fringe' as a whole, and this issue opens up, in turn, the problem of internal colonialism. For a schematic account see Michael Hechter, *Internal Colonialism: The Celtic Fringe in British National Development, 1536–1966* (1975).

11 The principal contributions to the peripheral thesis are: Ronald Robinson, 'Non-European Foundations of European Imperialism: Sketch for a Theory of Collaboration', in Roger Owen and Bob Sutcliffe, eds. *Studies in the Theory of Imperialism* (1972); and idem, 'The Excentric Idea of Imperialism with or without Empire', in Mommsen and Osterhammel, *Imperialism and After.* J.S. Galbraith, 'The "Turbulent Frontier" as a Factor in British Expansion', *Comparative Studies in Society and History,* II (1960), is an early contribution of lasting value. For a broad survey emphasising the periphery, see D.K. Fieldhouse, *Economics and Empire, 1880–1914* (1973).

12 D.C.M. Platt, *Finance, Trade and Politics in British Foreign Policy, 1815–1914* (1968).

13 See especially Platt's article 'British Policy During the New Imperialism', *Past and Present,* 39 (1968). Surveys of the literature which include discussions of this question are: W. Roger Louis, ed. *Imperialism: The Robinson and Gallagher Controversy* (1976); P.J. Cain, *Economic Foundations of British Expansion Overseas, 1815–1914* (1980); C.C. Eldridge, ed. *British Imperialism in the Nineteenth Century* (1984). A fine textbook by Bernard Porter, *The Lion's Share: A Short History of British Imperialism, 1850–1970* (2nd edn 1984), employs a theoretical structure derived from Robinson and Gallagher but gives greater emphasis to the role of economic anxiety in creating a climate for imperialist action after 1870.

14 See, for example, W.G. Hynes, 'British Mercantile Attitudes Towards Imperial Expansion', *Hist. Jour.*, XIX (1976).
15 P.J. Cain and A.G. Hopkins, 'The Political Economy of British Expansion Overseas, 1750–1914', *Econ. Hist. Rev.*, 2nd ser. XXXIII (1980).
16 See Platt, *Finance, Trade and Politics,* Pt. I.
17 For an astute presentation of this approach see Fieldhouse, *Economics and Empire,* Ch. 13.
18 Our first attempts to express our new position were made in 'Gentlemanly Capitalism and British Expansion Overseas, I: the Old Colonial System, 1688–1850', *Econ. Hist. Rev.* 2nd ser. XXXIX (1986); and II. 'New Imperialism, 1850–1945', ibid. XL (1987).
19 For critiques of Marxist theories of imperialism see Brewer, *Marxist Theories of Imperialism*; Norman Etherington, *Theories of Imperialism: War, Conquest and Capital* (1984), Chs. 6 and 7; Bill Warren, *Imperialism: Pioneer of Capitalism* (1980); and V.G. Kiernan, *Marxism and Imperialism* (1974), Chs. 1–3, 5 and 6.
20 Joseph Schumpeter, 'The Sociology of Imperialism', in idem, *Imperialism and Social Classes* (1951), p. 92.
21 Ibid.
22 See Thorstein Veblen, *The Theory of Business Enterprise* (1904); *Imperial Germany and the Industrial Revolution* (1915); and *An Inquiry into the Nature of Peace and the Terms of Its Perpetuation* (New York, 1919), pp. 249, 288, 290. Neither Schumpeter nor Veblen has attracted much attention from scholars in recent years in their role as imperial theorists. Veblen in particular is virtually an untapped source in this regard. An exception to this neglect can be found in Etherington, *Theories of Imperialism,* Ch. 8. There is also a useful chapter in Tom Kemp, *Theories of Imperialism* (1967).
23 J.A. Hobson, *Imperialism: A Study* (1988 edn), p. 59.
24 For an introduction to Hobson as an imperial theorist see Brewer, *Marxist Theories of Imperialism,* Ch. 4; Etherington, *Theories of Imperialism,* Chs. 3 and 4; Peter J. Cain, 'J.A. Hobson, Financial Capitalism and Imperialism in Late Victorian and Edwardian England', *Jour. Imp. and Comm. Hist.*, XIII (1985); and idem, 'Variations on a Famous Theme: Hobson, International Trade and Imperialism, 1902–38', in Michael Freeden, ed. *Reappraising J.A. Hobson: Humanism and Welfare* (1990).
25 Fernand Braudel, *Capitalism and Material Life, 1400–1800* (1973); Wallerstein, *The Modern World System* (New York, 1974).
26 The seminal modern statement, now neglected but still well worth reading, is Allen G.B. Fisher, 'Capital and the Growth of Knowledge', *Econ. Jour.*, 43 (1933).
27 See, for example, C.H. Lee, 'The Service Sector, Regional Specialisation, and Economic Growth in the Victorian Economy', *Jour. Hist. Geog.*, 10, (1984); Clyde G. Reed, 'Transactions Costs and Differential Growth in Seventeenth-Century Western Europe', *Jour. Econ. Hist.*, 33 (1973); and Douglass North, 'Ocean Freight Rates and Economic Development, 1750–1913', *Jour. Econ. Hist.*, 18 (1958).
28 The standard texts on modern British economic history tend to treat services as being incidental to other more important activities and rarely discuss the role of the service sector. This is true even of the two capacious volumes edited by Roderick C. Floud and Donald N. McCloskey, *The Economic History of Britain Since 1700* (Cambridge, 1981). Pioneering studies of the service sector have been made by Clive Lee, whose detailed research has been brought together in *The British Economy Since 1700* (Cambridge, 1986). See also P.K. O'Brien, 'The Analysis and Measurement of the Service Economy in European Economic History', in R. Fremdling and P.K. O'Brien, eds. *Productivity in the Economies of Europe* (Stuttgart, 1983). The importance of traded services in boosting per capita incomes in Britain (as opposed to France) is emphasised by Patrick O'Brien and Caglar Keyder, *Economic Growth in Britain and France, 1780–1914* (1978), pp. 63, 66, 75–6, 163–4, 197.
29 For example: T.P. Hill, 'On Goods and Services', *Review of Income and Wealth,* 23 (1977); Irving B. Kravis, *Services in the Domestic Economy and in World Transactions* (Geneva, 1983); and Ronald K. Shelp, *Beyond Industrialisation: Ascendancy of the Global Service Economy* (New York, 1981). In view of the general argument advanced in the present study, it is particularly interesting to note that economists now place considerable emphasis on the

potential for developing traded services in Third World countries. Introductions to the recent literature include: Andre Sapir, 'North–South Issues in Trade and Services', *World Economy*, 8 (1985); Jagdish Bhagwati, 'Splintering and Disembodiment of Services and Developing Nations', in idem, *Essays in Development Economics*, Vol. I (Oxford, 1985), and Gary Sampson and Richard Snape, 'Issues in Trade in Services', *World Economy*, 8 (1985).

30 This is a prominent theme in the writings of economists from Smith to Kaldor (whose influence was partly responsible for the introduction of Selective Employment Tax, which was designed to halve the growth of service employment).

31 Bhagwati, 'Splintering and Disembodiment'.

32 Unlike the French *gentilhomme*, whose status was determined solely by birth or royal appointment. The definitive historical study of the English gentleman has yet to be written. Introductions include: Philip Mason, *The English Gentleman: The Rise and Fall of an Ideal* (1982); and David Castronovo, *The English Gentleman: Images and Ideals in Literature and Society* (New York, 1987).

33 On this subject, and particularly on its nineteenth-century manifestations, see the outstanding and underused study by Mark Girouard, *The Return to Camelot: Chivalry and the English Gentleman* (New Haven, Conn., 1981). We have also made much use of John Scott, *The Upper Classes: Property and Privilege in Britain* (1982).

34 Thorstein Veblen, *The Theory of the Leisure Class: An Economic Study of Institutions* (1924 edn), pp. 37–8.

35 R. Bendix, *Max Weber* (1966 edn), p. 366.

36 The quotations are taken from Jonathan Powis, *Aristocracy* (1984), pp. 88–9. See also the powerful essay by Joseph Schumpeter, 'The Rise and Fall of Whole Classes', in his *Imperialism and Social Classes.*

37 Randall Collins, *Weberian Sociological Theory* (Cambridge, 1986), pp. 129ff.

38 Max Weber, *Economy and Society: An Outline of Interpretive Sociology* (ed. G. Roth and C. Wittich, 1978), Ch. IV: 'Status Groups and Classes'. The word 'acquisitive' is used instead of 'entrepreneurial' or 'commercial' in A.M. Henderson and Talcott Parsons' translation of Max Weber, *The Theory of Social and Economic Organization* (New York, 1947). Helpful interpretations of Weber's sociology include: Frank Parkin, *Max Weber* (1982): Reinhart Bendix, *Max Weber: An Intellectual Portrait* (1959); Seymour Martin Lipset, 'Social Stratification and Social Class', *International Encyclopaedia of the Social Sciences* (1968), and idem, 'Values, Patterns, Class and the Democratic Polity: the United States and Great Britain', in Reinhart Bendix and Seymour Martin Lipset, eds. *Class, Status and Power: Social Stratification in Comparative Perspective* (2nd edn 1967); Talcott Parsons, 'The Professions and Social Structure', in *Essays in Sociological Theory: Pure and Applied* (Glencoe, Ill., 1949); John Rex, 'Capitalism, Elites and the Ruling Class', in Philip Stanworth and Antony Giddens, eds. *Elites and Power in British Society* (Cambridge, 1974).

39 Weber, *Economy and Society*, p. 307.

40 This idea is, to some extent, the result of reading David Lockwood, *The Black Coated Worker: A Study in Class Consciousness* (1958), esp. pp. 202ff; and W.G. Runciman, *Social Science and Political Theory* (Cambridge, 1965), pp. 137–8. There are also some suggestive comments in Geoffrey Ingham. *Capitalism Divided? The City and Industry in British Social Development* (1984), pp. 240–3.

41 Powis, *Aristocracy*, pp. 28–9.

42 For an engaging introduction to City life from an early-twentieth-century perspective see Ronald Palin, *Rothschild Relish* (1971).

43 There is no study of the relations between high finance and high politics in Britain to compare with Fritz Stern, *Gold and Iron: Bismarck, Bleichröder, and the Building of the German Empire* (1977), from which we have learned a great deal. On this theme, see also the interesting comment on financial power in Collins, *Weberian Sociological Theory*, p. 137.

44 Parkin, *Max Weber*, p. 96.

45 The modern formulation of this debate is associated with the work of Ralph Miliband, *The State and Capitalist Society* (1969) and Nicos Poulantzas, *Political Power and Social*

Classes (1973) and subsequent discussion, especially in the *New Left Review.* For further references see Poulantzas, 'The Capitalist State: a Reply to Miliband and Laclau', *New Left Review,* 95 (1976).

46 John Goldthorpe, 'On the Service Class, its Formation and Future', in Antony Giddens and G. Mackenzie, eds. *Social Class and the Division of Labour* (Cambridge, 1982).

47 As it remains today: 'British political administration is concentrated spatially as well as numerically . . . if you are not in (or within easy reach of) London, you are politically nowhere. Success in political administration depends upon judgements of your fellows and to be judged you must get to London. In a hundred different ways, the provincial can reveal that he is not intimately acquainted with current wisdom'. See H. Heclo and A. Wildavsky, *The Private Government of Public Money* (2nd edn 1981), pp. 7–8.

48 Ibid. pp. 2–3.

49 Although we shall refer to gentlemen as a group which shared certain defining characteristics, we recognise of course that a full social history would pay more attention to intra-group differences as well as to the distinction between gentlemen and others. Here, it is sufficient for us to make the point that gentlemen were not identical. In principle, it was possible to be a gentleman by living up to the moral code of gentility; hence the phrase 'one of nature's gentlemen' and its attendant hope that shared rules of conduct would bind the nation as one. In practice, being a gentleman (and being accepted as a gentleman) was a matter of bearing as well as behaviour, and this was a quality bought at considerable cost in both time and money through informal and formal education. Even so, there were intangible but instantly recognisable gradations of gentility among those who had succeeded in embellishing nature: Asquith, who qualified by most criteria as being a gentleman above the majority of gentlemen, was nevertheless regarded for many years as being 'not quite a gentleman' by those who felt that his education at the City of London School was not fully redeemed by his sojourn at Balliol. See Girouard, *Return to Camelot,* p. 263.

50 See, for example, N. McKendrick, J. Brewer and J.H. Plumb, *The Birth of a Consumer Society* (1982), and P.B. Munsche, *Gentlemen and Poachers: The English Game Laws, 1671–1831* (Cambridge, 1981).

51 This theme is pursued by Homai J. Shroff, *The Eighteenth-Century Novel: The Idea of the Gentleman* (New Delhi, 1978).

52 Quoted in Harold Nicolson, *Good Behaviour* (Gloucester, Mass., 1955), p. 194.

53 Cain and Hopkins, 'Gentlemanly Capitalism and British Expansion Overseas, I: the Old Colonial System, 1688–1850', pp. 512–13.

54 And some had defined themselves. See Ralph Strauss, *Lloyds': The Gentlemen at the Coffee House* (New York, 1938), pp. 69, 73.

55 John Brewer, 'English Radicalism in the Age of George III', in J.G.A. Pocock, ed. *Three British Revolutions: 1641, 1688, 1776* (Princeton, NJ, 1980).

56 Quoted in Nicolson, *Good Behaviour,* p. 195.

57 The authoritative source is Girouard, *Return to Camelot.*

58 Two recent valuable contributions to this theme are: David Eastwood, 'Robert Southey and the Intellectual Origins of Romantic Conservatism', *Eng. Hist. Rev.,* CIV (1989); and Peter Mandler, 'Tories and Paupers: Christian Political Economy and the Making of the New Poor Law', *Hist. Jour.,* 33 (1990).

59 See David Cannadine, 'The Context, Performance and Meaning of Ritual: the British Monarchy and the "Invention of Tradition", c.1820–1927', in Eric Hobsbawm and Terance Ranger, eds. *The Invention of Tradition* (Cambridge, 1983). The comment by W.L. Arnstein, 'Queen Victoria Opens Parliament: the Disinvention of Tradition', *Hist. Research,* 63 (1990), is interesting but does not disturb the point made here.

60 P. Langford, 'Old Whigs, Old Tories and the American Revolution', in P. Marshall and G. Williams, eds. *The British Atlantic Empire Before the American Revolution* (1980).

61 See Boyd Hilton, *Corn, Cash and Commerce* (Oxford, 1977); and idem, 'Peel: a Reappraisal', *Hist. Jour.,* 22 (1979).

62 Edward Collins, *Marquis and Merchant,* Vol. I, p. 171; Quoted in Ivan Melada, *The Captain of Industry in English Fiction, 1821–1871* (Albuquerque, 1970), p. 186.
63 See Robin Gilmore, *The Idea of the Gentleman in the Victorian Novel* (1981), and Norman Russell, *The Novelist and Mammon: Literary Responses to the World of Commerce in the Nineteenth Century* (Oxford, 1986).
64 H. A. Taine, *Notes on England* (8th edn 1885), pp. 174–5.
65 J.A. Mangan, *The Games Ethic and Imperialism* (1985).
66 See, for example, Alan Sandison, *The Wheel of Empire* (1967), and G.D. Killam, *Africa in English Fiction* (1968). It is interesting to find that the celebrated French colonial administrator, Lyautey, had a high regard for the qualities of the English gentleman as a ruler of alien people; the *Ecole coloniale* was founded in 1899 to raise the standards of French administrators to similar levels. See Louis Hubert Lyautey, *Lettres du Tonkin et de Madagascar, 1894–1899* (Paris, 1920), pp. 71–2.
67 Quoted in Mason, *The English Gentleman,* p. 214.
68 These are well-known themes in the novels of Waugh and Wodehouse, and they were pursued by social commentators such as Harold Laski, *The Danger of Being a Gentleman and Other Essays* (1939), and Simon Raven, *The English Gentleman* (1961).
69 Tom Paine, *Rights of Man,* in *The Political and Miscellaneous Works of Thomas Paine* (1819), I, p. 75.
70 Weber, *Economy and Society,* p. 307.
71 For an attempt to employ Veblen's concept of conspicuous consumption in an historical context see Roger S. Mason, *Conspicuous Consumption: A Study of Exceptional Consumer Behaviour* (1981). Conspicuous consumption and group intermarriage, like exclusive education, are means towards what Weber calls 'social closure', a phenomenon examined by Frank Parkin, *Marxism and Class Theory: A Bourgeois Critique* (1979).
72 The distinction originates with Adam Smith, *An Inquiry into the Nature and Causes of the Wealth of Nations* (eds. R.H. Campbell, A.S. Skinner and W.B. Todd, Oxford, 1976), Bk. II, Ch. III.
73 This theme is discussed in Douglass C. North, *Structure and Change in Economic History* (Toronto, 1981), Chs. 12–13.
74 D.C. Coleman, 'Gentlemen and Players', *Econ. Hist. Rev.,* 2nd ser. XXVI (1973).
75 In 1914 Britain was the only European country, save Hungary, not to have manhood suffrage. See H.C.G. Matthew, R.I. McKibbin and J.A. Kay, 'The Franchise Factor in the Rise of the Labour Party', *Eng. Hist. Rev.,* XCI (1976), pp. 723–6.
76 'The complete rule of industrial capital was not acknowledged by English merchant's capital and moneyed interests until after the abolition of the duties on corn etc'. Karl Marx, *Capital,* III (1909 edn), p. 385, n. 47. Ch. 38 and pp. 385ff are also of interest in this context.
77 François Crouzet, *The First Industrialists: The Problem of Origins* (Cambridge, 1985), p. 44.
78 Powis, *Aristocracy,* p. 10.
79 Crouzet, *The First Industrialists,* p. 81.
80 Samuel Smiles, *Self Help* (ed. A. Briggs, 1958), p. 29 and Ch. XIII.
81 This point is made by Weber in *Economy and Society,* pp. 931–2. We are aware of the fact that some services, notably transport, were heavily unionised by the late nineteenth century and subject to the same pressures as mechanical industry. But finance and the professions were much less affected by this problem.
82 Crouzet, The *First Industrialists,* Chs. 5 and 7.
83 On this problem see Mancur Olsen, *The Logic of Collective Action,* (Cambridge, Mass., 1965). Growing concentration in finance and distribution, on the other hand, was not only a rational response to economic opportunity, but also politically efficient. For a discussion of the relationship between economic fragmentation and political influence in a contemporary setting see Robert H. Bates, *Markets and States in Tropical Africa* (Berkeley, Calif., 1981).
84 It is instructive to find that, even in 1990, the 'most an industrialist can usually hope for is to become a baron, the lowliest form of peer', and that industrialists 'generally receive the

lowliest form of knighthood too – the knight bachelor, a title awarded in medieval times to those knights too young or too poor to display their own banners', *Financial Times,* 29 December 1990.

85 A point made strongly by M. Daunton, 'Gentlemanly Capitalism and British Industry, 1820–1914', *Past and Present,* 122 (1989), pp. 137–40.

86 W.K. Hancock, *Wealth of Colonies* (Cambridge, 1950), p. 1.

87 The case is neatly put by Robert C. Stalnaker, 'Events, Periods and Institutions in Historians' Language', *History and Theory,* 6 (1967).

88 J.R. Seeley, *The Expansion of England* (1883), p. 8.

89 We make this point to avoid misunderstandings of the kind expressed in Andrew Porter's article, 'The South African War (1899–1902): Context and Motive Reconsidered', *Jour. African Hist.,* 31 (1990), p. 51, which would have gained from using Peter Cain, 'Capitalism, War and Internationalism in the Thought of Richard Cobden', *Brit. Jour. Internat. Stud.,* 5 (1979).

90 This observation is both obvious and neglected; its conceptual ramifications have only recently attracted the attention of economists. See, for example, Jagdish N. Bhagwati, 'Trade in Services and the Multinational Trade Negotiations', *World Bank Economic Review,* 1 (1987).

91 Manifested separately or in combination. Imperial eccentrics, it might be said, were those who took one aspect of the empire-building role to hitherto unknown extremes. Lawrence, for example, was gripped by medieval legends and crusading fantasies which were topped up by reading the *Morte d'Arthur* during his desert campaigns and personified by his loyal Arab 'knights' and 'squires'. His ability to represent the world in terms of his idea of it made him a master of legendary truth as well as, eventually, a legend himself. See Lawrence James, *The Golden Warrior: The Life and Legend of Lawrence of Arabia* (1990). For a fascinating French perspective see Maurice Larès, *T.E. Lawrence, la France et les français* (Paris, 1980). Lawrence studied in France between 1907 and 1910 and wrote a dissertation on the castles of the crusaders.

92 The empire is, of course, wheeled on stage from time to time, especially at moments of crisis. But it has neither a permanent nor a central place in the major debates on the evolution of modern British history and its exclusion, usually without explicit justification, is characteristic of both right- and left-wing approaches to the past.

93 We should note at this point that we have decided against aligning our interpretation with any one of the contending possibilities offered by international relations theory. We are greatly indebted to this source for helping to clarify the assumptions and connections of our argument. In the end, however, we came to the conclusion that our thesis could be made to fit all or none of the approaches currently on offer, and that to engage in a dialogue with what is now a voluminous literature while also trying to control our main historical theme would create more difficulties than it would solve. The extent of these difficulties cannot be laid out fully here. In the present context, we must confine ourselves to observing that there is first of all a problem as to what constitutes international relations theory, the answers being different in the United States, Britain and France – the three leading producers. Secondly, the most influential body of work, that generated in the United States, is itself divided between realist, neo-realist and other schools, and deploys a terminology respecting regimes, hegemons and other entities which needs to be considered carefully and therefore at some length. Finally, since international relations theory is culturally specific (though aiming at universality), potential users are perhaps justified in exercising caution before adopting a viewpoint that may be more parochial than its advocates imagine. The current debate over the decline of the United States as a world power, for example, is beginning to reveal that many supposedly timeless and objective notions were in fact the product of a brief period of global dominance and were fashioned for the purpose, albeit by an art that concealed art, even from the artificers. Isabelle Grunberg, 'Exploring the "Myth" of Hegemonic Stability', *International Organization,* 44 (1990), provides a penetrating analysis which can be compared to the critiques that brought down modernisation theory in the early 1970s.

94 The question of the costs and benefits of imperialism has been assessed by Lance E. Davis and Robert A. Huttenback, *Mammon and the Pursuit of Empire: The Political Economy of British Imperialism, 1860–1912* (Cambridge, 1986).

95 A. Arato, 'Lukacs's Theory of Reification', *Telos,* 11 (1972) provides a valuable discussion of this problem.

96 Along the lines set out by W.H. Walsh, 'Colligatory Concepts in History', in W.H. Burston and D. Thompson, eds. *Studies in the Nature and Teaching of History* (1967).

97 Two helpful summaries of the issues are: W. Outhwaite, *Understanding Social Life: The Method Called Verstehen* (1975), and Patrick Gardiner, ed. *The Philosophy of History* (Oxford, 1974).

98 Appearances can also deceive, as readers of Agatha Christie know well.

99 See, for example, Michael W. Doyle, 'Thucydidean Realism', *Review of International Studies,* 16 (1990), and Steven Forde, *The Ambition to Rule: Alcibiades and the Politics of Imperialism in Thucydides* (Ithaca, NY, 1989).

2

PROSPECTIVE

Aristocracy, finance and empire, 1688–1850

Starting points have origins which lie beyond the antecedents chosen to define them. A plausible case could be made for beginning this study in the late sixteenth century, as this would encompass the Elizabethan explorers, the foundation of the East India Company, and the establishment of the first colonies in the New World. In taking the Glorious Revolution as our point of departure instead, we do not intend to minimise the importance of these events, to suggest that our argument is incompatible with them, or indeed to claim that 1688 was itself a cataclysmic year in the making of imperial history. We do, however, wish to argue that the Revolution brought together and lent impetus to forces that left a deep imprint not only on domestic history, as is well known, but also on the character and course of colonial development – a proposition that is less well appreciated. By taking this additional step, we hope to establish a systematic connection between British and imperial history from the outset of our study; by tracing the evolution of this relationship, we hope to show how one phase in the history of the empire dissolved into another in the nineteenth century.

Historiographical perspectives

To reach this point we need first to define our position with respect to the existing historiography. As far as Britain is concerned, this means choosing between interpretations which emphasise the persistence of an *ancien régime* dominated by an oligarchy of landowners from 1688, or even from 1660, down to 1832 or even beyond, and those which emphasise evidence of change as demonstrated, variously, by the Revolution of 1688, the Hanoverian succession, the rise of a 'polite and commercial' middle class, the growth of an impolite radicalism, the American and French Revolutions and, finally, industrialisation.[1] Our contribution to this wide-ranging but also highly specialised debate can be only a modest one. It appears to us that the boundaries of discussion have been drawn too narrowly around political, constitutional and ideological issues and have not fully incorporated the results of recent research into economic history, even where reference is made to the Industrial Revolution. Our purpose in including this dimension, however, is not to renovate an argument about industrialisation but to emphasise the continuing importance of agriculture and the significance of innovations in finance and commercial services. In claiming that these innovations made headway because they were compatible with the 'traditional' social order, we shall indicate how an argument for change can be combined with one emphasising continuity without, we hope, collapsing the case into generalities.

The imperial perspective also needs to be brought into focus. At present, the mainland colonies are the only part of the empire to appear either prominently or regularly in the controversy over the direction taken by eighteenth-century Britain, principally because constitutional issues carried contemporary debate over political rights and duties across the Atlantic. The empire as a whole, however, does not feature systematically in the discussion, and its role is often pared down to the point at which near-sighted observers might begin to doubt its existence.[2] This anomaly has persisted despite the fact that Britain's presence abroad was substantially enlarged in the course of the eighteenth century. Territorial advances were made in India and in the North American settlements that were to become Canada; the West Indies rose to head the list of Britain's trading partners; commercial ties with the mainland colonies increased down to the War of Independence, survived the creation of the United States, and prospered thereafter. Imperial assertiveness was neither dimmed by the loss of the American colonies nor extinguished by the resumption of peace in 1815 after the long war with France. Colonies of settlement were promoted in New South Wales from the 1780s, in the Cape after the turn of the century, and in New Zealand from the 1840s. During and after the French Wars a chain of naval bases, some within the empire and others outside it, was established to police the ocean routes and to create points of entry into tropical Africa, South America, the Persian Gulf, south-east Asia and the Far East. Forceful diplomacy, occasionally accompanied by house-breaking, continued to be used to bend the world overseas to Britain's will and reached a new peak of intensity with the exercise of Palmerston's muscular authority during the 1830s and 1840s.

The omission of these sizeable developments from serious consideration of the course of British history after 1688 is to some extent the result of an excess of specialisation that affects all fields of historical study. But it can also be explained by the fact that imperial historians themselves have long been unsure about what role to assign the empire in the evolution of the mother country. Despite the creation of what is now a voluminous and impressive body of literature, no general interpretation of the eighteenth-century empire has succeeded either in commanding acceptance or in generating the creative dissent needed to inspire a superior alternative.[3] Imperial historians have themselves become divided by a common empire: specialists on North America have devised one set of controversies and dates; those working on India have evolved another. The outcome of these separate inquiries, valuable though it is, has contributed more to an understanding of the history of the states that arose from the debris of empire, whether British or Mughal, than to an awareness of a common imperial purpose. In these circumstances, it is easy to draw the conclusion that no common purpose and no significant unity existed, and thereby to make a virtue out of what, on closer inspection, might be a weakness in historical analysis.

There was a time when this problem appeared to have a satisfactory solution. On the assumption that the history of the empire was defined by events affecting its constitutional standing, it was acceptable for the *Cambridge History of the British Empire* to regard the creation of the United States as marking the termination of the 'old' empire.[4] However, as it became apparent that this criterion excluded too much that was relevant to an understanding of the realities of imperial relations and international power alike, increasing attention was paid to influences other than those defined by constitutional considerations. The weightiest statement of the revisionist case was presented in Vincent Harlow's *The Founding of the Second British Empire, 1763–1793,* which sought to reduce the importance attached to 1783 and to suggest that the real turning point in Britain's imperial relations occurred with the successful conclusion of the Seven Years' War 20 years earlier in 1763.[5] This date symbolised both the achievement of British naval supremacy and the emergence of new expansionist forces based on incipient industrialisation and characterised by a quest for markets and raw materials rather than for territorial possession. Harlow's argument thus contained elements of the idea of informal empire that Gallagher and Robinson applied to the mid-Victorian period.[6] In effect, Harlow's interpretation created what might be called the long nineteenth century, whereby 1763 became the starting point for the industrial-based, free-trading imperialism that was to prevail until the neo-mercantilist policies of rival powers disrupted it at the close of the nineteenth century.

Had this interpretation held, historians of empire would have a thesis to offer the wider world. However, it is generally accepted that Harlow's argument created more difficulties than it could resolve. Important though it was, Britain's success in 1763 signified neither her ascendancy as a naval power nor the elimination of the French challenge. Harlow's emphasis on the part played by the process of industrialisation is also at variance with current assessments of the chronology of the Industrial Revolution, which have moved the turning point forward to the close of the eighteenth century rather than back to 1763. Similarly, in underlining the significance of early experiments with free trade, Harlow was left with the problem that protectionism remained in place until well into the nineteenth century. This difficulty entailed another: in stressing the shift of policy towards trade rather than dominion, Harlow was unable to account adequately for Britain's continuing expansion within the formal empire in British North America, the West Indies and India, while his idea that there was a 'swing to the cast' following the loss of the mainland colonies minimised the enduring importance of economic ties with the United States as well as with the Atlantic economy generally.

These weaknesses have yet to be overcome either within the liberal tradition of scholarship or outside it.[7] Indeed, as far as imperial history is concerned, the contribution made by those opposed to 'bourgeois' scholarship has proved to be disappointingly conventional. Andre Gunder Frank, for example, claimed that the Industrial Revolution 'began with the year 1760', and that the last quarter of the eighteenth century marked the transition from mercantile to industrial capitalism.[8] Wallerstein's treatment is far more detailed, but the result falls into a familiar pattern. He, too, distinguishes between mercantile capitalism, which occupied the 'long' seventeenth century (1600–1750), and industrial capitalism, which predominated thereafter. The point of transition is symbolised by the year 1763, which saw 'the victory of certain segments of the world bourgeoisie, who were rooted in England, with the aid of the British state'.[9] But this date, as we have seen, had already been selected by Harlow and been criticised subsequently, and Wallerstein is unable to substantiate his additional claim that the bourgeoisie rose (finally) to power in the mid-eighteenth century. If, today, historians of all persuasions are more likely to halt in 1776 or 1783, it is not because the conventional case for doing so is convincing but because the alternatives are even less persuasive; and one result of this decision is that the period between 1783 and 1815 is covered imperfectly or not at all.[10]

It should be evident by now that we cannot simply present a summary of an acceptable interpretation of eighteenth-century imperialism because it does not lie readily to hand; if we adopt any of the existing approaches we are likely to drive through signs warning of the hazards surrounding concepts such as mercantilism, free trade and the Industrial Revolution. The problem is to devise a route that offers a plausible way of connecting the history of Britain to the history of the empire. There are, no doubt, a number of possibilities. But the one that appears to us to have the greatest explanatory power is that which begins by focusing on the structure of authority installed by the Revolution of 1688 and its attendant property rights, rewards and sanctions, and views imperialism as an attempt to export the Revolution Settlement (and hence to entrench it at home) by creating compliant satellites overseas. Domestic and imperial developments were joined in various ways, but none was more pervasive than the bond created by finance. As the financial revolution underwrote the new regime at home, so it helped to fund settlement, export-production and trade overseas: the evolution of the credit and revenue-raising system provides a means of tracing not only the fortunes of the revolution settlement itself but of the empire as well.

The financial revolution: private interests and public virtues

The period 1688–1850 owes its unity to the economic and political dominance of a reconstructed and commercially progressive aristocracy which derived its power from land. Agriculture remained the most important economic activity for the greater part of the period, whether measured by its share of national income, its contribution to employment, or by its ability to generate large fortunes.[11] In

1790, no less than three-quarters of all agricultural land was owned by no more than 4,000–5,000 aristocrats and gentry, who presided over a series of innovations which raised productivity, increased incomes from rents, and helped to lift land values.[12] Down to the 1760s the prosperity of agriculture, especially in the south-east, was boosted by foreign demand, which drew grain exports out of the country; thereafter, the growth of the domestic market ensured that investment in agriculture remained high and that farm incomes stayed buoyant.[13] Throughout the eighteenth century, purchasing power derived from agricultural rents and wages formed the basis of consumer demand for both domestic manufactures and imports, including colonial products.[14] As we shall see, the dominance of agriculture was not seriously questioned until the 1820s; even so, its decline was protracted and became irreversible only with the measures opening Britain to free trade at the close of the 1840s.

As the landed interest threw off the last traces of feudalism, eliminating the threat not of a rising bourgeoisie but of conservative farmers, so too its representatives increased their grip on the levers of power in the aftermath of the Civil War. Following the Revolution of 1688, the magnates consolidated their political authority as they consolidated their estates.[15] These 'great oaks', as Burke called them, shaded the country because they possessed, in land, a form of wealth that also carried the supreme badge of authority, being permanent, prestigious and allowing time for the affairs of state. In dominating parliament, the landed interest also gathered together the main lines of authority, notably the legal system, public expenditure, and defence, which joined the seat of government in London to the most distant provinces. The control exercised by the peerage over the House of Commons remained undisturbed before 1832 and was only slowly eroded thereafter, while its dominance of the executive lasted well beyond 1850.[16] Social exclusiveness was maintained by in-group marriage, ideological cohesion was demonstrated by a commitment to the Church of England, and cultural homogeneity was shaped by the public schools, whose pupils, 'the glory of their country' in Defoe's judgement, were set apart from their contemporaries, 'the mere outsides of gentlemen', who were educated by other means.[17] None of this is to suggest, even in a summary as compressed as this, that the country was run by an oligarchy which became somnolent because it was allowed to rest undisturbed: opposition sprang from different quarters and was sometimes powerful enough to trouble the repose of the most complacent members of the government. But opposition that was Tory or urban middle class in origin remained within constitutional limits, at least after 1745; and, when radical protest broke the bounds of law and convention, it was brought under control.[18] At such moments, the instinct of self-preservation sharpened the quality of political judgement and caused property-owners to sink their differences in their common interest.

The most important development outside agriculture in the eighteenth century was the financial revolution of the 1690s centred on the foundation of the Bank of England and the creation of the national debt.[19] These innovations were linked to wider developments within the financial sector: the recoinage of 1697 and the establishment, thereafter, of a *de facto* gold standard; the evolution of specialised merchant banks in the City; the growth of a market in mortgages; the increasing use of bills of exchange to settle domestic and international obligations; the rise of the stock exchange; the development of marine and fire insurance; and the appearance of a financial press.[20] The early eighteenth century saw the expansion of the East India Company and the South Sea Company, the two great companies whose shares formed a sizeable part of the stock market, the growth of Lloyds as the international centre of underwriting, and the formation of new insurance companies, such as the Sun Fire Office (1708) and the Exchange Assurance Company (1720).[21] The external effects of these innovations were felt, in turn, on other activities in the service sector. Improvements in credit and commercial services boosted the shipping industry, promoted overseas trade and assisted the balance of payments by generating invisible earnings.[22] The expansion of overseas commerce encouraged the rise of large mercantile firms whose size enabled them to mobilise the capital and credit needed for long-distance trade.[23] As the eighteenth century witnessed the consolidation of large estates and their perpetuation through the male line, so it saw the growth of a merchant oligarchy and its 'entailment' through commercial dynasties. It was during this period, too, that non-commercial branches of the service sector were expanded and defined. Official employment, especially in new or reformed departments, such as the Board of Trade and the Treasury, became associated with a concept of public duty that was the hallmark of gentility and was handed on, often from father to son, while in the private sector a number of prominent occupations acquired the status of professions and their members became acknowledged as gentlemen.[24]

All of these developments came together in London, and gave further impetus to the growth of what was already a large and expanding urban centre.[25] The great institutions which supported the financial revolution, and indeed the Glorious Revolution too, were based in the City, where they benefited from the externalities generated by geographical proximity and overlapping functions. As the leading port, London itself was already distinguished by the wealth and cosmopolitan character of its merchant community, and was well placed to launch new ventures overseas. London's manufactures also came to reflect the expansion of the financial and service sector: older industries, such as silk and cloth, lost ground to foreign and provincial competitors, but new industries, ranging from sugar-processing to the production of high-quality furniture, arose to meet the needs of the country's most important concentration of wealthy consumers as well as its largest mass market.[26] No other town experienced such a striking development of consumer-oriented industries that relied so heavily on wealth derived ultimately from overseas trade and government expenditure; and no other town evolved such refined gradations of status as were found among London's service class of gentlemen's gentlemen, superior shopkeepers, clerks and the semi-employed attendants of the great and the pretenders to greatness.

This is not to say that London was unique: recent work on provincial towns as well as the long-established record of outports, such as Liverpool, Bristol and

Glasgow, indicates that both the financial revolution and the elite-consumer tastes that accompanied it spread beyond the metropolis in the course of the eighteenth century.[27] But imitation flattered the power of the centre rather than diluted it: London remained outstanding not only in its size but also in the qualitative differences that separated so many of its functions from those of even the largest provincial towns. There was only one Bank of England, one Lloyds and one national debt, and they were all found in London. Moreover, the City was distinguished from the outset by its close involvement with government finance and by its pronounced overseas orientation. The long-term capital market, as it emerged in London, was already separated from the rest of the country; provincial needs were met by local credit networks.[28] If the supremacy of the metropole was underpinned by powerful economic causes, it owed much of its distinction to the fact that London was the capital as well as the main port. The proximity of the City to parliament, to the departments of state and to the court provided opportunities for gaining access to information and for influencing policy that simply did not exist elsewhere. Provincial business could compete at the same level only by relocating its headquarters in London, as happened increasingly after 1850.

The causes of the financial revolution cannot be examined here in any detail. But it is clear that the pre-conditions had long been present in the shape of the City's merchants and goldsmiths, its cosmopolitan connections and its already extensive international trade. By the late seventeenth century, it was apparent, too, that dear money had placed Britain at a disadvantage in her struggle with the Dutch, and that improved credit was a vital part of her defence strategy – which included overseas expansion.[29] A further perception, which was to be realised fully in the course of the next three centuries, was that invisible earnings had an important contribution to make to the balance of payments, especially at a time when commodity exports (in this case woollen textiles) were experiencing difficulties in overseas markets.[30] However, no fundamental revolution was possible before 1688 because James II's pro-French and pro-Catholic policies frightened the predominantly Protestant bankers and investors whose support it required. The gentlemanly revolution of 1688 removed this fear by installing not just a new monarch but a new type of monarchy. The financial independence of the crown was destroyed: to secure an adequate income the king was compelled to govern through parliament and thus to acknowledge the political dominance of the landed interest.[31] The price that had to be paid was participation in the continental wars of the new ruler and his successors, and it was the demand for war finance after 1688 that precipitated the expansion of the national debt.

The distinctiveness of these innovations also needs to be emphasised. The extensive literature on economic growth defines 'early start' and 'late start' countries almost exclusively with reference to the development and spread of industry. What has still to be fully appreciated is the extent of Britain's lead in the area of finance and commercial services and the degree to which it set her apart from her rivals, as well as the role of these activities in the history of economic development.[32] The suggestion that Britain was about a century ahead of France in evolving modern financial institutions[33] is supported by recent detailed research on public finance and monetary policy.[34] Both the form taken by the public debt and its management were far more advanced in Britain than they were in France. During the final conflict between the two powers from 1793 to 1815, Britain was able to borrow extensively and efficiently because investors had confidence that their money would be returned, whereas France was forced to rely much more heavily on taxation because creditors were unimpressed by the government's record in honouring its obligations. Moreover, confidence in sterling enabled Britain to leave the gold standard in 1797 and adopt an emergency monetary policy without provoking a flight from the currency. What part this difference played in the outcome of the wars is impossible to say, but its existence needs to be stressed, not least because superior credit facilities, in helping to make Britain an international power, had given her a considerable stake to defend, as well as the means of doing so.

If the developments that flowed from the financial revolution seem recognisably modern, so they were. Contemporaries were universally impressed and often greatly disturbed by the far-reaching implications of the financial revolution, and their reactions gave rise to a debate that still echoes today in discussions of Britain's economic problems. Swift's alarm at the rise of the moneyed interest led him to argue that financiers had encouraged the flow of capital abroad to the detriment of the country's real interests, which lay in preserving the value of productive investments in agriculture:

> I have known some People such ill Computers as to imagine the many Millions in Stocks and Annuities are so much real Wealth in the Nation; whereas every Farthing of it is entirely lost to us, scattered in Holland, Germany and Spain.[35]

Defoe drew attention to another recurring feature of the debate, one that also struck Hobson nearly two centuries later: the division between a highland, pastoral and industrial north and west and a lowland, arable and commercial south and east.[36] In making this distinction, Defoe also underlined London's special function as a centre of finance and commercial services. His aim, however, was not to attack the capital, but rather to defend the role of services in maximising employment and adding value to economic activities.

As these contrasting interpretations suggest, the rise of the moneyed interest was the subject of one of the principal controversies of the eighteenth century.[37] To some observers, the new financiers were patriots whose expertise in organising low-cost credit funded the defence of the realm, overseas expansion and domestic employment. To others, they were upstarts who threatened to undermine the established social order by importing 'avarice' into a world that depended on 'virtue' to guarantee good government. As Bolingbroke, the most eminent of the City's critics in the early eighteenth century, put it: 'the landed men are the true owners of our political vessel; the moneyed men, as such are but passengers in it'.[38] The question of ownership was indeed central because the activities of the moneyed interest created

new forms of property, essentially paper instruments representing financial claims and obligations, that appeared to be insubstantial but were in practice powerful and invasive. The national debt became a particular focus of attention partly because it was readily identifiable and partly because it continued to expand throughout the century. On one view, the debt saved Britain from defeat at the hands of France; on another, it subverted the kingdom from within by attracting capital away from agriculture, by advancing representatives of the City to positions of privilege previously held exclusively by the landed interest, and by threatening the nation with bankruptcy. Not surprisingly, the debate joined by Swift and Defoe was carried on by Hume, Smith and Burke later in the century and by Southey and his contemporaries in the 1820s.[39]

However, the debate was being resolved even as it was being continued. As the eighteenth century advanced, the new financial institutions and services took root, and leading members of the moneyed interest were accepted into the inner circles of political and social influence.[40] The economic argument for incorporating the City was compelling because its expertise was vital to financing the wars that were the price of upholding the Revolution Settlement.[41] The national debt was also directly profitable to the small minority who could afford to invest in it – mainly substantial bankers, merchants and landowners, most of whom lived in London or the Home Counties (or had a residence there).[42] The growing integration of land and finance was symbolised by the action of the Earl of Bath, reputedly one of the wealthiest magnates in the country, who lent his weight in 1737 to a successful move to prevent a reduction in the interest paid on the national debt because his wife's considerable capital was invested in government stock.[43] In addition, the debt helped to fund the patronage system, which gave light work to many potentially idle hands, especially younger sons of landed families. In 1726 about one-quarter of the peerage held government or court office; in the second half of the century it became increasingly acceptable for the younger sons of aristocrats to take posts in the colonies, including placements arranged by the East India Company.[44] Outside the national debt, important connections between the country's large landowners and the City were formed by apprenticing younger sons to the leading merchant houses, especially those involved in the prestigious import and export trades,[45] and by the growth of the mortgage market, which developed rapidly as mortgages became the recognised means of obtaining credit on the security of land.[46] In these ways, the fortunes of the magnates who made the Revolution of 1688 and the merchant bankers who underwrote it became increasingly entwined both in the definition of the national interest and in matters of personal finance.

Social integration was necessarily a gradual process, but it was greatly helped by affinities in the life-styles of leading City figures and magnates at their meeting points in London, and by the subsequent gentrification of new money through the purchase of land, inter-marriage and the acquisition of titles.[47] This process led to the assimilation of recent immigrants, such as Jacob Houblon, who founded a City dynasty, bought a country estate, and finally entered parliament during the reign of

George II – who was also, of course, a member of a successful immigrant family.[48] It assisted established banking families, too, such as the Hoares, who gained impetus from the financial revolution, married into the English and Irish peerage, and thereafter combined broad acres with service to the City and to the crown.[49] Old money also prospered from new opportunities: Henry Lascelles, came from a family of Yorkshire landowners but he made his own fortune from colonial trade (principally imports from Barbados), entered parliament, and at his death in 1753 was worth an estimated £284,000 in land, the national debt, and loans to planters in the West Indies.[50] His son, Edwin, became a baron in 1796, and his grandson became Earl (and Viscount) Harewood in 1812.[51] By the close of the eighteenth century, the principle of the national debt had won general acceptance, though there was continuing concern about its size, and the avarice that Bolingbroke had associated with the moneyed interest had become virtuous in public service and in enhancing the private wealth of the magnates who managed the country. Bankers became gentlemen not least because gentlemen needed bankers.

Manufacturers were already important and familiar figures on the landscape in 1688, and their role expanded thereafter, as is well known. The woollen industry made a sizeable contribution to domestic employment, export earnings and state revenues in the eighteenth century, and the cotton industry performed a similar function, on an even larger scale, in the nineteenth century. At the same time, it must also be acknowledged, in the light of recent research, that industrialisation was a much slower process than was once thought: it now seems unlikely that there was a marked upward shift in the contribution made by manufacturing to national output in the 1740s; the spurt of the 1780s was confined largely to cotton goods; it was not until the 1820s that the quantitative weight of new industries imposed itself on the economy as a whole.[52] Only then did investment in industry become significantly larger than in agriculture; even so, the greater part of manufacturing output still came from small-scale, traditional (often household) units of production. Given the persistence of low productivity in so much of the manufacturing sector, it ought not to be surprising to find that industrial producers were content to shelter behind protectionist barriers for most of the period under review.[53] Even in branches of industry where productivity was growing impressively, such as cotton goods, the risks associated with new manufacturing techniques inspired a high degree of caution with respect to free trade.[54] Moreover, productivity gains in manufacturing still had to be realised in rising sales; and, as the home market became saturated, manufacturers found themselves relying increasingly on the worldwide system of distribution organised and financed from London.[55]

The success of the new industrial forces was therefore highly qualified, even in 1850. The number of large fortunes amassed by industrialists did not compare with those derived from land and from the financial and service sector.[56] Moreover, manufacturers did not make money in acceptable ways, and were not considered to be suitable candidates for entry into what Hume called 'that middling rank of men who are the best and finest basis of public liberty'.[57] In the eighteenth century, members of the banking and mercantile elite gained a degree of social approval for their activities that was 'not accorded to the captains of industry, whose profit-making inhibited the pursuit of pleasure, and whose petty bourgeois origins created formidable social barriers'.[58] It is true that sections of the landed interest benefited as producers from connections with industry, most obviously by supplying wool to textile manufacturers or by leasing mineral rights; but in general they used the capital they raised in London to improve their estates, and few landed magnates derived much of their income from investment in manufacturing, even in the nineteenth century.[59] Successful bankers and merchants were also disinclined to involve themselves in manufacturing, and showed a consistent preference for investments in urban property and country estates.[60] Indeed, there is evidence to suggest that landowners responded to the rise of the new industries by distancing themselves from them at the close of the eighteenth century, while merchants who expanded their operations were more likely to move into banking, shipping and allied services than into manufacturing.[61]

Industry's direct political influence also remained limited, even after the constitutional reforms of 1832. This was partly because the Bounderbys of the Midlands and the north of England (as they were increasingly portrayed by spokesmen in the south) had neither the time nor the social connections to shape national policy, and partly because they were rarely able to present a united front when they decided to make the attempt. A General Chamber of Manufacturers was formed in 1785, but its one great success – aborting Pitt's Anglo-Irish treaty – was motivated by timid protectionism rather than bourgeois self-confidence. Divisions among manufacturers on the issue of freer trade destroyed their unity in the following year, when the Anglo-French commercial treaty was negotiated, and led to the demise of the Chamber in 1787.[62] Thereafter, it proved impossible to pull the manufacturing interest together, except on an *ad hoc* basis, until the 1830s, and even then unity tended to follow the business cycle in emerging at times of slump and dissolving with the return of prosperity.

An alliance between land and money was firmly in place well before the economic and political consequences of industrialisation compelled attention. When the new industries eventually made their presence felt, their importance in generating income from overseas trade and in creating employment was widely acknowledged in government circles. But their representatives never took control of policy: they were claimants among others whose interests had to be balanced and mediated, not a force whose time had finally come. As far as international policy was concerned, their claims fitted into government priorities rather than challenged them. To adapt a phrase, the industrial bourgeoisie played an evolutionary part, at least in the period down to 1850.

The evolution of the military-fiscal state

At the centre of the state that emerged from the Revolution of 1688 stood a strong government which proved itself capable of greatly increasing the funds at its disposal, of sustaining warfare for long periods, and of maintaining political unity. The alarms were many and real, from the Jacobite threat at home to the Jacobin threat from abroad, and fissures opened at moments of crisis; but the galleon of state sailed on, leaving the loss of the mainland colonies to one side, moving steadily, if also anxiously, through the French Wars, negotiating the transition to free trade and avoiding revolution in 1848, Europe's year of universal upheaval. Property rights, especially land and financial claims, were defended by the law, as enacted by a parliament dominated by landed interests, by financial inducements, notably patronage, and by a powerful military presence based on an expanded army and navy and bolstered by substantial subsidies to continental allies. If legal measures were relatively costless, patronage was less so, and the military presence was an insatiable consumer of resources. Consequently, it ought not to be surprising to find that the fastest growing sector in the eighteenth century as a whole was probably government and defence rather agriculture or manufacturing.[63] Increased public expenditure imposed revenue demands which, in turn, ensured that high priority was given to managing public credit efficiently, to expanding the tax base, and to improving its administration, from the Treasury down to the excise collection. The result was a state characterised by a form of military-fiscalism, but one that sought to create additional revenues by market-oriented policies and not merely by diverting them from other sources.[64]

This enterprise, as we have seen, was launched on a raft of credit, and it was kept afloat by maintaining a judicious, if often uncertain, balance between revenue and expenditure. This balance, in turn, depended upon matching the needs of the Treasury with those of political stability, which set the ultimate limit to fiscal demands. If taxation provoked civil unrest, property values would be placed at risk and investors would lose confidence in the government and sterling. The financial revolution undoubtedly created opportunities for speculation, and these could easily produce crises and instability. But the longer-term interest of the managers of the financial system lay in curbing these tendencies, and their efforts eventually led to the emergence of what subsequently became an orthodoxy: the idea that sound money and sound government stood together.

The necessary balancing act was achieved by striking a series of bargains with key pressure groups. One set of bargains took the form of buying in or incorporating a limited number of powerful interests, principally the City and the country gentry. The City, which was tied into the regime through its investment in the national debt, began to exert considerable influence on policy at the point where public borrowing requirements met foreign policy, and was assimilated in the course of the eighteenth century in ways that we have touched upon.[65] Members of the provincial gentry who had Tory sympathies were encouraged to keep their hostility to the national debt within bounds by being offered rewards that were already available to Whig loyalists. The land tax was held at low levels, efforts were made to bring defence expenditure under control following the Peace of Utrecht in 1713, and steps were taken to curb excesses of financial speculation after the South Sea Bubble in 1720.[66] Finally, from the middle of the century increasing numbers of Tories were readmitted to public office, and thus had their independence compromised by the comforts of patronage.[67] Out of these measures emerged a highly regressive system of taxation, a growing commitment to financial orthodoxy, and a renewed sense of solidarity among the landed interest.

A second set of bargains bought off or accommodated particular interests by offering concessions that were designed to keep them content but also at arm's length. Manufacturers, for example, wanted import tariffs fixed at levels that would protect domestic industry. Given the general importance of manufacturing to the economy, their request was listened to: no government wished to damage wealth-creating activities, and members of parliament were sensitive to the fact that increased unemployment had consequences for local rates (which would have had to rise to pay for poor relief) and civil order.[68] In this case, however, a high-tariff regime was already favoured as a means of generating revenue to service the national debt, and manufacturers were thus able to benefit from policies that were devised for a wider purpose.[69] Out of concessions of this kind emerged a complex of commercial regulations that entered into what can be termed 'mercantilism' – providing this is thought of less as a coherent 'system' than as an accretion of separate deals, albeit one with a degree of hard-headed logic behind it.[70]

There is no simple way of charting the evolution of this military-fiscal system because the study of some of its main ingredients, especially credit and taxation, has only recently begun to attract detailed research.[71] The most obvious and most important theme is that joining public expenditure and war: expenditure increased rapidly during the major wars of the eighteenth century and did so on a rising trend which culminated in the massive costs of the French Wars between 1793 and 1815.[72] In 1700 the national debt stood at £14m.; in 1748 it was £78m.; by 1763 it had jumped to £133m.; by 1783 it had grown to £245m.; and in 1815 it reached £700m.[73] Interest payments on the national debt swallowed more than 50 per cent of public expenditure in peace time and in consequence assumed massive proportions: one calculation suggests that they were equivalent to about half the value of total exports in the eighteenth century.[74] It is now apparent that the real burden of taxation was heavier in England than in France both on a per capita basis and as a share of national income, and that it increased as the century advanced.[75] It is also clear that the bulk of the tax burden was borne by the mass of consumers, principally in the form of excise and customs duties, while the land tax supplied a small and diminishing proportion of the total.[76] The social incidence of taxation identifies the chief beneficiaries of the Revolution Settlement: the landed interest, which voted itself valuable tax benefits; the bond-holders in London and the Home Counties, who gained from transfers made by taxpayers in the country as a whole; and the merchants trading overseas (in association with shipowners, contractors and members of the armed services), who profited from the drive to increase earnings and revenues from the colonies.[77]

Although the principle of the national debt gradually became accepted, its size preoccupied commentators to an increasing extent as the century advanced. After the Seven Years' War (1756–63) in particular, concern about Britain's ability to service the debt prompted successive governments to take steps to improve the efficiency of tax-gathering at home and to search for new sources of revenue abroad.[78]

The fact that revenue was raised mainly by indirect taxes made payment marginally less painful than it would otherwise have been, and opposition to the growing weight of taxation was generally held within constitutional limits. Nevertheless, the tax burden fuelled the radical movements that developed from the 1760s: it had a place in the spontaneous protests that appeared at moments of crisis, when it merged with more immediate problems, such as unemployment (often arising out of credit failures) and food shortages; it entered the organised radicalism of Wilkes in the 1760s and 1770s and of Wyvill in the early 1780s.[79] The regional and social bases of the movements led by Wilkes and Wyvill were very different, but between them they mounted a comprehensive attack on the unrepresentative character of the legislature, the power of the executive and the operation of the patronage system, and they had in common demands for greater accountability and efficiency in public affairs. The eighteenth-century amalgam of patronage and protection was also criticised at this time by commentators who perceived that expanding commercial services and new industries could gain from measures that promoted more competitiveness in the market and less interference from the state. Pitt's tentative moves towards 'economical reform' and freer trade in the 1780s were a response to these criticisms. In taking these steps, however, Pitt was not preparing to launch a bourgeois revolution but trying to reinforce an oligarchic order by increasing revenues from customs duties, curbing the growth of the national debt, and placating irate taxpayers.[80]

Reformers failed at the point where the prospect of success appeared to threaten property values or, in the case of Pitt's experiments, when the outbreak of the French Wars created a state of emergency. The revolt of the American colonies had already caused property-owners to draw together in defence of established authority. The conflict with France raised the prospect of invasion by republicans and Jacobins, and greatly magnified the danger to order and property. These challenges, both at home and from abroad, were met by elaborating a brand of 'new conservatism' which brought property-owners together in defence of the status quo.[81] By the close of the century the defenders had become a formidable group: the landed interest had already been strengthened by the readmission of Tory sympathisers, and holders of new forms of property in paper credits and commercial wealth had also won acceptability, with the result that they took up positions inside the castle rather than with the besiegers. In the event, the need to place the economy on a war-footing postponed reform, and the immense cost of the French Wars carried the national debt to new heights. In 1815 the structure of 'Old Corruption' not only was still in place but also had been considerably enlarged.

Radical criticism was countered partly by suppressing it and partly by appealing to the solidifying forces of patriotism – a step that also involved elevating the dignity of the monarchy.[82] These moves were accompanied by an ideological refurbishment that helped to guide the propertied interest into and through the nineteenth century. Burke, among others if also above them, elaborated a political philosophy that defended inequalities in the ownership of property, justified the right of a minority to determine the government of the country and emphasised the importance of manners (and hence deference) in establishing rules of conduct.[83] But it was left to a revitalised Christianity to undertake the moral rearmament of the nation by anchoring behaviour to standards set by enduring biblical principles, thus insulating society from the wayward novelties propagated by those whom Burke referred to, disapprovingly, as the 'enterprising talents' of the country. The message advertising spiritual equality was also designed to produce social solidarity, which in turn formed a line of defence against the spread of subversive ideas proclaimed in France. It is interesting to find that only one reform of note, the celebrated measure outlawing the slave trade in 1807, was passed in Britain during the period of the French Wars.[84] This Act, promoted chiefly by evangelicals and humanitarians, rallied public opinion behind the Godly notion of the equality of man. It held out the promise of improvement for those who were denied minimal human rights, but it also preserved the principle of social inequality among all free men, and any disturbance caused by its enactment affected societies outside Britain. At home, the classical precept still marked the way forward: justice was knowing one's place; temperance was keeping it.

Nevertheless, even as Old Corruption continued to expand, important changes were taking place, some of them behind the scenes, and these created acute tensions between supporters of the status quo and those who saw the need to reshape policy both to deal with the size of the national debt and to cope with the new forces released by rapid economic change. After about 1800, there was a growing awareness in government circles that Britain's ability to defend herself against larger powers depended critically on the pace of economic development. It was recognised, too, that development had indeed been taking place over a long period, though no special emphasis was attached at the time to the new mechanised industries.[85] Moreover, it was generally agreed that this process was a result of the considerable degree of freedom enjoyed by the domestic economy, and that this was one of the liberties guaranteed by the Glorious Revolution.[86] In the eyes of those who discussed and determined policy, Britain's strength and stability relied on continuing capitalist development, which was held to be in the interest of the poor, the 'middling orders' and the rich alike. The brand of capitalism in question was thought to rest upon a foundation of law and custom which the gentlemanly elite could fairly claim to have created and sustained. As the French Wars drew to a close, the central issue was not whether the gentlemanly order would have to yield to a rising industrial bourgeoisie, but what direction policy would have to take to carry that order into the nineteenth century.

It was at this point that uncertainties about the shape of future economic policy came to the surface. The debate over the renewal of the East India Company's charter in 1813, for example, provides a rare insight into the split within the City at this time between those who supported the Company and the regulative system in general, and those who were eager to abolish restrictions and to open up new opportunities.[87] The Corn Law of 1815, on the other hand, was a wholly conservative measure that reflected the assumption that agriculture and the landed interest remained central to the economy and society.[88] In the event, the direction of policy as a whole came to be determined by the forward-looking members of the post-war Tory government who realised that the burden of the national debt, which consumed nearly 80 per cent of public revenue in the immediate post-war years, the weight of taxation entailed by debt service, and the persistence of monopoly endangered Britain's prospects for both economic growth and social stability.[89] The deep cuts in public spending after 1815, the return to the gold standard in 1819, the reductions in tariff rates in the 1820s and the progressive withdrawal of the government from direct participation in the economic process were all initiated by the gentlemanly elite. Their central purpose was to restore the confidence of investors and other property-holders in the credit system and hence in the credibility of the government. From one point of view, these moves can be seen as a reaction to the fiscal excesses imposed by the French Wars. In a longer perspective, they also represented an extension of the pressures for accountability, efficiency and 'economical reform' that had manifested themselves before the outbreak of the wars but had been postponed by them. The difference was that, after 1815, reform ceased to be associated mainly with radical and 'country' outsiders and acquired the general support of the propertied interest, and it did so for the compelling reason that it was seen to be necessary to the preservation of the gentlemanly order.[90]

Yet these acts of self-preservation should not be treated as if they were merely mechanical reactions to unpleasant stimuli. In engineering a sizeable shift in economic policy, progressive Tories and Whigs both sought to establish an ideological link between commercial society and improvement and between improvement and the advance of civilisation. By occupying the moral high ground, the reformers showed their awareness of the need to establish a legitimising ideology that would validate the changes they sponsored and also attract new supporters. The details of how this was achieved have still to be fully understood, though it is apparent that the problem can no longer be cast in terms of simple dualities, whether between Whigs and Tories or between free trade and mercantilism.[91] Burke's defence of property and privilege had to be refurbished in the light of the defeat of France, the diminished fear of Jacobinism, and the increasingly visible presence of manufacturing industry. Above all, there was a need to demonstrate that the brand of capitalism that had carried Britain through the eighteenth century retained its vitality, and that changes in economic policy were not only natural but also authorised adjustments to its trajectory. Only in this way was it possible for the landed interest to distance itself from Old Corruption while still keeping one step ahead of critics who wanted more radical reform. This was done partly by updating the eighteenth-century debate over the means of reconciling private interests with civic virtue, and partly by adding new elements, drawn, to take two very different examples, from the Scottish Enlightenment and from evangelical Anglicanism. In repositioning itself to direct a form of economic change that offered, so it seemed, the best chance of maintaining those elements of inequality that Burke wished to preserve, the gentlemanly order took account of the rise of industry but stopped short of embracing it. Industry was to be harnessed and therefore controlled; and, as we have seen, early in the nineteenth century a new generation of urban gentlemen began to be fashioned, principally from the service sector, to assist in the management process.[92]

Only an elite whose gentlemanly traditions were permeated by capitalist assumptions could have attempted such a dramatic shift in policy and could have responded so flexibly to pressures from below. Only an elite with these qualities, moreover, could have recognised in the 1820s that the looming imbalance between population growth and domestic sources of food supply was weakening the dominance of agriculture and increasing the need to move towards a more open economy.[93] At the same time, Britain's policy-makers also realised that there was a growing need to provide new industries, especially cotton goods, with overseas markets to deal with problems of foreign competition and domestic unemployment.[94] The link between the difficulties experienced by both agriculture and industry was provided by the City and its associated international services: if tariffs were reduced, imported corn would solve the problem of food supply, suppliers would have the purchasing power to buy British manufactures, and the ensuing expansion of trade would be financed, insured and transported principally by London. Increased trade would generate additional revenues, thus allowing the tax burden to be eased and the national debt to be reduced to manageable proportions. The policy changes which followed from this analysis, like the political concessions made in 1832, were astute moves to prevent the erosion of landed power by placating and partly incorporating the most successful representatives of the new wealth produced by economic development.[95] In implementing reform, the landed interest was thus responding to the results of economic advance on a broad front and not just to the rise of mechanised industry, important though that was. The Reform Act of 1832, for example, put the seal of political acceptance on new property in the south of England as well as on that created by the Industrial Revolution in the provinces.

The legislation of 1840–60, which finally installed free trade, established 'Gladstonian orthodoxy' in public finance, and ended the reign of the last chartered companies, was the logical outcome of the measures introduced by Lord Liverpool's government after 1815.[96] At the same time, it is evident that the assertiveness of provincial industry, spearheaded by the Anti-Corn Law League, increased dramatically in the final stages of this process.[97] However, industry's commitment to reform is to be read less as an expression of its triumphant advance than as an indication of its gathering difficulties. Fierce competition and falling prices, both at home and abroad, meant that rapid economic growth, in boosting the importance of mechanised industry in the economy, also contributed to a continuing crisis of excess capacity and low profitability.[98] This crisis was at its worst in the depression of 1837–42, when a sharp rise in urban unemployment fuelled the unrest which expressed itself in the Chartist movement.[99] The failure to solve these problems by assertive imperialist actions served only to encourage industry's interest in free trade as a means of creating markets and cutting costs.[100] Consequently, free trade was pushed further and faster than was thought expedient by the bulk of the landed interest. The budgets of 1842 and 1845 introduced additional modifications to what remained very largely a protectionist system, and as late as 1843 Peel was still trying to expand overseas trade by adjusting tariff preferences.[101] But the repeal of the Corn Laws in 1846 was a surrender to free trade which, a generation later and despite Peel's hopes, began to erode the profitability of agriculture and with it the particular form of gentlemanly capitalism, based on the wealth and power of the landed interest, which had arisen out of the Revolution Settlement of 1688.[102]

Even at this point, however, the decline of the landed interest did not deliver economic policy into the hands of the representatives of British industry, though in the 1840s this must have seemed a strong possibility. Ultimately, the chief beneficiaries of the strategy based on free trade, the gold standard and balanced budgets were the City of London and its associates in the service sector, though this outcome could not have been predicted with certainty even as late as 1850. Down to 1815, the City had tied much of its fortunes to the national debt and, indirectly, to the network of patronage which radicals labelled Old Corruption. Cutting these profitable ties was unwelcome and painful. Lord Liverpool's reform programme was designed partly to emancipate governments from excessive dependence on the City and was deeply resented there.[103] As noted earlier, the debate over the East India Company's charter in 1813 revealed that the City was uncertain whether to support the old order or to anticipate the new one, and its ambivalence weakened its influence with the government.[104] Attacks on the chartered companies also threw an unwelcome degree of light on the role of the Bank of England in directing monetary policy, and led to checks upon its powers.[105] In 1850, the City appeared to be less certain than industry of the road to follow.[106]

Nevertheless, the City, as the centre of a dynamic service economy, became the leading beneficiary of the reforms initiated after 1815. The return to gold and the moves towards freer trade were designed to turn Britain into the warehouse of the world rather than its workshop. The skills developed in domestic finance early in the eighteenth century helped to launch sterling on its international career at the close of the century, when invisible earnings began to assume importance in the balance of payments. Impetus was given to this development by the decline of Amsterdam, which enabled London to emerge as the world's leading financial centre from the 1790s, by the influx during the French Wars of refugee bankers, who enhanced the City's international expertise, and by Britain's role as chief paymaster of the allies.[107] In the 1820s, overseas finance assisted the post-war reconstruction of Europe and began to fund development projects further afield. Thereafter, foreign investment, combined with new domestic opportunities, such as railway construction, provided the basis of rentier fortunes as the eighteenth-century edifice of public debt and patronage was gradually dismantled.[108] Free trade also benefited the City by transforming London into a great entrepôt for world trade in foodstuffs and raw materials, thus boosting shipping services, marine insurance, specialised commodity exchanges, and wholesaling and commission agencies. In the course of this transformation, many prominent export industries became dependent on

City credits to finance their operations; in the case of cotton textiles the degree of dependence seriously impaired the industry's profits.[109]

By the mid-Victorian period, free trade and overseas investment were propelling the City towards the leadership of a global economy instead of merely a colonial one. The Bank of England, the pivotal institution in the Square Mile, took on a new lease of life as the accepted regulator of the intricate network of international payments that arose to meet the needs of specialised, multilateral trading ties. Moreover, once committed to a world role, the gentlemen of the City were well placed, by virtue of social and physical proximity, to carry their interests into the corridors of power in London, unlike British industry, which suffered from being heterogeneous, small scale and provincial. Later in the century, as Britain's overseas investments reached unprecedented heights and as her export industries began to feel the pressure of foreign competition, the City's international dominance gave it an authority in the economic affairs of the nation that was second to none.

Exporting the Revolution Settlement

In the most general terms, the empire created before the mid-nineteenth century represented the extension abroad of the institutions and principles entrenched at home by the Revolution of 1688. The export version of the new order was compelled to adjust to the conditions it encountered overseas, but it remained a recognisable reflection of its domestic self. Indeed, the various crises of empire helped to define the profile of the gentlemanly order in Britain more clearly both by revealing and by determining the limits of its flexibility.

The imprint of the landed interest was felt most obviously in the colonies of settlement, especially in the New World, which was the most important growth area for British trade and influence in the eighteenth century. The planters in the West Indies and the gentry in the mainland colonies saw themselves as being Britons and wanted to remain so.[110] If they distanced themselves from some aspects of the emerging British way of life, they also espoused gentlemanly ideals, succumbed to the 'irresistible lure' of London,[111] and employed the rhetoric of the 'country' opposition to express their dissent and their preferences.[112] Even in regions where white settlement was unimportant, such as India, extensions of imperial control were accompanied by systematic attempts to establish property rights in land, and the new rulers instinctively looked to indigenous landholders to provide steady support for civil order.[113] In settled and non-settled parts of the empire alike, the patronage system provided employment for the younger sons of magnates and gentry, and endowed authority with a military bearing and a paternal style that survived long after 1850.[114] The influence of the City and the newer forces thrown up by the financial revolution was very evident too, especially in the impetus given to overseas trade by improved credit facilities, by the expansion of the mercantile marine, powerfully supported by the Navigation Acts, and by advanced forms of commercial capitalism, such as the East India Company, with its close links with Westminster and its predominantly City-based investors.[115] Overseas expansion was backed by other important interest groups: manufacturers who needed a vent for their surplus products, export merchants who handled their goods, and import merchants and their associates who dealt with the re-export trades.[116] Expansion abroad also conferred indirect benefits on the home government, which gained from enlarged customs revenues, on the landed interest, which in consequence enjoyed favourable tax treatment, and on investors in the national debt, whose returns rose when borrowing and interest rates increased.[117]

The pursuit of what Adam Smith termed 'opulence' merged with the interests of defence to produce Britain's long-serving 'Blue Water' policy.[118] Since Britain could not hope to control continental Europe and felt herself to be threatened by the emergence of any large single power there, she capitalised on her geographical location and her comparative advantage in services by building up her naval power instead. The Navigation Acts, as we have seen, boosted British shipping, which in turn fostered both trade and defence. This policy commended itself because it was cheap, and hence kept taxation within acceptable bounds and avoided the need for a standing army, which was a highly sensitive option on political grounds as well as a costly one. By commanding the seas, Britain hoped to prevent France from blockading her trade with the continent and to frustrate any attempt at invasion. By the middle of the eighteenth century, these calculations had already been made and acted on. In the 1750s, Pitt was well aware that the threat of invasion endangered both financial and political stability. He observed that 'paper credit may be invaded in Kent', and anticipated the 'consternation that would spread through the City, when the noble, artificial yet vulnerable fabric of public credit should crumble in their hands'.[119] However, Britain's focus on naval defence did not mean that she was isolated from the continent. On the contrary, both diplomacy and money were devoted to the task of creating allies in Europe, especially among the smaller states that were conscious of their vulnerability in the face of larger neighbours. But the balance of advantage lay in the blue water and overseas; and one of the consequences of this decision was to elevate the standing of those who supported it, so that in time they became defenders of the national interest and not merely advocates of sectional advantage.

The most striking commercial results of the Blue Water strategy in the eighteenth century can be seen in the changing direction of British trade.[120] Continental Europe's share of Britain's home-produced exports fell from 82 per cent in 1700–1 to 40 per cent in 1772–3, while imports from Europe declined from 68 per cent of the total to 47 per cent during the same period. Over a rather longer term, Europe's share of Britain's total overseas trade dropped from 74 per cent in 1713–17 to 33 per cent in 1803–7.[121] This fundamental reorientation of British commerce was prompted by two considerations. In the first place, it seems likely that down to the third quarter of the century Britain's foreign trade was propelled primarily by import-led demand, especially for new colonial products, such as sugar, tea and tobacco, and was driven by rising incomes in London and south-east England, which in turn derived from wealth generated from arable farming and from finance and services.[122] The second influence was the difficulty of increasing sales of manufactured goods (chiefly woollens) in Europe and the need, consequently, to prise open new markets elsewhere. These were found chiefly in the mainland colonies, where competition was limited, rather than in Asia, where British goods were unable to make headway against local substitutes.[123]

The import bill was met partly by pushing manufactures into new corners of the world, and partly by capturing the re-export trade, that is by selling colonial products in continental Europe. The re-export trades made a notable additional to Britain's own exports: they accounted for about one-third of the value of all exports during the first three-quarters of the eighteenth century and played a vital part in closing the gap that would otherwise have opened up in Britain's visible trade balance. Britain's competitive advantage in the transactions sector thus made it possible for her to solve the formidable problems posed by the limited competitiveness of woollen textiles and by the array of protectionist barriers that hampered access to the major markets on her door-step in continental Europe, and also to dominate the rapidly expanding trade in overseas products. In doing so, she forged a chain of multilateral links that spanned the world and enabled a system of compensating balances to function long before the better-known settlements pattern of the nineteenth century came into being.[124] Even as the Industrial Revolution was beginning, Britain was already becoming the warehouse and shop-window of the world.

With the development of the cotton industry from the 1780s, Britain finally had a product that gave her a competitive edge in major markets, and exports became a powerful 'engine of growth' of national income for the first time.[125] The rate of export expansion rose steeply, and the ratio of exports to national income doubled between 1783 and 1801, when it reached 18 per cent. Cotton products accounted for about 53 per cent of the increase in total export values between 1784–6 and 1814–16. By 1804–6, cotton goods were responsible for no less than 42 per cent of the value of total exports, and in 1805–7 more than two-thirds of the value of the cotton industry's output was exported. The main markets were found outside the empire, in Western Europe and the United States, and after 1806 (when Napoleon's blockade closed much of Europe to British exports) in Latin America. However, these impressive developments did not signal the 'triumph of industry' or even the triumph of one particular industry. By the close of the eighteenth century, Europe and the United States had already reached the peak of their relative importance as markets for British cotton goods, and early in the new century manufacturers were again seeking new outlets for their products.

After 1815, despite the resumption of peace, exports failed to act as an engine of growth, as they had done after 1780. The volume of exports increased rapidly between 1815 and 1850, but values grew much more slowly as productivity gains reduced manufacturing costs and cut export prices. But falling prices did not enable Britain to hold on to her share of major markets: exports of cotton goods lost ground in Europe and the United States, where import-substitution aided by protection severely limited the prospects of foreign suppliers. Consequently, as we noted earlier, the cotton industry suffered from bouts of excess capacity and from reduced profit margins during the 1820s and 1830s.[126] Exports of other finished goods, notably woollens and metal products, did increase in Europe and the United States; but the overall tendency, even at this early date, was for Britain to become a supplier of semi-finished manufactures, such as yarn, to her rivals (especially those in Europe), thus aiding their industrialisation.

The inadequate rate of growth of exports, combined with rising demand for imports (fuelled by increased population), caused the trade gap to widen, especially in the late 1830s and early 1840s. Since income from shipping services increased only slowly, a trade-plus-services gap also appeared.[127] From the mid-1820s Britain depended upon rapidly increasing returns on foreign investments in Europe, North America and the Middle East to provide a small current-account surplus and to hold imports of raw materials at a level that would maintain domestic employment. In the period after 1815 the City therefore began to assume a fully international role and to perform a key function in balancing Britain's payments. During this period, too, London's finance and commercial services continued to play a vital part in creating markets for Britain's staple exports and in securing the resources needed as inputs into industry. In the case of exports, for example, no less than four-fifths of the increase in values that occurred between 1816–20 and 1838–42 arose from sales to new markets in Asia, Latin America and Africa.[128]

We turn, finally, to the ways in which the impulses we have described so far, in shaping British history and the course of overseas trade, also shaped the history of the empire. The installation in 1688 of a cohesive government, whose supporters had seen instability and were determined to avoid it, expressed itself in centralising tendencies that aimed at bringing all of the outer provinces under closer central control. Scotland was incorporated by the Act of Union in 1707, the Welsh, who were already incorporated, were subjected to renewed Anglicising influences, and Ireland was placed under the management of an Anglo-Irish, protestant gentry.[129] Further afield, the mainland colonies came under firmer direction from the Board of Trade and from a new generation of military governors, and were integrated more closely with the developing Atlantic economy managed from London.[130]

Whether or not this flurry of activity was followed by a period of 'salutary neglect' is a matter of dispute.[131] It is equally plausible to suggest that, once the initial institutional changes had been made, Britain's main interest lay in developing trade and increasing revenues, and that this priority is not captured by measures of administrative activity. However, the failure of overseas trade to grow at a pace that met the expectations of powerful mercantile lobbies in London helped to push Walpole into war with Spain between 1739 and 1748; and the Seven Years' War that followed in 1756 witnessed the further development of an ideology of aggressive commercial expansion.[132] When the war came to an end in 1763, France had been driven out of Canada and India, and Britain had emerged as a major colonial and commercial power. In the course of this struggle, Britain had tightened her hold on the colonies in order to secure her defences. After the war, as the costs of victory began to be counted, she extended her grip in searching for ways of balancing the budget and servicing the national debt. This quest led to increased revenue demands both at home, as we have seen, and in the colonies, where it was accompanied by a spirit of assertiveness that was one of the legacies of military success.[133] Since Britain's fiscal problems were not offset by domestic economic growth or by foreign trade during the 1760s and 1770s,[134] there was some anxiety about her ability to maintain the level of re-exports needed to settle the import bill, and at moments of crisis doubts were also expressed about her credit-worthiness.[135] It is against this background that Britain's changing relations with India and her mainland colonies in the third quarter of the century can best be approached.

Until the mid-eighteenth century, Britain's interests in India were represented by the East India Company and associated private traders, and were almost exclusively commercial.[136] From the 1720s, however, the Company's trade in its main spheres of activity in western India and Bengal began to run into difficulties. The problem stemmed principally from the dislocation caused by the break-up of the Mughal empire, but was compounded by competition from French companies and by military costs incurred during the conflict with France in the middle of the century. The attempt to resolve these problems, by restructuring trade relations to improve profitability and by using local revenues to subsidise the Company's activities, produced two important initiatives. The first, prompted by Clive's enterprise, led in 1757 to the Battle of Plassey, which delivered Bengal into British hands and a fortune into his own.[137] The second resulted in 1759 in the capture of Surat, which gave Britain a commanding position on the west coast.[138] The British government's interest in these advances was aroused by a desire to annex some of the Company's gains for its own budgetary needs:[139] 'Plassey plunder' did not fund the Industrial Revolution, as was once supposed, but it did enable Britain to indigenise the national debt by purchasing foreign (especially Dutch) holdings.[140] Thereafter, the quest for revenues to pay for military costs became a permanent one, and it greatly distorted the Company's commercial operations. As the East India Company began to generate debts and not just revenues in the 1770s, the British government found itself drawn further into the task of controlling the Company's administration and, in this way, of managing India too.[141]

Britain was not pulled into India simply by a breakdown of 'law and order'. The decline of central authority disrupted existing relations, but it did not lead to anarchy and it spawned a cluster of independent and semi-independent states whose ambitions sometimes cut across Britain's own purposes. Nor was Britain's advance the product of new industrial forces at home. The role of private traders expanded in the second half of the century, but their interest lay in selling Indian rather than British manufactures.[142] It is more plausible, we suggest, to view the move into India as being the result of competition between two military-fiscal organisations, one represented by the Mughals and their successor states and the other by the Company and the British government.[143] Both sides sought revenues to bolster trading profits, and both became involved in territorial expansion as a result. The outcome was strongly influenced by the military resources that the two were able to mobilise, and this in turn depended largely upon finance. The key decisions in this respect were made by local merchant bankers, who stood at the point of intersection between British and Indian commercial and political systems. In the end, the British were able to present themselves as the side likely to succeed, if not deserving of success: they won the support of the 'great moneyed men' of Surat before capturing the port;[144] and the balance of advantage in Bengal tilted in the Company's direction when local financiers deserted the nawab in 1756 and jeopardised his control of provincial treasuries.[145] Clive's actions were not directed from London; but they cannot be understood unless they are placed in the broader context of the financial revolution, the expansionist forces that it generated, and the problems these forces experienced on distant frontiers, where credit lines were fully stretched and where the junctions made with representatives of indigenous financial and fiscal systems were a necessary precondition of commercial success.

Similar influences – the search for revenue and the extension of commercial credit – were at work in the New World too, the main difference being that in North America they ran into young states that were being built up, whereas in India they were entangled with an ancient empire that was breaking down.[146] Just as the war with France had heightened an awareness of the importance of the empire, so the coming of peace in 1763 was accompanied by a determination to strengthen Britain's grasp on the mainland colonies. Mercantilist regulations were tightened by a battery of controls designed to raise revenues and to limit the independent economic development of the colonies.[147] As Charles Jenkinson, the Secretary of the Treasury, put it in 1765, the idea was to administer the colonies 'in such a manner as will keep them useful to the Mother Country'.[148] Exactly how burdensome Britain's demands proved to be is a matter of debate; but the point to emphasise in the present context is that they were resented partly because they disappointed the expectations of the colonists, who anticipated being rewarded for their loyalty during the war with France, and partly because they were perceived to be unjust on grounds of principle. At the same time, key interest groups in the mainland colonies also found themselves subjected to pressures arising from developments in the private sector. The massive expansion of overseas trade that had occurred in the course of the century had been financed largely by advances made by merchant bankers in London.[149] When trading conditions deteriorated in the 1760s and 1770s (and especially after the financial crisis of 1772), relations between creditors and debtors came under very considerable strain, not least because the colonists felt that indebtedness limited their sense of personal independence as well as their profits. These pressures were imprinted particularly strongly on Massachusetts and Virginia, the two colonies that were in the forefront of opposition to Britain's impositions. Merchants in Boston who jibbed at the demands made upon them became advocates of a less regulated market system;[150] planters in Virginia mounted what was, in effect, an agrarian revolt in defence of their gentlemanly status and against attempts to tax them and to call in outstanding debts.[151]

As a result of these developments, Britain lost the allegiance of vital sections of the colonial elite in the mainland colonies. Lack of patronage contributed to this outcome by limiting the number of loyalist supporters, and so did a progressive break-down in communications, which deprived the elite of effective representation in London.[152] Much more important, however, was the fact that the mainland colonies were developing aspirations of their own which were neither readily diluted by patronage nor easily contained within a regulated colonial system.[153] The colonists were becoming more confident of being able to manage their own affairs, though independence was not their first choice until it was, in a sense, thrust upon them. Population and wealth were expanding, and there were signs that trade relations could be diversified.[154] Furthermore, segments of the elite were acquiring expansionist ideas of their own which were further encouraged after 1763 by the removal of the threat from France.[155] In Massachusetts, Virginia and Carolina, these aspirations were hurried into political shape by the need to take control of a more radical strain of opposition which, in representing the discontents of poor whites, also posed a threat to property and privilege in the colonies.[156] A comparison with the West Indies is instructive, for there the planters did not rebel, even though they suffered many of the same frustrations.[157] The difference was that Jamaica and Barbados were truly dependent. The planters there were few in number and many of them were absentees. They relied heavily on British finance and totally on the British navy, and could envisage no alternative to either. In the West Indies, independence was simply not possible, even if it had been conceived.

The assertiveness which characterised imperial policy in the 1760s and 1770s not only survived the loss of the mainland colonies but also was reaffirmed after the event and then further reinforced by the French Wars. Lord North's government fell in 1782 not because its policies towards the mainland colonies were unpopular but because they failed.[158] Thereafter, the consolidation of 'new conservatism' in Britain combined with the need to put the economy on a war footing were translated directly into imperial policy. The aristocratic, military element placed itself in the vanguard of the imperial presence, colonial patronage was greatly extended, and the empire acquired a Christian purpose as an instrument of moral defence against Jacobinism. Extensions of authority in British North America, Australia, the Cape, Ireland, the West Indies, India and south-east Asia reinforced the empire and strengthened Britain's defence against foreign aggressors. No more colonies were to be lost through the error, as Lord Thurlow saw it, of allowing them too much 'political liberty'.[159] The Canada Act of 1791 imposed a conservative constitution on Quebec; unruly colonists in New South Wales and the Cape were disciplined by a succession of authoritarian governors; and insurrection in Ireland in 1798 was first forcefully put down and then dealt with by the Act of Union in 1801.[160] The West Indies were marked out as suppliers of cotton to replace the United States, India was to become a bastion of landed values and a model of agrarian improvement, and the Straits Settlements were to guarantee free passage for the resulting exports from Bengal and for imports from China.[161]

As far as commercial policy was concerned, the immediate reaction to the loss of the American colonies was to repair the breach in the protectionist wall by means of the Navigation Act of 1786. The French Wars which followed in 1793 emphasised the continuing importance of colonial supplies to national security. Shifts in the direction of exports to Europe and North America from the 1780s undoubtedly helped to bring about some liberalisation of trade with the United States, and in 1794 the Jay Treaty acknowledged the significance of extra-colonial ties by according ships from the United States the same rights as British vessels in trade with the West Indies.[162] However, this was a matter of making a virtue out of necessity: it was a grudging modification to a system which remained resolutely protectionist in intent, rather than an early sign of a confident move towards free trade. Similarly, the modification of the East India Company's monopoly of Indian trade in 1793 and its abolition in 1813 were aimed at developing trade with the Far East so that India could improve its contribution to the imperial system, not at assisting foreign traders to gain entry to regions opened by British enterprise.[163] Down to 1815, policy-makers in Britain were as much agreed on the need to maintain protected colonial outlets for goods and services as they were on the importance of liberalising the home market.

After 1815, the role of the empire was adjusted, slowly and hesitantly, to fit the changing priorities of the metropole. Having helped the war effort, the empire was mobilised – not for the last time – in the cause of winning the peace. The reforms set in train at home left their mark on the empire too as Britain set about designing an international regime that would make the world safe for the monarchical, propertied, gentlemanly order that had survived, providentially, the threats of republicanism and secularism. The empire was to be adapted, not abandoned, to meet this new challenge, above all by putting in place a set of 'like-minded', co-operative elites who would demonstrate that the British view of the world could and should be reproduced elsewhere, and that economic progress was compatible with, indeed required, individual liberty, differential property rights, and political stability. As Goderich, the Colonial Secretary, declared in 1833, Britain's aim was 'to transfer to distant regions the greatest possible amount both of the spirit of civil liberty and of the forms of social order to which Great Britain is chiefly indebted for the rank she holds among the civilised nations'.[164] India was the most prominent illustration of this policy, despite the fact that 'improvement' was imposed by paternal rather than liberal means.[165] The colonies of settlement, though still at an early stage of development, also had an important place in this design.[166] They offered openings for migrants as well as for capital and commerce, and were thought to be the most promising launching points for the 'Anglicising' mission.[167] In the 1820s the Colonial Office planned to 'create and uphold an opulent gentry' in Australia, as in the other colonies of white settlement;[168] in the troubled 1830s and 1840s considerable interest was shown in the possibility of taking government action to promote factor flows to the colonies, and especially to widen the 'field of employment' for the middle class as the apparatus of state contracted at home.[169]

These changes occurred within a structure that was still based on colonial preferences, even though these were being modified from the 1820s. Indeed, the vigorous protectionist policies adopted in Europe and the United States after 1815 appeared to confirm the wisdom, or at least the necessity, of adhering to Britain's traditional policy. By limiting access to major markets, the new mercantilism adopted by foreign powers also prompted Britain to take an interest in extending trade to underdeveloped areas that lay outside her formal control. The extension of informal influence after 1815 is best understood, not as an alternative to the old colonial system, but as an addition to it which reflected the increasingly cosmopolitan character of Britain's trade and finance and the growing ambivalence of her commercial policy during the period of transition to free trade. This means of expansion was made possible by the elimination of the French naval threat, which greatly reduced the need for direct British political influence abroad and made the pursuit of new markets compatible with the drive for cheap government.[170] Castlereagh and Canning believed that the steady liberalisation of trade with new partners, especially in Latin America, would naturally promote British influence, and that this would extend beyond commerce: British experts were at hand to supply appropriate constitutions for new states; British missionaries stood ready to convert the heathen; and the City was beginning to explore the prospects of funding this programme of world development.[171]

By the 1830s, Canning's successor as Foreign Secretary, Lord Palmerston, was more aware of the obstacles to achieving this desirable state of affairs as a result of the growth of competition from Europe and the United States and the urgent need to find new markets for industry and commerce in the underdeveloped world. Palmerston's almost instinctive commitment to free-market economics ought not to be surprising, given that he inherited beliefs espoused by the gentlemanly elite at the beginning of the century. But the effort he put into extending Britain's trade and influence in the extra-European world needs to be emphasised because it is still underplayed by diplomatic historians. Palmerston was determined to 'export abroad the same self-regulating system which was transforming British society'.[172] To this end, he was willing to impose free trade on reluctant rulers, to evict recalcitrant ones, and to advance 'legitimate commerce' by putting down the African slave trade.[173] Behind this grand design, which aimed at creating a cluster of economic satellites managed by foreign beneficiaries of English culture, stood Palmerston's persistent concern about the possibility of social breakdown in the 1830s and 1840s, when industry was severely depressed and Chartism was at its height.[174] It is no coincidence that Palmerston's interventionist policy reached new levels of intensity during this period. The war against China, the bombardment of slave ports on the west coast of Africa, the treaties with Turkey and Egypt and the attack on Argentina's protectionist policies,[175] all reflected his concern to find overseas solutions to domestic problems and his particular belief that 'it is the business of government to open and secure the roads for the merchant'.[176]

Palmerston carried into the mid-nineteenth century the peculiarly British mixture of economic liberty and gentlemanly paternalism that had its origins in the late seventeenth century. He also infused these ideas with a renewed sense of mission: the belief that the British model of development could be exported overseas and the conviction that it had to be exported if it were to be preserved at home. Unfortunately for Britain, this strategy ran into serious difficulties. The colonies of settlement made slow and disappointing progress, India resisted or frustrated modernisers as much as she was bent to their will, and the penetration of other underdeveloped countries was confined very largely to coastal regions.[177] The abortive attempt to integrate the Latin American republics more firmly into the international economy in the 1820s was indicative of the problems Britain faced, and the losses suffered then remained as a warning for a generation of City bankers. Development and influence alike awaited the coming of the railway and the opening of the interior during the second half of the century. Meanwhile, the failure to extend Britain's economic reach by these informal, if also forceful, means increased the pressure to adopt complete free trade in the 1840s, and brought nearer the demise of the particular brand of gentlemanly capitalism that Palmerston so aptly represented.

Conclusion

The dominance of the landed interest and its aristocratic leaders provides a unifying theme for the years between 1688 and 1850 and points to an underlying continuity covering a period of one and a half centuries. But this claim does not lend support to the 'continuity thesis', if that is taken to mean the perpetuation into the nineteenth century of an *ancien régime*. On the contrary, our interpretation suggests that the regime founded in 1688 was substantially new and that much of its innovative character stemmed from the financial revolution it helped to sponsor. The result, as we have described it, was the creation of a form of capitalism headed by improving landlords in association with improving financiers who served as their junior partners. This joint enterprise established a tradition of modernisation and was itself the product of a modernisation of tradition that both conserved gentlemanly values and carried them forward into a changing world.

The various challenges made and encountered by the new regime indicate subdivisions which break the continuity of the period, though they do not destroy its unity at a much higher level of historical generalisation. In particular, we have tried to show how the historical contours of the gentlemanly order were shaped by the need to service the national debt, to fund patronage and to manage the political system in ways that preserved privilege, civil peace and the constitution. These imperatives drove the machinery of state through the eighteenth century and into the era of reform. In turn, they go far towards explaining the gentlemanly elite's commitment to economic growth and its interest first in constructing a system of commercial protection and national credit, and then in moving towards free trade and a wider role for British finance. This transformation was bound up with a complex realignment of cultural values which involved legitimising new activities by converting private interests into public virtues, harnessing the monarchy to buttress political stability, and calling upon the Church to stiffen the moral fibre of the nation.[178] By distinguishing in these ways between changes within a social system and changes to the system itself, it becomes possible to see how the former contribute to the latter and thus to devise an analysis that takes account of both continuity and change.

We have also tried to demonstrate how the constellation of forces that was entrenched and released by the Glorious Revolution found expression in Britain's international policy and overseas presence. From this perspective, imperialism was a means of defending the Revolution Settlement by building a strong navy and by creating satellites that gave Britain a measure of independence from powerful neighbours on the continent of Europe. Equally, it was a means of exporting the Revolution Settlement by promoting a propertied interest abroad and by capitalising on Britain's comparative advantage in finance and commercial services to supply credit, carriage and insurance, and thus to capture an increasing share of world trade. Aside from our particular argument on this subject, we have also put a general case for reintegrating the history of the empire with that of the metropole during this period. In doing so, we are returning to a perspective which contemporaries regarded as being uncontroversial, though it has now been diminished by the specialisation required of modern scholarship. Tom Paine, among many others, was well aware of these global connections. He had a shrewd appreciation of the relationship between the national credit and political order, and he saw, too, that there was a link between the fortunes of empire in Asia and in the New World. As he observed of the government's attempt to rescue the East India Company's declining fortunes in 1773 by giving it a monopoly of tea: 'it is somewhat remarkable that the produce of that ruined country, transported to America, should there kindle up a war to punish their destroyer'.[179] It is not necessary to accept Paine's interpretation of the causes of the revolt of the mainland colonies to agree with him on the wisdom of keeping in view the relationship between the parts and the whole.

Successful expansion, reinforced by colonial acquisitions, generated profits and revenues, helped to service the national debt, and contributed to employment and political stability. In this guise, imperialism was expansive and often aggressive. The extension of credit and the search for revenue led to collisions on diverse peripheries, while the contest for colonies and for control of world trade played its part in causing the large-scale wars that began in 1739 and culminated in 1815. By that date the costs of war had expanded the national debt to the point where it was threatening to topple the structure it was supposed to support. Once France had been defeated, a new campaign had to be mounted to bring public expenditure under control, to generate extra revenue and to create employment at home. This exercise committed Britain to a new overseas development drive which sought to mobilise the empire while also adding a cosmopolitan element to it by moving progressively towards free trade. The aim in both cases was to secure resource pools, to open markets and to put in place a set of allies who would ensure that the values defended by war were reinforced by a lasting peace.

The survival of mercantilism in the nineteenth century was therefore not the result of its success in meeting Britain's needs. Platt's argument that the imperial system was more or less self-sufficient down to the 1840s underestimates both the acute difficulties experienced by the export industries during this period and the growing urgency of problems arising on the domestic front.[180] As we have suggested, it was the inadequacy of the regulated system inherited from the eighteenth century that prompted renewed overseas expansion and the accompanying moves to reduce protectionism after 1815. But this does not mean, either, that the period saw the creation of a form of free-trading imperialism arising out of the expansive and confident forces generated by new industries and technology.[181] Britain's intentions in seeking to extend her informal influence were perfectly clear, but the results were very limited down to the middle of the nineteenth century. As we have seen, it was Britain's inability to solve her problems either within the existing empire or by informal means that provoked Palmerston's final burst of bellicosity and impelled Peel's risky lunge towards free trade.

After 1850, free trade destroyed the old colonial system and, in combination with the rise of new wealth, ensured the gradual demise of the landed aristocracy, thus bringing one phase of gentlemanly capitalism to an end. But the new economic and political structures that arose – and the imperialism that flowed from them – were still not dominated by industrial capitalism. From the middle of the nineteenth century, the main area of growth was the service sector, and the most rapidly developing region in Britain was the south-east. The City was at the heart of both. London stood at the centre of a well-developed network of international services, and these were destined to expand rapidly as world trade increased in the second half of the century. Even before 1850, financial flows from the City were an important determinant of the rhythm of development in the colonies.[182] Beyond formal empire, London's influence as the main source of long-term finance had begun to spread to Europe and North America after 1815, and was poised to increase dramatically after 1850, as the age of the steamship and railway began.[183] The City and the service sector overcame their hesitations, supported the introduction of free trade and proved, down to 1914, to be its chief beneficiaries. They also carried into free-trading Britain many of the cultural values acquired in the course of their long apprenticeship to the landed aristocracy. After 1850, as one form of gentlemanly capitalism began to fail another arose to take its place.

Notes

1 The continuity thesis has been restated by J.C.D. Clark, *English Society, 1688–1832: Ideology, Social Structure and Political Practice during the Ancien Regime* (Cambridge, 1985). Statements of the alternative view are too numerous to be listed, but for the one quoted here (and for further references) see Paul Longford, *A Polite and Commercial People: England, 1727–1783* (Oxford, 1989).

2 See Philip Lawson, 'The Missing Link: the Imperial Dimension in Understanding Hanoverian Britain', *Hist. Jour.*, 29 (1986), and the agenda drawn up by J.G.A. Pocock, 'British History: a Plea for a New Subject', *Am. Hist. Rev.*, 87 (1982).

3 See the judgements of I.K. Steele, 'The Empire and Provincial Elites: an Interpretation of Some Recent Writings on the English Atlantic, 1675–1740', in Peter Marshall and Glyn Williams, eds. *The British Atlantic Empire Before the American Revolution* (1980), p. 2, and Peter Marshall, 'The British Empire in the Age of the American Revolution', in William M. Fowler and Wallace Coyle, eds. *The American Revolution: Changing Perspectives* (Boston, Mass., 1979), p. 193.

4 J. Holland Rose, A.P. Newton and E.A. Benians, eds. *The Old Empire From the Beginnings to 1783* (Cambridge, 1929). See also Sir Reginald Coupland, *The British Empire After the American Revolution* (1930).
5 Vol. I, *Discovery and Revolution* (Oxford, 1952), and Vol. II, *New Continents and Changing Values* (Oxford, 1964). The discussion that follows draws especially on Vol. I, pp. 1–11, 147–8, 154, 158 and 647, and Vol. II, pp. 1–3, 259, 782–6 and 792–3, and on two valuable guides: Peter Marshall, 'The First and Second Empires: a Question of Demarcation', *History,* 44 (1964), and Ronald Hyam, 'British Imperial Expansion in the Late Eighteenth Century', *Hist. Jour.,* 10 (1967). There is also a perceptive review of Vol. I by Richard Pares in *Eng. Hist. Rev.,* LXVIII (1953).
6 J. Gallagher and R.E. Robinson, 'The Imperialism of Free Trade', *Econ. Hist. Rev.,* 2nd ser., VI (1953).
7 Starting points other than that advanced by Harlow have been put forward: 1748 is one; the 'middle of the eighteenth century' is another. But these suggestions have not been accompanied by a thesis encompassing the 'first' empire as a whole. Harlow's argument therefore deserves to retain its place in the historiography of the eighteenth-century empire, despite the fact that it now has few advocates.
8 *Dependent Accumulation and Underdevelopment* (1978), pp. 72–3 and the discussion of periodisation on pp. 7–10.
9 Immanuel Wallerstein, *The Modern World System,* Vol. II, *Mercantilism and the Consolidation of the European World Economy, 1600–1750* (New York, 1980), p. 258 and the discussion of periodisation on pp. 2–9.
10 A recent exception, which should encourage imperial historians to look more closely at this neglected period, is C.A. Bayly, *Imperial Meridian: The British Empire and the World, 1780–1830* (1989).
11 We follow here N.F.R. Crafts, 'British Economic Growth, 1700–1831: a Review of the Evidence', *Econ. Hist. Rev.,* 2nd ser. XXXVI (1983); idem, 'British Industrialization in an International Context', *Jour. Interdisc. Hist.,* 19 (1989); and C.H. Feinstein, 'Capital Formation in Great Britain', in Peter Mathias and N.M. Postan, eds. *The Cambridge Economic History of Europe* (Cambridge, 1978), VII, Pt. 1.
12 J.V. Beckett, 'The Pattern of Landownership in England and Wales, 1660–1880', *Econ. Hist. Rev.,* 2nd ser. XXXVII (1984); J.R. Wordie, 'Rent Movements and the English Tenant Farmer, 1700–1839', *Research in Economic History,* 6 (1981); P.K. O'Brien, 'Quelle a été exactement la contribution de l'aristocratie britannique au progrès de l'agriculture entre 1688 et 1789?', *Annales,* 42 (1987).
13 A.H. John, 'The Course of Agricultural Change, 1660–1760', in L.S. Pressnell, ed. *Studies in the Industrial Revolution Presented to T.S. Ashton* (1960), pp. 125, 130–2; and for the stimulus provided by the corn bounties, idem, 'English Agricultural Improvement and Grain Exports, 1660–1765', in D.C. Coleman and A.H. John, eds. *Trade, Government and Economy in Pre-Industrial England: Essays Presented to F.J. Fisher* (1976), pp. 48–50.
14 Patrick O'Brien, 'Agriculture and the Home Market for English Industry', *Eng. Hist. Rev.,* C (1985).
15 See, for example, Geoffrey Cannon, ed. *The Whig Ascendancy* (1981); G.E. Mingay, *English Landed Society in the Eighteenth Century* (1963), pp. 10–11, 111–13.
16 M.W. McCahill, *Order and Equipoise: The Peerage and the House of Lords, 1783–1806* (1978); J. Slack, 'The House of Lords and Parliamentary Patronage in Great Britain, 1802–32', *Hist. Jour.,* 23 (1980); John Cannon, *Aristocratic Century: The Peerage of Eighteenth-Century England* (Cambridge, 1984); Ellis Archer Wasson, 'The House of Commons, 1660–1945: Parliamentary Families and the Political Elite', *Eng. Hist. Rev.,* CVI (1991).
17 Quoted in Cannon, *Aristocratic Century,* p. 39.
18 See, for example, Linda Colley, *In Defiance of Oligarchy: The Tory Party, 1714–60* (Cambridge, 1982); idem, 'Eighteenth-Century Radicalism Before Wilkes', *Royal Hist. Soc. Trans.,* 31 (1981); John Stevenson, *Popular Disturbances in England, 1700–1870* (1979); and John Brewer, 'English Radicalism in the Reign of George III', in J.G.A. Pocock,

ed. *Three British Revolutions* (Princeton, NJ, 1980). The constituencies and the towns are dealt with by Frank O'Gorman, *Voters, Patrons and Parties: The Unreformed Electorate of Hanoverian England, 1734–1832* (Oxford, 1989), and Nicholas Rogers, *Whigs and Cities: Popular Politics in the Age of Walpole and Pitt* (Oxford, 1989).

19 Our thinking on this subject, and on the period as a whole, owes a great deal to two very different but complementary books: P.G.M. Dickson, *The Financial Revolution in England: A Study in the Development of Public Credit, 1688–1756* (1967), and J.G.A. Pocock, *The Machiavellian Moment: The Florentine Contribution to the Atlantic Republican Tradition* (Princeton, NJ, 1975). See also idem, 'The Machiavellian Moment Revisited: a Study in History and Ideology', *Jour. Mod. Hist.*, 53 (1981); idem, *Virtue, Commerce, and History* (Cambridge, 1985); and Julian Hoppitt, 'Attitudes to Credit in Britain, 1680–1790', *Hist. Jour.*, 33 (1990).

20 A.E. Feaveryear, *The Pound Sterling: A History of English Money* (2nd edn 1963), pp. 154–7; J. Sperling, 'The International Payments Mechanism in the Seventeenth and Eighteenth Centuries', *Econ. Hist. Rev.*, 2nd ser. XIV (1962); D.M. Joslin, 'London Private Bankers, 1720–1785', *Econ. Hist. Rev.*, 2nd ser. VII (1954), pp. 175–9, 184; Dickson, *Financial Revolution*, pp. 225–8, 493, 505–6, and Ch. 20; Larry Neal, 'The Rise of a Financial Press: London and Amsterdam, 1681–1810', *Bus. Hist.*, 30 (1988). Recent research drawing attention to the importance of the service sector in the eighteenth century is summarised by N.F.R. Crafts, *British Economic Growth during the Industrial Revolution* (Oxford, 1985), pp. 12–13, 16–17.

21 Dickson, *Financial Revolution*, Ch. 16; P.G.M. Dickson, *The Sun Insurance Office, 1710–1960* (1960); B.E. Supple, *The Royal Exchange Assurance: A History of British Insurance, 1720–1970* (Cambridge, 1970); A.H. John, 'Insurance Investment and the London Money Market of the Eighteenth Century', *Economica*, 20 (1953).

22 Ralph Davis, *The Rise of the English Shipping Industry in the Seventeenth and Eighteenth Centuries* (2nd edn. 1972), pp. 389–90; Simon Ville, 'Michael Henley and Son, London Shipowners, 1775–1830: With Special Reference to War Experience', (Ph.D. thesis, London University, 1983).

23 Jacob M. Price, 'What Did Merchants Do? Reflections on British Overseas Trade, 1660–1790', *Jour. Econ. Hist.*, 49 (1989), pp. 273, 278–82.

24 John Brewer, *The Sinews of Power: War, Money and the English State, 1688–1783* (1989), Ch. 3 (which also discusses the relationship between public service and patronage); Geoffrey Holmes, *Augustan England: Professions, State, and Society, 1680–1730* (1982). Our formulation (see also Chapter 1) suggests that some occupations in the private sector were compatible with gentlemanly status and therefore refines the contrast drawn by Brewer, *Sinews of Power*, p. 206.

25 E.A. Wrigley, 'A Simple Model of London's Importance in Changing English Society and Economy, 1650–1750', *Past and Present*, 37 (1967), and the pioneering studies by F.J. Fisher now gathered together in *London and the English Economy, 1500–1800* (1990). For the concentration of wealth and service-sector employments see James Alexander, 'The Economic Structure of the City of London at the End of the Seventeenth Century', *Urban History Yearbook* (1989); L.D. Schwartz, 'Social Class and Social Geography: the Middle Class in London at the End of the Eighteenth Century', *Social History*, 7 (1982); and John A. James, 'Personal Wealth Distribution in Late Eighteenth-Century Britain', *Econ. Hist. Rev.*, 2nd ser. XLI (1988).

26 A.E. Musson, 'The British Industrial Revolution', *History*, 67 (1982), pp. 257–8. See also Neil McKendrick, John Brewer and J.H. Plumb, *The Birth of a Consumer Society* (1982), though the precise date of birth is open to discussion, as the title of Joan Thirsk's study of the seventeenth century suggests: *Economy, Policy and Projects: The Development of a Consumer Society in Early Modern England* (Oxford, 1978).

27 See, for example, P.J. Corfield, *The Impact of English Towns, 1700–1800* (Oxford, 1982); Peter Borsay, *The English Urban Renaissance: Culture and Society in the Provincial Town, 1660–1770* (Oxford, 1989); and the important essay by J.A. Chartres, 'Cities and Towns, Farmers and Economic Change in the Eighteenth Century', *Hist. Research*, 64 (1991).

28 Peter Mathias, *The Transformation of England* (1979), pp. 91–4; B.L. Anderson, 'Provincial Aspects of the Financial Revolution of the Eighteenth Century', *Bus. Hist.,* 11 (1969), pp. 11–12; and idem, 'Money and the Structure of Credit in the Eighteenth Century', *Bus. Hist.,* 12 (1970).

29 Dickson, *Financial Revolution,* pp. 4–6, 304–5.

30 Davis, *Rise of the English Shipping Industry,* p. 300; Dickson, *Financial Revolution,* pp. 304–5. It ought to be noted here that 'mercantilist' writers were well aware of the importance of invisible items in the balance of payments: see Jacob Viner, *Studies in the Theory of International Trade* (1937), pp. 13–15.

31 Clayton Roberts, 'The Constitutional Significance of the Financial Settlement of 1690', *Hist. Jour.,* 20 (1977).

32 This subject has been put on the agenda of historical inquiry by Patrick O'Brien and Caglar Keyder, *Economic Growth in Britain and France, 1780–1914* (1978). Contemporaries were well aware of the disparity: François Crouzet, 'The Sources of England's Wealth: Some French Views in the Eighteenth Century', in P.L. Cottrell and D.H. Aldcroft, eds. *Shipping, Trade and Commerce: Essays in Memory of Ralph Davis* (Leicester, 1981), pp. 71–2.

33 Charles P. Kindleberger, 'Financial Institutions and Economic Development: a Comparison of Great Britain and France in the Eighteenth and Nineteenth Centuries', *Expl. Econ. Hist.,* 21 (1984).

34 D. Weir, 'Tontines, Public Finance and Revolution in France and England, 1688–1789', *Jour. Econ. Hist.,* 49 (1989); Michael D. Border and Eugene N. White, 'A Tale of Two Currencies: British and French Finance During the Napoleonic Wars', *Jour. Econ. Hist.,* 51 (1991); and a source that might easily be overlooked in this connection, Gilbert Faccarello and Philippe Steiner, eds. 'La pensée économique pendant la révolution française', *Economies et sociétés,* 13 (1990), Pt. 4.

35 *The Conduct of the Allies* (1711), quoted in Dickson, *Financial Revolution,* p. 26.

36 Peter Earle, 'The Economics of Stability: the Views of Daniel Defoe', in Coleman and John, *Trade, Government and Economy,* pp. 277–8; and idem, *The World of Daniel Defoe* (1976), Pt. 3.

37 In addition to the references given in n. 19, there is a particularly valuable set of essays in J.G.A. Pocock, ed. *Three British Revolutions: 1641, 1688, 1776* (Princeton, NJ, 1980).

38 Quoted in Donald Winch, *Adam Smith's Politics* (Cambridge, 1978), p. 123. Isaac Kramnick, *Bolingbroke and his Circle* (Cambridge, Mass., 1968), has provoked methodological criticism but remains the classic statement.

39 Pocock, *Virtue, Commerce, and History*; Winch, *Adam Smith's Politics*; David Eastwood, 'Robert Southey and the Intellectual Origins of Romantic Conservatism', *Eng. Hist. Rev.,* CIV (1989).

40 For a broad survey of these tendencies see P.J. Corfield, 'Class by Name and Number in Eighteenth-Century Britain', *History,* 72 (1987).

41 For one example see Larry Neal, 'Interpreting Power and Profit in Economic History: a Case Study of the Seven Years War', *Jour. Econ. Hist.,* 37 (1977).

42 This remained the case right down to 1815. See Dickson, *Financial Revolution,* pp. 58–9, 285, 295, 297–8. 302; Alice Carter, *Getting, Spending and Investing in Early Modern Times* (Assen, The Netherlands, 1975), pp. 19, 66–75, 136–7; also J.R. Ward, *The Finance of Canal Building in Eighteenth-Century England* (oxford, 1974), pp. 140–2, 171–2. For the very similar composition of the original subscribers to the Bank of England, see Dickson, *Financial Revolution,* p. 256.

43 R.S. Neale, 'The Bourgeoisie, Historically, has Played a Most Important Part', in Eugene Kamenka and R.S. Neale, eds. *Feudalism, Capitalism and Beyond* (1975), P. 90.

44 Mingay. *English Landed Society,* pp. 71–6; P.J. Marshall, *East India Fortunes: The British in Bengal in the Eighteenth Century* (1976), pp. 9–14.

45 Richard Grassby, 'Social Mobility and Business Enterprise in Seventeenth-Century England', in Donald Pennington and Keith Thomas, eds. *Puritans and Revolutionaries: Essays in Seventeenth-Century History Presented to Christopher Hill* (Oxford, 1978), pp. 355–7, 365–6, 378–9. The direct connection with trade may have declined in the

course of the eighteenth century as more attractive openings arose in public service, but at the highest levels ties between land and trade remained close, especially in London: Nicholas Rogers, 'Money, Land and Lineage: the Big Bourgeoisie of Hanoverian London', *Soc. Hist.*, 4 (1970), pp. 444–5.

46 Dickson, *Financial Revolution,* pp. 5–7; Neale, 'The Bourgeoisie', p. 98.

47 Dickson, *Financial Revolution,* p. 282; Carter, *Getting, Spending,* p. 106; Rogers, 'Money, Land and Lineage', pp. 444–7; G.C.A. Clay, 'The English Land Market, 1660–1770: the Role of the Moneyed Purchasers'. We are grateful to Dr Clay for allowing us to cite his unpublished paper. As F.M.L. Thompson points out, the purchase of a country estate did not necessarily mean that the new owner left the town or his business: 'Desirable Properties: the Town and Country Connection in British Society Since the Late Eighteenth Century', *Hist. Research,* 64 (1991).

48 Derek Jarrett, 'The Myth of "Patrotism" in Eighteenth-Century English Politics', in J.H. Bromley and E.H. Kossman, eds. *Britain and the Netherlands,* Vol. 5 (The Hague, 1975), p. 124. For the background see Daniel Statt, 'The City of London and the Controversy over Immigration, 1660–1722', *Hist. Jour.,* 33 (1990).

49 G.C.A. Clay, 'Henry Hoare, Banker, and the Building of the Stourhead Estate'. We are grateful to Dr Clay for allowing us to cite his unpublished paper on this subject.

50 Richard Pares, 'A London West India Merchant House', in idem, *The Historian's Business* (Oxford, 1961).

51 Thereafter, the family was prominent in public service, especially the army. Its eminence was crowned in 1922, when the 6th earl married Princess Mary, the only daughter of George V.

52 Crafts, *British Economic Growth*; idem, 'British Industrialization'; C.K. Harley, 'British Industrialisation Before 1841: Evidence of Slower Growth during the Industrial Revolution', *Jour. Econ. Hist.,* 42 (1982). Peter H. Lindert, 'Remodelling British Economic History', *Jour. Econ. Hist.,* 43 (1983).

53 Contemporary views are discussed by Michael Kammen, *Empire and Interest: The American Colonies and the Politics of Mercantilism* (Philadelphia, Pa, 1970).

54 Mathias, *Transformation,* pp. 23, 31; D.J. Jeremy, 'Damming the Flood: British Government Attempts to Check the Outflow of Technicians and Machinery, 1780–1843', *Bus. Hist. Rev.,* 51 (1977); Douglas Farnie, *The English Cotton Industry and the World Market, 1815–96* (Oxford, 1979), p. 97. On the benefits of protection to special interests see, for example, N.B. Harte, 'The Rise of Protection and the English Linen Industry, 1690–1790', in N.B. Harte and K.G. Ponting, eds. *Textile History and Economic History* (Manchester, 1973).

55 S.D. Chapman, 'British Marketing Enterprise: the Changing Role of Merchants, Manufacturers and Financiers, 1700–1860', *Bus. Hist. Rev.,* 53 (1979).

56 W.D. Rubinstein, 'The Victorian Middle Classes: Wealth, Occupation, and Geography', *Econ. Hist. Rev.,* 2nd ser. XXX (1977); idem, 'Wealth, Elites, and the Class Structure of Modern Britain', *Past and Present,* 76 (1977). Information on the eighteenth century is less systematic, but see, for example, Brewer, *Sinews of Power,* pp. 208–9.

57 Quoted in Thomas A. Horne, *The Social Thought of Bernard Mandeville* (1978), p. 95. See also Winch, *Adam Smith's Politics,* p. 99.

58 Rogers, 'Money, Land, and Lineage', p. 453.

59 Dickson, *Financial Revolution,* p. 203; Mingay, *English Landed Society,* pp. 197–8; David Spring, 'English Landowners and Nineteenth-Century Industrialisation', in J.T. Ward and R.G. Wilson, eds. *Land and Industry: The Landed Estate and the Industrial Revolution* (Newton Abbot, 1971), pp. 39–42, 51–3.

60 See n. 44. Also John, 'Insurance Investment', p. 157; Joslin, 'London Private Bankers', p. 185; Thompson, 'Desirable Properties'.

61 François Crouzet, *The First Industrialists: The Problem of Origins* (Cambridge, 1985), pp. 68, 77, 80–4; Michael W. McCahill, 'Peers, Patronage and the Industrial Revolution, 1760–1800', *Jour. Brit. Stud.,* 16 (1976); David Spring, 'English Landowners', pp. 51–2.

62 On the General Chamber see Donald Read, *The English Provinces, 1760–1960: A Study in Influence* (1964), pp. 22–33. However, in scoring their success it seems likely that the manufacturers were manipulated by Pitt's opponents, who supplied the Chamber with alarming and possibly misleading information about the proposed Irish treaty. See J. Ehrman, *The Younger Pitt: The Years of Acclaim* (1969), pp. 207–9; and Harlow, *Founding of the Second British Empire,* 1, p. 608.

63 Crafts, 'British Economic Growth, 1700–1831: A Review of the Evidence', *Econ. Hist. Rev.,* 2nd ser. XXXVI (1983), Table 5, p. 187. We have phrased our comment to take account of R.V. Jackson, 'Government Expenditure and British Economic Growth in the Eighteenth Century: Some Problems of Measurement', *Econ. Hist. Rev.,* 2nd ser. XLIII (1990). Given that the problems of data and definition are so formidable, we have not attempted to tie our argument closely to one particular set of figures.

64 We refer here to an idea mentioned in our article, 'Gentlemanly Capitalism and British Expansion Overseas, I: the Old Colonial System, 1688–1850', *Econ. Hist. Rev.,* 2nd ser. XXXIX (1986), p. 521 and n. 112, and developed independently and with greater authority by Brewer, *Sinews of Power,* and Burtton Stein, 'State Formation and Economy Reconsidered', *Mod. Asian Stud.,* 19 (1985). Brewer's point of reference is continental Europe; Stein's is eighteenth-century India. There would appear to be scope for putting the two together in order to define the term more closely and to explore its historical exemplars more fully.

65 For examples of the City's influence (a subject that needs looking at in greater detail) see Lucy S. Sutherland, 'The City of London in Eighteenth-Century Politics', in R. Pares and A.J.P. Taylor, eds. *Essays Presented to Sir Louis Namier* (Oxford, 1956); Dickson, *Financial Revolution,* pp. 228–33, 239; H.T. Dickinson, *Walpole and the Whig Supremacy* (1973), pp. 108–9.

66 The best account of the South Sea Bubble is in Dickson, *Financial Revolution,* Chs. 5–8. It is important to note, though we cannot pursue the point, that the South Sea Bubble was also the first international financial crisis of modern times. On the progressive integration of financial markets see E.S. Schubert, 'Innovations, Debts and Bubbles: International Integration of Financial Markets in Western Europe, 1688–1720', *Jour. Econ. Hist.* 48 (1988), and the further references given there. The evolution of financial crises in England is charted by Julian Hoppitt, 'Financial Crises in Eighteenth-Century England', *Hist. Jour.,* 39 (1986).

67 Jarrett, 'The Myth of "Patriotism"', pp. 124–34, 138–40.

68 Joyce Oldham Appleby, *Economic Thought and Ideology in Seventeenth-Century England* (Princeton, NJ, 1978), pp. 127–8, 166–7; Stevenson, *Popular Disturbances,* pp. 70–2, 113–16, 118–19.

69 Ralph Davis, 'The Rise of Protection in England, 1669–1786', *Econ. Hist. Rev.,* 2nd ser. XIX (1966).

70 The pragmatic aspects are emphasised by D.C. Coleman, 'Mercantilism Revisited', *Hist. Jour.,* 23 (1980), and the logic by Cosimo Perrotta, 'Is the Mercantilist Theory of the Favourable Balance of Trade Really Erroneous?', *Hist. Pol. Econ.,* 23 (1991).

71 The pioneering study is Peter Mathias and Patrick O'Brien, 'Taxation in Britain and France, 1715–1810: a Comparison of the Social and Economic Incidence of Taxes Collected for the Central Governments', *Jour. Eur. Econ. Hist.,* 5 (1976). Important recent contributions are: Patrick O'Brien, 'The Political Economy of British Taxation, 1660–1815', *Econ. Hist. Rev.,* 2nd ser. XLI (1988); and J.V. Beckett and Michael Turner, 'Taxation and Economic Growth in Eighteenth-Century England', *Econ. Hist. Rev.,* 2nd ser. XLIII (1990).

72 The clearest guide (given in constant prices) is in Jackson, 'Government Expenditure', Figs. 1–2, pp. 222–3.

73 Brewer, *Sinews of Power,* pp. 114–16, provides a convenient summary.

74 Peter Mathias, *The First Industrial Nation: An Economic History of Britain, 1700–1914* (2nd edn. 1983), p. 38.

75 Mathias and O'Brien, 'Taxation in Britain and France'; Beckett and Turner, 'Taxation and Economic Growth', pp. 388–91; Brewer, *Sinews of Power,* pp. 126–34.

76 Although excise duties became the chief source of tax revenue, they cannot be distinguished readily from customs duties because excise duty was also levied on a number of imports and not just on goods produced at home. See J.V. Beckett, 'Land Tax or Excise: the Levying of Taxation in Seventeenth- and Eighteenth-Century England', *Eng. Hist. Rev.,* C (1985).

77 Mathias, *Transformation of England,* p. 126. Some interesting comparisons are made by Hilton L. Root, 'The Redistributive Role of Government: Economic Regulation in Old Regime France and England', *Comp. Stud. in Soc. and Hist.,* 33 (1991). The most obvious comparison, however, is with the broadly similar distribution of gains suggested for the nineteenth century (after the introduction of income tax) by Lance E. Davis and Robert A. Huttenback, *Mammon and the Pursuit of Empire: The Political Economy of British Imperialism, 1860–1912* (Cambridge, 1987), Chs. 7–8.

78 Brewer, *Sinews of Power,* Ch. 4 and p. 124; James C. Riley, *International Government Finance and the Amsterdam Capital Market, 1740–1815* (Cambridge, 1980), pp. 103–8.

79 John Brewer, 'English Radicalism in the Reign of George III', in Pocock, ed. *Three British Revolutions*; John Torrance, 'Social Class and Bureaucratic Innovation: the Commissioners for Examining the Public Accounts, 1780–87', *Past and Present,* 78 (1978). A related facet of popular dissent during this period has been revealed by James E. Bradley, *Popular Politics and the American Revolution in England: Petitions, the Crown and Public Opinion* (Macon, Ga, 1986).

80 John Ehrman, *The British Government and Commercial Negotiations with Europe, 1783–93* (Cambridge, 1962), p. 193. For the pragmatic and selective use made of Adam Smith see C.R. Ritcheson, 'The Earl of Shelbourne and Peace with America, 1782–1783: Vision and Reality', *Internat. Hist. Rev.,* 5 (1983); and John E. Crowley, 'Neo-Mercantilism and *The Wealth of Nations*: British Commercial Policy after the American Revolution', *Hist. Jour.,* 33 (1990). N. 54 refers to the reluctance of the industrial bourgeoisie to play the heroic role so often assigned to them by subsequent commentators.

81 Paul Langford, 'Old Whigs, Old Tories and the American Revolution', in Peter Marshall and Glyn Williams, eds. *The British Atlantic Empire Before the American Revolution* (1980); Linda Colley, 'The Apotheosis of George III: Loyalty, Royalty and the British Nation, 1760–1820', *Past and Present,* 102 (1984); Thomas Philip Schofield, 'Conservative Political Thought in Britain in Response to the French Revolution', *Hist. Jour.,* 29 (1986). The expansion of the concept and content of what constituted acceptable forms of property is considered by Paul Langford, *Public Life and the Propertied Englishman, 1689–1798* (Oxford, 1991).

82 Clive Emsley, *British Society and the French Wars, 1793–1815* (1979); Ian R. Christie, *Stress and Stability in Late-Eighteenth-Century Britain: Reflections on the British Avoidance of Revolution* (Oxford, 1984); H.T. Dickinson, *British Radicalism and the French Revolution, 1789–1815* (1985); Colley, 'The Apotheosis of George III'. There was also, of course, the exit option – emigration.

83 J.G.A. Pocock, 'The Political Economy of Burke's Analysis of the French Revolution', *Hist. Jour.,* 25 (1982); Schofield, 'Conservative Political Thought'. If manners maketh man, their further refinement into politeness helped to make gentlemen. For a study of this process (at an earlier point in the century) see Lawrence E. Klein, 'Liberty, Manners and Politeness in Early Eighteenth-Century England', *Hist. Jour.,* 32 (1989); and on an allied subject, Frank O'Gorman, 'Electoral Deference in "Unreformed" England, 1760–1830', *Jour. Mod. Hist.,* 56 (1984).

84 The massive literature which this subject has now generated can be approached through Barbara L. Solow and Stanley L. Engerman, eds. *British Capitalism and Caribbean Slavery* (Cambridge, 1987), and the references given there. The important point to note from the present perspective is that abolition was not promoted by a rising industrial bourgeoisie seeking to reach the goals of liberty and free trade set for it by a later generation of Whig historians.

85 J.E. Cookson, 'Political Arithmetic and War in Britain, 1785–1815', *War and Society,* 1 (1983).
86 Idem, 'British Society and the French Wars, 1783–1815', *Australian Journal of Politics and History,* 31 (1985).
87 Anthony Webster, 'The Political Economy of Trade Liberalization: the East India Company Charter Act of 1813', *Econ. Hist. Rev.,* 2nd ser. XLIII (1990).
88 Boyd Hilton, *Corn, Cash and Commerce: The Economic Policies of the Tory Governments, 1815–1830* (Oxford, 1977), Ch. 1.
89 On these themes see Hilton, *Corn, Cash and Commerce.*
90 Hilton, *Corn, Cash and Commerce,* Chs. 4–7, and pp. 305–6; Norman Gash, 'After Waterloo: British Society and the Legacy of the Napoleonic Wars', *Trans. Royal Hist. Soc.,* 5th ser. 28 (1978); and A.D. Harvey, *Britain in the Early Nineteenth Century* (1978), p. 312.
91 Recent work has opened up some important new lines of inquiry: Eastwood, 'Robert Southey'; Peter Mandler, 'Tories and Paupers: Christian Political Economy and the Making of the New Poor Law', *Hist. Jour.,* 33 (1990); J.W. Burrow, *Whigs and Liberals: Continuity and Change in English Political Thought* (Oxford, 1988); and Boyd Hilton, *The Age of Atonement: The Influence of Evangelicalism on Social and Economic Thought, 1795–1865* (Oxford, 1988). Norman Gash (*Eng. Hist. Rev.,* CIV (1989), pp. 136–40) offers a perceptive review of the issues raised by Hilton's study. For an assessment of economic opinion in 1820 see William D. Grampp, 'Economic Opinion When Britain Turned to Free Trade', *Hist. Pol. Econ.,* 14 (1982).
92 See Chapter 1, pp. 31–4.
93 Hilton, *Corn, Cash and Commerce,* Ch. 4.
94 The difficulties of the cotton industry in the 1820s are dealt with by S.D. Chapman, 'Financial Restraints on the Growth of Firms in the Cotton Industry, 1790–1850', *Econ. Hist. Rev.,* 2nd ser. XXXII (1979), pp. 55–8. On government perceptions of the importance of international services see Hilton, *Corn, Cash and Commerce,* p. 63.
95 M. Brock, *The Great Reform Act* (1973) remains the standard work. See also O'Gorman, 'Electoral Deference'.
96 Hilton argues that the Whigs could not afford to make concessions on economic policy 'because the only hope of winning office was by economic bribes to the country gentry'. Consequently, economic reform was postponed during the 1830s. The Tories, on the other hand, tried to stave off political reform in the 1820s and again in the 1840s by making economic concessions to the enemies of the landed interest. Hilton, *Corn, Cash and Commerce,* pp. 306–7.
97 William D. Grampp, *The Manchester School of Economics* (Stanford, Calif., 1960), Ch. 5; Lucy Brown, *The Board of Trade and the Free Trade Movement, 1830–42* (Oxford, 1958), pp. 108–10, 121–3, 132–3. For a recent view see T.J. McKeown, 'The Politics of Corn Law Repeal and Theory of Commercial Policy', *Brit. Jour. Pol. Sci.,* 19 (1989).
98 R.A. Church, ed. *The Dynamics of Victorian Business* (1980), Ch. 1; J.K.J. Thompson, 'British Industrialization and the External World: A Unique Experience or Archetypal Model?', in M. Bienefeld and M. Godfrey, eds. *National Strategies in an International Context* (1982).
99 The cyclical crises of the period are still best described by R.C.O. Matthews, *A Study in Trade Cycle History, 1833–1842* (Cambridge, 1954), esp. pp. 209–17.
100 See pp. 99–100.
101 By increasing the preferences allowed to Canadian wheat, for example. See R.L. Schuyler, *The Fall of the Old Colonial System* (1945), pp. 142–4.
102 D.C. Moore, 'The Corn Laws and High Farming', *Econ. Hist. Rev.,* 2nd ser. XVIII (1965). Peel believed that arable farming could survive if it became more responsive to market forces. As it happened, domestic cereal prices were seriously affected by foreign competition before the 1860s, as Wray Vamplew has shown: 'The Protection of English Cereal Producers: the Corn Laws Reassessed', *Econ. Hist. Rev.,* 2nd ser. XXXIII (1980). However, it cannot be assumed that protection would have helped the landed interest to retain power for very long. Protection would have retarded economic

growth, reduced real wages and, by intensifying social conflict, might have brought demands for sweeping changes to property relations. On the connection between free trade and economic growth see Donald N. McCloskey, 'Magnanimous Albion: Free Trade and British National Income, 1841–1881', *Expl. Econ. Hist.*, 17 (1980); P.J. Cain, 'Professor McCloskey on British Free Trade, 1841–1881: Some Comments', ibid., 19 (1982); and McCloskey's reply, ibid. The repeal of the Corn Laws was followed, in 1849, by the repeal of the Navigation Acts. This was a significant but also a symbolic measure because the Acts had already been modified in the 1820s. On this subject see Sara Palmer, *Politics, Shipping and the Repeal of the Navigation Laws* (Manchester, 1991).

103 Hilton, *Corn, Cash and Commerce,* pp. 56f.

104 See n. 87 and R.W. Hidy, *The House of Baring in American Trade and Finance* (Cambridge, Mass., 1949), pp. 17–20.

105 See pp. 143–8.

106 For Rothschild's views see B. Davis, *The Rothschilds* (1983), pp. 68–9. The exact role of the City in the debates of the 1830s and 1840s needs further investigation. Meanwhile, we have adopted a cautious position to avoid reading into the past more than the evidence currently justifies.

107 Riley, *International Government Finance,* pp. 195–200; S.D. Chapman, 'The International Houses: the Continental Contribution to British Economic Development, 1800–1860', *Jour. Eur. Econ. Hist.*, 6 (1977); J.M. Sherwig, *Guineas and Gunpowder: British Foreign Aid in the Wars with France, 1793–1815* (1969).

108 See W.D. Rubinstein, 'The End of "Old Corruption" in Britain, 1780–1860', *Past and Present,* 101 (1983); and, for a case study, James Raven, 'The Abolition of the English State Lotteries', *Hist. Jour.*, 34 (1991).

109 S.D. Chapman, 'British Marketing Enterprise', pp. 321–3; idem, 'Financial Restraints on the Growth of Firms', p. 58. There is some evidence that industrialists were already putting their savings into safe foreign and home investments marketed in the City. See Mary B. Rose, 'Diversification of Investment by the Greg Family, 1800–1914', *Bus. Hist.*, 21 (1979), p. 89.

110 See Nicholas Canny and Anthony Pagden, eds. *Colonial Identity in the Atlantic World, 1500–1800* (Princeton, NJ, 1987); Carl Bridge, P.J. Marshall and Glyndwr Williams, 'Introduction': a "British" Empire', *Internat. Hist. Rev.*, 12 (1990).

111 Richard L. Bushman, 'American High-Style and Vernacular Cultures', in Jack P. Greene and J. R. Pole, eds. *Colonial British America: Essays in the New History of the Early Modern Era* (Baltimore, Md, 1984), p. 367.

112 Richard Pares, *A West India Fortune* (1950); idem, *Merchants and Planters* (Cambridge, 1960); Tamara P. Thornton, *Cultivating Gentlemen: The Meaning of Country Life Among the Boston Elite, 1785–1860* (New Haven, Conn., 1989); and Pocock, *Three British Revolutions,* 'Introduction', and Chs. 8, 10 and 11.

113 For two contrasting cases see Rajat Roy and Ratna Roy, 'Zamindars and Jotedars: a Study of Rural Politics in Bengal', *Mod. Asian Stud.*, 9 (1975); and Neil Rabitoy, 'System v Expediency: the Reality of Land Revenue Administration in the Bombay Presidency, 1812–1820', *Mod. Asian Stud.*, 9 (1975).

114 Stephen S. Webb, *The Governors-General: The English Army and the Definition of Empire, 1569–1681* (Chapel Hill, NC, 1979); Paul David Nelson, *William Tryon and the Course of Empire: A Life in British Imperial Service* (Chapel Hill, NC, 1990); Marshall, *East India Fortunes,* pp. 9–14; Bayly, *Imperial Meridian,* pp. 133–6.

115 The Navigation Acts were reinforced in 1696 and the East India Company, founded in 1600, was restructured in 1708. On the capitalist qualities of the Company see K.N. Chaudhuri, *The Trading World of Asia and the English East India Company, 1660–1760* (Cambridge, 1978), and Hoh-cheung Mui and Lorna H. Mui, *The Management of Monopoly: A Study of the English East India Company's Conduct of its Tea Monopoly, 1784–1833* (Vancouver, 1984). Complementary views are expressed in Leonard Blusse and Femme Gastra, eds. *Companies and Trade: Essays in Overseas Trading Companies During*

the Ancien Regime (The Hague, 1981). The investors have been analysed by H.V. Bowen, 'Investment and Empire in the Later Eighteenth Century: East India Stockholding, 1756–1791', *Econ. Hist. Rev.,* 2nd ser. XLII (1989). While Dr Bowen is in agreement with the main direction of our argument, he questions (pp. 195–6) our claim that gentlemanly capitalism was a 'formidable mixture of the venerable and the new' on the grounds that there were few landowners among the East India Company's stockholders. We accept his evidence but not his conclusion. Our claim does not depend on showing that landowners were stockholders in the Company but on a broader set of connections arising from the financial revolution and the increased degree of social integration that it encouraged – as we have suggested earlier in this chapter.

116 On mercantile lobbies see Brewer, *Sinews of Power,* pp. 169, 231–49. We acknowledge that there is a gap in the literature at this point: there is no study of the eighteenth century to match the detailed work undertaken on the seventeenth century by Robert Brenner, *Merchants and Revolution: Commercial Change and Political Conflict in the London Merchant Community, 1550–1660* (Princeton, NJ, 1992), and on the turn of the century by D.W. Jones, *War and Economy in the Age of William III and Marlborough* (Oxford, 1988).

117 Consumers, especially but not exclusively in London and the south-ecast, also benefited from the increased availability (at steadily falling prices) of imports of colonial products.

118 See Richard Pares, 'American Versus Continental Warfare, 1739–63', in idem, *The Historian's Business* (Oxford, 1961); W.A. Speck, 'The International and Imperial Context', in Jack P. Greene and J.R. Pole, eds. *Colonial British America: Essays in the New History of the Early Modern Era* (Baltimore, Md, 1984); Daniel A. Baugh, 'Great Britain's "Blue Water" Policy', *Internat. Hist. Rev.,* 10 (1988); and, for a view that extends beyond strategic considerations, J.S. Bromley, 'Britain and Europe in the Eighteenth Century', *History,* 66 (1981).

119 Quoted in Pares, 'American Versus Continental Warfare', p. 144. See also ibid. pp. 140–3.

120 The trade data summarised in the following five paragraphs derive principally from: Ralph Davis, 'English Foreign Trade, 1700–1774', in W.E. Minchinton, ed. *The Growth of English Overseas Trade in the Seventeenth and Eighteenth Centuries* (1969); idem, *The Industrial Revolution and British Overseas Trade* (Leicester, 1979); François Crouzet, 'Toward an Export Economy: British Exports during the Industrial Revolution', *Expl. in Econ. Hist.,* 17 (1980); Jacob M. Price, 'New Time Series for Scotland's and Britain's Trade with the Thirteen Colonies and States, 1740–1791', *William & Mary Quarterly,* 32 (1975); and Crafts, 'British Economic Growth'. A slightly fuller commentary is given in P.J. Cain and A.G. Hopkins, 'The Political Economy of British Expansion Overseas, 1750–1914', *Econ. Hist. Rev.,* 2nd ser. XXXIII (1980), pp. 470–8. Additional references will therefore be given selectively.

121 Seymour Drescher, *Econocide: British Slavery in the Era of Abolition* (Pittsburgh, Pa, 1977), p. 20.

122 On import-led growth see F.J. Fisher, 'London as an Engine of Growth', in J.S. Bromley and E.H. Kossmann, eds. *Britain and the Netherlands,* 6 (1971); and Davis, 'English Foreign Trade', p. 108.

123 Chaudhuri, *Trading World,* Chs.10–11.

124 See Davis, *Industrial Revolution,* pp. 53–61, 73, 85; and the neglected study by C.J. French, 'The Trade and Shipping of the Port of London, 1700–1776', (Ph.D. thesis, Exeter University, 1980), Ch. 2. By the middle of the eighteenth century contemporary writers had distinguished between the balance of trade and the balance of payments, and soon afterwards David Hume published his celebrated analysis, 'Of the Balance of Trade', in his *Essays and Treatises on Several Subjects,* Vol. I (1772). At the close of the century, Paine made a characteristically scathing reference to the 'motley amphibious-charactered thing called the balance of trade', which, he said, was deployed to deceive members of parliament whose understanding of 'fox-hunting and the game laws' was somewhat ahead of their knowledge of economics. See Paine, *Complete Works,* p. 492.

125 Crouzet, 'Toward an Export Economy'.
126 See pp. 80–4.
127 Cain and Hopkins, 'Political Economy', p. 475.
128 Calculated from A.H. Imlah, *Economic Elements in the Pax Britannica: Studies in British Foreign Trade in the Nineteenth Century* (New York, 1958), Table 12.
129 For a recent survey see J.C.D. Clark, 'English History's Forgotten Context: Scotland, Ireland, Wales', *Hist. Jour.*, 32 (1989).
130 I.K. Steele, *The Politics of Colonial Policy: The Board of Trade in Colonial Administration, 1696–1720* (Oxford, 1968); Webb, *The Covernors-Ceneral*; and, for colonial reactions to first royal absolutism and then Whig oligarchy, the essays by Murrin and Lovejoy in Pocock, *The British Revolutions.*
131 James A. Henretta, *'Salutary Neglect': Colonial Administration Under the Duke of Newcastle* (Princeton, NJ, 1972); and the commentary in Speck, 'The International and Imperial Context'.
132 For a summary and further references see Brewer, *Sinews of Power,* pp. 173–8, and H.T. Dickinson, *Walpole and the Whig Supremacy* (1973), Ch. 6 and pp. 105–6, 135–7.
133 On the mood of assertiveness that took hold in the 1760s see P.J. Marshall, 'Empire and Authority in the Later Eighteenth Century', *Jour. Imp. and Comm. Hist.*, 15 (1987); and for the perception (by others) that Britain was the main threat to peace and stability after 1763 see H.M. Scott, *British Foreign Policy in the Age of the American Revolution* (Oxford, 1990).
134 For the abysmal performance of Britain's exports during this period see Crouzet, 'Toward an Export Economy', p. 52.
135 For example, Riley, *International Government Finance,* pp. 123–5.
136 The detailed literature has now been brought together in two complementary studies: P.J. Marshall, *Bengal: The British Bridgehead. Eastern India, 1740–1828* (Cambridge, 1987), and C.A. Bayly, *Indian Society and the Making of the British Empire* (Cambridge, 1988). We should like to express our debt to Prof. Marshall for the comments and advice he has generously supplied over many years on the subject of British interests in India in the eighteenth century.
137 We are aware that we are over-compressing an episode that began rather than ended with Plassey, which was more of a coup than a battle. Subsequent developments culminated in the more important military engagement at Buxar in 1764. On Clive see Huw V. Bowen, 'Lord Clive and Speculation in East India Company Stock, 1766', *Hist. Jour.*, 30 (1987). We are grateful to Dr Bowen for discussing these and related issues; we hope that any differences that remain are those of perspective rather than of substance.
138 Lakshmi Subramanian, 'Capital and Crowd in a Declining Asian Port City: the Anglo-Bania Order and the Surat Riots of 1795', *Mod. Asian Stud.*, 19 (1985), relates the problems of the 1790s to commercial and financial difficulties that first surfaced in the middle of the century. On the subsequent shift of influence from Surat to Bombay see Pamela Nightingale, *Trade and Empire in Western India, 1784–1806* (Cambridge, 1970).
139 Huw V. Bowen, 'A Question of Sovereignty: the Bengal Land Revenue Issue, 1765–67', *Jour. Imp. and Comm. Hist.*, 16 (1988).
140 Marshall, *East India Fortunes,* p. 256; Davis, *The Industrial Revolution,* pp. 55–6.
141 The principal measures were the Regulating Act of 1773, Pitt's India Act of 1784, and the Charter Act of 1793. The political background to the first of these measures has now been reappraised by H.V. Bowen, *Revenue and Reform: the Indian Problem in British Politics, 1757–1773* (Cambridge, 1991).
142 See, for example, P.J. Marshall, 'Economic and Political Expansion: the Case of Oudh', *Mod. Asian Stud.*, 9 (1975); and Anthony Webster, 'British Export Interests in Bengal and Imperial Expansion in South-East Asia, 1780–1824: the Origins of the Straits Settlements', in Barbara Ingham and Colin Simmons, eds. *Development Studies and Colonial Policy* (1987).
143 On the Mughal empire as a patronage state that was ceasing to deliver, see Richard B. Barnett, *North India Between Empires: Awadh, The Mughals and the British, 1720–1801* (Berkeley, Calif., 1980).

144 The relative power of the Company and the banias (and much else of consequence) is debated by Lakshmi Subramanian, 'Banias and the British: The Role of Indigenous Credit in the Process of Imperial Expansion in Western India in the Second Half of the Eighteenth Century', *Mod. Asian Stud.*, 21 (1987), and Michelguglielmo Torri, 'Trapped Inside the Colonial Order: the Hindu Bankers of Surat and their Business World during the Second Half of the Eighteenth Century', *Mod. Asian Stud.*, 25 (1991). See also Subramanian's reply in ibid.

145 We base ourselves here on J.D. Nichol's important study, 'The British in India, 1740–1763: a Study in Imperial Expansion into Bengal', (Ph.D. thesis, Cambridge University, 1976), pp. 62–75, Chs. 3–4, and pp. 163–71. There is a published discussion of these issues, but it is at a rather general level and does not include an assessment of Nichol's research: Karen Leonard, 'The Great Firm Theory of the Decline of the Mughal Empire', *Comp. Stud. in Soc. and Hist.*, 21 (1979); J.F. Richards, 'Mughal State Finance and the Pre-Modern World Economy', ibid. 73 (1981); and Leonard's reply in ibid.

146 We have benefited particularly from Greene and Pole, *Colonial British America*; Peter Marshall and Glyn Williams, eds. *The British Atlantic Empire before the American Revolution* (1980); and Pocock, ed. *Three British Revolutions.* J. McAllister, 'Colonial America, 1607–1776', *Econ. Hist. Rev.*, XLII (1989), surveys the economic history of the period.

147 Summarised by Jack P. Greene, 'The Seven Years' War and the American Revolution: the Causal Relationship Reconsidered', in Marshall and Williams, *British Atlantic Empire,* pp. 90–5. For a case study see Thomas C. Barrow, *Trade and Empire: The British Customs Service in Colonial America, 1760–1775* (Cambridge, Mass., 1967).

148 Quoted in Greene, 'The Seven Years' War', p. 90.

149 On these topics see Jacob M. Price, 'The Transatlantic Economy', in Greene and Pole, *Colonial British America*; idem, *Capital and Credit in British Overseas Trade: The View from the Chesapeake, 1700–1776* (Cambridge, 1980); and Mira Wilkins, *The History of Foreign Investment in the United States to 1914* (Cambridge, Mass, 1989), pp. 14–15.

150 John W. Tyler, *Smugglers and Patriots: Boston Merchants and the Advent of the American Revolution* (Boston, Mass., 1986); William Pencak, 'Warfare and Political Change in Mid-Eighteenth-Century Massachusetts', in Marshall and Williams, *British Atlantic Empire.*

151 T.H. Breen, *Tobacco Culture: The Mentality of the Great Tidewater Planters on the Eve of Revolution* (Princeton, NJ, 1985).

152 Alison, G. Olson, 'The Board of Trade and London-American Interest Groups in the Eighteenth Century', in Marshall and Williams, *British Atlantic Empire.*

153 Jack. P. Greene, *Peripheries and Center: Constitutional Development in the Extended Polities of the British Empire and the United States, 1607–1788* (Athens, Ga, 1986); Pocock, *Three British Revolutions.*

154 Marc Egnal, 'The Economic Development of the Thirteen Continental Colonies, 1720–1775', *William & Mary Quarterly,* 32 (1975); James F. Shepherd, 'British America and the Atlantic Economy', in Ronald Hoffman, et al. eds. *The Economy of Early America: The Revolutionary Period, 1763–90* (Charlottesville, Va, 1988); Peter A. Coclanis, 'The Wealth of British America on the Eve of the Revolution', *Jour. Interdisc. Hist.*, 21 (1990); Julian Gwyn, 'British Government Spending and the North American Colonies, 1740–1775', in Marshall and Williams, *British Atlantic Empire,* pp. 82–3.

155 Marc Egnal, *A Mighty Empire: The Origins of the American Revolution* (Ithaca, NY, 1988).

156 T.R. Clayton, 'Sophistry, Security and Socio-Political Structures in the American Revolution: Or Why Jamaica did not Rebel', *Hist. Jour.*, 29 (1986); Gary Nash, *The Urban Crucible: Social Change, Political Consciousness and the Origins of the American Revolution* (Cambridge, Mass., 1979).

157 Clayton, 'Sophistry, Security'.

158 Marshall, 'Empire and Authority', pp. 114, 119–20.

159 Thurlow to Grenville, 1–10 Sept. 1789. Quoted in David Milobar, 'Conservative Ideology, Metropolitan Government and the Reform of Quebec, 1782–1791', *Internat. Hist. Rev.*, 12 (1990), p. 51.

160 Milobar, 'Conservative Ideology'; Alan Atkinson, 'The Little Revolution in New South Wales, 1808', *Internat. Hist. Rev.,* 12 (1990); Stanley Trapido, 'From Paternalism to Liberalism: the Cape Colony, 1800–1834', *Internat. Hist. Rev.* 12 (1990); R.B. McDowell, *Ireland in the Age of Imperialism and Revolution, 1760–1800* (Oxford, 1979); Thomas Bartlett, '"A People Made Rather for Copies than Origina"': the Anglo-Irish, 1760–1800', *Internat. Hist. Rev.,* 12 (1990).

161 Drescher, *Econocide,* pp. 56–60; Bayly, *Imperial Meridian,* pp. 121–6, 155–60, 209–11; Marshall, *Bengal,* pp. 140–58; Webster, 'British Export Interests in Bengal', pp. 166–7.

162 D.L. Mackay, 'Direction and Purpose in British Imperial Policy, 1793–1801', *Hist. Jour.,* 17 (1974). On the effort made to incorporate the trade of the United States into the system see Gerald S. Graham, *Sea Power and British North America, 1783–1820* (Harvard, Mass., 1941); and S.G. Checkland, 'American Versus West Indian Traders in Liverpool, 1793–1815', *Jour. Econ. Hist.,* 17 (1958).

163 P.J. Marshall, *Problems of Empire: Britain and India, 1757–1813* (1968), pp. 95–101. This question is referred to in Chapter 10 of the present study.

164 Quoted in J.J. Eddy, *Britain and the Australian Colonies, 1818–31* (1969), p. xiii.

165 For the emergence of the idea that sound money, free markets and good government marched together see Neil Rabitoy's study of Bombay, 'The Control of Fate and Fortune: the Origins of the Market Mentality in British Administrative Thought in South Asia', *Mod. Asian Stud.,* 25 (1991).

166 A.G.L. Shaw, 'British Attitudes to the Colonies, c.1820–1850', *Jour. Brit. Stud.,* 9 (1969).

167 This term came into use in the late eighteenth century, when it was applied principally to French Canadians and Afrikaners. See James Sturgis, 'Anglicisation at the Cape of Good Hope in the Early Nineteenth Century', *Jour. Imp. and Comm. Hist.,* 11(1982).

168 Eddy, *Britain and the Australian Colonies,* p. 224.

169 Wakefield's list of possible beneficiaries of a policy of systematic colonisation makes interesting reading. See 'A Letter from Sydney', in E. Lloyd Prichard, ed. *Collected Works of E.G. Wakefield* (Glasgow, 1968), p. 165.

170 The naval aspects are dealt with by Gerald S. Graham, *Tides of Empire: Discursions on the Expansion of Britain Overseas* (1972), pp. 80f.

171 C.J. Bartlett, *Castlereagh* (1966), pp. 235f; P.J.V. Rolo, *George Canning: Three Biographical Studies* (1965), pp. 254–8.

172 See R.J. Gavin's important and unfortunately still unpublished study, 'Palmerston's Policy Towards East and West Africa, 1830–1865', (Ph.D. thesis, Cambridge University, 1958), pp. 16–48.

173 This is the theme of Sir Thomas Fowell Buxton's *The African Slave Trade and its Remedy* (1840). The best study of these developments remains Jack Gallagher, 'Fowell Buxton and the "New African Policy", 1838–1842', *Cambridge Historical Journal,* 10 (1950). See also A.G. Hopkins, 'Property Rights and Empire Building: Britain's Annexation of Lagos, 1861', *Jour. Econ. Hist.,* 40 (1980).

174 R.J. Gavin, 'Palmerston and Africa', *Jour. Hist. Soc. Nigeria,* 6 (1971), p. 94. Palmerston was particularly upset by French expansion in north Africa. There was also a close connection between the difficulties experienced by British exports, unemployment and social unrest, and the aggressive stance taken towards Argentina during the Uruguayan dispute in 1841–5. See H.S. Ferns, *Britain and Argentina in the Nineteenth Century* (Oxford, 1960), Ch. IX; Peter Winn, 'British Informal Empire in Uruguay in the Nineteenth Century', *Past and Present,* 73 (1976), pp. 104–8; and V.G. Kiernan, 'Britain's First Contacts with Paraguay', *Atlante,* 3 (1955).

175 These matters are dealt within greater detail in Chapters 9 and 11–13.

176 C.K. Webster, *The Foreign Policy of Palmerston,* II (1951), pp. 750–1.

177 See Chapters 9–13.

178 We take this opportunity to express our broad agreement with Bayly, *Imperial Meridian,* p. 253, and to add that we had insufficient space to examine the cultural aspects of gentlemanly capitalism in the article to which he refers: Cain and Hopkins, 'Gentlemanly

Capitalism'. We hope that we have gone some way towards remedying this defect in the present study.

179 Paine, *Complete Works,* p. 98.

180 D.C.M. Platt, 'The National Economy and British Imperial Expansion Before 1914', *Jour. Imp. and Comm. Hist.*, 2 (1973/4). See also the more extended comment in Cain and Hopkins, 'Political Economy', p. 476.

181 Gallagher and Robinson, 'Imperialism of Free Trade'.

182 For examples of networks of trade and factor movements connecting the City with the colonies during this period see Frank J.A. Broeze, 'Private Enterprise and the Peopling of Australia, 1831–50', *Econ. Hist. Rev.,* 2nd ser. XXXV (1982); and W.E. Cheong, *Mandarins and Merchants: Jardine Matheson & Co., a China Agency of the Early Nineteenth Century* (Malmo, 1978), Chs. 6–7.

183 Insights into the growth of British overseas credit operations and investments can be found in D.C.M. Platt, *Foreign Finance in Continental Europe and the U.S.A., 1815–70: Quantities, Origins, Functions and Distribution* (1984).

PART TWO

The gentlemanly order, 1850–1914

3

'SOMETHING PECULIAR TO ENGLAND'

The service sector, wealth and power, 1850–1914[1]

When historians of British imperialism have taken any serious note of the work of economic historians, they have concentrated mainly upon the slowing rate of growth of the British economy in general, and of industrial growth in particular, after 1870 and the more rapid growth of other industrialising nations. Generally speaking, these trends are well attested in the literature, although some of the implications of the growth figures for overseas expansion have not been drawn out.

Economic growth

Contemporaries were apt to divide the period 1850–1914 into three parts: a 'Great Victorian Boom' between 1850 and 1873; a succeeding Great Depression until the mid-1890s; and then a return to prosperity culminating in a vigorous full-employment boom between 1910 and 1913. These labels were attached on the basis of limited knowledge of the movement of prices and profits, and are often misleading. In their pioneering work, Deane and Cole found that, apart from one or two short exceptional periods, rates of growth of GNP and national income in the United Kingdom accelerated until the 1890s and then fell off markedly.[2] Deane's later estimates of GNP modified this, arguing for a peak in growth rates in 1858–73 followed by a sharp deceleration and interrupted by a brief revival in the 1890s.[3] Feinstein's early work also indicated a slow-down in growth in the 1870s and an equally sharp dip at the end of the century.[4] The latest available estimates are much more emphatic in placing the decisive break in the growth of domestic product around 1900, and reveal no obvious turning point in 1870. Evidence about productivity trends is much more tentative but the indications are that total factor productivity (the share of growth which cannot be accounted for simply by additional labour and capital inputs) fell off decisively only around the turn of the century (Table 3.1). If the most recent work on earlier periods is included, the picture that emerges is of a steady acceleration in the growth of both productivity and output between the late eighteenth century and about 1870, at which point there is some evidence of deceleration, a partial upsurge in the 1890s and a more decisive fall after 1900.[5] The relative decline of the economy is also marked, at least for the period after 1870. Growth rates in the United States and Germany were bound to be higher than in Britain because of considerably higher rates of growth of population. But the evidence of international productivity comparisons also shows that Britain was lagging after 1890, and the lag is only partly explained by the ability of the late-starters to call on a much larger pool of low-productivity agricultural labour than was available at the time in Great Britain.[6]

Sectorally, the most dramatic event was the decline of agriculture, where output actually fell between 1865–82 and 1889–99.[7] The movement of manufacturing output was closer to that of output as a whole. The Hoffman-Lomax index of industrial production shows a break below 3 per cent per annum growth in the 1870s with a significant revival in the 1890s.[8] Another series, which removes cotton textile production from the total in order to eliminate the distortions introduced by

TABLE 3.1 Rates of growth of output and productivity, cyclical peak to cyclical peak: United Kingdom, 1856–1913 (per cent per year)

	GNP	*GDP*[b]	*TFP*[a] *(GDP)*	*Manufacturing Output*	*TFP*[a] *(Manuf)*
1856–60	1.6	1.7	0.4	2.5	1.2
1860–65	3.0	2.0	0.6	1.7	–0.1
1865–73	2.7	2.4	1.1	3.2	1.3
1873–82	1.6	1.9	0.6	2.3	1.1
1882–89	1.9	2.2	0.9	1.9	0.4
1889–99	2.3	2.2	0.8	2.3	1.1
1899–1907	1.8	1.2	–0.3	1.6	0.1
1907–13	1.6	1.6	0.3	1.0	0.3
1856–73	2.5	2.2	0.8	2.6	0.9
1873–99	2.0	2.1	0.7	2.2	0.9
1899–1913	1.7	1.4	0.0	1.4	0.3

Sources: First column (GNP): P. Deane, 'New Estimates of Gross National Product for the United Kingdom, 1830–1914', *Review of Income and Wealth,* XIV (1968), pp. 106–7. Rest of table: CA. Feinstein, R.C.O. Matthews and J.C. Odling-Smee, 'The Timing of the Climacteric and its Sectoral Incidence in the United Kingdom, 1873–1913', in C.P. Kind-leberger and Guido di Tella eds. *Economics in the Long View: Essays in Honour of W.W. Rostow,* Vol. II, Pt I, (Basingstoke, 1982), pp. 175, 178; R.C.O. Matthews, C.H. Feinstein and J.C. Odling-Smee, *British Economic Growth, 1856–1973* (Oxford, 1982), App. L, pp. 606–7.

Notes:

[a] Total Factor Productivity (see p. 108).

[b] Composite figures based on a number of different estimates.

the cotton famine in 1861–5, dates the deceleration in growth from the 1860s: but figures for industrial production per head show a downturn after 1900 as well as 40 years earlier.[9] The latest figures also suggest a decline in the rate of growth of output after 1875, a revival after 1890 and a decisive fall in the Edwardian period, though the productivity figure points to 1900 as being the climacteric (see Table 3.1).[10] What is more important from our perspective is the extent of the growth of services after 1850. The growth rate of commerce (weighted by its share in Gross Domestic Product) was on a par with that of manufacturing over the period as a whole and its contribution to productivity was broadly similar. Transport and communications and public and professional services also made contributions to growth which were as significant as that made by mining.[11]

Agricultural decline

Despite Peel's optimistic assumption, free trade was a sentence of execution on British agriculture; but the sentence was not carried out immediately. Before world-wide rail and steamship links were established, domestic farming enjoyed a degree of natural protection and flourished in the generation after the repeal of the Corn Laws as income and output in Britain grew rapidly.[12] Even so, imports of cereals were sufficiently high to keep prices down and encouraged a steady shift from arable to pasture.[13] From the 1860s the effects of the world-wide application of new transport technology began to be felt, and cheap cereals poured in from Russia, Eastern Europe and the United States. The price of wheat fell by about half in 30 years and other grain prices were almost as badly affected because the intensity of competition was aggravated by the slow growth of demand.[14] Farmers and landlords who were dependent on arable saw their incomes and rents tumble. The gross value of arable output fell from £104m. in 1867–9 to £62m. in 1894–1903 and much land went out of cultivation or reverted to pasture.[15] Most of the strain was taken up by the landed interest itself since rents fell more rapidly than overall income.[16] Even so, the pastoral sector continued to prosper, despite growing foreign competition, largely because of rapidly increasing demand for meat and dairy produce in the expanding cities and towns. Income from pastoral farming actually rose between 1870 and 1900, signalling a shift in the locus of agricultural power from the wheat-growing south to the pastures of the north.[17] While arable landlords suffered sharp falls in income, large owners of pastoral land, like the Earl of Derby, improved their positions. Overall, though, the decline in arable marked the end of agriculture's crucial role in the economy. Its share of national income declined from about one-fifth in 1850 to one-sixteenth in 1900; and income from farm ownership fell from roughly one-fifth of all property income in 1856 to one-twentieth by 1913.[18]

Britain also moved, in the same space of half a century, from practical self-sufficiency in basic foodstuffs to a dependence on imports for roughly half her annual consumption. This represented at one and the same time a sublime faith in her ability to export enough to pay for this additional import burden and to protect her overseas commerce through naval supremacy. Arable agriculture was the first outstanding victim of Britain's mid-century commitment to the international division of labour, one momentous consequence of which was the decline in the wealth and influence of the landed aristocracy who had hitherto been the dominant component of gentlemanly capitalism.

Industry after 1850

If arable agriculture was the first significant casualty of Britain's economic internationalism after 1850, some segments of manufacturing industry also began to show signs of difficulty in coping with free trade. Throughout the period, industrialists remained chronically pessimistic about profit margins and markets, except in brief periods of breakneck boom, such as 1849–53, 1869–73 and 1910–13. The pessimism before 1880 was grounded in the fierceness of domestic competition[19] and, after that, confirmed by the growing threat posed to both domestic and foreign markets by industrialising rivals.[20] As industrialisation spread abroad, often behind protectionist barriers, the transformation of industry in Britain was steady rather than dramatic. Textiles, iron, steel and other metals, coal and engineering dominated industry in 1914 as they had in 1850. Though textiles had declined in relative importance, steel output had outpaced iron and Britain had developed the world's most efficient shipbuilding industry. Also, despite the rapid spread of steam technology across industry in the late nineteenth century[21] and the rise of the joint-stock form of enterprise, big business was slow to appear in Britain and the typical firm in 1914 was still small by the standards of Germany or the USA. When compared with these developing rivals, British industry was showing disturbing signs of technological and organisational backwardness in some key industries like steel by the 1890s, and the take-up of innovative technology in new fields – chemicals and electricals, for example – was slow.

Some of the statistical research on manufacturing suggests that overall rates of growth of output and productivity did not decline until after 1900, though the rate of growth of both should have risen rather than stagnated in the late nineteenth century, given the extent to which Britain could import technology from others after 1870.[22] However, there is little doubt that the downturn in the performance of many of the older, export-oriented staples of provincial England occurred much sooner. Rates of growth of output and productivity in textiles, for example, declined precipitately in the 1870s and revived only very modestly in the great export boom before 1913;[23] the metal trades, especially iron, showed similar trends.[24] Relative decline must also be dated at least as far as back as 1870 and probably before. In 1870 Britain still produced one-third of world manufacturing output, but her share had fallen to one-seventh at the outbreak of World War I.[25] In steel production, one of the key activities of the time, the relative decline was more alarming. Britain's share of output fell from just over one-third in the late 1870s to one-tenth by 1909–13, at which point Germany produced twice as much as Britain, and the United States twice as much again.[26]

The service sector

Even though British industrialism had passed its zenith in world terms late in the nineteenth century, it is still taken for granted that industry dominated British economic life after 1850 and provided the main economic dynamic before World War I. This judgement would be unexceptionable if it were applied to, say, southern Scotland and Wales, north and north-west England, the West Riding and the west Midlands, but it is difficult to sustain if applied to the whole country. The share of mining, manufacturing and building in national income rose from 34 per cent to 40 per cent of the total between 1841 and 1911 but most of that expansion was accounted for by mining, especially coal, and manufacturing's share was stagnant. The manufacturing sector's share of total employment was also stable, at around one-third of the total, after 1841.[27] The chief compensation for agricultural decline after 1840 came not from industry but from services.[28]

The share of services in employment was higher in Britain in the nineteenth century and early twentieth centuries than anywhere else save the Netherlands,[29] and, as Table 3.2 shows, that share was increasing steadily from the mid-nineteenth century. The table also makes clear the concentration of service employment in the south-east of England: that region alone accounted for one-third of all service employment in Britain in 1841 and two-fifths in 1911.

Looking at manufacturing and service employment in isolation from each other does not give a true picture of the complex nature of development in Britain after 1850 or of the importance of the south-east. Lee has recently identified three crucial areas of growth in terms of output and employment: those connected with mining; the staple export trades and heavy industries; and a third group in which a complex of services and linked consumer-goods industries was the dominant form, and of which London and its environs was the greatest exemplar.[30] This third group was growing more rapidly than the others as early as the 1840s. At that date, it was dominant only in London, Middlesex and Surrey but its influence grew thereafter until, by the outbreak of war in 1914, it had encompassed all of what we now call the Home Counties, as the agricultural frontier in the south-east of England retreated.[31] The pre-eminent position of the south-east within this service-consumer industry complex was very marked. The whole group accounted

TABLE 3.2 Share of services in employment, 1841–1911 (per cent)

Region	*1841*	*1881*	*1911*
North-west	20.0	24.9	26.9
South-east	35.8	41.8	45.8
Great Britain	26.3	30.2	33.1

Source: C.H. Lee, *British Regional Employment Statistics, 1841–1971* (Cambridge, 1979), Series A, employment categories 22–27: transport; distribution; insurance, banking, financial and business services; professional and scientific; miscellaneous; public administration and defence.

for 55 per cent of British employment in 1841 and 65 per cent 70 years later. Of the employment in the south-east, 71 per cent fell into this category at the first date and 85 per cent at the second, at which point the region was responsible for 37 per cent of all employment in the group.[32] Not only was employment rising faster in the south-east than elsewhere but also the London-centred area was more closely integrated economically than the others, which were more dependent on exports either to other regions or abroad.

Moreover, although the development of services was often an adjunct of industrial development in the provinces, the reverse was true in the south-east. There, the growth of consumer manufactures was often stimulated directly by the growth of service income and employment.[33] A case in point was the engineering sector, an area of rapid technological change: nearly half of all the new jobs created in instrument engineering in this period, and over two-fifths of those in electrical engineering, were found in the south-east.[34] Also, under the stimulus of rising real wages after 1870, consumer industries and services offered some of the most impressive examples of dynamic entrepreneurship in Britain,[35] including the massive transformation which took place in retail trading and the rapid development – much of it involving complex technical change – of the finance and banking sector.[36]

At the heart of this highly successful service economy was London, a city which, while shedding many of its old-established industries (like shipbuilding) under pressure from the provinces,[37] was as much a magnet for people, wealth and power in 1900 as it had been in 1750. In 1801 London contained 12 per cent of the population of England and Wales; by 1901 the figure had risen to 20 per cent. It grew faster than any other conurbation in Great Britain after 1850 and, by 1911, its population was equivalent to the six other great centres of population combined.[38] Indeed, London's growth after 1850, like the growth of the south-east region itself, was a reassertion of an ancient dominance rather than a novel force in British life. As Dyos expresses it, 'the shift of resources into the exploitation of the northern provinces, and others, in the eighteenth and nineteenth centuries might be represented simply as an interlude in a much larger historical trend'.[39] If, between 1750 and 1850, the economic tide had run in favour of the industrial provinces it swung decisively back again, to the traditional centre of wealth and power, in the Victorian and Edwardian epoch.

The new gentlemanly capitalists

Before 1914, aristocratic ideals and life-styles retained a powerful appeal in Britain despite the relative decline of land as an economic force. The peerage was still highly visible and active, culturally and socially, and landed gentlemen played a leading role in high politics until the outbreak of war. Even in 1900, members of parliament with landed backgrounds had a disproportionate share of government posts and Lord Salisbury's last administration was known as the 'Hotel Cecil', so strong was the imprint of his own family upon it.[40] It was not so obvious, however, that this pervasive aristocratic presence betokened real power and influence. In recent years, both Marxist and 'liberal' historians have disagreed among themselves and with each other about whether the continued prominence of the landed elite reflected a real aristocratic dominance or whether aristocratic government and cultural norms were merely convenient veils behind which the 'bourgeoisie' could work its will undisturbed.[41] Our argument will be that aristocratic power was in clear decline but that power and prestige devolved more upon a new gentlemanly class arising from the service sector than it did upon the industrial bourgeoisie. The landed aristocracy could mitigate their economic difficulties after 1870 only by reaching an accommodation with other forms of wealth, but the links they made were largely with non-industrial rather than industrial sources, as we shall see. And, insofar as their political and social power was on the wane, their successors were gentlemen from the service sector or from finance rather than manufacturers from the industrial provinces.

As the basis of Britain's economic fortunes shifted from the land and agriculture to urban-based manufacturing and service activities, the transformation was registered unambiguously in the sources of top wealth holding (Table 3.3). From our perspective what is important is that, as land declined as the chief source of great fortunes, especially after 1880 when arable agriculture felt the full force

TABLE 3.3 Non-landed fortunes at death, 1860–1919 (£0.5m. or more)

	1860–79	*%*	*1880–99*	*%*	*1900–19*	*%*
Manufacturing and mining	44	35.7	82	36.7	124	34.2
Food, drink and tobacco	3	2.4	36	16.1	48	13.2
Finance	40	32.5	47	21.1	79	21.9
Commerce	29	23.5	47	21.1	101	27.9
Other	7	5.6	11	4.9	10	2.8
Total (non-landed)	123		223		362	
(Land)	(280)		(174)		(140)	

Source: W.D. Rubinstein, Men of Property: The Very Wealthy in Great Britain Since the Industrial Revolution (1981), Tables 3.3, 3.4, pp. 60–6.

Notes:
A small percentage of landed fortunes covers the period 1858–79 but not enough to change the total in column 1 significantly.
It must be emphasised here that Rubinstein's statistics do not include the value of the land of those whose property was subject to legal settlements forbidding sale and in which any particular owner had only a life interest.
The compilation of the groups is as follows: *Manufacturing and mining* comprise columns 1–11 of the tables; *Food, drink and tobacco,* columns 12–15; *Finance,* columns 16–18 and 22–3; *Commerce,* columns 19–21 and 24–5; *Other,* columns 26–32.

of foreign competition, commerce and finance more than held their own, with industry, as replacements. The predominance of non-landed wealth over land was not apparent until the end of the century; but since the statistics are for fortunes declared at death it can usually be assumed that the greater part of this wealth had been accumulated a generation earlier and that 1880 is roughly the point at which land ceased to be the outstanding source of great wealth in Britain. Working on the same generational principle, it is also apparent that there was a strong surge in the growth of large fortunes made in manufacturing, if the food, drink and tobacco industries are included, but that these sectors did not make further relative gains during the next 30 years. Moreover, if account is taken of all the industrial regions of the provinces, then their share of peak wealth-holding stayed at around three-tenths of the total throughout the period 1850–1914, with the rise of fortunes in areas like South Wales in the late nineteenth century being compensated by the declining importance of the Manchester region (Table 3.4). The fact that the industrial regions did not perform more strongly overall probably reflects not only the growing strength of trades unionism, which cut into profits, but also the

TABLE 3.4 Geographical origins of non-landed fortunes, 1858–1919 (£0.5m. or more)

	1858–79	%	*1880–99*	%	*1900–19*	%
City	51	41.5	51	22.9	82	22.7
Other London	12	9.8	32	14.3	47	13.0
Lancashire	13		22		24	
Yorkshire	9		8		25	
North-east	6		11		26	
Midlands	6		20		25	
Northern Ireland	–		1		3	
South Wales	4		2		7	
Total, industrial	38	30.9	64	28.7	110	30.5
Clydeside[a]	8	15.5	15	13.9	28	15.8
Merseyside[a]	11		16		29	
Others	3		45		66	
Grand total	123		223		362	

Source: Rubinstein, *Men of Property*, Tables 3.11 and 3.12.

Note:

[a] Merseyside and Clydeside have been listed separately from the industrial areas because of the predominance there of commercial fortunes.

persistence of the small firm and the growth of the foreign challenge both at home and in markets overseas after 1880. Where some form of monopoly did exist, the manufacturing wealthy multiplied. No fewer than six of the sixteen millionaire fortunes declared at death in Scotland between 1873 and 1913 came from members of the J.P. Coats sewing-thread combine; twenty of the thirty-four millionaire fortunes made in food, drink and tobacco between 1860 and 1919 came from that traditional big business, brewing. They were the exceptions, and textiles were more typical of manufacturing as a whole. Only fifteen millionaires and twenty-five half-millionaires were produced by the whole of cotton manufacturing in Britain between 1860 and 1919.[42]

Commerce and finance were traditional sources of non-landed wealth and declined sharply in relative importance in the third quarter of the century (Table 3.3). The City of London, the centre of these activities,[43] suffered from this trend, its relative share falling from two-fifths to just over one-fifth (Table 3.4). At the same time, fortunes made in the rest of London became more prominent, partly because of its association with the food, drink and tobacco industries, especially brewing,[44] which were an important part of the consumer goods sector so strongly associated with the south-east of England. In the late nineteenth and early twentieth centuries, commerce and finance more than held their own as producers of great wealth, and London and the City retained their relative shares: in terms of millionaire fortunes alone the City actually made important relative gains at the latter end of the period. The concentration of wealth within the City is indicated by the fact that merchant banking alone produced 22 millionaire and 29 half-millionaire fortunes between 1860 and 1919, a better record than the vast cotton textile industry could boast. The preponderance of the City is even more marked if attention is focused on the tax statistics. Of incomes over £5,000 per annum assessed for tax under schedule D in 1879–80, the number originating in Metropolitan Middlesex and London was 1,210 as against 730 for the three major English industrial areas – Lancashire, Yorkshire and Warwickshire/Staffordshire – combined. The City alone accounted for 630 of the metropolitan incomes or just over one-half of the total. Furthermore, at over £41m., the total income assessed for tax in the City was four times as high as in Manchester and ten times greater than in Birmingham.[45]

One reason for this concentration of wealth was London's dominance of the international side of the service economy and, within that, the pronounced importance of a few major institutions. Joint-stock banking amalgamations put power into the hands of no more than a dozen leading companies by 1914,[46] a degree of concentration unparalleled in Britain outside of transport. Moreover, a large share both of the market for short-term credit and of the far more lucrative loan flotation business was controlled by a handful of merchant banks. Although competition from the joint-stock banks was increasing by 1914, seven of the major merchant banks were responsible for about one-third of all the acceptance credits in the market in 1913[47] and many of the old established houses had a dominant role in the issue business for particular countries: for example, the Rothschilds held first place in regard to Brazil and Chile, while Barings were the predominant force in Argentina and Canada.[48] The confidence inspired by the outstanding merchant banks and merchant houses gave them a virtual monopoly of the business of many of their clients. As Bagehot put it: 'an old established bank has a "prestige" which amounts to a "privileged opportunity"; though no exclusive right is given it by law, peculiar power is given it by opinion'; and he went on to emphasise that 'the "credit" of a person – that is the reliance which may be placed on his pecuniary fidelity – is a different thing from his property'.[49] Consequently, the most prestigious financiers were able to handle vast amounts of other people's money while putting relatively small amounts into the business as capital, with the result that the most successful could earn profits which were immense by the standards of most industrial capitalists.[50]

The City was the point at which the international economy intersected with the service capitalism of the south-east. It is fairly certain that the south-east always had a higher per capita income than other parts of the country but its lead had probably narrowed in the early nineteenth century, only to widen again towards 1900.[51] Schedule D income tax per capita averaged £16.41 in Britain in 1879–80 but £22.49 in the south-east,[52] an indicator not only of the vast fortunes to be made in the City but also of the large number of the 'servant-keeping classes'[53] living in the Home Counties in late Victorian England. One-third of all adult males in London in 1860 paid tax as opposed to about 10 per cent in northern industrial towns, and the middle-class share of London's population grew significantly later in the century.[54]

Just as the south-east was the most dynamic sector of the economy in the late nineteenth century, so too it was the region where an invigorated elite adapted aristocratic cultural norms to suit more modern conditions. One fundamental blow to aristocratic power was loss of control over the gentlemanly professions in government, Church and army as a result of reforms in the recruitment system and the beginning of meritocratic selection between 1850 and 1870.[55] Nonetheless, the final collapse of the old patronage system did not provoke a social revolution but merely handed over power to a large, non-industrial middle class which was mainly resident in the London region[56] and eager to secure genteel employment. The examination system acted as a rationing device for this class, which had already benefited considerably from patronage.[57] The reconstruction of these traditional professions was accompanied by the transformation of others, such as medicine and engineering, all of which were reorganised in such a way as to restrict supply and increase income.[58]

Despite this capitalist exploitation of their own intellectual property rights,[59] the professions as a whole saw themselves as gentlemen, or at least aspired to be such, and assumed the possession, in Matthew Arnold's words, of 'fine and governing qualities'.[60] In order to meet these new needs the leading public schools and the ancient universities became manufactories for the creation of public servants and professionals who blended the aristocratic ideal of leadership and service with the new administrative abilities and techniques demanded by a complex urban society[61] to produce that characteristic mixture of amateurism and efficiency which was the mark of the English establishment well into the twentieth century.[62] This newly formed gentlemanly class, paternalist in its assumptions and held together by the club-like spirit which resulted from a common educational and social background, was deeply suspicious both of landed indolence and of the world of trade and everyday work.[63] But, though they had to break free of aristocratic control in order to develop, both the ideology[64] and the practice of these service-based professions were much closer to aristocratic ideals than they were to those of industry,[65] especially as regards their control over their own time, their ability to charge fees rather than to depend upon salaries or wages,[66] their contempt for mere money-making and the personal rather than mechanical nature of their work. They also acted as the transmitters of gentlemanly cultural norms to the lower levels of service capitalism inhabited by the likes of Pooter[67] and the clerking heroes of H.G. Wells, who combined an ethic of extreme economic individualism with an almost desperate desire for a status untainted by 'Trade'.[68]

The connection went deeper than the mere cultural influence of the great upon the small. Although most recruits into the highest ranks of the public service, the Church and other professions were from families in the south of England already connected with the service sector, they were frequently drawn from the lower income end of the taxpaying spectrum, finding their way to the top through a combination of parental determination to pay for public school education and their own ability to exploit the Oxbridge scholarship system.[69]

Gentlemanliness was, therefore, a marked feature of those parts of the 'official mind' which were closely concerned either with the management of government finances, such as the Treasury,[70] or with Britain's overseas responsibilities and possessions. The Foreign Office, and more particularly the diplomatic service, retained throughout the period a much more aristocratic flavour then other sections of government: applicants for the diplomatic service, for example, had to have private means.[71] The Foreign Office also retained a wider patronage network than was available elsewhere, especially through the consular service which, even in the twentieth century, remained 'a harbour of refuge for retired army officers and for failures whose only recommendation was aristocratic, official or personal influences'.[72]

The gentlemanly class formed the backbone of the Colonial Office[73] and of the administration which ruled India after 1850 and then spread its influence into south-east Asia and into Africa after partition. Most British colonial governors, for instance, 'came from the south-eastern part of England or were educated there' at public schools and then perhaps went on to Oxbridge; and they were, generally speaking, the sons of other civil servants, professional men, army officers or – most frequently – clergymen.[74] Their narrow educational background and social origins offered them a code of honour which ensured that governors were 'gentlemen both in the sociological and ethical meaning of the word'.[75] The ordinary district officers were of similar social and cultural backgrounds and, like their leaders, saw their roles as bringing 'law and order' and endowing local elites with the same leadership qualities – and the same educational institutions – as they possessed themselves. They were vigorous proponents of the telegraph, the railway and all the other infrastructual investments without which civilisation – and good careers for the 'sons of gentlemen' – could not be advanced, but they tended to despise business and modern urban life.[76] Their natural economic links were with the City rather than industry. The Crown Agents, for example, who handled most of the economic transactions between Britain and the colonies on capital account, belonged 'to the social universe of the universities, the great government departments and the clubs', and they operated via an informal, even secretive, network of financial institutions in the City 'on the basis of trust of a kind that could only exist in a society where private business and public administration were linked by informal ties of school, class and clubland'.[77]

The City of London and gentlemanly capitalism

Links between the Crown Agents and the City provided one small instance of the fact that, in the evolving world of gentlemanly culture focused on London, in which aristocracy was still an important element, finance – or at least City finance – had a place while industry still lacked one. The City of London had a traditional importance as the financier of aristocratic governments in Britain, with the Bank of England acting as chief intermediary between the two; and the bonds between the world of finance and of politics and power were strengthened by daily contact in the metropolis. As the power of the land declined and gentlemanly capitalism established itself anew, the City maintained its position as banker to governments while evolving in ways which made it the financial headquarters of elite wealth and elevated a part of the City itself into the gentlemanly capitalist sphere.

The gentlemanly capitalist City was to a large extent dominated by the great merchant banking houses which, having acquired vast wealth in commerce, had then graduated to become financiers of British and overseas governments. It was the link with governments which brought the leading houses into the world of power and diplomacy. Through their dealings with government, they also moved into the overlapping world of superior social connections, becoming bankers to the aristocracy and personal friends and intimate advisers of the politically powerful. This position at the centre of elite society was the basis of the prestige Bagehot pointed to as being the hallmark of the most successful banking organisations, a prestige that made them, to some degree, the arbiters of what was or was not acceptable in the City. Many, though not all, of these great houses were represented on the Court of the Bank of England, the official channel of communication between governments and City, which supplemented the more informal relationships that existed between merchant banker and politician.

At its most fruitful, City life combined great wealth with freedom from continuous work. 'Banking', as Bagehot put it, 'is a watchful, but it is not a laborious trade'; it allowed, he thought, for the 'educated refinement' which had characterised the life of many London private bankers.[78] The private banks were dying fast after 1870, swallowed by the joint stocks: but their leaders often lived on as directors of the larger banks[79] and Bagehot's observation was true also of the great merchant banking families like the Rothschilds, Barings and Grenfells. Peerages came to many of these City dynasties much sooner than to industrialists and they often lived, and worked, in a style appropriate to great landed wealth.[80] The leading figures in the banking world were not idle but they operated in a world where leisure was often difficult to distinguish from work. A new recruit to the London house of Morgan wrote to tell Alfred Milner that 'the City does not involve long hours or much fatigue. But it means incessant presence and attention. You never know when you may be called upon'.[81] He was describing a world which, like that of high politics, depended as heavily upon networks of social intercourse as it did upon formal structures. The City magnate operated in an intricate world where business, social life and political intrigue all overlapped,[82] one where these activities were so entwined that the members of great City families who were not involved directly in the business could nonetheless bring great benefits to it because of the information they gathered and the connections they forged.

Many of the leading City figures were Jewish in origin, members of families which had been attracted to London because of its pivotal position in world finance. The extended families of the Jewish bankers stretched across the globe, giving them a superb information network and also providing them, *in extremis,* with extensive lines of credit. The City was, simultaneously, both a British institution and a cosmopolitan one. The great Jewish families epitomised this duality, combining country houses, sons at Eton and Harrow, and outspoken loyalty to the crown and the empire with a global spread of personal and economic connections which stretched well beyond the limits of formal British influence. In addition, close relationships among the ramifying cousinhood meant that there was a better chance of finding the new entrepreneurial talent necessary to the vitality of the houses across the generations. This left others free to devote themselves to the artistic life, to politics or to sport, or to keeping the family in the social swim by entertaining royalty.[83]

The employees of the great were frequently gentlemen themselves, and their working hours could be even shorter than Hilaire Belloc's celebrated Peter Goole, who toiled

> All day long from 10 till 4!
> For half the year or even more;
> With but an hour or two to spend
> At luncheon with a city friend.[84]

Leisure came not simply from the wealth generated by the principal bankers but from the nature of their business in the City, which was conducted among a small, close-knit group of people who shared a similar public-school education and life-style,[85] and whose gentlemanly code allowed transactions to be entered into and honoured, informally, without the need for elaborate bureaucracy.[86] Like the higher professions, the nature of much City business at this level was personal rather than mechanical and it allowed the amateur spirit full play.[87]

At the beginning of the period, although land and City could even then be seen as 'dividing . . . the social empire of the kingdom between them',[88] the aristocracy still thought of intermarriage as an occasional irksome necessity.[89] By the 1890s, the great merchant bankers not only shared a similar educational background with aristocrats and leading professionals but also were regularly intermarrying with the landed interest and, at the highest social levels, the great financiers and the aristocrats had begun to merge.[90] There is considerable truth in the contemporary view that

> The great merchant banker of today is an English gentleman of the finished type. He is possibly a peer, and an active partner in a great City firm: if he is not a peer, the chances are he is a member of the House of Commons. He is a man of wide culture. . . . There is in fact but one standard of 'social position' in England and it is that which is formed by the blending of the plutocratic and the aristocratic element.[91]

Certainly, 'Society', which acted as an upper-class information network as well as conferring social distinction on its members, had widened considerably beyond its original aristocratic limits by 1880, and the weightier City men were by then an intrinsic part of the system.[92]

The great majority of those who worked in the City were not a part of the web of gentlemanly connection any more than the majority of those who worked in the professions were a part of it. The Stock Exchange, run by former public schoolboys in a club-like atmosphere and ruled by gentlemanly codes of behaviour, was rising in the social scale by this time. Its prestige was enhanced by the informality of its proceedings and by the fact that business could be discussed 'effectively and lucratively round dinner tables or at a shoot'.[93] On the other hand, even such an important group as the managers of the large and growing joint-stock banks, whose work was characterised as bureaucratic and time-consuming, failed to qualify as gentlemen at all and this was emphasised by their exclusion from the Court of the Bank of England, which was dominated by the merchant bankers.[94] Even the latter were not an homogeneous or unchanging group by any means. Among those who established a permanent presence in the later nineteenth century were new firms, such as Kleinworts and Schroders, whose business ethics and life-style had more in common with northern industrialists than with the banking aristocracy and who disliked the Bank of England and its coteries. This new wave of immigrants from the continent made large inroads into the bill-acceptance business of the established merchant bankers though, unlike the Anglo-American invaders, Morgans, they made little impact on the much more lucrative and prestigious business of issuing stocks and bonds.[95]

The rise of new wealth is a reminder of the dynamic nature of the Victorian and Edwardian City, which had to change continuously in order to retain London's leading position in the world economy.[96] City wealth was often precarious: firms with an established reputation and great prestige in the Square Mile could falter or even fail suddenly if a partner decided to withdraw his capital, if the business fell into the hands of ineffective or uninterested sons, or if there was no one to inherit.[97] Even the mighty could stumble, as the Baring Crisis of 1890 clearly demonstrates. The same process of change also raised new wealth and could catapult individuals or firms into great prominence with amazing speed. The City was so much a part of the life of London's elites by the late nineteenth century that it was easy for spectacular wealth to make an impact socially.[98] But to move into the highest circles, where society and politics overlapped, it was insufficient simply to consume conspicuously in the style of Julius Wernher, the South African mining magnate.[99] Needed also were friends in high places and the willingness and the ability to do the state some service, perhaps by using influence or lending money in politically sensitive arenas like the Middle East, when the usual intermediaries, like the Rothschilds, did not care to involve themselves. Both attributes were outstanding features of the meteoric rise of Ernest Cassell and the Sassoons to prestige and authority around the turn of the century.[100]

Taking the City as a whole, it would be fair to describe it in 1850 as 'an intimate club of familiar people undertaking easily recognisable tasks', whereas by 1900 it had grown spectacularly and was populated mainly by 'hordes of specialists each making out their own peculiar contribution to an increasingly complex process' that few understood in the round.[101] Most of the 40,000 firms which populated the City around the turn of the century had a short life, and they and their 350,000 employees worked and lived in an atmosphere with which any small industrialist would have been familiar. These were not conditions which conduced to a gentlemanly life or which attracted social honours and prestige. But the wide range of occupations did mean that the City of London housed a broad spectrum of society from aristocrats at one end to £100-a-year clerks at the other; through its vast chain of institutions, it linked the powerful with the marginal and even with the shady and dishonourable.[102] Moreover, through its enormous commercial sector, the City provided a connection between domestic and international economic life and between high finance on the one side and industry on the other. It was this diversity of institutions, practices and ideas which allowed the few who could speak for the City to claim, with some plausibility, that it was representative of national interests and that what was good for the Square Mile was necessarily good for Britain.

Although the composition of the City changed over time and the complexity of its operations increased, at the end of the period it was still led by a small cohesive elite, centred on the Bank of England, which was wedged firmly into the British 'establishment' in the late nineteenth century.[103] The power of this elite was also growing. Before the last quarter of the nineteenth century the bankers were an adjunct to aristocratic control; after 1914 financial power was clearly more potent than that of the land. The period 1880 to 1914 was one of precarious equipose, when the power of finance, growing increasingly cosmopolitan, reached a transitory equality with that of land, whose agricultural base was being slowly undermined by the free trade internationalism on which the City flourished.[104]

Industry, provincialism and power

The representatives of industry did not achieve the same degree of prestige and power in the period before World War I.[105] Although the number of 'self-made men' was diminishing and there was a strong hereditary element in business by 1914, the average manufacturer was too small and too provincial (at a time when power was beginning to focus even more strongly on London)[106] to make an impact at the centre.[107] Among this class in the regions there could still be found a strong tradition of hostility to the established Church, landed monopoly and royalty, and grave misgivings about London-based finance. Even in these circles mere 'money-grubbing' was frowned upon and there was a growing emphasis upon the importance of service to the community and of the value of cultural achievement, which provided a bridge between industrialists and gentlemanly life-styles.[108] Among the wealthiest manufacturers, the tendency to conform to gentlemanly norms of conduct was stronger. Where firms were bigger than average, as in steel, wealth was more concentrated and public school and Oxbridge influences were felt early:[109] indeed, some large firms began to acquire gentlemanly directors in the manner of joint-stock banks.[110] It has been claimed that if manufacturers often bought land they usually acquired only enough to establish themselves in a good house with a decent park. However, new evidence shows that the wealthiest at least bought substantial quantities of land with the idea of improving their status or founding a dynasty: only the childless seemed uninterested in land purchase.[111] But, even among the super-rich, most manufacturers had no wider ambitions than to concentrate their political and social talents on their localities.[112] So provincial were they – even the far from negligible number who were Anglican, Tory and deeply respectful of aristocracy[113] – that gentlemanly governments found it hard to assimilate them after 1860, when manufacturing wealth began to multiply rapidly and to become politically more visible. When the question of honours for industrialists was seriously broached in the 1880s, the Liberal government of the day reacted 'almost as if they were talking about some remote, foreign tribe which they believed to be important but of whose intentions they were suspicious and which they were uncertain how to treat'[114].

Gladstone's hesitations about granting peerages to cotton capitalists reflected the assumption that what was quintessentially 'English', what was nationally regarded as significant or otherwise, was something that gentlemen had a right and duty to define.[115] Matthew Arnold's famous proposal for a common public-school education for the children of both gentlemen and the industrially wealthy was a serious attempt to create a unified bourgeois elite in the face of aristocratic decline. However, his greatest fear was that power would fall into the hands of the 'Philistines' of industrialism, and his proposals were intended to ensure that the cultural norms of industrialism would give way to gentlemanly ones. Gentlemen ought to learn some science and be given some understanding of the world of trade, but industrialists were expected to embrace 'sweetness and light', as currently defined in the public schools and ancient universities, and, more importantly, to learn that leadership was a different and far more elevated art than that of mere money-making.[116]

Gentlemanly capitalism and politics

Direct aristocratic influence upon high politics also declined before 1914. In mid-century, the aristocracy's command of the House of Commons was still overwhelming: even among the Liberals, the party in which radicalism found a home, nearly half of all the members of parliament (MPs) who sat in the House between 1859 and 1874 were either large landowners or 'gentlemen of leisure'.[117] But, by 1914, the number of MPs with non-landed economic interests had risen very rapidly. Landowning ceased to be the majority interest in the House among both parties, as is illustrated by the figures available for the occupations of members in 1914 and by the prominence of professional men (mainly lawyers), manufacturers and other businessmen by that time (see Tables 3.5 and 3.6 (Appendix One)).

Even in mid-century, the Tory Party had a greater share of aristocratic MPs than the Liberals, and the landed interest's adherence to the right in British politics became stronger over time. Simultaneously, the south, and especially the south-east, of England hardened its support for Conservatism.[118] The large, non-industrial middle class in London and the Home Counties, much of it directly connected with City finance, had a dominating influence over its non-unionised and more deferential workforce; it was their brand of gentlemanly capitalism which shaped the Conservative Party and ensured that the aristocracy still had a prominent role to play at the highest levels of politics.[119] Liberal strength increased the further north one travelled[120] and rested to a large degree on the industrial towns, where provincial manufacturers and workers often shared a hostility to gentlemanly culture and the status quo it represented. Not surprisingly, manufacturing interests were always larger among Liberal MPs than among Tories (Appendix One).

There is no doubt, though, that after 1870 there was some drift of all business interests, not just landed ones, towards the Conservative Party. The extension of the franchise in 1867 and 1884 roused fears for property in general and these were confirmed by the growth of trade unionism and of anti-capitalist, as well as anti-aristocratic, ideas among working men. Gladstone's Irish legislation in the 1880s and his subsequent conversion to Home Rule[121] also offended the remaining Whig aristocrats within the Liberal Party and alarmed business interests, which feared the disintegration of the empire and a wholesale attack on property rights. Among MPs with City credentials, Liberalism finally went out of favour in the 1880s (Table 3.6); those with financial interests who still adhered to Liberalism after this time tended to have their economic roots in the provinces rather than in London.[122] The drift of business and landed interests away from Liberalism forced the party into a more radical stance in order to appeal to the new mass electorate in the provinces.[123] The sharpness of the attack on land and the 'unearned increment' in Chamberlain's Unauthorised Programme of the 1880s – which was aimed at City wealth as well as at the aristocracy[124] – and in the Newcastle Programme a decade later reflects this. It also represents a determined attempt to focus on non-industrial targets in order to keep the Liberal electorate united, and to divert attention from direct conflicts between workers and manufacturing interests in the Liberal Party's provincial strongholds.[125]

Although the Liberals remained the favoured party of the manufacturing interest up to 1914, the drift to Conservatism among them was quite marked (Table 3.6) and was accentuated by the disputes over protectionism after 1880, as we shall see. The spread of economic interests across the parties by 1914 was such that it was impossible to speak of either as 'representing' industry. Moreover, MPs from constituencies in manufacturing areas often saw themselves as representing their locality rather than as attempting to make a mark on the national stage. Even in the Liberal Party, leadership almost automatically devolved on the remaining gentlemanly capitalists and the professional politicians, and the direct influence of the business element was limited.[126] Liberalism had not become identified with industry to quite the extent that the Conservative Party had become the political arm of the aristocracy, the City and the gentlemanly capitalism of the south-east.

Aristocratic power was in steady decline during this period,[127] and what authority it still exerted in 1914 was dependent upon its role within a wider gentlemanly capitalist culture which had grown dramatically over the previous 50 years. Industry and industrialists did not play starring roles in the evolution of this new ideology of gentlemanliness, nor did they have the same degree of control over political power which the aristocrats, the City financiers and the professional classes of London and the Home Counties possessed. This is not to say that they had been suborned by some aristocratic ideal of ruralism and leisure, as has been claimed.[128] Small scale and indelibly provincial as they were, most industrialists in Britain were untouched by the aristocratic ideal. As Rubinstein has expressed it:

> In Britain, the net effect of the industrial revolution was systematically to advantage the older and more conservative, rather than the newer and most radical, sectors of the British wealth structure – above all the great landowners and the bankers and merchants of the City of London, rather than the manufacturers and industrialists, a circumstance which had the most profound effects on the evolution of British society and its class system.[129]

Cobden had thought of the coming of Free Trade as the prelude to the triumph of industrialism in Britain. But Cobdenite ideologies could not prevail because his chosen people did not have sufficient wealth and influence to make them dominant either economically or ideologically. Suitably modified, the aristocratic ideal survived because it was adopted and supported by the gentlemanly class which arose from the service sector in the nineteenth century and proved to be the most successful and dynamic element in British economic life between 1850 and 1914.[130]

APPENDIX ONE

Economic interests and occupations of members of parliament, 1868–1914

The economic interests of MPs on both sides of the House are given in Table 3.5. 'Professional service' consists mainly of lawyers but also newspaper proprietors. Brewing is subsumed under manufacturing; merchants are included with commerce and finance. The shift from landed (and military) interests is marked.

MPs could, and often did, have more than one economic interest, so the number of interests is greater than the numbers of MPs.

One way of gauging the extent to which a particular economic interest was stronger in one party than in another is by using the 'associative index' developed by Perkin, which counteracts the influences of electoral swing upon the share of different interests in parliament. An index of the strength of particular interests in the Liberal Party can be found by using the following formula:

$$\frac{\text{Liberal members of interest}}{\text{Conservative members of interest}} \times \frac{\text{Conservative MPs}}{\text{Liberal MPs}}$$

TABLE 3.5 Economic interests of MPs, 1868–1910 (per cent for each party)

	1868		*1892*		*1910 (Jan)*	
	Lib	*Con*	*Lib*	*Con*	*Lib*	*Con*
Landowning	26.1	45.9	9.0	24.1	7.2	21.6
Military service	6.9	13.6	1.8	8.6	2.6	9.5
Finance, commerce	16.4	10.3	16.5	22.5	16.9	20.9
Professional service	17.3	9.4	29.5	18.3	28.5	16.1
Manufacturing	12.0	4.4	24.8	12.1	27.3	20.1
Transport	13.0	13.6	8.9	10.5	9.5	8.7

Sources: J.A. Thomas, *The House of Commons, 1832–1901: A Study of its Economic and Financial Character* (Cardiff, 1939); idem, *The House of Commons, 1906–1911: An Analysis of its Economic and Social Character* (Cardiff, 1958).

Any resulting number above 1.0, for example, would indicate that, at any particular time, the Liberal share of the interest was greater than the Liberal share of the MPs of the two parties and vice versa. This formula produces the result shown in Table 3.6.

Table 3.6 clearly shows the predominance of Conservatism among landowners, those with military interests, and in finance and commerce as early as 1880. It also illustrates the drift of manufacturing interests and merchants towards Conservatism after 1868.

Interests are unsatisfactory as indices of economic alignment because they are not weighted: landowners with £10,000 per annum in farm rents and £500 in an investment trust would register two interests but they are hardly comparable. So it is useful to supplement the interest tables with information on occupations. Unfortunately, this information is scarce: the only usable table, for 1914, is reproduced as Table 3.7.

TABLE 3.6 Liberal MPs: associative index, 1868–1910

	1868	*1880*	*1892*	*1900*	*1906*	*1910**
Landowners	0.66	0.54	0.36	0.44	0.48	0.30
Military service	0.59	0.46	0.20	0.27	0.32	0.25
Finance and commerce	1.86	0.92	0.71	0.58	0.75	0.73
Transport services	1.11	1.06	0.81	0.97	0.66	0.99
Merchants	3.57	2.45	2.26	1.42	2.22	2.02
Professional services	2.14	1.99	1.58	1.61	1.97	1.52
Manufacturing	3.19	2.10	1.97	1.69	1.25	1.22

Sources: As Table 3.5, and Harold Perkin, *The Structured Crowd: Essays in English Social History* (Brighton, 1981), pp. 128–31.

* The election of January 1910 only.

TABLE 3.7 Occupations of members of parliament, 1914 (per cent share in each party)

	Unionist	*Liberal*
Landowning	22.1	6.1
Military and government service	20.8	9.1
Professional services	34.0	42.1
(of which, lawyers)	(26.7)	(26.9)
Commerce and finance	13.2	15.5
Industry	9.9	24.2
Working men	–	3.0

Source: J. Ramsden, *The Age of Balfour and Baldwin, 1902–1940* (1978), Table 5.1, pp. 98–9. The table does not include the occupations of all MPs, some of which are unknown. Merchants are included in Commerce and finance. Industry includes building and brewing.

Table 3.7 does show the concentrations of landed wealth and of military personnel in the Conservative and Unionist Party and also the continued prominence of manufacturers among the Liberals. But if the table of economic interests perhaps overstresses the importance of finance, the occupational table probably underrates it. Few MPs were financiers but very many had substantial financial holdings.

Notes

1 The quotation in the title is taken from Robert Henry Super, ed. *The Complete Prose Works of Matthew Arnold* (Ann Arbor, Mich., 1965), Vol. II, p. 88.

2 Phyllis Deane and W.A. Cole, *British Economic Growth, 1688–1959: Trends and Structure* (Cambridge, 1964), pp. 282–4, 311.

3 Phyllis Deane, 'New Estimates of Gross National Product for the United Kingdom, 1830–1914', *Review of Income and Wealth,* XIV (1968), esp. Table 2, p. 98.

4 C.H. Feinstein, *National Income, Expenditure and Output of the United Kingdom, 1955–1965* (Cambridge, 1972), Table 7, p. 19; see also D.N. McCloskey, 'Did Victorian Britain Fail?', *Econ. Hist. Rev.,* 2nd ser. XXIII (1970); D.H. Aldcroft, 'McCloskey on Victorian Growth: a Comment', *Econ. Hist. Rev.,* 2nd ser. XXVII (1974), pp. 272–3; and McCloskey, 'Victorian Growth: a Rejoinder', ibid. pp. 275–7. The last three articles are reproduced in Donald N. McCloskey, *Enterprise and Trade in Victorian Britain: Essays in Historical Economics* (1981). An early essay stressing the importance of 1900 as a turning point is R.C.O. Matthews, 'Some Aspects of Post-War Growth in the British Economy in Relation to Historical Experience', *Transactions of the Manchester Statistical Society* (1964–5) and reprinted in Derek H. Aldcroft and Peter Fearon, eds. *Economic Growth in Twentieth-Century Britain* (1969).

5 N.F.R. Crafts, *British Economic Growth during the Industrial Revolution* (Oxford, 1985), p. 45. See also C.H. Lee, *The British Economy Since 1700: A Macro-Economic Perspective* (1986), Ch. I.

6 Angus Maddison, *Economic Growth in the West: Comparative Experience in Europe and North America* (1964), esp. Table 1.1, p. 28, and Table 1.3, p. 30.

7 C.H. Feinstein, R.C.O. Matthews and J.C. Odling-Smee, 'The Timing of the Climacteric and its Sectoral Incidence in the United Kingdom, 1873–1913', in Charles P. Kindleberger and Guido di Tella, eds. *Economics in the Long View: Essays in Honour of W.W. Rostow,* Vol. 2, Pt. I (1982), Table 8.4, p. 178.

8 K.S. Lomax, 'Growth and Productivity in the United Kingdom', in Aldcroft and Fearon, *Economic Growth,* Table 2, p. 12.

9 D.J. Coppock, 'The Climacteric of the 1890s: a Critical Note', *Manchester School,* XXIV (1956), pp. 7–8.

10 For a general discussion of nineteenth- and early twentieth-century growth patterns see R.A. Church, *The Great Victorian Boom, 1850–1873* (1975); S.B. Saul, *The Myth of the Great Depression, 1873–1896* (1969); François Crouzet, *The Victorian Economy* (1982), Chs. 2 and 3; Sidney Pollard, *Britain's Prime and Britain's Decline: The British Economy, 1870–1914* (1989), pp. 1–17.

11 R.C.O. Matthews, C.H. Feinstein, and J.C. Odling-Smee, *British Economic Growth, 1856–1973* (Oxford, 1982), pp. 222–3, 288–9, App. L., pp. 606–7; Lee, *The British Economy since 1700,* Table 1.4, p. 12.

12 See E.L. Jones, *The Development of English Agriculture, 1815–73* (1968), pp. 17–30. For an overview of the agricultural industry within the context of landed society see F.M.L. Thompson, *English Landed Society in the Nineteenth Century* (1963).

13 Wray Vamplew, 'The Protection of English Cereal Producers: the Corn Laws Reassessed', *Econ. Hist. Rev.,* 2nd ser. XXXIII (1980), esp. p. 391; Church, *The Great Victorian Boom,* pp. 60–1; E.L. Jones, *Agriculture and the Industrial Revolution* (1975), Ch. 9.

14 M. Tracy, *Agriculture and Western Europe* (1964), Table 10, p. 49.

15 T.W. Fletcher, 'The Great Depression of English Agriculture, 1873–96', *Econ. Hist. Rev.,* 2nd ser. XIII (1960–1), reprinted in P.J. Perry ed. *British Agriculture, 1875–1914* (1973). See Appendix, p. 54.
16 Tracy, *Agriculture and Western Europe,* Table 9, p. 48.
17 Fletcher, 'The Great Depression', passim.
18 Deane and Cole, *British Economic Growth, 1688–1959,* Table 76, p. 291; Matthews, Feinstein and Odling-Smee, *British Economic Growth,* Table 6.1, p. 164.
19 Roy A. Church, ed. *The Dynamics of Victorian Business* (1980), Ch. 1.
20 There is some evidence that the share of profits in GNP at current prices rose in the period 1850–70 and fell thereafter. See Matthews, Feinstein and Odling-Smee, *British Economic Growth,* Table 6.1, p. 164. The influence of foreign competition in squeezing profits is discussed in ibid. p. 196.
21 A.E. Musson, 'Industrial Motive Power in the United Kingdom, 1800–70', *Econ. Hist. Rev.,* 2nd ser. XXIX (1976), esp. p. 436.
22 Matthews, Feinstein and Odling-Smee, *British Economic Growth,* pp. 535–7.
23 Crouzet, *The Victorian Economy,* pp. 191, 197; D.A. Farnie, *The English Cotton Industry and the World Market, 1815–1896,* (Oxford, 1979), Table 9, p. 199, argues for sharp declines in productivity in the industry from the 1850s. Matthews, Feinstein and Odling-Smee, in *British Economic Growth,* also suggest a sharp fall in productivity growth in textiles as a whole, c.1860 (p. 450).
24 See, for example, the data on iron and steel production in Crouzet, *The Victorian Economy,* p. 246.
25 League of Nations, *Industrialization and World Trade* (New York, 1945), p. 13.
26 P.L. Payne, 'Iron and Steel Manufactures', in D.H. Aldcroft, ed. *The Development of British Industry and Foreign Competition, 1875–1914: Studies in Industrial Enterprise* (1968), p. 72.
27 Deane and Cole, *British Economic Growth, 1688–1959,* Table 31, p. 143, and Table 37, p. 166.
28 The latest statistical work indicates that 'during the second half of the 19th century, structural change in Britain involved principally a shift of resources from agriculture to services, rather than to manufacturing'. See N. Gemmell and P. Wardley, 'The Contribution of Services to British Economic Growth, 1856–1913', *Explorations in Economic History,* 27 (1990), p. 302. Crouzet, while recognising the importance of service growth for both employment and income after 1840, still tends to see this growth as being subservient to that of the industrial sector, which is assumed to be the dominant force in economic life. In this he reflects received opinion: *The Victorian Economy,* pp. 68–71, 188.
29 P.K. O'Brien, 'The Analysis and Measurement of the Service Sector in European Economic History', in R. Fremdling and P.K. O'Brien, eds. *Productivity in the Economies of Europe* (Stuttgart, 1983), p. 82. For further analysis of the differences in structure between Britain and other European countries see Gemmill and Wardley, 'The Contribution of Services', pp. 300–2.
30 C.H. Lee, 'Regional Growth and Structural Change in Victorian Britain', *Econ. Hist. Rev.,* 2nd ser. XXXIV (1981).
31 Ibid. pp. 442–3.
32 The calculations are based on material in C.H. Lee, *British Regional Employment Statistics, 1841–1971* (Cambridge, 1979).
33 Lee, 'Regional Growth and Structural Change in Victorian Britain', pp. 449–50; Pollard, *Britain's Prime and Britain's Decline,* pp. 51–2.
34 Lee, *The British Economy since 1700,* p. 135.
35 There is much evidence for this in Charles Wilson, 'Economy and Society in Late Victorian Britain', *Econ. Hist. Rev.,* 2nd ser. XXIII (1965).
36 A distinguished modern economist has recently highlighted these two sectors in an attempt to overcome the view of most of his colleagues that services are not technically progressive and are inevitably areas of low productivity. Jagdish Bhagwati, 'Splintering

and Disembodiment of Services and Developing Nations', in Bhagwati, *Essays in Development Economics,* I (Oxford, 1985), pp. 98–9. For a positive, if tentative, view of the importance of services to productivity growth after 1870 see Gemmell and Wardley, 'The Contribution of Services to British Economic Growth', pp. 307, 317.

37 This is one of the themes of Gareth Stedman Jones's now classic account, *Outcast London: A Study in the Relationship between Classes in Victorian Society* (Oxford, 1971), pp. 152–5.

38 H.J. Dyos, 'Greater and Greater London: Notes on Metropolis and Provinces in the Nineteenth and Twentieth Centuries', in J.S. Bromley and E.H. Kossman eds. *Britain and the Netherlands,* Vol. IV, *Dominion and Provinces* (The Hague, 1971), pp. 100–1. Also Crouzet, *The Victorian Economy,* pp. 95–8; Francis Sheppard, 'London and the Nation in the Nineteenth Century', *Trans. Royal Hist. Soc.,* 5th ser. 35 (1985), pp. 54–5; Pollard, *Britain's Prime and Britain's Decline,* p. 52.

39 Dyos, 'Greater and Greater London', pp. 91–2.

40 J.P. Cornford, 'The Parliamentary Foundations of the Hotel Cecil', in R. Robson, ed. *Ideas and Institutions of Victorian Britain* (1968); see also F.M.L. Thompson, 'Britain', in D. Spring ed. *European Landed Elites in the Nineteenth Century* (Baltimore, 1977). The changing fortunes of the landed classes have now received authoritative treatment in David Cannadine, *The Decline and Fall of the British Aristocracy* (1990).

41 The importance of the continued existence of a landed aristocracy and the culture derived from it has been a matter of lively debate in Britain during the last twenty years. Without attributing our own views to any single historian, we can say that we have found the following very stimulating: Perry Anderson, 'Origins of the Present Crisis', *New Left Review,* 33 (1964); E.P. Thompson, 'The Peculiarities of the English', *The Socialist Register,* 11 (1965) and reprinted in *The Poverty of Theory and Other Essays* (1978); J.R.B. Johnson, 'Peculiarities of the English Route: Barrington Moore, Perry Anderson and English Social Development', (University of Birmingham, Centre for Contemporary Cultural Studies, Occasional Paper, History Series, 26, 1975); Tom Nairn, *The Break-up of Britain,* (2nd edn, 1981), Ch. 1; Martin J. Weiner, *English Culture and the Decline of the Industrial Spirit, 1850–1980* (Cambridge, 1981); David Cannadine, *Lands and Landlords: The Aristocracy and the Towns* (Leicester, 1980); Arno Mayer, *The Persistence of the Old Regime: Europe to the Great War* (1981); and, most recently, Perry Anderson, 'The Figures of Descent', *New Left Review,* 161 (1987). For a useful discussion of the debate see also Paul Warwick, 'Did Britain Change? An Inquiry into the Causes of National Decline', *Jour. Contemp. Hist.,* 20 (1985).

42 R. Britton, 'Wealthy Scots, 1876–1913', *Bull. Inst. Hist. Research,* LVIII (1985). W.D. Rubinstein, *Men of Property: The Very Wealthy in Britain Since the Industrial Revolution* (1981), Table 3.3, pp. 62–3, and Table 3.4, pp. 64–5.

43 Rubinstein, *Men of Property,* Table 3.10, p. 88.

44 Ibid. pp. 62–5.

45 W.D. Rubinstein, 'Wealth, Elites and the Class Structure of Modern Britain', *Past and Present,* 76 (1977), p. 110.

46 On bank amalgamations see Joseph Sykes, *The Amalgamation Movement in English Banking, 1825–1924* (1926). The clearing banks, which earned high profits before the war, were mostly controlled by the elite of merchant banks in the City via directorships. On clearing-bank profits see Youssef Cassis, 'Profits and Profitability in English Banking, 1870–1914', *Revue internationale d'histoire de la banque,* 34–5 (1987).

47 Stanley Chapman, *The Rise of Merchant Banking* (1984), App. 4, p. 209. In accepting bills, merchant banks were guaranteeing them and thus making them more saleable. For further details on the international money market see Chapter 5.

48 Ibid. pp. 86–7.

49 Walter Bagehot, 'Lombard Street', in *Collected Works* (ed. Norman St J. Stevas, 1978), IX, pp. 171, 191.

50 Ibid. pp. 171–2. On banking profits and fortunes see also Youssef Cassis, *Les Banquiers de la City à l'époque eduardienne (1890–1914)*, (Geneva, 1984), Ch. V.

51 Lee, *The British Economy Since 1700,* pp. 130–2.
52 C.H. Lee, 'The Service Sector, Regional Specialization and Economic Growth', *Jour. Hist. Geog.,* 10 (1984), Table 7, p. 149.
53 H. Pelling, *Social Geography of British Elections,* 1885–1910 (1967), p. 83.
54 W.D. Rubinstein, 'The Size and Distribution of the English Middle Class in 1860', *Historical Research,* 144 (1988), esp. pp. 79–80. By 1911–12 London had 14 per cent of the population of Britain but contained 44 per cent of its taxable income. The corresponding figures for 1848–9 are 12 per cent and 29 per cent respectively. See W.D. Rubinstein, 'Education and the Social Origins of British Elites, 1800–1970', *Past and Present,* 112 (1987), pp. 199–200.
55 For the army and the Church see P. Razzel, 'Social Origins of Officers in the Indian and British Home Armies, 1758–1962', *British Journal of Sociology,* 14 (1963); C.B. Ottley, 'The Social Origins of British Officers', *Sociological Review,* new series XVIII (1970); D.N.J. Morgan, 'The Social and Educational Background of Anglican Bishops: Continuity and Change', *Brit. Jour. Soc.,* 20 (1969).
56 Rubinstein, 'Education and the Social Origins of British Elites', pp. 197–8.
57 J.M. Bourne, *Patronage and Society in Nineteenth-Century England* (1986), esp. Ch. II.
58 On the development of service professionalism in general see W.J. Reader, *Professional Men: The Rise of the Professional Class in Nineteenth Century England* (1966), esp. pp. 185ff; Harold Perkin, *The Rise of Professional Society: England Since 1880* (1989), Chs. 3 and 4; T.R. Gourvish, 'The Rise of the Professions', in T.R. Gourvish and Alan O'Day, eds. *Later Victorian Britain* (1988). On engineering as a profession see R.A. Buchanan, 'Gentlemen Engineers: the Making of a Profession', *Victorian Studies,* 26 (1982–3).
59 Perkin, *The Rise of Professional Society,* p. 123.
60 Arnold was speaking in evidence to the Taunton Commission on public schools in 1868: Perkin, *Rise of Professional Society,* pp. 83, 529. In this context see also H.B. Thomson, 'The Choice of a Profession', in B. Dennis and D. Skilton, eds. *Reform and Intellectual Debate in Victorian England* (1987), pp. 67, 70–1; and T.W. Heyck, *The Transformation in Intellectual Life in Victorian England* (1982), pp. 20–2.
61 Rupert Wilkinson, *The Prefects. British Leadership and the Public School Tradition: A Comparative Study* (1964). For the connection between professions and public schools see also Rupert Wilkinson and Thomas Bishop, *Winchester and the Public School Elite: A Statistical Analysis* (1967), and T.W. Bamford, *The Rise of the Public Schools* (1967). For Oxbridge in this context see especially, Sheldon Rothblatt, *The Revolution of the Dons: Cambridge and Society in Victorian England* (Cambridge, 1981), and for universities in a more general framework, Heyck, *The Transformation of Intellectual Life.* A pioneering attempt to see the professional classes as a new gentry can be found in G. Kitson Clark, *The Making of Victorian England* (1962), pp. 251–74.
62 See in particular here W.L. Burn, *The Age of Equipoise* (1964), pp. 253ff and esp. p. 264; and Geoffrey Best, *Mid-Victorian Britain, 1851–1875* (2nd edn 1973), pp. 168–78.
63 Perkin, *The Rise of Professional Society,* pp. 119–121.
64 Perkin (ibid., p. 119) appears to argue that the professional ideal was often mistakenly associated with pre-industrial ideas, but he does not emphasise sufficiently the extent to which the professional ethic in society owed its power to the fact that it was an updated version of traditional gentlemanly attributes. See also Gourvish, 'The Rise of the Professions', pp. 34–5.
65 They were also better paid than most industrial or mining managers. See Reader, *Professional Men,* p. 202. As Reader points out, the pay of many professionals had less to do with their actual skills than with their status as gentlemen (p. 203).
66 L.H. Gann and P. Duignan, *The Rulers of British Africa, 1870–1914* (1978), p. 200.
67 As in George and Weedon Grossmith's *Diary of a Nobody,* first published in 1892.
68 See Geoffrey Crossick, ed. *The Lower Middle Class in Britain, 1870–1914* (1977), esp. Crossick's overview essay, pp. 39–46.
69 Rubinstein, 'Education and the Social Origin of British Elites', passim; Perkin, *The Rise of Professional Society,* pp. 87–92.

70 Henry Roseveare, *The Treasury: The Evolution of a British Institution (1969),* Ch. 6. For a view of the whole process see Peter Gowan, 'The Origins of the Administrative Elite', *New Left Review,* 162 (1987).
71 Zara S. Steiner, *The Foreign Office and Foreign Policy, 1898–1914* (Cambridge, 1969), p. 21. On the Foreign Office in general see Valerie Cromwell and Zara S. Steiner, 'The Foreign Office Before 1914', in Gillian Sutherland, ed. *Studies in the Growth of Nineteenth-Century Government* (1972); and R.T. Nightingale. 'The Personnel of the British Foreign Office and Diplomatic Service, 1851–1929', *American Political Science Review,* 24 (1930).
72 D.C.M. Platt, *The Cinderella Service* (1971), p. 22.
73 Richard M. Kesner, *Economic Control and Colonial Development: Crown Colony Financial Management in the Age of Joseph Chamberlain* (Oxford, 1981), pp. 53ff.
74 Gann and Duignan, *The Rulers of British Africa,* pp. 174–5. Also, C.A. Hughes and J.F. Nicholson, 'A Provenance of Pro-Consuls: British Colonial Governors, 1900–60', *Jour. Imp. and Comm. Hist.,* 4 (1975).
75 Gann and Duignan, *The Rulers of British Africa,* p. 181.
76 Ibid. pp. 199–200 and p. 53; Cyril Erlich, 'Building and Caretaking: Economic Policy in British Tropical Africa, 1890–1960', *Econ. Hist. Rev.,* 2nd ser. XXVI (1973), pp. 650–1; R.C. Bridges, 'Europeans and East Africans in the Age of Exploration', *Geographical Journal,* CXXXIX (1973), pp. 227–9.
77 Gann and Duignan, *The Rulers of British Africa,* p. 69.
78 Bagehot, 'Lombard St.', pp. 183–4. For an insight into the business of a private bank, Williams, Deacon & Co., which survived into the late nineteenth century, see E.J.T. Ancaster, '20 Birchin Lane, London. Mr. Newman's Entrance, 1883', *The Royal Bank of Scotland Review,* No. 155 (1987).
79 Y. Cassis, 'Management and Strategy in the English Joint-Stock Banks, 1890–1914', *Bus. Hist.,* XXVII (1985), pp. 302–4.
80 Ronald Palin, *Rothschild Relish,* (1970), pp. 40–2, 63.
81 The writer was Dawkins, fresh from the colonial service. See Kathleen Burk, *Morgan Grenfell: The Biography of a Merchant Bank, 1838–1988* (Oxford, 1989), p. 58.
82 The friendship between Natty Rothschild and Lord Randolph Churchill, although unusually intense, is illustrative of the intimacy of some of these relationships. R.F. Foster, *Lord Randolph Churchill: A Political Life* (Oxford, 1981), pp. 30, 194–5, 277, 290–1, 331, 375, 395. This is a good point at which to say how much our understanding of the interrelations between finance and politics has been illuminated by Fritz Stern, *Gold and Iron: Bismarck, Bleichröder and the Building of the German Empire* (New York, 1977).
83 The Rothschilds obviously fit this pattern to some degree, but a more spectacular example is provided by the Sassoon dynasty. See Stanley Jackson, *The Sassoons: Portrait of a Dynasty* (1989).
84 From *Cautionary Verses,* first published together in 1940 but written before World War I. Compare this with George Littlehales, a senior manager at Rothschilds in the 1920s, who lived too far away to be expected to come in regularly: 'When he did turn up it was usually about noon. He would spend the next hour prodding his men into greater diligence, at one o'clock he went to lunch and at 2.30 he caught his train home from Liverpool St.'. Palin, *Rothschild Relish,* p. 91. See also Chapman, *The Rise of Merchant Banking,* p. 169.
85 Youssef Cassis, *La City de Londres, 1870–1914* (Paris, 1987), pp. 154ff; also idem, *Les Banquiers de la City,* Ch. VII.
86 See the shrewd comments of Palin, *Rothschild Relish,* on Colonel Scott of the cashier's department at Rothschild's (p. 49). For a wider viewpoint see also Michael Lisle-Williams, 'Beyond the Market: the Survival of Family Capitalism in English Merchant Banks', *Brit. Jour. Soc.,* XXXV (1984).
87 For an example see Arncaster, '20 Birchin Lane, London', p. 41.
88 The quotation is from *The Book of Snobs,* first printed in Punch in the late 1840s. See *The Works of William Makepeace Thackeray,* Vol. XIV (1884), p. 41.

89 'It used to be the custom of some very old-fashioned clubs in this city, when a gentleman asked for change for a guinea, always to bring it to him in washed silver: that which had passed immediately out of the hands of the vulgar being considered "as too coarse to soil a gentleman's fingers". So, when the City Snob's money has been washed during a generation or so; has been washed into estates, and woods, and castles, and town-mansions, it is allowed to pass current as real aristocratic coin' (ibid. pp. 42–3).
90 Y. Cassis, 'Bankers and English Society in the Late Nineteenth Century', *Econ. Hist. Rev.*, 2nd ser. XXXVIII (1985); idem, *Les Banquiers de la City,* Ch. VI.
91 T.H.S. Escott, *England: Its People, Polity and Pursuits* (1885), pp. 314–5.
92 On the importance of Society see the excellent book by Leonore Davidoff, *The Best Circles: Society, Etiquette and the Season,* (1973), pp. 36–7 and Ch. V. Society's constituents in the 1880s were listed by a contemporary as royalty, the aristocracy, diplomats, the representatives of high finance, 'Turf and Stock Exchange', judges, lawyers and other eminent professional men including politicians and artists. The only figure with any direct contact with industry who received a mention was Joseph Chamberlain. See [T.H.S. Escott], *Society in London: By a Foreign Resident* (5th edn, 1885). Escott made particular note of the importance of financial wealth and the links between City figures such as the Rothschilds and senior politicians (pp. 86–7, 90).
93 W.J. Reader, *A House in the City: A Study of the City and the Stock Exchange based on Records of Foster and Braithwaite, 1825–1975* (1979) p. 82; Cassis, *La City de Londres,* pp. 167–70.
94 Cassis, 'Management and Strategy', pp. 309–10. It should be noted that, the Rothschilds apart, only three firms of Jewish origin, which had been thoroughly anglicised, had representatives on the Bank of England's directorate.
95 Chapman, *The Rise of Merchant Banking,* pp. 121–4 and Ch. 10; idem, 'Aristocracy and Meritocracy in Merchant Banking', *Brit. Jour. Soc.*, XXXVII (1986); Stephanie Diaper, 'Merchant Banking Growth in the Second Half of the Nineteenth Century', *Revue internationale d'histoire de la banque,* 34–5 (1987). On Morgan's see Burk, *Morgan Grenfell,* Ch. 2. Chapman makes much of the fact that Kleinworts had far more capital in the business by 1900 than, for example, Rothschilds. The acceptance business depended crucially upon capital, but issues depended on prestige. The fact that firms like Rothschilds and Morgans could do so much business on so little capital is a sign of their key role as gentlemanly capitalists. See Burk, *Morgan Grenfell,* pp. 67–8, 71–2.
96 R.C. Michie, 'Dunn, Fischer and Co. in the City of London', *Bus. Hist.*, XXX (1988).
97 M.J. Daunton, 'Inheritance and Succession in the City of London in the Nineteenth Century', *Bus. Hist.*, XXX (1988), and idem, 'Firm and Family in the City of London in the Nineteenth Century: the Case of F.G. Dalgety', *Historical Research,* 148 (1989).
98 Escott pointed to the link in Society between sport, gambling and the City: 'When it is not the Turf, it is the Stock Exchange, and perhaps this is one reason why the City plays so large a part in the arrangements of the West End'. See *Society in London,* pp. 117–18.
99 Prof. Perkin argues as if all forms of new wealth were equally conspicuous in society, though his own evidence shows how important finance was. He also does not distinguish between those, like Wernher, who were noticeable and those who were powerful. See *The Rise of Professional Society,* esp. pp. 63–76. For an interesting study of new wealth in Edwardian Britain see Jamie Camplin, *The Rise of the Plutocrats: Wealth and Power in Edwardian England* (1978).
100 Pat Thane, 'Financiers and the British State: the Case of Sir Ernest Cassell', *Bus. Hist.*, XXVII (1986). See also Jackson, *The Sassoons,* pp. 90–1.
101 Michie, 'Dunn, Fischer and Co.', esp. p. 196.
102 On this theme see, Dilwyn Porter, '"A Trusted Guide to the Investing Public": Harry Marks and the *Financial News,* 1884–1916', *Bus. Hist.*, XXVII (1986). City corruption, involving minor members of the aristocracy, was a major theme in Anthony Trollope's novel, *The Way We Live Now,* first published in 1875. Overseas finance was sometimes raised by eccentric aristocrats who could coax money from the gentlemanly classes to

invest in companies run by characters whom the well-bred would never acknowledge socially. Richard Davenport-Hines and Jean Jacques van-Helten, 'Edgar Vincent, Viscount D'Abernon, and the Eastern Investment Company in London, Constantinople and Johannesburg', *Bus. Hist.*, XXVII (1986).

103 For further interesting light on the social role of the City in the late nineteenth and early twentieth centuries, see Y. Cassis, 'Merchant Banks and City Aristocracy', *British Journal of Sociology,* XXXIX (1988), pp. 114–19; S.D. Chapman, 'Reply to Youssef Cassis', ibid. pp. 121–5; and S.D. Chapman, *Merchant Enterprise in Britain: From the Industrial Revolution to World War I* (Cambridge, 1992).

104 José Harris and Pat Thane, 'British and European Bankers, 1880–1914: an "Aristocratic Bourgeoisie"?', in Pat Thane, Geoffrey Crossick and Roderick Floud, eds. *The Power of the Past: Essays for Eric Hobsbawm* (1984), p. 228.

105 Donald Coleman and Christine McLeod, 'Attitudes to New Techniques: British Businessmen, 1800–1850', *Econ. Hist. Rev.,* 2nd ser. XXXIX (1986), p. 609.

106 David J. Jeremy, 'Anatomy of the British Business Élite, 1860–1980', *Bus. Hist.,* XXVI (1984), Table 9, p. 19.

107 For example, hosiers, who were in a small-scale, extremely competitive business, were less likely to have privileged backgrounds or to obtain the 'right' education. See Charlotte Erikson, *British Industrialists: Steel and Hosiery, 1850–1950* (Cambridge, 1959), Ch. IV.

108 Business success was often linked with nobility of character by Smiles. In her famous novel, *The Manchester Man* (1876), Mrs Linnaeus Banks went further than this. The hero, Jabez Clegg, although self-made, turns out to be a lost member of a business family with long-standing gentlemanly connections who remind him that there is more to life than work.

109 Erikson, *British Industrialists,* Ch. II.

110 D.C. Coleman, 'Gentlemen and Players', *Econ. Hist. Rev.,* 2nd ser. XXVI (1973).

111 Nineteenth-century land purchases by non-aristocratic buyers is a complex subject. W.D. Rubinstein, 'New Men of Wealth and the Purchase of Land in the Nineteenth Century', *Past and Present,* 92 (1981), argues that land was too expensive for most non-landed wealthy to buy in quantity. Lawrence Stone and Jeanne C. Fawtier Stone go further in *An Open Elite? England, 1540–1880* (abridged edn, Oxford, 1986), and claim that industrialists did not buy land because the status of industry was so low and they knew that they would not be accepted in 'society'. They also admit, however, that industrialists may not have wished to enter 'society' (pp. 195–6). The contrary case has recently been put by F.M.L. Thompson, 'Life after Death: How Successful Nineteenth-Century Businessmen Disposed of their Fortunes', *Econ. Hist. Rev.,* 2nd ser. XLIII, (1990). For further insights see idem, 'English Landed Society in the Nineteenth Century', in Thane, Crossick and Floud, *The Power of the Past,* pp. 209–11; David Spring and Eileen Spring, 'Social Mobility and the English Landed Elite', *Canadian Journal of History,* XXI, 3 (1986); and R.C. Michie, 'Income, Expenditure and Investment of a Victorian Millionaire: Lord Overstone, 1823–1883', *Bull. Inst. Hist. Research,* LVII (1985), pp. 67–8. Rubinstein's latest views on this question can be found in 'Gentlemen, Capitalism and British Industry, 1820–1914', *Past and Present,* 132 (1991). pp. 159–64. For a good example of localism see Anthony Howe, *The Cotton Masters, 1830–1860* (Oxford, 1984), pp. 252–4.

112 For some insight into provincial industrial culture and political life see A.J. Kidd and K.W. Roberts, eds. *City, Class and Culture: Studies of Cultural Production and Social Policy in Victorian Manchester* (Manchester, 1985); D. Smith, *Conflict and Compromise: Class Formation in English Society, 1830–1914* (1982); also John Garrard, *Leadership and Power in Victorian Industrial Towns, 1830–80* (Manchester, 1983). Some of the differences between provincial industrialism and gentlemanly culture were expressed through the creation of the 'redbrick' universities at the turn of the century. The best introduction to this development is M. Sanderson, 'The English Civic Universities and the "Industrial Spirit", 1870–1914', *Hist. Research,* 144 (1988).

113 There was a startlingly high proportion of men of Anglican religious faith among the very wealthy. See Rubinstein, *Men of Property,* Ch. V. For Tory paternalism among cotton manufacturers see Patrick Joyce, *Work, Society and Politics: The Culture of the Factory in Later Victorian England* (1980), Ch. 6, and n. 52 above.

114 Bourne, *Patronage and Society,* p. 46. See also H.J. Hanham, 'The Sale of Honours in Late Victorian England', *Victorian Studies,* III (1960).

115 Phillip Dodd, 'Englishness and the National Culture', in Robert Colls and Phillip Dodd, eds. *Englishness: Politics and Culture, 1880–1920* (1986).

116 Reader, *Professional Men,* p. 113. In many ways, Arnold's ideal type was the new professional class of the south-east of England. He was aware of the development of 'a large class of gentlemen in the professions, the services, literature, politics – and a good contingent is now added from business also. This large class, not of the nobility but with the accomplishments and taste of an upper class, is something peculiar to England'. Arnold was speaking at the time at the Royal Institution in London and felt that, 'of this class I may probably assume that my present audience is in large manner composed'. Super, *The Complete Prose Works of Matthew Arnold,* Vol. II, pp. 88–9. See also F.G. Walcott, *The Origins of Culture and Anarchy: Matthew Arnold and Popular Education in England* (1970), esp. p. 45.

117 John Vincent, *The Formation of the British Liberal Party, 1857–68* (1976), p. 3. When Lord Derby joined the Cabinet in 1882, he noted that nearly all his colleagues were 'large' or 'moderate-sized landowners' or 'connected with the Whig aristocracy' or with the 'landowning class'; he was satisfied that 'it would be difficult to find a Cabinet with less admixture of anything that in France would be called democracy'. Quoted in Marvin Swartz, *The Politics of British Foreign Policy in the Age of Disraeli and Gladstone* (1985), p. 145.

118 On the emergence of regional voting patterns and the growing Conservatism of the south-east see Pelling, *Social Geography,* Chs. 2 and 3; Hanham, *Elections and Party Management,* pp. 225–7; T.J. Nossiter, *Influence, Opinion, and Political Idioms in Reformed England: Case Studies from the North-East, 1832–74* (Brighton, 1975), pp. 185–92; J.P.D. Dunbabin, 'British Elections in the Nineteenth and Twentieth Centuries: a Regional Approach', *Eng. Hist. Rev.,* XCV (1980); Martin Pugh, *The Making of Modern British Politics, 1867–1939* (1982), Chs. 3 and Table 3.1, p. 43.

119 Lord Salisbury was impressed by the power of what he called 'Villa Toryism'. Peter Marsh, *The Discipline of Popular Government: Lord Salisbury's Domestic Statecraft, 1881–1902* (Brighton, 1978), p. 36.

120 This is clear from the work of Nossiter, Dunbabin and Pelling cited in n. 118, and from Pugh, *The Making of Modern Politics, 1867–1939,* p. 64. The two anomalies as far as the Liberals were concerned were the west Midlands after 1886 – largely explained in relation to Joseph Chamberlain – and Lancashire, where a working-class electorate showed a surprisingly strong tendency to vote Conservative until, as one might expect, the free trade issue pushed them towards Liberalism in 1906. Lancashire Toryism was greatly influenced by the reaction of Protestant locals to Irish Catholic immigrants. This was in part an economic issue since the Irish were seen to be a threat to wages and employment in the indigenous community. In addition, Joyce has recently emphasised the extent to which Toryism might reflect the politics of a particularly dominant cotton master who often had the same paternalist relationship towards his workforce as the landed aristocracy had, and who also received the same kind of loyal support. On Lancashire politics in general see Pelling, *Social Geography,* Ch. 12, and P.F. Clarke, *Lancashire and the New Liberalism,* (Cambridge, 1971). On the influence of employers on political choice in certain areas see Patrick Joyce, 'The Factory Politics of Lancashire in the Later Nineteenth Century', *Hist. Jour.,* XVIII (1975).

121 For the effects of Irish policy on English political economy see T.W. Heyck, 'Home Rule, Radicalism and the Liberal Party, 1886–95', *Jour. Brit. Stud.,* XXIII (1974); and Pugh, *The Making of Modern Politics,* pp. 33–9.

122 Cassis, *La City de Londres,* Table 18, p. 171, for the political affiliations of banker MPs after 1892; also G.R. Searle, 'The Edwardian Liberal Party and Business', *Eng. Hist. Rev.,* XCVIII (1983), pp. 44–6.

123 The substantial literature on the anti-privilege elements in liberalism and the character of its electorate and policies includes: Nossiter, *Influence, Opinion and Political Idioms in Reformed England,* esp. Ch. 10; J.R. Vincent, *Pollbooks: How Victorians Voted* (Cambridge, 1967), esp. pp. 15ff; J. Chamberlain, et al., *The Radical Programme* (ed. D. Hamer, Brighton, 1971), esp. the introduction; Michael Barker, *Gladstone and Radicalism: The Reconstruction of Liberal Policy in Britain, 1885–94* (Brighton, 1975); Harold Perkin, 'Land Reform and Class Conflict in Victorian Britain', in his *The Structured Crowd: Essays in English Social History* (Brighton, 1981), Ch. 7; Bentley B. Gilbert, 'David Lloyd George: Land, the Budget and Social Reform', *American Historical Review,* LXXXI (1976); idem, 'David Lloyd George: the Reform of British Landholding and the Budget of 1914', *Hist. Jour.,* XXI (1978); Avner Offer, *Property and Politics: 1870–1914, Landownership, Law, Ideology and Urban Development in England* (Cambridge, 1981), Chs. 20–3; Searle, 'The Edwardian Liberal Party and Business', pp. 47–8. On the economic theory behind die anti-land movement after 1870 see Avner Offer, 'Ricardo's Paradox and the Movement of Rent in England, c. 1870–1910', *Econ. Hist. Rev.,* 2nd ser. XXXIII (1980).

124 Perkin, *The Structured Crowd,* 117–18.

125 Pugh, *The Making of Modern Politics,* p. 32.

126 Searle, 'The Edwardian Liberal Party and Business', p. 46. Also Douglas Farnie, 'The Structure of the British Cotton Textile Industry, 1846–1914', in Akio Okochi and Shin-Ichi Yonekawa, eds. *The Textile Industry and Its Business Climate* (Tokyo, 1982), p. 71.

127 The loss of aristocratic power over local government in industrial areas was more marked than at the national level. On local government, see J.M. Lee, *Social Leaders and Public Persons: A Study of County Government since 1888* (Oxford, 1963), Pts. I and II. Aristocrats sometimes made spirited attempts to retain influence in urban areas where they were extensive property owners. See Cannadine, *Lands and Landlords,* passim.

128 By Weiner, in *English Culture and the Decline of the Industrial Spirit,* passim.

129 W.D. Rubinstein, 'Entrepreneurial Effort and Entrepreneurial Success: Peak Wealth-Holding in Three Societies, 1850–1930', *Bus. Hist.,* XXV (1983), p. 17. See also Sidney Pollard, *Britain's Prime and Britain's Decline: The British Economy, 1870–1914* (1989), pp. 227–35.

130 Rubinstein's methods of assessing wealth-holding and the conclusions he has drawn from his evidence have been sharply criticised recently by N.J. Morgan and M.S. Moss, 'Listing the Wealthy in Scotland', *Bull. Inst. Hist. Research,* LIX (1986), and by B. English, 'Probate Valuations and the Death Duty Registers', ibid. LVIII (1984). Their reservations are summarised in M.J. Daunton, '"Gentlemanly Capitalism" and British Industry 1820–1914', *Past and Present,* 122 (1989), pp. 128–9. Rubinstein's response, reasserting his position in debate with Daunton, is in *Past and Present,* 132 (1991). In reply, Daunton argues that, even if Rubinstein is correct about wealth distribution, he assumes too easily that wealth confers power. 'It does not necessarily follow that the financial and commercial middle classes dominated the formation of economic policy because they left large fortunes and paid more income tax' (ibid. p. 182). We entirely agree that wealth, power and status are related in complex ways: it is precisely for this reason that we have suggested the concept of gentlemanly capitalism to explain why some forms of capitalist wealth confer more prestige and authority on their owners than do others.

4

GENTLEMANLY CAPITALISM AND ECONOMIC POLICY

City, government and the 'national interest', 1850–1914

In previous chapters we have tried to show that, as the wealth, cultural standing and political authority of the aristocracy diminished, the reformed gentlemanly class that arose in the course of the nineteenth century achieved greater wealth and social status than the manufacturers who were associated with the major staple industries of Britain. It remains for us to demonstrate that this economic and social superiority was reflected in the making of economic policy after 1850, and in its chief modifications after 1880.

Gladstonian finance

The great cry for a generation after 1850 – as it had been for over a generation before – was for a small state and 'cheap government'.[1] The demand is inexplicable unless placed in the context of the unprecedented success and dynamism of the private economy in Britain over nearly 200 years. The tremendous buoyancy of 'natural society' and the widespread 'middling' wealth which it entailed discredited government as an economic agent. Government was unnecessary because it diverted income and savings from their 'natural' channels, and it was corrupt because it spent the taxpayer's money lavishly and on behalf of those with political influence. The desire for freedom of individual economic choice merged readily into a general hostility to aristocratic government, the national debt and 'Old Corruption', providing a common anti-aristocratic focus for both middle-class and working-class radicals which occasionally overrode their own mutual antagonisms and appeared as a common element in the works of thinkers as far apart as Tom Paine and J.S. Mill.[2] It was this broadly-based consensus which lay behind the drastic cuts in expenditure at the end of the Napoleonic Wars, established the view that government expenditure should be low and budgets balanced, and led to the return to the gold standard in 1819 on the assumption that the need to maintain convertibility into gold would force inflation out of the system and make financial discipline at the centre unavoidable. Government expenditure (including central funds allocated to local authorities) fell from an equivalent of 29 per cent of GNP in 1814 to 11 per cent in 1841 and 9 per cent in 1870.[3] The share of national debt repayment as a percentage of total expenditure also fell sharply over this period.[4]

Agreement among the non-aristocratic propertied classes and a large section of the working population on a limited role for the state helps to explain Gladstone's extraordinary success as Chancellor and Prime Minister in mid-century and beyond. In keeping such a tight hold on expenditure, and in completing the transition to free trade begun in the 1820s, Gladstone believed that he was releasing the economy from unnatural restraint and allowing, at one and the same time, the maximum degree of liberty for individuals and the most rapid and widespread economic growth, as well as eliminating the chief source of corruption in public life.[5] As a result, his popularity transcended class divisions, and he became the 'People's William' – the man who epitomised a liberal consensus centred on middle-class property, both industrial and non-industrial, but who also respected aristocratic and gentlemanly values and appealed to the artisan classes with their deep hostility to the state as an engine of repression and as a 'tax-eater'.[6] Gladstone, with his gentlemanly background, thus had an authority and a following denied to Cobden and other radical industrialists who, despite their association with free trade and cheap government, were isolated, on the one hand, by the depth of their antipathy to aristocracy and, on the other, by the class bitterness which separated them from the working masses.

Free trade and cheap government had different origins. But it is clear that, after 1840, both Peel and Gladstone accepted the view that free trade, like low taxation, was vital to stamp out corrupt vested interests, to remove politics from the contaminating influence of commerce and to confer a benefit – cheap food – which, being seen as universal, would damp down social conflict and lead to class reconciliation. Free trade also narrowed the sources of taxation and led to the reintroduction of income tax in 1842. From then on, the propertied interest had an incentive to try to curb public spending. Extravagance might mean either higher direct taxes or the reintroduction of protection. The first posed a threat to the cardinal virtue of thrift; the second could be construed as an attack on the 'poor man's breakfast table', and was popularly associated with a profligate attitude to government expenditure.[7] Once it was clear that the revocation of free trade was equivalent to political suicide, the aristocrats of the Conservative Party recognised that they had to curb expenditure or face tax increases which would hurt them badly. Although Disraeli and Salisbury were less stringent than Gladstone in the application of the principles of 'sound' finance, they felt obliged to follow the same general policy.[8]

Gladstonianism, the Bank of England and the gold standard

Gladstonianism gave a considerable boost to the power of two emerging gentlemanly institutions, the Treasury, the supervisor of government spending, and the

Bank of England which, as guardian of the gold standard, was the most important element in determining the money supply in Britain. Gladstone ruthlessly centralised the process of budgetary decision-making, and encouraged the newly meritocratic Treasury to exercise and extend its dominance over individual departments of state which often had an easy attitude to spending the nation's revenues.[9] The Bank's progress towards modernity was less simple.[10] It attracted a great deal of hostility from industrialists and middling property-owners because of its historic role as the financier of Old Corruption, and its power and privileges were under constant attack after 1815. The return to gold in 1819 was undertaken partly to curb the influence of the government's banker by reducing expenditure; and, after a bitter struggle, the Bank lost its monopoly of joint-stock status in the legislation of 1825 and 1833. Governments thus showed some sympathy with the argument that the Old Lady's monopoly had been responsible on occasion for an oversupply of money and for inflation.

Yet the Bank survived. Governments could accept the demise of other chartered monopolies, such as the East India Company, because they had ceased to have an interest in influencing commerce and could happily leave it to the mercy of the market. In contrast, no government was prepared to relinquish ultimate control of the money supply, and not all the considerable force and propaganda of the 'free banking' school could make headway against this conviction. Given the Bank's size and importance in the money market, and their own intimate relations with it, governments had to decide whether to utilise the Bank as an instrument of public policy in a more formal manner than hitherto or whether to replace it with new institutions. But throughout the 1820s and 1830s the Bank remained in an awkward position as a private institution with important but ill-defined public responsibilities, while governments alternated between complaining about its discretionary power and exhorting it to use those powers to help the system out of crisis.

One solution, popular with elements in the industrial provinces who distrusted the Bank's freedom of action, was to create a new central bank with purely administrative control over a money supply mechanically related to gold holdings, leaving the Bank of England to operate purely as a private concern. Peel was sympathetic to the aims of these reformers but felt that he could achieve them by an easier route. In the Bank Charter Act of 1844, he adapted the structures of the Bank in order to eliminate its schizoid tendencies. Working on the bullionist assumption that gold and notes were the key factors in money supply, Peel set up a rigidly controlled Issue Department within the Bank while also ensuring that, in due time, the note-issuing powers of other banks in England would cease. On the other hand, the Banking Department was left to act freely in the market. Unfortunately, the bullionist definition of money was too limiting in leaving aside bank deposits and in ignoring the rapid development of the cheque system. In these circumstances, the commercial activities of the Banking Department had an important influence upon the money supply, interest rates and flows of gold. Having reluctantly given up its influence over the issue of currency, the Bank could still exercise a profound authority in the market by different means; the intricate and confused argument about where its private role ended and its public one began continued unabated.

The Bank remained for a time an object of suspicion outside its own circle of intimates in the City. Those hostile to it often perceived the Bank as being no more than 'a relic of feudalism',[11] and this hostility was shared by Gladstone, who was deeply suspicious of traditional 'money power'.[12] His creation of a Post Office Savings Bank in 1861 was expressly designed to give the Treasury access to funds independent of the Bank. At one point, he even considered amending the Bank Charter Act to allow the Treasury to create bonds in financial crises, thus loosening the Bank's grip on the money supply and on interest rates.[13]

The Act of 1844 largely absolved the Bank from the obligation to manage the nation's money and, after 1850, its interventions in the market were dictated largely by a concern for profit rather than by any sense of wider public duty.[14] As the biggest player in the London market, the Bank's chief general interest was the retention of the gold standard on which City cosmopolitanism and Britain's rising invisible income depended. Gold was the basis of the credit system, and London's ability to supply gold at all times at fixed rates of exchange was the foundation of confidence in City credit and vital to its business. In theory, the system worked automatically: changes in foreign trade and payments induced inflows and outflows of gold which led in turn to rises or falls in money supply and interest rates. In fact, the Bank never had enough gold to allow for automaticity, mainly because it was a competitive animal with no desire to hoard large stocks of non-earning metal. Also, leaving the market completely to its own devices might have led to devastating credit crises: a heavy drain of gold and a sharp contraction in money supply could have brought the whole system down or rendered it politically unacceptable.[15] The Bank had to intervene on occasion and it learned to do so pragmatically. Faced with a drain of gold, the Bank could raise its interest rate, Bank Rate, and use its power over the commercial banks' reserves to force a restriction of credit, thus deflating the economy, discouraging imports, correcting the balance of payments and stopping the drain. In these conditions the joint-stock banks would usually call in their own short-term loans to the discount houses, the chief actors in the commercial bill market, forcing a contraction of activity there and also ensuring that the discount houses would have to borrow from the Bank of England at Bank Rate, thus making the new, higher rates effective.

In the early years of the period the strategy did not work well. A dispute with one of the leading bill acceptors, Overend and Gurney, in 1858 caused the Bank to withdraw its facility of rediscounting for the market in a crisis, and this made it difficult to use Bank Rate as a disciplinary measure. The Bank was also extremely reluctant to accept the classic central banker's role as lender of last resort. The market was bailed out in the 1866 crisis because the Bank recognised that a complete collapse of confidence would have undermined London's position in the world. But there was little general confidence that the Bank would act in this way again, and the joint-stock banks were left to assume that the Bank might not accept the ultimate responsibility. This concern forced them to remain highly liquid, to eschew long-term lending to industry and to keep a large percentage of their assets on call in the London market, thus adding to the internationalist bias of the monetary system.

Uncertainty about Bank policy also played its part in galvanising amalgamations among the joint-stock banks, for banks with nationwide networks of branches were less liable to large fluctuations in business and to crises of confidence. Indeed, by the 1890s the biggest joint-stock banks were much larger than the Bank of England. The latter still competed strenuously for business, and thus kept its gold stocks low. The result was that, when drains occurred, the Bank had to take swift action which could disrupt credit and anger the clearers. After the shock of the Baring Crisis in 1890, the Bank made more strenuous efforts at control by competing less and restoring its discounting function in the bill market. Besides exhorting the joint-stock banks to keep adequate reserves, the Bank also evolved new management techniques designed to protect its gold reserves without too great a restriction upon domestic credit. A number of strategies were tried over the years: among the most prominent were the 'gold devices' whereby the Bank raised its gold price in order to attract the metal to London and offset drains, both internal and external. This was superseded, around the turn of the century, by a much more sophisticated use of the Bank Rate, not so much to discipline domestic credit as to attract holders of surplus funds in Europe into sterling in time of need.[16] London's power to attract funds in this way reflected the unique nature of the bill market there and the ability, aided by the growth of foreign banks in London, to draw easily upon the short-term capital of the continent. De Cecco has claimed that the system was moving towards breakdown after 1900 because Britain's ability to command gold was threatened as other nations absorbed it in vast quantities and refused to allow it to circulate freely.[17] But this does not really come to terms with the evidence that the monetary authorities did discover increasingly sophisticated ways of defending the reserves and attracting gold without drastic effects on domestic credit.[18]

Dissent over the priority given to external criteria (that is, the maintenance of London's international financial position) in deciding economic policy never disappeared entirely. The joint-stock banks' resentment at London's control of monetary policy and the Bank's monopoly of the gold reserve was one aspect of the implicit difficulty involved in reconciling the needs of the domestic economy with those of sterling viewed as an international asset and as a medium of exchange. The conflict was made worse by the social distance which, before 1914, separated the largely provincial joint-stock bankers from the public-school gentlemen who ran the merchant banks and accepting houses and provided the bulk of the Bank's directors. The chief antagonist of the Bank of England was the Midland Bank, which would have liked to redistribute financial power by holding its own gold reserve; the Midland was the only one of the great joint-stock banks which could fairly claim to have close links with industry. Anything like a showdown was deferred until the outbreak of war in 1914, when a very sharp increase in Bank Rate led the joint-stock banks to question the whole basis of financial authority.[19] The Bank's instinctive defence of the international role of sterling in the war crisis of 1914 foreshadowed its stance in the 1920s, when convertibility became an issue for the first time in a century.[20]

The City of London and the national interest

The success of Gladstonianism rested upon policies that took management of the economy out of the hands of party politicians and transferred it to the Treasury and the Bank of England, which could be said to be beyond the reach of everyday political conflict. This new alignment, together with the esoteric nature of financial management, gave these gentlemanly institutions a certain political invisibility. There were, of course, disputes about policy and who should control it, as we have seen, but most of these took place behind closed doors in the small space between Whitehall and Threadneedle Street.[21]

Government and industry were not totally separated, as the Factory Acts and a host of other legislative enactments show. Interference increased as the century progressed, and sometimes to good effect, though there is little sign that gentlemen in Whitehall had any real understanding of what industry was about.[22] Everyday contacts with the private market were made through the City of London, whose major institutions became increasingly entwined in gentlemanly culture after 1850. The main intermediary between the politically powerful and finance came via the Bank of England, whose directorate, as we have seen, was dominated by the leading City merchant banks and merchant houses. And it was the City, as the financial fulcrum of the service sector, which benefited most obviously from Gladstonian policies. Although the end of Old Corruption lost the City a great deal of business, it also forced its members further into the international financial arena, where they scored their greatest success. Although paradoxical, this transformation was not altogether unintended by policy-makers: in the 1820s Huskisson had expected invisible trade to be the chief beneficiary of tariff revision and, by the 1850s, it seems to have been taken for granted that free trade was important not just for the sake of manufacturing but because Britain was 'the great Emporium of the commerce of the World'.[23]

Nonetheless, the City's success owed far more to the gold standard and to stern control of public expenditure than it did to free trade. As Goschen, Chancellor of the Exchequer and a leading figure in the City, put it in 1891, London's position as an international service centre rested on the fact that 'it is known that any obligations held payable in England mean absolutely and safely so much gold'. This confidence gave the City 'the command of capital from abroad' and made it possible 'to tap the continent for cheap money'.[24] Without convertibility at a fixed rate, the use of sterling in world trade would have been much reduced by uncertainty. With it, traders and investors had an incentive not only to use sterling but also to hold sterling assets, which had the advantage of yielding a rate of return related to Bank Rate, while gold did not.[25] Next to convertibility, low direct taxation was of prime importance. After 1850, Britain was lightly taxed compared with her European neighbours,[26] and capital came to Britain for that reason as well as to find the security guaranteed by the navy and by the stability of her political and social structure.[27]

In its success, the City developed a strong sense of self-esteem and, not surprisingly, assumed that its own interests were those of the nation's. So fundamental was this belief that it was only rarely expressed as, for example, during the budgetary crisis of 1909, when the head of Barings, Lord Revelstoke, lamented that the Liberal government was ignoring 'the extent to which the prosperity of the nation has been due to its great capital resources, its heritage of financial supremacy, its unshaken credit'.[28] Lord Rothschild was even blunter: without the City, he claimed, 'England could not exist'.[29] In less apocalyptic terms, financier-politicians like Goschen could take it for granted that the City's international success was bound to be for the good of the whole domestic economy.[30]

Industrialists often made similar claims for their own activities. But, despite Gladstone's early doubts, it was the City which became accepted in governing circles at its own valuation. The City possessed a coherence, a concentration and a geographic centrality which industry could not match. Moreover, as the century progressed, the leading bankers in the City became integrated into elite culture. All this, together with the City's freedom from the class hostility which so reduced the ability of industrialists to appear as credible political leaders and made City advice seem comparatively disinterested, explains why governments in need of counsel turned instinctively to the City rather than to the industrial provinces.[31]

The bimetallic controversy of the 1880s and 1890s provides an excellent insight into the nature and extent of City influence, and is worth close examination in this context, even though it cannot be dramatised simply as a battle between 'producers' and 'rentiers'.[32] The demand for a bimetallic standard was provoked by the slide in silver prices as silver production increased after 1880 and as a growing number of countries abandoned silver and adopted the gold standard. One effect of the collapse of silver prices was to revalue sterling against silver-based currencies, making it harder to export to silver-standard countries and easier to buy imports from them.[33] The obvious remedy, according to the supporters of bimetallism, was to reach an international agreement which would fix the ratio of gold to silver prices, thus halting the steady devaluation of silver-based currencies.

Those who championed the retention of the existing gold standard stressed the fact that Britain's commerce had flourished under it. They also pointed out that sterling's revaluation against non-gold currencies increased Britain's invisible income (since payments for invisibles had to be made in sterling) and helped to raise real incomes and living standards by lowering import prices.[34] On the other side, alarm was widespread among agriculturalists, who were already suffering acutely from foreign competition;[35] but it is more difficult to detect a 'producers' alliance' of manufacturers and trade unionists who were united in opposition to the gold standard. The main centre of provincial hostility to gold was Lancashire, where fears for the future of the cotton export trade with India became acute as the silver rupee began to fall steadily against sterling; many ferocious attacks upon the evils of London's money power and the rentier mentality emanated from there, especially during the depression of the early 1890s.[36] The intensity of support from other industrial areas is more problematic; even within Lancashire itself, the most voluble critics of orthodoxy were merchants and local bankers with interests in the cotton trade. Some manufacturers did join with trade unionists to condemn the gold standard, but just as many thought that Lancashire's problems were more likely to be solved by cutting wages than by raising prices.[37] There was also support for bimetallism in the City, especially among businesses dependent on trade with the Far East.[38] There was, therefore, no consensus for bimetallism among producers and not all men of commerce and finance were adamant for the gold standard. On the other hand, while industry proved to be a 'babel of voices'[39] on this issue as on many others, opinion in the City was heavily weighted in favour of orthodoxy, and this was probably the crucial reason why there was never any realistic chance that the bimetallists would win the day.

Bimetallism was important because it raised in acute form the question of 'the relative worth of productive and service interests to the economy'.[40] By adhering to the gold standard, governments were assenting, sometimes explicitly, to the City view that it was vital to Britain's command of international commerce and finance, which were the central activities of the economy and the key to the prosperity of the domestic economy as a whole. Despite the presence of a bimetallist element in the Liberal Party, mainly Lancastrian in origin, the party was convinced that the gold standard was the 'sheet anchor' of the British economy. The true political home of monetary radicalism was the Conservative Party, where there was considerable support for bimetallism among its leaders, including Salisbury and Balfour. Nonetheless, Conservative Chancellors proved as impeccably orthodox as their Liberal counterparts, and this reflected City pressures. Defence of orthodoxy among the most influential City figures was so strong that Hamilton, the Gladstonian Under-Secretary at the Treasury, thought that it would be impossible for any politician with bimetallic sympathies to be Chancellor. As he noted, a crucial qualification for the post, which involved working closely with the City, was a belief that the prosperity of the country depended above all on Britain's commercial supremacy and on the banking system which supported that commerce. A Chancellor who was a bimetallist would be seen as challenging this position and would be unable to gain the City's confidence.[41]

Gentlemanly elites in the City could also rely on the support of the official class: a large number of the permanent officials at the Treasury and at the Board of Trade gave their blessing to the powerful, City-based Gold Standard Defence Association because they saw clearly that bimetallism was an attack on the internationalism and openness which had been the hallmark of British economic policy for over half a century.[42] In fact, the influence of the City and its administrative allies was so pervasive that it is doubtful if bimetallism would have surfaced as an issue at national level had there not been elements within the Square Mile who were dissatisfied with gold.[43] Nonetheless, if the City's claim to represent the nation was somewhat exaggerated, the victory of the supporters of the gold standard cannot be represented as some kind of Hobsonian financial conspiracy. By the 1890s, when the bimetallic agitation was at its height, the City was the financial hub of the most dynamic part of the economy. Moreover, the cosmopolitan economic policy which the City favoured also suited the interests of large sections of Britain's export industries. Gentlemanly finance had political influence not only because it was embedded within elite decision-making structures but also because it represented enormous economic strength.

The Baring Crisis and its resolution

The bimetallic controversy illustrates, among other things, the informality of the relationship between City elites and government and the 'empathy' between them. But the swift and decisive way in which the Baring Crisis of 1890 was handled is, perhaps, the best illustration both of the City's capacity for coherent action and of the strength of its connection with political power.

In 1890, the firm of Baring Bros, one of the most prestigious in the City, found itself in great difficulties. The firm had underwritten several loans to Argentina during the previous few years and was unable to meet its obligations. Had Barings failed, the consequence for international credit would have been extensive and a world liquidity crisis, with ramifications impossible to foresee or to control, might have been inevitable. The crisis was aborted, however, by the swift action of the Bank of England, in conjunction with the leading acceptance houses in the City, and with government approval. Before Barings' plight became known outside the intimate circle within the City, a guarantee fund to cover their obligations, totalling £17m., was subscribed, and knowledge of this fund was sufficient to prevent either Barings' failure or a widespread collapse of credit when their difficulties became common knowledge.[44]

The Baring Crisis offers perhaps the most revealing picture of the close relationship between government, the Bank of England and the City elite in the pre-1914 period. The increasing intimacy of the connection becomes clear when the crisis of 1890 is compared with that of 1866. The crucial difference between the two crises appears to be that, while Overend and Gurney were insolvent, Barings were merely illiquid. Overend's insolvency was the result of dishonesty as well as stupidity, whereas Barings had simply been imprudent. Nonetheless, once the 'lock up' had occurred, and before Barings were forced to consult the Bank, *The Economist* did not think that they had acted very honourably, and Clapham seems to agree.[45]

Secondly, Overend and Gurney were one, albeit the biggest, of a number of joint-stock finance companies in trouble in 1866: in 1890, Barings were the only major house with a critical problem. In 1866, the Bank was faced with the very difficult task of how to handle a whole spate of dubious financiers and found it easier to do this by letting them default, meeting the subsequent panic by acting as 'lender of last resort' and obtaining government approval to suspend the 1844 Act, which restricted the Bank's ability to lend. In 1890, they could nip the crisis in the bud by helping out one company.[46]

On this evidence, it appears that the 1866 and the 1890 crises were not, as De Cecco implies, similar and that there was a prima facie case for the Bank to react to them in very different ways. Nonetheless, the Bank's instinctive response to both crises was not quite as impartial as its leading officials no doubt believed that it was.

The Bank not only was prepared for the 1866 crash (its reserves were built up in advance) but also was quietly pleased to see Overend fail. This reflected both a reasonable distaste for Overend's activities between 1860 and 1866 and the long-standing rivalry between the Bank and the Corner House: the bitterness left behind by the Bank's decision on rediscounting in 1858 and Overend's retaliatory action in 1860 was very marked.[47] *The Economist's* argument, that one reason why Overend's went down and Barings survived, was that the former did not approach the Bank for help in time, rather glosses over the problem of Overend's bad relations with the Bank and fails to emphasise the fact that Barings enjoyed much closer ties with authority.[48]

The closeness between Barings and the Bank raises the wider question of the intimate nature of crisis management in 1890. The almost automatic, informal intercourse between government, Treasury, Bank and merchant houses, and the great speed with which decisions were taken, does give the impression of a gentleman's club at work.[49] Goschen, the Chancellor of the Exchequer, was put in the picture immediately the Bank became aware of Barings' plight. He, and other members of the Cabinet, resisted the Bank's initial demand for direct financial assistance, partly because this would have involved parliament and precipitated the financial panic that the authorities and the City both wished to avoid.[50] Instead, Goschen urged the Bank to organise a guarantee fund with which to pay Barings' creditors and maintain faith in the City. If this was done then 'the government would help the Bank with the difference between what it could raise and what it needed to give Barings if this proved necessary'.[51] All the initial negotiations on the guarantees involved only that part of the City most closely associated with the Bank. The clearing banks were brought in very late and more or less confronted with a *fait accompli*; when, not surprisingly, there were murmurs of dissent they were suppressed by Lidderdale, the Governor of the Bank, with what in banking terms was brute force since he threatened to close the accounts at the Bank of England of those banks which felt that Barings should be left to their own devices. Powell was right to claim that the Baring Crisis was met by a new spirit of cooperation, but some of that cooperation – or rather the form which it took – was forced on those outside the Bank's immediate circle.[52]

It was said by Clapham that the problem in 1866 was a domestic one[53] while most authorities on the Baring Crisis assume that the matter was international in scope and, by implication, one requiring more drastic intervention. Kindleberger, at least, does not think that Clapham was right about 1866,[54] but it is probably true that the 1890 crisis, had it broken, would have had more serious repercussions on London's world role. It is possible, given Barings' enormous international reputation, that their fall could have triggered a global panic of unprecedented proportions, especially since the foreign banking presence in London was much greater in 1890 than in 1866.[55] The elite merchant banking fraternity was certainly aware that the 1890 crisis posed a direct threat to them; the hysteria which Goschen detected on his visit to the City at the beginning of crisis week[56] reflected the very real fear of people like Rothschild that their own businesses would be permanently damaged.[57]

What was at stake in 1890 was the position of London as an international financial centre: the Bank of England's swift, even ruthless, reaction reflected its instinctive recognition of this weighty fact. The Bank's moves, while clearly intended to prevent a general conflagration hurtful to the whole international business community, also seem to have maximised the advantages of the international houses closely associated with it. The feeling that the Bank's solution to the crisis had benefited some interests more than others was fairly widespread once the first shock was past. The joint-stock banks in particular felt that the Bank was using the crisis as a way of both increasing its power over them and of enhancing its position as a competitor. There was also a great deal of resentment about how well Barings had done out of the resolution of the crisis and a general feeling that no one could be expected to be bailed out in the same way again.[58] The solution to the Argentine debt crisis, reached in 1891, also appears to have been heavily influenced by the Rothschild Committee's, and the Bank's, determination to get the best deal for Barings and the guarantors rather than to find a solution which treated all Argentina's creditors equitably.[59] This involved the Bank in some rather 'indelicate' activity[60] clearly related to the illiquidity problems which beset it as a result of its quick action to save Barings.[61]

There was no Marxist inevitability about the solution found: with a weaker governor than Lidderdale in charge the crisis might have engulfed the City and changed its history. Again, we are not saying that the Bank ought necessarily to have allowed the crisis to develop and then met it by suspending the Bank Charter Act, as in 1866. Rather, our argument is that, given Lidderdale's outstanding abilities, the Bank was able to find a solution to the crisis which not only prevented an international panic, but also helped to reinforce existing structures of power and influence within the City. The Bank's actions were not conspiratorial: the governor genuinely believed that the best way of meeting the crisis was by building up the strength of the informal networks which made gentlemanly capitalist control of finance possible.

Industry and economic policy

Industrialists were not at the centre of economic policy-making before 1914, nor did they aspire to be, as Cobden and Bright were reluctantly forced to admit. Manufacturing interests made themselves felt at the centre in the form of 'pressure from without', either on specific issues which affected them directly or at times of acute economic crisis, when fears of social upheaval inspired a hunger for new markets and brought Chamber of Commerce delegates down to London to importune the gentlemenly statesmen of the day. The Victorian economy lurched erratically between periods of high boom and deep depression, and there were severe slumps in economic activity every seven to ten years on average, with troughs in 1858, 1868, 1879, 1886, 1893, 1903–4 and 1908–9.[62] The crises from the 1870s onwards were felt more severely than earlier ones because of falling prices and the dramatic increase in the pressure of foreign competition. At these times of slack demand and unused capacity, industrialists were especially fearful of the penetration of 'backward areas' by foreign countries which would then use protection to exclude British trade. There is strong evidence that pressure in times of economic crisis for an extension of British authority in Asia and Africa to safeguard markets for British traders influenced the shaping of policy in these areas, as we shall see.[63]

Nonetheless, this success needs to be put in perspective. First, the process required the provinces to seek the attention of governments and highlights the extent to which they were generally outside the normal circles of power. Second, the pressure from the provinces for action in Africa and Asia was frequently supplemented by pressure from the City, which often shared the enthusiasm for imperial expansion in these circumstances.[64] Third, and more important, in the traditional empire of the white colonies and India, in Latin America, Egypt and South Africa, where the potential economic benefits were considerably greater than those in the new territories of tropical Africa, industry was not the dominant economic force behind the British presence. In these regions, and in the ageing and fragile empires of Turkey and China, British financial and commercial penetration were the foundations of her expanding power, as we shall see.

City and government in the nineteenth century

In the eighteenth century the British state was, to adapt a Marxist phrase, little more than a managing agency for the aristocracy; the City of London and the Bank of England found their rationale as the commercial and financial agents of the landed order. In the early part of the nineteenth century this order was challenged by new social and economic pressures, forcing the aristocracy and its allies on to the defensive; and the battle was complicated by the fact that existing elites not only were under attack from outside but were themselves split between the supporters of tradition and others willing, and even eager, to allow the fresh winds of economic change to fill their sails. In the City, this tension between conservative elements surrounding the chartered companies and more liberal ones moving in the direction of free trade, occasionally led to paralysis. In these circumstances, as competing interests clashed and became deadlocked, there were many openings for forceful governments to act independently of the great interests and to determine policy. It was by no means inevitable that this would occur; but the elites who controlled the state apparatus did, on the whole, accept the need for change and acted with decision, coming to terms with modernity as the aristocratic order gave way slowly to a more widely based gentlemanly one, accommodating the new industrialism on the way. The leading financial institutions of the nation were similarly renewed rather than replaced. In 1815, the City was still a centre of traditional money, closely identified with chartered monopolies and the financing of an extravagant state, but it responded remarkably to new opportunities offered by the growth of the international economy.

If the state stood against a divided City to some degree after 1815 and forced it to accept the disciplines of the gold standard and parsimonious government and to adjust to competition, the adaptation had taken place completely by 1880. Legislation which had been seen initially as a burdensome interference in Liverpool and Peel's time was, by then, regarded as the foundation stone of the prosperity of both the City and the nation; no clear line could be drawn between gentlemanly governments and a united gentlemanly City over matters of fundamental importance in economic and financial policy, as the authority of the Bank of England over monetary policy, the failure of the bimetallist agitation and the inter-party consensus on budgetary matters all indicate.

Notes

1 Norman Gash, *Pillars of Government and Other Essays in State and Society, c.1770–c.1880* (1986), pp. 43–54.
2 Some aspects of this issue are dealt with in Peter J. Cain, 'Hobson, Wilshire and the Capitalist Theory of Capitalist Imperialism', *History of Political Economy,* 17 (1985), pp. 457–8.
3 A.T. Peacock and J. Wiseman with J. Veverka, *The Growth of Public Expenditure in the United Kingdom* (Princeton, 1961), Table 1, p. 37.
4 J. Veverka, 'The Growth of Government Expenditure in the United Kingdom since 1790', *Scottish Journal of Political Economy,* X (1963), Table 3, p. 119.
5 John Morley, *The Life of William Ewart Gladstone* (1908 edn) Vol. I, Bk. V, Ch. IV: 'The Spirit of Gladstonian Finance'.
6 Gladstone's attempt to maintain a balance between direct and indirect taxes was a crucial element here. See H.C.G. Matthew, *Gladstone, 1809–74* (Oxford, 1986), pp. 121–8. For a short but useful summary of the principles of Gladstonianism see S.G. Checkland, *The Gladstones: A Family Biography, 1764–1851* (Cambridge, 1971), pp. 398–9. For a more detailed account see H. Roseveare, *The Treasury: The Evolution of a British Institution* (1968), Ch. 7. There is also an interesting comment from a modern perspective by Barry Baysinger and Robert Tollison, 'Chaining Leviathan: the Case of Gladstonian Finance', *Hist. Pol. Econ.,* 12 (1980).
7 For the link between free trade and budgetary restraint see Roseveare, *The Treasury,* p. 187.
8 A.N. Porter, 'Lord Salisbury, Foreign Policy and Domestic Finance, 1860–1900', in Lord Blake and Hugh Cecil, eds. *Salisbury: The Man and his Policies* (1987), pp. 155–9; also P.R. Ghosh, 'Disraelian Conservatism: a Financial Approach', *Eng. Hist. Rev.,* XCIX (1984).
9 Roseveare, *The Treasury,* pp. 183–6; Matthew, *Gladstone,* pp. 110–11.
10 The main sources of information on the Bank are Boyd Hilton, *Corn, Cash and Commerce: The Economic Policies of the Tory Governments, 1815–1830* (Oxford, 1977); Frank W. Fetter, *The Development of British Monetary Orthodoxy, 1797–1875* (Cambridge, Mass. 1965); Lawrence H. White, *Free Banking in Britain: Theory, Experience and Debate, 1800–1845* (Cambridge, 1984); Michael Collins, *Money and Banking in the United Kingdom: A History* (1988).
11 On this see Fetter, *The Development of British Monetary Orthodoxy,* pp. 253–5.
12 Morley, *Life of Gladstone,* I, pp. 608–9.
13 Ibid. pp. 386, 512–13; Matthew, *Gladstone,* pp. 117–18; Richard Shannon, *Gladstone, Vol. I, 1809–65* (1982), pp. 287–9, 296, 319, 332, 417, 425, 431–2.
14 M. de Cecco, *Money and Empire: The International Gold Standard, 1890–1914* (Oxford, 1974), p. 83. See also Deiter Ziegler, *Central Bank, Peripheral Industry: The Bank of England in the Provinces, 1826–1914* (Leicester, 1990). The standard accounts of the Bank's development are Sir John Clapham's highly readable study, *The Bank of England: A History,* Vol. II (Cambridge, 1944), and R.S. Sayers, *The Bank of England, 1891–1944,* 2 vols (Cambridge, 1976).

15 This was *the* central concern of Walter Bagehot's famous *Lombard Street,* first published in 1873.

16 On the working of the gold standard system see R.S. Sayers, *Central Banking After Bagehot* (Oxford, 1957), pp. 8–19; idem, 'The Bank in the Gold Market, 1890–1914', in R.S. Sayers and T.S. Ashton, eds. *Papers in English Monetary History* (1953), pp. 132–50; W.M. Scammell, 'The Working of the Gold Standard', *Yorkshire Bulletin of Economic and Social Research,* XVII (1975); C.E.A. Goodhart, *The Business of Banking, 1890–1914* (1972), pp. 218–19; I.A. Bloomfield, *Short Term Capital Movements Under the Pre-1914 Gold Standard, 1900–1913* (Princeton Studies in International Finance, No. 24, 1969), pp. 42–57; B. Eichengreen, *The Gold Standard in Theory and History* (1985), pp. 3–19; and Ian M. Drummond, *The Gold Standard and the International Monetary System, 1900–1939* (1987), Ch. 1.

17 de Cecco, *Money and Empire,* Chs. 5 and 6.

18 In this context we should also emphasise that the development of a sophisticated credit mechanism in London meant not only an extension of the importance of sterling but also a considerable economy in gold use and in gold flows, except in times of crisis. This point has recently been emphasised by R.C. Michie, 'The Myth of the Gold Standard: an Historian's Approach', *Revue internationale d'histoire de la banque,* 32–3 (1986).

19 de Cecco, *Money and Empire,* pp. 100–2 and Ch. 7.

20 For interesting recent discussions of the role of the Bank see Sidney Pollard, *Britain's Prime and Britain's Decline: The British Economy, 1870–1914* (1989), pp. 245–50, and Zeigler, *Central Bank, Peripheral Industry,* pp. 129–37.

21 On this theme see Geoffrey Ingham, *Capitalism Divided? The City and Industry in British Social Development* (1984), esp. Chs. 5 and 6.

22 Pollard, *Britain's Prime and Britain's Decline,* pp. 250–1.

23 Sir John Graham quoted in Olive Anderson, *A Liberal State at War: English Politics and Economics During the Crimean War* (1967), p. 252.

24 G.J. Goschen, *Speech at Leeds on the Insufficiency of Our Cash Reserves and of Our Central Stock of Gold* (1891), quoted in S. Ambirajan, *Political Economy and Monetary Management: India, 1766–1914* (New Delhi, 1984), p. 120.

25 On the use of sterling as international money see H. van B. Cleveland, 'The International Monetary System in the Inter-War Period', in B.M. Rowland, ed. *Balance of Power or Hegemony: The Inter-War Monetary System* (New York, 1976), pp. 18–22.

26 Gash, *Pillars of Government,* p. 53.

27 In 1909 Lord Rosebery, a City man as well as an aristocrat, based his opposition to Lloyd George's supertax proposals on the proposition that it would scare foreign capital away from Britain. *Parliamentary Debates* (Lords), IV, 1909 cc. 947–9, 24 Nov. 1909.

28 Ibid. c. 799, 22 Nov. 1909. It was this, he said, which had made Britain 'the Bank and the workshop of the world', which itself is revealing about his order of priorities.

29 Ibid. c. 1153, 29 Nov. 1909.

30 Ibid. c. 1277, 29 Nov. 1909. The City's image of its own importance comes out strongly in a valuable recent thesis by S.R. Smith, 'British Nationalism, Imperialism and the City of London, 1880–1900' (unpublished Ph.D. thesis, London University, 1985).

31 S.G. Checkland, 'The Mind of the City, 1870–1914', *Oxford Economic Papers,* new ser., IX (1957).

32 The best introduction to die controversy is by E.H.H. Green, 'Rentiers versus Producers? The Political Economy of the Bimetallic Controversy', *Eng. Hist. Rev.,* CIII (1988). See also Checkland, 'The Mind of the City', pp. 262, 276; Y. Cassis, *La City de Londres, 1870–1914* (Paris, 1987), pp. 177–81; Ambirajan, *Political Economy and Monetary Management,* p. 121; Pollard, *Britain's Prime and Britain's Decline,* pp. 237–8.

33 Michael Collins, 'Sterling Exchange Rates, 1847–1880', *Jour. Eur. Econ. Hist.,* 15 (1986), pp. 521ff.

34 Green, 'Rentiers versus Producers?', p. 595.

35 Ibid. pp. 598–9.

36 Ibid. pp. 595–602.

37 A.C. Howe, 'Bimetallism, c.1880–1898: a Controversy Re-opened', *Eng. Hist. Rev.,* CV (1990), pp. 381–2; Edward R. Wilson, 'Lancashire Cotton and the Bimetallic Controversy of the 1890s', (M. Soc. Sci. Diss., University of Birmingham, 1990), pp. 162, 178–80, 191–4. Wilson does not believe that bimetallism was a popular cause in other industrial centres (pp. 180–1).

38 Daunton, 'Gentlemanly Capitalism and British Industry, 1820–1914', *Past and Present,* 122 (1989); Wilson, 'Lancashire Cotton', pp. 196–8.

39 E.E.H. Green, 'The Bimetallic Controversy: Empiricism Belimed or the Case for die Issues', *Eng. Hist. Rev.,* CV (1990), pp. 672–4.

40 Ibid. pp. 679–80.

41 Cassis, *La City de Londres,* p. 181. For the political alignment see Howe, 'Bimetallism', p. 389; Wilson, 'Lancashire Cotton', pp. 165–72.

42 Green, 'Rentiers versus Producers?', p. 611.

43 Howe, 'Bimetallism', p. 383–4.

44 The most authoritative account of the crisis can be found in L.S. Pressnell, 'Gold Reserves, Banking Reserves and the Baring Crisis of 1890', in C.R. Whittesley and J.S.G. Wilson, eds. *Essays in Money and Banking in Honour of R.S. Sayers* (Oxford, 1968), pp. 192–207. See also Roy A. Batchelor, 'The Avoidance of Catastrophe: Two Nineteenth-Century Banking Crises', in Forrest Capie and Geoffrey E. Wood, eds. *Financial Crises and the World Banking System* (1986); and Philip Zeigler, *The Sixth Great Power: Barings, 1762–1929* (1988), pp. 244–66. We would also like to thank Prof. Pressnell for causing us to rethink our position on this issue. What follows amplifies and modifies our previous highly compressed statement, which followed de Cecco's analysis rather too closely. See P.J. Cain and A.G. Hopkins, 'Gentlemanly Capitalism and British Expansion Overseas, II: New Imperialism, 1850–1945', p. 5; de Cecco, *Money and Empire,* pp. 80–2, 89–95. Batchelor, 'The Avoidance of Catastrophe', pp. 43, 71, lends credence to this view. The Argentine aspects of the crisis are dealt with in Chapter 9, pp. 292–7.

45 *The Economist* thought some of Barings' dealings in Argentina were 'of doubtful character' (22 Nov. 1890, p. 1465) and 'shady' (13 June 1891, p. 757). Clapham, *The Bank of England,* II, p. 325.

46 E.T. Powell, *The Evolution of the Money Market, 1385–1915: An Historical and Analytical Study of the Rise and Development of Finance as a Centralized, Co-ordinated Force* (1915: 1966), pp. 400–7, 523–31; W.T.C. King, *History of the London Discount Market* (1936), pp. 242–55, 307–9; J.H. Clapham, *The Bank of England,* II, pp. 260–9, 325–36; R.G. Hawtrey, *A Century of Bank Rate* (1938), pp. 109–110; *The Economist,* 22 Nov. 1890, p. 1465.

47 Clapham, *Bank of England,* II, pp. 242–6; King, *History of the London Discount Market,* pp. 193, 213–15.

48 *The Economist,* 22 Nov. 1890, p. 1466. It is worth noting that one of the emissaries sent by the Bank to assess whether or not Barings could be helped, agreed with 'some reluctance' that they could, since he knew that if he withheld his assent 'the Governor would be unable to take further action': Zeigler, *The Sixth Great Power,* p. 249. A well-informed, if anonymous, writer later claimed that 'The Great House was supported because it was a Great House'. See 'The Recent Criticism of the Bank of England', *Econ. Jour.,* IV (1894), p. 348.

49 The best indications of this are the accounts in Pressnell, 'Gold Reserves, Banking Reserves and the Baring Crisis of 1890', pp. 200–4; Hon. A.D. Elliot, *The Life of George Joachim Goschen, First Viscount Goschen,* II (1911), pp. 170–2 and pp. 183–4; Clapham, *Bank of England,* II, pp. 328–33; Roger Fulford, *Glyn's, 1753–1953: Six Generations in Lombard St.* (1953), pp. 207–17.

50 Elliot, *The Life of George Joachim Goschen,* II, p. 172; Zeigler, *The Sixth Great Power,* p. 249.

51 Pressnell, 'Gold Reserves, Banking Reserves and the Baring Crisis of 1890'., p. 201.

52 Powell, *The Evolution of the Money Market,* pp. 526–8; Joseph Wechsberg, *The Merchant Bankers* (1967), p. 141.

53 Clapham, *Bank of England,* II, p. 268.

54 Charles P. Kindleberger, *Keynesianism v. Monetarism and Other Essays* (1985), p. 199.

55 L.S. Pressnell, 'Comment', in Capie and Wood, *Financial Crises and the World Banking System,* p. 76.

56 Elliot, *Life of J.G. Goschen,* II, pp. 170–1.

57 Pressnell, 'Gold Reserves, Bank Reserves and the Baring Crisis of 1890', pp. 200, 202. When the Bank asked for a contribution to the guarantee fund, Rothschild complied reluctantly, perhaps because he felt that locking up more of his firm's capital might make his own position even more difficult. See Fulford, *Glyn's, 1753–1953,* p. 210. In persuading him to help, his City colleagues emphasised that by saving Barings he was saving himself: Zeigler, *The Sixth Great Power,* p. 253. Also Pressnell, 'Gold Reserves, Banking Reserves and the Baring Crisis of 1890', pp. 217–19; Clapham, *Bank of England,* II, p. 336; Fulford, *Glyn's, 1853–1953,* p. 211; Anon, 'The Recent Criticism of the Bank of England', p. 348; *The Economist,* 22 Nov. 1890, p. 1,466, 13 June 1891, p. 757, 12 Jan. 1895, p. 44.

58 It should be noted that, though Barings were saved, they did suffer considerable capital loss; although they eventually re-established themselves in the international loan business they never had quite the same predominance as before. On Latin American and other loans, they often had to share the spoils with Morgans. See Zeigler, *The Sixth Great Power,* pp. 260–3, 294–319; Kathleen Burk, *Morgan Grenfell: The Biography of a Merchant Bank, 1838–1988* (Oxford, 1989), pp. 54–7.

59 *The Economist,* 17 June 1893, pp. 721–2.

60 Ibid. 15 Sept. 1894, p. 1,126.

61 A. Crump, 'The Baring Financial Crisis', *Econ. Jour.,* I (1891), pp. 393–4.

62 R.S. Sayers, A *History of Economic Change in England, 1880–1939* (1969), Ch. 3.

63 W.G. Hynes, 'British Mercantile Attitudes Towards Imperial Expansion', *Hist. Jour.,* XIX (1976).

64 On this see Smith, 'British Nationalism, Imperialism and the City of London, 1880–1914', passim.

5

'THE GREAT EMPORIUM'

Foreign trade and invisible earnings, 1850–1914[1]

Commodity trade and foreign competition

The steady shift in the epicentre of British economic activity after 1850 from north to south, and from the traditional staples of the Industrial Revolution to services, is reflected in the changing composition of British foreign trade. The period witnessed a steady increase in the importance of 'invisible' income from trade in services and from the returns on overseas investments, while 'visible' exports suffered from increased competition and the slow pace of transformation of Britain's industrial base.

Between 1850 and the early 1870s exports grew with great speed both in volume (except for a brief pause during the cotton famine of 1861–5) and value. Growth in values was sharply halted in the late 1870s and remained low until the end of the century. The decline in the rate of growth of volumes was less precipitous but still fell to very low levels in the 1890s. After 1900, however, there was a return to growth rates of pre-1870 dimensions (Table 5.1). Exports grew at a faster rate than income between 1840 and 1870 and after 1900, and at a slower rate between 1870 and 1900: the ratio of exports to Gross National Product at current prices rose from 10 in 1841 to 20 in 1870, fell to 15 in 1901 and then rose again to 21 in 1912.[2] Changes in the pace of growth of exports closely followed those in world trade as a whole.[3]

In the third quarter of the century growth was rapid and also evenly spread. European demand for British products increased at a faster than average rate between 1846–50 and 1871–5. The most rapid growth area of all was north and north-eastern Europe (mainly Scandinavia and Denmark), which became increasingly dependent upon the British market for primary exports; but the growth of exports to industrial Europe was also high. This was a period of 'take off' in Western Europe, and Britain benefited by being able to supply the 'inputs for

TABLE 5.1 British domestic exports: growth between cyclical peaks, 1856–1913 (per cent per year)

	By value	*By volume*[a]
1856–60	4.1	3.6
1860–65	4.1	0.0
1865–73	5.3	5.6
1873–82	–0.7	3.0
1882–89	0.4	2.5
1889–99	0.7	1.0
1899–1907	6.1	4.0
1907–13	3.6	2.9
1856–73	4.7	2.7
1873–99	0.1	2.1
1899–1913	5.1	3.6

Sources: B.R. Mitchell and P. Deane, *Abstract of British Historical Statistics* (Cambridge, 1962); A.H. Imlah, *Economic Elements in the Pax Britannia* (New York, 1958).

Note:
[a] Volumes have been calculated from Imlah's export price index with 1880 as the base year.

TABLE 5.2 Exports of British produce by region, 1846–1913 (quinquennial averages, per cent)

	1846–50	*1871–75*	*1881–85*	*1896–1900*	*1909–13*
North and north-east Europe	3.9	5.9	4.7	7.8	6.8
Industrial Europe[a]	23.0	28.1	23.3	24.2	21.8
United States	17.9	13.2	11.6	7.4	6.5
Newly settled countries[b]	18.7	21.2	25.0	24.4	28.5
Underdeveloped countries	35.6	31.6	35.4	36.2	36.2

Sources: Mitchell and Deane, *Abstract; Statistical Abstract of the United Kingdom* (HMSO).

Notes:
[a] Industrial Europe consists of the 'North-west Europe' and 'Central and Southeast Europe' groups in Mitchell and Deane.
[b] Includes South Africa, Australia, Canada, New Zealand and Central and South America.

industrialization'[4] – semi-finished manufactures such as yarns and pig-iron rather than finished manufactures – at a time when, albeit often for political reasons, the trend in Europe was towards freer trade.[5] The United States was at a similar stage of development as the railway system pushed out from the eastern states, but export growth was muted by continued high protection and by the effects of the Civil War in the early 1860s (Table 5.2).[6] Despite the buoyancy of industrial markets, Britain's chief manufactured export, cotton piece-goods, was increasingly being driven out of Europe and America. Exports of piece goods to these areas fell from 29 per cent of the total in 1840 to only 12 per cent in 1870,[7] and, by the latter date, the cotton trade had become extremely dependent on markets in newly settled countries and

TABLE 5.3 Exports of British produce to the empire, 1846–1913 (quinquennial averages, per cent)

	1846–50	*1871–75*	*1881–85*	*1896–1900*	*1909–13*
British settlement colonies[a]	8.7	12.0	16.2	16.7	17.5
India and Burma	9.4	8.9	12.9	11.8	11.9
Rest of empire	9.2	5.9	5.9	5.6	5.6
British empire	27.3	26.8	35.0	34.1	35.0

Source: Mitchell and Deane, *Abstract; Statistical Abstract of the United Kingdom* (HMSO).

Note:
[a] Includes South Africa.

the underdeveloped world: two-thirds of Britain's exports to India and Turkey in 1871–5 were cotton manufactures.[8] Nonetheless, in this period, the overall growth of markets in underdeveloped countries (including those within the empire) was slower than the average. The development of the white colonies, on the other hand, was rapid (Tables 5.2 and 5.3).

Between 1875 and 1900 the growth of international trade was much slower and export values increased very sluggishly as prices fell. It is probable that the enormous boom of 1869–73 created considerable excess capacity in world industry and that this increased competition, lowered prices and inhibited investment.[9] The development of Western Europe and the United States had reached the point where Britain was subject to fierce competition in neutral markets and, by 1900, in some cases, such as iron and steel, even in her own market and in the empire. Her problems were aggravated by the growth of protectionism in other industrial countries and by the steady fall in primary produce prices as the first phase of world railway building in mid-century came to fruition. Since primary produce prices fell faster than the price of manufactured imports, the terms of trade moved in Britain's favour; but this advantage may have been more than offset by the reduction in the demand for British exports from the primary exporters whose incomes were squeezed as prices fell.

As industrialism spread, British exports to other developed countries fell in value quite sharply. Markets in north and north-east Europe kept up well, but they were mainly primary producers dependent on the British market and on British capital and financial institutions. Loss of position in the American market and in industrial Europe was marked. Compensation was found in increased exports to the newly settled parts of the white empire (except Canada, where growth was relatively slow and United States' competition keen) and India. Textiles were still the key to growth in Indian markets, though that growth itself was alarmingly slow in the world trade crises of the late 1870s and the early 1890s. The increased importance of India is the chief reason for the rising share of underdeveloped countries in Britain's export economy after 1870 (Table 5.1). Most of the increase in the share of India and the white settlement colonies took place in the late 1870s, when the share of the empire as a whole rose from just over one-quarter to more than one-third; but the empire's relative significance did not increase much further before World War I (Table 5.3).

By contrast, industrial Europe and the United States took 41 per cent of British exports in 1871–5 and only 32.2 per cent in 1896–1900. The fall in exports to Europe would undoubtedly have been greater had it not been for the demand for British coal. Coal provided only 2 per cent of exports in 1851, rising to 9 per cent by 1910;[10] coal exports to European industrial countries were crucial in offsetting the effects of competition and rising protectionism on British industrial exports. In the case of Germany, for example, exports of coal accounted for 42 per cent of all the increase in the value of exports from Britain between 1872 and 1913; the corresponding figures for France and Italy were 57 per cent and 80 per cent respectively.[11] But the dependence of the world's first industrial nation upon exports of coal by 1900 was a serious worry to contemporaries. Britain's share of world trade in manufactures declined markedly after 1870;[12] it is possible that, by strengthening the balance of payments and keeping up the price level, coal exports may have speeded the process.[13]

This relative decline was the result of a heavy commitment of resources to commodities whose growth rates were slowing down.[14] When, in 1850, over half of British exports were textiles this was a sign of modernity; the fact that textiles still represented a quarter of the total in 1910 was a cause for concern, as was Britain's underrepresentation in high growth areas such as chemicals and electrical goods in comparison with Germany and the United States.[15] Moreover, the basis of export strength was extremely narrow: 14 per cent of British exports in 1913 were textiles destined for India and the Dominions.[16] The empire also supplied a bolt-hole for a number of industrial exports which were finding competition in Europe and elsewhere too difficult to meet;[17] several other extra-European markets which were dependent upon Britain economically and fell within the orbit of her informal control served the same purpose. Britain's problems were eased by a rapid increase in the growth of exports after 1900; but this was the result of a boom in world trade, and Britain's share of world trade in manufactured goods continued to fall. The recovery of exports also took place within an economy suffering from low growth and stagnant productivity.

The relationship between the changing fortunes of British manufacturing output and the output of the economy as a whole is complex and will be given detailed treatment later. But it is clear that the fortunes of exports were of crucial significance to many of the traditional industrial areas and were intimately bound up with their decline. The fall in growth rates of cotton textile exports after 1860 was particularly sharp. In the main, this problem was the result of the fact that the industry was fully mechanised by this time, had few openings for further increases in productivity without radical technological change, and its comparative advantage was beginning to slip away as industrialisation spread. Even by 1870, the loss of markets in other industrial countries was severe and the dependence on exports to underdeveloped lands very marked. In the face of chronic overproduction after 1890 – a condition aggravated by the smallness of the average firm and the fiercely competitive nature of the industry – the importance of empire markets, especially India, and the eagerness for new ones, whether in Africa or China, can hardly be overemphasised.[18] Other traditional industries, like metals, also suffered seriously from the decline in export growth after 1870. In their case, the decline was the result of an emerging lack of competitiveness which kept costs at too high a level; their uncompetitiveness was a threat to their possession of both the domestic market and that in the empire, so much so that their leaders often became devotees of protection and imperial preference.

Import volumes rose a little faster than export volumes before 1875 but much faster from then until 1900, though the effect was mitigated by a favourable shift in the terms of trade. Imports of 'manufactures and miscellaneous goods' actually rose from just over 3 per cent of the total in 1860 to 25 per cent by 1900.[19] At constant prices, manufactured imports were equivalent to 10 per cent of manufactured exports in 1854 rising to one-third in 1913, and the growth of imports was so rapid that, between 1870 and 1913, *net* manufactured exports (exports minus imports) grew at only 0.4 per cent per annum.[20]

Net exports of manufactures to foreign countries rose in the 1860s but then fell with alarming rapidity until the turn of the century, apart from a brief recovery in the 1880s. In 1902, according to contemporary Board of Trade figures, they fell to their lowest point of slightly less than £20m.; and, at that time, Britain was actually in deficit to foreign countries in trade in the most highly finished goods. There was a recovery from 1903 onwards; but despite the hectic boom in world trade just before the war, net exports showed a tendency to stagnate after 1906 and, in 1913, the recovery had taken Britain back only to the position she held in 1870. By contrast, net exports to the empire increased steadily until the 1880s, marked time in the following decade, and then rose to previously unrecorded heights just before World War I (Table 5.4).

Nonetheless, a crude division between the fate of manufacturing trade with foreign countries and with the empire gives a misleading impression of the importance of the latter since most of Britain's imports of manufactured goods came from a handful of newly industrialising and developing countries. In 1913, when manufactured imports accounted for 25 per cent of all imports, two-thirds of the total (£112.3m.) came from four European countries with which Britain had heavy deficits on manufacturing trade (Table 5.5). Only £58m. came from other foreign countries, and the United States accounted for nearly one-half of that (£26.4m.). Britain also exported nearly as much to 'other foreign countries' as she did to the empire and her net export position with them was nearly as healthy as it was with her own possessions. Part of this surplus on manufactured trade was with other advanced countries, including the Netherlands and the United States – to which Britain sold £6.7m. more than she bought in 1913 – but most of it was gained in trade with the non-industrial periphery including Latin America and the Middle and Far East. This is another way of emphasising how much Britain had come to depend upon exports not just to the empire but to a wide range of what Arthur Lewis has called 'semi-industrial' countries in this period. By 1913, Germany sold

TABLE 5.4 Net exports of British manufactures, 1860–1913 (£m.)

	Foreign countries		*British empire*	
	(a)	*(b)*	*(a)*	*(b)*
1860	68.5		34.8	
1870	94.4		41.3	
1880	72.0		72.1	
1890	80.9		70.0	
1900	40.5		68.1	
1901	25.3		79.4	
1902	19.3		84.1	
1903	26.3		87.2	
1904	35.3		87.6	
1905	54.0		88.1	
1906	64.0	80.9	92.5	93.6
1907	98.0	84.9	106.1	108.7
1908	68.8	76.3	97.6	100.5
1909		71.1		102.6
1910		93.7		119.6
1911		88.1		127.9
1912		85.8		142.8
1913		88.6		157.6

Sources: Figures for (a) 1860–1908 are from Board of Trade, *Statistical Tables and Charts Relating to British and Foreign Trade and Industry* PP. 1909, Cd4954, and for (b) 1906–13 are from the *Statistical Abstract of the United Kingdom* (HMSO).

TABLE 5.5 British trade in manufactures, 1913 (£m.)

	Imports	*Exports and re-exports*	*Net exports*[a]
Germany	–56.1	+30.2	–25.9
Belgium	–17.4	+9.0	–8.4
France	–29.6	+19.2	–10.4
Switzerland	–9.2	+4.4	–4.8
Total[b]	–112.3	+62.8	–49.5
Other foreign countries	–58.0	+196.0	+138.0
All foreign countries[c]	–170.3	+258.8	+88.5
British empire	–23.4	+181.0	+157.6
Total[d]	–193.7	+439.8	+246.1

Source: Annual Statement of Trade and Navigation.

Notes:

[a] Difference between imports and exports/re-exports.

[b] Total for Germany, Belgium, France and Switzerland

[c] Total for Germany, Belgium, France, Switzerland and other foreign countries.

[d] Total for all foreign countries plus British empire.

TABLE 5.6 Visible trade balance: Britain, 1851–1913 (annual averages, £m.)

	Exports and re-exports	*Imports*	*Balance of trade*[a]	%[b]
1851–75	195	–246	–51	–26.2
1876–1900	291	–411	–120	–41.2
1901–13	467	–620	–153	–31.2

Source: Mitchell and Deane, *Abstract*.

Notes:
[a] Difference between exports/re-exports and imports.
[b] Balance of trade divided by sum of exports and re-exports.

more manufactured goods in Europe than did Britain – $925m. worth as opposed to $624m. – and matched Britain's performance in sales to the very poorest of non-industrial countries. However, to the semi-industrial group – which included Australia, New Zealand, South Africa, India, Brazil, Argentina, Chile, Colombia, Mexico and Turkey – Britain sold $810m. worth of manufactures, nearly four times as much as Germany, and equivalent to two-fifths of all her manufactured exports.[21] This reflected a cosmopolitanism which no other trading nations of the time could match or even seriously challenge;[22] it also formed an important element in an economic imperialism which ranged far beyond a concern with the Scramble for Africa and even with 'formal' empire as a whole.

The rise in manufactured imports was one of the principal influences on the size of the balance of trade deficit which the British ran during this period. The trade gap was partly filled by re-exports, which ran at between 12 per cent and 16 per cent of gross imports between 1850 and 1913, but the gap remained considerable, as Table 5.6 shows. It widened markedly during the period 1875–1900, as export growth slowed down and manufactured imports began to rise sharply, before narrowing again after 1900 when, for the first time since the boom of 1868–73, exports rose faster than imports. This gap was more than filled by 'invisible' exports, or exports of services, which were the international expression of the growing importance of the service sector whose structures we have already described.

Trade in services

There are few generalisations about Victorian and Edwardian Britain which are more firmly based than the assertion that, as Britain's manufacturing industries began to decline in relative importance and exports became less competitive, a more than adequate compensation was found through the growth in 'invisible' exports. As Arthur Lewis put the matter over 30 years ago: 'having ceased to be able to command an abnormal share of world trade in manufactures, Britain temporarily maintained her balance of payments by achieving an abnormal share of the world's shipping, insurance, and, other commercial services', which 'developed so

TABLE 5.7 Invisible trade and balance of payments: Britain, 1851–1913

	1851–75	*1876–1900*	*1901–13*
Balance of trade	−51	−120	−153
Business services[a]	+24	+35	+49
Shipping	+35	+58	+87
Balance of services[b]	+59	+93	+136
Overseas investment income	+26	+80	+151
Balance of payments[c]	+34	+53	+134

Source: Imlah, *Economic Elements in the Pax Britannica*. We have preferred Imlah's figures to those produced by C.H. Feinstein, *Statistical Tables of National Income, Expenditure and Output, 1855–1965* (Cambridge, 1972), because Feinstein's series begins only in 1870 and does not distinguish shipping from other services.

Notes:

[a] Business services include insurance and are net of some miscellaneous expenditure on services, including government spending abroad.

[b] Business services plus shipping.

[c] Balance of trade plus balance of services plus overseas investment income.

considerably that a large surplus was still left to finance a growing export of capital, the accumulated stores of which themselves provided Britain with an ever growing income from interest and dividends'.[23] The sources of, and broad movements in, Britain's invisible income are summarised in Table 5.7.

Shipping income rose steadily throughout the period 1850 to 1914 (Table 5.7). In the wake of the repeal of the Navigation Acts, competition from the American and Scandinavian merchant marines was acute – the British proportion of the tonnage of shipping cleared in cargo through British ports fell from 70 per cent in 1848 to 60 per cent in 1858 – although in absolute terms tonnage grew rapidly. The rise of the iron ship, in which the British had a competitive edge, and the adverse effects of the Civil War on American shipping gave Britain a relative advantage over other shipping nations, and her share of the tonnage using British ports rose to over 70 per cent again by the late 1890s. Britain's share began to decline towards World War I, as did her share in the world's steam tonnage. This had risen steadily from 26 per cent in 1860 to around 60 per cent in 1890 before falling off sharply to just over 40 per cent in 1914. The steeper fall in Britain's share of steam tonnage than in her share of tonnage in British ports probably indicates the unsurprising fact that Britain was losing out more in non-British trade than she was in her own. In the British trade, too, shipping felt the benefits of empire. Britain's share in shipping services with British possessions trading in British ports actually rose from 87 per cent in 1880–4 to 96 per cent in 1905–9.[24] The growth of shipping income was, of course, intimately related to the growth of other forms of invisible income, such as re-exports, which came mainly from the empire, where British shipping was dominant, and the shipping insurance business, of which London was the world centre.

Britain's income from shipping was large because her trade was large: the value of her net imports in 1860 was about 30 per cent of the rest of the world's exports and her share was still 17 per cent in 1913.[25] This high share was partly the result of free trade: the openness of the British market encouraged the growth of Britain as a re-export centre. But it is also evident from the size of the merchant marine that Britain's shipping was extensively used for non-British trade, and the same was true of 'foreign trade services' (Table 5.7).

As Britain was the world's outstanding international trader and the greatest free market in the world, the main British ports, and especially London, became great warehouses for the primary commodity trade of the world, the chief centres for the buying and selling of everything from precious stones to basic foodstuffs. This immense traffic was the source of the business in international short-term credits for which the City of London was justly famed.[26] After 1860, there was a decline in the use of the internal bill of exchange as a means of trade payment, and it was superseded by the use of the cheque system provided by the rapidly developing joint-stock banking network.[27] The discount houses in the London market, which had hitherto dealt mainly in domestic paper, shifted their attention to international credit, the 'bill on London'. Many of the leading merchant bankers, whose more prestigious activities included the issue of foreign loans, nonetheless made a good living in 'acceptance' business, that is in guaranteeing bills which could then be more easily placed in the discount market. The latter was dependent on using funds provided by the joint-stock banks, which regarded the money laid out in the London market as an ideal pool of near-liquid but profitable assets.[28] This market in short-term credit was the City of London's most unique feature. Its power is indicated by the extent to which foreign merchants, trading between their own countries and Britain, often found it profitable to operate from London, where they could more easily utilise the sterling credits that trade depended upon: the City was constantly absorbing foreign firms and foreign talent in this way. Many other foreign banking institutions, lacking the same local facilities where money was both easily available and also earning a return, found London an ideal place for their spare assets, which then formed part of the vast pool of liquidity keeping world trade on the move.

One very important source of overseas funds for the market was provided by the international and imperial banks, which had their headquarters in the City. These banks first became prominent in the white colonies in the 1830s and had become global in scope by the 1860s. The spread of joint-stock banks at home was paralleled by an enormous extension of their influence abroad. After various legislative hindrances were removed in the late 1850s and early 1860s, their orbit became world-wide. George Goschen, gentlemanly banker and Chancellor of the Exchequer during the Baring Crisis of 1891, could claim in the 1880s

> that English and French banking principles are on a crusading tour throughout the world. . . . Banks abound whose familiar names in every

> variety suggest the one pervading fact of the marriage of English capital with foreign demand. There is the Anglo-Austrian Bank, the Anglo-Italian Bank, the Anglo-Egyptian Bank. There is the English and Swedish Bank; there is the British and Californian Bank, there is the London and Hamburg Continental Exchange Bank; there is the London and Brazilian Bank, the London Buenos Ayres and River Plate Bank, and even a London and South American Bank.[29]

These banks, raising their capital in Britain and their deposits locally and using them as a basis to extend trade credit, were extremely important in spreading British trade and finance, and British influence, around the globe and in integrating large parts of the world into the international economy under Britain's leadership.[30] This trade credit was supplemented by the creation of 'finance' or 'accommodation' bills, based upon no particular trading transaction, but important in extending liquidity in many smaller countries, including some in Europe, like Denmark, which relied heavily on trade with Britain.

Foreign investments

Despite considerable growth, the returns on invisible services and shipping were insufficient, after the mid-1870s, to fill entirely the deficit on visible trade (Table 5.7), and Britain's ability to generate a balance of payments surplus came to depend increasingly upon the returns on investments abroad.

Britain was at the centre of the market for international finance after 1850. Numerous attempts have been made to estimate the accumulated total of British assets abroad since the pioneering work of Paish undertaken before World War I. Until recently, assessments by different methods had led to a broad agreement that British investments overseas were worth £195m.–230m. in the mid-1850s, rising to about £700m. in 1870, over £2,000m. by 1900 and to between £3,500m. and £4,000m. by 1913. The periods of most rapid growth were 1869–73, the late 1880s and 1909–13, with low points in the late 1870s and the 1890s. By 1913, these assets are said to have produced an income of roughly £200m., equivalent to about one-tenth of the national income.[31] These figures have been strongly challenged by D.C.M. Platt. His argument is that because Britain marketed foreign securities it should not be taken for granted that British investors either bought them or, if they did buy them, that they held on to them for long periods, and that all previous estimates are exaggerated because, like Paish's, they fail to recognise this. So, whereas Paish's estimate just before the war was for an accumulated holding of about £4,000m., Platt argues that this figure should be reduced to £3,100m. or just over three-quarters of the generally accepted total.[32]

In some ways, Platt's claims are a sophisticated modern version of criticisms of Paish's estimates voiced by contemporaries such as Keynes, and there is some substance in them.[33] The most recent survey of shareholdings of companies which raised money in London for overseas ventures shows that, on average, nearly 17 per cent of the shares of firms operating in foreign countries were held abroad. Moreover, although only about 3 per cent of the shares of firms located in the empire were so held, 8 per cent of shares in firms located in the empire were held in the empire itself.[34] The importance of foreign participation in loans raised in the City of London is also clear from the detailed records of particular issues. Of the £1.5m. raised in 1888 for the Argentine North-Eastern railway company, around two-fifths at least were raised in Paris and Berlin, though the syndicate underwriting the loan was organised by the London merchant bankers, Antony Gibbs and Son.[35] Similarly, when Barings organised a loan for the Argentine government in 1907, only 43 per cent of the money was raised in London: 31 per cent came from France and 26 per cent from Germany.[36] It is also true that foreign loans originally purchased by Britons were often repatriated: many of the stocks of American railroads bought in Britain in the 1880s found their way back to the United States over the next 30 years.[37]

On the other hand, Platt may have underestimated the extent to which British investors subscribed to loans raised in foreign centres such as Paris. But a more important difficulty with his position is that he assumes that the bulk of the capital raised on the London Stock Exchange before 1913 was portfolio investment – that is, loans issued by foreign or imperial firms or governments over which the British buyer of stock had no control. Platt estimates that a total of £2,600m. of portfolio investment was outstanding in 1913 compared with only £500m. worth of direct investments resulting from the creation of British-owned companies overseas. Of other recent global estimates, however, one suggests that direct investments were around 35 per cent and another that they were between 44 per cent and 60 per cent of the total of accumulated assets by 1913: a similarly high proportion of direct investment has been found in a detailed analysis of British investments in Argentina.[38] If these estimates are correct, then the likelihood that the bulk of the capital would be owned and retained by British nationals is strong. Beside this, Platt's revisions of the direct estimates of foreign investment made by Paish and others conflict with the indirect one made by Imlah. The latter was based upon the accumulated balance of payments surpluses calculated from his revision of British visible and invisible trade income. Platt is critical of Imlah's figures,[39] but offers no alternative to them.

Platt's achievement is to cast doubt on the legitimacy of all estimates, including his own. This is evident from Davis and Huttenback's recent work. They concentrate on the export of finance raised in London, and deliberately avoid the problem of how much of this finance represented long-term foreign investment. Yet they still manage to offer three different sets of estimates: a minimum one based on issues taken up entirely in the United Kingdom plus two others which allow for, *inter alia,* calls on capital made in foreign countries. As a result, Davis and Huttenback produce estimates ranging from a low of £3,165m. to a maximum of £4,779m.; all three estimates carry the proviso that 'the actual totals are almost certainly higher than the figures reported' in their main source, the financial press.[40] For all these reasons, it is difficult to accept that the original estimates should be replaced without further detailed research,[41] although Platt's emphasis on Britain as an international service centre as well as a lender is a salutary one.

Recent disputes over the size of Britain's foreign investments have not really disturbed conventional judgements on their geographical location or their composition by enterprise.[42] Before about 1870, loans to central governments were predominant and were mainly placed in Europe and the Middle East, though even at that stage railway investments in Europe, North America and India were significant. After 1870, as capitalism spread across the globe, communications improved steadily and a truly international economy came into being. Vast infrastructural investments were made in South America, Australasia and Asia as well as the United States. By 1913, 65 per cent of British investments were in newly settled countries, including the white settled colonies, but ranging far beyond them: over the period 1865–1914, roughly three-fifths of all the money raised in London went to foreign countries and two-fifths to the empire, with the centre of gravity in the latter area shifting steadily from India to the white colonies.[43] In addition, whereas half of the money raised in Britain for foreign or empire activities in 1865–72 went to governments, two-thirds of new funds in 1909–13 were raised for private concerns; of the reduced government portion, much more was issued by municipalities and provincial authorities in 1913 than in 1870, a sign in particular of the growing strength and complexity of capitalist organisation on the newly settled frontier. Railways remained the first preference of British investors placing money abroad. Only about 15 per cent of investments went directly into mining or manufacturing industry just before the war.[44]

The increased predominance of British loans abroad and of Britain as a market for international funds, was part of the rapid internationalisation of the economy after 1850. And, as the free-trade regime established itself, Britain grew in importance as banker, moneylender, insurer, shipper and wholesaler to the world at large. As a result, the demand for Britain's currency, sterling, was widespread. Sterling developed into the most important international currency, and circulated in the world, or at least outside Europe, almost as freely as it did at home. Confidence in sterling was maintained by its convertibility into gold or other currencies at a fixed ratio, which made it easy to hold and to use; sterling also benefited from the fact that the British navy secured the safety of British trade and protected the island from invasion, making Britain 'the strong box and the safe of Europe'.[45] In addition, foreigners could be induced to hold sterling because it earned interest if it was held in British financial institutions, whereas gold itself, the basis of the system, was sterile. Sterling's use was further enhanced by strong links between the markets for short-term credits and those for bonds. Funds in London for trading or similar purposes, if temporarily unemployed, could find a home in some safe, easily saleable stock marketed on the Stock Exchange,[46] which had a range and a liquidity unmatched in the world at that time. Hence, it is reasonable to argue that, before 1914, there was a sterling standard in operation rather than a gold standard;[47] and confidence in sterling clearly increased the desire to buy British goods and British services.

TABLE 5.8 Balance of payments on current account: ratios to GDP, 1856–1913 (per cent)

	1856–73	*1874–90*	*1899–1913*
Exports of goods	17.9	18.4	17.7
Imports of goods	–20.9	–23.9	–23.8
Balance of trade[a]	–3.0	–5.5	–6.1
Net services income	4.7	5.1	4.3
Balance of trade and services[b]	1.7	–0.4	–1.8
Net income for abroad	2.8	5.4	6.8
Balance of payments on current account[c]	4.5	5.0	5.0

Source: R.C.O. Matthews, C.H. Feinstein and J.C. Odling-Smee, *British Economic Growth, 1856–1973* (Oxford, 1983) p. 442

Notes:
[a] Difference between exports and imports.
[b] Balance of trade plus net services income.
[c] Balance of trade and services plus net income for abroad.

The openness of the economy encouraged the growth of the service economy, and the continuance of free trade was important to its success. Free trade meant that all those who had payments to make in Britain, whether in return for British exports or in payment for loans or services, could earn sterling by selling commodities in the British market. Britain's deficit on her visible trading account was a necessary function of the part which she played as an international mart and banker.[48] In turn, the service sector generated an increasingly large invisible income which filled the visible trade gap, left a surplus on the current account of the balance of payments and thus provided the means to swell British assets abroad and increase rentier incomes. This is clear from Table 5.6 and also from Table 5.8, which looks at foreign trade in the context of the growth of gross domestic product.

Table 5.8 demonstrates both the inability of services alone – at between 4 per cent and 5 per cent of GDP – to fill the widening trade gap, and the growing dependence on income from foreign assets, which had reached the equivalent of almost 7 per cent of GDP in the 20 years before the war. Using Feinstein's figures, we can look at this from a different angle. Between 1870 and 1913 income from trade in services usually bought about one-sixth of gross imports; at the same time, income from assets owned abroad rose from around 15 per cent of gross imports in 1871–5 to 27 per cent in 1909–11.[49] The income from services may be underestimated,[50] and that from foreign investment exaggerated, as we have seen; but the growing importance of invisible income, at a time when industrial exports were weakening and manufactured imports rising, cannot be in doubt.

Commerce, finance and free trade

Finally, it is worth emphasising that the interconnections between the 'invisible' elements in the account and between invisible and visible trade were highly complex and important. As we have already seen, the use of sterling encouraged the role of London as a banking centre and as a 'strongbox' for world saving, and this in turn enhanced London's ability to lend abroad. Overseas loans also encouraged the use of British banking and commercial facilities abroad[51] and British shipping and insurance. The re-export trade, which was equivalent to between 12 and 16 per cent of gross imports, depended on Britain's position as an international wholesale market and on her credit and financial network. It was London's pre-eminent role as an entrepôt for trade – a result of Britain's unique economic development and her policy of free trade – which made her the outstanding centre for trade credit and insurance. The vast commerce of London was the solid base on which the 'bill on London', and sterling's supremacy, rested. The outcome was a short-term credit market which was unique in the world and capable of attracting money from many other foreign banking centres on the look-out for safe but highly liquid openings for their spare funds.[52]

Britain's shipping was also tied in with her function as a financial centre: it was a testimony to the extent and ramification of the monetary network that between one-fifth and one-quarter of all British-owned ships rarely entered British ports.[53] Links with industry were close as well, since even Britain's greatest industrial success story of the post-1850 period, shipbuilding, was in many ways a function of the creation of her invisible empire of commerce and the demand for her mercantile marine that this helped to stimulate. The size of the market was a factor in British technological superiority: it allowed 'different yards to specialize in certain types of ships, to apply mass production methods to some processes and to use their capital assets to the maximum'.[54]

The relationship between the overall flows of British foreign investment and the movement of British commodity exports was more complex.[55] British loans were never tied: exports and loans came, as we shall see in Chapter 6, from two different income streams, two different regional economies. But British governments in the dependent empire often used loans to finance projects in which the purchase of British goods and services was taken for granted. And exports sometimes followed in the slipstream of foreign investment elsewhere because of close kinship relations – as in the white colonies – or because of Britain's overall dominance of the financial and trading network, as occurred in some parts of Latin America. But the relationship between capital export and commodity exports weakened over time as competition increased. This fact raises the wider question (which we shall address in Chapter 6) of whether Britain's extensive foreign investments were of overall benefit to the economy.

Notes

1 The phrase is Sir John Graham's, when First Lord of the Admiralty during the Crimean conflict in 1854. Quoted in O. Anderson, *A Liberal State at War: British Politics and Economics During the Crimean Conflict* (1967), p. 252.

2 François Crouzet, *The Victorian Economy* (1982), p. 112. For selected figures see Paul Bairoch, *Commerce extérieur et développement économique de l'Europe au XIXe siècle* (Paris, 1976), pp. 193, 209.

3 William Ashworth, *An Economic History of England, 1870–1939* (1960), p. 148.
4 Ralph Davis, *The Industrial Revolution and British Overseas Trade* (Leicester, 1979), p. 34. Albert H. Imlah, *Economic Elements in the Pax Britannica: Studies in British Foreign Trade in the Nineteenth Century* (New York, 1958), Table 9.
5 Charles P. Kindleberger, 'The Rise of Free Trade in Western Europe', *Jour. of Econ. Hist.*, XXXV (1975), pp. 36ff.
6 On British trade with the United States see Jim Potter, 'The Atlantic Economy, 1815–60', in L.S. Pressnell, ed. *Studies in the Industrial Revolution Presented to T.S. Ashton* (1960).
7 Thomas Ellison, *The Cotton Industry of Great Britain* (1886), p. 64.
8 These figures are derived from the *Annual Statement of Trade and Navigation.*
9 This was the view of the *Majority Report of the Royal Commission on Depression in Trade and Industry,* PP 1886, C 4893.
10 Phyllis Deane and W.A. Cole, *British Economic Growth, 1688–1959* (Cambridge, 1962), Table 9, p. 31.
11 These figures have been calculated from the statistics in the *Annual Statement of Trade and Navigation.*
12 W. Arthur Lewis, 'International Competition in Manufactures', *American Economic Review: Papers and Proceedings,* XLVII (1957), p. 579; S.B. Saul, 'The Export Economy, 1870–1914', *Yorkshire Bulletin of Economic and Social Research,* XVII (1965), p. 12; R.C.O. Matthews, C.H. Feinstein and J.C. Odling-Smee, *British Economic Growth, 1856–1973* (Oxford, 1982), Table 14.5, p. 435.
13 Matthews, Feinstein and Odling-Smee, *British Economic Growth,* p. 455.
14 H. Tysinski, 'World Trade in Manufactured Commodities, 1899–1950', *Manchester School,* XIX (1951).
15 See Deane and Cole, *British Economic Growth, 1688–1959,* Table 9, p. 31.
16 Werner Schlote, *British Overseas Trade From 1700 to the 1930s* (Oxford, 1952), pp. 154, 172–3.
17 Ibid. pp. 166–7.
18 R.E. Tyson, 'The Cotton Industry', in D.H. Aldcroft, ed. *British Industries and Foreign Competition*; L.G. Sandberg, *Lancashire in Decline: A Study in Entrepreneurship, Technology and International Trade* (Columbus, Ohio, 1974); D.A. Farnie, *The English Cotton Industry and the World Market, 1815–96,* (Oxford, 1979), pp. 171ff; J. Nicholson, 'Popular Imperialism and the Provincial Press: Manchester Evening Newspapers, 1895–1902', *Victorian Periodicals Review,* XII (1980), pp. 85, 89–90.
19 Deane and Cole, *British Economic Growth, 1688–1959,* p. 33.
20 W. Arthur Lewis, *Growth and Fluctuations, 1870–1913* (1978), pp. 118–19.
21 Ibid. p. 121.
22 Two-thirds of all British exports went to extra-European destinations in 1909–11. The corresponding figure for Germany was 26 per cent. See Paul Bairoch, 'Geographical Structure and Trade Balances of European Foreign Trade from 1800 to 1970', *Jour. Eur. Econ. Hist.*, III (1974), p. 566.
23 W. Arthur Lewis, *Economic Survey, 1919–39* (1949), p. 77.
24 These figures are taken from Board of Trade, *Memoranda on Foreign Trade,* Cd 4954 (1909).
25 Imlah, *Economic Elements in the Pax Britannica,* p. 191.
26 An overdue reminder of the *commercial* basis of the City of London's financial operations has recently been provided by Geoffrey Ingham, *Capitalism Divided? The City and Industry in British Social Development* (1984), p. 5.
27 S. Nishimura, *The Decline of Inland Bills of Exchange in the London Money Market, 1855–1913* (Cambridge, 1971).
28 M. de Cecco, *Money and Empire: The International Gold Standard, 1890–1914* (Oxford, 1974), Ch. 5.
29 G.J. Goschen, *Essays and Addresses* (1905), p. 23.
30 A.S.J. Baster, *The Imperial Banks* (1929) and idem, *The International Banks* (1934) are still extremely valuable studies. See also Youssef Cassis, *La City de Londres* (Paris, 1987), pp. 37–40, and idem, 'Competition Advantage in British Multinational Banking since 1890', in Geoffrey Jones, ed. *Banks as Multinationals* (1990). On investment banks, which were

often explicitly designed to transfer capital abroad, see P.L. Cottrell, 'London Financiers and Austria, 1863–75: the Anglo-Austrian Bank', *Bus. Hist.*, XI (1969), and idem, 'The Financial Sector and Economic Growth: England in the Nineteenth Century', *Revue internationale d'histoire de la banque,* 4 (1971).

31 On the rise of British foreign investments overseas see P.L. Cottrell, *British Overseas Investment in the Nineteenth Century* (1975), and M. Simon, 'The Pattern of New British Portfolio Foreign Investment, 1865–1914', in J.H. Adler, ed. *Capital Movements and Economic Development* (1967), reprinted in A.R. Hall, *The Export of Capital from Britain, 1870–1914* (1968); and, most recently, Lance E. Davis and Robert A. Huttenback, *Mammon and the Pursuit of Empire: The Political Economy of British Imperialism, 1860–1912* (Cambridge, 1987), Table 2.1, pp. 40–1. For George Paish's original estimates of overseas investment see: 'Great Britain's Capital Investments in Other Lands', *Journal of the Royal Statistical Society,* LXXII (1909); and 'Great Britain's Capital Investments in Individual Colonies and Foreign Countries', ibid. LXXV (1911).

32 D.C.M. Platt, *Britain's Investment Overseas on the Eve of the First World War* (1986), Table 2.3, p. 60. For similar argument see idem, 'British Portfolio Investment Overseas Before 1870: Some Doubts', *Econ. Hist. Rev.*, 2nd ser. XXXIII (1980).

33 J.M. Keynes, 'Great Britain's Foreign Investment (1910)', in *Collected Works of John Maynard Keynes,* XV (Cambridge, 1971); pp. 57–8; E. Crammond, 'International Finance in Times of War', *Quarterly Review,* 425 (1910), p. 317; also B.R. Tomlinson, 'The Contraction of England: National Decline and the Loss of Empire', *Jour. Imp. and Comm. Hist.*, XI (1982), pp. 63–4.

34 Davis and Huttenback, *Mammon and the Pursuit of Empire,* Table 7.5, p. 209.

35 Chapman, *The Rise of Merchant Banking,* p. 159.

36 Cassis, *La City de Londres,* p. 119.

37 Platt, *British Investments Overseas,* pp. 116–26. A considerable turnover in assets is indicated by research on British investments in overseas land and on the dealings of the British Assets Trust. See A.J. Christopher, 'Patterns of British Overseas Investment in Land, 1885–1913', *Institute of British Geographers Transactions,* 10 (1985); and R.C. Michie, 'Crisis and Opportunity: the Formation and Operation of the British Assets Trust, 1897–1914', *Bus. Hist.*, XXVI (1983).

38 Peter Svedberg, 'The Portfolio-Direct Composition of Private Foreign Investment in 1914 Revisited', *Econ. Jour.*, LXXXVII (1978); Mira Wilkins, 'The Free-Standing Company, 1870–1914: an Important Type of British Foreign Direct Investment', *Econ. Hist. Rev.*, 2nd ser. XLI (1988); Irving Stone, 'British Long Term Investment in Latin America, 1865–1913', *Bus. Hist. Rev.*, XLII (1968).

39 Platt, *British Overseas Investments,* pp. 17–21.

40 Davis and Huttenback, *Mammon and the Pursuit of Empire,* pp. 35–6 and Table 2.1, p. 40.

41 See, in addition, W.P. Kennedy's review of Platt in *Econ. Hist. Rev.*, 2nd ser. XL (1987); and, more recently, the criticisms of Platt's estimates in Charles Feinstein, 'Britain's Overseas Investments in 1913', *Econ. Hist. Rev.*, 2nd ser. XLIII (1990).

42 The best discussion of the geographical and institutional distribution of overseas investments remains Simon's 'The Pattern of New British Portfolio Foreign Investment', cited above and idem, 'The Enterprise and Industrial Composition of New British Portfolio Investment, 1865–1914', *Journal of Development Studies,* III (1967). His overall picture is not seriously disturbed by the new surveys by Davis and Huttenback, *Mammon and the Pursuit of Empire,* Ch. II, and Platt, *British Overseas Investments,* Chs. V and VI.

43 Davis and Huttenback, *Mammon and the Pursuit of Empire,* Table 2.1, pp. 40–1.

44 Simon, 'Enterprise and Industrial Composition', p. 289. Davis and Huttenback, *Mammon and the Pursuit of Empire,* pp. 53ff, indicate a considerable interest in agriculture, mainly plantations, in the empire. See also Platt, *British Overseas Investments,* Table 6.2, p. 114.

45 The words of Lord Rosebery in *Parliamentary Debates* (Lords), 1909, IV, 22 Nov. 1909, c.947–8.

46 R.C. Michie, 'Options, Concessions, Syndicates and the Provision of Venture Capital, 1880–1913', *Bus. Hist.*, XXIII (1981), pp. 158–9; also idem, 'Different in Name Only? The London Stock Exchange and Foreign Bourses, c.1850–1914', *Bus. Hist.*, XXX (1988).

47 W.M. Scammell, 'The Working of the Gold Standard', *Yorkshire Bulletin of Economic and Social Research,* XVII (1965).
48 S.B. Saul, *Studies in Overseas Trade, 1870–1914* (Liverpool, 1960), Chs. 3–4; R. Skidelsky, 'Retreat from Leadership: the Evolution of British Economic Foreign Policy', in B.M. Rowland, ed. *Balance of Power or Hegemony* (New York, 1976).
49 These calculations are derived from C.H. Feinstein, *Statistical Tables of National Income, Expenditure and Output of the U.K., 1855–1965* (Cambridge, 1973), Table 15.
50 Saul, 'The Export Economy', p. 10.
51 For imperial and international banks as conduits for overseas investment see Goschen, *Essays and Addresses,* pp. 22–3.
52 R.J. Truptil, *British Banks and the London Money Market* (1936), pp. 125–6.
53 Crouzet, *The Victorian Economy,* p. 313.
54 Ibid. pp. 253–4.
55 Bairoch, *Commerce extérieur et développement économique,* pp. 110–111, and 199–200, argues for a correlation between merchandise exports and capital export; but compare this claim with Sidney Pollard, 'Capital Exports – Harmful or Beneficial?', *Econ. Hist. Rev.,* 2nd ser. XXXVIII (1985), p. 508. See also idem, *Britain's Prime and Britain's Decline: The British Economy, 1870–1914* (1989), pp. 103–4.

6

TWO NATIONS? FOREIGN INVESTMENT AND THE DOMESTIC ECONOMY, 1850–1914

The sharp increase in the share of British savings going abroad after 1850 was a response both to new demands created by a growing world economy and to the pressures of increased supply. Edelstein's comprehensive survey of fluctuations in British investment overseas suggests, firstly, that the upward trend in foreign investment from 1850 to the 1870s was due, in the main, to the demands of countries such as the United States who were embarking on heavy infrastructural investments and lacked adequate savings of their own. Foreign investment in the early part of the period was, therefore, the result of the 'pull' of attractively high interest rates abroad. This influence was still felt after 1870: Australia, Argentina and the United States played the most prominent role in the foreign investment boom of the 1880s and Canada proved to be the most important market for British capital just before World War I. After 1870, though, the pull of foreign demand was supplemented increasingly by changes in the structure and the growth of the British economy which tended to 'push' savings out into foreign fields. The general tendency was for the weight of savings to push down the rate of interest in Britain and drive investors to look for more profitable opportunities abroad, as the economy adjusted after 1870 to a permanently lower rate of growth. This latter phenomenon flowed from the convergence of a number of major influences, including the secular decline in the birthrate and the consequent slower growth in the demand for major population-sensitive investments such as housing.[1] It was also very obviously connected with the fact that, as savings rose rapidly after 1870, industry did not change in ways that created a sizeable demand for new investment.

The City and foreign investment

The role of the City, in this context, was to act as a channel through which savings that would once have gone into the national debt or into railways in Britain now

TABLE 6.1 Relative holdings of overseas stocks (by occupation), 1865–1914 (UK = 100)

Occupation	*Foreign firms*	*Empire firms*
Merchants	173	76
Manufacturers	24	13
Professional and Management	66	64
Miscellaneous Business	100	41
All business	86	45
Financiers	228	97
Military	63	76
Miscellaneous Elites	200	260
Peers and Gentlemen	97	166
All Elites	115	153

Source: Lance E. Davis and Robert A. Huttenback, Mammon and the Pursuit of Empire: The Political Economy of British Imperialism, 1860–1912 (Cambridge, 1987), Table 7.6, p. 212.

found their way into similar investments offering a steady return abroad. The bulk of these savings came from the gentlemanly capitalist class and from the service sector of the south-east. This is borne out by the most recent evidence, Davis and Huttenback's analysis of 80,000 shareholders in 260 firms, operating both in Britain and abroad between 1883 and 1907, which at some time raised money in the City.[2] One particularly striking finding of their research is that investors with a background in business much preferred home to foreign investments and, perhaps even more surprising, foreign stocks to imperial ones (Table 6.1). The only exceptions to this generalisation were merchant investors, who showed a greater interest in foreign companies: for every £100 they invested in domestic securities, they put £173 into foreign concerns. Nonetheless, they, too, preferred domestic investments to those available in the empire. Manufacturers, for their part, were four times more likely to invest in a British-based company than one in a foreign land and seven times more interested in domestic than in imperial firms. Overall, the business class (which includes the professions – law, management, medicine, education, etc.) was responsible for one-half of the investment in British-based companies but rather less than one-third of those in foreign countries or the empire. Investors with a background in manufacturing accounted for less than 6 per cent of Britain's overseas loans.[3]

In contrast, Davis and Huttenback's 'elite' category – which corresponds roughly to our gentlemanly capitalist class, though it omits some of the professional groups we would include in this class – had a much greater predeliction for cosmopolitan investments. The financiers among them were indifferent between domestic and imperial outlets but had a massive preference for foreign investments over both.

'Peers and gents', on the other hand, were marginally more favourable to domestic than to foreign investment but preferred empire investments to both by a very wide margin. 'Miscellaneous elites', including ecclesiastics, government officials and some parliamentarians, had a decided preference for both foreign and empire stocks over domestic ones; among elites, only military men showed an inclination to favour domestic stocks (Table 6.1).

Although there was some overlap between the groups, the kinds of investments chosen by businessmen and elites were often sharply different. Business investors, especially manufacturers, insofar as they ventured abroad at all, were much more inclined than elites to favour firms working in agriculture, mining or industry, thus making investments abroad similar to those they chose at home. Elites preferred banks, public utilities, transport and other infrastructural investments as well as government paper – again searching outside Europe for the kinds of investments they tended to favour in Britain.[4] Among elite groups, 'peers and gents' were dominant, accounting for around one-fifth of all investors in British-based companies in Davis and Huttenback's sample and no fewer than one-quarter of the stockholders in both foreign and empire-based firms.[5] Investors in this sociological category were also among the largest stockholders. Of the 35 largest identified by Davis and Huttenback, 22 were peers or gentlemen, 10 were merchants and 3 were bankers.[6]

The importance of this group as overseas investors dovetails neatly with evidence from other sources concerning the business behaviour of the aristocracy in response to the decline in rents from arable agricultural land which set in after 1870. The 8th Duke of Devonshire shifted assets out of both agriculture and industry after 1890 and invested heavily in overseas railways and government stocks, which provided a considerable part of his income before 1914, and the major part of it by the 1920s.[7] Similarly, the Earl of Leicester, also one of the top 50 income-earners in Britain in the late nineteenth century, offset falling rent rolls by putting a large amount of his surplus income into railways both at home and in the empire after 1870.[8] There are other examples of adjustments to rural adversity which involved foreign investment,[9] and some of them were doubtless inspired by the new educational and social ties which brought landed gentlemen into close touch with gentlemanly City bankers. Earls Grey and Wantage benefited in this way from connections in the Square Mile;[10] and the funding of many of the investment trusts, formed at the end of the century and spearheaded by merchant banks and merchant houses, came from the traditionally wealthy.[11] The preference which peers and gentlemen showed for empire was probably a result of their social connections since many of them had relations or friends in government or colonial administration or had served abroad themselves. As Michie notes,

> the Empire found it easier and less expensive to borrow in Britain than foreign countries, as the British investor was more inclined to trust those who belonged to the wider British community, though the actual security offered might be identical.[12]

TABLE 6.2 Geographical distribution of stockholders, 1865–1914 (per cent of value held)

Residence of stockholders	*UK*	*Location of firms Foreign*	*Empire*
Foreign	0.4	16.7	2.6
Empire	0.1	0.1	8.5
London	20.8	50.9	58.5
Non-metropolitan England	59.1	25.8	21.2
Scotland, Wales and Ireland	19.5	6.2	9.1
Unknown	–	0.3	0.1
	100	100	100

Source: Davis and Huttenback, *Mammon and the Pursuit of Empire*, Table 7.5, p. 209.

That trust must have been much increased through the intimate contacts between members of the gentlemanly class, who were the 'natural leaders' in both Britain and large parts of the empire.

The non-industrial basis of most overseas investments is revealed with equal clarity through an examination of the geographical spread of stockholding (Table 6.2). Shares in domestic firms were widespread, but London dominated overseas investment. London investors took one-fifth of the shares of the domestic companies but over one-half of those operating overseas. For every £100 invested at home, provincial English and Celtic investors were prepared to place only £50 abroad, whereas Londoners put £156 and £161 in foreign or imperial companies respectively. Most of the direct investment overseas of the late Victorian age flowed from the metropolis. One emerging trend after 1870 among City firms which had long been engaged in the finance of trade in primary products from the furthest corners of the globe, was to react to the challenge of falling mercantile profits (caused by the telegraph and other technical innovations) by investing in the production of the commodities they serviced. This investment in mines, plantations and similar activities abroad involved the creation of firms which were organised and managed at the point of production, but their direction remained firmly in London hands.[13]

London's cosmopolitanism was such that even its resident manufacturing class was heavily biased in favour of overseas investment, as were its professional investors. It is also noticeable that regions close to London were more inclined to invest overseas than were the provinces, while the Home Counties themselves had a very positive leaning in favour of imperial investments.[14]

Overseas investment did not offer very high average returns either in foreign lands or the empire. Edelstein concluded that, during the whole period from 1870 to 1913, returns on foreign investment were higher than on domestic investment but by only a small margin: domestic securities in Britain brought in 4.6 per cent on average, the equivalent foreign stocks 5.72 per cent. Furthermore, domestic investment was a better financial bet in 1870–6, 1887–96 and 1910–13.[15] Davis and Huttenback, on the other hand, argue that foreign and empire stocks did better than domestic stocks before 1880, but from then until Edwardian times domestic returns were higher. For the whole period 1860–1914 they conclude that foreign investment was slightly less fruitful than domestic. Empire investments performed marginally better than both, but the big benefits from imperial investment were gained before 1880 and before the Scramble for Africa had really got under way.[16]

It could be inferred from this evidence that overseas investment, after 1880 at any rate, was simply irrational or misguided;[17] but in view of what has already been said about the lack of interest among industrialists and other provincial businessmen in new sources of finance, this would be too hasty a judgement. Elites were enmeshed in one 'social web of investment' centred upon London, provincial businessmen in others.[18] Elites were looking for investments which were compatible with a gentlemanly life-style and found them abroad when they ceased to be available in sufficient quantity at home; provincial businessmen, on the whole, found their own domestic network satisfactory before 1914 without needing to invade, on a large scale, those dominated by their social betters. As Davis and Huttenback express it, 'Britain was not one capital market but two'.[19]

Given this social segregation of investment opportunities, it is hardly surprising that non-industrial investors needed to look abroad in the late nineteenth century to find outlets for their surplus capital. As well as the traditional gentlemanly classes already discussed, institutional investors, such as banks and insurance companies, were faced by serious problems which more or less forced them to look abroad to maintain income, especially after 1890. Agricultural mortgages were a losing game after the decline of arable agriculture under the stress of foreign competition; 'Gladstonian' government finance limited severely the amount of new government paper on the market and helped to push down the rate of interest on government stock;[20] new issues by those traditional favourites, domestic railway companies, were in short supply after 1870, and the profitability of the companies was also under severe pressure from the 1890s.[21] The obvious response, in the absence of any dynamic industrial demand at home, was to find similar investments abroad.[22] The shift towards overseas government stocks and foreign and imperial railway company bonds and shares is very marked, for example, in the records of the leading insurance companies, whose overseas holdings often increased from under 10 per cent of total assets in 1870 to 40 per cent or more by 1913.[23] The joint-stock banks, too, became considerably more adventurous in their investment policies especially in the 1890s, when the rate of return on traditionally secure investment at home began to fall rapidly, and by 1913 'bonds of all kinds came to be grist to the banker's mills'.[24]

Had the share of savings going abroad not increased, returns on some domestic investments – government stock for instance – might have fallen to starvation levels. It is also possible that, given the barriers to industrial investment, a lack of foreign outlets might have produced severe crises of oversaving. Although

Edelstein's analysis of overseas investment flows is principally based on neo-classical assumptions about the downward tendency of the rate of interest on domestic investment in response to limited home opportunities and a rising supply of savings, he does pinpoint two short periods, in the late 1870s and in 1901–3, when 'desired' savings overshot 'desired' domestic investment opportunities considerably. In his judgement, these bouts of Hobsonian oversaving may have triggered off the great overseas investment booms of the 1880s and 1905–13.[25] Without foreign outlets, these savings might have lain in idle balances and caused severe depressions.

The extension of foreign investment often involved an increase in risk-taking as the emphasis shifted over time from government-backed loans to investment in private railway companies in an ever-widening range of countries.[26] But it would be wrong to overemphasise the risks associated with many of Britain's foreign investments after 1850, for these were often ideally suited to the needs of a growing body of landed and other rentier and gentlemanly investors looking for safe, fixed interest securities.[27] Their incomes might have fallen to alarmingly low levels without a marked movement into foreign stocks, especially after 1870.[28] As Vincent has pointed out, a great deal of wealth in mid-nineteenth-century England was concentrated 'not in the hands of entrepreneurs and captains of industry, but in the hands of widows, spinsters, rich farmers, clergymen, academics, squires and rentiers claiming gentility',[29] that is, the cast of characters who populate the pages of Mrs Gaskell's *Cranford* rather than the philistine industrialists of *Hard Times,* or those with whom Karl Marx was obsessed. These gentlemanly investors, like the landed aristocracy, inhabited a cultural universe very different from that of industrialists and had few openings for secure investment outside land, railways and the national debt before 1870.[30] The shift to safe foreign investments was one way of maintaining both the income and the status of the non-industrial wealthy and their supporters. Foreign investments were important, too, along with directorships of companies, mining royalties and ground rents, in extending the power and influence of the landed interest longer than would otherwise have been possible.[31] Foreign investments also gave new life to a commercial and financial middle class centred on the City, which transformed itself between 1850 and 1914 into the centre of an international service economy. And it was landed wealth, together with returns on overseas investments, which provided the foundation for the rapid growth of the service economy in London and the south-east and gave the region pre-eminence before 1914.[32]

Foreign investment and industry

Whether foreign investment was a positive force in British economic development or whether it was merely a symptom of economic decline has been a matter of controversy for some years. The simplest response to the problem is to assume that markets behaved optimally and that, since resources were fully employed in Britain, capital going abroad was merely seeking a higher return than that available locally.[33] But the assumption of a fully employed economy after 1850 is probably unrealistic; if it is removed, the problem becomes much more difficult to determine, even when it is allowed that capital export, besides bringing in a direct return of around 5 or 6 per cent annually, stimulated commodity exports, lowered the cost of imports and also increased national income by making the terms of trade more favourable.[34] Given potentially very high rates of return on domestic investment,[35] some modern historians have claimed that, if Britain had employed the capital and labour which left her shores after 1850 at home, the growth rate after 1870 could have been as high or higher than that achieved during the 'Mid-Victorian Boom'.[36] It is tempting to conclude that the reason for Britain's relatively poor performance after 1870 was not so much that her savings were lower than those of her rivals but that, whereas Germany and the United States invested about 12 per cent of their annual income domestically, Great Britain put only 7 per cent of hers back into the national economy and sent another 4 or 5 per cent abroad.[37]

One reason frequently alleged for this low rate of domestic investment was the failure of the financial establishment to adjust to new industrial circumstances. It is certainly true that the major banking and financial institutions did not develop as a part of an emerging finance capitalism in the style of the United States or Germany; there was no welding of the joint-stock banks, money markets and Stock Exchange with provincial manufacturing industry.[38] Banks with a primary interest in long-term industrial investment did appear in the 1860s and 1870s, but their lives were brief. As Kennedy puts it:

> a point had been reached where the entire system had either to be reorganized to withstand the greater risks of steadily enlarging industrial requirements or the system had to withdraw from long-term industrial involvement. The system withdrew.[39]

After 1870, the major joint-stock banks preferred the liquidity brought by increasing contact with the London money market to long-term involvement with industry. At the outbreak of war in 1914, they were not holders of industrial equity;[40] neither they nor the merchant banks of the City of London had concerned themselves much with the issue of securities for manufacturing companies. As for their impact on the Stock Exchange, only 600 of the 5,000 stocks quoted in 1910 were of industrial and commercial origin and a good many of those were overseas-based concerns.[41] The share of British-based companies in the money raised in London was, indeed, falling before 1914. Davis and Huttenback's survey found that one-third of domestic and foreign finance went to British-based companies or home governments between 1865 and 1914, but the proportion was 47 per cent in 1865–9 and it fell to just over one-fifth in 1909–13.[42] Of the money raised for British-based projects, only about 18 per cent went into manufacturing on average during the years 1865 to 1914, or about £29m. per annum. This represented roughly 6 per cent of all the finance raised in London in these years. In sharp contrast, something like one-quarter went into railway companies operating in the empire or foreign countries.[43] It is not surprising that this disparity has been seen as a failure on the City's part. Even the leading historian of Britain's merchant banks believes that they, like other financial intermediaries, were 'incredibly slow' to react to opportunities offered by industry before 1914.[44]

But were these opportunities actually available? Is it correct to speak, in Kennedy's words, of 'steadily enlarging industrial requirements' and to argue that the bias of the capital market towards overseas investments meant that potential investors had only scanty knowledge of 'new industries' and were unable to assess them adequately?[45] The financial needs of provincial industry continued to be met, as in the early and mid-nineteenth century, not by London but by a complex of methods including provincial stock exchanges and a host of private, local sources so widespread and so informal that contemporaries found it hard even to guess at the level of investment in domestic industry before 1914.[46] No great changes, either geographical or technical and organisational, occurred among the traditional staple industries after 1870 sufficient to disturb these financial relationships seriously or to render them obsolete. Capital remained abundant in areas of well-established industrial strength such as Lancashire.[47] Indeed, the ease and cheapness with which capital could be raised for established industrial concerns by traditional methods was probably one of the chief reasons for the maintenance of a high degree of competition in British industry and the persistence of the small firm.[48] Severe competition meant that the need to produce high dividends for shareholders lowered the incentive to plough back profits and increase investment ratios, and inhibited the growth of the large firm.[49]

As a result, the joint-stock banks, for example, were given no great incentive to offer anything other than their time-honoured services to industry – principally overdraft facilities and short-term credit[50] – and the City and the Stock Exchange remained similarly remote from industrial investment. It is true that merchant bankers and other City financiers were often unjustifiably suspicious of limited liability industrial companies, but this was a prejudice they shared with many industrialists.[51] They and their partners on the Exchange were clearly better fitted to handling the large loans floated by national and municipal governments or large corporations than to raising the small sums required by the typical British firm. They usually came into contact with home industry only on those relatively rare occasions when a substantial loan was floated as part of a company's conversion from partnership to joint-stock status.[52] Even joint-stock flotation was used more as a way of preserving the individuality of particular firms than as a means of promoting rationalisation or creating a corporate structure.[53]

In other words, it is difficult to blame the City for failing to adapt to industry when the industry it was supposed to serve did not put forth radical new demands for its services.[54] This lack of demand for new sources of finance was one result of the slowness of the evolution of Britain's industrial structure, explanations of which are legion. Britain's difficulties can be ascribed to the peculiar strength of trade unionism, which inhibited the replacement of labour by capital and led to overmanning in many industries.[55] Alternatively, they may be attributed to her 'early start' as an industrial power and her 'overcommitment' to the labour-intensive phase of economic development based on textiles, steam-power and the small firm,[56] a phase much lengthened by the ease with which the staple industries could continue to find markets in the empire and other parts of the globe subject to British influence. Relative decline can also be explained in terms of entrepreneurial failure:[57] the steel industry provides some excellent examples.[58] But whatever explanation is offered (and some of the more complex ones include all the approaches noted here and more besides),[59] it is obvious that Britain's industrial crisis after 1870 can be understood as a series of events largely uninfluenced, for good or ill, by the City and its institutions. There are some instances of new industries finding it hard to raise money in London or being forced to raise it in a non-optimal manner because they could not penetrate conventional financial barriers;[60] but there is little evidence of any general shortage of funds. New industries in Britain before 1914 often found it difficult to raise capital, not because London financiers were unwilling to open their doors to them but because demand for their services was small and their prospects were often uninviting – a consequence perhaps, of the massive commitment to the older industries and traditional sources of energy in Britain after 1870.

In an ideal world, new industry might have prospered on long-term finance backed by the state, but this was out of the question, politically and ideologically, in Britain before 1914. Had British industrial growth been faster, then the City and the banks would have been faced with the challenge of transforming themselves to meet new opportunities. Whether they could or would have done so cannot be known; but it is idle to complain that no finance capitalism on a German model developed in Britain in the late nineteenth century when British industry did not grow and change as rapidly as it did on the continent. Finance capitalism arose in response to a crisis of industrial funding in Germany: in Britain this crisis never developed, at least before 1914.[61]

Foreign investment and economic growth

That the bias in London financial markets was a natural one in the circumstances and reflected, in a very real sense, the configuration of the economy does not, of course, necessarily mean that heavy overseas investment did not have long-run deleterious effects. The very ease with which capital could be sent abroad and the virtual certainty of the returns probably had an influence in tempering entrepreneurial drive[62] by creating a level of prosperity which put off the need for fundamental industrial change. It is possible, too, that an oversavings crisis, however painful, might have been the prelude to dynamic industrial growth had not overseas investment provided relief from the need to change.

The most recent statistical work does provide some evidence that, after 1870, high foreign investment was inimical to overall industrial growth. Before 1870, home and foreign investment fluctuated more or less in unison and in conformity with the familiar seven-to-nine-year trade cycle. After that date, the paths of home and foreign investment diverged, each setting into a pattern of swings approximately 20 years in length which were inverse to each other.[63] The peaks of capital export in the late 1880s and in 1909–13 were periods of low domestic investment, while troughs in foreign investment in the late 1870s and the 1890s were accompanied by a strong upsurge in capital formation at home.[64] When foreign investment was high, exports and the export regions boomed,[65] but domestic investment as a whole and, it appears, manufacturing investment as well were low, and total output grew more slowly. The overall growth of manufacturing output and investment was far more dependent upon changes in domestic activity than it was on changes in exports.[66] The sharp fall in foreign demand in the downswing after 1873 affected overall manufacturing growth only slightly: the temporary cessation of foreign investment and the miserably slow growth of exports in the 1890s were accompanied by a revival of the rate of growth of manufacturing, of productivity and of growth as a whole.

If bursts of foreign investment had short-run beneficial effects on exports, they may have retarded the development of export industries in the longer term by cushioning them against the need for technical and organisational change. If, for whatever reason, there had been less foreign investment, then staple export industries might have been forced to adapt themselves more quickly and investors would have had a greater interest in other domestic opportunities – with radical effects on the structure of capital markets and financial institutions.[67] Foreign investment, like formal empire, proved to be a considerable force in favour of conservatism in industry, not only by keeping up overseas sales of traditional manufactures from a number of export-producing regions but also by offering easy alternatives to new and risky domestic ventures.

Despite provincial industrialists' general aversion to overseas opportunities, capital export was a significant feature of investment decisions in Lancashire and industrial Scotland. While growth was slowing and the textile industry was losing its technological lead,[68] Lancashire was producing a surplus of capital, some of which flowed abroad. Lancashire capitalists provided 8 per cent of the capital placed in the foreign-based firms in Davis and Huttenback's sample, and the region had a greater taste for foreign than for home investment after 1880.[69] Slower growth after 1870, low industrial investment and a high rate of foreign investment also coexisted in lowland Scotland. Between 1870 and 1914, the Clyde was the most important location for shipbuilding and heavy engineering in Britain. But, as profits fell under the stress of competition after 1870, the tendency was for manufacturers to put more of their savings abroad. An estimated 10 per cent of Scotland's national income went abroad every year. Scottish capitalists were particularly interested in the empire, for which they provided about 8 per cent of the capital in this period.[70] In both Lancashire and industrial Scotland it is probable that capital export reinforced the natural tendency to technological conservatism that was further encouraged by the maintenance of export demand, especially in empire markets. By 1914, the whole set of relationships must have posed a formidable barrier to change.[71]

Britain's initial success, both as a provider of the new industrial commodities and of services like shipping, credit and insurance produced a large balance of payments surplus in the latter half of the nineteenth century. This surplus was the basis for her extensive capital exports. As the value of assets held abroad increased, the stream of dividend and interest payments increased likewise. Until the 1870s, the flow of new investment abroad exceeded the value of in-payments. After that date, save for the late 1880s and the few years before World War I, when overseas flows were exceptionally high, the position was decisively reversed. Over the whole period 1870–1913, incoming payments exceeded capital exports by roughly £1 billion.[72]

To accommodate this massive inflow, Britain had to allow a high and rising level of imports since this was the only way in which the borrowers could meet their debt obligations. Free trade was a necessary adjunct to the repayment of foreign debts, but, in allowing increasing levels of primary produce to enter Britain, free trade also exposed her to competition from her industrial rivals. This reduced industrial profitability, investment and growth, especially in those new industries which could not compete in world markets as easily as cottons or other more traditional exports. However, in reducing the rate of growth of British exports, foreign competition performed the same function as rising imports in helping Britain to solve her invisible repayments problem because a decelerating rate of growth of exports decreased the demand for sterling and improved the ability of overseas debtors to meet payments on accumulated loans. Had the rate of growth of exports been higher, Britain's balance of payments surplus would have been larger and, in lieu of higher foreign investment (which, in the long term, would only have made the repayment problems worse), might have led to a grand international liquidity crisis as the world ran out of sterling.

This economy, founded on free trade, capital export and high imports, was not best fitted to the needs of export manufacturers. Foreign investment booms undoubtedly produced benefits for traditional export industries such as textiles, but in doing so they reinforced Britain's commitment to industries which were no longer at the forefront of world industrial change. At the same time, the free-trade policy inevitably subjected the newer industries to the full blast of competition from Germany, the United States and elsewhere, retarded their progress and inhibited investment. Britain's export sector was not well prepared to meet the needs of the second industrial revolution, whose transforming power after the 1870s was to be far greater than that of the first.[73] A low rate of industrial investment contributed to technological and organisational backwardness in key areas, such as chemicals and engineering, and to an excessive commitment to the time-honoured and the traditional – something for which the British eventually paid a heavy price after 1945, when the international economy, held back by two world wars and an intervening Great Depression, finally took off and left Britain behind.[74]

On the other hand, this open economy was entirely compatible with the rise of the complex of services and consumer industries we have already described.

These activities developed particularly rapidly in London and the south-east region and gained perhaps their greatest stimulus from the income generated by foreign investment. The open economy was also entirely supportive of the commercial and financial sector, and especially of the City of London, since the huge inflow of imports under free trade and the large outflows of capital, which were characteristic of the British economy in this period, were the basis of its success after 1850.[75]

Foreign investment and gentlemanly capitalism

There was a considerable degree of overlap between the world of services and consumer goods in the south-east and that of the heavily industrialised provinces, and it is undoubtedly true that the City of London and the northern export staples had a common dependence on international trade. Nonetheless, Davis and Huttenback felt constrained to argue, as we have seen, that in terms of investment preferences Britain was sociologically divided; and it is important for us to emphasise, at this juncture, that the gentlemen who were the chief overseas investors were also the leading lights in the service economy which was, in many ways, culturally as well as economically, distinct from provincial, industrial Britain. Despite his obvious animus against gentlemanly elites, his rather too clear-cut distinction between north and south, and his failure to recognise the dynamic nature of the development of south-eastern England, J.A. Hobson caught something of the flavour of the division. He distinguished between 'Producers England', where industry set the tone of life and 'Consumers England', which he described in the following manner:

> The Home Counties, the numerous seaside and other residential towns, the cathedral and University towns, and in general terms, the South are full of well-to-do and leisured families whose incomes, dissociated from any present exertion of their recipients, are derived from industries conducted in the North or in some oversea country. A very large share, probably the major part, of the income spent by these well-to-do residential classes in the South, is drawn from investments of this nature. The expenditure of these incomes calls into existence and maintains large classes of professional men, producers and purveyors of luxuries, tradesmen, servants and retainers, who are more or less conscious of their dependence upon the goodwill and patronage of people 'living on their means'. This class of 'ostentatious leisure' and 'conspicuous waste' is subordinated in the North to earnest industry: in the South it directs a large proportion of the occupations, sets the social tone, imposes valuation and opinions. . . . Most persons living in the South certainly have to work for a living, but much of their work is closely and even consciously directed by the will and demands of the moneyed class.[76]

The society led by the 'moneyed class' had evolved over the previous 50 years of high overseas investment. The mid-century squads of genteel investors listed by

Vincent were an elite of that part of British society still agricultural at base, still dominated by landed capitalism and cut off from the industrialism that was transforming a large part of provincial England and the Celtic fringes. Trapped within the cultural norms of this rural and small town society, the only acceptable and accessible investment outlets open to this elite were land and government stock. As the world economy expanded and opportunities for foreign investment grew, the numbers of socially acceptable investment outlets multiplied and the vast flows of returning income which resulted helped first to reproduce this gentlemanly elite and then, slowly, to recreate it in a new form. In other words, the nature of the new economic society which emerged in London and the south-east in the latter half of the nineteenth century was moulded by the social and cultural preferences of a gentlemanly class which was itself changed by the process.

The City of London was the economic powerhouse of this service sector and of the gentlemanly order which dominated it. As such, it was a part of gentlemanly capitalism itself. There have been some fascinating debates between Marxists in recent years about the extent and nature of the power of the City of London. Despite many marked disagreements among them, they all begin with the assumption that the City's position depended entirely upon its wealth, and they fail to investigate the extent to which that wealth was created in a particular social context that set the limit upon both its nature and its extent.[77] In practice, after 1850, City wealth was determined to a large degree by the continuing weight of landed wealth and by the size of gentlemanly investment abroad, which were the two chief driving forces behind the evolution of the distinctive Victorian and Edwardian economy already described in this chapter.

The peculiar path of development adopted by the British had, therefore, more than mere economic significance. The growth and predominance within Britain of the service sector and of wealth based on foreign investment meant also the continued dominance of a non-industrial elite. The older gentlemanly elite based on land was losing its power, though this loss was slowed down by the transference of assets from land into services and abroad. From the late nineteenth century the landed interest was forced to share this power, with industrialists to some degree, but more often with the bankers, financiers and professionals who rose to influence and prestige as the service sector grew in importance. Out of this union of land and service wealth the new gentlemanly capitalist class was born.

Notes

1 Michael Edelstein, *Overseas Investment in the Age of High Imperialism, 1850–1914* (New York, 1982), passim. There is a convenient summary of his principal findings on pp. 288–311.

2 Lance E. Davis and Robert A. Huttenback, *Mammon and the Pursuit of Empire: The Political Economy of British Imperialism, 1860–1912* (Cambridge, 1987), pp. 195–6.

3 Ibid. Table 7.33, p. 204.

4 Ibid. Table 7.7, p. 213.

5 Ibid. Table 7.33, p. 204.

6 Ibid. p. 206.

7 David Cannadine, 'Landowner as Millionaire: the Finances of the Dukes of Devonshire, c.1800–c.1926', *Agricultural History Review,* CCV (1977).

8 Susan W. Martins, *A Great Estate at Work: The Holkham Estate and its Inhabitants in the Nineteenth Century* (1980), pp. 58–65 and App. II.

9 David Spring, 'Land and Politics in Edwardian England', *Agricultural History,* 58 (1984), pp. 22–6. It was still the case in 1914 that the majority of the landed aristocracy depended mainly upon these rentals for survival and reacted to the depression by selling land and by introducing economies. See Andrew Adonis, 'Aristocracy, Agriculture and Liberalism: The Politics, Finance and Estates of the Third Lord Carrington', *Hist. Jour.,* 31 (1988), pp. 881–3.

10 R.C. Michie, 'The Social Web of Investment in the Nineteenth Century', *Revue internationale d'histoire de la banque,* 18–19 (1979), pp. 164–8.

11 S.D. Chapman, 'British-Based Investment Groups before 1914', *Econ. Hist. Rev.,* 2nd ser. XXXVIII (1985).

12 Michie, 'The Social Web of Investment', p. 173.

13 Mira Wilkins, 'The Free Standing Company 1870–1914: an Important Type of British Foreign Investment', *Econ. Hist. Rev.,* 2nd ser. XLI (1988), passim. On this theme see also Chapman, 'British-Based Investment Groups'. For a good regional example see R.T. Stillson, 'The Financing of Malayan Rubber', *Econ. Hist. Rev.,* 2nd ser. XXIV (1971). See also Charles Harvey and Jon Press, 'Overseas Investment and the Professional Advance of British Metal Mining Engineers, 1851–1914', *Econ. Hist. Rev.,* 2nd ser. XLII (1989). It has recently been emphasised that, in the case of overseas mining investment, the initiative came mainly from the periphery and that 'the pull from the periphery was at its strongest in territories of increasing British influence', Charles Harvey and Jon Press, 'The City and International Mining, 1870–1914', *Bus. Hist.,* XXXII (1990), p. 113.

14 Davis and Huttenback, *Mammon and the Pursuit of Empire,* Table 7.8, pp. 214–15 and p. 215.

15 Michael Edelstein, 'Realized Rates of Return on U.K. Home and Overseas Portfolio Investment in the Age of High Imperialism', *Expl. Econ. Hist.,* 13 (1976), Table 7, p. 314; and idem. *Overseas Investment in the Age of High Imperialism,* Ch. 5.

16 Davis and Huttenback, *Mammon and the Pursuit of Empire,* Ch. 3, esp. p. 107, and App. 3.2, p. 117. On this topic see also Sidney Pollard, 'Capital Exports, 1870–1914: Harmful or Beneficial?', *Econ. Hist. Rev.,* 2nd ser. XXXVIII (1985), pp. 495–8.

17 One consequence of Davis and Huttenback's work has been a renewal of interest in the old question of whether the empire paid. On this see, especially, P.K. O'Brien, 'The Costs and Benefits of British Imperialism, 1846–1914', *Past and Present,* 120 (1988); A.G. Hopkins, 'Accounting for the British Empire', *Jour. Imp. and Comm. Hist.,* XVI (1988), and Andrew Porter, 'The Balance Sheet of Empire, 1850–1914', *Hist. Jour.,* 31 (1988).

18 Michie, 'The Social Web of Investment', passim.

19 Davis and Huttenback *Mammon and the Pursuit of Empire,* p. 211. They also argue that elites benefited in particular because they paid a disproportionately small amount of the taxes necessary to defend overseas investment while receiving a larger share of the gains. Ibid. pp. 244–52.

20 Thus allowing the conversion of consols in the 1880s. C.K. Harley, 'Goschen's Conversion of the National Debt and the Yield on Consols', *Econ. Hist. Rev.,* 2nd ser. XXIX (1976). Government stocks accounted for 38 per cent of the value of all stocks quoted on the Exchange in 1873 and for only 9 per cent by 1913. Youssef Cassis, *La City de Londres, 1870–1914* (Paris, 1987), Table 5, p. 49.

21 The major companies did not experience difficulties in raising money until after 1900. See R.J. Irving, 'British Railway Investment and Innovation, 1900–14: an Analysis with Special Reference to the North Eastern and London and North Western Railway Companies', *Bus. Hist.,* XIII (1971).

22 W.P. Kennedy, *Industrial Structure, Capital Markets and the Origins of British Economic Decline* (Cambridge, 1989), pp. 145, 148–9.

23 B. Supple, *The Royal Exchange Assurance* (Cambridge, 1970), pp. 330–48; B.L. Anderson, 'Institutional Investment Before the First World War: die Union Marine Insurance

Company 1897–1915', in S. Marriner ed. *Business and Businessmen: Studies in Business, Economic and Accounting History* (Liverpool, 1978); J.H. Treble, 'The Pattern of Investment in the Standard Life Assurance Company, 1875–1914', *Bus. Hist.*, XXII (1980).

24 C.A.E. Goodhart, *The Business of Banking, 1891–1914* (1972), pp. 127–41. The flurry of interest in overseas investment after 1909 may have had some connection with the fears of swingeing increases in taxation threatened by the Liberal Chancellor of the Exchequer, Lloyd George: Hartley Withers, *Stocks and Shares* (2nd edn 1917), pp. 295–9. See also *Parliamentary Debates* (Lords), IV (1909), cols. 745 (Lansdowne), 796–8 (Revelstoke), 1,155 (Rothschild). Joint-stock banks became increasingly interested in direct participation in overseas loan flotations before 1914. See A.R. Hall, *The British Capital Market and Australia, 1870–1914* (Canberra, 1963), p. 72; Cassis, *La City de Londres,* Table 10, p. 115.

25 Edelstein, *Overseas Investment in the Age of High Imperialism,* pp. 177–95.

26 R.C. Michie, 'Options, Concessions, Syndicates and the Provision of Venture Capital, 1880–1913', *Bus. Hist.*, XXIII (1981), pp. 149–50.

27 On the rentier character of British overseas investment after 1870 see W.P. Kennedy, 'Foreign Investment, Trade and Growth in the United Kingdom, 1870–1913', *Explorations in Economic History,* II (1974), pp. 425–39; D.R. Adler, *British Investment in American Railways, 1834–98* (Charlottesville, Va, 1970), pp. 197–8; H.W. Richardson, 'British Emigration and Overseas Investment, 1870–1914', *Econ. Hist. Rev.,* 2nd ser. XXV (1972), pp. 109–10.

28 Supple, *Royal Exchange Assurance,* p. 335.

29 John Vincent, *Pollbooks: How Victorians Voted* (Cambridge, 1967), p. 41.

30 An excellent illustration of the narrow nature of investments considered suitable for gentlemen is provided by R.C. Michie, 'Income, Expenditure and Investment of a Victorian Millionaire: Lord Overstone, 1823–1883', *Bulletin of the Institute of Historical Research,* LVII (1985). Overstone, however, was rather more conservative than the average in his later years. It is interesting to note that by Edwardian times E.M. Forster's middle-class, cultivated, rentier heroines were heavily into 'Foreign Things'. See *Howards End* (1910), p. 11.

31 G.D. Phillips, *The Diehards: Aristocratic Society and Politics in Edwardian England* (Cambridge, Mass, 1979), pp. 39–44; C.H. Lee, *The British Economy Since 1700: A Macro-Economic Perspective,* (Cambridge, 1986), pp. 36–7. Some landowners also developed interests of an industrial kind. See Harold Perkin, *The Rise of Professional Society: England since 1800,* (1989), pp. 67–9.

32 C.H. Lee, 'The Service Sector, Regional Specialization and Economic Growth in the Victorian Economy', *Journal of Historical Geography,* 10 (1984), p. 154.

33 This is assumed, for example, by D.N. McCloskey, 'Did Victorian Britain Fail?' *Econ. Hist. Rev.,* 2nd ser. XXIII (1970). See also idem, 'No It Did Not: A Reply to Crafts', in ibid. XXXII (1979).

34 Michael Edelstein, 'Foreign Investment and Empire, 1860–1914', in Roderick Floud and Donald McCloskey, eds. *The Economic History of Britain since 1700. Vol II: 1860 to the 1970s* (Cambridge, 1981), pp. 84–7.

35 If there was less than full employment then the upper limits on returns to domestic investment would be determined by the capital-output ratio, which is estimated at 4:1. R.C.O. Matthews, C.H. Feinstein and J.C. Odling-Smee, *British Economic Growth, 1856–1973* (Oxford, 1982), pp. 135–7. This would allow for average returns of up to 25 per cent.

36 See especially here Kennedy, 'Foreign Investment, Trade and Growth in the United Kingdom, 1870–1913'; and idem, 'Economic Growth and Structural Change in the United Kingdom, 1870–1914', *Jour. Econ. Hist.*, XLII (1982).

37 Pollard, 'Capital Exports 1870–1914, p. 489; B.J. Eichengreen, 'The Proximate Determinants of Domestic Investment in Victorian Britain', *Jour. Econ. Hist.*, XLII (1982).

38 The classical description of finance capitalism is, of course, Rudolf Hilferding, *Finance Capital: A Study of the Latest Phase of Capitalist Development,* (English edn 1982).

39 W.P. Kennedy, *Industrial Structure, Capital Markets and the Origins of British Economic Decline,* p. 122. See also idem, 'Institutional Response to Economic Growth: Capital Markets in

Britain to 1914', in L. Hannah, ed. *Management Strategy and Business Development: An Historical and Comparative Study* (1976), p. 160.

40 Goodhart, *The Business of Banking, 1891–1914,* p. 135.

41 Cassis, *La City de Londres,* p. 48.

42 Davis and Huttenback, *Mammon and the Pursuit of Empire,* Table 2.1, p. 40.

43 Ibid. Table 2.6, p. 54.

44 Chapman, *The Rise of Merchant Banking,* p. 103.

45 Kennedy, *Industrial Structure, Capital Markets and the Origins of British Economic Decline,* Ch. 5.

46 Keynes, 'Great Britain's Foreign Investment', p. 58.

47 Farnie, 'The Structure of the British Cotton Industry, 1846–1914', in Akio Okochi and Shin-Ichi Yonekawa, eds. *The Textile Industry and its Business Climate* (Tokyo, 1982), p. 55.

48 Lance Davis, 'The Capital Market and Industrial Concentration: the U.S. and the U.K., a Comparative Survey', *Econ. Hist. Rev.,* 2nd ser. XIX (1966).

49 For an example see Wayne Lewchuk, 'The Return to Capital in the British Motor Vehicle Industry, 1896–1939', *Bus. Hist.,* 27 (1985).

50 P.L. Cottrell, *Industrial Finance, 1830–1914: The Finance and Organization of English Manufacturing Industry* (1980), pp. 210–44.

51 Stanley Chapman, *The Rise of Merchant Banking* (1984), p. 99; Michael H. Best and Jane Humphries, 'The City and Industrial Decline', in Bernard Elbaum and William Lazonick, eds. *The Decline of the British Economy* (Oxford, 1986), p. 227. It should be noted, however, that for the aristocratic merchant bankers, like Barings, acceptances were the 'bread and butter' business and issuing foreign loans the 'jam'; and 'the financing of British industry was fare for the servants' hall or, worse still, fit only for the dogs', Philip Zeigler, *The Sixth Great Power: Barings, 1762–1929* (1988), p. 290.

52 Keynes, 'Great Britain's Foreign Investments', p. 58; Hall, *The London Capital Market and Australia,* esp. Ch. 1; Ranald C. Michie, *Money, Mania and Markets: Investment Company Formation and the Stock Exchange in the Nineteenth Century* (Edinburgh, 1981), esp. Pt. V; Edelstein, *Overseas Investment in the Age of High Imperialism,* Ch. III.

53 Best and Humphries, 'The City and Industrial Decline', p. 226; Farnie, 'The Structure of the British Cotton Industry, 1846–1914', p. 74. For a more detailed study of the joint-stock movement in Lancashire see D.A. Farnie, *The English Cotton Industry and the World Market, 1815–1896* (Oxford, 1979), Chs. 6 and 7.

54 For other surveys of the vast literature on this topic see Best and Humphries, 'The City and Industrial Decline', pp. 223–9; Pollard, 'Capital Exports, 1870–1914', and idem, *Britain's Prime and Britain's Decline: The British Economy, 1870–1914* (1989), Ch. 2.

55 D. Coleman and C. MacLeod, 'Attitudes to New Techniques: British Businessmen, 1800–1950', *Econ. Hist. Rev.,* 2nd ser. XXXIX (1986), pp. 605–9, for a critical survey of the relevant literature.

56 See especially, H.W. Richardson, 'Retardation in Britain's Industrial Growth, 1870–1913', *Scottish Journal of Political Economy,* XII (1965), and idem, 'Over-Commitment in Britain before 1930', *Oxford Economic Papers,* XVII (1965). Both are reprinted in Derek H. Aldcroft and Harry W. Richardson, eds. *The British Economy, 1870–1939* (1969). Also: William Ashworth, 'The Late Victorian Economy', *Economica,* new ser. XXXIII (1966); Bernard Elbaum and William Lazonick, 'The Decline of the British Economy: an Institutional Perspective', *Jour. Econ. Hist.,* XLIV (1984). For a discussion of similar themes in a wider perspective see Mancur Olsen, *The Rise and Decline of Nations* (1982).

57 There is a vast literature on this theme, and for a thorough survey a reader should consult P.L. Payne, *British Entrepreneurship in the Nineteenth Century* (1988). See also A.L. Levine, *Industrial Retardation in Britain, 1880–1914* (1967) and Coleman and McLeod, 'Attitudes to New Techniques', passim. The comments of Matthews, Feinstein and Odling-Smee, *British Economic Growth,* also show some agreement with an entrepreneurial interpretation on pp. 381–2, 539–40. For a spirited contrary argument see Donald McCloskey and Lars Sandberg, 'From Damnation to Redemption: Judgements on the Late Victorian Entrepreneur', *Explorations in Economic History,* IX (1971).

58 On the steel industry, see Donald McCloskey, *Economic Maturity and Entrepreneurial Decline* (Cambridge, 1974), and, especially, Robert Allen, 'Entrepreneurship and Technical Progress in the North-East Coast Pig-Iron Industry: 1850–1913', in Paul Uselding, ed. *Research in Economic History,* 6 (1981).

59 See, for example, the comprehensive surveys by François Crouzet, *The Victorian Economy* (1982), Ch. 12, and P. Mathias, *The First Industrial Nation: An Economic History of Britain, 1700–1914* (2nd edn. 1983), pp. 369–93; also Pollard, *Britain's Prime and Britain's Decline,* passim, and the *Oxford Review of Economic Policy,* 4 (1988).

60 For example: A.E. Harrison, 'F. Hopper and Co. – The Problems of Capital Supply in the Cycle Manufacturing Industry, 1891–1914', *Bus. Hist.,* 24 (1982); Kennedy, 'Institutional Response to Economic Growth'; John Armstrong, 'Hooley and the Bovril Company' *Bus. Hist.,* XXVIII (1986).

61 Lee, *British Economic Growth since 1700,* pp. 66–70, is worth consulting here. For a comprehensive survey of the literature on finance and industry in Britain see Michael Collins, *Banks and Industrial Finance in Britain, 1800–1939* (1991).

62 Matthews, Feinstein and Odling-Smee, *British Economic Growth,* p. 355; Pollard, 'Capital Exports, 1870–1914', p. 512.

63 The best explanation of the emergence of the twenty-year cycle is given by H.J. Habakkuk, 'Fluctuations in Housebuilding in Britain and the United States in the Nineteenth Century', *Jour. Econ. Hist.,* XXII, (1962), reprinted in A.R. Hall, *The Export of Capital from Britain, 1870–1914* (1968).

64 The best introduction to the vast literature on this subject is P.L. Cottrell, *British Overseas Investment in the Nineteenth Century* (1975), pp. 35ff.

65 There is a detailed examination of the relationship between long swings in investment and exports in A.G. Ford, 'The Transfer of British Foreign Lending, 1870–1913', *Econ. Hist. Rev.,* 2nd ser. XI (1958–9), and idem, 'Overseas Lending and Internal Fluctuations, 1870–1914', *Yorkshire Bulletin of Economic and Social Research,* XVII (1965). On the alternation in the level of activity between export regions and other parts of the economy see J. Parry Lewis, *Building Cycles and Britain's Growth* (1965), esp. Chs. 5–7.

66 Matthews, Feinstein and Odling-Smee, *Britain's Economic Growth,* Table 9.10, and p. 282.

67 Ibid. pp. 254–6.

68 On this question see William Lazonick, 'Industrial Organization and Technological Change: the Decline of the British Cotton Industry', *Bus. Hist. Rev.,* 57 (1983).

69 Davis and Huttenback, *Mammon and the Pursuit of Empire,* Table 7.5, p. 209, and Table 7.8, p. 214. An example of Lancastrian overseas investment is provided by M. Rose, 'Diversification of Investment by the Greg Family', *Bus. Hist.,* XX (1979), esp. p. 91.

70 Davis and Huttenback's figures are for the whole of Scotland rather than just industrial Scotland, and tome of the overseas investment must have come from non-industrial, mainly landed, sources. Roughly one-third of all those who died worth £100,000 or more in Scotland in this period were landowners, but the bulk of the wealthy came from manufacturing origins. R. Britton, 'Wealthy Scots, 1873–1913', *Bull. Inst. Hist. Res.,* LVIII (1985), pp. 79, 81–2.

71 For the Scottish example see Tony Dickson, ed. *Scottish Capitalism: Class, State and Nation from Before the Union to the Present* (1980), esp. pp. 248–55; B. Lenman, *An Economic History of Modem Scotland, 1660–1976* (1977), esp. pp. 192–3; and B. Lenman and K. Donaldson, 'Partner's Income, Investment and Diversification in the Scottish Linen Area, 1850–1921', *Bus. Hist.,* XII (1971).

72 Pollard, *Britain's Prime and Britain's Decline,* Table 2.6, p. 69.

73 Douglass C. North, *Structure and Change in Economic History* (New York, 1981), Chs. 12 and 13.

74 For two ways of generalising this experience see W. Arthur Lewis, *Growth and Fluctuations, 1870–1913* (1978), Ch. 5, and Michael Beenstock, *The World Economy in Transition* (1983 edn), Ch. 6.

75 The last two paragraphs have been greatly aided by the work of Pollard, *Britain's Prime and Britain's Decline,* pp. 108–10; and by Kennedy, *Industrial Structure,* pp. 153–63, which

also offers a Hobsonian-type demand-deficiency argument for slow industrial growth not utilised here, as does idem, 'Notes on Economic Efficiency in Historical Perspective the case of Britain, 1870–1914', in Paul Uselding, ed. *Research in Economic History,* 9 (1984).

76 J.A. Hobson, 'The General Election: a Sociological Interpretation', *Sociological Review,* 3 (1910), p. 113.

77 For a good example see Geoffrey Ingham, *Capital Divided: The City and Industry in British Social Development* (1984) passim and the recent controversy between Ingham and Barratt Brown, on which see Michael Barratt Brown, 'Away with all the Great Arches: Anderson's History of British Capitalism', *New Left Review,* 167 (1988), and Ingham's 'Commercial Capital and British Development: A Reply to Michael Barratt Brown', ibid. 172 (1988). There is also an interesting contribution to this debate from D. Nicholls, 'Fractions of Capital: the Aristocracy, the City and Industry in the Development of Modern British Capitalism', *Social History,* 13 (1988).

7

CHALLENGING COSMOPOLITANISM

The tariff problem and imperial unity, 1880–1914

What eventually undermined the Gladstonian consensus and threatened the ability of governing elites to keep economic policy out of the public eye were rising defence costs and the new demands made upon civil expenditure by policies designed to meet the needs of the more democratic electorate created by the 1867 and 1884 Reform Acts. Gladstone's great budgetary feats were made possible by neglecting defence spending and by the luck which enabled Britain, given the state of Europe, to enjoy naval supremacy on the cheap.[1] The extent of the luck was made plain during brief periods of adversity like the Crimean War, when soaring military expenditure pushed up direct taxation sharply, Bank Rate rose steeply to stem a drain of gold, governments were forced to add to the national debt and even free trade was threatened before the war came abruptly and unexpectedly to an end in 1856.[2] Half a century later, the Boer War also triggered off a similar financial crisis, which threatened orthodoxy and the City's supremacy.[3] Like the earlier conflict, it also led to sharp criticism of the amateurism and inefficiency of Britain's governing institutions.[4] The Crimean conflict was a set-back to Gladstonianism soon retrieved: by 1900 the Boer conflict only exacerbated the tendency for defence, especially naval expenditure, to grow in response to the threat posed to the Pax Britannica by first French and Russian and, later, German expansion.

When faced with rising bills for defence and a growing demand for welfare expenditure, the Liberals remained strong in their free-trade faith and thus had to rely on increases in direct taxation. But in order to maintain their middle-class vote in the industrial provinces they tried to avoid penalising income from foreign investment and kept income tax increases down by directing most of their fire at the landed aristocracy.[5] Lloyd George's 1909 budget, the House of Lords crises of 1909–11 and the Liberal land campaign that followed were a direct outcome of the attempt by Gladstone's successors to wrestle with the new problems of rising public spending – problems that could be resolved only by reducing even further the Liberal connection with the landed interest.

As defenders of aristocracy and the status quo, the Conservatives, faced with the need to improve Britain's defences, resisted direct tax increases. But they were forced in return to resort to tariffs, a commitment clearly made by 1910.[6] The City, as part of the Conservative interest, moved in the same direction. City influence on naval rearmament – a necessary 'insurance premium' to safeguard British commerce and finance – was impressive,[7] but the City did not relish paying for what was so clearly in the nation's interest as well as its own and, when forced to choose, preferred to spread the burden by accepting increased indirect taxation. If the choice was between maintaining free trade or suffering higher direct taxation, which might scare capital away from London, the City by 1910 was clear about its priorities.[8]

Free trade and empire unity

Given that the Conservatives had always been less committed to free trade than the Liberals and that, by the turn of the century, the temptation to raise indirect taxes was becoming almost irresistible, it seems surprising that Chamberlain's Tariff Reform campaign, launched in 1903, should have split the party and allowed the Liberals their first real taste of power for 20 years. The failure of Chamberlain's campaign may seem the more puzzling in that it was based on a passionate desire for imperial economic unity. Since Disraeli's time, the Conservatives had always been the party identified both with the desire for closer unity with the white empire and with a more aggressive line on expansion in Africa and Asia than the Liberals, many of whom were infected with 'little Englandism', inherited from Cobden and Gladstone.

Although he was by no means a 'no foreign policy' man, Gladstone did lean more towards Cobden's view of the universe than he did to the 'free trade imperialism' of Palmerston.[9] This stance was probably reflective of northern, urban Liberalism which, before the 1880s, was relatively confident in Britain's ability to sell its wares world-wide. Gladstone tended to take Britain's power for granted. He once argued that if all Britain's overseas possessions and means of influence abroad were suddenly removed we should, simply because of the physical and mental powers of the British people, soon re-establish ourselves as world leaders. In his view, Britain's strength lay in Britain, not in her empire, and his superb confidence in Britain's intrinsic power meant that he had very little sympathy for those who worried about military and naval security. He did not believe, for instance, that the possession of formal empire was important. India, he argued, was not a source of strength and profit to Britain and our presence there could be justified only if we could show that we were leading the Indians towards civilisation. His attitude to the white colonies was that they should grow up and shoulder their own responsibilities as soon as possible though, at the same time, he hoped that a close but informal affinity would continue to bind Britain and her 'children' together.[10] Gladstone did not, of course, propose to leave India and, like most other radicals, he assumed that the economic dependence of the white colonies would continue irrespective of the nature of the political tie. Nonetheless, his determined attempt to cut expenditure on colonial defence after 1868 provoked a great uproar, not at first in the Conservative Party itself, which was slow to react, but among colonial intellectuals, journalists and professional men, many of whom resided in London and were not always representative of their homelands.[11] It is useful to look at the main ideas spawned by the agitation of 1869–71 because a number of them endured and became part of the stock-in-trade of imperialists before 1914.

Many of those who opposed Gladstone's policies were struck by the rapid growth of other 'empires', especially the federated states of Germany (created in 1870) and the United States. They were impressed by the large populations and geographical spread of these youthful great powers and fearful of their potential for future growth. It was clearly an article of faith among many Conservatives after 1870 that Britain might be dwarfed by these nations in the future. Hence, Britain needed the strength given by her empire and in particular should look to unification with the white colonies. The growth potential of the white colonies was expected to be similar to that of the United States, and many observers clearly believed that, together with Great Britain, they would one day provide a level of population and wealth sufficient to maintain the empire's position as a great power. Another emphasis of the time was that the ideal of universal free trade was no longer realisable, that protectionism was increasing again and that the white colonies would become critically important as markets before long. If they were cut adrift abruptly they might easily be absorbed by other powers.[12]

There is no doubt that rising fear of the might of other great powers – illustrated by the power of the North in the American Civil War and by Germany's defeat of France in 1870 – had much to do with the reaction to Liberal colonial policy in 1869–71. There is no doubt, either, that Gladstone's own vision of the world depended crucially upon Britain's ability to maintain her economic supremacy over all her rivals. But, 'once doubt had been cast on the Manchester School's prophecy of an era of universal peace and free trade, dominated industrially by Great Britain, the value of overseas possessions once again became a completely open question'.[13] If Britain's security was threatened, it began to seem madness to some commentators for her to acquiesce in a colonial policy which allowed the empire slowly to fragment. Froude's conception of the empire, surrounded by a tariff wall, self-subsisting, strong in population and wealth and with the flow of migrants to her potential enemy, the United States, diverted to the empty lands within the Queen's jurisdiction, began to have a wide appeal at this juncture.[14] Modern communications, it was felt, made such a united empire a possibility and offered a shelter against a hostile world, which was increasingly seen in social Darwinist terms.[15]

Disraeli, astute politician that he was, sensed this change in the political wind earlier than most of his colleagues and, as leader of the Conservative Party, turned on the Liberals and accused them of weakening the empire and sapping the strength of Britain. His strident imperialism at this time has often been seen as a typically cynical piece of political manoeuvring, merely a convenient way of discrediting

Gladstone and winning the election of 1873. It has also been claimed that much of Disraeli's imperialism was designed to provide a political sideshow which would keep the minds of the newly enfranchised masses off their domestic woes rather than to achieve specific goals overseas.[16] But, if proponents of imperial unity before 1870 were unfashionable, they still existed, and Disraeli was prominent among them. His advocacy of empire unity had often been vague but it was consistent.[17] The popularity of his views after 1870 probably had something to do with the changing nature of the Conservative Party itself, whose southern British base was increasingly connected with empire through colonial employment and investment in empire railways and governments.

In his famous Crystal Palace speech of 1872, Disraeli offered the Conservative Party as the repository of tradition and national honour and the true home of gentlemanly capitalism, while the Liberals were damned as upholders of 'cosmopolitan principles imported from the Continent'. The Conservatives had three aims: to uphold the traditional institutions of the country such as the established Church and the landed aristocracy; to elevate the conditions of the mass of the people; and 'to uphold the Empire of England' which, Disraeli claimed, Liberalism had tried to destroy.

Deftly ignoring the convergence of policy of both Tory and Liberal administrations over the previous 20 years, Disraeli argued that self-government for the white colonies was obviously right but that it ought to have been associated with

> a great policy of Imperial consolidation, it ought to have been accompanied by an Imperial tariff, by securities for the people of England for the enjoyment of the unappropriated lands which belong to the sovereign as their trustee and by a military code which shall have precisely defined the means and responsibilities by which, if necessary, the country should call for aid for the colonies themselves. It ought further to have been accompanied by the institution of some representative council in the metropolis which should have brought the colonies into constant and continuous communications with the Home Government.[18]

Leaving aside the question of the disposal of colonial lands, the main items on the agenda in the discussions between Britain and the white colonies over the next 40 years are all here.

If, as we have seen, there was a strong convergence between the parties on economic policy, it was also the case that something like a consensus on imperial questions began to emerge, at least at Cabinet level. Liberals remained wedded to free trade and were thus deeply suspicious of any attempts at uniting the empire economically. The party also retained its Cobdenite wing, which was hostile to any extension of the boundaries of empire and ready to pillory the interests, political or economic, they believed were conspiring to force on the nation a policy of imperial aggression. Nonetheless, Gladstone's lofty disdain for empire clearly stopped short of any desire to dismember it. Moreover, denunciations of expansion helped to disguise a partly subconscious acceptance of Britain's economic leadership and of her informal influence, and thus failed to confront the awkward question of what might have to be done should such relationships begin to collapse. The financial crisis of the early 1880s in Egypt – to whose stocks, marketed in the City, Gladstone was an enthusiastic subscriber – and its resolution by military force followed by occupation, was notable in bringing this implicit Liberal imperialism into the political light.[19] And Gladstone's successor, Rosebery, whose City affiliations were more direct, was happy enough to pursue a forward policy in Africa in the 1890s, despite misgivings among his political colleagues.

On the Conservative side, it has recently been claimed that the fear of high taxation, aimed at landed wealth, among the party's aristocratic leadership was so great that they were driven to oppose highcost enterprises like imperial expansion.[20] As we have already seen, however, Gladstonian financial rectitude was no real barrier to painting more corners of the world red. The argument also ignores the extent to which the Tory leadership, of which Salisbury was a prime example, had been emancipated from a dependence on income from agriculture and had come to see itself as the protector of a wide band of propertied interests, many of them involving overseas income and the extension of British power abroad.[21] Furthermore, just as the Liberals provided a traditional home for anti-imperialist sentiment, so the Conservative Party acted as a time-honoured refuge for imperial enthusiasts. Conservatives were the main force behind bodies like the Imperial Federation League in the 1880s;[22] they showed the most alarm at the rise of continental tariffs from the late 1870s;[23] and they were the first to consider seriously the possibility of bringing in imperial preference.[24] But they could not unite behind Chamberlain to oppose the New Liberalism which was replacing Gladstonianism. On the fiscal question the leadership had anyway to manoeuvre with great delicacy since a frontal attack on free trade could spell political disaster. Despite his hostility to Peel and his strong views on imperial unity, Disraeli had led the Conservatives away from protectionism as early as 1852 for electoral reasons. Salisbury also kept the issue out of the public gaze as far as possible when anti-free trade sentiment began to arise in the 1880s and for similar reasons, as we shall see. Chamberlain broke with tradition in making tariffs a matter of central concern in 1903 and, in so doing, he split the party, which had long ceased to depend either upon land or protection. Indeed, what made Chamberlain's initiative so devastating to the Conservatives was that it could easily be construed as an attack on the complex of gentlemanly economic forces which were in control of the party by the turn of the century.

Chamberlain and protectionism

The two periods when anti-free trade movements became important politically – the early 1880s and after 1903 – both followed rapid increases in manufactured imports in the previous decade and falls in net exports of manufactures. Both movements, the National Fair Trade League in the 1880s and early 1890s and then the Tariff Reform campaign, voiced strong criticisms of existing economic policy and of the economic structures they believed this policy helped to produce. The League was extremely critical of the effects of a high level of British foreign investment on manufacturing industry:

> An important effect of the combined influence of foreign tariffs and free imports is to discourage and lessen the investment of capital in the development of our agriculture and manufactures and to stimulate and increase its investment in foreign land and securities and foreign industrial enterprises: the inevitable consequence being that a large and increasing amount of food, clothing and other commodities is imported in payment of income due to owners of foreign investments here resident, and therefore without a corresponding export of the production of our own industry. This directly operates to limit the employment of labour in the country. We think that this important feature of our economic position has not hitherto received the attention it deserves.[25]

Fair Traders were wrong to assume that much British foreign investment went into industrial enterprises abroad; but they were correct in thinking that the effect of the returning income, in connection with the policy of free trade, was to increase competitive pressures on both agriculture and industry in Britain. The main thrust of the campaign in the 1880s was for tariffs to be used as diplomatic weapons in the struggle to reduce the protective barriers erected by Britain's rivals in the depression of the late 1870s. This reflected both the conviction that Britain could compete easily in a free-trade universe and the belief that protection in Germany and other industrial countries prevented British exports from penetrating their markets and, at the same time, allowed foreign rivals to dump their surplus produce in Britain below cost price without fear of retaliation.[26]

Chamberlain and the Tariff Reformers also stressed the link between free trade, low domestic investment and a high rate of capital export. But they did so with a greater sense of urgency and with wider industrial support since, by 1900, the erosion of Britain's industrial superiority had gone further and the demand for protection, as well as for retaliatory tariffs, had become distinctly stronger. The Tariff Reformers raised the spectre of a de-industrialised Britain, where crucial industries like steel, vital for defence and for great power status as well as for wealth creation, were lost; they pointed to the time when Britain could no longer maintain her position in the world and would be faced with a breakdown in social order as industry disintegrated.[27] The campaign of 1903–6 was, in fact, a concerted attack on the whole drift of economic policy in Britain after 1850, since the Tariff Reformers argued that the ultimate result of a policy of free trade would be the creation of a rentier-dominated service economy which would be impotent in the face of its enemies. As Chamberlain put it in 1904

> whereas at one time England was the greatest manufacturing country now its people are more and more employed in finance, in distribution, in domestic

> service and in other occupations of the same kind. That state of things is consistent with ever increasing wealth. It may mean more money but it means less men. It may mean more wealth but it means less welfare; and I think it worthwhile to consider – whatever its immediate effects may be – whether this state of things may not be the destruction ultimately of all that is best in England, all that has made us what we are, all that has given us our power and prestige in the world; whether it will not be bad for these qualities if we sink into the position of Holland which is rich – richer than it ever was before – but still an inconsiderable factor in the world.[28]

In the 1880s the Fair Traders wanted a small duty on manufactured imports and they put some emphasis on the need for closer links with the empire, suggesting small preferential duties in favour of the white colonies.[29] Chamberlain was more empire-minded than his predecessors because he was even more convinced that the industrial future lay with great empires and federations, such as Russia and the United States, with their huge populations and vast natural resources. Many Tariff Reformers firmly believed that it was only by uniting Britain with her white colonies – whose populations were expected to expand enormously in the twentieth century – and by using their joint power to exploit the underdeveloped parts of empire, that industrial leadership and great-power status could be retained. Chamberlain himself constantly claimed that a system of imperial tariffs would be crucial in linking Britain's destiny with those parts of the empire whose growth potential was far greater than that of the motherland.[30] When Colonial Secretary in the late 1890s, he demonstrated his interest in imperial economic integration by trying to increase state economic involvement in the development of the dependent empire in order to encourage a more secure supply of imports and better markets for British goods.[31] In 1896, the same reasoning prompted him to suggest creating a free-trade empire with a common tariff against foreign countries, which he hoped would form the economic basis for greater unity.

The *Zollverein* idea fell foul of free-trade opinion in Britain and also offended the white colonies, which feared that their recently won economic independence would be infringed. Instead, the colonies advocated a system of mutual preferences which would allow them to protect their own industry. Chamberlain and his supporters fell back upon their proposals as being the most politically plausible. The hope was that, if the electorate could be persuaded to accept them, a united empire would eventually arise which would compensate for Britain's own economic decline.[32] In 1903, when he began his campaign, Chamberlain was convinced that the empire issue ought to be the paramount one in British politics; but he soon became aware that domestic protection had a broader popular appeal than empire preference. His campaign was designed to educate the electorate, but, not surprisingly, as it developed Chamberlain's speeches also began to reflect the protectionist concerns of those who rallied to Tariff Reform, even though empire economic unity remained his primary aim.[33]

The National Fair Trade League had considerable support within the Conservative Party in the 1880s and its policy could possibly have become established as the Tory answer to urban Liberalism. This did not happen partly because industry was hopelessly split over the protectionist issue and partly because the Home Rule crisis brought a large draft of Liberal Unionists, most of them solidly free trade in sympathy, into alliance with the Conservatives after 1886. Conservative leaders were also keen to marginalise the Fair Trade campaign for fear of its electoral implications.[34] Chamberlain's attempt to overturn economic orthodoxy and to change the nature of the political debate after 1903 was more challenging since, as one of the leading politicians of his day, he had the power to put the tariff question at the centre of political controversy. The tariff campaign gave the Conservative Party a modern 'cry', a new way of attracting the votes of the working men enfranchised in 1884.[35] It offered a programme of 'social imperialism' designed to unite property with labour in the cause of empire and to head off the formation of a mass party dedicated to socialism. But, had Chamberlain achieved his ambition, he might have overturned the existing hierarchy in the Conservative Party and threatened gentlemanly leadership in general.[36]

Chamberlain had begun his career as a radical industrialist hostile to the landed class. He combined his radicalism with a strong sense of the need for empire and empire markets: his opposition to Irish Home Rule in 1886 forced him out of the Liberal Party and compelled him, if only to maintain his influence, to take his Midlands support into an alliance with the Conservative Party, which at least shared his enthusiasm for empire. The hostility which his unorthodox attitudes to state spending as Colonial Secretary provoked within the Conservative Party,[37] and its indifference to industrial concerns, convinced him that the party, like the Liberals, was not an ideal vehicle for his views or for the interests he represented. It is doubtful if the Tariff Reform campaign[38] was expressly designed to overthrow the existing leadership of the Conservative Party, but it was nevertheless a danger to it. The campaign could have succeeded only if the Conservatives had made large electoral gains in provincial industrial areas at the expense of the Liberals. Had they done so on the basis of a programme which put industrial concerns at the forefront of politics, the centre of gravity of Tory politics would have shifted from the south to the north, from services to industry. More important, success for Tariff Reform would have transformed the party's ideological stance from one based on gentlemanly capitalism to another inspired by an aggressive, industrial radicalism. Like his famous brand of municipal socialism in the 1870s and his 'Unauthorised Programme' of the early 1880s, Chamberlain's tariff campaign was an attempt to create a 'producers' alliance' of industrial capitalists and their workforce which, besides muting industrial class conflict, was also expressly designed to encourage industry to assert itself and to take the nation's destinies out of the hands of the gentlemanly class. Since Chamberlain was making a direct assault on gentlemanly culture, it was inevitable that he would be condemned, in similar terms, by traditional leaders on both sides of the political divide. Almost instinctively, his attempt to place industrial wealth creation and its problems at the head of the political agenda was condemned as 'utterly sordid'[39] because it catered for the 'ignoble passions' of 'vulgarity and cupidity'.[40]

Industry, the City and free trade

Although Tariff Reformers were often determined to dramatise a split between industry and the service sector from which gentlemanly capitalism drew much of its strength, they did not succeed in doing so. As we have already seen, support for tariffs often came from traditional sources in the Conservative Party who saw them as a better way of raising revenue than increasing direct taxation. On the other side, faced with preferences on food, many industrial workers were more impressed by the danger of the 'dear loaf' than they were by promises of more employment and better wages in an imperial economy. The representatives of industrial capital were almost as divided about Tariff Reform as they had been by Fair Trade. There were strong pockets of support for tariffs in iron, steel and engineering, for example, where foreign competition was keenly felt. Cotton textiles, on the other hand, faced little challenge either at home or abroad and stood by free trade, while shipbuilding prospered on the cheap imports which the steel masters wanted to check.[41]

Similarly, although some industrialists were deeply frustrated by traditional methods of raising finance and were critical of the City's role in channelling British savings abroad, the tariff campaign did not reveal any fundamental rift between London finance and provincial industry. Industrial critics of the City were few and the extent of foreign investment became a national issue in 1909 only because discontented aristocrats and leading City men on the Conservative side combined to complain that the Liberals' proposals for supertax were driving capital abroad and hurting the domestic economy. The implication of this argument, however, was that without such an unnecessary stimulus – and even with a tariff to raise revenue instead – the natural balance between foreign and home investment would be found again with only 'surplus' capital continuing to flow abroad. Liberals, in their turn, dismissed the claims about the effects of taxation on capital export. They emphasised that industrial investment was raised largely outside the City and underlined the importance of capital export to the health of British foreign trade.[42]

In the election campaign of 1910, Churchill rallied Lancashire's industry behind free-trade Liberalism by vigorously denying protectionist claims that foreign investment harmed home industry.[43] Mindful, perhaps, of the large local commitment to foreign investments, he ridiculed the idea that capital for domestic industry was difficult to find and claimed that, in Lancashire at least, foreign investment was an important method of diffusing surplus capital. He argued that capital sent abroad encouraged the development of cheap imports of food and raw materials rather than fostered foreign industrial competition, as protectionists believed, and also that it left Britain 'almost entirely in the form of British exports'. In conclusion,

Churchill clearly identified the interest of foreign investment with the interests of industry and with the nation as a whole, claiming that:

> foreign investment and its returns are a powerful stimulus to the industrial system of Great Britain, that they give to the capital of the country a share in the new wealth of the whole world which is gradually coming under the control of scientific development, and that they sensibly enlarge the resources on which the state can rely for peaceful development and war-like need.[44]

Not a great many Conservatives would have objected to this: as one Liberal leader put it in 1909, the beneficial nature of foreign investment was 'a ground of common agreement'[45] between the parties. Chamberlain himself, when speaking in the City in 1904, came as one who saw 'the future of the country as a country of production, as a creator of new wealth and not merely the hoarder of invested securities',[46] but he did not suggest that there was any fundamental antagonism between the City and industry. Rather, he linked the fortunes of City and industry together and then claimed that both depended on the future development of the empire under a regime of tariffs. He admitted that some firms in the City took a cosmopolitan view of economic affairs and that to these, 'the fate of our manufacturers therefore is a secondary consideration: that provided the City of London remains, as it is at present, the clearing house of the world, any other nation may be its workshop'. But he felt he could appeal to a larger group in the City who would recognise a symbiotic relationship between finance and industry and between these two and empire development:

> You are the clearing-house of the world. Why? Why is banking prosperous among you? Why is a bill of exchange on London the standard currency of all commercial transactions? Is it not because of the productive energy and capacity which is behind it? Is it not because we have hitherto, at any rate, been constantly creating new wealth? Is it not because of the multiplicity, the variety, and the extent of our transactions? If any one of these things suffers even a check, do you suppose that you will not feel it? Do you imagine that you can in that case sustain the position of which you are justly proud? Suppose – if such a supposition is permissible – you no longer had the relations which you have at present with our great Colonies and dependencies, with India, with the neutral countries of the world, would you then be its clearinghouse? No, gentlemen. At least we can recognize this – that the prosperity of London is intimately connected with the prosperity and greatness of the Empire of which it is the centre. Banking is not the creator of our prosperity, but is the creation of it. It is not the cause of our wealth, but it is the consequence of our wealth; and if the industrial energy and development which has been going on for so many years in this country were to be hindered or relaxed, then finance, and all that finance means, will follow trade to the countries which are more successful than ourselves.[47]

He went on from this to argue that, since the development of industry depended upon the empire, and the development of empire upon the abandonment of free trade, the City had good reason to support his campaign.

Chamberlain's audience would hardly have accepted his assumption that industry was the central source of national wealth. But Chamberlain was right to believe that there were those in the City who were sympathetic to the view that finance and industry were interdependent and that the empire had a special part to play in maintaining Britain's economic position in the world. City men had been interested in the question of imperial federation and imperial unity from the 1880s and had put their weight enthusiastically behind imperial expansion at the time of the Scramble for Africa.[48] Some of the leading figures remained passionately in favour of free trade after 1903, convinced that tariffs would undermine City cosmopolitanism and threaten invisible earnings.[49] However, there were others who saw no such danger and some who were behind Chamberlain's campaign because they, too, felt that industrial decline was occurring and that it would inevitably undermine the City's position in the world economy.[50] Most fell between these extremes. Balfour's election as a City MP in 1906 suggests a cautious approach to the question because the Conservative leader deliberately adopted a stance halfway between the free-trade and Chamberlainite wings of the party when he argued that tariffs could be used as a retaliatory device.[51] The City's pragmatism no doubt indicates a degree of uncertainty about the merits of the contending parties. It also reflects the fact that the issue was not regarded as one of outstanding importance by most prominent men in the City: the movement away from free trade proposed by the Tariff Reformers was probably too small to change either the pattern or the volume of world commerce very much and, in any case, the City was far more interested in keeping the gold standard than in maintaining free trade.

Chamberlain and other prominent Tariff Reform supporters insisted that City wealth depended, in the final analysis, upon the prosperity of British industry; but they never succeeded in convincing either educated opinion or the electorate in general that free trade and a high level of foreign investment were harmful to the industrial structure. Many of their Conservative opponents and a large section of the electorally victorious Liberal Party denied that there was any fundamental industrial problem, while even those who shared Chamberlain's misgivings about Britain's future often refused to accept the argument that preferences and protection were the key to industrial revival. Some of his antagonists also went out of their way to stress the importance of overseas investment to exports and, by extension, to industrial development. Indeed, the overall effect of the debate on free trade was to highlight the significance of the City to the whole economy and to strengthen its perceived position as the rock upon which British economic strength was built. In so doing, it reinforced the tendency of governments to rely on the City for advice and left the policies upon which the City depended most, notably the gold standard, untouched except for behind-the-scenes criticism from some of the joint-stock bankers.

The Tariff Reform campaign of 1903–6 failed because the Chamberlainites, despite adding a protectionist layer to the original argument about preferences for the empire, could not unite industry and the industrial workforce. The spread of interests, both industrial and non-industrial, which favoured free trade and internationalism was too great to make the policy electorally successful. The campaign split the Conservatives in 1903–6, led to their disastrous defeat in the 1906 election and contributed to further defeats in the two elections of 1910. One of its effects, for example, was to rally free-trade business interests to the side of Liberalism and to halt, to some extent, the drift of industrialists to the political right (see Appendix Two).

The Fair Trade movement and the Tariff Reform campaign were, in their way, cries of alarm about the drift of the British economy in the direction of services and the implications of this drift for the domestic economy and Britain's world position. Had Chamberlain managed to unite industry behind him, his campaign might have succeeded. His failure to do so, like that of the Fair Traders before him, illustrates both the power of the perceived connection between free trade, foreign investment and industrial strength and also the fragmented nature of industry in Britain, which could never speak on any major issue with one voice. Tariff Reform gathered considerable support from the 'newer' end of British industry, that most hurt by German competition and impressed by German success. Many of the entrepreneurs in this sector argued not just for protection, but for greater state involvement in business on continental lines. They were also deeply frustrated by traditional methods of raising finance and by the exclusion of industrialists from policy-making.[52] Ideologically, however, they were far apart from traditional industrialists, like those in cotton textiles, where free-trade sentiment was still strong, where worries about City finance of domestic industry were an irrelevance and where government was still viewed with deep suspicion (see Appendix Two). Since a large section of industry was content with the status quo, gentlemanly hegemony over economic policy was unlikely to be seriously threatened.[53] Had industrial imports continued to flood in after 1903 at the rate of the previous ten years, the anti-free-trade forces might have gained more momentum; but Chamberlain had the ill-luck to begin his attack just as exports recovered and began to grow at a rate higher than any time since the early 1870s.[54]

After the 1906 election, the Tariff Reformers briefly dominated the Conservative Party, controlling two-thirds of the remaining 157 MPs.[55] Nonetheless, in the longer term, the 1903–6 campaign failed to change the nature of the Conservative Party. This became clear from 1909 onwards when the Liberals, faced with rising expenditure, decided to introduce higher taxation. As Chancellor of the Exchequer, Lloyd George was keen not to alienate his own middle-class support and he was also made aware of the link between Britain's high levels of foreign investment, the buoyancy of foreign trade and the customs revenue which gave him the leeway both to pay for social reform and to build Dreadnoughts as the German naval threat grew.[56] He concentrated his attack mainly on unearned income, especially land, provoking the great budgetary crisis of 1909 and the constitutional crisis of

1909–11. The Conservatives failed to head off the Liberal attack, which reduced the power of the House of Lords, losing both elections in 1910. But they made a strong recovery from the débâcle of 1906, rallying their southern vote in defence of the status quo rather than winning more of the northern vote, as the Tariff Reformers had hoped. After 1910, the cry of industrial regeneration and protection was almost drowned in the noises emanating from opponents of Irish Home Rule, from discontented aristocrats and gentry (who, like the City and other financial interests, feared Liberal tax policies), and from the rising anti-plutocratic and militaristic radical right – many of them forces which Chamberlain would have liked to eject from the party or subject to the will of industry.[57]

The fact that, by 1910, most Conservatives, including those in the City, were advocating tariffs meant only that they recognised the need for new sources of revenue: it certainly did not mean either that they were converted to a strategy of industrial regeneration or that a cosmopolitan view of economic policy was seriously threatened. Imperial preference, Chamberlain's pet idea, fell from prominence. It was obvious to the Conservatives after 1910 that, if they were to win another election and safeguard the status quo from future Liberal attack, they had to gain a bigger share of the northern urban vote. They set out to do this in 1913 by abandoning imperial preference because the 'dear loaf' cry raised against them by the Liberals in 1906 and again in 1910 had been so successful.[58] In 1914, the two main parties still represented a solid wall of opposition to any fundamental changes in Britain's internationalist economic policy. It was a wall which the Tariff Reformers could neither scale nor demolish.

Cosmopolitanism and industrial decline

It would be difficult to argue that the protectionists represented the national interest more faithfully than did the advocates of economic orthodoxy; but, as the Tariff Reformers foretold, sticking to orthodoxy had some grim consequences for Britain's position as an industrial and world power. This does not mean that the Tariff Reform solution to Britain's industrial plight would necessarily have worked. Many of the more intelligent free-trade critics were quick to point out that protection and preference might simply provide bolt-holes for uncompetitive firms, slowing down rather than increasing the pace of technical change.[59] This was a charge that the Fair Traders and Tariff Reformers found hard to repudiate at the time, and empire markets certainly provided a home for an uncomfortably large share of the exports of many of Britain's staple industries. It is true, too, that policies of protection and preference would have been assured of success only had they been combined with a more wide-ranging attack on economic policy and with radical measures of state intervention in industry. These were steps which most Tariff Reformers, as good capitalist businessmen, were unwilling to contemplate. Nonetheless, complaints by Tariff Reform and Fair Trade supporters that domestic industry had been starved of funds by excessive foreign investment were, as we have seen, not altogether misleading.

A protectionist strategy might also have raised the rate of profit in the more important capital-intensive industries such as steel and helped to bring about some shift in the relative proportions of domestic and foreign investment, and in the balance between services and heavy industry in Britain.[60] In addition, Chamberlain's campaign had the merit of highlighting the extent to which, in an economy dedicated to cosmopolitanism, the fate of arable agriculture could eventually be shared by important sectors of industry, posing grave problems for employment and for Britain's ability to sustain an empire and a world role. Perhaps only the defeat of so many of her industrial rivals in the two world wars saved Britain from the consequences of openness for so long: much of what the protectionists predicted has come to pass since 1945.

The beginnings of the industrial decline which worried the Tariff Reformers also posed a threat to Britain's financial empire, though in ways that were not really appreciated by contemporaries. It has recently been argued that the use of sterling as a reserve asset in place of gold after 1900 was a sign of growing weakness. Britain's overseas loans were not entirely matched by her current surplus on the balance of payments so that her 'basic balance' (current account surplus less spending on capital account) was in deficit. This deficit exceeded Britain's small reserves of gold. According to Lindert, the problem was solved by inducing other countries, especially those within the empire, to hold sterling assets rather than gold, a solution which cannot be explained 'without reference to the familiar story of Britain's loss of export markets and the steady advance of imports'.[61] The rise of sterling reserve assets after 1900 probably did cushion the country against the need for internal adjustment in crises, and the size of the reserves was partly a function of Britain's imperial power; but their existence was not in itself a sign of weakness. A comparison between the outflows of portfolio investment and the current account surplus in the 1890s and after 1900 suggests that the basic balance was stronger in the latter period, when sterling reserves were accumulating;[62] large sterling holdings may have arisen, not from any discernible weakness in the balance of payments, but from growing confidence in sterling as London refined its techniques of international monetary management and became increasingly accepted as a repository for other nations' spare international assets.

If sterling was under threat by 1914, the threat certainly had an industrial origin but it was of a more obscure and complex kind than Lindert considers. In the 1870s, Britain's balance of trade deficits were fairly evenly spread between developed and underdeveloped countries alike, and her account with the countries of recent settlement (including the white colonies) was more or less in balance (Table 7.1). Since Britain had a considerable surplus on invisibles with nearly all her trading partners, she had no acute settlement problems with any country or group of countries. After 1870, her balance of trade deficit with industrial Europe and the United States grew very rapidly. Imports of food and manufactures from these countries leapt up while her own exports faltered because of uncompetitiveness and protectionism. Britain paid off these huge deficits with her industrial competitors partly through her invisibles and partly via a complex system of multilateral settlements. Industrial

TABLE 7.1 British balance of trade surpluses (+) and deficits (–): by region, 1871–1913 (£m.)

	1871–5	*1896–1900*	*1913*
Industrial and developed countries	–32	–156	–157
Newly settled countries	–3	–18	–29
Underdeveloped countries	–28	+13	+52
World total	–63	–161	–134
British white colonies	0	–18	–12
Rest of empire	–11	+11	+29
British empire	–11	–7	+17

Sources: B.R. Mitchell and P. Deane, *Abstract of British Historical Statistics* (Cambridge, 1962); and *Statistical Abstracts of the United Kingdom* (HMSO).

Note: South Africa is included in British white colonies and newly settled countries.

Europe and the United States had deficits with the underdeveloped and newly settled worlds. Since Britain had surpluses there, she could pay off her debts to her industrial rivals by settling their debts with her creditors in the underdeveloped world. Towards 1914, many of Britain's surpluses with countries in the newly settled world began to diminish as their exports of primary produce to Britain swelled and as her exports grew less competitive in their markets. Britain's ability to meet her deficit with Europe and the United States thus came to depend more and more upon the invisible surplus as a whole and on her ability to export manufactured commodities, mainly textiles, to a limited range of underdeveloped countries many of which, like India, were within the empire (Table 7.1). Insofar as Britain's traditional exports were growing slowly in world trade and competition was increasing, the multilateral settlement pattern was under threat. Had it broken down, confidence in the whole sterling-based system could have been undermined.[63] As Chamberlain had claimed, the fate of the City and of British industry were closely connected, but in ways which neither he nor most of his contemporaries understood.

APPENDIX TWO

Manufacturing interests in parliament, 1868–1910

Some indication of the impact of the Tariff Reform campaign on industrial opinion can be gathered from data on the political affiliations of MPs with a background in manufacturing. In Table 7.2, numbers above 1.0 indicate that the Liberal share of the manufacturing interests concerned was greater than the Liberal share of the total number of Liberal and Conservative MPs. Numbers below 1.0 show that the Conservative share of the interest was greater than the Conservative share of the total number of Liberal and Conservative MPs.

The table indicates that, over the whole period, manufacturing interests in Parliament were shifting steadily away from the overwhelming adherence to Liberalism evident in the 1860s. However, the most decisive movement towards Conservatism occurred among businessmen connected with heavy industry, including metal manufacture and engineering. The Tariff Reform movement appears to have accentuated this drift. In contrast, Chamberlain's campaign appears to have reversed the

TABLE 7.2 Liberal MPs associative index: manufacturing interests, 1868–1910

	1868	*1880*	*1892*	*1900*	*1906*	*1910★*
Heavy industry	3.96	2.23	2.04	1.75	0.96	0.87
Textiles	5.40	1.72	2.89	2.33	4.78	5.04
Other manufacturing	4.66	5.56	1.90	2.01	1.22	1.27
All manufacturing	3.19	2.10	1.97	1.69	1.29	1.22

Sources: Harold Perkin, *The Structured Crowd: Essays in English Social History* (Brighton, 1981); J.A. Thomas, *The House of Commons, 1832–1901: A Study of its Economic and Financial Character* (Cardiff, 1939); idem, *The House of Commons, 1906–1911: An Analysis of its Economic and Social Character* (Cardiff, 1958).

★ The election of January 1910 only.

decline in allegiance to the Liberals among those MPs with an interest in textiles, as it also did among those MPs with a background in merchanting. In both these cases, the threat to free trade reinforced a commitment to liberalism.

Notes

1 C.J. Bartlett, ed. *Britain Pre-eminent: Studies in British World Influence in the Nineteenth Century* (1969), p. 173; Gerald S. Graham, *Tides of Empire: Discursions on the Expansion of Britain Overseas* (1972), p. 82. A survey of British naval history, placing it within the context of a changing economy, is Paul Kennedy, *The Rise and Fall of British Naval Mastery* (1976). See also Bernard Semmel, *Liberalism and Naval Strategy: Ideology, Interest and Sea Power during the Pax Britannica* (Boston, Mass., 1986).

2 Olive Anderson, *A Liberal State at War: English Politics and Economics During the Crimean War* (1967), Chs. 6–8.

3 Clive Trebilcock, 'War and the Failure of Industrial Mobilization, 1899–1914', in J.M. Winter, ed. *War and Economic Development: Essays in Memory of David Joslin* (Cambridge, 1975), pp. 141, 143. See also the important new study by Aaron L. Friedberg, *The Weary Titan: Britain and the Experience of Relative Decline, 1895–1905* (Princeton, NJ, 1988), Ch. 3.

4 Anderson, *A Liberal State at War,* Chs. 3 and 4; G.R. Searle, *The Quest for National Efficiency, 1899–1914: A Study in British Politics and National Thought* (Oxford, 1971).

5 There is a wide literature on these aspects of the political economy of Liberalism in Edwardian England. Particularly useful in this context are H.V. Emy, 'The Impact of Financial Policy on English Party Politics Before 1914', *Hist. Jour.,* XV (1972); Bentley B. Gilbert, 'David Lloyd George: Land, the Budget and Social Reform', *Am. Hist. Rev.,* LXXXI (1976); idem, 'The Reform of British Landowning and the Budget of 1914', *Hist. Jour.,* XXI (1978); B.K. Murray, *The People's Budget, 1909–1910: Lloyd George and Liberal Politics* (Oxford, 1980); Avner Offer, *Property and Politics, 1870–1914: Landownership, Law, Ideology and Urban Development in England* (Cambridge, 1981); and idem, 'Empire and Social Reform: British Overseas Investment and Domestic Politics, 1908–1914', *Hist. Jour.,* XXVI (1983).

6 See Emy, 'The Impact of Financial Policy on English Party Politics'.

7 This is one of the major themes of S.R. Smith, 'British Nationalism, Imperialism and the City of London, 1880–1900' (unpublished Ph.D., Univ. of London, 1985), pp. 169–97, 314–56. See also Peter Stansky, *Ambitions and Strategies: The Struggle for Leadership of the Liberal Party in the 1890s* (Oxford, 1964), pp. 24, 34. The fact that Gladstone resigned as Prime Minister over the question of the naval estimates in 1894 is symbolic of the transformation of the economic basis of politics and of the City's decisive shift away from Liberalism.

8 On City pragmatism in the matter of tariffs see below, pp. 217–18.

9 For Cobden's views see Peter Cain, 'Capitalism, War and Internationalism in the Thought of Richard Cobden', *British Journal of International Studies,* V (1979); and Oliver McDonagh, 'The Anti-Imperialism of Free Trade', *Econ. Hist. Rev.,* 2nd ser. XIV (1961–2).

10 W.E. Gladstone, 'England's Mission' *The Nineteenth Century,* IV (1878).

11 C.C. Eldridge, *England's Mission: The Imperial Idea in the Age of Gladstone and Disraeli, 1868–80* (1973), Ch. 4.

12 Ibid. Ch. 5. See also C.A. Bodelsen, *Studies in Mid-Victorian Imperialism* (1960), Pts. II and III.

13 Eldridge, *England's Mission,* p. 126.

14 J.A. Froude, 'England and her Colonies', and 'The Colonies Once More', in *Short Studies on Great Subjects* (1871).

15 On the changing ideological background see John Roach, 'Liberalism and the Victorian Intelligentsia', *Cambridge Historical Journal,* XIII (1957); and, for a contemporary example, E. Dicey, 'Our Route to India', *The Nineteenth Century,* I (1877).

16 On Disraeli's supposed cynicism about the white Empire see Robert Blake, *Disraeli* (1966), pp. 455, 523–4. A 'social imperialist' streak in Disraelian imperialism has been detected by Freda Harcourt, 'Disraeli's Imperialism, 1866–68: a Question of Timing', *Hist. Jour.*, 23 (1980), and to a lesser extent by P.J. Durrans, 'A Two-Edged Sword: the Liberal Attack on Disraelian Imperialism', *Jour. Imp. and Comm. Hist.*, X (1982), esp. pp. 267, 277–9. Harcourt's position is similar to that taken up by Joseph Schumpeter in Ch. 2 of his famous *Imperialism* (1951), which sees imperialism as 'the catch phrase of domestic politics'. For a criticism of Harcourt's analysis of Disraeli see Nini Rodgers, 'The Abyssinian Expedition of 1867–8: Disraeli's Imperialism or John Murray's War?', *Hist. Jour.*, 27 (1984).

17 Stanley R. Stembridge, 'Disraeli and the Millstones', *Journal of British Studies,* 5 (1965).

18 T.E. Kebbel, ed. *Selected Speeches of the late Rt. Hon. The Earl of Beaconsfield* (1882), Vol. II, pp. 523–35.

19 H.G.C. Matthew, ed. *The Gladstone Diaries,* Vols. X and XI, (Oxford, 1990), pp. lxxi–lxxii. See also below, pp. 362–9.

20 A.N. Porter, 'Lord Salisbury, Foreign Policy and Domestic Finance, 1860–1900', in Lord Blake and Hugh Cecil, eds. *Salisbury: The Man and his Policies* (1987).

21 John France, 'Salisbury and the Unionist Alliance', and F.M.L. Thompson, 'Private Property and Public Policy', in Blake and Cecil, *Salisbury: The Man and his Policies.*

22 On the imperial unity movement as a whole see J.E. Tyler, *The Struggle for Imperial Unity, 1868–95* (1938); Nicholas Mansergh, *The Commonwealth Experience,* Vol. 1, (2nd edn 1981); W.D. McIntyre, *The Commonwealth of Nations: Origin and Impact, 1869–1971* (Oxford, 1977); and W.K. Hancock, *Survey of British Commonwealth Affairs,* Vol. I (Oxford, 1937), Ch. 1.

23 J. Gastan, 'The Free Trade Diplomacy Debate and the Victorian European Common Market Initiative', *Canadian Journal of History,* XXII (1987).

24 L. Trainor, 'The British Government and Imperial Economic Unity, 1890–5', *Hist. Jour.*, XIII (1970).

25 *Minority Report of the Royal Commission on Depression in Trade and Industry,* PP 1886, C 4893, para 59. See also Sidney Pollard, *Britain's Prime and Britain's Decline: The British Empire, 1870–1914* (1989), p. 236.

26 The most useful studies of the Fair Trade movement are: Tyler, *The Struggle for Imperial Unity,* which places Fair Trade in the context of the wider movement for imperial unity at the time; J.H. Zebel, 'Fair Trade: an English Reaction to the Breakdown of the Cobden Treaty System', *Journal of Modern History,* XII (1940); and Benjamin H. Brown, *The Tariff Reform Movement in Great Britain, 1881–95* (1943). There is an excellent regional study by Roger J. Ward, 'The Tariff Reform Movement in Birmingham, 1877–1906', (Unpublished MA thesis, London University, 1971).

27 For a brief discussion of the Tariff Reform case see Peter Cain, 'Political Economy in Edwardian England: The Tariff Reform Controversy', in Alan O'Day, ed. *The Edwardian Age: Conflict and Stability, 1900–1914* (1979), pp. 41–4. A wider and still very readable discussion of the politics and economics of Tariff Reform is Bernard Semmel, *Imperialism and Social Reform: English Social Imperialism, 1895–1914* (1960). The most recent survey is by Friedberg, *The Weary Titan,* Ch. 2. Imports of steel in 1913 were equivalent to 45 per cent of exports by value. P.L. Payne, 'Iron and Steel Manufacturers', in D.H. Aldcroft, ed. *British Industry and Foreign Competition, 1870–1914* (1968), p. 75.

28 Joseph Chamberlain, *Speeches* (ed. C.W. Boyd, 1914), Vol. II, pp. 267–8. For another speech in a similar vein, Jim Tomlinson, *Problems of British Economic Policy, 1870–1945* (1981), p. 54; for similar sentiments see W.J. Ashley, *The Tariff Problem* (1903), pp. 112–13. Ashley was by no means the only intellectual interested in the growth of services and concerned with the problems which we now call 'deindustrialisation'. For other contributions which contain material germane to this theme see H.J. Mackinder, 'The Great Trade Routes', *Journal of the Institute of Bankers,* XXI (1900), and W.S. Hewins, *Apologia of An Imperialist: Forty Years of Empire Policy,* I (1929), pp. 56ff.

29 *Minority Report of the Royal Commission on Depression in Trade and Industry,* Paras 129, 137.

30 Julian Amery, *Life of Joseph Chamberlain,* Vol. VI (1968), p. 540; Chamberlain, *Speeches,* Vol. II, pp. 231–2.

31 S.B. Saul, 'The Economic Significance of "Constructive Imperialism"', *Jour. Econ. Hist.,* XVII (1959); R.M. Kesner, *Economic Control and Colonial Development: Crown Colony Financial Management in the Age of Joseph Chamberlain* (Westport, Conn., 1981); Robert V. Kubicek, *The Administration of Imperialism: Joseph Chamberlain at the Colonial Office* (Durham, NC, 1969).

32 For the background of Chamberlain's 'conversion' to a preferential policy see Amery, *Life of Joseph Chamberlain,* Vol. V (1951), and Vol. VI (1968); Peter Fraser, *Joseph Chamberlain* (1966), esp. Chs. 10–12; Elie Halévy, *History of The English People in the Nineteenth Century,* Vol. V (1961 edn), pp. 285–331; J.H. Zebel, 'Joseph Chamberlain and the Genesis of the Tariff Reform Campaign', *Jour. Brit. Stud.,* VII (1967); W.K. Hancock, *Survey of British Commonwealth Affairs,* Vol. II, Pt. I (Oxford, 1940), pp. 72ff; and, more recently, Richard Jay, *Joseph Chamberlain: A Political Study* (Oxford, 1981), Chs. 8 and 9.

33 A.J. Marrison, 'The Development of a Tariff Reform Policy during Joseph Chamberlain's First Campaign, May 1903 – February 1904', in B.M. Ratcliffe, ed. *Trade and Transport: Essays in Economic History in Honour of T.S. Willan* (Manchester, 1977). For Chamberlain's views see Amery, *Life of Joseph Chamberlain,* V, pp. 409–10, 415; VI, p. 473. For his shifting views by 1905 see ibid. VI, p. 725.

34 Ward, 'The Tariff Reform Movement in Birmingham', pp. 296–7; Tyler, *The Struggle for Imperial Unity,* Ch. 6.

35 E.H.H. Green, 'Radical Conservatism: the Electoral Genesis of Tariff Reform', *Hist. Jour.,* XXVIII (1985); Amery, *Life of Joseph Chamberlain,* V, p. 311.

36 This wider aspect of the Tariff Reform campaign has not been considered in any depth. The most thorough political account of the movement, Alan Sykes, *Tariff Reform in British Politics, 1903–13* (Oxford, 1979) deals mainly with Westminster infighting, and Semmel's *Imperialism and Social Reform,* despite its many virtues, does not really explore this theme either. There are some suggestive hints in Peter Fraser, 'Unionism and Tariff Reform: the Crisis of 1906', *Hist. Jour.,* V (1962), and in the interesting review of Sykes's book by Dilwyn Porter, 'Fiscalitis: a Suitable Case for Treatment', *Moirae,* 6 (1981). See also Pollard, *Britain's Prime and Britain's Decline,* pp. 241–2.

37 This comes out most clearly in a particular case study, that by R.E. Dumett, 'Joseph Chamberlain, Imperial Finance and Railway Policy in British West Africa in the Late Nineteenth Century', *Eng. Hist. Rev.,* XC (1975).

38 Apart from the sources mentioned already, there is a wide literature upon the political development of the Tariff Reform campaign including: Richard A. Rempel, *Unionists Divided: Arthur Balfour, Joseph Chamberlain and the Unionist Free Traders* (Newton Abbot, 1972); A.K. Russell, *Liberal Landslide: The General Election of 1906* (Newton Abbot, 1973), pp. 65–73, 80, 83–91, 172f; K.D. Brown, 'The Trade Union Tariff Reform Association', *Jour. Brit. Stud.,* XI (1970); Neal B. Blewett, *The Peers, The Parties and the People: The General Elections of 1910* (1972); Richard J. Scally, *The Origins of the Lloyd George Coalition: The Politics of Social Imperialism, 1900–18* (Princeton, NJ, 1975).

39 Robert Cecil, quoted in Dennis Judd, *Balfour and the Empire: A Study in Imperial Evolution, 1874–1932* (1968), p. 93.

40 The sentiments of Campbell-Bannerman in a letter to Bryce, quoted in Amery, *Life of Joseph Chamberlain,* VI, p. 541.

41 For the split in industry see the interesting article by A.J. Marrison, 'Businessmen, Industries and Tariff Reform in Britain, 1903–30', *Bus. Hist.,* 25 (1983). For the reaction of the workers see Brown, 'The Trade Union Tariff Reform Association'.

42 See the fascinating debate in the House of Lords in *Parliamentary Debates* (Lords), Vol. IV, 1909, Cols. 745–904, 22 Nov., and Cols. 947–1328, 24 Nov.

43 W.S. Churchill, *The People's Rights* (1909, 1970), pp. 104ff.

44 Ibid. p. 110.

45 Lord Crewe's words. See *Parl. Deb.* (Lords), IV (1909), c. 1327.

46 Amery, *Life of Chamberlain,* VI, p. 535.

47 Ibid. p. 536. For Chamberlain's London associations and his own links with the City see Ronald Quinault, 'Joseph Chamberlain: a Reassessment', in T.R. Gourvish and Alan O'Day, eds. *Later Victorian Britain* (1988).

48 Smith, 'British Nationalism, Imperialism and the City of London, 1880–1900', pp. 209ff.

49 See, for example, F. Huth Jackson, 'The "Draft on London" and Tariff Reform', *Econ. Jour.*, XV (1904).

50 R.H. Inglis Palgrave, 'The Economic Condition of the Country', *National Review*, 42 (1903–4); idem, 'The Industrial Condition of the Country', ibid. 45 (1905). For some shrewd general comments on the City's attitude to the tariff campaign see Youssef Cassis, *La City de Londres, 1870–1914* (Paris, 1987), pp. 181–3, and idem, *Les Banquiers de la City à l'époque edouardienne, 1890–1914* (Geneva, 1984), pp. 357–64.

51 For Balfour's views, which were based on the notion that tariffs were acceptable as retaliatory devices, see his *Economic Notes on Insular Free Trade* (1903). There are extracts from this in W.H.B. Court, *British Economic History, 1870–1914: Commentary and Documents* (Cambridge, 1965), pp. 452–9.

52 For a good example of a Tariff Reform businessman and his background, see R.P.T. Davenport-Hines, *Dudley Docker: The Life and Times of a Trade Warrior* (Cambridge, 1985), Chs. 3 and 4. For other examples of aggrieved manufacturers see Scott Newton and Dilwyn Porter, *Modernization Frustrated: The Politics of Industrial Decline in Britain since 1900* (1988), pp. 11–12, 37, and D. Porter, 'The Unionist Tariff Reformers, 1903–14' (Unpublished Ph.D. thesis, Manchester University, 1976), pp. 19–36, 206–8.

53 There were some highly tentative negotiations involving Lloyd George and the successors of Chamberlain, such as Milner, in 1910 about the possibilities of combining the 'progressive' sections of both parties to form a new social imperialist political force in Britain. Had it succeeded, such a combination could well have brought industrialists nearer to the forefront of British politics; but the chances of success, given the bitterness of the party disputes of the time, were always extremely small. See Scally, *Origins of the Lloyd George Coaltion*, especially the introduction and pp. 375–86. Nonetheless, under the hammer of Lloyd George's 'socialism', many traditional Liberal businessmen were beginning to wonder by 1913 whether modest protection from the Conservative Party was not better than free trade and increased direct taxation under the Liberals. See P.F. Clarke, 'The End of Laissez-Faire and the Politics of Cotton', *Hist. Jour.*, XV (1972).

54 This was recognised by contemporaries. See Amery, *Life of Joseph Chamberlain*, V, p. 320.

55 Ibid. Vol. VI, p. 789.

56 On this important theme see Offer, 'Empire and Social Reform: British Overseas Investment and Domestic Politics, 1908–1914'.

57 Sykes, *Tariff Reform in British Politics, 1903–13*, Ch. 13; G.R. Searle, 'Critics of Edwardian Society: the Case of the Radical Right', in O'Day, *Edwardian England*.

58 Semmel, *Imperialism and Social Reform*, pp. 124–7.

59 For a summary of the argument on the free trade side see Cain, 'Political Economy in Edwardian England: the Tariff Reform Controversy', pp. 44–5.

60 Michael Edelstein, *Overseas Investment in the Age of High Imperialism: The United Kingdom, 1850–1914* (1982), p. 222.

61 P.H. Lindert, *Key Currencies and Gold, 1900–1913* (Princeton Studies in International Finance, No. 24, 1969), p. 75.

62

	Money Calls (£m. annual av.)	*Current Account Surplus (annual av.)*	*2 as % 1*
1891–1900	60.7	45.5	82.2
1901–1913	134.5	124.4	92.5

The figures for money calls are from M. Simon, 'The Pattern of New British Portfolio Investment, 1865–1914', in J.H. Adler, ed. *Capital Movements and Economic Development*

(1967), Table II. The current account surplus is from C.H. Feinstein, *Statistical Tables of National Income Expenditure and Output in the UK, 1855–1865* (Cambridge, 1973). Lindert himself recognises the force of this argument to some extent in *Key Currencies and Gold*, p. 74.

63 For the classic account of this multilateral mechanism see S.B. Saul, *Studies in British Overseas Trade, 1870–1914* (1960), Chs. 3 and 4. There is also a concise summary of the major themes in François Crouzet, 'Trade and Empire: the British Experience from the Establishment of Free Trade until the First World War', in B.M. Ratcliffe, ed. *Great Britain and her World, 1750–1914: Essays in Honour of W.O. Henderson* (Manchester, 1975).

PART THREE

The wider world, 1815–1914

8

'AN EXTENSION OF THE OLD SOCIETY'

Britain and the colonies of settlement, 1850–1914[1]

One of the outstanding features of the economic history of the second half of the nineteenth century was the enormous increase in international trade and international specialisation which took place principally under Britain's leadership. The rapid growth of world trade was part of a much wider process of change in the international economy involving a great movement of factors of production – capital and labour – across the globe. In Europe, the decline of agriculture and the shift to industry and services in the towns led to a vast displacement of peoples both within the continent and overseas; the latter movement brought the 'new world' of America, Australasia and southern Africa firmly into the capitalist net, settling them with emigrants from Europe and shaping them into centres of primary produce for export to the industrialising world.

The international economy and the New World

If we look at this complex extension of capitalism from Britain's angle, its main elements can easily be identified. Britain was a country with a shortage of land and, therefore, primary produce had a high price. She also had an abundance of labour, both skilled and unskilled, and of capital too by world standards; but she faced the Ricardian-Malthusian nightmare that, in the long run, her development might be choked off by a shortage of agricultural land. On the other hand, the newly colonised areas had such an abundance of land that it was often practically a free good, but they lacked the labour and capital needed to bring their natural resources into full production. Imports of primary produce by Britain under free trade were the equivalent of extending her own land area; in the newly settled country, imports of manufactured commodities and of services embodied the capital and labour in short supply domestically. But without a massive shift of capital and labour from Britain (and other parts of Europe) to these new lands, the process of trade interaction could not have taken place so rapidly; and a network of transport and utilities had to be built in these areas before they were equipped to play their part.[2] It was the extension of railway and shipping networks, embodying many technological improvements over half a century, which brought the price of transport tumbling down and made it possible, by the 1890s, for wheat to be brought thousands of miles from the newly settled frontier to Britain and sold at a price which was half that ruling in the British market 20 years earlier.

The place occupied by the newly settled countries in this global upheaval in economic relations, and their importance to Britain, must not be overstated. The 35 million people who left Europe for the new world after 1870 still represented only about two-fifths of its total population increase.[3] Vast quantities of the capital exported from European countries found other European homes, as was the case particularly with French loans which poured into Eastern Europe and Russia.[4] Besides this, the factor movements out of Europe were, on a global scale, only a part of a wider movement which also distributed millions of Indians, Chinese and other non-Europeans throughout Asia.[5] New sources of primary products in the world economy were also manifold, including a range of commodities from the tropics and significant contributions from Europe. Britain herself became the world's most important exporter of coal in the second half of the century and she took in large supplies of Russian wheat, German sugar beet, Scandinavian iron and timber and Danish dairy produce – to mention only a few of the most prominent European items. Denmark's development in this context is particularly interesting in that, as a small country, she was crucially dependent for growth on British demand for her agro-industrial products. Britain took 38 per cent of Denmark's exports in 1873 and three-fifths at the end of the century and, by 1913, Denmark was Britain's biggest food supplier after the United States and Argentina. She was also part of the sterling system, and British investors were important in funding Denmark's railways – all of which suggests that Denmark was just as much within the orbit of Britain's overseas economic influence as were the smaller, newly settled countries.[6]

Britain provided about two-fifths of the world's total of exported capital between 1870 and 1914,[7] and most of that went to the new lands, as did the bulk of her migrants. Some areas – the white colonies of Australia, New Zealand, Canada and South Africa as well as the United States – took both migrants and capital from Britain; but Britain's capital exports to Argentina and Brazil went along with migrants from Southern Europe, and, in the case of Chile, substantial investment by Britain and other European nations induced hardly any migrant flow at all.

In the case of the largest newly settled country, the United States, there was no question of her economic relationship with Great Britain involving any form of economic subordination. In the late nineteenth century the United States already had a population equivalent to that of the great European powers and a large and rapidly growing industrial sector based on the home market. The capital which she borrowed from Britain provided her with only a small portion of her investment needs. Britain's position *vis-à-vis* the United States is best illustrated by her tactical retreat over Canada, which we shall examine later in this chapter, and by her inability to give any substantial aid to the free-trade, cotton-growing South in the American Civil War. In the smaller new countries, however, the impact of Britain, via factor movements and trade, was often a decisive element in their development. Some idea of this can be gauged from the fact that the four principal countries with which we deal – Australia, New Zealand, Canada and Argentina – together accounted for about 17 per cent of both Britain's exports and imports in 1913, while their trade dependence on Britain was altogether greater.

All the small, newly-settled countries had high ratios of trade to national income, and this is a clear indication of the importance of the international economy in their development – an importance emphasised from the time of Gibbon Wakefield to the so-called 'staple' theorists of modern times.[8] Australia's development, for example, has recently been described in terms of a succession of staple exports – from whaling in the early nineteenth century, wool after 1820, gold at mid-century and dairy produce in the 20 years before World War I – which created internal demand linkages and attracted foreign capital and migrants.[9] Export-led growth does not, of course, tell the whole story of the development of new countries. It gives little clue, for example, to the reasons for economic progress in the French Canadian province of Quebec, which was much less affected by Canadian links with the international economy than were other provinces;[10] generally speaking, too heavy a concentration on external stimuli can obscure important domestic sources of growth and change. An emphasis on the crucial role of exports may also invert the process of economic development. In Canada, during the wheat boom of 1900–14, it would be hard to argue that grain exports were the key to growth. Britain was by far the largest purchaser of wheat internationally, but her imports accounted for only 10 per cent of the total production of all the wheat-exporting countries in the late 1880s and 5 per cent in 1909–13. Britain's demand for Canadian wheat could not have added more than 2 per cent to Canada's per capita income at the time, and the boom, like other phases of rapid development in new countries, must be explained in terms of its domestic origins.[11]

Nevertheless, if export to Britain was not the immediate cause of growth, Britain still had a decisive part to play. Rapid internal growth in new countries soon ran up against ceilings imposed by capital and labour shortages and an inability to meet domestic requirements without a soaring import bill. Development had to be sustained by immigration and financed by borrowing which, on a per capita basis, was often massive by European standards. The capital inflow, most of it from London sources, was crucial in sustaining booms; but it had to be paid for eventually by the creation of export income. In the long term, therefore, the pace and extent of economic growth in new countries depended upon immigration, the ability to borrow extensively in Europe and success in finding exports to finance the loans.[12] In the Canadian case, much of what she borrowed from Britain between 1900 and 1914 was paid for by exporting wheat and other commodities to Britain during World War I and in the 1920s.

Whether growth was export-led or whether it occurred as a result of the roundabout process described above, rapid change in many small, newly settled countries could be achieved only at the cost of dependence on British capital and, ultimately, conformity to the rules of the economic game as set in London. This was as true of the emergent Dominions as it was of Argentina or Chile,[13] despite the fact that the former were making steady progress towards political independence from Britain from the 1840s. What we must first show is that the constitutional freedom of the emerging white Dominions was gained at the same time as their economic development bound them more closely to the financial system based on London and that, in this sense, the white colonies exchanged a position of political dependence for a place in a wider and looser framework of 'free-trade imperialism' – even if the latter was only apparent clearly in times of economic crisis.

Political liberty and financial dependence

In recent years there has been a considerable revision of historical opinion concerning British attitudes to colonies of new settlement in the mid-nineteenth century. Most of the participants in the debate have been political historians, and the economic dimension of Anglo-colonial relationships after 1850 has been somewhat neglected. The trade dependence of many white colonies has been noted, of course, but the implications of this dependence within the context of an evolving system of 'responsible government' have not been seriously considered in Britain for many years. Our intention here is to spell out some of the consequences of colonial dependence on capital supply from Britain from mid-century, first in general terms, and then by looking briefly at two specific issues: the economic evolution of Australasia and the creation of a Canadian state independent of the United States.

The assumption that there was a simple connection between the form taken by Anglo-colonial economic relations at any one time and the kind of governmental authority exercised by Britain in the settlement colonies has a long history. Adam Smith's opinion was that political control of the colonies from London was essential to force the mercantilist system upon them. 'The maintenance of this monopoly', he wrote, 'has hitherto been the principal, or more properly perhaps, the sole end and purpose of the dominion which Great Britain assumes over her colonies'.[14] Similarly, until quite recently it was generally believed that the abandonment of the preferential system between 1846 and 1860 led logically to the ending of Britain's interest in controlling colonial destinies.[15] It has now become apparent, however, as a result of extensive research undertaken on the background to the granting of responsible government, that those who expressed strong anti-imperial sentiment in mid-century were mainly vociferous, but unrepresentative, free-trade radicals. Indeed, in 1953 Gallagher and Robinson went so far as to claim that the granting of political liberty represented merely a transition from formal to informal methods of controlling settlement colonies and that:

> responsible government, far from being a separatist device, was simply a change from direct to indirect methods of maintaining British interests. By slackening the formal political bond at the appropriate time, it was

> possible to rely on economic dependence and mutual good feeling to keep the colonies bound to Britain while still using them as agents for further British expansion.[16]

Gallagher and Robinson believed, therefore, that free trade and responsible government were simply the economic and the political aspects of the same policy, though one which marked a decisive shift, not from imperialism to colonial freedom, as their predecessors had believed, but from one form of imperialism to another.

There is no doubt that some contemporary statesmen dearly felt that responsible government was compatible with maintaining, even strengthening, the colonial tie. Earl Grey, for example, did not see responsible government as a step on the road to imperial fragmentation. He gloried in 'the global union which linked the mother country with her children in the colonies', and took it for granted that Britain would continue to exercise authority within the empire of settlement even after political liberty had been granted, partly to ensure that free trade would be maintained.[17] But Grey's clarity of vision was unusual. Most of the statesmen and officials who took the decisions were more hesitant and often held a bewildering variety of opinions on colonial subjects.[18] A good many took refuge in the image of Britain as the 'mother country' whose 'children' would eventually grow up, leaving open the question of how rapid the process of growth might be and how colonies which had achieved adult status might relate to their parent.[19] Very few observers had a clear idea of the future of Anglo-colonial relations: in retrospect, the granting of responsible government, like political reform at home, was something of a leap into the unknown.

Under the old system of colonial administration, power rested with the governor and with councils which, although partly elected, were mainly composed of officials supported by patronage and by the wealthiest elements in the local colonial society who, whether representing land or commerce, were dependent upon the British connection. This elite was, in every sense, 'an extension of the old society' and only too well aware of the importance of imperial power and imperial favour.[20] As the colonies grew in size and complexity so did the desire for greater freedom from direct British control. This was enhanced, after 1815, by the decline of British patronage as Parliament became more critical of expenditure on colonies: the plea for greater local autonomy grew commensurately with rising levels of local taxation. The great catalyst for change here was the Canadian rebellion of 1837–8, which inspired the famous Durham Report of 1840. However, Durham proposed only a very limited form of local control: in his plan, Britain would have retained the final say not only in foreign affairs but also in the disposal of colonial lands and in tariff policy, both of which local politicians were eager to control.[21] Had Durham's views prevailed, the colonies could have expected little more than what Wakefield termed 'municipal self-government',[22] and tension between London and the periphery would have grown more acute.

In practice, from the late 1840s the British bowed to local pressures and, in line with observed constitutional changes taking place in Britain herself, accepted the idea that, in mature colonies, governors should in future form ministries from the majority elements in elected legislatures. In doing so, they moved faster and further than traditional colonial elites wished to travel. In Australia in the early 1850s, for example, a concerted effort was made by the old, wool-rich rural elite – the 'squattocracy' – to fashion a constitution which would allow an hereditary upper chamber, modelled on the House of Lords, to check the democratic excesses of the more popular lower house. This failed, less because of local opposition which, in the turmoil of the gold rush era, hardly had time to cohere, than because the British determined on a swift move to the kind of institutional arrangements already emerging in Canada. These allowed for a conservative second chamber but of a more moderate variety than envisaged by vested economic interests in the colonies themselves.[23] As in the Canadian provinces, the movement to self-government could be achieved only at the cost of reducing both the power of the traditional sources of British influence in the colonies, which adhered to the land, to government and to administration, and the economic activities which had flourished under the protectionist system.

Gallagher and Robinson's belief that the granting of political liberties made no essential difference to Britain's imperial power in the colonies needs careful qualification. Responsible government did mean a devolution of power to the periphery, 'comparable in its way with the decolonization of Africa a century later'.[24] The tacit acceptance, around this time, of the colonists' right to dispose of their land even though, in legal terms, it was often under the authority of the British crown, is evidence enough of this. Ward argues, additionally, that the British 'did not expect the liberties granted with full responsible government to be offset by colonies of settlement becoming increasingly dependent on the mother country for money, markets or men'.[25] This is undoubtedly correct; but there is a danger that emphasising it may obscure how economically dependent the white colonies were and how much their dependence was already taken for granted in Britain. Britain's economic superiority and leadership were simply assumed, and expected to endure, even by radicals.[26]

Metropolitan assumptions about colonial economies certainly helped to shape perceptions of when and where to grant political liberty. One important point which has emerged from the modern debate, for example, is that the coming of colonial self-government followed the recognition, by Britain, that many of the white colonial societies were reaching levels of maturity that were incompatible with direct rule. Burroughs, writing of the Canadian colonies, claims that Grey, then Colonial Secretary, had realised by 1846 that 'circumstances now imperatively demanded the acceptance of self-government in communities with adequate population, wealth, social stability and political experience'.[27] Similarly, Ward argues in more general terms that responsible government came to be seen 'as an evolutionary process of constitutional change, in which Britain shared the advanced conventions of her own political life with colonies that became substantial British communities overseas'.[28] Statesmen who had already learned that domestic political adjustments, like the 1832 Reform Act, were necessary to accommodate widespread social and economic change were also capable of appreciating the need for similar moves in mature colonies of settlement and of recognising that withholding political freedoms at this point would only have provoked resentment and unrest. But what 'maturity' meant to the British, among other things, was that some of the colonies in Canada and Australia had developed into well-ordered capitalist societies capable of functioning as satellite economies without direct intervention.

Responsible government certainly brought with it a remarkable degree of freedom, and quickly too. Within three years of achieving self-government the Australian states of New South Wales and Victoria had decided upon a democratic voting system, despite Britain's disapproval of a measure which could only reduce her direct influence; by 1859, the province of Canada had adopted protection, despite the hostile incredulity of statesmen in the metropolis, where free trade was assuming the status of natural law.[29] Nor did any British government seriously attempt to influence policy on colonial land sales, despite the fact that, legally speaking, colonial land was at the disposal of the crown.[30] Interference at this level would have been counter-productive as British statesmen, remembering the revolt of the 13 American colonies, were quick to recognise.

Britain retained considerable power over the white colonies, including the right to veto discriminatory tariffs and to supervise colonial legislation on immigration and shipping,[31] but her most important sphere of direct authority was international relations, a dimension of political life which the colonists were happy to ignore, partly out of ignorance and incapacity and partly because the implication of Britain's supremacy here was that she would pay the costs of imperial defence. Despite drastic pruning of expenditure by Gladstone's Liberal government in the early 1870s,[32] Britain's defence expenditure remained high by the standards of other industrial countries. Between 1860 and 1912 the British spent an annual average of £1.14p per capita on defence, a sum which amounted to 37 per cent of central government expenditure. By contrast, colonies which either already had responsible government or achieved it in this period, spent around 12p per head on defence, a mere 3 or 4 per cent of their annual budgets.[33]

Britain's assumption of the defence burden meant that the colonies could devote the bulk of their own savings to social and economic development.[34] High levels of domestic investment were pushed even higher by the colonies' ability to borrow in London cheaply. Empire investments, including those in the white colonies, were much sought after by British investors though, as we shall see, at different times one or other of the colonies might be out of favour with the London market. Capital could be borrowed cheaply by comparison with the rates of interest offered to even the most eligible foreign borrowers; and it was made cheaper still by various legislative enactments, especially the Colonial Stocks Act of 1900, which allowed trustees, who had hitherto been restricted in their purchase of investments on their clients' behalf to certain British and Indian stocks, to add some colonial securities to their portfolios.[35]

The British preference for empire stocks, especially those of the white empire, may have owed something to patriotism rather than to pure market forces. Returns on private capital placed in the empire, including private railway investments, were higher than returns on corresponding investments in Britain or in foreign countries before the mid-1880s, but performed less well over the succeeding 30 years.[36] Nonetheless, the somewhat fragmentary evidence which exists does indicate that returns on stocks issued by public authorities in the empire were better than on corresponding British securities.[37] Nearly three-fifths of the borrowings of colonies of responsible government between 1865 and 1914 were on public account,[38] and they provided an ideal vehicle for investors looking for safe outlets abroad. Default was unheard of in these British territories, whether directly controlled or not. This is one of the key reasons why the colonies could borrow cheaply: they offered almost complete safety at a rate of return higher than that on standard British investments, such as consols.[39]

With the British to protect them and to supply them with migrants and with capital, it is not surprising that the white colonies should have grown rapidly, in terms of both population and output, or that they should have achieved average living standards which were well in advance of those in the parent country in the late nineteenth century. At the same time, and inevitably, the nature of this development was such as to bring them into a dose economic and financial dependence upon Britain. In a very real sense, the colonies became part of the 'invisible' financial and commercial empire which had its centre in the City of London.[40]

Ward is right to maintain that politicians did not anticipate any strengthening of economic ties between metropole and frontier after responsible government was granted, but it is still the case that, although there was little awareness of it in higher political circles, the economic bonds between metropole and colonies were tightening just as the political ones were slackening. Habakkuk is one of the few British historians to have recognised this.[41] Free trade, he claimed, came about partly because the old, restrictive colonial system had failed to satisfy fully Britain's international needs as her economy expanded; but British possessions, including settlement colonies, did find a more important niche as markets and sources of supply in the cosmopolitan structure which arose after 1850. Major shifts in the economic relations between the imperial centre and the colonies of settlement were early examples of that great transformation of the world economy in which the industrialising countries became locked into a much more complex international division of labour with the agricultural periphery than hitherto. Growing links between Britain and the newly settled world, including the white colonies, were one of the most dynamic features of this development, which involved not only a greatly extended trade but also the export of British capital and labour.[42] Britain's ability to supply the colonies with development finance, either from home sources, or through London's position as a channel for European savings, was a crucial element in the chain of connection and often indispensable to colonial growth. With the capital came new forms of control, as Habakkuk recognised:

> Down to the 'fifties, and while the export of capital to the colonies was still unimportant, the colonies were economically dependent upon the United Kingdom, but their economic activity was not directly controlled by it. This

> applies in large measure even to India. But when in the 'fifties the colonies drew largely on British capital supply, they found they had neither the means nor the administrative capacity to redeem and carry on with ease the public works which they desired. England had to supply not merely the original capital but the permanent direction. The companies formed to build railways, found banks and cultivate tea had their headquarters in London and worked their properties from England. The Empire had become in a new sense an integral part of the British economic system.[43]

The white colonies could have chosen a different future for themselves, one which relied less on exports and less on imported capital and migrants. Had they done so, they would have enjoyed greater autonomy but growth would have been markedly slower. In practice, neither the 'staple' approach to rapid development, nor the need for British markets and factors of production which this development entailed, was ever seriously brought into question. Australasia and Canada were dominated by 'ideal prefabricated collaborators' who were concerned, above all else, 'to keep export markets open and capital flowing'.[44] Local politics often involved little more than faction fighting, based on regional differences or disputes over tariff policy between groups otherwise unquestioningly committed to the export economy: 'formal political life became a contest between those groups who accepted the logic of export-led development'.[45] Given this almost instinctive commitment, white colonial growth was limited by the need to conform to the expectations of British financiers and by the need to play the game by London's rules, even though colonial economies emerged from the tutelage described by Habakkuk to a large extent, and the British preference for portfolio investment gave colonial recipients a greater control over capital flows than more direct investment would have done.[46]

The influence of British finance was pervasive. Sometimes, as in Australasia, it took the very obvious form of the large Anglo-colonial banks; but, even in Canada, where the influence of the Anglo-banks was much more limited, the banking system was created on British lines and was geared mainly to the needs of primary production, transport and foreign trade. Moreover, in both Australasia and Canada, economic power rested on urban rather than rural bases after 1850 and was in the hands of commercial and financial groups centred on the foreign trade sector, rather than those of manufacturers or agriculturalists, as was the case in Britain itself.[47] The acceptance of conservative English financial practices, especially as regards long-term lending, made dependence on imported capital greater.[48] It was the predominant influence of the export sector in these countries which ensured that budgetary orthodoxy on British lines was adhered to and fostered an 'internationalist' approach to economic management.

After 1850, the old ruling groups, based on imperial patronage and mercantilist commerce lost influence. However, the new elite which flourished under free trade, although shorn of the gentlemanly accoutrements which were out of tune with the brash democratic certainties of colonial life, remained dependent upon the financial favours of gentlemanly capitalists in London; and local economic ideologies were shaped to British standards, particularly City ones. This explains why default was unthinkable and why, in consequence, colonial securities were seen as such good investments in Britain. The extent of this practical and ideological dependence upon the British economy in general, and upon the City of London in particular, is best understood by taking a brief look at the economic history of the Australian colonies and of New Zealand, especially during those periods of financial stringency when dependence was more starkly demonstrated.

Australasia

The first Australian colony of New South Wales was formed in 1788 as a penal settlement, and its development was for many years propelled by direct British subsidy.[49] As late as 1831 the subsidy added a quarter to the Australian national income.[50] While transportation and emancipated convicts were the dominant influence on development, the growth of domestic agriculture was rapid[51] and it was not until the 1830s that wool, and the export of wool, became a major galvanising force in the economy. It was the wool industry which first attracted private British capital to Australia in large quantities and brought enthusiastic City of London support for the various land-sale and emigration schemes promoted both by individuals and by governments striving to foster local economic development.[52] The establishment of British-based banks in Australia in the 1830s was also a 'response to the desire of the British investor for a larger share in and more direct control over the golden fleece'.[53] Their successful competition with local banks provoked hostility in Australia, where it was feared that the remittance of profits to Britain would drain Australia of investible funds. In the crisis of the early 1840s, when many local banks went under, the Anglo-banks became the dominant financial force on the continent.[54] Australian banks made a vigorous comeback after 1850 and this meant that the share of commercial bank assets held by British-owned banks fell from two-thirds of the total in 1851 to two-fifths in 1890. The British banks retained their competitive edge in financing Anglo-Australian trade; it is noticeable that the most successful Australian-owned banks were the 17 which opened offices in London in order to obtain direct access to City finance, expertise and business connections.[55]

The dependence of Australian prosperity after 1850 upon the international economy, and upon links with Britain in particular, was very marked. Australia was a trade-dependent nation: foreign trade per head of population in 1912 was nearly £34, slightly higher than Britain's but over twice as large as Germany's and four times as large as that of the United States. In 1912, Britain took 40 per cent of Australia's exports and supplied half of her imports. Although Britain's share had declined since the early 1860s, when she had taken 60 per cent of Australia's exports and supplied 75 per cent of her imports, the mother country was still overwhelmingly important to Australia's international success.[56]

Of more fundamental significance, though less generally appreciated, was the fact that, like New Zealand's, Australia's money supply and, therefore, her long-run growth was determined by her economic relations with Britain. Banks in Australia, whether local or imperial, regulated credit according to the level of their London balances. When these balances rose, the banks in Australia expanded credit, and when they fell, the money supply was contracted. In other words, the level of Australian credit depended upon the state of the balance of payments; this was chiefly a function of Australia's trade and payment relations with Britain.[57]

On this basis, it is tempting to reduce Australian economic history to a crude description of her staple exports and to see prosperity purely as a function of success in selling gold, other minerals and wool on London markets. But the links between colony and parent were more subtle. Had Australia relied entirely on exports for her success, Britain's cyclical fluctuations would have been transmitted to her more directly via the mother country's fluctuating demands for Australian exports. Yet Australian growth, a few minor interruptions apart, was almost continuous between 1850 and 1890 and, at an average of about 5 per cent per annum, was considerably higher than in Britain.[58] Moreover, when Australia fell into deep depression in the 1890s, exports from Australia to Britain were rising rapidly after stagnating in the previous decade (Table 8.1). Australia's ability or inability to borrow in London was as crucial to the pace and the stability of her economic growth as were the changing fortunes of her export industries.

The gold rushes of the 1850s – classic export-led booms – had a weighty influence upon the future of Australia. Population in the colonies rose from less than 500,000 in 1850 to 1.2 million ten years later.[59] Together with the very high levels of per capita income created in gold mining, this increase triggered off a demand for infrastructural investment, construction and services. It also led to a marked growth in some sectors of manufacturing industry since Australia's remoteness from Europe gave her a degree of natural protection.[60] The gold era had a strong influence on the economy well into the 1880s, when the 'echo' effect of the population explosion of

TABLE 8.1 Balance of payments and net capital imports: Australia, 1881–1900 (quinquennial averages, £m.)

	1	*2*	*3*	*4*	*5*	*6*	*7*	*8*	*9*
	GDP at factor cost	*Exports*	*Imports*	*Interest and dividend payments*	*Bullion and specie movement*	*Balance of payment (net capital import) (2–3–4+5)*	*Col. 4 as % of Col. 2*	*Col. 2 as % of Col. 1*	*Col. 3 as % of Col. 1*
1881–85	158.2	28.8	36.9	6.7	0.2	−14.6	23.3	18.2	23.3
1886–90	194.1	27.9	37.3	10.0	−0.1	−19.5	35.8	14.4	19.2
1891–95	163.1	35.8	28.6	12.7	−0.8	−6.3	35.5	22.0	17.5
1896–1900	172.4	42.2	36.0	12.1	0.6	−5.4	28.7	24.5	20.8

Sources: Column 1: N.G. Butlin, *Australian Domestic Product: Investment and Foreign Borrowing, 1861–1900*. (Cambridge, 1962), Table 1, p. 6; Columns 2–6: E.A. Boehm, *Prosperity and Depression in Australia, 1887–97* (Oxford, 1971), Table 7, p. 15.

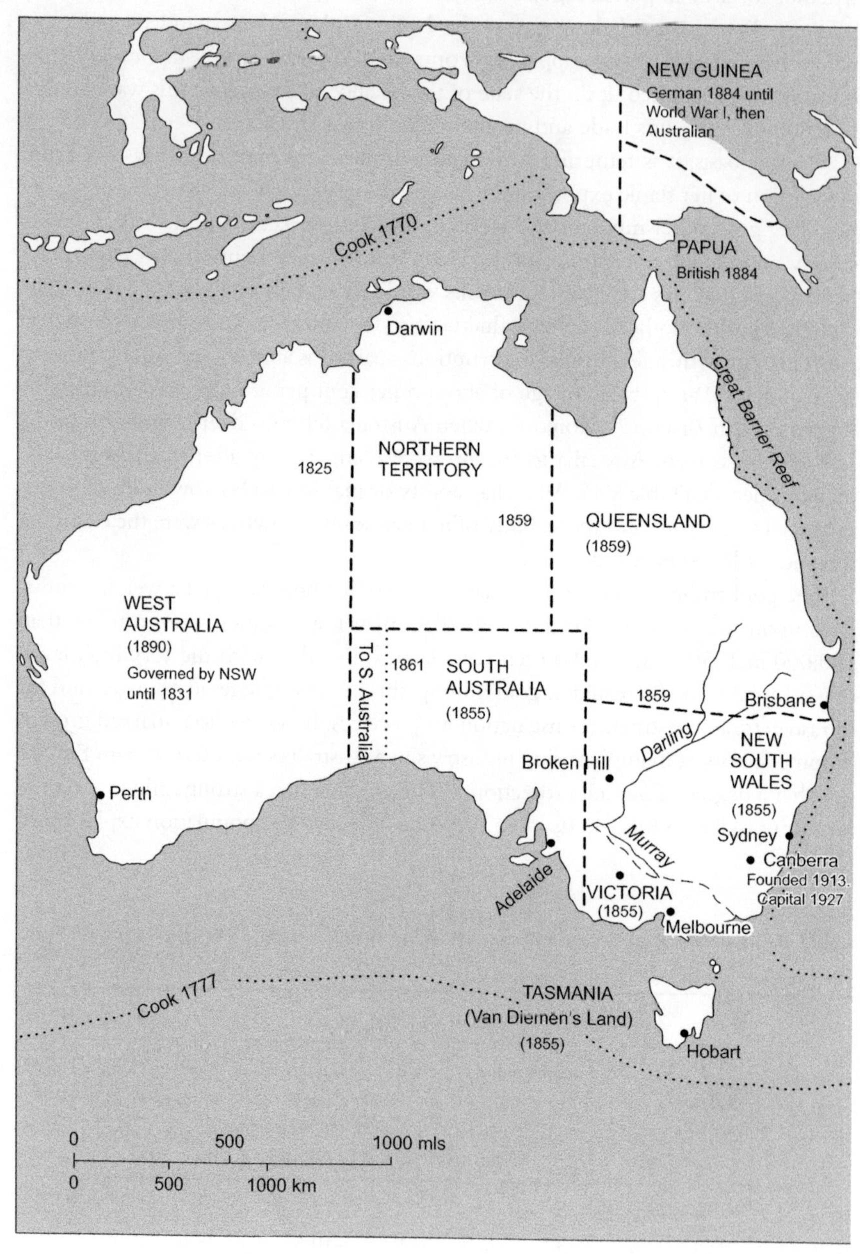

MAP 2 Australasia, 1825–1914

After: J.O. Lloyd, *The British Empire, 1558–1933* (Oxford, 1984)

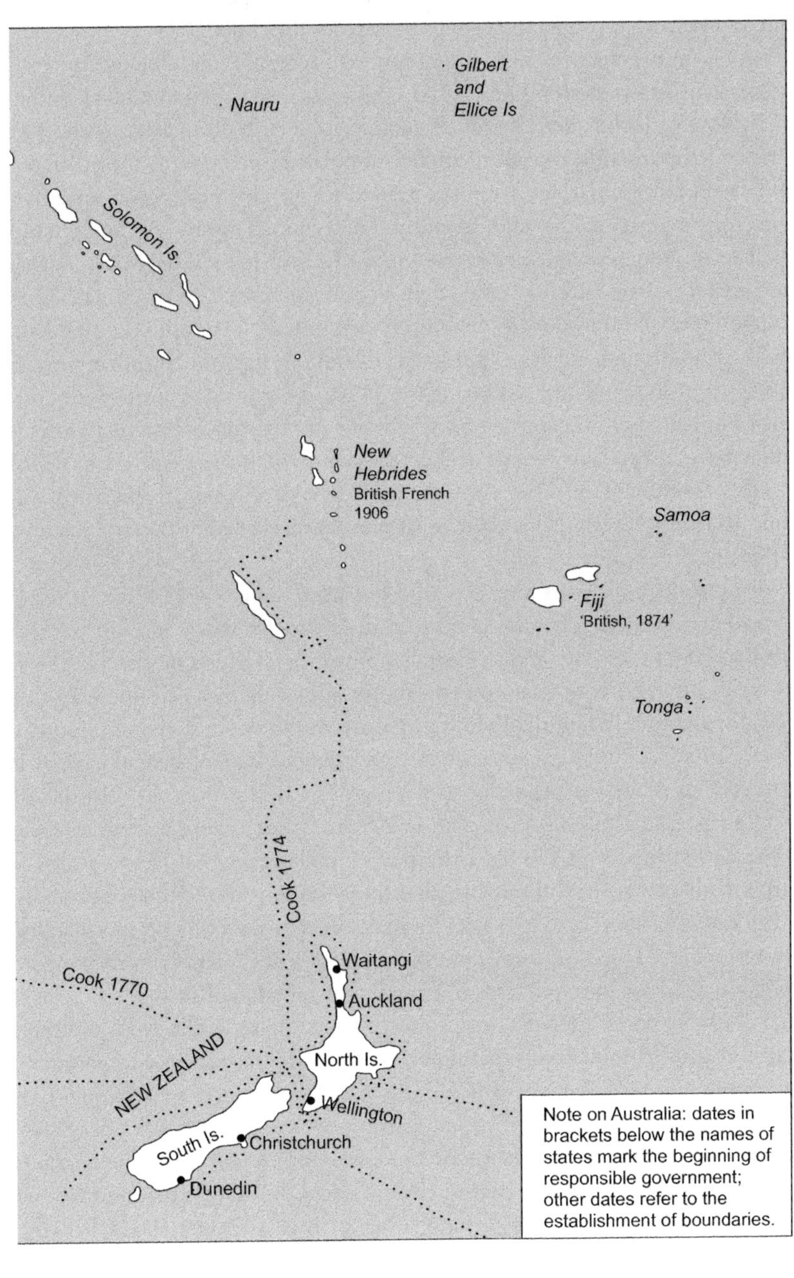

Gilbert
and
Ellice Is
Nauru
Solomon Is.
New
Hebrides
British French
1906
Samoa
Fiji
'British, 1874'
Tonga
Cook 1774
Waitangi
Auckland
Cook 1770
NEW ZEALAND
North Is.
Wellington
South Is.
Christchurch
Dunedin
Note on Australia: dates in brackets below the names of states mark the beginning of responsible government; other dates refer to the establishment of boundaries.

the 1850s underlay a sharp increase in the demand for 'population-sensitive' investment and helped to propel the economy into another boom.[61]

From our perspective, it is important to recognise that the hectic pace of development between 1860 and 1890 could not have been sustained without a large inflow of labour and capital. Immigration, mainly from Britain and Ireland, accounted for roughly one-third of the population increase in these 30 years.[62] Capital exports from Britain were of even greater proportional significance. Accustomed to prosperity in the gold decade and determined to preserve living standards which were probably higher than anywhere else save the United States, Australian voters expected the state to supplement private initiatives by investing heavily in public utilities and transport to open up the continent. The resulting high levels of growth created a demand for imports which could be met only by borrowing, especially in the 1860s and 1880s. During the 1870s, when wool exports were buoyant, capital imports could be kept at low levels, but in other decades capital flows from Britain were heavy. Borrowings in the 1860s and 1880s were equivalent to half of the gross investment made in Australia and most of the capital imported was on public account.[63] Sterling-standard constraints were rarely felt because borrowings kept balances in London healthy.

For more than 30 years after the gold bonanza, the colonists found it relatively easy to borrow. Gold gave the continent an Eldorado image; kinship offered the British a sense of security about Australian investment which meant that the colonies could often borrow when foreign supplicants were frowned upon. In the late 1870s, for example, when the British economy was in depression and imports were falling, Australia could have been severely affected but was rescued, in part, by British interest in Australian securities as a refuge in a troubled world.[64] In the 1880s, when 'push' factors began to operate in Britain,[65] borrowing became even easier for the Australians. It was in the latter part of this decade that clear signs of overborrowing began to show themselves as pastoral stations were pushed into marginal territory, construction activity began to shade off into frenetic land speculation, and railway-building failed to stimulate external economies.[66] Heavy borrowing in the 1860s was paid for by rapid export growth, but investment in the 1880s failed to generate the exports needed to pay for Australia's loans. In the wool industry, the chief source of export income between 1860 and 1890, costs rose as marginal land was pressed into service at the same time as world wool prices were falling. Exports were about 27 per cent of GDP by value in 1861–5, but only 14 per cent in 1886–90.[67] Overseas debt payments, on the other hand, were equal to 19 per cent of the value of exports in 1881 and 39 per cent in 1891 (Table 8.1).[68] Given the case with which money could be borrowed, an irrational air of high expectations in Sydney and Melbourne, and the downward trend in primary produce prices as a whole in the 1880s, it was perhaps inevitable that a great deal of investment should go into areas remote from the export sector and that the process should end eventually in a balance of payments crisis – just as it did in Argentina and Brazil.[69]

There is no doubt that the initial downturn in activity in the key construction sector was triggered off by purely Australian problems;[70] but the crisis entered its most acute phase after 1891 when, in the wake of the Baring Crisis, the British lost interest in new investments in Australia. Even in the late 1880s, Australian exports were moving so slowly that, given the accumulating interest on debt which had to be paid annually, increasing amounts of British capital were needed merely to maintain the high level of imports reached in the early part of the decade (Table 8.1). After 1891, the Australians were faced with the need to finance the import bill, on which the level of domestic activity crucially depended, entirely from export earnings already deeply bitten into by the need to service existing debt.[71] Exports did rise in the early 1890s, bolstered by the output of newly discovered gold-mines in Western Australia; but the effects of this were partly cancelled out in the latter part of the decade by the long drought which affected wool production and exports.[72] Consequently, a large part of the adjustment forced by reduced capital imports had to be achieved by cutting commodity imports, which fell by roughly a quarter between 1886–90 and 1891–5. Capital imports dropped from an average of £19m. a year in the late 1880s to about £5m. at the turn of the century (much of it placed in Western Australian gold) while debt repayments, which were only £5m. in 1881, rose to over £12m. per annum in the 1890s (Table 8.1).

By the late 1890s, the Australians not only had to manage without large scale capital imports but also were using a portion of their own savings on debt repayments. Reduced sterling balances in London led inevitably to a severe squeeze on domestic credit. GDP fell sharply in the 1890s and did not reach its 1890 level again until 1903.[73] What helped incomes to recover after this experience was industrial growth based on import substitution and the opening up of the market for refrigerated meat and dairy produce in Britain and Europe.[74] Exports also rose rapidly enough between 1900 and 1910 for the Australians to finance capital formation and to service debts without importing capital; but imports leapt up again after 1910 and the rise in borrowing from Britain just before the World War I indicated that Australia was still dependent on access to the London capital market when her economic activity approached full employment levels.[75]

The Australian depression was intensified in the mid- and late 1890s by the loss of liquidity following the banking crisis of 1893. Confidence in the system was lost because too many institutions had locked up money, borrowed on short loan, in real assets such as land, which proved unsaleable after 1890. Numerous land and mortgage companies collapsed after 1891 and many of the banks which had financed them were also brought down. It was once believed that the banking crisis was precipitated by the withdrawal of British-held banking deposits – which had increased dramatically in the 1880s – but there is little evidence of this.[76] It is interesting, however, that those banks which raised their capital in London came out of the crisis in better shape than those which raised funds locally. Of the twenty-eight joint-stock banks existing in 1890, only four were British but two of these, the Australasia and the Union Bank, were of particular importance, accounting for one-fifth of all bank deposits in Australia. In 1893, nineteen of the twenty-eight banks were forced to close their doors at least temporarily. Of these nineteen, two were the smaller

British-owned banks and, of the nine survivors, only three were large banks and two of them were the Australasia and the Union.[77]

We have already seen that London-based banks played an important role in Australian finance from the 1830s onwards and that, although they raised their deposits locally, they provoked resentment in Australia, as elsewhere, because they repatriated their profits. Local banks often established themselves, from the 1850s onwards, by taking advantage of this antagonism.[78] But all the Australian banks, like other colonial banks, were British in one sense, whether they raised their capital in London or not, because they owed their origins to regulations laid down by the British Treasury, and the most important of them had opened London offices. Also, as already noted, their domestic role was constrained by the sterling system and the cosmopolitanism this forced upon them.

As in Britain, the banks were mainly concerned with the short-term finance of commerce and trade. But, although they eschewed long-term lending to industry, the major Australian banks were tempted into accepting land and other fixed assets as security against advances, although this practice had been frowned upon initially by officialdom in Britain.[79] One reason for the survival of the Anglo-banks was their conservatism in lending in this way, and, ironically enough, their prudence in refusing to accept a great many deposits from British sources when many local banks used them to extend credit to a dangerous extent after 1885. Another vital element in their survival was their more extensive links, often via interlocking directorships, with the City of London, which offered them credit lines right up to the Bank of England itself.[80]

Bank reconstruction (paying off depositors, including the British, over an extended period of time) locked up a great deal of capital in Australia in the 1890s and both deepened and prolonged the depression. The financial crash had even wider ramifications. It gave a strong impetus to the federation movement, from which the Commonwealth of Australia emerged in 1901, since it convinced business interests of the need to unify and extend the internal market.[81] It was also a decisive moment in the evolution of the Australian labour movement, helping to create not only its structures but also its ideological stance, by focusing attention on the 'soulless money-bags', both indigenous and British, who had shattered the working man's dream.[82] This labourite *cri de coeur* reflected the plain fact that the bankers, merchants and other businessmen who dominated Australian economic policy saw no way out of the crisis other than to play the game London's way. Angered by rumours, some emanating from Britain, of possible default, the Chief Secretary of New South Wales claimed in 1893 that:

> The abhorrence which any suggestion of repudiation always provokes here need not be dwelt upon. Time will prove that no such word shall ever with justice be applied to any Australian Colony.[83]

Foreigners might threaten not to pay, but repudiation was out of the question as far as the politically powerful in Australia were concerned. Gladstonianism was practically a reflex action in the crisis.[84] Australian governments were anxious not only to demonstrate their monetary orthodoxy but also to trim their tariffs in the 1890s to please Britain and they even made some grudging concessions on contributions to imperial naval defence – all with the aim of improving their credit in London and re-opening the possibilities for further borrowing.[85]

The debt burden affected Australian attitudes towards closer relations with Britain in another direction. As in Canada, political independence was asserted and tariff autonomy realised as early as 1870.[86] Tariffs were imposed mainly for revenue purposes, but they did have some impact in encouraging manufacturing employment, especially in Victoria, and the manufacturing base was economically and politically significant by the 1890s.[87] The need to economise on imports in the 1890s reinforced this interest and, by the time that the Commonwealth of Australia was founded in 1901, it had become axiomatic that protection (along with the exclusion of cheap labour through the white Australia policy) was vital to create jobs and maintain traditionally high living standards.[88] Australia objected strongly to political unity in the empire and to a free-trade empire which would expose her industries to greater British competition. After 1895, though, the Australian appetite for a system of preferential tariffs within the Empire grew, since a privileged position in the British market would have supported export income and eased the problem of debt repayment. As Richard Jebb, the Chamberlainite propagandist, put it in 1905:

> In Australia the object is financial independence of the British bondholder. The reduction and ultimate liquidation of the Australian public debt, whatever the means adopted to effect it, obviously will be facilitated by the development of direct trade with the creditor country. . . . Hence the preferential system, if it helps to retain the major portion of Australia's foreign trade in the channel through which interest and principal find their nearest way to the British bondholder, naturally commends itself to those who desire the financial emancipation of their country.[89]

Preferences were also important to the colonies as a whole because it was only by generating export income that they could keep the level of internal demand high enough to sustain a market for locally produced manufactures.[90] Maintaining local industry was vital to both living standards and employment in a continent where, despite its dependence on primary exports, the bulk of the population lived in urban areas. The most industrialised state, Victoria, protected its manufacturing sector in the late nineteenth century and, after 1901, the Commonwealth government did likewise. British exporters thus had to face the irritant of a colonial tariff as well as increasing competition from third countries in Antipodean markets.[91] One result of this was a growing interest in the possibility of mutual preferences within the empire, with colonial privileges in the British market being offset by discriminating favours for British exports in the white empire.

New Zealand provides a further dramatic instance of growth shaped by British economic dominance. The islands' dependence on trade with Britain actually increased in the period under review. In the 1860s, trade with Australia was more important than trade with Britain: economically, New Zealand was merely an offshoot of her larger neighbour. Rapid growth was accompanied by a more direct commercial and financial relationship with Britain, which accounted for 40 per cent of New Zealand's trade in the early 1860s, rising to around 80 per cent from the early 1880s to World War I.[92]

Like Australia, New Zealand had its gold bonanza and its spectacular immigrant rush in the 1860s; here again, the enormous boom in public investment after 1870, funded to a large extent by London, was an attempt to build up an infrastructure to cope with rapidly rising numbers and to maintain high living standards in a country where voters expected politicians actively to promote their economic welfare.[93] As in the Australian case, New Zealand's desire to borrow and Britain's willingness to lend were only tenuously related to any immediate criterion of market efficiency, though there was never any question of default.[94] Public debt increased from about £9m. in 1870 to £39m. in 1893, or from £44 per head to over £60, much of it borrowed when the price of wool, the principal export, was falling: exports per head fell from £22 to £12 between 1863 and the early 1880s.[95] In the mid-1880s Britain turned her attention to Australia and Argentina, and New Zealand found borrowing more difficult. The outcome was a prolonged economic depression ending in a banking crisis in the mid-1890s similar to that already described for Australia.[96] The scale of New Zealand's debt was so great by the 1890s that even a large surplus of exports over imports of £55m. between 1887 and 1914 covered only about one-half of the country's external debt obligations and outward flows of private capital, and the gap had to be plugged by further borrowing.[97] As in Australia's case, the problem of debt repayment forced New Zealand to adopt a deflationary policy which kept down imports.[98] New Zealand also benefited from import substitution; and the rapid rise in exports, once refrigeration was established in the 1890s, made it possible for the country to grow and at the same time to become less dependent on capital imports.

Both Australia and New Zealand were vulnerable because of their smallness and their commercial and financial dependence. The political autonomy which responsible government gave them has to be weighed against their status as economic, and especially financial, satellites of Britain when assessing the degrees of freedom achieved after 1850. Britain's informal financial imperialism was masked, in New Zealand before 1885 and in Australia before 1890, by the ease with which the colonists could raise capital in London and, therefore, keep imports at a level which allowed rapid growth to take place. What was, in effect, a privileged access to City funds fostered, to some degree, the illusion of economic autonomy in the same way that Britain's own defence umbrella and the remoteness of the Antipodes from the main centres of military conflict encouraged some colonists to believe that they were free of European squabbles and beyond the control of the great powers. Lending was not, of course, an arbitrary process. Although the Baring Crisis influenced British attitudes to all foreign lending, the drying up of loans to New Zealand and Australia also reflected the declining profitability of major activities in both countries.[99] In that sense, the crises described were internally generated rather than wilfully imposed from without. Nonetheless, what the crises did illustrate vividly was that development which failed to produce sufficient export income would ultimately lead to disaster and to the tightening of London's grip on colonial economic life.

The upheavals of the 1880s and 1890s certainly left a permanent mark on Australasian society. In the case of Australia, it has been argued that the crisis gave birth to a 'national bourgeoisie' capable of organising industrial growth under the shelter of protection and simultaneously lessening Australia's dependence on Britain.[100] The growth of manufacturing before 1914 was significant, as was the development of a national capital market.[101] However, Australia's ability to meet her own needs for capital after 1890 partly reflected the low level of economic activity and of investment: when, after 1910, the economy began to move towards full employment, British investment in Australia rose rapidly again. And, as we shall see, Australia borrowed heavily in London in the 1920s. It is also important to remember that the growth of import substitution under protection was a necessity if Australians were to meet financial obligations in London at a time when their credit was poor: local production reduced imports and released sterling for debt repayments. Australian industrialism, in that sense, complemented Britain's own peculiar capitalist structure. So, although the influence of domestic manufacturing increased over time, it would be difficult to argue that it resulted in any marked reorientation of policy or greatly disturbed the links between Australia's overseas interests and London finance. The crisis of the 1890s also sharpened class antagonisms in Australia and promoted the development of Labour parties, at both state and Commonwealth levels. These parties supported protection and a white Australia policy, and were suspicious of the imperial link and of Britain as 'the headquarters of the Money Power'.[102] But, once in office, Labour did little to alter the fundamentals of the Anglo-Australian economic relationship.

In New Zealand, where the population was too small to support as important a manufacturing sector as in Australia, wool and land exerted a greater sway. The traumas of the 1880s and 1890s gave a shattering blow to their social and political authority, and 'the old "Establishment" dominated by squatters, speculators, merchants, British gentlemen and their ladies' collapsed as wool declined in significance and dairy farming, dominated by small farmers, became the leading industry.[103] By the 1890s, New Zealand was ruled by a radical party with a mandate to create a welfare state, and the political dominance of the local gentry was over. But the dairy farmers were as dependent as the wool growers upon the British market, the problem of debt repayment remained as anxious and unremitting as in the past, and further heavy borrowings were necessary before 1914.[104]

In the sequel, both countries came out of depression with more efficient and diversified export sectors and both developed a greater ability to finance their own investment needs, although growth, especially in Australia, was much slower after 1890 than in the previous 30 years.[105] Depression brought home the importance of exports to prosperity and to financial stability as never before. It was inevitable that, by the 1890s, Australia and New Zealand should be at the forefront of demands for a preferential position in the British market.[106] From the colonial perspective, the logical consequence of extensive trade and financial commitments to Britain was that the parent country should abandon free trade.

Canadian unity and British finance

If Australia and New Zealand were economic satellites of Britain after 1850 in the manner described, this was not true in the same sense of the North American colonies, which were less successful as exporters of staples until around 1900 and where the influence of the United States was already strong at mid-century. Even in 1850, despite the growth of a banking system on the British model which eschewed American-style industrial lending, and despite British predominance in Canadian trade, only one important bank was British in origin, and the colonies held their reserves not in London but in New York.[107] What can be said is that the independence of the colonies from the USA and the creation of British North America in its modern form would have been most unlikely if the former had been unable to tap capital sources in London and if British governments had not occasionally been willing to use the leverage which London's financial predominance gave them. North America presented particularly acute problems for imperial statesmen who recognised the need for self-government, but feared its consequences in the age of free trade.

Geographically, the colonies were no more than the northerly fringes of the rapidly expanding United States,[108] and only common dependence on the preferential system had given them any sense of unity. After the Napoleonic Wars, the province of Upper Canada (Ontario) had flourished as its agricultural frontier expanded and as its population increased fivefold between 1815 and 1850.[109] But much of the prosperity of the province – and of the small but cosmopolitan community centred on Montreal in the French-speaking province of Lower Canada (Quebec) – depended upon the ability to use the St. Lawrence Seaway as a conduit for trade between Britain and the mid-west of America.[110] To this end, large sums were spent, both privately and publicly, upon the construction of a series of canals to improve the competitiveness of the seaway. Capital for these purposes was in short supply in the late 1830s, and the British government turned this to its political advantage in 1841 by offering a guarantee of interest on a loan for canal construction as an inducement to the provinces of Lower and Upper Canada to unite under the name of Canada. In the process, Britain hoped both to improve the colony's credit rating in London and to subordinate and assimilate the fractious French in a British-dominated union.[111] The importance of the seaway was further underlined in 1842, when the British offered a substantial preference on wheat shipped from Canadian ports.[112]

The ending of preferences after 1846 badly hurt many North American export industries, including the timber trades of the Maritime Provinces of Nova Scotia and New Brunswick, and triggered a movement in Montreal, the financial and commercial centre of the St Lawrence trading system, in favour of joining the

United States. The problem was compounded by the growing power of the United States, as the frontier swept westwards and as the Union's manufacturing and military might grew with frightening speed, threatening to pull the small colonial outposts irresistibly into its orbit. One manifestation of American power was the rapid spread of railways south of the border, which increased the competitiveness of the east coast ports. Together with the loss of the wheat preference, this threw the future of the 'commercial empire' of the St Lawrence into doubt and threatened to leave the province of Canada with enormous unproductive debts.

At the same time, British governments were reluctantly recognising that Britain's political presence in North America was a constant provocation to the United States and that the colonies could not be defended against her in the long term.[113] In any case, public opinion in Britain was impatient of high military expenditure in North America, partly because the costs of defence appeared to cancel out the benefit of the connection, and partly because of the assumed correspondence between political freedom and military self-help. When the colonies claimed political freedom, the British authorities argued that, in return, the local communities should assume more of their own defence burden. Not surprisingly, the Canadians, while eagerly claiming the political privileges, baulked at the economic price. Wrangles over the issue of the distribution of military burdens between Britain and Canada harmed relations for years and provoked the most famous outbursts of anti-imperial and anti-colonial sentiment in mid-Victorian Britain.[114] There was also a feeling in some business circles in Britain that it would be madness to antagonise, or at the worst go to war with, Britain's best customers for the sake of a few, relatively unimportant possessions[115] and that abandoning them to their fate was a small price to pay for continued American goodwill.

A few radicals might be prepared to abandon the empire: no English ministry could take such a cavalier attitude. Keeping Canada independent held open a potentially valuable market, maintained a British presence on the American continent, slowed down the otherwise inevitable rise of the United States to world power status and limited the spread of its dangerously republican philosophy. As Russell, then Prime Minister, argued in 1849, 'the loss of any great portion of our Colonies would diminish our importance in the world, and the vultures would soon gather to despoil us of other parts of our Empire, or to offer insults to us which we could not bear'.[116]

The question before a succession of concerned British statesmen and officials was, therefore, a difficult one: how to ensure Canadian independence from the United States and to maintain as much as possible of the British presence in North America, while supervising political and military withdrawal and tacitly recognising United States' hegemony on the American continent? The answer was to use British political and economic influence to sustain, and enhance the fortunes of, those collaborative agents in Canada who had a vested interest in the imperial link.

British support for North American independence would have been unavailing had it not met with an enthusiastic local response. Colonial governments and the business elites who supported them needed a British presence in Canada. Despite

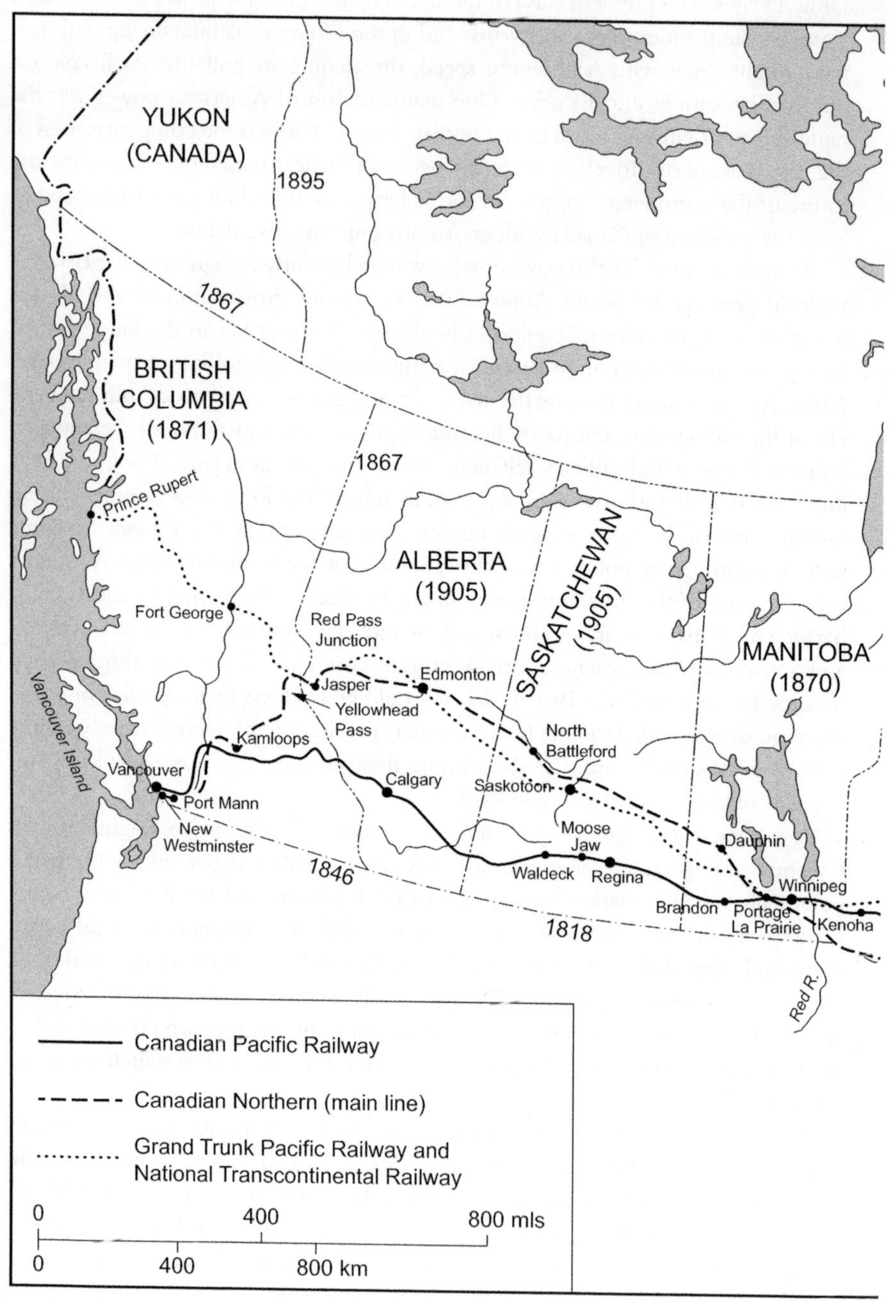

MAP 3 The Canadian transcontinental railways, 1916. The dates of the creation of the Western provinces are given in brackets

After: W.J. Easterbrook and H.G.J. Aitken, *Canadian Economic History* (Toronto, 1956)

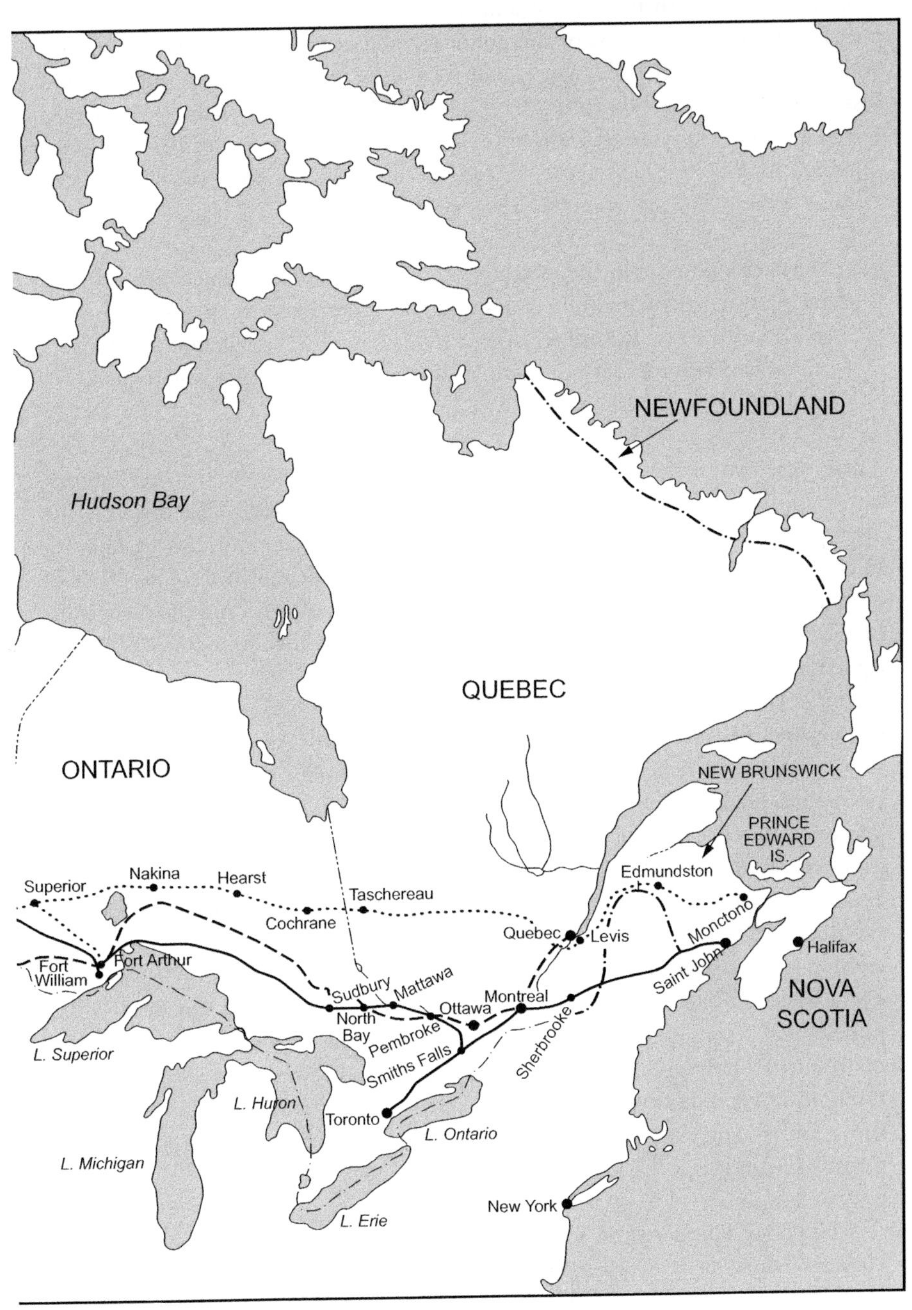
NEWFOUNDLAND
Hudson Bay
QUEBEC
ONTARIO
NEW BRUNSWICK
PRINCE
EDWARD
IS.
Edmundston
Superior
Nakina
Hearst
Taschereau
Cochrane
Quebec
Levis
Moncton
Halifax
Fort
William
Fort Arthur
Sudbury
Mattawa
Ottawa
Montreal
Saint John
NOVA
SCOTIA
North
Bay
Pembroke
Sherbrooke
L. Superior
Smiths Falls
L. Huron
Toronto
L. Ontario
L. Michigan
New York
L. Erie

a brief flirtation with the idea of annexation to the United States when preferences came to an end, most of the politically and economically powerful groups had benefited from the old system and were keen to avoid the competition and loss of prestige which absorption by the United States might entail.[117] They preferred independence; but that was possible only with the support of British capital, whether publicly or privately subscribed. As an American historian of Canadian railway development has recently expressed it:

> The decision to opt for British rather than American dominance reflected the persistence of traditional ties and the more lucrative British market. Because of traditional sentiment and geographical separation, British capital and control was not commonly perceived as foreign dominance: similar American participation was.[118]

There were two main phases in Canadian development in which Britain's 'indirect imperialism'[119] helped to shape a distinctive North America. The first was the attempt between the late 1840s and the early 1860s to achieve growth through closer economic ties with the United States; the second included the emergence of a united Canada from the British North America Act of 1867 and the acceptance of the reality of Confederation by the United States in the Treaty of Washington signed in 1871.

In the late 1840s both Grey, as Colonial Secretary, and Elgin, the Governor General, realised that the independence of the British North American colonies from the United States depended ultimately upon their ability to maintain economic prosperity. Reciprocity – free trade in natural products with the United States – was one way of achieving growth since it offered the chance of channelling the products of the American mid-west up the St Lawrence Seaway. The British government undertook to negotiate with the United States on the colonies' behalf, and the Reciprocity Treaty was signed in 1854.[120] Fostering colonial unity was seen as another important means of encouraging a viable economy. After 1846, Grey and Elgin tried to barter an imperial guarantee for the building of a Quebec–Halifax railway against an acceptance by the Canadians of the responsibility for the bulk of their own military expenditure. A united Canada would have a good credit rating in London: both Grey and Elgin recognised that lack of capital was one of the colonies' crucial problems and that, initially, only government help could give Canadian enterprises the standing which would make them credit-worthy in the City of London.[121]

The policy foundered on intercolonial squabbles, the inability to agree on the colonies' contribution to their own defence and parliamentary cheeseparing over guarantees for railway capital. But, despite hostility to the colonies in some quarters in Britain, proposals of the kind favoured by Grey and Elgin remained on the Anglo-Canadian agenda throughout the 1850s and 1860s.[122] In the early 1850s, prompted by legislation guaranteeing returns on railway investment passed by the Canadian Parliament[123] and by the world economic boom driven by gold discoveries in the

United States and Australia, private capital began flowing to North America in abundance. British savings poured into the Grand Trunk and other railways built by British contractors and run by British managements; as much capital per head was invested in North America in the 1850s as in the days of the famous wheat boom of 1900–14.[124]

The great mediators between the City and the colonies at the time, and for many years after, were the banking families of Barings and Glyn, Mills, who acted as agents for the colonies in London.[125] Without their help the Grand Trunk might never have been completed, and their willingness to hold its securities, and those of colonial governments, often kept up the price of North American stocks: in 1860, for example, Barings were effectively subsidising the Grand Trunk to the extent of £1.2m. through loans and holdings of its securities.[126] Whether this was a very profitable business for the bankers is doubtful; but holding the agency of governments, even impoverished ones, and involvement in high profile projects such as the Grand Trunk, brought a degree of prestige which enhanced business in general.[127] The power of the bankers was also considerable. After protests by both Barings and Glyn, Mills, Canada passed an Act in 1851 which declared that the province would not increase its debt 'without the consent of the Agents through whom loans may have been negotiated in England, or the previous offer to pay off all debentures then outstanding'.[128] Ten years later, hints by Barings and Glyn's that they would jointly take possession of the Grand Trunk's property in lieu of debts galvanised the government of Canada into action to help the railway out of its financial difficulties.[129]

The strategy based on Reciprocity and the Grand Trunk began to collapse in the late 1850s, beginning with the financial crisis of 1857, after which capital and trade flows both slowed significantly. The basis of this 'American' policy was also destroyed by the Civil War, when victory by the protectionist northern states doomed the Reciprocity Treaty and aroused new fears of American expansion into the north. The Confederation of the colonies under a strong Dominion government in 1867 was, on the Canadian side, the direct outcome of their failure to tap the American market successfully.[130] With their mid-west ambitions blocked, the colonists turned to their only alternatives – unity and a concerted effort to develop the Canadian west before it was absorbed by their neighbour. Such a grandiose project required immense capital resources, mainly for railways, and Confederation was one means of attracting them. Harold Innis, the famous Canadian economic historian, once wrote: 'The constitution of Canada, as it appears on the statute book of the British Parliament, has been designed to secure capital for the improvement of navigation and transport'.[131]

In other words, Confederation like the union of Quebec and Ontario in 1840 was, among other things, a way of improving Canada's credit rating in London after the railway schemes of the 1850s had ended in disappointment. Or, as a more cynical historian has put it:

> Canadian 5 per cent bonds had fallen seriously in London to the level of 71 . . . [but] on the day the Confederation resolution reached London they

> rose to 75. When the full texts arrived they rose to 92, lending considerable credence to the view that the Baring Bros. were the true fathers of Confederation.[132]

Support for a federal solution to Canada's difficulties also took on a new urgency in Britain in the mid-1860s. Colonial military expenditure had to be trimmed to meet Gladstone's need for budgetary stringency and in recognition of new threats in Europe, just when the possibility of a conflict over Canada with an angry and militarily awesome Northern United States was at its height.[133] Confederation – a strong, united but independent Canada – suited Britain's needs; after 1863, when the colonists began to take what the British considered to be a more mature attitude to their own military responsibilities, London was willing to improve its offer of financial help to British North America considerably. Without this offer the Quebec–Halifax or Intercolonial Railway, completed in 1871, would not have been built and the Maritimes would not have agreed to Confederation. Without Confederation, it would have been impossible to raise the funds to buy out the Hudson's Bay Company and to begin the conquest of the western prairies, which were so vital to the development of an independent Canadian economy. In pursuit of the objective of union, the Liberal government in Britain was not averse to applying a good deal of economic and political pressure on doubtful or hesitant elements in Canada.[134]

The main support for the new Dominion of Canada came from the wealthiest province, Ontario, and was composed of:

> ambitious, dynamic, speculative and entrepreneurial business groups who aimed to make money out of the new business community or to install themselves in the strategic positions of power within it – the railway promoters, banks, manufacturers, land companies, contractors.[135]

They provided the collaborating economic elite who clung to, and depended upon, British power and British capital. The British government gave them strong support and was not afraid to bully or cajole other colonists who had their doubts about the benefit of a united North America. The Canadian Liberal, Edward Blake, looking back from 1876, felt that Confederation had been 'prematurely forced' on the colonies and that 'N[ew] B[runswick] was frightened into it, N[ova] S[cotia] coerced into it, the North West, B[ritish] C[olumbia] and P[rince] Edward Island bought into it'. Blake was rather disenchanted by the time he wrote this, but it is an exaggeration, not a wild untruth.[136]

Confederation would have had poor prospects without the acquiescence of the United States. The Treaty of Washington in 1871 underwrote the decision of 1867 since the United States accepted Canadian political independence in return for a tacit recognition of its own military hegemony in Northern America – implied by British military withdrawal – and improved fishing rights for American vessels in Canadian waters.[137] The latter concession deeply offended the Maritime provinces, and the Dominion government could be induced to accept it only in return for a guarantee by Britain of a considerable part of the initial expenditure on the Canadian Pacific Railway, the key both to Canadian control of the Western Prairies and to the incorporation into the union of the most westerly settlement, British Columbia.[138]

Tariffs also made a significant contribution to the process of organising and maintaining a united Canada. In the late 1850s, tariffs were justified as a way of raising revenue to pay debts and hence of maintaining the credit-worthiness of the public authorities. The British disliked the tariff immensely: Grey was particularly hostile.[139] But free trade seemed incompatible with the development of an independent Canada, and in the face of this conundrum the British quietly abandoned their opposition, even though the tariff gave some protection to local manufacturing.[140]

Protection took on a heightened significance in the 1880s. The vague developmental ideas which lay behind Confederation broadened into the so-called 'National Policy' of Macdonald's Conservatives in 1879, when the project of western development took on its final shape. The west could not be conquered without the Canadian Pacific Railway, and a steady supply of settlers was needed to produce the wheat which would ultimately pay for the capital raised in London for prairie investments. Success on the prairies also required a high-tariff policy to raise resources for the Dominion, which underwrote a great many of the new projects, and to protect the industry in eastern Canada which would supposedly thrive on western growth.[141] Recently, some Marx-inspired historians have argued that the commercial and financial oligarchs who were the chief architects of the National Policy designed it specifically to encourage direct US industrial investment and to limit the power of Canadian manufacturing.[142] Although the importance of the bankers and merchants in Canada's political economy is not in doubt,[143] it must be remembered that the invasion of Canada by American industrial capital did not begin in earnest until after 1900 and that the tariff gave an immediate fillip to import substitution.[144] Insofar as the rise of manufacturing aided Canadian growth, it also swelled the tax revenues of the Dominion and provincial governments and eased the growing burden of debt repayments, including those due in London. Nor, given the overall importance of Canada to British trade and finance, would it have been wise for British governments to support the complaints of their manufacturers too strongly or to 'allow particular manufacturing interests in Britain to overrule the general interests of British capital'.[145]

For a generation after Confederation the National Policy gave Canadians something to fight over rather than offering them a sense of shared achievement. While the grain frontier remained south of the Canadian border, the western frontier of the United States was a magnet for migrants and capital. Slow development in western Canada meant a high burden of public indebtedness: about £170m. worth of capital was imported between 1870 and 1895, roughly 5 per cent of national income at that time (Table 8.2); it also brought high tariffs and lower living standards, especially for those dependent on imported goods.[146] Given many financial as well as technical problems, the building of the Canadian Pacific took much longer than expected and, although the company was formed in Canada, the project might

TABLE 8.2 Net capital inflows: Canada, 1871–1915

	$m	*% of GNP*
1871–75	166	7.0
1876–80	93	3.3
1881–85	167	5.2
1886–90	242	6.4
1891–95	202	4.6
1896–1900	124	2.5
1901–05	317	5.3
1906–10	784	9.2
1911–15	1515	12.4

Source: W.L. Marr and D.G. Paterson, *Canada: An Economic History* (Toronto, 1980), Table 9.1, p. 267.

have foundered without London's support and particularly much timely help from Barings. Barings marketed a considerable amount of Canadian Pacific stock, around £10m. all told in the 1880s, and often held parts of it for considerable periods when the London market was averse to Canadian securities.[147]

Resentment against the National Policy threatened the unity of the Dominion and fuelled an interest in free trade and in closer links with the United States in the 1880s.[148] This movement failed because of the extent of the interests tied to the National Policy, especially in the relatively highly populated manufacturing centres of Eastern Canada which benefited from protection, and because of constant fears of United States' annexationist designs. Macdonald, the leading force behind the National Policy, continually emphasised its compatibility with the British connection;[149] in 1891, he tried to revive enthusiasm for it by arguing for a preference in the British market, pulling Canada away from the United States, guaranteeing export markets and ensuring the payment of debts.[150] The National Policy was, indeed, the clearest expression of the fundamental fact that 'the empire was no longer held together by diplomatic bonds but by the financial commitments made by many influential British investors'.[151]

Macdonald's Liberal successors, who held power in the late 1890s, were more interested in free trade; but the National Policy and its aims were so entrenched in Canada by this time that the Liberals ended by offering the British preferential concessions on imports in 1897 in the hope of stimulating similar concessions on Canadian exports to Britain.[152] Besides its economic advantages, enthusiasm for the imperial cause was also a useful way in which Canadians could emphasise their distance from the United States, as support for Britain in the Boer War illustrates.[153] Given the extent to which Canada's determination to avoid the American embrace put her in the hands of the London money market, it is clear that the Canadians, when they had to choose, preferred informal economic dominance from London to political control by the United States.[154] On the British side, it was rapidly recognised after 1867 that any overt interference in the Dominion's internal affairs would only breed resentment and hostility, and endanger imperial relationships.[155]

From 1895, when the grain frontier shifted across the 49th parallel, the National Policy began to pay off. The great wheat boom[156] was initially developed by Canadian savings and Canadian labour but, given the initially slow growth of exports and the rapid rise in imports as infrastructural investment increased, it could be sustained, after the turn of the century, only by large inflows of capital and labour. Migration from Britain rose sharply in the decade before the World War I;[157] between 1900 and 1914, Canada imported about $2,500m. (or £500m.) of capital, 70 per cent of which came from Britain. Capital imports were equivalent to about one-half of domestic capital formation in the last few years before the war,[158] or 12 per cent of gross national product (Table 8.2). A large percentage of British capital went into railway investment: 10,000 miles were opened for traffic in 1911–15,[159] by which time Canada was showing alarming signs of the over-borrowing which had earlier afflicted Australia and New Zealand.

The economic integration of east and west after 1870 formed the basis for an independent Canadian state in the twentieth century; and it was financed to a large degree by London bankers. Looking back at three generations of economic change in Canada, one Canadian historian has claimed that US investment, especially in industry, goes unrecognised here along with Canadian entrepreneurs' own considerable contribution to growth; but the quotation is useful in highlighting the often underrated significance of British investment not only to Canada's growth but also to its existence as an independent entity.

> It was not the Fathers of Confederation but Lombard Street which built the canals, the railways, financed the lumber and grain trades, the mines and the industries without which Canadian provinces would now be states in the American union.[160]

London's stake in the wheat boom only emphasised the extent to which Canada had become dependent on the City over the previous two generations. By 1913 Canada was paying roughly £20m. a year in interest to Britain on investments in railways and other public utilities.[161] British manufacturers had done less well. Canadian tariffs ensured debt repayment but also brought heavy competition. The British also found it increasingly difficult to meet the American import challenge. Britain's direct investment in Canada was small compared with that of the United States, and attempts by British manufacturers to get behind the tariff were neither frequent nor very successful.[162] Britain's share of Canadian imports fell steadily, despite the preferences of 1897 and the flow of British capital into Canada, while Britain's share of Canadian exports, necessary to debt payment, rose significantly after 1870 (see Table 8.3). Even between 1911 and 1913, when British capital was flooding in, Britain's share of Canada's exports failed to improve.[163] Much of Canada's borrowings

TABLE 8.3 Shares in Canadian foreign trade, 1851–1911 (%)

	1851[a]	*1860*[a,b]	*1870*[a]	*1880*	*1890*	*1900*	*1911*
Imports for consumption							
UK	59.3	44.4	57.1	47.8	37.5	24.2	24.3
USA	37.0	51.1	32.2	40.0	46.4	60.1	60.9
Others	3.7	4.5	10.7	12.2	16.1	15.7	14.8
Exports of foreign and domestic produce							
UK	58.8	38.1	43.3	54.6	50.5	53.9	48.2[c]
USA	35.3	57.1	44.8	37.1	41.2	36.4	37.9[c]
Others	5.9	4.8	11.9	8.3	8.3	9.7	13.9[c]

Sources: O.J. Firestone, 'Canada's Foreign Trade, 1851–1900', in *Trends in the American Economy in the Nineteenth Century,* Table 3, p. 766; M.C. Urquhart and K.A.H. Buckley, *Historical Statistics of Canada* (Cambridge, 1965), pp. 181–2.

Notes:

[a] The figures for 1851, 1860 and 1870 are for the four major colonies only.

[b] Figures for 1860 are strongly influenced by the short-lived Reciprocity Treaty with the United States.

[c] Export of domestic produce only.

were spent on imports from the United States and became part of the burden of dollar settlements in the multilateral system described earlier.[164] Besides the natural geographical advantage possessed by the United States, the erosion of Britain's position as a manufacturing exporter to Canada was also due to local protectionism and lack of competitiveness.[165] Nonetheless, in Canada as in Australia, the rise of import-substituting manufactures, insofar as they reduced imports, made it easier for the colonies to find the sterling with which to pay interest on their debts and thus strengthened the financial side of the imperial equation.

The Dominion of Canada was an artificial creation. Its chief motive force was undoubtedly local, but without substantial British support, particularly the support of British capital, it is doubtful if the enterprise could have been sustained. From the British angle, a politically independent, but economically dependent, Canada was an excellent offset to the rising power of the United States on the American continent and brought both political and material gains. On the other hand, a united Canada was not possible without protection; it was the effects of this protection, and of declining manufacturing competitiveness, which were rapidly undermining Britain's commodity exports by 1914, while finance, commerce and services sustained her informal economic empire in Canada.

Britain and the white empire after 1850

Britain's economic influence upon the white colonies was exercised via factor movements and her predominant position in world trade. It was powerful enough to sustain a range of collaborative groups whose leverage on the colonial frontier was sufficient to keep these countries within the international system dominated by Britain. There were many prominent figures in these colonies who felt that 'national pride and economic security were both jeopardized by reliance on a few export staples'; but 'when it came to the point, the rulers of the prairies and the villages would take only such measures as were compatible with the needs of export production and the demands of export producers'.[166] The 'point' usually came when countries experienced balance of payments crises or ran into other problems over borrowing in London and repaying debt: it was then that London could exact ultimate authority over their economic policies, since it was only by playing by the City's rules that the dominant economic elites could re-establish their credit-worthiness and retain their credibility locally.

Dependence upon Britain and upon the world economy was certainly not incompatible with rapid growth, nor was the diversification of the economy out of primary production impossible. In terms of the production of manufactured goods per head of population, Canada, Australia and even New Zealand ranked higher than Germany in 1913.[167] Also, given strong local pressures for reducing dependence on primary output, diversification was no bar to a smooth relationship with Britain. In the Canadian case, the very process of creating a state strong enough to resist the pressures of the United States meant a National Policy within which protection and industrialisation were indispensable. In addition, the enormous annual debt payments which the future Dominions had to make gave them an added reason to succour local manufacturers since keeping down the rate of growth of imports was one way of generating the export surplus needed to pay their creditors. This is a further reason, other than slower growth and the rise of competition why, after 1880, the white colonies proved to be a disappointment to English manufacturers. Leaving aside South Africa, their 14 per cent share of British domestic exports in 1881–5 was not achieved again until 1911–13. In the same period, their share of Britain's imports rose from 9.2 per cent to 11.9 per cent.

The relentless pressure of debt repayment and dependence upon the British market also lay behind the colonies' growing interest in economic privileges within the empire and helped to define the precise character of this interest. An imperial tariff, if it meant, as Chamberlain hoped, a free-trading empire discriminating against foreigners, alarmed them deeply since it would have exposed their manufactures to British competition. Mutual preferences, however, offered them a more secure place in Britain's market and did not imperil their right to protect their manufacturers. It was the only practical kind of unity in which the white colonies were really interested and it is an eloquent expression in itself of the complex nature of their dependence upon Britain. Before 1914, of course, the British electorate rejected Chamberlain's attempt to persuade them to accept such a system of preferences, and British governments felt embarrassed when, first Canada and then Australia and New Zealand, granted them to the mother country. The range of Britain's economic interests was much wider than simply the empire: from a metropolitan perspective, if the imperatives of debt repayment and dependence upon the British for export markets were the criteria for preferences then they ought to have been offered to Argentina as well as to Australia or New Zealand.[168] It was only after 1918, when Britain had become more dependent on her economic connections with the empire, that a preferential system began to seem worth while to more than a minority of her own economic interest groups. Even then, the benefits could be obtained only at the expense of some valuable links with non-empire countries such as Argentina and Denmark.

The international system in the late nineteenth and early twentieth centuries was compatible with the diversification of white colonial economies, and in some ways encouraged it. By the same token, the cosmopolitan economic policy of Britain may have harmed the growth of her own manufacturing industry in the long run by exposing it to competition both at home and in colonial markets. Peripheral industry was not suppressed for the sake of metropolitan capitalism; instead metropolitan industry, as Chamberlain realised, was to some extent sacrificed to the interests of metropolitan finance.

Notes

1 The quotation is taken from E.G. Wakefield, 'A Letter from Sydney', in E. Lloyd Prichard, ed. *The Collected Works of Edward Gibbon Wakefield* (Glasgow, 1968), p. 165.

2 This 'factor endowment' approach to international trade, found in the work of Adam Smith, is expounded succinctly by D.P. O'Brien, *The Classical Economists* (Oxford, 1975), pp. 170–2. It is also at the heart of the Wakefieldian argument for colonisation, on which see Donald Winch, 'Classical Economics and the Case for Colonization', *Economica,* new ser. 30 (1963). A factor endowment approach is much more realistic in this context than one based on Ricardian or orthodox neo-classical theory, since the latter cannot account for the importance of international factor movements. The best exposition of the contrast between the two positions remains J.H. Williams, 'The Theory of International Trade Reconsidered', *Economic Journal,* 39 (1929).

3 Frank Thistlethwaite, 'Migration from Europe Overseas in the 19th and 20th Centuries', in Herbert Moller, ed. *Population Movements in Modern European History* (1964). See also I. Ferenczi, 'A Historical Study of Migration Statistics', *International Labour Review,* XX (1929). There is now a comprehensive review of English and Welsh experience in Dudley Baines, *Migration in a Mature Economy: Emigration and Internal Migration in England and Wales, 1861–1901* (Cambridge, 1985).

4 On the distribution of French overseas investment in 1900 and 1914 see Herbert Feis, *Europe, The World's Banker, 1870–1914* (Clifton, NJ, 1974), p. 51. French investment in Europe is dealt with by René Girault, *Emprunts russes et investissements français en Russie, 1887–1914* (Paris, 1973), and Raymond Poidevin, *Les relations économiques et financières entre la France et L'Allemagne de 1898 à 1914* (Paris, 1969).

5 W. Arthur Lewis, *Growth and Fluctuations, 1870–1913,* (1978) pp. 185–8.

6 B.N. Thomsen and B. Thomas, *Anglo-Danish Trade, 1661–1963* (Aarhus, 1963), pp. 175–6, 297–8, 344.

7 Brinley Thomas, 'The Historical Record of International Capital Movements to 1913', in J.H. Adler, ed. *Capital Movements and Economic Development* (1967), p. 10.

8 For an introduction to the staple theory of economic growth see Douglass C. North, 'Location Theory and Regional Economic Growth', *Journal of Political Economy,* LXIII (1955); Albert O. Hirschmann, *The Strategy of Economic Development* (New Haven, Conn., 1958), Ch. VI; Melville H. Watkin, 'The Staple Theory of Economic Growth'. *Canadian Journal of Economics and Political Science,* XXIX (1963).

9 There is an abundance of material on Australian growth which adopts the staple approach. The pioneering work was by J.W. McCarty, 'The Staple Approach in Australian Economic History', *Business Archives and History,* IV (1964) and Geoffrey Blainey, 'Technology in Australian History', ibid. V (1965). See also McCarty's, 'Australia as a Region of Recent Settlement in the Nineteenth Century', *Australian Economic History Review,* 12–13 (1972–3). A widely used textbook which adopts this approach is W.H. Sinclair, *The Process of Economic Development in Australia* (Melbourne, 1976), esp. Ch. 1. For Canada see Watkin,'The Staple Theory of Economic Growth'; R.E. Caves and R.H. Holton, *The Canadian Economy* (Cambridge, Mass., 1961); Richard Pomfret, *The Economic Development of Canada* (Toronto, 1984), Ch. 3; and William L. Marr and Donald G. Paterson, *Canada: An Economic History* (Toronto, 1980), pp. 10–18.

10 Kenneth A.H. Buckley,'The Role of Staple Industries in Canada's Economic Development', *Jour. Econ. Hist.,* XVIII (1958).

11 See Mancur Olson, 'The U.K. and the World Market in Wheat and Other Primary Products', *Explorations in Economic History,* XI (1973–4).

12 An early example of this is described by Douglas McCalla,'The Wheat Staple and Upper Canadian Development', in J.M. Bumstead, ed. *Interpreting Canada's Past,* Vol. I, *Before Confederation* (Toronto, 1986). An emphasis on the complexity of development on new frontiers in the later nineteenth century can be found in Richard Pomfret, 'The Staple Theory as an Approach to Canadian and Australian Economic Development', *Austral. Econ. Hist. Rev.,* 21 (1981).

13 The only major work which looks at newly settled countries in a comparative context is Donald Denoon, *Settler Capitalism: The Dynamics of Dependent Development in the Southern Hemisphere* (Oxford, 1983), which covers Australia, New Zealand, South Africa, Argentina, Uruguay and Chile. Denoon's general views on the relationship between the settlement countries and Great Britain seem to be compatible with our own. We would also like to direct attention to C.B. Schedvin. 'Staples and Regions of Pax Britannica', *Econ. Hist. Rev.,* 2nd ser. XLIII (1990), which appeared too late to he incorporated into our arguments.

14 Adam Smith, *The Wealth of Nations,* ed. R.H. Campbell, A.J. Skinner and W.B. Todd (Oxford, 1976), II, p. 614.

15 The classic accounts here are C.A. Bodelsen, *Studies in Mid-Victorian Imperialism* (1960), and R.L. Schuyler, *The Fall of the Old Colonial System: A Study in British Free Trade, 1770–1870* (New York, 1945).

16 J. Gallagher and R.E. Robinson,'The Imperialism of Free Trade, 1815–1914', *Econ. Hist. Rev.,* 2nd ser. VI (1953), p. 4.

17 Earl Grey, *The Colonial Policy of Lord John Russell's Administration* (2nd edn 1853), I, pp. 281–2. See also Peter Burroughs,'The Determinants of Local Self-Government', *Jour. Imp. and Comm. Hist.,* VI (1978), pp. 321–2; and A.G.L. Shaw, 'British Attitudes to the Colonies ca. 1820–50', *Jour. Brit. Stud.,* IX (1969), pp. 84–85.

18 The pioneer studies included J.S. Galbraith, 'Myths of the "Little England" Era', *Am. Hist. Rev.,* LXVII (1961–2), and Richard Koebner and Helmut Dan Schmidt, *Imperialism: The Story and Significance of a Political Word* (Cambridge, 1964). The latest survey is Stanley R. Stembridge, *Parliament, the Press and the Colonies, 1846–1880* (1982). See also Ged Martin, *The Durham Report and British Policy* (Cambridge, 1972).

19 Koebner and Schmidt, *Imperialism,* p. 76; Ged Martin, 'Anti-Imperialism in the Mid-Nineteenth Century and the Nature of the British Empire, 1820–1870', in Ronald Hyam and Ged Martin, *Reappraisals in British Imperial History* (1975), pp. 101–06.

20 Peter Burroughs, *The Canadian Crisis and British Colonial Policy, 1828–1841* (1971), pp. 20–21. For a good example of a colonial elite, see Robert E. Saunders, 'What was the Family Compact?', in J.K. Johnson, ed. *Historical Essays on Upper Canada* (Toronto, 1975).

21 For the substance of Durham's recommendations see A.B. Keith, ed. *Speeches and Documents on British Colonial Policy, 1763–1917* (Oxford, 1961 edn), I, pp. 113–72. The best modern commentary is Martin, *The Durham Report.* See also the latest scholarly sum-

mation in respect of North America: Philip A. Buckner, *The Transition to Responsible Government: British Policy in British North America* (Westport, Conn., 1985).

22 Martin, *The Durham Report,* p. 61.

23 John M. Ward, *Empire in the Antipodes: The British in Australasia, 1840–1860* (1966), Ch. 7; Ged Martin, *Bunyip Aristocracy: The New South Wales Constitutional Debate of 1853 and Hereditary Institutions in the British Colonies* (1986). For an interesting comment on the failure to establish a colonial aristocracy on the English model see G.C. Bolton, 'The Idea of a Colonial Gentry', *Historical Studies: Australia and New Zealand,* 13 (1967–9).

24 Peter Burroughs, 'Colonial Self-Government', in C.C. Eidridge, ed. *British Imperialism in the Nineteenth Century* (1984), p. 62.

25 John M. Ward, *Colonial Self-Government: The British Experience, 1759–1856* (1976), p. 289.

26 Martin, 'Anti-Imperialism in the Mid-Nineteenth Century', pp. 111–14.

27 Burroughs, 'The Determinants of Local Self Government', p. 241. For a similar line of argument see B.A. Knox, 'Reconsidering Mid-Victorian Imperialism', *Jour. Imp. and Comm. Hist.,* I (1972–3).

28 Ward, *Colonial Self-Government,* p. 289.

29 For the correspondence between the colonies and Britain on this issue see Keith, *Speeches and Documents,* II, pp. 51–83.

30 Martin, *The Durham Report,* pp. 59–69.

31 Beverly Kingston, *The Oxford History of Australia, 1860–1900*: Vol. III, *Clad, Confident Morning* (Oxford, 1988), pp. 295–6.

32 C.C. Eldridge, *England's Mission: The Imperial Idea in the Age of Gladstone and Disraeli, 1868–80* (1973), Ch. 3.

33 Lance E. Davis and Robert A. Huttenback, *Mammon and the Pursuit of Empire: The Political Economy of British Imperialism, 1860–1912* (Cambridge, 1987), Table 5.1, p. 161. Britain's average expenditure per capita over the whole period was almost double that of France and Germany (Table 5.2, p. 164). For an interesting general discussion of the (usually vain) attempts to persuade colonists to contribute to imperial defence see ibid. pp. 145–160.

34 Ibid. p. 163.

35 David Jessop, 'The Colonial Stocks Act of 1900: a Symptom of the New Imperialism?', *Jour. Imp. and Comm. Hist.,* IV (1976); Davis and Huttenback, *Mammon and the Pursuit of Empire,* pp. 168–9.

36 Davis and Huttenback, *Mammon and the Pursuit of Empire,* pp. 104–10, esp. Table 2.15, p. 107, and their comments on p. 171. Also, L.S. Pressnell, 'The Sterling System and Financial Crisis before 1914', in Charles P. Kindleberger and Jean-Pierre Laffargue, eds. *Financial Crises: Theory, History and Policy* (Cambridge, 1982), p. 150.

37 A.K. Cairncross, *Home and Foreign Investment, 1870–1913* (Cambridge, 1953), pp. 217–30; Michael Edelstein, 'Realized Rates of Return on U.K. Home and Overseas Portfolio Investment in the Age of High Imperialism', *Explorations in Economic History,* 13 (1976), p. 319.

38 Davis and Huttenback, *Mammon and the Pursuit of Empire,* Table 2.6, p. 54.

39 Ibid. p. 171. Australian state bonds were known in the nineteenth century as 'colonial Consols'. N.G. Butlin, Alan Barnard and J.J. Pincus, *Government and Capitalism: Public and Private Choice in Twentieth-Century Australia* (Sydney, 1982), p. 16.

40 The phrase 'invisible empire' is in Leland H. Jenks, *The Migration of British Capital to 1875* (1927; 1963), p. 1.

41 H.J. Habakkuk, 'Free Trade and Commercial Expansion, 1853–70', *Cambridge History of the British Empire,* II (Cambridge, 1940).

42 See Denoon, *Settler Capitalism,* passim, for this process.

43 Habakkuk, 'Free Trade and Commercial Expansion', pp. 798–9.

44 Ronald Robinson, 'Non-European Foundations of European Imperialism', in Roger Owen and Bob Sutcliffe, eds. *Studies in the Theory of Imperialism* (Oxford, 1972).

45 Denoon, *Settler Capitalism,* p. 223; Cf. Geoffrey Bolton, *Britain's Legacy Overseas* (Oxford, 1973), p. 128.
46 R.T. Naylor, 'The Rise and Fall of the Third Commercial Empire of the St. Lawrence', in Gary Teeple, ed. *Capitalism and the National Question in Canada* (Toronto, 1972).
47 W. Armstrong, 'The Social Origins of Industrial Growth: Canada, Argentina and Australia, 1870–1913', in D.C.M. Platt and Guido di Tella, eds. *Argentina, Australia, Canada: Studies in Comparative Development, 1870–1965* (1985), pp. 87–91. Throughout the pre-1914 period, pastoral and agricultural occupations were dominant among peak wealth-holdings in Australia. But after 1860, when free land-selection policies were introduced, many of the rural wealthy became dependent on the banks because they were forced to bid higher for land; and through the banks they became more directly dependent both upon urban, commercial Australia and upon the City of London. See W.D. Rubinstein, 'The Top Wealth Holders of New South Wales, 1817–1939', *Australian Economic History Review,* XX (1980), esp. Table 5, p. 148; and Kingston, *Oxford History of Australia,* pp. 263–5.
48 R.T. Naylor, *The History of Canadian Business, 1867–1914, I: The Banks and Finance Capital* (Toronto, 1975), p. 68.
49 The best modern introductions to Australian history which put economic developments in the context of wider currents of historical change are Kingston, *Oxford History of Australia,* Vol. III; Stuart McIntyre, *Oxford History of Australia,* Vol. IV, *1901–1942* (Oxford, 1986), Chs. 1–6, and M. Dunn, *Australia and the Empire: From 1788 to the Present* (Sydney, 1984). An interpretation of Australian economic development based on neo-Marxist under-development theory is provided by Philip McMichael, *Settlers and the Agrarian Question: Capitalism and Colonialism in Australia* (Cambridge, 1984). A similar treatment is provided by Peter Cochrane, *Industrialization and Dependence: Australia's Road to Economic Development, 1870–1939* (St Lucia, 1980). See also J.D.B. Miller, ed. *Australians and British: Social and Political Connexions* (North Ryde 1987), and A.F. Madden and W.H. Morris-Jones, eds. *Australia and Britain: Studies in a Changing Relationship* (1980). On New Zealand, the best general introduction remains K. Sinclair, *A History of New Zealand* (1980 edn). There is also useful coverage of Australasian history in Ronald Hyam, *Britain's Imperial Century, 1815–1914: A Study of Empire and Expansion* (1976), Ch. 11.
50 N.G. Butlin, 'Contours of the Australian Economy, 1788–1860', *Austral. Econ. Hist. Rev.,* XXVI (1986), pp. 101–4. For the estimates on which this conclusion is based see N.G. Butlin and W.A. Sinclair, 'Australian Gross Domestic Product, 1788–1860: Estimates, Sources and Methods', in the same issue of the *Review.*
51 Butlin, 'Contours of the Australian Economy, 1788–1860', p. 118.
52 On the City of London connection see Frank J.A. Broeze, 'Private Enterprise and the Peopling of Australia, 1831–50', *Econ. Hist. Rev.,* 2nd ser. XXXV (1982). The role of government in economic development is considered in J.J. Eddy, *Britain and the Australian Colonies, 1818–1831: The Technique of Government* (Oxford, 1969), and Peter Burroughs, *Britain and Australia, 1831–55* (Oxford, 1967).
53 S.J. Butlin, *The Foundations of the Australian Monetary System, 1788–1851* (Melbourne, 1953), p. 258. The principal British banks are discussed on pp. 259–68.
54 Ibid. pp. 264–5, 345–55, 378.
55 D.T. Merrett, '"Paradise Lost?" British Banks in Australia', in G. Jones, ed. *Banks as Multinationals* (1990), pp. 63–71.
56 D.C.M. Platt, *Latin America and British Trade, 1806–1914* (1972), pp. 107, 111; N.G. Butlin, *Investment in Australian Economic Development, 1861–1900* (Cambridge, 1964), p. 28. An excellent introduction to Australian experience in foreign trade can now be found in Barrie Dyster and David Meredith, *Australia in the International Economy in the Twentieth Century* (Cambridge, 1990).
57 A.H. Tocker, 'The Monetary Standards of Australia and New Zealand', *Economic Journal,* 34 (1924).

58 Butlin, *Investment in Australian Economic Development,* p. 16. For a good overview of Australian economic growth in the late nineteenth century set W.A. Sinclair, *The Process of Economic Development in Australia* (Melbourne, 1976).
59 For the gold rush period the best accounts remain Geoffrey Blainey, *The Rush That Never Ended: Mining in Australia* (Melbourne, 1963), and E.V. Portus, 'The Gold Discoveries of 1850–60', in the *Cambridge History of the British Empire,* VII, Pt. I, (Cambridge, 1933).
60 N.G. Butlin, 'Some Perspectives on Australian Economic Development, 1890–1965', in Colin Forster, ed. *Australian Economic Development in the Twentieth Century* (1970), p. 299.
61 Alan C. Kelley, 'Demographic Change and Economic Growth in Australia, 1861–1911', *Explorations in Entrepreneurial History,* V (1967–8); A.R. Hall, 'Some Long Period Effects of the Kinked Age-Distribution of the Population of Australia, 1861–1961', *Economic Record,* XXXIX (1963).
62 Butlin, 'Some Perspectives on Australian Economic Development', Table 6.8, p. 289.
63 See N.G. Butlin, 'Colonial Socialism in Australia', in H.G.J. Aitken, ed. *The State and Economic Growth* (New York, 1959); idem, *Investment in Australian Economic Development,* p. 29. See also Dyster and Meredith, *Australia in the International Economy,* Table 2.6, p. 34. The average amount borrowed by the Australian colonies between 1865 and 1914 was roughly £7m. per year of which £5.6m. was by public authorities. See Davis and Huttenback, *Mammon and the Pursuit of Empire,* Table 2.4, p. 48. For a detailed study of one state's borrowings in Britain, see P.N. Lamb, 'Early Overseas Borrowing by the New South Wales Government', *Business Archives and History,* IV (1964). Between 1856 and 1868 £6.6m. was raised in London as against £2.3m. in Sydney (p. 61). For further details on Australia and the London money market see R.S. Gilbert, 'London Financial Intermediaries and Australian Overseas Borrowing', *Austral. Econ. Hist. Rev.,* XI (1971), esp. pp. 41–5.
64 J.D. Bailey, *Growth and Depression: Contrasts in the Australian and British Economics, 1870–1880* (Canberra, 1956), Ch. V and pp. 123–36.
65 M. Edelstein, *Overseas Investment in the Age of High Imperialism: The United Kingdom, 1850–1914* (1982), Ch. XI.
66 Butlin, *Investment in Australian Economic Development,* p. 37 and pp. 407–24. On the problems of the pastoral companies see the articles by Neville Cain, 'Capital Structure and Financial Disequilibrium: Pastoral Companies in Australia, 1880–93', and 'Pastoral Expansion and Crisis in New South Wales, 1880–93: the Lending View', both in *Australian Economic Papers,* II (1963).
67 Butlin, *Investment in Australian Economic Development,* Table 7, p. 28 for the 1861–5 figures; the 1886–90 estimates are Butlin's figures as revised by E.A. Boehm, *Prosperity and Depression in Australia, 1887–1897* (Oxford, 1971), Table 43, p. 187. See also H. Coombs, 'Balance of Payments Problems: Old and New Style', in N.H. Drohan and J.H. Day, eds. *Readings in Australian Economics* (Melbourne, 1966), pp. 72–3.
68 Calculated from Boehm, *Prosperity and Depression in Australia,* Table 7, p. 15.
69 A.R. Hall, *Australia and the London Capital Market, 1870–1914* (Canberra, 1963), Ch. VIII. See also B.L. Bentick, 'Foreign Borrowing, Wealth, and Consumption: Victoria, 1873–93', *Economic Record,* 45 (1969).
70 Emphasis on the domestic roots of the depression can be found in Butlin, *Investment in Australian Economic Development,* Ch. VI; and in W.A. Sinclair, 'The Depression of the 1980s and the 1890s in Australia: a Comparison', in Drohan and Day, *Readings in Australian Economics,* pp. 85–90. Modern interpretations of the crisis are discussed in Dyster and Meredith, *Australia in the International Economy,* pp. 44–9.
71 On the balance of payments crisis see Coombs, 'Balance of Payment Problems', pp. 75–6, and Boehm, *Prosperity and Depression in Australia,* Ch. VII.
72 A vivid picture of the crisis produced by drought and over-capitalisation of marginal stations is given in Neville Cain, 'Companies and Squatting in the Western Division of New South Wales, 1896–1905', in Alan Barnard, ed. *The Simple Fleece: Studies in the Australian Wool Industry* (Parkville, Victoria 1962).

73 N.G. Butlin, *Australian Domestic Product, Investment and Foreign Borrowing, 1861–1938/39* (Cambridge, 1962), Table 1, p. 6.

74 W.A. Sinclair, 'Aspects of Economic Growth, 1900–1930', in A.H. Boxer, ed. *Aspects of the Australian Economy* (Melbourne 1965). See also Dyster and Meredith, *Australia in the International Economy,* pp. 49–59.

75 Butlin, *Australian Domestic Product, Investment and Foreign Borrowing,* Table 265, p. 444. The figures suggest that, just before World War I, Australia was about to feel the effects of another steep upswing in population growth of the kind experienced in the 1880s. Kelley, 'Demographic Change and Economic Growth', Table 1, p. 214. In 1914, when national income was roughly £80 per head, Australian borrowings from Britain were equivalent to £75 per person. McIntyre, *Oxford History of Australia,* 4, p. 42.

76 Boehm, *Prosperity and Depression in Australia,* pp. 302–12.

77 S.J. Butlin, *The Australia and New Zealand Bank: The Bank of Australasia and the Union Bank of Australia Ltd., 1828–1951* (1961), p. 279; and Boehm, *Prosperity and Depression in Australia,* Table 65, pp. 272–3.

78 A.J.S. Baster, *The Imperial Banks* (1929), pp. 59–60, 138–40; Geoffrey Blainey, *Cold and Paper* (Melbourne, 1958), pp. 5–7.

79 Baster, *The Imperial Banks,* p. 40; Butlin, *The Australia and New Zealand Bank,* pp. 249–51.

80 Butlin, *The Australia and New Zealand Bank,* p. 281.

81 C.M.H. Clark, *A Short History of Australia* (Sydney, 1963), p. 173. Before Federation in 1901, the economic links between the colonies were small compared with their contacts with Britain. See Kingston, *Oxford History of Australia,* Ill, p. 298. An important collection of essays on this topic is A.W. Martin, ed. *Essays in Australian Federation* (Melbourne, 1969). See also H.M. Schwartz, *In the Dominions of Debt: Historical Perspectives on Dependent Development* (Ithaca, NY, 1989), Ch. 3; and Dyster and Meredith, *Australia in the International Economy,* pp. 60–4.

82 Richard Jebb, *Studies in Colonial Nationalism* (1905), pp. 203–8; C.M.H. Clark, ed. *Select Documents in Australian History, 1851–1900* (Sydney, 1955), pp. 305–10. See also Peter Love, *Labour and the Money Power* (Melbourne, 1984).

83 Sir E. Dibbs, quoted in Clark, *Select Documents in Australian History,* p. 311.

84 Boehm, *Prosperity and Depression in Australia,* pp. 178, 190, 207.

85 Luke Trainor, 'The Economics of the Imperial Connexion: Britain and the Australian Colonies, 1886–96' (Institute of Commonwealth Studies, Seminar Paper, University of London, 1979). It is worth noticing, too, that the Act of the British Parliament which created the Australian Commonwealth in 1901 was shaped in important particulars by the need to soothe the fears of British investors. See B.K. de Garis, 'The Colonial Office and the Commonwealth Constitution Bill', in Martin, *Essays in Australian Federation.*

86 W.A. Sinclair, 'The Tariff and Manufacturing Employment in Victoria, 1860–1900', *Economic Record,* XXXI (1955); idem, 'The Tariff and Economic Growth in Pre-Federation Victoria', ibid. XLVII (1971).

87 On manufacturing industry see A. Thompson, 'The Enigma of Australian Manufacturing, 1851–1901', *Australian Economic Papers,* IX (1970).

88 Ian Turner, *Industrial Labour and Politics: The Labour Movement in Eastern Australia* (Cambridge, 1965), Chs. I and II; Robin Gollan, *Radical and Working Class Politics: A Study of Eastern Australia, 1850–1910,* (Parkville, 1965), Ch. 9. A recent study of white nationalism is Avner Offer, 'Pacific Rim Societies: Asian Labour and White Nationalism', in John Eddy and Deryck Schreuder, eds. *The Rise of Colonial Nationalism* (Sydney, 1988).

89 Jebb, *Studies in Colonial Nationalism,* pp. 230–1.

90 Ibid. Australia tried to stimulate British interest in preferences by offering her own from 1906. See Dyster and Meredith, *Australia in the International Economy,* pp. 65–6.

91 For increased foreign competition in the Australian market see I.W. McLean, 'Anglo-American Engineering Competition, 1870–1914: Some Third Market Evidence', *Econ. Hist. Rev.,* 2nd ser. XXIX (1976).

92 G.R. Hawke, *The Making of New Zealand: An Economic History* (Cambridge, 1985), Fig. 3.4, p. 58.

93 The best accounts of New Zealand's economic history from our perspective are Hawke, *The Making of New Zealand*; C.G.F. Simkin, *The Instability of a Dependent Economy: Economic Fluctuations in New Zealand, 1840–1914,* (Oxford, 1951); and R.C.J. Stone, *Makers of Fortune: A Colonial Business Community and its Fall* (Auckland, 1973). See also Schwartz, *In the Dominions of Debt,* Ch. 5.

94 J.A. Dowie, 'Business Politicians in Action: the New Zealand Railway Boom of the 1870s', *Business Archives and History,* V (1965); F. Capie and K.A. Tucker, 'Foreign Investment in New Zealand, 1870–1914' (unpublished MS, 1976).

95 Simkin, '*The Instability of a Dependent Economy*', p. 24.

96 Hawke, *The Making of New Zealand,* pp. 71–83. The New Zealand banking system was heavily influenced by both British and Australian institutions. Ibid. pp. 60–4.

97 W. Rosenberg, 'Capital Imports and Growth, the Case of New Zealand: Foreign Investment in New Zealand, 1840–1958', *Econ. Jour.,* LXXI (1961), Tables III and IV, pp. 95–6. New Zealand earned a persistent surplus on her balance of trade from the late 1880s onwards. Details can be found in J.B. Condliffe, 'The External Trade of New Zealand', *New Zealand Official Year Book* (1915), pp. 875–6.

98 Rosenberg, 'Capital Imports and Growth', pp. 107–8.

99 For the New Zealand case see Hawke, *The Making of New Zealand,* p. 82.

100 This is a simplified version of the thesis argued by Schwartz, *In the Dominions of Debt,* Ch. 4.

101 Ian M. Drummond, 'Government Securities on Colonial New Issue Markets: Australia and Canada, 1895–1914', *Yale Economic Essays,* I (1961).

102 Love, *Australia and the Money Power,* p. 47. On the rise of Labour after 1890 see McIntyre, *Oxford History of Australia,* IV, Chs. 3 and 4.

103 Sinclair, *History of New Zealand,* p. 166. On changes in land ownership and use see J.D. Gould, 'The Twilight of the Estates, 1891–1910', *Austral. Econ. Hist. Rev.,* X (1970).

104 On New Zealand see also Schwartz, *In the Dominions of Debt,* Ch. 5. For a more global perspective see Denoon, *Settler Capitalism,* Ch. 3.

105 Growth of GDP was estimated at 4.7 per cent per year for 1861–90 and at 2.4 per cent for 1891–1913. Rates of growth of GDP per capita were 1.2 per cent and 0.4 per cent per annum respectively. See Butlin, 'Some Perspectives on Australian Economic Development', Table 6.6, p. 284.

106 The pressures for preferences in New Zealand are discussed in Sinclair, *History of New Zealand,* pp. 223–4.

107 As early as 1851, the Canadians had adopted the decimal system and the dollar. The connection between the USA and Canada had become so intimate by the 1870s that Canadian banks, taking advantage of legislative restrictions on their American counterparts, were setting up branches in New York and playing a significant role in the finance of Anglo-American trade. See E.P. Neufeld, ed. *Money and Banking in Canada: Historical Documents and Commentary* (Toronto, 1964), pp. 128–9 and 163–9. On the banking system as a whole see Pomfret, *The Economic Development of Canada,* pp. 168ff; Marr and Paterson, *Canada: An Economic History* pp. 249–52; Naylor, *The History of Canadian Business,* I, Ch. III; and Craig McIvor, *Canadian Monetary, Banking and Fiscal Development* (Toronto, 1958).

108 The best general histories of Canada are by Pomfret and by Marr and Paterson cited in n. 9, and by W.J. Easterbrook and H.G.J. Aitken, *Canadian Economic History* (Toronto, 1956). See also H.G.J. Aitken, 'Defensive Expansionism: the State and Growth in Canada', in Aitken, *The State and Economic Growth*; O.J. Firestone, *Canadian Economic Development, 1867–1953* (Income and Wealth Series, VII, 1958); and idem, 'Development of Canada's Economy, 1850–1900', in *Trends in the American Economy in the Nineteenth Century* (Studies in Income and Wealth, XXIV, Princeton, NJ, 1960). See also the discussion of Canada in the context of a wide review of Anglo-American relations in Hyam, *Britain's Imperial Century,* Ch. 6.

109 Marr and Paterson, *Canada: An Economic History,* pp. 87–95; Aitken, 'Defensive Expansionism', pp. 88ff.

110 The classic study here is Donald G. Creighton, *The Commercial Empire of the St. Lawrence* (Toronto, 1937).

111 Marr and Paterson, *Canada: An Economic History,* p. 98; Easterbrook and Aitken, *Canadian Economic History,* p. 269. On the importance of the canals in stimulating demand for British capital see H.C. Pentland, 'The Role of Capital in Canadian Economic Development before 1875', *Canadian Journal of Economics and Political Science,* XVI (1950).

112 Easterbrook and Aitken, *Canadian Economic History,* p. 352.

113 At the same time as they were facing the problem in the north, the British were withdrawing from central America under US pressure. See Kenneth Bourne, *Britain and the Balance of Power in North America, 1815–1908* (1967), Ch. 6. On Britain's tacit recognition of the need to withdraw from the North American continent, see W.L. Morton, *The Critical Years: The Union of British North America, 1857–1873* (Oxford, 1964), p. 216. The most recent detailed study of US–Canadian relations from this angle is R.C. Stuart, *United States Expansionism and British North America, 1775–1871* (Chapel Hill, NC, 1988).

114 Stembridge, *Parliament, the Press and the Colonies,* passim.

115 See, for example, Richard Cobden's speech at Manchester in 1849, quoted in George Bennett, *The Concept of Empire, 1774–1947* (1953), pp. 169–70.

116 Russell to Grey in Grey Papers, University of Durham, quoted in John B. Ingham, 'Power to the Powerless: British North America and the Pursuit of Reciprocity, 1846–1854', *Bulletin of Canadian Studies,* VIII (1984), p. 125.

117 Gerald J.J. Tulchinsky, *The River Barons: Montreal Businessmen and the Growth of Industry and Transportation, 1837–53* (Toronto, 1977), Ch. 13.

118 Peter Baskerville, 'Americans in Britain's Backyard: the Railway Era in Upper Canada, 1850–1880', *Bus. Hist. Rev.,* LV (1981) p. 324.

119 Ibid. p. 335.

120 D.G. Masters, *The Reciprocity Treaty of 1854* (Toronto, 1963); Robert Ankli, 'The 1854 Reciprocity Treaty', *Canadian Journal of Economics,* 4 (1971); Ingham, 'Power to the Powerless', passim. For the British recognition of the importance of the treaty at this crisis point in Canadian history see A.G. Doughty, ed. *The Grey–Elgin Papers, 1846–52* (Ottawa, 1937), pp. 363–413, 465–66, 471.

121 For something of the flavour of the arguments and proposals which preoccupied Grey and Elgin see Doughty, *The Grey–Elgin Papers, 1846–52,* pp. 26, 37, 252–4, 257–61, 263, 266–7, 276–7, 349, 351, 392, 419, 437, 448, 608–12, 1591, 1593. See also W.P. Morrell, *Colonial Policy in the Age of Peel and Russell* (Oxford, 1930), pp. 436–44.

122 Donald Roman, 'The Contribution of Imperial Guarantees for Colonial Railway Loans to the Consolidation of British North America, 1847–65' (unpublished D. Phil thesis, Oxford, 1978). J.A. Gibson, 'The Duke of Newcastle and British North American Affairs, 1859–64', *Canadian Hist. Rev.,* XLIV (1963); and P.B. Waite, 'A Letter from Leonard Tilley on the Intercolonial Railway, 1863', *Canadian Hist. Rev.,* XLV (1964), give insights into particular episodes.

123 For some interesting aspects of this see Michael J. Piva, 'Continuity and Crisis: Francis Hincks and Canadian Economic Policy', *Canadian Hist. Rev.,* LXVI (1985).

124 Penelope Hartland, 'Factors in the Economic Growth of Canada', *Jour. Econ. Hist.,* XV (1955), p. 14.

125 On the origins of the British bankers' concern with Canada see M.L. Magill, 'John H. Dunn and the Bankers', in Johnson, *Historical Essays on Upper Canada.*

126 Roger Fulford, *Glyn's, 1753–1943: Six Generations in Lombard St.* (1953), p. 155; Philip Ziegler, *The Sixth Great Power: Barings, 1762–1929* (1988), p. 226; D.C.M. Platt and J. Adelman, 'London Merchant Bankers in the First Phase of Heavy Borrowing: the Grand Trunk Railway of Canada', *Jour. Imp. and Comm. Hist.,* XXVIII (1990), pp. 218–23.

127 On accepting the Agency in 1837, Glyn wrote that 'there is no salary or emolument but it is a feather': Glyn to Sir George Grey, 10 June 1837, quoted in Fulford, *Glyn's,* p. 146.

On the other hand, it is arguable that, by the late 1850s, Barings and Glyn's commitment to the Grand Trunk was such that they had to support it because their reputations were linked with its survival. Platt and Adelman, 'London Merchant Bankers in the First Phase of Heavy Borrowing', p. 221.

128 Quoted in Fulford, *Glyn's,* p. 153. See also Platt and Adelman, 'London Merchant Bankers in the First Phase of Heavy Borrowing', p. 216.

129 Ziegler, *The Sixth Great Power,* p. 226. For a Canadian view of the role of English bankers in North America at the time see Naylor, *History of Canadian Business,* I, pp. 23–8. On the Grand Trunk itself see George Parkin de Twenebroker Glazebrook, *A History of Transportation in Canada,* I (Toronto, 1967), pp. 152ff; and Archibald William Currie, *The Grand Trunk Railway of Canada* (Toronto, 1957).

130 Masters, *The Reciprocity Treaty,* Ch. 6 and pp. 130–6.

131 Harold A. Innis, *Essays in Canadian Economic History* (Toronto, 1956), p. 395; cf. also p. 174. For similarly forthright statements see Donald G. Creighton, *British North America at Confederation* (Toronto, 1939), p. 9; and Peter J. Smith, 'The Ideological Origins of Canadian Confederation', *Canadian Journal of Politics,* 20 (1987), p. 28.

132 Naylor, 'The Rise and Fall of the Third Commercial Empire of the St. Lawrence', p. 15.

133 C.P. Stacey, 'Britain's Withdrawal from North America, 1864–1871', *Canadian Hist. Rev.,* XXXVI (1955); idem, *Canada and the British Army, 1846–1971: A Study in the Practice of Responsible Government* (Toronto, 1963).

134 A.B. Erickson, 'Edward T. Cardwell: Peelite', *Transactions of the American Philosophical Society,* NS, XLIX, Pt. II (1959), pp. 35–9; D.M.L. Farr, *The Colonial Office and Canada, 1867–87* (Toronto, 1955), Ch. 3; P.B. Waite, 'Edward Cardwell and Confederation', *Canadian Hist. Rev.,* 4 (1962). For the direct pan played by British investors in shifting attention to the idea of linking Canada and the Maritimes with the Pacific Coast see John Bartlett Brebner, *North Atlantic Triangle: The Interplay of Canada, the United States and Great Britain* (New Haven, Conn., 1946), pp. 174–7; Glazebrook, *A History of Transportation,* II, p. 3; Arthur R.M. Lower, *Colony to Nation: A History of Canada* (Toronto 1964), pp. 316–17; and Elaine Allen Mitchell, 'Edward Watkin and the Buying-Out of the Hudson's Bay Company', *Canadian Hist. Rev.,* 34 (1953).

135 Frank H. Underhill, *The Image of Confederation* (Toronto, 1964), pp. 24–26.

136 Blake to McKenzie, 1 July 1876, in *Dufferin-Carnarvon Correspondence, 1874–78* (Toronto, 1955), p. 397. As a leading historian of the white empire recently put the matter: 'the gentlemen who made mid-Victorian policy conveyed their intentions through the velvet glove rather than the bludgeon, and were adept at hinting that it might contain metal'. See Ged Martin, 'Launching Canadian Confederation: Means and Ends, 1836–1864', *Hist. Jour.,* 27 (1984), p. 601.

137 Morton, *The Critical Years,* pp. 250–8, links the treaty firmly with Confederation. For the wider context of Anglo-American relations see M.M. Robson, 'The Alabama Claim and the Anglo-American Reconciliation, 1865–71', *Canadian Hist. Rev.,* 42 (1961).

138 Morton, *The Critical Years,* pp. 266–7; Farr, *The Colonial Office and Canada,* pp. 85–91. On the earlier incorporation of British Columbia within the empire see B.M. Gough, '"Turbulent Frontiers" and British Expansion: Governor James Douglas, the Royal Navy, and the British Columbia Gold Rushes', *Pacific Historical Review,* XLI (1972).

139 Though, in supporting the Reciprocity Treaty idea, Grey and other British statesmen were acquiescing in a policy which allowed Canada to impose discriminatory duties on Britain and other countries. See Masters, *The Reciprocity Treaty,* pp. 5–8.

140 On tariff policy see Masters, *The Reciprocity Treaty,* pp. 64–7: the connection between thinking on the tariff issue in the 1850s and the later National Policy is stressed in Morton, *The Critical Years,* pp. 65–7, and in A.A. den Otter, 'Alexander Galt, the 1859 Tariff and Canadian Economic Nationalism', *Canadian Hist. Rev.,* LXIII (1982).

141 The best introduction to the National Policy is still probably V.C. Fowke, 'The National Policy – Old and New', *Canadian Jour. Econ. and Pol. Sci.,* XVIII (1952); 'The National Policy and Western Development in N. America', *Jour. Econ. Hist.,* XVI (1956), and *The National Policy and the Wheat Economy* (Toronto, 1957).

142 Naylor, 'The Rise and Fall of the Third Commercial Empire of the St. Lawrence', pp. 19ff.

143 Judith Teichmann, 'Businessmen and Politics in the Process of Economic Development: Argentina and Canada', *Canadian Jour. Pol.,* 15 (1982), pp. 56–7.

144 L.R. McDonald, 'Merchants against Industry: An Idea and its Origins', *Canadian Hist. Rev.,* LVI (1975); Glen Williams, 'The National Policy Tariffs: Industrial Underdevelopment through Import Substitution', *Canadian Jour. Pol.,* 12 (1979), pp. 333–8. For another interesting comment on the Naylor thesis see Pomfret, *The Economic Development of Canada,* pp. 142–5. For the attitudes of Canadian businessmen to the penetration of American capital see Michael Bliss, *A Living Profit: Studies in the Social History of Canadian Business, 1883–1911* (Toronto, 1974), pp. 109–111.

145 Williams, 'The National Policy Tariffs', p. 361.

146 Charles M. Studness, 'Economic Opportunity and the Westward Migration of Canadians during the late 19th Century', *Canadian Jour. Econ. and Pol. Sci.,* XXX (1964). For various criticisms of the National Policy, both contemporary and recent, see Melville H Watkin, 'Economic Nationalism', ibid. XXXII (1966); Ian Grant, 'Erasmus Wiman: a Continentalist Replies to Canadian Imperialism', *Canadian Hist. Rev.,* LIII (1972); and Goldwin Smith's famous *Canada and the Canada Question* (1891).

147 D.C. Masters, 'Financing the CPR, 1880–5', *Canadian Hist. Rev.,* XXIV (1943); Ziegler, *The Sixth Great Power,* pp. 227–8; Glazebrook, *History of Transportation,* II, pp. 77, 85–9.

148 This is a major theme of Robert Craig Brown, *Canada's National Policy, 1883–1900: A Study in Canadian-American Relations* (Princeton, NJ, 1964). See also Bliss, *A Living Profit,* pp. 97–106.

149 In 1881 Macdonald claimed that, 'if our scheme is carried out, the steamer landing at Halifax will discharge its freight and emigrants upon a British railway, which will go through Quebec and through Ontario to the Far West, on British territory, under a British flag, under Canadian laws and without any chance of either the immigrant being deluded or seduced from his allegiance or proposed residence in Canada'. Quoted in Fowke, 'National Policy and Western Development in N. America', p. 476.

150 Brown, *Canada's National Policy,* Ch. 7. See also Edward Vickery, 'Exports and North American Economic Growth: "Structuralist" and "Staple" Models in Historical Perspective', *Canadian Jour. Econ.,* 7 (1974).

151 A.A. den Otter, *The Galts and the Development of Western Canada* (Edmonton, 1982), p. 43.

152 Brown, *Canada's National Policy,* Ch. 8; Norman Penlington, *Canada and Imperialism, 1896–1899* (Toronto, 1965), pp. 45–52.

153 Penlington, *Canada and Imperialism,* pp. 218–60.

154 Penlington argues that the interest in imperial unity represented a tacit Anglo-Canadian alliance to prevent Canada being swallowed up by the United States. 'It was the condition of Canada's freedom and potential nationhood during the country's dejected and difficult childhood in the last decades of the nineteenth century'. See *Canada and Imperialism,* p. 261.

155 Farr's book, *The Colonial Office and Canada,* explores the emergence of a relationship with Britain which, in Lord Carnarvon's words, was 'political rather than colonial' (p. 309).

156 For studies of the wheat boom see John Archibald Stovel, *Canada in the World Economy* (Cambridge, Mass., 1959), pp. 104–24; A.K. Cairncross, *Home and Foreign Investment, 1870–1913* (Cambridge, 1953), Ch. III; D.C. Corbett, 'Immigration and Economic Development', *Canadian Jour. Econ. and Pol. Sci.,* XVII (1951); and G.M. Meier, 'Economic Development and the Transfer Mechanism: Canada, 1859–1913', ibid. XIX (1953); Robert E. Ankli, 'The Growth of the Canadian Economy, 1896–1920: Export-led and/or Neo-Classical Growth', *Expl. Econ. Hist.,* 17 (1980).

157 A small but significant proportion of migrants to Canada could be classed as English gentlemen. As public school numbers increased, competition in Britain for places on the land (suffering from the effects of agricultural depression) and in the professions

was so great that, after 1870, around 10 per cent of the products of the 'best' schools were going abroad to seek their fortunes. Emigration to Canada appealed to the young, the athletic and the adventurous: 'in the minds of many of the emigrants, Canada was simply a remote, somewhat rugged, part of Great Britain'. It offered the prospect of landownership – land could be had for a penny an acre in the west in the early days – and other eligible gentlemanly occupations. Sport was another attraction, the coyote taking the place of the fox on the frontier. Public-school migrants kept in close touch with home, attracting investment and providing openings for new waves of gentlemanly emigration. They were concentrated enough in some places to set the social tone as in, for example, Victoria, British Columbia. These 'older established communities provided social diversion, financial security, and enough novelty to keep life interesting', and, in return, they 'provided Canada with a cultured white collar labour force . . . which was . . . vital in turning the cogs of the nation's commercial and administrative machinery'. Patrick A. Dunae, *Gentlemen Emigrants: From the British Public Schools to the Canadian Frontier* (Vancouver, 1981). Quotations are from pp. 67 and 79.

158 Stovel, *Canada in the World Economy,* Table 9, p. 12. There are annual estimates of portfolio investment in Canada in Matthew Simon, 'British Investments in Canada, 1865–1914', *Canadian Jour. Econ.,* III (1970). The limited nature of the market for securities in Canada itself is emphasised in R.C. Michie, 'The Canadian Securities Market, 1850–1914', *Bus. Hist. Rev.,* 62 (1988).

159 Kenneth A.H. Buckley, *Capital Formation in Canada, 1896–1930* (Toronto, 1955), Table XII, p. 30. British investors dominated the Canadian market in railway and government stocks. They held 60 per cent of the shares of the CPR in 1913. Michie, 'The Canadian Securities Market', pp. 38–41.

160 Magill, 'John H. Dunn and the Bankers', p. 214.

161 This is based on the assumption of an average return of 5 per cent on British investment in Canada.

162 Donald G. Paterson, *British Direct Investment in Canada, 1890–1914: Estimates and Determinants* (Toronto, 1976).

163 G.L. Reuber, *Britain's Export Trade with Canada* (Toronto, 1960), Table I, p. 6. The failure of British manufacturers to take maximum advantage of the flow of British capital to Canada after 1900 was noted by contemporaries with alarm. *Royal Commission on the National Resources, Trade and Legislation of Certain Portions of His Majesty's Dominions,* Minutes of Evidence, Pt. I (Cd 8458) 1917, p. 416; and ibid. *Fifth Interim Report* (Cd 8457) 1917, paras. 23–5.

164 S.B. Saul, *Studies in British Overseas Trade, 1870–1914* (Liverpool, 1960), p. 186.

165 Ibid. Ch. VII.

166 Denoon, *Settler Capitalism,* p. 223.

167 Lewis, *Growth and Fluctuations,* Table 7.1, p. 163.

168 'Argentina and parts of China were more closely linked with Britain through trade and investment in 1913 than were Canada and the West Indies': Saul, *Studies in Overseas Trade, 1870–1914,* p. 228.

9

CALLING THE NEW WORLD INTO EXISTENCE

South America, 1815–1914[1]

Britain's relations with South America in the nineteenth century are recognised by historians of all persuasions as providing the crucial regional test of theories of informal imperialism. With the minor exception of Guyana (a seventeenth-century settlement which was reinforced during the French Wars), Britain neither sought nor acquired territorial rights on the South American mainland. Consequently, the argument that Britain exercised imperialist control over the continent can be sustained only if it can be shown that the newly liberated states became card-carrying, if not flag-waving, members of her informal empire. Gallagher and Robinson's celebrated article made precisely this claim by suggesting that Britain aimed at 'indirect political hegemony' in South America in order to promote her commercial interests there.[2] However, Platt has demonstrated that British governments intervened in South America's internal affairs only when international law had been broken or when British lives and property were at risk.[3] It is possible to argue that Platt's own reading of the evidence follows the workings of the official mind rather too closely; additional sources and a different perspective have revealed instances where the rules were indeed bent in order to defend Britain's economic interests.[4] Nevertheless, on the evidence presently available, Platt's case would seem to hold for most of the continent and for the greater part of the period under review.

If, then, Britain did found an informal empire in South America, it must have been based on forms of collaborative interaction which encouraged independent states to become subordinate partners of the metropolitan power. Evidence of this development might be sought in the growth of 'complementary satellite economies';[5] it might also appear in the guise of 'cultural imperialism', whereby 'the values, attitudes and institutions of the expansionist nation overcome those of the recipient one'.[6] From this perspective, Britain's sway in South America derived from a combination of overwhelming economic power and mesmerising liberal ideology.

In these circumstances, direct political interference by Britain was either unnecessary or else was likely to be counter-productive in stirring nationalist feelings.

This seemingly promising line of inquiry has also run into serious opposition. Detailed research undertaken (or directed) by Platt in particular has concluded that South American states retained economic as well as political sovereignty during the period under review.[7] Economic relations between Britain and South America were entered into freely because both sides wanted an open door for commerce and capital. International exchange was mutually beneficial because competitive pressures prevented Britain from establishing a monopolistic and hence an exploitative grip on markets and resources. If South America's economic prospects came to rely on a narrow range of exports, it was because specialisation followed the logic of comparative advantage and not because imperialist forces imposed deviations from the 'natural' path of development. Just as British governments avoided political interference in South American affairs, so too the unofficial mind of imperialism neither envisaged nor imposed a form of 'business imperialism' on the continent. Far from moulding South American societies in a European image, the Europeans themselves often had to adapt to the shape of local institutions.

Evaluating these claims and counter-claims has been made more difficult by the fact that the debate has shown signs of fission in recent years.[8] On the one hand, the proliferation of local studies, while correcting stereotypes of the periphery associated with conventional metropolitan-based theories of imperialism, has made it harder to generalise responsibly about the continent as a whole. On the other hand, the notion of informal empire has been lifted out of its original mid-nineteenth-century setting and attached to high-flying versions of the dependency thesis. One consequence has been to introduce a number of broad and often poorly specified propositions into the discussion; another has been to tempt participants on both sides into mixing judgements about the results of dependence with explanations of the causes of imperialism, a procedure which has an immediate appeal but which is dubious in terms of both logic and the use of historical evidence.

These trends have underlined the need for a restatement of the causes of British imperialism which shows an awareness of new research on the history of countries in South America and which is also anchored in a particular institutional setting, rather than derived from very general assumptions pertaining to European capitalism as a whole. Specifically, we shall apply our interpretation of imperialism to the South American case by examining how Britain administered the 'rules of the game' in her dealings with the principal players in the new states during the century after 1815. We shall return, in the conclusion, to the question of whether the game itself, as well as the way it was refereed, constituted a form of external control and, if so, whether this can be said to have been imperialistic.

A continental perspective

As the French Wars altered the map of Europe, so too they moved the boundaries of Europe's overseas empires. The Spanish empire in Latin America fell apart between

1810 and 1824, some 300 years after its foundation.[9] The equally antique Portuguese empire effectively divided itself in 1807, when the Prince Regent was hastily shipped to Brazil under British protection to escape the liberating imperialism of Napoleon's armies. The subsequent diversification of Brazil's political and commercial ties, particularly her reorientation towards Britain, provoked a conservative reaction in Portugal which in turn led Brazil to declare independence in 1822.[10] If the stages of imperial decline now appear to have been both more protracted and more complex than was once thought, they have also revealed a sequence of events which prompts comparison with other colonial systems in their terminal state: the growth of a degree of 'informal emancipation' seen in the burgeoning aspirations of colonial interest groups and the loosening of economic ties with the metropole; the attempt to impose a form of 'new imperialism' characterised by tighter centralisation and increased taxation; and the dogged failure of imperial governments to recognise political realities until long after they had materialised and been given permanent illumination.[11]

The opportunities presented by these events were not lost on British policymakers; but they were regarded as setting the scene for extending influence rather than dominion. In 1807, in the aftermath of an unauthorised and unsuccessful attempt to annex the estuary of the River Plate,[12] Castlereagh decided that the British should present themselves in future as 'auxiliaries and protectors' rather than as conquistadors.[13] This principle was endorsed by Canning, his successor at the Foreign Office, and, with a few exceptions at moments of crisis or misjudgement, it was to guide British policy towards South America throughout the nineteenth century. Military intervention presented daunting logistical problems; it was also counterproductive in rousing opposition among nationalists whose hostility to colonial rule scarcely needed further advertisement. Persuasion rather than coercion was required if the emerging new states of Latin America were to become, in Canning's well-known phrase, both free and English.[14] Thus was a role found for South America in Britain's plans for a new world order after 1815. Liberal reforms would preserve monarchy, property and order at home, check what Canning referred to as 'the evils of democracy', and defuse the time bombs of revolution.[15] Commercial expansion abroad would deliver prosperity, and prosperity would fix in place a string of friendly states which would help to maintain stability in a world caught between the old, 'worn out' monarchies of continental Europe and the 'youthful and stirring' nations headed by the United States.[16]

Transplanting liberal principles proved to be more complicated than was originally supposed. Britain's hopes that a clutch of viable but also pliable monarchies would arise from the debris of the Iberian empires were quickly disappointed.[17] Brazil alone preserved a monarchical system, but it rested on slavery and the slave trade, which Britain was committed to abolish. Elsewhere, British liberalism had to make its way in the new republics, where democratic and populist sentiments also flourished. If eminent members of the first generation of South American leaders, notably Bolívar and O'Higgins, were dazzled by liberal principles, their successors were more inclined to draw on a *mélange* of ideas, using ingredients from France and

USA
MEXICO
(1821)
Mexico
Havana
BAHAMA Is.
CUBA
DOM. REP.
BR. HONDURAS
GUATEMALA
HONDURAS
JAMAICA
HAITI
PUERTO RICO
LEEWARD Is.
EL SALVADOR
NICARAGUA
COSTA RICA
TRINIDAD
Caracas
PANAMA
Georgetown
Paramaribo
VENEZUELA
(1821)
Br
Neth
Cayenne
Fr
GUIANA
Bogotá
COLOMBIA
(1819)
Negro R.
Quito
Amazon R.
ECUADOR
(1830)
Amazon R.
Manaus
Tapajós R.
Xingu R.
Tocantis R.
Madeira R.
Recife
PERU
(1821)
BRAZIL
(1822)
Lima
Salvador

MAP 4 Latin America in 1913

After: Peter Morris, ed. *Africa, America and Central Asia: Formal and Informal Empire in the Nineteenth Century* (Exeter, 1984)

the United States as well as from Britain, and were ready at times to capitalise on conservative reactions to liberalism.[18] Against the promise of new 'quasi-colonies' of European settlement, stood social realities which did not fit the template of the British political system. The societies which emerged from the struggles for independence possessed neither a solid urban middle class nor a progressive aristocracy, and their open frontiers encouraged a form of extreme democracy which soon began to throw up strong men, usually on horseback, whose purpose was to bring discipline to the unruly world of the gauchos.[19] None of this was quite what Canning had envisaged. Hobbes's wilderness was not easily made into Locke's garden.

Commercial progress was also disappointing. There was undoubtedly some promise and much enthusiasm during the first years of independence. Commercial treaties with Argentina in 1825 and Brazil in 1827 boosted British interests, and by 1850 Britain was firmly established as South America's leading trading partner.[20] But the volume of commerce remained small, partly because Britain's conversion to free trade was still incomplete, and partly because limitations of transport (and allied services) put much of the mainland beyond the reach of external influences.[21] In the republics, moreover, economic development was also hampered by the extreme social fluidity and continuing political uncertainty which characterised the years after independence. Consequently, the period was marked less by the penetration of capitalism than by checks to its advance, including in some instances a flight into self-sufficiency.[22]

A similar sequence of optimism and disillusion was experienced by British investors. The achievement of independence in the early 1820s encouraged a speculative boom which reached its peak in 1825 with the formation of the British Churning Company, whose alleged purpose was to export Scottish milkmaids to tend Argentine cows.[23] When the market began to trade in fantasies of this order, a crash was inevitable. It duly came in 1826, and was followed by widespread default, withdrawal and protracted debt negotiations.[24] Short-lived though it was, the investment boom provided some interesting anticipations of the future. It was, first of all, an early experiment in extending the British system of lending money to the state in the expectation that it would eventually be returned.[25] As such, it has to be seen in the context of the moves towards free trade in the 1820s and the beginnings of the diversification of British capital flows abroad. The boom also underlined the importance of the link between overseas investment and nation-building. Britain's interest in promoting stable and progressive governments in South America, as elsewhere, was financial as well as political. Since there could be no sovereign debt without sovereignty, political unification was a prerequisite of loans to foreign governments, and Britain's recognition of new states was crucial to their creditrating.[26] The resulting mutual interest in government finance created bonds between the representatives of foreign creditors and the leaders of new states which foreshadowed the relationship that was to develop more fully later on.[27]

It was in the second half of the century, following the growth of the international economy, that South America became, from the British point of view, a success story. During this period, the principal states developed classic export economies, shipping cereals, beef, coffee and minerals, and importing a range of manufactures, beginning with textiles and progressing to capital goods for railways and other public utilities.[28] As a result, Britain's total trade with Latin America experienced a threefold increase in value between 1865 and 1913.[29] Looked at from another angle, Latin America received about 10 per cent of Britain's exports (and re-exports) between 1850 and 1913, and accounted for about the same proportion of Britain's retained imports during the same period.[30] These shares were larger than those of any other continent or country within the empire, apart from India.

Even more striking was Latin America's role as a recipient of British capital.[31] In the case of publicly issued capital (for which reasonable measures exist), British holdings in Latin America rose from a modest £81m. in 1865 to a massive £1,180m. in 1913. The rate of growth of investment was much faster than in the case of commodity trade; it was also more significant in proportionate terms, for in 1913 Latin America accounted for approximately 25 per cent of all British publicly issued overseas assets, a figure which put the continent in the first rank of international debtors in the non-industrialised world. Given that privately placed direct investment was also growing rapidly, especially from the 1890s, it is evident that, on financial grounds alone, Latin America merits close attention in any study of Britain's overseas interests and policy in the nineteenth century.[32]

This mountain of British investment stood behind South America's economic development down to World War I. Cheap manufactured goods had been available since the 1820s, but sales to South America could not expand until her exports found a market. This constraint was overcome by investment in low-cost transport and credit facilities which, in turn, was encouraged by the adoption of free trade in the 1840s. Regular steamship services (and falling freight rates) brought a generation of specialised, competitive merchants to South America.[33] The first wave of joint-stock banks and insurance companies soon followed (stimulated, too, by the Companies Acts of 1858–62). Submarine cables, the latest aids to market perfection, were laid in the 1860s and 1870s.[34] Improvements in communication spread an awareness of new opportunities far beyond business circles and encouraged a swelling number of immigrants, mostly from Spain and Italy, whose mobility and vigour played a vital part in speeding urbanisation and in colonising South America's abundant land resources.[35]

Economic growth also gave decisive impetus to the development of the state. The expansion of exports raised yields from tariffs, provided the means of servicing foreign loans, and thus created an effective revenue basis for the exercise of centralised political authority. The rise of large estates and ranches, and the spread of urban business and professional employments, both consolidated new property rights and defined the principal political constituency in the republics. From this confluence of economic and institutional trends emerged the landed and urban elites who exercised power in the second half of the century. In matters of overseas business, external policy and cultural orientation, the elites became closely associated with the representatives of foreign interests whose financial support played a crucial role in sustaining the configuration of economic and political power in South America. The liberal hour, which Canning had so eagerly anticipated, had finally come.

However, the growth of new opportunities in South America also attracted foreign competition, especially from the 1880s, and there followed a 'scramble' for influence in the continent which suggests comparisons with other parts of the world, though these have yet to be given serious consideration by historians of imperialism.[36] Admittedly, overt diplomatic confrontation was confined to the Venezuela boundary dispute, which threatened to become a major crisis in 1895 and again in 1902–3, and to the passing possibility of external involvement in the War of the Pacific (1879–83), though it is interesting to note that there were widespread fears in South America, especially at times of financial crisis in the 1890s, that Britain, the major creditor, might resort to formal intervention.[37] The principal manifestations of international rivalry were less visible, but no less important, and took the form of a struggle for control of trade and finance. The United States, continuing its slow southwards advance, attempted to capture Brazil's export trade.[38] Germany made a bid for informal influence by mounting an export drive consisting of manufactures, military aid, and settlers backed by the Deutsche Ueberseeische Bank (1886), which aimed at freeing German trade from its dependence on British finance.[39] France, capitalising on long-standing connections and republican sympathies, also tried to enlarge her share of trade and investment, particularly through the agency of the Crédit Mobilier and the Banque de Paris et des Pays Bas.[40]

Britain reacted vigorously to this new foreign challenge by tightening her grip on areas which were considered to be worth holding, very much as she did in the Ottoman Empire, China and Africa. Hence, attention was concentrated increasingly on the three most important countries, Argentina, Brazil and Chile, which, on the eve of World War I, accounted for 85 per cent of Latin America's foreign trade and 69 per cent of all publicly issued British capital placed in the continent.[41] Diplomatic support for British interests was strengthened, though selectively and discreetly, and British firms pushed further into the economies of these countries by stepping up direct investment in utilities, export production, and manufacturing, and by securing banking business which previously had been considered to lie beyond the bounds of conservative practice.[42]

Although it is impossible in the present state of knowledge to reach precise conclusions about the outcome of this contest, the broad trends are reasonably clear. On the eve of World War I, Britain still dominated the export sectors of the three leading South America countries, but her share of overseas trade had fallen from the peaks reached in the third quarter of the nineteenth century, when foreign competition was limited, and she had virtually given up some of the smaller and more difficult markets. Even in the cases of Argentina and Brazil, Britain's share of the import trade had dropped from over 50 per cent in the middle of the century to 31 per cent and 25 per cent respectively in 1912, whereas Germany, advancing from an insignificant base, supplied 17 per cent of the goods imported into each of these markets.[43] Admittedly, data pointing to relative decline have to be seen in the context of very substantial increases in total trade; but it is possible, nevertheless, to link the evidence to theories which seek to explain industrial retardation in the late-Victorian era and, by extension, to use it to support the conventional view that Britain was a waning imperial power whose hardening arteries prevented her from keeping up with younger, fitter rivals.

By concentrating on commodity trade, however, this perspective neglects a vital consideration, namely that Britain's competitors were unable to dent her supremacy in finance and commercial services. In 1914, the City and sterling still dominated short-term trade finance and the market for long-term development capital. The City's discount rates were cheaper than those available elsewhere, and the London capital market was simply too big and too well organised to allow its smaller and less experienced competitors to make much headway.[44] The principal British banks retained their leading positions in South America in both established and developing sectors of the economy;[45] British shipping stayed well ahead of its rivals in the carriage of South America's overseas trade.[46] The United States was able to move into Mexico and Central America, but made little progress further south before World War I.[47] Trade between Germany and South America also expanded, but much of it, too, depended on British finance.[48] Germany and France made modest inroads into Britain's share of the large and rapidly expanding long-term loan business, but their advance fell far short of expectations. Too often they were pushed into less enticing countries or riskier sectors of the economy, along with members of the City fringe.[49] Although British finance and commercial services continued to support Britain's share of exports to South America, they played an increasing role in promoting the exports of rival powers, as well as exports from the continent itself.[50] This development, the product of Britain's position as a mature creditor, was both a measure of the strength of Britain's financial sector and a recognition of the need to provide debtors with the means of meeting their obligations. It underlined, once again, the crucial importance of free trade in sustaining Britain's multilateral ties and generating the invisible earnings which had become such a vital entry in the balance of payments.

We can now reduce the scale of the enquiry to consider how Britain maintained her position in the three most important countries: Argentina, Brazil and Chile. This change of focus will supplement our generalisations with a measure of disaggregation and add detail to our broad historical characterisation of the continent as a whole.[51]

Argentina

It is evident from the commercial data alone that Britain's position in South America depended heavily on her ability to retain her stake in Argentina. By 1913, the republic was responsible for 42 per cent (a total of £23m.) of Britain's annual exports and re-exports to Latin America. Argentina's share of the import trade was even more striking, and in 1913 amounted to 58 per cent (£43m.) of the total entering Britain from Latin America, a figure which placed Argentina above any of the white-settled parts of the empire.[52] In 1913, too, Argentina accounted for no less than 41 per cent (£480m.) of all publicly-issued capital directed to Latin America from Britain.[53] Free trade gave Argentina's wheat and beef entry to Britain; Argentina's relatively open economy provided a market for British manufactures. Although Argentina's industrial sector was beginning to increase its share of national output, import substitution had not proceeded very far by 1914, and the market for Britain's traditional staple, cotton goods, remained strong.[54] Admittedly, Britain did not enjoy the same advantages in Argentina as she did in Canada and Australia, where kinship ties strengthened consumer loyalty. In Argentina, where the majority of immigrants came from southern Europe, competition was bound to be fiercer;[55] as Britain's share of Argentina's foreign trade began to be squeezed, especially after 1900, a number of British firms turned to safer, imperial markets.[56] Nevertheless, in 1914 Britain's position in Argentina remained substantially intact because it rested on supports which newcomers could neither match nor overturn: British finance and commercial services, and the co-operation of the wealthy and politically powerful Anglo-Argentine elite in Buenos Aires.[57]

Commercial expansion brought considerable gains to both Britain and Argentina, though the precise relationship between private profits and social benefits is not easily determined. On the British side, the developing connection with Argentina provides a prime example of the extension abroad of the financial and service interests centred on London and the Home Counties, and of their (increasingly ambiguous) alliance with provincial export industries. Argentina's willing acceptance of British finance was symbolised by the appointment of Barings as bankers to the government in 1857 and by the settlement (with interest) in the same year of the defaulted Buenos Aires loan of 1824.[58] The resumption of foreign borrowing in the 1860s encouraged British merchants in Buenos Aires to begin to specialise in finance and in commercial services other than handling goods,[59] and it also influenced the moves which led to the formation of the London and River Plate Bank in 1862.[60] The Bank's investors were drawn initially from the ranks of City merchants and bankers, and subsequently from a wider circle encompassing London's 'professions and gentlemen'.[61] Their risk was well taken: the Bank was not only the first but also the most consistently profitable of the foreign commercial banks in Argentina.[62]

A representative, if unusually successful, example of these new interests was Charles Morrison (1817–1909), a City-based financier who became one of the wealthiest Englishmen of his generation, having a fortune of nearly £11m. at the time of his death, as well as extensive landed property.[63] Morrison and his business associates made their money through a mixture of overseas and home-based ventures, all of which were in the fields of banking, handling and communications (and none of which came very close to manufacturing or mining). Morrison began to focus on Argentina in the 1860s, when circumstances favoured new inflows of foreign capital. He acquired the Mercantile Bank of the River Plate in 1881, invested directly in a range of public utilities in the 1890s, and by 1900 controlled nearly 10 per cent of all British investment employed in Argentina. Evidently, the investment was profitable; but it was also principled. Morrison was a liberal idealist who viewed

Argentina as a great democratic republic in the making, a new United States which would realise and renew the virtues of individualism, private property, and minimal government. He never turned to British officialdom for support in Argentina, but preferred, like Canning, to place his faith in the emergence of independent but culturally subservient satellites. In helping to fashion this destiny, Morrison also began to interfere, like his contemporaries in India and Africa, in the lives of those he sought to liberate.

The ability to borrow on a massive scale and to make repayment through exports of primary products became the basis of the power and prosperity of the 400 or so wealthy landed families who formed the Argentine elite, and also of their allies in banking and commerce.[64] General Rosas had tamed the gauchos in the 1830s and 1840s, but in doing so had increased the burden of taxation and decreased his popularity; his removal in 1852 symbolised a commitment to a pacific and outward-looking economic programme which aimed to raise revenues less painfully, through export expansion, and thus to minimise the risk of political discontent.[65] Having settled the defaulted debt of 1824, Argentina's new leaders used fresh foreign loans to complete the unification of the republic in the 1860s and to 'pacify' the Indians in the following decade. Both measures were crucial to improving Argentina's credit-rating and to expanding the land available for export production.[66] Thereafter, policy continued to favour agricultural exports rather than local industries: low duties were applied to external trade, internal tariffs were reduced or eliminated, and financial guarantees were given to a number of railway projects which aimed at enlarging the export sector.[67] These developments were accompanied by a process of cultural assimilation which steadily absorbed key members of the elite. Rosas, having left Argentina with British help, enjoyed a long retirement 'very like a country gentleman' on his Hampshire estate.[68] Under his successors, Britain's civilising mission reached its highest stage: Pellegrini, who was related to John Bright, was educated at Harrow; Roca and Juárez Celmán, among others, sent their children to English public schools and built English-style mansions on the pampas; a replica of Harrods, a shrine for elite consumers, was opened in Buenos Aires in 1912.[69]

The wisdom of adhering to a cosmopolitan policy based on free trade aroused opposition in both countries, particularly in the provinces, which resented the power of the centre and jibbed at the idea that the alliance between two privileged capital cities was in the best interests of society as a whole. As some manufacturers in the British Midlands became attracted to tariff reform, so leading figures in a number of 'secondary cities' in Argentina began to argue for a policy of indigenisation.[70] These reactions were undoubtedly significant in pointing the way towards future developments, but they made little impression on the status quo before 1914. Argentina's international commercial policy continued to be formulated in Buenos Aires, where differences between Argentine and British interests involved a questioning not so much of the relationship itself as of the distribution of the benefits.[71]

The central requirement of the commercial pact between Britain and Argentina was that sovereign debts should be honoured. Exceptional circumstances demanded flexibility, but the rule itself was not to be broken. Argentina's acceptance of this principle, first signified by repaying the defaulted loan of 1824, was next tested by the world financial crisis of 1873, which trapped a number of primary-producing countries between fixed obligations and falling revenues. President Avellaneda immediately declared that Argentina would 'willingly suffer privations and even hunger' to maintain the international reputation and credit-rating of the national government, and he lost no time in introducing an austerity programme.[72] Both the declaration and the policy were welcomed by the City, which produced a vital short-term loan (advanced by Barings in 1875–6) enabling Argentina to continue to service its debts.[73]

The crisis of the mid-1870s also provides an insight into the way in which the central government clamped down on provincial discontent, when it was seen to threaten the national interest.[74] As Argentina's exports faltered in the world recession, doubts were raised about the stability of several local banks which had advanced money on the security of mortgages and other fixed assets in the province of Santa Fe. Anxious customers in the port of Rosario began to move deposits from the Banco National and the Provincial Bank of Santa Fe to the London and River Plate Bank, which had followed a more conservative policy in the years before the slump. The provincial government tried to halt the drain by forbidding the London and River Plate Bank to issue notes, by taxing its operations (but not those of its rivals) and by seizing its gold reserves. Britain's threats to use the navy to restore the Bank's property left both national and provincial governments unmoved. What persuaded Buenos Aires to act was partly the fact that the closure of the London and River Plate Bank had brought trade in Rosario to a stand-still, thus depriving the national government of customs revenue at a vital moment, but mainly the realisation that the dispute would severely damage Argentina's standing in the City. The matter was finally settled when the Argentine government made a loan to the Santa Fe authorities in exchange for an agreement that it would return the London and River Plate Bank's gold reserves and allow it to resume operations. What British naval power had failed to do, the implied threat of the withdrawal of financial aid in London had accomplished instead.

The Argentine elite was also quick to see where its interest lay in the more severe economic blizzard which blew up with the Baring Crisis in 1890.[75] During the 1880s, when the financial problems of the previous decade had been overcome, British investors poured capital into Argentine government stocks, railways and utilities on an unprecedented scale. Since returns on investments in infrastructure were invariably delayed, there was a danger that Argentina would run into a development crisis if external obligations leaped too far ahead of export earnings. In 1890, when the cost of servicing the foreign debt had risen to 60 per cent of the value of Argentina's export earnings, and with export prices falling, the alarm bells began to ring. The fact that Argentina's economic policy had become increasingly detached from the discipline of the gold standard undoubtedly made matters worse. The initial response of Juárez Celmán's government (1886–90) was to appease domestic interests by allowing the peso to depreciate and by printing inconvertible paper money. Given that Argentina's external debts were payable mainly in gold or gold-backed currencies, this course of action, if pursued, would have led to default. However, to the extent that there was a crisis of management as well as of development, a heavy responsibility also lay with the expatriate banks, which entered too willingly into the cavalier spirit of the times.[76] Barings in particular had become caught up in what the *Bankers' Magazine* aptly called 'gaucho banking', and had taken exposed positions, partly in the belief that the boom had still some way to run and partly in response to growing competition from foreign banks.[77] In November 1890, Barings suddenly found themselves holding massive quantities of Argentine government bonds which the market no longer wanted. The Baring Crisis struck at the heart of the British financial system: if the unthinkable happened and Barings were made bankrupt, large segments of the City of London, including the Bank of England, might also be pulled down. In this way, Baring's imprudence tested the strength of the whole financial edifice which had been built in London in the course of the nineteenth century.[78]

From the British perspective, the solution to the crisis fell into two connected parts: one centred on keeping Barings afloat; the other depended on persuading Argentina to co-operate in paying its debts. Barings was saved by an impressive example of self-help when the joint-stock and private banks in the City formed a fighting fund of £17m., backed by the Bank of England and, unofficially, by the Treasury, to meet its most pressing obligations. Thus were the entrenched precepts of *laissez-faire* swiftly discarded in favour of rapid official intervention: the government simply could not allow one of the most prestigious merchant banks in the City to go into liquidation. The second step was more difficult and involved delicate negotiations to safeguard the interests of creditors without provoking a nationalist reaction, and with it the threat of repudiation. Although some senior employees of British banks made an unofficial and rather vague request for intervention at a moment when alarm turned to panic in 1891, the leading figures in the City and in Whitehall held consistently to the view that a satisfactory outcome would emerge from discussion rather than from coercion. Consequently, though Lord Salisbury was prepared to nudge the Argentines from time to time, he would not prejudice negotiations over the debt by appearing to threaten the use of force.[79] Argentina was not, in any sense, Egypt.

This strategy amounted to a vote of confidence in the Argentine elite. Even before the crisis broke, Juárez Celmán's administration had shown signs of conversion to fiscal rectitude by trying to cut public expenditure. Indeed, Celmán's tentative reforms were largely responsible for generating the opposition which led to his downfall in 1890. Pellegrini, his successor, moved swiftly to reassure foreign creditors. On hearing news of Baring's imminent collapse, he declared: 'rather than suspend service on the debt I would prefer to renounce the presidency',[80] and his economic programme was designed to 'scrape up every loose peso in the Republic in order to meet government costs and hasten the day when Argentina's obligations to its foreign creditors could again be met'.[81] *The Times* nodded approvingly: 'all the wisest Argentine citizens are anxious to secure the credit of their country, and they are setting about it in the proper way'.[82] The election of Sáenz Peña, the nominee of the landed interest, to replace Pellegrini in 1892 further strengthened the confidence of foreign creditors. Sáenz Peña's victory not only eliminated an opposition candidate who stood for a far less cooperative programme, but also brought to office Juan Romero, who was regarded by the British Minister in Buenos Aires as being 'a sure guarantee towards a sound and honest administration of the Ministry of Finance'.[83]

When negotiations over the debt began, at the close of 1890, British interests were entrusted to a committee led by Lord Rothschild, whose immediate concern was to protect the value of the bonds held by Barings and other British investors.[84] The German and French banks were aware that their own claims took second place in this British design, but they were unable to shape the negotiations to suit their own interests. In essence, Rothschild devised what today would be called a rescheduling agreement: a limited advance was made to enable Argentina to meet her short-term liabilities and to postpone the resumption of full debt service for three years, thus avoiding default; in exchange, the Argentine government entered into an implicit agreement to adopt deflationary policies to bring the balance of payments into equilibrium. Rothschild's deal undoubtedly preserved Britain's financial standing and saved Baring's position in Argentina. The alternative, allowing substantial new borrowing, would have undercut the price of Baring's bonds and would also have given opportunities to foreign banks at a moment when the City was unwilling to make new loans to Argentina. By the same token, however, the transfer of funds was not large enough to refuel the Argentine economy, and the imposition of deflationary policies provoked an anti-British reaction which led to Pellegrini's fall in 1892.

A new settlement was reached in the following year.[85] As the immediate threat of default and liquidation receded, both sides were willing to take a longer view of the debt problem. Much of the initiative for the Romero Arrangement, as it was called, came from Argentina, though it is worth noting that British interests were represented by the reconstituted and revived firm of Barings, a fact which suggests that the City was ready to resume business as usual. Under the Romero Arrangement, Argentina was allowed to settle its outstanding external debts by making reduced interest payments for five years and by suspending payments on the sinking fund for a decade. By adjusting Argentina's repayments to suit her capacity, Britain acknowledged the difficulties of the republic's economic situation; by assigning revenues to debt payments, and by pursuing cautious domestic fiscal and monetary policies, Romero's plan was reassuringly orthodox. The fact that the plan worked, however, owed much to the coincident revival of the export economy, which boosted foreign exchange earnings and government revenues. Good management and good luck enabled Argentina to resume full interest payments in 1897, one year ahead of schedule, and to return to the gold standard in 1899 after an absence of twenty years. Thus purged, and with her credit-worthiness restored, Argentina was ready to begin borrowing heavily again during the boom years which lasted to 1913.[86]

The wider consequence of the Baring settlement was to facilitate the penetration of the Argentine economy by British firms, thus giving impetus to a process which had been under way since the 1860s, when the large joint-stock banks began a financial advance which gave British companies a substantial stake in railways and public utilities, as well as in banking and insurance.[87] The Baring Crisis brought down the two large Argentine banks, the National and the Banco de la Provincia, and left the London and River Plate Bank in a virtually unassailable position. As the economy revived, the London and River Plate took the lion's share of renewed business, and was able to return consistently impressive profits down to 1914.[88] The crisis also put an end to Argentina's attempt to build a nationally owned rail network. The need to cut expenditure and generate income during the 1890s forced the Argentine government to 'privatise' much of the railway system by selling state companies to foreign, principally British, firms.[89] A review of the railway code in 1907 (the Mitre Law), produced a new set of favourable conditions for the further expansion of the private rail network, and with it of British control.[90] Argentina's tariff policy was equally friendly to foreign business interests, and was aimed principally at collecting the revenues needed to fund the administration and to service external debts. From the 1890s onwards Argentina developed a sizeable surplus on her visible trade with Britain, and this was needed to meet obligations on her invisible and capital accounts. Preserving the openness of the economy was an essential element in the smooth flow of international payments, even though it limited the extent to which tariffs could be used to protect local industries.[91]

Argentina's almost automatic orthodoxy in financial matters after 1892 symbolised the recognition by the elite that its hold on power depended on the ability of both government and private firms to continue to raise funds in London. Alternative sources in Paris, Berlin and New York were tried but found wanting.[92] Had good relations with the City broken down, the Argentine government would have been forced to finance its development programme from domestic savings, a course which was so fraught with economic problems and political risks that it was scarcely contemplated, even by the country's emerging radical and socialist parties.[93] Britain's instincts, refined by decades of experience in appraising foreign debtors, proved correct: in the end, and despite attempts at deviation, Argentina played by the approved rules of financial orthodoxy. The expansionist years which followed the Baring Crisis delivered considerable rewards. They confirmed the dominance of the Anglophile elite in Argentina, underwrote the political stability of the republic, and softened criticism of the inequalities generated by the export sector. In Britain, the boom produced steady profits on secure investments for a sizeable complement of investors. The fact that British investment in Argentina financed an increasing volume of manufactured imports from rival industrial powers was a disappointment for the Midlands and the north of England which the Home Counties were well able to tolerate.[94]

Brazil

Brazil and Chile were in many respects very different from Argentina, as well as from each other: Brazil was Portuguese-speaking, and it was also a monarchical, slave-holding society for the greater part of the nineteenth century; Chile, though

Spanish-speaking like Argentina, looked towards the Pacific instead of the Atlantic and depended on mining rather than on agriculture for its prosperity. Nevertheless, from the point of view of the present study, the interest of these countries lies in the fact that, despite their differences, they entered and participated in the international economy on broadly similar terms, which in both cases were drawn up principally by Britain.

In many ways, Brazil was Britain's most accommodating and most successful satellite in South America during the first half of the nineteenth century.[95] The weak monarchy, which owed its presence to British support, readily bent before Britain's demands by conceding a one-sided Commercial Treaty in 1827, and a congenial alliance emerged thereafter between an oligarchy of slave-holding sugar and coffee producers and British import-export merchants. Brazil also behaved as a model debtor, surviving the financial crisis of 1825 and, uniquely, continuing to service her foreign loans. Throughout this period, the government adhered to orthodox fiscal and monetary policies, retained its credit-worthiness, and had no difficulty in raising money in the City when loans to South America resumed in the 1850s.[96] It is scarcely surprising that Brazil has been referred to, during its first phase of independence, as being a virtual British protectorate.[97]

However, it has also been claimed that British influence declined in the second half of the century, as Brazil regained tariff autonomy after 1844, as Britain's share of commodity trade fell thereafter, and as her diplomatic standing suffered as a result of conflict over the abolition of the slave trade and the growing presence of the United States.[98] This argument is open to question. Replacing special commercial privileges with most-favoured-nation treatment was fully in line with Britain's move towards free trade and also generated goodwill in Brazil; Britain's performance with respect to commodity trade has to be set in the context of her increasing role as a supplier of capital;[99] the dispute over abolition, though serious, did not hamper Britain's position in the long run; and the United States was unable to upset British parmountcy before 1914. In fact, as we shall try to show, the expansion of finance and commercial services after 1850 both enlarged Britain's stake in Brazil and boosted her influence there.

Britain achieved in Brazil what she failed to bring about in Africa: the conversion of a slave-holding state to one capable of sustaining new and much expanded forms of 'legitimate' commerce on terms which were still consistent with the maintenance of sovereign independence. During the 1840s, Brazil found herself on the receiving end of Palmerston's renewed efforts to put down the slave trade and open new markets, and in 1851, after considerable opposition, the emperor agreed to implement measures which brought slave imports to an end.[100] Depriving the oligarchy of one of its main economic props was scarcely a popular act among privileged circles in Rio de Janeiro. At the same time, it made the Brazilian government even more dependent upon British support and ensured that it cooperated in maintaining an open commercial regime which was attractive to foreign firms and pursued orthodox fiscal and monetary policies which won the approval of the City'.[101] Signs of the emergence of a new 'alliance for progress' quickly made their appearance. Rothschilds became official bankers to the Brazilian government in 1855, complementing the position of Barings in Argentina, and the London and Brazilian Bank was founded in 1862 by merchant-financiers in the City and in Rio to channel funds into the 'modern' sector of the economy.[102] A flow of new loans (though still on a small scale) soon followed, first to refinance government debt and then to promote railway construction.[103] The country's excellent credit record and continuing good relations with Rothschilds paid its own dividend: when the world financial crisis struck South America in 1873, Rothschilds were able to place a large issue of Brazilian bonds on the London market which enabled the government to continue to service its external debts and thereby retain its stability.[104] Not surprisingly, differences between Britain and Brazil were settled informally and in the knowledge that 'adverse publicity' would 'injuriously affect' the standing of Brazil's credit in the London money market.[105]

During the period which followed the abolition of the slave trade, Brazilian elites, outside the diminishing band of slave-owners, imbibed liberal values with undiluted enthusiasm. Brazilian ministers in London were so Anglophile that Lord Salisbury even joked of one of them that he could speak no Portuguese.[106] Rio de Janeiro like Buenos Aires, was strongly influenced by the values and style of London and Paris, and English (replacing French) became the preferred language of commerce.[107] Brazilian entrepreneurs, such as André Rebouças, had no doubts about the beneficial effects of foreign capital, 'which comes principally from London, which, thanks to the wisdom of the Anglo-Saxon race, is the treasury of the whole world'.[108] Politicians, too, became standard-bearers of British liberalism, absorbing its anti-democratic slant while also deploying arguments against royal absolutism first devised in seventeenth-century England. As the celebrated abolitionist, Joaquim Nabuco, put it: 'When I enter the Chamber [of Deputies] I am entirely under the influence of English liberalism, as if I were working under the orders of Gladstone. This is really a result of my political education: I am an English liberal . . . in the Brazilian Parliament'.[109]

If Britain's relations with Brazil were cordial to the point of warmth, they were also circumscribed by the relatively slow pace of economic development. The prohibition of imports of slaves had created a growing problem of labour supply which could not be met, while the institution of slavery persisted, by free immigrant labour. In the 1870s and 1880s labour scarcity became the crucial bottleneck to export-led growth, and the failure of the aged emperor to introduce the necessary reforms undermined support for his government, especially among the new and increasingly important coffee-producers in the São Paulo region.[110] The abolition of slavery in 1888 came too late to save either the monarch or the monarchy; by then, discontent in influential civil and military circles had acquired too much momentum. The proclamation of the first republic in 1889, and the constitution introduced in 1891, confirmed the accession to power of a modernising but also conservative oligarchy, which, broadly speaking, represented the interests of the elites of São Paulo and Rio de Janeiro and (by devolving a degree of authority) the most prominent of their counterparts in the provinces.[111]

This considerable upheaval, far from signalling the decline of British influence, offered fresh opportunities to City and service interests. Despite its long association with the Brazilian monarchy, the City did not allow sentiment to extend to the point of backing a loser. British interests detached themselves from the *ancien régime,* supported the abolition of slavery, funded the transition to free labour, and (after an initial period of customary caution) favoured the creation of the Republic as being the best means of combining economic progress with political stability.[112] On this point agreement was mutual. The new rulers were particularly anxious to secure Britain's recognition of the Republic because, as the British ambassador noted, 'it is in London that they doubtless hope to raise further loans'.[113] Subsequently, they demonstrated the extent of their 'like-mindedness' by the resolute measures they took to maintain the open economy and to hold the confidence of foreign investors.[114] They were rewarded by the rapid expansion of the export sector, driven by flows of foreign capital, and by a sharp rise in living standards among elite groups in the years down to World War I.

Britain's share of Brazil's foreign trade continued to fall during this period. As far as the import trade was concerned, the decline was gradual rather than dramatic: Britain supplied about one-third of Brazil's imports during the last years of the monarchy, and her share dropped to about one-quarter (though of a much larger total) on the eve of World War I.[115] In the case of the export trade, the fall was much more pronounced: Britain's share dropped from 23 per cent to 13 per cent between 1880 and 1900 following the growth of coffee and rubber exports, which went increasingly to the United States.[116] But, as in the case of Argentina, trends in commodity trade provide an imperfect index of Britain's presence and influence. It was in Britain's interest as a mature creditor to encourage Brazil to find markets for her exports, wherever they might be, so that she could acquire the foreign exchange needed to service her debts, as well as to buy imports (including manufactures from Britain). And, as Brazil became a mature debtor, the proportion of export receipts devoted to debt service grew, while that spent on commodity imports declined. Moreover, the financing, shipping and insuring of Brazil's overseas trade remained overwhelmingly in British hands down to 1914, irrespective of its destination.[117] Above all, Britain continued to be responsible for the major share of the vastly expanded flows of foreign capital (portfolio and direct) which accompanied the creation of the Republic and continued down to the final boom on the eve of World War I.[118]

As in the case of Argentina, British claims and Brazilian responses are well illustrated by the tests of conduct and policy imposed by financial crises, the most important of which occurred in 1898 and 1913.[119] Brazil escaped the wash created by the Baring Crisis, despite having borrowed heavily in the late 1880s, because her credit rating was supported by buoyant coffee prices. However, a fall in coffee prices from the mid-1890s combined with a depreciation of the *milreis* (a legacy of currency inflation during the early years of the Republic) presented the government with a considerable transfer problem.[120] The official response was entirely orthodox, if also unsuccessful. A deflationary programme was drawn up in 1894, but serious political disorder prevented it from being implemented. In 1895 the government used a loan of £7.2m., originally raised in London, to defend the exchange rate, and followed this in 1896 with large tariff increases and a credit squeeze. However, when coffee prices slumped further in 1896 and 1897 so did the *milreis*. In 1898 the service charge on Brazil's external debt accounted for half the federal budget, and the Republic faced a major balance of payments crisis. At this point, having failed to solve the problem by itself, the government was forced to turn to the City for assistance.

The Funding Loan of 1898 was very similar to the loan devised for Argentina in 1891, and was also arranged by Lord Rothschild. The Brazilian government was advanced £10m. over three years to cover its debt service, and was allowed to suspend amortisation payments until 1911. With the good news came the bad: in return, Brazil was obliged to impose severe deflationary measures and to pledge the whole of her receipts from customs duties to meet debt payments. Lord Rothschild, anticipating that the resolve of the recipients might weaken, took care to point out, in a manner which was unauthorised but managed to sound authoritative, that the alternative, repudiation, would involve not only 'the complete loss of the country's credit' but might also 'greatly affect Brazil's sovereignty, provoking complaints that could arrive at the extreme of foreign intervention'.[121] Brazil's President, Campos Sales (1898–1902), responding to both carrot and stick, duly administered the medicine: harsh deflationary policies were applied; the radical opposition to foreign influence was broken; coffee prices fortuitously recovered; the *milreis* rose; and debt payments were resumed on time.

The most important single consequence of the crisis of 1898 was to draw both government and creditors further into the economy. Brazilian governments adopted interventionist policies in order to have more effective means of maintaining a liberal trade regime – a paradox already worked out within the British empire by the Government of India; and foreign creditors collected additional gains from Brazil's indebtedness in much the same way as they did in Argentina and (in a somewhat different form) in China. Both trends were an indication of the central and expanding role of external finance in Brazil's economy and, indirectly, in the politics of the Republic too.

The priority attached to maintaining Brazil's credit-worthiness can clearly be seen in the measures taken by Rodrigues Alves, a 'conspicuous advocate of deflationary policies', who replaced Campos Sales as President in 1902.[122] Alves masterminded Brazil's return to the gold standard by reorganising the Banco da Republica (which became the Banco do Brasil in 1905) and by setting up a complementary body, the Treasury Conversion Office, in the following year.[123] The Banco do Brasil, which was under government control, had most of the powers of a central bank and was charged particularly with managing the exchange rate; the Conversion Office, as its name implies, issued notes against equivalent gold deposits in much the same way as the Currency Boards did in Britain's colonies.[124] The aim was to give greater stability to the exchange rate by holding it between fixed gold import and export points, and to provide an automatic adjustment for movements beyond these points by linking the balance of payments to the supply of money and credit in the domestic economy, ultimately by moving gold in and out of the country. These measures, it was hoped, would boost the confidence of foreign investors, maintain inflows of foreign capital, and enable Brazil to steer clear of financial crises of the magnitude which had struck in 1898. The commercial banks, encouraged to operate freely in this congenial climate, made more than hay: the leading British concerns (the London and Brazilian and the London and River Plate) attracted business from local banks, which had suffered during the crisis of 1898 and in its aftermath, and by 1913 held about one-third of all deposits in the Brazilian banking system.[125]

Other important government initiatives taken during the period 1898–1914 can also be seen to have complemented the primary aim of supporting Brazil's international credit rating. The nationalisation of a number of railway lines in 1901, far from striking a blow at expatriate control, was favoured by foreign investors because it reduced the burden on the state budget caused by the need to provide private companies with subsidies.[126] The substantial tariff increases which occurred in 1895 and 1906 were imposed principally for revenue purposes, not as concessions to local manufacturers, and were viewed by investors as being necessary for budgetary stability. Any protectionist effects were secondary; and if protection harmed some of Britain's manufactured exports, it also created opportunities for British financiers and entrepreneurs who were prepared to accept the risks of direct investment.[127] Finally, it is now clear that even the scheme devised in 1906 to stabilise coffee prices was aimed mainly at reassuring external creditors that funds would be available for debt service.[128] The initial plan favoured coffee producers, but it was condemned by Lord Rothschild, among others, as being 'an artificial expedient', and quickly withdrawn.[129] The plan eventually approved by Congress fell well short of the demands of producers, and also had to be backed by foreign loans, which the City obligingly supplied. In this way, Brazil lost control over its coffee sales, which in 1908 passed to a committee based in London (and headed by Baron Schroder). A measure of the London committee's success in determining coffee prices is that it finally provoked the United States into taking antitrust proceedings in 1912.

Despite its exemplary fiscal and monetary policies, Brazil experienced a second major financial crisis in 1913, when swelling debt commitments, encouraged by a decade of export expansion, intersected with falling export proceeds.[130] When foreign creditors took fright in 1912, Brazil was unable to attract fresh capital from abroad, despite her good record and continuing adherence to orthodox policies. A financial mission sent by Rothschilds in 1913 eventually raised a large loan of £20m. from an international consortium. But the conditions were as severe as those imposed in 1898, and even went beyond them in demanding direct control of important instruments of Brazilian policy. These requirements were reinforced by the Foreign Office, which instructed the British Legation in Rio de Janeiro to 'press the Brazilian Government to meet outstanding British claims out of the proposed new loan and to point out that a continued failure to settle is likely seriously to impair Brazilian credit in England'.[131] The Brazilian government wriggled but could not escape, and finally accepted the terms offered. In the event, the agreement did not become operative; but it was the outbreak of war, not the decline of imperial energies, that saved Brazil from greater subjection to foreign control.

Chile

A similar story of British dominance can be told in the case of Chile. The period after independence in 1818 was marked by a push for export growth, and by the emergence of an oligarchy which depended on international trade for its affluence and power.[132] In this process the British, the master craftsmen of nation-building, were ever at hand, supplying the principles of political economy, the international trade connections, and the loans which helped to shape the render mentality and aristocratic authoritarianism of Chile's almost gentlemanly elite, the appropriately named Bigwhigs. After a slow start, as elsewhere in South America, the economy entered a period of more rapid growth from the middle of the century, as a result of the shift to free trade and increased demand for Chile's principal exports, first copper and silver, and then nitrates. British merchants handled most of Chile's imports and exports, British shipping carried the trade, British banks financed both commerce and transport, and the City dominated the expanding government loan business.[133] The noted Chilean historian and publicist, Benjamin Mackenna, observed in 1880 that:

> There does not exist in the whole globe a country whose prosperity or adversity has a more direct influence as regards Chile than that which affects the welfare of the vast Empire of Great Britain, the Modem Rome.[134]

Mackenna gave particular emphasis to the role of British capital, and commented with some pride that the republic's debts were repaid with 'English punctuality'.[135] A visitor from the United States put the matter rather more tersely: 'this city', he said of Valparaiso in 1885, 'is nothing more than an English colony',[136]

The extent to which Chile's fortunes, indeed her very existence, had become bound up with the international economy was demonstrated dramatically during the 1870s, which began with a trade depression and ended in warfare.[137] Although Chile escaped the immediate consequences of the global financial crisis of 1873, export prices fell and the debt burden rose as the 1870s advanced, causing serious hardship and generating opposition to the ruling oligarchy's resolutely orthodox economic policies. By the close of the decade, the financial situation had reached a critical stage: in 1877 debt service absorbed 44 per cent of public expenditure, and in the following year Chile's reserves dropped to such a low point that the government was forced to suspend convertibility and raise import tariffs.[138] The Minister of Finance tried to reassure Britain of Chile's continuing commitment to 'the liberal principles which form the basis of our customs system', but the City feared that default was imminent and refused to bail out the government by issuing a new loan.[139] After a brief interlude of fantasy, occupied by a memorable scheme for turning copper into gold, the government faced up to a hard choice: it could either implement internal reforms, which meant imposing income tax and capital gains taxes on the wealthy, or it could gamble on an external solution to its domestic problems. Predictably, perhaps, it chose the latter.

The War of the Pacific, which began in 1879, was a struggle between Chile on the one side and Bolivia and Peru on the other for control of rich nitrate and guano deposits in the provinces of Atacama and Tarapacá.[140] Although Atacama belonged to Bolivia and Tarapacá to Peru, Chile had invested heavily in both, and all three countries viewed the resources of these provinces as providing a solution to their desperate financial problems. Domestic impulses were greatly complicated by external involvement. British investors in Chile stood to gain from a Chilean victory; but British creditors in Peru, struggling to salvage something from that country's massive default in 1876, were concerned to protect their assets there. In addition, British policy had to take account of the French presence, as a creditor in Peru and as a power with wider ambitions on the Pacific coast, and of opposition from the United States to any further extension of European influence in South America. Given these complex elements of causation and momentum, the claim that the conflict was 'an English war' provoked by a conspiracy of financial interests is now seen to be far too crude.[141] What can be said is that, once the war was under way, Britain's antennae searched for a solution which protected her financial interests in both Chile and Peru. Early signs of Chile's success led in 1880 to an informal agreement whereby Chile would look after the claims of British creditors in Tarapacá in exchange for Britain's benign neutrality in the conflict. As a result, Chile also secured the active backing of bondholders in London as well as support locally from British firms which were likely to benefit from an extension of Chile's borders.[142]

British policy paid dividends. When the war ended, with Chile's victory in 1883, the nitrate provinces were delivered into Chilean hands. Thereafter, Chile's revenues grew rapidly, the position of the ruling elite was re-established, and her policy of co-operation with foreign interests was confirmed and extended. But Chile had to share her triumph by fulfilling her bargain with Britain. Consequently, the newly conquered Peruvian nitrate fields were returned to private foreign ownership, a move which placated the bond-holders even if it did not solve all their problems.[143] But, as the Chilean government realised, repudiating their claims would have seriously damaged the country's credit-rating in London.[144] Moreover, revenue considerations, and the urgent need to service the external debt, made concessions to foreign mining companies imperative. The imposition of a uniform tax on nitrate exports eliminated most of the small Chilean firms and enabled expatriate companies to dominate the industry. By 1890, Britain owned 69 per cent of the capital employed in the nitrate industry and took 80 per cent of Chile's exports.[145] Britain's financial and cultural dominance had been consolidated, French ambitions had been frustrated, and Washington's fears of the spread of London's influence had been realised.

Among those who did well out of the war was John North, a British engineer turned entrepreneur whose shrewd investment in the Tarapacá mines enabled him to build up a syndicate which in 1890 accounted for about 68 per cent of the authorised capital of all British firms engaged in the nitrate industry.[146] North's entrepreneurship was in the cavalier style appropriate to a man who bestowed upon himself the honorary title of colonel. But he mastered the intricacies of the stock exchange as well as the challenges of the frontier, cultivated the friendship of Nathan Rothschild and Randolph Churchill, and stoked the excitement which produced the mania for shares in nitrate companies in the late 1880s. Yet North, like Rhodes, was too much of a 'mushroom gentleman' to acquire significant influence in top circles in the City. His business interests intersected with those of senior members of the merchant-banking fraternity at certain points, which was significant in itself, but he was never fully accepted in 'society', despite the lavish hospitality he offered visitors to his estate in Kent in an effort to earn the spurs to match his assumed rank.

North's share-dealings made him, briefly, a controversial figure in London when the nitrate bubble burst in 1891, while allegations that he was behind the conspiracy which overthrew President Balmaceda in the same year brought him permanent notoriety in Chile. Both episodes have their importance. But the interest of the second lies less in determining North's exact role, than in demonstrating the extent to which the fortunes of the political elite, and the shape of politics itself, had become bound up with the development of the nitrate industry.[147] By the close of the 1880s, North had extended his activities into railways and banking, and was using his control of freight rates to increase his dominance of the mining industry, a strategy that was given added urgency by the collapse of nitrate prices in 1890. At this point, however, North's plans ran into President Balmaceda's attempts to increase Chile's share of the profits from nitrates and to redirect them away from Congress and towards his own supporters. These conflicts led to civil war in 1891, and to the overthrow of Balmaceda later in the same year. There is no proof that North had a direct part in the president's downfall, though it is clear that he favoured Congress, and that his sympathies were shared by British business and the navy, which 'rendered material assistance to the opposition and committed many breaches of neutrality'.[148]

The establishment of parliamentary government in 1892 returned to power members of the elite who held a more tolerant view of foreign enterprise. British investment rose rapidly during the 1890s, British firms increased their involvement in nitrate mining, and British banks retained their supremacy.[149] Nevertheless, North was unable to impose himself on Chile, as, with weighty political associates, the mine-owners were able to do in the Transvaal. The rewards of victory were shared, after 1892 as after 1883. The new government frustrated North's planned railway monopoly, and the cartels he organised in the nitrate industry were not very successful. In any case, in the years following North's death in 1896, Chilean capital began to play a larger part in the industry, and the government itself became more sympathetic to the idea of rigging the market, if possible. In fact, the Chilean elite gained greatly from Britain's control of the nitrate industry, which produced 43 per cent of all government revenues between 1880 and 1920, allowed foreign borrowing to take place, and enabled debt service to be sustained without raising internal taxes.[150] But this does not mean that the economy and the elite were independent of Britain. As in the cases of Argentina and Brazil, the maintenance of affluence and authority in Chile still depended ultimately on fulfilling a set of policy requirements which met the needs of the senior partner and external creditor.

The spread of informal influence

South America had its place, with other continents, in Britain's grand design for a creating a developing yet stable world system after 1815. But results failed to match intentions, and the post-imperial order was not transformed into a new empire of informal sway. South America was indeed free but she was not, in the mid-Victorian period, English. From 1850, however, the position began to change, and after 1875 the extension of finance and commercial services gave Britain a much more visible and effective presence in the republics.

The expansion of British interests was part cause and part consequence of a hitherto underestimated 'scramble' for South America which merits comparison with the rivalry of the great powers for control of Africa, the Ottoman Empire and China during the same period. As elsewhere, Britain's role was not merely passive and reactive. She was creating a position not simply defending one, and she took vigorous, if largely unofficial, action to promote her interests. The main impulses for expansion came from the centre, specifically from the rapid growth of foreign lending and the subsequent integration of the republics into recurrent cycles of development debt. Crises on the periphery were basically symptoms of this evolution, even though (as in the case of North's activities in Chile) they often assumed a semi-detached character. This is not to suggest that British policy was determined by bond-holders or mine-owners; it is rather to recognise the extent to which economic policy and political alliances in the republics had become shaped by external considerations, and above all by the need to retain the confidence of British creditors. But it is also true, in South America as in other parts of the world, that the Foreign Office departed increasingly from its non-interventionist ideals, not just in response to new foreign rivals, but in acknowledgement of the fact that Britain's economic stake in South America had reached a size which compelled attention and sometimes action too.

There was, of course, no formal partition of South America. Considerations of cost, logistics and diplomacy were always on hand to restrain the major powers at moments of crisis. Far more important, however, was the fact that official political intervention was rarely demanded by economic interests; nor was it seen by the Foreign Office to be appropriate. The Latin American republics were treated as countries of white settlement, rather like the Dominions, and were regarded as having much greater potential both for economic development and for 'responsible' government than the 'oriental' societies which caused Lord Salisbury to furrow his brow and harden his heart. Consequently, as we have seen, British strategy relied on self-policing and self-regulating mechanisms, and especially on the disciplines imposed on South American governments by their need to remain credit-worthy.

This does not mean that the recipients were conditioned by ideological training to accept a subservient role. The elites of Argentina, Brazil and Chile were responsible for their own decisions and they acted in what they took to be their own interests. Cultural imperialism did not produce economic dependence. At the same time, the emergence of the remarkable degree of 'like-mindedness' among the principal creditors and debtors greatly assisted the process of understanding and conforming to the rules of the game. When the rules were broken, the penalties were severe: Peru was ostracised by the City following its bad default of 1876, and its subsequent economic development was seriously hampered by its inability to borrow abroad; elsewhere, financial crises were met by the standard penalties of retrenchment and deflation which were imposed, directly or indirectly, by external creditors.

Britain emerged from the 'scramble' with her position strengthened in a number of key areas. The fact that she reduced her presence in several of the smaller republics was less a sign of weakness or failing purpose than a recognition of the much greater potential of Argentina, Brazil and Chile. And evidence of Britain's declining share of commodity trade has to be set in the context of her expanding role as South America's chief foreign lender. Successive debt crises gave Britain more, not less, influence in the three major republics. Private investors moved further into the economy through purchases of public utilities and banks, and by investing directly in manufacturing and processing activities, while in the public sector fiscal and monetary priorities were set by borrowing requirements which were linked to the needs of open, export economies. Consequently, public expenditure, tariffs and the exchange rate, as well as the supply of money and credit to the domestic economy, were all profoundly affected by foreign influences.[151] Moreover, as we have seen, both the expansion of the public sector and the purpose of state intervention were significantly shaped by external considerations, as, beyond this, were the structure of elite politics and the ebb and flow of party rivalries.[152]

This degree of penetration, direct and indirect, must surely be seen as infringing the sovereignty of the recipients, even as it boosted their incomes. If Gallagher and Robinson overestimated the extent of Britain's informal empire in the mid-Victorian era, Platt has underestimated its size during the Edwardian period. The argument that the republics entered the international economy freely, profited from overseas commerce, and gained from competition among the expatriate firms does not prove that the relationship between Britain and South America was simply one of interdependence based on mutual business interests. It is misleading to suppose, for example, that Argentina's growing balance of trade surplus after 1900, and the weakening position of Britain's exports, are evidence that the republic was beginning to free itself from economic dependence. When returns on investments and other invisibles are included, Britain still had a comfortable surplus on the balance of payments (current account) in 1913. Moreover, as we argued earlier, the appearance of a trade deficit with the republics was a necessary function of Britain's development as a mature creditor: without open access to the British market, South American exporters could not have earned enough sterling to pay their debts, to maintain their credit-worthiness, and hence to support the free trade-foreign investment syndrome in Britain. It is an ironic comment on this system, as it had evolved in the late nineteenth century, that, had Britain's manufactured exports become more competitive, they might have damaged London's position at the centre of the international economy by reducing the ability of borrowers, like Argentina, to pay their debts. Similarly, the fact that, in times of boom, the republics often ran economic policies which would have horrified Gladstone is not to be read as evidence of growing economic freedom. In periods of prosperity, inflationary policies were no obstacle to debt repayment; in periods of depression they were, and conformity to norms which satisfied London was both expected and usually achieved.

The argument that relations, being interdependent, were approximately equal is also hard to sustain.[153] British financiers, like Morrison, thought of Argentina as being subservient, and even Anglophile leaders, like Pellegrini, feared British intervention at times of crisis. It has yet to be suggested that South American entrepreneurs saw Britain as a satellite or that Queen Victoria's ministers were much exercised by the prospect of Argentine troops occupying the City. Interdependence is clearly consistent with wide variations in degrees of independence and dependence. Britain invested heavily in the United States in the nineteenth century but contributed only a very small percentage of the republic's total capital formation, and consequently had less influence there than in countries such as Australia, Canada and Argentina, which relied more heavily on British finance. Approximately half of Argentina's fixed capital assets (excluding land) were foreign-owned in 1913, principally by the British,[154] whereas hardly any British assets were held by Argentine investors. Argentina also depended on Britain for about 28 per cent of her foreign trade in 1913, while Britain conducted less than 5 per cent of her overseas trade with Argentina.[155]

None of this is to be read as an attempt to resurrect crude versions of the dependency thesis; as pointed out earlier, the fact of dependence ought to be separated from a consideration of its consequences for economic development and social welfare. But, if the historian's task is to explain the structures of the past, then the evolution of Argentina, Brazil and Chile since independence cannot be understood without reference to the pervasive effects of British influence in the period down to 1914. Clearly, Britain's power was not felt in South America as it was in India and Africa, but Britain's influence was exercised in much the same way as it was in Canada and Australia.[156] Argentina was shortly to be thought of as an 'honorary dominion', and that is probably as accurate a description as the imperfect terms available to historians of imperialism will allow.

Notes

1 'I called the New World into existence to redress the balance of the Old'. Canning, 1826, quoted in William W. Kaufmann, *British Policy and the Independence of Latin America, 1804–1828* (New Haven, Conn., 1951), p. 220. The present chapter deals with the continental mainland and therefore refers to South America. The larger entity, Latin America, which also covers Central America, Mexico, and (in some usages) parts of the Caribbean, is referred to only where other sources cited here have

used it as their unit of analysis. We are grateful to Dr Rory Miller for his helpful comments on this chapter.

2 J. Gallagher and R. Robinson, 'The Imperialism of Free Trade', *Econ. Hist. Rev.,* 2nd ser. VI (1953), p. 8.

3 D.C.M. Platt, 'British Diplomacy in Latin America Since the Emancipation', *Inter-American Economic Affairs,* 21 (1967), pp. 21–41; idem, 'The Imperialism of Free Trade: Some Reservations', *Econ. Hist. Rev.,* 2nd ser. XXI (1968), idem, *Finance, Trade, and Politics in British Foreign Policy, 1815–1914* (Oxford, 1968), Ch. 6; and the important case study by W.M. Mathew, 'The Imperialism of Free Trade: Peru, 1820–70', *Econ. Hist. Rev.,* 2nd ser. XXI (1968), though it should be noted, in the context of the argument developed here, that Britain's tolerant view of Peru's guano monopoly was shaped partly by the need to ensure that Peru could continue to service her debts: ibid. pp. 575–7.

4 Peter Winn, 'British Informal Empire in Uruguay in the Nineteenth Century', *Past and Present,* 73 (1976), argues that informal rule was established in the second half of the century. George E. Carl, *First Among Equals: Great Britain and Venezuela, 1810–1910* (Ann Arbor, Mich., 1980), offers an interpretation which is far more critical of Platt's position than that adopted by Miriam Hood, *Gunboat Diplomacy, 1895–1905: Great Power Pressure in Venezuela* (1975: 2nd edn, 1983, appears not to have been influenced by Carl's work). See also Holger H. Herwig, *Germany's Vision of Empire in Venezuela, 1871–1914* (Princeton, NJ, 1987).

5 Gallagher and Robinson, 'Imperialism of Free Trade', p. 9.

6 Richard Graham, 'Sepoys and Imperialists: Techniques of British Power in Nineteenth-Century Brazil', *Inter-American Econ. Aff.,* 23 (1969), p. 29; and idem, 'Robinson and Gallagher in Latin America: the Meaning of Informal Imperialism', in Wm Roger Louis, ed. *Imperialism: The Gallagher and Robinson Controversy* (1976). This approach also appears in Michael Monteón, 'The British in the Atacama Desert: the Cultural Bases of Economic Imperialism', *Jour. Econ. Hist.,* 35 (1975).

7 D.C.M. Platt, 'Economic Imperialism and the Businessman: Britain and Latin America Before 1914', in Roger Owen and Bob Sutcliffe, eds. *Studies in the Theory of Imperialism* (1972); idem, ed. *Business Imperialism, 1840–1930: An Enquiry Based on British Experience in Latin America* (Oxford, 1977). This view was anticipated by H.S. Ferns, *Britain and Argentina in the Nineteenth Century* (Oxford, 1960), pp. 487–91. More recently, Platt has also emphasised the role of local sources of development finance: 'Domestic Finance in the Growth of Buenos Aires', in Guido di Tella and D.C.M. Platt, eds. *The Political Economy of Argentina, 1880–1946* (1986).

8 A valuable introduction to the subjects touched on in this paragraph is Christopher Abel and Colin Lewis, eds. *Latin America, Economic Imperialism and the State: The Political Economy of the External Connection from Independence to the Present* (1985), Chs. 1–3. See also Colin Lewis, 'Latin America: From Independence to Dependence', in Peter Morris, ed. *Africa, America, and Central Asia: Formal and Informal Empire in the Nineteenth Century* (Exeter, 1984), and, for a succinct survey of the economic history of the period, Bill Albert, *South America and the World Economy from Independence to 1930* (1983). For a more general but also comprehensive guide to recent research see Leslie Bethel, ed. *The Cambridge History of Latin America,* Vols. I and II (Cambridge, 1984), Vol. III (Cambridge, 1985), and Vols. IV and V (Cambridge, 1986).

9 See particularly John Lynch, *The Spanish American Revolutions, 1808–1826* (2nd edn 1987), and Michael P. Costeloe, *Response to Revolution: Imperial Spain and the Spanish American Revolutions, 1810–1840* (Cambridge, 1986). Timothy E. Anna, *Spain and the Loss of America* (1983) emphasises the decline of central authority rather than the rise of 'nationalism'.

10 Kenneth R. Maxwell, *Conflicts and Conspiracies: Brazil and Portugal, 1750–1808* (Cambridge, 1973) deals with the antecedents; A.J.R. Russell–Wood, ed. *From Colony to Nation: Essays on the Independence of Brazil* (Baltimore, Md, 1975) explores the consequences.

11 It is true that the Portuguese empire survived until the mid-twentieth century, but since it was barely animate for much of its existence it seems permissible to treat the

loss of Brazil as an episode in the story of the gradual subsidence of central authority. At all events, the foregoing comments are intended to suggest comparisons which, strangely, Latin Americanists themselves do not normally pursue (perhaps because, like other scholars in different contexts, they are already burdened by the weight of their own specialisation).

12 Kaufmann, *British Policy,* pp. 23–33.
13 Quoted in Ferns, *Britain and Argentina,* p. 48.
14 Canning to Granville, 17 Dec. 1824, quoted in Kaufmann, *British Policy,* p. 178. The intention was noted by others too. In 1843, the United States' chargé d'affaires in Brazil observed that British support for the independence of the Spanish and Portuguese colonies was 'for the purpose of making these the quasi colonies of Great Britain without the expense of their maintenance as such'. Hunte to Webster, 31 March 1843, quoted in Kinley J. Brauer, 'The United States and British Imperial Expansion, 1815–60', *Diplomatic History,* 12 (1988), pp. 23–4.
15 Canning to A'Court, 31 Dec. 1823, quoted in Kaufmann, *British Policy,* p. 203. Bentham was fascinated by the changes taking place in Spanish America and by the prospects of realising a utilitarian utopia there. He maintained a weighty correspondence with leaders of the new states, notably Rivadavia and Bolívar, and supplied them with constitutions designed to have universal applicability. See Mirian Williford, *Jeremy Bentham on Spanish America* (Baton Rouge, La, 1980).
16 Canning to Frere, 8 Jan. 1825, quoted in ibid. p. 201.
17 Kaufmann, *British Policy,* p. 38.
18 See, for example, Rivadavia's experiments in Argentina in the 1820s, discussed by Ferns, *Britain and Argentina,* pp. 111–18, and for the transition from liberalism to conservatism Simon Collier, *Ideas and Politics of Chilean Independence, 1808–1833* (Cambridge, 1967).
19 On these subjects Ferns, *Britain and Argentina,* remains as fresh and perceptive as when it was first published in 1960. See especially pp. 84–6 and Chs. 7 and 10; also idem, 'Latin America and Industrial Capitalism – The First Phase', *Sociological Review,* Monograph No. 11 (1967). The rise of Argentina's first important strong man is also well covered in John Lynch, *Argentine Dictator: Juan Manuel de Rosas, 1829–1852* (Oxford, 1981).
20 On the treaty with Argentina see Ferns, 'Latin America and Industrial Capitalism', pp. 13–17. The terms imposed on Brazil (which were more favourable to Britain) are described by Alan K. Manchester, *British Preëminence in Brazil: Its Rise and Decline. A Study in European Expansion* (Chapel Hill, NC, 1933), Ch. 8. British trade is dealt with by D.C.M. Platt, *Latin America and British Trade, 1806–1914* (1972).
21 Platt, *Latin America and British Trade,* p. 37; François Crouzet, 'Angleterre-Brésil, 1697–1850: un siècle et demi d'échanges commerciaux', *Histoire, Economie et Société,* 2 (1990).
22 Abel and Lewis, *Latin America,* pp. 96–7;See also Platt, *Latin America and British Trade,* pp. 3–34, and the case study by William Paul McGreevey, *An Economic History of Colombia, 1845–1930* (Cambridge, 1971), which shows that economic change was very limited until the 1890s.
23 Kaufmann, *British Policy,* p. 180.
24 Frank G. Dawson, *The First Latin American Debt Crisis: The City of London and the 1822–25 Loan Bubble* (New Haven, Conn., 1990); C. Marichal, *A Century of Debt Crises in Latin America: From Independence to the Great Depression, 1820–1930* (Princeton, NJ, 1989), Ch. 2.
25 Ferns, *Britain and Argentina,* pp. 133–44.
26 Ibid. pp. 121, 314–21.
27 Marichal, *A Century of Debt,* pp. 34–5, 40–1. On the links between Barings and Rivadavia in the 1820s see Ferns, *Britain and Argentina,* pp. 134–44.
28 On these subjects see Platt, *Latin America and British Trade.*
29 B.R. Mitchell and P. Deane, *Abstract of British Historical Statistics* (Cambridge, 1962), pp. 321–3. As we have noted in other contexts, the quantitative data need to be used cautiously and as measures of broad tendencies only. Some of the main difficulties are

discussed by D.C.M. Platt, 'Problems in the Interpretation of Foreign Trade Statistics Before 1914', *Jour. Latin Am. Stud.*, 3 (1977).

30 Mitchell and Deane, *Abstract,* pp. 321–3; Platt, *Latin America and British Trade,* pp. 251, 275–6.

31 See Irving Stone, 'British Direct and Portfolio Investment in Latin America Before 1914', *Jour. Econ. Hist.*, 37 (1977); and, for greater detail, idem, *The Composition and Distribution of British Investment in Latin America, 1865–1913* (1987).

32 Although Platt has produced revised and reduced figures for British investment overseas, he has also confirmed South America's importance as a recipient of British capital. See D.C.M. Platt, *Britain's Investment Overseas on the Eve of the First World War* (1986).

33 Robert G. Albion, 'British Shipping and Latin America, 1806–1914', *Jour. Econ. Hist.*, 11 (1951); Robert Greenhill, 'Shipping, 1850–1914', in D.C.M. Platt, ed. *Business Imperialism, 1840–1930* (Oxford, 1977); Juan E. Oribe Stemmer, 'Freight Rates in the Trade Between Europe and South America, 1840–1914', *Jour. Latin Am. Stud.*, 21 (1989).

34 The pioneering study of British banking is David Joslin, *A Century of Banking in Latin America* (1963). The starting point for more recent studies is the important work of Charles Jones. See, for example, 'Commercial Banks and Mortgage Companies', in Platt, *Business Imperialism,* and 'Insurance Companies', in ibid.

35 Nicolás Sánchez-Albornoz, 'The Population of Latin America, 1850–1930', in Bethel, *Cambridge History of Latin America,* Vol. 4, Ch. 4.

36 This is a curious omission, given the importance attached by historians of imperialism to the debate on informal empire earlier in the century. There is room for a book synthesising existing case studies and setting them in a wider context.

37 For the Venezuelan crisis see the references in n. 4. The point of departure for studies of the war between Chile and Peru is now William F. Sater, *Chile and the War of the Pacific* (Lincoln, Nebr., 1986). On South America's fear of intervention (a subject neglected by historians of imperialism) see Joseph Smith, *Illusions of Conflict: Anglo-American Diplomacy Toward Latin America, 1865–1896* (Pittsburgh, Pa, 1979), pp. 179, 186–7, 205–9.

38 Smith, *Illusions of Conflict,* pp. 118–21, 130–4, 143–55.

39 Ian L.D. Forbes, 'German Informal Imperialism in South America Before 1914', *Econ. Hist. Rev.*, 2nd ser. XXXI (1978); Warren Schiff, 'The Influence of the German Armed Forces and War Industry on Argentina, 1880–1914', *Hisp. Am. Hist. Rev.*, 52 (1972); Jürgen Schaefer, *Deutsche Militärhilfe an Südamerika: Militär-und Rüstungsinteressen in Argentinien, Bolivien, Chile vor 1914* (Düsseldorf, 1974) similarly emphasises the link between military aid and the growth of the munitions industry in Germany.

40 Andres M. Regalsky, 'Foreign Capital, Local Interests and Railway Development in Argentina: French Investments in Railways, 1900–1914', *Jour. Latin Am. Stud.*, 21(1989).

41 The figures relate to 1910 and 1913 respectively. See Platt, *Latin America and British Trade,* p. 276, and Stone, 'British Direct and Portfolio Investment', Table 2, p. 695. On the trend towards concentration see Platt, *Latin America and British Trade,* pp. 116–21, 276.

42 Smith, *Illusions of Conflict,* pp. 179, 196; Charles Jones, 'The State and Business Practice in Argentina, 1862–1914', in Abel and Lewis, *Latin America,* pp. 184–98.

43 Forbes, 'German Informal Imperialism', p. 398.

44 As German businessmen, among others, acknowledged. See Forbes. 'German Informal Imperialism', p. 393.

45 Marichal, *A Century of Debt,* p. 147, and (for a helpful guide to the main foreign banks) pp. 257–68; Jones, 'Commercial Banks', pp. 26–9, 37–9, 47, 52; idem, 'The State and Business Practice', pp. 184–98. Banking also remained highly profitable: see Joslin, *A Century of Banking,* pp. 108–11.

46 Platt, *Latin America and British Trade,* pp. 120–1; Greenhill, 'Shipping', p. 120.

47 Platt, *Latin America and British Trade,* pp. 277–8; Smith, *Illusions of Conflict,* pp. 45–6, 118, 140–1, 153, 166–7, 190.

48 See Holger Herwig's critical review of R. Fiebig-von Hase, *Lateinamerika als Konfliktherd der deutsch-amerikanischen Beziehungen, 1890–1903: vom Beginn der Panamerikapolitik bis zur Venezuelakrise von 1902/3* (Göttingen, 1986), *Hisp. Am. Hist. Rev.*, 68 (1988), p. 400.

49 Platt, *Latin America and British Trade,* p. 120, and the illustration given by Regalsky, 'Foreign Capital', p. 452. On the speculators see W.R. Reader and J. Slinn, *A House in the City: Foster and Braithwaite, 1825–1975* (1980), pp. 70–9, and Harris G. Warren, 'The Golden Fleecing: the Paraguayan Loans of 1871 and 1872', *Journal of Inter-American Economic Affairs,* 26 (1972), pp. 11–13.
50 Joslin, *A Century of Banking,* p. 107; Platt, *Latin America and British Trade,* pp. 283–4, 293.
51 If space allowed, this exercise would be carried much further, though it is worth noting that even historians who specialise on South America have not yet fully colonised the area between high-level generalisations about the continent as a whole and low level studies of particular regions or countries. The acknowledged starting point for such an exercise is Fernando Henrique Cardoso and Enzo Faletto, *Dependence and Development in Latin America* (Berkeley, Calif., 1979). See also the suggestive contributions by Carlos F. Díaz Alejandro, 'Open Economy, Closed Polity?', *Millennium,* 10 (1981), and Ian Roxborough, 'Unity and Diversity in Latin American History', *Jour. Latin Am. Stud.,* 16 (1984).
52 Mitchell and Deane, *Abstract,* pp. 321–3.
53 Stone, 'British Direct and Portfolio Investment', Table 2, p. 695.
54 E. Gallo, 'Agrarian Expansion and Industrial Development in Argentina, 1880–1930', *St. Antony's Papers,* 22 (1970), p. 50. Roger Gravil, *The Anglo-Argentine Connection, 1900–1939* (Boulder, Colo., 1985), pp. 88–9.
55 The population of Argentina more than doubled (from 1.8 million to 4 million) between 1869 and 1895, principally as a result of immigration. Reber, *British Mercantile Houses,* p. 34.
56 Platt, *Latin America and British Trade,* p. 166. Platt's study has now to be considered in the light of Gravil, *Anglo-Argentine Connection,* who takes a more critical view of the marketing performance of British firms. On the business community see Reber, *British Mercantile Houses,* Ch. 3.
57 On the relationship between exports of capital and exports of goods, see A.G. Ford, *The Gold Standard, 1880–1914: Britain and Argentina* (Oxford, 1962), S.B. Saul, *Studies in British Overseas Trade, 1870–1914* (Liverpool, 1960), pp. 72–95, and Gravil, *Anglo-Argentine Connection,* pp. 102–3.
58 Marichal, *A Century of Debt,* p. 92; D.C.M. Platt, 'Foreign Finance in Argentina for the First Half Century of Independence', *Jour. Latin Am. Stud.,* 15 (1983), pp. 32–3.
59 Reber, *British Mercantile Houses,* pp. 33, 58, 72, 123, 140–3.
60 Joslin, *A Century of Banking,* Ch. 3.
61 Ferns, *Britain and Argentina,* pp. 335–6; also Reber, *British Mercantile Houses,* pp. 120–22, 158.
62 Joslin, *A Century of Banking,* pp. 108–11.
63 Charles A. Jones, 'Great Capitalists and the Direction of British Overseas Investment in the late Nineteenth Century', *Bus. Hist.,* 22 (1980).
64 David Rock, *Politics in Argentina, 1890–1930: The Rise and Fall of Radicalism* (Cambridge, 1975), pp. 2–3; A. Ferrer, *The Argentine Economy* (Berkeley, Calif., 1967), p. 98.
65 Ferns, 'Latin America', pp. 18–21.
66 Ferns, *Britain and Argentina,* Chs. 10–11; idem, *Argentina* (1969), pp. 92–6; Platt, 'Foreign Finance in Argentina', pp. 32–3.
67 Donna J. Guy, 'Carlos Pellegrini and the Politics of Early Argentine Industrialization, 1873–1906', *Jour. Latin Am. Stud.,* ll (1979); idem, 'Dependency, the Credit Market, and Argentine Industrialization, 1860–1940', *Bus. Hist. Rev.,* 58 (1984); Colin M. Lewis, *British Railways in Argentina, 1857–1914: A Case Study of Foreign Investment* (1983), pp. 10–12.
68 Ferns, *Britain and Argentina,* pp. 217, 286.
69 Ibid. pp. 402–3, 423. Julio Roca was President from 1880 to 1886 and from 1898 to 1904; Miguel Celmán (his brother-in-law) from 1886 to 1890; and Carlos Pellegrini from 1890 to 1892. On Harrods see Gravil, *Anglo-Argentine Connection,* pp. 94–5.

70 On the provincial towns, see James Scobie, *Secondary Cities of Argentina: The Social History of Corrientes, Salta, and Mendoza, 1850–1910* (Stanford, Calif., 1988), which complements his *Buenos Aires: From Plaza to Suburb, 1870–1910* (Oxford, 1974).
71 Rock, *Politics in Argentina,* p. 7.
72 Marichal, *A Century of Debt,* p. 105.
73 Ibid. pp. 105–6.
74 For the episode which follows see Joslin, *A Century of Banking,* pp. 45–50; and Ferns, *Britain and Argentina,* pp. 381–4.
75 A full account is given by Ferns, *Britain and Argentina,* pp. 102–20. See also his *Argentina,* pp. 94–114, 119, 124, and for a different perspective, based on local sources, John E. Hodge, 'Carlos Pellegrini and the Financial Crisis of 1890', *Hisp. Am. Hist. Rev.,* 50 (1970). A valuable recent appraisal is Marichal, *A Century of Debt,* Ch. 14. The fundamental economic analysis remains A.G. Ford, 'Argentina and the Baring Crisis of 1890', *Oxford Economic Papers,* 8 (1956), and, for the wider context, idem, *The Gold Standard.*
76 Driven partly by foreign rivalries. See Charles Jones, 'Commercial Banks', pp. 37–9; and idem, 'The State and Business Practice in Argentina, 1862–1914', in Abel and Lewis, *Latin America, Economic Imperialism,* pp. 185–90.
77 Quoted in Marichal, *A Century of Debt,* p. 151.
78 For reactions in London see pp. 153–8.
79 Joslin, *A Century of Banking,* pp. 103–4; Ferns, *Britain and Argentina,* pp. 464–7.
80 Quoted in Marichal, *A Century of Debt,* p. 159.
81 Hodge, 'Carlos Pellegrini', p. 509, n. 35.
82 21 Aug. 1891. Quoted in Smith, *Illusions of Conflict,* p. 188.
83 Welby to Rosebery, 14 Sept. 1892. Quoted in Ferns, *Britain and Argentina,* p. 471.
84 Marichal, *A Century of Debt,* pp. 159–60.
85 A good account is in Marichal, *A Century of Debt,* pp. 159–70. Albert Fishlow, 'Lessons from the Past: Capital Markets During the Nineteenth Century', *International Organization,* 39 (1985), pp. 410–11, correctly stresses the part played by the revival of exports in the success of the Arreglo Romero.
86 Succinct overviews of this period can be found in Tulio Halperin, 'The Argentine Export Economy: Intimations of Mortality, 1894–1930', and David Rock, 'The Argentine Economy: Some Salient Features', both in Guido di Tella and D.C.M. Platt, eds. *The Political Economy of Argentina, 1880–1946* (1986).
87 These developments have been traced in a series of important essays by Charles Jones: 'Commercial Banks' and 'Insurance Companies', in Platt, *Business Imperialism;* 'The State and Business Practice', in Abel and Lewis, *Latin America;* and 'Great Capitalists'. See also Reber, *British Mercantile Houses,* Ch. 4, and Joslin, *A Century of Banking,* Ch. 4. British purchases of public utilities after the Baring Crisis are dealt with by Linda and Charles Jones and Robert Greenhill, 'Public Utility Companies', in Platt, *Business Imperialism.*
88 Joslin, *A Century of Banking,* Chs. 6–7; Jones, 'Commercial Banks and Mortgage Companies'.
89 This was part of a deal, approved by the City, which ended government subsidies to a number of railway lines. See Lewis, *British Railways,* pp. 86–7, 118–20; and Marichal, *A Century of Debt,* pp. 168–9.
90 Regalsky, 'Foreign Capital', pp. 447–52. Lewis, *British Railways,* pp. 193–6, underlines the wider significance of the Law in cementing relations between British investors and the Argentine government.
91 Guy, 'Carlos Pellegrini', and idem, 'Dependency'.
92 These efforts merely underlined the supremacy of British finance. See Ferns, *Britain and Argentina,* pp. 69, 108–9; Gravil, *Anglo-Argentine Connection,* pp. 24–7; Marichal, *A Century of Debt,* p. 161. After the failure of negotiations with the United States in 1892, the US Consul in Buenos Aires reported ruefully that the British were involved in 'everything, except politics, as intimately as though it were a British colony'. Quoted in Smith, *Illusions of Conflict,* p. 190.

93 Rock, *Politics,* Chs. 3–4. Indeed the rapidity of socio-economic change in Argentina began to provoke a conservative, anti-development reaction after 1900. See David Rock, 'Intellectual Precursors of Conservative Nationalism in Argentina, 1900–1927', *Hisp. Am. Hist. Rev.*, 67 (1989). Provincial resentment at foreign control undoubtedly found expression in disputes over the way in which railways and other public utilities were operated. But discontent was contained before 1914, partly at least because of the need to retain the confidence of the City.

94 On the growing divorce between British investment and British exports see Gravil, *Anglo-Argentine Connection,* pp. 95–104.

95 Manchester, *British Preëminence.* For the wider context see G. Clarence Smith, *The Third Portuguese Empire, 1825–1975: A Study in Economic Imperialism* (1985).

96 Marichal, *A Century of Debt,* pp. 34–5, 48–9, 55, 80.

97 Manchester, *British Preëminence,* p. 220. The definitive account of the institutional underpinnings of Brazil's dependence is Richard Graham, *Patronage and Politics in Nineteenth-Century Brazil* (Stanford, Calif., 1990).

98 See, for example, Nathaniel H. Leff, *Underdevelopment and Development in Brazil,* II (1982), Ch. 4, which develops the main theme of Manchester's study, *British Preëminence.*

99 As Manchester himself was careful to point out in *British Preëminence,* pp. vii–viii, 336, 341.

100 His decision was strongly influenced by the need to maintain Brazil's creditrating in London in readiness for war with Argentina and Uruguay. See Graham, *Britain and the Onset of Modernisation,* pp. 162–9. For further references see Seymour Drescher, 'Brazilian Abolition in Historical Perspective', *Hisp. Am. Hist. Rev.,* 68 (1988), and Robert Levine, 'Turning On the Lights: Brazilian Slavery Reconsidered One Hundred Years After Abolition', *Latin Am. Research Rev.,* 24 (1989).

101 Joslin, *A Century of Banking,* pp. 62–71.

102 Ibid. pp. 64–5, 70–2.

103 Marichal, *A Century of Debt,* pp. 80, 92, 94–7.

104 Ibid. pp. 104–6.

105 F.O. memo. by Davidson, 25 Jan. 1888, FO 13/642. Quoted in Smith, *Illusions of Conflict,* p. 18.

106 Graham, *Britain and the Onset of Modernisation,* pp. 100–2.

107 Ibid. Ch. 4. See also Jeffrey D. Needell, *A Tropical Belle Epoque: Elite Culture and Society in Turn-of-the-Century Rio de Janeiro* (Cambridge, 1988).

108 Quoted (1883) in Graham, *Britain and the Onset of Modernisation,* p. 202.

109 Quoted (n.d.) in ibid. p. 263.

110 See particularly Stanley J. Stein, *Vassouras: A Brazilian Coffee County, 1850–1900* (Cambridge, Mass., 1957), pp. 250–76, and Warren Dean, 'The Green Wave of Coffee: Beginnings of Tropical Agricultural Research in Brazil (1885–1900)', *Hisp. Am. Hist. Rev.,* 69 (1989).

111 Eugene W. Ridings, 'Class Sector Unity in an Export Economy: The Case of Nineteenth-Century Brazil', *Hisp. Am. Hist. Rev.,* 58 (1978), and idem, 'Business, Nationality and Dependency in Nineteenth-Century Brazil', *Jour. Latin Am. Stud.,* 14 (1982). For a fascinating study of the adaptations made by one of the 'great families' over four generations see Darrell E. Levi, *The Prados of São Paulo, Brazil: An Elite Family and Social Change, 1840–1930* (1987).

112 Graham, *The Onset of Modernisation,* pp. 172–85; Smith, *Illusions of Conflict,* pp. 169–80; R.F. Colson, 'European Investment and the Brazilian Boom, 1886–92: the Roots of Speculation', *Ibero-Amerikanishes Archiv,* 9 (1983); Marshall C. Eakins, 'Business Imperialism and British Enterprise in Brazil: The St. John d'el Rey Mining Company Limited, 1830–1960', *Hisp. Am. Hist. Rev.,* 66 (1986).

113 Wyndham to Salisbury, 24 July 1890, FO 13/666. Quoted in Smith, *Illusions of Conflict,* p. 162.

114 The United States tried to create a 'special relationship' with Brazil by negotiating a reciprocal trade treaty in 1891, but this was unsuccessful and was annulled in 1894. See Smith, *Illusions of Conflict,* pp. 143–53, 164–9.

115 Forbes, 'German Informal Imperialism', p. 398; Platt, *Latin America and British Trade,* pp. 98–9.
116 Leff, *Underdevelopment,* II, p. 85.
117 Platt, *Latin America and British Trade,* pp. 291–3; Greenhill, 'Shipping', in Platt, *Business Imperialism,* p. 120; Joslin, *A Century of Banking,* p. 110; Graham, *The Onset of Modernisation,* pp. 88–91, 94–7, 303.
118 Leff, *Underdevelopment,* Table 43, p. 77; Platt, *Latin America and British Trade,* pp. 286–93; Marichal, *A Century of Debt,* pp. 126–7. According to Peter Uwe Schliemann, *The Strategy of British and German Direct Investors in Brazil* (Farnborough, Hants. 1981), p. 99, Britain's share of foreign investment in Brazil fell from 78 per cent of the total in the period 1860–1902 to 53 per cent in the period 1903–13. However, we know from Stone, 'British Direct and Portfolio Investment', pp. 710–20, that the 11 per cent attributed by Schliemann to Canada for the latter period was in fact raised by the City, and Albert estimates that Britain's share was 62 per cent in 1914 (*South America,* p. 21).
119 Special mention must be made of the important contributions of Topik and Fritsch, which have made possible a reappraisal of the history of fiscal and monetary policy during this period. See Steven Topik, 'The Evolution of the Economic Role of the Brazilian State, 1889–1930', *Jour. Latin Am. Stud.,* 11 (1979); 'State Intervention in a Liberal Regime: Brazil, 1889–1930', *Hisp. Am. Hisp. Rev.,* 60 (1980); 'The State's Contribution to the Development of Brazil's Internal Economy, 1850–1930', *Hisp. Am. Hist. Rev.,* 65 (1985); *The Political Economy of the Brazilian State, 1889–1930* (Austin, Tex., 1987); and Winston Fritsch, *External Constraints on Economic Policy in Brazil, 1889–1930* (1988).
120 See Topik, 'The Evolution of the Economic Role', pp. 330–1; Fritsch, *External Constraints,* pp. 4–11; Graham, *The Onset of Modernisation,* pp. 103–5; and the illuminating essay by Jeffrey D. Needell, 'The *Revolta Contra Vacina* of 1904: the Revolt Against "Modernisation" in *Belle Epoque* Rio de Janeiro', *Hisp. Am. Hist. Rev.,* 67 (1987).
121 Quoted in Topik, 'The Evolution of the Economic Role', p. 331.
122 Fritsch, *External Constraints,* p. 10.
123 Argentina set up a similar Conversion Office in 1899 to maintain the stability of the peso. Joslin, *A Century of Banking,* p. 139.
124 Brazil's reserves, like Argentina's, were also held in London.
125 And over one-quarter in Argentina and Chile. Joslin, *A Century of Banking,* p. 110.
126 Topik, 'The Evolution of the Economic Role', pp. 335–7. Other lines were 'privatised', as in Argentina, to raise capital and to economise on running costs.
127 Graham, *The Onset of Modernisation,* pp. 110–11 and Ch. 5.
128 Fritsch, *Economic Constraints,* Ch. 2.; Topik, 'The Evolution of the Economic Role', pp. 330–4.
129 Quoted in Fritsch, *Economic Constraints,* p. 14.
130 Ibid. pp. 28–31.
131 Robertson to Grey, 9 July 1914, FO 371/1916. Quoted in Fritsch, *Economic Constraints,* pp. 218–19.
132 Thomas F. O'Brien, *The Nitrate Industry and Chile's Crucial Transition, 1870–1891* (1982), Ch. 1; Luis Ortega, 'Economic Policy and Growth in Chile from Independence to the War of the Pacific', in Abel and Lewis, *Latin America.*
133 Rothschilds became official bankers to the Chilean government, as they did in Brazil. The role of British merchants is discussed by John Mayo, *British Merchants and Chilean Development, 1851–1886* (Boulder, Colo., 1987), Chs. 1–5. See also idem, 'Before the Nitrate Era: British Commission Houses and the Chilean Economy, 1851–80', *Jour. Latin Am. Stud.,* 11 (1979), and Thomas F. O'Brien, 'The Antofagasta Company: A Case Study of Peripheral Imperialism', *Hisp. Am. Hist. Rev.,* 60 (1980), (and the debate in ibid. pp. 676–84). Valuable information can also be found in William M. Mathew, *The House of Gibbs and the Peruvian Guano Monopoly* (1981).
134 Quoted in Mayo, *British Merchants,* p. 236.
135 Ibid.
136 Ibid.

137 On these events, see William F. Sater, 'Chile and the World Depression of the 1870s', *Jour. Latin Am. Stud.*, 5 (1979); idem, *Chile and the War,* O'Brien, *The Nitrate Industry,* Chs. 2–3; and Luis Ortega, 'Nitrates, Chilean Entrepreneurs and the Origins of the War of the Pacific', *Jour. Latin Am. Stud.*, 16 (1984).
138 Ortega, 'Economic Policy', p. 159.
139 Quoted in ibid. p. 164.
140 The standard account is now Sater, *Chile and the War.*
141 This contemporary claim (made especially by the United States) is evaluated in V.G. Kiernan, 'Foreign Interests and the War of the Pacific', *Hisp. Am. Hist. Rev.*, 35(1955).
142 The Peruvian debt was a major issue in its own right which cannot be covered in the space available here. The authoritative study is by Rory Miller, 'The Making of the Grace Contract: British Bondholders and the Peruvian Government, 1885–1890', *Jour. Latin Am. Stud.* 8 (1976). See also idem, 'British Firms and the Peruvian Government, 1885–1930', in Platt, *Business Imperialism,* and 'The Grace Contract, the Peruvian Corporation and Peruvian History', *Ibero Amerikanisches Archiv,* 9 (1983). Miller shows that the settlement finally reached in 1890 involved considerable intervention by the Foreign Office, and was made possible on the Peruvian side by the realisation that future economic development depended on restoring credit-worthiness in London.
143 Chile's Minister of Finance was well aware that the bond-holders had been influential in Europe in 'preventing the Peruvians from acquiring war materials and creating for us a beneficent atmosphere in the opinion of these peoples'. Malte to Sotomayor, 6 Feb. 1880. Quoted in O'Brien, *The Nitrate Industry,* p. 51.
144 O'Brien, *The Nitrate Industry,* pp. 52–5.
145 Joseph R. Brown, 'The Frustration of Chile's Nitrate Imperialism', *Pacific. Hist. Rev.*, 32 (1963), p. 389; Thomas F. O'Brien, 'Chilean Elites and Foreign Investors: Chilean Nitrate Policy, 1880–82', *Jour. Latin Am. Stud.*, 11 (1979); Smith, *Illusions of Conflict,* p. 192.
146 On North see Harold Blakemore, *British Nitrates and Chilean Politics, 1886–1896: Balmaceda and North* (1974), pp. 38–42; O'Brien, *The Nitrate Industry,* pp. 64–77, 113–22; Robert Greenhill, 'The Nitrate and Iodine Trades, 1880–1914', in Platt, *Business Imperialism,* pp. 236–8; and Monteón, 'The British in the Atacama Desert', pp. 127–33. The estimate of North's holding is taken from O'Brien, *The Nitrate Industry,* p. 119.
147 The most detailed attempt to demonstrate North's involvement is by Osgood Hardy, 'British Nitrates and the Balmaceda Revolution', *Pacific Hist. Rev.*, 17 (1948). Blakemore, *British Nitrates,* argues that the war was essentially a matter of internal politics. O'Brien, *The Nitrate Industry,* presents an excellent synthesis of external and internal causes. See also Michael Monteón, *Chile in the Nitrate Era: The Evolution of Economic Dependence, 1880–1930* (Madison, Wis., 1982), pp. 41–7. The earlier literature is assessed by Harold Blakemore, 'The Chilean Revolution of 1891 and its Historiography', *Hisp. Am. Hist. Rev.,* 45 (1965). It is curious that obvious comparisons and contrasts with events in South Africa have yet to be explored.
148 Kennedy to Sanderson, 15 Sept. 1891, FO 16/266. Quoted in Smith, *Illusions of Conflict,* p. 196.
149 O'Brien, *The Nitrate Industry,* p. 144; Joslin, *A Century of Banking,* pp. 110, 185. The rise to prominence of British banks and insurance companies was also bound up with the development of the nitrate industry. See Mayo, *British Merchants,* pp. 201–7. Britain's share of Chile's import trade began to slip after the turn of the century, as Germany, in particular, made her presence felt. But (as we have argued for Argentina and Brazil) this trend was related to the expansion of Britain's role as a creditor and is not to be seen as a sign of a general decline in her influence.
150 Joseph R. Brown, 'Nitrate Crises, Combinations and the Chilean Government in the Nitrate Age', *Hisp. Am. Hist. Rev.*, 43 (1963); Greenhill, 'The Nitrate and Iodine Trades'; Brown, 'The Frustration of Chile's Nitrate Imperialism', p. 396. Moreover, after a brief stay on the gold standard (1895–8), Chile reverted to inconvertible paper. This can be read as an indulgence for exporters and as a lapse from the City's ideal of the perfect debtor, but it did not alter the fact that debts still had to be serviced promptly.

151 Charles Jones, '"Business Imperialism" and Argentina, 1875–1900: a Theoretical Note', *Jour. Latin Am. Stud.*, 12 (1980).

152 This is well brought out by Fritsch's discussion of the relationship between the balance of payments, the exchange rate, and interest-group politics in Brazil (*External Constraints,* Chs. 1–2).

153 We disagree here with Ferns (*Britain and Argentina,* pp. 487–9) as well as with Platt.

154 Ferrer, *The Argentine Economy,* p. 103.

155 Platt, *Latin America and British Trade,* p. 111.

156 For some illuminating comparisons, drawn principally from the perspective of economic development problems, see Barrie Dyster, 'Argentine and Australian Development Compared', *Past and Present,* 84 (1979); D.C.M. Platt and Guido di Tella, eds. *Argentina, Australia and Canada: Studies in Comparative Development, 1870–1965* (1985); and Carl E. Solberg, *The Prairies and the Pampas: Agrarian Policy in Canada and Argentina, 1880–1930* (Stanford, Calif., 1987).

10

'MEETING HER OBLIGATIONS TO HER ENGLISH CREDITORS'

India, 1858–1914[1]

When Disraeli dubbed India a 'jewel in the Crown of England', both the example and its symbolism were well chosen, as the subsequent popularity of the phrase amply confirms.[2] In the mid-nineteenth century, even observers of the political scene who were generally indifferent to empire could scarcely overlook Britain's connections with India. The sub-continent had already acquired the special value that attaches to ancient possessions; the weight of its presence within the empire ensured that discussion of its future readily transcended the levels occupied by particular pressure groups and entered the sphere reserved for matters of national interest. From this point onwards, moreover, the history of India under the Raj showed 'the face of the future' to much of the rest of the empire as she passed from acquisition to colonial management and on to the transfer of power. Theorists of empire may bypass Tonga and may regard Uganda as being an exception to the rule, whatever it may be, of imperial growth and decay; but no serious account of British imperialism can omit India or treat her as an anomaly, and no plausible explanation of the purpose of empire-building can afford to stumble over the sub-continent.

Interpretations of the imperial purpose

Not surprisingly, the numerous historians who have appraised India's role in the empire during the nineteenth century have all agreed upon her importance, whether they have chosen to stress economic ties with the metropole, the contribution made by the Indian Army, or the political and diplomatic commitments entered into by London (and its sometimes wayward representatives on the frontier) in pursuit of strategic priorities.[3] Nevertheless, the substantial scholarly literature which has illuminated these and allied subjects has yet to resolve the central question of the determinants of the British presence in India. This is partly because much recent work on the imperial connection has been concerned with rather different issues, such as techniques of colonial management and the costs and benefits of British rule, but it is principally because the main thrust of research during the past generation has been directed towards investigating the internal history of India. The results of this sustained effort constitute a remarkable historiographical advance. But one consequence of this concentration of interest has been that wider issues concerning the nature of the British presence in India and the purpose of imperial policy have become unfashionable and consequently have lost the central place in the literature that they once enjoyed.[4]

Of the global theories of imperialism that have dealt with India, Marx's analysis is outstanding among those advanced by contemporary observers, and it remains a powerful influence today.[5] The 1850s were for Marx a decisive moment of transition, a time when the obstructive 'moneyocracy' and 'oligarchy' of City and landed interests yielded to the progressive 'millocracy' of Manchester and its allies. Marx viewed the Indian Mutiny of 1857, and the transfer of administrative control from the East India Company to the crown in the following year, as symbolising an important stage in the global spread of industrial capitalism. Ending the East India Company's powers of patronage would deprive aristocratic families of administrative and military places for their younger sons; opening India to the full blast of competition from modern manufactures would fuel Britain's economic development, enhance the power of the rising industrial bourgeoisie, and stimulate the process of modernisation in India herself. Until recently, Marx argued:

> the interests of the moneyocracy which had converted India into its landed estates, of the oligarchy who had conquered it by their armies, and of the millocracy who had inundated it with their fabrics, had gone hand in hand. But the more the industrial interest became dependent on the Indian market, the more it felt the necessity of creating fresh productive powers in India, after having ruined her native industry.[6]

It was now time for the Indian economy to be refashioned:

> The millocracy have discovered that the transformation of India into a reproductive country has become of vital importance to them, and to that end it is necessary above all to gift her with means of irrigation and of internal communication.[7]

Despite its vision and incisiveness, Marx's interpretation fits uncomfortably with the evidence now available, principally because it overstates the role of the forces associated with industrialisation. In reality, industrialists exerted only limited influence on policy-making in Britain, and modern manufacturing itself made slow progress in India.

The most prominent liberal theory, on the other hand, has explained nineteenth-century imperalism without fully incorporating India.[8] This oddity has arisen because attention has been focused on the concept of informal empire and on the transition to formal rule. One result of this emphasis, less remarked than perhaps it ought to be, has been to move India to the margins of the debate over the causes of British imperialism in the nineteenth century. Since India was already part of the empire, it is clearly unsuitable territory for discussing either the existence of informal influence or the shift to formal rule during the last quarter of the century. Participants in this controversy tend to treat India as part of the furniture of empire, an eighteenth-century legacy whose provenance is to be explained by specialists of that period. Consequently, attention has been directed away from causation and towards questions of colonial management and its effects on India. Given that India's weighty presence within the empire is acknowledged by historians of varying persuasions, the minor part assigned to her by current theories of nineteenth-century empire-building remains a troublesome paradox. Furthermore, if the partition of Africa is to be presented as 'a gigantic footnote to the Indian empire', as one celebrated analysis claims,[9] it becomes doubly necessary to examine Britain's purpose in the sub-continent.

The view advanced here dissents from both of the foregoing interpretations. India was neither a vehicle for the industrial bourgeoisie nor a fixture that had to be defended simply because she had already been acquired by eighteenth-century enthusiasts. We shall argue instead that the longevity of Britain's presence in India provides a particularly apposite illustration of our argument about the long-run evolution of gentlemanly capitalism. The demise of the East India Company in 1858 can still be treated as a turning point in Anglo-Indian relations; but the event signified the extension abroad of the new service order following the transition from Old Corruption, rather than the triumph of the industrial bourgeoisie, as Marx supposed. The new class of officials and investors did not eject the landed and military interests which, with the East India Company, had dominated British India since the mid-eighteenth century; nor did they seek to do so. Instead, there was a progressive change in the complexion of the British presence in India which reflected the realignment of socio-economic forces that was taking place at home after 1815. As Pitt's quest for 'economical reform' eventually had its issue in Gladstonian finance, so the principles of sound money, free trade and efficient administration were slowly impressed on India. And, as peculation gave way to speculation, and speculation to serious long-term investment, so the official mind became increasingly concentrated on maintaining the credit-worthiness of the Raj and on ensuring that India's mounting external financial obligations were met. These priorities, as we shall see, were a reflection of India's growing importance in London's management of the international economy, and they provided a compelling motive for continuing to control the sub-continent and for defending it from the various external threats that preyed on the minds of successive Viceroys.

This argument does not presume that the history of the Raj stands as a proxy for the history of India. As recent research has demonstrated, pre-British India extended long lines of continuity into the nineteenth century, entangling the new rulers and helping to shape English liberals into oriental despots.[10] But it has also shown that they were aware of the paradox and made good use of it. The managers of the

Raj took readily to India partly because they were able to merge their own rent-seeking and capitalist purposes with the apparatus of 'military fiscalism' left by the Mughals,[11] and partly because their programme of 'economical reform' recognised the importance of grounding political stability in existing institutions in other parts of the world, as it did at home. Moreover, gentlemen fashioned for leadership in a society that was only just beginning to move, slowly and reluctantly, towards democracy, took readily to paternalism abroad, and they reconciled their belief in individualism with the adoption of increasingly *dirigiste* policies by arguing that firm direction was needed to prepare 'backward' societies for a more liberal order. Thus, as the British adapted to India, they also imposed on her by selecting from what they found there, and by seeking to reinforce, discard and invent traditions in the manner of those who were accustomed to applying Whig measures for Tory purposes.

Prelude, 1757–1857

The slow and discontinuous acquisition of India spanned nearly a century, beginning with the take-over of Bengal after the Battle of Plassey in 1757 and culminating in a clutch of acquisitions in the middle of the nineteenth century: Sind and the Punjab in 1843 and 1849; Berar and Oudh in 1853 and 1856.[12] Although the chronology of Britain's advance into India provides an approximate match with the timing of the Industrial Revolution, it has proved difficult, despite numerous heroic attempts, to demonstrate that the growth of empire in India was either a cause or a result of the rise of modern manufactures in England. It was not until the 1840s that products of the Industrial Revolution began to feature prominently among India's imports, and it was only in the second half of the century, after territorial annexations had been made, that this trade assumed weighty proportions.[13] If this evidence suggests that standard theories of economic imperialism are poorly aligned with the results of modern research, it has also given further impetus to the argument that the causes of expansion are to be found on the periphery rather than in the metropole.[14] The application of the 'excentric' thesis to India has the considerable merits of incorporating evidence from local studies and of drawing attention to various forms of sub-imperialism promoted by expansionists on the turbulent frontiers of empire. But, as we noted at the outset of this study, sub-imperialism does not explain imperialism, and to show that actions on the frontier were not always directed from London is not to explain why the actors were there in the first place.

A more illuminating approach, we suggest, is to view expansion into India from the mid-eighteenth century as illustrating the extension abroad of the social forces that dominated the polity at home after 1688. The emerging but still incomplete alliance between land and money in eighteenth-century England created a state that centred power on landed property and funded it by means of a fiscal system that was designed to support privilege without provoking discontent on a scale sufficient to overturn it. These aims, and the values that accompanied them, were extended to India: power was to be founded ultimately on the land, and revenue became

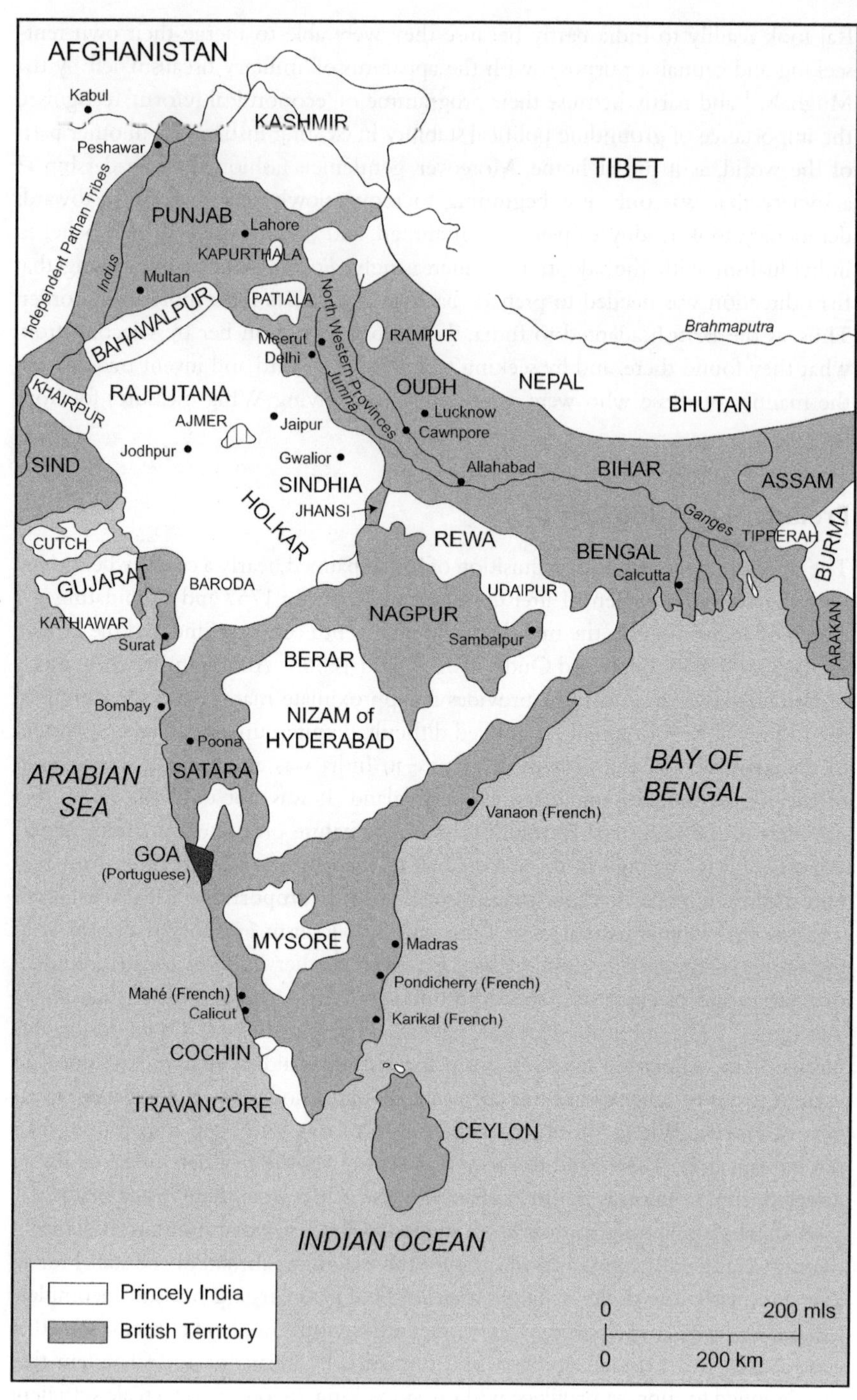

MAP 5 India on the eve of the Indian Mutiny, 1857

After: C.C. Eldridge, *Victorian Imperialism* (1978)

and remained the central preoccupation of policy, the more so because India's role was to be that of a tributary province. The main problem addressed by successive generations of administrators was not how to open India to British manufactures, but how to secure the revenue base of Britain's rule. The principal oscillations in policy, which swung from defending the East India Company to abolishing it, and from introducing Benthamite reforms to entrenching India's many princes, can all be traced to this enduring fiscal imperative.

The East India Company was undoubtedly the most impressive overseas manifestation of the alliance between land and finance in the eighteenth century. Initially, the Company was the vehicle of City merchants rather than of large landowners, but both groups had political interests, centred on London and the court, in its fortunes, and their joint commitment was reinforced as the century advanced by the Company's growing preoccupation with raising the revenue to pay for its administrative and military overheads.[15] Moreover, during the second half of the century, the landed families who were the chief beneficiaries of patronage came to appreciate the Company's job-creating potential once it had scoured the treasuries of the nawabs and had fastened upon the remnants of Mughal administration.[16] Thereafter, as government accompanied commerce in India, so policy was increasingly influenced by the values of the magnates who controlled the English state in the eighteenth century. They exported their notions of property rights to India, looked to agriculture to generate rents, and tried to identify or create an indigenous gentry and a compliant yeomanry who would both work the land and police it.[17] By the close of the century, Company rule had come to advertise the moral virtues as well as the political imperatives of military discipline and obedience to central authority. In this respect, too, Britain's presence in India reflected the changing contour of events at home, as the experience of the American Revolution and the French Wars promoted a brand of 'new conservatism' which sought to discipline the unpropertied and the un-Godly, and readily endorsed the use of force to maintain civil order and to uphold the inequalities of the 'balanced' constitution.[18]

It is important to emphasise at this point that the Company can no longer be portrayed as being a creaking, mercantilist monopoly whose historic role was to impede the progressive forces of British industry before finally being destroyed by them. It has now been shown that the Company was a much more innovative and efficient organisation than it has been given credit for.[19] It was undoubtedly a privileged club, but it was also a capitalist enterprise that generated as well as recycled wealth and achieved striking productivity gains in the transactions sector. In short, the Company provides an excellent example of the innovations we have identified as constituting the commercial and financial revolution of the eighteenth century. To the extent that the Company produced and integrated income streams from different countries, it can also be seen as forming a prototype for the multinational corporations that were to develop in the twentieth century. Imperfections in the Company's monopoly allowed private traders to make their way into new markets, whether by licence or by unauthorised enterprise, and the Company's inability to police all of its expanding frontiers meant that it was unable to hold back further commercial innovation, even if it wanted to. Both the Company and the private traders dealt with and sometimes borrowed from bankers and merchant princes who represented an indigenous, Indian brand of commercial capitalism. But they also enjoyed a growing competitive advantage in finance and distribution, as well as in techniques of coercion. Indian handicrafts were able to resist competition from British manufactures during the first half of the nineteenth century, whereas Indian banking and shipping were displaced from international commerce during this period.[20]

How far the Company could have extended its commercial efficiency into the nineteenth century is now a hypothetical question because its fortunes became increasingly bound up with the obligations it had assumed in administering India on behalf of the home government. The extension of empire and the financial health of the Company formed a circle that was both virtuous and vicious: territorial expansion was undertaken commonly to secure additional revenue, and thus to enable the Company to meet its financial obligations; but the costs of expansion frequently ran ahead of the estimates, and thus threatened to wreck rather than rescue the Company's finances. Naturally, London expected the Company's officials to create virtuous circles and avoid vicious ones, and important changes of policy towards the Company and the administration of India were invariably designed to achieve this result. When the Company's accumulating failures demonstrated its inability to achieve the near-impossible task it had been set, its powers were finally transferred to the crown in 1858.

The need to keep remittances flowing to London became a fixed priority in Britain's relations with India from the late eighteenth century onwards. Clive commandeered the revenues of Bengal for this purpose in the 1760s, and continuing fiscal imperatives go far towards explaining the territorial acquisitions made by his successors, their preoccupation with improving India's system of taxation, and official concern to develop an export surplus. During the first half of the nineteenth century, £3m.–4m. a year was required to meet official obligations (mainly pensions and equipment) and to pay dividends to the Company's shareholders in London, an additional amount (ranging from £0.5m. to £1.5m.) was needed for private remittances, and a further sum (which is not easily calculated) had to be found to settle India's invisible imports, such as freight charges, insurance and banking services.[21] The growth of India's external financial obligations at this time foreshadowed the future of countries which were drawn into Britain's orbit as overseas debtors later in the century; it also helps to account for the development of a multilateral trading system and for an emerging commitment to free trade during the first half of the nineteenth century.[22]

The revisions made to the East India Company's charter in 1813 and 1833 provide a clear illustration of the role of fiscal priorities in determining policy. The abolition in 1813 of the Company's formal monopoly of trade with India was essentially a wartime measure which was implemented principally to improve the flow of Indian commodities to Britain. The decision was not taken at the behest of a lobby representing Britain's new manufactures (though exports of cotton goods began to grow thereafter), but with one eye on placating provincial outports and the other on the ambitions of London merchants whose commercial interests had outgrown the bounds set by Company control.[23] In this respect, the action taken in 1813 pointed towards the regime of freer trade that Lord Liverpool's government began to install in the 1820s, and marked a further step towards shifting the responsibility for generating an export surplus away from the Company and towards private traders.

Similar considerations underlay the decision to end the Company's remaining commercial privilege, its monopoly of trade with China, in 1833.[24] An economic depression in Britain in 1829 hit the price of India's exports, especially indigo, and brought down many of the Agency Houses, the large, private commercial firms which financed the planters. This crisis came at a time when the Company was trying to cope with a legacy of heavy military expenditure, and it raised doubts about India's ability to meet her external obligations. The need to secure the means of maintaining the flow of remittances to London provided a strong incentive for promoting exports, and led in particular to attempts to open up trade with China. The end of the Company's last monopoly was not the outcome of pressure exerted by Manchester's manufacturers but the result of efforts made by merchants based in London and India who were keen to open markets for Indian cotton goods and opium in south-east Asia and the Far East. These pressures continued after 1833, and eventually culminated in the Opium War of 1839–42.[25] Meanwhile, the Company responded to the loss of its monopoly of trade with China by expanding into Sind and the Punjab in the 1830s and 1840s in the hope of annexing new sources of revenue.

The amendments to the East India Company's charter accompanied wider experiments in what, today, would be called development policy.[26] Even the Wellesleys, whose instinct was to preserve British interests in India by installing an effective despotism backed by 'salutary terror',[27] were keen to expand trade for revenue purposes and acknowledged the desirability of making London 'the throne of commerce of the world'.[28] The next generation of rulers, represented by Bentinck and Dalhousie, envisaged the 'improvement' of India through the application of utilitarian principles which would strengthen both the institutional basis of political stability and the means of funding British rule.[29] The attack on corrupt practices, like the quest for efficiency, was part of a programme which aimed at establishing a stable but also progressive propertied order in India. Bentinck, who was Governor-General between 1828 and 1835, hoped to open India to white settlers and foreign capital, and also to 'raise a middle class of native gentlemen' who would act as agents of development.[30] In the 1840s, when optimism about the speed of India's development had been dulled by a heightened awareness of the obstacles to change, talk of 'founding British greatness on Indian happiness',[31] gave way to more pragmatic considerations. Dalhousie, the Governor-General from 1848 to 1856, continued to plan for development, but concentrated on the application of Western technology, especially to the field of communications.[32]

Two features of this development programme deserve emphasis in the context of the argument advanced here. To begin with, it is important to note that the experiments practised on India were very similar to those attempted on other parts of the world, where Britain made equally determined, if less direct, efforts to establish compliant satellites during the first half of the nineteenth century. Furthermore, policies of 'improvement' in India, as elsewhere, were projections abroad of the changes occurring in Britain following the first tentative moves towards free trade, fiscal discipline and political reform in the aftermath of the Napoleonic Wars. India was still marked out as the patrimony of aristocrats and gentlemen, but estate management was to be conducted more responsibly than in the days of Clive and Hastings.[33] Although Company servants continued to be appointed through the patronage network, increasing numbers of them bore the imprint of Haileybury, absorbed the spirit of improvement, and stiffened it with the moral fibre of evangelical Christianity.[34] The second aspect of the reforming endeavour that needs to be stressed is its limited success. Beyond the rhetoric and the firm intentions lay a sub-continent that had been affected but not transformed by a century of British rule. The settlers' frontier proved to be abortive; the attempt to raise an indigenous 'middle class' touched a handful out of millions; and the alliance with land-holders weighed heavily on the taxable peasants who were supposed to be candidates for improvement. Above all, India's economic potential remained, if not untapped, unrealised: export growth was still restricted, difficulties remained in transferring remittances to London, and the City showed itself to be reluctant to place sizeable long-term investments in the sub-continent. In these respects, Britain's formal authority was rather more extensive than her informal influence, and the limitations of her ambitious development programme were manifest in India as they were in other parts of the world.

The extension of the gentlemanly order

Placed in this long perspective, the Indian Mutiny in 1857 and the transfer of civil authority from the East India Company to the crown in the following year can be seen as the culmination of a long transition which complemented, not the Industrial Revolution, but the demise of Old Corruption and the adoption at home of a peculiarly British brand of conservative reform. The end of the Company's official role in governing India was the final act in a process that had seen the progressive separation of economic and political powers in India and the growing specialisation of functions that Adam Smith and Max Weber regarded, from different standpoints, as being the hallmark of the modern world. Exactly why the Mutiny occurred is a much-debated issue that cannot be explored here; but it seems clear that the general failure of policies of development and reform provoked one kind of discontent and their modest success among particular social groups and in specific regions another, and that the two came together momentarily in 1857.[35] The resulting upheaval discredited the Company and finally forced London to take greater control of India's affairs by making the Governor-General directly accountable to the Secretary of State and parliament, not least, as we shall see, in matters of finance.[36]

The settlement which followed the transfer of power in 1858 reinforced the traditional priorities of British policy and put in place more effective means of achieving them. The creation of a new Government of India backed by an imperial guarantee upgraded the credit-rating of the state, increased the confidence of overseas investors, and greatly improved the prospects of raising foreign loans. Public finance was remodelled on Gladstonian lines and economic policy was tied to the universal principles of balanced budgets, sound money, free trade, and non-discriminatory revenue taxes.[37] One of the principal items of expenditure, the Indian Army, was brought under government control and at the same time placed on the official payroll, thus increasing the security and attractiveness of military employment. These measures gave renewed impetus to India's faltering development programme, but they also kept it on the pragmatic lines laid down by Dalhousie. British rule remained interventionist, but departures from the ideal of minimal government were justified in the case of India (as of 'backward' countries in general) by the authority of John Stuart Mill, among others, and had their rationale in the need to raise revenue as well as to keep order.[38]

After 1858, however, intervention assumed an increasingly economic character: the search for revenue led the government to promote mining and manufacturing activities as well is public utilities, especially railways and irrigation. Military intervention, on the other hand, lost its place as an established means of enlarging the treasury. It was a tempting strategy, but it had also proved to be a costly one, and after the Mutiny no government was prepared to risk actions that might stir the deep waters of Indian society. On the contrary, the Mutiny drew the Government of India into a closer partnership with land-holders and princes.[39] The result, a conservative 'alliance for progress', aimed at winning political support by picking a route to economic development that was consistent with social stability. In this respect, policy in India can be compared to that adopted towards other 'oriental societies', as Lord Salisbury called them, during the second half of the nineteenth century, when the idea of the brotherhood of man gave way to the notion of a hierarchy of racial types, each arranged into appropriate social classes, whose spiritual and material improvement were to be entrusted to the paternal direction of gentlemanly rulers.

From the 1850s, India became a notable outpost of the new service and financial order which had come to prominence in Britain following the demise of Old Corruption and the growth of sterling's role as a world currency.[40] The main instruments of British policy in India, the army and the civil service, employed only a small number of white officials. But their hands were on the levers of power: they controlled the means of coercion, they collected and allocated India's vast revenues, and their values helped to shape policy and its execution. From the 1850s, military and civil appointments in India became a large, vested interest of the educated upper middle class. In 1913–14, for example, the Government of India devoted no less than £53m. (65 per cent of the total budget of £82m.) to the army and the civil administration.[41] Imperial service enabled the mainly southern, professional and public-school culture to reproduce itself abroad and also, as we shall see, to create facsimiles among elites in the new colonies established in Asia and Africa.

Despite outspoken criticism from Manchester radicals, who deplored the 'waste' of Indian revenues on military expenditure,[42] the Indian Army remained vital to Britain's presence in Asia, both for reasons of internal security and for policing the vast region stretching from the Eastern Mediterranean to China. Without the Indian Army, and the Indian revenues that sustained it, Britain would not have been able to maintain her position east of Suez, and her status as a great power would have been seriously impaired.[43] From the 1850s onwards, the officer class was drawn mainly from the sons of professional families clustered in and around London and from the provincial gentry, though room was also found for recruits from the 'Celtic Fringe'.[44] In 1853, Cobden observed that 'our system of military rule in India has been widely profitable to the middle and upper classes in Scotland, who have more than their numerical share of its patronage', a fact that, in his view, partly explained their lack of interest in the Peace Society.[45] Colonial service helped to incorporate the articulate products of Scottish and Irish universities into a predominantly English-run enterprise and gave them a stake in defending national, that is to say British, interests. The social fusion, via public schools, of segments of the gentry and the middle class produced a formidable British hybrid: the Christian gentleman who combined measured refinement with licensed muscularity.

Parallel developments affected the Indian civil service after the East India Company's patronage machine was dismantled in the 1850s. Following an uncertain start, the introduction of an examination-based, meritocratic system forged close links between public schools, universities and colonial service, and created new employment opportunities, especially for professional families in south-east England.[46] Three-quarters of the recruits who entered the Indian Civil Service through the examination system between 1860 and 1874 were drawn from this class and a further 10 per cent came from the aristocracy and the landed gentry.[47] The competitive apparatus was not designed to open the corridors of power to ordinary citizens, and it created only limited opportunities for aspirants who saw in colonial service a means of attaining gentlemanly status.[48] The aim, as stated by Gladstone in 1854, was to 'strengthen and multiply the ties between the higher classes and the possession of administrative power'.[49] Emphasis was placed on the continuing vitality of the notion that gentlemen were uniquely qualified to become ideal administrators because of 'their capacity to govern others and control themselves, their aptitude for combining freedom with order, their love of healthy sports and exercise'.[50] The reformed civil service was more an act of management than an abrogation of privilege.[51] It was a response by the political elite to criticism of the patronage system, and it anticipated the expansion of demand for employment from the newly enfranchised middle classes. In the manner of British reforms, it looked more radical than it was. The army officer in India thus had his counterpart in the civil servant: both shared a common set of values and carried a blueprint, joining universal principles with worldly pragmatism, of how society – any society – ought to be governed.

A renewed effort was also made after the Mutiny to regroup India's large landholders behind the Raj and to reinforce their position in the great chain of command which joined London to the sub-continent's far-flung provinces. This was achieved by endorsing their privileges and incorporating them as junior partners into the imperial enterprise.[52] As the cult of royalty was elaborated at home, so the panoply of nobility was revived in India. The two came together in 1877, when the Queen was proclaimed empress of India and a huge 'royal assemblage' was staged in Delhi to pay homage to the monarch and to impress her subjects.[53] Lytton, the Governor-General and prospective Viceroy, had no doubt about the material value of this political ritual: 'the cost of the Assemblage', he calculated, 'will really be very moderate, and the effect of it may save millions'.[54] The new generation of mighty but loyal subjects was also educated for its imperial role. Those who were to exercise authority under British supervision were to be 'brought up as a gentleman should be' by establishing 'an Eton in India'.[55] In fact, several Etons were founded in India during the last quarter of the century with the aim of inculcating 'a healthy tone and manly habits' among future leaders.[56] In India, as elsewhere in the empire, team games became a means of moral instruction and not merely of physical exercise. The belief that sport was an allegory of life, and that life, like the body politic, was a matter of balancing individual rights and public duties through a mixture of effort and discipline was successfully conveyed to the children of India's elite, who learned the 'rules of the game' through the patient art of cricket.[57]

It is not surprising to find that the aims of the official 'caste' in India closely resembled those of the political elite at home, given the strong element of homogeneity in the recruitment and training of both. The central dilemma of policy remained unchanged after 1858, as before: how to produce sufficient revenue to meet India's financial obligations and defence commitments without provoking internal discontent on a scale that would raise the costs of maintaining order and unnerve foreign investors. After the Mutiny, however, the problem could no longer be attacked by tribute-gathering military expeditions; and the land tax could not be increased without raising the spectre of social protest and civil disorder. One solution was to raise agricultural productivity, but this was a gradual as well as a formidable task. A more promising alternative was to promote the export sector by a series of official 'pump-priming' development initiatives (which had the advantage of keeping the political and social consequences of economic policy in view), and to increase the proportion of revenue derived, directly or indirectly, from foreign trade.[58]

Judged by indices of volume and value, the export drive produced impressive results. India's overseas trade grew rapidly in the second half of the nineteenth century as she became fully incorporated into the international economy. Export values increased nearly five times between 1870 and 1914, as jute, cotton, indigo and tea flowed to Europe and rice and opium to the Far East.[59] In exchange, India absorbed increasing quantities of manufactured goods, especially from Britain. Her share of Britain's exports jumped from about 8 per cent in the early 1870s to about 13 per cent in the early 1880s, a figure that was almost maintained (though not exceeded) down to 1914.[60] This was a sizeable proportion, given Britain's numerous world-wide trading connections, and it made India her most important market in the empire.[61] It also made Britain India's principal trading partner: she supplied about 85 per cent of India's imports in the 1890s, and the proportion, though falling, was still over 60 per cent on the eve of World War I.[62] About two thirds of Britain's exports to India in 1880–84 consisted of cotton goods, and the figure was still around three-fifths in 1913. Moreover, the volume and value of cotton goods exported to India grew much faster than to other markets in the second half of the century. In terms of value alone, India's share of Britain's exports of cottons rose from 18 per cent in 1850 to a peak of 27 per cent in 1896, and was still around 20 per cent in 1913.[63]

How far this impressive record is to be attributed to official policy and how far to wider developments stimulating the international economy is a matter that needs dissecting, though it is not an operation that needs to be performed here. Evidently, some weight has to be attached to the rise of consumer demand in Europe, to railway construction in India from the 1850s, and to the opening of the Suez Canal in 1869.[64] It is equally clear that Britain's export industries gained greatly from the extension of British sovereignty over India and in particular from the transfer from Company to crown rule in 1858. As Dilke observed in 1869:

> Were we to leave Australia or the Cape, we should continue to be the chief customers of these countries: were we to leave India or Ceylon, they would have no customers at all; for, falling into anarchy, they would cease at once to export their goods to us and to consume our manufactures.[65]

Given that 'anarchy' could mean no more than India's refusal to cooperate with the international commercial order which Britain policed on behalf of the 'civilised' world (as the fate of Egypt subsequently made clear), Dilke's assessment was probably correct. The full value of British rule, the return on political investments first made in the eighteenth century, was not realised until the second half of the nineteenth century, when India became a vital market for Lancashire's cotton goods and when other specialised interests, such as jute manufacturers in Dundee and steel producers in Sheffield, also greatly increased their stake in the sub-continent.

Manchester's role is particularly relevant here because it provides a crucial test of the extent to which industrial lobbies were able to influence imperial policy. Increasing reliance upon the Indian market undoubtedly gave Manchester a keen interest in the development of the sub-continent, even though the link between commerce and empire-building remained a constant embarrassment to the Gladstonian wing of the Liberal Party.[66] At times of crisis, when raw cotton was in short supply or when export markets sagged, Manchester banged the drum for development and campaigned vigorously for increased spending on public works, for a guaranteed return on capital invested in Indian railways, and for low and non-discriminatory tariffs.[67] Given the importance of the Indian market, it is not surprising that Manchester's antennae were particularly sensitive to tariff issues. In 1859, for example, when the Government of India doubled the import duties paid on cotton goods as a means of meeting the heavy costs of the Mutiny, Lancashire protested vigorously and the tariff was reduced in 1862.[68] In 1874, Manchester was faced with a further threat to its prosperity, when a downturn in international trade coincided with the growth of competition from import-substituting manufactures in India. The Lancashire lobby pressed for the removal of duties on imported cottons, and in 1882, after a period of sustained agitation, the Government of India obliged.[69] When budgetary difficulties forced the government to reintroduce import duties in 1894, cotton goods and yarn were at first exempted. When they were included, later in the same year, strong representations from Manchester ensured that the duty was held at a low level (and was reduced in 1896), and that a 'countervailing' excise was imposed on Indian cotton manufactures.[70]

The activities of the textile lobby deserve emphasis because they provide a clear indication of the ways in which a major manufacturing interest could influence imperial policy at moments when it felt particularly threatened. Nevertheless, it would be mistaken to conclude from this evidence that the 'millocracy' had won a dominant role in the formulation of economic policy, even in the mid-Victorian era, when its influence was probably at its height, and even in India, where its stake was greater than in any other part of the empire. An assessment of the benefits derived by British exporters from the possession of India needs to be related to the aims and ambitions of India's rulers, both in Britain and in the sub-continent. Seen from this perspective, the Lancashire lobby appears to have been far less powerful than Marx supposed; its successes were achieved largely because its aims were congruent with those of India's rulers.

Manchester did indeed press for 'public works', but these were already part of the Government of India's development plans, and had been since at least the 1820s. Governments did not need to be persuaded of the importance of railways in 'opening up' the country because they were an integral feature of the Victorian conception of civilisation and improvement. If the main lines were built to assist economic development, they were also designed to serve the wider administrative and military needs of government, including increasing India's revenue potential.[71] Temporary inducements were offered to help prime the pump, but they were quickly discarded when fiscal problems arose. The Government of India refused to provide financial guarantees for the construction of new railway lines during the period of financial stringency which followed the Indian Mutiny, despite the fact that pressure from Manchester was then at its height, because balancing the budget was a higher priority.[72] In fact, Manchester had virtually no success in directing economic policy along paths that were not already marked out. It was unable to achieve significant representation on the Council of India (the body set up in 1858 to advise the Secretary of State), and its attempts to shape policy towards land, settlement and administration failed, as – predictably – did its effort to secure reductions in the 'large salaries' paid to India's rulers.[73] When accumulated frustration led Manchester to campaign for the removal of the Secretary of State, Sir Charles Wood, in 1862–3, the manufacturing interest was put firmly in its place. Palmerston shared Wood's opinion of 'parvenu capitalists', and he fully endorsed Wood's view that 'India was governed for India and . . . not for the Manchester people'.[74]

Even in the area of tariff policy, Manchester's success was heavily qualified. When the Government of India increased tariffs, it was not because it disagreed with Manchester over the principle of free trade, but because it was driven by fiscal need. This was the case in both 1859 and 1894. In cutting the rate from 10 per cent to 5 per cent, the concession made in 1862 merely returned traders to the position they had been in before the emergency brought about by the Mutiny. The outcome of the negotiations of 1894–6 cannot be counted as a victory for Manchester either, and was not seen in this light by contemporaries, because it established the principle that, in times of need, the Government of India could and would impose a tariff on imports from Britain.[75] Manchester 'reluctantly acquiesced' in the final deal, tried to have it revised, and was defeated in 1903.[76] When tariffs were reduced, it was largely because minimal rates were regarded as being the natural goal of commercial policy, and not because a reluctant government was bent to the will of the industrial lobby.[77] This reasoning undoubtedly applied to the cuts made in 1882, which were allowed only because the government's budgetary position had improved.

A full analysis, which cannot be pursued here, should also place these episodes in the wider context of the evolution of Anglo-Indian relations in the late nineteenth century.[78] In reducing India's tariffs in 1882, for instance, the British government was seeking both to increase the grip of the metropole at a time when the Indian administration appeared to be strengthening its autonomy and to capture the important Lancashire vote at a moment of extreme political fluidity. Similarly, by reimposing duties on imported cotton goods in 1894 and frustrating Manchester's attempts to curtail local competitors, the Government of India was showing an awareness of the need to blunt the edge of nationalist opposition by extending its appeal to progressive elements in India.[79] Even Manchester's least qualified successes have to be viewed as part of a process whereby liberal, free-trading interests were given a stake in empire and consequently had their opposition to imperialist expansion compromised. Concessions over tariffs helped to mute potentially serious criticisms of the burdens placed on the Indian budget by the army and the bureaucracy, and persuaded anti-imperialists to acquiesce in the wider aims of the Raj. Gladstone's anguish, as he saw his cosmopolitan principles transformed into imperialist actions, was only the most public example of a process that infected an increasingly vocal segment of the Liberal Party and eventually spread far beyond it.

It is important to recognise, too, that neither Manchester nor industry as a whole ought to be used as a proxy for British business in India. Other sizeable commercial interests, notably in finance and shipping, were also growing rapidly in the second half of the century.[80] After 1858, India attracted an increasing flow of investment from London, and accounted for approximately £286m. of the capital raised on the London stock market between 1865 and 1914.[81] This figure was about 18 per cent of the total placed in the empire, and made India second only to Canada as a recipient of British investment. India's share was even higher at the beginning of the period, when the railway boom was at its peak, but underwent a decline towards the close of the century as other regions (such as Australia) came to the fore, though the total invested annually continued to increase. In addition, substantial sums entered

India as direct investments, typically in commerce, services and plantations, though in this case the total can scarcely be guessed at.[82] Thus, as the patronage system served by the East India Company withered away, there arose a new, larger vested interest which relied on rentier incomes from safe overseas investments. Manchester may have pushed hard to secure financial guarantees for railway construction, but the principal beneficiaries were middle-class investors in London and the Home Counties.[83] This constituency of southern investors, and its institutional representatives in banking and shipping, fell in readily behind the flag of empire and gave full support to policies of free trade and sound money. If British rule in India was helpful to British industry, it was vital to British investment.

The growth of British trade and investment in the second half of the century was bound up with important institutional changes in banking and finance, though these have only recently begun to receive the historical attention they deserve.[84] India's external commerce had long suffered from inadequate credit facilities, and this problem had impaired the smooth functioning of multilateral trade and especially the transfer of funds to London. A solution to these difficulties was a central part of the settlement which followed the end of Company rule. The new administration developed an efficient system of making remittances by using Council Bills, which were sold in India for rupees and redeemed in London for sterling, redefined the role of the four semi-official Presidency Banks to bring them into line with sound banking principles, and pressed on with measures to standardise India's currencies.[85] It also created a climate of confidence which encouraged the spread of private commercial banks. Out of the banking boom that followed in the 1860s and 1870s emerged the National Bank of India, which was founded in Calcutta in 1863.[86] The National Bank began as a rupee-based bank and with a complement of Indian and expatriate directors. But it soon moved its headquarters to London (in 1866), denominated its reserves in sterling and steadily anglicised its personnel and ethos. Besides financing overseas trade, the National Bank invested in the production of tea, coffee, cotton and indigo, and, significantly, in Indian cotton mills. By 1900 the Bank had 19 principal offices spanning Ceylon, Burma and East Africa, as well as India. By then, too, the Bank had become part of the City hierarchy and had developed ties with Whitehall and the Indian Civil Service which led to seats on the Board of Directors for a number of retired officials.

The transition from Company to crown control also provided a boost to shipping services, which were needed for government business as well as for private trade. When Sir William Mackinnon's shipping group secured the official mail contracts for India in the early 1860s, the government provided him with a maritime subsidy that paralleled the inducements offered on land to investors in the railway system, except that it lasted a good deal longer.[87] Consequently, Mackinnon was well placed to take advantage of the growth of trade that followed the opening of the Suez Canal in 1869, and his firm, Mackinnon Mackenzie, also spread into various land-based enterprises, including jute and cotton mills. Mackinnon's official connection gave him ready access to policy-making circles in India, and he established a particularly close relationship with the Governor of Bombay,

Bartle Frere, a like-minded imperialist who was equally keen to capitalise on the link between profit and patriotism.[88] In the 1870s, Mackinnon shifted his head office from Clydeside to London, where he cultivated connections in Whitehall and acquired directorships in the City, including a seat on the board of the National Bank of India.

When Mackinnon died in 1893, his empire was inherited by James Mackay (later Lord Inchcape), who showed himself to be equally skilled in using political contacts to oil the machinery of commerce.[89] In the 1890s, Mackay became President of the Bombay Chamber of Commerce and a member of India's Legislative Council, and he established a privileged relationship with Lansdowne, who was Viceroy from 1888 to 1894. After the turn of the century, Mackay, like his predecessor, acquired directorships of leading banks in London, and he also became a tireless and ubiquitous member of numerous Whitehall committees. He received a knighthood for his work on Indian currency reform, and a peerage in 1911 as compensation for failing to become Viceroy two years earlier. He was Morley's choice but he received Asquith's veto. Intimate though the connections between acceptable commerce and high politics had become, there were still lines to be drawn, and Asquith did not intend to appoint a businessman to the viceroyalty, even one who had once been a prominent member of the Bombay Hunt.

The twin imperatives of holding the Raj together and keeping faith with external creditors exercised a pervasive, almost determining, effect on British policy in India. Between 1858 and 1898 India's remittances to external creditors averaged nearly half the value of her exports: about 30 per cent of the total represented payments for private services, including interest on investments and repatriated profits, and the remaining 20 per cent was accounted for by official obligations, the 'Home Charges', which consisted of pension and leave payments, bills for military equipment and stores, and interest on the public debt.[90] Successive Viceroys frightened themselves with the recurring nightmare that India might default on her external obligations. The fear was graphically expressed by Lord Mayo in 1869:

> We hold India by a thread. At any moment a serious danger might arise. We owe now £180 millions, more than 85 per cent of which is held in England. Add £100 millions to this and an Indian disaster would entail consequences equal to the extinction of half the National Debt. The loss of India or a portion of it would be nothing as compared to the ruin which would occur at home.[91]

Although the budgetary position improved in the 1880s, by the 1890s external obligations were rising faster than income from customs duties and the land tax, and could no longer be covered by the export surplus. As a result, India was able to balance her payments only by further borrowing.[92] Failure to service these obligations would have been disastrous for British rule in India and would have had far-reaching repercussions on the international economy and on Britain too, as Mayo clearly saw.

To prevent Mayo's nightmare from becoming a reality, India had to generate a sizeable export surplus and keep a firm grip on expenditure. Export earnings could not be boosted by bilateral exchange because India ran a growing trading deficit with Britain from the 1870s. The great merit of free trade, the quality which made it a much-prized orthodoxy, was that it allowed India to settle her trade deficit with Britain by using profits from exports shipped to countries elsewhere in Asia and in continental Europe. Moreover, this surplus was vital to the maintenance of the pattern of multilateral settlements which enabled Britain, in turn, to settle more than two-fifths of her own trading deficits, principally with Europe and North America.[93] The essence of this relationship was fully appreciated by contemporaries, as a memorandum from the India Office made clear in 1907:

> The aggregate exports from India to Asiatic and African ports, including the Crown Colonies of Ceylon, the Straits Settlements, and Mauritius, exceed in value her export trade with the continent of Europe. The balance of trade in both cases is largely in India's favour, and represents the sources from which she satisfies the heavy balance against her on her trading, debt, and administrative accounts with the United Kingdom.[94]

The India Office also noted that India had 'a large net balance in its favour on its trade with America as a whole, which no doubt finds its way to the United Kingdom in adjustment of international trade'.[95] The memorandum concluded that 'as a debtor country India requires the freest possible market for its exports, and as a poor country it requires cheap imports', and that 'any diminution of India's trade with those foreign countries that are the largest buyers of her exports would at once lessen her power of buying English produce and meeting her obligations to her English creditors'.[96]

The priority attached to upholding the multilateral payments system by means of free trade greatly reduced the scope for concessions to British industry. The India Office foresaw that, if British manufacturers were given preferential treatment in India, it 'would be likely to give rise to demands for other changes in the fiscal system of the country which would be very difficult to refuse', and in particular would encourage agitation in support of India's own import-substituting industries.[97] Consequently, successive Viceroys were unresponsive to Manchester's pleas for action to control India's burgeoning textile industry. When the Lancashire lobby attempted to eliminate the competitive advantage of its Bombay rivals by imposing factory legislation on India in 1891, the Viceroy devised an alternative that offered some safeguards to Indian workers but none to Manchester, and was accordingly received favourably by nationalist opinion.[98] Indeed, since local manufactures economised on imports, helped to balance the budget and hence maintained the confidence of overseas investors, the Government of India had good reason for encouraging them. As Lord Northbrook observed in 1874: 'I am very happy also on the progress of Indian manufactures ultimately. Whisper it not in Manchester'.[99] In the 1880s, Lord Ripon's policy of favouring local manufacturers for government purchases stimulated a wide range of industries and culminated in the development of a state-operated iron and steel plant.[100] Curzon's efforts to promote manufacturing in India after the turn of the century aroused renewed alarm in Lancashire. But the textile lobby's representations were again ineffective because the Viceroy's policy, though interventionist, was not protectionist and did not endanger budgetary stability.[101]

The need to keep a tight grip on expenditure had an influence that extended beyond the realm of economic policy and into administration and defence. As noted earlier, considerations of cost encouraged the adoption of cheap methods of internal control based on indirect rule and the mystique of racial supremacy.[102] After the Mutiny, fiscal imperatives also hastened moves towards political decentralisation which aimed at defusing opposition and generating fresh sources of revenue in the provinces.[103] In the manner of colonial solutions, this strategy created new problems by lending impetus to the formation of the Indian National Congress in 1885, and it prompted further constitutional concessions (the Morley-Minto reforms) after the turn of the century.[104] In essence, Britain's aim was to group conservative elements (Muslim and Hindu) behind the Raj and to head off militant nationalists by promoting a 'loyal opposition' in the hope of incorporating it.[105] Unrest, it was widely believed, was bad for investment. The need to hold defence expenditure down left its mark on India's external relations too. The cost of stabilising frontiers with Persia, Afghanistan and Tibet, for example, acted as a check on military action and eventually pushed Britain into an agreement with Russia in 1907, against the wishes of an influential group which favoured a more bellicose stance.[106]

The Government of India's internal fiscal and monetary reforms were complemented by a policy that aimed at stabilising the external value of the silver rupee to ensure the smooth payment of international obligations and to maintain the confidence of foreign investors. The process of internal reform was completed in the late 1850s and in the 1860s, as part of the administrative settlement that followed the abolition of Company rule. But serious problems arose on the external account from the 1870s, when falling world prices for silver led to the progressive depreciation of the rupee against sterling.[107] The Government of India found itself in difficulties because it raised its revenues in rupees and had to make payments in London in sterling. Initially, the budgetary consequences of this adverse trend were offset to some extent by the fact that the depreciation of the rupee raised the price of imports, encouraged import-substitution, and boosted India's exports.[108] From the mid-1880s, however, taxes had to be increased to secure the additional rupees needed to meet external obligations, and there were worrying signs that taxpayers were beginning to feed their discontent into the embryonic nationalist movement. Investors were also losing confidence in the rupee, and the expatriates who ran the Indian Civil Service and the Indian Army were becoming anxious about their declining ability to purchase sterling assets. By the 1890s, the effective devaluation of the rupee had reached a point where action had to be taken to protect the value of external payments, and the problem was eventually resolved, after a formidably complicated and protracted debate, by moving the rupee to a gold-exchange standard from 1898.

The interest of this outcome, in the present context, lies in the evidence it provides about the motives of contending parties to the debate and about their influence on policy. Sterling's growing strength against the rupee presented British industrialists, headed by Manchester, with an increasingly difficult market. Manchester wanted a solution that would help to restore its position in the Indian market and also undercut the competitive advantage of Bombay cottons in the Far East. After some uncertainty, the Manchester interest put its weight behind a bimetallist solution as being the one best calculated to achieve this result and also to prevent the Government of India from raising import duties.[109] This proposal, though propelled with considerable force, left scarcely a mark on the defenders of monetary orthodoxy: not only was bimetallism rejected, but also duties were imposed on imported cotton goods in 1894, as we have seen.[110] The Government of India favoured the introduction of a gold standard, which it considered to be the most effective way of overcoming the problem of remitting the Home Charges and of protecting the salaries of its officials.[111] The alternative was to compensate for the decline of the rupee by further tax increases, but senior officials in India opposed this course of action because they feared its political consequences.[112] Their arguments carried considerable weight in Whitehall and the City, where monetary orthodoxy held sway and where there was a strong vested interest in safeguarding the value of funds transferred from India to Britain.[113]

In the event, a gold-exchange standard was established in preference to a gold standard, partly because it was cheaper and partly because Whitehall was concerned that the adoption of a full gold standard would increase the independence of the authorities in India.[114] Manchester's defeat brought only incidental compensation: raising the exchange rate of the rupee against silver reduced the currency advantage of Bombay's textile exports, but the adjustment was insufficient to halt the advance of competition from Indian manufactures.[115] The Government of India secured its principal objectives, though it was not immediately reconciled to a gold-exchange system without a local, gold-based currency. The City's gains were considerable and unqualified: the new arrangements drew India more firmly into the orbit of London finance and did so at minimum cost and risk; and the removal of uncertainty over remittances encouraged a flow of new investment into the sub-continent.[116] The result was a triumph for the Gold Standard Defence Association, an alliance of City bankers and Whitehall officials whose purpose was to block deviations from orthodoxy of the kind proposed by Manchester and its allies.[117]

On the eve of World War I, India was still the largest market for Britain's exports in the empire, and was particularly important for the older staple manufactures, such as textiles and metal products.[118] Yet India, like many other parts of the empire, disappointed the expectations of a generation of British industrialists in the period before 1914. As we have seen, India's share of Britain's exports reached a peak early in the 1880s, while Britain's share of India's imports fell steadily during the second half of the nineteenth century.[119] To some extent, of course, the expectations of manufacturers were, as ever, exaggerated, not least because India remained resolutely poor and the new frontiers opened by the railway either lacked potential or were slow to realise it. Nevertheless, it is hard to avoid the conclusion that free trade provided ambiguous benefits for British industry in India, as indeed elsewhere. The open door offered a market for British goods, but it allowed entry to foreign rivals, too, and it did nothing to halt the development of indigenous competitors.[120] Moreover, India's need to generate an export surplus to fund her remittances to London gave the Government of India an incentive to restrain imports, where possible, and to promote import-substituting activities. But Manchester was tied into free trade as she was tied into the empire: had Britain adopted protectionism, India would have followed suit, and Manchester would have suffered more from the change than from continuing to endure the rigours of free trade.[121] Similarly, although Manchester found few favours within the empire, its prospects were still better there than in countries that were neutral but uncongenial, or unfriendly and therefore forbidding.

Financial imperatives and British rule

Despite the insights that he offered into events in India, Marx was mistaken in supposing that the demise of the East India Company symbolised the rise of the 'millocracy'. British policy towards India cannot be understood on the assumption that the industrial bourgeoisie finally grasped the levers of power in 1858. But this does not imply that 'economic' explanations of empire-building ought to make way for 'political' alternatives, still less that this polarity provides a satisfactory framework of analysis. Nor does it mean that the causes of Britain's presence in India can be left to historians of the eighteenth century, while historians of the nineteenth century concentrate on techniques of control and the consequences of imperial rule.

It is more plausible to interpret India's enlarged role within the imperial system between 1858 and 1914 as representing the extension abroad of the financial and service interests that had achieved prominence at home following the demise of Old Corruption and protectionism. These interests had already begun to shape India's international trade and the character of the Raj before 1858. The transition to crown rule after that date marked the assumption of authority by the new gentlemanly meritocracy and its 'like-minded' associates in finance and commercial services, the quantitative expansion of the economic influences they represented, and the installation of the Gladstonian orthodoxies of free trade, sound money and balanced budgets. In India, as in other parts of the empire which had to make large remittances to London, financial priorities overrode the claims of British industry. Moreover, since the multilateral trade regime was crucial to settling Britain's balance of payments, the gains accruing to finance and commercial services from free trade could also be presented as being of national rather than merely of sectional importance. British governments were concerned to keep industry content, especially at times of crisis, but in the last resort it was more important that India's debts were settled than that British goods were bought.

British industry, especially textiles, also gained from Britain's control of India and from the transfer from Company to crown rule in 1858. But Manchester's power was limited, even in India, the case which ought to provide an impressive illustration of the ability of manufacturers to shape imperial policy. The influence of the industrial lobby reached its height in the middle of the century rather than later on, when the new service interests had taken a firm grip on the formulation of policy and on the shape of India's international economic relations. Even so, manufacturers gained most where their aims were congruent with those of the civil and commercial service elite, whose main concern was to ensure that there were no impediments to the flow of India's multilateral trade and remittances. As the manufacturing interest became tied into the empire, so it lost its anti-imperialist stance; as it was offered a large new market, so too it lapsed into a conservative reliance on old staples. And, just as India became firmly incorporated into Britain's burgeoning service economy, so Manchester's fortunes came to depend increasingly on the southern-based diaspora whose leaders in London and far-flung representatives east of Suez were at once strong advocates and principal beneficiaries of the Raj.[122]

India, then, is no exception to the rules of imperial expansion: it offers, as it ought to do, a prime example of the gentlemanly forces which promoted expansion in the eighteenth century and, in their stronger, reconstructed form, shaped the Raj in the nineteenth and twentieth centuries. Moreover, the chronology of expansion in India fits the pattern of causation identified in this study in reflecting not only the shift from Old Corruption and protectionism to the new meritocracy and free trade, but also in demonstrating the limits to the realisation of imperialist intentions before the mid-nineteenth century and the greater extent to which they were implemented thereafter. In offering this long perspective, India provides a unique illustration, outside the white empire, of British imperialism untrammelled by foreign rivals. The British worried permanently about unstable frontiers, but inside India their policies were shaped without reference to the interests of foreign powers. The Indian example, we suggest, reveals the priorities of policy particularly clearly, and in doing so erects a signpost to other cases of imperialism where Britain's motives were complicated and often clouded by the presence of foreign rivals. Of course, motives identified in India cannot be transported to explain other episodes; but, where similarities already exist, it is instructive to bear the Indian case in mind, given the tendency of current interpretations, especially of the partition of Africa and the scramble for China, to assume that Britain was a defensive if not a declining power and to treat her actions as being reactions to initiatives taken by more athletic rivals.

This analysis suggests that India ought to be reincorporated into the study of empire-building in the nineteenth century rather than treated as a special case or as an imperfectly explained legacy of the eighteenth century. If this argument has merit, then India's significance for theories of imperial expansion extends far beyond her own frontiers: the multilateral trading ties and financial flows that Britain established with the sub-continent foreshadowed bonds of incorporation that were forged with other parts of the underdeveloped world and with the colonies of white settlement during the second half of the nineteenth century; the defence of vital interests in India, once they are defined, helps to explain how Britain's imperial design came to be tacked on to parts of the Middle East, south-east Asia and China. These ramifications cannot be explored here, but the comparison with the many other countries that experienced the 'debt crisis' of the late nineteenth century needs to be firmly identified, if only to suggest a route for future research. In Australia, New Zealand and Argentina, which were on a gold standard, devaluation was ruled out at times of crisis and deflationary policies were imposed. In Egypt and the Ottoman Empire, as we shall see, the bailiffs were sent in to deal with default. In India the bailiffs were already present, and 'sound' management combined with the unplanned depreciation of the silver rupee enabled the government to escape the most extreme consequences of indebtedness – economic chaos and political upheaval. The case of China, which was also on a silver standard, is particularly interesting in this connection. The depreciation of China's silver currency appears not to have stimulated exports to any noticeable extent, but it does seem to have aroused concern among external creditors about the security of their investments, and it may have encouraged them to try to take a firmer grip on the management of China's finances.

At this point speculation runs ahead of research: but it should at least be clear from the foregoing comments that gentlemanly interests were very much to the fore in India, and that, in forging India's links with the international economy, they created, and often foreshadowed, relations of the kind that Britain established elsewhere in the world after 1850. By perceiving these connections, we can improve our appreciation of the value of the jewel in the crown and the reasons for keeping it polished and protected.

Notes

1 The quotation is taken from an India Office Memorandum, 1907, cited on p. 342.

2 George Earle Buckle, *The Life of Benjamin Disraeli: Earl of Beaconsfield* (1920), V, p. 195.

3 References to this literature can be found in C.A. Bayly, 'English-Language Historiography on British Expansion in India and Indian Reactions since 1945', in P.C. Emmer and H.L. Wesseling, eds. *Reappraisals in Overseas History* (Leiden, 1979); Neil Charlesworth, *British Rule and the Indian Economy, 1800–1914* (1982); Sumit Sukar, *Modern India, 1885–1947* (New Delhi, 1983); R.J. Moore, 'India and the British Empire', in C.C. Eldridge, ed. *British Imperialism in the Nineteenth Century* (1984); and William A. Green and John P. Dewey, 'Unifying Themes in the History of British India, 1757–1857: an Historiographical Analysis', *Albion,* 17 (1985).

4 For a valuable synthesis of research on the role of the periphery see C.A. Bayly, *Indian Society and the Making of the British Empire* (Cambridge, 1988). Some of the consequences of over-specialisation are considered in Irfan Habib's review of Dharma Kumar, ed. *The Cambridge Economic History of India, II, 1757–c.1970* (Cambridge, 1983): 'Studying a Colonial Economy – Without Perceiving Colonialism', *Mod. Asian Stud.,* 19 (1985).

5 For a stimulating account of Marx's views on India see V.G. Kiernan, *Marxism and Imperialism* (1974). The debate about the relationship between early and late Marx is treated by Suriti Kumar Ghosh, 'Marx on India', *Monthly Review,* 35 (1984).

6 Karl Marx and Frederick Engels, *Collected Works,* XII (1979 edn), pp. 154–5.

7 Ibid. pp. 218–19.

8 J. Gallagher and R. Robinson, 'The Imperialism of Free Trade', *Econ. Hist. Rev.,* 2nd ser. VI (1953).

9 R.E. Robinson and J. Gallagher,'The Partition of Africa', in F.H. Hinsley, ed. *New Cambridge Modern History,* XI (Cambridge, 1962), p. 616.

10 See, for example, Eric Stokes,'The First Century of British Rule in India', *Past and Present,* 58 (1973); P.J. Marshall, *Bengal: The British Bridgehead: Eastern India, 1740–1828* (Cambridge, 1987); and C.A. Bayly, *Imperial Meridian: The British Empire and the World, 1780–1830* (1989).

11 On this theme see the important contributions by D.A. Washbrook, 'Law, State and Agrarian Society in Colonial India', *Mod. Asian Stud.,* 15 (1981), and Burton Stein,'State Formation and Economy Reconsidered', *Mod. Asian Stud.,* 19 (1985).

12 To which must be added Burma. See Oliver B. Pollack, *Empires in Collision: Anglo-Burmese Relations in the Mid-Nineteenth Century* (Westport, Conn., 1979).

13 K.N. Chaudhuri,'India's Foreign Trade and the Cessation of the East India Company's Trading Activities, 1828–40', *Econ. Hist. Rev.,* 2nd ser. XIX (1966).

14 Bayly, *Indian Society,* presents the view from the periphery; idem, *Imperial Meridian,* links the periphery to developments in the metropole in ways that are, we believe, consistent with the view expressed here.

15 H.V. Bowen,'Investment and Empire in the Late Eighteenth Century: East India Stockholding, 1756–1791', *Econ. Hist. Rev.,* 2nd ser. XLII (1989). We are grateful to Dr Bowen for his advice on this subject.

16 P.J. Marshall, *East Indian Fortunes: The British in Bengal in the Eighteenth Century* (Oxford, 1976), Chs. 1, 7, 8, 9.

17 For example: Rajat Ray and Ratna Ray,'Zamindars and Jotedars: A Study of Rural Politics in Bengal', *Mod. Asian Stud.,* 9 (1975); Michael H. Fisher,'Indirect Rule in the British Empire: the Foundations of the Residency System in India (1764–1858)', *Mod. Asian Stud.,* 18 (1984); Michelle B. McAlpin, 'Economic Policy and the True Believer: the Use of Ricardian Rent Theory in the Bombay Survey and Settlement System', *Jour. Econ. Hist.,* 44 (1984). Broader studies include: W.J. Barber, *British Economic Thought and India, 1600–1858* (Oxford, 1975), and Thomas R. Metcalf, *Land, Landlords and the British Raj* (Berkeley, Calif., 1979).

18 P. Langford,'Old Whigs, Old Tories and the American Revolution', in P. Marshall and G. Williams, eds. *The British Atlantic Empire Before the American Revolution* (1980); Linda Colley, 'The Apotheosis of George III: Loyalty, Royalty and the British Nation, 1760–1820', *Past and Present,* 102 (1984).

19 On the rehabilitation of the Company's commercial performance see K.N. Chaudhuri, *The Trading World of Asia and the English East India Company, 1660–1760* (Cambridge, 1978), and Ho-cheung Mui and Lorna H. Mui, *The Management of Monopoly: A Study of the East India Company's Conduct of its Tea Trade, 1784–1833* (Vancouver, 1984).

20 Frank Broeze, 'Underdevelopment and Dependency: Maritime India during the Raj', *Mod. Asian Stud.,* 18 (1984). The debate on handicrafts is summarised in Charlesworth, *British Rule,* pp. 32–6. See also Colin Simmons,'"De-industrialisation", Industrialisation and the Indian Economy, 1850–1947', *Mod. Asian Stud.,* 19 (1985).

21 Bayly, *Indian Society,* pp. 116–17; Marshall, *Bengal,* pp. 104–5; Chaudhuri,'India's Foreign Trade', pp. 355–60.

22 Marshall, *Bengal,* pp. 105–6, 118–19, 133; Rudrangshu Mukherjee,'Trade and Empire in Awadh, 1765–1804', *Past and Present,* 94 (1982), pp. 89–90, 99–100; Chaudhuri,'India's Foreign Trade', pp. 355, 358–63.

23 Anthony Webster,'The Political Economy of Trade Liberalisation: the East India Company Charter Act of 1813', *Econ. Hist. Rev,* 2nd ser. XLIII (1990), and the further references given there.

24 Amales Tripathi,'Indo-British Trade Between 1833 and 1847 and the Commercial Crisis of 1847/8', *Indian Hist. Rev.,* I (1974), pp. 306–11; Chaudhuri,'India's Foreign Trade', pp. 345–6, 349–50, 361–2; Anthony Webster,'British Export Interests in Bengal and Imperial Expansion into South-East Asia, 1780–1824: the Origins of the Straits Settlements', in Barbara Ingham and Colin Simmons, eds. *Development Studies and Colonial Policy* (1987), pp. 138–74; Douglas M. Peers,'Between Mars and Mammon: the East India Company

and Efforts to Reform its Army, 1796–1832', *Hist. Jour.*, 33 (1990); idem, 'War and Public Finance in Early Nineteenth-Century British India: the First Burma War', *Internat. Hist. Rev.*, 11 (1989).
25 See below, pp. 424–6.
26 This theme can be followed in W.J. Barber, *British Economic Thought and India, 1600–1858: A Study in the History of Development Economics* (Oxford, 1975).
27 Douglas M. Peers, 'The Duke of Wellington and British India during the Liverpool Administration, 1819–27', *Jour. Imp. and Comm. Hist.*, XVII (1988), p. 20. Wellington (then Arthur Wellesley) saw active service in India between 1796 and 1805.
28 Richard Wellesley, Governor-General from 1798 to 1805, quoted in Bayly, *Indian Society*, p. 83.
29 The classic study is Eric Stokes, *The Utilitarians and India* (Oxford, 1958).
30 John Rosselli, *Lord William Bentinck: The Making of a Liberal Imperialist* (Berkeley, Calif., 1974), p. 208; P.J. Marshall, 'The Whites of British India, 1780–1830: a Failed Colonial Society?', *Internat. Hist. Rev.*, 12 (1990). The career of the most famous of India's western-style entrepreneurs of the period, Dwarkanath Tagore (1794–1846), is placed in a comparative context by Rhoads Murphey, *The Outsiders: The Western Experience in India and China* (Ann Arbor, Mich., 1977), pp. 73–6. On the pursuit of Bentinck's reforms in the late 1830s see Dayal Dass, *Charles Metcalf and British Administration in India* (New Delhi, 1988).
31 Bentinck, quoted in Hyam, *Britain's Imperial Century*, p. 216.
32 Suresh Chandra Ghosh, 'The Utilitarianism of Dalhousie and the Material Improvement of India', *Mod. Asian Stud.*, 12 (1978).
33 J. Majeed, 'James Mill's "The History of British India" and Utilitarianism as a Rhetoric of Reform', *Mod. Asian Stud.*, 24 (1990); Ram Parkash Sikka, *The Civil Service in India: Europeanisation and Indianisation under the East India Company (1765–1857)* (New Delhi, 1984); Marshall, 'The Whites of British India'.
34 The pioneering study is B.S. Cohn, 'Recruitment and Training of the British Civil Servants in India, 1600–1860', in R. Braibant, ed. *Asian Bureaucratic Systems Emergent from the British Tradition* (Durham, NC, 1966). An important example is Peter Penner, *The Patronage Bureaucracy in North India: The Robert M. Bird and James Thomason School, 1820–1870* (Delhi, 1986).
35 The vast literature on the Mutiny can be approached through Bayly, *Indian Society*, Ch. 6 and the references given on pp. 222–3.
36 A summary of the constitutional changes is given in R.J. Moore, *Liberalism and Indian Politics, 1872–1922* (1966), pp. 6–8.
37 The main changes were made in 1859–60 by James Wilson, the first Indian Finance Member of the Council of India (and also the founder of *The Economist*). See Sabyasachi Bhattacharyya's valuable (and rather neglected) study, *Financial Foundations of the British Raj* (Simla, 1971), pp. xlviii–li, and 3–4; and, more generally, Raymond W. Goldsmith, *The Financial Development of India, 1860–1977* (New Haven, Conn., 1983). For the policy in action see, for example, Edward C. Moulton, *Lord Northbrook's Indian Administration, 1872–1876* (Bombay, 1968), Ch. 2.
38 Bhattacharyya, *Financial Foundations*, p. lxxv.
39 There is now a huge literature exploring the regional variations of the post-Mutiny settlement. See, for example, Thomas Metcalf, *Land, Landlords and the British Raj* (Berkeley, Calif., 1979). The Punjab is a particularly good example in the present context because it remained conspicuously loyal in 1857 and was rewarded thereafter. The Punjab also became the most important source of military recruitment for the Raj, and accounted for three-fifths of the Indian Army in 1914. See I. Talbot, *Punjab and the Raj, 1849–1947* (New Delhi, 1988). The 'princely states', however, have been unduly neglected. See S.R. Ashton, *British Policy Towards the Indian States* (1982), and John Hurd, 'The Economic Consequences of Indirect Rule in India', *Indian Econ. and Soc. Hist. Rev.*, 12 (1975).

40 On the London headquarters see Arnold Kaminsky, *The India Office, 1880–1910* (Westport, Conn., 1986). The Permanent Under-Secretary from 1883 to 1909, Sir Arthur Godley (later Lord Kilbracken), was educated at Rugby and Balliol College, Oxford, and had previously served as Gladstone's Private Secretary.

41 *Statistical Abstract of British India, 1911–12 to 1921–22* (1923), p. 126. The most thorough analysis of government expenditure during the period under review is A.K. Banerji, *Aspects of Indo-British Economic Relations, 1858–1898* (Bombay, 1982).

42 R.J. Moore, 'Imperialism and Free Trade Policy in India, 1853–4', *Econ. Hist. Rev.*, 2nd ser. XVII (1964), p. 139. For official salaries see Banerji, *Aspects,* p. 145.

43 On the connection between finance and defence see B.R. Tomlinson, 'India and the British Empire, 1880–1935', *Indian Econ. and Soc. Hist. Rev.*, 12 (1975).

44 P.E. Razzell, 'Social Origins of Officers in the Indian and British Home Army, 1758–1962', *Brit. Jour. Soc.*, 14 (1963). The aristocracy found employment in the Home Army more congenial.

45 Cobden to McLaren, 15 Sept. 1853. Quoted in J. Morley, *The Life of Richard Cobden*, II (1881), p. 144.

46 B.B. Misra, *The Bureaucracy in India: An Historical Analysis up to 1947* (Delhi, 1977); J.M. Compton, 'Open Competition and the Indian Civil Service, 1854–76', *Eng. Hist. Rev.*, LXXXIII (1968), pp. 265–84; C.J. Dewey, 'The Making of an English Ruling Caste: The Indian Civil Service in the Era of Competitive Examination', *Eng. Hist. Rev.*, LXXXVIII (1973); R.J. Moore, *Sir Charles Wood's Indian Policy, 1853–66* (Manchester, 1966), Ch. 6. See also Philip Mason, *The Men Who Ruled India* (1985).

47 Bradford Spangenberg, *British Bureaucracy in India: Status, Policy and the I.C.S. in the Late Nineteenth Century* (New Delhi, 1976), pp. 19–20. (On the question of the wider interpretation of the data, we may note in passing that Spangenberg's undoubtedly healthy revisionism appears not to have converted specialists. Broadly similar criticisms of the stereotype of selfless, Platonic guardians have been made with more restraint by Misra, *The Bureaucracy,* Ch. 3 and pp. 200–10, whose assessment is consistent with the argument advanced here.)

48 Ibid. pp. 256–7.

49 Quoted in Compton, 'Open Competition', p. 266.

50 Quoted from a Parliamentary Paper of 1854 by Compton, 'Open Competition', p. 269.

51 J.M. Bourne, *Patronage and Society in Nineteenth-Century England* (1986), pp. 45–6, 127, 181.

52 See n. 39 above.

53 Alan Trevithick, 'Some Structural and Sequential Aspects of the British Imperial Assemblages at Delhi, 1877–1911, *Mod. Asian Stud.*, 24 (1990). The important general study is Bernard Cohn, 'Representing Authority in Victorian India', in Eric Hobsbawm and Terence Ranger, eds. *The Invention of Tradition* (Cambridge, 1983).

54 Lytton to Morley, 29 Oct. 1876, quoted in Trevithick, 'Structural and Sequential Aspects', p. 563.

55 J.A. Mangan, *The Games Ethic and Imperialism* (1986), p. 125.

56 Ibid. p. 133. The Etons were complemented by Oxfords, whose origins have been studied by Robert Frykenberg, 'Modern Education in South India, 1784–1854: its Roots and Role as a Vehicle for Integration Under Company Raj', *Am. Hist. Rev.*, 91 (1986).

57 Donald Linster-Mackay, 'The Nineteenth-Century English Preparatory School: Cradle and Creche of Empire?', in J.A. Mangan, ed. *Benefits Bestowed? Education and British Imperialism* (Manchester, 1986). In England, it was also possible to explain the Holy Trinity in terms of three stumps and one wicket (ibid. p. 69).

58 On the oscillations of policy between the twin objectives of development and stability see D.A. Low, *Lion Rampant: Essays in the Study of British Imperialism* (1973), Ch. 2, and Barber, *British Economic Thought.*

59 Charlesworth, *British Rule,* pp. 48–9.

60 Mitchell and Deane, *Abstract of Historical Statistics,* pp. 324–6.
61 Tomlinson, 'India and the British Empire', p. 339.
62 Calculated from K.N. Chaudhuri, 'Foreign Trade and the Balance of Payments (1757–1947)', in Kumar, *Cambridge Economic History,* II, pp. 832–7.
63 D. Farnie, *The English Cotton Industry and the World Market, 1815–1896* (Oxford, 1979), Table 5, p. 91, Table 6, p. 98, Table 7, p. 118, and the authoritative discussion in Ch. 3.
64 John Hurd, 'Railways and the Expansion of Markets in India, 1861–1921', *Expl. Econ. Hist.,* 12 (1975); J. Forbes Munro, 'Suez and the Shipowner: the Response of the Mackinnnon Shipping Group to the Opening of the Suez Canal, 1869–84', in Lewis R. Fischer and Helge W. Nordwick, eds. *Shipping and Trade, 1750–1950: Essays in International Maritime Economic History* (Pontefract, 1990).
65 C.W. Dilke, *Greater Britain,* I (1868), pp. 394–5.
66 W.E. Gladstone, 'Aggression on Egypt and Freedom in the East', *Nineteenth Century,* II (1877), p. 153.
67 See D. Thorner, *Investment in Empire: British Railway and Steam Shipping Enterprise in India, 1825–1849,* (Philadelphia, Pa, 1950), Ch. 1; Moore, 'Imperialism and "Free Trade" Policy', pp. 135–45; idem, *Sir Charles Wood,* Ch. 6; A.W. Silver, *Manchester Men and Indian Cotton, 1847–72* (Manchester, 1966); Peter Harnetty, *Imperialism and Free Trade: Lancashire and India in the Mid-Nineteenth Century* (Manchester, 1972); and Dwijendra Tripathi's assessment of the cotton supply problem during the American Civil War: 'Opportunism of Free Trade: Lancashire Cotton Famine and Indian Cotton Cultivation', in Sabyasachi Bhattacharya, ed. *Essays in Modern Indian Economic History* (New Delhi, 1987). See also Ian Inkster, 'The "Manchester School" in Yorkshire: Economic Relations Between India and Sheffield in the Mid-Nineteenth Century', *Indian Econ. and Soc. Hist. Rev.,* 23 (1986).
68 Peter Harnetty, 'The Imperialism of Free Trade: Lancashire and the Indian Cotton Duties, 1859–1862', *Econ. Hist. Rev.,* 2nd ser. XVIII (1965).
69 Harnetty, *Imperialism and Free Trade,* Ch. 2; Ira Klein, 'English Free Traders and Indian Tariffs, 1874–96', *Mod. Asian Stud.,* 5 (1971).
70 Peter Harnetty, 'The Indian Cotton Duties Controversy, 1894–1896', *Eng. Hist. Rev.,* LXXVII (1962); Klein, 'English Free Traders'.
71 W.J. MacPherson, 'Investment in Indian Railways, 1845–75', *Econ. Hist. Rev.,* 2nd ser. VIII (1955), p. 179; R.O. Christensen, 'The State and Indian Railway Performance, 1870–1920. Part II: The Government, Rating Policy and Capital Funding', *Jour. Transport Hist.,* 3 (1982).
72 MacPherson, 'Investment', p. 186; Harnetty, *Imperialism and Free Trade,* p. 81; C.J. Dewey, 'The End of the Imperialism of Free Trade: the Eclipse of the Lancashire Lobby and the Concession of Fiscal Autonomy to India', in C.J. Dewey and A.G. Hopkins, eds. *The Imperial Impact: Essays in the Economic History of India and Africa* (1979), pp. 58–9.
73 Silver, *Manchester Men,* pp. 109–11, 152, 249–54; Arthur Redford, *Manchester Merchants and Foreign Trade,* II, *1850–1939* (Manchester, 1956), p. 29.
74 Silver, *Manchester Men,* pp. 144, 222 and Ch. 7; Moore, *Sir Charles Wood,* is important for policy as a whole during this period.
75 Tomlinson, 'India and the British Empire', p. 345.
76 Redford, *Manchester Merchants,* p. 43.
77 Tomlinson, 'India and the British Empire', pp. 342–5; Klein, 'English Free Traders', pp. 251–71; Dewey, 'The End of the Imperialism of Free Trade'.
78 Dewey, 'The End of the Imperialism of Free Trade', pp. 35–44, 50–2, 55–65. Dewey's study, referred to in full in n. 72, provides an excellent account of this context and one, moreover, that has important implications for the study of British imperialism beyond the realm of Anglo-Indian relations.
79 On official awareness of the need to placate nationalist feeling see Marc Jason Gilbert, 'Lord Lansdowne and the Indian Factory Act of 1891: a Study in Indian Economic Nationalism and Proconsular Power', *Journal of Developing Areas,* 16 (1982); Ira Klein, 'Politics and Public Opinion in Lytton's Tariff Policy', *Jour. Indian Hist.,* 45 (1967); and

Howard Brasted, 'Indian Nationalist Development and the Influence of Irish Home Rule, 1870–1886', *Mod. Asian Stud.*, 14 (1980). On the growth of competition from Bombay see Farnie, *English Cotton Industry,* pp. 111–12.

80 For an introduction to the history of expatriate business in India from the mid-nineteenth century see B.R. Tomlinson, 'British Business in India, 1860–1970', in R.P.T. Davenport-Hines and Geoffrey Jones, eds. *British Business in Asia Since 1860* (Cambridge, 1989).

81 Lance Davis and Robert A. Huttenback, *Mammon and the Pursuit of Empire: The Political Economy of British Imperialism, 1860–1912* (Cambridge, 1986), Table 2.1 (intermediate estimate), pp. 40–1, and 43–53; D.C.M. Platt, *Britain's Investment Overseas on the Eve of the First World War* (1986), pp. 88–9.

82 Platt, *Britain's Investment,* pp. 54–7; Tomlinson, 'British Business', pp. 114–16.

83 MacPherson, 'Investment in Indian Railways', pp. 181–4. MacPherson's evidence on India fits neatly with the broader conclusions reached by Davis and Huttenback, *Mammon,* Ch. 7.

84 Tomlinson, 'British Business', pp. 93–4.

85 B.R. Tomlinson, 'Exchange Depreciation and Economic Development: India and the Silver Standard, 1872–1893', in Clive Dewey, ed. *Arrested Development in India: The Historical Dimension* (Manohar, 1988), pp. 223–38 (on the use of Council Bills); Amiya Kumar Bagchi, 'Anglo-Indian Banking in British India: From the Paper Pound to the Gold Standard', *Jour. Imp. and Comm. Hist.*, XIII (1985). On the early history of banking see Amiya K. Bagchi, *The Evolution of the State Bank of India: The Roots, 1806–1876, I, The Early Years, 1806–1860,* and II, *Diversity and Regrouping, 1860–1876* (Bombay, 1987). On currencies see S. Ambirajan, *Political Economy and Monetary Management: India, 1766–1914* (New Delhi, 1984), pp. 76–85 and Ch. 6; and John S. Deyell and R.E. Frykenberg, 'Sovereignty and the "Sikha" under Company Raj: Minting Prerogative and Imperial Legitimacy in India', *Indian Econ. and Soc. Hist. Rev.*, 19 (1982).

86 Geoffrey Tyson, *100 Years of Banking in Asia and Africa* (1963). Frank H.H. King, *A Concise Economic History of Modern China* (New York, 1968), Ch. 3, traces the links between banks operating in India and China. Unfortunately, there is no equivalent study for India of King's monumental history of the Hongkong and Shanghai Bank (which we have used extensively in Chapter 13).

87 J. Forbes Munro, 'Shipping Subsidies and Railway Guarantees: William Mackinnon, Eastern Africa and the Indian Ocean, 1860–93', *Jour. African Hist.*, 28 (1987); idem, 'Scottish Overseas Enterpise and the Lure of London: the Mackinnon Group, 1847–1893', *Scottish Econ. and Soc. Hist.*, 8 (1988); and Stephanie Jones, *Two Centuries of Overseas Trading: The Origins and Growth of the Inchcape Group* (1986).

88 See pp. 387–90.

89 Stephanie Jones, *Trade and Shipping: Lord Inchcape, 1852–1932* (Manchester, 1989).

90 The fullest account of the 'Home Charges' and of the associated 'Drain' from India is in Banerji, *Aspects,* Chs. 4 and 8 and Appendix II. See also K.N. Chaudhuri, 'India's International Economy in the Nineteenth Century: an Historical Survey', *Mod. Asian Stud.*, 2 (1968), B.R. Tomlinson, *The Political Economy of the Raj, 1914–1947* (Cambridge, 1979), Ch. 11 and Table 1.1. p. 18, and James Foreman-Peck, 'Foreign Investment and Imperial Exploitation: Balance of Payments Reconstruction for Nineteenth-Century Britain and India', *Econ. Hist. Rev.*, 2nd ser. XLII (1989).

91 Mayo to Argyll, 17 May 1869, quoted in S. Gopal, *British Policy in India, 1858–1905* (Cambridge, 1965), pp. 91–2.

92 Banerji, *Aspects,* Table 34, pp. 168–9, Table 38, p. 220, and Tables 40a and 40b, pp. 236–7; Dietmar Rothermund, *An Economic History of India* (1989), p. 43.

93 S.B. Saul, *Studies in British Overseas Trade, 1870–1914* (Liverpool, 1960), Chs. 3–4, and the discussion in Banerji, *Aspects,* pp. 18–23. India's multilateral settlements are considered further in A.J.H. Latham, 'Merchandise Trade Imbalances and Uneven Economic Development in India and China', *Jour. Eur. Econ. Hist.*, 7 (1978), pp. 37–40.

94 India Office, 'Memorandum on Preferential Tariffs in their Application to India', in *Papers Laid Before the Colonial Conference, 1907,* Cd 3524 (1907), p. 1,155. We are indebted to Dr B.R. Tomlinson for providing this reference.

95 Ibid. p. 1,155.
96 Ibid. p. 456.
97 Ibid. pp. 456–7.
98 Gilbert, 'Lord Lansdowne', pp. 357–72.
99 Northbrook to Clerk, 27 Feb. 1874, quoted in Gopal, *British Policy,* p. 109.
100 Sunil K. Sen, 'Economic Measures of Lord Ripon's Government, 1880–84', in Bhattacharya, *Essays in Modern Indian Economic History,* pp. 217–23.
101 Clive Dewey, 'The Government of India's "New Industrial Policy", 1900–1925: Formation and Failure', in K.N. Chaudhuri and C.J. Dewey, eds. *Economy and Society: Essays in Indian Economic and Social History* (Delhi, 1979), pp. 231, 238.
102 See, for example. Michael H. Fisher, 'Indirect Rule in the British Empire: the Foundations of the Residency System in India (1764–1858)', *Mod. Asian Stud.,* 18 (1984); Robert Frykenberg, 'Elite Groups in a South Indian District, 1788–1858', *Indo-British Review,* 10 (1983); Frances M. Mannsakar, 'East and West: Anglo-Indian Racial Attitudes as Reflected in Popular Fiction, 1890–1914', *Victorian Studies,* 24 (1980).
103 Tomlinson, 'India and the British Empire', pp. 347–9.
104 A. Seal, *The Emergence of Indian Nationalism* (Cambridge, 1968); Gordon Johnson, *Provincial Politics and Indian Nationalism: Bombay and the I.N.C., 1880–1915* (Cambridge, 1973); Stanley Wolpert, *Morley and India, 1906–1910* (Berkeley, Calif., 1967); and Pardaman Singh, *Lord Minto and Indian Nationalism, 1905–1910* (Allahabad, 1976).
105 This is well brought out by Singh, *Lord Minto.*
106 Ira Klein, 'The Anglo-Russian Convention and the Problems of Central Asia, 1907–1914', *Jour. Brit. Stud.,* 11 (1971); Sheh Mahajan, 'The Problems of the Defence of India and the Formation of the Anglo-Russian Entente, 1900–1907', *Jour. Indian Hist.,* 58 (1980).
107 Ambirajan, *Political Economy,* Ch. 7; Banerji, *Aspects,* Ch. 10. See also Arnold Kaminski, '"Lombard Street" and India: Currency Problems in the Late Nineteenth Century', *Indian Econ. and Soc. Hist. Rev.,* 17 (1980).
108 Banerji, *Aspects,* Ch. 10; Chaudhuri, 'India's International Economy', pp. 47–50. To the extent that the decline in the value of the rupee represented an adjustment to a chronic balance of payments deficit, as well as to a fall in the price of silver, it would have reinforced the trend towards higher import prices and given further encouragement to import-substitution.
109 Redford, *Manchester Merchants,* pp. 34–42.
110 Ambirajan, *Political Economy,* pp. 119–20, 130–2, 144–5. Powerful interests involved in India's export trade (notably the British-dominated tea industry) wished to retain the silver standard, but they, too, were disappointed. See Tomlinson, *Political Economy,* p. 17.
111 Ambirajan, *Political Economy,* pp. 100, 178.
112 Ibid. pp. 100, 108, 128–9, 137, 142, 178.
113 This is not to suggest that there was a unanimous view in the City of how this could be achieved. For a summary of the discussion see pp. 151–3.
114 Ambirajan, *Political Economy,* pp. 152–7, 164–9, 182. On the difficulties of establishing a full gold standard see ibid., Ch. 6 and p. 123, and Banerji, *Aspects,* p. 225.
115 Farnie, *English Cotton Industry,* pp. 111–13.
116 Ambirajan, *Political Economy,* pp. 100, 167–71, 176; Banerji, *Aspects,* pp. 115–18; Chaudhuri, 'India's International Economy', pp. 47–50; and the data in Davis and Huttenback, *Mammon,* pp. 41, 44–5.
117 E.H.H. Green, 'Rentiers versus Producers? The Political Economy of the Bimetallic Controversy', *Eng. Hist. Rev.,* LIII (1988).
118 Tomlinson, *Political Economy,* pp. 2–3.
119 Calculated from Chaudhuri, 'Foreign Trade', pp. 832–7. See also Tomlinson, 'India and the British Empire', p. 339.
120 Belgian iron and steel products and German textiles provided increasing competition after about 1900; whatever the fate of Indian handicraft workers earlier in the century,

the new textile industry in Bombay made considerable headway under British rule from the 1880s onwards. See M.D. Morris, *The Emergence of an Industrial Labour Force in India: A Study of the Bombay Cotton Mills, 1854–1947* (Berkeley, Calif., 1965); and Makrand Mehta, *The Ahmedabad Cotton Textile Industry: Genesis and Growth* (Ahmedabad, 1982).

121 As contemporaries were well aware: Redford, *Manchester Merchants,* p. 46.

122 The commitment of the educated classes to the imperial cause was emphasised by H.N. Brailsford, *The War of Steel and Gold* (1915), pp. 86–8.

Note: Genesis of the White colonies

It is worth noting that the so called white colonies of North America (i.e. those which became the United States and Canada) Australia, New Zealand, South and East Africa were in chronological terms pre-figured by the Elizabethan and Stewart plantations formed in Ireland in the 16th and 17th centuries.

Prior to that time, the Norman Kings of England (eg. Edward I, who still spoke Norman French at court) had as a result of his military conquests awarded land to his Lords in Wales, Ireland and Scotland in the 12th Century. Prior to that, Henry II had done so in Ireland. When these lords, or their nominated placemen took up the fief they did so with a considerable number of retainers and so became a colony of England in Wales, Ireland and Scotland. In the case of the latter, Edward I, after his invasion, awarded land to the Scottish Lords and magnates in England and land to his English/Norman Lords in Scotland with the express purpose of incorporating the Scottish Lords into the political system in England and setting up the English Lords with their retainers as English colonies in Scotland.

And, of course, the 12th Century Anglo Normans, themselves, were the descendants of Northmen from north western Europe who invaded France in the 10th Century under Rolf the Ganger/Rollo and wrested north western France, later known as Normandy, from the Frankish French kings.

So the 'colony system' whereby groups of people from England/Britain were sent to other, sometimes distant, geographical locations around the world with the express purpose of creating colonies loyal to the mother country has lengthy antecedants in English/British history.

11

'THE IMPERIOUS AND IRRESISTIBLE NECESSITY'

Britain and the partition of Africa, 1882–1902[1]

Nowhere does the weight of historiography press so insistently upon the study of imperialism as in the case of the partition of Africa. So much has been written on this theme on behalf of so many competing theories that few interpretations, even of points of detail, can resist the absorptive power of the existing literature.[2] Given that the quality of this research is as impressive as its weight, it might be thought that the subject now requires fine-tuning rather than thorough reappraisal. However, the growth of knowledge has had the perplexing result of making it easier to say what is wrong with current interpretations than what is right. Historians who wish to move beyond this point appear to face a choice between retreating to the high ground of deductive certainty and taking shelter in the empirical undergrowth. Yet, as we shall try to show, the anomalies in the literature can be resolved once the assumptions underlying existing interpretations are removed.

Marxist and Marxisant interpretations have performed particularly badly, despite some excellent research on specific subjects, largely because of their failure to relate partition to the realities of capitalist development in the late nineteenth century. Because the trail taken by the agents of advanced industrial capitalism bypassed much of Africa, the hounds seem to have lost the scent. Aside from tentative attempts to treat partition as being an expression of feeble capitalist influences and atavistic social forces (a view that brings Marx uncomfortably close to Schumpeter),[3] most work in the Marxist tradition has fallen back upon very broad generalisations associating capitalism with imperialism. There is at present no study of partition from a Marxist perspective which combines a recognition of the analytical weaknesses of parts of the theory of capitalist imperialism with a detailed knowledge of the empirical literature.

Liberal interpretations, by contrast, have flourished on the diversity revealed by recent research, both on Africa and on policy-making in Europe. This evidence has been used to underline the inadequacies of standard Marxist accounts and to construct various alternatives, the most coherent, and certainly the most celebrated, being that advanced by Robinson and Gallagher.[4] However, this interpretation has now become a casualty of the work it has inspired. It commands unanimous respect among specialists but only their qualified support. To claim that imperialism was the result of crises on the periphery is to report the symptoms, not to diagnose the cause; to attribute British intervention to the actions of European rivals is to assign to others impulses which might properly be looked for at home. Indeed, were it not for the fact that metropolitan-based explanations of imperialism have been discredited by the poor performance of Marxist theories, it is unlikely that interpretations of British policy would have come to rest quite so heavily on decisions taken by other countries. However, Robinson and Gallagher's critics have in turn become victims of their own success, for they have provided explanations for every episode and often for every event, with the result that the repertoire of possibilities has become so extensive that it is almost impossible to comprehend the subject as a whole.

Disarray may well be a faithful representation of historical reality; and it also accords with a view of history which denies that there is a whole to be grasped. Nevertheless, an awareness of diversity is consistent with an explanation of partition which seeks to reconstruct the context within which numerous individual actions took place; and in our view, it is also compatible with the historian's obligation to try to advance beyond accounts which rely on 'the interplay of the contingent and the unforeseen',[5] or make a virtue of surrendering in the face of the infinite complexity of events. The problem, as defined here, is to explain how Britain's changing interest in Africa influenced her presence there in the second half of the nineteenth century with the result that she moved from being a power on the coast to being a power in the land and, more than this, the most important of the continent's colonial powers. Our suggested solution will be presented in two parts. We shall begin by showing how Africa as a whole was touched by Britain's plan for harmonious world development in the nineteenth century, and how this programme was recharged and also reshaped by the extension of finance and services to Africa after 1850. The regional implications of this new impetus will then be considered by looking at Egypt, southern Africa and tropical Africa. These examples are not comprehensive, but they cover Britain's principal areas of interest, before and after partition, and thus provide a crucial test of any general interpretation of the scramble for power in Africa.

Britain's first development plan for Africa

The decision taken in 1807 to outlaw the slave trade initiated a new era in Britain's long-standing relations with Africa.[6] Thereafter, there began a campaign to 'regenerate' the continent by promoting the 'civilising' values of commerce and Christianity.[7] This endeavour, as we have seen, touched every continent, if not quite every country. The utilitarians cut their teeth, and more besides, on India's ancient institutions; a new generation of commercial crusaders laid siege to the Sublime

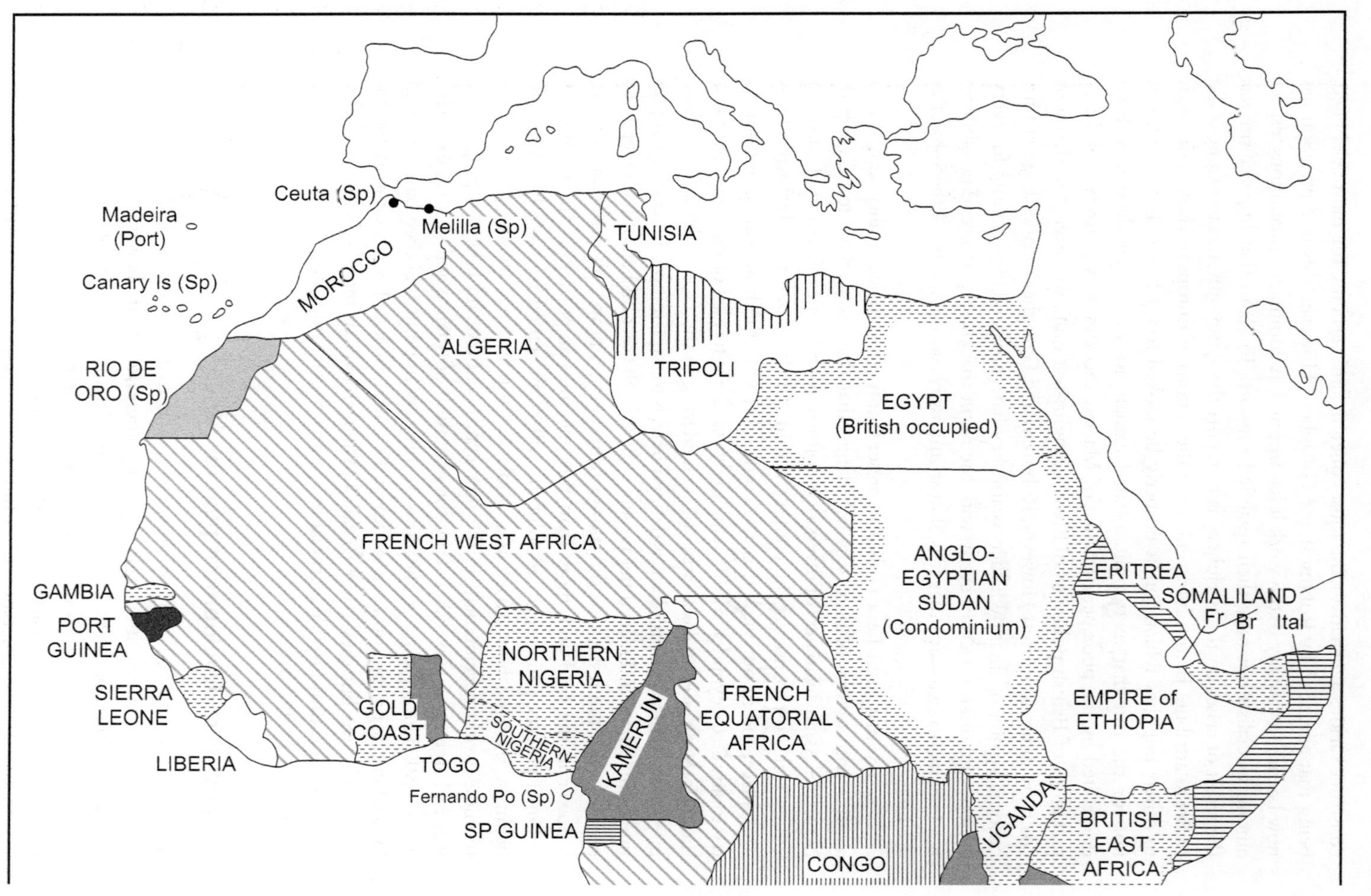

Madeira (Port)
Canary Is (Sp)
Ceuta (Sp)
Melilla (Sp)
MOROCCO
RIO DE ORO (Sp)
ALGERIA
TUNISIA
TRIPOLI
EGYPT (British occupied)
FRENCH WEST AFRICA
ANGLO-EGYPTIAN SUDAN (Condominium)
ERITREA
SOMALILAND
Fr
Br
Ital
EMPIRE of ETHIOPIA
GAMBIA
PORT GUINEA
SIERRA LEONE
LIBERIA
GOLD COAST
TOGO
NORTHERN NIGERIA
SOUTHERN NIGERIA
KAMERUN
FRENCH EQUATORIAL AFRICA
Fernando Po (Sp)
SP GUINEA
CONGO
UGANDA
BRITISH EAST AFRICA

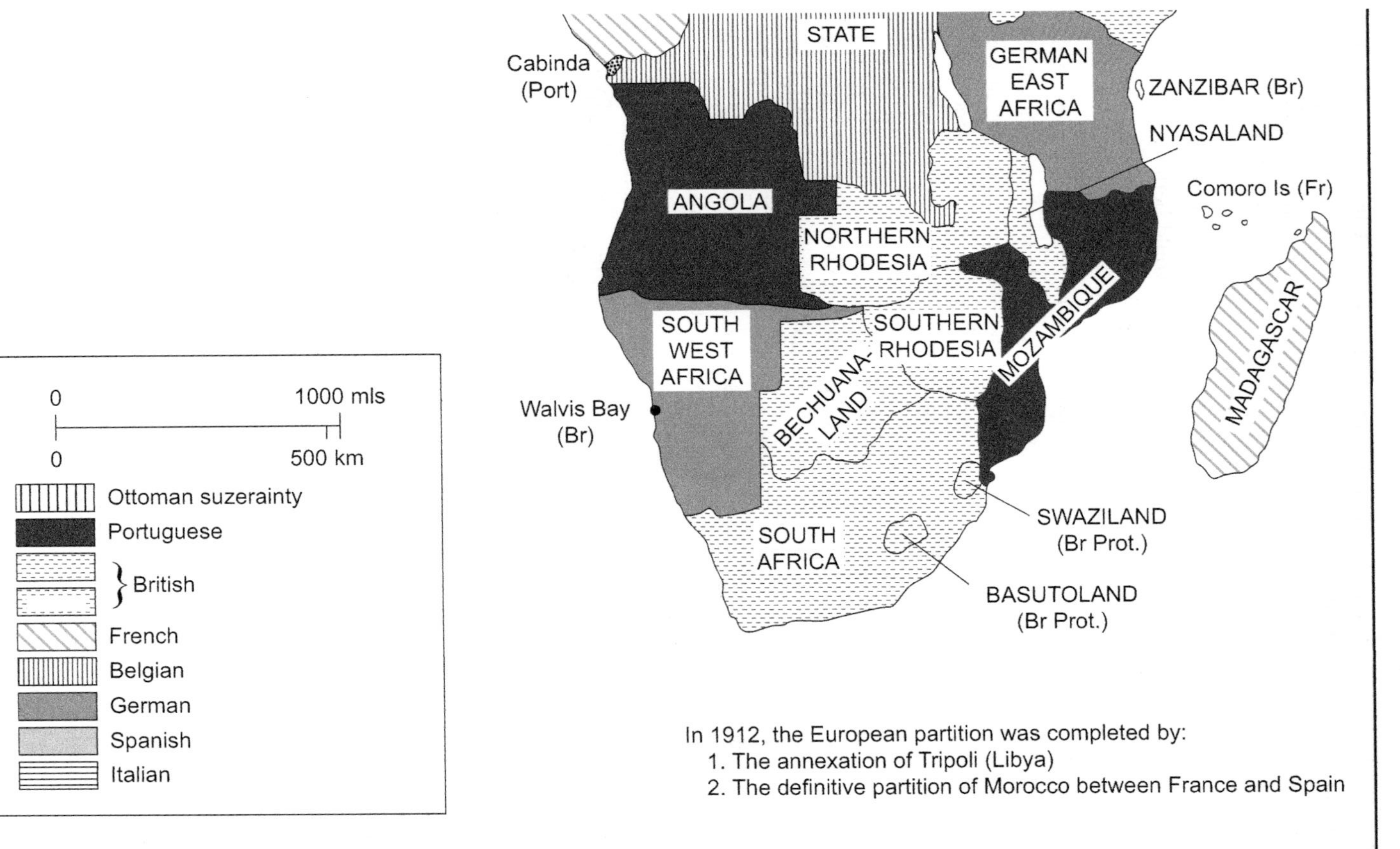

MAP 6 The partition of Africa, 1902

After. A.D. Roberts, ed. *The Cambridge History of Africa,* 6 (Cambridge, 1985)

Porte, and Christian missionaries knocked presumptuously at China's ancient doors. But Africa, the Dark Continent, had a special appeal; for there, in the aftermath of the Atlantic slave trade, it seemed that economic backwardness and moral degeneration had reached the lowest possible levels, and it was there, consequently, that the ultimate test of the supremacy of Western culture and skills was to be found.[8] The comprehensiveness of the new programme, and its confident belief that a combination of approved values and appropriate technology would both transform the world and cause it to be grateful, had no rival until the United States (unmindful of the precedent) promulgated a similar set of doctrines after 1945.

The most obvious effects of this endeavour were to be seen at points on the African coast that were designated as centres of diffusion. In southern Africa, it was expected that white settlers would play the role of 'like-minded' agents of metropolitan policy.[9] Here, strategy and commerce were closely entwined, both as means and ends, from the outset. A dependable colonial community was the best long-term defence of the route to India; a prosperous and progressive colony would remain dependable and would also promote trade, spread enlightened values, and ultimately become self-supporting. Spurred by this prospect, Britain reinforced the Cape after the French Wars by assisting emigration in 1819, and then attempted to 'Anglicise' the colony in the 1820s by crossing the social values of the English gentleman with the business ethic of the middle class.[10] Measures were taken against the slave trade and (after 1833) against the institution of slavery, and experiments with 'legitimate' commerce produced exports of wine, wool, grain and sugar.[11]

In other parts of Africa, where there were no white settlers, the universal ideals of the early and mid-Victorian periods had to be implanted into indigenous societies which themselves had very different characteristics. In west Africa, a new generation of educated, Christian Africans, who were intended to be the progenitors of a compliant middle class, arose in the main ports, and legitimate commodities, notably palm oil, began to flow from the hinterland in exchange for British cotton goods.[12] In north and east Africa, Britain had to negotiate her way in a more alien milieu. As there was no realistic prospect of making use of either white settlers or black Christians, working relationships were established with Muslim centralisers in Egypt and Zanzibar. In these cases, necessity imposed the virtue of tolerance, subject only to Palmerston's basic requirement that the state concerned should be 'well-kept' and 'always accessible'.[13] A combination of commercial self-interest and menace fostered the expansion of trade in raw cotton and manufactures with Egypt from the 1820s.[14] With greater effort, it also began to check the east African slave trade and encouraged a modest growth in exports of ivory, cloves and sugar.[15] In these diverse ways, new impulses from Britain touched the edges of the continent and sowed the seeds of the 'green revolution' which was eventually to produce the export-crop economies of colonial Africa.

Nevertheless, during the first half of the nineteenth century reform and development made disappointingly slow progress in Africa, as indeed elsewhere. The belief that unfree labour was incompatible with modern capitalism, though morally appealing, proved to be mistaken. The external slave trade, far from withering away, continued to flourish while it remained profitable, and the institution of slavery was strengthened as slave labour was redirected within the continent to produce new, 'legitimate' exports.[16] Consequently, the transition to legal forms of trade turned out to be far more protracted than the abolitionists had anticipated, and far more costly than successive British governments, committed to a 'leaner, fitter' public sector after 1815, had bargained for. The export of Christian values, never a serious prospect in north Africa, made disappointingly slow progress south of the Sahara. Efforts to convert Boer farmers to liberalism hastened their migration from British influence from the 1830s and generated conflicts over access to land and supplies of labour.[17] Attempts to create model settlements in the tropics were overwhelmed by the environment they were supposed to transform.[18] As it became clear that progress required more than a short course in applied ethics, Britain's official presence became more visible: naval squadrons were strengthened; diplomatic commitments were increased by establishing consulates in ports along the coast; and political acquisitions were made at strategic points, such as Aden (1839) and Natal (1842). But coastal bases 'opened up' very little of the interior, and the increase in legitimate trade was to levels that were still trivial.[19] There was no lucky strike and no 'quick fix' before 1850. As disillusion set in, the planners began to blame the recipients rather than the plan. Some felt that the continent should be abandoned to its fate; others that it required firmer direction.[20]

This situation changed during the second half of the century in ways that are important for understanding partition. The demise of the external slave trade was complemented by a new impulse: the extension to Africa of Britain's burgeoning financial and service sector. Investment in a few promising parts of the continent, principally Egypt and South Africa, grew rapidly, and soon drew in modern banking facilities as well. The beginning of regular steamship services in the 1850s increased the capacity and cut the cost of ocean transport; and the appearance, particularly from the 1880s, of 'megamerchants' and investment groups introduced forms of commercial organisation which were designed to be more successful than their predecessors in penetrating the interior.[21] In the British case, the 'large firm' emerged in the transactions sector much earlier than it did in manufacturing. The impetus for this development, as we have seen in other parts of the world, came from Britain's unique role and continuing dynamism in international commerce. Steamship, mining and trading companies all had to become larger in the late nineteenth century if they were to be successful, especially on the frontiers of empire. Small firms lacked the resources to buy and run steamships, to finance and manage complex mining operations, and to act as quasi-bankers, advancing credit, often over long periods, to indigenous traders and producers. Moreover, large firms operating in frontier conditions readily acquired political connections and often official functions too, both of which were helpful in reducing risk and suppressing competitors. Steamship companies secured subsidies in return for services to imperial communications; large commercial firms were sometimes awarded royal charters for acting as proxies for officialdom, and particularly for meeting protection costs which the Treasury was unwilling to bear.

The men who created these firms were adventurers as well as entrepreneurs. They were rarely gentlemen by birth, and their willingness to cut corners on the frontiers of empire was often frowned on in London. But, being on the make, they were also gentlemen in the making. As such, they took readily to the imperial mission and helped to rejuvenate it in the second half of the nineteenth century. Imperialism, however, was much more than a cover for new business interests: it gave private ambitions a wider purpose and enhanced their standing. The most successful of the entrepreneurs who descended on Africa carried the gentlemanly code with them. They saw themselves as being Christian knights engaged in a civilising mission and performing a patriotic duty, which in turn expressed their loyalty to the crown – and hence their acceptance of the social order it represented.[22] At the highest levels, business success and social advancement required connections in London, principally within the City and parliament. Thus, Goldie made use of first a Baron (Aberdare) and then an Earl (Scarborough) as chairmen of the Royal Niger Company, and Mackinnon mobilised the Duke of Sutherland to promote the Imperial British East Africa Company. As might be expected, Rhodes went a step further: he acquired a brace of Dukes (Abercorn and Fyfe), and cultivated good relations with Lord Rothschild. Currie, the shipping magnate whose steamers dominated the routes to South Africa, enjoyed Gladstone's friendship and also took a direct path to influence by becoming a Liberal MP in 1880.[23] In return came a good deal of local authority in Africa, a sprinkling of knighthoods, and some recycling of wealth into estates, usually in the south of England.[24]

If Africa's colonial entrepreneurs were proto-gentlemen, their associates, the explorers and the representatives of the Church Missionary Society, tended to be drawn from established gentry families and from the professional classes of southern England.[25] They, too, helped to revitalise the development drive in the second half of the century. A society that had given up protection for free trade took readily to the need to open new frontiers and gave explorers considerable status; one that had committed itself to creating 'like-mindedness' (where it could not readily be found) was also likely to inspire missionary activity. Not surprisingly, reports from both sources were cast in the image of metropolitan society, and were accompanied by renewed optimism about Africa's potential and Britain's ability to push the frontiers of economic growth inland, especially by means of the railway and the telegraph – 'the keys to the continent', as Rhodes called them.[26] Societies which showed signs of gentility were marked out as being ready for development by settlement or assimilation; those which did not were deemed to require developing by others. This more assertive attitude was endorsed by the Church Missionary Society, whose vision of spiritual egalitarianism retreated before the advance of militant evangelical influences in the late nineteenth century, and by the new academic disciplines of anthropology and phrenology, which lent scientific credence to the congenial view that the service class of the Home Counties was destined to dominate the world.[27] These ideas, and others linking racism to patriotism, were translated by the new popular press in a manner which encouraged statesmen to give increasing consideration to the use imperial issues might serve in an era of semi-democratic politics.

This argument is not to be read as disparaging the part played by manufacturers, who undoubtedly showed a keen awareness of the need to open markets for old staple exports outside Europe and the United States, particularly in the last quarter of the century.[28] But to an extent which has been underestimated, the manufacturing interest rode on the back of the new expansionist wave rather than created it. By the late nineteenth century the manufacture of cotton goods, the principal export to Africa, had ceased to be characterised by striking productivity gains, and further growth had come to depend increasingly on improvements in the transactions sector, especially transport and finance. Expansion also required political influence, in Africa and in London, and here too manufacturers relied to a considerable degree on the representations and actions of financial and commercial houses, while also, of course, making use of their own trade organisations and members of parliament.

The combination of capital and commercial innovation undoubtedly made inroads into Africa during the second half of the nineteenth century, though the poor quality of the data does not allow the results to be traced with any degree of precision.[29] Some approximate orders of magnitude are provided by Austen's calculations, which show that Africa's share of British exports (excluding trade with Egypt) rose from less than 3 per cent in the middle of the century to 4.3 per cent in 1890 and to 8.3 per cent in 1906.[30] The proportions were indeed small, and the striking gains came after partition rather than before. But these are not reasons for dismissing the importance of Britain's trade with Africa on the eve of partition. The fact that the proportion was rising shows that Africa was a growth area for Britain's exports, and such areas were in short supply in the late nineteenth century. Moreover, since Britain's total exports were expanding globally, the increasing share taken by Africa represents a considerable gain in absolute terms. However, the real significance of the data lies in their regional basis., In the 1880s three-quarters of Britain's direct trade with Africa (imports and exports amounting to about £30m. a year) was conducted with Cape Colony, Natal and Egypt.[31] This figure (£22.5m.) was larger than Britain's trade with the whole of China (including Hong Kong) during this period and slightly more than half the value of her trade with Latin America. When it is remembered that these were also the areas of Africa that attracted British investment after 1850, the significance of a regional approach to partition becomes apparent. This was certainly the perspective adopted by contemporary business opinion in London, which had no doubt that South Africa and Egypt were the parts of the continent that really mattered.[32]

The pace of commercial expansion during the second half of the century had profound effects on the African side of the frontier, though these are still imperfectly understood. However, research now available suggests that the various 'crises on the periphery' which have attracted the attention of historians of partition derived from structural changes to societies which were adapting to the demands of the new international economic order, and that these adjustment problems were greatly magnified by the renewed development push after 1850. The evidence also indicates that African polities produced a cluster of hybrid and often assertive responses to external forces and were not simply 'undermined' by them to the extent that 'law and order' had to be reimposed. Slave-raiders in west Africa achieved some success in adjusting to the palm oil trade and to competition from new small producers; hunters in east Africa momentarily held back the clock of history by making windfall gains during the ivory boom. Ismail in Egypt and Kruger in the Transvaal actively sought to use external influences to reinforce their independence. The problem was not that societies in Africa were unresponsive, but that Britain's presence was marked by increasing demands and diminishing tolerance in the second half of the century. From that point onwards the machinery of adjustment became vulnerable to short-term fluctuations in international trade, transmitted mainly by falling export prices and credit restrictions, and to random influences on the domestic economy, such as the size of the harvest and the incidence of disease. When these struck, as they did in different parts of Africa during the last quarter of the century, local crises were easily precipitated. In these circumstances, it was virtually impossible for African states to pass Palmerston's test: those which ran into difficulties failed because they were no longer 'well-kept', while those which turned Cobden's international principles to national advantage failed because they had ceased to be 'always accessible'.

This assessment suggests the need to question the conventional view that Britain's policy towards frontier disputes was essentially restrained and reactive. This characterisation undoubtedly represents the ideal of a low-cost, harmonious international order which inspired in the official mind a degree of coherence and a sense of purpose that it might otherwise have lacked. But in the real world the rules had long been bent where they had not been broken, despite Britain's aversion to territorial acquisition and desire for economy in public expenditure. To cite just a few examples from different parts of Africa: Britain had established a colony in Lagos in 1861 and had fought wars with Asante in 1863 and 1874; she had invaded Ethiopia in 1867–8 and had appointed a Consul-General at Zanzibar in 1873; she had annexed Griqualand West in 1871, the Transvaal in 1877, and Walvis Bay in 1878; and she had fought one war with the Zulu in 1879, and another with the Boers in 1880–81. These events certainly looked (and felt) aggressive from an African point of view. Although their precise causes are open to discussion and need to be attuned to particular circumstances, the fact that they occurred at all can be understood only in the context of the quickening beat of impulses transmitted from the metropole, which placed Britain in a position where circumstances 'forcing' her to take action on the frontiers of empire were much more likely to arise.

For the same reasons, it is also necessary to pause before assigning the responsibility for Britain's actions to foreign rivals. This exercise is partly flawed by its circularity: British historians tend to blame the French; but French historians tend to accuse Germany or Belgium; and German and Belgian historians are inclined to attribute responsibility to Britain and France.[33] This line of argument also suffers from empirical difficulties. It has to be remembered that Africa's most important commercial, financial and diplomatic ties in the period down to partition were with Britain, not France (still less with Germany, Belgium or Portugal). The entry of foreign rivals was undoubtedly a complication for British policy. But France and Germany had more influence in tropical Africa, at the margins of Britain's interests, than in Egypt and South Africa, which were central to her position in the continent. Britain had her own reasons for safeguarding her position in Africa. Appearances did not deceive; the tail did not wag the dog.

The general direction of the argument should now be clear. The next step is to consider its application to different parts of the continent. Schematically, Britain's presence in Africa can be considered along two axes: one, running from north to south, charts the extension abroad of the new financial and service sector; the other, drawn more tentatively from west to east across the tropics, represents less substantial speculative and manufacturing interests. This division, we suggest, reflects the realities of British capitalism because it gives appropriate weight to the influence exerted by the gentlemanly complex in London and the Home Counties. It also accords with the realities perceived by British diplomats. Since the continent was not united, even in the loose sense that applied to the Ottoman Empire and China, there could be no 'one Africa' policy. Officials had divided Africa in their minds long before they had begun to partition it in reality. As we shall now see, Britain fastened upon the most promising parts of the continent, where her economic and political purposes were more or less congruent, and did not let go.

The occupation of Egypt

The first, decisive advance inland on the route which Rhodes was later to envisage joining the Cape to Cairo took place in 1882, when British troops occupied Egypt.[34] This event sparked a lively debate among contemporaries, and it has made a distinctive contribution to theories of imperialism from that time to the present day. As far as modern scholarship is concerned, the Egyptian case is best known for the central role assigned to it by Robinson and Gallagher in *Africa and the Victorians*.[35] In their view, the occupation of Egypt was the product of a crisis on the periphery prompted by a proto-nationalist revolt. Britain was reluctant to intervene, but did so because the breakdown of law and order posed a threat to her strategic interest in the Suez Canal, which guarded the route to India. This decision had far-reaching consequences: it destroyed the informal understandings which had governed the major powers in their dealings with Africa, drove the French to seek compensation in west Africa, and pushed the British up the Nile and into east Africa in pursuit of strategic security. Southern Africa was too remote to become the final domino in this particular 'great game', but British policy towards the Boer republics nevertheless exemplifies the paramountcy of 'excentric' and strategic considerations in understanding the essentially defensive imperialism of the late Victorians.

Robinson and Gallagher's view of events is indeed very close to the official interpretation put forward at the time.[36] The question, however, is whether the authorised version also provides an acceptable explanation of the problem under review, and the evidence now available suggests that it does not. As we shall see, the official account was formulated with at least one eye on the need to ensure that the controversial decisions taken by Britain presented her in a favourable light; the other was uninterested in recording causes of actions which lay beyond the immediate reasons given for them by the participants themselves. A more plausible interpretation, we suggest, is one that sees the crisis of 1882 as a moment of conjuncture arising out of the long-term interaction between the expansion of British interests and the aspirations of Egypt's rulers.

Britain's commercial ties with Egypt grew rapidly after 1815. Manchester's quest for new markets coincided with the modernising policies of Egypt's ruler, Mohammed Ali, and led to the development of a sizeable export sector based on the exchange of cotton goods for raw cotton.[37] However, this emerging complementarity could not disguise the fact that Mohammed Ali was a centralising autocrat who favoured state monopolies and protectionism, and had expansionist ambitions of his own, whereas Britain was treading a path towards free trade and minimal government, and needed to create obedient and pacific satellites. The spread of cash crops had already begun to have destabilising consequences within Egypt in the 1820s, and these led, indirectly, to expansionist ventures in the 1830s.[38] After 1838, when Britain imposed free trade on the Ottoman Empire (of which Egypt was formally a part), Mohammed Ali's chances of achieving economic independence disappeared. State monopolies were destroyed, military expansion was checked, and Egypt's rulers were forced to rely increasingly on internal taxation and foreign borrowing.

The assimilation of Egypt into Britain's free-trading regime generated a substantial increase in foreign trade and investment from the 1840s onwards. One manifestation of the growth of European influences was the rapid expansion of the principal port, Alexandria, which became a colonial enclave long before Egypt became, effectively, a colony.[39] The French presence was sizeable and pervasive; but Britain was the most important foreign trading partner, and in 1880 took 80 per cent of Egypt's exports and supplied 44 per cent of her imports.[40] Commercial expansion was accompanied by railway and harbour construction and by the installation of industrial machinery, all of which gave employment to British manufacturers and personnel. Export growth was funded largely by private capital flows, which came chiefly from British sources. State bonds began to be marketed externally from 1862, principally to finance the construction of the Suez Canal and to underwrite the military budget. British investors held more than half the public debt in 1873, shortly before a rash of short-term loans temporarily raised the proportion held by the French. Even so, the funded debt remained largely in British hands. Moreover, Britain's financial stake in Egypt increased following Disraeli's purchase of the Egyptian government's shares in the Suez Canal in 1875 and the consolidation of the public debt in 1880, which led many French investors to sell their unified bonds in London.

Britain was therefore the principal creditor when Egypt subsided into bankruptcy in 1876.[41] However, it does not follow, as a matter of logic or necessity, that financial considerations played a determining part in subsequent events leading to the occupation of Egypt in 1882. This possibility, like others, must stand or fall by empirical tests. In fact, British governments were reluctant to give guarantees to private investors because they rightly feared the consequences of signing blank cheques for City speculators.[42] At the same time, governments also acknowledged a general obligation to support Britain's interests, including her economic interests, abroad. A case for intervention could be made, for example, where British lives or property were endangered by the break-down of law and order. As far as Egypt was concerned, the British government had a formal commitment to ensure that the loans made to the Ottoman Empire in the 1850s would be repaid, and recognised, too, that default would have sizeable consequences for financial and manufacturing interests in Britain. The Egyptian case was one among an increasing number of others in the late nineteenth century which left open the possibility of intervention providing that the reasons were weighty and respectable, either in reality or in presentation.

It now seems clear that Britain adopted a much more assertive policy towards Egypt than Robinson and Gallagher allowed.[43] In resolving to make Egypt pay her debts, Disraeli's Conservative government (1874–80) soon blurred the line between official neutrality and unofficial assistance. The banker, Goschen, was given semi-official support in negotiating the agreement which led to the establishment of Dual (Anglo-French) Control over Egyptian finances in 1876. Harsh measures were imposed to balance the budget and to enable debt service to be resumed; when these provoked opposition in Egypt in 1879, the British government came very close to taking military action. In the event, the Khedive was deposed, the system of dual control was tightened, and the Law of Liquidation was passed in 1880. This measure consolidated the public debt and rescheduled repayments: it also bound the European signatories to see that it was carried out.

The advent of the Liberal government in 1880 altered the tone but not the direction of policy. Gladstone was vaguely in favour of the 'nationalists' in Egypt; but, unlike his fellow Liberal, John Bright, he was not against intervention at any price.[44] In this particular case Gladstone himself had good reason to calculate the cost because no less than 37 per cent of his total portfolio was invested in Egyptian stock in 1882.[45] This is not to say that Gladstone was motivated by crude self-interest; but it does suggest that he was likely to see the creditors' point of view with some clarity if it could be presented as an issue of principle, and especially one that was in the wider public interest. Gladstone was also out-manoeuvred by the hawks in his government, headed by Hartington and Dilke, who were keen to shift the Liberals towards a strong foreign policy as a means of showing that the party could be as patriotic as the Conservatives in defending Britain's interests abroad.[46] This group began to devise ways of imposing an aggressive policy in opposition to Gladstone's internationalism, and sought specifically to replace Dual Control by British supremacy. In this aim the militants were well supported by the 'men on the spot', particularly Colvin, the British Controller-General, and Malet, the British Consul, who sent increasingly lurid reports purporting to show that Egypt would soon be governed by an authoritarian military clique dedicated to the elimination of European influences unless Britain took decisive action.

In addition, the City's involvement reached to the highest levels, and included a weighty contribution by Rothschilds, who had given substantial financial support in 1879, when Egypt's external debt was being reorganised in preparation for the Law of Liquidation.[47] Lord Rothschild himself was active in representing the interests of British investors, and so, too, was the Corporation of Foreign Bondholders, which mobilised *The Times,* the financial press, and the considerable number of members of parliament (besides Gladstone) who had a financial stake in the Egyptian economy.[48] There is little doubt that the government's purchase of shares in the Suez Canal, combined with increasing evidence of semi-official support for the various steps taken to improve the efficiency of Egypt's finances after 1875, had greatly encouraged British investors by providing an implied guarantee which, in appropriate circumstances and on a favourable interpretation, could be said to be a matter of principle.[49]

The budgetary rigours imposed by Britain and France eventually provoked a reaction in Egypt. In September 1881 Urabi, the nationalist leader, led a protest against the rapid spread of European influence, and shortly afterwards joined with the newly revived Chamber of Notables to challenge European financial control. The Chamber accepted Egypt's obligations to its external creditors, but wanted to manage parts of the budget that were not assigned to the foreign debt. The Controllers-General interpreted this demand as being the prelude to wider claims, and immediately raised the alarm. When this happened, Dilke and his associates felt ready to act. The Joint Note issued by Britain and France in January 1882 was deliberately provocative; Granville, the moderate Foreign Secretary, was won over in March by the fear that Britain's financial interests would be damaged by the determined stance taken by the nationalists; in June Hartington threatened to split the Liberal government by resigning unless a forward policy was adopted.[50] At this point Gladstone himself agreed to sanction some form of intervention, having been persuaded that action was justified by growing 'disorder' in Egypt. An Anglo-French naval presence was planned to intimidate the nationalists. In the event, the force became a British one and it had the predictable result of strengthening Egyptian unity and increasing tension in Cairo and Alexandria. When riots broke out in Alexandria, Admiral Seymour was let off the leash: the port was bombarded, and the occupation of Egypt began. Dilke was delighted with the outcome; Malet, writing to congratulate the Foreign Secretary, observed that the action had given the Liberals 'a new lease of popularity and power'.[51]

Not surprisingly, the official version told a very different story. The Foreign Office removed a passage from the draft of the public statement admitting that intervention had been brought about by Egypt's attempts to exercise control over the budget, and instead provided a set of explanations which were calculated to impress international opinion and to soothe the sensitivities of Liberal supporters.[52] According to the authorised view, Britain was reluctant to take action but was compelled to do so by the breakdown of law and order, which put British lives and property in danger and posed a threat to the Suez Canal. Even so, Britain found herself embroiled in Egypt largely as a result of the assertiveness of the French. Milner, whose experience of Egypt formed a prelude to the acts of colonial brinkmanship he was to perform in southern Africa, helped to propagate the myth, subsequently repeated by many others, that it was the French who, 'after dragging us into the Egyptian imbroglio in 1882, shirked at the last moment and left us to settle the whole matter alone'.[53]

Not one of these explanations can carry the weight attached to it.[54] Despite the pressures on the Egyptian polity, it is now apparent that Egypt was not descending into anarchy on the eve of the British occupation. Law and order were maintained until the riots in Alexandria in June 1882. Furthermore, the riots were a response to the intrusion of Europe, not a cause of it, and they were far less serious than the official version of events held them to be. Their real significance was psychological and political: they catalysed the anxieties of European residents and foreign investors, and caused them to reach for the alarm cord.[55] These anxieties had grown, not because Egypt was in a state of chaos, but because the British decided that they could not trust Urabi and the nationalists. The disorder they feared was financial; and fiscal anarchy was a moral issue, not just an economic one. Resolving the confusions of Egyptian finances became, for Gladstone, a 'holy subject' – and thus a matter of principle.[56]

The Suez Canal was not at risk in 1882; nor was it thought to be the cause of intervention by Gladstone or his Foreign Secretary, Granville, or by the Admiralty (which in any case based its strategy on the Cape route until the 1890s), or by the mercantile shipping lobby.[57] The Canal did not become an issue in the public mind until two weeks before the bombardment of Alexandria, and it was only after this event that the possibility of retaliatory action in the region of Suez arose. As for the French, it is now evident that they were indeed worried about safeguarding their interests between 1875 and 1880, when their investments were in a highly exposed position. After 1880, however, French policy towards Egypt was marked by restraint. The Law of Liquidation took care of the worries of French investors. Some sold their holdings and departed. Those who remained were quite happy to have their protection provided by the world's largest security organisation – Great Britain. Moreover, after 1881 France was preoccupied by the invasion of Tunisia. The French did not lead Britain into the 'Egyptian imbroglio'. Their fleet was withdrawn from Alexandria precisely because France did not want to be dragged into Egypt by Britain.

If, in its final stages, the crisis on the Egyptian periphery displayed clear signs of stage-management, its deeper origins lay in the expansion of European trade and investment after 1838, and especially in the growth of public-sector borrowing from the 1860s. British policy was assertive not because policy-makers were in the pockets of the bond-holders, but because they recognised the need to defend Britain's substantial economic interests in Egypt, and because they thought that these could be secured by a quick and inexpensive strike that would also produce political benefits at home. The outcome was what Milner called a 'veiled protectorate', which enabled Britain to retain control over the budget in much the same way as the Ottoman Public Debt Administration (with rather less power) managed the finances of the Sublime Porte. The other major consequence of the occupation of Egypt was to draw Britain into the Sudan. This further extension of British influence cannot be explored here.[58] But it is worth noting that Britain's involvement in the Sudan stemmed much more from Egypt's indebtedness than it did from a concern with the need to protect the Suez route to India. The collapse of Ismail's regime in 1879 weakened Egypt's hold over the Sudan and opened an opportunity for a coalition of slave-traders and taxpayers to unite against the reforms which Britain had tried to impose through Cairo's authority. It is understandable that the Mahdists opposed foreign influence and aimed at creating an independent Muslim state with its own fiscal system; it is not surprising either that the British decided that they could not allow 'disorder' to persist in the Sudan when it endangered the settlement they had just imposed on Egypt.

Crisis and war in South Africa

As Egypt was being occupied, so Britain was beginning to grapple with problems at the other end of the continent that were to lead, somewhat later and by an even more complex route, to the acquisition of the greater part of southern Africa. The impulses which carried Britain northwards into central Africa, culminating in the Boer War and the eventual Union of South Africa under British rule in 1910, also inspired among contemporaries a debate over the causes of imperialism which continues to stimulate scholars today.[59] At one extreme is the interpretation, formulated by Hobson, that events in southern Africa were driven by a conspiracy of financiers who hijacked the apparatus of state power in the interests of private profit; at the other extreme is the view that agents of the state on the periphery of empire harnessed both Whitehall and the mine-owners for their own (greater or lesser) ends. In between stand many floating voters who see the complexity of events rather more clearly than their underlying purpose. The principal problem, as in the case of Egypt, is to trace the ties that bound economics, strategy and private ambition, without also collapsing the argument into poorly specified generalities about the defence of British supremacy.

The extension of free trade from the 1840s and the advent of banking and steamship services during the 1860s gave fresh impetus to the Cape's agricultural exports (notably wool) and offered a small but growing market for British manufacturers.[60] By promising to underpin the prosperity of the settler community, these developments also held out the hope of securing Britain's strategic interest in the route to the Far East. This concern was enhanced as Britain's financial and commercial stake expanded, particularly in India, during the second half of the nineteenth century, and the Cape route retained its high priority, even after the opening of the Suez Canal in 1869.[61] Nevertheless, the vision of self-supporting communities of loyal settlers failed to materialise. Degrees of self-government were indeed conferred, but the trekkers in the Transvaal and the Orange Free State were given independence (in 1852 and 1854) because they could not be Anglicised and because they were thought to be unimportant; and the Cape's qualifications for 'responsible government' were hurried on in 1872 so that it could play its part in sustaining Britain's interests without also remaining a burden on the defence budget.[62]

Recent research on southern Africa has revealed in considerable detail the processes by which the expansion of agriculture and pastoralism in the second half of the nineteenth century increased competition for land and labour and generated economic disputes which rapidly assumed a political form.[63] It has also shown how exposure to free trade hit agricultural exports from the 1870s and stepped up pressure from farmers to cut labour costs, and how this turn of events became caught up with the natural disasters of drought and rinderpest which struck much of southern Africa after 1869.[64] In the Western Cape, wine producers and wheat farmers facing the cold winds of free trade and indebtedness were also confronted with the unbending orthodoxy of imperial finance in the shape of the Standard Bank. These developments cut into the support which the colonial government had built up during more prosperous times, generated demands for protection and for 'country' banks, and helped to stimulate Afrikaner nationalism.[65] A broadly similar picture has emerged from research on Natal, where depressed exports, difficulties over labour supply and rural indebtedness also promoted political disaffection.[66] It is now apparent that turbulence on the southern African frontier after 1850 resulted not only from attempts to escape the forces of modernisation but also from the consequences of their ambiguous embrace.

The issues facing British policy from the 1870s extended beyond the control of uncertain frontiers and centred increasingly on securing the economic base of the colony itself. The discovery of diamonds in 1867 and the exploitation of the rich reserves at Kimberley from 1870 appeared to be the 'lucky strike' that policy-makers had long been waiting for. By annexing Griqualand West in 1871, Britain gained control of the principal mines and with them a means of funding responsible government at the Cape, and the imperial government seized the opportunity to uncouple the colony from its reliance on the Treasury and to link it instead with the London money market.[67] However, the lucky strike did not produce an instant solution to the problem of marrying economic resources to political authority. The diamond mines quickly generated a substantial demand for labour which was met initially from settler farming areas, thus adding to the difficulties which agriculture was already experiencing.

It was the attempt to deal with this question that underlay Carnarvon's drive for a South African Confederation after he became Colonial Secretary in 1874.[68] Carnarvon's design was to turn central Africa and Mozambique into labour reserves for the mines and farms of the south. This strategy was linked to a revival of the anti-slavery campaign in East Africa and to the spread of steamship and banking services northwards along the south-east coast of Africa; it culminated in the annexation of the Transvaal in 1877.[69] Carnarvon's plan failed because of the hostile reactions it provoked in South Africa, and because diamonds were unable to generate the resources needed to carry Confederation through, with the result that independence had to be restored to the Transvaal in 1881.[70] But the plan deserves emphasis for the way it foreshadowed the future in recognising the centrality of the labour question and in seeking to solve the Cape's economic problems by mounting a 'big push' inland. It was a conscious expansionist scheme directed from the metropole, albeit with support from business interests in South Africa, and not merely an aberrant reaction to chance events occurring spontaneously on the periphery.

The problems raised by the shift from agricultural to mineral exports became both more complex and more intractable after the discovery of gold on the Rand in 1886.[71] The ensuing gold rush greatly hastened the pace of economic change by attracting foreign capital, manufactures and settlers, and by drawing more labour away from the hard-pressed farming communities whose prosperity and loyalty were supposed to uphold Britain's interests in southern Africa. By the close of the 1890s the Rand had become the largest single producer of gold, being responsible for over one-quarter of world output; by 1906–10 gold accounted for about two-thirds of the value of South Africa's exports.[72] In 1899, on the eve of the Boer War, investment in the gold-mines stood at about £74m.: recent research has drawn attention to the sizeable stake held by French and German investors, but it has also underlined the continued paramountcy of Britain, which was responsible for 60–80 per cent of the total.[73] Similarly, though Britain's share of South Africa's external trade declined under the pressure of foreign competition, in 1900 she still supplied two-thirds of the rapidly expanding import trade, which, with a value of £15m., made South Africa her largest single market in the continent.[74]

The discovery of gold made it clear that prosperity and authority in South Africa would in future rest on minerals rather than agriculture. However, since the richest gold deposits were located in the Transvaal, the Boer Republic which Britain had recently fought, annexed and relinquished for the second time in the century, a sizeable political obstacle stood between Britain and the realisation of this new potential. The discovery of gold gave the Republic the resources to underwrite its political independence, and the Boer leaders, headed by Kruger, took the opportunity to embark on a programme of modernisation and expansion.[75] The prospect of being able to finance a railway link to Lourenço Marques promised to give the Transvaal an independent route to the sea; the new-found prosperity of the Republic strengthened ties with the Orange Free State and encouraged the depressed farming areas of the Cape and Natal to look northwards for their future, thus threatening to deprive Cape Town of a large part of its hinterland.[76] Had Britain's interests in southern Africa been purely strategic, she might have been able to tolerate these developments. But her commitments, like her ambitions, had spread far beyond the narrow confines of a naval base. The Transvaal could no longer be ignored: the question now was how to bring it into line with British interests.

In the absence of a sturdy Anglophile yeomanry, and in the face of a new mining frontier populated by entrepreneurs whose activities were some way removed from gentlemanly norms and conduct, British policy took a further turn away from cultural idealism and towards political realism. Two main strategies were adopted from the 1880s: one made use of British finance to re-establish Britain's influence within the Transvaal: the other involved licensing colonial agents, above all Rhodes, to curb the Republic's expansionist tendencies outside its frontiers.

Although British governments could not direct British finance, they could reasonably hope that the Transvaal's dependence upon the London money market would cause Kruger, as it had caused others, to think twice before embarking on policies that were inimical to British interests. This hope was not left entirely to chance. In 1892, for example, official encouragement was given to Rothschilds when they sought City support in raising a loan (of £2.5m.) for the Transvaal, and the terms of the loan gave Britain a degree of leverage over the Republic.[77] But Kruger countered Britain's financial influence by attracting German capital, which assisted the formation of the National Bank of the South African Republic in 1894, despite Britain's opposition.[78] Moreover, Kruger's programme of nation-building operated against the large and predominantly British mining interest on the Rand by raising freight rates and the cost of dynamite, by impeding moves to increase the supply (and hence reduce the price) of labour, and by threatening to apply a tourniquet to Britain's plan for creating a free-trade area throughout southern Africa.[79] While it is hard to assign precise weights to the various difficulties confronting the mining industry, it seems clear that they grew more rather than less important, and that they became particularly contentious in 1895, when there was a slump in the gold market.[80]

In devising a more assertive policy towards Boer expansionism, Britain was caught in the familiar dilemma of trying to reconcile ambition and parsimony. The solution, which had its counterparts elsewhere in Africa, was to appoint an inexpensive instrument of policy by granting a royal charter to Cecil Rhodes's British South Africa Company in 1889.[81] In securing this privilege, Rhodes was greatly assisted by Sir Hercules Robinson, the Governor of the Cape, who had sizeable investments in Rhodes's companies and who was economical with the truth in presenting the Company's credentials.[82] Rhodes had made his fortune from diamonds in Kimberley, where his success in a series of heavyweight contests with local rivals had been greatly helped by the London branch of Rothschilds, and particularly by the consolidation of De Beers in the early 1880s.[83] Subsequently, however, Rhodes was slow to recognise the potential of the Rand and failed to lay hands on the most promising goldfields. Commercial disappointment led him to search for a second Rand further north, and it was at this point that his potential as an agent of imperial policy manifested itself. Rhodes had already played a part in the negotiations which led to the acquisition of Bechuanaland, to the west of the Transvaal, in 1884–5. His subsequent manoeuvres, especially his cavalier use of military and political means to boost his company's sagging fortunes, brought Mashonaland and Matabeleland (to the north) under British control between 1888 and 1893.[84] As it happened, none of these vast acquisitions yielded a second Rand, and in 1894 Rhodes fixed his gaze firmly on the Transvaal, where gold-production was beginning to shift from outcrop to deep-level operations.[85] Rhodes's own company, Consolidated Goldfields, in association with Wernher Beit, the largest of the mining firms, was this time well placed to take advantage of the industry's need for finance and of the process of amalgamation which accompanied it by drawing on his valuable City connections and his particular association with Rothschilds.[86] He was now in a good position to contemplate the industry's growing differences with Kruger and to consider a solution that would also further his wider political ambitions.

It was in these circumstances that Jameson, Rhodes's lieutenant, mounted his ill-judged coup against the Transvaal in 1895. The Jameson Raid was a wild attempt, launched by 'men on the spot', to solve disputes arising on the 'turbulent frontier' of empire; but its significance extended far beyond the actions of local buccaneers. Rhodes undoubtedly used his royal charter and his position as Prime Minister of the Cape for his own complex purposes, which included dreams of re-annexing the United States as well as plans for painting the map red in Africa and adding hugely to his own business empire there.[87] Yet to confine the explanation of this episode to Jameson or even to Rhodes is to adopt an excessively narrow view of causation. Sections of the mining interest were heavily implicated too.[88] Firms such as Wernher Beit, which had made long-term investments in both deep and outcrop mining, saw a chance to install a regime that would settle their immediate grievances, deal with the problem of labour supply, and provide a political framework favourable to international investment. Successive British governments also played a considerable part in bringing about an event which they had not planned. In granting a royal charter to the British South Africa Company, the imperial government took a conscious risk: the hope was that the aristocrats on the board of directors, combined with Lord Rothschild's influence, would make Rhodes an obedient agent of empire, and a chance was taken on the consequences that might follow if Rhodes slipped the leash when his territorial instincts were aroused. Moreover, it is now clear that the British government, under Salisbury's direction, was tightening the screws on Kruger in 1894–5, and was coming round to the view, always ominous for the prey of empire, that the Transvaal was an anomaly which, in a properly ordered world, ought to be governed by Englishmen.[89] Chamberlain, the Colonial Secretary, may not have connived in the Raid, but he gave 'indirect private encouragement to the plotters',[90] who, since they had already been used to encircle the Transvaal, might reasonably have concluded that they were now being encouraged to go over the top.

The chain of causation thus stretches back to the metropole. British governments were not the tools of mining magnates, nor were British financiers keen to fund Rhodes's political ambitions. But their hands were in the pot. As the wealth of the Transvaal drew in British capital and trade, so Kruger's policies made it increasingly unlikely that indirect means would suffice to winch the Republic back into Britain's sphere of influence. The conditions developing in the mid-1890s were such as to encourage men of Jameson's stamp to put up schemes of the kind he in fact concocted. The temptation of a quick and cheap solution to the Transvaal 'problem' was not easily turned down, and the notion that a change of government would also be popular within the republic gave a quasi-liberal tinge to the venture. The conspirators themselves were only a small group, but there were others, in higher places, who were looking elsewhere when the Raid took place.

The failure of the Jameson Raid diminished Rhodes as a political force, and ultimately widened the gulf between Britain and the Transvaal. In the short run, however, it led to renewed efforts to control the republic by more peaceful means under the supervision of London. The Colonial Office continued to make use of the 'good offices' of the City, especially Rothschilds, and tried in particular to limit the Transvaal government's access to foreign capital.[91] In 1898, when Milner, the British High Commissioner, learned of the Transvaal's plans for raising money in Europe, he asked the Colonial Office, 'through the international influence of big financial houses in London, to make difficulties for the Transvaal government in borrowing money'. The Colonial Office, having consulted Lord Rothschild, replied that 'any loan could be stopped and would be in London and possibly in Paris, but we cannot influence the market in Holland or Germany'.[92] In the event, £2m. was raised, largely in Germany, where the City's writ did not run, and the Transvaal was able to stiffen its defences and its foreign policy. There was a possibility, too, that the mine-owners might strike a deal with the Transvaal which, in settling their complaints, would also enhance British influence. Kruger's response to this prospect was to set up an Industrial Commission in 1897; but his attempt to win over the mine-workers by criticising their employers, his incomplete implementation of the Commission's recommendations in 1898–9, and the Randlord's insistence on linking the industry's problems to wider political issues ensured that no reconciliation took place.[93] The final means of exercising indirect influence depended on the Trojan Horse containing the *uitlanders* (foreigners). Chamberlain and Milner quickly developed a commitment to these predominantly British settlers in the Transvaal, and pressed for an end to the economic and political discrimination which they suffered.[94] Their hope was that an enlarged electorate would provide a constituency for more liberal Boer political figures and would swing the Republic back into Britain's orbit. But Kruger could not extend the franchise far without risking political defeat, and his re-election in 1898 damaged Britain's plans for applying this essentially Gladstonian formula of voluntary and low-cost political reform.

The failure to control the Transvaal by informal means opened the door to the advocates of force. Foremost among these was Milner, whose short fuse was readily set alight, and whose impatience was quickly communicated to others. But this does not mean, as some scholars have argued, that the Boer War was caused primarily by Milner and his policies.[95] Although Milner helped to stir the pot, he did not supply the ingredients. More important agents were the imperial government and, indirectly, the mine-owners. Neither wanted war; both exerted the pressures that brought it about. The imperial government knowingly adopted a high-risk policy.[96] Salisbury and his Cabinet were not driven off course by the men on the spot. Although they did not want a costly war, they accepted the possibility of hostilities, they continued to apply pressure to Kruger, and they became more insistent after 1898, when the Anglo-German agreement removed the Transvaal's best chance of securing external support.[97] Britain's determined stance owed little to strategic considerations: by the 1890s her interests and ambitions in South Africa had far outgrown the requirements of a naval base, as Lord Selborne's memorandum, written from the Colonial Office in 1896, makes quite plain.[98] In any case, it was not necessary to go to war with the Transvaal in order to protect Simonstown, which was 800 miles to the south and not under any threat.[99] As for the randlords, they had been tempted by the prospect of a quick, cheap coup in 1895, but they also had good reason to stop short of war in 1899 because a major conflict would have interrupted output and damaged investment. Nevertheless, the mine-owners played their part in a dangerous game. They pressed their grievances against Kruger's government in 1899, generalised them to include political questions, and associated themselves with Milner to an extent that compromised the search for a peaceful settlement.

A full appreciation of the motives behind Britain's determination to go to war in 1899 requires a longer perspective than that provided by the events of the previous few years. What Carnarvon strove for in the 1870s, Salisbury, Chamberlain and Milner achieved, if at a high cost, twenty years later. Carnarvon himself had played a significant part in steering through parliament the British North America Act, which brought the Dominion of Canada into being. The Act of 1867 was the culmination of a highly successful strategy which aimed at keeping Canada within Britain's economic orbit for much longer than would otherwise have been possible, given the rising influence of the United States.[100] Carnarvon tried to apply the same formula to South Africa, and for the same reasons, namely that unity was thought to be a prerequisite of local prosperity, sound credit and political stability under British authority, and would add to the strength of the empire.

Selborne's influential memorandum of 1896 was based on the same assumptions. What had changed since Carnarvon's time was that the power and potential of the Transvaal had greatly expanded, and the prospect of a Canadian solution to Britain's problems in South Africa was now threatened by the emergence of a rival possibility: the creation of a 'United States of South Africa' under Afrikaner control.[101] This prospect not only stirred up uneasy memories of colonial revolt but also aroused anxieties about a weakening of Britain's economic and political influence in the world. Union under the imperial flag was intended to forestall such a calamity by bringing the aspirations of the Afrikaners under control in much the same way as the problem of the French settlers in Canada had been dealt with; that is, by winning their loyalty through the creation of prosperity and by giving them the opportunity to cooperate, politically as well as economically, in the imperial adventure. These wider considerations enabled British politicians to generalise the issues in dispute and to present them in terms of the national interest. In September 1899 Chamberlain could claim that 'What is now at stake is the position of Great Britain in South Africa – and with it the estimate formed of our power and influence in Colonies throughout the world'.[102] Comforted by their own propaganda, policy-makers discounted the opposition; at this point the drums began to roll.

Selective acquisitions: tropical Africa

Compared to the weight of Britain's interests in Egypt and southern Africa, tropical Africa was scarcely able to turn the scales. Despite its vast size, this region accounted for only a minute share of Britain's overseas trade and had very limited strategic significance. Nevertheless, Britain secured two large slices of west Africa, Nigeria and the Gold Coast, and a substantial chunk of east Africa, based on Kenya and stretching inland to include Uganda. If the partition of tropical Africa has long posed a problem for theorists of imperialism committed to the quest for 'surplus capital', it has also raised difficulties for those who have turned to alternative geopolitical explanations of empire-building. These dilemmas can be resolved, we suggest, once it is recognised that Britain was prepared to promote her interests in tropical Africa, but was constrained (as in the Middle East and China) by the extent to which private enterprise was willing to fund the maintenance or extension of British claims. Since the City took a generally unfavourable view of tropical Africa, advocates of a forward policy faced an uphill struggle, and large parts of the region were taken over by foreign rivals who had been denied more attractive opportunities elsewhere. In general, Britain enlarged her sphere of influence in areas where the value of existing trade indicated that expansion would be self-supporting, or where anticipated returns, combined with arguments about the national interest, enabled committed pressure groups to squeeze a limited measure of support from the 'Gladstonian garrison' in the Treasury.

Early expectations that the 'Bible and plough' would transform the societies and economies of west Africa were disappointed. 'Legitimate' commerce expanded after 1807, but the rate of growth was modest and was hampered in particular by the persistence of the overseas slave trade.[103] Moreover, Britain's political and cultural influence was confined to a handful of entrepôts, which provided indirect and very limited control over affairs in the interior.[104] After 1850, however, the pace of change quickened, and the value of west Africa's external trade doubled between 1865 and 1885 as a result of the elimination of the overseas slave trade, the advent of regular steamship services, and buoyant prices for 'legitimate' exports.[105] These developments were also accompanied by an increase in the volume of commercial capital tied up in goods and advances to local merchants. From the City's perspective, however, the region still deserved its zero credit-rating: African states were in no position to attract foreign capital, even if they wanted to; and private investment inland awaited firm evidence, which never materialised, of the existence of a tropical Klondike.

During the last quarter of the century, commercial expansion was checked by falling export prices and reduced rates of growth.[106] Although import prices fell too, the indications are that the (net barter) terms of trade moved against primary producers.[107] These trends, transmitted from the metropolitan centres of demand, squeezed profit margins on the periphery and sharpened commercial conflict between merchants and producers. The declining performance of the export sector needs also to be seen in a longer perspective of structural change which affected both production and distribution. The shift to 'legitimate' commerce encouraged the rise of small export producers, caused large producers to intensify the use of slave labour, and had far-reaching social and political repercussions within west Africa which have still to be fully explored.[108] However, it seems clear that the fall in export prices reduced the chances of an orderly commercial transition and provided material for the claim, made by Europeans on the coast, that Africans were incapable of 'running their own affairs'. The growing volume of trade after 1850 had important consequences for the distributive system because it increased the credit requirements of the export sector and generated a demand for improved harbours and expanded on-shore facilities, including railways, to reduce the cost and hence restore the profitability of west African trade.[109] Credit became an especially critical issue because of the existence of non-convertible currencies, such as cowries, which were rapidly depreciating in value, and because of the lack of acceptable forms of security, such as transferrable land.[110] The periodic dips in export performance in the last quarter of the century caused acute problems for European wholesalers who, in the absence of modern banks, were also the principal suppliers of commercial credit on the west coast.

Deteriorating conditions of trade intersected with international rivalries, sharpening tensions among the major powers and in turn being aggravated by them.[111] The French began to advance inland from Senegal in 1879 and stepped up their efforts to control the lower Niger in the early 1880s; the Germans laid claim to Togo and Cameroun in the mid-1880s.[112] These moves aroused both cupidity and anxiety among Britain's representatives in west Africa: the optimists began to propagate the idea that the interior was an area of vast and easily realised potential; the pessimists expressed fears that it would soon be absorbed into protectionist regimes which would discriminate against British trade and cut into the revenues supporting Britain's outposts on the coast.

As the evidence began to indicate that the grand experiment in 'legitimate' commerce was faltering and might even founder, merchants and officials on the west coast started to agitate for a more overt defence of Britain's position to fend off the encroachments of foreign rivals and to promote a new development drive which would carry the commercial revolution inland.[113] Successive British governments responded to these pressures in two ways: by trying to preserve a large free-trade zone in west Africa, and by annexing regions that were particularly important for British commerce.

The threat to free trade had to be taken seriously because Britain was west Africa's principal foreign trading partner and consequently had interests throughout the region. Moreover, as we have seen in other parts of the world, Britain had a general interest in maintaining the open door because she had a powerful stake in preserving the pattern of multilateral settlements that underpinned her own position as the world's largest international trader and supplier of capital. In west Africa, as with the Congo, Portuguese Africa and south-west Africa, the Foreign Office was concerned less with sovereignty than with access: if foreign rivals could be persuaded not to discriminate against British goods and capital, then Britain's interests could be upheld without the burdens of territorial responsibility.[114] In pursuit of this goal, the Foreign Office embarked on a campaign of perpetual negotiation to secure agreements on tariffs and, by association, on boundaries too.[115] This strategy was hampered because the resources available for diplomacy were limited. No counterpart to the Hongkong and Shanghai Bank stood alongside the Foreign Office in tropical Africa because, in contrast to China, indigenous states in the west and east of the continent were unable to fund sizeable foreign loans. Nevertheless, Britain's negotiators achieved impressive results: a series of agreements, beginning in 1882 and culminating in the Anglo-French settlement of 1898, went a long way towards preserving an open door to west Africa, principally by limiting the extension of the discriminatory system in force in Senegal.

In the areas that were to become the colonies of Nigeria and the Gold Coast, the balance of costs and returns appeared to justify a more vigorous policy. On the lower Niger there were indications that mercantile enterprise could become self-supporting. Goldie's United African Company, formed in 1879, had engaged the French firms in economic warfare and had emerged victorious in 1885.[116] With its London base and its complement of aristocrats and reputable financiers, the National African Company, as it had (significantly) become in 1882, was an acceptable candidate for an official charter.[117] It duly became the Royal Niger Company in 1886, and was granted extensive commercial rights in exchange for repelling further French incursions.[118] In Lagos, Governor Carter was allowed to mount an expedition into Yorubaland in 1892, following considerable mercantile pressure and after agreement had been reached to pay for the campaign by raising import duties.[119] When Joseph Chamberlain became Colonial Secretary in 1895, a firmer line was taken towards reserving the remaining areas of British interest. Britain's new frontiersmen, coordinated by what Lugard called the 'Birmingham Screw Policy', subdued the Asante in the central region of the Gold Coast and took hold of northern Nigeria, thus pushing the French into the 'lighter soils' of the desert edge.[120] Beyond this point, however, Chamberlain's plans for cultivating his 'undeveloped estates' had only limited success. The advocates of subsidised development in the tropics were no match for the defenders of fiscal orthodoxy in the Treasury.[121] Chamberlain's defeat on this question, as on the larger issue of tariff reform, confirmed the supremacy of the principles of free trade and sound money and made clear to assailants the high price that would be exacted for attacking them.

British policy towards east Africa was broadly similar to that applied to the west coast, though in the eastern part of the continent the development of 'legitimate' commerce occurred later and was on a much smaller scale. The aspirations, however, were much the same: the Foreign Office identified a promising entrepôt and agent in Zanzibar and its sultan, imposed anti-slave-trade treaties in 1839 and 1845, and stood back to observe the anticipated expansion of 'legitimate' commerce. Both the principal exports, ivory and cloves, responded to the growth of external demand, but neither was capable of serving as the basis of long-term export development. Ivory depended upon essentially finite resources, which began to decline from the mid-1870s, while the production of cloves was confined to coastal estates which continued to employ slave labour.[122] As in the case of the west coast, abolitionist measures initially weakened or diverted the slave trade without destroying it, and caused serious discontent among slave-holders and traders.[123] One result was a political crisis in Zanzibar which drew in British intervention in 1859–61 but left the problem of reconstructing the export economy unresolved. With the completion of the Suez Canal in 1869 and the advent of the steamship, the pressure for change began to quicken. The prospect of 'opening up' the east coast attracted entrepreneurs who saw the potential of improved communication with Europe and of closer integration with the Indian Ocean economy. It also helped to revitalise the abolitionist movement by stimulating both the navy and the missions, and it merged with the activities of explorers to contribute to the 'Afromania' which infected influential segments of public opinion during the period of the scramble.[124]

This renewed effort to pull east Africa into line with British policy was signalled by the appointment of Sir John Kirk as Consul-General and Political Agent at Zanzibar in 1873. It has long been known that Kirk made a determined effort to use the Sultanate as an instrument of British policy by securing a new treaty abolishing the slave trade and by backing it with naval and military force.[125] What has only recently been revealed, however, is the extent to which the growing assertiveness of official policy was both matched and influenced by the attitude of private interests.

One important source of support for an expansionist policy came from southern Africa, where the mining firms were quick to see a possible connection between ending the east African slave trade and developing a flow of cheap labour for the mines.[126] In the 1870s, Frederick Elton, a former Indian Army officer who was involved in diamond-mining with one of Rhodes's brothers, made himself a powerful advocate of the need to advance 'commerce and civilisation' in east Africa. Elton was used as an unofficial consultant to the Foreign Office on central and east African affairs, became Britain's Consul in Mozambique in 1875, and lent strong support to Carnarvon's drive for a south African confederation in the late 1870s.

A second connection was with British shipping and mercantile interests in India, and particularly with William Mackinnon, who founded the British and India Steam Navigation Company in 1862 and had substantial commercial interests in the firm of Smith, Mackenzie.[127] Mackinnon recognised the implications of the opening of the Suez Canal and moved swiftly to secure prime positions in east Africa, linking Aden and Zanzibar by steamer in 1872 and extending his trading activities to Zanzibar shortly afterwards. Mackinnon had close ties with Elton and also with the governor of the Cape, Sir Bartle Frere, both of whom supported his schemes for controlling the shipping lanes of the east coast, and he was intimately associated, too, with the Church of Scotland mission in Livingstonia. Mackinnon, however, was much more than a sub-imperialist on the margins of empire. His close associates in Britain included James Hutton, the wealthy and politically active Manchester businessman who had a particular interest in tropical Africa, and the Duke of Sutherland, an enthusiast who was prepared to cover the world with railway lines, and sometimes to finance them. Moreover, in the mid-1870s Mackinnon himself moved his headquarters from Glasgow to London because he wanted to have better access to the City's commercial services and to the higher circles of political influence.[128] Mackinnon provides a good example of a particular type of business imperialist who was emerging in the second half of the nineteenth century as a result of the extension abroad of the new service sector: he supported free trade but also relied on imperial contracts and subsidies; he stood for private enterprise but also bent the arm of government when he could; he pursued profit but also invested in philanthropy and placed them both under the banner of an onward-marching Christianity.

It is now evident that there was a vocal and growing lobby of private and official interests pushing an expansionist policy in east Africa from the 1870s onwards.[129] In 1877 Mackinnon declared himself ready to take on the administration of the whole region from the coast to Lake Victoria; in 1884 Harry Johnston, a young proconsul in the making, wrote lyrical, almost chimerical, reports on the region, extolling its market potential, its unfathomed resources, and its suitability for European settlement; more important still, by 1884 the Foreign Office was making quantitative assessments of cast Africa's commercial potential, and had also persuaded itself that the indigenous population would welcome the establishment of good government – a sure sign that the Titans of officialdom were preparing to accept yet another burden. But, if interest in east Africa was more economic than strategic, it was also largely speculative.[130] Britain's commercial stake there was minuscule, even compared to west Africa, and there was little financial interest beyond that involved in foreign trade. Advocates of expansion spoke of a new India and a new Australia, but the City's scepticism and the Treasury's opposition combined to prevent this Atlantis from materialising.

As in the case of west Africa, the aims of the commercial lobby were helped along by the actions of foreign rivals. In 1885, when Germany declared protectorates over a region which included some of the principal trade routes to Zanzibar, the opponents of British expansion could no longer rely on traditional arguments for nonintervention.[131] In the following year, an agreement was reached with Germany which divided the hinterland of Zanzibar between the two powers (largely at the sultan's expense), preserved the principle of free trade in both spheres, and allocated the northern section (later to become Kenya) to Britain. Mackinnon and his associates did not gain all they wanted, but they did secure the area which was thought to have the greatest potential.[132] In a further agreement, reached in 1890, Germany effectively recognised Britain's paramount position in east Africa in exchange for Heligoland, an island in the North Sea which, in the eyes of the Foreign Office, was even less valuable than tropical Africa.[133]

The administration of this huge territory was assigned to a new chartered company, the Imperial British East Africa Company, which was formed by Mackinnon in 1888.[134] Mackinnon's company extended its domain inland in the hope of annexing the fabled (and indeed mythical) wealth of the interior, headed off German expansion, and laid claim to Uganda; but it failed to draw in either capital or settlers, and by 1890 was virtually bankrupt. When Mackinnon appealed for a financial guarantee to build a railway from Mombasa to Lake Victoria, parliament turned the proposal down, and in 1892 the company threatened to withdraw from Uganda unless it received a subsidy to cover its administrative overheads. This was a threat that Gladstone in particular welcomed, but the Prime Minister was again out-manoeuvred, as he had been in the case of Egypt, by the forward party in the Cabinet, this time led by the Foreign Secretary, Rosebery, who dusted off and deployed much the same arguments as Hartington and his associates had used in 1882.[135] In this case, 'anarchy' in the interior was linked not only (and improbably) to the claim that Uganda was strategically important to Egypt, but also to the alleged revival of the slave trade and the danger to Christian missions in the region. The press responded, public opinion was aroused, and the government appointed a commissioner to recommend a solution.[136] The Commissioner, Sir Gerald Portal, was Consul-General in Zanzibar and was therefore familiar with the issues. He had two other qualities: he was an ambitious imperialist who saw himself running a 'vast equatorial empire' and he was Rosebery's nominee.[137] The result, in the words of another well-placed imperialist, was 'a foregone conclusion'.[138] Uganda became a British protectorate in 1894, and Mackinnon's much-prized and hugely expensive railway followed soon afterwards, with some assistance from Joseph Chamberlain. Mackinnon's ambition had given Britain a stake in Uganda; Rosebery's ensured that it was firmly planted. It was left to others to try to create a viable unit out of what some contemporaries had already characterised as being a white elephant.[139]

From partition to paramountcy

From the perspective of this study, there is an argument to be made for reducing the attention customarily paid to the partition of Africa because the importance of the continent, as measured by trade and financial flows, did not give it a high ranking among Britain's international trading partners or even among regions that felt the force of her imperialist ambitions. Moreover, Africa was not a single state with one central government but a continent with numerous very different states, and this presents a problem of categorisation that is either not found or is far less prominent in the other cases we have considered. This degree of diversity suggests that it might be illuminating to repartition the literature on the scramble, so that Egypt is considered with the Ottoman Empire, southern Africa with regions of white settlement (including Latin America), west Africa with other tropical export economies, and east Africa with the expanding Indian Ocean complex. However, given that partition has been treated for so long as a subject with continental boundaries and is so firmly entrenched in the literature as the classic case of late-nineteenth-century imperialism, there are compelling historiographical reasons why we have situated our own interpretation in the context of the existing literature, and have tried to provide an adequate, if compressed, account of the voluminous research which the subject has generated.

By 1900, when the dust of partition had settled, it could be seen that Britain had secured the most valuable parts of Africa and had also preserved access to large parts of the continent that were not under her direct control. This outcome is not immediately apparent from the map of Africa, which shows that large areas were allocated to other colonial powers; but size is a poor measure of value, and there is no doubt that the continent's trade and finance were concentrated overwhelmingly on British territories, and remained so during the colonial era.[140] Moreover, Britain achieved considerable success in preserving access to regions which fell under foreign control: Belgium, Portugal, Germany and even France were all bound, albeit in different ways, to preserve elements of the open door in their African colonies.

Agreements to maintain free trade, though qualified in a number of respects, fitted the needs of Britain's system of multilateral payments and enabled her finance to flow readily over foreign boundaries.[141] This point deserves emphasis because it is commonly underestimated in studies of partition which are concerned, understandably but also incompletely, with the formal division of territory.

Britain's success is not readily explained by the existing historiography, despite its richness and refinement, because it remains tied too closely to the arguments mobilised by contemporary observers – often for a moral or political purpose.[142] Current interpretations either fasten a misleading stereotype of capitalist development on to Africa or assign too much weight to other parties, whether foreign rivals or proto-nationalists. Just as there are well-known difficulties in finding 'surplus' capital and conspiracies of bond-holders, so there are equally serious problems with the currently influential view that Britain was an ageing, defensive power struggling to fend off new challenges to her dominance. France and Germany complicated Britain's pursuit of her interests, but were not the main cause of her actions, and their chief influence was felt in tropical Africa, at the margins of Britain's principal areas of involvement. Strategic arguments have also been greatly overestimated. They were used mainly as a legitimation for action in Egypt and east Africa, were largely irrelevant in south Africa, and were non-existent on the west coast. As for proto-nationalism, while it is undeniable that there were numerous crises on the African frontier during the period of partition, an examination of their origins indicates that their prime cause lay in Europe rather than on the periphery.

This does not mean that we are obliged to fall back on the argument that partition was 'a remarkable freak' in the annals of imperialism.[143] The central fact which needs to be explained is that Britain began and ended partition as the dominant foreign power in Africa. To assume that she was ageing, declining and retreating is unhelpful; to invoke the flexible laws of chance is to abandon the possibility of providing a systematic account of a momentous historical event. The interpretation advanced here suggests that Britain had independent reasons for taking action to increase her grip on Africa. The impulses motivating policy can be traced to the metropole, and particularly to the expansion after 1850 of the gentlemanly occupations and values we have identified. Indeed, Britain's actions in partitioning Africa followed the contours of this development: the main weight of her interests lay in Egypt and southern Africa, where City and service interests were most prominently represented, and it was there that Britain showed the greatest vigour in promoting her claims.

The occupation of Egypt was closely linked to restoring the health of public finance. The course of treatment was connected, in turn, to the internal politics of the Liberal Party, through which it was generalised as an issue of principle and elevated to the status of a national interest. The occupation of southern Africa was also a result of Britain's growing stake in the region, where her investments had risen substantially following the discovery of minerals. But the Anglo-Boer War was not fought at the behest of the mine-owners any more than it was fought to secure a naval base or to realise the dreams of an ambitious proconsul. The decision was made because Britain was an expanding power which sought to create in Africa a dynamic economic and political satellite of the kind already in evidence in Australia, Canada, New Zealand and, it should be added, Argentina. Kruger's plans for achieving greater political independence cut across the trajectory of British policy by threatening to confine Britain's influence to the Cape and by perpetuating uncertainties about the long-term future of the mining industry. Whether war was necessary to achieve Britain's purpose, or was even desired by those who were responsible for bringing it about, are questions that this study can put to one side. But it is hard to imagine that Britain would have involved herself to the point where war became inevitable had the Transvaal been devoid of resources; and it is worth observing that Lord Salisbury was quite content to leave the French to federate vast areas of desert and savanna in west Africa.

In tropical Africa the shortage of investment limited Britain's presence and handicapped her diplomacy, in much the same way as it did in Persia. In the absence of a powerful City interest, the Foreign Office had to rely on chartered companies, which in turn required subsidies (in the shape of commercial rights and guarantees) in exchange for political services. Organisations such as the Royal Niger Company and the Imperial British East Africa Company represented gentlemanly capitalist interests in a dilute form. In these circumstances, they acted in association with or alongside other mercantile and shipping interests, and with the missions, to a greater extent than was usual elsewhere. In west Africa, mercantile pressure groups also joined with British Chambers of Commerce representing manufacturers who were keen to preserve markets for their goods. But this example is an exception that proves the rule: policy in Britain's principal spheres of interest throughout the world was not made by the manufacturing lobby and was influenced by it only to a limited extent. Even in west Africa, manufacturing interests made headway only because their demands were consistent with free trade and, in general, with principles of sound finance.[144] This loose coalition of pressure groups nevertheless managed to secure a substantial part of its demands, principally because the financial and diplomatic cost of acceding to them was very limited. The commercially attractive parts of west Africa were retained, and the most promising parts of east Africa were marked out for future use. Even when only half exerting herself, Britain was still able to outdistance her new foreign competitors.

In retrospect, we can now see that the problem was not that Britain's informal empire had broken down but that it had never come into being except, for an illusory moment, in Egypt. Elsewhere, political alliances were transitory where they were not abortive: sultans and chiefs were too often weak reeds; the Boers were too strong to be bent. The difficulty was rather that the rapidity of economic change affecting Africa after 1850 outpaced the rate of institutional adjustment needed to support it. The old staple industries may have begun to seek refuge in tropical markets, but the dynamic and highly competitive sector of the economy in London and the south-east was pushing back new frontiers at an unsettling speed. Viewed from this perspective, Britain was an advancing not a retreating power. It was not the arteries that hardened but the pulse that quickened. None of this meant that

Britain was bent on annexation, but it did mean that attempts to exert influence and to ensure that small states were 'well kept' and 'always accessible' were more likely to create conditions which placed annexation on the agenda. Men like Colvin, Rhodes, Goldie and Mackinnon undoubtedly made sure that it stayed there. Nevertheless, the crucial decisions were taken in London. Salisbury, Hartington, Rosebery and Chamberlain knew what they were doing even if they did not always entirely approve of their own actions or control all of the consequences. Accidents did indeed occur during the partition of Africa, but they can be understood only in the context of an event that was not, in itself, accidental.

The causes of actions must not be inferred from their consequences; at the same time, it is surely not fanciful to see, in the colonial settlement, the resolution of the problems which had led to partition. In Egypt, Baring's tax-gathering efficiency and rigorous control of expenditure balanced the budget and encouraged renewed flows of foreign capital from the 1890s onwards.[145] In South Africa, the period of post-war reconstruction witnessed the abolition of the most contentious of the Transvaal's monopolies, the implementation of measures to improve the supply of labour to the mines, and the accommodation of mining and political interests.[146] Carnarvon's long-sought confederation was achieved by an act of reconciliation that was dazzling and economical, even if it was not magnanimous: the Transvaal was granted self-government in 1906, and the management of the Union of South Africa was entrusted to a predominantly Afrikaner leadership in 1910.[147] In west Africa, the creation of new colonial states and the revival of international trade after 1900 provided the tax basis for raising foreign loans and accelerated the process of export-led growth. In east Africa, house-breaking also gave way to house-keeping, though in this case the City's judgement proved to be correct: there was some potential and more big game, but also white elephants to be preserved.

Notes

1 The quotation is from the Earl of Cromer (Evelyn Baring), Ancient and Modern Imperialism (1910), pp. 19–20. This study, which draws on Baring's long experience in Egypt, deploys many of the ideas which today are associated with modern studies of the 'official mind' of imperialism.

2 The fullest and most recent survey is R.A. Oliver and G.N. Sanderson, eds. *The Cambridge History of Africa,* Vol. 6, *1870–1905* (Cambridge, 1985). See in particular the important contributions by Sanderson, Hargreaves, Marks, and Lonsdale, and the extensive bibliographical essay.

3 See, for example, the interesting essay by Catherine Coquery-Vidrovitch, 'De l'impérialisme britannique à l'impérialisme contemporain: l'atavar colonial', in Jean Bouvier and René Girault, eds. *L'impérialisme français d'avant 1914* (Paris, 1976).

4 Ronald Robinson and John Gallagher with Alice Denny, *Africa and the Victorians: The Official Mind of Imperialism* (1961; 2nd edn 1981).

5 Fisher's widely quoted phrase has come to stand for a form of liberal individualism in historical writing and in opposition to the 'scientific' history written by Toynbee and others. See H.A.L. Fisher, A *History of Europe* (1936), p. v.

6 The substantial revisionist literature on this subject can be followed through Barbara L. Solow and Stanley L. Engerman, eds. *British Capitalism and Caribbean Slavery* (Cambridge,

1987); and David Eltis, *Economic Growth and the Ending of the Transatlantic Slave Trade* (Oxford, 1987).

7 J. Gallagher, 'Fowell Buxton and the New African Policy, 1838–1842', *Cambridge Hist. Jour.*, 10 (1950) is the starting point for what is now a substantial literature on this theme.

8 For this aspect of European perceptions of Africa see A.G. Hopkins, 'Of Africa and Golden Joys', *Genève-Afrique,* 23 (1985).

9 Stanley Trapido, 'From Paternalism to Liberalism: the Cape Colony, 1800–1834', *Internat. Hist. Rev.*, 12 (1990).

10 James Sturgis, 'Anglicisation at the Cape of Good Hope in the Early Nineteenth Century', *Jour. Imp. and Comm. Hist.*, XI (1982).

11 Robert Ross, 'The Relative Importance of Exports and the Internal Market for the Agriculture of the Cape Colony, 1770–1855', in G. Liesegang, H. Pasch and A. Jones, eds. *Figuring African Trade* (Berlin, 1986). The local currency, the Rixdollar, was tied to sterling from 1827. The 'rising gentry' also used coerced labour, as Clifton Crais has shown: 'Gentry and Labour in Three Eastern Cape Districts, 1820–1865', *South Afr. Hist. Jour.*, 18 (1986).

12 A.G. Hopkins, *An Economic History of West Africa* (1973; 1988), Ch. 4.

13 Quoted in M.E. Chamberlain, *The Scramble for Africa* (1974), p. 36.

14 E.R.J. Owen, *Cotton and the Egyptian Economy, 1820–1914* (Oxford, 1969).

15 E.A. Alpers, *Ivory and Slaves in East Central Africa* (1975); Abdul Sheriff, *Slaves, Spices and Ivory in Zanzibar: Integration of an East African Commercial Empire in the World Economy, 1770–1873* (1987).

16 See, for example, Paul O. Lovejoy, 'The Characteristics of Plantations in the Sokoto Caliphate (Islamic West Africa)', *Am. Hist. Rev.*, 84 (1979); Frederick Cooper, *Plantation Slavery on the East Coast of Africa* (New Haven, Conn., 1977), and Robert Ross, *Cape of Torments* (1983).

17 The causes of 'turbulence' on the frontier during this period have been the subject of important recent research. See, for example, J.B. Peires, *The House of Phalo* (Johannesburg, 1981), and Timothy Keegan, 'Dispossession and Accumulation in the South African Interior: the Boers and Tlhaping of Bethulie, 1833–61', *Jour. African Hist.*, XXVIII (1987). The phrase itself derives from John S. Galbraith's pioneering essay, 'The "Turbulent Frontier" as a Factor in British Expansion', *Comparative Studies in Society and History,* 11 (1960).

18 Most famously in the case of the Niger expedition. See C.C. Ifemesia, 'The "Civilising Mission" of 1841', *Jour. Hist. Soc. Nigeria,* 2 (1962).

19 The disillusion of the time is well captured by John S. Galbraith, *Reluctant Empire: British Policy on the South African Frontier, 1834–54* (1963). Problems of quantifying African trade during this period are discussed in Liesegang, Pasch, and Jones, *Figuring African Trade.*

20 A very similar sequence characterised the development drive which followed World War II.

21 A.G. Hopkins, 'Imperial Business in Africa, Part II: Interpretations', *Jour. African Hist.*, 18 (1976); S.D. Chapman, 'British-Based Investment Groups Before 1914', *Econ. Hist. Rev.*, 2nd ser. XXXVIII (1985), and the discussion in ibid. XL (1987).

22 Rhodes's mixture of hard-headedness and fantasy is well known, but see, too, D.J.M. Muffett, *Empire Builder Extraordinary: Sir George Goldie and His Philosophy of Government and Empire* (Douglas, I.o.M., 1978).

23 Alfred Jones, whose companies controlled British shipping to West Africa was less interested in high society. But he recognised the need to represent his interests in London and he was prepared (exceptionally) to cut his profit to secure a knighthood. See P.N. Davies, *Sir Alfred Jones: Shipping Entrepreneur Par Excellence* (1978), pp. 69–70.

24 A neat and little known example is provided by Frederick Stow, one of the founders of De Beers, who retired to Sussex and became a landed gentleman and supporter of the local hunt, though he also maintained his interest in the 'white man's cause' in South Africa.

See Rob Turrell, 'Sir Frederick Philipson Stow: The Unknown Diamond Magnate', *Bus. Hist.*, 28 (1986).

25 On this subject see the important article by Roy C. Bridges, 'The Historical Role of British Explorers in East Africa', *Terrae Incognitae,* 14 (1982).

26 Lois A.C. Raphael, *The Cape to Cairo Dream: A Study in British Imperialism* (New York, 1936), pp. 69–70.

27 On the changing mood of the missions see Andrew Porter. 'Cambridge, Keswick and Late Nineteenth-Century Attitudes to Africa', *Jour. Imp. and Comm. Hist.* V (1976); and idem, 'Evangelical Enthusiasm, Missionary Motivation and West Africa in the Late Nineteenth Century: the Career of G.W. Brooke', ibid. 6 (1977).

28 W.G. Hynes, *The Economics of Empire: Britain, Africa, and the New Imperialism, 1870–95* (1979). The authoritative account of Manchester's difficulties at this time is D.A. Farnie, *The English Cotton Industry and the World Market, 1815–1896* (Oxford, 1976), Ch. 5.

29 See Leisegang, Pasch and Jones, *Figuring African Trade.*

30 Ralph A. Austen, *African Economic History: Internal Development and External Dependency* (1987), pp. 277–80.

31 Colin Newbury, 'On the Margins of Empire: the Trade of Western Africa, 1875–1890', in Stig Forster, Wolfgang Mommsen and Ronald Robinson, eds. *Bismarck, Europe and Africa* (Oxford, 1988), pp. 41, 49.

32 Newbury, 'On the Margins', p. 50.

33 An illuminating (and probably chastening) historiographical study of the application of national traditions to international history could be written on this subject.

34 The interpretation which follows is based on A.G. Hopkins, 'The Victorians and Africa: a Reconsideration of the Occupation of Egypt, 1882', *Jour. African Hist.,* 27 (1986), and the references given there. The account presented here makes use of some additional sources, and has also benefited from advice generously offered by Profs. G.N. Sanderson and Juan Cole.

35 Set out in Chapter 4 and followed in subsequent chapters.

36 See, for example, Cromer, *Ancient and Modern Imperialism.*

37 E.R.J. Owen, *Cotton and the Egyptian Economy, 1820–1814* (Oxford, 1969).

38 See, for example, Fred H. Lawson, 'Economic and Social Foundations of Egyptian Expansionism: the Invasion of Syria in 1831', *Internat. Hist. Rev.,* 10 (1988).

39 Michael J. Reimer, 'Colonial Bridgehead: Social and Spatial Change in Alexandria, 1850–1882', *Int. Jour. Middle East Stud.,* 20 (1988).

40 Hopkins, 'The Victorians and Africa', p. 379.

41 On default see Roger Owen, *The Middle East in the World Economy, 1800–1914* (1981), pp. 122–8; and D.S. Landes, *Bankers and Pashas: International Finance and Economic Imperialism in Egypt* (1958), Chs. 1–2.

42 This point has been firmly established by D.C.M. Platt, *Finance, Trade and Politics in British Foreign Policy, 1815–1914* (Oxford, 1968), pp. 154–80. In the case of Egypt, investors overestimated both the number of years of uninterrupted debt service available to them and the extent of the losses that would follow from default. See Gershon Feder and Richard Just, 'Debt Crisis in an Increasingly Pessimistic International Market: the Case of Egyptian Credit, 1862–1876', *Econ. Jour.,* 94 (1984).

43 Hopkins, 'The Victorians and Africa', pp. 379–83.

44 Intellectual permissiveness had already been justified, as Joseph H. Udelson's neglected study has shown: 'Britain, Russophobia and the Egyptian Question of 1882: a Study in the Philosophy of History and Linguistics', (Ph.D. thesis Vanderbilt University, 1975), pp. 326, 330, 482–4, 659 and Ch. 4.

45 H.C.G. Matthew, ed. *The Gladstone Diaries,* Vols. X and XI, *January 1881–December 1886* (Oxford, 1990), pp. lxxii. Gladstone wisely sold some of his stock in 1884, when prices had recovered.

46 M.E. Chamberlain, 'Sir Charles Dilke and the British Intervention in Egypt in 1882: Decision-Making in a Nineteenth-Century Cabinet', *Brit. Jour. Internat. Stud.,* 11 (1976).

47 B.R. Johns, 'Business Investment and Imperialism: the Relationship Between Economic Interest and the Growth of British Intervention in Egypt, 1838–82' (Ph.D. thesis, Exeter University, 1981), pp. 75–92, 107, 215, 281–2.
48 W.S. Blunt, *A Secret History of the British Occupation of Egypt* (1907: 1969), pp. 240, 294–5; Paul F. Meszaros, 'The Corporation of Foreign Bondholders and British Diplomacy in Egypt, 1876–1882', (Ph.D. thesis, Loyola University, 1973), Ch. 5; Johns, 'Business investment', pp. 329, 376–7.
49 Johns, 'Business Investment', pp. 250–54.
50 Blunt, *A Secret History,* pp. 221–2.
51 Quoted in John S. Galbraith and Afaf Lufti al-Sayyid-Marsot, 'The British Occupation of Egypt: Another View', *Int. Jour. Middle East Stud.,* 9 (1978), p. 478.
52 Chamberlain, 'Sir Charles Dilke', pp. 238–9.
53 Alfred Milner, *England in Egypt* (5th edn, 1894), p. 416.
54 See the evidence cited in Hopkins, 'The Victorians and Africa', pp. 373–9.
55 See Juan R.I. Cole, 'Of Crowds and Empires: Afro-Asian Riots and European Expansion, 1857–1882', *Comp. Stud. in Soc. and Hist.,* 31 (1989).
56 Matthew, *The Gladstone Diaries,* p. lxxvi.
57 Ibid. p. lxx; Udelson, 'Britain, Russophobia', p. 579. Lord Randolph Churchill's opinion, expressed in 1884, was that 'the Suez Canal was at no time in the smallest danger'. Quoted in Chamberlain, *Scramble for Africa,* p. 114.
58 See G.N. Sanderson, *England, Europe, and the Upper Nile, 1882–1899* (Edinburgh, 1965); Robert O. Collins, *King Leopold, England and the Upper Nile, 1899–1909* (New Haven, Conn., 1968); idem, *Land Beyond the Rivers: The Southern Sudan, 1898–1918* (New Haven, Conn., 1971). An illuminating example of recent research is Yitzhak Nakesh, 'Fiscal and Monetary Systems in the Mahdist Sudan, 1881–1898', *Int. Jour. Middle East Stud.,* 20 (1988).
59 See Iain R. Smith, *The Origins of the South African War, 1899–1902* (London, 1996). See also his overview: 'The Origins of the South African War (1899–1902): a Reappraisal', *South African Historical Journal,* 22 (1990). See, too, Shula Marks, 'Scrambling for South Africa', *Jour. African Hist.,* 23 (1982), and idem, in Oliver and Sanderson, *The Cambridge History of Africa,* Vol. 6, Chs. 7–8.
60 The spread of 'legitimate' commerce in southern Africa is dealt with by Malyn Newitt, 'Economic Penetration and the Scramble for Southern Africa', in Peter Morris, ed. *Africa, America and Central Asia: Formal and Informal Empire in the Nineteenth Century* (Exeter, 1984). See also A.G. Hopkins, 'Imperial Business in Africa, Part II: Interpretations', *Jour. African Hist.,* 18 (1976); and on specific themes Andrew Porter, *Victorian Shipping. Business and Imperial Policy: Donald Currie, the Castle Line and Southern Africa* (Woodbridge, 1986), and V.E. Solomon, 'Money and Banking', in F.L. Coleman, ed. *Economic History of South Africa* (Pretoria, 1983), pp. 141–2.
61 D.A. Farnie, *East and West of Suez: The Suez Canal in History, 1854–1856* (Oxford, 1969), pp. 293–4, 334, 455.
62 The antecedents are dealt with by Basil A. Le Cordeur, *The Politics of Eastern Cape Separatism, 1820–1854* (Cape Town, 1981).
63 Only a selection of recent important work can be cited here: William Beinart, *The Political Economy of Pondoland, 1860–1930* (Cambridge, 1982); Philip Bonner, *Kings, Commoners and Concessionaires: The Evolution and Dissolution of the Nineteenth-Century Swazi State* (Cambridge, 1983); Colin Bundy, *The Rise and Fall of a South African Peasantry* (1979); Peter Delius, *The Land Belongs to Us: The Pedi Polity, the Boers and the British in the Nineteenth-Century Transvaal* (1984).
64 C. Van Onselen, 'Reactions to Rinderpest in Southern Africa, 1896–7', *Jour. African Hist.,* 13 (1972); Charles Ballard, 'The Repercussions of Rinderpest: Cattle, Plague and Peasant Decline in Colonial Natal', *Int. Jour. African Hist. Stud.,* 19 (1986).

65 These developments are discussed in important contributions by Hermann Giliomee, 'The Beginnings of Afrikaner Nationalism, 1870–1915', *South Afr. Hist. Jour.*, 19 (1986), and idem, 'Western Cape Farmers and the Beginnings of Afrikaner Nationalism, 1870–1915', *Jour. Southern African Stud.*, 14 (1987). See also Arthur Webb, 'Early Capitalism in the Cape: the Eastern Province Bank, 1839–73', in Stuart Jones, ed. *Banking and Business in South Africa* (New York, 1988).

66 Peter Richardson, 'The Natal Sugar Industry, 1849–1905: an Interpretative Essay', *Jour. African Hist.*, 23 (1982), pp. 522–6; Ritchie Ovendale, 'Profit or Patriotism: Natal, The Transvaal and the Coming of the Second Anglo-Boer War', *Jour. Imp. and Comm. Hist.*, VIII (1980).

67 Andrew Porter, 'Britain, the Cape Colony, and Natal, 1870–1914: Capital, Shipping and the Colonial Connexion', *Econ. Hist. Rev.*, 2nd ser. XXXIV (1981).

68 The historical significance of Carnarvon's plan has been emphasised by Norman Etherington, 'Labour Supply and the Genesis of South African Confederation in the 1870s', *Jour. African Hist.*, 20 (1979). See also R.L. Cope's important contributions: 'Strategic and Socio-Economic Explanations for Carnarvon's South African Confederation Policy: the Historiography and the Evidence', *History in Africa,* 13 (1986), and 'The Sources of Lord Carnavon's South African Confederation Policy', *Int. Jour. African Hist. Stud.*, 20 (1987). An additional dimension is revealed by John Wright and Andrew Manson, *The Hlubi Chiefdom in Zululand-Natal* (Ladysmith, 1983).

Henry Herbert (1831–90), the 4th Earl of Carnarvon, was educated at Eton and Oxford and held posts in every Conservative government between 1858 and 1886, including the office of Colonial Secretary in 1886–87. Carnarvon was a Tory grandee dedicated to maintaining his estates (amounting to nearly 36,000 acres), to securing the future of his dynasty, and to the survival of the great landowners in an era of free trade and increasingly democratic politics. As an aristocrat and a gentleman, he believed that the 'duties of property' were linked to the 'right to rule'. The agricultural depression caused him to channel funds into securities and land in the colonies from the late 1870s. His son, the 5th earl, married a daughter of Alfred de Rothschild in 1895, principally 'to induce solvency'. See A. Adonis, 'The Survival of the Great Estates: Henry, 4th Earl of Carnarvon and his Dispositions in the 1880s', *Hist. Research,* 64 (1991).

69 Norman Etherington, 'Frederick Elton and the South African Factor in the Making of Britain's East African Empire', *Jour. Imp. and Comm. Hist.*, IX (1980).

70 Exactly how much independence was restored was to become a matter of dispute: Britain subsequently claimed that the Transvaal was independent in internal but not external affairs. See D.M. Schreuder, *Gladstone and Kruger: Liberal Government and Colonial Home Rule, 1880–85* (1969).

71 The best single guide to this vast subject is Peter Richardson and Jean Jacques Van-Helten, 'The Gold Mining Industry in the Transvaal, 1886–99', in Peter Warwick, ed. *The South African War: The Anglo-Boer War, 1899–1902* (1980).

72 Jean Jacques Van-Helten, 'Empire and High Finance: South Africa and the International Gold Standard, 1890–1914', *Jour. African Hist.*, 23 (1983), p. 536; Peter Richardson and Jean Jacques Van-Helten, 'The Development of the South African Gold Mining Industry, 1895–1918', *Econ. Hist. Rev.*, 2nd ser. XXXVII (1984), p. 19.

73 R.V. Kubicek, *Economic Imperialism in Theory and Practice: The Case of South African Gold Mining Finance, 1886–1914* (Durham, NC, 1979); Van-Helten, 'Empire and High Finance', p. 539; Richardson and Van-Helten, 'Development of the South African Gold Mining Industry', pp. 21–2.

74 Jean Jacques Van-Helten, 'German Capital, the Netherlands Railway Company and the Political Economy of the Transvaal, 1886–1900', *Jour. African Hist.*, 29 (1978), p. 376.

75 For a summary of the revisionist view of Kruger, which now views him as trying to combine the defence of traditional rural Akrikaner interests with a programme of state development, see Richardson and Van-Helten, 'The Gold Mining Industry', pp. 30–35; and, for a detailed illustration, Van-Helten, 'German Capital'.

76 Ovendale, 'Profit or Patriotism'. The position of the Orange Free State has been rescued from unjust neglect by Timothy Keegan, who has shown that the republic was balanced between an urban, commercial and professional English-speaking community and rural Afrikaner communities led by magnates who stood to gain from rising demand for food in the Transvaal: 'The Political Economy of the Orange Free State, 1880–1920', Institute of Commonwealth Studies, London, S. African History Seminar, 1977.

77 Robert Vicat Turrell, '"Finance . . . The Governor of the Imperial Engine:" Hobson and the Case of the Rothschilds and Rhodes', *Jour. Southern African Stud.*, 13 (1987); Kenneth Wilburn, 'The Nature of the Rothschild Loan', *South African Journal of Economic History*, 3 (1988).

78 Van-Helten, 'German Capital'.

79 Richardson and Van-Helten, 'The Development of the South African Gold Mining Industry', pp. 27–35; A.N. Porter, *The Origins of the South African War: Joseph Chamberlain and the Diplomacy of Imperialism, 1895–1899* (Manchester, 1980), pp. 53–6.

80 We are aware that Patrick Harries has argued that the problem of labour supply has been exaggerated: 'Capital, State and Labour on the Nineteenth-Century Witwatersrand: a Reassessment', *South Afr. Hist. Jour.*, 18 (1986). Accordingly, we have not singled out this question for special emphasis; but there seems little doubt that it remained a continuing sore. See Norman Levy, *The Foundations of the South African Cheap Labour System* (1982), p. 133. We are grateful to Prof. W. Worger for his advice on this point. There is no evidence that British policy at this time was driven by fears about the security of gold supplies. See Russell Ally, *Gold and Empire: The Bank of England and South Africa's Gold Producers, 1886–1926* (Johannesburg, 1994).

81 John S. Galbraith, 'Origins of the British South Africa Company', in John E. Flint and Glyndwr Williams, eds. *Crown and Charter: The Early Years of the British South Africa Company* (Berkeley, Calif., 1974). The most recent biography is Robert I. Rotberg, *The Founder: Cecil Rhodes and the Pursuit of Power* (Oxford, 1988).

82 Kenneth O. Hall, *Imperial Proconsul: Sir Hercules Robinson and South Africa, 1881–1889* (Kingston, Ontario, 1980).

83 C.W. Newbury, 'Out of the Pit: the Capital Accumulation of Cecil Rhodes', *Jour. Imp. and Comm. Hist.*, X (1981); idem, 'Technology, Capital, and Consolidation: the Performance of De Beers Mining Company Limited, 1880–1889', *Bus. Hist. Rev.*, 61 (1987); and R.V. Turrell, 'Rhodes, De Beers and Monopoly', *Jour. Imp. and Comm. Hist.*, 10 (1982).

84 The precise relationship between Rhodes's business fortunes and his political activities during this period has still to be determined. See I.R. Phimister, 'Rhodes, Rhodesia and the Rand', *Jour. Southern African Stud.*, 1 (1974), and idem, *An Economic and Social History of Zimbabwe, 1890–1948* (1988), pp. 4–19; but also Jeffrey Butler, 'Cecil Rhodes', *Int. Jour. African Hist. Stud.*, 10 (1977), pp. 265–9. We are grateful to Prof. Phimister for his advice on this phase of Rhodes's career.

85 Richardson and Van Helten, 'The Development of the South African Gold Mining Industry', pp. 28–9; Phimister, 'Rhodes', p. 80.

86 Chapman's attempt to minimise the role of Rothschilds and of London generally is hard to sustain against the evidence advanced by Turrell and Van-Helten. Rothschilds feared the economic consequences of Rhodes's political ambitions, but they remained heavily committed to his business ventures. See S. Chapman, 'Rhodes and the City of London: another View of Imperialism', *Hist. Jour.*, 28 (1985); R.V. Turrell and Jean Jaques Van-Helten, 'The Rothschilds, the Exploration Company, and Mining Finance', *Bus. Hist.*, 28 (1986); Turrell, '"Finance, the Governor of the Imperial Engine"', pp. 427–31, and Van-Helten, 'Empire and High Finance', pp. 539, 541–2. On the complexities of the process of amalgamation see Richardson and Van-Helten ('The Development of the South African Gold Mining Industry'), who also point out that the industry remained dependent on foreign finance until *after* the Boer War (pp. 334–6).

87 On Rhodes's political exploits see Paul Maylem, *Rhodes, the Tswana and the British: Colonialism, Collaboration and Conflict in the Bechuanaland Protectorate, 1885–1902* (1980), and

A. Keppel-Jones, *Rhodes and Rhodesia: The White Conquest of Zimbabwe, 1884–1902* (Kingston, Ontario, 1984).

88 The best account of this question is Richard Mendelsohn, 'Blainey and the Jameson Raid: the Debate Renewed', *Jour. Southern African Stud.*, 6 (1980). Mendelsohn's conclusion is endorsed by Richardson and Van-Helten, 'The Development of the South African Gold Mining Industry', p. 326.

89 This point is firmly established by Porter, *The Origins of the South African War,* pp. 53–7, 73.

90 Ibid. p. 80; see also pp. 69, 79–85.

91 Turrell, '"Finance . . . The Governor of the Imperial Engine"'.

92 Quoted in Van-Helten, 'German Capital', p. 384.

93 Smith, 'Origins of the South African War'.

94 Diana Cammack, 'the Politics of Discontent: the Grievances of the Uitlander Refugees, 1899–1902', *Jour. Southern African Stud.,* 8 (1982); Porter, *The Origins of the South African War,* pp. 104–5.

95 For example, Thomas Pakenham, *The Boer War* (1979).

96 Porter, *The Origins of the South African War,* pp. 17, 253. Porter also argues, against the 'peripheral' view of empire building, that politicians were becoming increasingly responsive to public opinion in the metropole (pp. 246–7).

97 Ibid. pp. 159–60. It was at this point, too, that German mining interests on the Rand shifted their support from Kruger and moved behind the idea of a British-dominated South Africa. See Van-Helten, 'German Capital', pp. 386–8. When the 'small war' became a big one, Britain had to turn to the New York money market for assistance. See Kathleen Burk, 'Finance, Foreign Policy and the Anglo-American Bank: the House of Morgan, 1900–31', *Historical Research,* 61 (1988), pp. 199–201.

98 Selborne's Memorandum, dated 30 March 1896, is quoted at length in Robinson and Gallagher, *Africa and the Victorians,* pp. 434–7.

99 Cope, 'Strategic and Socio-Economic Explanations', is decisive on this question.

100 See pp. 261–6. The application of these ideas to South Africa is well brought out by J.S. Marais, *The Fall of Kruger's Republic* (1961).

101 Selborne's Memorandum (see n. 98) is evidence of this concern, which is also apparent in Chamberlain's Cabinet Memorandum of 6 Sept. 1899, quoted in J.A.S. Grenville, *Lord Salisbury and Foreign Policy: The Close of the Nineteenth Century* (1964), pp. 257–8.

102 Colonial Office Memorandum, 7 Sept. 1899, quoted in Ovendale, 'Profit or Patriotism', p. 226.

103 David Eltis and Lawrence Jennings, 'Trade Between Western Africa and the Atlantic World in the Pre-Colonial Era', *Am. Hist. Rev.* 93 (1988).

104 Martin Lynn, 'The "Imperialism of Free Trade" in West Africa, c. 1800–c. 1870', *Jour. Imp. and Comm. Hist.,* 15 (1986).

105 Newbury 'On the Margins of Empire', pp. 41–2; Martin Lynn, 'From Sail to Steam: the Impact of the Steamship Services on the British Palm Oil Trade with West Africa, 1850–1890', *Jour. African Hist.,* 30 (1989).

106 The analysis here broadly follows A.G. Hopkins, *An Economic History of West Africa* (1973: 1988), Ch. 4, and the work of Hargreaves and Newbury cited in n. 111.

107 Newbury, 'On the Margins of Empire', offers a valuable assessment of the relationship between commercial fluctuations and political action.

108 Hopkins, *Economic History of West Africa,* Ch. 4. The most important recent work is that undertaken by Robin Law, of the University of Stirling, 'The Historiography of the Commercial Transition in Nineteenth-Century West Africa', in Toyin Falola, ed. *African Historiography: Essays in Honour of Ade Ajayi* (1991).

109 C.W. Newbury, 'Credit in Early Nineteenth-Century West African Trade', *Jour. African Hist.,* 13 (1972); idem, 'On the Margins of Empire', p. 39.

110 Jan S. Hogendorn and Marion Johnson, *The Shell Money of the Slave Trade* (Cambridge, 1986) is the definitive account. For one detailed study of the decline of cowrie currency see A.G. Hopkins, 'The Currency Revolution in South-West Nigeria in the Late Nineteenth Century', *Jour. Hist. Soc. Nigeria,* 3 (1966). On the attempt to introduce British

ideas of rights in land see A.G. Hopkins, 'Property Rights and Empire Building: Britain's Annexation of Lagos, 1861', *Jour. Econ. Hist.*, 40 (1980).

111 Historians of West Africa are heavily indebted to the authoritative work of Hargreaves and Newbury on this subject, though only a selection of their important contributions can be referred to here. See, in particular: J.D. Hargreaves's trilogy, *Prelude to the Partition of West Africa* (1973), *West Africa Partitioned: The Loaded Pause, 1885–1889* and *West Africa Partitioned; The Elephants and the Grass* (1985); and C.W. Newbury, *The Western Slave Coast and its Rulers* (Oxford, 1966), 'The Tariff Factor in Anglo-French West African Partition', in Prosser Gifford and William Roger Lewis, eds. *France and Britain in Africa* (New Haven, Conn., 1971), and 'Trade and Authority in West Africa from 1850–1880', in Lewis Gann and P. Duignan, eds. *Colonialism in Africa,* Vol. I (Cambridge, 1969).

112 It is now clear that the French decision to advance inland from Senegal was taken before Britain's occupation of Egypt in 1882 and therefore cannot have been caused by it. See C.W. Newbury and A.S. Kanya-Forstner, 'French Policy and the Origins of the Scramble for West Africa', *Jour. African Hist.,* 10 (1969).

113 William G. Hynes, *The Economics of Empire: Britain, Africa and the New Imperialism, 1870–95* (1979); B.M. Ratcliffe, 'Commerce and Empire: Manchester Merchants and West Africa, 1873–95', *Jour. Imp. and Comm. Hist.,* 6 (1979).

114 For examples of the ways in which capital and trade crossed colonial boundaries see: W.G. Clarence Smith, ed. 'Business Empires in Equatorial Africa', *African Econ. Hist.,* 12 (1983); Ronald Dreyer, 'Whitehall, Cape Town, Berlin and the Economic Partition of South-West Africa: the Establishment of British Economic Control, 1885–94', *Jour. Imp. and Comm. Hist.,* XV (1987); Richard A. Voeltz, 'The European Economic and Political Penetration of South-West Africa, 1884–1892', *Int. Jour. African Hist. Stud.,* 17 (1984); S.E. Katzenellenbogen, 'British Businessmen and German Africa, 1885–1919', in B.M. Ratcliffe, ed. *Great Britain and her World* (Manchester, 1975), pp. 258–9; and A.G. Hopkins, 'Big Business in African Studies', *Jour. African Hist.,* 28 (1987), pp. 130–1.

115 The progress of this campaign can be followed through the work of Hargreaves and Newbury cited in n. 111 above.

116 C.W. Newbury, 'The Development of French Policy on the Lower and Upper Niger, 1880–98', *Jour. Mod. Hist.,* 31 (1959), pp. 16–26.

117 The Chairman, Lord Aberdare, was a prominent Liberal politician and a close friend of Gladstone and Lord Granville, the Foreign Secretary. Charles Mills of the leading merchant bank, Glyn, Mills & Currie, was also on the board. See J.E. Flint, *Sir George Goldie and the Making of Nigeria* (1960), pp. 45–6.

118 Flint, *Sir George Goldie,* Ch. 4.

119 A.G. Hopkins, 'Economic Imperialism in West Africa: Lagos, 1880–1892', *Econ. Hist. Rev.,* 2nd ser. XXI (1968).

120 Hargreaves, *West Africa Partitioned: The Elephants and the Grass,* pp. 201–8, 208–24, 224–35.

121 R.E. Dumett, 'Joseph Chamberlain, Imperial Finance and Railway Policy in British West Africa in the Late Nineteenth Century', *Eng. Hist. Rev.,* XC (1975). See also the perceptive comment by Hargreaves, who points out that Lord Salisbury had a larger as well as a sounder view of which parts of the world were of economic value: *West Africa Partitioned: The Elephants and the Grass,* pp. 230–31.

122 These subjects have been well covered by Abdul Sheriff, *Slaves, Spices and Ivory in Zanzibar: Integration of an East African Commercial Empire into the World Economy, 1770–1873* (1987), and F. Cooper, *Plantation Slavery on the East Coast of Africa* (New Haven, Conn., 1977).

123 Unfortunately, the ramifications of these changes in the East African interior have yet to be studied in the detail needed to sustain a plausible generalisation on this subject. Interesting case studies include: Charles H. Ambler, *Kenyan Communities in the Age of Imperialism: The Central Region in the Late Nineteenth Century* (New Haven, Conn., 1987); Ronald R. Atkinson, 'A History of the Western Acholi of Uganda, c.1675–1900' (Ph.D. thesis Northwestern University, 1978); and Thomas J. Herlehy, 'An Economic History

of the Kenya Coast: The Mijkenda Coconut Palm Economy, 1800–1980' (Ph.D. thesis, Boston University, 1985). There are many suggestive comments in John Lonsdale's important contribution, 'The European Scramble and Conquest in African History', in Oliver and Sanderson, *The Cambridge History of Africa,* Vol. 6, which deserve further research. On the slave trade set W.G. Clarence Smith, ed. 'The Economies of the Indian Ocean Slave Trade', *Slavery and Abolition,* 9 (1988).

124 R.J. Gavin,'The Bartle Frere Mission to Zanzibar, 1873', *Hist. Jour.,* 5 (1962); Raymond Howell, *The Royal Navy and the Slave Trade* (1987); R.M. Githige, 'The Issue of Slavery: Relations Between the C.M.S. and the State on the East African Coast Prior to 1895', *Journal of Religion in Africa,* 16 (1986); Bridges, 'The Historical Role of British Explorers'.

125 R. Coupland, *The Exploitation of East Africa, 1856–1890* (1939), Ch. 12.

126 Etherington, 'Frederick Elton'.

127 Our understanding of Britain's imperial interests in East Africa during this period is being transformed by J. Forbes Munro's research on Sir William Mackinnon. See 'Shipping Subsidies and Railway Guarantees: William Mackinnon, Eastern Africa and the Indian Ocean, 1860–93', *Jour. African Hist.,* 28 (1987); and 'Suez and the Shipowner: the Response of the Mackinnon Shipping Group to the Opening of the Suez Canal, 1869–84', in Lewis R. Fischer and Helge W. Nordvick, eds. *Shipping and Trade, 1750–1950: Essays in International Maritime Economic History* (Pontefract, 1990). Mackinnon also had dose connections with the National Bank of India, which established a branch in Zanzibar in 1892. See Geoffrey Tyson, *100 Years of Banking in Asia and Africa* (1963), pp. 111–13. His business interests in Smith, Mackenzie are dealt with by Stephanie Jones, *Two Centuries of Overseas Trading: The Origin and Growth of the Inchcape Company* (1986), Ch. 4.

128 J. Forbes Munro, 'Scottish Overseas Enterprise and the Lure of London: the Mackinnon Group, 1847–1893', *Scottish Econ. and Soc. Hist.,* 8 (1988).

129 This point has been established by M.E. Chamberlain in an important and still unjustly neglected article: 'Clement Hill's Memoranda and the British Interest in East Africa', *Eng. Hist. Rev.,* LXXXVII (1972). See also Hynes, *The Economics of Empire,* pp. 77–83, 127–9. In the mid-1880s the lobby was able to call upon Lord Aberdare (see n. 117), Chamberlain, Dilke, Kimberley (the Secretary of State for India), and a clutch of Lancashire MPs; it also had the sympathy of Lord Rothschild.

130 The idea (associated with Robinson and Gallagher, *Africa and the Victorians*) that Britain's concern in East Africa was largely strategic not only neglects the economic considerations summarised here, but also is hard to reconcile with the fact that Britain was unperturbed by the French acquisition of Madagascar in 1883–5, and that the Admiralty had no interest in making use of Mombasa at this time. There were plenty of bases: the real test was controlling the high seas. See Chamberlain, *The Scramble,* pp. 63–4.

131 As H.P. Merritt has shown, the British were not alone in being dazzled by the commercial potential of East Africa: 'Bismarck and the German Interest in East Africa', *Hist. Jour.,* 21 (1978).

132 Chamberlain, 'Clement Hill', pp. 545–6.

133 William Roger Louis, 'The Anglo-German Hinterland Settlement of 1890 and Uganda', *Uganda Jour.,* 27 (1963).

134 J.S. Galbraith, *Mackinnon and East Africa, 1878–95* (Cambridge, 1972) remains the most detailed account, though it must now be read in the light of Munro, 'Shipping Subsidies'.

135 However, contrary to an often-repeated statement, he did not threaten to resign: Gordon Martel, *Imperial Diplomacy: Rosebery and the Failure of Foreign Policy* (1986), pp. 80–6.

136 Anthony Low, 'British Public Opinion and the Uganda Question: October-December, 1892', *Uganda Jour.,* 18 (1954); Gordon Martel, 'Cabinet Politics and African Partition: the Uganda Debate Reconsidered', *Jour. Imp. and Comm. Hist.,* XIII (1984).

137 Martel, *Imperial Diplomacy,* p. 87.

138 Harry Johnston, *The Uganda Protectorate* (1904), p. 234.

139 Cartoon in *Punch,* 22 Oct. 1892.

140 See below, p. 608.

141 This theme is explored in the references given in n. 114. The case of South West Africa, where German rule was dependent on British capital, is particularly telling – and has been well told: Dreyer, 'Whitehall, Cape Town'; Richard A. Voeltz, *German Colonialism and the South-West Africa Company, 1894–1914* (Athens, Ohio, 1988).

142 For the origins of the most influential radical and liberal interpretations of partition see Hopkins, 'The Victorians and Africa', pp. 364–70; and for an assessment of the applicability of Hobson's views see P.J. Cain, *Hobson and Imperialism: Radicalism, New Liberalism and Finance* (Oxford, 2002), pp. 255–60.

143 R.E. Robinson and J. Gallagher, 'The Partition of Africa', in *New Cambridge Modern History,* Vol. XI (Cambridge, 1962), pp. 593–4.

144 Typically by raising customs duties to pay for military operations and the costs of administration.

145 Bent Hanson, 'Interest Rates and Foreign Capital in Egypt under British Occupation', *Jour. Econ. Hist,* 43 (1983).

146 Diana Cammack, 'The Johannesburg Republic: the Reshaping of a Rand Society, 1900–01', *South Afr. Hist. Jour.,* 18 (1986); Alan. Jeeves, *Migrant Labour in* South Africa's Mining Economy: The Struggle for the Gold Mines' Labour Supply, 1890–1920 (Kingston, Montreal, 1985). The precise nature of this accommodation is currently under discussion, and no doubt will remain so: see Donald Denoon, 'Capital and Capitalists in the Transvaal in the 1890s and 1900s', *Hist. Jour.,* 23 (1980). A valuable guide to this period is Deryck Schreuder, 'Colonial Nationalism and "Tribal Nationalism": Making the White South African State, 1899–1910', in John Eddy and Deryck Schreuder, eds. *The Rise of Colonial Nationalism* (Sydney, 1988). Ronald Hyam and Ged Martin, *Reappraisals in British Imperial History* (1975), Chs. 8–9.

147 Ronald Hyam and Ged Martin, *Reappraisals in British Imperial History* (1975), Chs. 8–9.

12

'WE OFFER OURSELVES AS SUPPORTERS'

The Ottoman Empire and Persia, 1838–1914[1]

The Ottoman Empire and Persia can be placed, with China, in a distinct category of regions that presented peculiar obstacles to European expansion in the underdeveloped world. The failure of societies in these three empires to produce modernising elites which were both powerful and cooperative limited their development as independent polities along Western lines. At the same time, the presence of large, antique, yet still death-defying political structures meant that indigenous authorities could not be taken over without promoting internal disorder, incurring massive expense and risking international conflict. The conundrum posed by the attempt to secure European interests without disrupting the Middle East became known in diplomatic circles as the Eastern Question. Policy-makers in Constantinople and Tehran grappled with a more desperate dilemma – the Western Question – of how to respond to intrusive European designs without losing their autonomy.[2]

Most of the historical literature on Britain's position in the Middle East has been harnessed to two opposed interpretations.[3] One emphasises the dominance of economic motives, both in Britain's presence in the region and in the formulation of policy in London; the other stresses the paramountcy of strategic considerations. The concern of the present study lies less with trying to reinforce one or other of these standpoints than with unravelling the ties between them. The danger of this approach is that it can readily become either over-complex and excessively narrow, or all-embracing and excessively vague. The account that follows has the specific aim of showing how the rise and retreat of British finance affected the instruments available to policy-makers and influenced both the purpose and the result of Britain's endeavours in the region.

During the first half of the period under review, economics and strategy found harmonious expression in Britain's spacious vision of a free-trading and progressive international order. Palmerston's grand design was intended to regenerate the fallen nations of the world and to uplift those which had never risen.[4] It was believed that Sultan and Shah alike would become converts to the new ideology of progress, would adopt liberal reforms and would thereby become congenial commercial clients and reliable political allies. During the last quarter of the century this optimistic view, already weathered by exposure to reality, was replaced by a colder set of calculations and accompanied by a less flattering image, especially of the Turks, whose capacity for moral improvement was downgraded after the publicity given to the Bulgarian 'atrocities'.[5] Thereafter, British policy aimed at sedation rather than conversion, and expansive plans for co-operation gave way to the calculated and admirably economical 'language of menace'.[6] As the City turned to more attractive areas of investment, so the Foreign Office was drawn further into the Middle East, meddling in local politics and trying to tempt reluctant businessmen into unpromising commercial opportunities in order to shore up Britain's strategic interests.

The growing divergence between economic and political commitments is an interesting indication of shifting priorities among segments of Britain's gentlemanly elite. But it is not to be treated, crudely, as demonstrating the ultimate primacy of 'strategic' over 'economic' motives. As we shall see, economic interests continued to be well represented through the Ottoman Public Debt Administration and through specific, if limited, commitments to particular regions and sectors in both the Ottoman Empire and Persia. Moreover, to the extent that successive British governments tried to prop up both states in order to safeguard the routes to India, it was because there Britain's economic stake *was* crucial to her status as a great power. The problem was that businessmen were not prepared to defend India by making essentially political investments in the Middle East. That burden was to be borne by governments, and governments were still constrained by cost, even though the tradition of non-intervention was steadily weakening. Informal ties between the City and government, though close, did not enable ministers of state to direct flows of funds overseas. Seen in this context, the Middle East offers a good example, not of the weakness, but of the strength and independence of the City. Bankers and traders paid the region the attention they thought its economic potential deserved; the Foreign Office gave it as much political commitment as the Treasury and the Government of India were willing to finance.

The Ottoman Empire: from free trade to foreign management

Britain's long-standing connections with the Middle East were greatly strengthened by success in the French Wars, which encouraged the belief that the region would readily fall into her orbit when conditions of peaceful competition returned.[7] The abolition of the Levant Company's monopoly in 1825 symbolised the transition from an era of restriction and patronage: thereafter, the number of British merchants and political representatives in the Middle East increased and the size of the Ottoman market for British manufactures expanded.[8] But the subsequent growth of trade, though welcome, was insufficient to offset serious problems posed by the rise of competition and protection in major outlets in Europe. It was against this background that Palmerston began his assertive quest for new markets in the late 1830s and early 1840s.[9] In the case of the Ottoman Empire, the breakthrough came in 1838, when a free-trade treaty was concluded in exchange for backing the Porte against its powerful satellite, Egypt.[10] The treaty was a typical example of its kind: tariffs were subjected to external control, state monopolies were eliminated, the capitulatory privileges of European minorities were confirmed, and Britain was guaranteed treatment as a most-favoured-nation. With the commercial treaty came a package of broader measures designed to promote institutional reforms and to support modernising elements within the Ottoman state.[11]

The Anglo-Turkish convention brought immediate and gratifying results. Ottoman foreign trade grew rapidly between 1840 and the outbreak of the Crimean War in 1854.[12] Britain's share of the total rose impressively, and Lancashire's cotton goods began to find a market worthy of their needs.[13] Moreover, Britain earned consistent surpluses on her visible trade with the Ottoman Empire and these contributed to her emerging pattern of multilateral settlements.[14] Nevertheless, the early optimism about the development potential of the Middle East was never fulfilled. Within the Ottoman Empire the reform movement made limited progress, and the most influential reformers turned out to be loyalists who wished to strengthen the empire against European incursions and to restrain the emergence of a comprador class which might become a compliant agent of foreign interests.[15] The Ottoman territories had difficulty generating exports to pay for additional imports, and the rate of growth of foreign trade began to slow from the 1850s once the early, easy gains from free trade had been realised.[16] As the mid-Victorian boom gathered pace, and as supplies from Russia and the United States were resumed following the Crimean War and the American Civil War, British exporters began to identify markets outside the Middle East as sources of future growth.[17]

Free trade also provided greater opportunities for British finance. In destroying state monopolies and in holding down tariff levels, the Anglo-Turkish Commercial Convention curtailed government revenues; in promoting reform it also imposed new burdens on the budget. The resulting fiscal balancing act had already become precarious when it was finally upset by the Crimean War, which drove the Ottoman government to seek external financial aid, thus anticipating a path followed by China after 1895. The fact that Britain and France decided to support the Ottomans against Russia is indicative of the importance they attached to the economic and political stake they had acquired in the Empire. Both governments encouraged subscriptions to the first Ottoman loan in 1854 and guaranteed the next one (floated by Rothschilds) in the following year.[18] This was the prelude to an extensive loan business which developed during the next 20 years to meet Ottoman needs for post-war reconstruction, 'modernisation' and – finally – current expenditure.[19] Foreign loans called into being novel agencies which specialised in attracting capital from a widening circle of investors around London (and Paris) to frontiers of risk beyond Europe.[20] The leading expatriate financial institution in the Empire, the Imperial Ottoman Bank, began its life in London as the Ottoman Bank in 1856 and received a state charter in 1863, when it became a joint Anglo-French concern.[21]

MAP 7 The Ottoman Empire, 1914

After: Marian Kent, ed. *The Great Powers and the End of the Ottoman Empire* (1984)

R U S S I A
CASPIAN SEA
BLACK SEA
Batum
Baku
Sinope
Samsun
Trebizond
Kars
Aras R.
Lake Van
ARMENIA
L. Urmia
Kharput
Tehran
Bozanti
Alexandretta
Nisibin
Mosul
Aleppo
Meskene
Dair-az-Zar
PERSIA
Hama
Homs
Euphrates R.
Baghdad
Tripoli
Beirut
LEBANON
Damascus
MESOPOTAMIA (IRAQ)
Tigris R.
The Shatt-el-Arab
PALESTINE
Jaffa
Aviv-Yafo
Amman
Basra
Jerusalem
Koweit (Kuwait)
Persian Gulf
TRANS-JORDAN
NEJD
Bahrain
Qatar
HEJAZ
Red Sea

The Bank was given special privileges, including a monopoly of issues of paper currency, which helped it to become the chief financial agent of the Empire; it was also the most visible manifestation of the extension abroad of the new financial instruments developed in Britain in the second half of the nineteenth century.

Initially, export proceeds were sufficiently buoyant to meet interest payments, and the level of capital flowing into Constantinople rose rapidly. By 1875 the public debt amounted to about £250m., and there was also a large, short-term floating debt.[22] However, little more than half the total nominally borrowed between 1854 and 1874 actually reached the Ottoman government, and a sizeable part of this sum was immediately recycled to repay existing loans. Much of the rest was channelled into military expenditures; some found its way into private pockets. It is over-simple to conclude that foreign loans were 'squandered' because it is now recognised that they helped to lay the foundation of a form of bureaucratic centralism that was to survive the demise of the Ottoman Empire.[23] But it is certainly true that they failed to produce the progressive, liberal reforms which commended themselves to European interests, and they may even have helped to avert them. By 1875 over half the Ottoman budget was assigned to servicing external obligations, and new loans were being raised to pay the interest on earlier debts. As the Empire's credit-worthiness dropped, interest rates rose; even so, it became harder to attract fresh capital. In 1875 the Ottoman government had to suspend payment on half its foreign debt, following a fall in export prices prompted by the financial crisis in the United States in 1873 and compounded by a series of poor harvests in Anatolia, which reduced government revenues after 1872. Default followed in 1876, and a formal declaration of bankruptcy was made three years later. The Ottoman Empire thus joined a clutch of countries, including its dissident province, Egypt, which had been pumped up by European capital from the middle of the century only to fall victim to the first major debt crisis of the 'developing world' in the 1870s.

The year 1875 marks, as well as any single date can, the end of mid-Victorian optimism about the development prospects of the Ottoman Empire. Britain remained the Empire's leading foreign commercial partner, but her share of Ottoman exports reached a peak of 29 per cent as early as 1850–2 and dropped gradually to 18 per cent in 1909–11; her slice of the import trade (which was concentrated heavily on textiles) fell from a high point of 45 per cent in 1880–2 to 24 per cent in 1909–11.[24] These proportions need to be considered against the slow growth of Ottoman foreign trade as a whole between 1873 and 1898, the decline in the external terms of trade (which made it harder for Ottoman exporters to buy imported goods), and the depressingly small scale of the market, which was unable to absorb more than 1 or 2 per cent of Britain's annual exports, despite half a century of firm persuasion. Trade with the Ottoman Empire was certainly not to be given up lightly, but there was scarcely a case for defending it heavily either. The costs of intervention were an ever-present and sensitive consideration at a time when public expenditure had become linked to democratic politics in Britain. Even when anti-Russian feeling reached a peak of stridency, as it did in 1877, Salisbury's judgement was that 'it no where rises nearly to Income-tax point', and he steered his course accordingly.[25]

Britain's financial interests underwent a more immediate reversal. The City was already becoming wary of Ottoman investments in the early 1870s; after the default of 1876 it became very difficult to tempt British capital into the region. Indeed, the longer-term trend was towards disinvestment, as British investors withdrew from the Ottoman Empire, often selling their holdings to French and German companies, and placed their money in more profitable and less risky openings elsewhere. After the 1880s, Britain ceased to be the leading source of new foreign finance in the Ottoman Empire. By 1913 her share of the Ottoman public debt had fallen to 13 per cent and her share of direct foreign investment to 15 per cent.[26] Britain's place was taken principally by her long-standing competitor, France, which held 53 per cent of the debt in 1914, and Germany, which held 21 per cent. France was also the dominant force behind the Imperial Ottoman Bank, which worked closely with the French government in expanding its activities from the 1890s, while Germany made increasingly effective use of its own financial agent in the Middle East, the Deutsche Bank.[27]

The events of 1875–6 led to a reappraisal of British policy towards the Ottoman Empire. It was now clear that the Empire was not going to become a progressive and self-supporting satellite bound to Britain by 'natural' ties of finance and commerce. The standing of the Empire, already damaged in British eyes by the harassment of Christian minorities, fell with its credit-rating to the point where the introduction of liberal government and institutional reforms was no longer considered to be a realistic expectation. There was even a feeling, in the 1870s, that the Empire ought to be allowed to disintegrate.[28] Ottoman bankruptcy and fear of Russian influence dictated otherwise, but disillusion with the Empire was accompanied by a stiffer and less tolerant attitude, summarised in Salisbury's view that British interests were best served by 'order and good government',[29] a formula that stood for political stability and sound finance. British governments continued to proclaim their support for the unity of the Ottoman Empire down to 1914, but they managed to combine this principle with the acquisition of semidetached and 'unstable' segments, notably Cyprus (in 1878) and Egypt (in 1882).[30]

The City was also keen to see the unity of the Ottoman Empire upheld in order to safeguard British investments there, though it, too, was sufficiently ambidextrous to back the take-over of both Cyprus and Egypt.[31] However, as Britain's capital stake in the Empire diminished after the turn of the century, the City became more willing to consider partition as being a practical means of safeguarding specific regional commitments. As the City's interest in Constantinople diminished, so too did the influence of the British government. After efforts to tempt British capital back into the Empire to strengthen the front against Russian expansionism had failed, the Foreign Office gave up the northern line of defence and pitched its tent in the south, where the main boundaries of commerce and investment had come to be drawn.

The City's involvement in the Ottoman Empire was therefore limited after 1875. But this does not mean that Britain's existing financial interests were abandoned. Once default had occurred, the overriding concern of British investors was to secure repayment of the Empire's outstanding obligations on the best possible terms. The Ottomans wavered, but they realised that a settlement was imperative if they were to resume borrowing, and their remaining hesitations were removed by a demonstration mounted by British warships in the Straits in 1879.[32] After lengthy negotiations, the Porte and its foreign creditors came to an agreement in 1881.[33] The outstanding debt was slightly reduced, consolidated and rescheduled; in exchange, the Ottoman government agreed to make the external debt the first charge on its revenues, to hand over the administration of a sizeable proportion of these revenues, and to cede control over tariff rates on imports and exports. The management of these concessions was entrusted to a new organisation, the Ottoman Public Debt Administration, which was established in the same year. This was a hybrid body: it was international, though in practice the two principal creditor countries, Britain and France, wielded the greatest influence; and it was private, though it also maintained very close links with official circles in Britain and France.

For the next 30 years, the Public Debt Administration was the most powerful economic agency in the Empire. In 1914 it had about 700 offices and 9,000 employees.[34] It virtually controlled central government finance, exerted great influence over railway concessions and other developmental projects (such as the silk industry), and received diplomatic support from the major powers and assistance from the principal foreign banks.[35] The Public Debt Administration proved to be an effective debt collecting agency: creditors were repaid in accordance with the terms agreed in 1881, and by the turn of the century the Ottoman government's credit-rating had improved to the point where it was able to float new loans. Indeed, the credit of the Empire came to rest largely on the prestige of the Public Debt Administration, which generated confidence among foreign investors and acted as a conduit for external finance.[36]

The City, however, remained sceptical, despite the persistence of several well-placed advocates. One, Edgar Vincent, was the British representative on the Council of the Ottoman Public Debt Administration in 1882–3 and Governor of the Imperial Ottoman Bank from 1889 to 1897.[37] Another, Vincent Caillard, replaced him on the Public Debt Council in 1883 and became its President (alternating with the French representative) until his retirement in 1898.[38] Vincent and Caillard are interesting examples of the new generation of financier-promoters thrown up by the growth of the City-service complex and its extension overseas after 1850. Both men came from families of substance in the south of England, were educated (together) at Eton, and found their way to the fringes of empire initially through careers in the army. They were not only officers and gentlemen, but also soldiers of fortune who became bankers of fortunes. Vincent served with the Coldstream Guards; Caillard won his spurs in the Egyptian campaign of 1882. When they entered financial administration, they combined, in a way that admirably captured the spirit of the period, a sharp eye for private profit with a more spacious view of Britain's imperial role, and they were tireless advocates of both causes. Their success owed much to their social connections. Vincent was a protégé of the Gladstone family and of George Goschen, the banker and prominent Liberal; Caillard drew upon distant family ties with Disraeli and close links with Dilke, the Liberal-imperialist. Both men had influence, but their speculative ventures led them into grey areas of international finance which did not inspire confidence in the highest banking circles.[39] In this matter the City's judgement was sound: Vincent steered the Imperial Ottoman Bank towards the rocks by making risky investments in South African gold-mines and had to resign in 1897; Caillard's constant intrigues and occasional misjudgements ensured that the leading merchant banks kept him at arm's length. The new clutch of Ottoman loans floated after the turn of the century attracted mainly French and German investors, and it brought them more headaches than profits.

As development prospects faded, British policy focused increasingly on the task of maintaining the stability of the Empire. This aim met the priorities of the Ottoman Public Debt Administration, which needed to control central revenues, and also of imperial strategy, which was preoccupied by the fear that foreign rivals would threaten India from bases in the Middle East. In countering this possibility, however, Britain was handicapped by her waning economic influence, as well as by her presence in Egypt and her moral support for Christian minorities within the Ottoman Empire, neither of which gave her a head start in the contest to gain leverage in Constantinople. Given these constraints, the Foreign Office fell back upon energetic diplomacy to bolster Britain's commercial presence and to create favourable alliances among rival powers and potential supporters in the region.[40]

A notable feature of this policy was the decision to step up official support for British investment in the hope that injections of capital would bolster Britain's political influence.[41] As the Foreign Secretary, Grey, observed in 1908: 'We shall make no progress till British capital of a high class takes an energetic interest in Turkey'.[42] Without formal guarantees, however, the City remained wary. Indeed, the rise of foreign competitors increased the uncertainty that already surrounded the political future of the Ottoman Empire and reinforced the cautious attitude of British investors. The closest the government came to success in the financial field was when the British-owned National Bank of Turkey was formed in 1909.[43] This was a private venture headed by Sir Ernest Cassel, another financier who was willing to engage in risky overseas loans in the hope of eventually gaining access to a higher grade of business.[44] On this occasion Cassel received support from Lord Revelstoke of Barings and encouragement from the Foreign Office. Grey had high hopes that the National Bank would spearhead a revival of British influence and counter the advance of Germany. The Foreign Office played an active part in channelling business towards the Bank and in warning off potential competitors. Nevertheless, the Bank was unsuccessful and ceased operations in 1913. This was partly because official support shackled as well as sheltered enterprise by subordinating commercial decisions to political priorities. But the main reason for the Bank's failure was its inability to win the confidence of British investors.[45] British governments could influence the City but not control it, and were rarely able to mobilise the market in support of the 'national interest'. In France and

Germany, law and custom gave governments greater power to direct private funds for political purposes; in Britain the City remained, in this sense, above politics.[46]

A more successful departure from mid-nineteenth-century principles of non-intervention followed the search for oil in Mesopotamia after the turn of the century.[47] This episode does not provide an example of capitalist investment on a scale that was generally lacking in the Ottoman Empire. On the contrary, the government intervened in 1908 to prop up a faltering concessionary company owned by a British subject, William D'Arcy. But it does demonstrate how economic resources were entwined with strategic priorities, and the extent to which the Foreign Office had accepted the need to reinforce private firms in areas of political sensitivity. Encouraged by the Admiralty, and with an eye on checking the advance of oil syndicates backed by the Deutsche Bank, the government supported the creation of the Anglo-Persian Oil Company in 1909 and acquired a controlling interest in it in 1914. Anglo-Persian was encouraged to buy out rival firms competing for oil concessions in Mesopotamia (including, ironically, one supported by the Foreign Office's other instrument, the National Bank of Turkey), and in 1912 it sponsored the Turkish Petroleum Company, which brought British and German oil interests in the region together but ensured that the Deutsche Bank group held only a minority share. Government intervention succeeded in this case because it fitted with the judgement of the market (especially after the discovery of large oil deposits in Persia in 1908), and because it involved material official participation rather than the less substantial offer of diplomatic and moral support.

Since Britain's own resources were insufficient to guarantee the friendly neutrality of the Ottoman Empire, she also defended her interests by striking bargains with rival powers. Until the close of the nineteenth century, competition with France was constrained by a common interest in the Ottoman Public Debt Administration and by Britain's concern to retain French goodwill in dealing with the Russians. From the 1890s, however, the resumption of foreign borrowing by the Ottoman Empire and the rise of German interest in the Balkans and Turkey set off a scramble for economic concessions and political influence which had parallels in other 'unclaimed' parts of the world, notably Africa and China.[48]

The chief focus of British anxiety was Germany's plan, devised between 1899 and 1903, for building a railway line between Berlin and Baghdad.[49] This ambitious scheme sounded alarms in London and Delhi because it threatened to pierce India's outer defences, and it quickly became a symbol of the global challenge which German expansion was thought to present. It therefore had to be resisted. One possibility, which arose in 1903, was to participate in the project, but this idea foundered on a mixture of anti-German feeling and dissatisfaction with terms of the proposed deal.[50] Another plan was to neutralise the German advance by combining with the French to promote alternative railway and development projects. This tactic received some impetus from the Anglo-French entente of 1904, but little was achieved in practice because official agreement was not backed by active support from either the Imperial Ottoman Bank or the City.[51] However, in 1906 Britain managed to persuade Constantinople to recognise her exclusive rights to build railways in parts of Anatolia, and the Foreign Office later gave strong backing to a British railway project in the western part of the province when it was challenged by a rival Italian concession.[52] In the event, the slow progress made by the Baghdad railway lowered anxiety levels in the Foreign Office, and Germany's growing preoccupation with European security strengthened the hand of British diplomacy in the Middle East. The outcome, the Anglo-German convention of 1914, was a satisfactory compromise which confirmed Britain's position in Mesopotamia and the Persian Gulf.[53]

An opportunity for creating an entirely new political alliance arose in 1908, when the Young Turks seized control in Constantinople and deposed the Sultan in the following year.[54] At first, the British were inclined to interpret the revolution as representing the resurgence of liberal constitutionalism and supposed that the new rulers would naturally turn to them for guidance. This expectation was encouraged by the promptness with which the provisional government expressed its willingness to co-operate with the Ottoman Public Debt Administration[55] and helped to provide official impetus for the formation of the National Bank of Turkey. However, once it became clear that the new government was bent on building an independent and centralised state with German rather than British assistance, the view from London changed. The Young Turks were then portrayed as a conspiracy of Freemasons and Jews with Jacobin intentions. Not surprisingly, this bizarre interpretation hardened attitudes on both sides. Far from promoting congenial allies for Britain, the advent of the Young Turks heightened tensions within the Ottoman Empire, encouraged regional defections, and brought the European powers closer to partition.

Persia: financial diplomacy – with limited finance

By 1914 the main weight of Britain's trade and finance had gravitated to the southern provinces of the Empire (apart from specific interests in Anatolia), and particularly to Mesopotamia, where they formed a bridge to her interests in Persia.[56] There, too, British governments had to come to terms with the City's reluctance to invest in unpromising areas, and were forced to adopt interventionist policies to ensure that imperial commitments were met.[57]

At the start of the nineteenth century Britain had a long-established commercial presence in the Persian Gulf, represented by the East India Company, and had also formulated plans to use Persia as a buffer in the defence of Wellesley's acquisitions in India.[58] With the end of the French Wars, Persia received the standard prescription of liberalism and coercion which Britain administered to weaker states, such as the Ottoman Empire and China, in pursuit of her economic and strategic goals. Piracy and slaving were suppressed in the Gulf, a free-trade treaty was signed in 1841, after a show of force, and a short war in 1856–7 curtailed Persia's imperial ambitions when they threatened India's land defences.[59] Thereafter the frontiers of progress were to be moved forward by private enterprise. Coastal trade was developed from the 1860s through the agency of the British and Indian Steam Navigation Company,

MAP 8 Persia, 1914

After: L.C.M. Platt, *Finance, Trade and Politics: British Foreign Policy, 1815–1914* (Oxford, 1968)

submarine cables were laid, and the opening of the Suez Canal in 1869 held out much promise.[60] The performance, however, proved to be disappointing. A very modest market for Manchester cottons was created, but Persia's export trade lacked the dynamism to raise import-purchasing power substantially.[61] Beyond the ports, the interior remained land-locked and unrewarding, and internal reforms made even less progress than in the Ottoman Empire.[62] The two principal concessions secured by British subjects both failed: de Reuter's comprehensive rights, obtained in 1872 (mainly for railway development), ran into opposition both within Persia and from Britain and Russia; Talbot's tobacco concession, granted in 1890, aroused such popular resentment in Persia that it had to be cancelled in the following year.[63] By the close of the century it was apparent that Persia offered neither rich pickings nor the conditions to support a sustained development drive.

The City did not like what it saw in Persia. The economy was hampered by a feeble export sector, a primitive transport system, and an unstable, silver-based currency, and Persian society showed little sign of producing a congenial comprador class.[64] The Shah's government was neither stable nor progressive and looked as if it might be submerged by dissidents from within or by Russian expansionism. Moreover, the history of the concessions granted to de Reuter and Talbot showed the face of Persian hostility to foreign influences and caused a loss of confidence in the City which was reflected in Persia's declining credit rating.[65] In these circumstances, it is not surprising that the City remained uninterested in Persia throughout this period, apart from a brief speculative flutter in 1909–11. Only two foreign loans were floated in London for the Persian government: one, a modest issue of £500,000 offered in 1892, met with a poor response; the other, a more substantial loan of £1.5m. launched in 1911, was well received largely because it had official backing. The flow of private capital was also very limited, and the leading British companies, the Imperial Bank of Persia and the Anglo-Persian Oil Company, both benefited from government support.[66] Yet, without pump-priming investment, the economy would remain backward and there was no prospect of creating a strong buffer state, and without government borrowing there was no easy way of ensuring the political dependence of the Shah. Consequently, British policy towards Persia in the late nineteenth century wavered between promoting a robust state, a strategy that required finance, and leaving the country to its own devices in the hope that its neutrality could be preserved by agile diplomacy.[67]

The cheap option depended upon the goodwill of other powers, and by the close of the nineteenth century it was clear that this was in short supply. After recovering from the Crimean War, Russia resumed her southern expansion. By the 1880s she dominated Persia's external trade (a position she retained until 1914), and had extended her railway network into central Asia and her political control south of the Caspian Sea.[68] Moreover, from the 1890s Russian capital was directed to the Persian government in a series of loans (totalling £7.5m. by 1905), which gave her considerable leverage in Tehran.[69] These developments were greeted with alarm in Britain, where it was thought that Russia's advance might stimulate disaffection in India and also pose a direct military threat in the Middle East itself.[70] As these fears multiplied, Britain responded by adopting a more interventionist approach to Anglo-Persian economic and political relations.

Early indications of this response can be found in the 1880s, when Salisbury began to stiffen British policy towards the defence of Persia. A modest start was made by subsidising steamship services on the Tigris and Karun rivers at the head of the Gulf from the 1880s.[71] A more significant development was the attempt to encourage British investment in Persia. This aim found concrete expression in the shape of the Imperial Bank of Persia, which was formed in 1889 with the backing of two highly reputable City houses, J. H. Schroder and David Sassoon & Co.[72] The Imperial Bank provides a good example of the composition and operation of Britain's burgeoning financial and service diaspora in the second half of the nineteenth century. J. H. Schroder was a well-known merchant bank run by a family which had found refuge in London during the French Wars at the beginning of the century. The Sassoons had made their fortune by accompanying the moving frontier of British influence in the Middle East, India and China before locating their headquarters in London in 1858 and establishing their reputation in the City thereafter. The family's acceptance into high society was marked by a knighthood for Albert Sassoon, the head of the firm, in 1872. The first chairman of the Bank was William Keswick, the former head of Jardine, Matheson & Co. and of the Hongkong and Shanghai Bank. The other banker on the board of directors was Geoffrey Glyn of Glyn, Mills, Currie & Co., the leading private bank in London specialising in overseas railway and banking ventures. As in the case of the Hongkong and Shanghai Bank, cosmopolitan origins gave way to a more homogeneous pattern of recruitment as the Bank became established. The English public school and its ethos soon infused the institution and its staff: hunting, shooting and racing were among the gentlemanly sports fostered in Persia, and by 1896 the Tehran branch was able to field its own cricket team.[73]

The Imperial Bank was a private undertaking but it received the valuable endorsement of a royal charter as well as the support of the British Minister in Persia, and it was given subventions to open branches in politically sensitive areas.[74] The Bank's political ties were readily established. Its royal charter, for example, was granted after the Foreign Office had exerted pressure on the Treasury, and the lever was pulled by Sir Henry Drummond Wolff, a career diplomat with strong connections in the City and Westminster, who was sent to the Middle East in 1888 to strengthen Britain's presence there. The Bank's board of directors soon began to include prominent retired officials from Whitehall and the Indian Civil Service – a pattern of recruitment that continued in the twentieth century and characterised all of the 'colonial' banks. For its part, the Foreign Office hoped to use the Imperial Bank as a conduit for British capital, and attached particular importance to the Shah's need for foreign investment in the 1890s. As the British Minister in Tehran observed of Persia in 1903: 'The more we get her into our debt, the greater will be our hold and our political influence over her government'.[75]

The purpose was clear, but the means remained elusive. The Baring Crisis and the Australian banking collapse in the 1890s added to the City's reluctance to respond to patriotic appeals to invest in Persia without formal guarantees, which successive governments were reluctant to offer.[76] The Imperial Bank itself struggled through the 1890s with some difficulty and little profit.[77] Safe overseas investments lay outside the Middle East, and speculators preferred to take their chance with South African or Australian gold-mining shares, where there was some prospect of a tangible return. In this situation the British government was forced to depart still further from its ideal of non-intervention. At the Foreign Office, Lansdowne developed a more active policy after 1900, authorising two small direct loans to the Persian government in 1903 and 1904, providing subsidies for private firms and giving official backing (including assistance from secret service funds) to the Persian Transport Company, which was established in 1902 to promote road building.[78] This pattern of interference was continued by his successor, Grey, who was also an advocate of sterling diplomacy: 'the broad principle upon which we must necessarily proceed', he emphasised in 1906, 'is to obtain leverage over the Persian government by assisting them in a financial sense'.[79]

The constitutional revolution of 1906 appeared to offer a chance for Britain to apply Grey's maxim. As in the case of the Young Turks, however, the British mistook incipient nationalism and dissident provincialism for Western-style liberalism, and greatly overestimated their chances of forging new political alliances within Persia.[80] Moreover, the revolution generated a great deal of internal instability and it was not until 1909 that victory over the Shah was assured. By that time, however, British policy was increasingly constrained by a desire to placate Russia, and this meant tempering support for reform. The need to reach a settlement with Russia stemmed from the British government's recognition that the costs of halting Russian expansion in Persia were unacceptably high, and that it had also become necessary to concentrate on the threat posed by Germany. Under the terms of the Anglo-Russian Convention of 1907, the two powers agreed to respect Persia's territorial integrity, but they also divided the country into spheres of influence: one in the north assigned to Russia, another in the south-east allotted to Britain, and a third, neutral zone between them.[81] Like the Anglo-Japanese alliance of 1902, the Anglo-Russian convention was essentially a way of reducing defence costs in the face of a challenge by a third power, in this case Germany. In 1911 Britain deserted the constitutional movement and endorsed Russia's successful demands for the dismissal of the Persian government's new American financial adviser, Morgan Schuster, and for the suppression of the Persian assembly, the Majlis.[82] The buffer state was to be preserved, but by policies that favoured stability rather than reform.

After 1907, therefore, sterling diplomacy was hampered by the need to work with the Russians as well as by the continuing caution of the City. Two joint Anglo-Russian loans were approved in 1908 and 1909 in an attempt to restore political stability to Persia, though Britain hoped that they would increase her influence with anti-Russian elements within the country as well.[83] But the Foreign Office also had to intervene in 1910 to prevent the City from lending to the Shah on one of the very rare occasions when it was prepared to do so, because a loan without political strings would have jeopardised Grey's Anglo-Russian policy.[84] In 1911, when a new Persian loan of £1.25m. was placed successfully in the City, it was issued via the Foreign Office's preferred vehicle, the Imperial Bank, and with official support, as well as with the agreement of the Russians.[85] By 1914 the British government had moved very far from its ideal of non-intervention in financial affairs. In doing so, it had also lent a helping hand to the Imperial Bank, whose fortunes improved as a result of official and semi-official support for Persian loans after the turn of the century.[86]

The success of this policy could be seen in the hold which Britain took on the south-eastern sphere of influence allocated to her by the Anglo-Russian Convention, and on the coastal area of the neutral zone, where British troops were stationed after 1911. Britain's presence here was firmly based on her dominance of coastal commerce and shipping, and on her control of the customs revenues of the Gulf ports, which served as security for foreign loans.[87] Inland, important initiatives were taken to promote oil-mining and railway construction, both of which were capital intensive and vulnerable to political uncertainty. As noted earlier, the British government rescued D'Arcy's failing oil concession in 1908, following representations from the Admiralty.[88] This move was the prelude to the formation of the Anglo-Persian Oil Company in 1909 and to government control of the new firm in 1914. The contrast between the *laissez-faire* attitude adopted towards de Reuter and the assistance granted to D'Arcy provides an apt measure of the change in government policy towards private enterprise in Persia between the 1870s and the 1900s. Railway-building was long prevented by 'sterilising agreements' between Russia and Persia. But these expired in 1910 and an opportunity then arose to promote Britain's strategic and commercial interests in the south. In the following year, the Foreign Office helped to put together the Persian Railways Syndicate, a consortium consisting of British oil interests in Persia, the Imperial Bank, the Persian Transport Company, Indian shipping interests, and investment trusts in London.[89] The Syndicate was given preferential treatment by the Foreign Office, though in the event no construction took place before World War I.

By 1914 it was evident that India's line of defence had shifted from Constantinople to the Gulf, where political priorities were more compatible with Britain's commercial and financial interests. But, if the geography had changed, Britain's grip had not loosened: her influence gave her a virtual protectorate along the Gulf coastline eastwards to India, and stretched westwards to Aden and on to Egypt.

Management without development

This assessment of the literature on British imperialism in the Middle East suggests revisions to the two leading interpretations referred to at the outset of the chapter. Historians who look for economic motives find themselves in difficulty when they reach the Middle East because the evidence now available fits awkwardly with the idea that British manufactures and finance swept all before them in either the Ottoman Empire or Persia. This problem has been seized upon by proponents of diplomatic or strategic interpretations of imperialism who have treated the efforts of successive British governments to mobilise business interests as vindicating the belief that politics dominated economics. The only point at which the two interpretations appear to touch is in agreeing that Britain was forced to retreat in the face of the gathering power of new foreign rivals. This perception can be incorporated into the notion that industrial capitalism entered a stage of crisis in the late nineteenth century; it can be attached with equal facility to the argument that, at a time when the metropolitan economy was beginning to suffer from hardening arteries, Britain remained ambulant in the international arena only because the athletes of the Foreign Office were capable of running simultaneously in all directions.

The interpretation presented here has taken a rather different course. We have tried to show that the Middle East fits with our other examples of Britain's ambitious policy of global development in the nineteenth century, and that it demonstrates, too, the extent to which the realisation of this vision depended on the extension abroad of the new financial and service sector after 1850. Throughout the period under review, governments of different complexions called upon financial instruments, rather than manufacturing interests, to act as agents of economic development and political strategy. The Public Debt Administration served in this capacity in the Ottoman Empire; the Imperial Bank did its duty in Persia. Indeed, the links forged between 'colonial' banks, such as the Imperial Bank of Persia and the Hongkong and Shanghai Bank, and the ties established between these groups and the metropolitan government, suggest that a new form of financial corporatism was emerging to service the international economy long before the large firm became characteristic of industry in Britain itself.

Nevertheless, Britain's great experiment met with limited success in the Middle East, and British policy was left without the economic underpinning it needed. The central cause of this failure was the City's judgement that the Middle East was an area of high risks and generally low returns which could not compete with alternatives that were opening up elsewhere, especially in the Dominions and South Africa, during the second half of the century. The turning point here was the Ottoman default of 1875–6, which was regarded in the City as being particularly reprehensible both because of its size and because it was thought to be the product of bad management rather than of bad luck. Thereafter, the Empire was moved steadily to the periphery of Britain's international economic relations, just as representatives there of the new financial and service class, such as Vincent and Caillard, remained on the fringe of inner City circles. The City itself was close to politicians but above politics: it could not be directed into investments that did not satisfy the judgement of the market. If the Ottoman Empire was in default, Persia was too poor to attract serious interest from the City. Consequently, British governments had to adjust their traditional attitudes towards intervention and had to supply subsidies, in one form or another, to draw investors into the region. The Imperial Bank and the activities associated with its operations in Persia provide good examples of the implementation of this policy. Although the tactic achieved a considerable measure of success, as we have seen, Britain's informal influence remained partial rather than complete, and in these circumstances diplomatic agreements were made to control rival powers, notably Russia.

Seen in this light, the Middle East offers an illustration both of the strength of the City and of the importance of strategy in imperial policy; and the two together provide little support for the view that Britain's power, however defined, was on the wane before 1914. But the City's caution is not to be taken as an indication of the weakness of British finance in the face of foreign competition. On the contrary, the small scale of Britain's investments in the Middle East was a sign of the City's strength in having a range of more promising investment opportunities available elsewhere, and in being able to resist political demands. Moreover, where they were present, the City's dispositions were shrewdly placed. The Public Debt Administration served British creditors well and also upheld Britain's wider interest in maintaining the unity of the Ottoman Empire. The Imperial Bank and related ventures in Persia benefited from official support, while other investments were made in the Gulf ports, where the returns were attractive, or secured by customs revenues.

These financial decisions undoubtedly set limits to the power behind British diplomacy in the Middle East. Even so, it is hard to reconcile the evidence with the assumption, influential though it is, that Britain was engaged in a series of rearguard actions in a long retreat from dominance. Palmerston's energetic policy was intended to open the way to informal influence; but, as we have seen, it is misleading to suppose that the result was an informal empire under British sway. It was not until the late Victorian era, when informal empire is conventionally said to have been in decline, that Britain was able to extend her grip on the Ottoman Empire and Persia. This happened, as we have shown in other cases, at the time when Britain's share of commodity trade was beginning to decline, and it is this trend which has attracted scholarly attention. A more important and somewhat less emphasised development, however, was the growing external indebtedness of first the Ottoman Empire and then Persia, which increased the leverage at Britain's disposal. As Lord Derby observed in 1879, three years after the Ottoman default: 'the daily surveillance of which Turkey is the object in her domestic affairs has reduced her sovereign authority to practically zero'.[90] Moreover, the City's caution did not, in the event, frustrate Britain's aims. It is certainly true that French, German and Russian banks increased their investments in the Ottoman Empire and the Middle East from the 1890s. But it has also to be emphasised that these investments were made at least partly because Britain's competitors did not have access to comparable opportunities in other parts of the world, that they were not particularly profitable, and that in 1914 the investors lost their money. At that point, Britain had been neither ousted from the region nor defeated in her purpose of defending India, despite the considerable effort and expenditure made by her rivals.

World War I destroyed the Ottoman Empire, but it also brought down Germany, diverted Russia and enabled Britain and France to influence the division of territory in ways that served their interests. Britain remained the dominant power in the new states that emerged from the southern provinces of the empire as well as in Persia, and she also controlled the region's important oil resources. After World War II, when Whitehall designed a new era of colonial rule, Britain aimed to reposition the empire in the Middle East and Africa. The end came in the 1950s; but its origins should not be traced so far into the past that evidence of successful expansion before 1914 is either minimised or translated, mistakenly, into the language of decline.

Notes

1 'The Porte, it is abundantly proved, is not strong enough to stand alone. It must be held up. We offer ourselves as supporters on the East, Austria on the West'. Lord Salisbury, 1878, quoted in C.J. Lowe, *The Reluctant Imperialists* (1969), Vol. I, p. 19.

2 For one variation on this theme see A.J. Toynbee, *The Western Question in Greece and Turkey*, (Boston, Mass., 1922). The indigenous point of view is put by L. Carl Brown, *International Politics and the Middle East* (Princeton, NJ, 1984), and M.E. Yapp, *The Making of the Modern Near East, 1792–1923* (1987).

3 A crisp summary is provided by D.C.M. Platt, *Finance, Trade and Politics in British Foreign Policy, 1815–1914* (1968), pp. 181–5. Helpful guides to the broader historiography of the region are John R. Broadus, 'Soviet Historical Literature on the Last Years of the Ottoman Empire', *Midd. East. Stud.*, 18 (1982); Rifaat Ali Abou-el Haj, 'The Social Uses of the Past: recent Arab Historiography of Ottoman Rule', *Int. Jour. Middle East Stud.*, 14 (1982); and William J. Olson, *Britain's Elusive Empire in the Middle East, 1900–1921: An Annotated Bibliography* (1982).

4 See Alan Cunningham's illuminating article, 'The Sick Man and the British Physician', *Midd. East. Stud.*, 17 (1981), and the wider commentary in Ronald Hyam, *Britain's Imperial Century, 1815–1914* (1976), Ch. 2.

5 The use made of the Bulgarian issue in British politics is dealt with by Marvin Swartz, *The Politics of British Foreign Policy in the Era of Disraeli and Gladstone* (1985), Ch. 2.

6 The phrase was coined by Lord Dufferin, a noted practitioner, in 1881. Quoted in H.S.W. Corrigan, 'British, French and German Interests in Asiatic Turkey, 1881–1913' (unpublished Ph.D. thesis, University of London, 1954), p. 8. Corrigan's thesis deserves credit for anticipating many of the conclusions of research published subsequently.

7 The economic history of the period is covered by Roger Owen, *The Middle East in the World Economy, 1800–1914* (1981), Charles Issawi, *An Economic History of the Middle East and North Africa* (Chicago, 1982); idem, ed. *The Economic History of the Middle East, 1800–1914* (Chicago, 1966), *The Economic History of Iran, 1800–1914* (Chicago, 1971) and *The Economic History of Turkey, 1800–1914* (Chicago, 1980).

8 A.G. Wood, *A History of the Levant Company* (Oxford, 1935), pp. 198–202; D.C.M. Platt, *The Cinderella Service: British Consuls since 1825* (1971), pp. 125–131.

9 P.J. Cain and A.G. Hopkins, 'The Political Economy of British Expansion Overseas, 1750–1914', *Econ, Hist. Rev.*, 2nd ser. XXXIII (1980), pp. 479–81.

10 The text is printed in Issawi, *The Economic History of the Middle East, 1800–1914*, pp. 38–40. See also Orhan Kurmus, 'The 1838 Treaty of Commerce Re-examined', in Jean-Louis Bacqué-Grammont and Paul Dumont, eds. *Economies et sociétés dans l'Empire Ottoman* (Paris, 1983).

11 Carter V. Findley, *Bureaucratic Reform in the Ottoman Empire: The Sublime Porte, 1789–1922* (Princeton, NJ, 1980); S. Shaw, 'The Nineteenth-Century Ottoman Tax Reforms and Revenue System', *Int. Jour. Middle East Stud.*, 7 (1975); Ehud R. Toledano, *The Ottoman Slave Trade and its Suppression, 1840–1890* (Princeton, NJ, 1983); Roderic H. Davison, *Reform in the Ottoman Empire, 1856–1876* (New York, 1973), Ch. 1.

12 Sevket Pamuk, *The Ottoman Empire and European Capitalism, 1820–1913* (Cambridge, 1987), Ch. 2. Pamuk's important study provides the most rigorous analysis yet made of the Ottoman foreign trade data.

13 Halil Inalcik, 'When and How British Cotton Goods Invaded the Levant Markets', in Huri Islamoglu-Inan, ed. *The Ottoman Empire and the World Economy* (Cambridge, 1987).
14 Pamuk, *Ottoman Empire*, p. 33.
15 Davison, *Reform*, pp. 49–51; Pamuk, *Ottoman Empire*, pp. 132–3.
16 Given the size and diversity of the Ottoman Empire, this is inevitably a generalisation which needs qualification. See, for example, Haim Gerber, 'Modernization in Nineteenth-Century Palestine: the Role of Foreign Trade', *Midd. East. Stud.*, 18 (1983).
17 Exports of Manchester cottons peaked in 1880. See Arthur Redford, *Manchester Merchants and Foreign Trade*, Vol. II (Manchester, 1956), p. 80.
18 O. Anderson, 'Great Britain and the Beginnings of the Ottoman Public Debt, 1854–5', *Hist. Jour.*, 7 (1964), pp. 47–8; Owen, *The Middle East*, pp. 100–1.
19 Pamuk, *The Ottoman Empire*, pp. 57–60, 176–81.
20 Leland H. Jenks, *The Migration of British Capital to 1875* (1927), Chs. 8–9; David Landes, *Bankers and Pashas* (1958), pp. 62–7; A.S.J. Baster, *The Imperial Banks* (1927).
21 A.S.J. Baster, 'The Origins of British Banking Expansion in the Near East', *Econ. Hist. Rev.*, 2nd ser. V (1934). We are grateful to Prof. Christopher Clay, who is writing a history of the Imperial Ottoman Bank, for advice on his subject. At present, a number of topics still have to be clarified, among them the timing of the Ottoman Empire's shift to an effective gold standard. It would seem that Pamuk (*The Ottoman Empire*, p. 13) minimises the extent to which the Empire remained on a bimetallic standard. Evidently, the Empire's ambivalence cannot have increased the City's confidence.
22 Jenks, *Migration*, pp. 294–300; Owen, *The Middle East*, pp. 101–5; Pamuk, *The Ottoman Empire*, Ch. 4.
23 Findlay, *Bureaucratic Reform*. The revisionist view of the Ottoman reform programme is well summarised by Yapp, *Making of the Modern Near East*, pp. 97–145. For a detailed study of reform in one area see David Kushner, 'The Ottoman Governors of Palestine', *Midd. East. Stud.*, 23 (1987).
24 Pamuk, *The Ottoman Empire*, Table 2.4, p. 32; idem, 'The Ottoman Empire in the "Great Depression" of 1873–1896', *Jour. Econ. Hist.*, 44 (1984), pp. 107–18.
25 Quoted in Swartz, *The Politics of British Foreign Policy*, p. 67.
26 Owen, *The Middle East*, p. 198; Issawi, *Economic History of the Middle East*, p. 69; Pamuk, *Ottoman Empire*, pp. 72–3, 76.
27 The definitive work on French investment is Jacques Thobie, *Intérêts et impérialisme français dans l'Empire Ottoman, 1895–1914* (Paris, 1977).
28 Swartz, *The Politics of British Foreign Policy*, pp. 28–30.
29 Quoted in Corrigan, 'British, French and German Interests', p. 4.
30 As Keith Wilson has shown, British policy did not desert Constantinople for Cairo: 'Constantinople or Cairo: Lord Salisbury and the Partition of the Ottoman Empire, 1886–1897', in Keith M. Wilson, ed. *Imperialism and Nationalism in the Middle East* (1983).
31 Swartz, *Politics of British Foreign Policy*, p. 99; A.G. Hopkins, 'The Victorians and Africa: a Reconsideration of the Occupation of Egypt, 1882', *Jour. African Hist.*, 27 (1986), pp. 379–85.
32 Donald C. Blaisdell, *European Control in the Ottoman Empire* (New York, 1929), Ch. 5.
33 On the settlement of 1881 see Blaisdell, *European Control*, Chs. 5–7; Owen, *The Middle East*, pp. 191–200; and Pamuk, *Ottoman Empire*, pp. 61–2.
34 Issawi, *Economic History of the Middle East*, p. 190.
35 Donald Quataert, 'The Silk Industry of Bursa, 1880–1914', in Islamoglu-Inan, *The Ottoman Empire*; Osman Okyar, 'A New Look at the Problem of Economic Growth in the Ottoman Empire (1800–1914)', *Jour. Econ. Hist.*, 16 (1987), pp. 40–1, 46; Pamuk, *Ottoman Empire*, pp. 16–17, 63–4.
36 Okyar, 'A New Look', p. 40; Blaisdell, *European Control*, pp. 152–3.
37 R.P.T. Davenport-Hines and Jean Jacques Van-Helten, 'Edgar Vincent, Viscount D'Abernon, and the Eastern Investment Company in London, Constantinople and Johannesburg', *Bus. Hist.*, 28 (1986). Vincent (1857–1941) was also Financial Adviser to the Egyptian government, 1883–9. After he left the Imperial Ottoman Bank, he was

recruited by the financier, Sir Ernest Cassel (see n. 44), entered parliament as Conservative MP for Exeter, and became a director of the armaments firm, Vickers. He was elevated to the peerage in 1926 and took his title from his home in Stoke D'Abernon, Surrey.

38 R.P.T. Davenport-Hines, 'The Ottoman Empire in Decline: the Business Imperialism of Sir Edgar Vincent', Institute of Commonwealth Studies, London, 1984. We are grateful to Dr Davenport-Hines for permission to cite his unpublished seminar paper. Caillard (1856–1930) also acquired a clutch of directorships after retiring from the Ottoman Public Debt Administration, and became President of the Federation of British Industries in 1919. He was given a knighthood in 1896 but failed, despite persistent efforts, to secure a peerage.

39 Davenport-Hines and Van-Helten, 'Edgar Vincent', p. 44; Davenport-Hines, 'The Ottoman Empire in Decline', pp. 5–7, 9; Corrigan, 'British, French and German Interests', pp. 59–61.

40 No attempt will be made here to provide a general survey of great-power rivalries during the final years of the Ottoman Empire. The best introduction to the voluminous literature on this subject is Marian Kent, ed. *The Great Powers and the End of the Ottoman Empire* (1984).

41 Corrigan, 'British, French and German Interests', pp. 148, 151–3, 174–5; David McLean, 'Finance and "Informal Empire" Before the First World War', *Econ. Hist. Rev.,* 2nd ser. XXIX (1976).

42 Quoted in McLean, 'Finance and "Informal Empire"', p. 294.

43 Marian Kent, 'Agent of Empire? The National Bank of Turkey and British Foreign Policy', *Hist. Jour.,* 18 (1975); McLean, 'Finance and "Informal Empire"', pp. 294–7.

44 Pat Thane, 'Financiers and the British State: The Case of Sir Ernest Cassel', *Bus. Hist.,* 28 (1986). See also Anthony Allfrey, *Edward VII and His Jewish Court* (1991). Cassell (1852–1921) was active in the Balkans, Egypt and China, as well as the Ottoman Empire. His friendship with the Prince of Wales turned out to be a profitable one: when the Prince succeeded to the throne as Edward VII, Cassel managed his portfolio and benefited in return from access to privileged information. He became known, predictably, as 'Windsor Cassel'. The family's royal connection was continued by his granddaughter, Edwina, who married Earl Louis Mountbatten, a great-grandson of Queen Victoria.

45 McLean, 'Finance and "Informal Empire"', pp. 294–7.

46 Corrigan, 'British, French and German Interests', pp. 66, 74–5; Swartz, *Politics of British Foreign Policy,* p. 88; Thobie, *Intérêts et impérialisme,* p. 719, and (for a case study) idem, 'L'emprunt Ottoman 4%, 1901–1905: le triptyque finance-industrie-diplomatique', *Relations Internationales,* 1 (1974).

47 Marian Jack, 'The Purchase of the British Government's Share in the British Petroleum Company, 1912–1914', *Past and Present,* 39 (1968); Marian Kent, *Oil and Empire: British Policy and Mesopotamian Oil, 1900–1920* (1976); Helmut Mejcher, 'Oil and British Policy Towards Mesopotamia, 1914–18', *Midd. East Stud.,* 8 (1972), pp. 377–91; idem, *Imperial Quest for Oil, 1910–1928* (1976); G. Gareth Jones, 'The British Government and the Oil Companies, 1912–1924: the Search for an Oil Policy', *Hist. Jour.,* 20 (1977). See also Geoffrey Jones, *The State and the Emergence of the British Oil Industry* (1981).

48 The differing perspectives of the European powers are well covered in Kent, *The Great Powers.* But it is worth underlining the fact that recent research suggests that it is oversimple to assign Britain's problems in the Middle East to German expansion, which did not match up to the alarmist expectations of contemporary observers. See Ulrich Trumpener, *Germany and the Ottoman Empire, 1914–18* (Princeton, NJ, 1968); H.S.W. Corrigan, 'German–Turkish Relations and the Outbreak of War in 1914: a Reassessment', *Past and Present,* 36 (1967), pp. 144–52; and Gregor Schöllgen, *Imperialismus und Gleichgewicht: Deutschland, England und die orientalische Frage, 1871–1914* (Munich, 1984).

49 The substantial literature on this subject is summarised in Kent, *The Great Powers,* which also provides a bibliography.

50 Richard M. Francis, 'The British Withdrawal from the Baghdad Railway Project in April 1903', *Hist. Jour.,* 16 (1973).

51 Keith A. Hamilton, 'An Attempt to Form an Anglo-French Industrial Entente', *Midd. East. Stud.*, 11 (1975).
52 David McLean, 'British Finance and Foreign Policy in Turkey: the Smyrna-Aidin Railway Settlement, 1913–1914', *Hist. Jour.*, 19 (1976).
53 The Agreement ensured that the Baghdad railway would not extend to the Gulf except under British auspices. This concession reflected the difficulties which the Germans had experienced in raising money for the project and their desire to conciliate Britain in the hope of keeping her out of the impending war with France. (For further details see the references cited in n. 48). Apart from increasing their share of the Ottoman public debt, which turned out to be a bad investment, the French, too, were less of a threat to Britain's economic stake in the Middle East than is indicated by scholars who emphasise her weakness in the face of foreign competition. See, for example, Wigwam I. Shorrock, *French Imperialism in the Middle East: The Failure of Policy in Syria and Lebanon, 1900–1914* (Madison, Wis., 1976).
54 Yapp, *The Making of the Modem Near East,* pp. 189–95, provides an excellent overview. See also Feroz Ahmad, 'Great Britain's Relations with the Young Turks, 1908–14', *Midd. East. Stud.* 2 (1966), and, for an interesting attempt to trace the roots of the movement, Carter V. Findley, 'Economic Bases of Revolution and Repression in the Late Ottoman Empire', *Comp. Stud. in Soc. and Hist.*, 28 (1986).
55 Blaisdell, *European Financial Control,* pp. 178–9.
56 R. Khalidi, *British Policy Towards Syria and Palestine, 1906–14* (1980); Stuart A. Cohen, *British Policy in Mesopotamia, 1903–1914* (Oxford, 1976); Owen, *The Middle East,* pp. 275–6.
57 The analysis which follows owes a good deal to David McLean's authoritative study, *Britain and her Buffer State: The Collapse of the Persian Empire, 1906–1914* (1979). We hope that our indebtedness to his work is consistent with the additional emphasis we have tried to supply. McLean was concerned to demonstrate that British governments adopted increasingly interventionist policies; we have tried to trace the relationship between this trend and the attitude of the City of London towards investing in the Middle East.
58 There is a vast literature dealing with strategies for defending India in the nineteenth century. Recent studies with good bibliographies include: D. Gillard, *The Struggle for Asia, 1828–1914* (1977); M.E. Yapp, *Strategies of British India* (Oxford, 1980); Edward Ingram, *Commitment to Empire; Prophecies of the Great Came in Asia, 1797–1800* (Oxford, 1981); and idem, *In Defence of British India: Great Britain and the Middle East, 1775–1842* (1985).
59 J.B. Kelly, *Britain and the Persian Gulf, 1795–1880* (Oxford, 1968); Gillard, *Struggle for Asia,* pp. 20–3; Mikhail Volodarsky, 'Persia and the Great Powers, 1856–1869', *Midd. East. Stud.*, 19 (1983); idem, 'Persia's Foreign Policy between the Two Herat Crises, 1831–56', *Midd. East. Stud.*, 21 (1981); Barbara English, *John Company's Last War* (1971).
60 Stephanie Jones, *Two Centuries of Overseas Trading; The Origins and Growth of the Inchcape Group* (1986), pp. 21–3 and Ch. 3.
61 For an example of one development see Ahmad Seyf, 'Commercialisation of Agriculture: Production and Trade of Opium in Persia, 1850–1906', *Int. Jour. Middle Fast Stud.*, 16 (1984).
62 McLean, *Britain and her Buffer State,* pp. 19–23; Yapp, *The Making of the Modem Near East,* pp. 162–72. See also Shaul Bakhash, *Iran: Monarchy, Bureaucracy and Reform under the Qajars, 1858–1896* (1978), and Guity Nashat, *The Origins of Modern Reform in Iran* (Champaign-Urbana, Ill., 1982).
63 Geoffrey Jones, *Banking and Empire in Iran: The History of the British Bank of the Middle East,* Vol. 1 (1986), pp. 3–25, 48–52; N. Keddie, *Religion and Rebellion in Iran: The Tobacco Protest, 1891–1892* (1966).
64 On the currency question see P.W. Avery and J.B. Simmons, 'Persia on a Cross of Silver, 1880–1890', *Midd. East. Stud.*, 10 (1974). Persia's currency (the Kran) lost more than half its value against sterling between 1850 and 1890.
65 Jones, *Banking and Empire,* pp. 49–51.
66 Issawi, *Economic History,* pp. 70–1; McLean, *Britain and her Buffer State,* pp. 61–3, 143–4.

67 McLean, *Britain and her Buffer State,* pp. 29–30.
68 Ibid. pp. 14–19.
69 Jones, *Banking and Empire,* p. 87.
70 M.A. Yapp, 'British Perceptions of the Russian Threat to India', *Modem Asian Studies,* 21 (1987).
71 McLean, *Britain and her Buffer State,* p. 7.
72 Jones, *Banking and Empire,* pp. 20–31. For the Bank's colonial connections see also D. McLean, 'International Banking and its Political Implications: the Hongkong and Shanghai Banking Corporation and the Imperial Bank of Persia, 1889–1914', in Frank H.H. King, ed. *Eastern Banking: Essays in the History of the Hongkong and Shanghai Banking Corporation* (1983).
73 Jones, *Banking and Empire,* pp. 110, 143, 153.
74 Ibid. pp. 90–2.
75 Quoted in McLean, 'Finance and "Informal Empire"', p. 297.
76 Jones, *Banking and Empire,* pp. 17–20; McLean, 'International Banking', p. 12.
77 Jones, *Banking and Empire,* pp. 49, 53–4, 66.
78 McLean, *Britain and her Buffer State,* pp. 59, 68–9, 133–4. Also L.P. Morris, 'British Secret Service Activity in Khorassan, 1887–1908', *Hist. Jour.,* 27 (1984).
79 McLean, *Britain and Her Buffer State,* p. 143.
80 The constitutional movement is summarised by Yapp, *The Making of the Modem Near East,* pp. 247–60. The most interesting recent work has focused on the socioeconomic causes of the revolution. See, for example, Gad Gilbar, 'The Big Merchants (tujjar) and the Persian Constitutional Revolution of 1906', *Asian and African Studies,* 2 (1976); idem, 'The Opening up of Qajar Iran: some Economic and Social Aspects', *Bulletin of the School of Oriental and African Studies,* 49 (1986); and Mohammed Reza Afshari, 'The Pīshivarān and Merchants in Precapitalist Iranian Society: an Essay on the Background and Causes of the Constitutional Revolution', *Int. Jour. Middle East Stud.,* 15 (1983). British policy is dealt with by Ira Klein, 'British Intervention in the Persian Revolution, 1905–1909', *Hist. Jour.,* 15 (1972).
81 Ira Klein, 'The Anglo-Russian Convention and the Problems of Central Asia, 1907–1914', *Jour. Brit. Stud.,* 11 (1971), pp. 126–4; and, on this subject generally, Firuz Kazemadeh, *Russia and Britain in Persia, 1864–1914: A Study in Imperialism* (New Haven, Conn., 1968).
82 McLean, *Britain and Her Buffer State,* pp. 83, 103–5; Robert A. McDaniel, *The Schuster Mission and the Persian Constitutional Revolution* (Minneapolis, Minn., 1974).
83 McLean, *Britain and Her Buffer State,* pp. 89–91.
84 Ibid. pp. 93–100; Jones, *Banking and Empire,* pp. 120–1.
85 Jones, *Banking and Empire,* pp. 120–4.
86 Ibid. pp. 110, 116, 122–3.
87 McLean, 'International Banking', pp. 7–8; Marian Kent, 'Great Britain and the End of the Ottoman Empire', in Kent, *The Great Powers,* pp. 179–80.
88 See pp. 408–9.
89 Jones, *Banking and Empire,* pp. 129–31; McLean, *Britain and Her Buffer State,* p. 119. For a case study of the diplomacy of railway-building see D.W. Spring, 'The Trans-Persian Railway Project and Anglo-Russian Relations, 1909–14', *Slavonic and East European Review,* 54 (1976).
90 Quoted in Blaisdell, *European Financial Control,* p. 26.

13

'MAINTAINING THE CREDIT-WORTHINESS OF THE CHINESE GOVERNMENT', 1839–1911[1]

Hobson was not alone among contemporaries in regarding the contest for influence in China at the close of the nineteenth century as being the prelude to an economic division or even a territorial partition which would alter the course of world history.[2] In the event, China defied the odds: her vast economy was insufficiently penetrated to be either developed or undermined by Western forces; formally at least, she managed to retain her political independence, despite the manifest frailty of successive Ch'ing governments and the ultimate collapse of the Manchu dynasty in 1911. This outcome contrasts with the experience of the South American republics, which were drawn into the West's economic and cultural orbit, and of Africa, where indigenous states lost their independence and became colonies of the European powers. However, this does not mean that China escaped from imperialist impulses. The public sector, especially finance, fell under external control and this, in turn, curtailed the political independence of the central government. The Chinese case is therefore closer to that of the Ottoman Empire than it is to South America or Africa, and it raises the question of whether imperialist designs on these centralised but also sprawling polities sprang from different impulses or whether broadly similar intentions were frustrated by a series of drawn games of diplomatic chess or by forces within indigenous society which remain, despite the advances of modern research, in part inscrutable.

In the case of China, most answers to this question emphasise the underlying continuity of Britain's economic and political aims in the Far East during the nineteenth century and focus instead on changes in the means required to uphold them.[3] Thus, current assessments give considerable prominence to the process by which Britain shifted from a low-profile, free-trading policy to a more interventionist stance following the Sino-Japanese War of 1894–5, and attribute the change primarily to the new, assertive policies of other powers. There is less agreement about the character of the interests that were defended by this move: some interpretations point towards economic motives, but do so in ways which, though avoiding notions of capitalist conspiracies, often lack specificity; others note the relatively minor role played by China in Britain's international commerce, and give primacy to the activities of the Foreign Office in mobilising economic forces for predominantly geo-political purposes.

It is impossible to provide a comprehensive assessment of the relevant literature in the space available here, not least because a full account would need to determine the role of the complex changes taking place within China itself in the nineteenth century, and this is a vast undertaking which has yet to be attempted by historians of European imperialism.[4] However, research on the foreign, 'barbarian' presence has also advanced greatly in recent years, notably through contributions to business history, and it is now possible to offer a view of events which builds on but also adapts the positions established so far.[5] We shall try to show that Britain's interest in China, far from being static, underwent an important shift of emphasis from an initial concern with markets for exports from India and Britain to a preoccupation with opportunities for finance. This trend was under way well before the Sino-Japanese War, and was an expression of developments within the international economy brought about by innovations stemming largely from British enterprise, and was not simply a response to external stimuli administered by foreign powers. The outcome was an effective if sometimes awkward collaboration between political and economic agents, principally the Foreign Office and the Hongkong and Shanghai Bank. This alliance drew the template for British policy towards China from the 1890s onwards, and was successful in its twin aims of upholding China's territorial integrity while also advancing Britain's economic, and especially financial, interests during a period of intense international rivalry in the Far East.

Experiments with informal influence, 1839–94

The peculiar mixture of compulsion and liberalism prescribed by the early Victorians as a remedy for universal ills was first applied to China in the 1830s.[6] The end of the East India Company's monopoly of the China trade in 1833 created further opportunities for private traders who were keen to expand sales of Indian cottons and opium.[7] Among them were William Jardine and James Matheson, who moved into the China trade in the late 1820s as 'free merchants' and formed what was to become one of the most famous expatriate firms operating in China, Jardine, Matheson & Co., in 1832.[8] At the same time, growing concern about providing outlets for British manufactures, which were experiencing serious difficulties in the late 1830s, generated wider interest in the potential of the fabled China market. Underlying these developments, however, was the problem that India was unable to meet her external obligations, including the Home Charges, by exporting directly to Britain, and counted on exports to China (principally opium) to balance her payments.[9] China's refusal to extend ports of entry beyond the narrow gate at Canton, combined with Commissioner Lin's ban on opium imports in 1839, therefore presented a serious threat to an emerging system of multilateral settlements and took the problem far beyond the grievances of China hands, old and new.

These issues provided the impetus behind the forceful policies which led to wars with China in 1839–42 and in 1858–60.[10] The first war ended with the Treaty of Nanking, which ceded Hong Kong, conferred rights of extraterritoriality on British citizens, opened five ports (including Shanghai) to free trade, and fixed tariffs at uniform and modest levels. These provisions were reinforced in 1854 by the creation of the Imperial Maritime Customs Administration, which placed China's tariffs under the direction of a British Inspector-General, who, according to one observer, 'came to enjoy more influence with the Foreign Office than did the British Minister in Peking'.[11] The Treaty of Tientsin, which ended the second war, opened more ports to international commerce, allowed foreign shipping to enter the Yangtse, legalised the opium trade, and levied indemnities on China which were to be paid from customs duties.

These impositions were intended to be a low-cost and ultimately self-financing means of unlocking the potential of the vast China market. Britain had no territorial designs on China: on the contrary, in exchange for concessions centred on the Treaty Ports, Britain acquired a commitment to support the government in Peking, which was thought to be the best guarantee of domestic stability and orderly commerce.[12] The Treaty Ports were to become bridgeheads to the interior, releasing the export potential of the hinterland and acting as funnels for a return trade in goods from Britain and India. Despite their apparent promise, these plans disappointed successive generations of China-watchers.[13] Britain undoubtedly came to dominate China's overseas trade, but the trade itself remained small and expectations of expansion had constantly to be revised.[14] Between 1840 and 1870 China supplied about 5 per cent of Britain's imports, but took less than 3 per cent of her exports. India's exports of opium increased, but the feverish calculations about clothing and equipping several hundred million Chinese turned out, not for the last time, to be fantasies. By 1896, after half a century of endeavour, China and Hong Kong between them accounted for only about 8 per cent of Britain's main export, cotton goods.[15] China's own export sector remained dependent on tea and silk, which, as we shall see, began to experience difficulties towards the close of the century. Foreign investment was also on a small scale and was confined mainly to the Treaty Ports. At the time when the Ottoman Empire was on the edge of bankruptcy, China had scarcely contracted her first foreign public loan.[16] Instead of acting as bridgeheads, the Treaty Ports became enclaves which strengthened Chinese merchants, notably the compradors, and incorporated the representatives of the West into a vibrant indigenous system of distribution.[17]

The reasons for the failure of this experiment in development derive from a mixture of economic constraints and public policy choices which lies beyond the scope of this study.[18] At the time, when the outcome was unclear, British merchants continued to hope that the China market could be prised open by a combination of railways and active diplomacy, and to fear that this strategy would first be applied by foreign competitors. British governments, however, began to take a more cautious view of China's development prospects from the 1860s.[19] The Foreign Office was not prepared to see Britain's position eroded, but it was also unwilling to adopt policies which, besides being costly, might weaken the authority of Peking and stimulate the territorial ambitions of rival powers.[20] As always, opportunities had to be weighed against costs and against alternatives which, fortuitously, arose elsewhere in the middle of the century following the revival of international trade and the expansion, in particular, of the Indian market.[21]

The manifest limitations of the development drive ought not to obscure the fact that significant changes took place among the firms representing Britain's economic interests in China during the second half of the century, principally as a result of the extension of new financial and commercial services to the Far East.[22] The foundation of the Hongkong and Shanghai Bank in 1865 greatly improved credit facilities; and the advent of regular steamship services in the 1870s, coupled with the extension of the telegraph (which reached Shanghai in 1871), reduced the time taken by commercial transactions and lowered their cost. These innovations attracted new traders (such as Butterfield & Swire) to the Treaty Ports and heightened business rivalries at a time when Western firms were unable to penetrate the interior.[23] Moreover, the main lines of trade became much less profitable in the 1870s and 1880s.[24] China's import-purchasing power was affected by a decline in the profitability of tea and silk exports during the last quarter of the century, largely as a result of competition from India and Japan. Although exports received some stimulus from the fall in the value of silver from the 1870s, this was offset by adverse movements in the barter and income terms of trade. The return business in British manufactured goods also began to suffer from competition: after 1883, for example, cotton yarn from India replaced British yarn in the China market.[25] The years preceding the Sino-Japanese war were particularly poor. At the close of 1886 the British Consul in Shanghai reported that the year had ended in 'a state of depression never before witnessed in the China trade'.[26] Matters did not improve: Russell & Co., the most prestigious of the United States' firms trading in China, collapsed in 1891;[27] the Hongkong and Shanghai Bank's chief comprador became bankrupt in the following year; and the Australian banking crisis shook business confidence in 1893.[28] According to Jardine, Matheson's agent, trade in the Far East had been 'disastrous for some time'.[29]

The leading import and export firms reacted to these trends by moving out of the old staple trades and by becoming managing agencies concerned increasingly with services, notably shipping, insurance and banking, and with an array of activities connected to property and utilities in the Treaty Ports.[30] Jardine, Matheson & Co. provides a good example of this shift of interest. Reacting to competition from newcomers to the China trade, and judging that Chinese merchants would continue to handle imports and exports outside the Treaty Ports, Jardines gave up the opium trade in the 1870s and turned to shipping, banking and allied services.[31] They also started to forge alliances with progressive elements in the Chinese bureaucracy, made several small loans for political purposes in the 1870s, and showed their willingness to co-operate with the modernising programme advocated by the 'self-strengthening' movement by entering into joint ventures with Chinese entrepreneurs.[32]

These changes in the organisation and performance of the export sector had important consequences for the Hongkong and Shanghai Bank, which had become the leading expatriate bank in the Far East by the close of the nineteenth century.[33] The Bank was founded by a cosmopolitan group of local merchants primarily to finance China's overseas trade but also in the expectation that the development of the Chinese economy was imminent, and that new business, including public loans, would then materialise.[34] From the 1870s, however, the Bank found itself grappling with unexpected problems as the profitability of trade declined and as the fall in the value of silver created difficulties in meeting sterling obligations. Moreover, from the 1880s the bank began to face competition, first from the Yokahama Specie Bank (1880) and then from the Deutsche-Asiatische Bank (1889).[35] The Bank had to manage its exchange dealings with great skill, and it also had to grow if it was to remain profitable and credit-worthy.

In these circumstances, the Bank was anxious to extend its business beyond its traditional concern with international trade and, if possible, into government loans.[36] The Bank had privileged access to official sources from the outset, since it acted as banker to the colonial government in Hong Kong and also to the Imperial Maritime Customs Administration, which controlled the principal security for public borrowing.[37] Only 'imperial' loans (those raised by the central government in Peking) could draw on this security which, in turn, was essential to winning the support of the London money market.[38] Not surprisingly, the Bank was keen to see the unity of China maintained, and it joined the Foreign Office in supporting the central government. However, the Ch'ing dynasty was reluctant to raise money from abroad, and did so only as a result of crises in foreign affairs, first with Japan over Formosa in 1874 and then following the Sino-French War of 1883–5. These events provided the Bank with the opportunity it had been waiting for: it issued China's first foreign loan in 1874, and followed this with further loans later in the decade and during the 1880s.[39] The first loan enabled the Bank to avoid making a loss in 1874–5; the others underpinned its profitability during a period of continuing trading difficulty.[40]

The growth of the Bank's foreign loan business also strengthened its ties with London. The Bank had the backing of the London and County Bank at the time of its foundation, and thereafter it took care to maintain close links, through its London office, with bankers of 'very high standing' in the City.[41] Its managers and shareholders became predominantly British, and its reserves were invested in British (and Indian) government securities.[42] Although the Bank lost some of its cosmopolitan origins, it remained international in its aspirations; it was never intended to serve or even to favour British industry.[43] By the 1890s, the Bank was considered to be part of the City community. At the Bank of England's request, it subscribed to the fund raised to help out Barings in 1890, when the General Manager, Thomas Jackson, received a knighthood for 'services to British commerce in the East'.[44]

During the last quarter of the century, the changing structure of trade and growing difficulties among the expatriate firms led to renewed demands for China to be opened to foreign enterprise. This pressure reinforced and expressed a wider concern in Britain with the effects of commercial depression and foreign competition, and in turn led the Foreign Office to reconsider the extent to which it was willing to act in support of business interests in China, as indeed elsewhere. This drift in official thinking can be discerned from two episodes which arose in the mid-1880s: the first drew attention to the political implications of new lending to China; the second tested Britain's reaction to the rise of foreign competition.

In 1884, when China was technically in default on a portion of her loan repayments, the Hongkong and Shanghai Bank asked Sir Harry Parkes, the British Minister in Peking, to intervene with the Chinese authorities.[45] Parkes, who had subscribed heavily to the Bank's loans to China, duly obliged and payment was resumed. His action prompted considerable discussion in Whitehall. As always, the Treasury was alarmed at the prospect of a back-door guarantee and the Foreign Office was equally worried about unauthorised intervention. However, Sir Julian Pauncefote, then an Assistant Under-Secretary at the Foreign Office and also a substantial shareholder in the Hongkong and Shanghai Bank, argued that 'diplomatic intervention in China is a necessity in many cases where it would not be resorted to elsewhere', and pointed out that formal communications concerning the loan had to be conducted through the Legation because this was the only channel which the Ch'ing government recognised.[46] Although no official departure from existing policy was sanctioned, the episode showed that the Foreign Office was edging towards more active backing for British interests in China. Parkes's action helped to maintain the confidence of British investors, and in doing so blurred the line between loans which were guaranteed and those which were not.

Two years later, reports that a powerful German syndicate was about to descend on China led to fears that British finance and manufactures would be pushed aside, and prompted a flurry of representations from Chambers of Commerce, the China lobby in the House of Commons, and influential private sources.[47] Once again, the official response was guarded; but the alarm was real and it produced a 'series of "unofficial" measures designed to support both the financial and the commercial interests of British firms in China and of British industry'.[48] This concern died away when the German venture faded in 1886, but the event offered a preview of the more serious rivalries which were to arise in the 1890s.

None of this is to suggest that big business was pushing for the partition of China; on the contrary, the large firms remained keen to cooperate with modernising elements within the bureaucracy and continued to hope that China would eventually develop along Japanese lines.[49] At the same time, the evidence now available indicates that the evolution of commerce since the mid-century had put British companies in a position where they had both the capacity and the need to develop more profitable business, that loans to Peking were seen as being a particularly attractive option, and that the Foreign Office, under both Liberal and Conservative governments, was willing to take a more assertive line on behalf of British business at times when it appeared to be under threat. The idea that British interests on the China coast remained quiescent until disturbed by the sudden outbreak of the Sino-Japanese War therefore misses a developing theme in British imperialism in the late nineteenth century, and in doing so it also presumes that policy was more reactive than was the case. As we shall now see, Britain's attitude towards China after 1894–5 was very much an extension of trends which had already begun to make their presence felt.

The scramble for China, 1894–1911

If the outbreak of the Sino-Japanese War in 1894 pushed British policy further along a path it was beginning to take, it nevertheless did so at a pace which caused the Foreign Office to shed a number of long-standing assumptions about the future of the Far East. The hope that China would experience a measured evolution, combining economic progress with political stability and led by Britain, suddenly began to look unrealistic. In its place was thrust the prospect that Britain, the sitting tenant, might be dislodged by upstarts who had no respect for her claims. China was one of Britain's minor trading partners, but the surplus generated by existing commerce made a useful contribution to the balance of payments,[50] and the potential, especially for finance and services, was irresistible. If the China market was finally going to be opened, Britain intended to cross the threshold as fast as other entrants. The principles of free trade and the open door were bent and at points abandoned in the rush; but the Foreign Office held firmly to the policy of supporting central authority in Peking both to safeguard the security for China's foreign loans and to prevent other powers from establishing exclusive rights that would damage Britain's cosmopolitan trading relationships.[51] In doing so, Whitehall became closely involved with British commercial interests, and particularly with the Hongkong and Shanghai Bank, which regarded the preservation of China's unity as being crucial to securing new business as well as to avoiding default on existing loans.[52]

The defeat of Ch'ing forces at the hands of Japan in 1895 signalled the start of a scramble for influence and territory in China. The immediate and also the most important result of the war was to compel the government to borrow from foreign sources on a far larger scale than before. As Charles Addis (then an aspiring sub-manager with the Hongkong and Shanghai Bank) was quick to realise, Japan's victory was an opportunity rather than a set-back for British policy. China now needed Britain's protection more than ever; the indemnity imposed by Japan would have to be financed in London; and Britain would then be in a position to influence the 'development of the material resources of China'.[53] This judgement may have underestimated the obstacles to opening up the hinterland, but it was also prescient: in the 21 years between 1874 and 1895 the Bank (the principal intermediary) raised about £12m. for the Chinese government; in the four years between 1896 and 1900 it provided no less than £32m.[54] British loans to the Chinese government continued to grow after the turn of the century, albeit at a slower rate, and almost doubled in value between 1902 and 1914.[55] Addis might also have predicted that

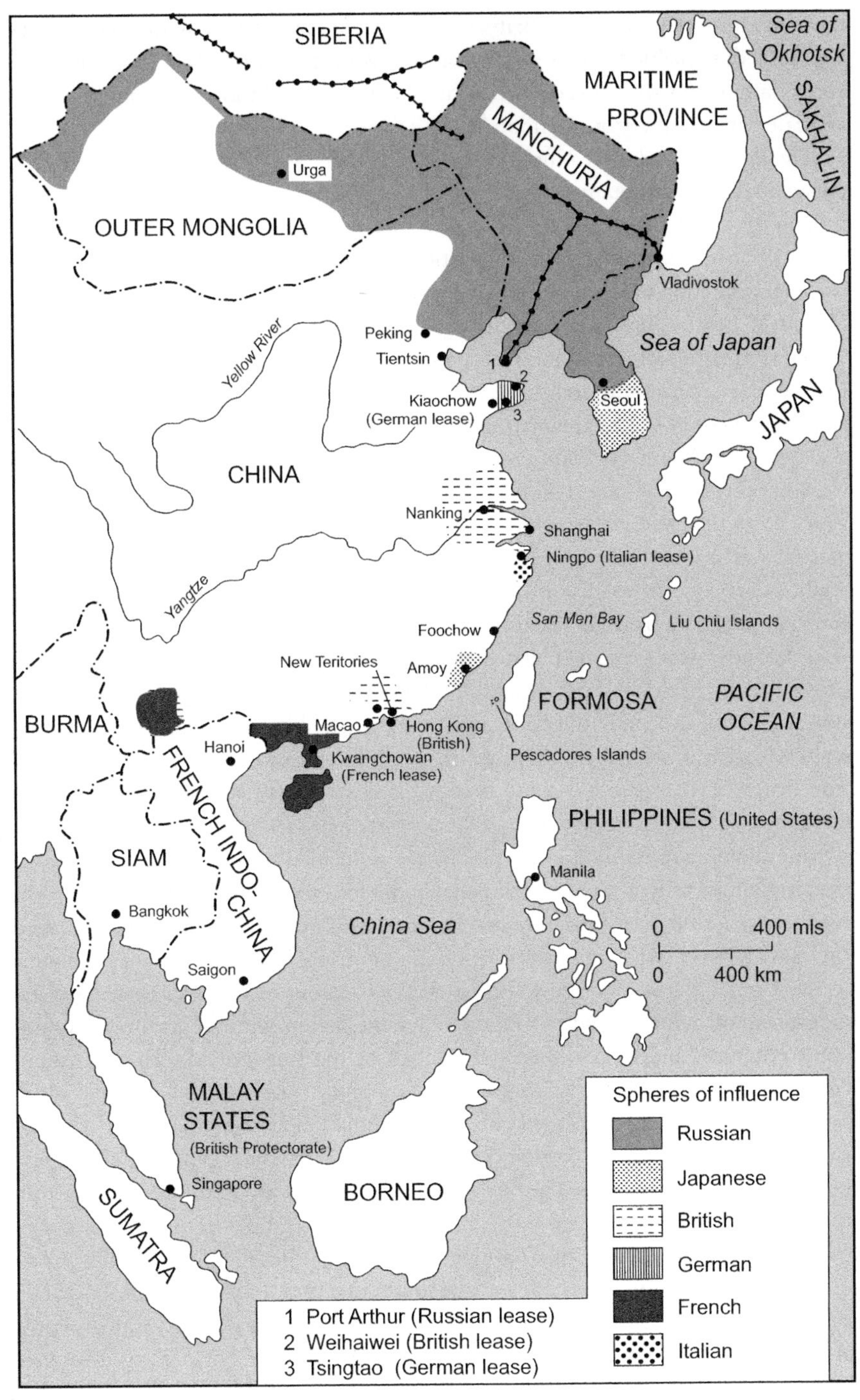

MAP 9 Foreign spheres of influence in China, c.1900

After: C.C. Eldridge, *Victorian Imperialism* (1978)

the indemnity would benefit British business with the victors as well as with the vanquished: it enabled Japan to move to the gold standard in 1897, improved her credit-rating, and thus helped her to attract substantial inflows of foreign capital, most of which came from London.[56]

The growing and increasingly overt convergence of politics and finance became apparent during negotiations over the three post-war loans that funded China's indemnity payments. In 1895, when the first loan was being discussed, the Foreign Office tried to create an international consortium that would hold China together and contain the ambitions of rival powers. The Hongkong and Shanghai Bank asked for official support, but the Foreign Office thought that formal action would simply provoke retaliation, and responded by calling on 'the assistance of the Rothschilds in preventing anything being done to prejudice British interests'.[57] The result was a cooperative agreement between the Hongkong and Shanghai Bank and the Deutsche-Asiatische Bank in conjunction with Rothschilds in London; but by the time this arrangement had been reached the loan had been won by a Russian syndicate, which had government backing (and French support). When the second loan was raised in the following year, the Anglo-German group was in place and ready to act. On this occasion the Bank of England agreed to inscribe the bonds, following pressure from the British government.[58] Addis, who was surely in a position to know, was satisfied that for practical purposes the Bank of England had provided 'one of the best guarantees'.[59] The group's bid was accepted, the flotation was successful, and the Hongkong and Shanghai Bank's profits jumped. The third loan, which was offered in 1898, was also given official backing, despite opposition from the Treasury, and it too was handled by the British-led consortium. As Curzon explained, in a statement that conveyed his sense of British superiority with undiplomatic frankness: 'the Government decided not merely that they were better qualified to lend the money than any others, but that in the interests of commercial expansion, which we also had in view, and in the interests of sound finance, the assistance was what might very properly be given'.[60] No doubt with the same interests in mind, the Foreign Office used the occasion to establish Britain's claim to a sphere of influence in the Yangtse Valley, the region with the greatest development potential, and to reinforce her control of the Imperial Maritime Customs Administration.[61]

International competition over shares in China's indemnity loans was complemented by a battle for railway and mining concessions which reached its height between 1895 and 1900. The scramble for concessions stemmed partly from the hope of finding new, profitable business, but also from the need to generate extra revenues to secure China's foreign loans, since the income from the Imperial Maritime Customs was fully pledged by the turn of the century.[62] Britain was well represented in the vast allocations which were made during this period, acquiring large holdings in the Yangtse Valley and securing concessions elsewhere to prevent rival powers from carving China into exclusive zones.[63] As in other parts of the world, the opening of the frontier was accompanied by the formation of new investment groups and syndicates.[64] The leading companies were not simply vehicles for expatriate firms on the China coast, but were backed by London finance and included prominent City bankers among their directors. The British and Chinese Corporation, founded in 1898, brought together Jardine, Matheson and the Hongkong and Shanghai Bank, and was connected to Rothschilds, Barings and other City banks. The Peking Syndicate (1897) and the Yangtse Valley Company (1901) were similarly constituted, and the former also included South African mining interests. These firms were essentially financial instruments rather than representatives of 'finance capital' in the sense of linking banks with industry.[65] Within the limits of prudence dictated by financial cost and diplomatic risk, the Foreign Office gave vigorous support to private enterprise in securing concessions and in diverting competitors to the fringes of the Chinese empire away from the main focus of British interests.[66]

Yet the estate remained undeveloped. Concessions were more easily won than exploited, and the attempt to move inland fuelled a reaction to foreign intrusion which culminated in the Boxer Rising in 1900.[67] Following the suppression of the Boxers, Britain consolidated her position in China by revising her treaty arrangements with the Ch'ing government. Under the terms of the Mackay Treaty (1902), China abolished certain duties on internal trade and in exchange was allowed to raise the tariff on imports.[68] Manchester opposed the increase but could make no headway against the Foreign Office and the Hongkong and Shanghai Bank, which recognised that Peking had to be provided with the means of servicing China's enlarged foreign debt. In fact, the Mackay Treaty was based upon a memorandum drawn up by Addis, now manager of the Hongkong and Shanghai Bank, and it also bound China to adopt a uniform currency, a national bank, and, when conditions allowed, a gold standard.[69]

After 1900, however, the City of London marked down the attractions of investing in China, partly because of the political risks and partly because of anxieties about the soundness of the security, which in turn reflected the increasing size of the public debt and the disappointing performance of the export economy.[70] The indemnities imposed by the foreign powers after the Boxer Rising were profitable fines which forced China into renewed borrowing, but they also reduced her ability to finance productive projects and made British investors wary of putting their money into risky, long-term development loans in China.[71] The Foreign Office complained endlessly about the lack of British enterprise, but it could neither alter the judgement of the market nor lead the City where it did not want to go. Exceptions to this rule arose only when the government provided sufficient support to reduce the risk or when the banks decided to treat particular loans as 'loss leaders' which would subsequently promote profitable business. Britain's rivals, on the other hand, generally had fewer investment opportunities and greater powers of direction over their money markets.[72] Consequently, there was growing apprehension that Britain would lose ground in the contest to win influence in Peking and to develop the mainland.

Britain's response to this challenge showed just how interdependent politics and finance had become. After 1900, intervention on behalf of British business in China became a regular feature of diplomatic activity. In 1903, for example, the Foreign Office helped to put together a syndicate to construct a railway along the Yangtse Valley, and provided official backing when it raised money in the City;[73] in the next year government encouragement was given to a loan for building the Shanghai–Nanking line.[74] Following the Boxer Rising, Britain also had to take account of the emergence of 'Young China'.[75] As with the Young Turks and the constitutionalists in Persia, the Foreign Office hoped that the reform movement was a sign that the long-awaited conversion to Western liberalism was at hand. Having loaned money to secure concessions after 1895, Britain was prepared to lend more money after the turn of the century to enable China to recover her rights, providing that the terms were suitable and that the results did not weaken central authority. In a complex deal in 1905, for instance, the Colonial Office arranged for the Hongkong and Shanghai Bank to lend £1.1m. to enable China to buy out American interests in the Canton–Hankow line, and then advanced a further £3m. to redeem the railway in return for the right to build a direct link between Hankow and Hong Kong.[76]

Financial considerations also entered into various schemes which the Foreign Office devised to conciliate other powers. An obvious case was the alliance formed with the Japanese in 1902, which helped the Treasury to control naval expenditure at a critical time by making Japan Britain's watchdog in the Far East.[77] In return for guaranteeing China's territorial integrity, Japan was let off the leash in Korea, which lay beyond the bounds of British interests. With regard to the mainland itself, the chief aim of the Foreign Office was to shepherd other powers into agreements which would uphold the principles of 'responsible lending' and prevent financial competition from degenerating into territorial acquisition. This task required the cooperation of the City, but because the government could not direct the merchant banks there was often a need to draw on foreign sources to supplement British capital. This problem played a part in the decisions first to share China's post-war indemnity loans with Germany, and then to cooperate with France, in harmony with the new entente, in financing Chinese railways after 1904.[78] An allied consideration was that, since rival powers had free access to the London capital market, they did not have to be penned in by the Foreign Office. Concern that Russia and Japan, which had weak capital markets and strong government support, might use the City of London to compromise British policy ensured that their claims for shares of China's loan business were listened to more carefully than would otherwise have been the case.[79]

These developments drew the Foreign Office and the Hongkong and Shanghai Bank into an even closer partnership, despite increasing criticism – the more embarrassing because it was justified – that this involved a departure from the principle of impartiality which government departments were supposed to apply in their dealings with private firms. This special relationship was the product of converging interests and was sealed by a process of osmosis which absorbed the Bank into gentlemanly culture.[80] The Bank never lost its Hong Kong base, which was the source of its strength in the Far East, but it was also steadily permeated by metropolitan values. From the 1880s, the Bank's main recruiting and training centre was located in London, and by the turn of the century it had become an institution for changing 'young gentlemen into bank clerks'.[81] Not surprisingly, the young gentlemen were drawn primarily from landed and professional families, and hardly at all from backgrounds in manufacturing. As in other parts of the empire, there was a strong admixture of promising young Scots who had been caught in the glutinously effective 'porridge trap'.[82] On both sides of the border, the Bank relied heavily on public schools to supply suitable new entrants, and it cultivated a sporting ethos which placed great emphasis on team games such as rugby and cricket. In these ways, the Bank nurtured a sense of solidarity which generated institutional loyalty among its employees, helped to define their sense of social identity, and justified the supremacy of the white man in his dealings with alien cultures. There were infrequent attempts to modify the rites of apprenticeship by attracting graduates and by encouraging Bank staff to learn Chinese, but they left little impression. Since the existing system produced satisfactory results, there seemed little reason to change the method: exchange bankers, it was said, 'were born not made'.[83]

The qualities prized by the Bank were personified by Charles Addis, the son of a Scots minister, who joined the Bank as a young clerk in 1880 and became London Manager in 1905.[84] On his return from the East, Addis was steadily absorbed into London banking and social circles, where his benefactors included Lord Revelstoke, the head of Barings. After 1905, Addis spent an increasing amount of time acting as a financial diplomat, travelling between London, Paris and Berlin on behalf of the Bank and keeping in close touch with the Foreign Office.[85] He received a knighthood in 1913, and he finished his career as a director of the Bank of England and as an adviser to the Treasury and the Cabinet on financial and Far Eastern affairs before retiring to his home in Surrey. Addis was a consistent supporter of free trade, the gold standard and stable exchange rates. His vision of international development allocated non-governmental organisations, principally banks, a leading role in financing modernisation, and he regarded the British empire as being the best means yet invented of realising these cosmopolitan aspirations. His was a world in which, ideally, capital knew no national frontiers; he had no time for protectionist sentiments or for the special pleading of industrial interests whose competitive power was in decline. His approach to China was that of the modern missionary whose faith was drawn from the universal principles found in Calvinism and economics. Addis hoped that China would remain strong and independent but also that it would be converted to progress through a programme of 'responsible lending', which Britain was uniquely qualified, and therefore morally obliged, to undertake.[86]

Cooperation between the Foreign Office and the Hongkong and Shanghai Bank reached a new peak of intensity during the critical period between the fall of the Manchu dynasty in 1911 and the appointment of Yuan Shi-k'ai as President of the Republic of China in 1912. The underlying causes of the revolution of 1911 lie beyond the scope of this chapter, and in any case are still much debated among specialists.[87] But it is clear that foreign incursions since 1895 had generated growing disaffection in the provinces, which resented the increased burden of taxation imposed by the central government to meet China's external financial obligations, and that their hostility merged with mercantile and popular opposition to railway and mining concessions and to the attempts to exploit them after the turn of the century. The Ch'ing government fell between its dislike of the barbarians (manifested in its support for the Boxers), and its belated recognition of the need for economic reform, which could be undertaken only with foreign assistance, given the reluctance of Chinese investors to back government-managed projects. For their part, the foreign powers, especially Britain, wanted to maintain the central government and one China, but the flow of loans which they supplied contributed to the downfall of both.

The immediate cause of the revolution was the outbreak of discontent which greeted the announcement of the Hukuang railway loan. The Foreign Office and the Hongkong and Shanghai Bank had been trying to tie the major powers into a general consortium to finance railway construction since 1909, and terms were finally agreed with the Ch'ing government in 1911.[88] The conditions of the Hukuang loan were not unusual, but they were agreed at a point when foreign indebtedness had become a highly sensitive political issue. Critics of the regime were also aware that the consortium was considering a further large loan to reform the Chinese currency and to assist China's long-debated transfer to the gold standard, a move that was intended partly to improve her credit-rating. As one revolutionary leader put it: 'China's present situation is that if it is not conquered by partition it will be lost by invisible financial control by foreign powers'.[89] From Britain's point of view, the events of 1911 overturned the regime supported by the foreign powers, raised the possibility of default on existing loans, and opened up the prospect of a renewed scramble for China.

Britain played a leading part in averting this outcome. In 1912, the Foreign Office and the Hongkong and Shanghai Bank led the way in forming an International Commission of Bankers to manage customs revenue, and hence to secure loan repayments, in enlarging the international consortium to include Russia and Japan (in the hope of controlling them), and in backing the provisional government under Yuan, a former Ch'ing general who had agreed to cooperate in maintaining the open door and in meeting China's external financial obligations.[90] In the following year, the consortium issued a Reorganisation Loan of £25m., which helped Yuan to gather support, become President of the Republic, and purge the democratic wing of the reform movement. The new loan was secured on specified revenues (principally the salt tax), which were to be administered by an official appointed by the international consortium. China's credit-rating was maintained, and the issue was a success. Investors looked forward to a new era of development; borrowers looked back on a long process by which external indebtedness, contracted by successive governments, had compromised China's independence.

It was during this period that the Hongkong and Shanghai Bank's virtual monopoly of official loans to China and of unofficial influence in Whitehall came under heavy attack from British manufacturers and their sympathisers. Pauling & Co., the large railway contractors, had already made an attempt in 1908 to ensure that loans to China were tied to the purchase of British manufactures.[91] Their campaign had the support of the British Minister in Peking, Sir John Jordan, and it gained impetus from anti-German feelings expressed in *The Times* and elsewhere. The Bank defended its cosmopolitan policy on conventional free trade grounds, and its position was endorsed by the Foreign Office. As a result, Pauling's plea was turned down. In 1912, with the prospect of new and lucrative loans to China, the Bank faced direct competition from a British financier, Charles Crisp, who was prepared to offer a loan to the provisional government.[92] Although Crisp was not in the top rank of City bankers, his challenge, like Pauling's, attracted attention because it merged with growing anxiety about foreign competition in manufactured goods and with the feeling that the Bank's cosmopolitan approach to lending was damaging British exports. Since Crisp could fairly claim to be acting in the spirit of free trade and private enterprise, his bid was an embarrassment to the British government. Nevertheless, the Foreign Office leant on him heavily to try to stop the issue, and made its displeasure known when it went forward, with the result that only 40 per cent of the £5m. offered in London was subscribed by the public.[93] The official view was that Crisp's loan would enable China to evade the controls needed for 'responsible lending', a phrase which applied not only to the security of the loan but to the reliability of the lenders. This was a dubious argument in terms of free-trade orthodoxy, but it demonstrated the extent to which the success of British policy towards China had come to rely on particular financial interests.

The Bank had to pay for its victory by agreeing to enlarge Britain's representation on the consortium, and thus reduce its share of loans to the Chinese government.[94] However, given that China needed some £60m. in new loans, this amendment did not have a serious effect on the Bank's position or prospects. Moreover, the newcomers to the consortium were all established City associates of the Bank, the most prominent being Barings. The loan business was opened up just enough to allow the Foreign Office to give exclusive support to the British group in the Consortium, but it was also kept in the family. Jordan continued to call for 'the organisation of British manufacturing and financial interests into one or two powerful syndicates equipped in such a way as to enable them to compete with the Associations which are being formed by our rivals'.[95] But, as the Foreign Office noted in 1914: 'It is extremely difficult to collect British firms to undertake business in China, especially mining. We are not really in touch with those sort of people'.[96] In fact, 'those sort of people' were divided among themselves as well as separated from the City. Railway interests may have been willing to ride on anti-German sentiment, but Manchester refrained from attacking either Germany or the Hongkong and Shanghai Bank's monopoly because over half of its exports to China were distributed by German firms, which were financed very largely by the City and the Bank.[97] If the future of British manufactures in China depended on the emergence of finance capitalism, then the outlook was indeed gloomy. But most of Britain's exports to China probably still gained more than they lost from free trade in 1914, even though the price was dependence on the City's financial and commercial services and exposure to foreign competition.

The new financial empire

Reflecting on Britain's relations with China, Charles Addis observed in 1905 that 'an imperial policy is essentially a commercial policy and to resent the intrusion of politics into business is to do injury to both'.[98] This assessment accords not only with other contemporary opinion, whether favourable or hostile to imperialism, but also with the evidence now available on Britain's involvement with China in the period between the Opium Wars and the fall of the Manchu dynasty. The commercial policy that Addis referred to was based essentially on a continuing belief in the merits of free trade. If, in 1839, policy was influenced by the needs of manufacturing interests, by 1911 it was quite clearly shaped by considerations of finance. Moreover, even at the outset of the period, the pressure to open China was driven by a concern to ensure that India had the means of meeting her financial obligations to Britain, and to this end markets were sought for Indian as well as for British exports. Of course, British industry remained an important element in policy-making, and the potential of the China market was a permanent feature of the calculations of the Foreign Office as well as of Manchester and Birmingham. But the China market remained more of a myth than a reality. Although the value of Britain's trade with China rose after the turn of the century, her share of the total fell sharply as rival powers made inroads into the larger market created by the revival of international commerce and the partial opening of the interior, and her manufactured exports suffered badly from Japanese competition.[99]

The dynamic force, in China as elsewhere, was the growth of investment, a process both symbolised and realised by the success of the Hongkong and Shanghai Bank. As Britain lost her place in commodity trade, so she strengthened it in the field of finance. This is not to say that capital flowed readily to China: the City was generally wary of investing in the Far East, apart from Japan, and China remained, in global terms, one of Britain's minor debtors. On the other hand, China had never defaulted on a major loan. Peking's credit remained good, and secure loans authorised by the central government or anchored in the Treaty Ports, were usually taken up. It was there, in centres of political authority and international trade, that British influence was most pronounced. By 1914, Britain's holdings of Chinese government stock had grown both absolutely and relative to other foreign powers.[100] The volume of private investment flowing from Britain had risen too, as had her share of the total, most of which found safe havens in shipping, property and utilities in the major ports. This investment helped British-registered shipping to retain its lead in the carrying trade between China and other countries and to hold its share of the enlarged inter-port carrying trade. In China, as in other parts of the world, invisible earnings had come to depend increasingly on moving goods other than those produced in or required by Britain.[101]

Strategic motives played little or no part in Foreign Office thinking because China was not on the route to anywhere of importance to Britain. The wider purposes of diplomacy could undoubtedly be seen in the slow-moving and endless bargaining which aimed at deflecting or accommodating rival powers by giving them slices of other people's property, but this was neither a unique nor a pre-eminent feature of British imperialism in the Far East. In addition, there were a number of crises at various points on the periphery where Britain and China met, but the most important of these, the Boxer Rising, followed rather than caused foreign intervention, and indeed prompted the major powers to adopt a more cautious stance in their dealings with Peking. Finally, while it can be acknowledged that other states, especially Japan but also Germany, France and Russia, had considerable influence on British policy, this does not mean that changes in Britain's presence in China were simply, or even largely, responses to external stimuli. The view that policy towards China was essentially reactive needs to take account of the fact that Britain was an expanding power which gained either territory or influence in other parts of Asia too in the late nineteenth century, most obviously in Burma and Malaya, but also in Thailand, North Borneo and Japan.

The scramble for China can therefore be placed in the global context shaped by the extension of Britain's finance and services during the second half of the nineteenth century. There were many reasons why China did not suffer the same fate as Africa, but prominent among them was the fact that the continuing authority of Peking was needed to guarantee foreign loans and to underwrite the Treaty Port system, whereas in Africa viable states and central authorities had to be created before foreign lending could begin. A closer comparison can be drawn between China and the Ottoman Empire: each had a recognised central authority and far-flung, poorly integrated domains; and Britain's chief interest, in both cases, lay in public-sector loans, which in turn gave her a strong commitment to the maintenance of political stability. In both cases, too, informal influence was exerted through government borrowing rather than through trade, and tended to grow rather than diminish as the period advanced. The principal difference was not of structure but of timing. The default of 1875 removed the Ottomans from the City's list of creditable borrowers and shifted its considerable influence towards debt collection, whereas China beckoned at the close of the century as a land of promise which required sizeable foreign loans for the first time and offered adequate security (much of it under British control) for repayment. The revolution of 1911, itself caused partly by foreign indebtedness, placed Peking even more firmly under the discipline of external creditors headed by Great Britain. It is true, as we have noted, that Britain had a greater strategic interest in the Middle East, which was on the route to India, than she had in China, but this was not, as is sometimes claimed, the determining influence on policy: preserving the open door and maintaining debt service were sufficiently weighty reasons in themselves for upholding the authority of both Constantinople and Peking.

At the same time, the City's reluctance to invest beyond well-defined limits played its part in China, as in the Ottoman Empire, in drawing the boundaries of British influence and in pushing the Foreign Office towards agreements with other powers. Valuable though it was, the Yangtse Valley was scarcely the Rand of the East, and its potential could be realised only at huge expense and considerable political risk. Consequently, Britain was unable to open a vast new market for her manufactures, but she did succeed in holding China together and in expanding opportunities for finance and commercial services there. In moving towards this goal, the Foreign Office and the Hongkong and Shanghai Bank cooperated so closely that it is misleading as well as unnecessary to speak of one dominating the other, not least because they were manned by 'the same sort of people'.

Notes

1 The quotation is taken from a review of general policy made by the Hongkong and Shanghai Bank at the close of the nineteenth century. See Frank H.H. King, *The History of the Hongkong and Shanghai Bank,* I (Cambridge, 1987), p. 18.

2 P.J. Cain, 'International Trade and Economic Development in the Work of J.A. Hobson Before 1914', *History of Political Economy,* 11 (1979); Ronald Hyam, *Britain's Imperial Century, 1815–1914* (1976), pp. 360–1.

3 Important discussions of these issues can be found in D.C.M. Platt, *Finance, Trade and Politics in British Foreign Policy, 1815–1914* (Oxford, 1968), Ch. 5; D.K. Fieldhouse, *Economics and Empire, 1880–1914,* Ch. 12; and in the work of David McLean cited below and summarised in 'Finance and Informal Empire Before the First World War', *Econ. Hist. Rev.,* 2nd ser. 29 (1976), pp. 300–04.

4 Though much progress has been made by historians of China. The best starting point is John K. Fairbank, ed. *The Cambridge History of China,* Vols. X and XI (Cambridge, 1978 and 1980). On the other hand, as Marie-Claire Bergère has observed, these advances have tended to widen the gulf between specialists on Chinese history and analysts of international relations: 'The Issue of Imperialism and the 1911 Revolution', in Eto Shinkichi and Harold Z. Schiffrin, eds. *The 1911 Revolution in China: Interpretative Essays* (Tokyo, 1984).

5 We are especially indebted to the work of King, *History of the Hongkong and Shanghai Banking Corporation,* Vols. I and II (Cambridge, 1987 and 1988), and Roberta A. Dayer, *Finance and Empire: Sir Charles Addis, 1861–1945* (1989). Important research on the history of expatriate and local financial institutions between 1895 and 1911 is currently being undertaken by Takeshi Hamashita of the University of Tokyo.

6 Michael Greenberg, *British Trade and the Opening of China, 1800–1842* (Cambridge, 1951); John K. Fairbank, *Trade and Diplomacy on the China Coast: The Opening of the Treaty Ports, 1842–1854* (Cambridge, Mass., 1964); Gerald Graham, *The China Station: War and Diplomacy, 1830–1860* (Oxford, 1978).

7 P. Harnetty, *Imperialism and Free Trade: Lancashire and India in the Mid-Nineteenth Century* (1972), Ch. 3; A. Tripathi, 'Indo-British Trade Between 1833 and 1847 and the Commercial Crisis of 1847/8', *Indian Hist. Rev.,* 1 (1974); W.E. Cheong. 'The Crisis of the East India Houses, 1830–1834', *Revue internationale de l'histoire de la banque,* 9 (1974).

8 Maggie Keswick, ed. *The Thistle and the Jade: A Celebration of 150 Years of Jardine, Matheson & Co.* (1982). It is interesting to note that the firm's headquarters were in London, where it had dose City connections. Alexander Matheson, the head of the affiliated London firm of Matheson & Co., became a director of the Bank of England in 1847.

9 Tripathi, 'Indo-British Trade', pp. 308–11.

10 P.W. Fay, *The Opium War, 1840–1842* (Chapel Hill, N.C., 1975); Douglas Hurd, *The Arrow War: An Anglo-Chinese Confusion, 1856–1860* (1968); Britten Dean, *China and Great Britain: The Diplomacy of Commercial Relations, 1860–1864* (Cambridge, Mass., 1974).

11 Quoted in Dayer, *Finance and Empire,* p. 8. On Sir Robert Hart, the long-serving Inspector General, see Stanley F. Wright, *Hart and the Chinese Customs* (Belfast, 1950).

12 Fairbank, *Trade and Diplomacy,* pp. 464–8; Dean, *China and Great Britain,* pp. 129–32, 141–4.

13 Rhoads Murphey, 'The Treaty Ports and China's Modernization', in Mark Elvin and G. William Skinner, eds. *The Chinese City Between Two Worlds* (Stanford, Calif., 1974); Shannon R. Brown, 'The Partially Opened Door: Limitations on Economic Change in China in the 1860s', *Mod. Asian Stud.*, 12 (1979); Thomas G. Rawski, 'Chinese Dominance of Treaty Port Commerce and its Implications, 1860–1875', *Explorations in Econ. Hist.*, 7 (1970); Robert Y. Eng, 'Chinese Entrepreneurs, the Government and the Foreign Sector: the Canton and Shanghai Silk-Reeling Enterprises, 1861–1922', *Mod. Asian Stud.*, 18 (1984).

14 Britten Dean, 'British Informal Empire: the Case of China', *Journal of Commonwealth and Comparative Politics,* 14 (1976), pp. 70–1.

15 Dean, 'British Informal Empire', p. 72; D.A. Farnie, *The English Cotton Industry and the World Market, 1815–1896* (Oxford, 1979), p. 91. Here, and throughout this chapter, we have confined our general comments on overseas trade (and investment) to broad indications of the principal trends. These are sufficient for our main purpose, though less accurate than we would like them to be. At present, however, the data contain too many uncertainties to allow a more precise analysis to be made without an extended justification, which is precluded by limitations of space. We are particularly indebted to the work of Hsiao Liang-lin, *China's Foreign Trade Statistics, 1864–1949* (Cambridge, Mass., 1974), to Hou Chi-ming, *Foreign Investment and Economic Development in China, 1840–1937* (Cambridge, Mass., 1965), and to Dr John Latham for his advice on this subject.

16 David J.S. King, 'China's First Public Loan: the Hongkong Bank and the Chinese Imperial "Foochow" Loan of 1874', in Frank H.H. King, ed. *Eastern Banking: Essays in the History of the Hongkong and Shanghai Banking Corporation* (1983). See also Shannon R. Brown, 'The Transfer of Technology to China in the Nineteenth Century: the Role of Foreign Direct Investment', *Jour. Econ. Hist.*, 39 (1979).

17 Hao Yen-p'ing, *The Comprador in Nineteenth-Century China: Bridge Between East and West* (Cambridge, Mass., 1970); idem, *The Commercial Revolution in Nineteenth-Century China: The Rise of Sino-Western Mercantile Capitalism* (Berkeley, Calif., 1986); Dean, 'British Informal Empire', p. 70.

18 For a lively introduction to some of the main issues see Philip C. Huang, ed. *The Development of Underdevelopment in China* (New York, 1980).

19 Mercantile and official views during this period are discussed by Nathan A. Pelcovits, *Old China Hands and the Foreign Office* (New York, 1948). This study is of lasting value, but the subject itself now needs to be reassessed in the light of the research produced since the early 1950s.

20 Marvin Swartz, *The Politics of British Foreign Policy in the Era of Disraeli and Gladstone* (1985), p. 14; Dean, 'British Informal Empire', p. 74.

21 Farnie, *English Cotton Industry,* pp. 96–106.

22 A valuable synthesis is Jürgen Osterhammel, 'British Business in China, 1860s–1950s', in R.P.T. Davenport-Hines and Geoffrey Jones, eds. *British Business in Asia since 1860* (Cambridge, 1989), pp. 190–200. See also Hao, *The Commercial Revolution,* Ch. 7; Motono Eiichi, 'The "Traffic Revolution": Remaking the Export Sales System in China, 1866–1875', *Modern China,* 12 (1986); Liu Kwang-ching, 'British-Chinese Steamship Rivalry in China, 1873–85', in C.D. Cowan, ed. *The Economic Development of China and Japan: Studies in Economic History and Political Economy* (1964); and Daniel Headrick, *Tentacles of Progress: Technology Transfer in the Age of Imperialism, 1850–1940* (Oxford, 1988), pp. 37–41.

23 On John Swire, see Sheila Marriner and Francis Hyde, *The Senior: John Samuel Swire, 1825–1898: Management in Far Eastern Shipping Trades* (Liverpool, 1967); and Shinya Sugiyama, 'A British Trading Firm in the Far East: John Swire & Sons, 1867–1914', in Shin'ichi Yonekawa and Hideki Yoshihara, eds. *Business History of General Trading Companies* (Tokyo, 1987). Swires joined the growing number of provincial overseas trading firms which moved their headquarters to London in the 1870s.

24 Hao, *The Commercial Revolution,* Ch. 11; Cheng, Yu-kwei, *Foreign Trade and Industrial Development of China* (Washington, D.C., 1956), pp. 258–9; Liu Kwang-ching, *Anglo-American Steamship Rivalry in China, 1862–1874* (Cambridge, Mass., 1962), pp. 117–18, 138–9, 150; Hou Chi-ming, *Foreign Investment and Economic Development in China, 1840–1937* (Cambridge, Mass., 1965), pp. 194–210, 231–2; Albert Feuerwerker, 'Economic Trends in the Late Ch'ing Empire, 1870–1911', in Fairbank, ed. *Cambridge History,* XI, Pt. 2, pp. 45–7; King, *History of the Hongkong and Shanghai Bank,* I, pp. 283–4, 426; Jerome Ch'en, *State Economic Policies of the Ch'ing Government, 1840–1895* (1980), pp. 116–20.
25 Farnie, *English Cotton Industry,* pp. 110–11.
26 Quoted in Hao, *The Commercial Revolution,* p. 324.
27 It is interesting to note that the firm was also a distant casualty of the Baring Crisis. See Hao, *The Commercial Revolution,* p. 324.
28 King, *History of the Hongkong and Shanghai Bank,* I, pp. 404–6, 433, 438–42.
29 Edward le Fevour, *Western Enterprise in Late Ch'ing China: A Selective Survey of Jardine, Matheson and Company's Operations, 1842–1895* (Cambridge, Mass., 1968), pp. 152–3.
30 Osterhammel, 'British Business in China', pp. 192–3. This completed an adjustment that was already under way: as early as 1851, one of the partners in Rathbone, Worthington & Co. observed that, in future: 'profits will be made as much in the management of the funds and exchanges as in any other way'. Quoted in S.G. Checkland, 'An English Merchant House in China after 1842', *Bull. Bus. Hist. Soc.,* 27 (1953), pp. 162–3. See also ibid. pp. 168, 170, 181.
31 Le Fevour, *Western Enterprise,* pp. 28–9, 48–9; Liu, *Anglo-American Steamship Rivalry,* pp. 138–9, 150; Hao, *The Commercial Revolution,* p. 173.
32 Le Fevour, *Western Enterprise,* pp. 52–3, 57–62, 125. Economic aspects of the 'self-strengthening' movement are covered by Wellington K.K. Chan, *Merchants, Mandarins and Modem Enterprise in Late Ch'ing China* (Cambridge, Mass., 1977).
33 King, *History of the Hongkong and Shanghai Bank,* I, Ch. 1.
34 Ibid. pp. 43–5, 86, 157–62, 353–5, 500–1, 523–4, 535. The career of the Bank's founder, (Sir) Thomas Sutherland, spanned banking, shipping (chairman of P&O in 1884) and politics (MP for Greenock, 1884–1900) in a way that was characteristic of imperial entrepreneurs from the second half of the nineteenth century onwards, and suggests comparison with figures such as Currie, Mackinnon and Inchcape.
35 Ibid. pp. 261–3, 283–4, 422, 451, 426, 440.
36 Ibid. pp. 266, 284, 298, 308–11.
37 Ibid. pp. 546–7.
38 Ibid. pp. 19, 98–100, 270, 303–4, 538–41, 546–7.
39 King, 'China's First Public Loan'.
40 Ibid. p. 261; King, *History of the Hongkong and Shanghai Bank,* I, pp. 266, 283, 308–11.
41 King, *History of the Hongkong and Shanghai Bank,* I, p. 100.
42 Ibid. pp. 98–100, 143–4, 270, 276, 311, 343.
43 Ibid. pp. 558–62.
44 Ibid. pp. 422–3, 565.
45 Ibid. pp. 546–7. See also Platt, *Finance, Trade,* pp. 269–70.
46 King, *History of the Hongkong and Shanghai Bank,* I, p. 547; King, 'China's First Public Loan', p. 247. Pauncefote (1828–1902) was appointed Ambassador to the United States in 1893 and became a peer in 1899.
47 David McLean, 'Commerce, Finance and British Diplomatic Support in China, 1885–86', *Econ. Hist. Rev.,* 2nd ser. XXVI (1973).
48 Ibid. p. 469.
49 King, *History of the Hongkong and Shanghai Bank,* I, p. 508; Le Fevour, *Western Enterprise,* pp. 67–9, 132–3. On the growth of manufacturing see Stephen C. Thomas, *Foreign Intervention and China's Industrial Development* (Boulder, Colo., 1984).
50 S.B. Saul, *Studies in British Overseas Trade, 1870–1914* (Liverpool, 1960), p. 58.
51 For a detailed study of these issues see L.K. Young, *British Policy in China, 1895–1902* (Oxford, 1970).

52 King, *History of the Hongkong and Shanghai Bank,* II, pp. 250–1, 264, 315, 506–7; Dayer, *Finance and Empire,* pp. 35–6. On the shared aims of bankers and diplomats generally see Clarence B. Davis, 'Financing Imperialism: British and American Bankers as Vectors of Imperial Expansion in China, 1908–1920', *Bus. Hist. Rev.,* 56 (1982).
53 Quoted in Dayer, *Finance and Empire,* p. 37.
54 King, *History of the Hongkong and Shanghai Bank,* II, pp. 242, 264, 312.
55 Hou, *Foreign Investment,* pp. 13–14; C.F. Remer, *Foreign Investment in China* (New York, 1933), pp. 19, 138. The data on foreign investment in China need to be treated with caution until the pioneering work of Remer and Hou has been updated.
56 R.P. Sinha, 'Unresolved Issues in Japan's Economic Development', *Scottish Journal of Political Economy,* 23 (1969), pp. 132–4; R.P.T. Davenport-Hines and Geoffrey Jones, 'British Business in Japan Since 1860', in idem, *British Business,* pp. 224–5. See also King, *History of the Hongkong and Shanghai Bank,* II, pp. 94–101.
57 F.O. Memo. by Sanderson, 20 May 1895, quoted in King, *History of the Hongkong and Shanghai Bank,* II, p. 269. On the episode as a whole, see ibid. pp. 264–75, and D. McLean, 'The Foreign Office and the First Chinese Indemnity Loan, 1895', *Hist. Jour.,* 16 (1973).
58 King, *History of the Hongkong and Shanghai Bank,* II, pp. 275–83.
59 Quoted in Dayer, *Finance and Empire,* p. 38.
60 Quoted in King, *History of the Hongkong and Shanghai Bank,* II, p. 286.
61 Young, *British Policy,* pp. 91–2; King, *History of the Hongkong and Shanghai Bank,* II, pp. 280–81.
62 King, *History of the Hongkong and Shanghai Bank,* II, pp. 350–1; Dayer, *Finance and Empire,* p. 39.
63 E.W. Edwards, *British Diplomacy and Finance in China, 1895–1914* (Oxford, 1987), pp. 4–6 and Ch. 2; Young, *British Policy,* pp. 77–85.
64 On the details which follow see King, *History of the Hongkong and Shanghai Bank,* II, pp. 295–303; Osterhammel, 'British Business', pp. 193, 197–200.
65 As such, they illustrate the financial and managerial innovations described by Mira Wilkins, 'The Free-Standing Company, 1870–1914: an Important Type of British Foreign Direct Investment', *Econ. Hist. Rev.,* 2nd ser. XLI (1988).
66 Platt, *Finance, Trade,* pp. 283–307; Ian H. Nish, *The Anglo-Japanese Alliance: The Diplomacy of Two Island Empires, 1894–1907* (1966), pp. 93, 233, 252, 276; and, for an example of the use of concessions to counter the expansion of other powers, A.L. Rosenbaum, 'The Manchurian Bridgehead: Anglo-Russian Rivalry and the Imperial Railways of North China, 1897–1902', *Mod. Asian Stud.,* 10 (1976).
67 For an introduction to recent research on the Boxer Rising (referred to in some studies as the Boxer Rebellion) see the special issue of *Chinese Studies in History,* 20 (1987). The geographical and social diversity of the movement is brought out well by Joseph W. Esherick, *The Origins of the Boxer Uprising* (Berkeley, Calif., 1987).
68 The Mackay Treaty also created several new Treaty Ports. The fullest account remains Pelcovits, *Old China Hands,* pp. 278–82.
69 King, *History of the Hongkong and Shanghai Bank,* II, p. 202.
70 Edwards, *British Diplomacy,* pp. 52, 63, 68, 70, 78, 83, 125; King, *History of the Hongkong and Shanghai Bank,* II, pp. 333, 351–3; Feuerwerker, 'Economic Trends', pp. 65–7.
71 King, *History of the Hongkong and Shanghai Bank,* II, p. 333.
72 Edwards, *British Diplomacy,* pp. 64–6, 85, 88, 130, 196–7; and, for the case of France, D. Gagnier, 'French Loans to China, 1895–1914: the Alliance of International Finance and Diplomacy', *Australian Journal of Politics and History,* 18 (1972).
73 D. McLean, 'Chinese Railways and the Townley Agreement of 1903', *Mod. Asian Stud.,* 7 (1973); King, *History of the Hongkong and Shanghai Bank,* II, pp. 331–7.
74 Edwards, *British Diplomacy,* Ch. 2, and pp. 64, 70. On the history of China's railways see Ralph W. Huenmann, *The Dragon and the Iron Horse: The Economics of Railroads in China, 1876–1937* (Cambridge, Mass., 1984).
75 On this subject see Chuzo Ichiko, 'Political and Institutional Reform, 1901–1911', in Fairbank, *Cambridge History,* XI; Lee En-han, *China's Quest for Railway Autonomy, 1904–1911* (Singapore, 1977); and, for case studies of the relationship between the economics

and the politics of reform, Yen Chin-hwang, 'Chang Yu-Nan and the Chaochow Railway (1904–1908)', *Mod. Asian Stud.*, 18 (1984); and D. Atwell, *British Mandarins and Chinese Reformers: The British Administration of Weihaiwei, 1898–1930* (Oxford, 1986).

76 Dayer, *Finance and Diplomacy*, pp. 57–8. As far as private risk-capital was concerned, however, the City took a guarded view of China outside the treaty ports, and this limited the extent of Britain's co-operation with the self-strengthening movement. The progress of the movement after 1900 is well covered by Chan, *Merchants, Mandarins.*

77 The standard work is Nish, *Anglo-Japanese Alliance.*

78 King, *History of the Hongkong and Shanghai Bank,* II, pp. 272–5, 353; Edwards, *British Diplomacy,* pp. 64–6, 76, 85, 88.

79 King, *History of the Hongkong and Shanghai Bank,* II, pp. 484–5.

80 What follows is based on King, *History of the Hongkong and Shanghai Bank,* I, Ch. 15, and II, Ch. 3; and Christopher Cook, 'The Hongkong and Shanghai Banking Corporation on Lombard Street', in King, ed. *Essays.*

81 Quoted in King, *History of the Hongkong and Shanghai Bank,* II, p. 173.

82 According to banking lore, the agents of banks operating in the Far East would dig large pits on desolate moors in Scotland, place bowls of porridge in them and thus trap unwary native youths who were searching for food. The captives were then sent down to London to be trained as bankers. See King, *History of the Hongkong and Shanghai Bank,* II, p. 173.

83 Ibid. p. 187.

84 See Dayer's excellent biography, *Finance and Empire,* and idem, 'The Young Charles Addis: Poet or Banker?', in King, ed. *Essays.*

85 King, *History of the Hongkong and Shanghai Bank,* II, pp. 412–14.

86 Ibid. pp. 517–19.

87 See, for example, Shinkichi and Shiffrin, *The 1911 Revolution*; E. Zurcher, 'Western Expansion and Chinese Reaction – A Theme Reconsidered', in H.L. Wesseling, ed. *Expansion and Reaction: Essays on European Expansion and Reactions in Asia and Africa* (Leiden, 1978); Mark Elvin, 'The Revolution of 1911 in Shanghai', *Papers on Far Eastern History,* 29 (1984); Richu Ding, 'Shanghai Capitalists Before the 1911 Revolution', *Chinese Studies in History,* 18 (1985); and compare the views of Feuerwerker, pp. 65–9 with those of Bastide-Brugière, pp. 592–9. in Fairbank, *Cambridge History,* XI.

88 Different judgements on the terms of the loan are given by Dayer, *Finance and Empire,* pp. 63–4, and King, *History of the Hongkong and Shanghai Bank,* II, Ch. 7. We have followed King's fuller statement. The international politics of the loan are dealt with by K.C. Chan, 'British Policy in the Reorganisation Loan to China, 1912–13', *Mod. Asian Stud.*, 5 (1971), and Anthony B. Chan, 'British Policy in the Reorganisation Loan to China, 1912–13', *Mod. Asian Stud.*, 6 (1977). There is also a disagreement between these two writers, but the difference is unimportant from the standpoint of the present study.

89 Quoted in Dayer, *Finance and Empire,* p. 64.

90 Liu Ming-te, 'Yuan Shih-k'ai and the 1911 Revolution', *Bull. Inst. of Mod. Hist.*, 11 (1982); and, for a biography, Jerome Ch'en, *Yuan Shih-k'ai, 1859–1916: Brutus Assumes the Purple* (Stanford, Calif, 2nd edn 1972).

91 Edwards, *British Diplomacy,* pp. 96, 120–1, 126, 131–5, 180.

92 King, *History of the Hongkong and Shanghai Bank,* II, pp. 490–8; Dayer, *Finance and Empire,* pp. 66–7.

93 Hou, *Foreign Investment,* p. 48; Platt, *Finance, Trade,* pp. 300–1.

94 King, *History of the Hongkong and Shanghai Batik,* II, pp. 453, 496.

95 Quoted in Edwards, *British Diplomacy,* p. 191.

96 Ibid. p. 193.

97 See King, *History of the Hongkong and Shanghai Bank,* II, Ch. 9 and especially pp. 523, 527, 531–2, 544–5, 605, 615. The Deutsche Asiatische Bank was established to finance German exports, but it remained dependent on the London money market because it was unable to discount bills of exchange at competitive rates.

98 Quoted in Dayer, *Finance and Empire,* p. 58.

99 Calculated from *Statistical Abstract for the United Kingdom, 1899–1913* (1914), and Hsiao, *China's Foreign Trade Statistics.* See also Oriental Economist, *The Foreign Trade of Japan: A Statistical Survey* (Tokyo, 1935); Cheng, *Foreign Trade*; and Hou, *Foreign Investment.* There was a decline, too, in the share of China's overseas trade handled by the 'imperial unit' of Britain, India and Hong Kong.

100 Remer, *Foreign Investment,* pp. 19, 138; Cheng, *Foreign Trade,* pp. 88–92; Hou *Foreign Investment,* pp. 16–17. Shipping data calculated from Hsiao, *China's Foreign Trade.*

101 And, as Osterhammel notes, British trade '*in* China was vastly more important than British trade *with* China': 'British Business', p. 215.

PART FOUR

Redividing the world

14

BRITAIN, GERMANY AND 'IMPERIALIST' WAR, 1900–14

In 1913 Britain was the only nation whose economic interests were global[1] and the only one whose status as a great power rested upon world-wide commitments. She had neither the sheer size of population and territory which gave a country like Russia great power, despite her relative economic backwardness, nor the enormous internal market and wealth of natural resources which fuelled the growth of the United States. It was a recognition of the strength and the vulnerability resulting from this world-wide system which dictated the general lines of British foreign policy.[2]

The economics of foreign policy

In the first place, Britain was determined to prevent the domination of the European continent by any one power or a close combination of powers. Checkmating her European rivals was of prime importance because, as a memorandum from the General Staff put it in 1911:

> Such domination or control would place at the disposal of the Power or Powers concerned a preponderance of naval and military force which would menace the importance of the United Kingdom and the integrity of the British Empire.[3]

In other words, much of the concern about Europe reflected worries about the fate of Britain's vast extra-European network upon which her economic strength – and therefore her world political status – depended. Britain's second great diplomatic concern was a close corollary of the first: the maintenance of the freest possible intercourse for trade and commerce throughout the world. Both of these aims could be achieved only through naval strength, which ensured her independence of Europe and gave her the leading position in the extra European world through control of a string of coaling stations and strategic outposts across the seas.

Besides the attainment of these diplomatic objectives, Britain had a more fundamental need, that of world peace. The whole intricate web of financial and commercial interests of which London was the centre depended upon adhering to an economic orthodoxy which would be severely tested and could even be overthrown by a protracted war or a sustained high level of defence expenditure.[4] The dangers of war were clear enough even during the brief Crimean conflict of the mid-1850s. Gladstone, one of the fathers of fiscal orthodoxy, was forced, as Chancellor of the Exchequer at the time, to borrow extensively and increase the national debt. Heavy war expenditure also led to a drain of gold and made the commercial community anxious about maintaining the convertibility of sterling, and about the high Bank Rate and the increased income tax which were necessary to stem the flow and pay for the troops. The Crimean War disturbed the status quo at a yet more fundamental level in that the disappointments of the campaign threatened to expose the amateurism of gentlemanly government and led to demands for changes which, had the war lasted longer, could have sparked off a social revolution.[5]

Britons had a long-standing aversion to large armies. Any attempt to produce a force which could rival that of the European powers would have involved conscription and an invasion of liberty that few politicians were willing to contemplate. Equally important in deterring militarism was the cost. A large standing army could have been created only by pushing taxation to levels that would have intensified social conflict and threatened Britain's role as an international financial market. So Britain had to rely upon the Indian Army to give her the status of a great land power; and the orbit of operations of that army was strictly limited for both political and economic reasons. What this meant in practice was that Britain's influence upon the balance of power in Europe was never as great as she often pretended. Even in Palmerston's time Britain lacked the power to enforce her will in Europe, and her bluff could be called, as was Palmerston's, by Bismarck over the Schleswig-Holstein crisis in 1863.[6] Britain's power lay outside Europe and rested upon her navy. Maintaining a large navy was the cheapest and most effective way of protecting her interests and was heartily supported not only by the political establishment but even by the City, which took it for granted that naval predominance was crucial to world peace, a form of insurance premium taken out on the wealth owned or controlled by Britain.[7]

The relationship between naval predominance, the security of Britain and her empire, and confidence in Britain as the world's banker and commercial intermediary, was very well understood before 1914. As one aristocratic member of the government expressed it during the Boer War: 'Its Credit and its Navy seem to me to be the two main pillars on which the strength of this country rests and each is essential to the other'.[8] Reconciling foreigners to this naval predominance was also thought to be a good reason for standing by free trade. As a senior member of the Foreign Office pointed out in 1907, the openness of the British market and Britain's opposition to discrimination in trade were ways of demonstrating that her control of the seas and her extensive empire were used for the benefit of others as well as herself.[9] The more Britain's international economic empire expanded and the greater the cost of defending it, the more the desire to settle conflicts with other powers by discussion and rational concession became part of the furniture of the minds of the political elite.[10]

Before 1880, the need to reconcile cheap government with naval supremacy did not prove too difficult and, given the lack of competition from the other great powers, Britain managed to rule the waves and penny-pinch simultaneously.[11] Competition began to hot up and Britain's defence commitments to expand alarmingly as the formal empire grew, just as her industrial growth prospects were becoming a matter of concern and as social welfare expenditure began to rise to meet the needs of voters enfranchised in 1867 and 1884.[12] By 1900, the expansion of Britain's overseas commitments was pushing up public expenditure to the point where the alarm bells were beginning to ring. The Boer War cost 14 per cent of the national income of 1902: £160m. was added to the national debt and Bank Rate had to be raised to 6 per cent (from an average of 2 or 3 per cent in the 1890s) in order to prevent a drain.[13] The war and the subsequent naval race with Germany also provoked a more general crisis in public expenditure, opening the door both to Chamberlain's protectionist and imperial ideas and to Lloyd George's radical budgeting of 1909–14.

Moreover, the South African conflict appeared to prove that Britain had no ally of any importance, while the number of contenders for great-power status was increasing rapidly; and it was recognised that the time had arrived when, in the interests of keeping down defence expenditure and policing her empire and her economic interests overseas, she ought to decide who were her friends and who were her enemies. The Hay-Pauncefote Treaty of 1901 with the USA and the Anglo-Japanese alliance of the following year delimited Britain's naval responsibilities in the Caribbean and Pacific respectively, helping both to head off potential conflicts and to narrow the area wherein the British had to find men and money to defend essential interests.[14] It was at this time, too, that hostility to, and fear of, Germany started to crystallise in Britain, as the former began to appear as a threat to Britain's standing in the world greater than any since that posed by France a century earlier. The conflict was analysed closely by contemporary Marxists and incorporated into their evolving critique of imperialism, a critique which perhaps deserves more attention than it has received from imperial historians during the last 30 years.[15]

Marxist theory and World War I

Marxists viewed the last part of the nineteenth century as the end of what Lenin termed the 'free capitalist' stage of development, when the small, self-financed firm was the characteristic unit. By the end of the century the world had been 'divided up' economically, politically and strategically on the basis of this free capitalist development. Britain, as the leading economic power, had been the chief beneficiary of the division. By 1900, the free capitalist phase was giving way to a more advanced stage: 'finance' or 'monopoly' capitalism. A succession of economic crises after 1870 had produced not only an oligopolistic economic structure in the most advanced nations but also a fusion between large-scale industry and banking capital. Changes in the structure of enterprise were accompanied by shifts in the geographic epicentre of capitalism: Germany and the United States superseded Britain as the front-runners in development. Whereas the growth of the United States was still largely within her own frontiers, Germany's expansion required the rapid extension of her trade, commerce and capital into the world at large and, therefore, into areas largely controlled by Britain and other countries, like France, which were in relative economic decline. To assert herself as a world power rather than remain merely a European one, Germany needed to acquire the kind of global political and military authority, the secure outlets for trade and capital, and the control of the institutions of finance and commerce which Britain had built up during the previous two centuries – and still enjoyed. This is why Marxist theorists spoke of the need to 'redivide' the world after 1900: world power relations had to change drastically to bring them into line with changes in the world economy wrought by the uneven development of capitalism.

When Hilferding and his fellow Marxists wrote about the need for redivision they were not making a simple identification between imperialism and colonialism, or concentrating on the struggle for colonies and spheres of interest in 'backward' parts of the world. The new phase of imperialism was the result of a change in capitalism as a whole and had global implications: it was a battle for hegemony between the great powers which involved a very wide spectrum of economic and political relationships, both formal and informal, within Europe itself as well as in Africa, Asia or Latin America.[16] The scramble was not a matter of overwhelming importance: African partition was a minor part of the process, occurring in the final stages of free capitalism rather than as a result of mature finance capital and, as such, was part of the original division of the world which had now to be destroyed.

Hilferding – whose understanding of these matters was subtler than that of his more politically embattled comrades, Bukharin and Lenin – recognised that, though Britain might be sliding into industrial backwardness by 1900, the way in which the economy had evolved internationally had helped to slow down her decline as a world power. The rapidity of internal development in the United States and Germany limited the capital resources they could devote to overseas expansion. Britain, lodged at an earlier stage of development and with finance and industry still separated, could use the resources of the City to create a world-wide service network, to support her industrial exporters and to fend off the competition of rivals abroad for longer than would otherwise have been possible.[17]

For Bukharin and Lenin, writing in 1915 and 1916, the war in progress was evidently the result of the uneven development of capitalism, with the Anglo-German conflict at the centre of the struggle.[18] Other radicals, and even some Marxists, doubted whether war was an inevitable outcome of the transformation of capitalism. Hobson, for example, felt that, in the longer run, the contending capitalist powers might be forced, simply by the growing internationalisation of capital, to replace war by 'inter-imperialism', a joint exploitation of the world's resources by the leading economic powers.[19] Kautsky, the leading German Marxist thinker, also believed that the costs of colonialism and militarism were becoming prohibitive and that the great colonial powers might renounce the arms race. The result would be a 'cartelisation of foreign policy' or 'holy alliance of the imperialists' and a peaceful division of the globe resulting from economic domination.[20] Neither Bukharin nor Lenin could accept this analysis. Temporary agreements for sharing out the spoils there might be; but, in an unevenly developing world, the fastest growing entities would always have an incentive to break those agreements and take what they wanted by force.[21]

But if the Hobson-Kautsky assumption of a global division of the world bringing permanent peace in its train seems far-fetched, there is no need to go as far as Lenin did and claim that the economic differences between Britain and Germany made war inevitable. What we can say, following Hilferding, is that they probably made fundamental conflict inevitable and, by doing so, drastically narrowed the scope for political and military agreement.[22] It was also the case that, should war break out for any other reasons, the conflict would inevitably become a battle between Britain and Germany for the controlling voice in the management of the world economy and a struggle for empire. The essence of this conflict was expressed with remarkable bluntness in 1907 by Viscount Esher, an important member of the Committee of Imperial Defence:

> Meanwhile the Germans proceed unabashed on their way, and have their objectives clearly in view. The German prestige, rising steadily on the continent of Europe, is more formidable to us than Napoleon at his *apogée*. Germany is going to contest with us the Command of the Sea, and our commercial position. She wants sea-power and the carrying trade of the world. Her geographical grievance has got to be redressed. She must obtain control of the ports at the mouths of the great rivers which tap the middle of Europe. She must get a coastline from which she can draw sailors to her fleets, naval and mercantile. She must have an outlet for her teeming population, and vast acres where Germans can live and remain Germans. These acres only exist within the confines of our Empire. Therefore, 'L'Ennemi c'est L'Allemagne'.[23]

Anglo-German rivalry and its effects

Even as late as the 1890s, Britain's most serious confrontations were with Russia and France rather than with Germany. Britain was at loggerheads with the French over imperial acquisitions in Africa and Asia, the contest culminating in the tense dispute at Fashoda in 1898. Fear of Russian ambitions was, if anything, greater: Britain confronted Russia in Turkey, Persia and Afghanistan where, directly or indirectly, Tsarist forces appeared to menace the stability of the Indian empire and the routes to the East. The accommodation between France and Russia in the 1890s was regarded with deep anxiety in Britain because it meant a conjunction of naval forces in the Mediterranean, and effectively ended her predominance there. It was this agreement, together with the expansion of the navies of other powers, which made the 1889 decision on the Two Power Standard – a determination to maintain a navy of greater strength than the combined forces of the next two largest naval powers – almost impossible to implement, even though it was not formally abandoned until 1912.[24]

Conflicts between Britain, France and Russia over imperial territory and imperial strategy meant that, in Salisbury's time, Britain tended to lean towards friendly relations with the Triple Alliance powers led by Germany. Under Bismarck, Germany was not an ambitious power outside Europe, despite her interest in colonies during the 1880s; the recognition that Bismarck was reasonably satisfied with the European status quo after 1870 also helped to keep relations between Britain and Germany cordial. Between 1898 and 1901, Chamberlain made several attempts to persuade his colleagues, and the Germans themselves, of the virtues of a close accommodation between the two powers, despite the Kaiser's open support for the South African republics during the Boer War.[25]

Germany's decision to build a large navy made an alliance or agreement with Britain impossible because an understanding could have been reached only if the Germans had been willing to accept permanent naval inferiority. German *Weltpolitik* was exceedingly tortuous in that it was reckoned to take at least 15 to 20 years to build a navy equivalent to Britain's, and this had to be done, if possible, without provoking too much British antagonism. The Germans feared obsessively that Britain might be tempted to thwart them by making a pre-emptive strike upon their naval force before it became a serious threat to the empire.[26] In the event, the British became convinced that Germany was planning to challenge their power and were also worried, as were France and Russia, about the possibility of a bid to establish German hegemony on the continent.[27]

Britain's sensitivity on the naval issue clearly indicated the connection between her diplomatic and military stance and her economic power. The navy was not only the key to the defence of Britain herself, but also the crucial safeguard for the enormously complex chain of economic interests which Britain had built up over centuries and without which she was just an offshore island of Europe rather than a great world power. It was for this reason that Grey, as Foreign Secretary, insisted that naval agreements with Germany could be made only on 'the basis of superiority of the British navy', since the German navy 'is not a matter of life and death to them as it is to us'. If Germany were to maintain a navy as large as Britain's, together with her enormous army, 'for us it would not be a question of defeat. Our independence, our very existence would be at stake'.[28]

In 1912, the Admiralty made almost exactly the same claims but expanded the argument, linking it with a possible bid for continental hegemony by Germany:

> There is practically no limit to the ambitions which might be indulged by Germany, or to the brilliant prospects open to her in every quarter of

> the globe, if the British Navy were out of the way. The combination of the strongest Navy with that of the strongest Army would afford wider possibilities of influence and action than have yet been possessed by any Empire in Modern times.[29]

Indeed, the extent of Germany's economic power, its overseas ramifications and the apparent attempt to combine her formidable military strength with a navy as powerful as Britain's, were felt to be a threat greater than anything Britain had faced in over a century. It was the clearest sign possible of Britain's own loss of industrial leadership, something which France and Russia, for all the difficulties they had caused on her imperial frontiers, had ineffectively challenged. The changes in diplomatic alignments following from this were political reactions to the consequences of uneven development and were a direct result of Germany's rise as an industrial power.[30]

The agreements of 1904 and 1907, made with France and Russia respectively, indicated clearly that they and Britain had a common and growing fear of German ambitions. The French, already ineradicably hostile to Germany on account of Alsace and Lorraine, were becoming increasingly anxious about Germany's colonial designs, especially in relation to Morocco. The agreement with Britain took the form of an attempt to clear up colonial conflicts and eliminate sources of friction. Britain, for instance, recognised France as the predominant power in Morocco in return for a French promise not to hinder British policy in Egypt – which had long been a source of dispute.[31]

Once the agreement had been reached, the French became anxious to see a similar settlement between their own ally, Russia, and Britain. During the Russian-Japanese War, the commitments made by France and Britain could have resulted in a conflict between them in support of their alliance partners. Russia herself had an interest in reaching agreement with Britain, partly because of her exhausted state after defeat by Japan and partly because of her own nervousness over German and Austrian ambitions in the Balkans. With the British keen to use Russia's temporary weakness to push her into agreement, the Anglo-Russian Convention of 1907 delimited the spheres of the respective powers in Persia and Afghanistan, and temporarily relieved Britain's fears about India. This was of particular importance to Britain since, once the Trans-Siberian Railway had been completed and before the defeat of Russia by Japan, the British had become increasingly gloomy about their ability to forestall a strong advance by Russia on the buffer states around the Indian Empire.[32]

There was very little positive commitment to joint action in these agreements and the British in particular were extremely wary of any formal alliance binding them to fight on the side of France and Russia in a European war. Indeed, given the strong Cobdenite element in the Liberal Cabinet after 1906, no formal commitment to fight could have been made without destroying the government. Nevertheless, Britain's support for France and Russia was stiffened considerably during the years 1906 to 1914 as a result of the naval conflict with Germany and because of the latter's clumsy and counter-productive attempts, particularly in the Moroccan crises of 1906 and 1911, to undermine the Anglo-French colonial settlement.[33]

Although this picture of the inevitability of conflict (rather than the inevitability of war) between Britain and Germany fits in reasonably well with the work of many prominent diplomatic historians, it is not unassailable. Starting from the premiss that the most pressing necessity of British policy around the turn of the century was the security of her Indian and Asiatic interests, it could be inferred that the essential route to this, given a shortage of resources, was an accord with Russia. But that accord could be reached only by way of agreement with Russia's ally, France; the result of this would, inevitably, have put Britain in opposition to Germany. From this perspective, the Anglo-German conflict was a simple by-product of an attempt to safeguard British imperial interests: paradoxically, Germany became the enemy precisely because she was the power least likely to pose a direct threat to the eastern empire.[34] It is true that the British reaction to the German navy in the early days was fairly mild and that the French and Russian ententes were also sought as ways of curbing mounting defence costs independently of any supposed provocation by Germany. Even so, this reading of the creation of the Entente does not really account for the intensity and the widespread nature of Britain's hostility to Germany in the years immediately before the outbreak of war. As the builder of a navy only a few hundred miles from Britain's shores, the Germans were bound to appear more directly threatening than either France or Russia.

German penetration of British and empire markets also contributed to the conflict. British alarm at German 'dumping' of manufactures in her market was much greater in the depressed mid-1890s than afterwards, when the problem was alleviated to some degree by the rapid growth of world trade.[35] Nonetheless, after 1900 Britain's fear of German penetration of her domestic market – and imperial ones – was never far below the surface; this antagonism emerged, unashamedly, into the light of day during the brief industrial slump of 1908–9.[36] Like the Fair Traders before them, the Tariff Reformers always gained adherents in depression, and elements within the movement were quite outspokenly anti-German. It is plain that the 'strategic' reasons for free trade espoused by the Foreign Office fitted in neatly enough with the interests of cotton barons and shipbuilders and those who believed that Britain's invisible earnings (which depended to a large degree on the level of world trade in general) were a crucial element in her defence strategy because of the command they gave over vital resources overseas. But, as we have seen, this did not make much impression upon those who felt that the same policy that encouraged the growth of invisibles also eroded the industrial base.

The protectionists and imperialists had no hope of persuading the Liberals to adopt their cause and they failed to win over the Conservatives; but, under the stress of acute depression, the mild revenue tariffs proposed by Conservatives just before the war could have hardened into a protectionist, anti-German weapon under some future government of the Right. Germany was intensely nervous of a possible British tariff and of imperial preference, and some high-ranking officials clearly felt that the introduction of protection by Britain would be a deliberately hostile, even warlike, act.[37] Any settlement of differences between Britain and Germany would have had to include guarantees for maintaining easy entry for German goods into British and imperial markets; there is some sense in Hoffman's claim of 50 years ago that 'the pressure of German business in British markets drove Great Britain towards protection and imperial preference while the drift towards Tariff Reform stimulated German navalism and imperialism'.[38] After 1900, hostility to Germany on the industrial front and the tariff question both became entangled with a wider, right-of-centre, political movement which sought to implement 'social imperialist' policies and to make Britain capable of meeting the challenge of German military and economic competition.[39]

Economic rivalry was fundamental to the dispute between Great Britain and Germany, and was muted only by the rapid growth of international trade just before 1914. It was also a rivalry which was global in scope. The occasional discussions over purely colonial matters and the desultory negotiations about sharing out the Dutch and Portuguese empires should they collapse, were of marginal significance, as contemporaries themselves were well aware.[40]

Once the war had begun, Britain had no real choice but to join in on the side of France and Russia, despite the lack of any formal commitments to give armed support and despite the pacifist inclinations of the majority of the Liberal government. The radical element in the party had been strong enough to prevent any categorical military pledge to Britain's allies and had helped to steer her away from any drastic measures, such as conscription, which would have given Britain's forces great weight in a continental battle.[41] They could not, however, prevent Britain from entering the war against Germany, and this can be explained in a number of ways. In the first place, the Liberal government knew that, had it resigned rather than face a declaration of war, an incoming Conservative government would have opted for belligerency anyway. In the circumstances the Liberals calculated that it was better to stay in power in the hope of retaining influence over the course of the war.[42] Next, although it is probably wrong to infer, as Mayer has done, the existence of a direct link between the various social crises which rent Britain between 1906 and 1914 and the decision to fight,[43] it is now clear that there was a strong, though not very articulate, popular feeling that Germany was the enemy and that Britain had to conquer to survive.[44] This grass-roots conviction, based partly on the alarm and anxieties provoked by German industrial competition, had a significant influence upon Grey's thinking in July and August 1914.

Britain was also committed in a different way. Any continental war from which Britain stood aside and which ended in a victory for Germany would have given the latter just that degree of superiority in Europe which it was the aim of British foreign policy to prevent. On the other hand, although a victory for France and Russia, unaided by Britain, might have been less immediately disastrous, it might still have brought a set of solutions for world problems which drastically reduced Britain's power.

Exactly how the British might fight the war was a more contentious matter, and it divided opinion even after hostilities began. 'Navalists', who felt that Britain's survival depended upon sea-power, went beyond the argument that the fleet was vital to keep open the channels of trade and to maintain supplies of cheap food for the masses lest they reject both the war and the social structures from whence it sprang. They believed, too, that naval predominance offered Britain a chance to contribute to an Allied victory by denying the enemy supplies, rather than by committing herself heavily to fighting on land. Navalist strategies were congenial to the Liberal Party with its abhorrence of conscription and struck a chord with all those who were fearful of wholesale military slaughter. They also appealed because, if Britain stayed on the periphery of the battle in Europe, there was a greater chance that the existing social and economic structure would survive. Opinion in the army, and in the Foreign Office, was different. There, it was felt that a blockade of Germany would incur the wrath of neutral countries, particularly the United States, without bringing the Germans to heel. Only a massive military commitment in Europe would bring victory. The 'continentalists' won in the end, one reason being that the enormous, and unexpected, enthusiasm for the war shown by the bulk of the population meant that a mass army was raised quickly and that the British could make a major impact on the European mainland.[45]

However hesitantly Britain entered the war, the conflict seemed to offer an ideal opportunity to destroy Germany's burgeoning overseas power, at least temporarily, and to preserve Britain's economic dominance overseas – a dominance without which she was of little account in the world.[46] In the event, the economic strain of war and the destruction of the international economy weakened the basis of Britain's world position: when the war ended, the United States was emerging to challenge Britain for the place in the world for which Germany had fought in vain.

Britain's eventual fate had been briefly foreshadowed during the Boer War. With the usual supplies of gold from the Transvaal cut off, the sharp rise in government spending pushed up interest rates rapidly and threatened a heavy drain of gold. In response, the Conservative government of the day decided that funds would have to be raised in New York as well as London. This aroused the 'intense jealousy'[47] of the City, not least because of the boost it gave to the prestige of the great Anglo-American merchant bank, Morgans. The longer-term significance of the episode was not lost on officialdom in Britain. Borrowing in the United States would be useful in a crisis but ought to be kept carefully in check for fear of the consequences. As a senior Treasury man put it in 1901: 'Our commercial supremacy has to go sooner or later; of that I feel no doubt; but we don't want to accelerate its departure across the Atlantic'.[48] That acceleration began in earnest in World War I: it is little wonder that the City was reluctant to go into battle in 1914.[49]

Nonetheless, despite her many problems, Britain was still formidably strong when war broke out. She had been overhauled as an industrial power and technological leadership had passed to others; but she had compensated by extending her commercial and financial influence across the world over the previous half-century. While remembering the pressures and difficulties presented by the spread of industrialisation, it is important not to forget how much Britain's power had grown and how much more she had to defend in 1914 compared with 1850. Moreover, although the war inevitably weakened Britain in the face of the challenge of the United States, its impact was not great enough to ensure American dominance of the world economy after 1918. Britain's service economy, and the gentlemanly elites who managed it, survived the war and subsequently renewed their bid for leadership with much ingenuity and some success. If Britain's inability to retain her position as an industrial leader proved, in the very long run, to be her undoing as an imperial power of the first rank, Hilferding was right to believe that her empire, her enormous accumulation of financial assets spread across the globe, and the banking and commercial skills of the City would be critical in keeping her at the centre of the world economic stage well into the twentieth century.

Notes

1 Between 1909 and 1911, 65 per cent of Britain's exports went outside Europe, and in 1910 55 per cent of her imports came from extra-European sources. The corresponding export figure for Germany, Britain's greatest trade rival, was 25 per cent. Paul Bairoch, 'Geographical Structure and Trade Balance of European Foreign Trade from 1800 to 1970', *Jour. Eur. Econ. Hist.*, III (1974), Tables 5 and 6, p. 573.

2 On British foreign policy generally see Paul Kennedy, *The Realities behind Diplomacy: Background Influences on British External Policy, 1865–1980* (1981), Pt. I; Bernard Porter, *Britain, Europe and the World, 1850–1982: Delusions of Grandeur* (1983); Kenneth Bourne, *The Foreign Policy ofVictorian England, 1830–1902* (Oxford, 1970); C.J. Lowe, *The Reluctant Imperialists: British Foreign Policy, 1878–1902,* 2 Vols., (1967); C.J. Lowe and M.L. Dockrill, *The Mirage of Power: British Foreign Policy, 1902–22,* 3 Vols., (1972); M.E. Chamberlain, *'Pax Britannica'? British Foreign Policy, 1789–1914* (1988). Marvin Swartz, *The Politics of British Foreign Policy in the Era of Disraeli and Gladstone* (1985) has also proved useful in relating foreign policy to domestic politics. There is a good short summary of the main principles of nineteenth-century foreign policy in Alun Davis, 'England and Europe', in J.S. Bromley and E.H. Kossman, eds. *Britain and the Netherlands in Europe and Asia* (The Hague, 1968).

3 Memorandum from the General Staff, 13 August 1911. PRO Cab. 38/19/47, reprinted in Lowe and Dockrill, *The Mirage of Power,* Vol. III, p. 445.

4 Paul M. Kennedy, 'Strategy versus Finance in Twentieth-Century Great Britain', *Internat. Hist. Rev.,* III (1981), pp. 45–52. This essay has been reprinted in *Strategy and Diplomacy, 1870–1945: Eight Studies* (1983). See also idem, *The Rise of the Anglo-German Antagonism, 1860–1914* (1980), pp. 295, 302–5.

5 Olive Anderson, *A Liberal State at War: English Politics and Economics in the Crimean War* (1967), Chs. 3, 4, 6, 7, and 8.

6 Porter, *Britain, Europe and the World,* pp. 26–7.

7 Kennedy, *The Rise of the Anglo-German Antagonism, 1860–1914,* p. 305; Peter Stansky, *Ambitions and Strategies: The Struggle for Leadership of the Liberal Party in the 1890s* (Oxford, 1964), pp. 19–35, esp. pp. 24, 34.

8 See the Cabinet Memo. of 16 Nov. 1901, written by Selborne, in Lowe, *The Reluctant Imperialists,* I, p. 5.

9 Eyre Crowe's memorandum on 'The Present State of British Relations with France and Germany', 1 Jan. 1907, printed in G.P. Gooch and H. Temperley, eds. *British Documents on the Origins of the War,* Vol. Ill (1928), App. A. The sections on free trade are reprinted in W.H.B. Court, *British Economic History, 1870–1914: Commentary and Documents* (Cambridge, 1965), pp. 469–70. See also Gerald S. Graham, *Tides of Empire: Discursions on the Expansion of Britain Overseas* (1972), p. 82.

10 P.M. Kennedy, 'Tradition of Appeasement in British Foreign Policy, 1865–1939', *Brit. Jour. Internat. Stud.*, II (1976); W.D. Gruner, 'The British Political, Social and Economic System and the Decision for Peace or War: Reflections on Anglo-German Relations, 1800–1939', ibid. VI (1980).
11 C.J. Bartlett, ed. *Britain Pre-eminent: Studies in British World Influence in the Nineteenth Century* (1969), p. 173; Graham, *Tides of Empire,* p. 80. A recent survey of British naval history which places it within the context of a changing economy is P.M. Kennedy, *The Rise and Fall of British Naval Mastery* (1976). See also Bernard Semmel, *Liberalism and Naval Strategy: Ideology, Interest and Sea Power During the Pax Britannica* (1986).
12 Harold Sprout and Margaret Sprout, 'The Dilemma of Rising Demands and Insufficient Resources', *World Politics,* XX (1968).
13 Clive Trebilcock, 'War and the Failure of Industrial Mobilization 1899–1914', in J.M. Winter, ed. *War and Economic Development: Essays its Memory of David Joslin* (Cambridge, 1975), pp. 141, 143.
14 G.W. Monger, *The End of Isolation: British Foreign Policy, 1900–1907* (1963), Chs. I and 3; Zara S. Steiner, *Britain and the Origins of the First World War* (1977), Ch. 2. For a recent analysis of the connection between crises over government expenditure and Britain's foreign policy stance see Aaron L. Friedberg, *The Weary Titan: Britain and the Experience of Relative Decline, 1895–1905* (Princeton, NJ, 1988).
15 The main texts are Rudolf Hilferding, *Finance Capital: A Study of the Latest Phase of Capitalist Development* (ed. T. Bottomore, 1981); N. Bukharin, *Imperialism and World Economy* (1972 edn) and V.I. Lenin, 'Imperialism, the Highest Stage of Capitalism' (1916), in *Collected Works,* XXXII (Moscow, 1964). Commentaries sympathetic to the approach taken here can be found in Eric Stokes, 'Late Nineteenth-Century Colonial Expansion and the Attack on the Theory of Economic Imperialism: a Case of Mistaken Identity?', *Hist. Jour.*, XII (1969), to which we owe a considerable debt. See also the important contribution by Norman Etherington, *Theories of Imperialism: War, Conquest and Capital* (1984).
16 See particularly Hilferding, *Finance Capital,* pp. 329–30; Bukharin, *Imperialism and World Economy,* pp. 120–1; and Lenin, 'Imperialism, the Highest Stage of Capitalism', pp. 268–9. There is also a clear recognition of 'informal empire' in Lenin, 'Imperialism', pp. 263–4.
17 Hilferding, *Finance Capital,* pp. 324–5, 331.
18 V.I. Lenin, *British Labour and British Imperialism* (1969), pp. 135–6. The analysis presented in this chapter does not imply that Marxist theories of imperialism are unassailable. This is particularly true of the Leninist approach, which limits imperialism to the finance-capitalist stage of development and ignores the importance of capital export before the turn of the century. Lenin was also woefully out of touch with reality when he suggested that finance capitalism was the last stage of capitalism and that the imperialist powers had lost their economic dynamism and were becoming parasitic upon the backward nations of the world. It is noticeable that Hilferding avoided these traps and that the subtitle of his book describes finance capital as being the *latest* stage of capitalist development. For a good critique of Marxist theories of imperialism see Anthony Brewer, *Marxist Theories of Imperialism: A Critical Survey* (2nd edn 1989), which is especially severe on Lenin's numerous errors of fact and logic, as is Bill Warren, *Imperialism: Pioneer of Capitalism* (1980), Chs. 3 and 4, which castigate Lenin for his assumption that capitalism had lost its dynamic and had reached its highest stage. In assuming that the imperialist states had become parasitic and decaying, and that their industry was already in decline as a result of the export of capital, Lenin (in *Imperialism,* pp. 276–85) relied heavily on British material and on Hobson. The influence of Hobson on Lenin's views is discussed in Peter Cain, 'J.A. Hobson, Financial Capitalism and Imperialism in Late Victorian and Edwardian England', *Jour. Imp. and Comm. Hist.* XIII (1985), pp. 10–11. For other critiques of aspects of Marxist theories of imperialism see V.G. Kiernan, *Marxism and Imperialism* (1975), Ch. 1; and Roger Owen and Bob Sutcliffe, eds. *Studies in the Theory of Imperialism* (Oxford, 1972), Chs. I and II.

19 J.A. Hobson, *Imperialism: A Study* (1988 edn), pp. 311–12. On this important aspect of Hobson's thought see P.J. Cain, 'International Trade and Economic Development in the Work of J.A. Hobson before 1914', *History of Political Economy,* XI (1979), pp. 410ff.
20 Karl Kautsky, 'Ultra-Imperialism', *New Left Review,* 59 (1970).
21 Lenin, 'Imperialism, the Highest Stage of Capitalism', pp. 275–6, 295; Bukharin, *Imperialism and World Economy,* pp. 141–2.
22 Hilferding, *Finance Capital,* pp. 331–2.
23 M.V. Brett, ed. *Journals and Letters of Reginald Viscount Esher* (1934), II, p. 267, quoted in Court, *British Economic History,* p. 471.
24 Arthur J. Marder, *The Anatomy of British Sea Power: A History of British Naval Policy in the Pre-Dreadnought Era* (New York, 1940), Ch. VII and pp. 509–14.
25 J.A.S. Grenville, *Lord Salisbury and Foreign Policy: The End of the Nineteenth Century* (1964), Ch. VII; Monger, *The End of Isolation,* Ch. 2.
26 Jonathan Steinberg, 'The Copenhagen Complex', *Jour. Contemp. Hist.,* I (1966).
27 For the importance of the naval issue in aligning Britain against Germany see P.M. Kennedy, 'German World Policy and the Alliance Negotiations with England, 1897–1900', *Journal of Modern History,* XLV (1973), and idem, *The Rise of the Anglo-German Antagonism,* pp. 415–16, 420–1, 423.
28 See Grey's speech in the House of Commons, 29 March 1909, printed in Sir Edward Grey, *Speeches on Foreign Affairs, 1904–14* (1931), p. 133.
29 Lowe and Dockrill, *The Mirage of Power,* III, p. 459.
30 This seems to be the drift also of Kennedy's argument in *The Rise of the Anglo-German Antagonism,* pp. 464–6. See also the interesting essay by C.A. Fisher, 'The Changing Dimensions of Europe', *Jour. Contemp. Hist.,* 1 (1966).
31 P. Guillen, 'The Entente of 1904 as a Colonial Settlement', in Prosser Gifford and W. Roger Louis, eds. *France and Britain in Africa* (New Haven, Conn., 1971).
32 Monger, *The End of Isolation,* Chs. 6, 7, 11; Steiner, *Britain and the Origins of the First World War,* Ch. 4.
33 S.L. Mayer, 'Anglo-German Rivalry at the Algeciras Conference', in Prosser Gifford and W. Roger Louis, eds. *Britain and Germany in Africa* (New Haven, Conn., 1967); J.S. Mortimer, 'Commercial Interests and German Diplomacy in the Agadir Crisis', *Hist. Jour.,* X (1967); Monger, *The End of Isolation,* Chs. 8 and 10.
34 For this argument see Keith Wilson, *The Policy of the Entente: Essays on the Determinants of British Foreign Policy* (1985); and idem, *Empire and Continent: Studies in British Foreign Policy from the 1880s to the First World War* (1987).
35 The *locus classicus* for the argument over German infiltration of the British domestic market for manufactures is E.E. Williams, *Made in Germany* (Brighton, 1973), first published in 1895. The standard scholarly account is R.J.S. Hoffman, *Great Britain and the German Trade Rivalry, 1875–1914* (1933). For more recent work see H. Neuberger and H.H. Stokes, 'The Anglo-German Trade Rivalry, 1887–1913; a Counterfactual Outcome and Its Implications', *Social Science History,* III (1979); Christoph Bucheim, 'Aspects of Nineteenth-Century Anglo-German Trade Rivalry Reconsidered', *Jour. Eur. Econ. Hist.,* X (1981); Steiner, *Britain and the Origins of the First World War,* pp. 29–32; and Kennedy, *The Rise of the Anglo-German Antagonism,* Chs. 15 and 16.
36 Hoffman, *The Anglo-German Trade Rivalry,* pp. 286–9.
37 Ibid. pp. 290–1.
38 Ibid. p. 285.
39 G.R. Searle, *The Quest for National Efficiency, 1899–1914: A Study in British Politics and Political Thought* (Oxford, 1971); idem, 'Critics of Edwardian Society: the Case of the Radical Right', in Alan O'Day, ed. *Edwardian England* (1979); Robert J. Scally, *The Origins of the Lloyd George Coalition: The Politics of Social Imperialism, 1900–16* (Princeton, NJ, 1975).
40 On the Portuguese negotiations see Grenville, *Lord Salisbury's Foreign Policy,* Ch. VII; Richard Langhorne, 'Anglo-German Negotiations Concerning the Future of the Portuguese

Colonies, 1911–14', *Hist. Jour.*, XVI (1973); and J.D. Vincent Smith, 'Anglo-German Negotiations Over the Portuguese Colonies in Africa, 1911–14', ibid. XVII (1974).

41 On the Radical influence on foreign policy see A.J.A. Morris, *Radicalism Against War, 1906–1914* (1972); Howard Weinroth, 'The British Radicals and the Balance of Power, 1902–14', *Hist. Jour.*, XXII (1974). For their enemies see A.J.A. Morris, *The Scaremongers. The Advocacy of War and Rearmament, 1896–1914* (1986).

42 K.M. Wilson, 'The British Cabinet's Decision for War, 2 August, 1914', *Brit. Jour. Internat. Stud.*, I (1975).

43 This is a part of Mayer's more general thesis on the relationship between the old aristocratic order and the coming of the war. See Arno J. Mayer, *The Persistence of the Old Regime: Europe to the Great War* (1981), esp. Ch. V. Also important in this context are Mayer's 'Domestic Causes of the First World War', in Leonard Kreiger and Fritz Stem, eds. *The Responsibility of Power* (New York, 1967); Donald Lammers, 'Arno Mayer and the British Decision for War', *Jour. Brit. Stud.*, XII (1973); and Michael R. Gordon, 'Domestic Conflict and the Origins of the First World War: the British and German Cases', *Jour. Mod. Hist.*, XLVI (1974).

44 Colin Nicholson, 'Edwardian England and the Coming of the First World War', in O'Day, *Edwardian England*.

45 Avner Offer, *The First World War: An Agrarian Interpretation* (Oxford, 1989), esp. Chs. 15–21.

46 Hoffman, *The Anglo-German Trade Rivalry, 1875–1914,* pp. 325–9. This subject is pursued further in the case studies which follow in Volume II of the present study.

47 Kathleen Burk, *Morgan Grenfell: The Biography of a Merchant Bank, 1838–1988* (Cambridge, 1989), p. 118.

48 Ibid. p. 119.

49 Kennedy, *The Realities Behind Diplomacy,* p. 137.

15

RETROSPECT

1688–1914

Our first and most general conclusion is that the character and purpose of Britain's presence on the moving frontiers of empire can be fully understood only by linking events in diverse parts of the world to causes that can be traced back to the metropole itself.[1] This claim may seem to be self-evident to readers who are not themselves working underground in one of the many deep shafts of historical research, but specialists will probably be willing to acknowledge that a process of continental drift has taken place in the course of the last thirty years and that the various subdivisions created by detailed research, for all their merits, have not provided an accessible route to an understanding of the larger issues that also demand our attention. The process of reunification poses formidable problems. It is necessary, on the domestic front, to penetrate far below the level of diplomatic exchanges and other direct representations of Britain's international interests; at the same time, it is now impossible to discuss events on the periphery with any pretence at adequacy without incorporating the results of the abundant new research produced in the period since decolonisation. In terms of scholarly output, the burdens of empire are heavier today than they have ever been. Once lifted, however, they become an indispensable asset, and one that future interpretations of imperialism must surely mobilise if they are to achieve credibility.

Our own interpretation attempts to connect metropole and periphery by linking innovations in the finance and service sector to the priorities that shaped both national policy and Britain's unofficial presence abroad. These innovations, symbolised by the foundation of the Bank of England, the creation of the national debt and the rise of associated gentlemanly activities centred on London, are far more important to an understanding of the economic history of modern Britain than is generally allowed. They were also translated, through wealth made in approved ways, into social status and, by a further transformation, into political authority. Beyond this, they entered into the notion of a wider British mission, one that was

Christian, civilised and civilising. These developments took concrete shape in the alliance cemented in the eighteenth century between the landed interest, headed by the aristocracy, and the new 'moneyed men' of the City, who had a common interest in the national debt, in forms of mercantile enterprise that gathered or generated revenue, and in the political system later known as Old Corruption. This coalition was reshaped in the nineteenth century, beginning after the defeat of France in 1815, when the leaders of the landed interest started to dismantle the system of political economy put in place following the Revolution of 1688 and to move towards cheap government and free trade. The transition gathered speed in the second half of the nineteenth century, when the balance of the coalition changed to give greater prominence to financial interests, the leading beneficiaries of economic reform, and when a social merger was effected by extending gentlemanly status to the higher ranks of the new urban middle class, who were coopted into the defence of property and order. Taken together, these realignments were designed to manage a distinctive form of conservative progress, one that safeguarded tradition and privilege while also upholding the rights of 'free-born Englishmen' and offering prospects of material improvement.

This compromise was inspired initially by the need to save the polity from an unacceptable choice between tyranny and anarchy. It was kept alive subsequently by fear of subversion from within, whether by Jacobites or, later, by the menacing forces of industrialisation and their offshoot, socialism, and by perceived threats from abroad, ranging from French republicanism to the dangers posed by new, expansive states, whether democratic, like the United States, or centralised, like Germany. However, the link between domestic developments and Britain's international policy and presence was not simply a defensive one: finance and services were expansive from the outset because the productivity gains derived from innovations in credit, shipping and commercial organisation could be fully realised only by increasing their international scope. The configuration of wealth, status and power that materialised in gentlemanly forms of enterprise was therefore outward-bound as well as inward-looking: in the most general terms, it can be said that the overseas empire and Britain's influence beyond it were extensions abroad of the forces first installed by the Revolution of 1688 and transmuted subsequently by the reforms of the nineteenth century.

In the eighteenth century these forces made their mark both on the colonies of white settlement, where deliberate attempts were made to reproduce and hence to reinforce British landed society, and on India, where efforts were made to raise up a class of indigenous land-holders and where the East India Company, one of the principal manifestations of the new commercial order, extended its sway. The subsequent history of the loss of the American colonies and the acquisition of India was closely bound up with the extension of commercial credit, the search for revenue, and the centralising tendencies of the British state. After 1815, and especially after 1850, City finance and associated services performed a vital, indeed historic, function of integrating countries that lacked adequate capital markets of their own. By funding export development overseas, the City enabled newly incorporated regions to raise and service an increasing volume of foreign loans; by generating a massive invisible income from these activities, the City made a crucial contribution to Britain's balance of payments. In this way, the City and sterling acquired a world role, and London became the centre of a system of global payments that continued to expand right down to the outbreak of war in 1914.

Our argument at this point emphasised the fact that the impulses drawing Britain overseas merged economic considerations with a wider programme of development that aimed at raising the standard of civilisation as well as the standard of living, and was accompanied, accordingly, by exports of liberal political principles and missionary enterprise. The underlying purpose of the venture was to nurture congenial allies at critical points of entry or passage for British trade and finance, thus tightening Britain's control over the system of multilateral exchanges on which her prosperity increasingly depended and strengthening her ability to ward off threats from old rivals in Europe and new competitors (notably the United States) further afield.

These expansionist impulses were pacific as well as imperialist in character; and the imperialist option was peaceful and informal as well as aggressive and territorially acquisitive. Broadly similar impulses therefore produced a range of outcomes that reflected the strength of British interests, the structure of the society concerned and the international environment at the time. The colonies of white settlement, for example, fell more firmly under British influence in the second half of the nineteenth century. As they increased their formal political independence, so they became reliant on flows of British capital to an extent that limited their freedom of action in crucial respects and tied export interests and their political representatives to policy norms, the rules of the game, set by London. A very similar pattern can be discerned in the case of the South American republics, where British finance was heavily involved in funding the apparatus of government as well as the growth of exports, thereby helping both to build new nation states and to subordinate them to external influences. As Disraeli observed, 'colonies do not cease to be colonies because they are independent'.[2] The subsequent history of the countries of white settlement, especially their response to mounting pressures for debt repayment from the close of the nineteenth century, attests to the continuing validity of this observation. Nor is the conclusion qualified by examples of the growth of manufacturing on some parts of the periphery towards the close of the period under review. This development undoubtedly limited the market for exports of British consumer goods, but it met the needs of the City because it economised on the import bill of the satellites concerned and helped to generate the export surplus required to service external debts.

Elsewhere, the application of Palmerston's test that non-European societies should be 'well kept' and 'always accessible' produced more candidates than successes.[3] As British finance and influence extended their range in the second half of the century, it became clear that indigenous societies were often unwilling to respond to external demands on the terms set by foreign interests, even when they were able to do so. India, of course, had already been incorporated into the empire and was managed by English gentlemen in ways that guaranteed conformity to priorities established in London. There, as we have seen, policy was directed towards ensuring that India's external obligations continued to be met: when a choice had to be made between the claims of finance and those of manufacturing, as was increasingly the case in the late nineteenth century, preference was given to the former. The most spectacular example of territorial annexation, the partition of Africa, offers a detailed illustration of how the penetration of British interests produced conditions that caused Palmerston's rules to be broken. In the two key cases, Egypt and South Africa, a preoccupation with finance and its attendant political implications provided powerful incentives for moving inland. The City's interests were also at the forefront of Britain's presence in areas of informal influence. Following the Ottoman default of 1875, the City's representatives became heavily involved in managing the empire's affairs to ensure that debt service was resumed, and at the same time less willing to supply new finance, with the result that the Foreign Office was hard-pressed to uphold Britain's wider interests in the region. The case of China demonstrates the central part played by finance in different circumstances, for China remained credit-worthy, and when gaps finally opened in the Great Wall after her defeat at the hands of Japan in 1895, British banks were the first to enter, and Britain became the dominant foreign influence on the Ch'ing regime thereafter.

This evidence points to the need to revise some of the central features of the historiography of British imperialism during the classic phase of nineteenth-century expansion. We have questioned the widespread and long-standing assumption linking the 'triumph of industry' to imperialist expansion, and have emphasised instead the role of finance and services. These activities, as we have noted, have long been either underestimated or neglected by historians, yet they arose before the Industrial Revolution, continued to expand during the nineteenth century and maintained their dynamic after manufacturing had entered its long period of relative decline. The representatives of British industry were less wealthy than their counterparts in the City, made their money in ways that did not meet the approval of their social superiors, and exercised only limited political influence at national level. Of course, to the extent that British finance and services were funding the distribution of British manufactures, the two had an important interest in common. But the City's activities were not simply an offshoot of industry; still less were they beholden to it. The international order that was erected on the basis of free trade and the gold standard served the purposes of finance and services rather better than it did those of manufacturing: the increasing scale and complexity of multilateral trade relations gave the City opportunities and commitments that extended far beyond the distribution of British manufactures. Moreover, where a choice had to be made, policy invariably favoured finance over manufacturing. The empirical evidence is compelling: the manufacturing lobby always put its case, but it rarely got its way, whereas the City's needs were very much to the fore in all the examples we have examined – in exercising informal influence, in acquiring territory and in formulating the principles of colonial administration.

This argument carries wider implications for assessing the influence of pressure groups on policy-making. Our study suggests that what is usually referred to, generically, as the 'business' lobby needs to be disaggregated to account for differences of the kind we have identified between the City and industry – a distinction, of course, that is itself open to further refinement. When this is done, the contrast commonly drawn between officialdom and business loses much of its validity because it is apparent that an important segment of the non-industrial business elite consisted of gentlemen who moved in the same circles and shared the same values as those who had their hands on the levers of power – and often managed their investments too. Imperial and imperialist policies did not issue from a conspiracy by a covert minority but from the open exercise of authority by a respected elite who enjoyed the deference of those they governed. Like-mindedness was certainly extended abroad, but it began at home.

Shifting the basis of causation has also required us to reconsider some of the standard categories and chronological divisions of imperial history. Linking imperialism to the process of industrialisation has produced a number of well-known landmarks: an informal empire in the mid-Victorian era followed by the defensive imperialism of a declining power is one; the 'new' imperialism generated by the crisis of advanced industrial capitalism in the late nineteenth century is another. The expansionist impulses we have identified suggest a very different picture. In the mid-Victorian period, informal empire was more of an ideal than a reality. This was not because Britain was self-sufficient and lacked incentives to expand; on the contrary, the record of attempted house-breaking attests to Britain's need to open up the world economy. It was rather that British manufactures were only just beginning to penetrate countries overseas, even at a time when foreign competition was still very limited, principally because they awaited lubrication from British finance and commercial services.

It was not until the second half of the century, after investors had diversified out of the national debt and when free trade had been installed, that capital flows began to accelerate and transport improvements started to deliver the benefits of cheap, bulk carriage. It was at that point, and not before, that countries beyond Europe could develop a sizeable export trade and hence generate the purchasing power to buy imported manufactures and the revenues to fund external loans. And it was only in the late Victorian period that these forces began to be felt in earnest. In other words, Britain's informal influence was growing at precisely the time when it is conventionally thought to have been in decline, and it continued to extend its reach right down to 1914. By plotting the relative performance of British manufactures, and by then using this measure as a proxy for Britain's standing as a world power, the hand has deceived the eye: historians have overlooked, where they have not minimised, the process by which Britain moved from being an early lender to becoming a mature creditor with an increasingly heavy stake in protecting cross-border property rights and the complex international trade flows that were essential guarantees of debt service. As our argument suggests, the most important examples of territorial acquisition in the late nineteenth century were overflows from these expansionist tendencies, not rearguard actions fought to delay decline.[4]

It is true that this was also the time when rival powers, especially France and Germany, were beginning to flex their muscles. Their activities on the world stage are usually linked to Britain's weakening industrial performance to support the conventional conclusion that her standing as an international power was on the wane. This argument, though now routine, is profoundly unsatisfactory. In the first place, it fails to give adequate recognition to the vigorous, expansionist forces we have identified, and thus neglects the possibility that foreign rivals were reacting to Britain's assertive and imperialist impulses as well as expressing claims of their own. Secondly, the thesis is overwhelmed by contrary evidence, which shows that rival powers failed to topple Britain from her dominant position in any of the contested areas of importance outside Europe. In the dominions and India there was scarcely a contest: even in Canada, which was wide open to influences from her large southern neighbour, British finance and services remained supreme. Elsewhere, besides swallowing the most valuable parts of Africa, Britain increased her grip on the leading South American republics and on China. If France and Germany made more headway in the Ottoman Empire, it was mainly because the City took an unforgiving view of the Ottoman default and had better opportunities in more attractive parts of the world. Despite the declining competitiveness of her manufactures, Britain's ability to impose her will within and beyond the empire was still unmatched in 1914 because the London capital market remained the largest, most efficient and hence most competitive in the world – as Germany and France were well aware.

On the eve of World War I, Britain remained a dynamic and ambitious power, fearful of the cost and wider implications of large-scale conflict, but nevertheless assertive in pursuit of her own expansionist aims. When war came in 1914, it brought many of the expected adverse consequences. But the conclusion that beckons should be resisted: the period between World War I and the end of empire was not simply a long retreat directed by faltering and increasingly weary Titans. Just as the causes and chronology of British imperialism need to be revised for the era before 1914, so too a different perspective is required for appraising imperialist impulses thereafter. The familiar story of Britain's decline as a world power merits reassessment in the light of evidence of her continuing imperialist aspirations and her underestimated successes. The circumstances of the period were different, but Britain's strategy still lay in the hands of officers and gentlemen whose vision of a world order managed from London remained undimmed. This next episode, being in many respects less familiar to historians of imperialism, contains attractions and hazards of its own: some of the existing boundary stones may need to be moved; others have yet to be put in place.

Notes

1 Readers should note that this is an interim statement summarising the position in 1914 and at the end of the first part of this study. A fuller conclusion, dealing with both parts of the book, is presented in Chapter 27.

2 Speaking in the House of Commons, 5 February 1863. *Parliamentary Debates* 3rd Ser. 169, c.81.

3 Quoted in M.E. Chamberlain, *The Scramble for Africa* (1974), p. 36.
4 An extension of our argument at this point would give fuller consideration to questions such as the definition and defence of property rights in an international setting, the applicability of the distinction between management debt and development debt, the exercise of what today would be called conditionality, and the possibility of establishing a more rigorous typology for understanding decisions to intervene and decisions to annex.

PART FIVE

The empire in the twentieth century

16

THE IMPERIALIST DYNAMIC

From World War I to decolonisation

Britain's position in the world, as we have described it, was much stronger in 1914 than is customarily thought.[1] This claim does not arise from counting heads or estimating acres within the British empire, sizeable though they were at the point when war broke out. It depends, rather, upon a reassessment of the basis of Britain's global influence in the pre-war era. Although Britain's manufactured exports were running into increasing difficulties in overseas markets, as is well known and widely emphasised, Britain's financial presence continued to grow and it remained strong, indeed pre-eminent, right down to 1914. Moreover, the financial presence, in the various forms we have discussed, dominated policy towards the management of the formal empire, and also gave Britain substantial interests and considerable influence outside it. Far from being in decline in the late nineteenth century, Britain's 'invisible empire' was expanding at precisely that point. To a degree that has often been underestimated, mounting international rivalries and growing nationalist resistance from this time onwards were symptoms less of the erosion of Britain's 'hegemonic' status than of the continuing extension of her global influence. On our interpretation, then, Britain remained a dynamic power, and the anxieties, alarms and difficulties which beset the builders of the second Rome, though real enough, need to be placed in the context of their strikingly successful record in upholding British interests throughout the world.

After 1914, the gentlemanly order was compelled to operate in a more hostile global environment. The war disrupted the international economy, enabled the United States to emerge as a competitor on a global scale and seriously damaged Britain's ability to act as banker to the world. Thereafter, the slow and incomplete recovery of international trade hampered Britain's efforts to return to 'normality' and checked her influence overseas. Exports and foreign investment dwindled during the war, and failed in the 1920s to recover the levels attained in 1913. The gold standard, the evocative symbol of Britain's power, had to be suspended in 1913 and was abandoned in 1919. Returning to gold in 1925 involved an immense effort which probably accelerated Britain's relative economic decline. The onset of the world slump in 1929 ensured that the 1930s were, in most respects, an even gloomier period. Export values fell to new levels and foreign investment was reduced to a trickle. In 1931 Britain was forced to abandon the gold standard again; in the following year she replaced free trade with a preferential commercial system centred on the formal empire.

It would be easy to infer from this catalogue of economic set-backs and disappointed expectations that the gentlemanly elite and its interests steadily lost ground during the inter-war years and that Britain was in irreversible decline as an imperial power. Indeed, this is the conclusion that is conventionally reached. Standard interpretations of the period after 1914 emphasise Britain's economic weakness, her faltering will-power and her diminishing ability to maintain political control inside the empire and influence beyond it. These judgements are not to be thrown aside, but there are grounds for thinking that they are not as robust as their frequent repetition might suggest. One temptation, easily entered into, is of reading the present into the past, so that contemporary preoccupations with Britain's loss of status as a great power encourage the search for ever more distant intimations of decline. The danger here is that, in seeking to verify the favoured hypothesis, other evidence regarding the continuing vigour of Britain's presence in the world may be minimised or overlooked, and with it alternative approaches to understanding both her present predicament and the end of empire. A further hazard, which historians are inclined to hit head-on, though frequently without seeming to notice the impact, consists of discussing decline without defining the concept or specifying how it is to be measured. One consequence of this procedure is that connections between, for example, economic performance and political strength are often assumed rather than demonstrated.

Our stress on the enduring vitality of British imperialism begins by emphasising the fact that the complex of services and consumer industries which sustained wealth in the south-east of England continued to flourish after World War I, thus providing the means of perpetuating gentlemanly values, status and power. The City of London retained its independence and its central position in British economic life throughout the inter-war period, despite the fall in income from overseas investment and the rise of large-scale manufacturing in Britain. The City was not absorbed into a monopoly-capitalist structure dominated by manufacturing in the way that banks had become linked to large-scale industry in Germany and the United States; its priorities continued to imprint themselves on economic policy and on the empire, as they had done before the war. It is true, of course, that the City could no longer mobilise funds with the ease that had made it the world's largest creditor before 1914, and in the 1930s foreign investment fell to very low levels. But even this limitation does not provide straightforward evidence that Britain's power was on the wane. Power, considered as a measure of the ability to influence others, is relative as well as absolute, and potential as well as real. The resources at Britain's disposal were less plentiful after 1914 than before, but relatively she still remained a long way ahead of her European rivals, while the United States, which could have deployed forms of economic and military might far in excess of Britain's, was only just beginning to emerge as a world power. Moreover, and partly for this reason, Britain's position in relation to her various satellites and dependencies also remained strong, either because they lacked alternative sources of external support or because, during a period of considerable difficulty for primary producers, they relied heavily on the British market or on finance and services provided by the City to gain access to other markets.

From this perspective, it becomes easier to see why policy-makers did not accept that Britain's future lay behind her after 1914. The strenuous efforts made in the 1920s to return to pre-war 'normality', both at home and abroad, represented a rational choice on the part of Britain's gentlemanly elite rather than a rearguard action against the tide of history. Britain had, after all, won the war, not lost it; although the conflict had raised the standing of the United States, it had also greatly reduced that of Germany and France. The war had dented Britain's resources, too, but it had stiffened her resolve to win the peace and given her the chance of doing so. The struggle to restore the gold standard, for example, demonstrates Britain's determination to repel the challenge of the United States and to reassert financial authority on the periphery as well as traditional orthodoxy at home. As our case studies show, Britain did not relax her grip on matters of vital interest within the empire, and she had considerable success in retaining or regaining her informal influence outside it. In seeking to reconstruct the pre-war international system after 1918, the gentlemanly order also rose to a higher challenge: the need to reinvigorate liberal capitalism both to frustrate predictions of its imminent demise and to ward off the new dangers presented by Bolshevism and, later on, fascism. After 1918, as after 1815, Britain's hard-headed policies were infused with an element of crusading zeal which rallied the gentlemanly elite and gave it a mission to accomplish.

Although Britain suffered in the world slump that began in 1929, she was far less affected than her rivals, including the United States, whose global economic influence shrank rapidly. Indeed, it is important to remember that Britain was the only truly world power of consequence in the 1930s. The decade saw a resurgence of her imperialist ambitions, as she pieced together the Sterling Area, which emerged as the most important international economic bloc, and encroached on positions that the United States had begun to occupy in Canada, South America and China. The overriding purpose of British policy, within the empire and beyond it, was to restore or enhance her financial influence. This priority gave direction and momentum to important decisions on international policy, from the Ottawa agreements to appeasement; it shaped Britain's other dealings with the Dominions and the colonies; it dominated her aims in South America and China. In pursuing these goals, Britain showed a degree of energy and agility that is hard to reconcile with the view that, by the close of the 1930s, she had become an elderly and arthritic power. She held on resolutely to her central overseas interests against the claims of Germany and Japan, as imperialist rivalries gathered pace from the mid-1930s; and she showed both determination in pursuing her debtors and flexibility in adjusting to developments on the periphery by investing in joint-ventures and by working with nationalists instead of against them.

What halted this promising strategy was not renewed American expansionism, which was only just reappearing at the close of the 1930s, but the coming of another world war. From the perspective of the present study, World War II itself was the culmination of international rivalries which accelerated under the pressures generated by the world slump. Failure to accommodate or control the 'have-not' powers of Germany and Japan finally made war inevitable and reduced Britain to financial dependence on the United States. Anticipations of this fate in London had done much to inspire efforts to keep the peace, to restrain defence costs, and thus to uphold the value of sterling and the prospects of a British-led recovery in international trade. After 1939, with these plans in ruin, Britain's gentlemanly capitalists became players, albeit important ones, in an orchestra conducted jointly in Washington and New York.

Nevertheless, the outbreak of World War II did not mark the end of Britain's long history of imperial expansion. Britain's war aims included regaining and regrouping the empire, and in this she was remarkably successful – given the desperate situation in 1940 and the fact that her main ally and chief paymaster was a former colony with an anti-colonial bias. As the principal component of the Sterling Area, the empire also made a vital contribution to Britain's post-war reconstruction plans in the decade after 1945. The acts of decolonisation which gathered pace from the late 1950s were neither fortuitous events nor the inevitable culmination of a long process of decay. In the end, as is well known, nationalist aspirations could not be contained at a price that was worth paying, or perhaps at any price. But by that time, too, as is less well appreciated, the empire had served its purpose. It did not simply fall apart but was taken apart by the proprietors as well as by its prospective new owners. However, even as the debris of deconstruction went overboard, the gentlemen of the City had already changed course and were heading towards new horizons, where global opportunities – above the nation state and beyond the empire – beckoned.

Note

1 Readers should note that a full statement of the argument, concepts and methodology deployed in this study can be found in Chapter 1.

PART SIX

The gentlemanly order, 1914–39

17

'THE POWER OF CONSTANT RENEWAL': SERVICES, FINANCE AND THE GENTLEMANLY ELITE, 1914–39[1]

Manufacturing, services and the south-east

The need to create a mass army and the disruption caused by the suppression of international trade led to a fall in total output in Britain after 1914. Pre-war levels of output were not recovered until the mid-1920s. Thereafter, despite the crisis of 1929–33, the economy grew at an average rate of over 2 per cent per annum until the late 1930s, a rate in excess of that achieved between 1870 and 1913.[2] Productivity rose sharply in wartime, too, partly to compensate for losses of manpower to the defence forces, and in the 1920s and 1930s increased at rates comparable with those of late Victorian Britain.[3] Another marked feature of the post-war economy was the rapid growth of manufacturing which, at over 3 per cent per year, was much higher than pre-war: by contrast, service growth was slower than before 1914. Manufacturing's share of output increased from around 30 per cent in 1913 to 35 per cent in 1937, while the share of services fell. Manufacturing productivity also rose at a much higher rate than previously, whereas productivity in services may well have declined.[4]

The output of industries dependent on export sales sometimes fell between the wars but this was more than compensated by the growth of manufactures based on domestic demand.[5] This rapid growth has led some historians to argue that, despite the difficulties produced by an ailing export sector, the inter-war period was one of far-reaching economic transformation led by new, technologically dynamic industries.[6] But the 'new industries', such as chemicals and motor vehicles, accounted for only one-fifth of manufacturing output in 1937. Also, much of the improved productivity performance in the 1930s was a result of the 'rationalisation' of older industries, like textiles, where employment fell faster than output.[7] Investment in manufacturing between the wars remained low: around 70 per cent of net investment between 1920 and 1938 was in housing.[8] This low level of industrial investment was a reflection of reduced profits compared with the period before 1914 and the uncertainty generated by severe cyclical fluctuations, as well as the capital-saving nature of some important innovations.[9] Despite mergers, rationalisation and the increasing significance of 'big business' in Britain, technological backwardness and managerial inefficiency remained features of much of British industry, including some of the more rapidly growing sectors, which needed protection in the 1930s to preserve their domestic market and could not compete abroad outside the confines of empire.[10] Although the United States' economy suffered greatly in the 1930s, the productivity gap in manufacturing between Britain and the USA was wider in 1939 than in 1914. Measured against her European neighbours, Britain held her own between the wars in terms of productivity, but no more than that.[11]

The rapid development of manufacturing in the inter-war period did not mean, either, that there was any change in the patterns of regional dominance which had established themselves before 1914. The south-east's share of manufacturing output rose from about one-fifth just after the war to over one-quarter thirty years later; this was the chief reason why the region's share of total employment also increased in the same period.[12] Of all new firms formed in industry, transport and services, 50 per cent took place in the south-east between the two wars, attracted by the well-established high levels of per capita income in the region;[13] in many ways the development of the south-east followed the same pattern as pre-1914, when high incomes generated in services increased the demand for locally produced consumer manufactures. The south-east had a higher concentration of new industries, a higher rate of employment growth and a lower rate of unemployment than any other region.[14] It also attracted the bulk of the direct industrial investment from overseas, mainly the United States, which flowed into Britain in this period.[15] The boom in private housing, which was so important in sustaining growth in Britain after 1918, was much more marked in the south-east than elsewhere, and was a direct result of the high concentration of income-taxpayers there.[16] Manufacturing had become a more important element within the economy than before 1914 but its development reinforced the influence of the south-east corner of Britain. Shifts in the location of industry fused the centres of manufacturing and service sector power more closely together; London's dominance, as registered by the locations of the head offices of firms, increased.[17]

Finance and industry after 1914

Before World War I there was, as we have seen, a divide between industrial capitalism and the major financial institutions, whose concentration in London became more marked over time. The bulk of industry remained self-financing up to 1914 or relied on local stock exchanges; even had they wished to do so, the majority of manufacturing firms would have been too small to benefit from the services offered by leading City issuing houses. On their side, the merchant bankers and the finance houses of the City were occupied with the business of government and public-utility finance either in Britain or overseas. The great clearing banks, reduced by amalgamation to the 'Big Five' in 1921, had, of necessity, a closer relationship with industry, but what they offered was short-term accommodation and overdraft facilities rather than long-term loans.

After 1914 the two spheres or 'fractions' of capital, as Marxists prefer to call them, came closer together. In one important respect this was an accidental process. In the great restocking boom of 1919–20, cotton, coal, shipbuilding and other major exporting interests made large additions to their capital in anticipation of rapid growth in overseas markets once 'normality' had been restored. The clearing banks often shared their customers' febrile optimism and offered accommodation on an unprecedented scale. When the new markets anticipated in 1920 proved non-existent, much of the new capital was wasted and, as profits collapsed, the banks were left with overdrafts which could be called in only at the risk of bankruptcy.[18]

At the end of the decade and in the 1930s, when the ailments of the export industries had proved to be chronic and heavy regional unemployment was a fixture, more positive efforts were made to marry finance with industry. Led by Norman, as Governor, the Bank of England launched a series of initiatives designed to bring City and provincial industry together. The Bank was acutely aware of the increasing criticism of financial policy in the 1920s. Norman, in particular, was convinced that the failure of the financial sector to show some interest in reviving older industries would give the green light to politicians, particularly Labour politicians, to interfere – with disastrous effects on the market system which the Bank supervised.[19] He also recognised, frankly enough, that in an age when opportunities for overseas investment were shrinking, City institutions needed to look more to the domestic market for business. As Norman put it in 1930:

> I believe that the finance which for 100 years has been directed by them abroad can be directed by them into British industry, that a marriage can take place between the industry of the North and the finance of the South.[20]

The Bank often urged the clearing banks to use their new financial position with major industries to impose mergers or more efficient management upon them. It also launched, in 1929, the Bankers Industrial Development Corporation, which brought City and industry together in an endeavour to promote 'rationalisation', especially in the steel industry;[21] it played a leading role in National Shipbuilders Security, which was designed to reduce capacity in shipbuilding and lower costs;[22] and in the late 1930s it took part, with the Treasury, in the Special Areas Reconstruction Association, a body composed of City and industrial firms which invested capital in areas of high unemployment.[23]

One of the Bank's main aims was the creation of efficient big business. The war, by effecting a coordination of output in many industries, and the intensity of international competition in the 1920s, gave a significant boost to the creation of oligopoly in Britain. The share of the leading 100 companies in British output rose from 15 per cent in 1907 to around 26 per cent in the later 1920s, though levels of concentration appear to have fallen slightly in the 1930s.[24] Many mergers in the 1920s were carried through with the aid of Stock Exchange finance[25] and, as the large corporations became more

TABLE 17.1 New capital issues, 1919–38 (quinquennial averages, £m.)

	Public	Industry and commerce	Total Domestic	Domestic %		Overseas %
1919–23	37.1	119.0	156.1	61.1	99.3	38.9
1924–28	55.1	96.4	151.5	55.2	123.3	44.8
1929–33	41.3	60.4	101.7	61.7	63.2	38.3
1934–38	47.5	90.7	138.2	82.3	29.7	17.7

Source: T. Balogh, *Studies in Financial Organizations* (Cambridge, 1947), Table XLVIa, pp. 249–50; W.A. Thomas, *The Finance of British Industry* (1978), Table 2.1, p. 27.

typical members of the British industrial landscape, there began to emerge a new class of managerial capitalists – Mond of ICI is a good example – who had a more central role in British economic (and political) life than hitherto.

Furthermore, domestic issues of capital on the Stock Exchange were a more dominant part of the capital market after 1919 and domestic industrial and commercial issues were the most prominent element. Domestic issues as a whole were over twice the value of overseas issues between the wars, whereas on average only two-fifths of all issues were raised for domestic concerns between 1865 and 1914 and, in the last few years before the war, only three-tenths (Table 17.1).[26] Some specialist firms arose to deal with domestic industrial finance,[27] but even the traditional merchant bankers responded to some degree to changing times. Although Barings remained primarily an overseas issuing house, they acted as advisers to Armstrongs, the armaments firm, and underwrote flotations for underground railways, breweries and even tyre firms.[28] Kleinworts were more adventurous and promoted issues for cotton firms and shipbuilders, while Morgan Grenfell could probably claim a greater involvement in industrial issues than any other firm between the wars.[29]

By 1939, the large corporation was well established in Britain, and finance and industry had intermingled to a novel degree; but whether the outcome could be described as 'finance capitalism', in Hilferding's sense of the term, is doubtful. Even in 1939 the large firms which had merged with the help of the London Stock Exchange still made little use of it for new capital, which was mainly raised internally,[30] and smaller firms still found London too expensive a place to find finance.[31] Nor did the closer involvement of the clearing banks in financing industry lead to fundamental changes in the relationship between them. Encouraged by the Bank of England, the banks most closely involved with cotton textiles did use their influence, via the Lancashire Cotton Corporation, to push through a policy of scrapping excess capacity owned by the firms beholden to them, on pain of having overdrafts withdrawn.[32] This action, however, was unusual: the clearers normally had little influence on industrial policy and wanted less. Norman's hope that they might use their position to force industry into efficiency did not materialise.[33] The clearers did not evolve into industrial banks and they were still dependent for their income on investment outlets dominated by the City of London and its money market. As such, they remained rather uneasily placed between provincial industry and the dominant financial sector in London centred on the Bank of England. Their status and their influence remained limited. Industry was given representation on the Bank of England's directorate in 1928; but the clearers had to wait until 1934 before one of their number was invited to join.[34]

Even successful industrial mergers often turned out to be no more than the bringing together of disparate elements which resisted fundamental change in managerial structures and methods.[35] As for the clearers, when profits rose in the 1930s, their advances to industry actually fell quite sharply.[36] This disengagement from industry can be interpreted either as a determination by the banks to free themselves to pursue their primary goal of maintaining a high degree of liquidity or as a conscious repudiation of long-term involvement with bank capital by industry.[37] Either way, the result was that the two sides of capitalism were not indissolubly committed to each other.

Like the clearers, the merchant banks often found that their experiences in industrial finance were unhappy ones: Kleinworts, for example, burned their fingers badly on occasions.[38] Stock Exchange investors were also wary of industry. The number of industrial companies quoted on the Exchange rose from 569 in 1907 to 1,712 in 1939 and their combined market value was five times greater in 1939 than before World War I.[39] But, partly because of the massive increase in public debt as a result of the war, industrial securities still made up only 10 per cent of the value of all quoted securities in the 1930s, as opposed to 8 per cent in 1913.[40] Although industrial issues were slowly increasing in importance, low returns on capital and the insecurities surrounding industrial profits were still powerful deterrents which inhibited outsiders from making long-term investments in manufacturing. The raising of new industrial finance on the Stock Exchange was also inhibited after 1914 by the growth of the national debt, which diverted income to rentiers whose inclination was to look for safer domestic investment outlets than industry could offer.[41]

It is important, too, not to magnify the novelty of the Bank of England's own initiatives in this field. It was resolutely opposed to providing much new money for industry;[42] it saw its role mainly as facilitating contacts with financiers and promoting self-help. Some of its schemes were, in fact, little more than gestures designed to divert criticism from financial policy in general and to keep the state at bay. Like the National Government itself, which encouraged industries to raise profits by concocting price and output schemes in the 1930s, the aim was to make industry help itself while preserving the orthodoxies of balanced budgets, low government spending and a strong pound, all of which found support in industrial circles.[43]

What little direct help the Bank of England or the Treasury did give often went to older industries because the underlying assumption of policy remained one of attempting to revive exports and the international economy.[44] London remained cosmopolitan in outlook. The Macmillan Committee's verdict of 1930, that 'in some respects the City is more highly organized to provide capital to foreign countries than to British industry',[45] was still correct at the end of the period. It is also possible that the chief result of Bank of England and government involvement in industry was to create a more conscious and vocal set of vested interests, dependent on cartelisation and protection, whose power was often used to forestall change rather than to encourage it.[46] Thus, the emergence of the large corporation in British industry did promote the growth of a more coherent, politically aware, industrial interest which had more influence than in the past and was closer to centres of power in London, where the head offices of these major companies were based. But the incorporation of industrial capital did not lead to any fundamental shifts in the structure of relations between the principal segments of capital in Britain and, as a consequence, it had little influence upon the distribution of power or any new, determining effect upon economic policy.

Wealth and power between the wars

Recent studies of the distribution of wealth in Britain all show a remarkable continuity between the inter-war period and preceding times. In the first place, landed wealth continued to decline in relative importance. In all fortunes of £0.5m. or above declared at death, the share of landed wealth was two-fifths in 1880–99 but fell to a mere 15 per cent by 1920–39 (Table 17.2). The rising importance of other sectors, land taxes and death duties, and the low level of agricultural prices and profits after wartime state support was removed, all contributed to this decline. Land sales were very high in the immediate post-war years. About one-quarter of all land changed hands, the main movement being from landlords to farmers who exchanged tenancy

TABLE 17.2 Non-landed fortunes at death, 1880–1969 (£0.5m. or more)

	1880–99	*%*	*1900–19*	*%*	*1920–39*	*%*	*1940–69*	*%*
Manufacturing and mining	82	36.7	124	34.2	153	30.4	164	32.1
Food, drink and tobacco	36	16.1	48	13.2	97	19.3	86	16.8
Finance	47	21.1	79	21.9	90	17.9	211	41.3
Commerce	47	21.1	101	27.9	138	27.4		
Other	11	4.9	10	2.8	24	4.8	50	9.8
Total	223		362		502		511	
(Land)	(174)		(140)		(91)		(n/a)	

Source: derived from W.D. Rubinstein, *Men of Property: The Very Wealthy in Great Britain Since the Industrial Revolution* (1981), Tables 3.3, 3.4 and 8.3.

Note: Rubinstein's figures do not include the value of the land of those whose property was subject to legal settlements forbidding sale and in which any particular owner had only a life interest. The compilation of the groups is as follows: *Manufacturing and mining* comprising columns 1–11 of the original tables; *Food, drink and tobacco*, columns 12–15; *Finance*, columns 16–18, 22 and 23; *Commerce*, columns 19–21, 24 and 25; and *Others*, columns 26–32.

for ownership. Most major landed estates survived, although with a diminished acreage, and the proceeds of sales were invested in other forms of economic activity, mainly financial, integrating the landed elite more firmly into the structures of a gentlemanly capitalism which contained them rather than being dominated by them.[47]

Secondly, despite the rapid growth of manufacturing output after 1914 and the tendency towards industrial concentration, the relative importance of manufacturers among top wealth-holders did not change much. The number of deceased half-millionaires who owed their fortunes either to manufacturing or to the food, drink and tobacco industries was always around one-half of all non-landed fortunes and, between the wars, the share of the purely manufacturing wealthy declined slightly (Table 17.2). A fall in the importance of wealth made in cottons and woollens was to be expected; but newer industries did not generate outstanding new concentrations of wealth. The engineering and chemical industries together produced 26 half-millionaire fortunes or above in 1880–98 and only 32 between 1920–39. Although the food, drink and tobacco sector was buoyant, this was partly due to the importance of traditional industries such as brewing and distilling, which produced 43 out of the 96 half-millionaire fortunes in this sector between the wars.[48]

Thirdly, as before 1914, commerce and finance provided about two-fifths of all large estates. Not surprisingly, merchant banking's dependence on the international economy caused a decline in its relative importance,[49] but banking in general, stockbroking, insurance and, most of all, shipowning more than compensated for this. Estates above £0.5m. in value derived from shipbuilding increased from 10 in 1880–99 to 24 in 1900–19, and then rose dramatically to 56 in 1920–39.[50]

Nor were there any notable changes in the geographical distribution of large fortunes (Table 17.3). London's share was stable at just under two-fifths: the City's share fell slightly but still amounted to well over one-fifth of the total in 1920–39. Given the increasing concentration of big business, both financial and industrial, between the wars and the growth of manufacturing in the south-east, it is surprising that London's share of great wealth did not increase. On the other hand, the major industrial areas did not improve their position *vis-à-vis* the metropolis, and because the south-east was the most dynamic centre of industrial development, the Midlands increased its share of top wealth only marginally (Table 17.3).

It can, of course, be argued that the estates of those dying in the period 1920–39 are a very inadequate index of wealth concentration between the wars since so many of those who left fortunes between the wars had made their mark on the pre-1914 economy, while many who made their fortunes between 1914 and 1939 died long after. However, what information there is on wealth at death in the period 1940–69 shows a very similar distribution, both by sector and by region (Tables 17.3 and 17.4). This evidence confirms that, despite the shift from overseas to domestic sources of income and wealth after 1914 and the rise of new industry, there were no sweeping changes in the nature of wealth-holding in Britain in the inter-war period. The south-east remained the most rapidly developing region; the service-consumer industry complex formed its central activities; the City of London remained the main source of its economic strength; its wealth provided the economic basis for the social and political

TABLE 17.3 Geographical origins of non-landed fortunes, 1900–39 (£0.5m. or more)

	1900–19	*%*	*1920–39*	*%*
City	82	22.7	106	21.1
Other London	47	13.0	67	13.4
Lancashire	24		36	
Yorkshire	25		38	
North-east	26		31	
Midlands	25		38	
Northern Ireland	3		6	
South Wales	7		6	
Total, industrial	110	30.5	155	30.9
Clydeside[a]	28	15.8	40	15.9
Merseyside[a]	29		40	
Others	66		94	
Grand total	362		502	

Source: Rubinstein, *Men of Property,* Tables 3.11 and 3.12.

Note:

[a] Merseyside and Clydeside have been listed separately from the industrial areas because of the predominance there of commercial fortunes.

TABLE 17.4 Geographical origins of non-landed fortunes, 1940–69 (£0.5m. or more)

	1940–69	*%*
City[a]	95	18.1
Other London[a]	85	16.1
Greater Manchester	17	
West Yorkshire	24	13.6
Greater Birmingham	31	
Clydeside[b]	28	10.4
Merseyside[b]	27	
Total[c]	526	

Source: Rubinstein, *Men of Property,* Table 8.4.

Notes:

[a] The number of large fortunes declared after 1940 is severely affected by taxation and estate-duty avoidance: the wealthy of the City were more adept at hiding their wealth than others. See Rubinstein, *Men of Property,* pp. 235–6.

[b] Merseyside and Clydeside have been listed separately from the industrial areas because of a predominance there of commercial fortunes.

[c] The total figure includes a number of fortunes made in Britain by foreigners.

power of the gentlemanly service class, which was one of the south-east's outstanding products.

There was an 'establishment' in Britain between the wars and, as before 1914, its material foundation was the service wealth which funded the activities of the 'service class' – the higher civil servants, lawyers and other professionals, clergy and military men. The establishment had a strong association with aristocracy (though the latter's direct power was fading), with Eton and Harrow, with Oxford and Cambridge; and its members filled many of the jobs at the 'commanding heights' of society.[51] But it was not a caste. As Bédarida has noted, what

> gave the top class the power of constant renewal and adaptation to change was its capacity to absorb and assimilate. It welcomed outsiders and, by investing them with its own aura, perpetuated itself. It knew how to inculcate its own norms and values on those it took under its wing.[52]

Indeed, the powerful and the influential in society were the top echelons of a complex structure of service employment, revolving around London and the Home Counties, which reached even farther down into the world of white-collar employment than before 1914. Upward mobility was a significant feature of this economy: bishops, higher civil servants, university figures and other leading professionals were often recruited from the lower reaches of the middle class, who had little capital and no connections, and whose careers mainly depended on success at public school and Oxbridge.[53] Power was meritocratic in origin rather than purely hereditary but, as before 1914, there was little recruitment from outside the service sector itself. Of Wykehamists born in the 1880s (who would have been at the height of their careers in the 1920s and 1930s) only 15 per cent had fathers in business or engineering and only one-fifth took up careers in these areas, most of them outside manufacturing.[54] The career paths of the products of other prestigious public schools were very similar: of boys entering Rugby and Harrow in 1880 only one-quarter and one-sixth respectively chose business careers, and the importance of business did not increase with time.[55] The concentration of both public school and Oxbridge recruits and the families of 'top people' in government and the professions around London and the south-east was also obvious since this was where the bulk of the service-sector middle class was found.[56] Bound together by a common background in service-sector capitalism and by a similar education, the establishment was the product of a system which preferred the security offered by bureaucratic or professional employment to the hazards of business.[57] Gentlemen continued to give 'service' rather than to make profits, and this ideal of service formed a bond of union across the whole professional class – from permanent officials in the Foreign Office to underpaid London clerks.[58]

The colonial service remained a strong branch of this particular culture up to World War II and indeed beyond. Between 1919 and 1948 recruitment was in the hands of one man, Sir Ralph Furse, assisted by two close and long-serving colleagues.[59] Furse came from an old and well-connected gentry family and was educated at Eton (where the future Lord Salisbury was his 'fag') and Oxford before entering the Colonial Office in 1910. His family links to Church and state (his grandfather had been Archdeacon of Westminster) were extended by his marriage to Sir Henry Newbolt's daughter, who was related to the Montagus. Furse's method of recruitment favoured selection by interview from a pool of candidates created very largely by his own actively cultivated contacts at Oxford and Cambridge, and his experience as an undergraduate gave him 'a keen eye for the merits of that admirable class of person whom university examiners consider worthy only of third-class honours'.[60] His life in London and his travels throughout the empire provide an insight into the continuing vitality of the gentlemanly diaspora: no matter where he went, Furse was certain to run into other men of influence who were known to him through family connections, Eton or Balliol. Furse's dedication and integrity were accompanied by a sense of purpose that was as unswerving as it was uncritical. His belief in England's mission was inspired by an Elizabethan spirit of adventure and directed by rules of conduct that were drawn from the disciplines of military life and team games, especially cricket. As soon as war broke out in 1939, Furse began to make plans for the recruiting drive that would be needed after it had been won.

The impressions evoked by Furse's autobiography have been confirmed by recent research.[61] An analysis of 200 colonial governors between 1900 and 1960 shows that they came predominantly from the south-east of England and had close family connections with the service sector. Virtually all of them were educated at public schools and over half had been to Oxford or Cambridge. Variations from this pattern occurred but were inconsiderable. As in the case of many other professional groups, the future governors emerged from a wide range of public schools and only a small minority (14 per cent) had been educated at the top nine 'Clarendon' schools. They also tended to come from the less affluent, non-industrial middle class. As one of their number wrote in retirement, they were

> mostly the younger sons of the professional middle class, and had been given a Sound Old-fashioned Liberal Education in the humanities at preparatory and public schools ending with an arts degree at one of the older universities.[62]

Insofar as they had any direct contact with business, it was likely to be with firms in the City;[63] and this was also true of other sections of the service elite.[64] Of all business centres, the City remained the one most thoroughly in touch with the world of gentlemanly employment. The proportion of merchant bankers and the chairmen of other leading banking firms going to Eton, or the other top public schools which educated so many of the political elite, was very high. The family connections between financiers remained much stronger than they were in other businesses;[65] despite the problems of some houses which were very dependent on overseas income, the levels of wealth attainable in the City were still much higher than in most of the manufacturing sector.

Some of the older houses felt the need to draw on outside talent after 1919 in order to increase their performance, but the gentlemanly quality of life in the City remained undisturbed.[66] In assessing London's virtues in the mid-1930s, Truptil thought that the concentration of a multitude of different commercial and financial activities in one small space was an important aid to efficiency because it allowed for 'economy of time and staff' and 'a multiplicity of contact between all the various people who have to work together'.[67] But, besides that, he emphasised that the City was characterised by 'closer personal relationships in which direct family ties were an important element but not outstandingly so, for to have been at the same college at Oxford or Cambridge frequently forms a far closer bond between two men then the fact that they may be cousins'. It was for this reason, Truptil believed, that the sense of community in London was much stronger than in Paris and made it possible, for example, for the Bank of England and the Treasury to operate embargoes on overseas loans without legal sanctions. 'Team spirit' and 'a sporting sense of discipline' could ensure a certain amount of self-regulation, solidarity and mutual self-help in the face of crisis.[68] The personal element in City business was one of the factors which gave financiers an affinity with the professionals and bureaucrats who ran the rest of the service sector and distanced them to some degree from the world of industry.[69]

The status of industry, though improving, still lagged somewhat behind that of the professions and the City. The broad swathe of industrialists whose firms were small, together with the growing managerial element in manufacturing, came from backgrounds that differed markedly from those of the leading members of the service sector. Jeremy's study of the 270 businessmen (mainly industrialists and industrial managers) who figure in the first volume of the *Dictionary of Business Biography* shows that only one-fifth of those born between 1870 and 1899 (and who would have been most active between the wars and immediately after that) went to public school, though the public school component for later birth cohorts was significantly higher. Only one-ninth of the group had been educated at one of the ancient universities and half had fathers who were craftsmen, clerks, tradesmen or were similarly occupied.[70]

Nonetheless, industrialists' links with centres of power certainly strengthened after 1914. As big business increased in significance, the connections between finance and industry became closer. The leaders of large manufacturing companies enjoyed an educational background similar to that of non-traditional members of the elite,[71] the chief difference being that, like top City men, these leading industrialists often came from rather wealthier backgrounds than did recruits to the professions.[72] On the whole, however, industrialists still lacked entry into the circles of influence to which the City had long been admitted.

There is no doubt that, as a result of the war and its effects, there emerged a new breed of industrialists who moved between manufacturing business on one side and finance and politics on the other to a degree unheard of before 1914. On the whole, though, it would seem that those who became more prominent at the centre of affairs were frequently absorbed by gentlemanly culture without making any major impact upon it. One excellent example of this was the eagerness with which industrialists accepted the honours system. After 1914, they played a much fuller part in this remnant of the 'gentlemanly meaning system of the nineteenth century', dignifying their calling by accepting status rewards in return for their 'services' to the community. In doing so, they joined the traditional gentlemanly elite in playing down the importance of the profit motive, notwithstanding the fact that, in Lloyd George's time at least, honours had to be bought rather than won.[73]

Among the bigger corporations, where integration had gone furthest, there is some evidence that the influence of gentlemanly values on industrial life was becoming strong enough to affect policy and attitudes. In many important boardrooms there was 'a vague but persistent belief that some things were indeed more important than profits', a view which may well have hindered innovation and adaptation to the times.[74] By contrast, the 'practical men', who still dominated the small firm or held important managerial or technical positions in the larger firms, were too close to the machinery of industry to possess high status and often lacked the broad vision which, at its best, a traditional liberal education could bring: a great many of those involved in industry thus remained 'provincial' not just in geographical terms but also in a cultural sense.

On the political front, the most noticeable feature from our perspective was the extent to which all kinds of propertied interests, gentlemanly or otherwise, herded together within the Conservative Party, as Labour replaced the Liberals and as working men began to enter Parliament in strength for the first time. The movement of provincial propertied interests from Liberalism to Conservatism, already evident before 1914, was registered strongly at the election of 1918, when nearly half of all new recruits to the Conservative-dominated coalition government were businessmen. Landed representation in Parliament fell sharply, never recovering its former levels, and the ranks of public school men and Oxbridge graduates were thinned.[75] Overall, the party became more of a coalition of propertied interests than it had been before 1914: the 181 Conservatives identified as directors of companies in 1939 held a vast range of appointments in which finance, transport, distribution and manufacturing were all well represented;[76] and the changes which took place in party composition were enough to provoke alarm among traditionalists.[77] Nonetheless, business interests, whether provincial or otherwise, were hardly dominant after 1918. Aristocrats remained heavily over-represented in Cabinets and, in 1937, 19 out of 21 Cabinet members were public-school men, a high proportion of them old Etonians.[78] In 1939 three-fifths of all Conservative MPs were from public school backgrounds; the same percentage had connections with the land, the professions or other service occupations. Of the remaining two-fifths, a commercial background was still far more common than an industrial one. It remained the case, too, that the safest seats went to those who came from traditionally privileged backgrounds.[79]

The Conservative Party – which was in power for most of the period, though sometimes under the guise of 'Coalition' or 'National' governments – needed a deeper well of support than that provided by a congerie of nation-wide propertied interests. As before 1914, the main source of Conservative strength was the south-east, where the middle-class population was extensive and trade unionism less influential. With one or two traditional exceptions, Conservatism was much weaker in areas where heavy industry was concentrated.[80] As Labour captured the industrial working-class vote and post-war industrial disputes became more bitter, manufacturing interests, big and little, were driven into Conservatism. In doing so, they became part of a movement whose heartland was the service-consumer industry complex of the south-east of England,[81] and they were contained within a traditional power structure whose cultural authority rested upon gentility and whose fulcrum of economic power was the City of London. 'The City counted on the party to provide the climate of political stability essential for its role as the world's financial capital; the party in turn relied on the City for financial advice and support'.[82] The intimacy between the two was such that the City could effectively veto 'unsuitable' candidates for the post of Chancellor of the Exchequer, as it had done before 1914.[83]

Notes

1 The phrase is taken from François Bédarida, *A Social History of England, 1850–75* (1979), p. 303.
2 R.C.O. Matthews, C.H. Feinstein and J.C. Odling-Smee, *British Economic Growth, 1856–1973* (Oxford, 1982), Table 2.1, p. 22.
3 Ibid. Table 7.3, p. 210.
4 Ibid. Table 8.3, pp. 228–9, and Table 8.1, pp. 222–3.
5 Ibid. Table 9.10, p. 281.
6 See Derek H. Aldcroft and Harry W. Richardson, *The British Economy, 1870–1939* (1969), pp. 190–288; H.W. Richardson, *Economic Recovery in Britain, 1932–39* (1967); D.H. Aldcroft, 'Economic Growth in the Inter-War Years: a Reassessment', *Econ. Hist. Rev.*, 2nd ser. XX (1967), reprinted in Derek H. Aldcroft and Peter Fearon, eds. *Economic Growth in 20th-Century Britain* (1969).
7 Nick Crafts, 'The Assessment: British Economic Growth in the Long Run', *Oxford Review of Economic Policy,* 4 (1988), p. vi; Neil K. Buxton, 'The Role of the "New" Industries in Britain during the 1930s: a Reinterpretation', *Bus. Hist. Rev.*, XLIX (1975); J.A. Dowie, 'Growth in the Inter-war Period: some More Arithmetic', *Econ. Hist. Rev.*, 2nd ser. XXI (1968).
8 C.H. Feinstein, *Domestic Capital Formation in the United Kingdom, 1920–38* (Cambridge, 1965), Table 3.40, p. 49.
9 Matthews, Feinstein and Odling-Smee, *British Economic Growth,* Table 6.1, p. 164, and pp. 383–6.
10 B.W.E. Alford, 'New Industries for Old? British Industry between the Wars', in Roderick Floud and Donald N. McCloskey, eds. *An Economic History of Britain, II: 1860 to the 1970s* (1981); Crafts, 'The Assessment', pp. vi–viii.
11 Stephen Broadberry, 'The Impact of the World Wars on the Long Run Performance of the British Economy', *Oxford Review of Economic Policy,* 4 (1988), Table 2, p. 27. Charles Feinstein, 'Economic Growth Since 1870: Britain's Performance in International Perspective', ibid. Table 3, p. 10. For a detailed study of British industry see N.K. Buxton and D.H. Aldcroft, *British Industry Between the Wars: Instability and Economic Development, 1919–1939* (1979).
12 Christopher M. Law, *British Regional Development Since World War One* (1980), Table 22, p. 110. The south-east's share of total employment rose from 28 per cent to over 31 per cent between 1911 and 1951. Figures from C.H. Lee, *British Regional Employment Statistics* (1979).
13 James S. Foreman-Peck, 'Seedcorn or Chaff? New Firm Formation and the Performance of the Inter-War Economy', *Econ. Hist. Rev.*, 2nd ser. XXXVIII (1985), Table 4, p. 412, p. 415 and Table 5, p. 416. See also C.H. Lee, *The British Economy since 1700: A Macroeconomic Survey* (Cambridge 1986), pp. 213–14, 230–1.
14 Law, *British Regional Development,* Table 12, p. 74; Sidney Pollard, *The Development of the British Economy, 1914–1980* (1983), Table 2.9, p. 78. On regional unemployment see M.E.F. Jones, 'The Economic History of the Regional Problem in Britain, 1920–1938', *Journal of Historical Geography,* 10 (1984). Contrary to the usual assumptions of historians, it has recently been suggested that unemployment was higher in the older industrial regions than

in the south of England before 1914 as well as after. This conclusion would be consistent with the idea, presented in this book, of a dynamic south-eastern economy both before and after 1914. See Humphrey R. Southall, 'The Origins of the Depressed Areas: Unemployment, Growth and Regional Economic Structures in Britain before 1914', *Econ. Hist. Rev.*, 2nd ser. XLI (1988).

15 Foreman-Peck, 'Seedcorn or Chaff?', p. 416; Law, *Regional Development*, pp. 175–7.

16 See J.L. Marshall, 'The Pattern of Housebuilding in the Inter-War Period in England and Wales', *Scottish Journal of Political Economy*, 15 (1968), Table 1, p. 185; and Mark Swenarton and Sandra Taylor, 'The Scale and Nature of the Growth of Owner-Occupation in Britain Between the Wars', *Econ. Hist. Rev.*, 2nd ser. XXXVIII (1985). A good example of linkage between services and industry is that between the growth of the professions, the suburbs and the motor car. See Bédarida, *Social History of England*, pp. 205–7.

17 David J. Jeremy, 'Anatomy of the British Business Elite', Table 9, p. 19.

18 Jeffrey H. Porter, 'The Commercial Banks and the Financial Problems of the English Cotton Industry', *Revue internationale d'histoire de la banque*, 9 (1974), pp. 1–10; Stephen Tolliday, *Business, Banking and Politics: The Case of British Steel, 1918–1939* (Cambridge, Mass., 1988), pp. 176–8.

19 Tolliday, *Business, Banking and Politics*, pp. 197–210; Carol E. Heim, 'Limits to Intervention: the Bank of England and Industrial Diversification in the Depressed Areas', *Econ. Hist. Rev.*, 2nd ser. XXXVII (1984), pp. 535, 543–4.

20 From Norman's evidence to the Sankey Commission 1930, quoted in Tolliday, *Business, Banking and Politics*, p. 183.

21 Ibid. Pt. II; Leslie Hannah, *The Rise of the Corporate Economy* (2nd edn, 1983), pp. 64–5. See also Stephen Tolliday, 'Steel and Rationalization Policies, 1918–50', in Bernard Elbaum and William Lazonick, *The Decline of the British Economy* (Oxford, 1986).

22 Tolliday, *Business, Banking and Politics*, pp. 238–9, 323–4.

23 Heim, 'Limits of Intervention', passim. For earlier overviews of Bank of England involvement see R.S. Sayers, *The Bank of England*, Vol. I (Cambridge, 1970), pp. 314–30; and Sir Henry Clay, *Lord Norman* (1957), Ch. VIII.

24 Hannah, *Rise of the Corporate Economy*, pp. 91–2, 180. For slightly different figures see Lewis Johnmann, 'The Largest Manufacturing Companies of 1935', *Bus. Hist.*, XXIV (1986), p. 229.

25 Hannah, *Rise of the Corporate Economy*, pp. 55–7.

26 Lance E. Davis and Robert A. Huttenback, *Mammon and the Pursuit of Empire: The Political Economy of British Imperialism* (Cambridge, 1986), pp. 40–1; R.C. Michie, 'The Stock Exchange and the British Economy, 1870–1939', in J.J. Van-Helten and Y. Cassis, eds. *Capitalism in a Mature Economy: Financial Institutions, Capital Export and British Industry, 1870–1939* (1989), p. 98.

27 W.A. Thomas, *The Finance of British Industry, 1918–76* (1978), p. 49.

28 Philip Zeigler, *The Sixth Great Power: Barings, 1792–1929* (1988), pp. 342–5.

29 Stephanie Diaper, 'Merchant Banking in the Inter-War Period: the Case of Kleinwort, Sons and Co.', *Bus. Hist.*, XXVIII (1986), pp. 57–60; Kathleen Burk, *Morgan Grenfell, 1838–1988: The Biography of a Merchant Bank* (1989), pp. 91–8, 157–66.

30 Hannah, *Rise of the Corporate Economy*, pp. 62, 66.

31 This is the famous 'Macmillan Gap'. See Thomas, *The Finance of British Industry*, pp. 116–21.

32 Porter, 'The Commercial Banks and the Financial Problems of the English Cotton Industry', pp. 11–16; Hannah, *Rise of the Corporate Economy*, p. 65; Tolliday, *Business, Banking and Politics*, pp. 197–9.

33 Tolliday, *Business, Banking and Politics*, esp. Ch. 9.

34 For a rather more positive view of relations with industry see Duncan M. Ross, 'The Clearing Banks and Industry – a New Perspective on the Inter-War Years', in Van-Helten and Cassis, *Capitalism in a Mature Economy*.

35 Michael H. Best and Jane Humphries, 'The City and Industrial Decline', in Elbaum and Lazonick, *The Decline of the British Economy*, p. 231.

36 Tolliday, *Business, Banking and Politics,* p. 184; Best and Humphries, 'The City and Industrial Decline', p. 230.

37 One chairman of a major clearing bank declared in 1930 that a commitment to an industrial policy by the banks would be wrong because 'it would militate against the liquidity of the banks and that would in turn militate against our large foreign earnings and that in turn would militate against our balancing our imports and exports'. Quoted in Ross, 'The Clearing Banks and Industry', p. 54. For a strong argument that banks did not offer long-term funding mainly because there was little demand from industry, see Thomas, *The Finance of British Industry,* pp. 74–5.

38 Diaper, 'Merchant Banking in the Inter-War Period', pp. 60–1; idem, 'The Sperling Combine and the Shipbuilding Industry: Merchant Banking and Industrial Finance in the 1920s', in Van-Helten and Cassis, *Capitalism in a Mature Economy.*

39 Hannah, *Rise of the Corporate Economy,* p. 61.

40 W.J. Reader, *A House in the City: A Study of the City and of the Stock Exchange Based on the Records of Foster and Braithwaite, 1825–1975* (1979), pp. 141–6. Investment trusts also took a greater interest in domestic industrial investment after 1919, but the amounts of capital involved were not large. See Youssef Cassis, 'The Emergence of a New Financial Institution: Investment Trusts in Britain, 1870–1939', in Van-Helten and Cassis, *Capitalism in a Mature Economy.*

41 As we have already seen, the investment of capital in domestic manufacturing was not high between the wars, despite high levels of output. For the effects of the national debt, see Michie, 'The Stock Exchange and the British Economy', pp. 105, 109.

42 Hannah, *Rise of the Corporate Economy,* p. 65.

43 For a profound study of these relationships see Tolliday, *Business, Banking and Finance,* Chs. 12–14.

44 Heim, 'Limits of Intervention', pp. 544–5.

45 *Report of the Committee on Finance and Industry,* Cmd 3897 (1931), para. 397. The merchant bankers were 'reproached for being better informed on conditions in Latin America than in Lancashire or Scotland'. Thomas, *The Finance of British Industry,* p. 48.

46 Tolliday, *Business, Banking and Finance,* pp. 330, 335–7.

47 On the fortunes of landed wealth after 1914 see F.M.L. Thompson, *English Landed Society in the Nineteenth Century* (1963), Ch. XII; John Scott, *The Upper Classes: Property and Privilege in Britain* (1983), pp. 133–4; John Stevenson, *British Society, 1914–45* (1984), esp. pp. 333–5; Perkin, *The Rise of Professional Society: England since 1880* (1989), pp. 251–5. See also Marion Beard, *English Landed Society in the 20th Century* (1989).

48 W.D. Rubinstein, *Men of Property: The Very Wealthy in Great Britain Since the Industrial Revolution* (1981), Tables 3.3 and 3.4.

49 S. Diaper, 'Merchant Banking in the Inter-War Period', pp. 69–70.

50 See Rubinstein, *Men of Property,* pp. 62–6. Why there should have been such a dramatic increase in top wealth in shipowning when world shipping was in the doldrums is not obvious, but it may have been related to high levels of concentration in the industry.

51 Scott, *The Upper Classes,* Ch. 7.

52 Bédarida, *A Social History of England,* p. 303.

53 W.D. Rubinstein, 'Education and the Social Origins of British Elites, 1880–1970', *Past and Present,* 112 (1986). Rubinstein points out (p. 203) that a significant number of recruits to elite positions did not come from public school backgrounds; but many of these came from traditional grammar schools which were strongly imbued with public school values.

54 Thomas J.H. Bishop and Rupert Wilkinson, *Winchester and the Public School Elite: A Statistical Analysis* (1967), Table 5, p. 106, and Table 10, p. 67. The occupations of 30 per cent of fathers of entrants born in 1880–9 could not be traced. The term 'Wykehamist' refers to someone educated at Winchester, whose founder was William of Wykeham (1323–1404).

55 Thomas William Bamford, *The Rise of the Public Schools: A Study of Boys' Public Boarding Schools in England and Wales from 1837 to the Present Day* (1967), Table 12, p. 210.

56 Rubinstein, 'Education and the Social Origins of British Elites', pp. 199–200.

57 W.D. Rubinstein, 'Social Class, Social Attitudes and British Business Life', *Oxford Review of Economic Policy,* 4 (1988).
58 See also Perkin, *The Rise of Professional Society,* pp. 258–66.
59 Sir Ralph Furse, *Aucuparius: Recollections of a Recruiting Officer* (1962). India, Ceylon and Hong Kong recruited by a separate system; so too did Malaya until the 1930s, when it came within Furse's remit. One of Furse's assistants was his brother-in-law, Francis Newbolt; the other was Greville Irby, who left in 1942 when he inherited the title and estates of his uncle, Lord Boston. Robert Heussler, *Yesterday's Rulers: The Making of the British Colonial Service* (New York, 1963) provides a fascinating commentary on Furse's career.
60 Furse, *Aucuparius,* p. 9.
61 I.F. Nicolson and Colin A. Hughes, 'A Provenance of Pro-Consuls: British Colonial Governors, 1900–1960', *Jour. Imp. and Comm. Hist.,* 4 (1974–5), Table VI, p. 97; See also A.H.M. Kirk-Greene, 'On Governorship and Governors in British Africa', in L.H. Gann and Peter Duignan, eds. *African Proconsuls: European Governors in Africa* (1978), pp. 196–9.
62 K. Bradley, *Once a District Officer* (1966), pp. 3–4, quoted in Nicolson and Hughes, 'A Provenance of Pro-Consuls', p. 104. For an example of the 'benign colonialism' which this training produced, see the autobiography of a former governor of Honduras and Fiji, Sir R. Garvey, *Gentleman Pauper* (1984).
63 Nicolson and Hughes, 'A Provenance of Pro-Consuls', p. 90.
64 Robert W. Boyce, *British Capitalism at the Crossroads, 1919–1932: A Study in Politics, Economics and International Relations* (Cambridge, 1987), p. 31.
65 Philip Stanworth and Antony Giddens, 'An Economic Elite: a Demographic Profile of Company Chairmen', in Philip Stanworth and Anthony Giddens, eds. *Elites and Power in British Society* (1973), pp. 92–3.
66 Ziegler, *The Sixth Great Power,* pp. 336–7. The new partners in Morgans were very much of the gentlemanly capitalist type: Burk, *Morgan Grenfell,* pp, 99–100, 159–60.
67 R.J. Truptil, *British Banks and the London Money Market* (1936), pp. 172–5.
68 Though the embargo did encourage British investors to take their capital to the New York market instead. Burk, *Morgan Grenfell,* pp. 88–9.
69 Truptil, *British Banks and the London Money Market,* pp. 196–7.
70 Jeremy, 'Anatomy of the British Business Elite', pp. 3–13.
71 Stanworth and Giddens, 'An Economic Elite', pp. 93–7.
72 Rubinstein, 'Education and the Social Origins of British Elites', pp. 180–2.
73 Scott, *The Upper Classes,* Ch. 6, esp. pp. 157, 160.
74 D.C. Coleman, 'Gentlemen and Players', *Econ. Hist. Rev.,* 2nd ser. XXVI (1973). The quotation is from p. 114.
75 John M. McEwan, 'The Coupon Election of 1918 and Unionist Members of Parliament', *Journal of Modern History,* 34 (1962), pp. 297–304.
76 Simon Haxey, *Tory M.P.* (1939), p. 37.
77 McEwan, 'The Coupon Election of 1918', p. 306.
78 Stevenson, *British Society, 1914–45,* pp. 349–50; Bédarida, *A Social History of England,* p. 237.
79 John Ramsden, *The Age of Balfour and Baldwin, 1902–1940* (1978), pp. 360–1.
80 J.P.P. Dunbabin, 'British Elections in the Nineteenth and Twentieth Centuries: a Regional Approach', *Eng. Hist. Rev.* XCV (1980), Table 3, p. 37.
81 On this south-eastern hegemony see the suggestive comments in W.J.M. Mackenzie, *Politics and Social Science* (1967), pp. 351–2.
82 The quotation is from Boyce, who also claims that the movement of industrialists into the party 'did more to turn industrialists into Conservatives than Conservatives into the party of industry': *British Capitalism at the Crossroads,* p. 21.
83 The City objected to the appointment of Sir Robert Horne as Chancellor in 1923 because of his association with groups which were sceptical about restoring the gold standard. Ibid. pp. 21, 72–3.

18

INDUSTRY, THE CITY AND THE DECLINE OF THE INTERNATIONAL ECONOMY, 1914–39

World War I devastated international trade, and recovery was slow and incomplete in the 1920s. Britain's invisible trade was as badly affected by this, by the succeeding great depression of 1929–33 and by the protectionism which characterised the 1930s, as was the export trade in manufactures. The problems of the latter were compounded by further competitive failures in markets which had been particularly important to Britain before 1914. Invisible exports were also threatened by increased competition, and New York proved to be an effective rival source of long-term international investment in the 1920s. In the 1930s, however, when neither London nor New York could lend abroad, the City of London remained the headquarters of the largest commercial and financial bloc in the world, the Sterling Area, and its development was restrained as much by lack of opportunity as by competition.

The tribulations of industrial exports after World War I are one of the best documented episodes in the history of inter-war Britain. Declining competitiveness, evident well before 1914, would have brought severe problems for Britain's traditional exporters eventually; but the shock of war, and of the depression which began in the late 1920s and ran across the globe like a virulent disease, accelerated the process of decline by closing down markets and encouraging import substitution. Exports of goods never regained their pre-war levels, in terms of volumes, before 1939. After a decade spent assuming that pre-1914 conditions could somehow be restored, it was generally accepted in the 1930s that the staple industries of provincial Britain would recapture no former international glories. Despite the rapid growth of manufacturing output, the 'new industries' were not competitive enough to do well outside the Sterling Area.

What is less well appreciated is the severity of the decline in income from 'invisible' exports, which were equally devastated by war and its aftermath: measured against the standards of 1913, the City of London was performing less well in the 1920s than were the much-maligned exporters of industrial goods. In the 1930s, just as industry became dependent on protection and imperial markets, so the City had to abandon cosmopolitanism and settle for dominance within a sterling bloc centred on the empire. In this sense, the overseas interests of industry and finance converged markedly after 1914 and especially in the 1930s.

Commodity trade

The value of exports was much higher after the war than before, averaging £718m. annually between 1925 and 1929 as against £455m. for 1909–13. But prices had risen sharply during the war and fell only slowly after it; an index of the volume of exports (1913 = 100) shows them running at 91 in 1909–13 against 80.5 by 1925–9 and 86.3 in 1929, the height of the post-war boom.[1] In 1914–18 some markets were lost because they were cut off, encouraging import substitution and allowing less harassed rivals, notably the United States and Japan, to take advantage of Britain's difficulties. The demands of the domestic economy in total war also reduced the volume of goods available for export. But, despite the rapid rise to prominence of the United States during the war, Britain's share of world trade may even have been higher in the early 1920s than it was in 1913; this reflected the economic dislocation of Britain's European rivals.[2] In the boom of 1924–9, however, Britain's share fell sharply. Lewis puts Britain's share of the world's manufactured exports at about 26 per cent in 1913, falling to 21 per cent by 1929; Germany's share was also lower in 1929 (19 per cent) than in 1913 (23 per cent), while the USA's share had gone up from 11 per cent to 18 per cent.[3] Britain's relative decline had been clear since the late nineteenth century and, in the 1920s, it continued for broadly similar reasons: the inability of the old staples to fend off competition and the failure to replace them adequately. The most obvious decline was in cotton textiles, Britain's leading commodity export, which accounted for £127m. or 25 per cent of exports in 1913, and maintained its share in 1924. But between 1924 and 1929 exports fell from £199.2m. to £135.4m., or 18.6 per cent of the total.[4]

During the 1920s most efforts in Britain, the United States and elsewhere were devoted to trying to make the pre-1913 world economy work again. After 1929, the system, so carefully patched up over the previous decade, suddenly fell apart. The world depression, centred on the collapse of the economies of the United States and of many leading primary producers, led to a severe contraction of world trade and to financial panic; protectionism and the bloc system took the place of the cosmopolitan world economy which still existed in 1929.

The value of exports fell in the depression and averaged £451m. in 1934–8, slightly less than the average for 1909–13. Volumes fell even further – from 80.5 in 1925–9 (1913 = 100) to 63.2 in 1934–8 and to 69.4 in the best year of the decade, 1937. But the slump was universal, and Britain's share of world trade actually rose a little in the early 1930s following the stimulus of devaluation in 1931 and, at

19.1 per cent in 1937, was only fractionally lower than in 1929.[5] The shift away from the nineteenth-century staple exports also continued in the 1930s. Cotton textiles' share of domestic exports fell to 13 per cent in 1937; on the other hand, 'new' industries – machinery, chemicals, electrical goods, vehicles and aircraft – accounted for 12 per cent in 1924, 16.5 per cent in 1929 and nearly 22 per cent in 1937.[6]

In contrast to exports, import volumes were higher after 1914 than before. They showed a 5 per cent rise over 1913 volumes in 1924, and were 16 per cent higher in 1929.[7] Part of this increase stemmed from the improvement in living standards which accompanied growth in Britain after 1919, and part was generated by increased demand for raw materials which could not be obtained at home (e.g. petroleum). But imports of manufactures also grew rapidly after 1924, when 'normality' was restored, moving from 21 per cent of gross imports in that year to 25 per cent in 1929 (Table 18.1). Net exports of articles wholly and mainly manufactured (exports and re-exports of British produce minus imports) did extremely badly in the mid- and late 1920s. Overall, net exports fell by about £85m. between 1924 and 1929. Practically the whole of that fall (£76m.) can be attributed to increased imports from foreign countries, although there was also a small fall in net exports to the empire.

TABLE 18.1 Imports and net exports of articles wholly or mainly manufactured, 1924–37[a]

	Imports (£m.)	*Share of gross imports (%)*	*Net exports[b] (£m.)*
1924	298.8	20.8	354.4
1925	318.7	21.8	330.0
1926	314.0	23.3	251.2
1927	321.8	24.4	268.1
1928	317.0	24.4	288.6
1929	333.6	25.0	269.9
1930	306.8	27.1	157.9
1931	261.3	28.3	48.8
1932	157.4	20.8	130.7
1933	150.4	20.7	142.2
1934	170.9	21.9	144.3
1935	184.5	22.6	157.6
1936	212.7	23.2	143.9
1937	274.9	24.4	154.1

Source: *Statistical Abstract for the United Kingdom* for 1939 (HMSO).

Notes:

[a] Figures are not strictly comparable with those for pre-1913.

[b] Exports of British produce and re-exports minus gross imports.

Import volumes fell in the depression from 116 in 1929 (1913 = 100) to 1913 levels in 1932 but then rose rapidly to a new high of 121 in 1937.[8] Manufactured imports increased sharply in 1929–31, when exports were falling fast, and reached 28 per cent of total imports in 1931. The rise in manufactured imports, partly induced by anticipations of protectionist measures, which duly came in 1932,[9] meant that net exports fell catastrophically from £270m. in 1929 to £49m. in 1931, and a net export surplus on manufactures with foreign countries of £25m. was converted into an import surplus of £66m. in 1931. Net exports of manufactures to empire countries also fell, by over 50 per cent in two years, as their income from exports of primary produce exports shrank. Once protection had been imposed on foreign manufactures in 1932, the share of manufactures in imports fell to less than 21 per cent in 1933, but then rose steadily to reach nearly 25 per cent again in 1937 (Table 18.1). Net exports of manufactures to foreign countries were positive in 1933–6, but a small import surplus appeared again in 1937. Over the whole period, and despite protection in the 1930s and the surge in manufacturing output in Britain between the wars, Britain's position as a manufacturing trader continued to worsen. The ratio of exports and re-exports of manufactures to imported manufactures, which was 2.27:1 in 1913 and 2.18:1 in 1924, fell sharply to 1.56:1 in 1937. Britain's comparative advantage still lay in the labour-intensive older staple industries which were in decline as traded goods, and her 'new' industrial output was not competitive enough to provide adequate compensation.[10]

What eased Britain's position as a trading nation after 1914 was a very favourable shift in the terms of trade. Import prices rose less than export prices during the war and fell more quickly during the 1920s. Despite favourable price movements, exports and re-exports bought only 60 per cent of gross imports in 1914–18, but after 1918 exports recovered some ground, aided by a world restocking boom, the devaluation of sterling below its fixed wartime level of $4.76 (it reached $3.40 in March 1920) and the disorganisation of European rivals. This trend, together with favourable terms of trade, sent the ratio of exports and re-exports to imports up to 85 per cent in 1919–23. The ratio then fell to 77 per cent between 1924 and 1928, when Britain revalued sterling on returning to the gold standard, when her European rivals were moving back to 'normality', and when competition in the old staple commodities was extremely fierce (Table 18.2). Although the buying power of exports in the 1920s was disappointing compared with the boom of 1911–13, it was on a par with experience in the 1890s (Table 18.2). In the 1930s, though, despite a further favourable shift in the terms of trade as import prices fell drastically from 1929 to 1933, exports and re-exports were only 69 per cent of the value of imports in 1929–33 and slightly less than that in 1934–8 (Table 18.2).

One of the most noticeable features of the inter-war period was the increased importance of trade with the empire, and more especially with the white Dominions

TABLE 18.2 Exports, re-exports and invisible surplus as percentage of gross imports, 1896–1948

	Net property income	*Other services*	*All invisibles*[a]	*Exports and re-exports*	*All credits*[b]
1896–1900	22.6	17.3	39.9	73.1	113.0
1901–05	22.4	13.5	35.9	73.0	108.9
1906–10	25.7	16.4	42.1	83.3	125.4
1911–13	27.6	16.2	43.8	87.7	131.5
1914–18	19.7	18.8	38.5	60.3	98.8
1919–23	15.1	13.6	28.7	85.2	113.9
1924–28	19.6	9.0	28.6	77.2	105.8
1929–33	21.9	8.6	30.5	69.0	99.5
1934–38	23.6	5.3	28.9	67.8	96.7
1939–43	14.4	–26.6	–12.2	40.9	28.7
1944–48	10.5	–21.2	–10.7	75.1	64.4

Source: C.H. Feinstein, *Statistical Tables of National Income, Expenditure and Output of the United Kingdom, 1856–1965* (Cambridge, 1972), Table 15.

Notes:
[a] Net property income plus other services.
[b] All invisibles plus exports and re-exports.

of Canada, Australia, New Zealand and South Africa (Table 18.3). In the 1930s, when world trade was collapsing, the British not only adopted protection for their manufactures but also created a preferential system centred on the empire, particularly the white colonies. Nonetheless, although the Ottawa agreements did increase British trade with the Dominions, it is clear that the 1930s preferential system merely formalised an interdependence which had been growing rapidly before 1914 and continued to expand in the 1920s. At the same time, however, as trade with the Dominions and with the more recently acquired parts of the underdeveloped empire was growing in relative significance, Britain's links with India slackened, especially in the 1930s. Moreover, the empire was only a part, albeit the largest part, of the Sterling Area which emerged in the 1930s and which included some of the smaller countries of Europe. The share of exports going to the area as a whole rose from just over one-half to three-fifths between 1929 and 1937, and European members contributed a significant part of the increase. In contrast, the erosion of Britain's position in industrial markets continued apace. Exports to four major Western European countries and the United States, which were 24 per cent of the total in 1913, fell to 21 per cent in 1929 and to 19.5 per cent in 1937, though the fall owed something to protectionism as well as a further decline

TABLE 18.3 Regional shares in British exports and imports, 1846–1938 (per cent)

				Regional shares in exports of British produce		
	1846–50	*1871–75*	*1896–1900*	*1909–13*	*1925–29*	*1934–38*
Developed countries	44.8	47.2	39.4	35.1	31.1	33.4
Newly settled countries	18.7	21.3	25.2	28.7	30.2	34.0
Underdeveloped countries	35.6	31.1	34.3	35.9	37.0	33.8
Dominions	8.7	12.0	16.7	17.5	20.6	25.9
India and Burma	9.4	8.9	11.8	11.9	11.6	8.0
Rest of British empire	9.2	5.9	5.6	5.6	5.0	7.4
British empire	27.3	26.8	34.1	35.0	37.2	41.3
				Regional shares in net imports into Britain		
	1846–50	*1871–75*	*1896–1900*	*1909–13*	*1925–29*	*1934–38*
Developed countries	n/a	48.1	61.8	49.9	46.2	38.2
Newly settled countries	n/a	17.7	17.7	24.9	28.0	34.5
Underdeveloped countries	n/a	34.1	20.1	24.7	25.3	26.4
Dominions	n/a	9.6	12.6	14.3	16.9	24.3
India and Burma	n/a	9.9	6.2	7.3	6.1	6.5
Rest of British empire	n/a	5.3	3.9	5.3	9.9	11.4
British empire	n/a	24.8	22.7	26.9	32.9	41.2

Source: B.R. Mitchell and P. Deane, *Abstract of British Historical Statistics* (Cambridge, 1962); and *Statistical Abstracts for the United Kingdom* (HMSO).

Notes: Eire has been treated as UK internal trade in 1925–9 and 1934–8 in order to allow comparisons with earlier years. South Africa appears under 'Newly settled' and 'Dominions' throughout.

in competitiveness.[11] In areas of traditional informal influence, trade performance between the wars was very poor. Latin America's share of British exports in the 1930s was lower than at any time since the 1870s. China, usually singled out as the area with the greatest potential for growth, proved even more disappointing: in 1934–8 China and Hong Kong together took 1.9 per cent of British exports as against 3.7 per cent in 1871–5.

A close look at the fate of trade in manufactures confirms the shrinkage of Britain's influence between the wars (Tables 18.4 and 18.5). What is remarkable is not the deficit on manufacturing trade with other industrial countries, which was worsening (a deficit on trade with the United States appeared after 1914), but the erosion of the British position in other areas, including some parts of the empire. Net exports to the European members of the Sterling Area kept up well, partly because Britain managed to sign some highly favourable treaties with them in the

TABLE 18.4 British trade in manufactures, 1924 and 1937 (£m.)

	Imports		*Exports and re-exports*		*Balance of trade*[a]	
	1924	*1937*	*1924*	*1937*	*1924*	*1937*
Industrial countries[b]	–222.9	–139.2	+178.2	+76.6	–44.8	–62.6
European Sterling Area[c]	–15.1	–19.4	+31.5	+39.7	+16.4	+20.3
Rest of Europe	–10.3	–13.1	+29.5	+26.6	+19.2	+13.5
Other foreign	–16.9	–40.8	+117.1	+67.7	+100.2	+26.9
All foreign[d]	–265.2	–212.5	+356.2	+210.6	+91.0	–1.9
Dominions[e]	–12.3	–35.3	+132.9	+118.5	+120.6	+83.2
India	–11.8	–13.0	+86.8	+35.7	+75.0	+22.7
Other empire	–10.5	–14.1	+76.9	+64.4	+66.4	+50.3
All empire[f]	–34.6	–62.4	+296.6	+218.6	+262.0	+156.2
Total trade[g]	–299.8	–274.9	+652.8	+429.2	+353.0	+154.3

Source: *Annual Statement of Trade of the United Kingdom*.

Notes:

[a] Difference between imports and exports/re-exports.

[b] Industrial countries comprise Germany, Belgium, The Netherlands, Luxembourg, France, Italy, Switzerland and the United States.

[c] European Sterling Area comprises Finland, Norway, Sweden, Denmark, Estonia, Latvia, Lithuania, Iceland and Portugal.

[d] Industrial countries plus European Sterling Area plus Rest of Europe plus Other foreign.

[e] Dominions include South Africa.

[f] Dominions plus India plus Other empire.

[g] All foreign plus All empire. These figures do not always tally with Table 18.1. Some rough estimates of the trade of small countries have had to be made because the tables in the *Statement* are not sufficiently specific.

TABLE 18.5 British trade in manufactures, 1924 and 1937: trade ratios (exports and re-exports ÷ imports)

	1924	*1937*
Industrial countries	0.80	0.55
European Sterling Area	2.09	2.05
Rest of Europe	2.86	2.03
Other foreign	6.93	1.54
All foreign	1.34	0.99
Dominions	10.81	3.36
India	7.36	2.75
Other empire	7.32	4.57
All empire	8.57	3.50
Total trade	2.18	1.56

Source: *Annual Statement of Trade of the United Kingdom*.

Note: In this table numerals less than 1 indicate a deficit on manufactured trade and above 1 indicate a surplus. Thus in 1924 Britain's exports to other industrial countries were only four-fifths the value of British imports from them. In the same year, exports to the Dominions were almost eleven times greater in value than imports from them. See also notes for Table 18.4.

1930s, as we shall see. But net exports to 'other foreign' countries fell very sharply between 1924 and 1937. This was due, to some degree, to the spread of industrialisation on the periphery and increased protectionism; but it also owed something to the decline of British competitiveness in areas of traditional informal influence such as Latin America, the Middle East and the Far East. More specifically, however, the erosion occurred across the 'semi-industrial' periphery identified earlier, which included countries within the empire. Net exports to India declined significantly following the demise of textile exports, and Britain developed a deficit with Canada on trade in manufactures in the 1930s. Trade with the Dominions as a whole was disappointing, especially in view of the preferential system brought in after 1932. Broadly speaking, it would be fair to say that Britain's exporters became increasingly dependent on Sterling Area countries after 1919, mainly because trade with them declined less dramatically than trade with other customers.

The City and invisibles

The decline of visible exports is a commonplace of inter-war history but the drastic slump in Britain's invisible income was of equal significance. In value terms, the invisible surplus was worth £317m. in 1913, £359m. in 1929 and £289m. in 1937.[12] In real terms, though, the decline in invisible income after 1913 was severe. Measured by pre-war prices, the purchasing power of invisible income was only three-fifths of the 1913 level in 1929 and 54 per cent of the pre-war level in 1937.[13] Invisible income had grown very rapidly before 1914, when the chief driving force was income from investments and property overseas. This income was badly affected by the war. Some investments were permanently lost, most notably those placed in Russia, which were repudiated by the Bolsheviks in 1917. Others had to be liquidated, especially those held in the United States, to pay for war supplies. British assets abroad were reduced by about £1bn. (roughly one-quarter) during the war.[14] In addition, the British government incurred a dollar debt of about £750m.[15] American debts, permanent loss of assets, the disruption of the world economy and, after 1919, the devaluation of sterling (in which invisible payments to Britain were made) all reduced net income on overseas property in the early 1920s. The invisible surplus was equivalent to 44 per cent of the value of imports just before World War I but was worth only 29 per cent of imports in the 1920s (Table 18.2). The return to gold in 1925, and the resumption of foreign lending by Britain in the 1920s, pushed up property income relative to imports. The improvement continued in the early 1930s, mainly owing to the tremendous fall in import prices and to the fact that very few of Britain's debtors actually defaulted on their loans, although many of them paid reduced rates of interest.

Other forms of invisible income suffered even more severely. Shipping income fell in the 1920s as competition increased and freight rates collapsed; it contracted even more sharply in the 1930s as the world economy shrank.[16] Returns on the provision of short-term credit and other business services were also badly hit by the war and by depression (Table 18.2). The war shook confidence in credit, and many assets were frozen for the duration. In 1914 many London firms could not have met their obligations on bills accepted without help from the Bank of England and the Treasury.[17] Those firms, such as the merchant banker, Kleinworts, which had been heavily involved in extending credit to Germany and other enemy powers, were most seriously affected by the crisis.[18] New business also declined drastically as international trade shrank: former customers, cut off from London credit, had to make new arrangements, and American competition proved keen.[19] During the war, business centred more and more on the handling of growing amounts of government short-term debt although, on the foreign front, some of the more prestigious houses, such as Barings, made a comfortable living by facilitating inter-allied financial arrangements.[20]

Once the war was over, continental business picked up quickly and, insofar as Britain became a centre for the operation of the gold exchange standard in the 1920s, this brought considerable funds into the London short market.[21] Nonetheless, most United States business was permanently lost;[22] confidence in London was never quite the same again. Merchant banks and discount houses involved in short-term credit adopted limited liability status in the 1920s – a clear sign of diminishing credibility.[23] Furthermore, a great deal of business during the decade was in the form of 'reimbursement credits' in which borrowers had their credit status guaranteed by their bankers before funds were made available in the City: the old system of doing business through contacts between City institutions, and their family and other personal contacts abroad, began to break down under the strain of war and the uncertainties that war left behind.[24] The absolute volume of bills in the London market in 1929 may have been similar to the pre-war figure[25] because world trade volumes were higher in the late 1920s than before 1914 and because the loss of American business had been compensated by increased volume in Europe.[26] Returns, however, were sharply lower than before the war because the discount houses and acceptance houses in London had to face competition not only from New York (and later in the decade, Paris) but also from the domestic clearing banks, which invaded this field of operations in the 1920s.[27]

In the succeeding decade, the commercial bill market shrank rapidly and, despite the fact that the joint-stock banks withdrew from direct competition with the specialist houses, competition between the latter was so fierce that returns were driven down to very low levels. Again, those most involved in European business were the worst affected: German assets were first frozen, then rigidly controlled later in the decade.[28] In all, net returns on 'financial and other services' were around £45m. in the 1920s, reached a low of £15m. in 1932 and had recovered only to £25m. by 1937.[29] Profits fell and survival for the bill specialists, such as the discount houses, depended on amalgamation, encouraged by the Bank of England, and opening new lines of business on the domestic front, especially in Treasury bills, government stock and even, after devaluation in 1931, currency speculation. For their part, the merchant bankers also turned to domestic industrial issues.[30]

The troubles of merchant bankers were shared by the British overseas banks, which faced greater local competition, often spiced with nationalist hostility, as well as a decline in international business. Many were bought out by British clearing banks which moved into international business for the first time between the wars and were encouraged in the 1930s by the Bank of England, which feared that some international banks would otherwise fail.[31] However, the removal of American competition, and very low interest rates in the 'cheap money' era after 1932, probably meant that London's comparative advantages in short-term credits increased in the 1930s.[32] The French financial expert, R.J. Truptil, writing in the mid-1930s, felt that, though New York and Paris had made up some ground on London in comparison with 1913, 'there can be little doubt that a return to stability in money matters will result in such a revival in the City that it will once more become the world centre for the financing of international trade'.[33] In practice, trade was so restricted in the 1930s that the City was forced to operate mainly within the confines of the empire and the Sterling Area.

The overall effect of the crisis in both visible and invisible trade after 1914 was that the large balance of payments surplus of the immediate pre-war period was much reduced in the 1920s and disappeared in the 1930s. The current account surplus of over £200m. was reduced by two-thirds in the late 1920s, and the deficit between 1934 and 1938 averaged about £25m. per annum.[34] The surplus was equivalent to nearly one-third of imports in 1911–13, fell to about 5 per cent in the mid-1920s and became negative in the 1930s, at which point Britain was having to reduce her assets overseas to cover payments on her imports (Table 18.2). In the 1920s the principal problem was invisible income, which fell more heavily than income from visible exports. In that decade, when Britain was attempting to lead the world back to pre-1913 'normality', commodity exports as a percentage of GDP actually rose compared with pre-war from an average of 17.7 between 1891 and 1913 to 18.2 in 1921–9; and the balance of trade deficit was lower on average in the second period than in the first. But the decline in the invisible surplus, from 11 per cent of GDP in the 20 years before the war to 7.3 per cent in the 1920s, reduced the overall balance of payments surplus from 5 per cent of GDP on average before 1913 to just over 2 per cent in 1921–9, a level lower than at any time since the early nineteenth century. In the 1930s during the world economic crisis, exports fell drastically as a proportion of GDP, but imports dropped almost as much and the balance of trade gap was only as great as that experienced in the period 1891–1913. Even so, when the deficit on commodity trade was added to a further fall in the contribution of invisibles to national income, the British found themselves disinvesting overseas at a rate equivalent to 1 per cent of GDP per year in the 1930s (Table 18.6).

It was recognised quite early in official circles that Britain's lending capacity would be much reduced compared with the heady days immediately before the war.[35] Overseas loans in the 1920s were running at roughly £100m. per annum, much below the levels of 1900–14, especially remembering that the price level was much lower before the war than in the 1920s (Table 18.7). Besides this, domestic issues were of greater significance than overseas issues after 1919, as we shall see.

TABLE 18.6 Balance of payments on current account, 1891–1964: ratios to GDP (average of annual percentages)

	Exports of goods	*Imports of goods*	*Balance of trade*[a]	*Net property income*	*Net other services*	*All invisible income*[b]	*Balance of payments on current a/c (new overseas investment)*[c]
1891–1913	17.7	–23.8	–6.1	6.8	4.3	11.1	5.0
1921–29	18.2	–23.3	–5.1	5.1	2.2	7.3	2.2
1930–38	10.9	–16.9	–6.0	4.2	0.9	5.1	–0.9
1952–64	16.6	–17.5	–0.9	1.3	0.2	1.5	0.6

Source: R.C.O. Matthews, C.H. Feinstein and J.C. Odling-Smee, *British Economic Growth, 1856–1973* (Oxford, 1983).

Notes:
[a] Difference between exports and imports.
[b] Net property income plus net other services.
[c] Balance of trade plus all invisible income.

The Bank of England used a great deal of unofficial pressure at times to persuade City institutions not to lend abroad lest the flow should jeopardise Britain's attempts to get back to gold before 1925 or to stay on gold after that date.[36] Barings had to refuse an offer to take up a large loan for Argentina in 1925 because of Bank of England disapproval, and other merchant bankers also responded to similar calls for restraint.[37] Despite embargoes, some foreign issues were positively encouraged by the authorities in the 1920s as part of the European reconstruction schemes which British governments and officials felt were crucial to the recovery of the world economy. Loans to Austria and Hungary fell into this category.[38] Moreover, in the late 1920s, when embargoes were lifted, foreign issues did increase in importance. But embargoes apart, the British lost a great deal of their traditional foreign loan business in the 1920s because the London rate on loans was often too high in comparison with that prevailing in New York, and much of the European business which did come London's way was of the 'second class' variety.[39] Trustee status (extended to underdeveloped parts of the empire in the late 1920s) ensured that the empire could still borrow in London at rates New York could not match;[40] embargoes on empire loans were rarely applied because 'empire development' was officially in vogue. As a result, empire issues came to predominate over foreign ones when Britain invested overseas (Table 18.7).

A further important change in the nature of foreign investment in the 1920s was the predominance of borrowing by public authorities compared with the position before the war. Public-authority borrowing accounted for about one-third of all foreign loans on average between 1865 and 1914 and just over one-half of imperial ones.[41] In the period 1918–31 the proportions rose to 47 per cent and 70 per cent respectively.[42] This change may reflect not only state reconstruction schemes after

TABLE 18.7 New capital issues, empire and foreign, 1900–38 (average per year)

	Empire		*Foreign*		*Total*	
	£m.	*%*	*£m.*	*%*	*£m.*	*%*
1900–14	53.5	39.1	83.9	60.9	137.4	100
1919–23	65.4	66.4	27.9	33.6	93.3	100
1924–28	72.5	58.8	50.8	41.2	123.3	100
1929–33	44.0	69.6	19.2	30.4	63.2	100
1934–38	25.6	86.2	4.1	13.8	29.7	100
1919–38	51.9	67.1	25.5	32.9	77.4	100

Sources: Calculated from T. Balogh, *Studies in Financial Organization* (Cambridge, 1947), Table XLVIa, pp. 249–50; L. Davis and R. Huttenback, *Mammon and the Pursuit of Empire: The Political Economy of British Imperialism 1860–1912* (Cambridge, 1987), pp. 40–1 (intermediate estimate).

the war but also a diminution in confidence in private borrowers after the traumas of 1914–18.

Despite lending on a reduced scale compared with the Edwardian age, Britain was still probably the world's largest overseas investor in 1929.[43] but it seems likely that she overstretched herself as a long-term lender in the 1920s. Allowing for the purchase of about 10 per cent of issues by foreigners and also adjusting for loan repayments, it has been estimated that Britain sent £542m. of new money abroad between 1924 and 1930.[44] Although this foreign investment probably had a positive influence on Britain's exports, the accumulated balance of payments surplus for these years was roughly £70m. less.[45] Britain had to borrow short in Europe in order to lend long to the empire. Although the short-term liabilities which resulted from over-extended, long-term lending were only a small fraction of all the short money held in London in the 1920s, worries about overcommitment undoubtedly contributed to the crisis which took sterling off gold in 1931.[46]

Overseas lending diminished after 1929 and reached levels on a par with early-nineteenth-century experience in the 1930s (Table 18.7). Borrowing was almost entirely confined to empire countries by the mid-1930s and the trickle of money going to foreigners went largely to those within the Sterling Area. Capital export was on a very tight rein in the 1930s and lending to the empire and to foreign countries fell sharply although, despite embargoes, governments did not attempt to prevent British investors from subscribing to stocks issued in foreign capitals. In fact, repayments on existing loans exceeded new issues in every year between 1932 and 1938 by a huge margin.[47]

Once the gallant attempt to restore a cosmopolitan economy in the 1920s had failed, finance and industry were forced into an increased dependence upon the Sterling Area and upon the domestic market as the free-trading, expanding world economy which had existed before 1914 disappeared. And just as, before 1914, visible and invisible trade had interacted in a dynamic way so, in the less favourable post-war atmosphere, the weakness of the one sometimes increased the difficulties of the other. Thus the reduction in the volume of exports affected shipping income and returns on commercial business and insurance. The smaller balance of payments surplus which resulted from this fall meant less foreign investment and hence fewer exports of goods. Similarly, attempts to maintain high levels of foreign investment in the 1920s meant that high interest rates had to be imposed to attract the short money which would ease the strain imposed by lending long: this inhibited the growth of investment in industries which were important contributors to exports. Most important of all, the attempt to restore London's position by returning to the gold standard led to an overvaluation of the pound which harmed Britain's export industries and encouraged manufactured imports.[48]

The City suffered as badly as industry and its area of effective control covered only the Sterling Area by the 1930s, but its long-term future was brighter. The concentration of commercial and financial power connected with overseas trade in London continued to grow between the wars, and London's dominance was shown by its increasing relative importance as a centre for import traffic and shipping.[49] Moreover, as already indicated, the City's problems over short-term credit instruments had more to do with the chaotic state of world trade than with lack of competitiveness; if Britain's own savings were much diminished and New York had the capital, London still had much to offer in terms of the 'expertise, the clients and the market' should the international economy revive.[50] In terms of both markets and policy, City and industry were more at one with each other in the 1930s than before; but if a protected Sterling Area was a necessity for uncompetitive industry it was more of a temporary refuge in hard times for the City.[51]

Moreover, given the continued influence of gentlemanly values upon government and administration, the main emphasis in international economic policy was on the problems of Britain's financial sector and how to overcome them. In the 1920s restoring London's position as the main international money market, fighting off the American financial challenge and encouraging the recovery of invisible income were the chief concerns. In the 1930s the most pressing matter was how the emerging sterling bloc could make payments on accumulated debt, when foreign trade had been devastated by depression and loans from Britain were few and small. This debt crisis posed a threat to the stability of the bloc and, as we shall see, the emergence of a new policy in the 1930s is understandable only in relation to it, and to the determination to win back the ground lost to the United States in the previous decade.

Notes

1 Volumes are arrived at by using the figures in B.R. Mitchell and Phyllis Deane's *Abstract of British Historical Statistics* (Cambridge, 1962), p. 284, and applying C.H. Feinstein's price indices, which can be found in *Statistical Tables of National Income, Expenditure and Output for the U.K., 1855–1965* (Cambridge, 1972), Table 64. The figures include trade with Eire from 1923 onwards. The most comprehensive study of British foreign trade in this period is still Alfred E. Kahn, *Britain and the World Economy* (1946). There are a number

of obvious discrepancies here and in other chapters between some of the trade and payments statistics quoted. The figures for the invisible items in the balance of payments and for the balance of payments surpluses and deficits are from Feinstein, *Statistical Tables.* Like the Bank of England's figures (*Quarterly Bulletin,* 12 (1972), pp. 345ff), they do not tally with the data presented in the *Statistical Abstracts* and in Mitchell and Deane. On the other hand, neither Feinstein's nor the Bank's figures allow for a geographical breakdown of the trade statistics. Since this is vital to our purpose, we have used the older statistics where necessary. It is comforting to note, however, that the trends shown in both the older figures and the newer estimates are very similar. Nonetheless, it is only by using Feinstein's figures that it is possible to conclude as readily as we do that the balance of trade gap in the 1920s was less than is usually assumed, that the performance of invisibles in the 1920s was worse than is usually assumed, and that invisibles did better in the 1930s than the conventional wisdom usually allows. The only real problem arises from the first of these judgements concerning the trade gap. There are simply no figures for invisibles to compare with those of Feinstein, and all serious work in this area must begin from his starting points.

2 Gerd Hardach, *The First World War, 1914–18* (1977), p. 148 and Table 18. This gives Britain's share of world trade in 1913 as 15.3 per cent compared with 16.3 per cent in 1924. World trade was, of course, lower in 1924 than in 1913.

3 W. Arthur Lewis, 'International Competition in Manufactures', *American Economic Review: Papers and Proceedings,* XLVII (1957), p. 579. For different figures, which nonetheless indicate similar trends, see: Alfred Maizels, *Industrial Growth and World Trade* (1963), p. 189; and H. Tysynski, 'World Trade in Manufactured Commodities, 1899–1950', *Manchester School,* 19 (1951), p. 286.

4 Figures from Mitchell and Deane, *Abstract,* pp. 305–6.

5 Lewis, 'International Competition in Manufactures', and other sources as in n. 3.

6 Derived from Mitchell and Deane, *Abstract,* pp. 305–6.

7 Figures obtained as for n. 1.

8 Figures obtained as for n. 1.

9 Forrest Capie, 'The Pressure for Tariff Protection in Britain, 1917–31', *Jour. Eur. Econ. Hist.,* 9 (1980).

10 N.F.R. Crafts and M. Thomas, 'Comparative Advantage in U.K. Manufacturing Trade, 1910–35', *Econ. Jour.,* 96 (1986); Alec Cairncross and Barry Eichengreen, *Sterling in Decline: The Devaluations of 1931, 1949 and 1967* (Oxford, 1983), pp. 32–3.

11 The four European countries are France, Germany, the Netherlands and Belgium. The percentages are computed from figures in Mitchell and Deane, *Abstract.*

12 Feinstein, *Statistical Tables,* Table 38.

13 These results are arrived at by deflating the current value figures by an index of the prices of consumer goods and services. See Feinstein, *Statistical Tables,* Tables 15 and 61.

14 United Nations, *International Capital Movements in the Inter-War Period* (1949), pp. 4–5.

15 Hardach, *The First World War,* Table 18, p. 148.

16 Shipping returns fell from just under £30m. per year on average during 1921–9 to around £15.5m. per year in 1930–8. See Feinstein, *Statistical Tables,* Table 38.

17 Thomas Balogh, *Studies in Financial Organization* (Cambridge, 1947), p. 243; Henry Roseveare, *The Treasury: The Evolution of a British Institution* (1969), pp. 236–8. See also the lucid 'eyewitness' account given by J.M. Keynes, 'War and the Financial System, August 1914', in *Econ. Jour.,* XXIV (1914).

18 Suzanne Diaper, 'Merchant Banking in the Inter-war Period: the Case of Kleinwort, Sons and Co.', *Bus. Hist.,* XXVIII (1986), p. 64.

19 Balogh, *Studies in Financial Organization,* p. 179. For Barings' experience see Philip Ziegler, *The Sixth Great Power: Barings, 1762–1929* (1988), pp. 321–4.

20 Ziegler, *The Sixth Great Power,* p. 328.

21 Balogh, *Studies in Financial Organization,* pp. 178, 247–8.

22 Diaper, 'Merchant Banking in the Inter-War Period', p. 64.

23 R.J. Truptil, *British Banks and the London Money Market* (1936), pp. 134–5.

24 Truptil, *British Banks,* p. 136; Diaper, 'Merchant Banking in the Inter-War Period', p. 66; Balogh, *Studies in Financial Organization,* p. 244.
25 Balogh (*Studies in Financial Organization,* p. 248) argues for this, but Gordon A. Fletcher claims that there was an absolute decline in the volume of bills. See his *The Discount Market in London: Principles, Operation and Change* (1976), pp. 39–40.
26 Ziegler, *The Sixth Great Power,* pp. 339–40. For the experience of some acceptance houses in the 1920s see Diaper, 'Merchant Banking in the Inter-War Period', p. 67; also Kathleen Burk, *Morgan Grenfell, 1838–1988: The Biography of a Merchant Bank* (Cambridge, 1989), pp. 85–6.
27 Balogh, *Studies in Financial Organization,* pp. 224–5; Diaper, 'Merchant Banking in the Inter-War Period', p. 66.
28 Diaper, 'Merchant Banking in the Inter War Period', pp. 67–9; Balogh, *Studies in Financial Organization,* pp. 263–5.
29 Feinstein, *Statistical Tables,* Table 38.
30 Fletcher, *The Discount Market in London,* pp. 35–41; Diaper, 'Merchant Banking in the Inter-War Period', pp. 57–61.
31 Geoffrey Jones, 'Competitive Advantages in British Multinational Banking since 1890', in idem, ed. *Banks as Multinationals* (1990), pp. 42–8.
32 Balogh, *Studies in Financial Organization,* pp. 178, 180.
33 Truptil, *British Banks and the London Money Market,* pp. 199–200.
34 Figures are from Feinstein, *Statistical Tables,* Table 15.
35 J.M. Atkin, *British Overseas Investment, 1918–1931* (1977), p. 53.
36 Idem, 'Official Regulation of British Overseas Investment, 191–31', *Econ. Hist. Rev.,* 2nd ser. XXIII (1970).
37 Ziegler, *The Sixth Great Power,* pp. 349–50. The Argentine business had originally been lost to the USA in the war (ibid. pp. 345–5). See also below, pp. 150, 155–6, 168.
38 Atkin, *British Overseas Investment,* pp. 93–7, 133–4.
39 Ibid. pp. 147–54.
40 Ibid. pp. 76–86. British investment by multinationals became most concentrated on the empire after 1914. Stephen J. Nicholas, 'British Multinational Investment before 1939', *Jour. Eur. Econ. Hist.,* 11 (1982).
41 Lance E. Davis and Robert A. Huttenback, *Mammon and the Pursuit of Empire: The Political Economy of British Imperialism, 1860–1914* (Cambridge, 1986), Table 2.2 pp. 44–5.
42 Atkin, *British Overseas Investment,* Table 14, p. 130.
43 United Nations, *International Capital Movements in the Inter-War Period* (Ney York, 1949), estimated total UK overseas assets in 1929 to be $16.86bn. as against $14.6bn. for the USA (p. 29).
44 Atkin, *British Overseas Investment,* p. 246. The figures probably underestimate the outflow since they do not cover some private direct overseas investment.
45 Feinstein, *Statistical Tables,* Table 37.
46 For the role played by the collapse of invisible income in precipitating a balance of payments crisis in 1931 see Donald Moggeridge, 'The 1931 Financial Crisis – A New View', *The Banker,* CXX (1970); and Cairncross and Eichengreen, *Sterling in Decline,* pp. 56–7. Of equal significance in our view was the £230m. shrinkage in the net export of manufactures between 1929 and 1931.
47 Kahn, *Britain in the World Economy,* pp. 188–95: Cairncross and Eichengreen, *Sterling in Decline,* p. 96.
48 M.E.F. Jones, 'The Regional Impact of the Overvalued Pound in the 1920s', *Econ. Hist. Rev.,* 2nd ser. XXXVIII (1985). The assumption that the pound was overvalued in the late 1920s has recently been attacked by K.G.P. Matthews, 'Was Sterling Overvalued in 1925?', ibid. XXXIX (1986). We do not find his argument convincing.
49 In 1913 the tonnage of shipping entered and cleared in London was 25 million tons; in Liverpool it was 23 million. By 1936 the figures were 42 million and 27 million respectively. The information is from the *Statistical Abstract of the United Kingdom.* The concentration of financial control of colonial trade in London between the wars is

evident in Kathleen Stahl, *The Metropolitan Organization of British Colonial Trade* (1951), pp. 295–6.

50 Burk, *Morgan Grenfell,* p. 86.

51 It is worth noting here that, although invisible income declined in the 1930s, the ratio of invisible exports to invisible imports was 2.58:1 in 1929, fell to 2.2:1 in 1933 and then rose to 2.64:1 in 1937. The ratio was, however, much more favourable to Britain before 1914. See Feinstein, *Statistical Tables,* Tables 38–9.

19

UPHOLDING GENTLEMANLY VALUES

The American challenge, 1914–31

Industry, the state, and war, 1914–21

When war broke out in 1914, and for some months afterwards, the British government assumed that fighting Germany was compatible with (in the words of Churchill) 'business as usual'. Britain's small expeditionary force would supplement the much larger French army and we would supply them and our other Allies with financial and material aid in what, it was confidently expected, would be a short campaign similar to the Franco-German conflict of 1870. By the end of 1915 these assumptions had been overturned. A mass army now had to be organised and the nation had to accept the prospect of a long, exhausting war and the mobilisation of all available material resources in order to survive. Under the strain, the market economy failed to deliver the goods and it was soon recognised that the state had to extend its authority to a degree unimagined in peace-time. Central allocation of resources and price fixing began with munitions and were then extended further and further into the economy to ensure adequate war supplies and a proper division of output between military and civilian needs. By 1918 two-thirds of the economy and nine-tenths of imports were subject to direction by bodies authorised by government.[1]

One inevitable outcome of this development was a much greater involvement of governing elites in the mechanics of the industrial production process, from which they had been so remote in 1914. Numerous ad hoc commissions and boards were set up in industry for the purpose of coordinating, and inevitably centralising, the production of hitherto scattered industries. These new bodies brought owners and managers, whose horizons had previously been irredeemably provincial, into intimate contact with each other and with authority in London.[2] One outcome of the war was an acceleration in the development of big business in Britain; another was the evolution of peak organisations to represent industrialists who were becoming conscious of themselves as an interest over against, not only labour, but also that traditional centre of economic power, London finance. The most important of these organisations, the Federation of British Industries (FBI), was established in 1916.[3]

The entry of provincial industry into the power structure after 1914 was made a great deal easier by the appearance in 1916 of Lloyd George's coalition government, which was free from the normal restraints of party allegiance.[4] By contrast, the influence of traditional finance and of the City in general was curbed by the war. The illiquidity crisis, involving the acceptance houses at the outbreak of war, was only resolved by government guarantees and was a grave blow to the City's self-confidence.[5] More important in its long-term effects was the rapid decline in the international service economy, and the permanent rupture of many of the delicate commercial and financial threads which had linked London with the world economy before 1914. The gold standard was virtually suspended at the outbreak of war and the control of the money supply slipped out of the grip of the Bank of England as government expenditure soared and the economy endured inflation at a rate unheard of since Napoleon's time. The Treasury strove mightily to contain expenditure but during the war the power of the main spending ministries, especially munitions, could not be controlled effectively.[6]

By 1917 there was a considerable body of support for the view that the role of the state in the economy should be greatly enhanced even in peacetime. In certain areas, state control appeared to promise more efficient production than the market; there was also a strong lobby which argued that the powers used to create weapons in war ought to be turned to the production of social amenities, once peace was declared, to reward the nation for its fortitude.[7] Equally if not more important than the zeal of the reconstructionists in focusing attention on the state was the fear that outright victory against Germany might not be achieved.[8] Any compromise peace might be followed by an economic assault from Germany as she tried to refloat her economy by a massive export drive and a policy of 'dumping', thus undermining British industry and producing heavy unemployment. It was this fear which led the principal Allies to sign the Paris Agreements in 1916. Here, the Allies pledged themselves to measures designed to counteract post-war German dumping and agreed to deny her and Austria most-favoured-nation status after the war. Plans were drawn up for coordinated Allied production and a common post-war reconstruction policy was promised.

To achieve their ends, the Allies were prepared to use extensive government intervention in the economy and heavy protection, and to draw on the resources of their empires through preferential tariffs and other forms of discrimination.[9] Protection had a general appeal to propertied interests by 1916 since it held out the prospect of raising revenues to pay off escalating war debts without placing too high a burden on personal taxation.[10] But the Paris Agreements were most enthusiastically received by pre-war supporters of Chamberlain's programme.[11] Within government, the pressures making for an 'imperial' strategy and for a renewed emphasis on the centrality of empire were enhanced by the presence of 'social imperialists', like Milner, in the war Cabinet after 1916. Social imperialists were ready to accept that Germany could not be completely defeated and were convinced that this did not matter fundamentally, provided that she was confined to Europe. To ensure her own independence Britain should, they believed, retire behind a heavily protected empire dominated by British industry. From this perspective, 'only the failure of "Britons" to make the empire strong and cohesive enough to ignore the balance of power in Europe had required war against German domination of the Continent'. What they now wanted was the freedom for the 'Southern British World . . . to go about its peaceful business without constant fear of German aggression'.[12] Germany would have to be relieved of her colonies and British naval predominance maintained: that apart, imperial self-sufficiency was the key to survival.

The rising power of the social-imperialist element in government in the latter part of the war was paralleled by an increased clamour from provincial businessmen, involved in engineering and other industries subject to severe pre-war German competition, who were strongly protectionist, empire-minded and often hostile to the City and to pre-war *laissez-faire*. They favoured a much enhanced role for the state after the war in order to repel German competition by tariffs and by creating new institutions to finance the export trade and to divert funds from overseas to home purposes. As one of their number expressed it, without protection Britain would soon be 'a national scrapheap'; he also voiced the usually unspoken resentments of many industrialists when he claimed that 'financiers' were 'a sort of nation apart, with the City of London for its metropolis, but possessing no territory and no sentiment'.[13]

Britain had already moved away from free trade in 1915, when the McKenna duties were placed on luxury goods for revenue purposes and to clear the shipping lanes for imported war supplies. By 1917 there was excited talk in 'imperial' circles about empire self-sufficiency in foodstuffs and about a strategy of planned emigration to the Dominions. At the Imperial Conference in 1917, an imperial emigration programme was proposed, and it was agreed that the Dominions should be allowed preferences on items that Britain felt needed protection.[14] A year later, the Balfour Committee on 'Commercial and Industrial Policy After the War' put its weight behind the Paris Agreements. Although it remained suspicious of a general tariff on efficiency grounds, the Committee advocated tariffs on a list of commodities assumed to be vital to national security and acknowledged the openings for imperial preference.[15] During the 1918 election campaign, Lloyd George's successful Coalitionists argued for imperial preference in principle. By this time, the dominant party within the Coalition, the Conservatives, were sure that imperial economic unity offered far greater benefits than the prospects of inter-Allied cooperation.[16]

Late in the war, therefore, a new economic policy was beginning to take shape based on close consultation between government, business and trade unions,[17] and offering industrial protection, closer union with the empire and far greater prospects of state intervention in the economy than would have been considered desirable before war broke out. But proposals that seemed to be moving to the centre of the political agenda in 1917–18 were no longer practical politics by 1921. By then, the economy had been almost entirely decontrolled; free trade was largely reaffirmed; restoring balanced budgets and the gold standard were again the chief aims of government; and the Treasury, the Bank of England and the City of London had reasserted their authority over economic policy. How did this come about?[18]

Four years of economic transformation were insufficient to eradicate the deep suspicion of government felt by many in business or to temper their eagerness to be rid of its influence as soon as the emergency was over.[19] What this reflected, in part, was a conflict between businessmen in older industries who were more inclined to accept traditional roles and ideologies, and those in the new industries who felt a need for drastic change. This split, together with that between the free traders, chiefly represented by cotton interests, and those on the receiving end of German competition, who favoured protection, seriously weakened the FBI, for example, and often made it impossible for it, or other industrial pressure groups, to speak with one voice, or even any voice at all, on matters of national importance.[20] Impatient with the apparent passivity of the FBI, some of the leading protectionist and imperially minded industrialists, such as Dudley Docker and Sir Alan Smith, tried to create organisations which could keep their ideas before the public; but they could not gather enough support on their own to be effective.[21] At the end of the war, British industry was still too small in scale, too fragmented and too bitterly competitive to allow any strategy to emerge which could match that offered by the City in terms of coherence and simplicity.[22] Even when industrialists did manage to offer a distinctive viewpoint, they found that the message failed to rise to the political heights because most channels of communication after 1918 were controlled by the traditional financial and commercial communities. Before the Cunliffe Committee in 1918, the FBI argued strongly that recreating the export economy should precede any attempt to reintroduce the gold standard. The Committee ignored this completely in its report arguing, mainly from the first principles of conventional wisdom, that restoring the standard was a prerequisite of Britain's economic success and that industry concurred with this view.[23]

The entry of the United States into the war in 1917, followed by Germany's unexpectedly rapid collapse in the following year, also undermined the position of those who advocated a revolution in economic management. Germany's comprehensive defeat made an 'economic war after the war' unnecessary, undermined the 'siege economics' of the social imperialists and made liberal normality seem plausible again, reinforcing the opinion of those who viewed the state's intrusion into economic life in wartime as being temporary and accidental.[24] Then in 1919 and 1920, many of those who had remained faithful to the idea that social and economic reconstruction was essential lost their credibility because the rapid inflation which accompanied the restocking boom gave the Treasury and the Bank their chance to reassert the need for discipline in government expenditure.[25] Inflation terrified the nation and drove it back to orthodoxy for, as Keynes wrote at the time, it meant that

> all permanent relations between debtors and creditors, which form the ultimate foundation of capitalism, become so utterly disordered as to be

> almost meaningless. Lenin was certainly right. There is no subtler, no surer means of overturning the existing bases of society than to debauch the currency.[26]

In this atmosphere, and with the Chancellor of the Exchequer in 1921 'prophesying ruin for the country if expenditure were not cut drastically',[27] those in power who were either imperialists or sympathetic to reconstruction schemes were panicked into assuming that the cure for the disease must be the traditional medicine administered by the usual gentlemanly doctors.[28]

Between 1918 and 1921 the policies proposed by radical industrialists and politicians were swept from the agenda. Immediately the war ended, despite formally accepting the message of the Cunliffe Committee, Lloyd George's coalition let the pound float down from its fixed wartime level of $4.76. Freed from the need to protect a fixed rate of exchange, the government could have gone wholeheartedly for a policy of social reform and imperial preference. Social reconstruction and an empire policy seemed to go naturally together for, as the Cabinet were informed early in 1919, 'if large sums of capital are locked up in slow maturing investments (e.g. housing) the trade of the country must be reduced and emigration on a large scale is necessary'.[29] In fact, as the incompatibility between these new policies and established financial rectitude became apparent, it was the dreams of imperial tariffs and state-led emigration schemes which were shattered first of all. Although the Conservative Party wavered briefly on the issue in 1923, the free-trade policy remained largely intact in the 1920s: only a few commodities were protected, in 1921, for the purposes of national defence and a few minor concessions were made on imperial preference.

Plans for a massive resettlement of Britons on the white imperial frontier also failed to materialise. Discussion of state-supported emigration had first arisen in the context of a debate on resettling ex-servicemen after the war. In the enthusiastic atmosphere of 1918–19, Milner and Amery had translated this mundane issue into a grand strategy for peopling the empty spaces of empire and encouraging inter-imperial flows of both labour and capital. The main colonial enthusiasts were the Australians, then busy planning a significant extension of their agricultural frontier. The Treasury's reaction was cold: spending on emigration would drain British savings, reduce domestic investment, raise interest rates and make a return to gold more difficult. In the atmosphere of 1921–2 this might have been enough to torpedo the scheme completely had not rising unemployment meant that assisting emigrants might be no more expensive than paying out additional unemployment pay. So the Treasury agreed reluctantly to spend between £1.5m. and £3m. per year for the next fifteen years to place British migrants on colonial land, and the Empire Settlement Act of 1922 was born.[30] Plans for social reconstruction lingered longer but were soon washed away in the tide of fear produced by the inflation of early 1920.[31] The pound fell to $3.4 and industrial unrest, aggravated by falling real wages, sent the propertied interests scuttling behind the barricades provided by ancient financial verities.

Orthodoxy triumphed because the Bank of England's determination to control the money supply, the Treasury's interest in curbing government spending, and the City's urgent demand that the international service economy be restored as quickly as possible, offered a consistent and well-established set of priorities and policies with which to meet the frightening problems of 1919–21. They owed their weighty appeal not only to their simplicity and coherence, which the radical critics of orthodoxy simply could not emulate, but also to the fact that the City and the controlling financial institutions were the visible manifestations of a dominant gentlemanly capitalist culture which still had control over the 'commanding heights' of the economy and a prestige which producers – industrialists and trade unionists alike – could not match. In the 1920s it was still possible for a City MP to claim 'that because of its national services, the City as a whole occupied a special position' in matters of political economy, and it was sincerely believed, as one historian has recently pointed out, that 'City parliamentarians were expected to preserve more independence from their political parties than most other MPs'.[32] The City still represented the nation: industry was seen as provincial and self-interested and this was inevitable as long as the latter remained fragmented and divided.

No complete 'return to 1913' was, of course, possible. The McKenna duties remained and several industries were given protection in 1921 because domestic production was thought to be vital in the event of another war. The Treasury, as we have seen, grudgingly supported a limited scheme of emigration to the empire; some measures of social reform in education, housing and social services survived the crisis of 1919–21. More important than this was the fact that industry and the trade unions were both more politically self-aware after 1919. Gentlemanly capitalists, in or out of government, now had to justify their policy preferences: the rules of the game had to be made explicit after the war and thus open to argument and contradiction. In pursuing financial discipline, too, it had to be accepted that budgets would balance only at much higher levels of expenditure in real terms than before the war, mainly because of the high level of the national debt and increased commitments to social services. If industrial peace after 1919 could be bought only at the price of a higher level of real wages than before 1914, a price also had to be paid for re-establishing financial peace: orthodoxy, at levels of taxation which did not provoke mutiny, was achievable only by ruthlessly cutting defence expenditure in the 1920s.

After the war, the problems of holding together a more fragile social and economic order pushed the British towards disarmament, towards appeasement of their former enemies and towards international economic liberalism, which offered the greater promise of peace.[33] This weakening of Britain's defence came at a time when her global dominance was also challenged by the United States, for whom the war proved to be an entry point into world power status. As we shall see, the rise of the United States proved more troublesome to Britain's gentlemanly capitalists than did the increased assertiveness of domestic industry.

The impact of the United States

For the gentlemanly capitalist class, the mushroom growth of the United States' influence after 1914 presented a serious and abiding challenge. To defeat Germany, Britain had to enlist first the financial, and then the military, strength of the United States with the result that there was a permanent shift in the world balance of power. After 1914 Britain faced a fresh global challenge, a renewed threat of a 're-division of the world', though one more subtle and more difficult to resist than that offered by the Kaiser's empire. The years 1917–19 apart, the American impact was not overtly political because of her strong tradition of isolationism. The pressure came largely from the unparalleled economic dynamism of the republic spilling out dramatically into the world in the shape of trade and finance, and undermining the British position just as surely as Britain's own market power had once undermined the economic foundation of the international power of Portugal, The Netherlands, Spain and France. So, although there were tense moments of naval rivalry, the central battle was between economies, Treasuries, central banks and stock markets rather than between armies and navies. For British elites, the battle was also confused in that the Americans were difficult to identify clearly as an enemy. They appreciated the importance of the global struggle for informal economic influence set in train after 1914. But the strident anti-imperialist ideology suitable to an ex-colony, which they feared and resented, was often accompanied by the language of an economic internationalism which the gentlemanly capitalist class could instinctively appreciate as the foundation of their own power and influence. Similarly, their hostility to the brashness and assertiveness of the United States was muted by a strong feeling that the republic was, after all, part of 'Anglo-Saxondom', a genuinely liberal state, one more like a Dominion than a foreign country.[34]

Wartime dependence on the United States stemmed from her crucial position as a supplier of vital war materials and from Britain's role as financier of her own, and the Allies', international needs.[35] Many British investments in the United States were liquidated and gold reserves run down in order to pay for supplies; but, as early as 1915, the British had a dollar problem which required extensive borrowing on Wall Street, using Morgans as their principal agent.[36] In 1916, the American authorities, unused to foreign lending, became sufficiently alarmed at the extent of the borrowing that they took steps to discourage investors. Had Britain been unable to continue borrowing then, her plight, and the Allied cause, would have been desperate: it is difficult to see how Germany could have been defeated without a liberal supply of American aid.[37] The situation might have been eased had Britain let the exchange rate fall from its fixed wartime level of $4.76. For the Treasury, however, this not only threatened inflation but also meant a loss of prestige 'equivalent to the loss of a major battle'.[38] The Allied cause was saved in 1917 by the United States' entry into the war, which opened the way to public, as well as to a renewal of private, loans. By the end of the war, the time-honoured financial relationship between Britain and the United States had been turned upside down, and the British had borrowed a total of $3.7bn.[39] Britain was now a 'permanent debtor' thus 'making it impossible for London alone to continue as the principal effective financial centre of the world'.[40]

It may not be too cynical to suggest that one motive for American intervention on the Allied side was to safeguard her loans and her burgeoning export markets, which would have been imperilled by an Allied defeat or by a stalemate peace among increasingly protectionist powers:[41] the United States raised her share of world exports from 13.5 per cent in 1913 to over 25 per cent by 1920.[42] The administration, and many export-minded business and financial circles in the United States, were certainly alarmed by the implications of the Paris Agreements, and entry into the conflict gave them the opportunity to put their weight behind a liberal solution to the world's problems. The fear that the United States' expanding economic interests would be curbed by rampant militarism and imperialism lay behind Wilson's demand for a liberal peace which would bring a democratised Germany back into the world economy quickly and, by preserving freedom of trade, would encourage the flow of American capital into Europe and elsewhere.[43] With British policy still under the influence of social imperialist sentiment, Anglo-American relations were often imbued with a deep economic antagonism even while the common fight against Germany continued; at one point, late in 1918, the British went so far as to slow down the shipment of American troops to the battlefield in order to release British shipping to counter American trade competition. Fear of American competition also influenced Britain's decision to seize the German merchant fleet after the war was over.[44]

Fortunately for the Allies, the war ended quickly enough to prevent the United States from attaining the overwhelming authority which ever-increasing Allied indebtedness would have given her. Germany's decisive defeat marked the end of the Paris Agreements but, as they faded from view, they were replaced by bitter and unreasoning demands that Germany should pay huge, if not precisely specified, reparations to cover Allied war costs.[45] After the German defeat, the 1918 general election in Britain was dominated by ideas of economic revenge:[46] it has been claimed that, at the Versailles Peace Conference, the British were, if anything, more intransigent than the French on this issue,[47] as Lloyd George dreamed of financing social reform by taxing the Germans 'till the pips squeak'.[48] The United States opposed reparations as being unworkable and as a sure recipe for continued antagonism between the Allies and Germany. But Wilson's ideas were ignored and the United States was also defeated on the colonial issue as Britain, encouraged by her Dominions, demanded a large share of the German empire as it was dismembered.[49] Nor could the Americans prevent the Allies from agreeing to discriminate against Germany in trade for five years after the war.[50]

British and American aspirations were still far apart in 1918. In Britain, reconstruction and empire unity remained part of the political agenda and the fear of American competition went with a fear of social disorder which a return to liberalism might bring. For the United States the chief economic worry at the end of the war was the possibility of a slump; this increased her determination to press for a liberal solution to European problems. Export markets had to be maintained and, since the domestic American market was protected by tariffs which no administration had the power to reduce, it was clear that American capital export would become a vital part of her expansion abroad. In an essentially free-market society the capital would have to be privately funded; these private funds would not flow into Europe until American investors were satisfied that peace there was well established and the liberal order permanently restored. Only then would the American economic invasion get under way and the English 'monopoly' of financial services be broken.[51]

From 1919 onwards, as we have seen, the 'industrial elite' who had strongly influenced the Coalition government in Britain and was responsible for its 'burst of economic nationalism' was in decline.[52] By 1921 the gentlemanly capitalists were in charge again, and their implicit internationalist assumptions once more guided British economic policy. This inevitably brought the United States and Britain closer together. Once convinced of the paramount need to restore a cosmopolitan world order rather than to retreat into their empire, the British gave up their futile attempt to stamp out Bolshevism in Russia, an attempt encouraged by imperialists fearful for Indian security, and began to think about how to tempt Lenin back into the liberal fold under British auspices.[53] On reparations, they were now of Keynes's opinion that huge exactions would hold back German recovery and damage the world economy. Their position thus shifted towards the United States and away from France.[54]

The reassertion of control by the gentlemen in Britain by no means eliminated all sources of conflict with the United States. One potent source of difficulty was the issue of war debts. Britain's position was that if her debts to the United States were scaled down she could be equally generous to her allied debtors and the pressure to collect reparations would be reduced.[55] No American administration would admit any connection between war debt and reparations and all insisted on full repayment. The British fear was that, if they had to pay, 'the effect of such payment would be to enable the American government to reduce taxation and so place the American manufacturer in a favourable position as regards British competition'.[56] In insisting on British payment, the Americans certainly appreciated this; they could not see why the British, whose imperial wealth they regarded as being unlimited, could not respond by liquidating other foreign investments or cutting down the flow of new loans, incidentally giving New York a further edge over London in the financial war. Finally, at the Washington Conference in 1922, the British repudiated their naval alliance with Japan and agreed to parity with the United States in capital ships, partly to reduce defence expenditure but partly also to influence favourably the American position on war debt. But in 1923, Britain had to accept full repayment, at a fairly high rate of interest, and a scaling down of her own demands on her former allies and Germany.[57]

The return to gold

Insistence on war debt repayment was one way of asserting New York's financial primacy;[58] a common belief in the need for a liberal world order stimulated rather than damped down the conflict between the two leading money markets. Britain's determination to restore the gold standard was a vital part of London's postwar rehabilitation. The United States supported the policy of restoration because it was seen as an essential step in recreating a fully functioning international system. But returning to the gold standard was acutely difficult. While the United States had huge stocks of gold, Britain's own holdings were small and the fear of the authorities was that, in order to achieve a balance of payments strong enough to give a restored gold standard credibility, such continuous and massive deflationary pressures would have to be applied that economic growth would be curtailed and the social order imperilled. This is why, at the Genoa Conference in 1922, the British authorities proposed that, in the wake of the war and post-war inflation, European currencies should be restabilised using either dollars or sterling as reserves rather than gold, as had been the case before 1914.[59]

Had this plan been universally accepted, Britain's problem as a financial centre in the 1920s would have been eased considerably and it would have been much easier to manage the gold standard after 1925. The system would have economised on gold and concentrated much of it in London. Increased gold reserves would have allowed for easier money and lower interest rates in Britain and given a stimulus to economic growth. The 'gold exchange standard', as it was known, would also have led, interestingly enough, to a considerable extension of the use of sterling in Europe, where Britain's financial writ had not run before 1914. In pre-war days the franc and, to a lesser extent, the mark had been the dominant currencies of Europe. The power of both had been destroyed by the war and the British, building on their position as wartime Allied paymaster, were keen to compensate themselves in Europe for the loss of financial position they had suffered in, for example, parts of Latin America at the hands of the United States. Not surprisingly, the gold exchange standard was bitterly opposed by the French, but it also fell foul of the United States, who viewed it with deep suspicion as being likely to produce inflation and were wary of supporting any proposal which looked likely to promote the power of the pound. It seems ironic in retrospect that the gentlemanly capitalists who preached deflation to the British voter and supported the gold standard with almost religious fervour were actually hoping to establish a different gold standard from that which existed in 1914, and one which could legitimately be attacked as being unorthodox and dangerous.

The universal acceptance of a gold exchange standard would have solved another puzzle for the British: how to attract American capital to Europe without surrendering their position at the centre of the world economy. To create a prosperous, liberal world economy and restore London's glory, a sustained recovery was necessary in Europe. This was impossible without United States' capital, but if that capital came would Britain and Europe become a part of an American economic empire? Britain's answer to this conundrum was given in the context of the Genoa discussions on the future of the Soviet Union.[60] The British proposed to create a financial consortium, led by themselves, to invest massively in the Soviet Union. Bolshevism would be killed off by kindness, the Soviet Union would be reintegrated into the world economy, benefiting in particular the Germans, whose trade links with Tsarist

Russia had been so important to her prosperity. In return for this capital, and for *de facto* recognition of their regime, the Bolsheviks were to acknowledge, rather than repay, their debts and allow foreign entrepreneurs to operate freely in the Soviet Union. The proposals failed. Lenin would not accept loans at the price of subverting communism, and the Soviet Union's creditors, especially the French, demanded repayment of old loans. The plan also failed because the United States' government believed, rightly, that the British were aiming at a settlement which would induce American private capital to flow to Europe through London channels (since shares in the proposed Consortium were to be issued in sterling), allowing Britain to extend her financial empire within Europe and turn the Soviet Union into a financial colony without having to raise much capital from her own diminished post-war stores.[61] The objections of the United States alone would have been sufficient to kill off this scheme for, without her tacit approval, no private capital would flow into Europe, and the British themselves were in no position to provide it.

Genoa was only the beginning of Britain's pursuit of a new empire for sterling in Europe. Under the leadership of Montagu Norman, its long-serving and highly influential Governor, the Bank of England organised a syndicate to buy up the ailing Anglo-Austrian bank and to establish a separate Anglo-Czech bank on similar lines. The creation of the latter was soon followed by a £10m. reconstruction loan orchestrated by Barings with encouragement from the Bank of England. Then, using his influence over the Financial Committee of the League of Nations, Norman took the lead in persuading London financiers to acquire the largest share in loans designed to bring financial stability to two of the war's greatest casualties, Austria and Hungary, in 1923–4.[62] In this endeavour, the Bank drew some support from American banking circles, including the Federal Reserve.

Norman was also keen to encourage the establishment of central banks throughout Europe. Like their prototype, the Bank of England, they would be free of political control and would manage the new financial order on the basis of informal cooperation:[63] the central banks proposed for both Austria and Hungary were strictly enjoined to be independent of government and their statutes disallowed financial entanglement with the state.[64] No doubt with their own history at the front of their minds, leading English bankers were convinced that 'if politicians would leave the financiers alone, they could solve the world's economic problems'; they would do so by relying 'on personal relationships rather than official structures, academic theory or statistics'.[65] Unfortunately, finance and politics could no longer be so easily separated. Outside some financial circles in the United States,[66] the impression remained strong that the British were using their power with the League to create a new Europe financed by New York but controlled in London.[67]

While spreading to Europe the gospel of sound money based on sterling reserves, the Bank of England was also encouraging the Dominions to think along the same lines. When the Imperial Conference of 1923 took place sterling was, of course, still floating and Dominion currencies, such as those of Australia and New Zealand, had actually begun to diverge in value from the British pound for the first time. At the Conference, the British urged the Dominions to accumulate sterling assets as

London funds, and assumed rather than argued that the latter would want to retain parity between their currencies and London. Ideally, it was claimed, the best way to do this would be to create central banks free of government control – South Africa had led the way in 1920[68] – which would cooperate with the monetary authorities in London in minimising fluctuations in exchange rates.[69] With Genoa in mind, the Bank of England was eager to train the colonial 'savages' in the niceties of financial management,[70] and was intent on setting up the same machinery to manage money in the Dominions as it was attempting to establish in Central Europe.

In 1923 there were 20 central banks holding sterling reserves compared with only four in 1914.[71] But none of these countries was an important economic power, save for Germany, whose financial future was still to be decided, and France, which was ready to remove the indignity of dependence on sterling as soon as the franc could be restabilised. The test case for the Bank of England's ability to make Europe dependent upon London finance was the restabilisation of the German mark in 1924. The French invasion of the Ruhr in 1923 – intended to exact reparations from Germany – not only gave an upward twist to spiralling German inflation but also simultaneously led to a collapse in the value of the franc. With French power reduced, Britain and the United States were able in 1924 to impose the Dawes Plan, which cut Germany's reparations bill and fixed payments over a long period of time.[72] But Germany could not be brought back to the centre of European affairs without the restabilisation of the mark. To accomplish this, the British revived their Genoa proposals and pressed Germany to hold sterling and dollars as reserve assets. Much German capital had fled to London during the great inflation; if Germany had adopted a sterling reserve system this would have made London the financial heart of Europe. Reconstructing the German central bank, the Reichsbank, was a crucial element in the policy of stabilisation, and the Bank of England hoped for an institution independent of government with which it could cooperate informally in managing an international economy free of the corrupting influence of politicians.[73] Nonetheless, it was the United States which subscribed the major part of the stabilisation loan and which also insisted on Germany holding at least three-quarters of her reserves in gold.[74] Washington feared that if Germany was pulled into a Sterling Area then Britain would have neither the incentive nor the desire to return to gold at all.[75] In this they were probably wrong, but the manner of the German stabilisation effectively ended Britain's bid to colonise the continent financially in compensation for her losses elsewhere, and it also meant that the gentlemanly capitalists could not avoid the implications of a return to a full gold standard.

The Dawes Plan and financial reconstruction offered the stability that the private investor craved, promised rapid development in Germany and general European growth, and loosed a flood of American capital on Europe. If London were to play a central part in this process, a quick return to the gold standard was imperative.[76] German stabilisation on gold made a similar British move unavoidable because Britain could not hope to retain world financial leadership with a floating currency when her close rivals were adopting stable exchange rates.[77] It is apparent also that the Dominions, especially South Africa, were becoming restless with a floating currency by 1924, and there were vague threats about stabilising on the dollar. Whether the Dominions, as primary exporters, would have received any benefit from transferring their allegiance from free-market Britain to the heavily protectionist United States is doubtful. However, the restlessness of the white empire seems to have influenced Churchill, as Chancellor of the Exchequer, and helped to convince him that the time for a return to $4.86 had come.[78]

Churchill still had his doubts; he would have preferred to leave sterling at its 1924 level of roughly $4.40 because this was better for exports and, he hoped, for employment. He was worried 'at the spectacle of Britain possessing the finest credit in the world simultaneously with a million and a quarter unemployed', and would have liked to 'see Finance less proud and Industry more content'.[79] The response from the Bank of England and the Treasury gave clear expression to hitherto unspoken gentlemanly assumptions on the nature of economy and policy. London had to remain the financial capital of the world because, as a Treasury official put it in 1924,

> mercantile business tends to be transacted at the centres from which it is financed. The greatest factor in the material prosperity of this country is not manufacturing, important as that is, but *commerce*. The diversion of commerce to other centres is the severest loss to which we could be exposed.[80]

This was the voice, not of crude and conspiratorial 'City interests', but of a whole, hugely successful, service economy dominated by gentlemen, in which the City of London, for whom industrialism and provincialism were synonymous, played the crucial coordinating role. Already condemned as marginal, manufacturers struggled – vainly – to be noticed. While some industrialists did offer support for the gold standard as the bringer of stability, there were deep worries in the provinces about deflation and high interest rates,[81] but both Churchill *and* the officials who advised him were effectively insulated from this branch of opinion.[82]

For officialdom, a return to $4.86 was a necessary means of disciplining all those, capitalists and workers alike, who apparently wished to use state economic power for their own, obviously selfish, ends. The gold standard was as important to the nation as 'A Police Force or Tax Collector': in returning to it, the views of 'the merchant, the manufacturer workmen etc should be considered (but not consulted any more than about the design of battleships)'.[83] The gentlemen who controlled policy never hesitated in their belief, nurtured by the successes of the pre-war era, that they alone understood what the true economic interests of the nation were: behind their confidence in their own authority lay generations of gentlemanly financial success.[84] If they could not have the gold exchange standard of Genoa, then the rigours of the full gold standard had to be faced. Industry might be hurt immediately by revaluation and the high interest rates needed to attract investors into sterling, but the benefits of stability and of London's prosperity would also, it was assumed, eventually rub off on them. Meanwhile, the imperative matter was London's ability to meet the challenge of New York and to recapture the invisible income lost during the war. By restoring the pre-1914 exchange rate regime, Britain was honouring her obligations in full, proving that a gentleman's word was his bond,[85] and, it was hoped, restablishing that confidence in London which was such a vital element in restoring its fortunes.

Confidence was indeed the key issue. Arguments by Keynes, for example, that Britain should have stabilised at a rate about 10 per cent below the old rate could be countered with the claim that this might have triggered off competing devaluations in Europe and undermined the stability which was the prime aim of policy.[86] Given industry's fragmentation and inability to come forward with a clear alternative strategy, and the general lack of interest in 'managed money', it is difficult, in retrospect, to see what other policy could in practice have been adopted in 1925, especially when one considers that a more flexible gold standard system – such as that proposed at Genoa – had been ruled out by international hostility. The gentlemanly capitalists who ran British economic policy were certainly arrogant in assuming that they knew what was good for industry, but industry was too divided to speak for itself with authority; it had no effective counter to the argument that a return to internationalism on the old terms was the most practical way of restoring Britain's economic fortunes.

Unfortunately, trying to maintain the gold standard after 1925 proved to be a constant, unrewarding struggle. At first, the British monetary authorities still had high hopes of establishing a viable gold exchange standard which would help to take the pressure off the pound.[87] The Belgian stabilisation of 1926 was successfully handled by London with Federal Reserve support.[88] But the attempts to steer countries such as Romania and Poland towards sterling fell foul of an increasingly assertive France, whose central bankers were not afraid to accuse the British of 'financial imperialism', a charge which seemed to leave the British genuinely hurt and rather baffled.[89] The French were supported in this by an increasingly suspicious United States, and Britain's endeavours came to very little.[90]

The restabilisation of the French franc at an undervalued rate in 1928 increased the pressure on London by making Paris as well as New York an attractive home for international funds. Bank Rate remained high in Britain, growth was below the world average and exports were sluggish. Discontent with the gold standard increased steadily in business circles though, again, it had few effective outlets and was muted by fear of labour unrest in the wake of the General Strike.[91] The pressure for government action to reduce unemployment was also mounting, as the Keynesian-inspired Liberal plan of 1929 and Mosley's imaginative initiative of 1930 for increasing public expenditure both show.[92] Neither proposal made much impact on policy. The official line, known as the 'Treasury View', was that public works merely diverted expenditure from private to public channels;[93] as budget deficits began to appear in the world depression after 1929, the financial authorities pressed for deflation and budget balancing. The aim was to impress upon foreigners the fact that $4.86 was safe in London's hands and to steer government away from the temptation to spend its way out of the crisis. In this the Treasury was supported by the Bank of England and by a wide spectrum of opinion. Beleaguered businessmen, conscious of falling profits, linked deficit financing with punitive taxation and inflation. Labour voters, on the other hand, were either terrified of inflation or criticised welfare spending and other government handouts as being an encouragement to 'spongers'.[94] If, as De Cecco claims, Keynes's historic achievement was to purge the English polity of its rentier assumptions on economic policy, his task had only just begun in 1930.[95]

The financial crisis, 1929–31

The major beneficiary of the 1925–9 boom, which accompanied Britain's return to gold, was the United States. Stabilisation under the gold standard offered American capital and trade the chance to begin an economic invasion of Europe.[96] Brief and unstable though it was, this stream of American goods, capital and institutions across the Atlantic was, in a sense, a trial run for the much greater and more permanent extension of the economic power of the United States in Europe after 1945. The transatlantic flow soon aroused fear and hostility:[97] a sense of the imminent Americanisation of the world, mingled with resentments about war debt repayments and American tariffs, lay behind the bitter Anglo-American naval disputes of 1927–8, for example.[98] The pressure of a high exchange rate and severe American competition also helped to stimulate demand for protectionism in Britain. Similar pressures were being felt across the continent. One reaction to the rise of the United States was the awakening of an interest in European economic union, and this was being actively canvassed by 1930. When the screw of American protectionism was given a further twist in 1929–30, a debate was sparked off across Europe on the iniquities of the huge American balance of payments surplus, its resolution via foreign investment and the resulting 'commercial imperialism'. When the French premier suggested forming a European Economic Union, the British were faced with the possibility, however remote, of being squeezed between two huge protected economic empires in North America and on the continent – foreshadowing their eventual fate in the 1960s.[99]

In 1930 a European accord on economic policy seemed remote. Besides, the British had an alternative available if the cosmopolitan economy should fail: empire unity, last seriously considered in the 1916–18 wartime emergency. As exports began to decline rapidly and the world economy started to disintegrate, the clamour for protection and for a retreat into empire increased. By then, not only much of industry but also large sections of organised labour were looking to the empire to save them from chaos.[100] More significantly, the City of London was also moving swiftly in the same direction, its cosmopolitanism worn down by competition from New York. The empire offered a safe haven, and 'protection was the price the City was prepared to pay to maintain sterling as a world currency'.[101] Thus for industry, unions and even finance, 'empire unity' provided an escape hatch down which they hoped to disappear in order to avoid the agonies of modernisation and restructuring as competition increased.[102] 'For many of its advocates an Empire strategy was attractive precisely because it was anti-development, a policy which protected the domestic industrial structure from new conditions in the world economy'.[103] Joining Europe was not an acceptable option; Britain's living standards might have had to fall to the continental level in order to compete. As Neville Chamberlain put it, succinctly and threateningly in 1929: 'If we do not think imperially, we shall have to think continentally'.[104] By the end of the decade, City and industrial interests were probably closer than at any time in their history, comrades in adversity as the world economy collapsed in ruins. If, by 1931, they could no longer manage a world economy, the British still aspired to run an empire.

As the groundswell of opinion in favour of protection increased, it spilled over into the centre of political life. In 1930 the Labour Cabinet was having to cling grimly to its traditional free trade beliefs as rank-and-file opinion changed rapidly, though it was strong enough to resist the white empire's call for preferences at the Imperial Conference of 1930.[105] The transformation on the Conservative side was more complete. In 1923, when the Ruhr crisis appeared to threaten the collapse of order in Europe, Baldwin had reacted by trying to sell protectionism and imperial preference to the electorate and had been roundly defeated.[106] But by 1930, with a virtual alliance on the backbenches between financiers and industrialists, the party could opt for a tariff with much greater confidence.[107]

The increased favour with which protection and empire policies were viewed in financial circles between 1929 and 1931 did not mean that orthodoxy had been abandoned. The Bank of England and the Treasury still regarded it as their duty – something far above the grubby game of party politics – to cajole, bully and even bounce governments, of any political stripe, into deflationary policies once budget deficits began to appear.[108] Discipline had to be maintained: foreign help was refused at times to ensure that pressure to deflate remained acute.[109] The gold standard had also to be defended *à outrance* for the sake of the 'honour' upon which the City placed such great store.[110] It may be, however, that by late 1930 or early 1931, the Bank had recognised that holding on to the standard would be impossible if New York and Paris continued to absorb gold and force deflation on the world economy. For a while Norman and his colleagues put their faith in the Bank of International Settlements, created in 1929, to act as a new way of extending the authority of sterling and of bringing about the informal central bank cooperation which was so dear to the Bank of England.[111] But, as this hope faded, they concentrated upon trying to force the Americans and French to recognise their 'responsibilities', while keeping a tight hold on the money supply in Britain. In this way they hoped both to demonstrate that they had played the game to the end, as gentlemen should, and also to ensure that, if gold was abandoned, financial discipline at home would not be relaxed.[112] In practice, the financial authorities felt they had been let down, not only by foreigners who would not play by the rules, but also by British industry, which had failed to respond to the stimulus of competition and thus to strengthen the balance of payments.[113]

The abandonment of the gold standard in September 1931 was a defeat for the City, for gentlemanly capitalism and for cosmopolitanism. But the impact of the depression was even greater in the United States, and her international economic sphere shrank markedly in the 1930s. As the United States retreated into economic isolationism, leaving wreckage strewn across the world, the British were left with the freedom to strike out on their own and to try to regain, within the confines of the empire and the Sterling Area, the power they had exercised before 1914 but which had eluded them in the 1920s.

Notes

1 For a useful summary of the evolution of the war economy see Sidney Pollard, *The Development of the British Economy, 1914–1980* (1983), pp. 14–47. See also G.C. Peden, *British Economic and Social Policy: Lloyd George to Margaret Thatcher* (1985), pp. 36–47; David French, 'The Rise and Fall of "Business As Usual"', in Kathleen Burk, ed. *War and the State* (1982); and an older, but still riveting, account in R.H. Tawney, 'The Abolition of Economic Controls, 1918–21', *Econ. Hist. Rev.*, 1st ser. XIII (1943).

2 Scott Newton and Dilwyn Porter, *Modernization Frustrated: The Politics of Industrial Decline in Britain Since 1900* (1988), pp. 37–8.

3 John Turner, 'The Politics of "Organized Business" in the First World War', in John Turner, ed. *Businessmen and Politics: Studies of Business Activity in British Politics, 1900–1945* (1984); R.T.P. Davenport-Hines, *Dudley Docker: The Life and Times of a Trade Warrior* (Cambridge, 1984), Ch. 5.

4 Newton and Porter, *Modernization Frustrated,* p. 32.

5 Henry Roseveare, *The Treasury: The Evolution of a British Institution* (1969), pp. 238–40; Teresa Seaborne, 'The Summer of 1914', in Forrest Capie and Geoffrey Wood, *Financial Crises and the World Banking System* (1986); also J.M. Keynes, 'War and the Financial System, Aug. 1914', *Econ. Jour.*, XXIV (1914).

6 Roseveare, *The Treasury,* pp. 238ff; Kathleen Burk, 'The Treasury: the Impotence of Power', in Burk, *War and the State.*

7 On reconstructionist ideas see Pollard, *The Development of the British Economy,* pp. 48–50; Peden, *British Economic and Social Policy,* pp. 47ff; Newton and Porter, *Modernization Frustrated,* pp. 45–54. There is also a highly detailed account in P.B. Johnson, *Land Fit For Heroes: The Planning of British Reconstruction, 1916–19* (Chicago, 1968).

8 Peter Cline, 'Winding Down the War Economy: British Plans for Peacetime Recovery, 1916–19', in Burk, *War and the State,* pp. 160–4.

9 Cline, 'Winding Down the War Economy', pp. 164–9; Robert E. Bunselmeyer, *The Cost of the War, 1914–18: British Economic War Aims and the Origin of Reparations* (Hamden, Corm., 1975), pp. 35ff. Details of the Paris Agreements can be found in Parliamentary Paper Cd 8271 for 1916 and in Albert O. Hirschman, *National Power and the Structure of Foreign Trade* (1945; 1980), App. B, pp. 163–5. See also V.H. Rothwell, *British War Aims and Peace Diplomacy* (Oxford, 1971), Ch. 8.

10 Bunselmeyer, *The Cost of the War,* pp. 13–17.

11 Ibid. pp. 24–32.

12 Paul Guinn, *British Strategy and Politics, 1914–18* (Oxford, 1965), pp. 193–4. For the strategic implications of the battle between the social imperialists and those – the Continentalists – who were more concerned with the need to defeat Germany, see Paul Kennedy, *The Realities Behind Diplomacy: Background Influences on British External Policy, 1865–1980* (1981), pp. 179–90.

13 Davenport-Hines, *Dudley Docker,* pp. 107–8 and Chs. 6 and 7.

14 Rothwell, *British War Aims,* p. 171; Ian M. Drummond, *Imperial Economic Policy, 1917–39: Studies in Expansion and Protection* (1974), pp. 25–6; see also idem, *British Economic Policy and the Empire, 1919–39* (1972), pp. 55–7, 143–50.

15 *Final Report of the Committee on Commercial and Industrial Policy After the War,* PP 1918 XIII (Cd 9035), Paras 317–52.

16 Bunselmeyer, *The Cost of the War,* pp. 47–51.

17 For this 'corporatist' strategy see Turner, 'The Politics of "Organized Business"', p. 2. There is detailed study in Keith Middlemass, *Politics in Industrial Society: The Experience of the British System Since 1911* (1974), Chs. 3–6.
18 The most comprehensive guide to the politics of the Coalition after the war is Kenneth O. Morgan, *Consensus or Disunity: The Lloyd George Coalition Government, 1918–22* (Oxford, 1979).
19 Newton and Porter, *Modernization Frustrated,* p. 39.
20 Davenport-Hines, *Dudley Docker,* pp. 117–19; Turner, 'The Politics of "Organized Business"', pp. 38–45.
21 Davenport-Hines, *Dudley Docker,* Chs. 5–7; John Turner, 'The British Commonwealth Union and the General Election of 1918', *Eng. Hist. Rev.,* XCIII (1978); Turner, 'The Politics of "Organized Business"', pp. 46–8; Terence Rodgers, 'Sir Alan Smith, the Industrial Group and the Politics of Unemployment, 1919–24', *Bus. Hist.,* XXXVIII (1986).
22 In *Modernization Frustrated,* Newton and Porter claim that one of the big weaknesses of the FBI was its failure to attract membership from consumer industries in the south of England (p. 56).
23 R.W.D. Boyce, 'Creating the Myth of Consensus: Public Opinion and Britain's Return to the Gold Standard in 1925', in P.L. Cottrell and D.E. Moggridge, eds. *Money and Power: Essays in Honour of L.S. Pressnell* (1988), p. 175; and idem, *British Capitalism at the Crossroads,* p. 31.
24 Cline, 'Winding Down the War Economy', pp. 171–7.
25 On the inflation and its effects see Susan Howson, 'The Origins of Dear Money, 1919–20', *Econ. Hist. Rev.,* 2nd ser. XXVII (1974); and on the boom, J.A. Dowie, '1919–20 is in Need of Attention', ibid. 2nd ser. XXVIII (1975).
26 *Collected Writings of J.M. Keynes,* IX (Cambridge, 1972), p. 57.
27 Burk, 'The Treasury', p. 101.
28 Newton and Porter, *Modernization Frustrated,* pp. 41–4.
29 Johnson, *Land Fit for Heroes,* pp. 364–76.
30 Drummond, *Imperial Economic Policy, 1917–39,* Ch. 2. See also his *British Economic Policy and the Empire,* pp. 70ff.
31 The best account of the whole episode remains S.M.H. Armitage, *The Politics of the Decontrol of Industry: Britain and the United States* (1969), pp. 8–15.
32 Phillip Williamson, 'Financiers, the Gold Standard and British Politics, 1925–1931', in Turner, *Businessmen and Politics,* p. 110.
33 For some of the wider political and defence implications of changing economic structures see Paul Kennedy, 'Strategy versus Finance in Twentieth Century Britain', in idem, *Strategy and Diplomacy* (1983); and Wolf D. Gruner, 'The British Political, Social and Economic System and the Decision for Peace or War: Reflections on Anglo-German Relations, 1800–1939', *Brit. Jour. Internat. Stud.,* 6 (1980).
34 The best recent overview of the relationship is D. Cameron Watt, *Succeeding John Bull: America in Britain's Place, 1900–1975* (Cambridge, 1984). Also helpful are David Reynolds, *The Creation of the Anglo-American Alliance, 1937–41: A Study in Competitive Co-operation* (1981), Ch. 1, which has many interesting general insights. A useful review article in this context is A.J. Thompson, 'From the Monroe Doctrine to the Marshall Plan', *Hist. Jour.,* 22 (1979).
35 Kathleen Burk, *Britain, America and the Sinews of War, 1914–1918* (1985); idem, 'The Diplomacy of Finance: British Financial Missions to the United States, 1914–1918', *Hist. Jour.,* 22 (1979).
36 Kathleen Burk, 'A Merchant Bank at War: the House of Morgan 1914–18', in Cottrell and Moggridge, *Money and Power.*
37 Keynes recognised in 1917 that without America's support 'the whole financial fabric of the Alliance will collapse'. See Kathleen Burk, 'J.M. Keynes and the Exchange Rate Crisis of 1917, *Econ. Hist. Rev.,* 2nd ser. XXXII (1979), p. 411. See also J.M. Cooper, 'The Command of Gold Reversed: American Loans to Britain, 1915–17', *Pacific Historical Review,* 45 (1976), p. 230.

38 Burk, 'A Merchant Bank at War', p. 164.
39 Gerd Hardach, *The First World War, 1914–18* (1977), Table 18, p. 148.
40 Max Beloff, *Imperial Sunset: Britain's Liberal Empire, 1897–1921* (1969), p. 178.
41 Roberta A. Dayer, 'Strange Bedfellows: J.P. Morgan and Co., Whitehall and the Wilson Administration during World War I', *Bus. Hist.*, XVIII (1978), pp. 130, 142–3.
42 Edward B. Parsons, 'Why the British Reduced the Flow of American Troops to Europe in August–October 1918', *Canadian Historical Review*, III (1977), p. 178.
43 Carl P. Parrini, *Heir to Empire: United States Economic Diplomacy, 1916–23* (Pittsburgh, Pa, 1969), esp. Ch. I; Michael J. Hogan, *Informal Entente: The Private Structure of Co-operation in Anglo-American Economic Diplomacy, 1918–1928* (Columbia, Miss., 1977), Ch. I.
44 Parsons, 'Why the British Reduced the Flow', passim.
45 For the evolution of thinking on reparations in Britain see Bunselmeyer, *The Cost of the War*, pp. 55–105.
46 Ibid. pp. 106–84; Seth P. Tillman, *Anglo-American Relations of the Paris Peace Conference of 1919* (Princeton, NJ, 1961), pp. 230–56. See also M.L. Dockrill and J.D. Goold, *Peace without Promise: Britain and the Peace Conferences, 1919–23* (1981), pp. 45–56.
47 Marc Trachtenberg, 'Reparations at the Paris Peace Conference', *Jour. Mod. Hist.*, 51 (1979).
48 On the link between reconstruction policy and reparations see Bunselmeyer, *The Cost of the War*, pp. 137–40.
49 On the German colonial issue see W. Roger Louis, *Great Britain and Germany's Lost Colonies* (Oxford, 1967), pp. 2–9, 108–35. As Louis observes, despite Wilson, German and Turkish colonies were divided in a manner that was similar to the scramble of the late nineteenth century (p. 155). See also Tillman, *Anglo-American Relations*, pp. 85–100; Dockrill and Goold, *Peace without Promise*, pp. 64–8; and below, pp. 211–13.
50 Tillman, *Anglo-American Relations.*
51 Parrini, *Heir to Empire*, Chs. 4 and 5. See also Frank Costigliola, *Awkward Dominion: American Political, Economic and Cultural Relations with Europe, 1919–1933* (Ithaca, NY, 1985), pp. 33–6, 38.
52 Cameron Watt, *Succeeding John Bull*, pp. 47–8.
53 On this fascinating sea-change see Stephen White, *Britain and the Bolshevik Revolution: A Study in the Politics of Diplomacy, 1920–1924* (1979), pp. 3–26; M.V. Glenny, 'The Anglo-Soviet Trade Agreement, March 1921', *Jour. Contemp. Hist.*, 2 (1970). When faced with the demand to carry on the fight against Bolshevism, Lloyd George argued that this would precipitate economic collapse in Britain and bring 'bankruptcy and Bolshevism in these islands'. C.J. Lowe and M.J. Dockrill, The *Mirage of Power: British Foreign Policy, 1902–1922* (1973), II, p. 324.
54 Dockrill and Goold, *Peace without Promise*, pp. 75–6, 85–6. Lowe and Dockrill claim that Britain adopted a conciliatory attitude towards Germany and Russia after 1920 because she saw them as being important to the world economy, while Turkey, a far less weighty economic entity, continued to be treated harshly. *The Mirage of Power*, II, p. 374.
55 Roberta Allbert Dayer, *Finance and Empire: Sir Charles Addis, 1861–1945* (1988), pp. 114–15.
56 A British Cabinet minute quoted in Roberta A. Dayer, 'The British War Debts to the United States and the Anglo-Japanese Alliance, 1920–3', *Pacific Historical Review*, 45 (1976), p. 584.
57 Apart from Dayer, the war debt issue is also treated in Hogan, *Informal Entente*, pp. 50–6 and Costigliola, *Awkward Dominion*, pp. 38–9, 81–6. Costigliola emphasises the fact that the British had to pay up in the end if they were to remain a great international financial centre (p. 106). For some strategic implications of the Washington Agreements see R.B. Holland, *Britain and the Commonwealth Alliance, 1918–39* (1981), pp. 11–15.
58 An excellent overview of the decade is given in Frank Costigliola, 'Anglo-American Financial Rivalry in the 1920s', *Jour. Econ. Hist.*, 37 (1977).
59 The Genoa Conference is now beginning to receive the attention it deserves from those interested in post-war British economic foreign policy. This account is based largely

upon Parrini, *Heir to Empire,* Ch. 6; Hogan, *Informal Entente,* pp. 45–7; Stephen V.O. Clarke, 'The Reconstruction of the International Financial System: the Attempts of 1922 and 1933' (Princeton Studies in International Finance, No. 33, 1978); Costigliola, *Awkward Dominion,* pp. 107–8; Costigliola, 'Anglo-American Financial Rivalry', pp. 913–20. See also the recent study by Anne Orde, *British Policy and European Reconstruction after the First World War* (Cambridge, 1990), Chs. 5 and 6; and Carole Fink, *The Genoa Conference: European Diplomacy, 1921–1922,* (Chapel Hill, NC, 1984).

60 As well as the sources referred to in n. 59, see White, *Britain and the Bolshevik Revolution,* Ch. 3.

61 Lowe and Dockrill, *The Mirage of Power,* II, p. 332.

62 R.S. Sayers, *The Bank of England, 1891–1944,* I (Cambridge 1976), pp. 163, 166–73; Hogan, *Informal Entente,* pp. 60–6; Orde, *British Policy and Reconstruction,* pp. 135–44, 266–74. See also Atkin, *British Overseas Investment,* pp. 93–7, and Kathleen Burk, *Morgan Grenfell, 1838–1988: The Biography of a Merchant Bank* (Cambridge, 1989), pp. 139–4. For a broad view of policy see W. Adam Brown, *The International Cold Standard Reinterpreted, 1914–1934,* I (New York, 1940), pp. 346–50.

63 Dayer, *Sir Charles Addis,* pp. 152–3; Clarke, 'The Reconstruction of the International Financial System', pp. 13–14.

64 Sayers, *Bank of England,* I, pp. 160, 168.

65 Dayer, *Sir Charles Addis,* pp. 173–4. On the Bank's role, see also Alicia Teichova, 'Versailles and the Expansion of the Bank of England into Central Europe', in N. Horn and J. Kocka, eds. *Recht und Entwicklung in Grossunternehmen im 19.und frühen 20. Jahrhundert* (Göttingen, 1979).

66 Norman was encouraged in his ideas of informal cooperation between central banks through his friendly relationship with Benjamin Strong, Governor of the Federal Reserve Bank. But the 'Fed.' did not have the authority in the United States possessed by the Bank of England in Britain. See Sayers, *The Bank of England,* I, pp. 154–62, and Dayer, *Sir Charles Addis,* p. 140.

67 Costigliola, *Awkward Dominion,* pp. 113–4.

68 Sayers, *Bank of England,* I, pp. 302–3.

69 Lyndhurst Falkiner Giblin, *The Growth of a Central Bank: The Development of the Commonwealth Bank of Australia, 1924–45* (Melbourne, 1951), pp. 17–18.

70 The word was used by Otto Niemeyer, then of the Treasury, later of the Bank of England. Dayer, *Sir Charles Addis,* p. 165.

71 Sayers, *Bank of England,* I, pp. 202–3.

72 Stephen A. Shuker, *The End of French Predominance in Europe: The Financial Crisis of 1924 and the Adoption of the Dawes Plan* (Chapel Hill, NC, 1976), pp. 383–93; Alan Cassells, 'Repairing the *Entente Cordiale* and the New Diplomacy', *Hist. Jour.,* 23 (1980).

73 See Sayers, *Bank of England,* I, pp. 181–3, and Burk, *Morgan Grenfell,* pp. 141–3.

74 For good accounts of this episode see Hogan, *Informal Entente,* pp. 66–71; S.V.O. Clarke, *Central Bank Co-operation, 1924–31* (New York, 1967), pp. 58–67.

75 Costigliola, *Awkward Dominion,* p. 128.

76 Boyce, *British Capitalism at the Crossroads,* pp. 57–60, emphasises this. Clarke argues that 'it is clear that Germany's imminent stabilization had put Norman under great pressure to commit himself to an early return', Clarke, *Central Bank Co-operation,* p. 66.

77 R.G. Hawtrey, then an economist at the Treasury, warned his colleagues in 1924 that 'the transition to a general gold standard may be a very short one, and London may be left isolated with a paper currency in a gold-using world. Should this occur, the danger to the position of London would be aggravated'. Quoted in Adrian Ham, *Treasury Rules: Recurrent Themes in British Economic Policy* (1981), p. 46.

78 Sources for this rather curious episode include L.S. Pressnell, '1925: the Burden of Sterling', *Econ. Hist. Rev.,* 2nd ser. XXXI (1978), pp. 71–3; Costigliola, 'Anglo-American Financial Rivalry', pp. 920–3; Costigliola, *Awkward Dominion,* pp. 128, 130–1; Dayer, *Sir Charles Addis,* pp. 170–1. See also Bruce Dalgaard, *South Africa's Impact on Britain's Return to Gold, 1925* (New York, 1981).

79 Quoted in D.E. Moggridge, *British Monetary Policy, 1924–31: The Norman Conquest of $4.86* (Cambridge, 1972), p. 76; also quoted in Costigliola, 'Anglo-American Financial Rivalry', p. 925.

80 Quoted in Boyce, *British Capitalism at the Crossroads,* pp. 65–6. These sentiments chimed in with deep worries about the level of invisible income (ibid. p. 67).

81 Ibid. pp. 79–90, and idem, 'Creating the Myth of Consensus', pp. 178–9, 181–7, 189–91. Also R.E. Catterall, 'Attitudes to, and the Impact of, British Monetary Policy in the 1920s', *Revue internationale d'histoire de la banque,* 12 (1976); and Geoffrey Ingham, *Capitalism Divided? The City and Industry in British Social Development* (Cambridge, 1984), pp. 175–87. For an earlier view see L.J. Hume, 'The Gold Standard and Deflation: Issues and Attitudes in the Nineteen Twenties', *Economica,* new ser. XXX (1963), reprinted in Sidney Pollard, ed. *The Gold Standard and Employment Policies Between the Wars* (1970). See also R.S. Sayers, 'The Return to Gold, 1925', in L.S. Pressnell, ed. *Studies in the Industrial Revolution* (1960), and W. Adams Brown, *England and the New Gold Standard, 1919–26* (1929), Ch. 10. Both are reprinted in Pollard, *Gold Standard.*

82 'The Chancellor finally decided in favour of a return to gold – partly as he himself said, because he knew that if he adopted this course Niemeyer [at the Treasury] would give him irrefutable arguments to support it, whereas if he refused to adopt it he would be faced with criticism from the City authorities against which he would not have any effective answer'. Frederick Leith Ross, *Money Talks* (1968), p. 92, quoted in Ham, *Treasury Rules,* p. 54. Leith Ross became Deputy Controller of Finance at the Treasury in 1925.

83 Norman, quoted in Moggridge, *British Monetary Policy,* pp. 270–1. See also the discussion of policy in ibid. pp. 64–70, and Hogan, *Informal Entente,* pp. 71–5.

84 For an interpretation of the return to gold as a restoration of authority by the Bank and the Treasury, see Jim Tomlinson, *Problems of British Economic Policy, 1870–1914* (1981), Ch. 6.

85 The City saw the return as 'a vindication of British financial integrity, and an assurance that British financial prestige and power would regain much that it had lost'. Brown, 'England and the New Gold Standard', in Pollard, *The Cold Standard,* p. 61.

86 Moggridge, *British Monetary Policy,* thinks that a 10 per cent devaluation would have been reasonable (pp. 233, 245–50). For sympathetic modem discussions of the policy adopted in 1925, see A.J. Youngson, *The British Economy, 1920–1966* (1967), pp. 23–35 and 171ff; and B. Williams, 'Montagu Norman and Banking Policy in the Nineteen Twenties', *Yorkshire Bulletin of Economic and Social Research,* 11 (1959–60).

87 Dayer, *Sir Charles Addis,* pp. 179, 181–2; Costigliola, *Awkward Dominion,* pp. 200–5.

88 Sayers, *Bank of England,* I, pp. 191–2.

89 Note the pained tone of Henry Clay, one of the Bank of England's advisers: 'For some years past it had been more than current comment in Europe, both in political and banking circles, that Governor Norman desired to establish some sort of dictatorship over the central banks of Europe and that I was collaborating with him'. Sir Henry Clay, *Lord Norman* (1957), p. 265.

90 Richard Hemmig Meyer, *Banker's Diplomacy: Monetary Stabilization in the Nineteen Twenties* (1970); J.L. Kooker, 'French Financial Diplomacy: the Inter-War Years', in Benjamin M. Rowland, ed. *Balance of Power or Hegemony* (New York, 1976); *Sayers, Bank of England,* I, pp. 191–5; Boyce, *British Capitalism at the Crossroads,* pp. 141–9, 158–66.

91 Boyce, *British Capitalism at the Crossroads,* pp. 90–5.

92 The classic text here is Robert Skidelsky, *Politicians and the Slump: The Labour Government of 1929–31* (1967). See also Alan Booth and Melvyn Pack, *Employment, Capital and Economic Policy: Britain, 1918–1939* (1985).

93 Donald Winch, *Economics and Policy* (1970), pp. 112–15, 118–22; Skidelsky, *Politicians and the Slump,* pp. 451–6; G.C. Peden, *Keynes, the Treasury and British Economic Policy* (1988), pp. 11, 27–9.

94 Skidelsky, *Politicians and the Slump,* esp. pp. 406–9.

95 M. De Cecco, 'The Last of the Romans', in Robert Skidelsky, ed. *The End of the Keynesian Era* (1977), pp. 18–24.
96 M.D. Goldberg, 'Anglo-American Economic Competition, 1920–1930', *Economy and History,* 16 (1973) provides a useful background.
97 Boyce, *British Capitalism at the Crossroads,* pp. 106–18, 176–84; Holland, *Britain and the Commonwealth Alliance,* p. 37.
98 Cameron Watt, *Succeeding John Bull,* pp. 56–7; B.J.C. McKercher, *The Second Baldwin Government and the United States, 1924–1929: Attitudes and Diplomacy* (Cambridge, 1984).
99 This is one of the main themes of Boyce, *British Capitalism at the Crossroads.*
100 Ibid. esp. pp. 232–3, 250–7. See also Forrest Capie, *Depression and Protectionism: Britain between the Wars* (1983), pp. 40–76.
101 Boyce, *British Capitalism at the Crossroads,* p. 253. On financial interests in protection see also Dayer, *Sir Charles Addis,* p. 217.
102 Michael Dintenfass, '"The Politics of Producers' Co-operation": the FBI–TUC–NCEO Talks, 1929–33', in Turner, *Businessmen and Politics,* pp. 84–7.
103 Holland, *Britain and the Commonwealth Alliance,* pp. 26–7.
104 R.W.D. Boyce, 'America, Britain and the Triumph of Imperial Protectionism in Britain, 1929–30', *Millennium,* 3 (1974), p. 63.
105 Boyce, *British Capitalism at the Crossroads,* pp. 257–66, 272–5.
106 Holland, *Britain and the Commonwealth Alliance,* p. 110. On the electoral politics of tariffs in the 1920s see C. Cook, *The Age of Alignment* (1971), pp. 140–78. For the imperial preference element see W.K. Hancock, *Survey of British Commonwealth Affairs,* Vol. II, Pt. I, (Oxford, 1940), pp. 143–7, and Drummond, *British Economic Policy and the Empire,* pp. 60–64.
107 Williamson, 'Financiers, the Gold Standard and British Politics, 1925–1931', pp. 119–20.
108 Ibid. pp. 120–9. See also his article, 'A "Banker's Ramp"? Financiers and the British Political Crisis of 1931', *Eng. Hist. Rev.,* XCIX (1984); Boyce, *British Capitalism at the Crossroads,* pp. 348–55.
109 Boyce, *British Capitalism at the Crossroads,* pp. 346–8.
110 See the comment of Keynes in *Collected Works,* IX, p. 245.
111 On the Bank of International Settlements (BIS) and its connection with the Young Plan of 1929 dealing with reparations see Dayer, *Sir Charles Addis,* pp. 352–8. There were some in the City who worried about the BIS as a 'super-bank' which might challenge London. See Boyce, *British Capitalism at the Crossroads,* p. 196; Burk, *Morgan Grenfell,* pp. 144–5.
112 See the argument in Dayer, Sir *Charles Addis,* pp. 217–30. Addis had been seriously worried by the deflationary consequences of the United States' thirst for gold in the late 1920s and had begun to recognise that the return to gold might have had adverse consequences for Britain (see pp. 199, 210–12).
113 Williamson, 'Financiers, the Gold Standard and British Politics', pp. 113, 117–18; Boyce, *British Capitalism at the Crossroads,* pp. 288–91. For a recent analysis of the causes of the 1931 crisis see Forrest Capie, Terrence E. Miller and Geoffrey E. Wood, 'What Happened in 1931?', in Forrest Capie and Geoffrey E. Wood, *Financial Crises;* and, for an extended treatment, Diane B. Kunz, *The Battle for Britain's Gold Standard in 1931* (1987). See also Burk, *Morgan Grenfell,* pp. 148–56.

20

'A LATTER-DAY EXPRESSION OF FINANCIAL IMPERIALISM'

The origins of the Sterling Area, 1931–39[1]

Financial crisis and economic orthodoxy

The pre-1913 international financial system, which the British strove mightily to reintroduce in the 1920s, depended on Britain's ability to maintain the convertibility of sterling at a fixed rate, to lend liberally and to maintain a free market for imports.[2] In the 1930s the pound went off gold, the balance of payments on current account lapsed into deficit, and overseas lending was severely limited. Free trade was abandoned in 1932, and was replaced by a tariff on manufactured imports and by a system of imperial preference supported by quotas and other bilateral arrangements with empire and foreign countries. Did this mean that Britain's traditional policies had been fully overthrown, and that the Tariff Reform dream of an imperial system supporting a revived industrial Britain had come fully into its own? The main purpose of what follows is to suggest that the answer to this question must be in the negative. The gold standard was abandoned in 1931 with extreme reluctance; tariffs were introduced in support of time-honoured monetary and financial policies both at home and overseas; and the Ottawa negotiations and the other trade arrangements of the 1930s make more sense if they, too, are considered as part of an attempt to salvage as much as possible of the traditional financial arrangements from the disasters of 1929–32.

The introduction of a tariff on manufactured imports in 1932 was not primarily, as historians have sometimes argued, a device designed to stem the growth of industrial unemployment as export values collapsed after 1929.[3] The central preoccupation of governments from 1929 was to maintain the external value of the pound; its defence was undertaken with the traditional complex of objectives in mind.[4] Without a stable currency, Britain's international leadership and her invisible earnings would be jeopardised.[5] Of equal importance was the recognition, as strong in the 1930s as in the run-up to the restoration of the gold standard in 1925, that a commitment to defending the pound would require severe monetary discipline: with no gold standard to defend, governments might easily give in to the temptation to spend their way out of a crisis. Even in the midst of the deflationary whirlwind of 1931, officials at the Bank of England were worried about inflation if the currency was allowed to float. One of Norman's advisers drew the obvious moral: 'with a floating rate control of domestic credit conditions must be even stricter than it is when the danger signal of weak exchange automatically compels credit restrictions'.[6] Financial discipline meant balanced budgets: the Treasury welcomed the cheap money policy made possible by falling interest rates in the wake of Britain's abandonment of the $4.86 rate chiefly because it allowed for a conversion of part of the national debt to the lower interest rates, cut government expenditure, made fewer demands on the taxpayer and made it easier to avoid deficits. By 1930 a tariff had other great attractions for those who stood by orthodoxy: it could, for example, help to restore confidence in sterling by improving the trade balance and increasing government revenue when other sources were drying up in a contracting economy.[7]

For the Labour Party, many of whose supporters strongly favoured free trade in the consumer's interest, the prospect of tariffs, like the prospect of deflation, proved disastrously divisive. The National Government, largely staffed by Conservatives, which took over in August 1931 had no such scruples. Support for the tariff was strong in sections of the Conservative Party and had been growing in the 1920s, as we have seen. What was new in 1931 was the call for a tariff on grounds of 'financial stability'.[8]

The National Government was formed to forestall devaluation. When, six weeks later, this proved impossible and Britain left gold in September 1931, fundamental policy objectives did not undergo radical change. Both government and officials adjusted rapidly to the idea that some devaluation of the pound against the dollar and other currencies had its advantages in making Britain more industrially competitive; the Exchange Equalisation Account, created under the auspices of the Bank of England to manage the currency, at first aimed at keeping sterling low against the dollar and the franc.[9] But a stable currency remained a priority. Although there was considerable disagreement initially about the most acceptable rate, all those in authority were determined to prevent a steady slide in the pound's value. Continuous depreciation would have increased the competitiveness of industrial exports but it would also have pushed up import prices, lowered real wages and, it was feared, set off a wage–price spiral ending in runaway inflation with the same consequences as in Europe in the early 1920s. Besides this, it was well understood that a government without a commitment of any kind to particular rates or bands of rates for the currency might give in to the eternal temptation to spend more money than it gathered in revenue, with similar inflationary consequences.[10] Insofar as tariffs, by cutting down manufactured imports in particular, helped to restore the trade balance and, therefore, to support the value of sterling, they were an aid to 'sound' finance. This was principally the reason why they were introduced, in emergency in 1931 and permanently the year after. The relative insignificance of the claims of industrial exports in the crisis can be gauged from the fact that the government believed, rightly or wrongly, that by raising the exchange rate tariffs would exacerbate the unemployment problem in the short run.

After devaluation, it was hoped that 'sterling would depreciate relative to the currencies of Britain's industrial competitors but [the British] encouraged the principal raw material suppliers to link their currencies to the pound at the traditional parity'.[11] Out of the last concern came the Sterling Area, a group of countries which were heavily dependent on the British market (Tables 20.1 and 20.2), did most

TABLE 20.1 British trade with the Sterling Area, 1929 and 1937 (£m.)

	Exports to	*Net imports from*	*Trade balance*	*Trade balance as % of exports*
1929				
European Sterling Area[a]	36.8	116.2	–79.4	–215.8
Argentina	29.1	81.9	–52.8	–181.6
British empire[b]	289.3	293.8	–4.5	–1.6
Rest of the Sterling Area[c]	21.0	29.0	–8.0	–42.9
Total Sterling Area[d]	376.2	520.9	–144.8	–38.5
Non-sterling trade	353.2	590.2	–237.0	–67.1
Total trade	729.4	1,111.1	–381.8	–52.4
1937				
European Sterling Area[a]	49.7	104.7	–55.0	–110.7
Argentina	20.0	59.5	–39.5	–196.9
British empire[b]	224.2	305.1	–80.9	–36.1
Rest of the Sterling Area[c]	14.5	22.1	–7.6	–52.4
Total Sterling Area[d]	308.4	491.4	–182.9	–59.3
Non-sterling trade	212.9	461.3	–248.4	–116.8
Total trade	521.3	952.7	–431.3	–82.7

Source: Trade figures are from B.R. Mitchell and P. Deane, *Abstracts of British Historical Statistics* (Cambridge, 1962) and *Statistical Abstracts for the United Kingdom* (HMSO). Total Sterling Area is the sum of European Sterling Area, Argentina, British empire and Rest of the Sterling Area. The list of Sterling Area countries is taken from De Vegh, *The Pound Sterling*, pp. 7–9. De Vegh defined three groups: first, 'those which hold all official international assets as sterling balances or securities, i.e. Australia, the British colonies (except Hong Kong, British Honduras, British Malaya) the British mandates, Eire and Siam. Second, 'countries which hold sterling but which feel free to alter their holdings', e.g. British Malaya, Denmark, Egypt, Estonia, Hong Kong, India and Burma, Iraq, Latvia, Lithuania, New Zealand, Portugal and South Africa. Third, those 'which hold official gold and/or other currency reserves as well as sterling reserves, but in actual practice peg their currencies to the pound sterling', e.g. Argentina, Finland, Norway and Sweden. De Vegh regarded the inclusion of Argentina and Sweden in this list as 'debatable', although this may be because he was writing at a time when the flight from sterling was becoming pronounced.

Notes:

[a] The European Sterling Area consists of Norway, Sweden, Denmark, Finland, Latvia, Lithuania and Estonia. Iceland is omitted.

[b] The British empire total includes Eire but excludes Canada and British Honduras.

[c] The Rest of the Sterling Area includes Portugal, Iraq, Egypt and Thailand (Siam).

TABLE 20.2 Share of the United Kingdom in the foreign trade of some Sterling Area countries, 1929, 1933 and 1937 (per cent)

	Exports			*Imports*		
	1929	*1933*	*1937*	*1929*	*1933*	*1937*
Australia	45	54	52	41	42	42
Denmark	56	64	53	15	28	38
Egypt	34	41	31	21	23	22
Eire	92	94	91	78	70	50
Estonia	38	37	34	10	18	17
Finland	38	46	43	13	21	19
India	21	30	32	42	41	32
Latvia	27	43	38	8	22	21
Norway	27	20	25	21	23	18
New Zealand	74	86	76	49	51	50
Portugal	23	22	22	27	28	18
Sweden	25	26	23	17	18	12
South Africa	66	78	79	43	50	43

Source: League of Nations, *International Currency Experience: The Lessons of the Inter-war Period* (Geneva, 1944), p. 48.

of their trade in sterling, fixed their own currencies in relation to the pound, and held some or all of their reserves in sterling. Membership of the area in the 1930s included not only the territories of the British Empire (except for Canada and British Honduras, which were in the dollar bloc) but also a large group of countries economically dependent on Britain, some of them in Europe.[12]

The holding of sterling as a reserve asset as well as for transactions purposes had begun well before 1913, as Lindert has shown,[13] and the Imperial Economic Conference of 1923 recommended that empire governments should increase the practice,[14] no doubt as part of Britain's attempt to follow up her Genoa proposals. So, there is something in the claim of Henry Clay, an adviser to the Bank of England, that the suspension of gold payments in 1931 'brought out the true nature of the Sterling Area'.[15] Apart from the dependent parts of the empire, which had no option, the rest of the countries which followed sterling after September 1931 were theoretically free to resist incorporation but, in practice, were forced into it because of a heavy dependence on British trade, or British credit, or both.[16]

> Not only would [these countries] have been faced with a serious loss [in their own currency] on the reserves they held in sterling, if they had refused to depreciate their own currency with sterling: they could not face the obstruction to their exports (and stimulus to imports) which an appreciation of their currency on sterling would have involved.[17]

The emergence of the Sterling Area marks an important stage in the decline of sterling from its position of 'Top Currency' before 1913 to the 'Master Currency' status within the empire that it held after World War II.[18] Its emergence had been anticipated by Keynes as early as August 1931 when, in giving up $4.86 for dead, he had urged the Labour government to take the initiative in forming a sterling bloc on the basis of a devalued pound. 'Many people in the City', he claimed, 'far more than might be expected . . . are now in favour of something of this sort'.[19] London had accepted that its orbit of operations was permanently reduced and was ready to make the best of it. After devaluation, the Treasury soon appreciated the value of creating conditions which

> make it easy for as many as possible of the unstable currencies to base themselves on sterling so that we may become leaders of a sterling block which, pending our stabilization on gold, would have the best opportunities for mutual trade and would give sterling a new force in the world.[20]

The necessary prerequisite was a stable pound, albeit at a lower parity than $4.86. If Britain could retain financial stability she would also retain the confidence of sterling-holders and 'the leadership of the block will be ours and the vital commercial business which it carries with it'.[21] Balanced budgets and the sterling bloc were intertwined from the beginning.[22] Throughout the 1930s the Treasury was worried about retaining the allegiance of sterling-holders, especially non-empire ones, and used this to hammer home its views on the need for financial restraint at home.[23]

In economic policy terms there was little change in fundamentals during the 1930s. Governments were not even Keynesian in drift, let alone philosophy. There was a great deal of intellectual debate, involving enlightened, younger members of both Conservative and Labour Parties, about the need for public works, redistribution of income and a new role for the state in regenerating depressed regions, where unemployment remained very high even at the height of the boom in 1937. But this discussion had little impact on the National Government which, under Treasury guidance, stuck firmly to the view that modernisation and recovery depended upon increased efficiency in the private sector and that the best aid the government could give was to keep taxation down and balance its books.[24]

Financial imperialism without gold

For most of the 1930s the countries of the sterling bloc were building up their reserves, so the demand for sterling was higher than was justified by current transaction needs.[25] The result of this additional demand for sterling was to offset, to some degree, the efforts of the Exchange Equalisation Account, created at the Bank of England, to keep the sterling rate below its pre-1931 level against other major currencies. Consequently, the terms of trade between Britain and the rest of world moved in Britain's favour, imports were encouraged and exports discouraged. Cheaper imports certainly raised real wages and living standards in Britain; however, it has been estimated that the use of sterling to build reserves rather than to purchase goods from Britain may have reduced British exports by between 6 per cent and 10 per cent between 1932 and 1938 and deepened the unemployment problem in the severely depressed export areas. The tendency to import more from, and export less to, sterling bloc countries was also reinforced by the decision of important members, such as Australia and New Zealand, to link their currencies with sterling at a devalued rate compared with the 1920s. In addition, by an intricate process, demand for sterling as a reserve reduced the money supply in Britain. The rise in sterling balances increased competition for Treasury bills between British and overseas banks, and reduced the British banks' supply of liquid assets as well as keeping Treasury bill rates low.[26]

As we have seen, industrial exports did less well out of the sterling system of the 1930s than invisibles, and this invites comparisons with experience before 1913. In saying this, it must be remembered that the overvaluation of sterling would have been reduced once sterling countries had built up sufficient reserve levels and that, in 1938, the shedding of sterling resources in the trade depression of that year pushed down the sterling rate and helped to cushion the impact of the depression on export values.[27] Moreover, the creation of the sterling bloc was valuable in maintaining liquidity in the crisis after 1929 and was an important element in the hesitant recovery of the world economy in the 1930s, thus making a considerable contribution to the growth of exports from their low point in 1932. Nonetheless, the reasoning behind the encouragement of the sterling bloc, like the argument for a tariff, shows how the defence of orthodox finance (and the assumption that the fortunes of industrial exports and the economic health of the older industrial areas were a direct consequence of this defence), was almost a reflex action among the political elite and their advisers.[28] As we shall see, these presuppositions about maintaining Britain's economic role in the world had a marked influence upon her trade negotiations with the empire countries after 1932 and with other sterling-bloc members.

When the tariff was permanently established in 1932, the crown colonies were exempted from its provisions; but the Dominions and India were only granted free entry pending negotiations with Britain at the Ottawa Conference about reciprocal concessions in their markets. At Ottawa the British hoped initially to persuade the Dominions to lower their tariffs and allow empire free trade. According to the British, this policy would stimulate exports, increase demand for Dominion produce in Britain and, by encouraging growth in Britain, allow for foreign investment.[29] In practice, no Dominion was willing to lower tariffs significantly and all of them decided instead to give Britain preferences in their markets in return for similar concessions for themselves in the British market.

As a result of Ottawa and subsequent negotiations, and despite taking measures to protect her own farmers from Dominion as well as foreign competition, Britain made more generous trade concessions to the Dominions than they made to her and received fewer benefits in return. Exports to the Dominions (including Canada, which received the benefit of empire status without being a member of the sterling bloc) had averaged £143m. in 1925–9 but had fallen to £111m., or 22 per cent, by 1934–8. Even when set against an overall fall in export values of 38 per cent in this period, the result was disappointing for British exporters. Against this, while net imports as a whole fell by 29 per cent, net imports from the Dominions rose from £183m. in 1925–9 to £189m. in 1934–8. Trade with India and the crown colonies showed the same trend. Exports from Britain were actually 44 per cent lower in 1934–8 than in 1925–9, while imports from them were only 15 per cent down on 1920s levels in the mid-1930s. This evidence fits with Drummond's rough estimate that, by 1937, the concessions won by Britain at Ottawa pushed up her exports to the Dominions by about 5 per cent, whereas the concessions she made may have added 10 per cent to her imports from the Dominions in the same year.[30] One result of this trend was that Britain's balance of trade deficit with her empire widened considerably.

The preferential system created as a result of the Ottawa Conference did not, of course, come up to the expectations of the Dominions.[31] Leaving aside permanent irritants such as Britain's determination, inexplicable to the Dominions, not only to support her own farmers but also to preserve some of the home market for foreigners like the Argentines and the Danes, the Dominions began to realise that the British market was not big enough, or growing fast enough, to ensure a level of export-led growth sufficient to solve their massive unemployment problems.[32] But the new arrangements were an even greater disappointment to British industrial exporters: it is worth asking why.

There are a number of obvious reasons why empire countries should have done better out of the preferential system than Britain. The collapse in empire primary produce prices in the depression was catastrophic, and recovery very slow, so that demand for British industrial goods was bound to suffer badly. On the other hand, Britain's national income fell relatively little in 1929–32, and was much higher in 1937 than in 1929, thus keeping import demand reasonably buoyant when compared with, for example, that of the United States. Given the persistence of balance of payments problems in the 1930s, and an inability to borrow as British overseas investment dried up, it is not surprising that recovery in the Dominions included a significant degree of import-substituting manufactures. The British underestimated the growing manufacturing interests in the Dominions, especially the power of the industrial lobbies in Canada and Australia and, in doing so, were grievously mistaken about the extent of the complementarity between the white settlement areas and the mother country. The British originally went to Ottawa believing that they could obtain tariffs on their exports to the Dominions and India low enough to allow them into empire markets on equal terms with domestic industry. Instead, after much haggling, they were given preferences which resulted from a further rise in Dominion tariffs on foreign goods.[33]

Besides this, however, there was also a wider sense in which it was necessary to the furtherance of the sterling system that Britain should accord the Dominions – and some other members of the Sterling Area – more generous treatment than they gave to her. In January 1932 H.D. Henderson, a prominent member of the

Economic Advisory Committee, made the point that the relationship between a British balance of trade deficit and the strength or weakness of sterling was not an obvious one: a big deficit need not necessarily imply a steadily falling pound. If, for example, Britain increased imports from the empire the deficit would increase too, but this would not put a strain on the sterling exchange rate because it would mainly result in an addition to the empire's London sterling balances

> with the result that the governments of India and Australia would find it easier to meet their sterling obligations without recourse to fresh borrowing. So far from weakening sterling, this would actually tend to strengthen it, by diminishing fears of eventual financial default by those countries, which form an intimate part of the British financial system.

He went on to say immediately:

> Conversely and for the same reasons, it would do nothing to strengthen sterling but something to weaken it, if we were to reduce our imports from India and Australia, whether by consuming less or by replacing these imports by home consumption.[34]

Empire countries were already good customers for British exports, and Britain's balance of trade with them was more favourable than it was with most other countries. Since the empire countries were often considerable borrowers and were dependent on British financial services and shipping, they had heavy bills to meet for invisible items. In the circumstances of the 1930s some of them would have had considerable difficulty in meeting their debt obligations and in building up sterling reserves unless access to sterling was improved. Default or repudiation could have destabilised sterling and might even have led to the collapse of the sterling bloc. Generous provision for the empire in British markets, and an adverse movement in the balance of her trade with the empire, were the price Britain had to pay for a smoothly functioning sterling bloc. Before 1913, Britain not only kept an open market which allowed debtors to acquire sterling, but also lent considerable amounts abroad and thereby allowed debtors to increase steadily their demands for British goods. In the 1920s the system still worked, though more sluggishly, as British overseas investment began to decline. In the 1930s overseas new issues declined to an average of only £33m. per year between 1932 and 1939 (of which £27m. per year went to the empire) and were tiny in comparison with repayments every year from 1933 onwards.[35] Faced with both a shrinking world market and a drying up of loans, the chief colonial debtors needed preferential treatment in the British market to obtain sterling, while simultaneously keeping tight control on imports of British goods. If, at Ottawa, the British had negotiated a better settlement for their industrial exporters in the Dominions, this 'success' could have imperilled the latter's ability to meet their sterling obligations.

Over the years, empire countries had been very important customers for British exporters and, from 1870 onwards, had often compensated the older industrial areas of Britain for declining markets elsewhere. But in the 1930s they could not keep up their demand for British commodities without threatening the whole sterling system. Some other members of the sterling bloc were, however, not quite in the same position. Some non-empire sterling holders had benefited as much as the others from the openness of the British market in the past, but lack of kinship relations and their independence of British capital markets had restricted their demand for Britain's exports. Unlike the empire countries, many of them had run heavy balance of payments surpluses with Britain in the 1920s. Given their dependence on the British market – which increased as other major markets contracted faster than Britain's after 1929 – and given that British exports to them could be increased substantially without precipitating balance of payment crises there, it was possible for Britain to make vigorous attempts to promote her industrial exports. In the 1930s it was relatively easy, too, for her to restrict their imports in favour of British farmers and those of the Dominions without fear of retaliation, and also to use the threat of further cuts to force these countries to take more British exports.

Immediately after Ottawa, for example, Britain signed an agreement with Denmark, 64 per cent of whose exports came to Britain in 1933 (Table 20.2). The agreement, signed in 1933, gave certain quotas for Danish produce in return for reduced duties on British exports to Denmark and an undertaking by the Danes to purchase specified quantities of certain industrial commodities, especially coal. As a result, the ratio between British imports of Danish produce and British exports to Denmark fell from 5.4:1 in 1932 to 2.2:1 in 1937.[36] Similar agreements were made with a number of other European countries including some, like the Soviet Union, which were not within the sterling group, but which had a large balance of trade surplus with Britain. These bilateral agreements were favourable to British exporters simply because the authorities could squeeze the European sterling-holders without precipitating a sterling crisis. Even here, though, success was limited. The share of the European sterling-holders in British exports rose from 5 per cent to 9.5 per cent between 1929 and 1937, but their share had already increased in the depression, reaching 7.2 per cent in 1932,[37] so the subsequent agreements confirmed a trend rather than established an entirely new one. Britain's gains were also limited because, in pushing her exports in these markets, she often displaced foreigners who found compensation by cutting into Britain's share of trade in the non-sterling world.[38]

Not all the non-empire countries dependent upon Britain were in this rather helpless position. There is no doubt, for example, that, despite her desperate need for markets for her beef, Argentina's debt position, her threat to hinder repayments and her operation of exchange controls, had some influence on commercial relations with Britain.[39] It is also worth noting that those countries, including Germany, which had frozen payments for British exports in the financial crisis, were treated by Britain in a very similar manner. In negotiating agreements with them, the main objective of the British government was to collect debts rather than to maximise trade flows; if necessary, imports from the debtors were encouraged and British exports suppressed in order to achieve this goal.[40]

Table 20.1 helps to confirm these findings. In those countries in the sterling bloc which, in 1929, were already good customers for British industrial exports – the empire countries – Britain had to offer entry into her market on easy terms but had to be restrained in pushing her own exports. Britain's share of the empire's markets rose but not as rapidly as did the empire's share of the British market, and Britain's balance of trade deficit with this imperial group increased significantly.[41] In those areas where export performance had been less satisfactory in the past, and where the countries concerned had strong balance of trade or balance of payments surpluses with Britain, imports could be restricted and there was some leeway for export promotion. Argentina, which had borrowed large amounts of British capital, could retain more or less the status quo in relative terms. The European members of the sterling bloc, who were more vulnerable because they were not heavy debtors, had their import share stabilised but also had to take a much larger share of British exports, and their trade surpluses with Britain were sharply reduced.

Emphasising the importance of sterling and the sterling bloc in the eyes of the British authorities in the 1930s alters some of the judgements made in the past about Britain's loss of economic influence within the empire in the 1930s. The use of tariffs to hamper British trade in India and the Dominions has led some scholars to wonder whether the British had any imperial authority at all,[42] whereas, as we have shown, concessions on tariffs were often a key part of the strategy for maintaining international financial stability. Within the orbit of the sterling bloc, Britain's power was still impressive. The creation of the bloc is a tribute to that; most members joined because they simply could not survive outside it. Hence South Africa, although keen on the retention of a gold standard because of her own exports of gold, was forced into line with sterling in 1933. This is hardly surprising considering that 78 per cent of her imports came from Britain in 1933 and 50 per cent of her own exports went to Britain in return (Table 20.2).[43]

Britain still aspired, and with considerable success, to maintain a high degree of financial authority within the sterling camp. Tariffs and trade were negotiable matters, but the British always took it for granted that finance was too important a matter to be left to mere colonials, even white ones. Imperial preference was in many ways Britain's substitute for the inability to lend – what meagre loans were available in the 1930s usually went to area members, often to help them build up sterling balances[44] – and a means of helping her own recovery, and that of the empire, without recourse to high government spending and other inflationary strategies in Britain and in the colonies.[45]

Throughout the 1930s the Bank of England was unceasing in its pursuit of central bank 'co-operation' within the empire, with the same ends in view. Central banking in the Dominions had begun in the 1920s in South Africa and Australia, and had been recommended for India. In the 1930s, as the search for economic stability intensified, central financial institutions in these countries were strengthened; Canada and New Zealand also felt the need for similar bodies. The Bank of

England had always wished to shape these institutions in its own image and pressed, with varying degrees of success, for private central banks whose freedom from competition with other banks and independence from government would enable them to manage the money supply on sound principles in the way that gentlemanly capitalists in Britain had long taken for granted.[46] In the 1930s, when the Bank's European plans had been shattered and when the Dominions began to emerge as the core of the overseas Sterling Area, Anglo-Dominion financial relations reached a new level of importance.[47] As one prominent Bank of England director, Sir Josiah Stamp, put it in 1934: 'the flow of capital funds' from London had once been the chief means of empire development but 'that great chapter may be regarded as closed' and 'the time has gone by when the Empire finance can be represented by the great financial institution in London' and their agencies abroad. With the rise of central banking, the Dominions were asserting 'an internal financial sovereignty', and doing it for reasons of domestic management.[48] It was vital to the future of the Sterling Area that these new institutions should learn to look outwards as soon as possible:

> We have perhaps hitherto looked upon co-operation between the foreign central banks as the first essential, to which co-operation between the Dominion Central Banks may be a useful auxiliary. But actually the priority should be reversed. The Dominions on a sterling exchange standard are critically interested in the fortunes of sterling and must join with Britain as custodians of the validity of sterling values especially if, as trade relations make most probable, the chief external reserves are in sterling. The Dominion banks as a whole even if not individually, at any moment are certain to hold large funds in London, and if they are moved and operated independently of each other and the Bank of England, then the difficulties of managing sterling must be all the greater. If the 'unknown' seller of sterling were a Dominion Bank, we might well find the resources of the Exchange Equalization Account being unnecessarily invoked to maintain sterling values, whereas fuller knowledge, by planning requirements correctly on a time basis, would obviate action in the dark.[49]

Stamp was at pains to stress that cooperation would not involve Bank of England dictatorship.[50] Nevertheless, the Bank did assume a right to leadership and did its best via advice, the recommendation of personnel and other means to influence financiers in the Dominions to its own way of thinking. In Britain the Bank's own strivings for independence were part of its determination to keep financial management as far as possible out of the political arena and prevent overspending. Similarly, as the Dominions began inevitably to exercise a greater conscious control over their economies, the temptation for governments, free of gold standard restrictions, would be to embark upon a course of monetary inflation which would eventually endanger trading and financial relations with Britain, make debt payment more difficult and perhaps imperil the stability of sterling. If, for example, rapid inflation should lead to a balance of payments problem in a Dominion, its sterling reserves would be run down, perhaps at a time when the pound was under severe pressure for other reasons. The more that Norman and other prominent Bank directors could persuade overseas governments to leave their central bankers alone, the more likely the latter were to resist these pressures and to remain 'dependent on traditional financial prospects, upon the trend of opinion in financial and business circles and upon the advice of the Bank of England itself'.[51]

What 'central banking co-operation' meant to the Bank of England in practice was the reinforcing of those export-oriented, London-facing trading and financial interests in the Dominions and other satellites which had thrived upon the old monetary orthodoxies in the past and which would automatically support the Sterling Area and hold out against economic nationalism in the colonies,[52] in the same way that the Bank, the Treasury and the traditional nexus of internationally minded economic interests were holding out against economic nationalism and the interventionist state in Britain. One Dominion economist with extensive governmental experience did not hesitate at the time to call this 'a latter-day expression of financial imperialism . . . the maintenance and extension of London's influence and control'.[53]

British politicians, and those who advised them, gave first priority to the restoration of the gold standard in the 1920s and defended their position until the last in the crisis of 1931. When they had to admit defeat they did not turn to a different set of objectives, but resurrected the old financial system on a reduced scale within what came to be known as the Sterling Area. Tariffs were broached in the first place to defend the gold standard and then to underpin the financial stability upon which the new sterling system, like the old, depended. Imperial preference, which was decisively rejected in 1930 at the Imperial Economic Conference before sterling fell, and then turned to in a panic when the collapse of the world economy was clearly apparent,[54] also found its chief significance in the 1930s as a part of the strategy for maintaining the viability of sterling as an international currency.[55] After 1931, as before, the preoccupations and prejudices of the British financial establishment were the base upon which British economic foreign policy was built. Like the gold standard regime which preceded it, the Sterling Area was controlled by traditional financial criteria and judgements which had an automatic, almost subconscious, priority. Industry, disappointed again, was already looking beyond Ottawa and towards a more multilateral trading world as early as 1936.[56]

The coming of the *Pax Americana*

The Sterling Area conferred many benefits on Britain, helping both to cushion her from some of the worst effects of the world depression and to retain her share of world trade after decades of relative decline. It also offered the City of London an international standing and influence which must have seemed unattainable in the desperate days of 1931. But the area was a spontaneous piece of crisis management aimed at salvaging as much of the old economic order as possible: it was simply not big enough or influential enough to offer a cure for an ailing world economy in the 1930s. Nor could it provide solutions to Britain's own fundamental foreign trade crisis stemming from the low demand for uncompetitive, old-fashioned labour-intensive exports in the regions, and the continuing lack of international competitiveness of the new industries of the Midlands and the southeast. Rapid growth in these areas, together with the concessions to the Dominions in particular which made the Sterling Area viable, meant that imports, including manufactures, recovered very quickly from depression despite protection in 1932. So, although invisible income rose steadily between 1932 and 1937 as the City reaped the benefits of the stable financial order in the Sterling Area, the current account of the balance of payments began to show persistent deficits from the mid-1930s onwards. Britain's inability to lend in the 1930s was the most potent sign of her weakening ability to influence the pace of change in the world economy.

Full international recovery, as the authorities began to recognise, now depended on what happened in the United States, the nature of her demands upon the world economy and whether or not American foreign investment would recover the levels reached in the 1920s. Moreover, the balance between the Sterling Area as a whole and the dollar bloc was precarious and could easily be disrupted. From the mid-1930s onwards, the steadily increasing threat of war with Germany pushed up the dollar imports of the Sterling Area significantly. This development, together with the nervousness induced in some sterling-holders by the threat of war, eventually led to capital flight and a falling pound. The international financial hegemony which had potentially been within the reach of the United States since 1918 was now achieved as Britain made the disagreeable, but inevitable, choice in favour of economic dependence upon the United States rather than military conquest by Germany.

The gentlemanly elite's perception of Britain's domestic and international economic weakness had a marked effect upon what was called 'appeasement' in the 1930s.[57] If appeasement means that a trading nation recognises its dependence on the world economy and tries to prevent the economic disruption arising from war by conciliating its potential enemies, then the British had been appeasers for generations.[58] But in the 1930s exceptionally heavy pressures were pushing the British in this direction to a much greater extent than in the past. It was widely recognised, in government and among the armed services, that Britain was 'overstretched' in the 1930s.[59] She had a huge burden of imperial defence commitments which had to be met from an economy relatively less powerful than before 1914, a less secure currency and small reserves of gold and foreign currencies. At the same time, Britain's enemies were numerous – Germany, Japan and Italy made a formidable list – and she had few plausible allies. France was in a state of internal economic and political disorder, and the Soviet Union was perceived to be both unreliable and ideologically unpalatable. In the run-up to the war, too, the prospect of military support from the United States was non-existent while, as we shall see, Britain was loath to rely on the Americans financially for fear of losing her economic independence.

This concentration of adverse circumstances meant that it was sensible for the authorities in Britain to try to solve their diplomatic problems by conciliating their enemies and avoiding all-out war. Besides this, it is clear that successive British governments in the 1930s were sympathetic to some of Germany's territorial claims. The policy of uniting as many Germans as possible within the Third Reich was not particularly offensive to many officials and politicians in key positions in Britain who still felt guilty over the supposed harshness of the Versailles settlement and were willing to accommodate Germany at the expense of some of the smaller nations created in 1918.[60] Moreover, an aggressive policy towards Germany, and towards Japan, was ruled out to some degree by the need to placate opinion in the empire. The Dominions in particular were adamant for appeasement right up until Munich and beyond; there is some plausibility in the argument that, in the event of war, Britain could be sure of their support, which was vital especially in relation to raw material and food imports, only when she had convinced them that every avenue for peace had been explored.[61]

The point at which economics and foreign policy most clearly converged, however, was on the question of rearmament. Financial orthodoxy had survived after 1918 only because the growing demands for expenditure on social services and education were compensated by severe cuts in defence, both naval and military. Rearmament had to be undertaken once Hitler seemed capable of launching Germany into war. At the same time, there was a pervasive fear in financial, administrative and political circles in Britain that a too rapid rate of rearmament would produce inflation, destroy the economic and social stability of the nation and wreck the Sterling Area by precipitating a financial crash equal to, or greater than, that of 1931. At the Treasury, the assumption was that rearmament diverted savings and industrial capacity from productive employment, provoked inflation, and reduced investment by pushing up taxes.[62] Inflation posed a danger to real wage levels and threatened an industrial relations crisis[63] that would not only affect output but also reduce Britain's image abroad as a strong and stable nation.[64] Moreover, assuming the ever-present need to balance budgets, it was feared that if government expenditure on defence rose too quickly welfare benefits would suffer, and this prospect had alarming implications for social order and morale.

Rapid rearmament also had deleterious effects upon Britain's balance of payments and put the existence of the Sterling Area in jeopardy. Rearmament widened the balance of payments deficit, putting downward pressure on sterling and opening the possibility of severe drains of gold and dollar reserves if a high rate of exchange was maintained. Given the need to import vital supplies in wartime, the Treasury was convinced that war readiness required that sterling remained strong.[65] This priority increased the emphasis upon tempering the arms build-up. The authorities hoped that enough would be done to deter Hitler and other potential enemies, and to interest them in some reasonable settlement of differences short of war, without having to accelerate the arms race to a point where a collapse of sterling and a flight from the currency undermined Britain's international economic position.

The rearmament programme was strongly influenced at all stages by these considerations, and foreign and military policy were shaped accordingly. The concentration on air power reflected the belief that this was the most cost-effective deterrent; the emphasis on economy meant that expenditure on the army and navy was limited. The services had been victims of economies ever since 1919, and the state of the army in the mid-1930s, for example, made it practically impossible for the British to produce any show of force on the continent. Similarly, naval economies meant that the policing of the empire in the Far East became an increasingly cosmetic affair.[66] In a more general perspective, there was a powerful link between economies in defence and foreign policy as a whole up until 1938:

> Based on the Treasury's firm belief that a continuance of the existing rate of rearmament would destroy Britain's economy and consequently her ability to defend herself, the Government's programme sought to limit the nation's expenditure on armaments while pursuing a foreign policy that would diminish the need for them. The policy by which defence spending was to be limited was known as rationing. The policy by which the nation's enemies were to be conciliated was known as appeasement.[67]

Deeply unsatisfied by the outcome of the Ottawa agreements, British industrialists were eager by the late 1930s for European-wide market sharing agreements with Germany and were actively encouraged in this endeavour by the National Government.[68] The City, too, had an active interest in loosening the economic restrictions of Hitler's Germany: many acceptance credits had been frozen in the depression and could be released only if Germany opened up her economy and earned more foreign exchange.[69] But appeasement was far more than an attempted rapprochement between sinister capitalist interests, encouraged by those who believed that Germany, like Italy, was a natural ally against Bolshevik Russia. Basically, it was an attempt to pull Germany away from autarky and warlike preparations and propel her towards economic liberalism and peace. The main target of the British appeasers were the German 'moderates' – including some of Hitler's senior aides – who, supposedly, were more interested in raising living standards than in building a war machine and who might produce a force within Germany sufficient to make war impossible if they received adequate support from outside. To this end, the British were willing to offer a range of economic concessions and benefits if the Germans would agree on disarmament and on a return to the liberal fold.[70] Many of these schemes were aimed at liberalising Anglo-German trade, including the 1934 Clearing Agreement (renewed annually thereafter), which left the Germans considerable freedom to use sterling to buy goods other than those produced in Britain or the empire.[71] Between 1935 and 1938, too, the British government actively considered making some colonial concessions to Germany and floated the idea of a central African consortium in which Germany would participate with other colonial powers in the exploitation of Africa's wealth.[72] When this failed to tempt Hitler, the British shifted the emphasis to south-east Europe, offering loans and trade agreements to help Germany achieve her economic objectives in that region without the need for force.

Nonetheless, the policy of economic appeasement had strict limits. Some elements in the Foreign Office, for example, put the blame for Germany's aggression on the growth of protectionism which followed the 1929–31 crisis, and saw a return to freer trade as being crucial to peace. But the majority view was that the Ottawa system must be preserved and that concessions could only be made in that context. There was also resistance to the idea that economic concessions should be handed out *gratis*: they were to be traded against concrete political guarantees on Germany's part.[73] Viewed in the round, the policy was intended to steer a course between either abandoning the Sterling Area and protection in an attempt to mollify the enemy, or embarking on a Churchillian policy of matching Hitler bomb for bomb, since it was widely believed that both policies would produce economic disaster and weaken Britain drastically should war be forced upon her. Following this cautious course put the British in a position where they felt sufficiently well-armed in 1939 to face the prospect of war with some military confidence.[74]

One other, very unwelcome, effect of rearmament was an increased dependence upon the United States both politically and economically.[75] Until the German menace became tangible, following Hitler's invasion of the Rhineland in 1936, Britain relished her freedom within the Sterling Area and resisted attempts by the United States to restore the gold standard. In an ideal world the British monetary authorities would have liked to return to gold;[76] but they were determined not to adopt a fixed rate of exchange for fear that it would have to be defended by high interest rates, thus losing the benefits of cheap money. So, at the World Economic Conference of 1933, when both France and the United States argued that Britain should return to gold at the 1925–31 rate, the British agreed – provided certain conditions were met. France and the United States, which had large balance of payments surpluses, would have to inflate their economies and lower their tariffs so as to increase their imports, raise commodities prices and release gold. Both were also expected to agree on measures for economising on gold, showing that the British still hankered after the gold exchange standard they had vainly pursued in the 1920s.[77] The proposals were put forward largely in the knowledge that neither France nor the United States would consider them, since both were wedded to deflation. The British had, anyway, already pre-empted the possibility of a cosmopolitan settlement of the world crisis by moving to the Ottawa system; Roosevelt gave the World Economic Conference its final and fatal blow by devaluing the dollar before the proceedings had begun. Nonetheless, the insistence on the need for American reflation as a prerequisite of any restored fixed exchange-rate regime meant that Britain had tacitly recognised that the future of the liberal world economy was at the mercy of the United States.

The devaluation of the dollar in 1933 brought the pound-dollar rate back to roughly the same level as under the old gold standard and the British authorities kept it there until 1938,[78] when the crisis began to overwhelm them, for fear that the United States would retaliate if the pound fell significantly. By 1936, with the

German problem intensifying, the British also began to weaken slightly in response to persistent American demands that they should stabilise the pound on gold again. In the Tripartite Agreement of 1936 Britain came together with the Americans and the French to agree on the extent and timing of a devaluation of the franc and to refrain from any competitive devaluation in response to French action.[79] Together with the French, Britain and the United States also agreed to settle central bank balances in gold on a 24-hour basis at a price based on the going exchange rate of their currencies relative to the dollar, the only currency which now had a fixed value in relation to gold: the dollar was becoming slowly, but effectively, the *numéraire* of the system.[80] The Agreement was the smallest concession to American demands the British felt they could decently make; they were still determined to avoid committing themselves to a fixed rate of exchange for fear that this might have to be defended by high interest rates, and so ruin the cheap-money policy.

By 1938 rearmament and the fear of war were seriously affecting the balance of payments and inducing a flight from sterling to the dollar. Even in the mid-1930s, the balance of payments of the Sterling Area with the Dollar Area was rather precarious. Britain's own large deficit with the United States was offset by the dollar earnings of the mainly underdeveloped parts of the empire and by exports of South African gold to an apparently insatiable American Treasury. This balance could easily be disturbed, as in 1937–8, when a recession in the United States led to a sharp cut-back in imports of empire commodities and put pressure on the sterling exchange rate.[81] Borrowing, together with rumours of war and the effects of preparations for war, which included heavy imports of supplies from the United States, meant dollar shortages and a recognition that, if war did break out, Britain's survival could well depend on her ability to borrow in the United States.[82] This could not be taken for granted: in Washington, Congress refused to allow loans to any nation which was in deficit on war debt – and Britain had stopped payment in 1934 – or any nation which was judged to be a belligerent in war.[83]

A need to keep on the right side of the American administration was the chief reason why Britain signed the Anglo-American reciprocity treaty in 1938.[84] Signing it did not imply that the British authorities had lost interest in the Ottawa agreements and were ready to dismantle the preferential system. Few concessions were made to American demands for entry into the British market and even these were made feasible only because Canada was willing to surrender some of her privileges in Britain in return for easier entry into the American market. Without Canada's flexibility, it is unlikely that a treaty would have been signed.[85] Britain stood by the preferential system and the delicate network of financial relations which held it together because, in the event of war, the system would be vital for survival. The direct benefits from easier trade conditions in the United States were few and the chief value of the agreement to Chamberlain and his government was political. The hope was that the agreement would signal to Hitler the unity of the democracies and deter him from further aggression, as well as increasing the chances of borrowing in the United States.[86] It certainly implied no real trust in the Roosevelt administration, since the British authorities were well aware that the

American campaign for reciprocity was rooted in a virulent hostility to the preferential system and to the imperialism which supposedly lay behind it.[87]

The lack of any real understanding or sympathy between the two great liberal powers was made plain during the sterling crisis which began early in 1938, even before Hitler's invasion of Austria. As sterling began to fall, the United States' reaction was to assume that the British were deliberately pushing down the rate in order to gain a competitive edge in export markets: it was hard for them to understand that the empire that they always believed was bursting with wealth, was actually chronically short of foreign exchange. Faced with the threat of retaliatory devaluation and worried about creating a bad impression in the United States when war seemed imminent, the British opted to hold the exchange rate up and allow their gold reserves to run down. Between the beginning of 1938 and the early months of 1939, Britain lost about half of her foreign exchange reserves to the United States.[88] By then, facing problems of inflation and labour unrest provoked by rearmament, and fearful that stringent controls would soon have to be placed on foreign exchange, there was a strong feeling in government circles that if Britain had to go to war at all, it were better sooner than later.[89]

Given the mutual suspicion and even hostility which existed between Britain and the United States, and the clear recognition in London that American help might be forthcoming only at the cost of emasculating the Sterling Area and accepting the 'open door' and the United States' economic supremacy,[90] it is no surprise that Chamberlain should have continued to put his efforts into reaching a settlement with Germany.[91] The exact rationale behind British foreign policy in 1938–9 is not easy to determine. After the absorption of Austria – a move with which he had no particular quarrel – Chamberlain stressed that Britain would go to war if the empire were attacked or if the territory of France, Belgium, Portugal, Iraq or Egypt were violated. Of the last three, Portugal had a certain strategic naval significance; Iraq was important for oil; and Egypt was also of strategic and economic value and under strong British informal influence. All three were members of the Sterling Area and this connection with Britain was bolstered by loans.[92] On eastern and south-eastern Europe, the British clearly felt they could find some *modus vivendi* with the Germans. Subsequent events are open to an interpretation based on traditional concerns about the balance of power. Although Czechoslovakia was dismembered at Munich in return for solemn guarantees of peace from Hitler, this seemed 'reasonable' in London because British interests in Europe were affected only marginally; but further aggression in eastern Europe was unacceptable to Britain because it would give the Germans control over resources large enough to allow them to dominate Europe. On this reading, British policy in 1938–9 was similar to that of pre-1914.[93] Other historians stress that, even after Munich, the British were quite willing to see Germany acquire further territory as part of a general settlement, but finally had to oppose Hitler's use of force.[94]

Whatever interpretation is favoured, it remains true that after Munich, and right up until the outbreak of war, the British carried on trying to deter Germany from war by offering trading and financial concessions in return for political guarantees.

It is very likely that Chamberlain's ultimate ambition was to secure a settlement which would stimulate European growth and keep Britain free from dependence on the United States: 'behind Chamberlain's idea for economic negotiations in 1938–9 may be seen the idea of a European Four-Power Directorate (Britain, France, Germany and Italy), serving to assure the continued prosperity and power of Europe in the face of the emerging superpowers',[95] that is, the United States and the Soviet Union. The United States certainly reacted with great alarm to these negotiations: Roosevelt believed that Chamberlain was 'attempting to engineer an Anglo-German money and trade deal . . . which would . . . exclude American trade from Europe, Africa and Latin America'.[96] Others in Washington spoke of the 'selfish City interests' intent upon carving up Europe at America's expense.[97]

Appeasement failed: the British assumed that German demands were rational and limited, whereas they proved to be irrational and boundless. As Chamberlain feared, war brought with it a severe challenge to the economic and social status quo. The war of 1914–18 had shaken gentlemanly capitalism in Britain; another war might extinguish it altogether by putting into question the whole social order on which gentlemanly capitalism had flourished. War also raised again, in a more menacing form, the prospect of a shift in the locus of economic power from the City to industry and organised labour, because when national survival was at stake, the role of the 'producing' part of the nation was much enhanced, as it had been during World War I.[98] At the same time, war would also bring the United States the economic dominance foreshadowed, but not fully achieved, between 1916 and 1918. In the early days of the war, the Chamberlain government did as much as it could to preserve the status quo. Mass mobilisation was deferred in the vain hope that it would not be necessary, and a fully fledged war economy was slow to appear. At the same time, exports were strongly encouraged in order to build up exchange reserves. The sudden fall of France in 1940 brought this phase of semi-commitment to an end. From then on the 'national interest' had, inevitably, to be defined in terms of full employment of all productive resources rather than financial orthodoxy regarding the position of sterling.[99] As early as 1940, Britain was desperately short of dollars and dependent upon American generosity for her survival.[100] By then she had fallen back on her 'special relationship' with the United States, preferring economic dependence upon her to military subjugation by Germany. This decision was

> essentially a response to weakness. Ever since the 1890s, the United States had seemed the least threatening of her competitors and, therefore, cutting her losses, the most attractive potential ally against the rest, especially given the similarities of language and culture.[101]

In 1939 the *Pax Britannica* was replaced by the *Pax Americana* and British gentlemanly capitalists had to adapt themselves once again, this time to serve under new masters. As they did so, however, they kept in view the prospect of 'educating' their dominant ally, and their determination to reinstate sterling and retain the empire remained strong, as we shall see.

Notes

1 The quotation is from A.W.F. Plumptre, *Central Banking in the British Dominions* (Toronto, 1940), pp. 191–2.

2 Robert Skidelsky, 'Retreat from Leadership: the Evolution of British Economic Foreign Policy, 1870–1939', in Benjamin M. Rowland, ed. *Balance of Power or Hegemony* (New York, 1976).

3 'The National Government itself believed that it was following an anti-unemployment policy': Ian M. Drummond, *Imperial Economic Policy 1917–39: Studies in Expansion and Protection* (1974), p. 179.

4 Most of what follows in the next three paragraphs is based upon B.J. Eichengreen, 'Sterling and the Tariff, 1929–32', (Princeton Studies in International Finance, No. 48, 1981), reprinted in idem, *Elusive Stability: Essays in the History of International Finance* (Cambridge, 1990).

5 This was why Keynes, the most persistent critic of the authorities' financial policy over the years, thought in 1931 that the $4.86 rate should be defended for as long as possible. Eichengreen, 'Sterling and the Tariff', p. 9.

6 Sir Henry Clay, *Lord Norman* (1957), p. 436.

7 Alan Booth, 'Britain in the 1930s: a Managed Economy?', *Econ. Hist. Rev.*, 2nd ser. XL (1987), pp. 503–10. On cheap money see Susan Howson, 'Cheap Money and Debt Management in Britain, 1932–51', in P.L. Cottrell and D.E. Moggridge, eds. *Money and Power: Essays in Honour of L.S. Pressnell* (1988).

8 Eichengreen, 'Sterling and the Tariff', p. 22. The shift in opinion was symbolised by the replacement of Snowden, an ardent free-trade Labourite, with Neville Chamberlain, heir to his famous father's tariff campaign, as Chancellor of the Exchequer in the National Government which was formed in August 1931.

9 Susan Howson, *Sterling's Managed Float: The Operation of the Exchange Equalization Account, 1932–9* (Princeton, NJ, 1980).

10 In a memorandum for the government, written in August 1931, Henry Clay pointed to 'The vicious circle of inflation, to which the departure from the Gold Standard lays us open' via import price increases and reckless government expenditure. 'The only way to stop it is to balance the Budget'. Quoted in Robert Skidelsky, *Politicians and the Slump; The Labour Government of 1929–31* (1967), pp. 414–15.

11 Eichengreen, 'Sterling and the Tariff', p. 26.

12 For the overlap between trade dependence and sterling bloc membership see Tables 20.1 and 20.2. The criteria for membership of the bloc are also listed by Brinley Thomas, 'The Evolution of the Sterling Area and its Prospects', in Nicolas Mansergh et al., *Commonwealth Perspectives* (Durham, NC, 1958), p. 180. Thomas has a slightly different list of countries and excludes Argentina. For De Vegh's detailed criteria for including countries in his list, see Table 20.1. The list of 15 principal sterling countries given by F.V. Meyer, *Britain, the Sterling Area and Europe* (Cambridge, 1952), p. 40, also excludes Argentina.

13 P.H. Lindert, *Key Currencies and Gold, 1900–13* (Princeton Studies in International Finance, no. 24, 1969).

14 Ian M. Drummond, *British Economic Policy and the Empire, 1919–39* (1972), p. 119.

15 Although he went on to say that 'observers may be pardoned for thinking that what they saw was something new and not something which had existed before without being apparent'. Sir Henry Clay, 'The Sterling Area', in Institute of Bankers, *Current Financial Problems and the City of London* (1949), p. 213.

16 League of Nations, *International Currency Experience: Lessons of the Inter-War Period* (1944), p. 48.

17 Clay, 'The Sterling Area', pp. 213–14. Some indication of the relationship between trade with Britain and national output levels for various sterling countries can be found in Ingvar Svennilson, *Growth and Stagnation in the European Economy* (Geneva, 1954), p. 198.

18 A 'Top Currency' is defined as 'the preferred medium of the international economy', something which derives from 'the issuing state's position of economic leadership', which 'inspires monetary confidence even amongst political opponents'. A 'Master Currency' is one imposed by an imperial or hegemonic state on countries which rely upon it, though whether the currency is forced on its subordinates or not depends upon the economic strength of the issuing state. See Susan Strange, *Sterling and British Policy: A Political Study of an International Currency in Decline* (Oxford, 1971), pp. 4–5.

19 Susan Howson, *Domestic Monetary Management in Britain, 1919–38* (Cambridge, 1975), p. 79, n. The City's interest is confirmed by Ian M. Drummond, *The Floating Pound and the Sterling Area, 1931–1939* (Cambridge, 1981), p. 14. For FBI support see Michael Dintenfass, '"The Politics of Producers' Co-operation": the FBI–TUC–NCEO Talks, 1929–1933', in John Turner, ed. *Businessmen and Politics: Studies in Business Activity in British Politics, 1900–1945* (1984), pp. 87–8.

20 Drummond, *The Floating Pound*, p. 10.

21 Ibid. p. 22. Strong support for the area also came from the government's own economic advisers. See Susan Howson and Donald Winch, *The Economic Advisory Council, 1930–1939* (Cambridge, 1974), pp. 257–8.

22 On this theme see also Roberta Allbert Dayer, *Finance and Empire: Sir Charles Addis, 1861–1945* (1988), pp. 238, 247, 292–3.

23 Ibid. p. 16.

24 There is a vast and growing literature on this subject. Particularly useful here are the summaries of the literature given in G.C. Peden, *Keynes, the Treasury and British Economic Policy* (1988); Scott Newton and Dilwyn Porter, *Modernization Frustrated: The Politics of Industrial Decline in Britain since 1900* (1988), pp. 78ff. See also W.R. Garside, 'The Failure of the "Radical Alternative": Public Works, Deficit Finance and British Interwar Unemployment', *Journal of European Economic History,* 14 (1985); and idem, *British Unemployment, 1919–39: A Study in Public Policy* (Cambridge, 1990).

25 Much of the next paragraph depends upon Meyer, *Britain, the Sterling Area and Europe,* pp. 36–46.

26 League of Nations, *International Currency Experience,* p. 61.

27 Meyer, *Britain, the Sterling Area and Europe,* p. 44.

28 Meyer notes that, had Britain joined the dollar bloc, stockpiling dollars would have reduced imports and lowered real incomes, 'though there might have been some stimulus to employment, especially in the export trades' (ibid. p. 44). Joining another bloc with all its implications for Britain's role in the world was, of course, unthinkable in the 1930s.

29 R.F. Holland, *Britain and the Commonwealth Alliance, 1918–39* (1981), pp. 130, 141.

30 Drummond, *British Economic Policy and the Empire,* p. 102.

31 The literature on the Ottawa conference and its implications, on which the next two paragraphs are based, is now considerable. Chapters 5–8 of Drummond's *Imperial Economic Policy* are very thorough, and there is a useful summary in his earlier book, *British Economic Policy and the Empire,* pp. 92–119. There are also excellent summaries and critical accounts in Skidelsky, 'Retreat from Leadership', pp. 178–83, and Holland, *Britain and the Commonwealth Alliance,* Ch. 8.

32 Holland, *Britain and the Commonwealth Alliance,* p. 145.

33 Drummond, *British Economic Policy and the Empire,* pp. 97, 100–1.

34 Hubert D. Henderson, 'Sterling and the Balance of Trade', in idem, *The Inter-War Years and Other Papers* (Oxford, 1955), p. 87. For a similar recognition of the importance of the sterling and debt questions in the Ottawa equation, see the comments by William Graham at the end of H.V. Hodson's article, 'Imperial Economic Policy', *International Affairs,* 14 (1935), pp. 542–3.

35 Howson, *Domestic Monetary Management,* p. 105. See also Alfred E. Kahn, *Britain and the World Economy* (1946), pp. 188–95.

36 B.N. Thomsen and B. Thomas, *Anglo-Danish Trade, 1661–1963* (Aarhus, 1963), pp. 364ff and esp. Table XV, p. 367. For a detailed study see T.J.T. Rooth, 'Limits

of Leverage: the Anglo-Danish Trade Agreement of 1933', *Econ. Hist. Rev.*, 2nd ser. XXXVIII (1984).

37 Political and Economic Planning, *Report on International Trade* (1937). The data are derived from Table 1, p. 288.

38 The best study of the trade relations between Britain and the European sterling countries is T.J.T. Rooth, 'Tariffs and Trade Bargaining: Anglo-Scandinavian Economic Relations in the 1930s', *Scandinavian Economic History Review*, XXXIV (1986). Also useful is the P.E.P. cited in n. 37, App. III. There are good sections in Carl Kreider, *The Anglo-American Trade Agreement: A Study of British and American Commercial Policies, 1934–1939* (Princeton, NJ, 1943), pp. 57–67; and J.H. Richardson, *British Economic Foreign Policy* (1936), pp. 101f. Most of the contemporary studies suggest how hard these countries were squeezed; but they did considerably better than non-sterling foreign countries in the British market. Drummond has noted, in passing, that in the bilateral agreements made from 1933 onwards, Britain 'in effect . . . promised not to squeeze the Argentinians, the Danes and the Swedes merely to make more room for the Dominions' foodstuffs' (*Imperial Economic Policy*, p. 311). For a detailed survey of British trade and financial policy at this time, see Tim Rooth, *British Protectionism and the International Economy: Overseas Commercial Policy in the 1930s* (Cambridge, 1993).

39 Argentina is dealt with in Chapter 7 in this volume. See the comment made by Robert Menzies, the Australian politician, on the fact that 'the Board of Trade . . . appears to be more pro-Argentinian than pro-Australian', in Drummond, *British Economic Policy and the Empire*, p. 224. Lord Beaverbrook also complained about 'the granting of Dominion status to the South American republic'. See F.C. Benham, *Great Britain under Protection* (New York, 1941), p. 136.

40 Henry Joseph Tasca, *World Trading Systems: A Study of American and British Commercial Policies* (Paris, 1939), pp. 94–6, 122–3, 146–51.

41 South Africa is an exception which proves the rule. Her gold exports – not included in the trade statistics – were very high in the 1930s, giving her a comfortable balance of payments surplus with Britain and allowing the latter to increase the value of her commodity exports to South Africa by nearly 30 per cent between 1929 and 1937.

42 Drummond, *British Economic Policy and the Empire*, p. 140, asks rhetorically, after examining Dominion and Indian tariff policies, who was exploiting whom.

43 See Table 20.2. See also Brinley Thomas, 'The Evolution of the Sterling Area', in Nicholas Mansergh, *Commonwealth Perspectives* (Durham, NC, 1958), p. 180.

44 R.B. Stewart, 'Instruments of British Policy in the Sterling Area', *Political Science Quarterly*, 52 (1937), pp. 184–91.

45 R.S. Sayers, *The Bank of England, 1891–1944* (Cambridge, 1976), II, pp. 449, 451.

46 See Norman's 'General Principles of Central Banking', as listed in Lyndhurst Faulkiner Giblin, *The Growth of a Central Bank: The Development of the Commonwealth Bank of Australia, 1924–45* (Melbourne, 1951), p. 40.

47 Sayers, *The Bank of England*, II, p. 513. For a contemporary recognition of the importance of imperial financial cooperation, see Howson and Winch, *The Economic Advisory Council*, pp. 258–60.

48 Sir Josiah Stamp, *Central Banking as an Imperial Factor* (Cust Foundation Lecture, Nottingham University, 1934), pp. 1–2, 7.

49 Ibid. pp. 21–2.

50 Ibid. pp. 22–3.

51 Plumptre, *Central Banking in the British Dominions*, pp. 191–2.

52 Ibid. pp. 196–7.

53 Ibid. p. 193.

54 Holland, *Britain and the Commonwealth Alliance*, pp. 120–2. There is a detailed treatment in Drummond, *Imperial Economic Policy*, Ch. 4, and a shorter one in his *British Economic Policy and the Empire*, pp. 67–9.

55 Drummond, in his early work, appreciates this to some degree when he argues that imperial policy was about 'sterling, debt service, the budget and unemployment', but

he puts rather too much weight on the last of these and the discussion of the financial aspects does not come out fully in the body of the work. See *Imperial Economic Policy,* pp. 422–5.

56 R.F. Holland, 'The Federation of British Industries and the International Economy, 1929–39', *Econ. Hist. Rev.,* 2nd ser. XXXIV (1981), pp. 287–300, which charts the growing interest of industrial lobbyists, like the FBI, in markets outside the empire, especially after 1936.

57 The literature on British diplomacy in the run up to the war is massive. For a short bibliographical guide see R.J. Overy, *The Origins of the Second World War* (1987). Interesting interpretations from our perspective can be found in Paul Kennedy, *The Realities Behind Diplomacy: Background Influences on British External Policy* (1980), Chs. 5 and 6; and Bernard Porter, *Britain, Europe and the World, 1850–1986* (1987), Ch. 4.

58 On this issue see the suggestive article by P.M. Kennedy, 'The Tradition of Appeasement in British Foreign Policy, 1865–1939', *Brit. Jour. Internat. Stud.,* 2 (1976).

59 This is one of the themes of Paul Kennedy's major work, *The Rise and Fall of the Great Powers* (1988).

60 Norman Medlicott, 'Britain and Germany: the Search for Agreement, 1930–37', in David Dilks, ed. *Retreat from Power: Studies in British Foreign Policy in the 20th Century,* Vol. I, 1906–39 (1981).

61 Richie Ovendale, *Appeasement and the English-Speaking World: Britain, the United States, the Dominions and the Policy of Appeasement, 1937–39* (Cardiff, 1975); and idem, 'Britain, the Dominions and the Coming of the Second World War, 1933–9', in Wolfgang J. Mommsen and Lothar Kattenacker, eds. *The Fascist Challenge and the Policy of Appeasement* (1983).

62 G.C. Peden, *British Rearmament and the Treasury, 1932–9* (Edinburgh, 1979), pp. 64–7, 71–92; F. Coghlan, 'Armaments, Economic Policy and Appeasement: Background to British Foreign Policy, 1931–7', *History,* 57 (1972); Robert Paul Shay, *British Rearmament in the Thirties: Politics and Profits* (Princeton, NJ, 1977), Chs. 1 and 4.

63 R.A.C. Parker, 'British Rearmament, 1936–39: Treasury, Trades Unions and Skilled Labour', *Eng. Hist. Rev.,* XCVI (1981).

64 On this complex theme see Gustav Schmidt, 'The Domestic Background to British Appeasement Policy', in Mommsen and Kattenacker, *The Fascist Challenge.*

65 R.A.C. Parker, 'Economics, Rearmament and Foreign Policy: the United Kingdom before 1939. A Preliminary Study', *Journal of Contemporary History,* 10 (1975), pp. 637–9. On government sensitivity to City opinion see Peden, *British Rearmament and the Treasury,* p. 95; Sayers, *Bank of England,* II, pp. 567–71.

66 Shay, *British Rearmament in the Thirties,* Ch. 2; P.M. Kennedy, '"Appeasement" and British Defence Policy in the Inter-War Years', *Brit. Jour. Internat. Stud.,* 2 (1976); Lawrence Roy Pratt, *East of Malta, West of Suez: Britain's Mediterranean Crisis, 1936–1939,* (Cambridge, 1975).

67 Shay, *British Rearmament in the Thirties,* pp. 195–6.

68 Holland, 'The Federation of British Industries and the International Economy', pp. 296–9.

69 On this problem see Sayers, *The Bank of England,* II, pp. 503–12; and Neil Forbes, 'London Banks, the German Standstill Agreements and "Economic Appeasement" in the 1930s', *Econ. Hist. Rev.,* 2nd ser. XL (1987).

70 C.A. MacDonald, 'Economic Appeasement and the German "Moderates", 1937–1939', *Past and Present,* 56 (1972); Berndt-Jürgen Wendt, '"Economic Appeasement" – a Crisis Strategy', in Mommsen and Kattenacker, *The Fascist Challenge,* pp. 163–4.

71 Wendt, '"Economic Appeasement"', pp. 168–9.

72 See pp. 586–7 and the references given there.

73 Gustav Schmidt, *The Politics and Economics of Appeasement: British Foreign Policy in the 1930s* (Leamington Spa, 1986), pp. 137–46, 195–225.

74 Overy, *The Origins of the Second World War,* p. 67.

75 For an excellent overview of the changing relationship see B.M. Rowland, 'Preparing the American Ascendency: the Transfer of Economic Power from Britain to the United

States', in Rowland, *Balance of Power or Hegemony,* and idem, *Commercial Conflict and Foreign Policy: A Study in Anglo-American Relations, 1932–1938* (New York, 1987).

76 Sayers, *Bank of England,* II, p. 450.

77 Clarke, 'The Reconstruction of the International Monetary System', pp. 19–40. See also Drummond, *The Floating Pound and the Sterling Area,* Chs. 6 and 7.

78 On exchange-rate policy see Howson, 'Sterling's Managed Float', passim, and Sayers, *Bank of England,* II, pp. 474–5. The advantages of the 1931 devaluation against the dollar were lost by early 1934 but, measured against all other currencies, the pound stayed below its 1929–30 level until 1936. John Redmond, 'An Indication of the Effective Exchange Rates of the Pound in the Nineteen Thirties', *Econ. Hist. Rev.,* 2nd ser. XXXIII (1980).

79 Blow-by-blow accounts of the origins of the Tripartite Agreement can be found in Drummond, *The Floating Pound and The Sterling Area,* Chs. 8 and 9; and idem, 'London, Washington and the Management of the Franc, 1936–9', (Princeton Studies in International Finance, No. 45, 1979). See also Stephen V.O. Clarke, 'Exchange Rate Stabilization in the Mid-1930s: Negotiating the Tripartite Agreement', (Princeton Studies in International Finance, No. 41, 1977); and Sayers, *The Bank of England,* II, pp. 475–81 and III, App. 28.

80 H. van B. Cleveland, 'The International Monetary System in the Inter-war Period', in Rowland, *Balance of Power or Hegemony,* pp. 53–6.

81 Kreider, *The Anglo-American Trade Agreement,* pp. 69–70.

82 For an interesting contemporary analysis of this see Imre de Vegh, *The Pound Sterling: A Study of the Balance of Payments of the Sterling Area* (New York, 1939), pp. 69–70, 107–12.

83 The modification of the last-named restrictions in the Neutrality Act of 1937, which allowed for sales of armaments to belligerents on a 'cash and carry' basis, may be seen as a bid by the United States to capitalize on Britain's dependence. See Warren F. Kimball, 'Lend Lease and the Open Door: the Temptations of British Opulence, 1937–1942', *Political Science Quarterly,* LXXXVI (1971), p. 239.

84 A useful study of the 1938 Agreement, which places it in the context of Anglo-American relations in the 1930s, is R.N. Kottman, *Reciprocity and the North Atlantic Triangle, 1932–1938* (Ithaca, NY, 1958).

85 Krieder, *The Anglo-American Trade Agreement,* pp. 104–7; Ian M. Drummond and Norman Hillmer, 'A Shaft of Baltic Pine: Negotiating the Anglo-American-Canadian Trade Agreement of 1938', in Cottrell and Moggridge, *Money and Power,* p. 204. For a more detailed study see Ian M. Drummond and Norman Hillmer, *Negotiating Freer Trade: The United Kingdom, the United States, Canada and the Trade Agreements of 1938* (Waterloo, 1989).

86 Drummond and Hillmer, 'A Shaft of Baltic Pine', pp. 205, 209. For a different perspective see Hans-Jürgen Schröder, 'The Ambiguities of Appeasement: Great Britain, the United States and Germany, 1937–9', in Mommsen and Kattenacker, *The Fascist Challenge.*

87 For an insight into the philosophy behind the American drive for reciprocity in the 1930s see A.W. Schatz, 'The Anglo-American Trade Agreement and Cordell Hull's Search for Peace', *Journal of American History,* 57 (1970–1).

88 R.A.C. Parker, 'The Pound Sterling, the American Treasury and British Preparations for War, 1938–9', *Eng. Hist. Rev.,* XCVIII (1983).

89 Parker, 'The Pound Sterling', p. 277; G.C. Peden, 'A Matter of Timing: the Economic Background to British Foreign Policy, 1938–1939', *History,* 69 (1984).

90 Callum A. MacDonald, *The United States, Britain and Appeasement, 1936–9* (1981), pp. 180–1.

91 For the 1938–9 discussions with German business circles and others, see MacDonald, 'Economic Appeasement and the German "Moderates", 1937–39', pp. 114–131.

92 Holland, *The Commonwealth Alliance,* p. 201. On Britain's policy towards foreign loans to these countries and to other sensitive areas, including Greece, Turkey and China, see

Simon Newman, *March 1939: The British Guarantee to Poland. A Study in the Continuity of British Foreign Policy* (Oxford, 1976), Chs. 3 and 4.

93 Newman, *March 1939,* pp. 107. This is compatible with the evidence concerning Britain's forceful policy in Romania, where control of oil was involved. See Philippe Marguerat, *Le IIIe Reich et le pétrole roumain, 1938–1940* (Geneva, 1977). For the considerable economic stake built up by Britain in south-east Europe after 1918 see Alicia Teichova, *An Economic Background to Munich* (Cambridge, 1974).

94 This is the view of David E. Kaiser, *Economic Diplomacy and the Origins of the Second World War: Germany, Britain, France and Eastern Europe* (Princeton, NJ, 1980).

95 Newman, *March 1939,* p. 7. See also John Charmley, *Chamberlain and the Lost Peace* (1989).

96 Watt, *Succeeding John Bull,* p. 81.

97 MacDonald, *The United States, Britain and Appeasement,* pp. 72–5; and idem, 'The United States, Appeasement and the Open Door', in Mommsen and Kattenacker, *The Fascist Challenge,* pp. 403–4.

98 There are some perceptive ideas on these themes in Schmidt, *The Politics and Economics of Appeasement,* and Maurice Cowling, *The Impact of Hitler* (1975).

99 On the coming of a war economy see Newton and Porter, *Modernization Frustrated,* pp. 90ff.

100 Kimball, 'Lend Lease and the Open Door', pp. 240–3. Also idem, '"Beggar My Neighbour": America and the British Interim Financial Crisis, 1940–1941', *Jour. Econ. Hist.,* XXIX (1969).

101 David Reynolds, 'Competitive Co-operation: Anglo-American Relations in World War Two', *Hist. Jour.,* 23 (1980), p. 245.

PART SEVEN

The wider world, 1914–49

21

MAINTAINING FINANCIAL DISCIPLINE

The Dominions, 1914–39

One of the best known themes in the history of the British empire between the wars is the steady movement of the white Dominions towards political independence.[1] The Balfour Report of 1926 gave birth to, and the Statute of Westminster in 1931 legally enshrined, the concept of equality of status between Britain and the major settlement colonies. But in many ways the notion of equality was no more than a polite fiction. All the white Dominions, save Canada, relied ultimately upon the power of Britain and her ability to defend them; Canada escaped this dependence only because she was protected by proximity to the United States.[2] In matters economic, the Dominions were similarly placed. Between the wars all of them were highly dependent for their prosperity on trade, despite tariff-aided import substitution during World War I and in the depression of the 1930s. Britain remained easily the most important trading partner of the Dominions throughout the period, the only exception being Canada, whose trade with the United States was of great importance (Table 21.1). The importance of the British market for Dominion exports diminished somewhat in the 1920s as the world struggled back to multilateralism and Britain made slow progress in comparison with her rivals. With the exception of South Africa, Britain's share increased again, dramatically, in the 1930s when depression struck and the Ottawa system was set in place. Similarly, while reliance on British manufactured goods in the Dominions was weakened after the war, especially in Canada, the 1930s saw a modest reversal of the trend.

Behind trade lay finance: if anything, Dominion dependence on Britain in this sphere was greater than in the case of trade, although this has not been well recognised by historians. As we have already seen, the money supply in Australia, New Zealand and South Africa before 1914 was determined largely by the state of the London balances of their banks which depended, in turn, upon the level of exports and the ability to borrow. Borrowing from Britain had, of course, played a crucial

TABLE 21.1 Britain's share of Dominion trade, 1913–38 (per cent)

	1913	*1929*	*1933*	*1938*
Exports from				
Canada	49.8	25.3	39.6	39.1
Australia	45.4	38.1	47.4	56.2
New Zealand	84.1	75.0	87.3	84.7
South Africa	78.8	48.4		38.8
Imports into:				
Canada	21.3	15.1	24.3	17.5
Australia	52.3	39.7	41.3	42.1
New Zealand	61.1	46.1	51.3	47.8
South Africa	56.7	43.9		43.9

Sources: F. Capie, *Depression and Protectionism: Britain between the Wars* (Manchester, 1983), Table 2.9, p. 30; *Statistical Abstracts of the United Kingdom* (HMSO).

part in the development of these colonies before the war. During the conflict, the London money market tap was turned off to a considerable degree; in the 1920s capital exports were low by pre-war standards, though the Dominions absorbed a larger share of them; in the 1930s they were reduced to a trickle. As a result, the Dominions were forced to rely more on their own savings for investment and growth, and local money markets developed accordingly.[3]

There is no doubt that after 1914 the Dominions became steadily aware of their own financial identity, not only because of greater self-reliance in terms of investment, but also because, for most of this period, Britain was not on the gold standard. Before 1914 the link between Australasian and South African currencies and London sterling, via the gold standard, was so close that it was difficult for the colonists to distinguish between them.[4] The floating of sterling from 1919 to 1925, and again after 1931, allowed for divergence; the precise relations between Dominion and British exchange rates became, for the first time, a matter of conscious management.[5] The Bank of England was quick to recognise the problem. In response, it encouraged the Dominions to establish central banks, which the Bank hoped would help to coordinate monetary policy in the empire, prevent embarrassing divergencies in exchange rates and make it easier for the Dominions to follow London if and when the gold standard was abandoned. Ideally, these peripheral central banks would be made in the Bank's own image, that is as essentially private institutions, free of government interference and independent in judgement, and able to exercise monetary control through their position as holders of the accounts of the government and of the local commercial banks. The Bank's great, if unspoken, fear was that, with 'automatic' discipline no longer possible and with increasing self-confidence in the Dominions, the role of the state in economic management on the white periphery would swell to intolerable proportions. In the worst case, radical governments might seize on central banks as ideal instruments for printing money to finance Utopian schemes. Inflation and economic collapse would be the inevitable result and the British trader and investor, whom the Bank had a duty to protect, would bear a considerable share of the burden. An independent status for central banks in the Dominions was thus regarded by the Bank as being a guarantee of sound money.

For their part, the Dominions recognised the importance of central banking in an age of managed currencies, and they were willing to take advice and even personnel from Threadneedle Street. On the other hand, in countries where the role of the state in economic development had been so much greater than was the case in Britain, it proved difficult to create effective central banking institutions by slavishly imitating the Bank of England. Moreover, Dominion governments and other interested parties were wary of imperial dominance and resented too much interference from London. Not surprisingly, what looked like independence to the Bank could seem like an arrogant metropolitan imposition when viewed from a colonial perspective.[6] In practice, this incipient clash between imperial and nationalist impulses did not matter much. With the exception of New Zealand in the late 1930s, Dominion governments followed an orthodox financial path. London balances remained of overwhelming importance to the money supply in all the Dominions save Canada. In the 1920s most governments still saw the ability to borrow in Britain as being vital to their country's development, and power remained in the hands of those who recognised the importance of the British economic connection and the need to satisfy London's criteria for sound financial management. After 1929, what bound the Dominions to London most effectively was the crushing weight of accumulated debt, when exports had collapsed and fresh loans were few and small. It has been noted that 'the Imperial Conference of 1930 resembled nothing so much as an interview between a bank manager and his improvident clients'.[7] The link connecting this crisis with the Ottawa preferential arrangements was a strong one for it was 'the prospect of a chain of defaults triggered in the first instance by primary producers overseas [which] seized the British of the need to shore up artificially the agricultural incomes of their closest partners'.[8]

The problems of the 1930s thus reinforced the financial dependence of the Dominions. We can see this most obviously in our first case study of Australia, the heaviest borrower in the 1920s and the most desperately indebted in the following decade. Then we look briefly at South Africa, whose dependence on British trade actually declined markedly in the inter-war period, but who could not shake off the dominance of London finance. Next, we examine New Zealand's belated and ultimately futile attempt, in the late 1930s, to break free of the restrictions imposed by membership of the Sterling Area. Lastly, we consider why it was that Canada, whose banking system did not depend on London sterling balances even before the war and who fell increasingly within the financial orbit of the United States in the 1920s, was tempted to join the Sterling Area in the worst years of depression.

The Australian debt crisis

After 1914 the symbiotic relationship between London funds and the Australian money supply still held:

> London funds appear to be the barometer of the system: if they rose to unusually high levels, this was the signal for an expansion of credit, if they fell to unusually low levels, this was the signal for a contraction of credit.[9]

All the major Australian banks, like their counterparts in South Africa and New Zealand, were heavily engaged in the London market. Funds built up rapidly in London at certain times of the year because of the seasonality of pastoral and agricultural exports to Britain and drained back only slowly to Australia to pay for the steadier flow of imports. In the mean time, the funds could be usefully employed either on the London Stock Exchange or in the discount market, with the result that the Australian banks were often responsive more to shifts in monetary policy and interest rates in Britain than they were to domestic conditions.[10] The banks tried to offset the effects of normal export seasonality on Australian credit and did not automatically respond to upward or downward shifts in metropolitan balances, but major changes in the latter were registered in Australia.[11] In 1921, for example, when imports rose with unusual rapidity, London balances fell sharply and the result was a severe, if temporary, contraction of credit in Australia.[12]

Despite the strength of the link between London finance and Australian credit – and the link was just as strong in the case of New Zealand and South Africa[13] – the British monetary authorities were anxious in the early 1920s to bring about a more conscious cooperation between themselves and Dominion bankers because, as we have seen, once sterling was floated after 1919, Dominion currencies and British sterling could diverge from each other more easily than in the past. At the 1923 Imperial Conference, the Dominions were urged to build up sterling balances in London, rather than hold gold reserves, in line with the Genoa proposals; the Bank of England also stressed the importance of monetary coordination and tried to promote central banking on traditional lines.[14] In the Australian case, this meant encouraging the view that the Commonwealth Bank should take on wider responsibilities.

The Commonwealth Bank had begun life in 1911 as a state bank, promoted by the Labour Party, trade unionists and other nationalists who were distrustful of the trading banks and their London connections and wished to see the new bank offer cheap credit as a challenge to the traditional 'money power'. But by the early 1920s the Commonwealth Bank's influence rested mainly upon its position as banker to the federal government, a role much enhanced during the war.[15] Despite its origins, the Bank was also fierce in its devotion to orthodoxy, sometimes to an extent which even London found uncomfortable to live with. In 1923–4, with Australian exports riding high and the banks flush with funds in London, the Bank used its newly won control over the note issue to slow down the expansion of credit in

Australia. Its main aim was to keep the Australian pound high with a view to an early return to the gold standard, which the Australians had abandoned in 1919 along with Britain. Since, at that time, London sterling was under pressure and falling against gold, a gap emerged between the value of the Australian pound and sterling. This development was embarrassing to the British, who were still extolling the virtues of a gold-exchange standard and who expected colonials to follow London's financial lead at all times.[16] But the outcome of the crisis was satisfactory to Britain. In 1924 new legislation prompted the Commonwealth Bank to allow a greater flexibility in the note issue. At the same time it received some of the powers of a central bank, including a measure of control over the reserves of the commercial banks and the right to discount their bills. The control over bank reserves was very limited and the Australian bill market small and immature, so the gain in authority was more theoretical than real: the trading banks still relied on London as the only market liquid enough to place their spare funds. But the 1924 regulations did indicate that politicians on the right of centre in Australia, who valued the British connection highly, were eager to try to model their own system of monetary management on London practice.[17]

In the late 1920s liaison between the Commonwealth Bank and the Bank of England was close, and the latter was not slow to offer advice.[18] The Commonwealth Bank was too competitive with the trading banks for the Bank of England's taste, but it did show a pleasing independence of government, despite governmental influence on its directorate, and demonstrated the same deep suspicions of politically motivated financial extravagance as animated the Old Lady herself.[19] This was not, perhaps, too surprising in a country where wealth based on primary exports, and its commercial and banking connections, was such a dominant force.[20]

Australian exports suffered during the war, which had drastic effects on shipping space and freights.[21] Government and banks had to help out with loans and in some cases, especially wool, the British authorities were content to buy up Australia's produce and let her set the price; but these were unusual circumstances.[22] The decline in exports was the chief reason for a wartime fall in Australian income,[23] but exports recovered in the post-war boom and, in the 1920s, the traditional assumption 'for which in the post-war period there was almost a national consensus', that the British market remained the key to Australian economic success was not disturbed.[24] Economic development in the 1920s was very much on pre-war lines. Resources were concentrated on extending the agrarian frontier to make space for a larger population and, simultaneously, to improve Australia's export performance. Rising incomes on the frontier would provide the stimulus to industry and services in the cities and guarantee balanced growth.[25] To implement this ambitious programme, the Australians required large-scale immigration and a considerable inflow of new capital to create the infrastructure needed on the new frontiers. In the event, export growth was slow in the 1920s: the world market for primary produce was sluggish and Britain's own tardy progress limited the expansion of demand.[26] Despite enthusiastic support for the Empire Settlement Act, the flow of immigrants never reached pre-1913 proportions.[27] Moreover, rapid development led to rising

TABLE 21.2 Balance of payments: Australia, 1909–39 (quinquennial averages, £m.)[a]

	Balance of trade	*Overseas debt payments*	*Other invisibles*	*Current account balance*[b]	*Overseas debt as % of exports*
1909–13	+17.8	–15.0	–3.1	–0.3	19.3
1919–20/1923–24	+18.4	–27.8	–8.6	–18.0	20.3
1924–25/1928–29	+6.9	–36.1	–10.6	–39.8	25.1
1929–30/1933–34	+29.9	–40.1	–6.4	–16.6	38.7
1934–35/1938–39	+35.7	–38.4	–9.6	–12.3	27.6

Source: I.W. McLean, 'The Australian Balance of Payments on Current Account, 1901 to 1964–5', *Australian Economic Papers*, 7 (1968), pp. 83–6. For similar estimates see Butlin, *Australian Domestic Product, Investment and Foreign Borrowing*, Pt. IV, Ch. XXXI.

Notes:

[a] We have included gold production in exports throughout and not treated it as an invisible item.

[b] Balance of trade plus overseas debt repayments plus other invisibles.

imports, a rise only marginally slowed by the progress of heavily protected, high-cost Australian industry.[28]

To pay for these imports Australians borrowed extensively in Britain;[29] overseas debt repayment rose from 17 per cent of export income in 1920 to 28 per cent by the end of the decade (Table 21.2).[30] Between 1925 and 1928 Australian borrowings accounted for over two-fifths of all overseas flotations in London;[31] Australian 'extravagance' – often involving state rather than federal spending – was the talk of the City of London. In 1929 the Bank of England was urging moderation on the Australians, much to the annoyance of local politicians of all shades of opinion, who felt that the Bank already had too much influence.[32] By the time of the Wall Street crash, the Australians were effectively borrowing to pay interest on previous loans, and the problem was compounded because a great deal of the borrowing was on overdraft and other forms of short-term credit and was difficult to roll over in a crisis.[33] Little wonder that the Australians were at the forefront of demands that Britain should offer the Dominions preferences in their markets for, without this particular boon, the development strategy of the 1920s was incomplete and potentially disastrous.

Disaster struck in 1929, when a mild upswing in the economy from a low point in 1926–7 was completely aborted by the rapid drop in export prices, which fell by 23 per cent between 1929 and 1930 and continued to fall heavily for the next three years.[34] The collapse in export income, combined with an inability to borrow, caused a drastic shrinkage in London funds and, after an interval,[35] a severe credit squeeze, a slump in imports and a cut in output, though, in real terms, the fall in the latter was not as severe as in the 1890s.[36] One immediate outcome of the collapse in the export sector was a crisis in overseas loan repayments, which was made much more acute by the short-term nature of much of the debt (Table 21.2).[37]

The problem of the floating debt was sufficiently serious in 1930 to attract the attention of the Bank of England, which was still fighting to keep Britain on the gold standard and feared the effect of default or deferment of debt payment on the position of sterling. The Labour government in Australia, elected to federal power in 1929, was also anxious to secure Bank of England aid in the immediate crisis,[38] and to help discipline state governments whose loan expenditures had been high in the previous decade. The outcome was a visit to Australia in 1930 by one of the Bank's leading figures, Sir Otto Niemeyer.[39] His recommendations were frigidly orthodox: Australia must deflate to keep imports down and take a cut in living standards in order to improve competitiveness in world markets and retain financial credibility which, in his view, also meant adhering to free trade and staying on gold.[40] But, in 1930, higher tariffs and quota restrictions to reduce imports, and a heavy devaluation of the Australian pound against sterling, proved inevitable.[41] Nonetheless, the banks, including the Commonwealth Bank – grateful for Niemeyer's moral backing, which it had actively sought[42] – hesitated over devaluation, were wholeheartedly in favour of meeting the crisis through deflation and balanced budgets, and were keen to head off any attempt by Labour to mitigate it by a wholesale creation of domestic credit.[43] The urge to strive for a solution to the monetary crisis which London would approve stemmed from the fact that 'it was important to impress Niemeyer with the financial orthodoxy of both the government and the banks, for assistance from the Bank of England and the future of Australian credit in London depended on his report'.[44]

In the event, the Bank of England did not offer the Australians immediate assistance to overcome their funding problem, but this only gave the representatives of orthodoxy, particularly the Commonwealth Bank, even greater cause to urge on the federal and state governments the need for monetary discipline of the kind finally espoused in the Premiers' Plan of 1931.[45] In the course of the crisis, the Commonwealth Bank's authority grew significantly. Its control over the trading banks increased greatly in 1930, when the Mobilisation Agreement brought their gold reserves under Commonwealth Bank control as part of the attempt to ensure that Australia's obligations in London were met.[46] The Bank also took on a much more strategic position within Australian finance in the early 1920s through its issue of Treasury bills, which helped the federal government over its immediate financial problems and produced an asset which the Commonwealth Bank could use to influence the liquidity and credit-creating power of the trading banks.[47] It was strong enough, too, with help both from the trading banks and the Bank of England, to see off an attempt, by Labour in 1930, to turn the Commonwealth Bank into a simple commercial concern and to hand over its main public functions to a new state-controlled bank;[48] and it led the chorus of complaint which ruled out the possibility of a mildly reflationary economic package being adopted by Labour in 1931.[49]

The pursuit of deflation provoked immense antagonism especially from organised labour, which saw Niemeyer as 'the Jewish bailiff from the Bank of England who had been sent to force down Australian living standards so that foreign bond-holders might get their pound of flesh',[50] and regarded the Australian bankers as evil collaborators in this process. In New South Wales the Labour government went so far as to threaten to reschedule overseas debts and reduce interest payments unilaterally, and there was angry, if vague, talk of default.[51] But these forces could not hold out against the enormous range of interests, political and economic, which looked to Britain and the international economy as the main support for Australian development. The Labour government, torn between imperial and nationalist ideologies, collapsed in 1931, with one section joining more conservative political groupings to form a national government devoted, among other things, to sound money.[52] Just as disputes over financing government broke Labour in Britain and led to the formation of a National Government, so similar disputes, based on competing ideologies, shattered a Labour government in Australia and put in power those who still saw Australia's relationship with Britain as a central fact of policy. As the leading authority on the depression has argued, 'the struggle to avoid default on public obligations underpins the entire history of the depression'.[53]

Economic policy followed traditional lines in the 1930s, and the Commonwealth Bank, which was more or less in tune with the Bank of England in the crises of 1929–32,[54] used its enhanced influence to ensure that an internationalist frame of reference was retained in economic and financial affairs. In the 1930s the Commonwealth Bank had greater influence over the exchange rate than hitherto and even hankered after restoring parity between the Australian pound and sterling, although it had, in practice, to accept that the Australian currency was actually pegged to sterling at the rate of £A125 to £100 sterling.[55] It is noticeable too, that in occasional moments of difficulty, the Bank of England was willing to help the Australians to maintain this rate, in contrast to its rigid policy in 1929–30, when Australia was wrestling with its short-term debt problem.[56] The Commonwealth Bank was also keen to phase Treasury bills out of the system once the worst of the depression was over because it saw them as being inflationary.[57] In doing this, it was, consciously or not, probably hindering the development of a separate Australian money market and enhancing the influence of London on the Australian financial system. It was, in short, offering just the sort of cooperation Norman, Stamp and other prominent money men in England hoped to elicit from the maturing Dominions once sterling had to be managed.[58]

In their struggle to retain the status quo in political economy and to fend off nationalist solutions to the depression, Australia's outward-looking and British-oriented elites were significantly helped by the Ottawa system. This gave the Australians a secure niche in the British market, especially for meat, fruit and dairy produce;[59] in return, Australia made relatively few concessions to British exporters. Faced with shrinking world markets and a drying up of loans, Australia needed significant help in the British market while keeping a tight control of imports because, as the chief colonial debtor, she had few other ways of generating the export surplus necessary to pay her obligations. In 1928 exports and imports of goods were both equal to about 18 per cent of Australia's national income, and her additional invisible payments, for debt-service and invisibles such as shipping, could be met only by

TABLE 21.3 British trade with the Dominions, 1909–38 (quinquennial averages, £m.)

		1909–13	*1925–29*	*1934–38*
Canada	Exports[a]	24.5	34.3	25.2
	Imports	27.2	60.6	72.3
	Balance of trade	–2.7	–26.3	–47.1
Australia	Exports[a]	33.8	61.1	23.4
	Imports	36.9	59.2	61.8
	Balance of trade	–3.1	+1.9	–38.4
New Zealand	Exports[a]	10.2	22.1	16.6
	Imports	19.4	47.9	43.8
	Balance of trade	–9.2	–25.8	–27.2
South Africa	Exports[a]	21.3	33.0	37.1
	Imports	10.7	22.7	14.3
	Balance of trade	+10.6	+10.3	+22.8

Source: B.R. Mitchell and P. Deane, *Abstract of British Historical Statistics* (Cambridge, 1962).

Note:

[a] Exports include re-exports.

borrowing. By 1937, when income per head had recovered the 1928 level, exports were still equivalent to 18 per cent of national income. Ottawa probably had a lot to do with this: Australian exports to Britain were higher in value terms in 1934–8 than they had been in 1925–9 despite heavy falls in the prices of primary produce (Table 21.3). In contrast, imports in 1937 were equivalent to only 13 per cent of national income and the rise in the trade surplus, together with some further borrowing, gave Australia the means to meet her invisible commitments more easily (Table 21.3). In Australia itself, the gap created by the suppression of imports was filled by domestic manufactures, aided by high tariffs and the devalued Australian pound.[60] The chief losers here were British manufacturers: Britain's exports to Australia were much lower in 1934–8 than they had been in the late 1920s (Table 21.3). Keeping Australia as a fully functioning member of the Sterling Area in the 1930s meant that her industrialisation was encouraged at Britain's expense. Had the Australians not been able to meet the crisis in this way, the landed exporters, and the commercial and financial interests in the urban areas to which they were tied, might have lost faith in the British connection and would have found it extremely difficult to resist the claims of those who demanded a more radical and a more inward-looking solution to Australia's economic difficulties.[61]

Antipodean politicians were always inclined to adopt an overconfident attitude towards the parent concern and frequently assumed, in the most aggressive manner, a right to favourable economic treatment.[62] They often claimed that preferences were no more than their due: had they not been offering Britain preferences in their market for years? They were also adept at identifying their own interests with imperial ones. At the time of Ottawa, 'the dominant feature was the conviction of Australian governments that their own interests were equivalent to imperial interests and that, since it was the duty of British governments to uphold imperial interests, it should do what Australian governments told it to do'.[63] In reality, of course, Australia was only one element, albeit an important one presenting special problems, within a complex, and still cosmopolitan, British financial and trading system. Once Ottawa had been put in place, the Australians were reminded, sometimes rudely, of the limits of their position. In 1933, for example, the federal government demanded a massive conversion of its loans to lower rates of interest, once cheap money had been established in Britain, and vague threats that default or unilateral reductions of interest payments might take place if Australian needs were not met were uttered, sometimes by prominent and respected men. The British response was cool: they had their own conversion operations under way and these took priority. They also knew that Australia was too dependent to take drastic action. The Dominion continued to borrow in London, though at a much reduced rate, throughout the 1930s. This facility, and the conversion operation, were possible only because Australians were seen in London to have responded to the crisis in the correct manner.[64] Conversion duly took place, but at a pace dictated by the British.[65] It brought much needed relief: annual debt payments fell from £28.4m. in 1930 to just over £20m. by 1939.[66]

On the trade front the Australians also found, in the latter half of the decade, that Britain was unwilling to give them the special place in the British market that they felt they deserved. Danes and Argentines were found seats at the British table, as well as the true sons of empire. Worse still, in 1936, when the Australians diverted trade from Japan and the United States towards Britain in the hope of winning further concessions from London, all they received was retaliation from an angry Japan.[67] No other episode in Anglo-Australian relations in the 1930s reveals better the essentials of the economic relationship between them:

> What seems to have lain behind the trade diversion policy was a numb fear in official quarters in Australia that if they allowed Japan to rout Lancashire in the sale of textiles to Australia, then they would be subjected by the government of the United Kingdom to a further substantial contraction of the British market for all types of agricultural produce.[68]

Lancashire was pleased, but the Australians accorded cotton too much importance. Seen from London, it was necessary for Australia to maintain her trade with Japan because this had a significant bearing on Australia's financial relations with Britain:

> Whatever might be the resentments of British manufacturers at the advance of competitors in the Australian market, British bondholders and the financial guardians of the British balance of payments had a desire that Australia

> should not default on her debt. And it was only by maintaining reasonable relations with her foreign trading partners that Australia could accumulate with some of them (and notably with Japan) the surpluses which she must thereafter transfer to London.[69]

Equally humbling to Australian pride was the Anglo-American Trade Agreement of 1938. To facilitate the Agreement, Australia was forced to give up a few privileges in Britain and to loosen restrictions on imports from the United States. In this respect, Australia was a 'sacrificial lamb' making an accord possible: 'she had surrendered preferences in the British market, ended trade diversions and made concessions to Canada and in return received nothing except faint praise for aiding the cause of world peace'.[70] By then, the Australians were grudgingly recognising that the intricate network of British overseas commitments made it impossible for the latter to go to endless lengths to satisfy the needs of Australian exporters.[71] By the mid-1930s the financial crisis which had given Australia her particular importance in the early days of world depression, had been mitigated through a combination of financial orthodoxy and the Ottawa agreements. From then onwards, Australia needed no special treatment from Britain and received none. Her role thereafter was to play her part in the Sterling Area, whose strength and stability depended on trading and financial relations ranging far beyond the bounds of empire.

Disciplining the Afrikaner

In Australia, despite the hostility of a large section of the Labour movement to British finance, there was never any real possibility that governments would adopt policies which threatened essential British interests. In South Africa the collaborative forces were weaker and anti-British nationalism was more politically overt and strident. Nonetheless, between the wars, British economic and financial power remained formidable and nationalist governments were forced to come to terms with it.[72]

Between 1902 and 1910, when the Union came into existence, an uneasy bargain was struck in South Africa whereby local freedoms were traded against an acceptance of British paramountcy in the region.[73] Afrikaner concerns centred on the maintenance of harmonious relations among the disparate groups making up the white population and on the question of white supremacy and the economic security needed to underpin it. This, in turn, depended on the prosperity and growth of the mining industry, which had a determinant influence on the rest of the economy, including agriculture, and also provided the state with the bulk of its revenues. The progress of mining itself required large supplies of cheap African labour, much of it found through sub-imperialist activity beyond the borders of the Union.[74] Mining's future was also, to a considerable degree, in British hands. Britain was South Africa's dominant trading partner and the City was the channel through which vital foreign investments flowed into mining and the rest of the

South African economy. This became obvious during World War I, when Britain virtually commandeered South Africa's supplies of gold.[75] In the inter-war period, South African prosperity remained heavily dependent upon gold exports[76] and the colony's trade was still tied to Britain, though the latter's importance diminished somewhat over the period as a whole (Table 21.3). Britain was also an important source of foreign capital, which accounted for two-fifths of net investment in the economy in the 1920s. Dependence on imported capital fell sharply in the 1930s, when external public borrowing ceased and some loans were repaid, but the private sector continued to rely on foreign investment, and the balance of payments showed a persistent deficit on current account.[77] In addition, the South African banking scene was dominated by two firms with headquarters in London, the Standard Bank and Barclays DCO, which, in 1926, took over the only 'local' bank of substance, the National.[78]

Falls in mining income, or a slowing down of overseas investment flows, could create white unemployment and cause outbursts of resentment against mining capitalists and the British connection behind them. Within the limits set by the need to maintain white political and economic hegemony, Smuts's South Africa Party was sympathetic to mining capitalists rather than to trade unions, and proud of the imperial link;[79] but one feature of the inter-war period was the rise of the National Party under Hertzog's leadership, which was much less openly collaborative. National Party politicians often took advantage of Afrikaner sentiment to demand greater local autonomy, but they had to take care not to scare off the capital which made white prosperity possible, and they also had to live with continued British trading and financial dominance. After 1918, one way that Nationalists could secure both white votes and room for manoeuvre internationally was by giving active support to a policy of rapid industrialisation under protection. As a result, employment opportunities grew rapidly, white living standards rose and import substitution reduced South Africa's dependence on British trade. It proved impossible, however, to shake off British financial imperialism before World War II broke out. Indeed, as was the case with other white colonies, the development of industry, insofar as it made it possible for South Africa to run a trade surplus, improved her ability to service returns on capital raised in London and took some of the strain out of financial dependence.

The hesitant world economic recovery of the early 1920s made it harder to underwrite the political compromise which held the Union together. Gold-mining was beset by rising costs and declining profitability, while agriculture made only a partial recovery from the post-war slump of 1920–1.[80] In these circumstances, nationalist demands, linking economic autonomy with political independence, had an increasing appeal. The first serious test of this platform came in 1919–20, when sterling was allowed to float. The banks adjusted their exchange rates for the South African pound so as to follow sterling. The price of gold rose in terms of paper currency, but since the banks were legally obliged to convert paper into gold on the old terms it became profitable to export gold from South Africa. There was a rapid gold drain and a contraction of credit which aggravated an already difficult economic situation in 1920. There were many calls in South Africa for a unilateral revaluation of the South African pound and a break in the link with sterling. But the opinion of the commercial bankers, including the South African-based National Bank, was that revaluation would ruin South Africa's trade with Britain, precipitate a balance of payments crisis and induce a capital flight from South Africa. These views prevailed: in 1920, South Africa left the gold standard and the pound was made inconvertible.[81]

One other outcome of the crisis was the creation of the first central bank in the Dominions, the South African Reserve Bank.[82] The Reserve Bank, like the Bank of England, was a private institution with sole rights of note issue, some control over the reserves of the commercial banks and the power to rediscount. Its first governor was a Bank of England man, and the Reserve Bank was clearly intended to be an institution with an independent voice in South Africa[83] which would cooperate with London in the novel and difficult task of ensuring that the South African pound did not get out of line with sterling. In practice, the Reserve Bank had little influence. Originally, it did not even hold the government's account and, as South Africa had only a rudimentary money market, the commercial banks still took most of their investment business to the City, where the Bank of England's influence was all-pervasive.[84]

Britain's decision to float sterling also weakened the demand for gold and increased the pressure on the mining industry to cut costs. Falling wages for white workers and reductions in the prices paid for supplies of foodstuffs alienated miners and farmers and led in 1922 to the Rand Revolt, a major strike of white miners which was crushed by the joint action of the government and the mining companies. The association between the pro-imperial South Africa party and mining capitalists during the strike lost Smuts the support of the electorate;[85] in 1924, Hertzog's Nationalists came to power with a mandate to improve the living standards of white workers and to reduce South Africa's dependence on Britain.[86] Hertzog's success was not welcomed in London: the National Party still had its roots in Afrikaner rural culture and there were fears that the new government would be anti-capitalist as well as anti-British.

Hertzog's administration undoubtedly felt an instinctive sympathy towards its agricultural constituency, but it also had a shrewd awareness of the need to work with and, if possible, to harness the forces of modernisation in South Africa.[87] Dependence on revenues from gold-mining ensured that the government cooperated with the mining firms in maintaining the flow of migrant labour; reliance on the London money market (despite the fact that new capital was in short supply in the 1920s) guaranteed that existing foreign debts would be serviced punctually. At the same time, the government pursued a vigorous and successful campaign of industrialisation. Tariffs, though limited by an obligation (inherited from before 1914) to give preferential treatment to Britain, were used to create manufacturing employment for whites; aspirations to economic independence were symbolised by the establishment of a prestigious state-sponsored enterprise, the Iron and Steel Corporation, in 1928.[88]

Perhaps the most telling illustration of the Nationalists' ambitions and limitations with respect to Britain in the 1920s was the attempt to wrest control of monetary policy from London. By 1924, pressure to take South Africa back to gold was building up again. With the British still uncertain about the date of return, the new Hertzog government decided to go it alone, despite Britain's clear preference for continuing the link with sterling.[89] Hertzog took advice from Kemmerer, the American 'money doctor', widely known as a champion of the gold standard, and from a Dutch central banker: the opinion of the City of London was deliberately unsought.[90] Again, the commercial banks protested that South Africa was too dependent on Britain to return to gold before her, and the English governor of the Reserve Bank was, generally speaking, in favour of South Africa retaining her link with sterling.[91] But, in this case, the banks were ignored for reasons that were primarily ideological and political: going back to gold alone would undermine British imperial power and broadcast South Africa's ability to survive outside the imperial circle.[92] South Africa's action also had wider implications, for 'when a Dominion broke from the fold Britain was in a poor position to expand its financial radius of power through infiltrating Central Europe'.[93] So, the South African decision – which the City of London met with profound silence in the hope of reducing its impact[94] – may, as already suggested, have had some influence on Britain's decision to return to gold in 1925, though the concurrent German stabilisation was of at least equal significance. In any event, Britain's return robbed the nationalists of their victory and left unanswered the anxious enquiries of the commercial banks as to whether or not South Africa was really able to strike out independently.

The world slump after 1929 and the financial crisis of 1931 gave added impetus to nationalist forces in South Africa, as elsewhere. Hertzog was a leading influence on the discussions which led to the Dominions being accorded 'equality of status' with Britain in 1931,[95] and legislative changes at home meant that, by the mid-1930s, South Africa had achieved a considerable degree of constitutional freedom. However, it proved more difficult to free the economy from its reliance on Britain. By the late 1930s, external trade was much more diversified than before 1914 and, contrary to the experience of other dominions, trade dependence on Britain continued to decrease in the depression decade (Table 21.1). However, as we have pointed out elsewhere, diversification of trade was consistent with (and often supported) continued financial dominance. Although the share of capital supplied to the gold-mining industry from local sources grew substantially during the 1930s,[96] the City's contribution to investment remained crucial.

The decisive test of South Africa's ability to manage its own economic affairs occurred after Britain left the gold standard in 1931.[97] Hertzog decided not to follow suit. Again, nationalist motives were prominent, but the government also genuinely feared that the rush to leave gold would prove the ruin of South Africa's most important industry. The consequences were disastrous. Agricultural exports, already hit by the world depression, suffered grievously from a high South African pound. There was also a considerable flight of capital as speculators anticipated that

South Africa would devalue. The commercial banks' London balances fell, and they responded in time-honoured fashion by squeezing credit in South Africa. This was deemed unpatriotic,[98] but the government, which tried vainly to counter capital flight by raising funds in New York and Amsterdam,[99] and the Reserve Bank, now firmly under Afrikaner influence, could do little to prevent it.

The Kemmerer-Vissering Commission which, in 1924–5, had advised the South African government to return to gold, had argued that the Reserve Bank's powers should be increased by allowing it to compete commercially, by giving it the government's account and by taking steps to create a bill market in South Africa.[100] All these reforms were attempted. However, no short-money market of significance developed in South Africa; acting as the government banker did not confer as much authority as it did in Australia or New Zealand because the role of the state in the South African economy was less significant. So, although the Reserve Bank proved helpful in lending to government at the height of the crisis, it had not the power to determine the money supply or to influence radically the exchange rate.[101] The country was still relatively small and underdeveloped. Despite her abundance of gold, South Africa was forced to accept in 1933 that she must allow her currency to go off gold and float with sterling: 'she was in fact on a sterling exchange standard and her gold exports were a means of keeping up her sterling reserves'.[102] South Africa was becoming more assertive in her relations with Britain but 'economic control outlived political control', and this was intimately connected with the hold which British financial institutions had on the country – a hold which, if anything, actually tightened in the inter-war years.[103]

Failure to remain on the gold standard had repercussions on domestic economic policy. The crisis weakened the Nationalists, who were forced into a coalition with Smuts's party, one consequence of which was to halt the further extension of protectionist tariffs.[104] Despite this, when the sharp rise in world gold prices after 1933 triggered off a boom in South Africa, industry prospered as much as mining. The latter, however, stayed at the centre of government concerns partly because, in the 1930s, it provided a rising proportion of state revenues; ensuring a steady flow of African labour for the mines thus remained a matter of great official concern. The coalition's alliance with mining interests, and its espousal of a 'practical' form of apartheid, was viewed with unease by purists who favoured absolute segregation and an almost equivalent degree of autonomy from foreign business.[105] But they had little influence at the time: in the 1930s the nationalist coalition worked with the mining companies, remained in the Sterling Area and paid its overseas debts without fuss. Its political independence was also problematic: the outbreak of World War II split the coalition, but it was Smuts, who supported Britain, who triumphed, and Hertzog, who wanted South Africa to remain neutral, who was defeated.

The settlement which shaped the Union of South Africa was a compromise between British and Afrikaner interests. Afrikaner politicians did not become merely servants of foreign business but, as in other settler colonies, political advance was associated with continued economic subordination, and nowhere more so than in matters of banking, capital investment and monetary policy. Profound though it was, the gulf between Briton and Afrikaner was spanned by the realisation that dependence with high wages was preferable to independence at lower standards of living. Acting on this appraisal was greatly helped by the fact that a large part of the costs of economic development and political stability could be transferred to the African labour force, which was both cheap and disenfranchised. This congenial formula worked for several generations: the accumulated bill is now being presented.

New Zealand breaks the shackles

The Afrikaner population was always big enough and influential enough to insert a strongly anti-imperial strand into South Africa's relations with the rest of the British empire. By contrast, New Zealand was traditionally the most docile of the Dominions.[106] Yet the strains imposed upon her by the depression of the 1930s eventually led her to challenge the basic premises upon which the Sterling Area was founded.

Of all the Dominions, New Zealand was the most trade dependent throughout the period (Table 21.1) and, with interest on debt running at twice the level of the export surplus in the 1920s, she was a persistent borrower throughout the decade.[107] Despite this, when international trade in primary products collapsed after 1929, New Zealanders were not faced with such an overwhelming balance of payments difficulty as beset their Australian neighbours because they did not have Australia's acute short-term debt problem and, probably as a result, found London more accommodating. Exports fell by two-fifths in value between 1929 and 1932 but this was more than balanced by a 50 per cent cut in import values in the same period. Only in 1930 and 1931 did New Zealand have to run down its balances in London, and then a certain amount of aid from the Bank of England was required. After 1932 exports started to recover, aided by the Ottawa concessions (Table 21.3), and New Zealand again began to run the balance of trade surpluses which had been characteristic of her economy since the 1890s.[108]

Nonetheless, export values did not regain their 1929 levels until 1936. To maintain her trade surplus and a healthy position as regards London funds, New Zealand had to suppress imports through devaluation, higher protection and a deflationary economic policy. National income fell by roughly three-tenths between 1929 and 1932.[109] It did not recover the 1929 level until the late 1930s,[110] and unemployment remained high throughout the decade. The fact that the mother country had failed to solve New Zealand's economic difficulties, and had even seen fit to put quota restrictions on New Zealand's exports in the 1930s, dealt a blow to the imperial sympathies of the remotest of Britain's 'children'. Unlike Australia, where those most hostile to the 'money power' were kept from political office, bitterness at the supposed iniquity of the bankers and rentiers resulted in the election, in 1935, of a radical government which made a gallant, even imprudent, attempt to assert the right to decide the country's economic future without reference to Britain's own economic priorities.[111]

Part of the new strategy of the late 1930s involved a radical use of the recently formed central bank, the Reserve Bank of New Zealand, whose origins lay in the early days of the world depression. Commercial banking in New Zealand and Australia was so closely related that, during the Australian exchange crisis of 1930, it seemed possible that the New Zealand pound might be devalued along with the Australian though, at that time, New Zealand's balance of payments problem was not so acute.[112] On a brief visit during his Australian trip, Niemeyer advised the New Zealanders that the solution lay in creating a central bank to manage their currency and credit, thus reducing the influence of the Australian banks and preventing a fall in the New Zealand pound. The Reserve Bank, built on lines approved by the Bank of England and with a Governor imported from Thread-needle Street, finally appeared in 1933, though too late to achieve its mission of preventing the devaluation of the New Zealand pound.[113]

In its earliest days, the Reserve Bank was the handmaiden of a government determined to adhere to monetary orthodoxy.[114] However, with the coming of a Labour government, this cautious and conservative institution was nationalised and used as one of the main instruments of a policy devoted to reducing unemployment, improving welfare and diversifying the economy, all of which required unprecedented levels of government expenditure.[115] By 1938 the policy was running into severe balance of payments constraints. Exports, which had risen rapidly in the world boom of 1937, fell sharply in the subsequent depression of 1938. Imports rose quickly as incomes increased in 1936–7 and marked time in 1938.[116] The balance of trade surpluses shrank with alarming speed and reserves held in London began to fall heavily in 1938–9. The position was greatly aggravated by a flight of capital as propertied New Zealanders took fright at 'socialism'.[117] Exchange and import controls had to be applied in 1938: exchange reserves in London fell by £34m. between 1935 and 1939,[118] and the government found it needed credit in London despite having come to power pledged to avoid making any more commitments to the 'bloodsuckers' of the City.

The British reaction to the crisis revealed the depths of gentlemanly distaste for those who refused to play the financial game by the normal rules.[119] In the Treasury, New Zealand's policy was described as 'a dreadful business' involving 'a degree of government control and of regimentation of industry which is intolerable except in a totalitarian system'.[120] However, given the mess that New Zealand was in by 1938, the Treasury preferred exchange controls to devaluation, which might have stoked up inflation in the Dominion and further threatened her ability to meet her obligations in London. When New Zealand applied for assistance in 1939, the Treasury was disinclined to help and made it clear to the colonial emissaries that there was little sympathy for antipodean socialism in the City. New Zealand responded by hinting at default. In normal times the British might well have called the New Zealanders' bluff. But in 1939 times were not normal, and it was recognised that Britain could not let default become an issue when sterling was under immense pressure. In the end, the New Zealanders got their loan, though on rigorous terms and in return for a promise to remove some of the more obnoxious restrictions placed on imports.

The Bank of England did its best to ensure a successful flotation to the extent of taking up about two-fifths of the loan itself. Had it not been for the imminence of war, New Zealand would most probably have been left, as Australia had been in 1930, to pay the price for its financial innovations without support from London.

Canada and sterling

If Australia, New Zealand and South Africa all presented Britain with a complex sum of financial problems, each one with its unique features, they had one quality in common: they were all more or less willing members of the Sterling Area. Canada, the oldest and most economically developed of the white Dominions, was not.[121] Canadian banks habitually kept their reserves in New York rather than in London. In the nineteenth century New York was favoured at least partly for its proximity. After 1900, though, the preference reflected the brute fact that the United States began to overtake Britain as Canada's chief economic partner. During the war and in the 1920s, the United States substantially increased her lead over Britain as a provider of Canadian imports and overtook her as a market for the Dominion's exports (Table 21.4). More fundamentally, the United States became Canada's chief source of imported capital after 1914. In 1914, Britain still owned three-quarters of all the foreign investment in Canada and the United States one-fifth.[122] By 1930 the British share had fallen to one-third and the American had risen to two-fifths. During the war, when Canadian exports to Britain rose sharply and Britain's exports to her fell, Canada was effectively exporting capital to Britain; when Britain left gold in

TABLE 21.4 Trade of Canada with various countries, 1911–39 (per cent)

	United States	*UK*	*Other Sterling Area*	*Others*
Imports				
1911	60.8	24.3	4.4	10.5
1926	66.3	16.3	5.0	12.4
1929	68.8	15.0	4.8	11.4
1937	60.7	18.2	11.0	10.1
1939	66.1	15.2	10.0	8.7
Exports				
1911	38.0	48.2	6.1	7.7
1926	36.3	36.4	7.6	19.7
1929	42.8	25.2	9.1	22.9
1937	36.1	40.3	10.4	13.2
1939	41.1	35.5	11.1	12.3

Source: H.G.J. Aitken et al., *The American Economic Impact on Canada* (Durham, NC 1959), Table 6, p. 155.

1919 and the Canadians stuck firmly to it, the fall in sterling gave Canada a chance to repatriate substantial amounts of British-held Canadian securities.[123]

Canada had its Anglophiles and others who, although not devoted to the imperial ideal, viewed the growth of American influence in Canada with alarm and hoped, as did metropolitan imperialists, that improved relations with Britain would act as a counterweight. In the 1920s common ground was hard to find. Canada wanted preferences but Britain hung on grimly to free trade. On the other side, the Canadians were unenthusiastic about granting further preferences to British manufacturers and were lukewarm on imperial emigration schemes.[124] The economic catastrophe of the early 1930s, however, forced Canada and Britain into a greater interdependence. The collapse of American demand after 1929 hit Canada extremely hard:[125] the Ottawa agreements provided partial compensation. Perhaps the worst hit group in Canada, the western prairie wheat farmers, received little advantage from the preferential system since Britain had little control over the price of wheat, or wool, and a number of other commodities exported by the empire.[126] But other Canadian exports, including manufactures, did well. Canada's exports to Britain fell from £57m. in 1929 to £35m. in 1931, but then rose rapidly again to £92m. by 1937 (Table 21.4). Britain's exports to the Dominion did much less well, hindered as they were by the depressed state of the Canadian economy and by high tariffs designed to protect local manufacturers.[127]

The overall effect of the depression and of the Ottawa agreements was to reverse the tendency for the American share of Canadian trade to increase. Not only did trade with Britain grow, but also the share of the rest of the Sterling Area in Canadian trade rose. Since Canada was not a member of the area, her inclusion in the preferential system was a sign that 'imperial' and sentimental factors had their place in British economic foreign policy in the 1930s. At the same time, it is probably the case that, if Canada was ever to be tempted to join the Sterling Area, something like the Ottawa system, and the shift it confirmed in Canadian trading patterns, was a necessary preliminary. Moreover, it was quickly recognised, both in Britain and Canada, that the weakening of the tie with the United States and the beginnings of the preferential system did open up the possibility of Canada joining the sterling bloc.

The Canadians left the gold standard in 1929, and unhinged their own dollar from that of the United States, though the abandonment was not recognised officially until 1932.[128] When sterling went off gold in 1931, Canada was thus left with the problem of whether to re-attach her currency to the dollar or to peg it to sterling. The alternative was to pursue an independent line of policy because Canada's money market was developed enough to allow some limited degree of independence. There were strong pleas from imperial enthusiasts in Britain, and a measure of support in banking circles in Canada, for a sterling peg system. Following sterling in 1932 and 1933 was tempting because it would have meant a significant devaluation against the American dollar and would have had beneficial effects on Canada's balance of trade with the United States, which was heavily adverse. But there was also a widespread fear that devaluation would have inflationary effects;

that it would increase the already heavy weight of repayments on American debt; and that it would reduce Canada's credibility in New York, the money market that really mattered to her, since loans from London were unlikely in the 1930s. These arguments were ultimately decisive in keeping Canada out of the sterling area, but she also avoided a fixed link with the American dollar and tried to steer an independent course on exchange rates throughout the 1930s.[129]

The question of managing the exchanges and the wider problem of dealing with the depression brought the issue of central banking into focus in Canada, and a Royal Commission was appointed in 1933 to investigate whether such a bank was necessary.[130] Two of the five members were British, including Sir Charles Addis, a Bank of England director and a confidant of its Governor. Under their influence, the Commission argued for a private institution similar to the Bank of England.[131]

These views were largely accepted when the Bank of Canada was formed in 1935,[132] with the express intent of keeping it free from political interference.[133] In their Report, the Commissioners explained that the most pressing task facing a Canadian central bank would be the exchanges since 'the need for international monetary co-operation is urgent and constant'. Order could be restored for the international economy only through 'the introduction of central banks working to harmonize national policy with the needs of the international situation'. The establishment of central banks in the empire was a key part of the process since they were 'the instrument of imperial monetary co-operation'. The whole Report was, in short, as clear an expression of the Bank of England's philosophy as could be wished, right down to the stress upon the primacy of the central banks' external role and the cautionary statement that a Canadian central bank 'would not be a source of unlimited credit for all borrowers on all occasions; indeed its operations might as often be restrictive as expansive'.[134]

The Bank of Canada's first Governor was on record as being sympathetic to the idea of Canada joining the Sterling Area;[135] the Bank's deputy governor was from the Bank of England. Furthermore, there is no doubt that the English members of the Royal Commission hoped that a Bank of Canada would serve as manager of a monetary system based on sterling. Addis, who described Canada in 1934 as 'an important component of the sterling group . . . which has not yet linked its currency to the pound',[136] and who saw the Royal Commission as a way 'to ensure that Canada was not wooed away from sterling by her American neighbour',[137] argued that a floating Canadian dollar could easily spark inflation. A return to gold would be ideal but, that apart, Canada's best option was to become part of 'an Imperial Sterling Union in which other countries might be invited to join' so that she could 'take part in an Imperial monetary policy in which every unit in the British empire might be called upon to co-operate as a means of defence against the menace to the whole Empire of the rapid economic nationalism of other countries'. Addis did not see Canada's mounting indebtedness to the United States as forming a barrier to her membership of the Sterling Area. Canada could get all the American dollars she needed in London in exchange for 'surplus sterling', and any difficulties could be overcome 'if a Canadian Central Bank, acting as a member of the Sterling

Union and in full knowledge of the movement of other currencies', took appropriate action. But to ensure this the Bank would have to be independent not only of governments – always likely to be hijacked by special interest groups promoting dangerous schemes involving 'funny money' – but also of the commercial banks, which could easily behave in a monopolistic and self-interested fashion.[138]

Needless to say, the extent of British influence on central banking in its early days generated much anxiety and hostility in Canada. This was particularly so on the prairies, the area worst affected by depression, where it was hoped that a central bank might be used to cheapen and extend credit. In 1934 one western politician, later to become a director of the Bank of Canada, wanted anxiously to know: 'Are we to have a Norman Conquest of Canada?'[139] The private nature of the original Bank certainly offended many in Canada: what looked like independence to Addis appeared as a dangerous freedom to many North Americans,[140] who had a more benign and positive view of the state's role in banking than did most Bank of England directors. With a change of government in 1936 came nationalisation.[141] However, this made no perceptible difference to the Bank's policy, which continued to be cautious and in line with government insistence on balanced-budget orthodoxy.[142] Nor did the Bank revive the opportunity to lead Canada into the Sterling Area: in exchange policy an independent course was steered between New York and London, a course made possible by the relatively advanced nature of the Dominion's money market.

After the disturbances of 1929–33, the British share of Canadian imports began to decline again. Despite Ottawa, Canadian exports to Britain did not expand rapidly enough to fill the gap left by the loss of exports to the United States and, by the mid-1930s, the Canadians were again looking south in the hope of improvement.[143] A liberalising agreement was made in 1935, and in 1938 came the Anglo-American trade agreement which, as we have already seen, was made possible because Canada was willing to forgo some of her privileges in the British market in order to make further inroads into that of the United States. Moreover, the Canadians began to run a balance of payments surplus with Britain in the late 1930s, partly as a result of the Ottawa agreements. Consequently, Canada was running an overall balance of payments surplus by the late 1930s and becoming a net exporter of capital.[144] The brief moment when Canada could have been enticed into the British financial camp had passed.

Imperial preference and British finance

In many ways the Ottawa preferential system was the logical outcome of decades of lending to the white dominions. While the world economy was buoyant, obligations could be met if Britain retained free trade; but once international trade ran into difficulties in the 1930s, free trade had to go because some degree of discrimination in favour of major debtors was necessary to prevent massive defaults. Even so, the preferential system proved inadequate to Dominion needs and its limitations provoked disappointment, even bitterness. By the late 1930s the pro-British elites on the white periphery, accustomed to treating Britain as a bottomless market for their produce and as an endless source of capital and migrants, were facing the hard truth that the mother country no longer had the strength and size to ensure rapid growth and full employment in the Dominions.

> In Canada, Australia, South Africa and even in gentle New Zealand the 1930s were characterised by moves to unscramble all those neat little imperial 'packages' which for decades had been an essential foundation of 'natural development'; they were rebound in ways that were internally more secreted and only loosely meshed into imperial networks, however relatively important the British remained as conventional trading partners.[145]

However, this process of 'ideal prefabricated decolonization'[146] had not gone far in 1939 and, from the international financial viewpoint, Britain still had a massive authority which was only just beginning to be questioned when war broke out again. The appearance of central banking in the Dominions registered both the beginning of the Dominions' attempts to further their own autonomy and Britain's determination to keep financial control in changing circumstances. If the Bank of England was only partially successful in ensuring that Dominion central banks would be created in its own image, the colonists remained, on the whole, orthodox in their monetary policies; the power of London balances and the money market of the City was still of overwhelming significance for most of the white periphery.[147] Indeed in the early 1930s, as the financial power of the United States waned, Britain seemed set to recover some of the ground lost by her in the previous twenty years, so much so that Canada was tempted to join the sterling group. Perhaps overwhelmed by the pressing nature of her debt problems, Australia was the most obedient Dominion in financial terms. A more aggressive nationalism in South Africa could not prevent conformity to the dictates of sterling; New Zealand's late surge of radicalism was a little more successful but in special circumstances. By the late 1930s impending world war and the resurgence of the United States meant that the problem for the Sterling Area was not so much expansion as survival: it is doubtful if New Zealand's cheeky attempt to buck the system would have been tolerated to the same degree if Hitler had not been ready to strike against Poland.

If the Dominions were beginning to take their first, rather hesitant, steps towards economic self-determination the process was, paradoxically enough, aided in the long run by the structure of the Sterling Area itself. The area could function properly only if the dependent members were able to meet their debt obligations and maintain adequate London balances. Now that British lending had virtually ceased, the main way of ensuring this was to produce, or increase the size of, Dominion balance of trade surpluses with Britain. This could be achieved through preferences in the British market. But, given the limitations on the size of the British market and the number of claimants to be satisfied, Dominion surpluses of a sufficient scale could be acquired only through the introduction of a fairly rigorous programme of import substitution which affected, most of all, British manufactured exports.

Asymmetry in the mutual preferences given, with Britain getting the worst of the deal, was probably essential if the Sterling Area was to work. The growth of industry on the white periphery was necessary to the functioning of the imperial economy, increasing the complexity of Dominion economies and hastening the time when they would become self-supporting enough to detach themselves from Britain's financial leading strings. British gentlemanly capitalism was steadily, if unwittingly, sowing the seeds of its own destruction at the very centre of the empire where its power was strongest.

Notes

1 Good general histories include: R.F. Holland, *Britain and the Commonwealth Alliance, 1918–39* (1981); D. Judd and P. Slinn, *The Evolution of the Modern Commonwealth, 1902–1981* (1982); P.N.S. Mansergh, *The Commonwealth Experience* (1969); W.K. Hancock, *Survey of British Commonwealth Affairs,* Vol. I (Oxford, 1936) and Vol. II, Pt. I (Oxford, 1940), is also excellent.

2 J.G. Darwin, 'Imperialism in Decline? Tendencies in British Imperial Policy between the Wars', *Hist. Jour.,* 23 (1980), pp. 665–7. In this context see also the classic text by A.P. Thornton, *The Imperial Idea and its Enemies* (1959), pp. 196ff.

3 A.W.F. Plumptre, *Central Banking in the British Dominions* (Toronto, 1940), pp. 9–13.

4 G.R. Hawke, 'New Zealand and the Return to Gold in 1925', *Austral. Econ. Hist. Rev.,* XI (1971), p. 49.

5 Plumptre, *Central Banking in the British Dominions,* p. 13.

6 Ibid. Chs. VI and VII.

7 Darwin, 'Imperialism in Decline?', p. 664.

8 R.F. Holland, 'Imperial Collaboration and Great Depression: Britain, Canada and the Wheat Crisis, 1929–35', *Jour. Imp. and Comm. Hist.,* XVI (1988), p. 115.

9 F.D. Guiney, 'Money Supply and Australian Trading Banks, 1927–39', *Austral. Econ. Hist. Rev.,* XI (1971), p. 165. See also J.S.G. Wilson, 'The Australian Trading Banks', in R.S. Sayers, ed. *Banking in the British Commonwealth* (Oxford, 1952), pp. 20–2, 27–8.

10 A.J.S. Baster, *The Imperial Banks* (1929), pp. 215–17, 243–50.

11 Guiney, 'Money Supply and the Australian Trading Banks', p. 166.

12 A.H. Tocker, 'The Monetary Standards of Australia and New Zealand', *Econ. Jour.,* 34 (1924), p. 570.

13 On South Africa in this context see S.H. Frankel, 'The Situation in South Africa', *Economic Journal,* 43 (1933), p. 106.

14 Lyndhurst Falkiner Giblin, *The Growth of a Central Bank: The Development of the Commonwealth Bank of Australia, 1924–1945* (Melbourne, 1951), pp. 17–18.

15 For the early history of the Bank see Peter Love, *Labour and the Money Power* (Melbourne, 1984), Ch. 2; R. Gollan, *The Commonwealth Bank of Australia: Origins and Early History* (Canberra, 1968); Giblin, *The Growth of a Central Bank,* pp. 2–6; Baster, *The Imperial Banks,* pp. 145ff; Plumptre, *Central Banking in the British Dominions,* pp. 86–8.

16 Giblin, *The Growth of a Central Bank,* pp. 6–13; Gollan, *The Commonwealth Bank of Australia,* p. 157; Geoffrey Blainey, *Cold and Paper: A History of the National Bank of Australia* (Melbourne, 1958), p. 313.

17 Giblin, *The Growth of a Central Bank,* pp. 13–23; Gollan, *The Commonwealth Bank of Australia,* Ch. 10; Baster, *The Imperial Banks,* pp. 162–5; J.S.G. Wilson, 'The Commonwealth Bank of Australia', in Sayers, *Banking in the British Commonwealth,* pp. 39–44; Plumptre, *Central Banking in the British Dominions,* pp. 88–91; Love, *Labour and the Money Power,* esp. pp. 84–7.

18 Giblin, *The Growth of a Central Bank,* pp. 37–46. See also the article by Sir Ernest Harvey, Comptroller of the Bank of England, in the *Economic Record,* 3 (1927). Harvey visited Australia to give advice in that year.

19 On the conservatism of bankers in general in Australia see C.B. Schedvin, *Australia and the Great Depression: A Study of Economic Development and Policy in the 1920s and 1930s* (Sydney, 1970), pp. 76–87. On independence from government see Giblin, *The Growth of a Central Bank,* pp. 50–1.
20 W.D. Rubinstein, 'The Top Wealth Holders of New South Wales, 1817–1939', *Austral. Econ. Hist. Rev.,* XX (1980), esp. pp. 148–50.
21 N.G. Butlin, Alan Barnard and J.J. Pincus, *Government and Capitalism: Public and Private Choice in Twentieth-Century Australia* (Sydney, 1982), p. 76.
22 Kosmas Tsokhas, 'W.M. Hughes, the Imperial Wool Purchases and the Pastoral Lobby, 1914–20', *Jour. Imp. and Comm. Hist.,* XVII (1989), tries to generalise about Anglo-Australian economic relationships, and in particular to deny the imperial element in them, on the basis of the wartime experience of wool sales without sufficiently considering the uniqueness of the times.
23 Stuart McIntyre, *Oxford History of Australia, 1901–1942,* Vol. IV (Oxford, 1986), p. 155.
24 W.H. Richmond, 'S.M. Bruce and Australian Economic Policy', *Austral. Econ. Hist. Rev.,* XXIII (1983), pp. 239–40. For interpretations of the 1914–29 period see M. Dunn, *Australia and the Empire: From 1788 to the Present* (Sydney, 1984); Peter Cochrane, *Industrialization and Dependence: Australia's Road to Economic Development, 1870–1939* (St Lucia, 1980), and Barrie Dyster and David Meredith, *Australia in the International Economy in the Twentieth Century* (Cambridge, 1990), Ch. 5.
25 W.A. Sinclair, *The Process of Economic Development in Australia* (1976), pp. 175–81; McIntyre, *Oxford History of Australia,* Vol. IV, Chs. 9 and 10; Richmond, 'S.M. Bruce and Australian Economic Policy', passim. Compare this with the import-substitution phase during the world war described by Sinclair on pp. 172–4.
26 E.A. Boehm, 'Australia's Economic Depression of the 1930s', *Economic Record,* 49 (1973), p. 609.
27 D.H. Pope, 'The Contours of Australian Immigration, 1901–30', *Austral. Econ. Hist. Rev.,* XXI (1981), esp. Table 1. For the imperial context see Ian M. Drummond, *British Economic Policy and the Empire, 1919–39* (1972), Ch. 2, and above p. 56.
28 Schedvin, *Australia and the Great Depression,* pp. 51–62; but cf. Boehm, 'Australia's Economic Depression of the 1930s', pp. 615–21. See also Butlin, Barnard and Pincus, *Government and Capitalism,* pp. 88–9.
29 The Commonwealth government also borrowed heavily in Britain during the war. See Dyster and Meredith, *Australia in the International Economy,* Table 5.3, p. 92. After 1914 Australians were just beginning to think in terms of borrowing elsewhere, but very little was achieved in this regard. During the war there was some talk, at both state and Commonwealth levels, of tapping the New York market. The Commonwealth government tried hard to suppress this initiative because it feared that, if the states could find new sources of finance, the Commonwealth government's fight against wartime inflation would be made more difficult. It is also doubtful whether money could have been raised on Wall Street at the time. See Bernard Attard, 'Politics, Finance and Anglo-Australian Relations: Australian Borrowing in London, 1914–1920', *Australian Journal of Politics and History,* 35 (1989), pp. 152–6. In 1921 the Queensland Labour government went further. It came to London to borrow but found the City hostile because Queensland pastoralists, who objected to local Labour Party legislation, had managed to convince the City that the proposed loans were risky. Labour responded by successfully raising funds in New York. But this proved an expensive business: by 1924 the government had compromised with its wool barons and it then found the City more obliging. On this episode, see: Gollan, *The Commonwealth Bank of Australia,* pp. 151–2; McIntyre, *Oxford History of Australia,* IV, pp. 231–2; B.C. Schedvin, 'G. Theodore and the London Pastoral Lobby', *Politics,* 6 (1971); Love, *Australia and the Money Power,* pp. 78–91. There were some successful attempts to organise state borrowings in New York in the late 1920s. On this see Dyster and Meredith, *Australia in the International Economy,* p. 119.

30 These figures are based upon statistics gathered by I.W. McLean, 'The Australian Balance of Payments on Current Account, 1901 to 1964–5', *Australian Economic Papers,* 7 (1968), pp. 84–7, and summarised in Table 21.2. Similar figures are given in Schedvin, *Australia and the Great Depression,* Table 13, p. 73, and in Dyster and Meredith, *Australia in the International Economy,* Table 5.10, p. 108. D. Clark, 'The Closed Book? The Debate on Causes', in Judy Mackinolty, ed. *The Wasted Years: Australia's Great Depression* (Sydney, 1981), offers rather lower ratios but they follow similar trends over time (p. 23). Dyster and Meredith show that public authorities' foreign debts rose from £364m. in 1918 to £631m. in 1929, with the states being the chief borrowers (Table 5.3, p. 93).

31 Schedvin, *Australia and the Great Depression,* Table 15, p. 100 and Ch. V. passim.

32 Richmond, 'S.M. Bruce and Australian Economic Policy', pp. 247–8; Clark, 'The Closed Book?', pp. 19–21; Schedvin, *Australia and the Great Depression,* pp. 103–4.

33 Schedvin, *Australia and the Great Depression,* p. 7; W.K. Hancock, 'Forty Years On', *Aus. Econ. Hist. Rev.,* XXII (1972–3), p. 73.

34 T.J. Valentine, 'The Course of the Depression in Australia', *Explorations in Economic History,* 24 (1987), p. 47. Besides Valentine and Schedvin there are valuable studies of the depression in: Boehm, 'Australia's Economic Depression of the 1930s'; W.A. Sinclair, 'Economic Development and Fluctuations in Australia in the 1930s', *Economic Record,* 51 (1975) (together with a reply by Boehm); Clark, 'The Closed Book?', and idem, 'Fools and Madmen', in Mackinolty, *The Wasted Years.* See also R.G. Gregory and N.G. Butlin, eds. *Recovery from the Depression: Australia and the World Economy in the 1930s* (Cambridge, 1989), and Dyster and Meredith, *Australia in the International Economy,* Ch. 6. There is an excellent discussion of the political economy of the crisis in McIntyre, *Oxford History of Australia,* IV, Ch. 11, and Love, *Australia and the Money Power,* Ch. 5.

35 Hancock, 'Forty Years On', p. 78. See also Schedvin, *Australia and the Great Depression,* pp. 204–10, which indicates the extent to which the banking system tried to delay the impact of falling London balances on Australian credit.

36 For G.D.P. figures see N.G. Butlin, *Australian Domestic Product, Investment and Foreign Borrowing, 1861–1938–9* (Cambridge, 1962), Table 13, p. 33. For comparisons with other countries' experiences, see Dyster and Meredith, *Australia in the International Economy,* Table 4.1, p. 84.

37 Schedvin, *Australia and the Great Depression,* pp. 90–1, 112–15.

38 Ibid. pp. 132–5.

39 We have learned a great deal about the origins of the Niemeyer visit from Bernard Attard, 'The Origins of the Niemeyer Mission: Anglo-Australian Financial Relations, 1921–1930', a paper read at the Sir Robert Menzies Centre for Australian Studies in the Institute of Commonwealth Studies, 24 May 1989. See also Schedvin, *Australia and the Great Depression,* pp. 134–7. Niemeyer's activities in South America are noted below, pp. 160, 166.

40 For Niemeyer's recommendations see Schedvin, *Australia and the Great Depression,* pp. 181–5. Also Peter Love, 'Niemeyer's Australian Diary and other English Records of his Mission', *Historical Studies,* 20 (1982–3), p. 261; Giblin, *The Growth of a Central Bank,* pp. 83–4; Love, *Australia and the Money Power,* pp. 100–1; Dyster and Meredith, *Australia in the International Economy,* pp. 135–6; E.D.G. Shann and D.B. Copland, eds. *The Crisis in Australian Finance, 1929–31* (Sydney, 1931), pp. 18–29.

41 On devaluation see Schedvin, *Australia and the Great Depression,* pp. 155–68, and on tariffs, pp. 141–4. The latter are also discussed in Butlin, Barnard and Pincus, *Government and Capitalism,* pp. 89–92.

42 Schedvin, *Australia and the Great Depression,* p. 135. The banks with London head offices resisted devaluation because they disliked 'the prospect of incurring substantial capital losses on their Australian assets'. The major 'local' bank, the Bank of New South Wales, was more worried about the effects of a high exchange rate on their customers. See M.W. Butlin and P.M. Boyce, 'Monetary Policy in Depression and Recovery', in Gregory and Butlin, *Recovery from the Depression,* pp. 201–4.

43 Ibid. pp. 183–4.

44 Ibid. p. 161. On this issue see also Neville Cain, 'Recovery Policy in Australia, 1930–2: Certain Native Wisdom', *Austral. Econ. Hist. Rev.*, 23 (1987), p. 202; and the statement by the Chairman of the Loan Council in February 1930, printed in Shann and Copland, *The Crisis in Australian Finance*, p. 10.

45 On the Premiers' Plan see Schedvin, *Australia and the Great Depression*, pp. 7–9, 244ff; Love, *Australia and the Money Power*, pp. 124–6. For recent debates on policy see Butlin and Boyce, 'Monetary Policy in the Depression and Recovery', and J. Pincus, 'Australia's Budgetary Policy in the 1930s', both in Gregory and Butlin, *Recovery from the Depression*. Dyster and Meredith claim that the premiers were 'overawed by the crisis [and] by the authority of the Bank of England'. See *Australia in the International Economy*, p. 137.

46 Ibid. pp. 8, 136–9; Giblin, *The Growth of a Central Bank*, pp. 69–70.

47 Giblin, *The Growth of a Central Bank*, pp. 121ff; Schedvin, *Australia and the Great Depression*, pp. 196–201; Dyster and Meredith, *Australia in the International Economy*, pp. 139–40.

48 Giblin, *The Growth of a Central Bank*, pp. 107–15; Schedvin, *Australia and the Great Depression*, pp. 172–6.

49 On Theodore's proposal and the opposition it aroused see Love, 'Niemeyer's Australian Diary', pp. 263–4; idem, *Australia an the Money Power*, pp. 114ff; Schedvin, *Australia and the Great Depression*, pp. 226–7, 239–43. Clark, 'Fools and Madmen', pp. 185ff, sees the plan in the context of other criticisms of orthodoxy. See also Cain, 'Recovery Policy in Australia', passim, and T. J. Valentine, 'The Battle of the Plans: A Macroeconomic Model of the Inter-War Economy', in Gregory and Butlin, *Recovery from the Depression*.

50 Love, 'Niemeyer's Australian Diary', p. 262. See also Schedvin, *Australia and the Great Depression*, pp. 186–7, 191–2. For trade union reactions see Shann and Copland, *The Crisis in Australian Finance*, pp. 58–61.

51 Clark, 'Fools and Madmen', p. 188; Schedvin, *Australia and the Great Depression*, pp. 186–8, 233–5, 269–70, 251–4; Love, *Australia and the Money Power*, pp. 104–7, 115–16; also Shann and Copland, *The Crisis in Australian Finance*, p. 182.

52 Schedvin, *Australia and the Great Depression*, esp. Ch. XIII. Lang's radical government in New South Wales was defeated at the polls in 1932. See Love, *Australia and the Money Power*, pp. 129–31; and Dyster and Meredith, *Australia in the International Economy*, pp. 143–4. For some insight into the tensions within the Labour Party in Australia see Shann and Copland, *The Crisis in Australian Finance*, pp. 61–5.

53 Schedvin, *Australia and the Great Depression*, p. 3. See also Butlin and Boyce 'Monetary Policy in Depression and Recovery', pp. 205–7. It has recently been argued that the defeat of even mildly reflationary measures demonstrates 'how much more important than elected ministries a determined coalition of domestic and foreign investors could be'. Dyster and Meredith, *Australia in the International Economy*, p. 140.

54 The Bank of England's approval of its Dominion counterpart is clear from Sayers, *The Bank of England*, I, p. 207.

55 Schedvin, *Australia and the Great Depression*, pp. 359–65. See also Giblin, *The Growth of a Central Bank*, pp. 136–50; Cain, 'Recovery Policy in Australia', pp. 209–11.

56 Giblin, *The Growth of a Central Bank*, pp. 142–3.

57 Ibid. pp. 159ff; Schedvin, *Australia and the Great Depression*, pp. 330–7. Schedvin notes that the funding of deficits meant that the funding policy succeeded in stabilising the amount of Treasury bills on the market only from 1932 (p. 337). See also Plumptre, *Central Banking in the British Dominions*, pp. 249–50, 322–24; and Butlin and Boyce, 'Monetary Policy in Depression and Recovery', pp. 208–11.

58 It is worth noting here that officials of the Commonwealth Bank tried to insist on the trading banks keeping a fixed proportion of their reserves with the Bank. This arrangement might have given the Commonwealth Bank greater indirect control over the London balances because these would have had to be run down to build up reserves with the Bank. But the Bank's policy was part of an internal power struggle with the commercial sector rather than a device to reduce the power of the London market over Australian finance. See Plumptre, *Central Banking in the British Dominions*, pp. 272–7.

59 Besides Drummond's comprehensive studies, see also R. Duncan, 'Imperial Preference: the Case of Australian Beef in the 1930s', *Economic Record,* 39 (1963), and Forrest Capie, 'Australian and New Zealand Competition in the British Market, 1920–1939', *Austral. Econ. Hist. Rev.,* XVIII (1978).

60 Schedvin, *Australia and the Great Depression,* p. 377; Mark Thomas, 'Manufacturing in Economic Recovery in Australia, 1932–1937', in Butlin and Gregory, *Recovery from the Depression.*

61 Schedvin, *Australia and the Great Depression,* pp. 373–5, for some general reflections on Australian financial orthodoxy. It may be worth noting here that, if the effects of devaluation are added to the tariff change of the early 1930s, protection against British imports was higher in 1939 than in 1930, despite Ottawa. Butlin, Barnard and Pincus, *Government and Capitalism,* p. 91.

62 J.D.B. Miller,'An Empire that Don't Care What You Do', in F.W. Madden and W. Morris-Jones, eds. *Australia and Britain: Studies in a Changing Relationship* (1980), pp. 92–4.

63 Ibid. p. 99.

64 Pincus, 'Australian Budgetary Policy in the 1930s', p. 177. In this context, Keynes's comments on the Australian debt problem in 1932 are worth remembering. He admitted that 'Australia has heavily overborrowed in the past and I have often advised that her securities be avoided'. But now, he claimed, London 'profoundly appreciates' the Australian determination 'to fulfil her bond'. In the coming era of 'ultra-cheap money', he felt that London would soon resume her position as an overseas lender and that 'respectable borrowers will be greatly sought after. . . . And why should not Australia be one of these? It lies within her power'. *Collected Works of John Maynard Keynes,* XXI (Cambridge, 1982), pp. 99–100.

65 Neville Cain and Sean Glynn, 'Imperial Relations under Strain: the British-Australian Debt Contretemps of 1933', *Austral. Econ. Hist. Rev.,* XXV (1985); see also Drummond, *The Floating Pound and the Sterling Area,* pp. 115–18.

66 Pincus, 'Australian Budgetary Policy in the 1930s', p. 184.

67 John B. O'Brien, 'Australia–British Relations during the 1930s', *Historical Studies,* 22 (1987), pp. 582–3; D.C.S. Sissons, 'Manchester v Japan: the Imperial Background of the Australian Trade Diversion Dispute with Japan, 1936', *Australian Outlook,* 30 (1976).

68 N.F. Hall, '"Trade Diversion" – An Australian Interlude', *Economica,* new ser., 5 (1938), p. 7. The episode is also treated by K.H. Burley, *British Shipping and Australia, 1920–1939* (Cambridge, 1968), pp. 135–44, and is seen from an Australian domestic perspective in Kosmas Tsokhas, 'The Wool Industry and the Trade Diversion Dispute with Japan', *Hist. Stud.,* 23 (1989).

69 Hancock, *Survey of British Commonwealth Affairs,* Vol. II, Pt. I, p. 253.

70 Ruth Megaw, 'Australia and the Anglo-American Trade Agreement, 1938', *Jour. Imp. and Comm. Hist.,* III (1975), p. 204.

71 For a revisionist approach to Anglo-Australian economic relations which is consistent with our line of argument see O'Brien 'Australia–British Relations', pp. 583–6; also Hancock, *Survey of British Commonwealth Affairs,* Vol. II, Pt. I, pp. 256–7.

72 For a general introduction to South African history see T.R.H. Davenport, *South Africa: A Modern History* (1977). Very useful surveys include A.P. Walshe and A.D. Roberts, 'Southern Africa', in the *Cambridge History of Africa,* Vol. 7 (Cambridge, 1986), and D.H. Houghton, 'Economic Development, 1865–1965', in Monica Wilson and Leonard Thompson, eds. *The Oxford History of South Africa,* Vol. II (Oxford, 1971).

73 The sizeable literature on this subject is surveyed by Deryck Schreuder, 'Colonial Nationalism and Tribal Nationalism: Making the White South African State', in John Eddy and Deryck Schreuder, eds. *The Rise of Colonial Nationalism* (Sydney, 1988). See also Ronald Hyam, 'The Myth of the "Magnanimous Gesture": the Liberal Government, Smuts and Conciliation, 1906', in Ronald Hyam and Ged Martin, *Reappraisals in Imperial History* (1976).

74 Alan H. Jeeves, *Migrant Labour in South Africa's Mining Economy: The Struggle for the Gold Mines' Labour Supply, 1890–1920* (Montreal, 1985); David Yudelman and Alan Jeeves,

'New Labour Frontiers for Old; Black Migrants to the South African Gold Mines, 1920–85', *Jour. Southern African Stud.*, 13 (1986). On South African sub-imperialism see Ronald Hyam, 'The Politics of Partition in South Africa, 1908–61', in Hyam and Martin, *Reappraisals in Imperial History*; and P.R. Warhurst, 'Smuts and South Africa: a Study in Sub-Imperialism', *South Afr. Hist. Jour.*, 16 (1984).

75 R. Ally, 'War and Gold – The Bank of England, the London Gold Market and South Africa's Gold, 1914–19', *Jour. Southern Afr. Stud.* 17 (1991).

76 Bruce R. Dalgaard, *South Africa's Impact on Britain's Return to Cold, 1925* (New York, 1981), Table 7, p. 28.

77 S.H. Frankel and H. Herzfeld, 'An Analysis of the Growth of the National Income of the Union in the Period of Prosperity before the War', *South African Journal of Economics*, 12 (1944), Table 8, p. 128 and Appendix I, p. 138.

78 On duopoly in South African banking see Stuart Jones, 'The Apogee of Imperial Banks in South Africa: Standard and Barclays, 1919–39', *Eng. Hist. Rev.*, CIII (1988). This development is put in the wider context of the growth of corporate banking and the increasing integration of Imperial and local banks within the empire in Baster, *The Imperial Banks*, pp. 223–243. See also A.C.L. Day, 'The South African Commercial Banks', in Sayers, *Banking in the British Commonwealth*, pp. 353–9.

79 The war against Germany was unpopular in many Afrikaner circles and the decision to invade German South-West Africa provoked a rebellion in sections of the army in 1914. Although this episode underlined the strength of local nationalist feeling in South Africa, it is important to note that the rebellion was suppressed by Afrikaner generals, including Smuts. See N.G. Garson, 'South Africa and World War I', in Norman Hillmer and Philip Wigley, eds. *The First British Commonwealth* (1980).

80 Maryna Fraser and Alan Jeeves, *All That Glittered: Selected Correspondence of Lionel Phillips, 1890–1924* (Cape Town, 1977), pp. 9, 284.

81 Dalgaard, *South Africa's Impact on Britain's Return to Gold*, pp. 45–50; J.A. Henry, *The First Hundred Years of the Standard Bank* (1963), pp. 176–84; also E. Cannan, 'South African Currency', *Econ. Jour.*, 30 (1920).

82 On the origins and original constitution of the Reserve Bank see G. de Kock, *A History of the South African Reserve Bank* (Pretoria, 1954); Dalgaard, *South Africa's Impact on Britain's Return to Gold*, pp. 51–2; Plumptre, *Central Banking in the British Dominions*, esp. pp. 59–60; H. Strakosch, 'The South African Reserve Bank', *Econ. Jour.*, XXXI (1921); E.H.D. Arndt, *Banking and Currency Development in South Africa, 1652–1927* (Cape Town, 1928); A.C.L. Day, 'The South African Reserve Bank', in Sayers, *Banking in the British Commonwealth*, pp. 373–7.

83 The commercial banks urged the need for the central bank to be independent. 'Those who gave this excellent advice in South Africa could scarcely be expected to realize how thoroughly the new Governor had been indoctrinated to the same effect in London': Henry, *The First Hundred Years of the Standard Bank*, p. 188.

84 Jones, 'The Apogee of the Imperial Banks in South Africa', pp. 894–5, 897, 907; Day, 'The South African Reserve Bank', pp. 373, 386; Plumptre, *Central Banking in the British Dominions*, p. 61.

85 On Smuts's attitudes towards mine-owners and mine-workers see Donald Denoon, *Settler Capitalism: The Dynamics of Dependent Development in the Southern Hemisphere* (Oxford, 1983), pp. 197–9.

86 Relations between government and workforce are dealt with by David Yudelman, *The Emergence of Modern South Africa: State, Capital and the Emergence of Organised Labour on the South African Gold Fields, 1902–1939* (Westport, Conn., 1983).

87 On Afrikanerdom's relationships with capitalism see Dan O'Meara, *Volkscapitalisme: Class, Capitalism and Ideology in the Development of Afrikaner Nationalism, 1934–1948* (Cambridge, 1983); and for a broad view of the politics of rural development, Timothy Keegan, 'The Dynamics of Rural Accumulation in South Africa: Comparative and Historical Perspectives', *Comp. Stud. in Soc. and Hist.*, 28 (1988).

88 W.G. Martin, 'The Making of an Industrial South Africa: Trade and Tariffs in the Interwar Period', *Int. Jour. African Hist. Stud.*, 23 (1990); Nancy Clark, 'South African State Corporations: the Death Knell of Economic Colonialism?', *Jour. Southern African Stud.*, 14 (1987).

89 Dalgaard, *South Africa's Impact on Britain's Return to Gold,* pp. 76, 158. For a general discussion of the anti-imperial element in monetary thinking see ibid. pp. 12–19.

90 Ibid. p. 86. For the Kemmerer-Vissering Commission's recommendations in detail see ibid. pp. 93–4, 102–4, and C.S. Richards, 'The Kemmerer-Vissering Report and the Position of the Reserve Bank of South Africa', *Econ. Jour.*, 35 (1925). Kemmerer's role in South America is noted below, p. 151.

91 Dalgaard, *South Africa's Impact on Britain's Return to Gold,* pp. 99–100; Richards, 'The Kemmerer-Vissering Report', p. 561.

92 Dalgaard, *South Africa's Impact on Britain's Return to Gold,* pp. 127–30.

93 Ibid. p. 157.

94 Ibid. p. 153.

95 Holland, *Britain and the Commonwealth Alliance,* pp. 54–5, 59.

96 Alan Jeeves, 'Migrant Labour and South African Expansion, 1920–1950', *South Afr. Hist. Jour.*, 18 (1986).

97 What follows is based largely on Drummond, *The Floating Pound and the Sterling Area,* Ch. 4. See also Henry, *The First Hundred Years of the Standard Bank,* Ch. 18; Plumptre, *Central Banking in the British Dominions,* pp. 398–402.

98 See Henry, *The First Hundred Years of the Standard Bank,* pp. 237–8.

99 Drummond, *The Floating Pound and the Sterling Area,* pp. 79–80. In 1931 the Reserve Bank appointed a new governor who lacked sympathy with Britain. See ibid. p. 78, and Henry, *The First Hundred Years of the Standard Bank,* pp. 241–2.

100 Dalgaard, *South Africa's Impact on Britain's Return to Gold,* pp. 94–6, 104.

101 Plumptre, *Central Banking in the British Dominions,* pp. 63–6, 403–5; Jones, 'The Apogee of the Imperial Banks', p. 899; Frankel, 'The Situation in South Africa', pp. 106–7.

102 Brinley Thomas, 'The Evolution of the Sterling Area' in Nicolas Mansergh et al., *Commonwealth Perspectives* (Durham, NC, 1958), p. 180.

103 Jones, 'The Apogee of the Imperial Banks', pp. 893, 915.

104 Martin, 'The Making of Industrial South Africa', pp. 82–4.

105 For an introduction to the literature on this theme see Shula Marks and Stanley Trapido, eds. *The Politics of Race, Class and Nationalism in Twentieth-Century South Africa* (1987).

106 A very useful general history of New Zealand for our purposes is Sinclair's *History of New Zealand.*

107 Wolfgang Rosenberg, 'Capital Imports and Growth, the Case of New Zealand: Foreign Investment in New Zealand, 1840–1958', *Econ. Jour.*, 71 (1961), pp. 97–8; Sinclair, *History of New Zealand,* pp. 254–5.

108 Hawke, *The Making of New Zealand: An Economic History* (Cambridge, 1985), pp. 128, 133–5.

109 Sinclair, *History of New Zealand,* p. 255.

110 Hawke, *The Making of New Zealand,* Figure 4. 5, p. 77.

111 Sinclair, *History of New Zealand,* pp. 260–2, 265–6.

112 This was first recognised by B.C. Ashwin, 'Banking and Currency in New Zealand', *Economic Record,* VI (1930). See also G.R. Hawke, *Between Government and Banks: A History of the Reserve Bank of New Zealand* (Wellington, 1972), pp. 18–22.

113 G.R. Hawke, *Between Government and Banks,* esp. Ch. 3; idem, 'The Government and the Depression of the 1930s in New Zealand: an Essay Towards a Revision', *Austral. Econ. Hist. Rev.*, XIII (1973), pp. 75–84; idem, *The Making of New Zealand,* pp. 151–2; Plumptre, *Central Banking in the British Dominions,* pp. 115–22, 185–7.

114 See Hawke, 'The Government and the Depression of the 1930s in New Zealand', pp. 86–7, and idem, *The Making of New Zealand,* pp. 150–1.

115 Hawke, *Between Government and Banks,* pp. 101–10; Sinclair, *History of New Zealand,* pp. 265–9.

116 Hawke, *The Making of New Zealand,* p. 128.
117 Plumptre, *Central Banking in the British Dominions,* p. 97. See also Hawke, *The Making of New Zealand,* pp. 163–6.
118 Hancock, *Survey of British Commonwealth Affairs,* Vol. II, Pt. I, pp. 283–4; Rosenberg, 'Capital Exports and Growth', pp. 98–9.
119 Drummond, *The Floating Pound and the Sterling Area,* p. 115. Our account is based largely on pp. 103–15 of this work, though Hancock, *Survey of British Commonwealth Affairs,* Vol. II, Pt. I, pp. 271–84, is still well worth reading.
120 The quotations are from Phillips, a leading British Treasury official, cited in Drummond, *The Floating Pound and the Sterling Area,* pp. 109, 107.
121 A useful general introduction to Canadian history in this period is provided by Robert Bothwell, Ian M. Drummond and John English, *Canada, 1900–1945* (Toronto, 1989). On Canadian economic history see the appropriate sections in Richard Pomfret, *The Economic Development of Canada* (Toronto, 1984): and William L. Marr and Donald G. Paterson, *Canada: An Economic History* (Toronto, 1980).
122 K.H. Buckley and M.C. Urquhart, eds. *Historical Statistics of Canada* (Cambridge, 1965), p. 169.
123 Hancock, *Survey of British Commonwealth Affairs,* Vol. II, Pt. i, p. 187; John Archibald Stovel, *Canada in the World Economy* (Harvard, Mass., 1959), p. 240.
124 Norman Hillmer, 'Personalities and Problems in Anglo-Canadian Economic Relations between the Two World Wars', *Bulletin of Canadian Studies,* III (1979), pp. 8–11; see also Holland, *Britain and the Commonwealth Alliance,* pp. 107–8; Drummond, *British Economic Policy and the Empire,* pp. 84–6.
125 On the depression see A.E. Safarian, *The Canadian Economy in the Great Depression* (Toronto, 1959), and Alan G. Green and Gordon R. Sparks, 'A Macro-Economic Interpretation of Recovery: Australia and Canada', in Gregory and Butlin, *Recovery from Depression.*
126 R.F. Holland, 'The End of the Imperial Economy? Anglo-Canadian Disengagement in the 1930s', *Jour. Imp. and Comm. Hist.* (1983), and idem, 'Imperial Collaboration and Great Depression'.
127 T.J.T. Rooth, 'Imperial Preference and Anglo-Canadian Trade Relations in the 1930s – the End of an Illusion', *British Journal of Canadian Studies,* 1 (1986), provides a comprehensive review of the statistical evidence.
128 The following paragraph depends heavily on Drummond, *The Floating Pound and the Sterling Area,* esp. pp. 64–71. See also Douglas H. Fullerton, *Graham Towers and His Times* (Toronto, 1986), pp. 28–31.
129 On the Canadian management of exchange rates see Michael D. Bordo and Angela Redish, 'Credible Commitment and Exchange Rate Stability: Canada's Interwar Experience', *Canadian Journal of Economics,* XXIII (1990); E.P. Neufeld, *Bank of Canada Operations, 1935–54* (Toronto, 1955), pp. 50–2; Plumptre, *Central Banking in the British Dominions,* pp. 408–21.
130 Fullerton, *Graham Towers and His Times,* pp. 33–9.
131 On Addis, see Dayer, *Finance and Empire: Sir Charles Addis, 1861–1945,* pp. 248–9; on Norman's influence in canvassing the idea of central banking, see Fullerton, *Graham Towers and His Times,* p. 42. The other English member of the Commission was Lord Macmillan, former chairman of the famous Macmillan Committee of 1930. See also Sayers, *Bank of England,* II, p. 514–15.
132 For a wide-ranging discussion of the origins of the Bank in the Canadian context see Michael D. Bordo and Angela Redish, 'Why Did the Bank of Canada Emerge in 1935?', *Jour. Econ. Hist.,* XLVII (1987); Craig McIvor, *Canadian Monetary, Banking and Fiscal Development* (Toronto, 1958), Ch. VII; Irving Brecher, *Monetary and Fiscal Thought and Policy in Canada, 1919–1939* (Toronto, 1957), Pt. III; G.S. Watts, 'The Origin and Background of Central Banking in Canada', *Bank of Canada Review* (1972); and R.B. Bryce, *Maturing in Hard Times: Canada's Department of Finance through the Great Depression* (1986), pp. 124–30, 135–44.

133 Plumptre, *Central Banking in the British Dominions,* p. 145–7. It should be noted that one Bank of England adviser to the Committee was happy to accept the idea of public ownership of a Canadian central bank, but Macmillan insisted on recommending a private company. Fullerton, *Graham Towers and His Times,* p. 44, 45–7.
134 All quotations are from the *Report of the Royal Commission on Banking and Currency in Canada,* Ch. V, (Ottawa, 1933), as reprinted in E.P. Neufeld, ed. *Money and Banking in Canada* (Toronto, 1964), pp. 234–46.
135 Fullerton, *Graham Towers and His Times,* pp. 31–2; Drummond, *The Floating Pound and the Sterling Area,* p. 65.
136 Dayer, *Sir Charles Addis,* p. 247.
137 Ibid. p. 133.
138 C.S. Addis,'Canada and Its Banks', *Quarterly Review,* 263 (1934), quotations are from pp. 51 and 53.
139 Fullerton, *Graham Towers and His Times,* pp. 48–9. On the prairie theme see T.D. Regehr, 'Banks and Farmers in Western Canada, 1900–1939', in John E. Foster, ed. *The Developing West: Essays in Canadian History* (Edmonton, 1983).
140 Ibid. pp. 49–50.
141 Ibid. pp. 67–70; Plumptre, *Central Banking in the British Dominions,* pp. 147–9. See also Neufeld, *Bank of Canada Operations,* pp. 3–15, on the attempt to define a degree of independence for the Bank in the late 1930s.
142 On Bank policy in general see Neufeld, *Bank of Canada Operations,* Ch. IV, and Fullerton, *Graham Towers and His Times,* pp. 71–86.
143 Holland,'The End of the Imperial Economy?', p. 172.
144 Her deficit on the balance of payments current account with the United States was more than offset by a large surplus with Britain. See H.G.J. Aitken et al. *The American Economic Impact on Canada* (Durham, NC, 1959), Table 13, p. 161; Stovel, *Canada in the World Economy,* Table 15, pp. 233–4; and Buckley and Urquhart, *Historical Statistics of Canada,* p. 160.
145 Holland,'Imperial Collaboration and Great Depression', p. 124.
146 Ibid.
147 For an effective summing up on this see Plumptre, *Central Banking in the Dominions,* pp. 422–5. See also P. Aldaheff,'Public Finance and the Economy in Argentina, Australia and Canada during the Depression of the 1930s', in D.C.M. Platt and Guido Di Tella, eds. *Argentina, Australia, Canada: Studies in Comparative Development, 1870–1965* (1985).

22

'A NEW ERA OF COLONIAL AMBITIONS': SOUTH AMERICA, 1914–39[1]

With the outbreak of World War I, South America sinks beneath the horizon of imperial history. Its disappearance, having won silent support with the passage of time, is now scarcely noticed. The elimination of a whole continent undoubtedly eases the task of historians of empire who are fully occupied in grappling with colonial nationalists after 1914, and it accords with the definition of the terms of the trade which confines empire to its constitutional parts. But the excision, being so radical, also fits oddly with the prominence given to South America in the debate on informal rule in the nineteenth century, and thus raises the question of whether the invisible empire (assuming that it existed) was simply destroyed in the upheaval brought by World War I, or whether it survived in some as yet unacknowledged form during the inter-war period.

To examine Britain's ties with South America after 1914 is therefore to peer into the outer space of imperial studies, and the results must be considered prospective rather than definitive. Fortunately, however, specialists on the history of the continent have produced important research on subjects which are closely related to the main theme of the present work. In drawing on this literature, we hope to make it known to a wider audience as well as to incorporate it into an argument for reintegrating South America into the study of British imperialism after 1914.[2] Specifically, we shall suggest that Britain's priority, after 1913 as before, was to maintain her position as banker to the world. During the 1920s this aim manifested itself in a series of determined efforts to steer South America back to pre-war conditions of normality; in the 1930s the banker turned debt collector while also trying to keep the republics 'sterling minded'.[3] Britain's exports of manufactures had a place in this strategy, but it was usually second place, and in the 1930s the old staples came to be regarded as more of a handicap than an asset. As the almost instinctive affinities which had smoothed relations in the pre-war era came under strain in the turbulence of war and depression, so Britain leant heavily on the republics, where and when she could, to try to hold them in their allotted place. These ambitions brought the British into conflict with rival powers, and helped to set the scene for a renewed scramble for influence in South America at the close of the 1930s which, we suggest, ought to command much greater attention from historians of imperialism than it has done so far.

A continental perspective

South America remained one of Britain's major trading partners between 1914 and 1939, accounting for about 9 per cent of her exports in 1928 and 7 per cent in 1937, and for about 9 per cent of her imports in the same years.[4] As in the pre-war era, British trade had a marked regional bias: Argentina, Brazil and (to a diminishing extent) Chile were responsible for no less than 80 per cent of Britain's exports to South America and for over 85 per cent of her imports from the continent in the inter-war period. As in the nineteenth century, too, Argentina was of overwhelming importance, receiving 49 per cent of all Britain's exports to South America in 1928 and 54 per cent in 1937, and supplying 67 per cent and 65 per cent of her imports from the continent in the same years. A more detailed view is provided by Svennilson's data on Britain's trade with her two principal partners (Table 22.1). Britain's exports staged a partial recovery in the 1920s, following the disruption caused by World War I, but suffered again in the 1930s, as a result of the slump, and by 1938 were well below the levels of 1913, as was trade to Argentina and Brazil as a whole. In default of a sustained growth in export values, the period was marked by an intense struggle for market shares.

Britain lost ground in this contest mainly because she still relied on traditional lines, such as textiles and railway equipment, which were experiencing problems of secular decline, but also because exports were hit at a critical moment of recovery by the overvaluation of sterling following the return to gold in 1925.

After 1914 Britain also faced serious problems in South America, as elsewhere, because she was unable to muster the capital needed to run the international economy at its pre-war level.[5] Investment in Argentina and Brazil (the principal recipients of British capital in the continent after 1914, as before) continued to

TABLE 22.1 Exports to Argentina and Brazil, 1913, 1928 and 1938 (millions of US dollars at 1938 prices)

	Exports to Argentina from			*Exports to Brazil from*		
	UK	*Germany*	*USA*	*UK*	*Germany*	*USA*
1913	131	87	48	72	65	45
1928	121	77	127	55	42	65
1938	80	57	76	21	58	50

Source: Ingvar Svennilson, *Growth and Stagnation in the European Economy* (Geneva, 1954), p. 190.

expand slowly during the 1920s, but the rate of return was generally lower than it had been in the pre-war era, and most of the new investment entering the republics in the 1920s was supplied by the United States. Once the world slump put an end to the modest recovery of the 1920s, inflows of capital from all sources virtually ceased until the close of the 1930s. Since income from shipping and insurance also suffered from falling profitability and reduced market shares after 1914, Britain could no longer rely on surpluses from South America to settle deficits with other parts of the world, and she even began to experience difficulties in balancing her payments with Argentina, her principal trading partner.[6] Nevertheless, and despite the advance of the United States, Britain remained the largest foreign investor in South America down to 1939. The continent still accounted for a sizeable share of the total stock of British capital placed abroad, and, in consequence, it continued to be an important source of overseas investment income. If the 1920s were spent preparing the ground for a resumption of foreign lending, the 1930s were devoted to safeguarding the capital that had already been invested.

World War I eliminated one of Britain's leading rivals, Germany, but it also presented opportunities to another, the United States.[7] As Britain's own plans for taking over Germany's share of South American trade were frustrated by the demands of the war effort in Europe, the United States was able to increase her economic influence in the continent by strengthening her commercial and financial ties with the republics.[8] The growing concern, shared by the Foreign Office and the City, that the dollar would replace sterling lay behind the de Bunsen trade mission, which showed the flag in South America in 1918, and also prompted a number of schemes, at once devious and optimistic, for mobilising funds from other countries to support British interests.[9] Far from being isolated by the disruptive effects of hostilities, South America, like China, became an arena for a fierce, if still pacific, power struggle which saw Britain's dominance in the large southern republics challenged, though not yet displaced, by the United States.[10]

The long-term significance of Anglo-American rivalry was revealed during the 1920s. Britain gave notice of her intention of resuming her pre-war role in South America, and the two largest banks operating in Argentina and Brazil strengthened their capital base to meet the testing uncertainties of the day.[11] But Britain's long-term goal also called for measures which, in the short run, proved counterproductive. Foreign lending was restrained in the early 1920s to assist the return to gold, and interest rates were raised in 1925 to support the chosen parity, with the result that the capital available for overseas loans was offered on terms which were less competitive than they had been before the war. In the absence of a sizeable stream of overseas finance from London, Britain found herself relying on funds raised in the United States to maintain the Atlantic triangle of trade and payments.[12] In the 1920s it was capital flows from New York that enabled the South American republics to pay their debts in London and thus helped Britain to settle her deficit with the United States.

The interest of the United States, on the other hand, lay less in acting as a spear-carrier in a great British epic than in managing the Atlantic triangle to her own advantage.[13] That this required the destruction of the financial dominance of London was fully appreciated in the United States, and it found concrete expression in the increasingly concerted efforts of the New York banks to capture South American business from the mid-1920s.[14] As British diplomacy pondered the delicate task of re-establishing the supremacy of London through the medium of New York, the financial power of the United States began to cut into the market share and the profits of British banks and commercial services at the close of the 1920s.[15] Surveying the casualty list in 1929, the British Ambassador in Argentina commented that 'the United States under Hoover means to dominate this continent by hook or by crook. It is British interests that chiefly stand in the way. These are to be bought out or kicked out'.[16]

It is important to recognise that this rivalry went far beyond the cut and thrust of normal business relationships, and became a battle for the 'hearts and minds of men' as well as for their pockets. The highly publicised visits of the eminent Princeton economist, Edwin Kemmerer, to South America in the 1920s acquired almost missionary status.[17] Animated by a spirit of scientific optimism, the 'money doctor' (as he became known) toured the Andean republics dispensing persuasive prescriptions for the ills of the time. The fact that his advice, which centred on fiscal reform and the adoption of the gold standard, was highly orthodox is less significant than his recommendation that the medicine should be bought from the United States, a prospect that caused a good deal of anxiety in London.[18] The gravitational pull of the United States also began to be felt at the level of popular culture through the spread of cinema, radio and newspaper services, a trend symbolised by the growing influence of Hollywood and by the creation of South America's first international superstar of light entertainment in the person of Carlos Gardel.[19]

With the onset of the world slump, the advance of the United States lost a good deal of its momentum. Capital flows dried up and renewed protectionism (installed by the formidable Hawley-Smoot Tariff of 1930) reinforced the ramparts of fortress America.[20] The transition from 'dollar diplomacy' to Roosevelt's Good 'Neighbor' policy was not a straightforward shift from informal expansion to effective isolation. But in the early 1930s the United States was temporarily less of a threat to Britain than was the renascent presence of Germany. Excluded from the British and French empires by a network of discriminatory measures, and grappling with a balance of payments deficit that was rapidly depleting her gold reserves, Germany pushed into neutral areas such as South America, seeking exclusive bilateral links, bartering exports for essential imports, where possible, and making striking gains in Brazil and some of the smaller republics.[21] The prospect that a string of fascist colonies might materialise in South America, combined with anxieties that membership of Britain's new sterling club might also be extended to the republics, prompted the United States to take a renewed interest in the continent at the close of the 1930s.[22] The passage of the Reciprocal Trade Agreements Act in 1934 and the creation of the Export-Import Bank in the same year were early signals of this intent.[23] As international rivalry intensified, it also took on a new aspect during this period, spreading beyond trade and finance to the control of airways and airwaves, as fascist propaganda, beamed initially at German and Italian immigrant communities, challenged the battered and still underfunded forces of liberalism.[24] As far as South America was concerned, World War II was very largely a continuation of these conflicts by other means, which suggests that more emphasis ought to be given to its imperialist origins.[25]

The leaders of South American states had no doubt that they were under threat from contending imperialist forces. It was commonly accepted by Brazilian commentators in the 1930s that the world was divided between 'colonizing peoples and colonizers', and that there was no room for intermediate categories.[26] Oswaldo Aranha, Brazil's astute Minister of Finance, predicted in 1935 that 'a new era of colonial ambitions, determined more by economic factors than strictly political ones, is going to take charge of universal destinies'.[27] Survival was seen to depend on manipulating these menacing expansionist forces by using one power to fend off another without allowing protection to become captivity – a dangerous game but one without alternatives.

While juggling with weighty foreign interests, South American governments also had to grapple with serious domestic problems, especially in the aftermath of the world slump, which brought widespread economic distress and caused a rash of defaults on foreign loans and a matching set of political and military coups.[28] Moreover, it became clear in the 1930s that these upheavals were not merely products of a temporary, if severe, crisis in the world economy, but were also connected to underlying long-run developments, notably the closing of the agricultural frontier and the continuing expansion of population, which posed acute problems of future sources of economic growth and employment, and also called into question the established alliance between export-interests and foreign firms.[29]

These developments and their policy implications have rightly been given considerable attention by specialists of the period who have examined the rise of radical nationalism, state intervention, and the growth of import-substituting industries. Yet, as recent work has also shown, powerful continuities survived amidst manifest signs of change, especially in the area of international economic policy, where liberal orthodoxy retained remarkable influence in unpropitious circumstances.[30] Admittedly, the fulsome pro-British proclamations of a Pellegrini or a Nabuco were rarely issued by their successors, but the appeal of liberal doctrines had always been pragmatic and was no less effective for being shorn of some accompanying rhetoric, however genuine. Open economies were maintained as far as possible and for as long as possible; debt service was continued to the point where default was a necessity rather than a matter of choice; and the republics generally cooperated in the various schemes put forward by foreign missions to reorder their fiscal and monetary policies. If the state became interventionist, it was largely to safeguard the existing division of labour, not to overthrow it, and the steps taken to promote local industries were motivated partly by the need to economise on imports so that foreign debts could be serviced. The new authoritarian regimes harnessed populism, but they also aimed to control radicalism. By the end of the period, the old export alliance had been jolted but not unseated, and some of the partners looked forward to riding again after World War II.

Argentina

Argentina remained by far the most important of Britain's commercial partners in South America after the war, as before, and indeed accounted for an increasing share of Britain's trade with that continent.[31] The republic took 42 per cent of Britain's exports to South America in 1913, 48 per cent in 1928–9, and 53 per cent in 1936–7. Imports from Argentina represented an even higher proportion, amounting to 58 per cent, 68 per cent and 63 per cent respectively of the value of goods shipped to Britain from the continent in the same years. In addition, well over half the stock of British capital in South America was held in Argentina, and at its peak in 1929 amounted to about £435m., which generated approximately 12 per cent of Britain's income from overseas investments.[32] Argentina was clearly a weighty commercial partner, ranking on a par with Canada, Australia and India, and not therefore one to be given up lightly.

Britain responded to the problems thrown up by World War I by subjecting Argentina to a degree of ungentlemanly pressure which infringed the republic's sovereignty and limited her freedom of choice.[33] Although Argentina refused to depart from neutrality, Britain tightened her grip on the direction of overseas trade by insisting that ties with Germany were cut and by contracting various purchasing agreements which committed the republic to supply the Allied powers with essential items. In some cases, these agreements were extended into the immediate post-war period – a helping hand which Vestey Bros, for example, used to improve their position in the meat trade.[34] The election of the Radical Party in 1916 was no more welcome in London than the accompanying anti-foreign rhetoric of the new President, Hipolito Yrigoyen, but these developments proved to be portents of a distant future rather than signals of immediate change. The essential planks of the Anglo-Argentine relationship survived the strains of war: the dividends of British firms continued to be remitted freely, and interest on the national debt was paid punctually, despite the hardship this caused in Argentina.[35]

Britain's plans for restoring the pre-war order were also shared by the most influential circles in Argentina after 1918.[36] Yrigoyen never pressed his attacks on British interests to the point where a major confrontation took place. His most publicised success was in preventing the British railway companies from increasing their rates in 1919; his less well publicised concession, in one of his last acts as president in 1922, was to allow the rise to take place.[37] His successor, Marcelo Alvear, was keen to maintain the Anglo-Argentine alliance, partly to secure a market for the republic's exports of foodstuffs at a time when over-supply in world markets was becoming a problem, and partly to have a counterweight to the growing influence of the United States. Consequently, in the 1920s Argentina adhered to open, free-trading policies which fitted with Britain's interests.[38] Tariffs remained low, foreign debts continued to be serviced, and relations between the Argentine government and the railway companies returned to congenial normality.[39]

The real threat to Britain's design at this time came from the advance of the United States rather than from the rise of Argentine nationalism. During the 1920s the United States began investing in Argentina on a sizeable scale for the first time, buying into public utilities and financing sales of new products, such as electrical goods and motor vehicles.[40] In 1929, when concern in London reached the point of alarm, the Foreign Office tried to stem the tide by dispatching a high-level trade mission to South America under the leadership of Edgar Vincent (metamorphosed as Lord D'Abernon), whose early career had been spent in the deep waters of Ottoman finances.[41] In a second metamorphosis, Yrigoyen, who had returned to office in 1928, kept his name but changed his opinions, and issued a series of reassuring, pro-British messages. Britain's railway investments, he declared, were 'sacred'. 'We have worked with the English and with English capital for fifty years. We know them and what they are. I see no reason of exchanging old friends for new'.[42]

The D'Abernon mission played on the president's fear of the United States and hinted that Argentina might be excluded from the various schemes for imperial preference then under discussion. In the hope of keeping the door open for Argentina's exports, Yrigoyen agreed to buy an additional £9m. worth of British manufactures, which was the equivalent of Britain's balance of trade deficit with Argentina at that time. To confirm the alliance, Britain allowed a loan of £5m. to be issued through Barings (though the arrangement was kept secret because the Treasury had just reimposed its curb on overseas loans). The agreement was regarded as a triumph for the British negotiators, though it is now clear that it also suited the interests of the Argentine government.[43] In the event, D'Abernon was denied his success. Yrigoyen was overthrown by a military coup in 1930, following the trade depression and ensuing revenue crisis, and his successor, General Uriburi, began his presidency by favouring the United States.[44] One of his first acts was to bury the D'Abernon agreement – much to the satisfaction of United States' business interests in Argentina.[45]

The D'Abernon mission had no practical significance, but it stands as a reaffirmation of Britain's determination to prevent the United States from taking over Argentina, and it can also be seen both as a holding operation pending the re-establishment of free trade and as an anticipation of the bilateral agreements which Britain deployed in constructing a smaller trading world in the 1930s. Either way, Britain's claim to enjoy a special relationship with Argentina remained unqualified. As the British ambassador in Buenos Aires put it: 'Without saying so in as many words, which would be tactless, what I really mean is that Argentina must be regarded as an essential part of the British empire'.[46]

Uriburu's expectations of the United States were rapidly disappointed by the abrupt cessation of foreign lending and by the revival of protectionism in 1930. Uriburu himself was quickly dispatched, and his successor, General Agustin Justo, who took office in 1930, reasserted the influence of the large landowners who had traditionally benefited from the Anglo-Argentine alliance. By this time, however, Britain was already moving towards a system of imperial preference, and Argentina faced the prospect that this door, too, would soon close. The republic still hoped to be treated as an 'honorary dominion', but the paid-up members, especially Australia, made sure that she was excluded from the Ottawa agreements, with the result that her exports to Britain came up against increased duties and quantitative restrictions.[47] These developments were particularly serious for the beef industry, which relied almost exclusively on the British market and which also formed the economic basis of the political power of the ruling elite.

These problems led to a series of discussions which produced the Roca–Runciman Pact in 1933 and set the course of Anglo-Argentine commercial relations for the rest of the decade.[48] The Pact was controversial at the time and it remains a lively issue among specialists today. On the one hand, it has been seen as an imposition which sacrificed Argentina's national development, especially the prospects for autonomous industrial growth, to the interests of a privileged minority; on the other, it has been regarded as a negotiated deal which was crucial to the economic recovery of the republic during the 1930s. The exploration of these questions stretches beyond the direct concern of this study. However, it is relevant to observe that the debate has suffered from a tendency to overemphasise the role of commodity trade; recent research, in revealing the importance of the financial aspects of the Pact, suggests that the priorities of the British side were those which, as we argued earlier, also underlay the Ottawa agreements.[49]

There seems little doubt that the Pact saved the Argentine beef industry by allowing meat exports access to the British market. Although the terms of entry were less generous than in the days of unrestricted free trade, the share of Argentine exports sent to Britain nevertheless rose from 28 per cent in 1927 to 36 per cent in 1939.[50] In return, Argentina reduced tariffs on goods imported from Britain, though with results that were not quite so clear cut. Britain's staple exports held on to business they would otherwise probably have lost, and her share of the import market increased, mainly at the expense of the United States. But the rise was modest (from 19 per cent in 1927 to 22 per cent in 1939),[51] and it is significant that local importers did not regard the Pact as giving Britain's traditional manufactures a new lease of life.[52] On the contrary, the members of the British Chamber of Commerce in Buenos Aires were beginning to move into local industries in the 1930s, and their interest in the old staples was steadily diminishing.[53]

The financial aspects of the Pact were much more significant from the British point of view and were an important consideration for the Argentine side too.[54] The financial crisis in 1931 had compelled Argentina to impose exchange controls to prevent the value of the peso from collapsing.[55] Blocking the repatriation of profits created serious difficulties for British firms and for an estimated 20,000 British investors who depended, to a greater or lesser degree, on incomes derived from capital placed in Argentina.[56] However, exchange controls could not be lifted without external financial assistance to support the peso. The problem was solved by a loan of £11m., known as the Roca Funding Loan, which was raised in London by Barings in 1933. Once the Funding Loan had been agreed, both sides were free to sign the more publicised Roca–Runciman Pact. Seen in this context, the Pact was significant less as an agency promoting British manufactures than as an instrument of debt collection which provided Argentina with the means of earning sufficient sterling to meet her foreign obligations.[57] Taken together, the Loan and the Pact were vital to maintaining Argentina's credit-worthiness, and to creating the conditions which enabled her, remarkably, to service her debts without interruption throughout the 1930s.[58]

It is clear that Argentine governments adopted a consistently orthodox response to the economic crisis and that they did so to preserve their markets and credit in Britain. Moreover, fiscal and monetary orthodoxy continued to characterise policy throughout the 1930s. Public expenditure was contained, import tariffs (and internal taxes) were raised when necessary to balance the budget, and the money supply was closely controlled to hold the value of the peso, as this was crucial to maintaining the confidence of external investors.[59] It was these considerations, rather than plans for wider development, that underlay the creation of the Central Bank in 1935, following advice from one of Britain's own money doctors, Sir Otto Niemeyer, a director of the Bank of England and a former senior Treasury official.[60] The Central Bank, one of several established during the 1930s in the empire and associated countries with strong ties to Britain, was in many respects an agent of British policy. Barings (who still acted as official advisers to the Argentine government) had well-placed contacts within the Bank itself, and representatives of British banks in the republic were on the Board of Directors.[61] Besides overseeing domestic monetary orthodoxy, the Bank was important in strengthening Argentina's ties with the emerging sterling bloc by pegging the peso to sterling and by holding the republic's currency reserves in London.[62]

The priority given by Britain to protecting existing investments during this period was implemented with notable tenacity in the case of the railways.[63] The railway companies, many of which were still British-owned, ran into serious difficulties in the 1930s as profits fell in the depression. When the companies tried to shore up their position by pressing for special concessions from the Argentine government, they met a hostile response. Given that the railways accounted for a very sizeable share of all British investment in Argentina, the Foreign Office did what it could to assist them, though in the event without much success. However, the outcome was not a defeat for British policy or for British investors. By 1935 the Foreign Office had reached the conclusion that the railways were becoming a lost cause, partly because of their managerial deficiencies, but mainly because of competition from motor transport, which developed rapidly in the 1930s following an aggressive marketing drive by US companies.[64] Moreover, by provoking a nationalist reaction, the railways were jeopardising wider financial interests as well as their own position.[65] With these considerations in mind, and with the cooperation of the companies, the Foreign Office began to negotiate the transfer of the railways to the Argentine government. Agreement was reached in principle in 1936, though the terms remained in dispute.

However, following the outbreak of World War II, Argentina accumulated large sterling balances which Britain effectively blocked in London until 1948, when they were finally released to enable the republic to buy the railways outright in a deal which met both the claims of popular nationalism and the interests of foreign investors.[66] Since Peron's government also used the occasion to pay off all outstanding bonds held in Britain, the date can be said to mark the end of a century of Anglo-Argentine relations which began with the outflow of capital from London and ended with its repatriation.[67]

Brazil

Britain's relations with Brazil in the period after 1914 deserve more attention than they have received, despite the appearance of some familiar signs of decline, because they illustrate with particular clarity the continuing priority attached to finance at a time of developing rivalry with the United States. The value of Anglo-Brazilian commerce fell steadily, and Britain's share of the republic's total overseas trade also dropped – in the case of the import market from 25 per cent in 1913 to 10 per cent in 1938 and in the case of exports from 13 per cent to 9 per cent during the same period.[68] By the close of the 1930s the United States and Germany had become Brazil's leading overseas trading partners. It is also true that most of the new foreign capital entering Brazil in the 1920s came from the United States, and that in the 1930s Britain was disinvesting, with the result that the total stock of British capital held in the republic dropped from about £291m. in 1929 to about £160m in 1938.[69] Nevertheless, Britain was still the largest foreign investor in Brazil in 1929, and possibly even in 1939 too. The British may have abandoned hopes of raising their share of commodity trade, but they mounted a spirited defence of their financial stake, while at the same time trying to keep the lid on the rising influence of the United States.

Initially, Britain expected to benefit from the elimination of Germany's trade with Brazil during World War I, though in the event the principal gains went to the United States.[70] British finance, however, was not so easily dislodged.[71] At the close of 1914, the long-standing connection with Rothschilds enabled Brazil to raise a large foreign loan (of £14.5m.), which made it possible for the republic to reschedule existing debts and hence to continue repayment, albeit at a reduced level. Two years later, opposition from the Rothschilds was sufficient to prevent Brazil from encouraging the United States to develop closer financial links with the republic.[72] As Britain's own financial position deteriorated, however, the United States made greater progress, and towards the end of the war the financing of the coffee trade began to shift from sterling to dollars and so from London to New York.[73] This development raised anxiety levels in London, but it was nevertheless seen as a trend that could be reversed once peacetime conditions had been restored.

The struggle to return to normality continued throughout the 1920s. Brazil's problems were intensified by the post-war slump of 1920–1, which pushed her into greater reliance on loans from the United States, initially to refinance existing obligations and subsequently to fund broader development projects, especially the expansion of public utilities and the purchase of foreign-owned railways.[74] As a result of these inflows, Brazil became by far the largest borrower in South America in the 1920s.[75] At the same time, the continuing fragility of Brazil's export sector and the uncertainties of a world which had yet to return to the gold standard prompted a set of reforms, beginning in 1921, which widened the powers of the Banco do Brasil and in particular authorised it to increase the money supply.[76] These changes were the outcome of considerable debate in academic and political circles in Brazil, and they followed similar experiments undertaken during the war. They were intended to bail out the republic at a critical time rather than to launch a drive for economic independence, but they were nevertheless departures which placed the principles of sound finance at risk.

Britain responded to these twin challenges by using her leverage over the funding of Brazil's scheme for supporting coffee prices. This was a crucial issue, both because coffee still accounted for about 50 per cent of the value of all Brazil's exports during the early 1920s and remained vital to the republic's ability to service its debts,[77] and because of the continuing political weight of coffee interests, which Britain had traditionally supported. Moreover, Britain's influence in this sensitive area of finance was enhanced by the fact that the United States refused to lend for this purpose on the ground that subsidies for coffee producers had to be paid for by American consumers (and voters).[78] The City used its advantage to the full. In 1922 a group headed by Schroder, Barings and Rothschilds raised a loan of £9m. to fund the coffee support scheme, and attached strings to it which greatly reduced Brazil's control over the market by placing sales in the hands of a committee of City bankers (as had happened in 1908).[79] Similar loans were made later in the 1920s, after the federal government had transferred responsibility for supporting coffee to São Paulo, and ensured that London's influence continued to be felt at a particularly sensitive point of juncture between the economy and political authority.[80]

An opportunity arose for London to take a firm grip on Brazil's finances in 1923, when continuing economic difficulties led the republic to approach Rothschilds for a substantial loan of £25m.[81] The City used the occasion to send a high-level mission, led by Edwin Montagu, a prominent banker and former Secretary of State for India, to curb government expenditure and put an end to the Banco do Brasil's experiments with inflationary finance by imposing 'some palatable form of control or advice'.[82] Not a man for half measures, Montagu sought to halt the development of the Brazilian steel industry, control railway policy and take over the Banco do Brasil.[83] While pressing the Brazilian government to sell its shares in the Bank, Montagu asked Rothschilds if they 'or their friends' would be interested in buying them, a proposal that was appreciated but wisely declined on the grounds that 'it would be most unpopular in Brazil for the national bank to be owned by foreigners'.[84] Nevertheless, as well as drawing up a package of stern measures for the public sector, the final deal incorporated a device for separating the Banco do Brasil from the government, and in June the loan was cleared for flotation.[85] However, Montagu was denied his triumph at the last moment by the embargo on foreign loans which the Bank of England had just requested. Although his mission failed, it stands as a very clear (and little-known) example of Britain's continuing imperialist ambitions in a country where they are generally supposed to have withered away.

On this occasion, however, the message survived the departure of the medium. Driven by the continued deterioration of the economy, and by the consequent need to attract foreign lenders, Brazil adopted a deflationary policy in 1924 and also freed the federal budget of an encumbrance by transferring the responsibility for supporting coffee prices to the state of São Paulo.[86] These reforms, culminating in Brazil's return to gold in 1927, fell short of Montagu's requirements, but they were sufficient to re-establish the republic's credit-worthiness and they enabled the federal government to approach both the United States and Britain (once the embargo on foreign loans was lifted at the end of 1925) for new finance. In the intense competition between London and New York which followed, London retained control over the funding of the coffee support scheme, now guaranteed by São Paulo, while the much larger federal loan, which was supposed to be shared between the two financial centres, went to New York. This outcome was the result of a fortuitous diplomatic complication which led the Foreign Office to ask the City to withdraw from the loan at the last moment, and it provides an interesting example of how special interests could be called upon to defer to higher priorities which were in the long-term interest of all parties concerned.[87] The British bankers pointed out that 'we have financed Brazil since her independence and to allow her to go to America would be a great loss to this country'.[88] The Foreign Secretary replied that his request was in the interests of 'peace, which I take to be the first of British interests and especially the first interest of the City of London'.[89] Following this appeal, the bankers agreed 'to respect his wishes loyally'.[90]

In Brazil, as in Argentina, these unsteady and protracted attempts to return to pre-war normality were destroyed by the world slump. As export prices collapsed and the flow of foreign capital ceased, Brazil faced a serious balance of payments crisis, mounting domestic discontent, and heightened political tension.[91] Yet, even as the international economic order broke up, the Brazilian government still held on to the gold standard, serviced its debts and allowed remittances to be made freely.[92] At the same time, the federal government approached Rothschilds, cap in hand, for a major loan to support the gold standard.[93] The City responded by laying down conditions which were essentially those sought by the Montagu mission; the Brazilian representatives twisted and turned, but in the end they accepted. Once again, the City was close to taking hold of Brazilian finances; once again it was frustrated, this time by the coup that brought Getulio Vargas to power at the close of 1930.

The central question now became the protection of British investments in a world which was beginning to take to the idea of default. Britain's immediate response was to dispatch Sir Otto Niemeyer to Brazil in 1931 to remind the government of the need to keep to the rules of the game. His report repeated the now standard British prescription in recommending tax increases, administrative reforms, a balanced budget, adherence to the gold standard, and the creation a central bank to maintain convertibility.[94] The medicine, however, was no longer acceptable: Vargas reacted by suspending payments on the foreign debt. Rothschilds, showing an impressive turn of speed, moved swiftly to limit the potential damage and (with the assistance of Niemeyer) managed to negotiate preferential treatment for the oldest and best secured loans, which were held principally by British investors.[95] When the Brazilian foreign debt was restructured in 1934, the partnership of Rothschilds and Niemeyer again succeeded in winning privileged treatment for British investors.[96]

In 1937, however, a further default occurred, this time in circumstances which revealed the extent to which foreign finance and foreign influence had become caught up in the gathering international rivalries of the immediate pre-war years.[97] From 1934 Germany had begun to make sizeable inroads into Brazil's overseas trade, principally by means of bilateral trade agreements. By ceasing to repay Brazil's existing debts, Vargas could afford to build up his 'new state' by diverting scarce foreign exchange to purchases of German capital goods and military supplies.[98] This strategy was possible only because Brazil's creditors were unwilling or unable to apply sanctions. The United States exercised restraint over debt collection mainly because she was trying to turn Brazil into a political ally. Britain had no such larger motives but no leverage either: she could neither tempt Brazil by dangling the prospect of fresh supplies of capital nor threaten her export trade, which did not depend on the British market and had in any case already suffered from imperial preference.[99] If Britain's frustration was evident, so was her purpose: by the late 1930s the Foreign Office had abandoned the defence of Britain's trade with Brazil, while the City was pressing the republic to cut back on imports and to move further into import-substitution so that more foreign exchange would be available for debt service.[100]

Prospects for repayment did not brighten until 1939, when the United States adopted a more active policy towards Brazil to counter the spread of Nazi influence.[101] With the outbreak of war, Brazil lost her German connection and was drawn further into the embrace of the United States. In these changed circumstances, it is not surprising that Brazil came to terms with her creditors or that the settlement favoured bond-holders in the United States rather than those in Britain.[102] Although this deal confirmed the emergence of the United States as the leading foreign power in Brazil, it did not signal the immediate eclipse of British influence. In fact, British finance, though not British trade, was rescued by the exigencies of war: Brazil's need for export markets led in 1940 to the Anglo-Brazilian Payments Agreement, which gave Brazil an outlet for her exports in exchange for sterling credits in London.[103] The improvement in Britain's bargaining position ultimately enabled her to reach a satisfactory settlement of the debt problem, as in Argentina, by transferring British-owned assets to the Brazilian government. As in Argentina, too, Britain hoped to keep Brazil 'sterling minded', and made plans to recapture her position in South America once the war had ended.[104]

Chile

Chile was far less important from Britain's perspective than were Argentina and Brazil, and the decline of British interests there was also much more precipitate. World War I damaged Britain's dominance of trade and finance in Chile to a far greater extent than in Argentina and Brazil.[105] Exports from the United States filled the space left by Germany's enforced withdrawal, and US capital and technology began to develop Chile's resources of copper, the export of the future. The United States continued its advance during the 1920s, buying up public utilities and supplying most of the capital which funded the development policies promoted by President Ibanez, the self-styled 'Chilean Mussolini', at the close of the decade.[106] Britain's interests, on the other hand, remained concentrated on the nitrate industry, which began to suffer from the development of synthetics in the 1920s and declined precipitously during the 1930s.[107] With the advent of the slump, Chile, like Argentina and Brazil, maintained debt service for as long as possible, but the removal of Ibanez in 1931 also brought down financial orthodoxy, and default quickly followed.[108] The republic became caught up in the revived imperialism of the late 1930s, as the resurgence of German influence first alarmed the United States and then prompted an economic and diplomatic reaction which continued throughout World War II. Britain's involvement in these increasingly weighty developments was both limited and diminishing. She gave up any hope of enlarging her share of Chile's import market in the 1930s, and concentrated on looking after her investments. A series of protracted negotiations ensued, beginning in 1932, when Chile redeemed part of the external debt, and continuing until 1948, when a final settlement was reached.[109]

Debt-collecting and control in South America

Far from giving up her claim to be the predominant foreign power in South America, Britain made a sustained attempt to retain her grip on Argentina and Brazil, the most important republics, after 1914. In the 1920s her paramount concern was to reassemble the pre-war international economic order, with London conducting the orchestra, and to this end strenuous efforts were made to strengthen the British connection, as the Montagu Mission to Brazil and the D'Abernon Mission to Argentina demonstrate. The shortage of capital also highlighted the importance, for balance of payments reasons, of holding on to markets for manufactures. In the 1930s policy became centred more or less exclusively on the defence of existing, and still very substantial, investments. This priority was bound up with the aim of keeping the republics, as far as possible, solvent and 'sterling minded', and it found concrete expression in the central banks promoted by Britain's travelling 'money doctors', and in the quasi-imperial ties which joined Argentina to Britain after 1933.

While it is correct to say that the Roca-Runciman Pact was negotiated rather than imposed, it is also apparent that Britain used Argentina's dependence on the British market to extract favourable treatment for her investments. This point becomes clear from a comparison with Brazil. There, Britain's bargaining position was much weaker because none of Brazil's exports relied on the British market.[110] The result was that the republic was able to treat her creditors with less deference than Argentina dared risk. From this perspective, the Pact should be seen primarily as a means of debt-collecting: Argentina, like the Dominions, had to be allowed space in the British market so that she could earn the exchange needed to meet her foreign obligations. This aim would have been frustrated if Britain had negotiated better terms for her exports of manufactures. In fact, as we have seen, Britain's old staple exports were being jettisoned in the 1930s by the Foreign Office, the City and the British Chamber of Commerce in Buenos Aires in favour of working with nationalist demands instead of against them. Moving into local manufacturing was beginning to make sense on economic as well as on political grounds, and to the extent that it held out the promise of assisting debt payments it found favour in the City too.

It is equally clear that the period after 1914 was characterised by intense imperialist rivalries over the 'unclaimed' regions of the world, the two outstanding examples being South America and China. This theme is bypassed by standard approaches to British imperialism which focus on the management of nationalism within the formal empire after World War I. As we have seen, the period witnessed a fierce struggle for financial control of the South American republics and for the markets that would fall to the successful power. The fact that the new conquistadors mobilised techniques of informal influence which made use of film, radio, cinema and the press, while also deploying tangible capital assets and the products of the second Industrial Revolution, adds to the distinctiveness as well as to the importance of this neglected phase of imperialist rivalry.

Britain's role in this contest was no more reactive than it was before 1914. She had sizeable commitments in South America which had to be developed as well as defended because they were integral both to her international system of trade and payments and, through this, to the structures of power and privilege at home. Consequently, Britain vigorously promoted her own interests as well as responded to the claims of Germany and the United States. Chile is one example of a number (especially among the smaller republics) where the takeover by the United States was comprehensive and seemingly irreversible soon after 1914, and it therefore showed the face of the future to contemporaries, even if they did not always recognise it. Elsewhere, however, Britain scored considerable success in looking after her interests in a world which no longer observed the rules of the game either instinctively or sometimes at all. If Argentina is the best example of a reliable (if sometimes reluctant) ally, it is also by far the most important one. It ought to be added, too, that Britain's performance in Brazil can be seen to have been much more impressive than is usually assumed, once attention is shifted from commodity trade to finance. Nor should the endless web-spinning diplomacy of the time be regarded as a rearguard action in the long retreat from empire. The descendants of the artificers who had galvanised Africa in the late nineteenth century did not see it that way, and in World War II, amidst the sound and debris of what might easily have become defeat, they held yet more meetings to design their re-entry in the post-war world. The timetable had slipped, but the plan remained intact.

Notes

1 The quotation is borrowed from Oswaldo Aranha: see below, pp. 152–3. We deal here, as in Chapter 9, with the continental mainland and not with the larger entity, Latin America.
2 The basic reference is now Leslie Bethel, ed. *The Cambridge History of Latin America*, Vols. IV and V, *1870–1930* (1986). Future volumes will cover the period after 1930.
3 Marcelo de Paiva Abreu, 'Anglo-Brazilian Economic Relations and the Consolidation of American Pre-eminence in Brazil, 1930–1945', in Colin Lewis and Christopher Abel, eds. *Latin America, Economic Imperialism and the State* (1985), p. 388.
4 The trade data are based primarily on the *Statistical Abstract for the United Kingdom, 1899–1913* (1914) and the *Statistical Abstract for the United Kingdom, 1913 and 1924 to 1937* (1948), and are best regarded as being no more than approximate measures of magnitude.
5 The basic source for this period remains the pioneering study by J. Fred. Rippy, *British Investments in Latin America, 1822–1949* (Minneapolis, Minn., 1959). As this is now regarded as being unreliable in a number of respects, it has been used with caution and checked against recent research on individual countries. Investments made by the United States are well covered by Barbara Stallings, *Banker to the Third World: U.S. Portfolio Investment in Latin America, 1900–1986* (Berkeley, Calif., 1987).
6 Roger Gravil, *The Anglo-Argentine Connection, 1900–1939* (Boulder, Col., 1985), p. 164, but also Michael Hilton, 'Latin America and World Trade', in Mark Abrams, ed. *Britain and her Export Trade* (1946), p. 178.
7 The definitive work is now Bill Albert, with the assistance of Paul Henderson, *South America and the First World War: The Impact of the War on Brazil, Argentina, Peru and Chile* (Cambridge, 1988). See also Juan Ricardo Couyoumdjian, *Chile y Gran Bretaña durante la Primera Guerra Mundial y la postguerra, 1914–1921* (Santiago, 1986). A seminal study for the wider context is Carl Parrini, *Heir to Empire: United States Economic Diplomacy, 1916–1923* (Pittsburgh, Pa, 1965).
8 Two case studies of particular relevance to our main theme are: Robert Mayer, 'The Origins of the American Banking Empire in Latin America: Frank A. Vanderlip and the National City Bank', *Journal of Inter-American Studies and World Affairs,* 15 (1973), and Emily S. Rosenberg, 'Anglo-American Economic Rivalry in Brazil during World War I', *Diplomatic History,* 2 (1978), pp. 143, 150–1. See also C. Marichal, *A Century of Debt Crises in Latin America: From Independence to the Great Depression, 1820–1930* (Princeton, NJ, 1989), pp. 180–1.
9 Gravil, *Anglo-Argentine Connection,* pp. 142–3; Rosenberg, 'Anglo-American Economic Rivalry', pp. 136–9.
10 Albert, *South America and the First World War,* p. 308.
11 Couyoumdjian, *Chile y Gran Bretaña,* p. 214.
12 Marichal, *A Century of Debt,* pp. 187–8.
13 Joseph S. Tulchin, *The Aftermath of War: World War I and United States Policy Toward Latin America* (New York, 1971), pp. 101–7.
14 Burton I. Kaufman, 'United States Trade and Latin America: the Wilson Years', *Journal of American History,* 58 (1971), pp. 345, 353, 355; Rosenberg, 'Anglo-American Economic Rivalry', pp. 136–7; Marichal, *A Century of Debt,* p. 182. Banking competition had been limited during the war by the fact that Morgan, the leading investment bank

in the United States, had respected Britain's sphere of influence. See Parrini, *Heir to Empire,* p. 55.

15 Rosenberg, 'Anglo-American Economic Rivalry', pp. 144–6, 150; Roger Gravil, 'British Retail Trade in Argentina, 1900–1940', *Inter-American Economic Affairs,* 29 (1970), pp. 8–10, 23; idem, *Anglo-Argentine Connection,* pp. 159–63.

16 FO memo. 25 October 1929. Quoted in Gravil, *Anglo-Argentine Connection,* p. 163. On the ambassador, Robertson, see ibid. p. 175, n. 41.

17 Paul W. Drake, *The Money Doctor in the Andes: The Kemmerer Missions, 1923–1933* (Durham NC, 1989). As we have seen (p. 131), Kemmerer's presence and influence extended beyond South America with consequences that prompted remedial action from Britain's own itinerant money doctors.

18 Drake, *Money Doctor,* Ch. 1. For the wider context of Anglo-US financial rivalry during this period see Roberta Allbert Dayer, *Finance and Empire: Sir Charles Addis, 1861–1945* (1988), pp. 109–17. Kemmerer's visit to South Africa in 1924 was greatly resented by the Bank of England (ibid. p. 168).

19 Tulchin, *Aftermath of War,* pp. 206–33; Simon Collier, *The Life, Music, and Times of Carlos Gardel* (Pittsburgh, Pa, 1986).

20 On the cessation of foreign lending see Stallings, *Banker to the Third World,* App. A.

21 There is considerable literature on Germany's relations with South America during this period. An accessible overview is Alton Frye, *Nazi Germany and the American Hemisphere, 1933–1941* (New Haven, Conn. 1967). More recent literature is cited in Jean-Pierre Blancpain, 'Des visées pangermanistes au noyautage hitlérien: la nationalisme allemand et l'Amérique latine (1890–1945)', *Revue Historique,* 281 (1989). On the important military connection see Frederick M. Nunn, *Yesterday's Soldiers: European Military Professionalism in South America, 1890–1940* (Lincoln, Nebr., 1983).

22 This re-entry is dealt with by David B. Haglund, *Latin America and the Transformation of U.S. Strategic Thought, 1936–1940* (Albuquerque, 1984).

23 Stanley E. Hilton, *Brazil and the Great Powers, 1930–1939* (Austin, Texas, 1975), pp. 39, 48–9, 71; Frederick C. Adams, *Economic Diplomacy: The Export-Import Bank and American Foreign Policy, 1934–1939* (Columbia, Miss., 1976).

24 Frye, *Nazi Germany.* Case studies include: Ricardo Silva Seitenfus, 'Ideology and Diplomacy: Italian Fascism and Brazil, 1935–38', *Hisp. Am. Hist. Rev.,* 64 (1984); Orazio A. Ciccarelli, 'Fascist Propaganda and the Italian Community in Peru during the Benvides Regime, 1933–39', *Jour Latin Am. Stud.,* 20 (1989), pp. 361–8. See also Fred. Fejes, *Imperialism, Media, and the Good Neighbor: New Deal Foreign Policy and the United States Shortwave Broadcasting to Latin America* (Norwood, NJ, 1986); William A. Burden, *The Struggle for Airways in Latin America* (New York, 1943); and Alfred Padula, 'Pan Am in the Caribbean: the Rise and Fall of an Empire', *Caribbean Review,* 12 (1983), pp. 24–7, 49–51.

25 The starting point for this subject, which has attracted a good deal of research in recent years, is now R.A. Humphreys, *Latin America and the Second World War,* Vol. I (1981), Vol. II (1982). For one of many case studies see Graham Taylor, 'The Axis Replacement Program: Economic Warfare and the Chemical Industry in Latin America, 1942–44', *Dip. Hist.,* 8 (1984).

26 Hilton, *Brazil and the Great Powers,* p. 183.

27 Quoted in ibid. p. 11.

28 Overviews include: Carlos F. Diaz Alejandro, 'Latin America in the 1930s', in Rosemary Thorpe, ed. *Latin America in the 1930s: The Role of the Periphery in World Crisis* (New York, 1984); Michael Twomey, 'The 1930s Depression in Latin America: a Macro Analysis', *Explorations in Economic History,* 20 (1983); and Marichal, *A Century of Debt,* Ch. 8.

29 Contemporary discussion of these questions is dealt with by Guido Di Tella, 'Economic Controversy in Argentina from the 1920s to the 1940s', in Guido Di Tella and D.C.M. Platt, eds. *The Political Economy of Argentina* (1986).

30 There is now a developing revisionist literature on this theme. See, for example, A. O'Connell, 'Free Trade in One (Primary Producing) Country: the Case of Argentina

in the 1920s', in Di Tella and Platt, *Political Economy*; Peter Alhadeff, 'The Economic Formulae of the 1930s: a Reassessment', in ibid.; Steven Topik, *The Political Economy of the Brazilian State, 1880–1930* (Austin, Tex., 1987); and Winston Fritsch, *External Constraints on Economic Policy in Brazil, 1889–1930* (1988). Fascinating insights by a contemporary and participant are given by Raúl Prebisch, 'Argentine Economic Policies since the 1930s', in Di Tella and Platt, *Political Economy*.

31 The data are derived from the sources given in n. 4 above, from Laura Randall, *An Economic History of Argentina in the Twentieth Century* (New York, 1978), pp. 224–5, and from Colin Lewis, 'Anglo-Argentine Trade, 1945–1965', in David Rock, ed. *Argentina in the Twentieth Century* (1975), p. 115.

32 See David Rock, *Argentina, 1516–1982* (1986), p. 192, and Rippy, *British Investments,* p. 161. However, it has to be said that this remains a very grey area. See also the estimates given in Albert, *South America and the First World War,* p. 147 (for 1913), Gravil, *Anglo-Argentine Connection,* p. 183 (for 1930), and Humphreys, *Latin America and the Second World War,* I, p. 30 (for 1936). There is at present no work on British investment during the period after 1914 to compare with Irving Stone's *The Composition and Distribution of British Investment in Latin America, 1865–1913* (New York, 1987).

33 Gravil, *Anglo-Argentine Connection,* Ch. 5; Albert, *South America and the First World War,* pp. 61–77, 143–56.

34 Gravil, *Anglo-Argentine Connection,* p. 133; but see also Albert, *South America and the First World War,* pp. 68–9.

35 Albert, *South America and the First World War,* pp. 155–6; Marichal, *A Century of Debt,* pp. 175–7.

36 This is not to underestimate the influence of the war in stimulating discussion of possible alternative paths of economic development. See Javier Villanueva, 'Economic Development', in Mark Falcoff and Ronald H. Dolkart, eds. *Prologue to Peron: Argentina in Depression and War* (Berkeley, Calif., 1975), pp. 58–9; and Randall, *Economic History,* p. 220.

37 Winthrop R. Wright, *British-Owned Railways in Argentina: Their Effect on Economic Nationalism, 1854–1948* (Austin, Tex., 1974), pp. 119–23.

38 O'Connell, 'Free Trade'.

39 The principal tariff increase (in 1923) was for revenue rather than for protectionist purposes. See O'Connell, 'Free Trade', p. 90. On the railways see Wright, *British-Owned Railways,* pp. 126–30.

40 Stallings, *Banker to the Third World,* pp. 125, 131, 134, 164, 170; Marichal, *A Century of Debt,* pp. 182–91; Gravil, *Anglo-Argentine Connection,* Ch. 6.

41 See below, pp. 376–7. On the D'Abernon Mission see Gravil, *Anglo-Argentine Connection,* pp. 163–72; Wright, *British-Owned Railways,* pp. 13–5; and Paul B. Goodwin, 'Anglo-Argentine Commercial Relations: a Private Sector View', *Hisp. Am. Hist. Rev.,* 61 (1981), pp. 37–41.

42 Quoted in Wright, *British-Owned Railways,* p. 133.

43 Goodwin, 'Anglo-Argentine Commercial Relations', pp. 39–40.

44 David Rock, 'Radical Populism and the Conservative Elite, 1912–1930', in Rock, ed. *Argentina,* pp. 84–7; Anne Potter, 'The Failure of Democracy in Argentina, 1916–1930: an Institutional Perspective', *Jour. Latin Am. Stud.,* 13 (1981).

45 Though the charge that Standard Oil played an important part in the coup is not supported by the evidence. See Rock, 'Radical Populism', p. 84, and Gravil, *Anglo-Argentine Connection,* p. 172.

46 Robertson to Henderson, 17 June 1929, FO 37/13460. Quoted in Wright, *British-Owned Railways,* p. 135.

47 Ian M. Drummond, *Imperial Economic Policy, 1917–1939* (1974), pp. 254–66; Gravil, *Anglo-Argentine Connection,* pp. 179–86.

48 See Gravil, *Anglo-Argentine Connection,* pp. 186–203, Marcelo de Paiva Abreu, 'Argentina and Brazil during the 1930s: the Impact of British and American Economic Policies', in Thorpe, Latin America; Arturo O'Connell, 'Argentina into the Depression: Problems of an Open Economy', in ibid.; Peter Alhadeff, 'Dependency, Historiography and Objections to the Roca Pact', in Christopher Abel and Colin Lewis, eds. *Latin*

America, Economic Imperialism, and the State (1985); idem, 'Economic Formulae', in Di Tella and Platt, *Political Economy.* Roca was Vice-President and 'an anglophile and a gentleman' (Wright, *British-Owned Railways,* p. 167); Runciman, the President of the Board of Trade, was a gentleman above most gentlemen. The Pact was renewed in 1936 and lasted until 1956.

49 See pp. 84–90.
50 Colin Lewis, 'Anglo-Argentine Trade, 1945–1965', in Rock, ed. *Argentina,* P. 115.
51 Ibid.
52 Goodwin, 'Anglo-Argentine Commercial Relations', pp. 32, 47.
53 Ibid. p. 49.
54 See especially Abreu, 'Argentina and Brazil', and Alhadeff, 'Dependency, Historiography'.
55 In 1929, the economic crisis had forced Argentina to close the Conversion Office and to suspend automatic convertibility, though gold exports were allowed so that the public foreign debt could continue to be serviced.
56 Board of Trade data published in the *South American Journal,* 4 March 1933, and cited in Alhadeff, 'Dependency, Historiography', p. 371.
57 Abreu, 'Argentina and Brazil', pp. 154–6; Alhadeff, 'Dependency, Historiography', pp. 369–71.
58 Alhadeff, 'Dependency, Historiography', p. 373; idem, 'Economic Formulae', pp. 109–11.
59 Alhadeff, 'Economic Formulae'; idem, 'Public Finance and the Economy in Argentina, Australia and Canada during the Depression of the 1930s', in D.C.M. Platt and Guido Di Tella, eds. *Argentina, Australia, and Canada: Studies in Comparative Development, 1870–1965* (1985).
60 Alhadeff, 'Economic Formulae', pp. 112–13.
61 Randall, *Economic History,* pp. 64–5; Jorge Fodor, 'The Origins of Argentina's Sterling Balances, 1939–43', in Di Tella and Platt, *Political Economy,* p. 158.
62 Philip W. Bell, *The Sterling Area in the Postwar World* (Oxford, 1956), p. xxiv.
63 Raúl Garc a Heras, 'Hostage Private Companies under Restraint: British Railways and Transport Coordination in Argentina during the 1930s', *Jour. Latin. Am. Stud.,* 19 (1987); Wright, *British-Owned Railways,* Chs. 10–11.
64 Raúl Garc a Heras, *Automotores noteamericanos, caminos y modernizac on urbana en la Argentina, 1918–1939* (Buenos Aires, 1985).
65 Heras, 'Hostage Private Companies', pp. 50–1, 60–1.
66 Raúl Garc a Heras, 'World War II and the Frustrated Nationalization of the Argentine British-Owned Railways, 1939–1943', *Jour. Latin. Am. Stud.,* 17 (1985); Wright, *British-Owned Railways,* Chs. 11–13; Fodor, 'Origins of Argentina's Sterling Balances', pp. 164–78; Lewis, 'Anglo-Argentine Trade', pp. 131–2.
67 Marichal, *A Century of Debt,* p. 217.
68 The data are derived from sources given in n. 4 above. See also Peter Uwe Schliemann's neglected study, *The Strategy of British and German Direct Investors in Brazil* (1981), pp. 104–5.
69 Albert, *South America and the First World War,* p. 309; Hilton, 'Latin America and World Trade', pp. 178–9; Rippy, *British Investments,* Ch. 13. Given the present state of research, these figures are best read as broad indicators of what is generally agreed to have been the main trend.
70 Albert, *South America and the First World War,* pp. 77–94, 130–43.
71 Fritsch, *External Constraints,* Ch. 3.
72 Ibid. p. 45.
73 Rosenberg, 'Anglo-American Economic Rivalry', pp. 131–2.
74 Marichal, *A Century of Debt,* pp. 173, 184, 197–9; Steven Topik, *The Political Economy of the Brazilian State* (Austin, Tex., 1987), pp. 127–8.
75 Marichal, *A Century of Debt,* pp. 184–5.
76 Principally by issuing fiat bank notes against short-term trade bills. See Fritsch, *External Constraints,* Ch. 4.

77 Fritsch, *External Constraints,* pp. 63, 70.
78 Marichal, *A Century of Debt,* pp. 195–6; Fritsch, *External Constraints,* p. 81.
79 Fritsch, *External Constraints,* pp. 67–8, 84.
80 Ibid. pp. 126–8, 154–7.
81 We are particularly indebted at this point to research by Winston Fritsch, who has rescued the Montagu Mission from undeserved obscurity. See 'The Montagu Financial Mission to Brazil and the Federal Economic Policy Changes of 1924', *Brazilian Economic Studies,* 9 (1985), and the slightly more compressed version in *External Constraints,* pp. 84–107.
82 Montagu to Rothschild, 26 December 1923. Quoted in Fritsch, *External Constraints,* p. 90. As noted below (p. 590) Montagu's constitutional innovations while Secretary of State were designed to strengthen Britain's grip on India. His team included Sir Charles Addis, the peripatetic Chairman of the Hongkong and Shanghai Bank, who watched over Britain's financial interests in the Far East. (See above, pp. 403, 548–9, and below, pp. 641–3).
83 Fritsch, *External Constraints,* pp. 89–90. It is worth noting that Montagu's opposition to Brazil's proposed steel industry was prompted not by concern for British exports but by anxiety about the consequences of increased public expenditure for the republic's ability to pay its external debts.
84 Ibid. pp. 90–1.
85 Ibid. pp. 94–100.
86 Ibid. pp. 104–11, 114.
87 The problem arose because Brazil's claim to be permanently represented on the Council of the League of Nations conflicted with Poland's application, which Britain supported. See Fritsch, *External Constraints,* p. 116.
88 Memo. by Wellesley, 19 April 1926, FO 371/11115, A2075/G. Quoted in Fritsch, *External Constraints,* p. 117.
89 Minute by Chamberlain, 16 April 1926, FO 371/11115, A2075/G. Quoted in ibid. p. 117.
90 As n. 88.
91 Fritsch, *External Constraints,* pp. 138–59.
92 Marichal, *A Century of Debt,* p. 203.
93 Fritsch, *External Constraints,* pp. 157–9; Marichal, *A Century of Debt,* p. 221.
94 Marichal, *A Century of Debt,* p. 220; Abreu, 'Anglo-Brazilian Economic Relations', pp. 381–2. Niemeyer also recommended a programme of economic diversification. See Fiona Gordon-Ashworth, 'Agricultural Commodity Control under Vargas in Brazil, 1930–1945', *Jour. Latin. Am. Stud.,* 12 (1980), pp. 87–8. This was significant because it recognised the need to modify the pattern of specialisation established in the nineteenth century.
95 Marcelo de Paiva Abreu, 'Brazilian Public Debt Policy, 1931–43', *Brazilian Economic Studies,* 4 (1978), pp. 112–18.
96 Between 1932 and 1937 Brazil paid £6m. to £8m. per year (about 20 per cent of the import bill) in public debt service, mainly to British creditors: Abreu, 'Brazilian Public Debt', p. 115.
97 The best guide is Hilton's valuable study, *Brazil and the Great Powers.* See also Ricardo A. Silva Seitenfus, 'Le Brésil de Getulio Vargas et la formation des blocs, 1930–1942' (Ph.D. thesis, University of Geneva, 1981.)
98 Abreu, 'Brazilian Public Debt', pp. 138–9. It is now acknowledged that Vargas made dextrous use of international rivalries to secure Brazil's interests; but this is not to say that Brazil was able to become independent of the major powers. See Hilton, *Brazil and the Great Powers,* Chs. 5–6, and, for the end of the story, idem, 'The Overthrow of Getulio Vargas in 1945: Diplomatic Intervention, Defense of Democracy or Political Retribution', *Hisp. Am. Hist. Rev.,* 67 (1987). On the 'new state' see, for example, Stanley Hilton, 'The Armed Forces and Industrialisation in Modern Brazil: the Drive for Military Autonomy (1889–1954)', *Hisp. Am. Hist. Rev.,* 62 (1982).
99 Hilton, *Brazil and the Great Powers,* pp. 133–9; Abreu, 'Anglo-Brazilian Economic Relations', pp. 381–3; idem, 'Brazilian Public Foreign Debt', pp. 134, 138–9.

100 Abreu, 'Anglo-Brazilian Economic Relations', pp. 382–3; idem, 'Argentina and Brazil', p. 149; idem, 'Brazilian Public Foreign Debt', pp. 115, 120–1.
101 Marichal, *A Century of Debt,* pp. 387–8; Abreu, 'Brazilian Public Foreign Debt', pp. 121–3; Hilton, *Brazil and the Great Powers,* pp. 195–7.
102 Abreu, 'Anglo-Brazilian Economic Relations', p. 387; idem, 'Brazilian Public Foreign Debt', pp. 122–5.
103 Abreu, 'Anglo-Brazilian Economic Relations', p. 387.
104 Ibid. p. 388; idem, 'Brazilian Public Foreign Debt', pp. 126–30. As Abreu has also shown, Britain manipulated Brazil's sterling balances to her own advantage: 'Brazil as a Creditor: Sterling Balances, 1940–1952', *Econ. Hist. Rev.,* 2nd ser. XLIII (1990). See also Hilton, *Brazil and the Great Powers,* p. 216.
105 Albert, *South America and the First World War,* pp. 95–105, 156–65; Couyoumdjian, *Chile y Gran Bretaña,* pp. 247–8.
106 Michael Montéon, *Chile in the Nitrate Era: The Evolution of Economic Dependence, 1880–1930* (Madison, 1982), Ch. 5; Thomas F. O'Brien, 'Rich Beyond the Dreams of Avarice: the Guggenheims in Chile', *Bus. Hist. Rev.,* 63 (1989); Marichal, *A Century of Debt,* pp. 173, 181–91; Humphreys, *Latin America and the Second World War,* I, p. 23.
107 Albert, *South America and the First World War,* pp. 98, 105.
108 Marichal, *A Century of Debt,* p. 212.
109 Humphreys, *Latin America and the Second World War,* I, pp. 6, 24–6; Marichal, *A Century of Debt,* p. 212.
110 The Peruvian case was very similar. See Bill Albert, 'Sugar and Anglo-Peruvian Trade Negotiations in the 1930s', *Jour. Latin. Am. Stud.,* 14 (1982).

23

'FINANCIAL STABILITY AND GOOD GOVERNMENT'

India, 1914–47[1]

After 1914, the study of India's history becomes increasingly preoccupied with political events and especially with charting the route to independence in 1947.[2] An older Whig tradition, invented to accompany the landmarks it described, purported to show that the transfer of power was the culmination of a sequence of well-judged constitutional reforms that set India on a progressive path toward liberal democracy. In more recent years, this interpretation has given way to an alternative which rejects the view that the road to independence consisted of a series of ordered steps, whether designed on high by imperial masterminds or hewn at ground level by dedicated nationalist leaders, and stresses instead the complexity of relationships among diverse political interests in Britain and India, and the uncertainty of their trajectory. In reaction to the element of uncritical self-approval that marked the older tradition, the newer approach emphasises the hard-headed bargaining that lay behind the idealised version of a stately procession towards independence; in harmony with the 'excentric' theory of imperialism, current thinking also allows room for the role of independent or semi-independent influences on the periphery. This aspect of recent historiography can be seen in the work produced by the school of 'subaltern studies', which has questioned perceptions of India's vast diversity formulated and represented by elites in Delhi and London, and has explored the many alternative worlds that existed in the provinces, underlining in the process the distinction between the ideals of policy and the realities of everyday practice.[3]

The contribution made by revisionist historians is rich and illuminating, and fits a broader trend in the study of 'late' colonialism in other parts of the British empire.[4] At the same time, the perspective remains predominantly political, even if much of the attention has shifted from officers to other ranks; and in some formulations it has posited an unnecessarily sharp distinction between interest and ideology. Accordingly, there remains room for a different kind of revisionism, one that seeks to reconsider the objectives of those who ran the Indian empire by relating economic to political considerations and by reappraising the metropolitan perspective on imperial management. This undertaking is not an attempt to turn the clock back by refurbishing an older-style of imperial history; nor is it in conflict with the view from the periphery. It simply suggests that questions relating to the direction of imperial policy towards India are historically significant, have become, in important respects, unfashionable, and need to be readvertised. The aim, however, is more easily formulated than executed because much of the work undertaken by economic historians, valuable though it is, has been inspired by a concern with economic development rather than with imperial purpose, and it, too, has tended to stay within sub-disciplinary boundaries. Nevertheless, sufficient research has been published in recent years to enable some of the links to be joined and for the following outline to be sketched.[5]

Our interpretation of the period after 1914 is essentially an extension of the argument we developed to explain Britain's purpose in India in the nineteenth century. Britain's traditional manufacturing interests, which were already beginning to suffer from free trade and from their inability to alter the priorities of policymakers in London, underwent a marked decline in India after World War I. As we have seen in other contexts, evidence of industrial decay has conventionally been used as an index of imperial decline too, and it forms the background to current debates about the management of Indian nationalism. This reasoning, as we have already argued, is misleading because it bypasses or underestimates a more important measure of value, that provided by fiscal priorities and the associated need to safeguard India's ability to fund her external financial obligations. These imperatives were determined not by a conspiracy of bondholders but by a concern for the probity of public finance, though this had the additional and congenial effect of providing security for private investors. As we shall see, fiscal priorities exerted a powerful influence on economic policy after 1914, as before. The doctrine of the balanced budget inhibited an expansionist development programme and was a target of nationalist criticism. But it also sought to maximise export earnings and to increase revenue by taxing imports and by promoting local industries, and these measures aroused opposition from British manufacturers, who became increasingly frustrated with policies that favoured Indian interests above their own. Amidst these cross-currents, policy-makers held steadily to their purpose: in the 1920s India was drawn into Britain's efforts to reconstruct the pre-war international economic order; and in the 1930s, when hopes of world recovery financed by new investment were replaced by strategies of debt-collecting, India was ordered into the sterling bloc on terms dictated by London.

These priorities had wide-ranging political ramifications. The choice of political alliances in India was determined largely by the need to promote groups that would support the government's fiscal and monetary policies. At the outset of the period under review, when the land tax was still the most important source of state revenue, the Government of India continued to regard the large landholders as being its principal allies.[6] However, as customs and excise duties assumed greater significance, Delhi attempted to win support from Indian representatives of the 'modern' economy in the hope that, by offering them a stake in the Raj, they could be detached from the nationalist movement. Limited constitutional reforms were introduced with the aim of controlling and redirecting opposition, not for the purpose of helping it on its way; radical political advance was constrained by the fear that the transfer of power would enable an independent government to renege on its external financial obligations. While these conditions held, Britain did not relax her grip on India any more than she did in the case of other debtor countries. Independence was eventually conceded when India became ungovernable, but the transition was greatly eased by the fact that, in 1947, the case for 'staying on' was no longer compelling. By then, India had ceased to be one of Britain's largest debtors and had joined the ranks of her creditors instead, while Britain's newer interest in joint ventures in manufacturing and other economic activities pointed to the wisdom of working with the nationalists rather than against them.

Patterns of trade and investment

We can begin to expand this argument by considering the data on foreign trade and investment.[7] After 1914, Britain's visible trade with India underwent a secular decline that extended throughout the period under review. On the eve of World War I, Britain still supplied about two-thirds of India's imports, but this figure dropped to about half in the 1920s, fell to nearly one-third in the 1930s (when Manchester cottons were virtually eliminated from the Indian market), and sank to one-quarter in 1940–41. Looked at from the perspective of the metropole, India accounted for about 13 per cent of all visible exports from the United Kingdom in 1913, about 11 per cent in the 1920s, 9 per cent in the 1930s and 8 per cent in the 1940s. In the 1920s the value of British exports achieved a measure of stability, though at levels that were approximately one-third lower than in the decade before World War I; but export values were cut by more than half between 1929 and 1937, and Britain's competitive position declined to a greater extent in India than in the world as a whole.

The corollary of Britain's loss of exports was the penetration of the Indian market by foreign rivals and the development of import-substituting industries. The combined share of the import market taken by Britain's main competitors, Japan, Germany and the United States, rose from just under 10 per cent in 1914 to just over 33 per cent in 1936–7. The advance of foreign rivals was particularly marked in the 1930s, when Japan became the leading supplier of cotton goods. At the same time, Britain took an increasing proportion of India's exports, especially following the trade agreements of the 1930s, and in 1938–9 her share rose to just over one-third of the total. The development of import-substitution was even more telling: in 1900 imports accounted for about 63 per cent of the market for cotton textiles, and virtually all of them were British; by 1936 only about 12 per cent of the market was supplied by imports, of which a mere 4 per cent came from Britain. The remaining

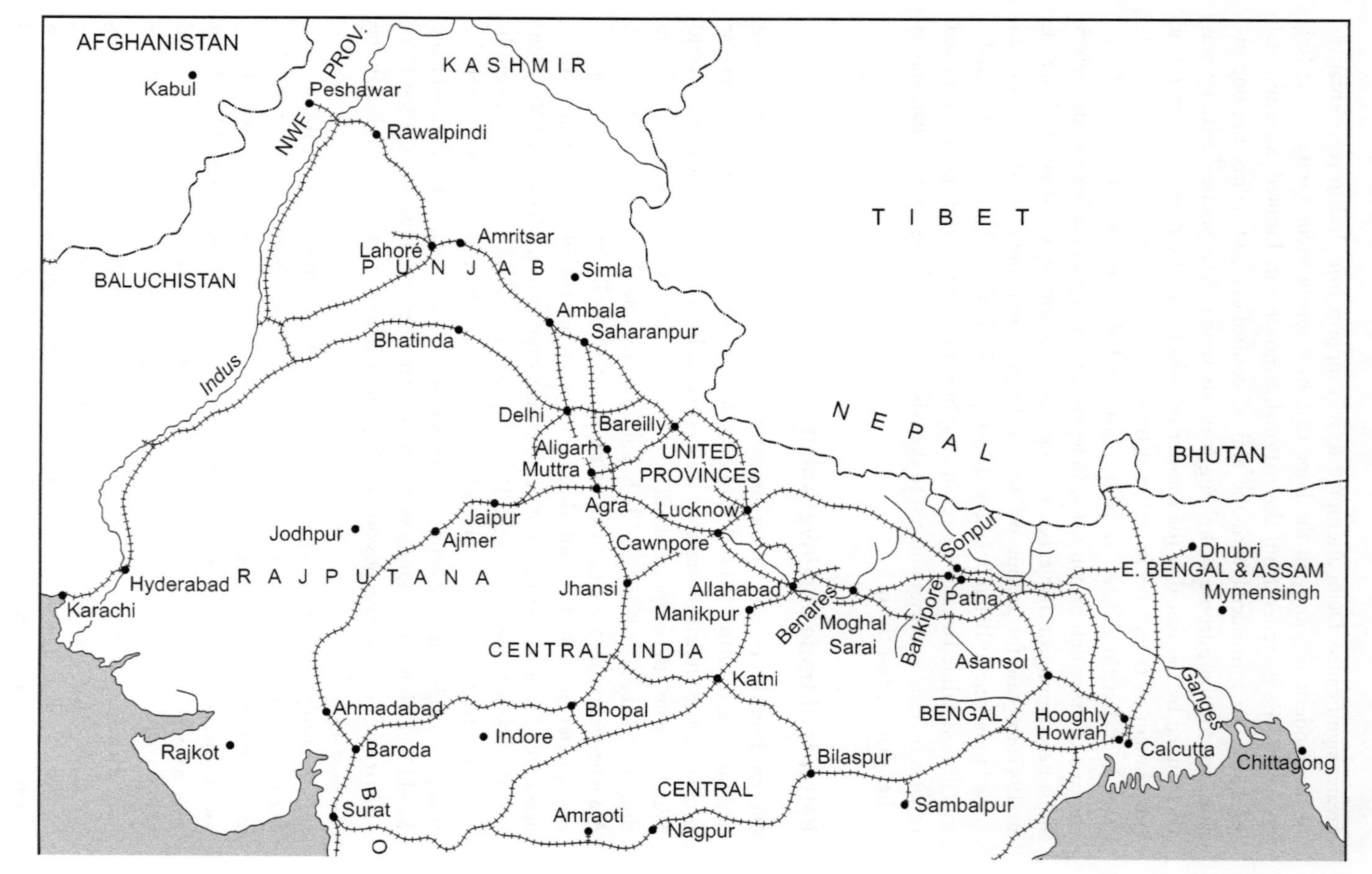
AFGHANISTAN
Kabul
NWF PROV.
Peshawar
Rawalpindi
KASHMIR
BALUCHISTAN
Lahore
Amritsar
PUNJAB
Simla
Ambala
Saharanpur
Bhatinda
Indus
TIBET
NEPAL
BHUTAN
Delhi
Bareilly
Aligarh
Muttra
UNITED PROVINCES
Agra
Lucknow
Jaipur
Ajmer
Jodhpur
Cawnpore
Sonpur
Dhubri
E. BENGAL & ASSAM
Mymensingh
Hyderabad
Karachi
RAJPUTANA
Jhansi
Allahabad
Manikpur
Benares
Moghal Sarai
Bankipore
Patna
Asansol
CENTRAL INDIA
Katni
Ganges
Ahmadabad
Bhopal
BENGAL
Hooghly
Howrah
Calcutta
Chittagong
Rajkot
Baroda
Indore
Bilaspur
CENTRAL
Sambalpur
Surat
Amraoti
Nagpur
B
O

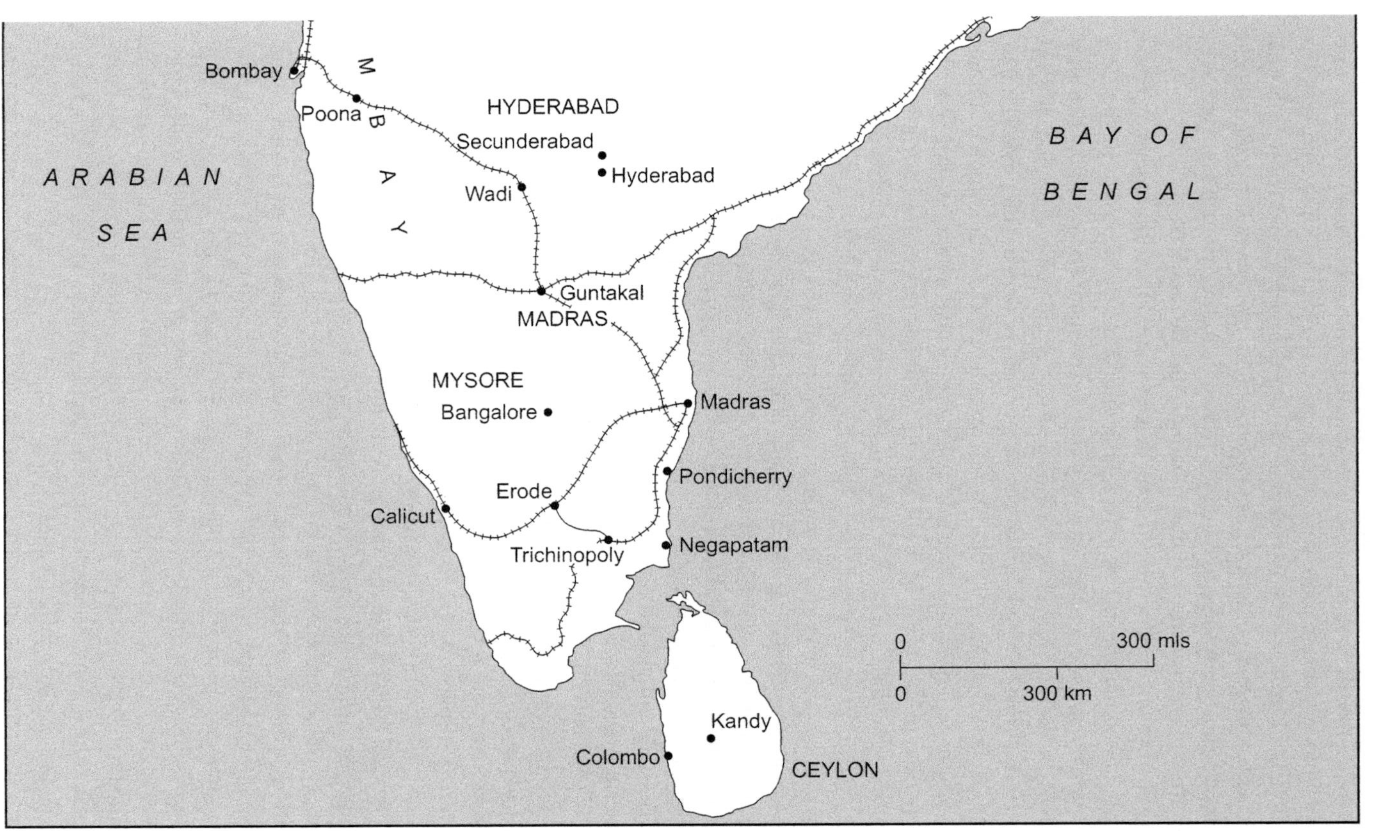

MAP 10 India: provinces and railways, 1931

After: Dharma Kumar, ed. *The Cambridge Economic History of India, c. 1757–c. 1970*, 2 (Cambridge, 1983)

88 per cent came from domestic sources: nearly two-thirds of this total were produced by modern textile mills. If benefits were conferred by British rule, very few of them found their way to Manchester during this period; and if the industrial bourgeoisie really did pull the wires of government, it is curious that they should have been so ineffective in defending their interests in India, which had long been one of their major markets, and was fully under British control.

British investment experienced a modest increase during the interwar period as a whole, though the rise was very limited and occurred mainly in the early 1920s, when there was a temporary revival of government borrowing.[8] Thereafter, decline set in: lack of growth in the Indian economy limited its attractions to British investors as the 1920s advanced; lack of revenue, combined with political unrest, made them positively wary in the 1930s. Nevertheless, the composition of foreign investment experienced an important qualitative change which we have observed in other parts of the world: in the 1930s and 1940s, when much of the infrastructure of state-building had been laid down, there was increase in the proportion of private foreign investment and a corresponding decline in public-sector loans. This shift was associated with the beginnings of structural change in the economy, as opportunities for developing import-substituting activities drew in multinational corporations and encouraged joint-ventures by private entrepreneurs. Despite the failure to generate substantial new flows of foreign capital, India remained one of the principal recipients of British foreign investment, and Britain still had a large stake to defend in the sub-continent.[9]

The full significance of these trends can be appreciated by looking at the balance of payments. Before 1914, Britain ran a surplus on her visible trade with India, and India settled the deficit through her exports to continental Europe and other parts of Asia.[10] This pattern of exchange survived in the 1920s, though in a less robust form, but it underwent a fundamental change in the 1930s, when India developed a surplus on her visible trade with Britain. The fact that Britain could no longer call upon substantial earnings from her commodity trade with India to settle her deficits with Europe and the United States was both a symptom and a contributory cause of her growing balance of payments problems in the inter-war period. To this extent, there is some truth in the view that India was less valuable to Britain in the 1930s than she had been before World War I. At the same time, however, India became a large net exporter of gold in the 1930s, and this item boosted her current account surplus and helped to service her foreign debt, pay the Home Charges and settle the deficit on the rest of her invisible trade. From this perspective, India remained highly prized: remittances from the sub-continent accounted for 15–16 per cent of Britain's total net invisible earnings in the 1930s and made a vital contribution to the stability of sterling and the balance of payments at a particularly difficult time.[11]

Transfers from India increased during the 1920s as a result of new government borrowing, and became more burdensome in the 1930s, when revenues were affected by the slump. Whereas in the late nineteenth century, debt service and the Home Charges accounted for about 16 per cent of India's current revenues, in 1933 they reached a peak of just over 27 per cent.[12] By then, India's surplus on her commodity trade with Britain had become increasingly necessary, both to pay for the growing proportion of imports drawn from other countries (notably Japan) and to meet her traditional obligations on her invisible account with Britain.[13]

The statistics on overseas trade and payments, fragmentary though they are in some respects, confirm that Britain's commodity exports were indeed of diminishing importance in her trade with India after 1914, whether measured by absolute value or by their contribution to the balance of trade and balance of payments. In the embattled commercial world of the 1930s, India remained a sizeable market for British goods, and it was not one to be given up lightly. But the collapse of sales of Manchester cottons further reduced the national significance and political influence of British manufacturers trading to the sub-continent. Invisible earnings and transfers of capital, on the other hand, became relatively more important and acquired greater weight in Britain's stake in India. This evidence suggests two hypotheses. One is that the Government of India was likely to have been preoccupied by the need to ensure that payments to Britain continued to flow smoothly, and that fiscal and monetary policy remained central to Britain's imperial purpose. The other is that financial priorities raised delicate issues of political control: they had to be applied without provoking discontent on a scale that would imperil the authority structures that were vital to the functioning of the imperial economy.

The gentlemen of the Raj

The argument derived from these hypotheses will be developed in the remaining part of this chapter. Before doing so, however, brief consideration needs to be given to the social background and cultural values of the men who managed India during the period under review. We have already suggested that the transition from Company to crown rule in 1858 created wider employment opportunities for members of professional families in the Home Counties, and is not to be seen as marking the triumph of the industrial bourgeoisie.[14] These recruits were either gentlemen or gentlemen in the making: accordingly, they tended to despise industry as well as to fear the spread of its influence, and they took more readily to activities that produced a means of support that was both substantial and virtually unseen. By upbringing and education, they had closer affinity with invisible income than with commodity trade, and they were enthusiastic agents of the fiscal and financial priorities of government as they emerged in India during the second half of the nineteenth century.

These values survived the decimation inflicted by World War I and continued to infuse policy in India (as in Africa and Malaya) down to the point where British rule was withdrawn, and in some respects they survived its passing. The pessimism that weighed upon intellectuals as they brooded over 'the decline of the West' in the inter-war period did not in general burden members of the Indian Civil Service (ICS). They remained men with a purpose united by shared values. If these had been challenged during World War I, they were reinvigorated thereafter.

The imperial mission continued to be a global advertisement for liberal capitalism and constitutional means of effecting change; as such, it had to be vigorously promoted to counter the powerful alternatives envisaged by Bolshevism, fascism and the pan-Islamic movements which appeared in different parts of the empire. In these circumstances, possessing an empire and defining a role were complementary, even inspirational, aims.

Gentlemanly norms continued to predominate: the ideal of the leisured amateur who undertook activities that had a general impact on the public mind remained unquestioned, as did the snobbery that was integral to the definition of social class in Britain and, when exported, turned members of the ICS into a caste in India. But gentlemen also aligned themselves to a code that stressed the virtues of honour, duty and public service, and they brought a moral certainty to the task of government that ought not to be discounted or treated as a disguise for material motives. This morality was derived from a particularly clear and sometimes militant brand of Christianity of the kind associated with the Round Table group and Exeter Hall.[15] Sir Arthur Hirtzel, the most important official in the India Office during the 1920s, was steeped in both the classics and Christian theology.[16] He believed, even after World War I, that the British empire was a greater, Christian version of the Roman imperial ideal, and that India's destiny under the Raj was bound up with her spiritual progress. An imperialist, he explained, was animated by the belief that 'the race to which he belongs is the noblest, and the civilization and ideals for which it stands are the highest – are, in fact, so high that all the world must needs accept them. Now, this is an outlook upon life that is at once familiar to the Christian'.[17] This vision does not merely qualify a crude, materialist interpretation of the imperial purpose, whether couched in political or economic terms, but suggests, more interestingly, ways in which principle and interest were joined. Both Sir Basil Blackett and Sir George Schuster, successively Finance Members of the Council of India during 1922–8 and 1928–34, were Christian exponents of economic rationality: financial management was for them an instrument of Christian rule, the balanced budget was the realisation of a state of spiritual harmony, and taxation was a powerful force for moral progress as well as a means of funding the Raj.[18] For such men, Christian faith and faith in the empire were spiritual and temporal dimensions of one integrated and superior system of belief.

As the values survived, so did the pattern of recruitment that supported them.[19] Members of the Indian Civil Service continued to be drawn overwhelmingly from upper- and middle-class families with professional backgrounds. With few exceptions, they were educated at public schools, and three-quarters of them had been to Oxford or Cambridge. The service was lifted from the depression that passed across it at the close of World War I, revitalised by a new sense of mission, and boosted by improvements in pay and conditions.[20] In the 1930s the ICS, having dealt firmly with Congress 'agitators', adapted to Congress governments; it also adjusted to a process of Indianisation, not least by assimilating Indian recruits to gentlemanly ideals.[21] The decline came during World War II, when lack of manpower allied to lack of will-power brought the machinery of government close to breakdown.[22] By

1945, however, Britain's interest in India had already begun to change; before then the gentlemen of the Raj did their duty effectively, as we shall now see.

The impact of World War I

World War I seriously disrupted India's international trade and payments.[23] Britain's exports were badly affected by shipping shortages, foreign competition (especially from Japan) and local import-substituting industries, and her surplus on visible trade with India disappeared.[24] British officials were alive to the threat posed by Japan, but recognised that she had to be allowed unfettered entry into India, even at the expense of Lancashire's textile exports.[25] Some inducement was needed to persuade Japan to acquiesce in the imperial presence in India at a time when she was tempted to encourage anti-colonial movements in Asia, and to bolster the Anglo-Japanese alliance, which was crucial to Britain's position in the Far East.[26] The war also dislocated India's gold exchange standard by severing the link between the level of currency in circulation and the value of the rupee.[27] Liquidity problems led to a growth in the money supply without a corresponding rise in India's reserves of silver bullion, and an increase in the world price of silver caused the bullion value of the rupee to rise above its established exchange rate. Consequently, the exchange rate became dependent on the sterling price of silver, while the level of currency in circulation was influenced by the government's financial needs. These needs mounted rapidly after 1914, principally because of the massive cost of stoking the British military machine.[28] India supplied over 1.5 million men for war service between 1914 and 1918; the expense placed a heavy burden on the Indian taxpayer and pushed the budget into deficit.[29]

Economic problems led readily to civil disorder and provided popular support for a new brand of assertive nationalism which drew inspiration variously from the Irish Home Rule movement, the Japanese economic miracle and the Russian Revolution, as well as from its own indigenous roots.[30] This heady mixture, stirred by German support, solidified as the war progressed into demands for self-government and for a new deal for India's economy. This was a formative time for a whole generation of nationalist leaders, from Argentina to China. It saw the emergence of Gandhi as the leader of the Indian National Congress, and it set the political agenda until independence was achieved in 1947.[31] Gandhi displaced the moderate leadership of Congress, and drew upon popular support to an extent that transformed the nature as well as the size of the political arena.[32] The non-cooperation movement of 1921–2, for example, was the first of a succession of similar popular protests, and the fact that it was launched after Germany had been defeated indicated that settling the peace was going to be an even more difficult task than winning the war.

Britain's response to these challenges provides a good guide to her priorities and a sound measure of her commitment to holding the Indian empire. The budgetary crisis was met in 1917 by allowing the Government of India to increase the tariff on imported cotton goods from 3.5 to 7.5 per cent (without also raising the countervailing excise on Indian textiles).[33] Manchester's opposition was fierce but unsuccessful, and the Government of India's independence in matters of tariff policy was confirmed by the Fiscal Autonomy Convention of 1919. The action taken in 1917 eased India's fiscal problems, assisted Bombay's cotton mills, and mollified nationalist feeling. Taken as a whole, the episode symbolised the waning power of the Lancashire lobby, and indeed of the provinces in British political life, and the growing influence on policy of forces within India; but it also emphasised the paramountcy of sound money principles, and hence of Treasury orthodoxy.[34]

Re-connecting the rupee to sterling proved to be a delicate and protracted operation, especially while sterling itself was floating against other currencies. But the aims of policy were quite clear from the report of the Babington-Smith Committee, which was appointed in 1919 to recommend a solution to the problem, even if their application was frustrated by the post-war slump of 1920–1.[35] The Committee was preoccupied by the need to conserve Britain's gold reserves and increase her credit in preparation for returning to prewar normality. Accordingly, it recommended a high exchange rate for the rupee against sterling in the hope of attracting silver to India rather than gold. This strategy was also deflationary, and it complemented the Government of India's efforts in the immediate post-war period to reduce the volume of currency in circulation and to regain budgetary stability. As Manchester was sacrificed to help balance India's budget, so India was drawn into a strategy for regaining Britain's pre-eminence in international finance.

Fiscal orthodoxy was accompanied by political concessions which were designed to win over moderate nationalist opinion.[36] Constitutional reforms were recommended by the Montagu-Chelmsford Report in 1918 and embodied in the Government of India Act in the following year. The principal concession centred on the devolution of various administrative functions to elected legislative assemblies in the provinces. Ostensibly, this was a step on the road to 'responsible' government, and was treated as such by a generation of liberal historians; but it is currently interpreted as being a device to perpetuate British power by dispersing opposition from the centre and by giving a larger number of Indians in the provinces a political stake in the Raj.[37] The reforms certainly did not imply any weakening of imperial resolve. As Montagu pointed out in the House of Commons in 1922, constitutional advance depended on continuing 'good conduct', and marks could be scored only by cooperating with the imperial mission.[38] Moreover, vital areas of policy, such as foreign affairs, defence and finance (including the most important sources of revenue) remained firmly in the hands of the Viceroy.[39] The need to maintain political stability was the proximate cause of constitutional reform,[40] but it is also important to recognise that in 1919, as in 1857, civil order sustained the credit as well as the credibility of the Raj.

The attempt to return to normality: the 1920s

The Montagu-Chelmsford reforms reinvigorated the imperial mission by giving it a renewed sense of purpose. In the 1920s the revitalised agents of the Raj set about 'nation-building' in the provinces, and they used the new constitution to reinforce their alliance with conservative land-holders and princes and to divide moderate nationalists from those who were not prepared to accept the new rules of the game.[41] This strategy rested on techniques of collaboration that have engaged much historical research, but it also involved coercive and other means of control that were not found in the liberal handbook. Current historiography may well underestimate this facet of British rule. Despite the fact that only a small number of white officials were present to hold the 'imperial facade' in place,[42] steps were taken to repress unconstitutional opposition and to censor subversive influences by blocking the inflow of anti-imperialist ideas, including American democratic republicanism as well as Soviet socialism.[43] It is interesting to note that Mazzini's autobiography (which was translated into Marathi in 1907) was banned in India shortly after it had been published and had sold out there, and it remained on the imperial index until 1947.[44] Mazzini had become a hero in England not least as a result of the writings of the Whig historian, George Macaulay Trevelyan.

These observations are made not to pass judgement on British rule but to underline Britain's determination to remain in charge of India's destiny. Early in 1922, Lloyd George informed the Cabinet that 'we were now masters in India, and we should let it be understood that we intend to remain so'.[45] Shortly afterwards, Montagu stamped on the belief that 'we regard our mission in India as drawing to a close, that we are preparing for a retreat. If such an idea exists', he added, 'it is a complete fallacy'.[46] These were not empty words: they marked a conscious commitment to re-establishing Britain's position as a world power, and matched similar statements of intent made about the South American republics, China and the African colonies. As the war had heightened public consciousness of the importance of the empire,[47] so the peace held out the prospect of taking out imperial insurance for the British way of life and of demonstrating its superiority over the alternatives that threatened it, both at home and abroad.[48]

Economic reconstruction in the 1920s was concerned, above all, with reestablishing India's place in the international payments system based on sterling. Accordingly, priority was given to balancing the Indian budget after the exigencies of war and to stabilising the exchange rate of the rupee. Sharp increases in taxation and severe retrenchment corrected budget deficits in 1918–19 and 1922–23 and enabled the Government of India to restore its credit-worthiness.[49] By then, however, it was apparent that the budget had to be expanded as well as balanced in order to fund the 'nation-building' projects that flowed from the Montagu-Chelmsford reforms. Given the prevailing monetary orthodoxy, there could be no big push for development, though some observers had begun to suggest that Britain's interests were ceasing to be served by India's backward agrarian economy, and even that they might gain from promoting local industry.[50] The only alternative was to increase the revenue from taxation. In practice, this meant augmenting the receipts from customs duties because the traditional source, the land tax, could not readily be expanded. Consequently, the general tariff on imports was increased from 7.5 per cent in 1917 to 11 per cent in 1921, and eventually reached 25 per cent in 1931.[51] Although this was a revenue tariff, it had a protective effect, and thus mollified Indian manufacturers while simultaneously increasing public revenues.

The main cost of this solution was borne by companies exporting to India. British firms were particularly hard hit because their Japanese rivals, besides having the advantage of high productivity, were also helped by the depreciation of the yen during the 1920s. Lancashire, the most notable casualty of the Government of India's tariff policy, was dealt a further blow in 1925, when the excise duty on Indian cotton goods was removed.[52] Officials had long resisted Indian demands for the abolition of the cotton excise on grounds of fiscal need, but finally gave way when agitation in Bombay threatened to turn an economic grievance into a political cause. The government had no wish to abandon Manchester's manufacturers, but the outcome was a damaging blow to their declining cause, and they were left with no more than a vague hope that they might benefit from imperial preference at some indeterminate point in the future.

In the 1920s, however, imperial preference had more appeal to Britain's ailing staple industries than to orthodox free traders in the City, who were bent on reconstructing the pre-war system of multilateral settlements, or to the Government of India, which was concerned about the budgetary consequences and political implications of trade restrictions. As a result, in 1924 India opted for 'discriminating protection' for a few industries rather than for imperial preference.[53] This policy gave a further boost to import-substituting industries, especially iron and steel, and also helped the budget by economising on imports.[54] Adjustments were made to incorporate differential duties on imports of iron and steel in 1927 and cotton goods in 1930, in response to pleas from British industry, but these were modest breaches of free trade which neither retarded the development of Indian manufactures nor checked the flow of imports from Japan.[55] The pursuit of fiscal objectives and the need to placate Indian opinion not only pushed the claims of British manufacturers down the list of policy priorities, but also induced the gentlemen of the Raj to overcome their distaste for industry to the extent of promoting it in India.

Stabilising the rupee was a more protracted and controversial process.[56] Fluctuations in the exchange rate during the immediate post-war period brought considerable uncertainty to commercial and official transactions, and involved the government in contentious problems of money management. Fixing the sterling value of the rupee was therefore a matter of high priority, though success ultimately depended on sterling's return to the gold standard. After a period when the exchange was allowed to float, the Government of India fixed the sterling rate at 1*s.* 6*d.* in 1924. This rate was endorsed by the Hilton-Young Commission of Inquiry in 1925; it was operative when sterling rejoined the gold standard, and it held until 1931.

The long haul back to a fixed exchange rate underlined the Government of India's determination to play its part in reviving the pre-war sterling system. The chosen rate, 1*s.* 6*d.*, was unpopular in India because it was thought to be too high. The result, so it was argued, was to boost the import trade and cheapen remittances to London, while also deflating the domestic economy.[57] It is now apparent, however, that Lancashire had no influence on the rupee rate and gained little if anything from the decision to fix it at 1*s.* 6*d.*[58] It is equally clear that, while the Bombay textile interest was able to secure concessions in the area of tariffs (not least because they suited the government's budgetary policy), it had no effect at all on monetary policy, despite vociferous lobbying. On the other hand, the rate undoubtedly assisted the payment of the Home Charges because fewer rupees were required to settle sterling debts. However, specific advantages such as this have to be set in the broader context of reestablishing sound money principles.[59] This meant restoring not only a stable exchange rate but also the automaticity of the monetary system and hence the confidence of external creditors. It was with this aim in mind that the Hilton-Young Commission (1925–6) recommended establishing a reserve bank to oversee the operation of the monetary system. Whether or not the rupee exchange rate was overvalued, the intention was to fix it at a level that would suit London's interests. A high exchange rate meant that India would continue to absorb silver rather than gold. Any deflationary consequences were the price that India had to pay for upholding monetary orthodoxy and avoiding the political effects of unbridled inflation. Sound money, a stable polity and moral order were an indivisible trinity. Britain had no intention of reproducing the experience of Weimar Germany either at home or in India.

By 1926 Britain had returned to the gold standard and silver prices had fallen. A high exchange rate for the rupee no longer implied that India would absorb silver rather than gold, and policy-makers in Whitehall reverted to pre-war techniques of managing India's gold exports, principally through exchange intervention. The high sterling exchange rate of the rupee now served a different purpose: it meant that India's gold import point was less likely to be reached and, accordingly, that a larger share of the empire's gold reserves could be placed at London's disposal. In this way, policy towards India continued to reflect Britain's wider purpose in seeking to reconstruct the pre-war international order based on the gold standard and the supremacy of sterling.

Economic crisis and political advance: the 1930s

In India, as elsewhere, the sustained effort to reconstruct the pre-war international economic order was brought to a halt by the onset of the world slump in 1929. Research on the impact of the slump on India and on imperial policy is comparatively recent, but the evidence now accumulating suggests that the predominantly political accounts which have dominated the historiography of the period, and particularly of the Government of India Act in 1935, need to be revised to give greater weight to economic influences on imperial policy.[60]

The most obvious manifestations of the slump in India were falling export prices, declining terms of trade, reduced profits in the overseas trade sector, and renewed budgetary problems for the government. These conditions heightened discontent in India, fuelled the nationalist movement and gave considerable impetus to the demand for constitutional progress.[61] The civil disobedience campaign led by Gandhi in 1930–1 included a boycott of British goods, and it unnerved expatriate business, caused a flight of capital from India and placed a question mark over the government's ability to maintain order. Since Congress was explicit in declaring that it would devalue the rupee and repudiate India's foreign debt, the alarm felt in London was well founded. But just as nationalist demands compelled attention, so pressures to balance the budget, to meet imperial financial obligations and to support British business mounted too. These contradictory claims concentrated the official mind, and the outcome provides as good a guide to official priorities as the imperfect historical record will allow. Once again, the Government of India gave first priority to sound money policies, and prescribed further bouts of retrenchment and deflation to maintain the external value of the rupee, to ensure the smooth flow of remittances and to guarantee India's international credit-worthiness. The measures that followed were carried through in the face of strenuous opposition both from nationalist opinion in India, which claimed that the government's monetary policy harmed the local economy, and from British exporters, whose interests were severely damaged by increased import duties.

Official priorities first expressed themselves during the rupee crisis of 1930–2.[62] As economic depression and political uncertainty exerted pressure on the exchange rate, the Government of India sought approval in 1931 for a modest devaluation of the rupee (to 1*s.* 4*d.*). But London turned down the proposal, fearing that the move would increase the rupee costs of meeting India's sterling obligations and would also turn out to be a short step on the road leading to more serious devaluation and even to bankruptcy. Default was unthinkable, given that India's sterling debt stood at over £350m. and the Home Charges at about £30m. a year. Commitments of this order had serious implications for the stability of sterling, which was itself becoming increasingly vulnerable. After much agonising in the Treasury and the India Office, it was eventually conceded that Britain would have to pick up the bill if India failed to meet her debt payments. As the India Office observed in 1931: 'There is no escape from the conclusion that as long as the British Government retains obligations which absorb so large a proportion of the total revenue of India, it must retain a direct interest in the financial administration of the country'.[63] Accordingly, Britain imposed a deflationary emergency budget on India in 1931 and made heavy calls on India's gold reserves to hold the exchange rate at 1*s.* 6*d.* When Britain left the gold standard in September of that year, London decreed that India should follow, and the rupee was placed on a sterling standard at the existing rate of 1*s.* 6*d.*

The integration of the rupee into the Sterling Area, combined with renewed gold flows to London following the depreciation of sterling and the rupee, restored confidence among investors and enabled India to meet her traditional financial commitments.[64] Only then was Britain prepared to consider further constitutional advance for India. Even so, the Government of India Act in 1935 gave the Viceroy final control over fiscal and monetary matters, committed the government to holding the exchange rate at 1*s.* 6*d.*, and ensured that currency reserves were ear-marked for sterling obligations.[65] The interesting development at this point was the decision to delegate key aspects of monetary policy to the new Reserve Bank of India, which had been founded in 1934.[66] The establishment of a Central Bank had been recommended by the Hilton-Young Commission in 1925, but it was not acted upon until the redivision of power contemplated in the Government of India Bill caused Whitehall and the City to reconsider ways of safeguarding Britain's financial interests. The Reserve Bank of India, like its counterparts in the Dominions, was designed to remove monetary policy from the political arena, or, to be precise, to prevent nationalists from tampering with monetary orthodoxy. Here, as elsewhere, the Governor of the Bank of England, Norman, played a key role in promoting the idea and implementing it.[67] Norman selected the first governor, Sir Osborne Smith, and groomed him for the position; when Smith was tempted into flirting with a lower exchange rate for the rupee, he was forced to resign in 1936. His successor, Sir James Taylor, had spent his career in the Indian Civil Service and was a man of proven loyalty: the exchange rate was held at 1*s.* 6*d.*, and there it remained until after India had been granted independence. From the British point of view, the results of these measures were wholly satisfactory: the confidence of overseas creditors was restored, the repatriation of capital was halted, the flow of remittances was maintained, and India's credit-rating remained at a level that enabled her to attract long-term private investment in the second half of the 1930s.

If the monetary policy imposed on India aroused intense opposition from Congress, the tariff policy adopted by the Government of India was much closer to nationalist demands. Even in tariff matters, however, the Government of India exercised the freedom of action it had won in 1919 in ways that supported Britain's financial priorities. As in the 1920s, deflationary budgets were accompanied by increased import duties, which hit Britain's manufactured exports and protected Indian industry.[68] Indeed, India's import-substituting manufactures experienced a decisive advance during the 1930s as a result of government support, indigenous enterprise, and the appearance of subsidiaries of transnational companies (such as Metal Box, Dunlop, Unilever and ICI).[69] Revenue imperatives were also a powerful motive for encouraging India's exports, as the international trade agreements of the 1930s clearly showed.[70] The crucial issue throughout these negotiations was the need to guarantee a market for India's exports so that she could continue to make remittances to London. This consideration ensured that India was treated on the same terms as the dominions at the Ottawa Conference in 1932. The labyrinthine negotiations that followed (leading to the Lees-Mody Pact on cotton goods in 1933, the Supplementary Agreement on steel in 1934 and the Anglo-Indian Trade Agreement of 1939), could scarcely conceal the fact that Britain was being forced to bargain with a dependent part of her empire or that India was the chief beneficiary.[71] In the course of the 1930s India achieved a visible trade surplus with Britain and also repaid much of the capital raised in the 1920s to promote provincial development.[72] Meanwhile, Lancashire's exports to India dwindled to insignificance, despite strenuous efforts to reserve a place for them in their former domain.[73]

The political implications of these trends unwound as the decade advanced. When it became clear at the close of the 1920s that further constitutional advances were needed to hold the loyalty of moderate nationalists and to amputate support from the 'extremists', the British government formulated a plan in 1931 for conceding a greater measure of self-government but containing it within a federal structure.[74] As we have seen in other cases (notably Canada and South Africa), federation was a well-tried imperial device for grouping territories that would otherwise be 'unviable', that is to say unable to raise the foreign loans needed to fund their development, without at the same time creating a powerful central government that might jib at continuing external management of important aspects of economic policy. The idea in the Indian case was to stop Congress from controlling the centre by drawing the princely states into a federal arrangement. This proposal ran into fierce opposition in India, and it also threatened to split the Conservative Party in Britain. In the early 1930s the constitutional concessions envisaged for India were opposed by a coalition consisting of about 50 Conservative MPs, led by Churchill, a band of Christian idealists, who believed that the British government was abandoning its historic mission, and leading representatives of Manchester's manufacturers, who thought that the country's industrial interests were being cast aside.[75] Encouraged by this unusual degree of political recognition, Manchester made an exceptional effort to present its case, notably by founding the Cotton Trade League in 1933, by pressing for the repeal of the Fiscal Autonomy Convention of 1919, and by opposing further constitutional concessions. The most significant result of this movement was its total failure. The die-hards, the idealists and the Lancashire lobby were comprehensively defeated, and Hoare's plan for salvaging British finance on a raft of constitutional reform was launched as the Government of India Act in 1935.[76]

The British scheme did not emerge without modification, but it was adjusted to fit Indian realities rather than pressures from Manchester manufacturers and their allies. The Government of India Act offered a large measure of self-government in exchange for financial and other safeguards, and it also made provision for a federation of Indian states. The federation, however, failed to materialise. The slump weakened the rural pillars of British rule by destroying the prosperity of agriculture and shifting the locus of development to the towns.[77] By the close of the 1930s, agrarian distress and criticism from Congress had cost the 'landed interest' and the princes much of their popular support, while their reluctance to cooperate in Britain's scheme for federation caused the agents of the Raj to question their value as political allies.[78] Casting about for durable alternatives, the Government of India tried to build up the Muslim League as a conservative counterweight to radical nationalism, and to attract Indian business interests by offering them protection against imports and by frightening them with the bogey of left-wing Congress socialism.[79] This strategy, in turn, had to be rethought in 1937, when elections set in train by the Government of India Act resulted in the defeat of the League and the installation of a Congress government.

Even at this stage, fortune or, as some imperialists would have put it, providence, lent a hand to the imperial cause. Once in power, Congress began to reach an understanding with Indian business by muting its proposals for nationalisation, and by controlling labour unrest in exchange for political and financial support.[80] At the same time, British firms also adopted a more cooperative attitude towards Congress, following the growth of joint ventures with Indian companies in the 1930s.[81] The short period of Congress government, from 1937 to 1939, was important for the shape of future political alliances because it showed that 'responsible government' did not necessarily have to be in British hands. The Government of India itself saw the experience as producing a new set of indigenous allies who could still be shaped to the imperial purpose. The Viceroy, Lord Linlithgow, gave little indication, even in his private correspondence, that he was in India to manage a retreat:

> After all, we framed the constitution as it stands in the Act of 1935 because we thought it the best way . . . of maintaining British influence in India. It is no part of our policy, I take it, to expedite in India constitutional changes for their own sake, or gratuitously to hurry the handing over of the controls to Indian hands at any rate faster than that which we regard as best calculated, on the long view, to hold India to the Empire.[82]

War, finance and independence

The outbreak of World War II derailed Britain's plans for training a new team of political allies. Despite windfall gains for parts of the economy, notably the import-substituting industries, the war had a generally adverse effect on India, bringing price inflation and famine, and causing heavy loss of life at the front.[83] India's international trade was disrupted, customs revenues suffered, and the government faced renewed budgetary problems. Discontent once again fed into powerful, though often conflicting, political forces, as Indian leaders tried to gauge the outcome of the war and to lay their bets accordingly. But Congress held together and became more militant, and Britain's plans for a federal India sank beyond the point where they could be salvaged. Britain's immediate reaction to these developments reflected her determination to retain control of India and with it her leadership of the empire. Although attempts were made to buy off Indian opposition with constitutional concessions, culminating in the much-publicised Cripps mission in 1942, the evidence now suggests that these were ploys approved by Churchill to gain time for Britain and to soothe anti-colonial feeling in the United States.[84] The main aim, championed by Churchill and the Viceroy, Linlithgow, was to use the opportunities presented by the war to reassert British paramountcy in both India and Burma.[85] The Government of India took advantage of its wartime emergency powers to suppress opposition, following the Quit India campaign of 1942–3, and coupled this with a further attempt to promote the Muslim League, which was regarded as being a more congenial associate than Congress.[86]

Britain's assertiveness failed to survive the war and Churchill's defeat in the general election of 1945. Repression could not be sustained indefinitely; nor, in the event, could the imperial mission be revived in India. By the end of the war, there was a loss of purpose at the very centre of the imperial system. The gentlemanly administrators who managed the Raj no longer had the heart to devise new moves against increasing odds, not least because after 1939 the majority of the Indian Civil Service were themselves Indian.[87] In 1945 the new Viceroy, Wavell, commented on the 'weakness and weariness of the instrument still at our disposal in the shape of the British element in the Indian Civil Service'.[88] The towns had been lost to opponents of the Raj; the countryside had slipped beyond control. Widespread discontent in the army was followed in 1946 by a mutiny in the navy. It was then that Wavell, the unfortunate messenger, reported to London that India had become ungovernable.[89] The days when 'every white skin automatically extracted a salute'[90] were now to be written about rather than experienced.

Yet to explain the transfer of power solely or even mainly in terms of personalities and the collective psychology of the bureaucracy is to miss a train of causation that began before the war and ran through to the terminal point at independence. By 1947 Britain ceased to have substantial economic motives for retaining India. The war destroyed what was left of India's value as a repository for Britain's old, staple manufactures. At the same time, it encouraged foreign investment to shift further into local manufacturing, with the result that by 1947 capital goods accounted for nearly half of Britain's exports to India.[91] The signals were clear: the future of British exports and investment lay in cooperating with Indian business interests and, through them, with Congress. As the Labour government rapidly discovered, cooperation meant conferring independence as soon as possible.[92] More important still, the war transformed Britain's financial stake in India as a whole: from being one of Britain's major debtors, India emerged in 1945 as her largest single sterling creditor. When Britain decided to rearm in the late 1930s, she reluctantly agreed to meet the expense of using the Indian army outside the sub-continent.[93] This cost and that of importing material supplies from India were settled during the war by means of paper credits, which were held as sterling balances in London. By 1945 India's balances amounted to approximately £1,300m.[94] Consequently, constitutional advance in India was no longer constrained by fear of default, as it had been in the 1930s.

In Britain's changed and desperate economic situation in 1945, India had ceased to be an imperial asset.[95] As far as visible trade was concerned, India was now in deficit with the United States and was no longer a net contributor to the Sterling Area's hard currency pool. Moreover, the British authorities were reluctant to promote exports to India partly because overseas demand for capital goods was thought to hamper domestic reconstruction, and partly because exports had to be directed to areas where they could earn dollars. The sterling balances were undoubtedly a problem because India, as the principal claimant, held no less than one-third of the total. The balances had to be freed because Britain was committed to restoring convertibility. However, if India drew on them at will, Britain's reserves would be depleted and an unacceptably large proportion of her exports would be drawn to the sub-continent. Moreover, if India left the Sterling Area, the damage would extend beyond Britain's hard currency position to the credibility of the area as a whole. The solution was found in an agreement that kept India in the Sterling Area and phased the withdrawal of the balances over a period that, in the event, extended to the close of the 1950s. In this way, the financial settlement acquired a political complement because agreement on the balances and on India's continuing membership of the sterling club greatly eased the transition to independence and to dominion status.[96]

Holding India to the empire

The evidence currently available suggests that the history of British rule in India does not fit easily into the conventional theory of imperial decline. The most general version of this theory is based on an implicit acceptance of an organic metaphor of growth, and is therefore readily inclined to trace the decay apparent in ancient states to defects accompanying their birth, to excesses of youth and to intimations of mortality appearing in middle age. Since this insight is a property of the historical model itself, it is unfortunate that it has often been treated as solving the problem rather than as revealing the important questions, which concern the definition of power, the measurement of decline, and the appropriateness of the life cycle of unnamed organisms for the study of human behaviour. These methodological issues extend far beyond the case of India and therefore cannot be explored here. But we have considered two specific and well-favoured illustrations of the thesis, and found them to be unconvincing. Socio-psychological arguments couched in terms of faltering will-power are not generally applicable to the Indian case until the very eve of the transfer of power, at which point they were also symptoms as well as causes of the termination of British rule. Explanations which draw on observations about Britain's economic decline are open to a different objection: signs of decline can indeed be found during the period under review and even before 1914; but, to the extent that they rest on the performance of Britain's staple manufactured exports, they are an imperfect measure of economic strength and a poor guide to the purposes of imperial policy.

Our own assessment agrees with the revisionist argument, referred to at the outset of this chapter, that policy-makers were much more concerned with perpetuating Britain's presence in India than with preparing themselves for immolation. However, the revisionist approach tends to emphasise the study of high politics in London and Delhi and to exclude or minimise wider considerations of the kind discussed here. This is partly a matter of specialisation, but it may also reflect a concern that giving weight to economic aspects of causation might be seen to offer too much to Marxist or Marxisant arguments. The account we have tried to construct describes the economic dimension of the imperial purpose and the policies it promoted without, we hope, being either narrow or deterministic.

From this perspective, it appears that British rule in India cannot be understood on the assumption that the agents of the Raj represented the executive arm of the industrial bourgeoisie. Despite its importance, the manufacturing lobby in Britain never came to direct policy towards India and it was rarely able to divert it from the path marked out to accommodate Britain's wider aims. Any argument to the contrary has to explain a formidable list of failures, from the Fiscal Autonomy Convention in 1919 to the Government of India Act in 1935, and it must also come to terms with the painful irony that policies adopted by the British Government of India often favoured Bombay more than Manchester. After 1914, Britain did indeed direct her energies and formidable manipulative skills to the task of retaining her grip on the sub-continent, not to loosening it. But policy remained firmly in the hands of gentlemen whose representation of the national interest gave first place to financial considerations. The exchange rate of the rupee was held at levels that were intended to assist debt service and to manage bullion movements; its deflationary consequences induced gold flows which helped to support Britain's balance of payments and sterling. When choices had to be made between competing claims, as was increasingly the case, Lancashire took second place to London because preserving textile exports was less important than defending sterling. The Indian budget was bent to this purpose, and political alliances were shaped to reinforce it. This priority reflected a power much greater than that exercised by a mere conspiracy of bond-holders: it stood for a form of capitalist enterprise that gave money-making social acceptability among the British elite; it upheld an interest that had become vital to the success of Britain's management of the global economic system; and it inspired and elevated the imperial mission by linking sound money with sound morality and joining both in a high-minded and therefore justificatory vision of human progress under the imperial aegis.

Accordingly, India can be placed in a broader imperial perspective rather than being sealed in its own historiography. The upsets caused by World War I, and Britain's determined reaction to them, were very similar to those found in other parts of the world, both within the empire (as in the case of Africa) and outside it (as in the cases of Argentina and China). As the war helped to revive the imperial mission, so the period of post-war reconstruction in the 1920s showed how India was expected to assist Britain's return to pre-war normality. The performance of this role explains the otherwise impenetrable wrangle over the exchange rate of the rupee, and it also accounts for the use made of tariff autonomy to balance the budget and, effectively, to create barriers to Britain's manufactured exports. Here, too, policy towards India was very similar to that adopted elsewhere. The closest comparison is probably with the Dominions, which used their tariff autonomy for much the same purpose, and tropical Africa, where monetary policy (as well as tariffs) was still tightly regulated by London. In this respect, India was a hybrid: a Dominion as far as tariffs were concerned, but a colony in monetary affairs.

When the world slump and the financial crisis of 1931 aborted the return to the pre-war cosmopolitan order, Britain concentrated on constructing a smaller version, which became the Sterling Area, and on salvaging her overseas investments by devising new techniques of debt collection. India was again representative of most of the empire in being attached to the sterling bloc: like tropical Africa, India entered on terms dictated by London whereas the dominions were able to negotiate a modest devaluation of their currencies against sterling; but these were variations along a continuum that still represented British control. Similarly, India's tariffs rose to protect the budget, import substituting manufactures were developed, and exports were given a favoured place in British markets – all with the aim of ensuring that debt service and other external remittances continued to flow. As Britain's exports went into steep decline, so British control was tightened.

The 1930s emerge as a period of particular interest because they mark the demise of old, nineteenth-century complementarities and the beginnings of a new economic relationship. The slump destroyed rural incomes, reduced the importance of revenues from land and cast doubt on the political value of the alliance between the Raj and the landed magnates, in much the same way as the merits of indirect rule in Africa came to be questioned at the close of the 1930s. At the same time, the growth of modern manufacturing, of joint ventures between expatriate and Indian entrepreneurs, of the proportion of deposits held in indigenous banks, and of a pragmatic alliance with Congress all pointed in a direction that was already being taken by the Dominions and was just being embarked upon by countries such as Argentina and China. The main obstacle to political independence remained India's indebtedness: fear of repudiation caused the Government of India Act to be hedged with restrictions and proscribed further constitutional advance. When, as a result of the war, the financial and monetary imperatives which had long underpinned the imperial mission were removed, the imperial presence quickly followed.

The role of powerful personalities, the failure of techniques of control, and the loss of confidence in London and Delhi must all have their place in any full assessment of the transfer of power. But if the analysis fails to identify the underlying purpose of policy and the ways in which changes in the relationship between Britain and India fulfilled that purpose or made it redundant, it will miss a central theme of causation – and one, moreover, that is not confined to the case of India.

Notes

1 The quotation is taken from a statement made by the Prime Minister (MacDonald) to the House of Commons in June 1931, and cited in B.R. Tomlinson, 'Britain and the Indian Currency Crisis, 1930–2', *Econ. Hist. Rev.,* 2nd ser. XXXII (1979), pp. 94–5: 'It will not be possible to introduce the proposed constitutional changes if financial stability is not assured and His Majesty's Government are determined not to allow a state of affairs to arise which might jeopardise the financial stability and good government of India'. We are grateful to Dr G. Balachandran for his helpful comments on this chapter. The forthcoming publication of his important research on inter-war monetary and fiscal policy will greatly advance our knowledge of these subjects.

2 Introductions to the recent literature are provided by John Gallagher and Anil Seal, 'Britain and India between the Wars', *Modern Asian Studies,* 15 (1981), and Sumit Sarkar, *Modern India, 1885–1947* (Delhi, 1983).

3 The best guide to the subject is Ranajit Guha, ed. *Subaltern Studies,* I–VI (Delhi, 1982–9). The approach can be compared to the literature on resistance in colonial Africa.

4 See also Chapter 24.

5 It will become apparent that we are particularly indebted to research undertaken by Dr B.R. Tomlinson, whose work has transformed as well as enlarged our understanding of the period.

6 On the land tax see Dharma Kumar, 'The Fiscal System', in idem, ed. *The Cambridge Economic History of India,* Vol. II, *c.1757–c.1970* (Hyderabad, 1984), pp. 916–19, 928–9. Land revenues accounted for 50 per cent of total revenues in 1850–9, for 23 per cent in 1920–1, and for 21 per cent in 1940–1.
7 The summary which follows is derived from: the *Statistical Abstract for the British Empire,* the *Statistical Abstract for the United Kingdom* (relevant years), K.N. Chaudhuri, 'Foreign Trade and the Balance of Payments (1757–1947)', in Kumar, *Cambridge Economic History,* Ch. X, and B.R. Tomlinson, 'Imperial Power and Foreign Trade: Britain and India, 1900–1970', in P. Mathias and J.A. Davis (eds.),*The Nature of Industrialisation, Vol.5, International Trade and British Economic Growth from the Eighteenth Century to the Present Day* (Oxford 1996). J.D. Tomlinson, 'Anglo-Indian Economic Relations, 1913–1928 with Special Reference to the Cotton Trade' (Ph.D. thesis, University of London, 1977) contains valuable data on its particular subject. The statistics are not robust enough to permit fine tuning but the broad trends are likely to be accurate. The underlying figures include Burma until 1937.
8 Evidence of the scale of private investment is fragmentary, but see A.K. Bagchi, *Private Investment in India, 1900–1939* (Cambridge, 1972); B.R. Tomlinson, 'Foreign Private Investment in India, 1920–1950', *Mod. Asian Stud.,* 12 (1978); and idem, 'Foreign Investment in India and Indonesia, 1920–1960', *Itinerario,* 10 (1986).
9 Tomlinson, 'Foreign Private Investment', p. 660.
10 See above, pp. 213–4, 306, 316–18.
11 B. Chatterji, 'Business and Politics in the 1930s: Lancashire and the Making of the Indo-British Trade Agreement, 1939', *Mod. Asian Stud.,* 15 (1981), p. 529; Sarkar, *Modern India,* pp. 258–60.
12 Kumar, 'Fiscal System', pp. 937–9; B.R. Tomlinson, *The Political Economy of the Raj, 1914–1947* (1979), p. 90.
13 Tomlinson, *Political Economy,* pp. 45–6.
14 See above, pp. 300–03, 308–11.
15 Gerald Studdert-Kennedy's illuminating study, *British Christians, Indian Nationalists and the Raj* (Delhi, 1991), provides an important corrective to accounts of British policy that concentrate on the process of bargaining and minimise the role of ideals and ideology.
16 Studdert-Kennedy, *British Christians,* Ch. 2. Hirtzel (1870–1937) was educated at Dulwich and Oxford, and was Assistant Under-Secretary of State at the India Office, 1917–21, Deputy Under-Secretary, 1921–4, and Permanent Under-Secretary, 1924–30.
17 Quoted in Studdert-Kennedy, *British Christians,* pp. 46–7.
18 Ibid. pp. 150–1, p. 240, n. 16, pp. 226–7, n. 33. Lugard held very similar views. Blackett (1882–1935), the son of a Nottingham vicar, was educated at Marlborough and Oxford. He was a leading City figure, and his directorships included the Bank of England, De Beers, and Cable and Wireless. Schuster (1881–1982) was educated at Oxford and enjoyed a successful career in the City before entering government service (in the Sudan) after World War I. Such men would repay further attention, not only for the interest of their Christian banking principles, but also because their advice and direction were felt in other parts of the empire besides India.
19 David C. Potter, *India's Political Administrators* (Oxford, 1986); T.H. Beaglehole, 'From Rulers to Servants: the I.C.S. and the Demission of Power in India', *Mod. Asian Stud.,* 11 (1977).
20 Ann Ewing, 'The Indian Civil Service, 1919–1924: Service Discontent and the Response in London and Delhi', *Mod. Asian Stud.,* 18 (1984).
21 Some fascinating records of this process have been set down by those who experienced it: Roland Hunt and John Harrison, *The District Officer in India, 1930–1947* (1980); Raj K. Niga, *Memoirs of Old Mandarins* (New Delhi, 1985); and S.Y. Krishnaswamy's gentle and self-deprecating *Memoirs of a Mediocre Man* (Jayanagar, 1983).
22 David C. Potter, 'Manpower Shortage and the End of Colonialism: the Case of the Indian Civil Service', *Mod. Asian Stud.,* 7 (1973).
23 The most valuable (and also curiously neglected) study is De Witt C. Ellinwood and S.S. Pradhan, eds. *India and World War I* (Manohar, 1978). Specialists on India might profit from Bill Albert, *South America and the First World War* (Cambridge, 1988).

24 See, for example, J.D. Tomlinson, 'The First World War and British Cotton Piece Exports to India', *Econ. Hist. Rev.*, 2nd ser. XXXII (1979).
25 See Thomas G. Fraser, 'India in Anglo-Japanese Relations During the First World War', *History*, 63 (1978).
26 Don Dignan, *The Indian Revolutionary Problem in British Diplomacy, 1914–1919* (New Delhi, 1983), Ch. 9.
27 B.R. Tomlinson, 'Monetary Policy and Economic Development: the Rupee-Ratio Question, 1921–1927', in K.N. Chaudhuri and Clive Dewey, eds. *Economy and Society: Essays in Indian Economic and Social History* (Delhi, 1979), pp. 200–1.
28 On the role of the Indian army see Jeffrey Greenhut, 'The Imperial Reserve: the Indian Corps on the Western Front, 1914–19', *Jour. Imp. and Comm. Hist.*, 12 (1983); Keith Jeffrey, *The British Army and the Crisis of Empire, 1918–22* (Manchester, 1984), Ch. 6; and S.D. Pradhan, 'Indian Army and the First World War', in Ellinwood and Pradhan, *India and World War I.*
29 Tomlinson, *Political Economy*, pp. 106–10.
30 On protest movements see Sakar, *Modern India*, pp. 147–64, Dignan, *The Indian Revolutionary Problem*, and (for a non-politicised example) David Arnold, 'Looting, Grain Riots and Government Policy in South India, 1919', *Past and Present*, 84 (1979).
31 Judith M. Brown, *Gandhi's Rise to Power: Indian Politics, 1915–1922* (Cambridge, 1972).
32 Judith M. Brown, 'War and the Colonial Relationship: Britain, India and the War of 1914–18', in Ellinwood and Pradhan, *India and World War I*; Stanley A. Wolpert, 'Congress Leadership in Transition: Jinnah to Gandhi, 1914–20', in ibid.
33 The key study here is Clive Dewey, 'The End of the Imperialism of Free Trade: the Eclipse of the Lancashire Lobby and the Concession of Fiscal Autonomy to India', in Clive Dewey and A.G. Hopkins, eds. *The Imperial Impact: Studies in the Economic History of India and Africa* (1978).
34 Arthur Redford, *Manchester Merchants and Foreign Trade*, II, *1850–1939* (Manchester, 1956), Ch. 22, charts the demoralisation and failures of the Manchester lobby from its own Chamber of Commerce records.
35 G. Balachandran, 'India in Britain's Liquidity Crisis: the Stabilization of 1920', *Occasional Papers in Third World Economic History*, No. 1 (SOAS, 1990); Tomlinson, 'Monetary Policy', pp. 199–201.
36 P.G. Robb, *The Government of India and Reform, 1916–1921* (Oxford, 1976); and for the longer period R.J. Moore, *The Crisis of Indian Unity, 1917–1940* (Delhi, 1974).
37 Gallagher and Seal, 'Britain and India', pp. 400–6; Sarkar, *Modern India*, pp. 165–8. The conservative features of the reforms are well brought out in David Page's study of the Punjab and the United Provinces: *Prelude to Partition: The Indian Muslims and the Imperial System of Control, 1920–1932* (Delhi, 1982).
38 Quoted in Tomlinson, *Political Economy*, p. 111. Edwin Montagu (1879–1924), the second son of the first Lord Swaythling, was educated at Clifton and Cambridge, and was Secretary of State for India from 1917 to 1922.
39 Neil Charlesworth, 'The Problem of Government Finance in British India: Taxation, Borrowing, and the Allocation of Resources in the Inter-War Period', *Mod. Asian Stud.*, 19 (1985), pp. 523, 530–6, 542–3.
40 As argued by Gallagher and Seal, 'Britain and India'.
41 On the conservative alliance see: Barbara N. Ramusak, *The Princes of India in the Twilight of Empire: Dissolution of a Patron–Client System, 1914–1939* (Columbus, Ohio, 1976); S.E. Ashton, *British Policy Towards the Indian States, 1905–1939* (1982); and Page, *Prelude to Partition.*
42 Judith Brown, 'Imperial Facade', *Transactions of the Royal Historical Society*, 26 (1976).
43 David Arnold, *Police Power and Colonial Rule: Madras, 1859–1947* (Delhi, 1986); S.T. Bashkaran, 'Film Censorship and Political Control in British India', *Journal of Indian History*, 54 (1976).
44 Dignan, *Indian Revolutionary Problem*, pp. xiv–xv.
45 Cabinet minute, 10 October 1922, quoted in Algernon Rumbold, *Watershed in India, 1914–1922* (1979), p. 279.

46 Quoted in Keith Jeffrey, '"An English Barrack in the Oriental Seas?" India in the Aftermath of the First World War', *Mod. Asian Stud.*, 15 (1981), p. 385.
47 John M. Mackenzie, *Propaganda and Empire: The Manipulation of British Public Opinion, 1880–1960* (Manchester, 1984).
48 The most important threat at this time was revolutionary socialism. The Indian dimension is covered by S.D. Gupta, *Comintern, India and the Colonial Question, 1920–37* (Calcutta, 1980), and Sada Nand Talwar, *Under the Banyan Tree: The Communist Movement in India, 1920–1964* (New Delhi, 1985). The Indian Communist Party, founded in 1920, followed Comintern directives and was strikingly unsuccessful, though this did not prevent it from being banned in 1934.
49 Tomlinson, 'Monetary Policy', pp. 200–1.
50 Lloyd George, for example, argued that: 'We must increase the wealth of India if we are going to make a success of a new system of government'. Quoted in John Gallagher, *The Decline, Revival and Fall of the British Empire* (Cambridge, 1982), p. 103. See also the Report of the Industrial Commission of 1916, cited in Dileep M. Wagle, 'Imperial Preference and the Indian Steel Industry, 1924–39', *Econ. Hist. Rev.*, 2nd ser. XXXIV (1981), p. 121.
51 Tomlinson, *Political Economy*, p. 62.
52 Basudev Chatterji, 'The Abolition of the Cotton Excise in 1925: a Study in Imperial Priorities', *Indian Econ. and Soc. Hist. Rev.*, 17 (1980).
53 Basudev Chatterji, 'The Political Economy of "Discriminating Protection": the Case of Textiles in the 1920s', *Indian Econ. and Soc. Hist. Rev.*, 20 (1983).
54 Tomlinson, *Political Economy*, pp. 61–4. Britain's exports of textiles and iron and steel were particularly badly affected. The only gains went to suppliers of machinery. See Colin Simmons, Helen Clay and Robert Kirk, 'Machinery Manufacture in a Colonial Economy: the Pioneering Role of George Hattersley and Sons Ltd. in India, 1919–43', *Indian Econ. and Soc. Hist. Rev.*, 20 (1983).
55 Wagle, 'Imperial Preference', pp. 120–31; Chatterji, 'Political Economy', pp. 268, 270.
56 See B.R. Tomlinson, 'Monetary Policy', and J.D. Tomlinson, 'The Rupee/Pound Exchange Ratio in the 1920s', *Indian Econ. and Soc. Hist. Rev.*, 15 (1978). Both authors, writing independently, reach broadly similar conclusions about the motives behind British policy towards this forbidding but important issue. Readers will recall that Miss Prism advised Gwendolen to omit the chapter on the Fall of the Rupee as it was 'somewhat too sensational'; she would probably have regarded its rise as going quite beyond the bounds of good taste and comprehension. On the other hand, it will also be remembered that Gwendolen was not very good at taking advice. Oscar Wilde, *The Importance of Being Earnest* (1895), Act II.
57 Tomlinson, 'Monetary Policy', pp. 204–5, 207.
58 Tomlinson, 'The Rupee/Pound Exchange Ratio', p. 145.
59 Tomlinson, 'Monetary Policy', pp. 208–9; Tomlinson, 'The Rupee/Pound Exchange Ratio', pp. 139, 147–9.
60 Recent surveys include: Dietmar Rothermund, 'The Great Depression and British Financial Policy in India, 1929–34', *Indian Econ. and Soc. Hist. Rev.*, 18 (1981); idem, 'British Foreign Trade Policy in India During the Great Depression, 1929–39', in ibid.; O. Goswami, 'The Depression, 1930–1935: its Effects on India and Indonesia', *Itinerario, 10* (1986); and Colin Simmons, 'The Great Depression and Indian Industry: Changing Interpretations and Changing Perceptions', *Mod. Asian Stud.*, 21 (1987).
61 See, for example, Christopher Baker, 'Debt and the Depression in Madras, 1929–1936', in Dewey and Hopkins, *Imperial Impact*; Arvind N. Das, 'Peasants and Peasant Organisations: the Kisan Sabha in Bihar', *Journal of Peasant Studies,* 9 (1982); Arvind Kumar Sharma, 'A Study of the Agrarian Discontent in the United Provinces, 1930–31, *Quarterly Review of Historical Studies,* 23 (1983); Sugata Bose, 'The Roots of "Communal" Violence in Rural Bengal: a Study of the Kishoreganj Riots, 1930', *Mod. Asian Stud.*, 16 (1982); David Baker, '"A Serious Time": Forest Satyagraha in Madhya Pradesh, 1930', *Indian Econ. and Soc. Hist. Rev.*, 21 (1984); and the general survey in D.N. Dhanagare, *Peasant Movements in India, 1920–1950* (Oxford, 1983).

62 B.R. Tomlinson, 'Britain and the Indian Currency Crisis'. Carl Bridge, 'Britain and the Indian Currency Crisis, 1930–2: a Comment', *Econ. Hist. Rev.,* 2nd ser. XXXIV (1981), raises interesting questions of emphasis but does not disturb the main point made here. See also B.R. Tomlinson's 'Reply', ibid.

63 Quoted in Tomlinson, *Political Economy,* p. 127.

64 Ibid. pp. 137–8; Basudev Chatterji, 'Lancashire Cotton Trade and British Policy in India, 1919–1939' (Ph.D. thesis, Cambridge University, 1978), p. 521. An interesting sidelight on imperial financial cooperation is provided by Frank H.H. King, *History of the Hongkong and Shanghai Bank,* Vol. III (Cambridge, 1988), pp. 195–6. Towards the close of 1931, when Britain was desperately trying to repay short-term credits advanced by Washington and Paris, the Bank of England made a secret deal (via the ubiquitous Sir Charles Addis) which authorised the Hongkong and Shanghai Bank to locate and buy gold in India and then ship it to London. This was duly done.

65 Tomlinson, *Political Economy,* pp. 128–31; idem, *The Indian National Congress and the Raj, 1929–1942* (1976), pp. 21–4. Sir James Grigg (1890–1964), who was Finance Member of the Council of India from 1934 to 1939 (in succession to Schuster), was deliberately chosen for his unwavering adherence to fiscal and monetary orthodoxy and for his well-known commitment to Britain's imperial mission.

66 See S.L.N. Simha, *All the Bank's Men: Management of the Reserve Bank of India* (Madras, 1975); E.P.W. de Costa, *Reserve Bank of India: Fifty Years (1935–85)* (New Delhi, 1985); Rajul Mathur, 'The Delay in the Formation of the Reserve Bank of India: the India Office Perspective', *Indian Econ. and Soc. Hist. Rev.,* 25 (1988).

67 R.S. Sayers, *History of the Bank of England,* I (1963), p. 204.

68 Charlesworth, 'The Problem of Government Finance', p. 525.

69 Rajar K. Ray, *Industrialisation in India: Growth and Conflict in the Private Sector, 1914–47* (Delhi, 1979), Ch. 6; Simmons, Clay and Kirk, 'Machinery Manufacture in a Colonial Economy'; B.R. Tomlinson, 'Continuities and Discontinuities in Indo-British Economic Relations: British Multinational Corporations in India, 1920–1970', in Wolfgang Mommsen and Jürgen Osterhammel, eds. *Imperialism and After: Continuities and Discontinuities* (1986), p. 163; idem, 'Foreign Investment', p. 148; and, for a longer perspective, idem, 'British Business in India, 1860–1970', in R.P.T. Davenport-Hines and Geoffrey Jones, eds. *British Business in Asia Since 1860* (Cambridge, 1989).

70 Ian M. Drummond, *British Economic Policy and the Empire, 1919–1939* (1972), pp. 121–40; Tomlinson, *Political Economy,* pp. 123–44; Chatterji, 'Business and Politics', pp. 550–1, 572–3.

71 Tomlinson, *Political Economy,* pp. 132–5; Chatterji, 'Business and Politics', pp. 550, 566–73.

72 Bagchi, *Private Investment,* pp. 438–9.

73 Chatterji, 'Political Economy', pp. 270, 274–5; idem, 'Business and Politics', pp. 560–5; Redford, *Manchester Merchants,* Ch. 22.

74 Carl Bridge, *Holding India to the Empire* (Delhi, 1986), Chs. 3–4 provides an excellent account of these developments. We should note here that we refer to the British government in a generic sense because there was a broadly bipartisan approach to India and indeed to colonial questions as a whole at this time. In the case of India, the only significant division occurred within the Conservative Party over the Government of India Bill.

75 Studdert-Kennedy, *British Christians,* Ch. 7; Redford, *Manchester Merchants,* pp. 283–90.

76 Sir Samuel Hoare (1880–1959): Harrow, Oxford; Secretary of State for India, 1931–35; Secretary of State for Foreign Affairs, 1935.

77 See, for example, C.J. Baker, *An Indian Rural Economy, 1880–1955* (Oxford, 1984), pp. 525–6.

78 Ashton, *British Policy,* Ch. 6. See also I.A. Talbot, 'Deserted Collaborators: the Political Background to the Rise and Fall of the Punjab Unionist Party, 1923–1947', *Jour. Imp. and Comm. Hist.,* 11 (1982); and Karen Leonard, 'Aspects of the Nationalist Movement in the Princely States of India', *Quarterly Review of Historical Studies,* 21 (1981–2).

79 Page, *Prelude to Partition,* Ch. 4; Ayesha Jalal and Anil Seal, 'Alternative to Partition: Muslim Politics between the Wars', *Mod. Asian Stud.,* 15 (1981); Claude Markovits, *Indian Business and Nationalist Politics, 1931–39* (Cambridge, 1985), Chs. 3–4.

80 Markovits, *Indian Business,* Chs. 5–6.
81 Chatterji, 'Business and Politics', pp. 540–2.
82 Linlithgow to Zetland, 21 December 1939, quoted in Bridge, *Holding India,* p. 153.
83 Tomlinson, *Political Economy,* pp. 92–100, 140–1, 160–1; Paul Greenough, 'Indian Famines and Peasant Victims: the Case of Bengal in 1943–44', *Mod. Asian Stud.,* 14 (1980).
84 This episode is covered by R. J. Moore, *Churchill, Cripps and India, 1939–1945* (Oxford, 1979), and idem, *Escape from Empire: The Attlee Government and the Indian Problem* (Oxford, 1983), Chs. 1–2. Gary Hess, *America Encounters India, 1941–47* (Baltimore, Md, 1971), suggests that, while Roosevelt was sympathetic towards Indian nationalism, he also felt that the nationalists should earn US support by demonstrating their loyalty during the war. This qualification removed much of the pressure that Britain would otherwise have experienced.
85 Moore, *Churchill, Cripps and India,* pp. 122–47. Linlithgow's stance is dealt with by Gowher Rizvi, *Linlithgow and India* (1978). On Britain's plans for Burma see Nicholas Tarling, 'A New and Better Cunning: British Wartime Planning for Post-War Burma, 1942–3', *Jour. South-East Asian Stud.,* 13 (1982), and idem, '"An Empire Gem": British Wartime Planning and Post-War Burma, 1943–44', ibid. The final phase of British rule is covered in an important article by Hugh Tinker, 'Burma's Struggle for Independence: the Transfer of Power Thesis Re-Examined', *Mod. Asian Stud.,* 20 (1986).
86 Sarkar, *Modern India,* pp. 388–405.
87 Potter, 'Manpower Shortage', pp. 68–9.
88 Quoted in Epstein, 'District Officers in Decline', p. 514.
89 See A.P. Thornton, 'With Wavell on to Simla and Beyond', in Norman Hillmer and Philip Wigley, eds. *The First British Commonwealth* (1980).
90 Epstein, 'District Officers in Decline', p. 496.
91 B.R. Tomlinson, 'Indo-British Relations in the Post-Colonial Era: the Sterling Balances Negotiations, 1947–49', *Jour. Imp. and Comm. Hist.,* 13 (1985), p. 156.
92 Gallagher, *Decline, Revival and Fall,* pp. 144–5; Tomlinson, *Political Economy,* p. 149.
93 Tomlinson, *Political Economy,* pp. 138–41.
94 Ibid. p. 140.
95 Tomlinson, 'Indo-British Relations', unravels Anglo-Indian economic relations in the period immediately after World War II.
96 On the diversification of India's external economic links after independence see Michael Lipton and John Firn, *The Erosion of a Relationship: India and Britain Since 1960* (Oxford, 1976).

24

'PLAYING THE GAME' IN TROPICAL AFRICA, 1914–40[1]

The study of African history has been transformed in the thirty years which have passed since the end of colonial rule. The history of the pre-colonial era has been extensively rewritten, and there is now a considerable literature on the diverse experience of Africans under colonial rule. To this novel history from below has been added, more recently still, a renewed interest in colonial policy – a history from above which went out of fashion in the immediate aftermath of independence.[2] Two large themes of relevance to the present study have emerged from this new historiography.[3] One treats colonial rule after 1914 as being a study in the management of imperial retreat in the face of nationalist advance; the other, influenced largely by Marxist and dependency theories, focuses on the relationship between capitalism and the 'colonial state' in Africa.[4] We shall comment on these themes here but not be led by them because our own analysis of the colonial presence starts from different assumptions. As will be apparent by now, we doubt whether the conventional hypothesis about imperial decline can carry the weight placed upon it, and we have reservations, too, about approaches which treat capitalism in an undifferentiated way or suppose that its relationship with either development or underdevelopment is unlinear.

We shall begin, instead, by identifying two qualities which set the tropical African colonies apart from the other cases we have examined and make them a particularly interesting test of our argument. From a political standpoint, the fact that the colonies were under direct control from London allowed impositions of will which were impossible in the self-governing parts of the empire and in regions of informal influence. Of course, all governments labour under constraints, and the formulation and implementation of colonial policy were no exception in being clouded by compromise and diluted by circumstance. Nevertheless, the colonial case is still the clearest available guide to the intended priorities of imperial policy. From an economic perspective, tropical Africa provides an example of a region where private finance lagged behind political control. Once again, this is a generalisation which requires qualification with respect to specific territories, sectors and periods. But the central point remains: the City was not prepared to pour money into tropical Africa, and no amount of rhetoric from imperial enthusiasts could conjure opportunities to compare with those available in South Africa and in other parts of the world.

It might be thought that these considerations call for an explanation which departs from our general interpretation, perhaps by stressing the independence of political issues from financial pressures or possibly by allowing the manufacturing lobby more scope in influencing policy. Neither departure, however, is necessary. On the contrary, we shall suggest that the appropriate model for Africa is one of colonial rule with limited supplies of capital. The need for external loans and the search for revenue ensured that fiscal problems had a permanent place at the centre of policy and made colonial governments more, not less, dependent on financial considerations. The City's caution was not, in these circumstances, industry's gain. Manufacturing interests made more noise than headway, and the few concessions they won were on the whole consistent with fiscal priorities. Moreover, financial discipline was infused with moral purpose. Injections of both invigorated the civilising mission and stiffened the imperial will, and in this way exercised a pervasive influence on all aspects of policy, including the doctrine of trusteeship. Thus sustained, Britain demonstrated her determination not merely to keep her empire but also to enlarge it; and, in the course of the fierce international rivalries that affected Africa between 1914 and 1945, she gained ground rather than surrendered it.

Trade, finance and economic policy: an overview

Our explanation of the partition of Africa stressed the fact that Britain's main interests lay in parts of the continent which were relatively well endowed with human and natural resources. The subsequent development of Africa, as measured by commercial and financial flows, confirms that Britain received the lion's share of the gains from colonial rule.[5] Nevertheless, it is important to recognise that these did not amount to very much when placed in a global context. In 1920 Britain's possessions throughout tropical Africa (including the newly acquired mandates) accounted for little more than 2 per cent of her total exports; although the share (but scarcely the value) increased, it was still not much over 3 per cent at its peak in 1938.[6] Moreover, Britain had a continuing interest in preserving free trade for her colonies so that they could maintain export earnings and service their debts. Consequently, though Britain remained their most important trading partner, the tropical African colonies conducted just over half of their overseas trade with other countries at the close of the 1930s, despite the rise of protectionism. British finance and commercial services, on the other hand, exercised a near monopoly of colonial business throughout the period under review.[7] Britain accounted for virtually all foreign investment in her tropical African colonies, limited though it was; she had almost complete control of banking; and she continued to dominate shipping services, even though foreign rivals cut into the re-export trade in the inter-war period.

Clearly, the economic significance of the African colonies is not to be found by measuring the absolute or even the relative value of their connection with the metropole. It lay, instead, in the contribution they made to Britain's balance of payments and to meeting the needs of special interest groups. Britain still ran a surplus on her visible trade with tropical Africa, and this was enhanced by returns on investment and by other invisible earnings. Taken together, the two made a useful, if still modest, contribution to settling Britain's international accounts. The colonies in tropical Africa also offered a refuge for Britain's older staples, such as textiles and metal goods, which had been pushed out of more attractive markets elsewhere; and they provided a haven for investors (especially larger investors in the Home Counties) who put their money and their faith in the empire because colonial government loans were backed by an imperial guarantee, which was implied where it was not also formally stated.[8] However, it is important to distinguish between these interests: manufacturers were given opportunities but few privileges; investors were singled out for favourable treatment. This difference was partly a reflection of the general bias of British policy, but it also recognised that the whole colonial enterprise would founder unless overseas investors could be persuaded to put their money into the Dark Continent.

The fundamental and persistent difficulty faced by colonial officials in tropical Africa was how to generate taxable resources in territories which were generally poor and rarely came with a ready-made tax base.[9] The fact that revenue was essential to pay for the colonial administration, the largest single item of expenditure, no doubt concentrated the minds and ordered the priorities of successive generations of officials. But it has also to be remembered that colonial governors were engaged in a large state-building exercise involving long-term capital investment.[10] To make the sovereignty they had acquired effective, the colonial authorities were obliged to build an infrastructure as well as to extend the machinery of state. An undertaking of this magnitude depended on foreign loans, and these could be raised only if revenues were available for debt-service and if investors were confident that there would be no wavering over repayment. The link between revenues and borrowing-power prompted the colonial authorities to take a keen interest in promoting exports because overseas trade was the most promising source of revenue and could be tapped efficiently by means of tariffs.[11] The poorer colonies were, by definition, those which failed to generate a sizeable taxable trade. There, colonial rule laboured on the harder and more contentious task of levying direct taxes, and borrowing-power was consequently severely constrained.

Although policy issued from the Colonial Office, commercial, monetary and fiscal matters were all subject to rules laid down by the Treasury, whose guiding principle remained that enunciated by Earl Grey in 1852: 'the surest test for the soundness of measures for the improvement of an uncivilised people is that they should be self-sufficing'.[12] Broadly speaking, the African colonies adhered to these principles: they maintained open economies to enable trade potential to be maximised, designed tariffs primarily to raise revenue rather than to encourage discrimination or protection, and were generally successful in balancing their budgets. It is true, of course, that policies of free trade were modified in the 1930s, but, as far as tropical Africa was concerned, the modifications were not very significant. The colonies were also expected to complement the British economy by exchanging raw materials for manufactured goods, but here, too, commercial policy was not fashioned to produce this result. Colonial officials offered minimal concessions to Manchester's demands for special treatment and they made few serious efforts to block the development of manufacturing in Africa, though they were equally reluctant to promote it.[13] If this measure of impartiality found its justification in the high doctrine of trusteeship, it also owed a good deal to the lower calculus of the budget, for officials were alert to the revenue costs of the trade distortions sought by special interests and to the fiscal implications of protecting infant industries in unpromising circumstances.

Financial policy, on the other hand, was tightly controlled. The orthodoxy which the Treasury and its allies hoped to spread throughout the world was most fully realised in the tropical colonies, which functioned as compliant subsidiaries of the sterling system.[14] The monetary regime was supervised by Currency Boards, which issued coin and paper currencies through the agency of authorised expatriate banks in the colonies and kept reserves (at reassuringly high levels) in London. Colonial currencies, though visually distinct from sterling, were held at parity with it and were freely convertible. Money supply was determined not by the colonial administration but by the balance of payments, and in essence by export earnings. A rise in earnings increased the supply of money by an amount which matched effective demand; a decline had the opposite effect. The Currency Boards were thus passive instruments, mediating as official money-changers between colonial currencies and sterling. These arrangements, combined with the principle of the balanced budget, produced a paradise of sound money in a wilderness of colonial backwardness, and ensured that the 'rules of the game' imposed by London were not bent by colonial politics or even by colonial governments. Devaluation was as unthinkable as it was impossible; the exchange rate was eternally predictable; deficit financing was unknown; fiscal autonomy was as distant a prospect as political independence.

The strict regulation of monetary and fiscal affairs was vital in giving investors confidence in a region that was otherwise generally unattractive. The link with sterling ensured that colonial business continued to be financed through London and also helped Britain to retain a large proportion of the trade itself.[15] Private investment was encouraged by holding royalties at low levels, by excusing company profits from colonial taxation, and by excluding the colonies from the embargoes which the Treasury imposed on overseas loans at critical times in the inter-war period.[16] In the public domain, the financial orthodoxy guaranteed by the imperial connection induced the City to raise money for colonial government loans, thus completing the link with revenue-gathering efforts in the colonies. Further assistance came from the Colonial Loans Act (1899), which enabled the colonies to borrow from the imperial government instead of from the open market, and from the Colonial Stock Act (1900), which allowed them to raise money on favourable terms by granting colonial loans trustee status.[17] Both measures departed from the ideal of non-intervention by calling upon taxpayers to provide incentives for investors, even though in practice their scope was limited.[18] In all of these measures of support, the Treasury and the Bank of England were intimately associated with the City and with the expatriate banks, which, in turn, were joined to the colonial administration by holding the government account and by acting as agents of the Currency Boards.[19]

Trusteeship and the trustees

These financial imperatives were fed into the machinery of formal rule and emerged, synthesised, in the concept of trusteeship.[20] As a term of imperial art, trusteeship had few rivals. In authorising both conservation and amelioration, it combined a respect for tradition with a commitment to progress: the former gave it a past; the latter held out the promise of a future. The idea that imperial rulers were trustees provided them with a validation as custodians of civilisation which stood above their own particular purposes. As Lugard, the leading imperial propagandist of the day, put it: 'We hold these countries because it is the genius of our race to colonise, to trade and to govern'.[21] The colonial contract could be justified by referring to abstract principles of legitimation, 'good government' could take the place of self-government, and taxation could be levied without representation on the eighteenth-century principle that the disenfranchised were 'virtually represented' by their betters. Trusteeship was not only firm of purpose, but also malleable with respect to time and circumstance, and this was an asset which the defenders of empire mobilised in response to domestic criticism of colonial rule. By updating and redefining the civilising mission, they were able to transform hostile forces, including Labour governments, into imperial trustees who found themselves improving the empire rather than trying to abolish it.[22]

To reduce trusteeship to economic motives is to mistake a part for the whole; but to translate the concept into forms of colonial rule without recognising the powerful influence of financial imperatives is to miss an essential element in the story. Even before 1914, the costs of occupation had caused the Treasury to call a halt to military expeditions, and problems of viability had helped to determine the boundaries of the new states of colonial Africa.[23] Thereafter, the precarious financial base of colonial rule led the authorities to extend the frontiers of their instinctive paternalism from housekeeping to a type of managerial entrepreneurship whose primary purpose was to solve the revenue question. At the same time, financial constraints set limits to action and reinforced the inherent caution of the bureaucracy. The trajectory of progress was not in doubt, but improvements were to be selective and modest in case they threw up forces which damaged the credit and the credibility of the overlords. From the perspective of trusteeship, fiscal discipline was a moral force

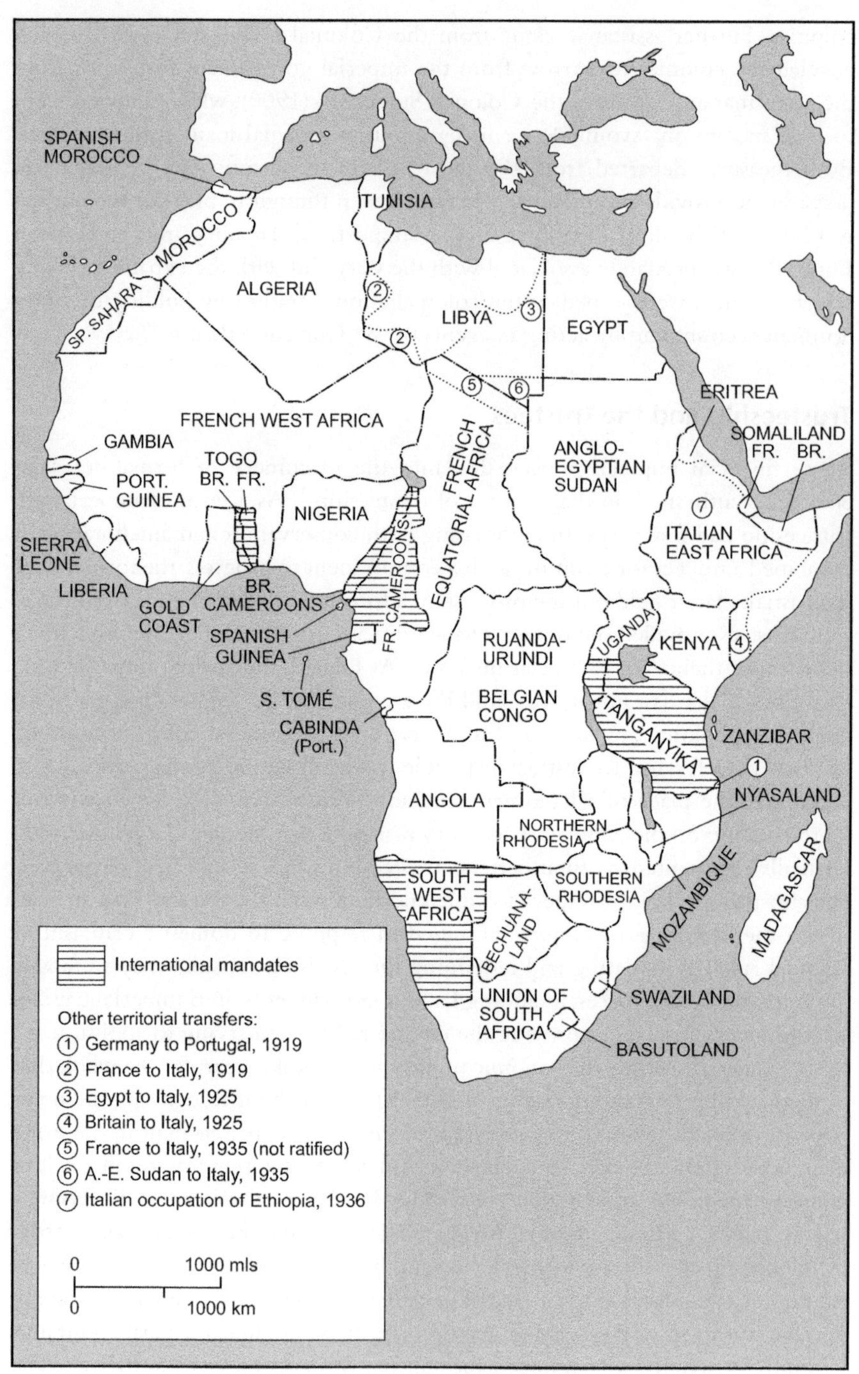

MAP 11 Colonial Africa in 1939

After: A.D. Roberts, ed. *The Cambridge History of Africa, 1905–1940*, 7 (Cambridge, 1986)

as well as a material necessity. As taxation fuelled the colonial machine, so it inculcated the work ethic, promoted individual responsibility and symbolised acceptance of the state.[24] Taxpayers, not surprisingly, often took a rather different view.

If the Indian Civil Service was the most impressive illustration of gentlemanly imperialism in its formal guise, the colonial service in Africa represented its highest stage because it was established later and survived in an undiluted form for longer. As recent research has shown, the rulers of British Africa came almost exclusively from the new urban gentry of southern England, and especially from the Home Counties.[25] The service was dominated by recruits from professional families who had been trained, expensively, at public schools and at Oxford and Cambridge to become enlightened guardians of the state, and who had been selected by a procedure which discriminated between members of the elite (largely on grounds of 'character') and effectively excluded competition from non-gentlemen.[26] Colonial service was relatively well paid, especially at the top of the hierarchy, and there were additional rewards of prestige, formalised through the honours system and liberally bestowed, which together compensated for the high entry costs.

Given their background, it is not surprising that Britain's representatives in Africa were champions of the gentlemanly values we described earlier. In its secular dimension, their sense of mission was shaped by Gladstonian orthodoxy and Treasury norms, by a distaste for industry and by a suspicion of commerce. Their closest links with the world of business were with the City and the colonial banks, and they showed little inclination to favour manufacturing interests.[27] Spiritually they were reinforced by the Church militant in Africa: conversion to Christianity implied acceptance of colonial values, even if it did not guarantee submission to colonial rule. The link between the worldly and the spiritual elements of gentlemanly imperialism had many personifications, but few were more memorable than Henry Gwynne, the crusading Bishop of Egypt and the Sudan.[28] Gwynne dedicated his life to the task of persuading the Sudanese to redeem themselves for the fate of General Gordon, whose death, elevated to martyrdom, became a symbol of Christian sacrifice in the performance of military duty and thus a manifestation of the permanent union of Church and state.

By 1914 the framework of colonial rule had been put in place. The first generation of officials assessed their subjects and administered, as new districts and provinces, the spaces allotted to them by partition. In parallel fashion, the expatriate firms established branches inland and divided markets in an unpublicised partition of their own.[29] The abolition of inland tolls created areas of free trade; the spread of colonial currencies aided commercial transactions and tax-gathering; the demand for labour in export-producing regions encouraged migration; railways cut the cost of moving goods and people, and hence hastened the development of the labour market. Buoyant prices for raw materials between 1900 and 1913 provided an incentive to expand exports and helped the new rulers to establish their authority by binding producers to the colonial economy, generating revenues and funding the first clutch of sizeable colonial loans. Underlying these developments were fundamental changes in property rights, especially over land and labour, which in turn were reflected in decisions made about the forms taken by trusteeship, notably the distinction between regions allocated to white settlers and those where indigenous rights were to be preserved. In these ways, the colonial frontier was defined and stabilised, if still not entirely occupied, and the shadowy imperial presence of the nineteenth century acquired substance and, so it seemed, permanence too.

World War I in tropical Africa

World War I threatened to bring down the newly built structures of British rule by exposing the African colonies to invasion and by disrupting the export sector.[30] The war itself was carried to sub-Saharan Africa, where hostilities centred on a struggle for control of the German colonies. The campaigns were of varying intensity and duration (being particularly marked and extended in East Africa), but by 1918 all of Germany's colonies had been occupied by allied forces.[31] By then, too, Britain's war aims had expanded to match the increasing cost and length of the conflict. As early as 1916, there was a popular argument to the effect that 'the Germans have no genius for the high task of colonisation', and that Britain had a duty as well as a right to take over Germany's African colonies when the war ended.[32] This view was shared by Harcourt, the Secretary of State for the Colonies, and was supported by influential imperialists, such as Curzon and Amery, who were busy redrawing the map of Africa in anticipation of a punitive peace settlement.[33] In 1918 Britain's imperial ambitions spread wider still and included a project for establishing a protectorate over Abyssinia, which was thought to offer scope for commercial concessions and white settlement.[34] The Abyssinian scheme, a piece of fantasy brought on by terminal war fever, was liquidated in 1919. But Britain achieved her other war aims: by adroit use of the mandate system she was able to establish colonies in camouflage, and thus avoided giving open offence to the United States.[35] Togo and Kamerun were divided with France, South-West Africa was managed by the Union of South Africa (as the reward for conquering it), and German East Africa was assigned to Britain, apart from the small region of Ruanda-Urundi, which was allocated to Belgium.

Britain's determination to acquire new colonies was matched by her firmness in holding those she already possessed. Although the demand for essential supplies for the war effort brought windfall gains for a fortunate minority of producers in Africa, the general dislocation of international markets also caused widespread hardship, discontent and, on occasion, open revolt.[36] Under these pressures, the machinery of colonial rule faltered at times but it never stalled. Political control was firmly maintained, taxes were collected and debts continued to be serviced. Indeed, the imperatives of war were used by imperial enthusiasts, like Milner, to expand government power in London and the colonies, initially to supply essential materials and then to establish a form of central direction which aimed at extending state enterprise into areas where private firms were reluctant to venture.[37]

This is not the record of a hesitant imperial power. On the contrary, the war enhanced the importance and popularity of the empire, and the additions made in 1919 provide evidence of Britain's continuing sense of imperial mission and appetite for territory. In the corridors of power, attitudes towards the disposition of other peoples' lands were essentially the same as they had been in the late nineteenth century, when the scramble for Africa began. From this perspective, the peace settlement was the final act in the partition of the continent.[38] Thereafter, policy towards the tropical colonies was enveloped in the broader aim of reconstructing the pre-war international order by trying to restore free trade and the supremacy of sterling. Opportunist schemes, devised under the stress of war, for extracting resources from the colonies were soon discarded as renewed supplies of tropical products quickly outpaced demand.[39] But other legacies of war remained: public awareness of the empire was heightened and greatly extended by novel techniques of publicity and propaganda;[40] air power, developed experimentally during the war, provided a new and effective means of colonial control in peacetime;[41] the 'imperial visionaries', headed by Milner, Amery and Cunliffe-Lister, carried their programme of empire development into the post-war period and ensured that it stayed in the public eye.[42]

Development and control in the 1920s

The main issue within policy-making circles in the 1920s was not commitment to the empire, which was generally accepted even by Labour governments, but the extent to which subsidies of various kinds should be given to fund colonial development and to strengthen links between the empire and the mother country.[43] The debates of the period can therefore be seen as episodes in a long-running saga which cast the Treasury and its allies against claimants who were trying to turn special interests into national policy. The imperialist lobby led by Milner and his disciples was especially adept at publicising the case for state-supported development, but it failed to convert colonial policy, and the concessions it won turned out to have more promise than substance. A programme of empire-settlement was widely advertised in the early 1920s, but its effect on the tropical colonies was very limited: increases in the number of white immigrants in Southern Rhodesia and Kenya owed more to perceived opportunities and to existing inducements than to hastily mixed schemes for providing lands fit for heroes.[44] Similarly, efforts to promote commercial ties with the empire by introducing tariff preferences aroused hope among the advocates of closer union and fear among third parties, but made little impression either on tropical Africa or on the direction of imperial trade as a whole.[45] Plans for channelling investment into the colonies through the Trade Facilities Acts (1921 and 1924), the East African Loans Acts (1924 and 1926), and the Colonial Development Act (1929) also produced results which fell far short of the ambitions of the promoters.[46]

A great deal could be said about all of these ventures, but for present purposes comment can be confined to the attempts to draw investment into tropical Africa.[47] Anxiety about unemployment in Britain provided the background to the legislation introduced in the 1920s, and to this extent it can be said that parliament was responsive to the needs of manufacturing interests, especially the older staple industries.[48] As in India, however, manufacturers made headway because their interests were congruent with larger policy aims rather than because they had laid hands on the machinery of state. In the early and mid-1920s, for instance, politicians were preoccupied by the fear that unemployment would lead to civil disorder and might even provoke revolution. In addition, policy throughout the decade was influenced by the prospect that increased colonial trade would help the dependencies to service their debts, assist Britain's balance of payments, and, in particular, reduce her obligations to the United States. The Colonial Development Act (1929), for example, was devised not only to cut unemployment in Britain but also to raise money to cover interest payments on existing debts contracted by the colonies, thus enabling them to float new development loans on the open market. Even so, the concessions made by the Treasury were very limited, and economic orthodoxy, represented by free trade, sound money and self-sufficiency, survived, if not intact, then with only a few dents. Apart from the fact that the sums involved in the various Acts were kept to modest levels, the Treasury succeeded in opposing the idea that the loans should be interest-free and instead offered a guarantee, which provided investors with the incentive they needed. Consequently the burden of repayment fell on African taxpayers, and colonial officials redoubled their tax-gathering efforts in the 1920s to ensure that budgets were balanced and debt service was maintained.[49] Not surprisingly, the anti-colonial protests of the period were often related to grievances about the weight of taxation.[50]

The promotion of the imperial mission after World War I was accompanied by a revitalisation of the principle of trusteeship. Particular prominence was given to the twin doctrines of indirect rule and 'native paramountcy', which affirmed the importance of preserving indigenous interests within the framework of colonialism. The point of reference for both concepts was what Lugard termed the dual mandate, which stressed the mutual interests of rulers and ruled and underlined the need to balance progress, in the form of economic development, against disruption, in the shape of untoward social change and the attendant danger of political instability.[51] This idea, like many other principles of imperial government, can be traced to Britain's experience in India. Lugard's contribution was to apply the notion of indirect rule with great vigour, and to exert his considerable influence to spread it from Nigeria to other parts of colonial Africa. By the close of the 1920s the process of administrative infill was complete, and indirect rule had been realised or planted in territories as distant and as different as Tanganyika, Uganda and the Sudan, as well as West Africa. As its name implies, indirect rule was based upon the use of indigenous authorities as agents of colonial government. This policy, in turn, involved restrictions on forms of foreign enterprise which might have undermined the social order and discredited chiefly authority by raising potentially explosive issues of land rights and labour use. In West Africa, to take the best known example, expatriate firms were kept out of primary production, with the exception of some mining operations, and confined largely to the import-export trades. On the traders' frontier, as it has been called.[52] there was no place even for a capitalist as powerful as W.H. Lever, whose schemes for palm-oil plantations in British West Africa were repeatedly turned down by the Colonial Office and had to be transferred to the Belgian Congo, where the climate, though still tropical, was also more receptive.[53]

Indirect rule was a construct that diverted the past in the name of tradition.[54] In practice, Lugard's 'traditional' chiefs were not on stand-by awaiting the call to colonial duty. If the emirates of Northern Nigeria came closest to his ideal of indigenous authority, too many other regions fell far short of it, lacking either centralised states or a political hierarchy which fitted readily into the colonial mould. The attempt to identify indigenous forms of authority often resulted in social engineering which invented as much as it codified 'native law and customs', increased an awareness of 'ethnicity' and 'tribalism', and created chiefs whose titles lacked historical legitimacy. These innovations had profound consequences for African societies, but they also had an important influence on colonial governments, making administrators more interventionist than the model of indirect rule envisaged, and encouraging forms of bureaucratic paternalism which survived the demise of colonial rule itself.

In the eyes of its advocates, indirect rule was both a necessity and a virtue. The poverty of most of tropical Africa, combined with the shortage of foreign capital, meant that colonial government had to be economical. Indirect rule recommended itself because it was cheap and, to the extent that it was self-policing, it was also unobtrusive. It was adopted either where settlers failed to materialise in sufficient numbers, as in Uganda and Tanganyika, or where export growth was already being promoted by 'native enterprise', as in Nigeria and the Gold Coast.[55] The distinction between traders' and settlers' Africa was not, therefore, simply a matter of climate: it also rested on judgements about the most cost-effective means of meeting the priorities of imperial policy.[56] However, judgement was a matter of principle as well as of interest. Africa's gentlemanly rulers saw themselves as conservationists – of people as well as of game.[57] They were inclined to idealise rural Africa, to identify with 'natural' pastoralists and cultivators, and to view urbanised and supposedly 'detribalised' Africans with a mixture of disdain and alarm. These perceptions mirrored their reactions to the spread of industrial society in Britain. In searching for 'lost tribes and vanished chiefs',[58] officials were trying to 'strengthen the solid elements in the countryside . . . before the irresponsible body of half-educated officials, students and town riff-raff takes control of the public mind'.[59]

Whereas in West Africa colonial policy prevented intrusions into 'native rights', in parts of East and Central Africa it lent support to white settlers. At the time of partition, as we have seen, East and Central Africa were thought to have considerable potential for white settlement, and there was extravagant talk of creating a new Australia in the Dark Continent. However, once the brief 'jungle boom' at the turn of the century had passed, more sober appraisals prevailed, and the City returned to its former caution.[60] Consequently, the number of settlers was limited and they also tended to be self-financing.[61] Kenya, for example, attracted a high proportion of officers and gentlemen from upper- and middle-class families whose backgrounds and values were very similar to those of members of the colonial service. Lord Delamere, the most famous of the founding settlers, acquired 100,000 acres in Kenya in 1903, following a hunting visit a few years earlier. He was joined by Lord

Cranworth and his brother-in-law, Mervyn Ridley, who arrived shortly afterwards with £1,500 and a pack of foxhounds.[62] Although Kenya never lost its aristocratic tinge, farming became a serious business with the development of maize, coffee and tea, and it is now clear that, amidst the dilettantes and the inefficient, there were many serious and shrewd entrepreneurs.[63] The gentlemen farmers of Kenya were escaping from the decline of agriculture, the growth of industry and the spread of democracy in Britain, but they were not refugees from all forms of capitalism.

The divergence in policy towards different parts of tropical Africa was largely a reflection of official calculations about the most appropriate means of realising the potential of various regions. In Kenya and Southern Rhodesia, the administration lent its weight to a form of imported agrarian capitalism by helping white farmers to secure access to supplies of land and labour. By controlling the market for the principal factors of production, colonial governments hoped to attract both well-capitalised settlers and those who needed to raise money on the strength of guaranteed land rights. But official support had its limits. The authorities had to balance the demands of settler farmers against those of expatriate commercial interests whose priorities were often different, and to do so without wholly ignoring the claims of indigenous societies.[64] The need to hold the ring against several contestants gave the administration a degree of independence from any one of them, even if this had then to be mortgaged to purchase a series of unequal and temporary compromises. More important still, colonial governments were instruments of imperial policy; as such, their primary task was to ensure that local interests of all kinds were subordinated to priorities laid down by the metropole. This mixture of encouragement and restraint can be seen very clearly in the handling of white nationalism in Kenya and Southern Rhodesia in the aftermath of World War I.

The formation of the colony of Kenya from the East Africa Protectorate in 1920 created important financial and political opportunities. As a colony, Kenya was able to take advantage of the favourable borrowing terms authorised by the Colonial Stock Acts, and immediately did so. The corollary, of course, was that the new colony was subjected to London in financial and monetary matters. The extent of this dependence became apparent in 1921, when the colony was struck by a serious currency crisis.[65] Kenya's currency, the silver rupee, appreciated significantly against sterling after 1918, when the pound was still floating against other currencies. This trend presented problems for sterling-holders in Kenya who had to make payments in rupees. The white settlers, supported by an indulgent governor, tried to introduce unorthodox currency reforms in a bid to cut the cost of their rupee payments. The response of the imperial banks in Kenya was immediate: they stopped the agitation in its tracks by threatening to call in local advances. The Colonial Office and the Treasury, with the support of the banks, then decided to resolve the problem by extending the Currency Board system to East Africa. In the ensuing discussions, the governor tried to fix an exchange rate with sterling which was more favourable to settler interests than that recommended by the banks and supported by the Colonial Office. The banks reacted by proposing to boycott all transactions in Kenya, and Whitehall imposed the rate approved in London.

The settlers also tried to use the new constitution to entrench their power, and in the early 1920s the militants among them began to make plans for self-government.[66] These ambitions ran into the aspirations of Indian settlers, who had been encouraged by recent constitutional concessions in India to claim equal rights in Kenya. The political crisis produced by the meeting of these forces culminated in an extraordinary plot, mounted by a group of white settlers in 1923, to kidnap the governor and install Lord Delamere as head of a provisional government. It is instructive to note that one of the principal instigators, Brigadier General Wheatley, came from a family of landed gentry which had held on to its respectability rather better than to its fortunes. Wheatley himself arrived in Kenya in 1919 under the auspices of the settlement scheme for ex-officers and set about turning his new estate into 'a real gentleman's place'.[67] Given his background, it is not surprising that Wheatley ranked as a die-hard, even by exacting settler standards, and advocated direct action to halt the threat to his plans to secure what he regarded as being his rightful social position.

The values represented by Wheatley and his associates were, broadly speaking, those of Whitehall too, but the planned insurrection broke the rules of the game. In 1923 London imposed a compromise, the celebrated Devonshire Declaration, which formally reserved Kenya for Africans.[68] This was something of a masterstroke in that it appeared to neuter both settler and Indian demands without actually giving the indigenous inhabitants anything that they did not have already. The settlers continued to hanker after self-government, and their claims resurfaced in the late 1920s. Again, however, the proponents of white supremacy were defeated, and the principle of native paramountcy was reaffirmed in 1929. The outcome was that the white settlers gained to the extent that their position in the White Highlands was confirmed and their Indian rivals were denied equality; but their wider ambitions were contained. Self-government was ruled out by the Colonial Office with the support of the India Office, the humanitarian lobby, and expatriate commercial interests which had begun to acquire a stake in low-cost production by African exporters. It was also opposed by the Treasury and the City, and by more sober minds among the settlers themselves, who realised that Kenya's credit depended upon imperial guarantees. Although the new constitution widened the scope for political activity, financial realities ensured that the colony remained bound firmly to London.

The settlers in Rhodesia, on the other hand, were granted self-government in 1923.[69] The concession was made partly because their numbers and viability were greater than in Kenya, but also because financial considerations there favoured rather than obstructed a larger degree of 'responsible' government. Down to 1923, the Rhodesias were administered by the British South Africa Company on behalf of the British government. By the early 1920s the Company was anxious to give up its administrative burdens and to be compensated for them, while the settlers were keen to advance their political claims. The Treasury, however, was determined to minimise the cost of devolution, and for this reason supported a scheme for linking the settlers to the Union of South Africa, which had thoughtfully offered to settle the British government's debt with the Company. The plan went awry in 1922, when the settlers voted for self-government with colonial status rather than for joining the Union. Nevertheless, the Treasury still charged a price for self-government, and insisted that Southern Rhodesia should meet half the Company's bill for administrative services. In an associated deal, completed in 1924, the British government confirmed the Company's mineral rights in Northern Rhodesia and transferred the territory to the Colonial Office. In exchange, the Company agreed to cancel its charges for past administrative services there.

The achievement of self-government in Southern Rhodesia was a success for settler aspirations, but it was not a defeat for British imperialism. The substance of Britain's interests remained untouched, and the new constitution was hedged with qualifications and restrictions. External affairs, including monetary and tariff policy, remained firmly under London's control. The new government continued to protect foreign investment, and showed itself to be a conservative and reliable successor to Company rule. Events in Kenya and Rhodesia made it clear that the major decisions were still being shaped by the metropole, and that the financial status of territories, especially their standing as debtors or creditors, exerted a powerful influence on their political fortunes.

Imposing and reappraising orthodoxy: the 1930s

In tropical Africa, as elsewhere, the slump put an end to hopes of reconstructing the pre-war international economic order.[70] By damaging the profitability of export production in the colonies, it also squeezed revenues and strained the principles of trusteeship. Moreover, it is now apparent that the downturn in the international economy transmitted by the industrial world coincided with longer-term structural problems in African economies which began to reveal the limits to further export expansion in the absence of an agricultural revolution.[71] This was a broad trend as well as a new one, and there were exceptions to it, both regionally and socially.[72] Nevertheless, the generalisation holds: the agricultural innovations which pulled parts of the African coast out of the crisis of legitimate commerce in the late nineteenth century were not repeated in the 1930s. The most profitable alternative, a 'lucky strike' of valuable minerals, was rarely made, and local manufactures were not a serious prospect in tropical Africa, as they were in the Dominions.[73] In these circumstances, it is understandable that producers responded to falling export prices by increasing output, not by reducing it, except in rare cases where they tried to control supplies through cartels or by exerting political pressure. Colonial governments therefore found themselves coping with the unforeseen consequences of previous developments in the international economy, which had vastly increased supplies of tropical raw materials on world markets, and which, in conditions of static or declining demand, had worrying implications for budgets, debt service and expectations.

The threat to the principle of self-sufficiency needs emphasising because it had an important, if indirect, influence on the approach to trusteeship and, in this way, on the whole imperial enterprise in Africa. As noted earlier, after 1900 the new African colonies contracted foreign loans to fund state-building activities, especially railways and administration. The money was raised by colonial governments at fixed rates of interest, and the debt was serviced from revenues which depended heavily on export earnings. In this phase of development debt, dominated by public-sector borrowing, the burden of repayment increased at times of depression, when earnings were reduced.[74] The problem of the rigidity of the debt structure in tropical Africa was compounded by the growth and increased cost (through higher interest rates) of public indebtedness after 1913. According to one estimate, the funded debt of all the British territories in Africa (apart from South Africa) grew by more than one-third in real terms between 1925 and 1935.[75] The link between increased debt and static or falling revenues during the slump is clearly illustrated by the history of public finance in two of the leading colonies in tropical Africa, Nigeria and Kenya, where the ratio of debt charges to gross revenue rose from 14 per cent and 18 per cent respectively in 1926 to 33 per cent and 34 per cent in 1934.[76] The financial problems of these important colonies concentrated the official mind to the extent of influencing the reappraisal of colonial rule which began in the late 1930s.

In the short run, however, the challenge to self-sufficiency was met by unwavering orthodoxy. Public expenditure was cut and the efficiency of tax collection was improved. There was neither a hint nor any prospect of devaluation: when the pound left the gold standard in 1931, the colonies automatically joined the sterling bloc at rates of exchange determined by London. Even in the depths of recession, the African colonies serviced their debts promptly and balanced their budgets with little or no assistance. On leaving Tanganyika in 1931, Governor Cameron declared that one of his proudest achievements was that the colony had paid its way since 1926 and had ceased to be a burden on the Treasury.[77] This record was matched by other struggling territories, such as the Sudan and Nyasaland.[78] Debts were not rescheduled, even where it was technically possible to do so. When the idea was mentioned by unofficial members of the Gold Coast Legislative Council in 1933, Governor Slater's response barely contained his apoplexy:

> If the rate of interest were to be compulsorily lowered before the expiry of the specified period, subscribers to the loan would have to accept a reduction in their income. The suggestion implies, therefore, that persons [British investors] who are already making enormous sacrifice in aid of their own country should accept yet another burden for the relief of persons in another country who have enjoyed all the benefits but will not accept their obligations.[79]

The governor concluded: 'I do not believe for one moment that the suggestion finds favour with the general public'.[80] This was an inherently improbable claim, though not one that could be tested directly in an undemocratic system. Nevertheless, there were manifest signs of discontent with low produce prices and of opposition to government exactions in colonial Africa during the 1930s (not least in the Gold Coast), and indications, too, that these were beginning to find a political voice outside the islands of white settlement.[81]

The priority attached to securing British capital and servicing the public debt also influenced international trade policy. Colonial governments became increasingly involved in export-marketing schemes during the 1930s, whether by sponsoring agricultural cooperatives or by approving cartels formed by mining interests, white farmers and the large expatriate trading firms.[82] The purpose in all cases was to raise export prices, either by improving quality or by restricting output, and hence to boost land values, incomes and revenues with the aim of averting the collapse of private credit and of meeting public-sector fiscal targets. Similar motives operated to shape the colonial tariff regime, which remained essentially an instrument of fiscal rather than of commercial policy. When imperial tariffs were renegotiated at Ottawa in 1932, the Colonial Office ensured that exports from the tropical colonies were allowed to enter Britain and the dominions on the most favourable terms. No significant preferences were given in return because most of the African colonies were committed by international agreements (made at the time of partition), to preserve free trade.[83] Sales of cheap goods from Japan and India expanded rapidly in the 1930s, especially in East Africa, and a number of British firms adjusted to commercial realities by becoming agents for Manchester's new competitors.[84]

The most publicised breach of free trade in tropical Africa occurred in 1934, when quotas were imposed on Japanese goods imported into Nigeria and the Gold Coast.[85] This was a clear case of official intervention in favour of British manufactures, and it demonstrates that colonial tariffs could be manipulated to an extent that was impossible in India or China, where Manchester's textile exports had been badly damaged by low-cost competitors in the 1920s. On closer inspection, however, it appears that government intervention was a gesture rather than a substantial measure of support for Britain's ailing staple industry. The quota system affected less than 5 per cent of the import trade of British West Africa, and fell far short of the Manchester lobby's pleas for comprehensive assistance. Japan found compensation elsewhere, and her share of the West African market was quickly filled by suppliers other than Britain. Manchester's cause was weakened partly by its own evident decline and partly by countervailing pressures from other powerful business interests which continued to favour free trade. More important still, however, was the fact that the Colonial Office had decided that existing commercial treaties suited the international trade and payments of both Britain and her colonies. This position was endorsed by the Foreign Office, which was concerned to avoid provoking Germany, Japan or the United States at a time when imperial policy had become entwined with negotiations for preserving world peace.

The international context of Britain's colonial policy can only be touched on here; but it is important to underline the point that the 1930s were a period of renascent imperialism in Africa, as they were in South America and China. The 'imperial problem', as defined by contemporaries,[86] was particularly acute in the case of Africa because the continent had been divided and parts of it reassigned comparatively recently. The 'problem' itself was not, as hindsight might misleadingly suggest, how to deal with nationalism, but how to accommodate the 'have-not' nations without weakening the empire. The 'have-nots', in the terminology of the day, were those deprived, not of food, but of colonies, and referred principally to Germany, Japan and (since demand for other people's territory was readily expandable) to Italy.[87] In dealing with claims from the rich but unsatisfied, Britain had also to fend off the attentions of the United States, which was both wealthy and anti-colonial. Neither group could be ignored: Germany's claims to her former colonies became tied up with wider issues of peace and stability in Europe; the United States was the British empire's leading foreign trade partner and the creditor of last resort should diplomacy fail and war follow.[88]

The attempted repartition of Africa began in 1935, when Italy invaded Ethiopia.[89] Although Britain did not favour this act of aggression, she was able to accommodate it because her own interests were not directly involved, and in 1938 she gave formal recognition to Italy's acquisition. This event had wider ramifications, stirring black nationalism in tropical Africa, raising questions about the nature of trusteeship and, more immediately, lending impetus to Germany's demands for the restoration of her former colonies. Between 1935 and 1938 the Foreign Office gave serious consideration to plans for making colonial concessions to Germany in the hope of securing a peace settlement in Europe. This policy has been treated as evidence that Britain was losing both the will and the ability to defend the empire. But Chamberlain never offered to transfer territory that was considered, by its constitution and longevity, to be an integral part of the empire. His idea was to give away other people's possessions by carving up portions of Germany's former colonies in tropical Africa and by spicing the offer with concessions in central Africa, which – *perfide Albion* – were to be made at the expense of Belgium and Portugal. Seen in this light, and leaving aside the lack of realism which pervaded the negotiations, Chamberlain's thinking demonstrates a fundamental continuity with the nineteenth century: Africa was still a continent to be divided and apportioned for the sake of greater European interests. While Chamberlain believed that Hitler was a Christian and a gentleman, he dealt with him as Salisbury dealt with Bismarck. After 1938, when it appeared that he was neither, concessions were no longer on the menu.

Further evidence that the British retained a strongly imperial cast of mind can be found in the extensive publicity campaign which accompanied diplomacy but also extended far beyond it.[90] In the 1930s the media were mobilised, officially and through private enterprise, to counter fascist propaganda and to disarm critics of empire in the United States and the League of Nations. The British Council was founded in 1934 specifically for this purpose; the BBC advanced its own characteristically restrained advertisement for the monarch and his empire; astute use was made of film to portray the white man, especially the white gentleman, in a favourable light; and a stream of publications, from comics and newspapers to histories of the empire written in approving, Whiggish style by high authorities in high places, combined to popularise and endorse the imperial mission. This process of moral rearmament won many converts, not least at home, and helped to prepare the

British for a war that would carry forward the imperial enterprise, as well as end the threat of fascism.

The continuing vitality of the imperial mission was associated, as both cause and consequence, with a far-reaching reappraisal of the concept of trusteeship at the close of the 1930s.[91] It was clear by then that indirect rule had failed to deliver economic progress or to contain social change. 'Native paramountcy' sounded well, but was an empty barrel, and its promise had been contradicted by the support given to white settlers and by the cavalier attitude taken towards the repartition of Africa – most glaringly in the case of Ethiopia. Expressions of political and economic unrest in Africa, though not a serious challenge to colonial rule, were bad publicity and caused thoughtful governors to question the assumptions of the Lugardian system.[92] The publication of Hailey's *African Survey* in 1938 revealed how much had still to be learned about the peoples and resources of colonial Africa and initiated a debate in official circles which was to divide policy-makers into preservationists and modernisers. Hailey's signal from Africa joined Macmillan's *Warning from the West Indies* (1936) and accompanied outbreaks of mass discontent in the Caribbean in 1937 and 1938.[93] The West Indies, ignored for so long, now commanded immediate attention because they were the 'show window'[94] of the branch of British colonialism closest to the United States, whose support against Hitler was becoming a vital consideration. As the Colonial Office recognised, the disturbances expressed, in acute form, a level of disaffection that was present elsewhere too, and the government feared a reaction that would ignite the whole of the colonial empire.

Underlying the unease with the colonial record in official circles was a growing realisation of the limitations of orthodox responses to the world slump and a perception that the tropical colonies had been set on a course of export development which had more of a past than a future. The fiscal rigour which characterised policy in the 1930s was successful in balancing budgets and servicing debts, but it also alienated key groups of producers and wage-earners who were already suffering from persistently low export prices, and it cast more than doubt on the claim that colonial rule was an improving influence. Logically, there were only two solutions to this problem: one was to abandon the colonies; the other was to give up the policies which had failed to fulfil their promise. Since the first possibility was never considered, it was the latter which was chosen. Once again, fiscal imperatives drove policy in novel directions. The search for revenue had first cast trusteeship in the form of indirect rule, and it now helped to bring about its downfall. The answer to the question of poverty in Africa and to the need to find new, secure sources of revenue was to be not less government but more.[95] The covert interventionism which already existed was to be made manifest, building was to replace caretaking, and a new ideology of development, a redefinition of trusteeship, was to be put in place. If these innovations appeared to steal newly fashionable radical clothing, and even to add a touch of what, in the half-light, looked like 'state socialism', so much the better.[96] There were plenty of precedents for laying hands on the untouchable and making it wholesome, and the imperial tradition had long come to terms with the paradox that freeing individuals from their pre-colonial past was a duty that required governments to take special and extensive powers.

Elements of the new thinking were already beginning to influence policy before World War II. In London, the Colonial Office prepared for its new role by becoming a larger and more specialised organisation.[97] On the ground in Africa, officials experimented with alternative ways of funding colonial rule which would also update the notion of trusteeship. In west Africa there was an emerging awareness of the need to promote research into tropical agriculture and of the importance, in the longer term, of encouraging wide-ranging innovations in land-management to raise productivity and taxable incomes.[98] In east Africa, the vulnerability of white farmers during the slump, combined with the costs of protecting settler agriculture thereafter, produced a significant shift in official thinking, especially in Kenya, where openings were created for low-cost African farmers whose taxable earnings were the mainstay of the colonial budget.[99] The significance of fiscal considerations was underlined by Sir Alan Pim, whose roving commissions in the late 1930s produced recommendations which criticised the status quo, pointed towards more active development policies (including more opportunities for Africans), and led to an event that was as notable for its symbolism as for its material impact: the imposition, finally, of income tax on white settlers in Kenya.[100]

These intimations of change were brought together in the Colonial Development and Welfare Act, which was passed in 1940 (but formulated before the outbreak of war).[101] The new Act differed in conception from the Act of 1929. It breached the principle of self-sufficiency, promoted the idea of social welfare, recognised the need for central initiatives, and made provision for expenditure on research. The Treasury resisted the measure, believing that the end of Gladstonian finance was at hand and fearing that the proposal would put the colonies 'on the dole from henceforth and forever'.[102] But MacDonald, the Colonial Secretary, argued that unless the Act was passed Britain might lose her colonies, and would certainly deserve to do so. Without new investment, the colonial economies would founder; without welfare measures to improve health and education, there was little prospect of renewing the loyalty of colonial subjects or of tempering criticism from the United States; and without a secure empire, Britain's global defence strategy was at risk. These arguments succeeded. By associating the colonial issue with the fundamental question of national survival at a time of acute international tension, the Colonial Office appeared to have cracked the Treasury safe and found a means, finally, of overcoming the shortage of capital that had confined colonial policy for so long.

Colonial rule with limited supplies of capital

It is plain that the vitality of British imperialism remained undiminished in Africa during the period under review. Anti-colonial protests undoubtedly gathered pace in the 1930s, but black nationalism was not yet a force to be reckoned with and white nationalism was managed in ways that left Britain's essential interests untouched, as the examples of Southern Rhodesia and Kenya have shown. Moreover, estimates of the importance of the nationalist movements, which have been exhaustively studied, have to be set against countervailing forces, still to be fully investigated, such as air power and radio communication, which did much to enable colonial governments to strengthen their grip after 1914. While dealing successfully with claims from within the empire, Britain also fought off challenges from rival 'have-not' powers and applied a policy of manipulative intent towards the United States with the aim of softening her anti-colonial stance. It has not been our purpose to discuss these international rivalries in any detail, but just enough has been said, it is hoped, to make the point that the 'age of imperialism' did not come to an end in 1914, and that the 1930s, in particular, witnessed a renewal of imperialist competition which needs emphasising both for its intensity and for the novelty of the techniques used, especially in the developing service industries, such as communications.

As to the purpose of the enterprise, the reason for 'staying on', we have suggested that this can best be viewed through the prism of trusteeship, a concept that was solid with respect to principle but flexible with regard to circumstance. The principles, material and moral, were those we have associated with the gentlemanly order in Britain, and, as we have now tried to indicate, with its extensions in tropical Africa. In escaping from industry and democracy, and in promoting a squirearchy in a tropical arcadia, the rulers of Africa were seeking to perpetuate 'traditional' British values and authority structures. But, with some notable exceptions, the white chiefs of Africa did not represent atavistic forces which were hostile to all forms of capitalism, despite their antipathy towards manufacturing industry. They were well aware that they lived in a material world of revenues, expenditures, salaries and pensions; they accepted liberal ideals of progress; and they acted in the belief that economic orthodoxies centred on Gladstonian finance and free trade would generate economic development and moral improvement. Their preference was for rural-based forms of capitalism which would make haste slowly without provoking social dislocation and civil disorder. This inclination, as we have argued, was powerfully reinforced by the shortage of capital needed to fund an alternative programme. This deficiency was turned to advantage: by claiming to promote both progress and conservation, Britain's version of trusteeship offered a vision of an international system which could compete with the appeal of Bolshevism and fascism. Although the world order envisaged by the British was neither democratic nor populist, the script for the civilising mission emphasised the merits of a multi-ethnic enterprise united in its diversity by long chains of loyalty which led ultimately to the imperial monarch.[103]

Flexibility in applying these principles can be seen by looking along the axes of space and time. The spatial axis shows that trusteeship could be invoked to defend both 'native paramountcy' and settler dominance. Each was viewed, in different regions, as being the most promising agent of conservative progress, including (by definition) the capacity to raise taxable incomes to meet administrative services and debt payments. The chronological dimension illustrates how the means of fulfilling the principles of trusteeship, including of course the maintenance of colonial control, shifted between 1914 and 1940 from indirect rule, with its assumption of gradual change, to direct government action to achieve rapid economic development. Once again, fiscal considerations were important in explaining this evolution: by the late 1930s indirect rule was bankrupt, and the treasuries of the colonies nearly so following their strenuous efforts to pay their way during the world slump. It was then that a radical change in policy presented itself as the only alternative to the loss, by subsidence, of the colonial empire, and the civilising mission was galvanised by becoming committed to an ambitious programme of state-led development.

The next chapter in this story cannot be written here. But it is worth noting that the interpretation we have advanced could be developed further for the period after 1940, for it is now known that World War II was fought to defend the empire as well as to defeat fascism, that the battle over the shape of post-war colonial policy was continued even as bombs fell on London, and that new development plans, controlled by enlarged bureaucracies, were set in motion as soon as peace returned.[104] In 1945, amidst a war-shattered Europe that had ceased to pose a threat but also appeared to offer little promise, Britain still saw her future as being at the centre of a revitalised empire. The African colonies, in particular, had proved their value during hostilities, and their resources (including their enlarged sterling balances) were regarded as being vital to Britain's post-war recovery. The new deal for the colonies offered them development funds, but it also bound them more closely to the sterling area and to directives from London. Treasury control, at risk in 1940, had been revised rather than abandoned.

Notes

1 The quotation is from F.D. (Lord) Lugard, *The Dual Mandate in British Tropical Africa* (1922, 3rd edn. 1926), p. 132. Referring to the qualities exhibited by the colonial service, Lugard observed that the public schools and universities had 'produced an English gentleman with an almost passionate conception of fair play, of protection of the weak, and of "playing the game"'. The term 'tropical Africa' is used here in a broad sense to include Nigeria, the Gold Coast, Sierra Leone, the Gambia, the Anglo-Egyptian Sudan, Kenya, Uganda, Nyasaland, Northern Rhodesia, the mandated territories of Tanganyika, Togo and Cameroun, and, stretching a point, Southern Rhodesia. Although their formal status varied, these territories were all effectively under direct control apart from Southern Rhodesia, which became self-governing in 1923. The main exclusions, therefore, are Egypt and the Union of South Africa.

2 Comprehensive guidance can be found in A.D. Roberts, ed. *The Cambridge History of Africa, 1905–1940,* Vol. 7 (Cambridge, 1986), Michael Crowder, ed. *The Cambridge History of Africa, 1940–1975,* Vol. 8 (Cambridge, 1985), and L.H. Gann and Peter Duignan, eds. *Colonialism in Africa, 1870–1960,* 5 vols. (Cambridge, 1969–75). Cyril Ehrlich, 'Building and Caretaking: Economic Policy in British Tropical Africa, 1890–1960', *Econ. Hist. Rev.,* 2nd ser. XXVI (1973), offers an illuminating interpretation; Terence Ranger, ed. 'White Presence and Power in Africa', *Jour. African Hist.,* 20 (1979), brings together a number of detailed studies; J. Forbes Munro, *Britain in Tropical Africa, 1880–1960* (1984) provides a concise account of economic relationships. All historians of colonial policy are indebted to W.K. Hancock's classic, *Survey of British Commonwealth Affairs,* Vol. II, Pts. 1 and 2 (1940 and 1942), and to Ian M. Drummond's important study, *Imperial Economic Policy, 1917–1939* (1974). A.D. Roberts, 'The Earlier Historiography of Colonial Africa', *History in Africa,* 5 (1978), draws attention to the work of an earlier

generation of scholars whose contributions have been neglected in recent years, despite their high quality.

3 And others which are not our concern, notably the question of the costs and benefits of colonial rule.

4 Although this designation is now widely used, it is often ill-defined. Older terms, such as 'colony' and 'colonial government', are more appropriate where the context allows specific meanings to be assigned.

5 Between 1907 and 1935, about 85 per cent of the value of exports from sub-Saharan Africa as a whole came from British territories, which also received about 77 per cent of all foreign capital invested in the region between 1870 and 1935. South Africa was pre-eminent in both trade and investment; but British territories were still predominant, even within tropical Africa. The starting point for this subject remains S. Herbert Frankel, *Capital Investment in Africa* (1938).

6 Calculated principally from *Statistical Abstract for the United Kingdom, 1913 and 1923–36* (1937); *Statistical Abstract for the British Empire, 1913 and 1924–29* (1931); *Statistical Abstract for the British Empire, 1929–38* (1939); and *Statistical Abstract for the British Commonwealth, 1933–39 and 1945–47* (1950). We should also like to acknowledge our indebtedness to F.V. Meyer's pioneering study, *Britain's Colonies in World Trade* (1948). It should be pointed out that the underlying data are fragile and that our summary statements are intended to provide orders of magnitude only.

7 Frankel, *Capital Investment,* pp. 193, 210; Peter Svedberg, 'Colonial Enforcement of Foreign Direct Investment', *Manchester School,* 50 (1981); Kathleen M. Stahl, *The Metropolitan Organization of British Colonial Trade* (1951), pp. 145, 204–6, 292–3, 295–6; Charlotte Leubuscher, *The West African Shipping Trade, 1909–1959* (Leiden, 1963), pp. 32–4, 55–6, 81–2.

8 John M. Atkin, 'British Overseas Investment, 1918–1931', (Ph.D. thesis, University of London, 1968), pp. 115–17, 120–1, 125.

9 In contrast to India, where land taxes made a fundamental contribution to government revenues. The history of taxation in colonial Africa remains a neglected subject. For a rare case study see Tijjani Garba, 'Taxation in Some Hausa Emirates, 1860–1939', (Ph.D. thesis, University of Birmingham, 1986); and for a comparison of tax burdens, David Fieldhouse, 'The Economic Exploitation of Africa: Some British and French Comparisons', in Prosser Gifford and William Roger Louis, eds. *France and Britain in Africa* (New Haven, Conn., 1971). Some long-run considerations are discussed by A.G. Hopkins, 'The World Bank in Africa: a Historical Perspective', *World Development,* 14 (1986).

10 This point is clearly brought out by John Lonsdale, 'The Conquest State of Kenya', in J.A. de Moor and H.L. Wesseling, eds. *Imperialism and War: Essays on Colonial Wars in Asia and Africa* (Leiden, 1989).

11 Frankel, *Capital Investment,* p. 188, appears to understate revenue from customs duties. Compare E.A. Brett, *Colonialism and Underdevelopment in East Africa: The Politics of Economic Change, 1919–1939* (1973), p. 192.

12 Quoted in Allan McPhee, *The Economic Revolution in British West Africa* (1926), p. 208. The two departments had their disputes, but kept them within the family. See Ronald Hyam, 'The Colonial Office Mind, 1900–1914', *Jour. Imp. and Comm. Hist.,* 8 (1979); and John M. Carland, *The Colonial Office and Nigeria, 1898–1914* (Stanford, Calif., 1985), pp. 199–200.

13 See, for example, Marion Johnson, 'Cotton Imperialism in West Africa', *African Affairs,* 73 (1974), pp. 178–87, and David Meredith, 'The British Government and Colonial Economic Policy', *Econ. Hist. Rev.,* 2nd ser. XXVIII (1975), pp. 495–7.

14 See, in particular, J. Mars, 'The Monetary and Banking System and Loan Market of Nigeria', in M. Perham, ed. *Mining, Commerce, and Finance in Nigeria* (1948); W.T. Newlyn and D.C. Rowan, *Money and Banking in British Colonial Africa* (Oxford, 1954); and Barbara Ingham, 'Colonialism and the Economy of the Gold Coast, 1919–45', in B. Ingham and C. Simmons, eds. *Development Studies and Colonial Policy* (1987). Additional historical detail is given in A.G. Hopkins, 'The Creation of a Colonial Monetary System:

the Origins of the West African Currency Board', *African Historical Studies,* 3 (1970); and Jan S. Hogendorn and Henry A. Gemery, 'Cash Cropping, Currency Acquisition and Seignorage in West Africa, 1923–50', *African Economic History,* 11 (1982).

15 Stahl, *Metropolitan Organization,* pp. 296–6.

16 Atkin, 'British Overseas Investment', p. 76.

17 Atkin, 'British Overseas Investment', pp. 14–15, 76, 83, 86; Sir Alan Pim, 'Public Finance', in Perham, ed. *Mining, Commerce, and Finance,* p. 245.

18 Joseph Chamberlain's efforts to direct public funds towards the empire were severely curtailed by the Treasury. See Richard M. Kesner, *Economic Control and Colonial Development: Crown Colony Financial Management in the Age of Joseph Chamberlain* (Oxford, 1981); and, more generally, R.V. Kubicek, *The Administration of Imperialism: Joseph Chamberlain at the Colonial Office* (Durham, NC, 1969).

19 Newlyn and Rowan, *Money and Banking,* p. 74; L.H. Gann and Peter Duignan, *The Rulers of British Africa, 1870–1914* (1978), pp. 48–53, 68–9; Richard Fry, *Bankers in West Africa: The Story of the Bank of British West Africa Ltd.* (1976), pp. 87–8, 94–6. Lord Milner was Chairman of the Bank from 1909 to 1916; his successor, Lord Selborne, was a former Under-Secretary of State at the Colonial Office and High Commissioner in South Africa.

20 On the antiquity of the concept see G.V. Mellor, *British Imperial Trusteeship, 1783–1850* (1951); and for assessments Kenneth Robinson, *The Dilemmas of Trusteeship: Aspects of British Colonial Policy Between the Wars* (1965), and Penelope Hetherington, *British Paternalism and Africa, 1920–1940* (1978). Different stages in the evolution of the idea are discussed by Ronald Robinson, 'The Moral Disarmament of African Empire', in Norman Hillmer and Philip Wigley, eds. *The First British Commonwealth* (1980); and J.M. Lee, *Colonial Development and Good Government: A Study of the Ideas Expressed by the British Official Classes in Planning Decolonization, 1939–1964* (Oxford, 1967). The interpretation offered here gives more weight to financial considerations than is customary.

21 Lugard, *Dual Mandate,* pp. 618–19.

22 See, for example, Robert Gregory, *Sidney Webb in East Africa: Labour's Experiment with the Doctrine of Native Paramountcy* (Berkeley, Calif., 1962).

23 Ronald Robinson, 'European Imperialism and Indigenous Reactions in British West Africa, 1880–1914', in H.L. Wesseling, ed. *Expansion and Reaction: Essays on European Expansion and Reactions in Asia and Africa* (Leiden, 1978); Colin Newbury, 'The Economics of Conquest in Nigeria, 1900–1920: Amalgamation Reconsidered', in Ecole des hautes études en sciences sociales, ed. *Etudes africaines offertes à Henri Brunschwig* (Paris, 1982).

24 Lugard, *Dual Mandate,* pp. 231–3, has some interesting comments on these relationships.

25 The literature on this subject is now too extensive to cite in full. Among the important contributions, which contain numerous further references, are: Gann and Duignan, *Rulers of British Africa*; idem, eds. *African Proconsuls: European Governors in Africa* (Stanford, Calif., 1978); and I.F. Nicolson and Colin A. Hughes, 'A Provenance of Proconsuls: British Colonial Governors, 1900–1960', *Jour. Imp. and Comm. Hist.,* 4 (1975). Studies of particular territories include: Robert O. Collins and Francis M. Deng, eds. *The British in the Sudan, 1898–1956* (Stanford, Calif., 1984); M.W. Daly, *Empire on the Nile: The Anglo-Egyptian Sudan, 1898–1934* (Cambridge, 1986); Henrika Kuklick, *The Imperial Bureaucrat: The Colonial Administrative Service in the Gold Coast, 1920–1939* (Stanford, Calif., 1979); and T.H.R. Cashmore, 'Studies in District Administration in the East African Protectorate, 1895–1914', (Ph.D. thesis, Cambridge University, 1965). On the spread of gentlemanly values through education in Africa, see, for example, R.J. Challis, 'The European Educational System in Southern Rhodesia, 1890–1930', *Zambezia,* 9 (1982), and J.A. Mangan, 'Gentlemen Galore: Imperial Education for Tropical Africa: Lugard the Ideologist', *Immigrants and Minorities,* 1 (1982).

26 The principal selector, Sir Ralph Furse (1887–1973), was educated at Eton and at Balliol College, Oxford. He published a revealing autobiography, *Aucuparius: Recollections of*

a Recruiting Officer (1962). For an assessment see Robert Heussler, *Yesterday's Rulers: The Making of the British Colonial Service* (New York, 1963). See also pp. 23–7 above.

27 The sources are given in notes 12, 13, 19 and 25 above. A particularly interesting case study of these values in action is G.N. Sanderson, 'The Ghost of Adam Smith: Ideology, Bureaucracy, and the Frustration of Economic Development in the Sudan, 1934–1940', in M.W. Daly, ed. *Modernization in the Sudan: Essays in Honour of Richard Hill* (New York, 1985), which is complemented by John Tosh, 'The Economy of the Southern Sudan under the British, 1898–1955', *Jour. Imp. and Comm. Hist.*, 9 (1981). Colonial governments began to work more closely with the large commercial firms in the late 1930s, but the alliance was largely a reflection of the conversion of 'big business' to bureaucratic ways of thinking and of the increasing concentration of decision-making in London. An important contribution to this unexplored subject is David Meredith, 'The Colonial Office, British Business Interests and the Reform of Cocoa Marketing in West Africa, 1937–1945', *Jour. African Hist.*, 29 (1988).

28 Collins and Deng, *The British in the Sudan*, Ch. 6. Gwynne (1863–1957) spent the whole of his career in the front line of empire, beginning as a missionary in Khartoum in 1899, and continuing as an itinerant bishop from 1908 to 1946.

29 This facet of the history of the expatriate firms has been neglected. For an exploratory account see A.G. Hopkins, 'Imperial Business in Africa. Part II: Interpretations', *Jour. African Hist.*, 18 (1976).

30 A good starting point is Richard Rathbone, ed. 'World War I and Africa', *Jour. African Hist.*, 19 (1978). See also Melvin Page, ed. *Africa and the First World War* (1987). As yet, there is no study of Africa to compare with Bill Albert, *South America and the First World War* (Cambridge, 1988), though Marc Michel, *L'Appel à l'Afrique: contributions et réactions à l'effort de guerre en A.O.F., 1914–18* (Paris, 1982), is important for French West Africa.

31 On East Africa see Geoffrey Hodges, *The Carrier Corps: Military Labor in the East African Campaign, 1914–1918* (New York, 1986), and Gregory Maddox, '"*Mtunya*": Famine in Central Tanzania, 1917–20', *Jour. African Hist.*, 31 (1990). On the campaign in South-West Africa (and the initial reluctance of Afrikaner officers to move against Germany), see N.G. Garson, 'South Africa and World War I', in Hillmer and Wigley, *The First British Commonwealth* (1980).

32 Albert F. Calvert, *The German African Empire* (1916), pp. xxi, and xxiii–xiv.

33 John S. Galbraith, 'British War Aims in World War I: a Commentary on Statesmanship', *Jour. Imp. and Comm. Hist.*, 13 (1984).

34 This little-known scheme has been disinterred by Peter J. Yearwood, 'Great Britain and the Repartition of Africa, 1914–19', *Jour. Imp. and Comm. Hist.*, 18 (1990).

35 Gaddis Smith, 'The British Government and the Disposition of the German Colonies in Africa, 1914–1918', in Prosser Gifford and William Roger Louis, eds. *Britain and Germany in Africa* (New Haven, Conn., 1967); William Roger Louis, 'The United States and the African Peace Settlement of 1919: the Pilgrimage of George Louis Beer', *Jour. African Hist.* 4 (1963). Italy's claims were largely brushed aside, as Robert L. Hess has shown: 'Italy and Africa: Colonial Ambitions in the First World War', *Jour. African Hist.*, 4 (1963). Benjamin Gerig, *The Open Door and the Mandate System* (1930) is still worth consulting for the legal and constitutional aspects.

36 For the contrast between winners and losers see J.D. Overton, 'War and Economic Development: Settlers in Kenya, 1914–18', *Jour. African Hist.*, 27 (1986), and Akinjide Osuntokun, *Nigeria in the First World War* (1979). Michael Crowder, *Revolt in Bussa: A Study in 'Native Administration' in Nigerian Borgu, 1902–1935* (1973), shows how wartime difficulties intersected with administrative changes to produce a rebellion in 1915.

37 Hancock, *Survey*, Vol. II, Pt. 1, Ch. 2; Suzanne Buckley, 'The Colonial Office and the Establishment of an Imperial Development Board', *Jour. Imp. and Comm. Hist.*, 3 (1974); David Killingray, 'The Empire Resources Development Committee and West Africa, 1916–20', *Jour. Imp. and Comm. Hist.*, 10 (1982).

38 At least in sub-Saharan Africa. There were worrying developments in Egypt, but these were managed in such a way as to safeguard Britain's essential interests. See John Darwin,

Britain, Egypt and the Middle East: Imperial Policy in the Aftermath of War, 1918–1922 (1981).

39 Hancock, *Survey,* Vol. II, Pt. 1, pp. 106–9, 113, 116, 122; Stephen Constantine, *The Making of British Colonial Development Policy, 1914–1940* (1984), Chs. 2–3.

40 In ways revealed in John M. MacKenzie's notable study, *Propaganda and Empire: The Manipulation of British Public Opinion, 1880–1960* (Manchester, 1984). A particularly relevant case study is Stephen Constantine, '"Bringing the Empire Alive": the Empire Marketing Board and Imperial Propaganda, 1926–33', in Mackenzie, *Imperialism and Popular Culture.*

41 David Killingray, 'A Swift Agent of Government: Air Power in British Colonial Africa, 1916–1939', *Jour. African Hist.,* 25 (1984); Robert L. McCormack, 'Airlines and Empires: Great Britain and the "Scramble for Africa"', *Canadian Journal of African Studies,* 10 (1976); David E. Omissi, *Air Power and Colonial Control: The Royal Air Force, 1919–39* (Manchester, 1990); and, for an illuminating comment by a contemporary, Raymond L. Buell, *The Native Problem in Africa* (New York, 1928), p. 717.

42 See Drummond, *British Economic Policy,* Ch. 2; Constantine, *The Making of British Colonial Development Policy*; and, for a sample of the programme, L.S. Amery, 'Economic Development of the Empire', *United Empire,* 16 (1925).

43 On the Labour Party's voyage towards empire during this period see Gregory, *Sidney Webb in East Africa.*

44 The authoritative treatment is in Drummond, *Imperial Economic Policy,* Chs. 2–3. See also Brett, *Colonialism and Underdevelopment in East Africa,* Ch. 6, and Paul Mosley, *The Settler Economies: Studies in the Economic History of Kenya and Southern Rhodesia, 1900–1963* (Cambridge, 1983), pp. 16–24.

45 Meyer, *Britain's Colonies,* pp. 10–11; United States Tariff Commission, *Colonial Tariff Policies* (Washington, DC, 1922).

46 Constantine, *The Making of British Colonial Development Policy,* Chs. 4–6.

47 George C. Abbott, 'British Colonial Aid Policy during the Nineteen Thirties', *Canadian Jour. Hist.,* 5 (1970), and the criticism by Ian M. Drummond, 'More on British Colonial Aid Policy in the Nineteen Thirties', *Canadian Jour. Hist.,* 6 (1971). Thereafter: Brett, *Colonialism and Underdevelopment,* pp. 131–3; and Meredith, 'British Government and Colonial Economic Policy', pp. 487–9. D.J. Morgan, *The Official History of Colonial Development,* Vol. I (1980), Chs. 5–6, says enough to suggest that this subject needs to be looked at afresh.

48 In the early 1920s Manchester was particularly exercised by problems of cotton supply and by the decline of its share of the Indian market. Its renewed interest in Africa, and the foundation of the Empire Cotton Growing Association in 1921, are examined by W.A. Wardle, 'A History of the British Cotton Growing Association, 1902–39, with Special Reference to its Operations in Northern Nigeria', (Ph.D. thesis, University of Birmingham, 1980), pp. 158–68. The most publicised experiment in cotton-growing is dealt with by A. Gaitskell, *Gezira: A Story of Development in the Sudan* (1959).

49 A sad tale, well told, is that by Leroy Vail, 'The Making of an Imperial Slum: Nyasaland and its Railways, 1895–1935', *Jour. African Hist.,* 16 (1975).

50 For example: Philip A. Igbafe, *Benin under British Administration: The Impact of Indirect Rule on an African Kingdom, 1897–1938* (1979), Ch. 9; Diana Ellis, 'The Nandi Protest of 1923 in the Context of African Resistance to Colonial Rule in Kenya', *Jour. African Hist.,* 17 (1976); Susan M. Martin, *Palm Oil and Protest: An Economic History of the Ngwa Region, South-Eastern Nigeria, 1800–1980* (Cambridge, 1988), Ch. 9.

51 Lugard, *The Dual Mandate.* Frederick Dealtry Lugard (1858–1945) was born in India and educated at Rossall School and Sandhurst. He made his career in the army and in the empire, especially in Africa and above all in Nigeria, from where he retired as Governor in 1919. Thereafter, he became an active publicist for empire and for his own ideas about how it should be governed. In action and thought, Lugard's military values marched with a strong sense of Christian ethics, which he derived from his parents, and particularly from his father, a chaplain in the East India Company. The standard

biography is Margery Perham, *Lugard,* 2 vols. (1956 and 1960), but more recent work takes the view that Lugard was better as a propagandist than as an administrator. See especially I.N. Nicholson, *The Administration of Nigeria, 1900–1960: Men, Methods, and Myths* (Oxford, 1969), and the valuable overview by John E. Flint, 'Frederick Lugard: the Making of an Autocrat (1858–1945)', in Gann and Duignan, *African Proconsuls.* For a French perspective see Claude Horrut, *Frederick Lugard et la pensée coloniale britannique de son temps* (Paris, 1975).

52 The distinction between traders' and settlers' frontiers has long been a central theme in the historiography of colonial Africa. The most influential statement, still unsurpassed, is in Hancock, *Survey of British Commonwealth Affairs,* Vol. II, Pt. 2, which in turn drew inspiration from the work of Frederick Jackson Turner on the United States.

53 Hancock, *Survey of British Commonwealth Affairs,* Vol. II, Pt. 2, pp. 173–200; and, for the subsequent history of Lever's interests, D.K. Fieldhouse, *Unilever Overseas: The Anatomy of a Multinational* (1978), Chs. 6 and 9.

54 There is now a sizeable revisionist literature on this subject. Illustrations of the comments made here include: A.E. Afigbo, *The Warrant Chiefs: Indirect Rule in Southern Nigeria, 1891–1929,* (1972); Ralph Austen, 'The Official Mind of Indirect Rule: British Policy in Tanganyika, 1916–1939', in Gifford and Louis, *Britain and Germany in Africa;* Martin Chanock, *Law, Custom and Social Order: The Colonial Experience in Malawi and Zambia* (Cambridge, 1985); D.C. Dorward, 'Ethnography and Administration: a Study of Anglo-Tiv "Working Misunderstanding"', *Jour. African Hist.,* 15 (1974); Cyril Ehrlich, 'Some Social and Economic Implications of Paternalism in Uganda', *Jour. African Hist.,* 4 (1963); Beverly Gartell, 'British Administrators, Colonial Chiefs, and the Comfort of Tradition: an Example from Uganda', *African Stud. Rev.,* 26 (1983); Owen J.M. Kalinga, 'Colonial Rule, Missionaries, and Ethnicity in North Nyassa District, 1891–1938', *African Stud. Rev.,* 28 (1985); Peter K. Tibenderana, 'The Irony of Indirect Rule in the Sokoto Caliphate, Nigeria, 1903–1944', *African Stud. Rev.,* 31 (1988); John Tosh, *Clan Leaders and Colonial Chiefs in Lango: The Political History of an East African Stateless Society c. 1800–1939* (Oxford, 1978); Landeg White, '"Tribes" and the Aftermath of the Chilembwe Rising', *African Aff.,* 83 (1984). For a comparative approach see E.J. Hobsbawm and T.O. Ranger, eds. *The Invention of Tradition* (Cambridge, 1983).

55 Thomas Taylor, 'The Establishment of a European Plantation Sector within the Emerging Colonial Economy of Uganda, 1909–1919', *Int. Jour. African Hist. Stud.,* 19 (1986); Jan S. Hogendorn, 'Economic Initiative and African Cash Farming: Pre-Colonial Origins and Early Colonial Developments', in Gann and Duignan, *Colonialism in Africa,* IV, Ch. 8.

56 The main issues are summarised in A.G. Hopkins, *An Economic History of West Africa* (1973), pp. 211–16.

57 On the latter see John M. Mackenzie's fascinating study, *The Empire of Nature: Hunting, Conservation, and British Imperialism* (Manchester, 1988). Conservation measures also enlarged the role of the state, as Ian Phimister, for example, has shown: 'Discourse and the Discipline of Historical Context: Conservationism and Ideas about Development in Southern Rhodesia, 1930–1950', *Jour. Southern African Stud.,* 12 (1986).

58 A phrase used by Sir James Currie (a former Director of Education in the Sudan and a critic of indirect rule) in 1926. Quoted in Daly, *British Administration,* p. 175.

59 Minutes of a meeting of Governors of Northern Sudan, 1920. Quoted in Daly, *British Administration,* p. 173.

60 Speculation in gold and rubber in West Africa at this time involved 'the shadier fringes of the Edwardian capital market'. See J. Forbes Munro, 'Monopolists and Speculators: British Investment in West African Rubber, 1905–1914', *Jour. African Hist.,* 22 (1981), p. 277. A similar boom in gold-mining shares in Southern Rhodesia collapsed in 1903.

61 By 1939 there were approximately 21,000 white settlers in Kenya and 63,000 in Southern Rhodesia. See Dane Kennedy, *Islands of White: Settler Society and Culture in Kenya and Southern Rhodesia, 1890–1939* (Durham, NC, 1987). M.P.K. Sorrenson, *Origins of European Settlement in Kenya* (1968), and Richard Hodder-Williams, *White Farmers in Rhodesia, 1890–1965* (1983), are also helpful.

62 Kennedy, *Islands of White,* p. 44.
63 Mosley, *The Settler Economies,* Ch. 2; Lonsdale, 'The Conquest State'. Also C.C. Wrigley, 'Kenya: the Patterns of Economic Life, 1902–1945', in Vincent Harlow and E.M. Chilver, eds. *History of East Africa* (Oxford, 1965).
64 There were differences of interest among farmers and also between farmers as a group and expatriate mine-owners (over labour supplies, for example). Commercial interests were represented by the Joint East Africa Board, on which see Stahl, *Metropolitan Organization,* pp. 189–98, and Brett, *Colonialism and Underdevelopment,* pp. 59–65. The juggling act is described in detail by John Lonsdale and Bruce Berman, 'Coping with the Contradictions: the Development of the Colonial State in Kenya, 1895–1914', *Jour. African Hist.,* 20 (1979).
65 Robert M. Maxon, 'The Kenya Currency Crisis, 1919–21 and the Imperial Dilemma', *Jour. Imp. and Comm. Hist.,* 17 (1989). See also R.M.A. van Zwanenberg with Anne King, *An Economic History of Kenya and Uganda, 1800–1970* (1975), pp. 281–7.
66 Robinson, 'Moral Disarmament'; C.J.D. Duder, 'The Settler Response to the Indian Crisis of 1923 in Kenya: Brigadier General Philip Wheatley and Direct Action', *Jour. Imp. and Comm. Hist.,* 17 (1989).
67 Duder, 'The Settler Response', p. 352.
68 Robinson, 'Moral Disarmament'; Jidlaph G. Kamoche, *Imperial Trusteeship and Political Evolution in Kenya, 1923–1963* (Washington, DC, 1981), Chs. 1–2. The activities of the 'humanitarian' pressure group are discussed by Diana Wylie, 'Confrontation over Kenya: the Colonial Office and its Critics, 1918–1940', *Jour. African Hist.,* 18 (1977).
69 Robinson, 'Moral Disarmament'; Ian Phimister, *An Economic and Social History of Zimbabwe, 1890–1948* (1988), Chs. 2–3; and, for the longer view, Martin Chanock, *Unconsummated Union: Britain, Rhodesia and South Africa, 1900–45* (Manchester, 1977).
70 Starting points for studying this subject include: Hopkins, *Economic History,* Ch. 7; 'L'Afrique et la crise de 1930', *Revue française d'histoire d'Outre-Mer,* 63 (1976); J.M. Lonsdale, 'The Depression and the Second World War in the Transformation of Kenya', in D. Killingray and R. Rathbone, eds. *Africa and the Second World War* (1986); and Ian Brown, ed. *The Economies of Africa and Asia in the Inter-War Depression* (1989).
71 See, for example, David Anderson, 'Depression, Dust Bowl, Demography and Drought: the Colonial State and Soil Conservation in East Africa during the 1930s', *African Affairs,* 83 (1984); and S.M. Martin, 'The Long Depression: West African Export Producers and the World Economy, 1914–45', in Brown, *The Economies of Africa and Asia.*
72 These are explored in Brown, *The Economies of Africa and Asia.*
73 Rich deposits of iron ore were found in Sierra Leone in 1933. Copper was already being produced in Northern Rhodesia, and the price fell in 1929. However, the development of new mines and the discovery of high-grade ore helped to pull the colony out of the slump in the late 1930s. The rise in the price of gold also encouraged new (and often marginal) mines to enter production: see Andrew D. Roberts, 'The Gold Boom of the 1930s in Eastern Africa', *African Affairs,* 85 (1986). Import-substituting manufactures are discussed by Brett, *Colonialism and Underdevelopment,* pp. 278–81, 298–9, and Gervase Clarence Smith, 'The Effect of the Great Depression on Industrialisation in Equatorial and Central Africa', in Brown, *The Economies of Africa and Asia.*
74 In contrast, where capital was provided mainly by private finance in the form of equities, as in the case of the South African gold-mines, reduced earnings were compensated to some extent by reduced dividend payments. See Frankel, *Capital Investment,* p. 179.
75 Frankel, *Capital Investment,* Table 36, p. 178.
76 Ibid. pp. 178, 181–3.
77 Sir Donald Cameron, *My Tanganyika Service and Some Nigeria* (1939), p. 280.
78 Daly, *Empire on the Nile,* pp. 194–5; Vail, 'The Making of an Imperial Slum'. Tanganyika's budget buckled in the early 1930s, but was soon straightened out. See Brett, *Colonialism and Underdevelopment,* pp. 143–5.
79 Quoted in N.A. Cox-George, *Studies in Finance and Development* (1973), p. 110.
80 Ibid.

81 J. Ayodele Langley, *Pan-Africanism and Nationalism in West Africa, 1900–1945* (Oxford, 1973).

82 A perceptive introduction is in Ian M. Drummond, *British Economic Policy and the Empire, 1919–1939* (1972), pp. 114–20. See also Meredith, 'The Colonial Office'. Examples of policy in Africa include: J.C. de Graft-Johnson, *African Experiment: Cooperative Agriculture and Banking in British West Africa* (1958); John McCracken, 'Planters, Peasants and the Colonial State: the Impact of the Native Tobacco Board in the Central Province of Malawi', *Jour. Southern African Stud.*, 9 (1983); and Kenneth Vickery, 'Maize Control in Northern Rhodesia', *Jour. Southern African Stud.*, 11 (1985).

83 Meyer, *Britain's Colonies,* pp. 10–11, 32–5; Brett, *Colonialism and Underdevelopment,* pp. 148–56.

84 Stahl, *Metropolitan Organization,* p. 212.

85 Followed by limited discriminatory measures in 1936. See Meyer, *Britain's Colonies,* pp. 64–6, 80–5; Brett, *Colonialism and Underdevelopment,* pp. 156–60; Charlotte Leubuscher, 'The Policy Governing External Trade', in M. Perham, ed. *Mining, Commerce, and Finance in Nigeria* (1948), pp. 158–63; Arthur Redford, *Manchester Merchants and Foreign Trade, Vol. II, 1850–1939* (Manchester, 1956), pp. 250–9.

86 The fullest statement is Royal Institute of International Affairs, *The Colonial Problem* (1937). See also Norman Angell, *The Defence of the British Empire* (New York, 1937), and idem, *Who Owns the British Empire?* (1942).

87 Norman Angell, *This Have and Have Not Business: Political Fantasy and Economic Fact* (1936); Douglas Rimmer, 'Have-Not Nations: the Prototype', *Economic Development and Cultural Change,* 27 (1979).

88 The importance of trade between the United States and the empire during this period has not been given its full emphasis. The starting point is Meyer, *Britain's Colonies,* Ch. 10.

89 This paragraph draws on: Wolfe W. Schmokel, *Dream of Empire: German Colonialism, 1919–1945* (1964); idem, 'The Hard Death of Imperialism: German and British Colonial Attitudes, 1919–1939', in Gifford and Louis, *Britain and Germany in Africa*; William Roger Louis, 'Colonial Appeasement, 1936–1938', *Revue belge de philologie et d'histoire,* 49 (1971); S.K.B. Asante, 'The Italo-Ethiopian Conflict: a Case Study in British West African Response to Crisis Diplomacy in the 1930s', *Jour. African Hist.,* 15 (1974); and Andrew J. Crozier, *Appeasement and Germany's Last Bid for Colonies* (Basingstoke, 1988).

90 Philip M. Taylor, *The Projection of Britain: British Overseas Publicity and Propaganda, 1919–1939* (Cambridge, 1981); John M. Mackenzie, ed. *Imperialism and Popular Culture* (Manchester, 1986); idem, *Propaganda and Empire*; J. Richards, 'Patriotism with Profit: British Imperial Cinema in the 1930s', in J. Curran and V. Porter, eds. *British Cinema History* (1983); Rosaleen Smyth, 'The Development of British Colonial Film Policy, 1927–1939, with Special Reference to East and Central Africa', *Jour. African Hist.,* 20 (1979); Andrew Roberts, 'Africa on Film to 1940', *History in Africa,* 14 (1987).

91 Lee, *Colonial Development,* Chs. 2–3; R.D. Pearce, *The Turning Point in Africa: British Colonial Policy, 1938–1948* (1982), Chs. 2–3; Robinson, *Dilemmas of Trusteeship.*

92 The most influential of the official critics in the late 1930s was Sir Bernard Boudillon (Governor of Uganda, 1932–35 and of Nigeria, 1935–9). See Robert Pearce, 'The Colonial Economy: Nigeria and the Second World War', in Ingham and Simmons, *Development Studies and Colonial Policy*; and idem, *Sir Bernard Bourdillon: The Biography of a Twentieth-Century Colonialist* (Oxford, 1987).

93 See Mona Macmillan, 'The Making of *Warning from the West Indies*', *Jour. Comm. and Comp. Pol.,* 18 (1980); and Hugh Macmillan and Shula Marks, eds. *Africa and Empire: W.M. Macmillan, Historian and Social Critic* (1989). On the situation in the West Indies see Howard Johnson, 'Oil, Imperial Policy and the Trinidad Disturbances, 1937', *Jour. Imp. and Comm. Hist.,* 4 (1975); and Maurice St Pierre, 'The 1938 Disturbances: a Portrait of Mass Reaction Against Colonialism', *Social and Economic Studies,* 27 (1978).

94 Howard Johnson, 'The West Indies and the Conversion of the British Official Classes to the Development Idea', *Jour. Comm. and Comp. Pol.,* 15 (1977), p. 66.

95 These trends in official thinking are discussed by Lee, *Colonial Government,* Chs. 2–3; and Pearce, *Turning Point,* Chs. 2–3.

96 On the 'state socialism' of a government formally dedicated to what it thought were the economics of Adam Smith, see the excellent discussion of policy-making in the Sudan in Sanderson, 'The Ghost of Adam Smith', pp. 101–11.

97 Lee, *Colonial Development,* Ch. 2; Robinson, *Dilemmas of Trusteeship,* p. 36. See also Charles Jeffries, *Whitehall and the Colonial Service: An Administrative Memoir, 1939–1956* (1972).

98 David Meredith, 'Government and the Decline of the Nigerian Oil-Palm Export Industry, 1919–1939', *Jour. African Hist.,* 25 (1984).

99 David Anderson and David Throup, 'Africans and Agricultural Production in Colonial Kenya: the Myth of the War as a Watershed', *Jour. African Hist.,* 26 (1985); idem, 'The Agrarian Economy of Central Province, Kenya, 1918–1939', in Brown, *The Economies of Africa and Asia*; Wolfgang Dopcke, '"Magorno's Maize": State and Peasants during the Depression in Colonial Zimbabwe', in Brown, *The Economies of Africa and Asia*; Lonsdale, 'The Depression and the Second World War', pp. 105–19.

100 Pim entered the Indian Civil Service in 1894 and turned his attention to Africa after taking formal retirement in 1930. His influence, like his reports, merits further study. His book, *An Economic History of Tropical Africa* (1940), is also unread today.

101 J.M. Lee and Martin Petter, *The Colonial Office, War and Development Policy* (1982), Ch. 1; Lee, *Colonial Development,* Chs. 2–3; Pearce, *Turning Point,* Chs. 2–3; Jane H. Bowden, 'Development and Control in British Colonial Policy with Reference to Nigeria and the Gold Coast' (Ph.D. thesis, University of Birmingham, 1981).

102 Quoted in Bowden, 'Development and Control', p. 103. On the bureaucratic fixing involved see Howard Johnson, 'The Political Uses of Commissions of Enquiry: the Imperial-Colonial West Indies Context', *Soc. and Econ. Stud.,* 27 (1978).

103 The creation of an 'ideology of loyalty' is discussed by Terence Ranger, 'Making Northern Rhodesia Imperial: Variations on a Royal Theme, 1924–1938', *African Aff.,* 79 (1980).

104 Starting points for what is now a sizeable literature include: William Roger Louis, *Imperialism at Bay: The United States and the Decolonization of the British Empire, 1941–1945* (Oxford, 1977); Michael Cowen and Nicholas Westcott, 'British Imperial Economic Policy during the War', in Killingray and Rathbone, eds. *Africa and the Second World War*; Herward Sieberg, *Colonial Development: Die Grundlegung moderner Entwicklungspolitik durch Großbritannien, 1919–1949* (Wiesbaden, 1985); Lee and Petter, *The Colonial Office*; and Pearce, *Turning Point.*

25

'THE ONLY GREAT UNDEVELOPED MARKET IN THE WORLD'

China, 1911–49[1]

With the fall of the Ch'ing dynasty in 1911, China ceases to feature in studies of British imperialism, as does South America after 1914. Neither region was incorporated into the formal empire, and it is generally assumed in both cases that Britain's invisible influence was irreparably damaged by World War I and by the quickening pace of her industrial decline thereafter. There is, of course, a substantial and valuable literature on diplomatic relations among the great powers, especially in the 1930s, when the Great Game in the Far East became one of the antecedents of World War II, but this rarely taps the domestic roots of policy-making in Britain, and only exceptionally does it set the problems of the Far East in the wider context of the history of imperialism.[2] Consequently, there is room for an account which shows how the evolution of Britain's continuing imperialist ambitions intersected with events in the Far East, and how this junction prompted significant changes in policy towards China during a turbulent period which began with one revolution and ended with another.

At the outset of the period under review, the central problem facing British policy-makers was the need to safeguard Britain's substantial investments in China without antagonising a queue of powerful and suspicious rivals. The rapid growth of foreign lending between 1895 and 1911 had concentrated China's fiscal system on Peking and given the major powers, especially Britain, a vested interest in upholding central authority there. However, the centralisation of financial and political power fed discontent in the provinces and stoked the opposition which led to the upheaval of 1911. The foreign powers, coordinated by Britain, responded by taking a tighter grip on government finance and by redoubling their efforts to hold China together. There was no withdrawal after the revolution; there was even room for a degree of optimism, despite the weighty uncertainties surrounding China's future in 1911, for the new regime was thought in some quarters to be more cooperative and more 'progressive' than its predecessor.[3] Seen from this perspective, the revolution of 1911 marked the end of one phase of imperialism, but not the end of imperialist ambitions.

World War I undoubtedly made heavy calls on Britain's resources of capital and manpower, but the evidence now available no longer supports the view that Britain had already begun a 'long retreat' from China,[4] or that she suffered a progressive 'diminution of will' during the inter-war period.[5] The myth of the China market continued to exert a powerful and unique influence on policy-makers and public opinion.[6] Experienced China-watchers had no illusions about the case of 'opening up' the interior, but they could not afford to be caught looking the wrong way in case the long-predicted, if also unexpected, event finally happened. Meanwhile, the reality of China's indebtedness and the need to secure repayment implied more foreign intervention, not less. Consequently, Britain made strenuous efforts to retain the dominant position she had held in China's affairs before 1911, first by trying to restore pre-war methods of control and then by adapting to the nationalist movement and to new economic opportunities, as she did in South America and India. During the 1930s this evolution became caught up, as in South America too, with renewed international competition between the 'have' and the 'have not' nations. In the case of China, however, international rivalries proved to be uncontrollable. Japan's invasion of China in 1937 marked the final breakdown of policies of cooperative imperialism and signalled the onset of a bid for territory which was the high point of aggressive imperialism in the Far East, the beginning of World War II, and the prelude to the revolution of 1949.

Trade and finance: an overview

Quantitative measures of Britain's economic stake in China are fragile and can easily deceive; consequently the data are better treated as orders of magnitude than as precise indices.[7] Contrary to received opinion, it is now becoming clear that the Chinese economy experienced both growth and structural change during this period, but that these developments were not fully reflected in China's overseas trade.[8] This was not only because the outside world accounted for only a very small part of China's total economic activity, but also because the domestic economy appears to have grown faster than the overseas sector, which remained sluggish for the greater part of the period under review. China's staple exports of tea and silk declined, and were replaced by a miscellany of agricultural exports; but none of these functioned as a leading sector in the process of development, even though they enabled the export economy to avoid the worst features of monoculture. From the standpoint of British manufacturers, China remained a land of unrealised potential which absorbed, almost without trace, a mere 2 or 3 per cent of Britain's total exports annually between 1911 and 1937. This was much the same as in 1889–93, on the eve of the scramble to open the interior. Moreover, Britain's share of China's imports continued to fall – from 17 per cent in 1913 to 8 per cent in 1931 – before recovering to 12 per cent in 1936.[9] The larger 'imperial unit' of Britain, Hong Kong and India performed more impressively, and accounted for about 31 per cent of

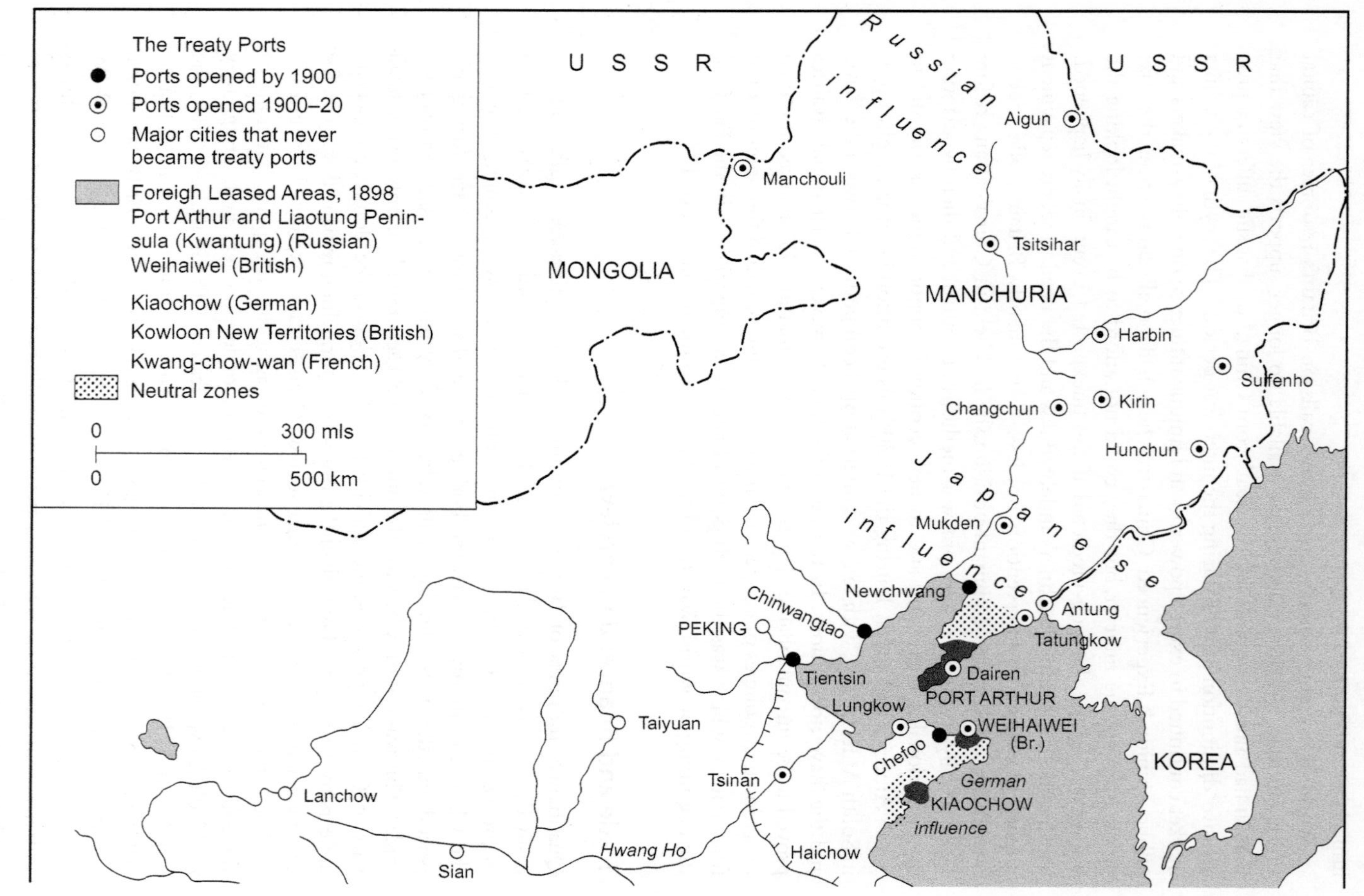
The Treaty Ports
Ports opened by 1900
Ports opened 1900–20
Major cities that never became treaty ports
Foreigh Leased Areas, 1898
Port Arthur and Liaotung Peninsula (Kwantung) (Russian)
Weihaiwei (British)
Kiaochow (German)
Kowloon New Territories (British)
Kwang-chow-wan (French)
Neutral zones
0 300 mls
0 500 km
USSR
USSR
Russian influence
MONGOLIA
MANCHURIA
Japanese influence
German influence
KOREA
Aigun
Manchouli
Tsitsihar
Harbin
Sufenho
Kirin
Changchun
Hunchun
Mukden
Newchwang
Antung
Tatungkow
Chinwangtao
PEKING
Tientsin
Dairen
PORT ARTHUR
Lungkow
WEIHAIWEI (Br.)
Chefoo
KIAOCHOW
Taiyuan
Tsinan
Lanchow
Sian
Hwang Ho
Haichow

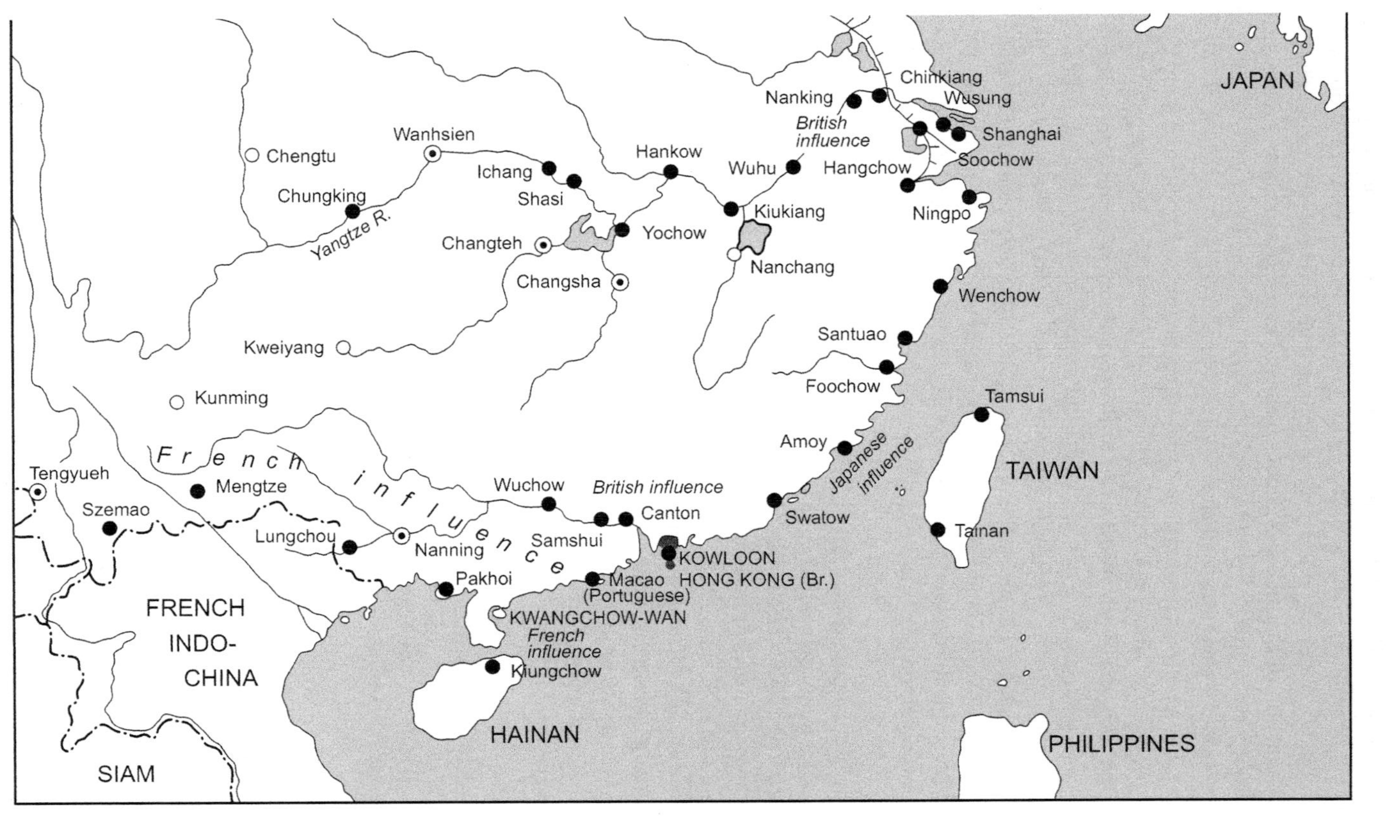

MAP 12 The foreign presence in China, c.1920

After. John K. Fairbank, ed. *The Cambridge History of China*, 12 (Cambridge, 1983)

China's imports in 1928–9. But this figure was also well down from the prewar total of 54 per cent in 1913, and it fell further – to about 16 per cent – in 1936. As far as commodity trade was concerned, the most striking feature of the early 1930s was the elimination of British cotton goods from the Chinese market, an event which put an end to a century of wishful thinking about clothing 400 million Chinese in textiles manufactured in Manchester.

Earnings from foreign investment and other invisibles also suffered after 1911, and even more so after 1914. Political instability made China less attractive to foreign investors, and World War I reduced Britain's ability to supply new capital for investment overseas. Nevertheless, China still received about 6 per cent of Britain's overseas investment in 1933,[10] and Britain's share of all foreign investment in China was little changed, amounting to 38 per cent in 1914, 37 per cent in 1931 and 35 per cent in 1936.[11] These figures mask an important and continuing shift away from government loans and towards direct private investment, which rose from 66 per cent of the total in 1913 to 81 per cent in 1930, and grew further, especially in the mid-1930s, when conditions at last began to favour new investment in China.[12] The main attractions, as in the past, lay in banking, commerce, property and, increasingly, local industry in and around the Treaty Ports, above all Shanghai. In the early 1930s foreign banks, headed by British firms and by the Hongkong and Shanghai Bank in particular, still financed over 90 per cent of the foreign trade of Shanghai, the greatest of China's ports.[13] But it is interesting to note that in 1936 Britain's investments in local manufacturing were also a long way ahead of those made by rival foreign powers, including Japan.[14] British-registered vessels, too, held on to the greater part of their share of the China market, and were responsible for about half the foreign shipping entering and clearing Chinese ports during the period under review, though they carried a decreasing proportion of British goods.[15]

Strategy and strategists

China was (with South America) the most tempting of the unclaimed regions of the world after 1914 – unclaimed, that is, except by the indigenous peoples, and in the Chinese case that did not carry much weight. China being the more vulnerable, it was there that imperialist rivalries became rampant both during the two world wars and in the inter-war years. From the British perspective, the main problem was to contain two major competitors, Japan and the United States, while pushing ahead, cautiously, with her own plans for controlling China's finances and development prospects. Japan posed the more serious problem because China was far more important to her than to the United States and because her expansionist ambitions on the mainland were readily transformed into aggressive imperialism.[16] The comparison made with Britain, the other island empire, suggested a measure of parity which was acceptable while the Anglo-Japanese alliance lasted, but later served to legitimise a degree of assertiveness which was eventually directed at Britain as well as at China. The United States, though beguiled by the myth of the China market, was less involved in the penetration of the interior and had limited political objectives.[17] She was concerned, nevertheless, to defend her interests in China and to frustrate Japan's ambitions once it became clear that they would jeopardise the principle of the open door. Russia offered less of a direct threat after 1917, though this did not prevent the capitalist states from frightening themselves with fears, imagined as well as real, about the spread of Bolshevism.[18] The German challenge lost momentum after 1918, but revived in the 1930s, when China became, briefly, part of Nazi plans for rearmament.[19]

British strategy centred upon ways of continuing her financial control, both to bind the Chinese government and to fetter rival powers. This priority explains the importance attached in the 1920s to the Second Consortium, which Britain saw as a device for restraining competitors by controlling political loans to China. When this strategy broke down in the 1930s, Britain used her leverage to secure financial reforms in China, made a bid to tie China to sterling, and adopted a more assertive policy in defence of her interests in central and southern China, while trying to divert Japan to marginal areas, such as Manchuria. As is well known, the failure to buy off Japan brought war nearer and drove Britain further towards a subordinate relationship with the United States. What is less well appreciated is the extent to which, on the eve of Japanese aggression in 1937, British policy had achieved a transformation which held out the prospect of continuing influence at a moment when China appeared, at last, to be entering a process of successful economic development.

The men charged with managing Britain's interests in China during this period of extreme turbulence and uncertainty, though far fewer in number than those involved with India and Africa, came from much the same stock and viewed the world from broadly similar perspectives. Victor Wellesley, who presided over the Far Eastern desk at the Foreign Office between 1925 and 1936, approached Chinese affairs with a degree of patrician detachment inherited from calmer times, when alien societies could be dealt with without being fully understood.[20] His inactivity in the face of China's political turmoil was less than masterly; but he was reinforced at a crucial moment by Sir John Pratt, whose determination to uphold British interests was informed by an unrivalled knowledge of Asian affairs.[21] Pratt's expertise, which was quite exceptional in the higher reaches of the Foreign Office during this period, did much to transform British policy towards China in the late 1920s. The British Legation continued to be stocked by career diplomats who viewed China from Peking as their colleagues at home viewed England from London, and who resisted Pratt's ultimately successful bid to alter traditional priorities. Lower down the hierarchy, the consular officials came mostly from professional, service and other gentlemanly families, though the unattractive salaries which resulted from rigorous Treasury control meant that recruits had to be drawn from the lower ranks of society too.[22]

The most influential of Britain's unofficial representatives were bankers, above all Sir Charles Addis, the London Manager of the Hongkong and Shanghai Bank.[23] The continuing importance of banking interests is not surprising, given the long-standing connection between finance and strategy in China; but after 1911 the problems thrown up first by World War I and then by the world slump encouraged leading bankers to aspire to an even more prominent role in international affairs. At such times, bankers tend to lose confidence in politicians and begin to imagine that international affairs can be managed by a small committee of businessmen led by themselves and guided by a set of universal principles based on free markets, sound money and solid security.[24] After Addis retired from the Bank in 1921, he continued his advocacy of these principles in his capacity as Britain's chief representative of the Second China Consortium and as an Adviser to the Governor of the Bank of England (of which he was also a Director). As an internationalist, Addis tried to draw Japan and the United States into a global fraternity of bankers; as an imperialist, he did his best to ensure that joint action served Britain's interests. The Hongkong and Shanghai Bank itself remained the most prominent foreign bank in China, notwithstanding Addis's departure, and it also retained close connections with leading firms in the City. After World War I, as before, the Bank provided a 'field of employment' for the products of public schools in England and Scotland, applying selection procedures which mirrored the principle of preferment by connection adopted by Sir Ralph Furse for the Colonial Service.[25]

Revolution, war and war-lords, 1911–18

The political uncertainty which followed the revolution of 1911 drew the foreign powers further into China's internal affairs. Central government had to be upheld to ensure that revenues continued to flow to Peking and that the external debt was serviced. This aim called for some astute diplomatic juggling: provincial aspirations had to be defused without being detonated, and central authority had to be warmed up without being allowed to escape from the bottle. Since stability took priority over schemes for democratic reform and economic development, the powers gave their backing to Yuan, the former Ch'ing general, rather than Sun Yat-sen, the liberal nationalist, whose idealism was thought to point too clearly in the direction of greater independence.[26] In this matter, as in so many others, the Hongkong and Shanghai Bank and the Foreign Office thought as one. Addis had already identified Yuan as the man for the job on the eve of the revolution, and the Foreign Office, in turn, had given the Bank virtually exclusive backing in negotiating a Reorganisation Loan in 1912.[27] These manipulations provoked a nationalist reaction which caused the loan to be postponed, but it was finally issued in 1913, when Yuan had subdued his opponents.[28] His political success, however, was bought at the cost of greater external financial dependence: the loan funded his regime, but was secured only by allowing the International Consortium of bankers to control the salt tax and to receive payments from customs duties directly from the revenue commissioners.[29] In these circumstances, the loan was viewed favourably by the City; coincidentally, Addis was given a knighthood in recognition of his sterling service in championing British interests in the Far East.[30]

World War I posed an obvious threat to Britain's leadership of the foreign powers in the Far East. The outbreak of war directed her attention and resources towards

Europe, unsettled the collective imperialism represented by the Consortium, and provided an opportunity for ambitious rivals, such as Japan and the United States, to promote their own interests. Britain's 'one China' policy was also jeopardised by President Yuan's death in 1916, which was followed by a period of internal instability that led, in turn, to the era of warlord politics.[31] Following the outbreak of war, Japan occupied Shantung, Germany's sphere of influence in China, and in 1915 announced the 21 demands, whose length and lack of guile left no doubt about her acquisitive intentions.[32] These actions were accompanied by a significant degree of commercial and financial penetration, including the secret Nishihara loans of 1917–18, which gave Tokyo considerable influence in Peking. The advance of the United States was pacific and more restrained, but was seen in London as a symptom of a wider and potentially greater threat to Britain's position as a world power.[33] No one in London (or perhaps even in Washington) knew exactly where the formula 'for God, for China and for Yale'[34] might eventually lead; but in China, as in South America, the first signs were of schemes to expand trade, establish banks and buy into British firms.[35]

Maintaining British influence: the 1920s

These developments raised the diplomatic stakes in the Far East and forced Britain's mandarins to join a risky game, which they played with habitual skill and considerable success until Japan broke the rules in the 1930s. Japan had to be controlled but not antagonised because the Anglo-Japanese alliance was vital to Britain's strategy of low-cost defence in the Far East. The cheapest and most effective way of restraining Japan was by drawing the United States into the imperialist club (under the guise of partnership in development) and using her financial power to buttress the one-China policy. The dangers were evident: an appeal to the United States might give offence to Japan; if successful, it might also end in subordinating Britain.

Initially, the Foreign Office mounted a holding operation, urging restraint on Japan while seeking, surreptitiously, to prevent the United States from developing a banking infrastructure in China.[36] However, the protraction of the war and Britain's growing financial dependence on the United States encouraged the Foreign Office to cast about for a more systematic solution, while continuing to work with the Hongkong and Shanghai Bank to maintain China's solvency.[37] The outcome was the Second China Consortium, which took embryonic shape in the closing stages of the war and was formally constituted in 1920, essentially to coordinate the financial dealings of the foreign powers with the Chinese government.[38] The Second Consortium, like the first, was the product of close cooperation between the Foreign Office and the Hongkong and Shanghai Bank. Addis, the manager of the British group in the Consortium, insisted on exclusive government support for his members, who represented 'the elite of City finance'.[39] The demand embarrassed the Foreign Office, which was supposed to remain impartial in matters of private business, but the price had to be paid, in 1920 as in 1911: financial power could not be commanded or directed from Whitehall, and without it Britain's influence in China would rapidly disappear.

The Second Consortium was Britain's chosen vehicle for the return to normality after World War I. In the case of China, the definition of normality was itself problematic; but in British eyes it meant maintaining a stable government which continued to honour its debts, and this implied continuing international supervision. Managing rival powers, however, became more difficult in the postwar years. Britain's own indebtedness to the United States made her vulnerable to pressure from Washington, and caused her to abandon the Anglo-Japanese Alliance when it came up for renewal in 1921.[40] This decision had far-reaching consequences: it knocked a hole in Britain's defence policy and did much to alienate Japan.[41] The Foreign Office hoped that, in return for calming anxieties in the United States about the growing power of Japan, Washington would take a lenient view of Britain's war debts. The prime consideration here was the need to restore Britain's creditworthiness at a time when London was trying to regain its position as the financial centre of the world. The hope was misplaced. What Washington grasped with one hand it also took with the other: the alliance was ended but Britain's war debts were not rescheduled.

Nevertheless, as Lloyd George told the Cabinet in 1921, the British had no intention of letting the Americans 'walk all over them in China',[42] and in the same year the morale of China hands was boosted by a diplomatic initiative that prevented a group of United States' firms from developing Canton as an alternative to Hong Kong.[43] Moreover, by drawing the United States into the Second Consortium, the Foreign Office had made her an honorary member of the imperial club, and in this way reduced the risk of an attack on Britain's overall strategy towards China as well as on important specific issues, such as extraterritorial rights. Addis, the manager of the Consortium, regarded it as a fraternity of 'responsible' lenders whose adherence to the universal principles of international finance enabled them to view the world from a perspective other than that provided by the projection of the nation state. This vision was turned to Britain's advantage: J.P. Morgan, the most important United States' bank in the Far East, had strong ties with the City and saw its business in China as complementing that of the Hongkong and Shanghai Bank.[44] The result was that plans devised in Washington for using the Consortium to advance the national interest were modified in New York by the bankers who were supposed to implement them. Washington was no more successful than Whitehall in directing the banking estate, and US finance flowed to Japan rather than to China.[45] Despite fears to the contrary, diplomatic management and market forces combined to ensure that the Americans did not 'walk all over' British interests in China after World War I.

The Consortium was more successful in perpetuating joint financial control than in promoting economic development. China continued to service her foreign debts after the revolution of 1911 and throughout World War I, but difficulties began to appear early in the 1920s. The solvency of the state depended on the health of revenues already assigned to foreign creditors, and government revenues were adversely affected by the post-war slump, by the limited growth of the export sector thereafter, and by the declining value of China's silver currency in terms of gold, all of which discouraged new lending and placed a question mark over China's ability to repay her existing debts.[46] The Consortium was also unable to control the centrifugal forces of Chinese politics. Continuing political instability damaged government finances and lowered China's credit-worthiness in the eyes of potential foreign investors. Provincial war-lords, freshly armed with surplus equipment from World War I, were not the first choice of foreign capitalists seeking partners for a peaceful development programme.[47] An alliance with westernised elements presented problems too: liberal reformers were preferred, but they were few in number and without a constituency;[48] nationalists had a larger following but their hostility to foreign control, and the fear that they were in league with Bolshevism (and even with Indian 'sedition'), made them deeply unattractive.[49] This appraisal flattered the organising skill, if not the vision, of the nationalist leaders; but it is true, nevertheless, that popular expressions of nationalist sentiment increased in China at this time, as they did elsewhere, in reaction to the growth of foreign influence during the war and to the imposition of foreign priorities on the peace settlement.[50] Sun Yat-sen revived the moribund Kuomintang in 1919, the Chinese Communist Party was founded in 1921, and there were serious protests at key points on the coast – a major strike in Hong Kong in 1922, persistent attempts to repossess the customs revenues of Canton between 1918 and 1924, and widespread riots in Shanghai in 1925 – which damaged Britain's trade and dented her image.[51]

By the mid-1920s it was clear that the means of restoring normality in China required review. The Consortium had kept the major powers in line, but it had been unable to mobilise new funds for China. Meanwhile, the continuing weakness of the central government shifted attention to provincial spheres of influence, compelled foreign interests to take nationalist demands seriously and cast doubt on the realism of the one-China policy. These problems prompted a fundamental reappraisal of British policy with the result that in 1926 the Foreign Office adopted a new strategy which set the course of British policy until Japan invaded China in 1937.[52] The new strategy had two elements: the first reordered Britain's international priorities in the Far East by favouring Japan rather than the United States; the second altered policy towards China by supporting the nationalist movement instead of trying to suppress it. This was not only a remarkable reversal but also a striking initiative for a power whose arteries had supposedly hardened.

The attempt to revive the alliance with Japan, albeit informally, recognised that she had become a far more powerful force in China than had the United States. This fact was brought home to China-watchers in 1924, when a new regime was installed in Peking with financial backing from Japan.[53] By that time, too, it had become apparent that Britain had achieved only limited success in persuading the United States to contribute either to the cost of China's development or to the defence of foreign interests there.[54] The deal envisaged with Japan aimed to divert her to northern China and Manchuria, leaving Britain free to consolidate her position in south and central China by controlling Canton and Shanghai. Thus, the traditional policy of supporting a united China under the authority of Peking was abandoned. Instead, the two 'island empires' would manage China from different points of influence as, in the Locarno formula, Britain and France planned to manage Germany.

The decision to cooperate with nationalist elements was even more radical, despite the precedents set in India.[55] To hold hands with Japan was to revive an old relationship; but courting Chinese nationalists was a departure from a tradition of gunboat diplomacy which went back to the 1840s. The fact that the nationalists could not be bombarded into submission was evidently one consideration; another was growing evidence that the anti-foreign movement was falling under Bolshevik influence.[56] From 1923 Sun Yat-sen began to expand his power base in Canton with help from Moscow, and in the following year the Soviet Union presented the acceptable face of international socialism by giving up Tsarist extraterritorial rights in China. Sun's death in 1925 offered an opportunity rather than removed a problem: his successor, Chiang Kai-shek, transformed the Kuomintang into the Nationalist Government of China in 1926 and extended its reach from Canton to the Yangtse; at the same time, the fall of the regime in Peking cast further doubt on the likelihood that Britain's aims would be realised by continuing support for a unitary state. These developments compelled the Foreign Office to rethink its established views about managing China.

It is now clear that the shift in British policy was initiated in London.[57] The 'men on the spot' in Hong Kong and Peking opposed the change, and urged that more effort should be made to hold China together and to put down the anti-imperialist movement. In Britain the election of a Conservative government in 1925 signalled a greater determination to restore Britain's pre-war dominance: hence the return to gold at pre-war parity, the conscious attempt to cut free from the influence of the United States and the priority given to defeating Bolshevism.[58] In Whitehall, Pratt's arrival at the Foreign Office, also in 1925, provided the expertise which enabled Britain's aspirations to be fitted to the evolution of events in China.[59] Towards the close of 1926, following Pratt's advice, the Foreign Office concluded that 'it ought to be a principle of our policy to sympathise with the best elements of the Kuomintang and try to get them on proper lines', and by doing so 'free ourselves from the shackles of Washington and recover our liberty of action'.[60]

The new policy, like the old, was closely bound up with financial considerations. Firms such as the Hongkong and Shanghai Bank, British and American Tobacco, Jardine Matheson, and Swires, which had substantial long-term investments in China, not only backed the new policy but also were independent advocates of it.[61] Following a visit to China in 1921–2, Addis himself had begun to question the wisdom of continuing to support Peking; by 1925 he was recommending a conciliatory policy towards the nationalists; in 1926 he advised the Foreign Office to recognise the government in Canton.[62] Thus, the new policy was not imposed by the Foreign Office but devised in consultation with firms whose importance it had long recognised. Pratt was quite clear which of these made the running: 'whereas financial interests have men of great influence, ability and fluency to speak for them, trade interests are for the most part struck dumb'.[63] Moreover, as Pratt's colleague, Strang, observed: 'the financial interests' did not have to rely on formal delegations because they had 'their own method of keeping in touch with us', and they also carried more weight in official circles than did representatives of other types of business activity.[64]

Why, then, should the banks and their associates press for a change of policy when, for the previous 30 years, their interests had been closely identified with the maintenance of one central authority in China? The answer to this question lies in alterations to the tactics required to defend Britain's investments in China.[65] In the 1920s Japan and the United States wanted to consolidate China's external debts so that the unsecured loans, which they had advanced during and after World War I, would be included in a comprehensive settlement. This scheme implied greater foreign control of Peking and of China's fiscal system. British banks and bond-holders had nothing to gain from consolidation because most of the money they had loaned to the Chinese government was secured on customs and other revenues, and these were now under direct foreign control. On the contrary, consolidation threatened to dilute their own share of China's repayments, while further interference with the fiscal system seemed likely to accelerate the anti-foreign movement and hence to place all debt service at risk. Consequently, Britain began to distance herself from Peking and to devise an alternative, provincial policy.

However, this decision was much more than a reaction to the consolidation plan and its ramifications. The centre-piece of the new strategy was a bold decision to concede tariff autonomy and to give the provinces a share of the revenues which, traditionally, had been paid to Peking.[66] The Foreign Office (or, to be exact, Pratt and Addis) calculated that this concession would help to win the southern nationalists from their Bolshevik allies, ward off the possible expropriation of Britain's sizeable private investments in Canton and Shanghai, and create the security on which new loans could be raised.[67] But Britain's conception of tariff autonomy did not include yielding administrative control of the pledged revenues or giving up extraterritorial rights. These were still seen to be crucial to servicing the foreign debt and to maintaining the confidence of overseas investors. The chief losers were British exporters, notably Manchester manufacturers, who opposed tariff autonomy because they foresaw, correctly, that import duties would be raised to ensure that debts could be serviced.[68]

Admittedly, the new policy was a leap in the dark, but Britain had been in the dark as far as China's politics were concerned since at least 1911. Moreover, in this case the Foreign Office landed on its feet: Chiang's forces took control of Nanking in 1927 and captured Peking in the following year. Equally significant, Chiang split from Moscow, conducted a savage purge of his communist supporters, and announced his commitment to honouring China's external debts.[69] The Foreign Office, reassured that 'the best elements' of the Kuomintang were now 'on proper lines', gave official recognition to Chiang's National Government in 1928 and lent substance to diplomacy by handing over control of tariff policy.[70] Far from being a step in a long retreat, the new strategy was a way of giving the nationalists a stake in the welfare of British investments in China; and by the close of the 1920s it had achieved a striking success.

Forging a new partnership: the 1930s

This vantage point also offers a different perspective on British policy in the 1930s, and in particular on the weighty decision made in 1937 to support China against Japan. On the assumptions that Britain's economic interests in China were waning and that her diplomacy generally lacked resolution, this decision has to be explained by a combination of special factors operating at the time.[71] However, if the assumptions are altered to take account of the strategy adopted by the Foreign Office in 1926 and its development in the 1930s, it becomes possible to put forward an additional argument which emphasises the continuity of Britain's priorities in China. The main issues, as in the 1920s, were financial, and centred on securing payments on existing debts and creating the conditions for new investment.

Deteriorating economic and political conditions meant that a number of China's external debts had fallen into temporary default by the late 1920s. As in India, tariff autonomy was conceded not only to mollify nationalists but also to provide the means of meeting foreign financial obligations. This step was necessary but not, by itself, sufficient, and additional fiscal and monetary measures were required to ensure that debt service was resumed.[72] Progress was made in bringing local banks into line with western practice after 1928; import duties were denominated in gold rather than in silver from 1930 to preserve the real value of government revenues; serious consideration was given to moving the currency on to a gold standard between 1928 and 1931. These reforms were a cooperative effort: foreign experts, such as Kemmerer, the flying 'money doctor', Salter, the former adviser to the League of Nations, and Addis, the ubiquitous banker, made important contributions; T.V. Soong, the Minister of Finance in the National Government between 1928 and 1933, was a westernised liberal who had studied economics at Harvard and was keen to attract outside expertise and funds for China's development.[73] Minds on both sides were concentrated by the knowledge that new loans would not be forthcoming until agreement on existing debts had been reached. Addis did his best to ensure that this sequence was followed by using the Consortium to control potentially 'irresponsible' lenders such as Japan (which had funds to lend) from stealing a march on Britain (which did not).[74] Amidst this considerable activity, Britain's old staple manufactures were quietly jettisoned. The leading export, cotton textiles, suffered a dramatic reverse: import duties rose sharply from 1929, and by the early 1930s sales of Manchester goods had been cut to insignificance, thus finally ending the hope that China would provide compensation for the loss of the Indian market.[75]

The most ambitious reform was the attempt to draw China into the emerging Sterling Area after Britain left the gold standard in 1931.[76] This plan was lent urgency by changing monetary conditions in China, which were themselves affected by the global financial crisis. The long decline in silver prices was reversed in 1931, when a rise in world demand began to draw silver out of China. The outflow threatened to deflate the economy and consequently to damage both the recovery of public finances, which had been in train since 1928, and the profitability of British investments.[77] Britain responded by dispatching a senior Treasury adviser, Frederick Leith-Ross, to China to devise a solution which would take the monetary system off the silver standard and also secure British interests.[78] The report drawn up by Leith-Ross and his team in 1935 recommended that China's currency should be linked to sterling, that a Central Reserve Bank should be established, and that the National Government should undertake to balance its budget.

Given that this was a composite package, taken from the shelf of universal banking verities, Leith-Ross had more success than local conditions might have allowed. China left the silver standard in 1935, and the new Chinese dollar (which had replaced the tael in 1933) was linked to sterling, as the Treasury, the Bank of England and Addis had hoped.[79] But the link was not exclusive; China wished to preserve her options, particularly the possibility of financial support from the United States, and so adopted a managed exchange standard, which in effect tied her currency to the dollar as well as to sterling. This decision required the cooperation of the foreign exchange banks and particularly of the Hongkong and Shanghai Bank, which played a vital part in helping to maintain the stability of the new system.[80] The Central Reserve Bank was created in 1936, and a member of the advisory team, Cyril Ross, remained in China to ensure that policy ran on lines laid down by the Bank of England. The National Government made considerable progress in balancing the budget, and a settlement of defaulted debts was reached in 1936. This cleared the way for new lending, and in 1937 Addis persuaded members of the Consortium to allow a substantial new railway loan to be issued in London. The decision drew China closer to Britain and, as Addis saw it, made her effectively 'a member of the sterling area'.[81]

The silver crisis and the ensuing monetary reforms also provide the key to understanding the wider relationship between the world slump and Britain's expanding stake in China in the 1930s. Recent research has made it clear that the Chinese economy as a whole was not seriously damaged by the severe depression in world trade after 1929, even though there was a fall in the value and profitability of overseas commerce between 1930 and 1936.[82] The explanation is not that China was isolated from the world economy, but that significant growth took place outside the 'traditional' export sector. Initially, the declining price of silver boosted China's exports and increased the cost of imports, thus reinforcing the protective effect of the new tariff regime and stimulating import-substituting activities. The rise in the price of silver after 1931 threatened to reverse these trends, and it was at this point that the monetary reforms acted to stabilise the economy as a whole. The success of the reforms limited the damage: China's money supply increased during the early 1930s, and the 'modern' sector (especially coal, textiles, electrical goods, utilities and banking) experienced significant growth as a result of the continuing buoyancy of the domestic economy.

These developments gave further impetus to Britain's new policy of cooperating with the Nationalist Government. In this case, as in others we have discussed, the implementation of official policy depended heavily on actions taken in the private sector, since the Foreign Office could neither coerce the Chinese government nor direct British business. Fortunately (and exceptionally) the strategy adopted by the expatriate firms operating in China in the 1930s is now known in some detail.[83] By that time, the China lobby was centred on a handful of large firms consisting of trans-national corporations, such as ICI, Unilever, British & American Tobacco, and Shell-BP, Far Eastern conglomerates, such as Jardine, Matheson, and the hardy perennial, the Hongkong and Shanghai Bank. These firms were fitted by their size and structure to meet the capital requirements and the risks of operating in the underdeveloped world; they also reflected impulses transmitted from Britain, where large firms and new industries were finally making their appearance. In essence, what happened in the 1930s was that the large expatriate firms began to move into the interior (especially the hinterlands of Shanghai and Canton), where new economic opportunities were associated with an acceptable level of political stability. There, they took advantage of the tariff protection which had eliminated imported Manchester goods and invested in the modern sector, often through joint ventures with Chinese entrepreneurs.

On the British side, these innovations signalled the end of the gunboat era and cleared the way for the surrender of extraterritorial rights, which had little relevance to activities outside the Treaty Ports; as far as China was concerned, they opened a new phase of cooperative enterprise with western firms.[84] China's entrepreneurs became incorporated by association into Chiang's bureaucratic and military regime, but they also won political protection and this lent support to their alliance with foreign business.[85] These developments began to realise the promise of a new deal for China and they go far towards explaining the optimism expressed by well-informed contemporaries in the mid-1930s. As Sir Louis Beale, Britain's Commercial Counsellor in Shanghai, observed in 1936:

> There has never been a time when we were so pre-eminent in prestige in China as we are today, and, if we adopt an enterprising policy of co-operation with China in the development of her vast potential resources, there is no reason why we should not stay permanently in the lead.'[86]

This judgement was echoed in the following year by the captain of Britain's official team in China: 'we are on a very good wicket here and we ought to take full advantage of it'.[87]

The process of reconstruction was both hurried on and ultimately brought down by foreign rivalries, especially with Germany and, above all, with Japan. Germany's revived presence began to make itself felt from the late 1920s, first through military links with the Kuomintang, and then through bilateral trade agreements, which played an important part in supplying raw materials for German rearmament in the 1930s.[88] Japan's interests in China were larger and more forcefully expressed. The end of the Anglo-Japanese alliance in 1921 had left Japan with a grievance and with more scope for remedying it; the world slump helped to convert her long-standing ambitions on the mainland into imperialist aggression.[89] The liberal policies of the civilian government were discredited, the search for markets became more urgent and power shifted towards the army.[90] Japan's invasion of Manchuria in 1931 signalled the transition from informal expansion to a form of militarist imperialism. Her withdrawal from the League of Nations in 1933 and the publication of the menacing Amau Statement in the following year were further signposts on the road to war. In 1936 the Anti-Comintern Pact brought Germany and Japan closer together, and gave Japan a freer hand in the Far East.[91] When Japan invaded China in 1937, all hopes for pacific development were sunk.

Despite the ending of the Anglo-Japanese alliance, the Foreign Office continued to base its policy towards the Far East on the assumption that Japan would not act aggressively, or at least not in a way that would damage Britain's interests. If this view seemed justified by events during the 1920s, it became instantly unrealistic after the invasion of Manchuria in 1931. From then on, Britain's mandarins struggled to reconcile the irreconcilable. The success of Britain's new policy towards China strengthened the Nationalist Government and hence checked Japan's influence. Britain was therefore seen in Tokyo to be taking an unfriendly attitude which helped, in turn, to legitimise an assertive response. The only sure way of restraining Japan was for Britain to step up her naval presence in the Far East, but the cost was daunting, if not prohibitive.[92]

This dilemma explains the increasingly intricate acts of contortion performed by the *artistes* of the Foreign Office as they tried to extend a hand to Japan without losing a grip on China. One idea, canvassed by the pro-Japanese lobby, was that Britain should fall in behind Japan's advance and collect some of the gains which would materialise once China had been reorganised and disciplined by an efficient, forward-looking regime.[93] This approach ran parallel to the Treasury's view that the stability of sterling required a low-cost defence policy, which meant, in effect, making concessions to Japan in the Far East.[94] The link between budgetary control, sterling and strategy gave the Treasury considerable prominence in foreign policy in the mid-1930s – much to the displeasure of the Foreign Office. Leith-Ross, for example, devised a banker's solution to the problem of containing Japan which involved giving her Manchuria and compensating China by offering her a loan on favourable terms. Moreover, the Treasury's view carried weight with Neville Chamberlain, who believed that the cost of rearmament was also unacceptable to the electorate and that, in consequence, Britain ought to adopt a low-cost defence strategy centred on Europe and based on the Air Force.[95]

Nevertheless, an alternative policy prevailed. As the 1930s advanced, it became clear that Japan wanted capitulation rather than concessions. When the scheme for recognising Japan's position in Manchuria failed in 1935, Britain began to adopt a firmer line.[96] The outbreak of the Sino-Japanese war in 1937 confirmed Britain's attitude and stiffened her resolve.[97] Yet the explanation of why Britain decided to support China against Japan ought not to be couched solely in terms of the way in which diplomatic realities gradually imprinted themselves on the official mind. The growing success of Britain's new policy towards China was a powerful consideration in the decision to confront Japan. It is now clear that the Hongkong and Shanghai Bank and the conglomerates which were investing heavily in China in the 1930s exerted strong pressure on the Foreign Office and on Chamberlain, and that their representations strengthened the government's determination to defend Britain's stake in China.[98] In the final analysis, Britain's interests in China were larger than those in Japan, and the Foreign Office also believed (albeit mistakenly) that, in the event of war between the two countries, China would win.[99] Wider considerations played their part, too, as friction between Britain and Japan spread beyond the Far East in the 1930s: faced with rising unemployment and a developing balance of payments problem, Britain could no longer watch benignly as Japan's manufactures penetrated imperial markets; Japan, on the other hand, resented the restrictions placed on her exports following the Ottawa Conference in 1932.[100] By the close of the 1930s, the 'two island empires' had not only ceased to be allies but had also embarked on a trade war which spread beyond Asia to Australia, the Middle East, and Africa.[101]

Britain's renewed support for the Chinese government took the traditional form of financial assistance. In 1935 Chamberlain was prepared to give official backing to Leith-Ross's scheme for raising a loan in the City to assist China. Two years later, Britain side-stepped the Second Consortium and supported an advance made by the Hongkong and Shanghai Bank to the Nationalist Government.[102] Export credits were granted to China in 1938, and a guaranteed currency stabilisation loan was issued in 1939.[103] These measures were firm evidence of Britain's intent, but they were limited in substance by the cost of the rearmament programme and by the sterling crisis of 1937–8. In 1938 the United States began to step up its support for the Chinese government at a rate that Britain could not match; and from 1941, when both powers declared war on Japan, US aid to China was increased still further.[104] As the stakes rose, Britain was left behind. To maintain her presence in China during World War II she had to fall back on what the Foreign Office termed 'unlimited flattery' (which included an Oxford doctorate for Chiang Kai-shek) as a substitute for material aid.[105]

Towards 1949

By 1945, China's foreign trade and finance, like Chiang himself, were firmly in the hands of the United States.[106] Even at this late stage, however, it is mistaken to suppose that Britain's ambitions in China had been extinguished or even that they were unrealistic. Britain fought World War II to retain her overseas possessions as well as to defeat Germany and Japan, and she made plans to re-establish her presence in the Far East as soon as peace returned. British firms were keen to secure their investments and to resume business, and the British government looked to China, as to other parts of the world beyond Europe, to assist in reconstructing the home economy.[107] By playing on fears in the United States about the spread of communism, the Foreign Office also persuaded Washington to allow Britain to reenter Hong Kong. Britain's plans were frustrated initially not by a loss of will, but by a deliberate policy decision which reflected the reordered priorities of international trade in the post-war years. In 1947 the Treasury ruled that trade with China could not be developed until Britain's position with respect to hard currency areas had improved and until the dollar gap in particular had been closed.[108] Since China's brief connection with the Sterling Area had been severed during the war, she was relegated to the basement of British commercial policy. After 1949, of course, events in China became the principal influence on Britain's presence there: the communist government nationalised foreign holdings, British business suffered the fate, which was rarer than might be thought, of being taken over without compensation, and investors learned the hard lesson that the value of portfolios not only can go down as well as up, but also can be eliminated.[109]

Safeguarding British interests in an age of revolution

The evidence presented above suggests that China ought to have a prominent place in the study of British imperialism in the period following the revolution of 1911. Its disappearance from the literature on this subject, though not justified explicitly, appears to derive from broad assumptions about the decline of British power, whether this is dated from the 1870s or after 1914. Yet, as we showed earlier, Britain's informal influence in China was limited in the middle of the nineteenth century and did not expand until after 1895, when new financial opportunities finally opened up. This influence was maintained and in some respects increased in the years between 1911 and 1937. Subsequent events, even those as momentous as World War II and the revolution of 1949, were treated in London as interruptions rather than as turning points. Imperialist powers are not easily deflected from their historic mission, and in the case of China there were precedents to suggest that Britain could survive war and revolution, and perhaps even gain from them. Of course, if exports of staple manufactures are treated as proxies of British power, then relative decline can indeed be traced to the late nineteenth century and absolute decline to the 1930s. But, as we have argued throughout the present study, this is in general a misleading indicator: in the case of China Britain's strength lay in her finance and commercial services rather than in her manufactured exports.

As we have seen in other contexts, financial leverage was also the more powerful weapon of policy. The ties which joined Whitehall to the City were much closer than those which ran to Manchester, as the example of Sir Charles Addis has shown. The claim that 'in democratic countries the real political power lies with big money and with a comparatively small circle of political wire-pullers' is perhaps too jaundiced and conspiratorial in tone to win acceptance; but, since it was the judgement of the former Deputy Under-Secretary of State at the Foreign Office in charge of Far Eastern affairs, it ought not to be discounted either.[110] The evidence now available confirms that finance had a central part to play in British policy towards China after 1911, as indeed before. As policy-makers relied heavily on financial power to influence the Chinese government, so bankers called upon political support for their own purposes. The two were fused in a particular conception of public interest which, by amalgamating national and imperial values, was able to rise above the level of mere sectional concerns.

The main aim of policy in the aftermath of revolution and world war was to safeguard Britain's investments by tightening her grip on Peking. This policy was successful but also limited, and in 1926 it was replaced by a 'new deal' which guided British policy towards China until 1937 and was not abandoned until the 1950s. The new policy established an alliance with suitably cooperative nationalists in the late 1920s, conceded tariff autonomy to the Nationalist Government, and expanded in the 1930s to encompass monetary reform, links with the sterling bloc and joint ventures with Chinese entrepreneurs. The purpose of these innovations was first to ensure that China could service her existing foreign debts and then to create conditions which would encourage a flow of new finance. The result enhanced Britain's presence and influence in China, even though it also damaged her traditional staple exports, especially cotton goods. The success of the alliance with the Nationalist Government gave experienced observers considerable optimism about Britain's future in China. Confidence was undoubtedly shattered by the outbreak of war in 1937, but until then it was not, for once, misplaced. The conventional view that Britain was a declining power expending its remaining energies on managing a 'long retreat' is not one that now draws persuasive support from the historical record.

The story of Britain's continuing and reinvigorated ambitions in China also fits into the wider argument of this study, which suggests that imperialist rivalries extended beyond 1914 and assumed new forms, especially in the 1930s, when there was a struggle for the airwaves and airways of the world. Even before Japan's invasion of Manchuria, foreign competition in China had long been imperialist in the sense of seeking domination rather than parity and in justifying the claim by referring to the duties and burdens of the civilising mission, whether in the guise of the western skills needed to impart the gift of progress or in the shape of the untried benefits of Japan's new Asian order. Each foreign state claimed to be more advanced than its rivals; all agreed that they were superior to China. It was this conviction which justified, in the minds of the outside powers, their right to impose and dispose. In this respect, the language and the mentality of diplomacy were much the same in the 1930s as they had been in the 1890s. What was missing from these calculations was the Chinese perspective; and in China the guardians of the Confucian tradition, even in retreat, looked upon the barbarians with a certainty, unremarked in London or Tokyo, that they, like their predecessors, would be eventually be absorbed and in due course civilised.

Notes

1 The quotation is from a comment made by D.G.M. Barnard of Jardine, Matheson & Co in 1936 and cited in Jürgen Osterhammel, 'Imperialism in Transition: British Business and the Chinese Authorities, 1931–37', *China Quarterly*, 98 (1984), p. 260.

2 Studies which we have found particularly helpful are listed in n. 71. In addition, and from a different perspective, guidance is now available from *The Cambridge History of*

China: Republican China, 1912–1949, Vol. 12, ed. John K. Fairbank (Cambridge, 1983), and Vol. 13, ed. John K. Fairbank and Albert Feuerwerker (Cambridge, 1986).

3 See, for example, Marius Jansen, 'The 1911 Revolution and United States East Asian Policy', in Eto Shinkichi and Harold Z. Shiffrin, eds. *The 1911 Revolution in China* (Tokyo, 1983).

4 Nicholas R. Clifford, *Retreat from China: British Policy in the Far East, 1937–1941* (1967) traces this to the Anglo-Japanese alliance of 1902.

5 Christopher Thorne, *The Limits of Foreign Policy: The West, the League and the Far Eastern Crisis of 1931–1933* (1972), pp. 46–7.

6 For this perception (and others) see William Roger Louis, *British Strategy in the Far East, 1919–1939* (Oxford, 1971).

7 The quantitative evidence summarised here is derived mainly from: *Statistical Abstract for the United Kingdom, 1913 and 1924–1937* (1939); Hsiao Liang-lin, *China's Foreign Trade Statistics, 1864–1949* (Cambridge, Mass. 1974); Cheng Yu-Kwei, *Foreign Trade and Industrial Development of China* (Washington, DC, 1956); Hou Chi-ming, *Foreign Investment and Economic Development in China, 1840–1937* (Cambridge, Mass., 1965). Mention should also be made of the pioneering work of Carl Remer, *Foreign Investments in China* (New York, 1933). The *Statistical Abstract* gives f.o.b. values for British exports and c.i.f. values for imports. On the difficulties of interpreting the data see Rhoads Murphey, 'The Treaty Ports and China's Modernization', in Mark Elvin and G. William Skinner, eds. *The Chinese City Between Two Worlds* (Stanford, Calif., 1974), and Ramon H. Myers, 'The World Depression and the Chinese Economy, 1930–36', in Ian Brown, ed. *The Economies of Africa and Asia in the Inter-War Depression* (1989).

8 Important revisionist research is contained in Loren Brandt, 'Chinese Agriculture and the International Economy, 1870–1930s: a Reassessment', *Explorations in Economic History,* 22 (1985); idem, *Commercialization and Agricultural Development: Central and Eastern China, 1870–1937* (Cambridge, 1990); and Thomas G. Rawski, *Economic Growth in Prewar China* (Berkeley and Los Angeles, Calif., 1989).

9 Japan's occupation of Manchuria in 1931 appears to have had little effect on this trend since Britain's trade was concentrated on south and central China. On Manchuria see Ramon H. Myers, *The Japanese Economic Development of Manchuria, 1932–1945* (New York, 1982).

10 Stephen L. Endicott, *Diplomacy and Enterprise: British China Policy, 1933–1937* (Manchester, 1975), p. 22.

11 Hou, *Foreign Investment,* p. 17.

12 Hou, *Foreign Investment,* p. 17, though Britain still dominated the government loans business: ibid. p. 229. See also Arthur N. Young, *China's Nation-Building Effort, 1927–1937: The Financial and Economic Record* (Stanford, Calif., 1971), pp. 365–6, 372–6, and Jürgen Osterhammel, 'British Business in China, 1860s–1950s', in R.P.T. Davenport-Hines and Geoffrey Jones, eds. *British Business in Asia Since 1860* (Cambridge, 1989), pp. 201–2.

13 Hou, *Foreign Investment,* pp. 54, 226.

14 Ibid. pp. 80–1.

15 Ibid. pp. 60–1; Peter Duus, Ramon H. Myers and Mark R. Peattie, eds. *The Japanese Informal Empire in China, 1895–1937* (Princeton, NJ, 1989), pp. 3, 28–9.

16 The best entry into this subject is now via W.G. Beasley, *Japanese Imperialism, 1894–1945* (Oxford, 1987), and Duus, Myers and Peattie, *Japanese Informal Empire.* On the broader setting, see Akira Iriye, *Pacific Estrangement: Japanese and American Expansion, 1897–1911* (Cambridge, Mass., 1972), and idem, *After Imperialism: The Search for a New Order in the Far East, 1921–1931* (Cambridge, Mass., 1965).

17 James J. Lawrence, *Organized Business and the Myth of the China Market: The American Asiatic Association, 1897–1937* (Philadelphia, Pa, 1981); Ernest R. May and John K. Fairbank, eds. *America's China Trade in Historical Perspective* (Cambridge, Mass., 1986).

18 It is easy today to underestimate the extent of the alarm felt in Britain during the 1920s. As with the fear of Jacobinism in the 1790s, there was acute anxiety about the spread

of an alien ideology which was not only anti-monarchical and anti-Christ but which also travelled 'on the wind' and so could cross the Channel. The need to produce an antidote to Bolshevism added to the determination to restore capitalism to health after World War I.

19 This theme is noted below and references given in n. 88. The French attempt to match British finance was belated and unsuccessful. See Nobutaka Shinonaga, 'La formation de la Banque Industrielle de Chine', *Le mouvement social,* 155 (1991).

20 Victor Wellesley (1876–1954) was a godson of Queen Victoria and a descendant of the first Duke of Wellington.

21 Sir John Pratt (1876–1970) was educated at Dulwich and Middle Temple, and spent his early career in the Consular Service in China before being transferred to the Foreign Office in 1925. He retired in 1938 but was active thereafter as an expert on the Far East. He published a number of books, the most interesting of which in the present context is *War and Politics in China* (1943).

22 P.D. Coates, *The China Consuls: British Consular Officers, 1843–1943* (Oxford, 1988). On the expatriate communities generally, see Albert Feuerwerker, *The Foreign Establishment in China in the Early Twentieth Century* (Ann Arbor, Mich., 1976).

23 There is now a valuable biography by Roberta Allbert Dayer, *Finance and Empire: Sir Charles Addis, 1861–1945* (1988).

24 This political aspiration reflects the fact that capital flows over boundaries as well as being generated within them. To say that capital 'knows no frontiers' makes a point; but it also underplays the extent to which overseas investment was nourished by the nation state in the period under review.

25 Frank H.H. King, *The Hongkong Bank Between the Wars and the Bank Interned, 1919–1945: Return to Grandeur* (Cambridge, 1988), pp. 5, 263–4, 318–24; Sir Ralph Furse, *Aucuparius: Recollections of a Recruiting Officer* (1962). Also above, pp. 23–7 and 210.

26 Roberta Allbert Dayer, *Bankers and Diplomats in China, 1917–1925: The Anglo-American Relationship* (1981), pp. 161–3. Washington shared London's doubts: Brian T. George, 'The State Department and Sun Yat-sen: American Policy and the Revolutionary Disintegration of China, 1920–1924', *Pacific Hist. Rev.,* 46 (1977). Sun's view of imperialism and development seems unexceptional today: indeed, his programme had much in common with the policies adopted by Chiang in the 1930s. See A. James Gregor and Maria Hsia Chang, 'Marxism, Sun Yat-sen and the Concept of Imperialism', *Pacific Affairs,* 55 (1982).

27 Dayer, *Addis,* pp. 64–5; King, *Hongkong Bank,* pp. 453, 464, 482–96, 506–7.

28 Anthony B. Chan, 'The Consortium System in Republican China, 1912–1913', *Jour. Eur. Econ. Hist.,* 6 (1977), pp. 597–640.

29 Dayer, *Addis,* pp. 69–70; King, *Hongkong Bank,* p. 471. Until then, the Inspector General (Hart), though an expatriate, had managed the Imperial Maritime Customs as an employee of the Chinese government.

30 Dayer, *Addis,* pp. 70–1.

31 The traditional view of the war-lord era has been reappraised in recent years. See, for example, Jerome Ch'en, *The Military-Gentry Coalition: China under the Warlords* (Toronto, 1979); C. Martin Wilbur, *The Nationalist Revolution in China, 1923–1928* (Cambridge, 1983); and Marie-Claire Bergère, *L'Age d'or de la bourgeoisie chinoise, 1911–1937* (Paris, 1986).

32 Dayer, *Bankers and Diplomats,* pp. 39–42. See also Albert A. Altman and Harold Z. Shrifrin, 'Sun Yat-sen and the Japanese, 1914–16', *Mod. Asian Stud.,* 6 (1972).

33 Dayer, *Bankers and Diplomats,* pp. 44–8. On the general theme see Carl Parrini, *Heir to Empire: United States Economic Diplomacy, 1916–23* (Pittsburgh, Pa, 1969).

34 Quoted in Jerome Michael Israel, *Progressivism and the Open Door: America and China, 1905–1921* (Pittsburgh, Pa, 1971), p. 19.

35 Dayer, *Bankers and Diplomats,* pp. 43–9; Noel H. Pugach, 'Keeping an Idea Alive: the Establishment of a Sino-American Bank, 1910–1920', *Bus. Hist. Rev.,* 56 (1982); Joan Hoff Wilson, *American Business and Foreign Policy, 1920–1933* (1971), p. 201.

36 Clarence B. Davis, 'Limits of Effacement: Britain and the Problem of American Co-operation and Competition in China, 1915–1917', *Pacific. Hist. Rev.,* 48 (1979).
37 Dayer, *Bankers and Diplomats,* Ch. 3; King, *Hongkong Bank,* Ch. 10.
38 Dayer, *Finance and Empire,* pp. 85, 98–9, 115.
39 Addis, quoted in Dayer, *Finance and Empire,* p. 123.
40 Roberta Allbert Dayer, 'British War Debts to the United States and the Anglo-Japanese Alliance, 1920–1923', *Pacific Hist. Rev.,* 45 (1976); John Milton Cooper, 'The Command of Gold Reversed: American Loans to Britain, 1915–1917', *Pacific Hist. Rev.,* 45 (1976). As President Wilson observed in 1917: 'When the war is over we will be able to force them [Britain and France] to our way of thinking, because by that time they will, among other things, be financially in our hands'. Quoted in A.J. Mayer, *Political Origins of the New Diplomacy* (New Haven, Conn., 1958), p. 332.
41 The implications have been considered at length by diplomatic historians. On the strategic aspects see Paul Haggie, *Britannia at Bay: The Defence of the British Empire Against Japan, 1931–1941* (Oxford, 1981), and the saga of the Singapore base recounted by James Neidpath, *The Singapore Naval Base and the Defence of Britain's Eastern Empire, 1919–1941* (Oxford, 1981).
42 Quoted in Dayer, *Bankers and* Diplomats, p. 74.
43 Ibid. pp. 89–92, 240.
44 Roberta Allbert Dayer, 'Strange Bedfellows: J.P. Morgan & Co., Whitehall and the Wilson Administration During World War I', *Bus. Hist.,* 18 (1976).
45 Wilson, *American Business,* pp. 201–3, 209–14, 222–3, 230–1. On the reorientation of US banks towards Japan after 1926 see Dayer, *Bankers and Diplomats,* pp. 123, 173–4, 178–9, 238.
46 Marie-Claire Bergère, 'The Consequences of the Post First World War Depression for the China Treaty Port Economy, 1921–3', in Ian Brown, ed. *The Economies of Africa and Asia in the Inter-War Depression* (1989); King, *Hongkong Bank,* pp. 69, 98.
47 Anthony B. Chan, *Arming the Chinese: The Western Armament Trade in Warlord China, 1920–1928* (Vancouver, 1982).
48 Eugene Lubot, *Liberalism in an Illiberal Age: New Cultural Liberals in Republican China, 1919–1937* (Westport, Conn., 1982).
49 Dayer, *Bankers and Diplomats,* pp. 125, 188.
50 China had declared war on Germany in 1917 largely in the hope of regaining Shantung, which in the event was transferred to Japan. On the intellectual ferment of the time see Robert A. Scalapino, 'The Evolution of a Young Revolutionary – Mao Zedong in 1919–1921', *Jour. Asian Stud.,* 42 (1982).
51 Dayer, *Bankers and Diplomats,* pp. 163–5, 217. See also Jessie G. Lutz, *Chinese Politics and Christian Missions: The Anti-Christian Movements of 1920–28* (Notre Dame, N.H., 1988).
52 The most important sources analysing this decision are two unpublished, underused and hence underestimated doctoral theses: Peter G. Clark, 'Britain and the Chinese Revolution, 1925–1927', (Ph.D. thesis, University of California at Berkeley, 1973), and William James Megginson, 'Britain's Response to Chinese Nationalism, 1925–1927: the Foreign Office's Search for a New Policy' (Ph.D. thesis, George Washington University, 1973).
53 Dayer, *Finance and Empire,* pp. 257–9.
54 Ibid. pp. 116, 144–5, 205, 210, 234, 254.
55 See, in addition to Clarke, 'Britain and the Chinese Revolution', and Megginson, 'Britain's Response', Edmund S.K. Fung, 'The Sino-British Rapprochement, 1927–1931', *Mod. Asian Stud.,* 17 (1983), and idem, 'The Chinese Nationalists and the Unequal Treaties, 1924–1931', *Mod. Asian Stud.,* 21 (1987).
56 The last gunboat action on the China coast mounted by the British navy was in September 1926 – just three months before the Foreign Office decided to co-operate with the nationalist movement. See Clark, 'Britain and the Chinese Revolution', pp. 250–61.
57 Clark, 'Britain and the Chinese Revolution', pp. 136–7, 149–65, 183–9, 205, 305, 399–405, 490–1.

58 Dayer, *Bankers and Diplomats,* Ch. 7.
59 Clark, 'Britain and the Chinese Revolution', pp. 136–7, 183.
60 FO minute by Wellesley, 1 October 1926. Quoted in Megginson, 'Britain's Response', p. 402.
61 Dayer, *Finance and Empire,* pp. 138–9, 260–4; King, *Hongkong Bank,* pp. 94–5; Clark, 'Britain and the Chinese Revolution', pp. 403–4.
62 Dayer, *Finance and Empire,* pp. 138–9, 234, 260–4.
63 FO minute by Pratt, 13 July 1926. Quoted in Clark, 'Britain and the Chinese Revolution', p. 188.
64 FO minute by Strang, 16 November 1925. Quoted in Clark, 'Britain and the Chinese Revolution', p. 188. On the trading community see ibid. p. 60.
65 The summary which follows is a reconstruction of an extraordinarily complex and obscure episode in the financial diplomacy of the period. In addition to Clark, 'Britain and the Chinese Revolution', Dayer, *Finance and Empire,* and King, *Hongkong Bank,* there is a great deal of valuable information in Young, *China's Nation-Building.* Arthur Young visited China as a member of Kemmerer's team in 1929 and stayed on as an adviser to the government. He subsequently produced a number of valuable accounts of the period, which he looked back on as a scholar and as a participant.
66 The question of tariff revision had been placed on the agenda at the Washington Conference in 1922.
67 Dayer, *Finance and Empire,* pp. 264–5; Young, *China's Nation-Building,* pp. 19–20, 48–54, 72–3, 92–3, 110, 116–1; Fung, 'The Sino-British Rapprochement', pp. 95–6.
68 Arthur Redford, *Manchester Merchants and Foreign Trade,* Vol. II, *1850–1939* (Manchester, 1956), pp. 229–31. There was absolutely no wavering on this point: customs duties had to be used to secure loans and the tariff had to be raised to ensure that repayments were made. See Megginson, 'Britain's Response to Chinese Nationalism', Ch. 18.
69 Clark, 'Britain and the Chinese Revolution', Ch. 7; Megginson, 'Britain's Response to Chinese Nationalism', Ch. 22; Dayer, *Finance and Empire,* pp. 269–72; Young, *China's Nation-Building,* p. 154; Osterhammel, 'Imperialism in Transition', p. 263.
70 The phrases are those of Victor Wellesley: see above, n. 59.
71 The considerable literature on the diplomatic history of this period can be approached through: Bradford A. Lee, *Britain and the Sino-Japanese War, 1937–1939* (1973); Peter Lowe, *Great Britain and the Origins of the Pacific War: A Study of British Policy in East Asia, 1937–1941* (Oxford, 1977); Aron Shai, *Origins of the War in the East: Britain, China and Japan, 1937–39* (1976); Christopher Thorne, *The Limits of Foreign Policy: The West, the League and the Far Eastern Crisis of 1931–1933* (1972); and Ann Trotter, *Britain and East Asia, 1933–1937* (Cambridge, 1975).
72 Young, *China's Nation-Building,* pp. 142–6, 177–83; Loren Brandt and Thomas J. Sargent, 'Interpreting New Evidence about China and U.S. Silver Purchases', *Hoover Institute Working Papers,* No. E-87–3 (Stanford, Calif., 1987), p. 23.
73 Kemmerer and Addis have been referred to earlier: see Drake, *Money Doctor in the Andes,* and Dayer, *Finance and Empire.* Arthur Salter (1881–1975) had been Director of the Economic and Finance Section of the League of Nations in the 1920s. His *Memoirs of a Public Servant* (1961) contain a chapter on his mission to China from 1931 to 1933. T.V. Soong (1894–1971) played a key role in linking the Shanghai business world to the Nationalist Government and in introducing Chinese banks to modern banking practices. Soong came from a wealthy Christian family, and his own talents were complemented by those of his sisters: one married Sun Yat-sen; the other Chiang Kai-shek. These advantages became handicaps in 1949, and Soong took refuge in the United States after the revolution.
74 Dayer, *Finance and Empire,* pp. 284–7, 292–5; King, *Hongkong Bank,* pp. 385–6.
75 Stephen L. Endicott, *Diplomacy and Enterprise,* pp. 42–3; Cheng, *Foreign Trade,* pp. 54, 59, 67; Osterhammel, 'British Business', p. 203. On metal goods see R.P.T. Davenport-Hines, 'The British Engineers' Association and Markets in China, 1900–1930', in idem, *Markets and Bagmen: Studies in the History of Marketing and British Industrial Performance, 1830–1939* (1986).

76 See, on this subject, Dayer, *Finance and Empire,* Ch. 11; Endicott, *Diplomacy and Enterprise,* Chs. 4–6; King, *Hongkong Bank,* Ch. 8; Young, *China's Nation-Building,* Chs. 9–10.
77 The established view of the causes of the silver crisis has been challenged by Brandt and Sargent, 'Interpreting New Evidence'.
78 Stephen L. Endicott, 'British Financial Diplomacy in China: the Leith-Ross Mission, 1935–1937', *Pac. Aff.,* 46 (1973/4). Leith-Ross (1887–1968) was Chief Economic Adviser to the British Government, 1932–46. His own account of the mission appears in Ch. 15 of his memoirs: *Money Talks: 50 Years of International Finance* (1968).
79 Dayer, *Finance and Empire,* pp. 278, 282–93; King, *Hongkong Bank,* p. 399.
80 King, *Hongkong Bank,* pp. 412–17, 442.
81 Addis, diary entry, 14 January 1937. Quoted in Dayer, *Finance and Empire,* p. 301.
82 Rawski, *Economic Growth,* pp. 171–8; Brandt and Sargent, 'Interpreting New Evidence'; Myers, 'The World Depression'.
83 Thanks largely to the authoritative work of Jürgen Osterhammel, *Britischer Imperialismus in Fernen Osten: Strukturen der Durchdringung und einheimischer Widerstand auf dem chinesischen Markt, 1932–1937* (Bochum, 1982). See also Osterhammel's important general studies, 'Imperialism in Transition' and 'British Business in China'. Osterhammel's work complements that of Endicott, *Diplomacy and Enterprise,* which is concerned more with the policy implications of economic change.
84 Extraterritorial rights were not to be given up lightly, but they had become a card to be played at the appropriate moment rather than a privilege to be defended at all costs. On their final surrender in 1943 see K.C. Chan, 'The Abrogation of British Extraterritorial Rights in China, 1942–43: a Study of Anglo-American-Chinese Relations', *Mod. Asian. Stud.,* 11 (1977).
85 The relationship between Chiang and China's modernising capitalists is a complex issue which in turn opens up the wider question of the connection between economic development and political representation. See Bergère, *L'Age d'or de la bourgeoisie chinoise*; Parks M. Coble, *The Shanghai Capitalists and the Nationalist Government, 1927–1937* (Cambridge, Mass., 1980); and Richard C. Bush, *The Politics of Cotton Textiles in Kuomintang China, 1927–1937* (New York, 1982).
86 Quoted in Osterhammel, 'Imperialism in Transition', pp. 260–1.
87 Knatchbull-Hugessen, the British Ambassador, to Cadogan, 3 March 1937. Quoted in Dayer, *Finance and Empire,* p. 301.
88 See Bernd Martin, ed. *Die deutsch Beraterschaft in China, 1927–1938* (Düsseldorf, 1981); John P. Fox, *Germany and the Far Eastern Crisis, 1931–1938* (Oxford, 1982); and William C. Kirby, *Germany and Republican China* (Stanford, Calif., 1984). These developments paralleled those in South America. See above, pp. 151–2.
89 Beasley, *Japanese Imperialism,* Ch. 10; Duus, Myers and Peattie, *Japanese Informal Empire*; Akira Iriye, *The Origins of the Second World War in Asia and the Pacific* (1987).
90 The shifts in political power in Japan at this time are dealt with by Kyozo Sato, 'Japan's Position Before the Outbreak of the European War in September 1939', *Mod. Asian Stud.,* 14 (1980). On the limited political influence of Japanese business see William Miles Fletcher, *The Japanese Business Community and National Trade Policy, 1920–1942* (Chapel Hill, N.C., 1989).
91 As Fox has shown, the Pact subordinated Germany's economic interests in China to Nazi ideological priorities favouring Japan: see Fox, *Germany and the Far Eastern Crisis.*
92 This dilemma has been thoroughly explored by Lowe, *Great Britain and the Origins of the Pacific War*; Trotter, *Britain and East Asia*; and Shai, *Origins of the War in the East.*
93 Endicott, *Diplomacy and Enterprise,* pp. 28–9; Trotter, *Britain and East Asia,* pp. 27–8, 115, 125–6, 129.
94 Endicott, *Diplomacy and Enterprise,* pp. 28–34; Trotter, *Britain and East Asia,* pp. 6–10.
95 Endicott, *Diplomacy and Enterprise,* p. 73; Trotter, *Britain and East Asia,* pp. 40–2, 88–92, 212–13.
96 Endicott, *Diplomacy and Enterprise,* 98–9, 150; Trotter, *Britain and East Asia,* pp. 115, 125–6, 131, 142–60. See also S. Olu Agbi, 'The Foreign Office and Yoshida's Bid for Rapprochement with Britain in 1936–1937', *Hist. Jour.* 21 (1978).

97 As did the Tientsin crisis in 1939. See Aron Shai, 'Le conflit Anglo-Japonais de Tientsin en 1939', *Revue d'histoire moderne et contemporaine,* 22 (1975).
98 Endicott, *Diplomacy and Enterprise,* pp. 30–4, 87–97, 173–85.
99 Trotter, *Britain and East Asia,* pp. 204, 217.
100 Ian M. Drummond, *British Economic Policy and the Empire, 1919–1939* (1972), pp. 27–40.
101 Trotter, *Britain and East Asia,* pp. 16–17, 29–32. Case studies include: D.C.S. Sissons, 'Manchester v Japan: the Imperial Background to the Australian Trade Diversion Dispute with Japan, 1936', *Australian Outlook,* 30 (1976); Yuen Choy Leng, 'Japanese Rubber and Iron Investments in Malaya, 1900–41', *Jour. South-East Asian Stud.*, 5 (1974); and Nicholas Tarling, '"A Vital British Interest": Britain, Japan, and the Security of the Netherlands Indies during the Inter-War Period', *Jour. South-East Asian Stud.*, 9 (1978).

102 Dayer, *Finance and Empire,* pp. 239–40.
103 Ibid, p. 305; King, *Hongkong Bank,* pp. 423–4; Lee, *Britain and the Sino-Japanese War,* p. 211.
104 Dayer, *Finance and Empire,* pp. 303–5; Chan, 'Abrogation of British Extraterritoriality', pp. 262–3; Michael Schaller, *The United States and China in the Twentieth Century* (Oxford, 1980), pp. 48–53.
105 Chan, 'Abrogation of British Extraterritoriality', pp. 263–5.
106 Cheng, *Foreign Trade,* p. 180.
107 On these issues see: Christopher Thorne, *Allies of a Kind: The United States, Britain and the War Against Japan, 1941–1945* (Oxford, 1978); Shai, *Britain and China*; and Osterhammel, 'British Business', pp. 212–13.
108 Shai, *Britain and China,* pp. 151–2.
109 T.N. Thompson, *China's Nationalisation of Foreign Firms: The Politics of Hostage Capitalism, 1949–1957* (Baltimore, Md, 1979); B. Hooper, *China Stands Up: Ending the Western Presence, 1948–1950* (Sydney, 1986); Aron Shai, 'Britain, China and the End of Empire', *Jour. Contemp. Hist.*, 15 (1980), pp. 287–97; and idem, 'Imperialism Imprisoned: the Closure of British Firms in the People's Republic of China', *Eng. Hist. Rev.*, 104 (1989).
110 Wellesley, *Diplomacy in Fetters,* p. 119.

PART EIGHT

Losing an empire and finding a role, 1939–2000

26

THE CITY, THE STERLING AREA AND DECOLONISATION

The last fifty years have seen profound changes in Britain's economy and society as well as her role in the world. Winning the war and losing the empire are the most immediately striking developments in the period; but adjusting to peacetime conditions and recoupling Britain with continental Europe are themes which are no less significant for being protracted and, in some respects, still incomplete. The mountain of commentary produced by these events ideally requires an evaluation of matching size. However, the main purpose of the present study is to explain the expansion of empire not its demise; consequently, the events of the post-war era, though a fascinating and important extension of our story, are not central to its main argument. At the same time, we recognise that the interpretation we have put forward carries implications for understanding the course of recent British history, and hence has a direct bearing on the analysis of contemporary issues. To avoid these matters entirely would be an unnecessary and perhaps a misleading act of discretion because, as we shall suggest, the gentlemanly interests which sustained the empire down to World War II also managed and to some extent planned its demise thereafter. Exactly why the relationship changed is a complex matter which we shall approach from the particular standpoint adopted in this study, though in summary fashion. As with the historical prologue surveying the eighteenth century, our object at this point is less to prove a thesis than to suggest how it might be constructed.

The essence of our argument is that a central preoccupation of British policy, even during the war and still more prominently thereafter, was the preservation of sterling's role in financing international trade and investment, and with it the maintenance of the earning power of the City of London. Between 1940, when the Sterling Area acquired formal status, and 1958, when full convertibility was restored, the pound was nursed within a framework of controls in which the empire, especially its dependent, colonial segment, had a starring if also involuntary role. The restoration of convertibility in the late 1950s then opened a second phase which relaunched sterling on what, in the event, turned out to be the final episode in its long career as an international currency of note. By the late 1950s policy-makers calculated that the City, and invisible earnings generally, had more to gain from emerging opportunities in the wider world than from remaining penned in the Sterling Area. As the value of the imperial component of the Sterling Area diminished, so did the economic obstacles to decolonisation. Indeed, by moving with the nationalist tide, Britain hoped to benefit from informal ties with the Commonwealth while simultaneously promoting sterling's wider, cosmopolitan role. This long-planned but short-lived venture ended with a series of sterling crises which culminated in the devaluation of 1967. By then, decolonisation was virtually complete and informal influence had faded.

The survival of the gentlemanly order

One of the fruits of victory in 1945 was the survival of Britain's cultural and institutional heritage. Heading the list of survivors were gentlemanly capitalists who, like the empire they controlled, were saved from liquidation in 1940 by American aid and then given a new role as junior partners in the American-dominated world after 1945. The complex of economic and social institutions and mores which supported the gentlemanly order also emerged intact from the conflict. The pace of economic change in Britain after 1945 was more rapid than hitherto but it often ran along familiar grooves, as the continued predominance of the service sector and of the south-east region indicates.[1] In these circumstances it is not surprising to find that changes in the structure of the British elite were evolutionary rather than dramatic. Corporations became more important than individuals in the processes of wealth-creation after 1945 and economic growth introduced many new ways of accumulating riches; but it is remarkable how much wealth was still concentrated in traditional areas, such as landownership and commercial and financial businesses, and also how dominant London, and in particular the City, remained in terms of economic power.[2] Continuities among service elites were equally marked: as the public sector grew and educational opportunities were widened, recruitment into the professions increased dramatically and selection became more a matter of merit and expert training; but it was still the case that 'top people' continued to come mainly from the service sector itself, particularly in the south-east of England, and were processed by the public schools and Oxbridge.[3] The dominance of Eton might not have been quite so obvious as before the war, but even as late as 1983 70 per cent of Conservative Members of Parliament were former public schoolboys.[4] The administrative arm of government remained similarly in the grip of tradition. The observation, made in 1926, that 'the English gentleman represents a specific and clearly marked type of humanity', could still be made of the generation which survived the war and managed the peace; while the claim that the gentleman was also 'an unrivalled primary teacher of peoples' remained plausible, too, as a self-description of those who set the timetable for decolonisation after the war.[5]

In the 1950s the City's place within these structures was little different from what it had been in the 1930s. The ties between City elites, the Bank of England, the political world and the wider 'establishment' were extremely close, as the Bank Rate tribunal of 1957 plainly revealed.[6] In the 1960s and 1970s, however, there arose a much more unified business elite than had existed before, and it has been argued that the dominance of finance in the old sense could no longer be expected in Britain since the fraction of capital represented by the City was merged with industry to the extent that the City became only one among a complex set of forces which determined the configuration of the economy and the outcome of policy. This conclusion may be misleading, even though the evidence does suggest that the economic elite became increasingly integrated after 1945.

Our own interpretation of the City's evolution is that financial markets fell steadily under the influence of big institutional investors such as insurance companies, pension funds and unit trusts. At the same time, these institutions became much more involved in raising finance for large-scale industry than was the case before the war, and in the processes of take-over and merger which became a far more important element in City life than hitherto. In practice, business as a whole, including manufacturing, came under the control of a relatively small group of financial managers who formed, via an intricate web of interlocking directorships, the chief decision-making body in the private economy by the 1970s. At the heart of this group were the gentlemanly directors of the clearing banks and merchant banks who were key intermediaries in the system because of the wide range of important directorships they held.[7] This commanding group was closely tied, through kinship and social connection, with the service-elites and the wider gentlemanly establishment; these links were reinforced over the years by the tendency of finance to call upon other professional skills such as law and accountancy, as business became a more bureaucratic and specialised matter.[8] So, although the channels of recruitment to top business positions, including those in the City, widened considerably and finance became steadily more professionalised,[9] the high-status connections of the principal participants in the world of British big business remained strong.

There is a very real sense in which the industrial sector in Britain was incorporated after 1945 into a structure dominated by traditional financial institutions and forced into conformity to their practices. One instance of this was the extent to which the emergence of the large firm through mergers and take-overs was shaped by the attractions of short-term financial gain rather than by a felt need for greater efficiency and more assured long-term profitability.[10] Another example was the reluctance of the major banks to follow the path taken by their counterparts in Germany and Japan and to lend to industry on a long-term basis, a reluctance which stemmed from the almost obsessive desire of the banks to stay liquid in the face of exacting demands from the Bank of England and the financial markets, set with international financial criteria in mind.[11] It is also worth noting in this context that banking profits were much higher in Britain than in countries where finance and industry were more closely allied.[12]

International economic policy, 1939–55

These continuities in elite formation and practice in the private sector were paralleled in the sphere of public policy although, as we have seen, the outbreak of war appeared to threaten the continuance of gentlemanly wealth and life-styles. After the fall of France, it became obvious that the national interest now had to be defined in terms of the full employment of all available productive resources and that traditional financial orthodoxy would have to be set aside, at least for the duration of the war. Keynesian budgetary techniques were in use as early as 1940 and the shift in priorities encouraged an alliance between government, industry and trades unions and depressed the influence of the financial authorities in the domestic arena. The creation, over the next few years, of a war economy also helped to convince the electorate that, when peace arrived, governments could act as a positive force in the economy and that profits for private industry were compatible with commitments to full employment and a welfare state. The Labour government of 1945 was the fruit of this conviction.[13] Nonetheless, despite the high profile of the producers in wartime and during the period of reconstruction which followed, the conduct of international economic policy remained the preserve of the gentlemanly elite. They were only reluctant converts to the Keynes-Beveridge policy consensus which began to emerge in these years. Although the crises of the time often revealed strong differences of opinion among the traditional authorities over tactics, there was little dispute over the main post-war objective of policy in this arena – a continued world role for sterling and for the City.

It was the gentlemen in Whitehall who were left to deal with the distasteful consequences of burgeoning American financial supremacy after 1940.[14] American aid was given on onerous terms. In 1942 Britain reluctantly agreed to consider abandoning trade discrimination after the war, though this would jeopardise the Ottawa system; British capital assets abroad often had to be sold, sometimes at ruinous prices, before aid was given and export capacity had to be run down, preventing the accumulation of reserves and forcing Britain to incur huge debts with Sterling Area countries. These sterling balances were, by 1945, equivalent to seven times the value of Britain's gold and dollar reserves.[15] Sterling had to be made inconvertible in 1939, when the loosely structured sterling bloc of the 1930s became the rigorously controlled Sterling Area of wartime emergency in which all dollar and gold earnings were pooled and rationed.[16] Convertibility had been vital to sterling's international position in its heyday and was maintained even in the crisis of the 1930s; but the huge overhang of sterling indebtedness meant that any return to convertibility in the immediate post-war period without American assistance would have led to an unsustainable drain on the gold and dollar reserves. American aid ceased abruptly at the end of the war;[17] the Bank of England felt that the best strategy for the immediate future was to reinforce the Sterling Area by attracting European adherents who might be tempted to join a defensive financial and trading alliance against the dollar.[18] For, although the sterling balances were burdensome liabilities, they also served, as we shall see, to emphasise the importance of both formal and informal overseas connections and of the need to maintain them in peacetime.

The principal opponent of this approach was Keynes, who had the tentative support of the Treasury. Keynes was well aware of the importance of both the empire and the Sterling Area, but believed that it was in Britain's interest to go along with American demands for rapid progress towards multilateralism at the end of hostilities. He did not expect that a tightly enclosed Sterling Area would be capable of maintaining Britain's income at levels compatible, in the long term, with the ambitious full employment and welfare schemes all British governments were now committed to introduce. Keynes also feared that, faced with a protective bloc organised around an inconvertible currency, the United States would use its trading power and 'dollar diplomacy' to lure away some of the Sterling Area's leading members. More positively, Keynes shared the gentlemanly assumption that the recovery of the City was of the 'greatest possible importance' to the nation and he was convinced that Britain's invisible trade would recover former glories only in a multilateral environment.[19]

His proposals for a new world monetary order, presented at the Bretton Woods conference in 1942,[20] were a daring attempt both to solve Britain's impending exchange crisis without disastrous deflation and to maintain an international role for sterling. A new currency, bancor, was to be created to replace gold as the basis of the world monetary system and to allow an extension of credit which would ensure a rapid revival of international trade financed, it was hoped, by the City after the war.[21] But even when the Americans killed the Keynes Plan and substituted a modified gold standard with only meagre credits available for a dollar-starved world, Keynes still argued that it was important to follow where the United States led. He expected that the post-war dollar crisis would be short lived as Europe quickly recovered its export capacity, and that the Sterling Area would soon be able to return to convertibility.[22] The upshot was the Anglo-American agreement of 1945, which traded a British promise of a return to convertibility in 1947 against a substantial dollar loan.[23] However, exports to the United States recovered only slowly, while reconstruction needs pushed up the demand for dollar imports substantially in 1947 with the result that the convertibility experiment lasted a mere three weeks.[24]

Britain's dependence on her empire had increased markedly in wartime and, as we shall see, the empire had an important part to play in plans for post-war reconstruction and in providing Britain with dollars. But the drive towards empire development could not, at first, be squared easily with support for the new world order promoted by the United States. Although American hostility to the preferential system and the Sterling Area began to diminish at the end of the war, in the immediate post-war period British advocates of a rapid return to multilateralism and convertibility were often seen as the enemies of empire or as unwitting collaborators in an American drive for world economic domination.[25] However, with the onset of the Cold War, American attitudes to colonialism softened. The British empire finally ceased to be an obstacle on the road to progress and became instead a bulwark against the Communist menace. Multilateralism remained the primary goal, but it was now recognised in Washington that reaching it would be a slow process that required massive American aid to Europe. As a result of this shift in priorities during 1947, it became easier for Britain to pursue an imperial policy in the style of Joseph Chamberlain,[26] while at the same time accepting that a return to convertibility was a desirable aim in the longer term.

Convertibility proved difficult to achieve. Despite Marshall Aid, which paid for a considerable portion of Britain's dollar imports between 1948 and 1952,[27] there were further balance of payments crises in 1949, which precipitated a large devaluation of sterling,[28] and in 1951–2, when the Korean War led to a sharp rise in import prices. The Korean crisis led to a significant change in the emphasis of policy. In 1951, with Marshall Aid nearing its end, both the Treasury and the Bank of England came to the conclusion that the dollar shortage would soon reappear; taking advantage of the arrival of a Conservative government pledged to restore greater market freedoms and ideologically more amenable to gentlemanly persuasion than its predecessors, they argued that the problem should now be approached by moving quickly towards convertibility rather than by relying on a restrictive form of imperialism. In the ROBOT scheme of 1951–2 the Treasury, with the support of the Bank, proposed a 1930s-style floating, convertible pound with the proviso that sterling balances would have to be blocked to avoid a repetition of the 1947 crisis.[29] The plan was scuppered eventually because it might have threatened the full employment policy to which the government was committed for good electoral reasons, but it was only the first of a number of schemes in the early 1950s designed to speed Britain's return to convertibility. All of them would have involved raising trade barriers against other European states since countries with non-convertible currencies would otherwise have directed their exports to Britain in order to gain dollars. This would have had severe repercussions upon the growth of world trade and harmed British commodity exports. But the authorities, with their eyes on the invisible account and intent upon restoring sterling to its rightful position in the world, apparently felt that the price was worth paying. Without convertibility, it was feared that sterling would soon fall irretrievably behind the dollar as an international currency; with it, there was a good chance that London would at least become the world centre for non-dollar trade, with large parts of Europe included in an expanded Sterling Area.[30]

The Korean War crisis soon evaporated. Balance of payments surpluses reappeared from 1952 and, despite the ending of Marshall Aid, the European dollar problem was eased by rising exports in a growing world economy and by the flow of American private investment. By the middle of the decade it was possible to convince wary politicians that convertibility was compatible with commitments to welfare and full employment; it was gradually introduced, at fixed rates, between 1955 and 1958.[31]

As in 1918–25, international economic policy was largely decided by gentlemen who clearly believed that re-establishing sterling internationally was more important than worrying about the fate of commodity exports or even the future of the empire both of which, it was assumed, would fall into place if the prior financial problem was solved. Indeed, there was even less opposition to the policy in the 1950s than there was to the return to gold in 1925, principally because, in marked contrast to the 1920s, rapid growth after World War II applied a powerful anaesthetic to criticism.

The empire in war and reconstruction

The war to defeat the Axis powers was also fought to defend, and even to extend, the British empire. As far as imperial policy was concerned, the immediate effect of hostilities was to strengthen links between Britain and the empire and to centralise decisions upon London, both to coordinate defence and to mobilise strategic resources. As the sterling bloc took formal shape as the Sterling Area in 1940, colonial trade was brought under the control of new government organisations and tightly regulated. Vital imports from the colonies were subjected to compulsory purchase; manufactured exports were strictly rationed.[32] Since Britain was unable to meet the cost of essential imports and overseas defence expenditures, suppliers in the Sterling Area (and certain associated countries) accumulated credits, or sterling balances, which were held in London.[33] These balances, which were essentially loans to Britain volunteered by creditors who had virtually no choice in the matter, were crucial to the war effort.

It is now clear that the cost of the war, mountainous though it was, did not crush Britain's belief in her role as a world power at the head of a great empire.[34] It is true, of course, that some parts of the empire had been overrun, and that others, notably India, had experienced widespread civil unrest. But, as recent research has shown, even at the darkest moment – after the fall of Singapore in 1942 – plans were being laid to recapture the occupied parts of the empire and to rejuvenate the imperial mission.[35] As seen from Whitehall, the question was not whether the British empire had a future but how and when it was to be realised. By 1945 Britain had regained Burma, had argued her way back into Hong Kong, Singapore and Malaya, had taken control of Italy's colonies in Africa and had extended her grip on Egypt.[36] Even the occupation of Germany was viewed from London as being an exercise in colonial administration that required expertise from India. Nor were areas of informal influence written off, despite experiencing a sharp fall in British trade and investment during the war. Britain still aimed to develop the promising position she had held in China before the Japanese invasion in 1937, to keep her special place in Argentina (despite hostility from the United States), and to enlarge her influence in key areas in the Middle East.[37]

The fact that the empire had proved its value during the war undoubtedly lent weight to traditionalists, such as Churchill, whose instruction to Eden at the close of 1944 left no room for misunderstanding: 'hands off the British empire is our maxim and it must not be weakened or smirched to please sob-stuff merchants at home or foreigners of any hue'.[38] But the renewed commitment to empire was as much a matter of calculation as it was of sentiment. Quite simply, the imperial option appeared to be far more promising than the alternatives, especially in war-torn

Europe. Among those who looked forward, rather than back, it was agreed that reform was essential if the empire was to be retained. By the close of the war, the Colonial Office had devised a development programme for the dependent empire: the Colonial Development and Welfare Act was renewed and enlarged, and agreement reached on replacing the hallowed but also creaking Lugardian system of indirect rule by an administrative structure staffed by a new generation of educated colonial subjects.[39] Moreover, this programme commanded bipartisan agreement. Once elected, the Labour Party hoisted the burdens of empire with all the enthusiasm of the converted, despite its long-proclaimed opposition to imperialism.[40] In seeing the light, Bevin, the Foreign Secretary, also saw the way: 'our crime', he observed of the empire, 'is not exploitation; it's neglect'.[41] There followed what has been termed the 'second colonial occupation', which was characterised by an intensive effort to press ahead with development and reform.[42] The array of wartime controls was adapted to the needs of peace, instead of being scrapped, the direction of imperial economic policy remained firmly in London, and the Colonial Office duly increased its size and strengthened its links with other ministries in Whitehall.[43] The result, in the most general terms, was to revitalise the imperial mission by giving it a new sense of purpose.[44]

The explanation of this transformation in colonial policy is both complex and, as yet, incomplete. The momentum for change had already begun to build up during the 1930s, as we have seen,[45] but the need to conciliate the United States caused the pace to quicken during the war. The story of how the United States shifted from overt anti-colonialism to tacit support for the more viable of the European empires has now been told in some detail.[46] In essence, the turning point came towards the close of the war, when fear of communism replaced fear of fascism and Washington was persuaded, by a mixture of self-induced anxiety and skilful British diplomacy, that a friendly empire spanning the globe would be a useful ally in containing the threat to what was becoming known as the Free World. Effectively, a compromise was reached: the United States agreed not to press for immediate decolonisation; in return, Britain undertook to modernise her empire.[47]

The onset of the Cold War confirmed this understanding. Following the acute sterling crisis in 1947, the United States realised that Britain needed to be buttressed if she was to stand firm as an ally in Western Europe. This perception implied that the Sterling Area had to be maintained and that the empire had to be encouraged to play its part in the recovery of the British economy by supplying essential raw materials and by earning much-needed dollars. This meant, in turn, that imperial preference, long an irritant in Washington, had to be left in place, at least in the short term.[48] Stafford Cripps, speaking for the Treasury in 1947, was therefore able to proclaim a doctrine of imperial complementarity which appeared to meet the needs of wider interests: 'the further development of African resources', he declared, 'is of the same crucial importance to the mobilisation and strengthening of Western Europe as the restoration of European productive powers is to the future progress and prosperity of Africa'.[49] President Truman nodded, and so too, one imagines, did Joseph Chamberlain. Suitably framed and implemented, Labour's new deal for the colonies also held out the prospect of satisfying the reformist, Fabian element in the party (and in Whitehall) and, with luck, of enabling Britain to keep pace with growing nationalist demands in the colonies.[50] Liquidation was not on the agenda: the empire was to be given a shot in the arm rather than in the head.

Calculations of advantage were based primarily upon a heightened awareness of the economic worth of empire during the period of post-war reconstruction. Of course, the empire itself was far from uniform, and the value attached to the component parts varied according to their ability to meet the needs of the metropole. The dominions could not be organised for peace as, by negotiation, they had been mobilised for war, though self-interest kept them within the Sterling Area.[51] India could no longer be controlled, despite Churchill's endeavours, and was granted independence in 1947 with a degree of haste which Mountbatten was charged to disguise as forethought. But this event, for all its significance in the history of Anglo-Indian relations, did not bring down the rest of the British empire; and its economic implications, as we have seen, were less important than might be supposed.[52] After 1945, India ceased to be vital to Britain's pressing needs, being neither a source of essential supplies nor a net contributor to the dollar pool.[53]

The displacement of India gave prominence to other, formerly less significant parts of the empire. Far from being abandoned after 1947, the empire was repositioned in Africa, Malaya, and, informally, in the Middle East.[54] These regions were sources of vital supplies; they contributed to the hard currency pool through their dollar earnings; and they were all directly or indirectly under British control. They also held sizeable sterling balances which could be manipulated more freely than was possible elsewhere. Britain's new colonial policy needs to be interpreted with these priorities in mind. The Colonial Development and Welfare Act of 1945, like the Colombo Plan of 1951, served not only to fund overseas development projects but also to manage expenditures drawn from the balances.[55] By retaining the balances of dependent territories at high levels, Britain controlled the amount available for their development plans while ensuring that they contributed to the reserves held in London and hence to support for the pound. By forming the Colonial Development Corporation in 1947, Britain hoped to promote the production of food and other raw materials urgently needed at home.[56] By then purchasing colonial exports through official marketing boards, Britain shifted part of her burdens as a debtor to satellites that were her creditors, and hence made the austerity suffered at home somewhat less severe than it would otherwise have been.[57]

None of these measures could have been imposed without London's political authority; it is no coincidence that the regions of greatest economic value in the period of reconstruction were also those where Britain's determination to perpetuate her control was particularly marked.[58] This was especially the case where Britain's presence was associated with white enterprise and capital, typically in mines and estates. In Malaya and Kenya, coercion tended to be the first resort of policy. The bogey of communism was invoked, where it was not already present, and this sufficed in the early stages of the Cold War to legitimise the use of force. Confrontation also occurred in colonies where production depended directly on the cooperation of a multiplicity of indigenous entrepreneurs, as in the Gold Coast in 1948. But in these areas confrontation was followed more readily by accommodation. Nationalists were designated 'agitators' rather than 'terrorists', and constitutional reforms were set in train with the aim of turning opponents into partners.[59] In the Middle East, which lay outside the empire, a combination of techniques was used: the region was strongly fortified, but the aim was to economise on defence costs by raising up a generation of like-minded leaders who would maintain political stability and keep the oil wells flowing.[60]

This neo-mercantilist system served its short-term purpose. Britain's ties with the overseas Sterling Area were greatly strengthened in the decade after 1945, and sterling itself remained a formidable force in world trade, accounting for about half of all international transactions at the close of the 1940s.[61] Devaluation in 1949, though not the first choice of policy, gave a fillip to exports. By then, too, the commodity boom was under way, propelled first by Europe's reconstruction needs, next by Marshall Aid, and finally by the Korean War. These developments eventually boosted the earnings of the Sterling Area and helped to close the dollar gap.[62] Britain's balance of payments remained fragile rather than robust, but by the mid-1950s policy-makers were ready to move towards convertibility on the assumption that sterling could extend its operations beyond its immediate post-war confines in competition with the dollar. As we shall see, this step entailed a reappraisal of the role of the empire and ultimately of the Sterling Area in the international order.

The Sterling Area: the final phase, 1955–72

When Britain decided to return to convertibility in the late 1950s it was assumed that the Sterling Area would provide the solid base from which the pound could launch itself into the wider world. But the decisions were also taken in the light of the fact that the Sterling Area was now shrinking in relative importance and that Britain's links with many of its members were weakening.[63] By the mid-1950s it was becoming evident that the most dynamic centres of growth were Western Europe and Japan and that trade between the great industrial powers themselves was now the crucial element driving world trade forwards. In the late 1940s Britain conducted about half of her foreign trade with the Commonwealth and with other members of the Sterling Area, and about one-quarter with Western Europe; by the early 1970s this position had been reversed.[64] This trend was already apparent in the 1950s, though it accelerated in the following decade. In fact, Britain's own trade with Western Europe increased so rapidly that by 1961 she felt obliged to apply for membership of the EEC, though she was not accepted into the fold until twelve years later. Moreover, despite the fact that the rate of growth of Britain's economy was high when judged by her own past record, it was low in comparison with that achieved in most other advanced countries,[65] with the result that countries once dependent on Britain in trade were pulled into the orbit of more dynamic economies. One typical outcome of these sea-changes in the world economy and Britain's relations with it was the rapid erosion of her trading links with the white

Dominions. In 1948 the four Dominions accounted for 25 per cent of British trade; by 1963 this had declined to 17 per cent. The process was particularly marked in the case of Australia. She had taken half her imports from the mother country in 1948–9 and exported 40 per cent of her own produce to Britain; by 1963–4 the figures were 28 per cent and 18 per cent respectively and Japan was on the brink of becoming Australia's chief trading partner.[66] If sterling was to have a secure future, it had to be found outside the traditional area of sterling dominance.

But, while the base was crumbling, Britain also found it difficult to establish sterling's credibility elsewhere. Widespread use of sterling depended on international confidence, which was constantly being undermined by balance of payments crises caused ultimately by Britain's relatively slow growth, poor export performance and increasing vulnerability to the penetration of manufactured imports. Governments found it impossible to maintain policies of full employment without inducing a level of imports which deranged the balance of payments; once a deficit showed itself, holders of sterling would precipitate a crisis by selling pounds for fear that the authorities would try to solve the problem by devaluation, as they had done in 1949.[67] Balance of payments difficulties were accentuated by policy. In the 1950s and early 1960s governments spent large amounts – equivalent at their peak to about 10 per cent of the value of exports – on defence abroad. Some of this expenditure was caused by lingering imperial obligations and emergencies, but it also reflected continuing gentlemanly fantasies about great-power status.[68] Ironically, sterling's problems were compounded by the resumption of the City's role as provider of investment funds for the empire. This was sometimes necessary to ensure that the more independent members remained loyal to sterling, but if heavy foreign investment brought in a useful income from abroad it also led to a sizeable outflow of funds at times when sterling was weak and aggravated crises by adding to drains on Britain's reserves of gold and dollars.[69]

When faced with a severe fall in the reserves, the almost invariable reaction of governments of whatever political colour was to defend the value of the pound by deflation, which reduced the rate of growth and curbed imports, and by high interest rates, which were designed to attract short-term capital to London and to repel speculative attacks on sterling. This policy has frequently been condemned as short-sighted and self-destructive because it lowered the rate of industrial investment and thus ensured that the industrial capacity of the nation was inadequate for its needs when boom conditions returned, the inevitable result being, it is alleged, that a further surge of industrial imports soon produced another trade deficit and a renewed crisis of confidence in sterling.[70] It has also been claimed that the stifling of home demand under the 'stop-go' regime gave the larger firms an incentive to invest abroad, turning Britain into a leading centre of multinational business, a process fostered by the vast network of overseas connections built up through the City in the past.[71]

Policy in times of crisis was certainly reminiscent of that adopted in defence of the gold standard in the 1920s; but it would be mistaken to assume that it was dictated by the 'City–Bank–Treasury nexus'[72] on entirely traditional lines. Government was now too big and complex, and all parties were too committed to welfare and to raising living standards, for it to be possible to invoke the simple balanced-budget verities of the pre-1939 era. The Labour government of the 1960s resisted devaluation not just on the City's behalf but because of fears that it might trigger a world economic crisis. In addition, although willing to deflate to prevent devaluation, Labour did so by curbing private rather than public spending, much to the annoyance of the Bank of England and the City. Moreover, given the electoral imperatives of the day, all governments were quick to ease credit and boost spending once a crisis had passed, despite Cassandra-like objections from the financial authorities.[73] Nonetheless, Labour no less than the Conservatives saw the defence of sterling as being a fundamental priority of economic policy; it was almost inconceivable that any strategy which challenged this or the position of traditional authority, such as the Treasury, could have been adopted. When industry, in the shape of the CBI and the trade unions, became dissatisfied with the failure to arrest relative decline and the Labour government adopted a modernising strategy, the plans failed because of resolute hostility from the Treasury.[74] Attempts by the Conservatives to break out of the weary round of currency crises in 1963–4 and 1972–3 also came to grief when they posed a threat to sterling. They decided to allow the economy to run at a level high enough to induce a surge in industrial investment in the hope that, by permanently enlarging capacity, exports would grow more quickly and the economy's appetite for imported manufactures would be blunted. This tactic failed, partly because in both cases balance of payments problems led to runs on the reserves which panicked the authorities into deflation before the medicine had had time to prove its worth.[75]

A succession of financial crises from the mid-1950s onwards culminated in the forced devaluation of 1967, an event which marked the beginning of the end of the Sterling Area.[76] Many countries that had dutifully followed Britain's lead in 1949 now failed to do so, and the Bank of England was driven to the undignified expedient of promising to indemnify sterling holders against the effects of further devaluations in the hope of rallying them to the cause. This tactic was not a great success; Australia, for example, contemplating shrinking trade links, Britain's courtship of the EEC and increasing dependence on American investment, resolutely refused to hold more than 40 per cent of her reserves in sterling after 1967.[77] The end of the Sterling Area finally came in 1972 when, in the wake of the collapse of the Bretton Woods fixed exchange-rate regime and the devaluation of the dollar, the pound was allowed to float.[78]

Global economic change and the end of empire

The empire which had been reconstructed with such determination after World War II began to fall apart in the mid-1950s. Within ten years the most important constituents had voted for independence, sometimes with their hands but more often with their feet; thereafter, Britain was concerned to hurry on the process of decolonisation with as much dignity as the pressures of nationalism and the need for economy would allow. The Sudan became independent in 1956, Malaya and the Gold Coast in 1957, Nigeria in 1960 and Kenya in 1963. The West Indies were bundled briefly into a federation in 1957 before Jamaica broke free in 1962. Long-held strategic bases were discarded: Cyprus in 1960, Malta in 1964 and Aden in 1967. Outside the empire, Britain lost ground in her most important remaining sphere of informal influence, the Middle East, a process which began in Egypt and Iran in 1951 and culminated in the Suez crisis five years later. As these events queued for attention, Whitehall's busiest department was stamping out new constitutions from the old Westminster model, and recently jailed 'agitators' were being released and turned into 'responsible leaders' with unprecedented speed. Some awkward and often sizeable issues had still to be resolved, notably in central Africa, but by the mid-1960s the outcome was not in doubt; shortly afterwards the empire sank, leaving only the ripples of the Commonwealth behind.

The question of why the empire became unstuck so soon after it had been reglued has engaged many minds and stimulated much excellent research.[79] It is probably fair to say, in the briefest summary possible, that most historians of decolonisation favour a multicausal explanation which features, with varying emphases, the decline of British power, the rising costs of empire, the loss of imperial will, the irresistible force of colonial nationalism and the pressures of international opinion, including of course the attitude of the United States. Our purpose here is not to attack or choose between existing approaches but rather to link them together by suggesting how our particular interpretation of imperial expansion bears upon the problem of imperial decline.

By the mid-1950s, as we have seen, there were grounds for thinking that the post-war crisis had been overcome and that Britain could create a wider role for sterling by moving towards convertibility, as indeed happened between 1955 and 1958. Fundamentally, this change of direction was the product of hard-headed, if narrow calculations about shifting opportunities in the international economy, though it also appealed to ritualistic assumptions which connected the strength of the pound to the virility of the nation. The perception was that convertibility would offer more opportunities for the City and for Britain's trade generally, and that the move would have to be made before the dollar, already powerful, became almighty. Two developments in particular pointed towards this conclusion: the declining value of the colonies and the rising importance of the industrial economies in Europe and elsewhere.

The end of the Korean War in 1953 brought the long boom in commodity prices to a close. Thereafter, the export earnings of countries producing raw materials were less buoyant and their import-purchasing power grew more slowly. As a result of these trends, an increasing number of Britain's colonies began to run deficits with the United States in place of the surpluses which had made them such a vital part of the Sterling Area in the crucial period of reconstruction after World War II.[80] These were not markets to be given up lightly, but their growth potential now appeared to be limited and they had ceased to provide a refuge for Britain's older staples.[81] Moreover, by the close of 1952 the Conservative government also recognised that imperial preference no longer had a part to play in extending the trade of the Sterling Area and had ceased to be an effective instrument of economic policy, even within the Commonwealth.[82]

The counterpart of these developments was the revival of the economies of continental Europe and Japan. This was not just a matter of renewed growth but involved structural change, promoted by the United States, which gave rise to a new set of complementarities linking the advanced, highly specialised economies of the world.[83] As we have seen, the trade of the Sterling Area shrank in importance and overseas investment flows shifted accordingly. Beginning in the 1950s, and with increasing rapidity thereafter, British capital was directed away from India, South America, China and the tropics, and towards Europe and the United States. Canada, Australia and South Africa remained attractive to British investors, but this was the result of economic incentives which were largely independent of Commonwealth membership.[84] By the close of the 1950s, it was apparent that Britain's future international economic policy could no longer be based on the Commonwealth, still less on its colonial component. That sterling had a future as an international currency was not doubted by policy-makers in London, but the value of the Sterling Area, as then constituted, was less certain.[85] If Britain was to take advantage of the new opportunities opening in Europe, and in doing so avoid falling further under the influence of the United States, she had to begin marching in step with her continental neighbours. In 1956 these considerations led to the formulation of Plan G, which became the basis of the European Free Trade Association in 1959, and in turn the prelude to Britain's application to join the European Economic Community in 1961.[86]

If sterling was to resume its historic role as a major international currency, action had to be taken to secure the reserves held in London. As far as colonial policy was concerned, this meant scrutinising overseas expenditure and controlling the rate at which the sterling balances were used. The need for economy, combined with the declining value of parts of the empire, encouraged the Treasury (in alliance with Conservative Chancellors of the Exchequer) to question the wisdom of investing in the colonies from the mid-1950s and to readvertise the merits of the traditional doctrine of self-sufficiency.[87] For the same reasons, moves were made to curb defence costs, with the result that coercion began to give way to persuasion, where circumstances allowed, in dissident parts of the empire and the semi-colonies. This shift of emphasis also fitted with the changing mood of the United States: as the Cold War entered a phase of 'competitive coexistence', it was all the more necessary to offer the subject peoples of the world something other than repression. If the promise of economic development was not now to be swiftly executed, then constitutional concessions offered a cheap and an ideologically congenial alternative, as well as being an increasingly necessary response to nationalist pressures. This adjustment recommended itself, too, as a means of dealing with the outstanding sterling balances, which had now become a problem instead of an asset.[88] Once sterling became fully convertible, the balances could be drawn on more freely, if not at will. Given that the most important colonies were on course for increasing degrees of self-government, convertibility raised the prospect of a raid on the reserves which would provoke a run on the pound.

Taken together, these considerations pointed in one direction: the route to be followed was that marked by negotiation, and the purpose of the exercise was to transfer power to friendly rather than to hostile nationalists. In this way, Britain hoped to keep the Commonwealth 'sterling-minded', and if possible to persuade other countries to join the club. By the close of the 1950s the new strategy for dealing with the all-important sterling balances was well under way. Not for the first time, Britain pressed home the argument that it was scarcely in the interests of newly independent states to take action which might jeopardise London's ability or willingness to fund their development programmes.[89] Simultaneously, and with practised diplomacy, Britain made plans to reduce official investment in the new Commonwealth and prompted members to seek other sources of long-term capital.[90] Piece by piece, agreement was reached on a phased run-down of the outstanding balances (as had happened in the case of India). At the close of 1954, Britain allowed the colonies to issue currencies on a fiduciary basis, thus freeing balances held in London for approved development purposes.[91] The colonies were also encouraged to establish central banks in the hope that they would serve as agents of 'responsible' management and check the ambitions of politicians whose promises could not be funded by orthodox means.[92] Finally, the Colonial Development and Welfare Act of 1959 was designed, among other purposes, to tie withdrawals from London to agreed projects. If one example has to be selected to summarise the remarkable transition of the 1950s then it must be that of Kwame Nkrumah and the Gold Coast. Nkrumah was first jailed in 1950 and then released in 1951 to become chief minister of a newly elected assembly. Thereafter, the mood was one of cooperation: Nkrumah agreed to respect the rules governing the Sterling Area in 1956, and he led his country to independence in the following year.[93]

None of these decisions was made in a mechanical fashion, and the trend is doubtless clearer in retrospect than it was at the time. The Conservatives, for example, were caught in a particularly painful dilemma because they championed the pound and the empire with equal fervour. When the interests of the two began to diverge, there was uncertainty over which way to jump. The significance of the Suez crisis, from the British perspective, was precisely in highlighting the contradiction between upholding sterling and funding the military operations needed at times to defend Britain's world role.[94] The Treasury's early warning about the effect of military action on sterling was ignored; the war led to an immediate run on the pound; and the United States refused financial help until Britain agreed to withdraw her troops. Faced with bankruptcy, Britain complied. This searing experience caused Macmillan to undergo spontaneous conversion: after 1956, the advocate of empire and coercion stood four-square for sterling and peace. One of his first actions as Prime Minister in 1957 was to order a round of defence cuts specifically to help the pound. This was followed between 1957 and 1960 by a series of high-level reviews of Britain's current position and future options as a world power.[95] The results, in general terms, confirmed the declining economic and military value of the Commonwealth. In 1959 Macleod was appointed Colonial Secretary to speed decolonisation, while Macmillan set about persuading his uncertain Cabinet to support Britain's application to join the European Economic Community. The wind of change was already blowing long before Macmillan named it, and if events in the 1960s formed less of a pattern than hindsight suggests, they nevertheless followed trends which had already emerged in the mid-1950s.

Far from being in decline, imperialism and empire were revitalised during the war and in the period of reconstruction which followed. The basic aim of policy was to harness the resources of the empire to metropolitan needs, and then to buy off colonial discontent with a programme of economic development. Since the first aim took precedence over the second, the original strategy had eventually to be revised. The result was that political advance, which was cheap, was offered as a substitute for rapid economic progress, though in stages which the Colonial Office still hoped to control. At the same time, the empire became progressively less important to Britain's needs and it became easier, even for Conservative policymakers, to envisage and then to speed the process of decolonisation. This sequence suggests that some revision to the orthodox chronology of imperial decline is required, and also that the underlying causation needs to be reviewed.[96] Our argument holds that calculations about the means of maintaining Britain's position as a major financial centre are a vital and an underestimated part of the explanation of rebuilding the empire and then of transferring power.[97] We are not claiming that they were the sole cause; only that existing interpretations ought to give more weight to this consideration, and that accounts which rely on broadly phrased formulations about the rising costs and diminishing returns of empire could gain from being specified in the way we have suggested.[98] This perspective helps to explain the 'paradox', noted by specialists, that the empire became more important shortly before the process of transferring power gathered pace. It also throws light on the argument that decolonisation was merely a smokescreen to cover neo-colonialism. From the standpoint adopted here, neo-colonialism could not have been planned in 1945 for the simple reason that decolonisation was not then envisaged. It was only later, in the 1950s, that serious thought was given to ways of perpetuating British influence in the post-imperial world, but by then Britain's aims were limited by her changing interests and not simply by the resources at her disposal.

Unfortunately for those who had so carefully planned to extend the global role of sterling by dissolving the connection between formal empire and the Sterling Area, the strategy did not work. All the elaborate attempts to persuade ex-colonies to contribute to the strength of the area came to nothing because, as we have seen, the pound rapidly ceased to be a currency of major international importance. The City had to face a new struggle for survival.

Epilogue: the City in the post-imperial world

By the early 1970s, then, Britain had finally lost the imperial power base which had sustained her position in the world for so long and was faced with the prospect of becoming 'once more nothing but an insignificant island in the North Sea'.[99] The only viable alternative was membership of the EEC, which threatened to intensify competition in the domestic market. At the same time, Britain's troubles were aggravated by the ending of the post-war boom and by the rapid inflation associated with the OPEC price rise.

This 'post-imperial crisis' eventually provided the opening for the success of the Thatcherite Conservatives with their potent combination of emotive nationalism (most evident during the Falklands War in 1982) and free market economics. They claimed that Britain's economic problems could be solved by reducing the role of the state and allowing market forces to work unhindered. Thatcher's first government came into office in 1979 convinced that excessive public expenditure had 'crowded out' private investment and that rigorous control of the money supply would remove inflation and encourage industrial revival.[100] Keynes and Beveridge were abandoned and public expenditure attacked with a fervour which would have enthused Gladstone. The regime of high interest rates, deflation and rising exchange rates adopted in 1979–81 was designed to separate sound businesses from those sickly creatures which depended for survival on the unnaturally high level of demand sustained by extravagant governments during the previous 30 years. The chief result of these policies was the destruction of a large slice of an already ailing manufacturing sector. Services, boosted by the income from North Sea oil, responded much better to Thatcherism, and the long-standing 'North–South divide' became more pronounced. Given the government's ideological assumptions and the fact that the south-east remained the chief area of Conservative electoral support, it was not difficult for Thatcherites to believe that the outcome, though unexpected, was for the best.[101]

The most successful adaptation to the new regime took place in the money market. By the early 1970s City gentlemen could no longer rely on either the empire or the Sterling Area to provide them with a world role. Yet the City survived as a global financial centre. As the good ship sterling sank, the City was able to scramble aboard a much more seaworthy young vessel, the Eurodollar.[102] From small beginnings in the late 1950s, the Eurodollar market expanded very quickly in the following decades, principally because it proved useful to the vast multinational companies which had become the main players in world trade and investment. City elites were quick to recognise the potential of this market and London was able to attract the bulk of the Eurodollar and Eurobond business mainly because it was, at the time, by far the most open money market in the world.[103] Competition for financial business became much fiercer from the late 1970s as the computer revolution began to make security markets truly international for the first time, and Tokyo and New York became more serious rivals. When, as a part of the Thatcherite programme, exchange controls were abolished in 1979, the Bank of England was shocked by the amount of business transferred to other centres. The City responded in 1986 by embracing 'Big Bang', a series of reforms which removed restraints on Stock Exchange membership and abolished many restrictive practices. Once again, gentlemanly capitalists demonstrated a remarkable ability to adapt to changing times. But there was a high price to be paid: the reforms encouraged a large number of foreign firms to establish themselves in London, and they rapidly became the dominant force in the market.[104]

As the imperial basis of its strength disappeared, the City survived by transforming itself into an 'offshore island' servicing the business created by the industrial and commercial growth of much more dynamic partners. And, as the already established dominance of the south-east and of services became yet more pronounced, the role of the City within the complex of service activities reached an unprecedented level of importance. Thatcherites had no natural affinity with the City and, indeed, were known to have an instinctive preference for 'enterprise which manufactures things to those which make money from money';[105] but, when the free market philosophy was applied to industry and finance, the former wilted under the strain while the latter embraced it with enthusiasm. Ironically, the pace of change in the international monetary sphere was so rapid that it exposed the contradictions within Thatcherite ideology and eventually precipitated a political crisis. The relentless pressure for greater European economic unity, for financial integration and for the creation of a single currency offended the nationalists among the Thatcherites and cost Mrs Thatcher the leadership of the Conservative Party in 1990.

Thatcher governments were not friendly to the gentlemanly element in British capitalism, especially since gentlemanly power after 1945 had often become closely associated with the extension of the role of the state. Ideologically, they had more in common with Cobdenite liberalism, and with the world of the small producer which inspired that brand of liberalism, than they had with the paternalist Tory tradition stretching from Disraeli to Macmillan. The gentlemanly element within the party was progressively ousted from power, and professional monopolies and privileges came under attack. Gentlemanly power in the City was also finally undone by the massive inflow of foreign capital after Big Bang. The City has now become much more a centre for multinational business and finance than a British financial market, and the most powerful institutions are based on American, Japanese or European capital, even if they still rely on the expertise of the locals.[106] After Big Bang, many time-honoured restrictions on the activities of British firms in the City were removed, giving them the opportunity to reorganise themselves and launch new careers as American-style investment banks: alternatively, some famous names found a niche for themselves as providers of specialist services which the giant American or Japanese firms did not supply.[107] There was still some room for gentlemen though most were now beholden to much less gentlemanly firms whose ultimate loyalties lay outside Britain.[108] However, the British firms in direct competition with the foreign giants were often too small to survive in the longer term, and their traditionally informal management structures and regulatory regimes were unable to cope with the shift from personal to on-screen trading which followed Big Bang. The collapse of the once-mighty Barings in 1995 was particularly momentous not only because it brought down other British firms in its wake but also because it marked the end of a peculiarly British form of financial capitalism.[109] The City prospered in the long boom of the 1990s. Yet as Lord Levene, who as both

Lord Mayor and head of the London arm of Deutsche Bank had good reason to know, there had been a 'Wimbledonisation of the City. We have the best courts, but few finalists are British nationals'.[110]

The decline in gentlemanly capitalist influence under the Thatcherite regime was particularly evident in the reduced condition of the Bank of England. In the 1960s the Bank was still the crucial intermediary between a socially cohesive City, whose power was based on Britain's position in the world, and governments which readily recognised the Bank's authority in money matters. Thatcherite administrations in particular diminished the Bank's authority by taking more direct control of money supply and interest rates and by breaking down the cartelisation of financial markets through which the Bank exercised some of its power. The flood of foreign capital into the City also undermined the Bank's moral authority in the market.[111] The Bank was restored to some of its former glory in 1997 when the incoming Labour government gave it back the power to set interest rates, but its role as a regulator has changed. The Bank now sees its primary task as defending the City's position in global markets rather than encouraging the survival of British business, gentlemanly or otherwise, in the Square Mile.[112]

Britain's power has declined, and it is no longer possible to provide the City with a British-dominated, world-wide arena based on formal and informal imperialism: the City can now function successfully only by acting as an intermediary for powers whose economies are far stronger than Britain's. Nevertheless, the economic importance of this newly evolving City within Britain is greater than in the past and its political influence is no less significant. Inexorably, it seems, even governments like Thatcher's, which began with a genuine commitment to encouraging industrial revival, soon fell into a pattern of decision-making which promoted the interests of the City. Yet the continuing economic and political importance of the City should come as no real surprise to those who are aware that it has been at the centre of the most dynamic region of the British economy for the last 150 years and that its leaders have had privileged access to the controllers of political power for twice as long. The empire has sunk leaving hardly a trace behind; the gentleman is fast disappearing from British business and political life; but the City adapts and survives.

Notes

1 The best introductions to the subject of economic growth and structure after 1945 are C.H. Lee, *The British Economy after 1700: A Macro-Economic Study* (Cambridge, 1986), Pt. III; and Sidney Pollard, *The Development of the British Economy, 1914–80* (1983), Chs. 6–8. For a brief but emphatic insight into the dominance of the south-east, see Michael Moran, *Politics and Society in Britain: An Introduction* (2nd edn, 1989), p. 9.

2 W.D. Rubinstein, *Men of Property: The Very Wealthy since the Industrial Revolution,* (1981), Ch. 8. In the list of the 200 wealthiest individuals printed in the *Daily Telegraph,* 25 February 1988, the number of aristocratic names is still remarkably large. Famous City names also proliferate and much of the 'new money' in evidence is City-based.

3 Rubinstein, 'Social Origins of British Elites'; François Bédarida, *A Social History of England, 1851–75* (1979), pp. 281–7. See also Hugh Thomas, ed. *The Establishment* (1959) for a contemporary critique of the venerability of the nation's ruling elites.

4 John Ramsden, 'Conservatives since 1945', *Contemporary Record* (Spring, 1988), p. 18.
5 These judgements came from the authoritative voice of the professor of international relations at Oxford: Alfred Zimmern, *The Third British Empire* (1926), pp. 102–3.
6 C.S. Wilson and T. Lupton, 'The Social Background and Connections of "Top Decision Makers"', *Manchester School,* 27 (1959); For an entertaining and penetrating description of the scandal see Paul Ferris, *The City* (1960), Ch. 7, a book which has many insights into the gentlemanly nature of the City in the 1950s. See, for example, his account of the relations between the bill-brokers and the Bank of England in Ch. 3. These characteristics of the City were also noticed by Richard Spiegelberg, *The City: Power without Accountability* (1973), pp. 7, 19, and pp. 125–6 in relation to the clearing-bank directors. It is worth quoting the comment of one young City executive that the top brass of the Square Mile 'are not so much members of the Establishment because they have succeeded in the City; they have succeeded in the City because they are members of the Establishment'. Victor Sandelson, 'The Confidence Trick', in Thomas, *The Establishment,* p. 139.
7 Spiegelberg, *The City,* pp. 65–6.
8 John Scott, *The Upper Classes,* pp. 139ff. Much of Scott's analysis is confirmed in detail in Spiegelberg, *The City,* Chs. 1 and 2. See also the views of Geoffrey Ingham, *Capitalism Divided? The City and Industry in British Social Development* (1984), Ch. 3.
9 Kathleen Burk, *Morgan Grenfell, 1838–1988: The Biography of a Merchant Bank* (Cambridge, 1989), pp. 191–2; Spiegelberg, *The City,* p. 19.
10 Spiegelberg, *The City,* Ch. 7.
11 Grahame Thompson, 'The Relationship between the Financial and Industrial Sector in the United Kingdom Economy', *Economy and Society,* VI (1977); John Carrington and George T. Edwards, *Financing Industrial Investment* (1979); Richard Minns, *Take Over the City: The Case for Public Ownership of Financial Institutions* (1982), pp. 21–6.
12 Minns, *Take Over the City,* p. 23.
13 Scott Newton and Dilwyn Porter, *Modernization Frustrated: The Politics of Industrial Decline in Britain since 1900* (1988), Ch. 4; Paul Addison, *The Road to 1945* (1975); Keith Middlemass, *Politics in Industrial Society: The British Experience since 1911* (1979), Ch. 10.
14 The most authoritative account of Anglo-American financial diplomacy is now L.S. Pressnell, *External Economic Policy since the War,* Vol. 1: *The Post-war Financial Settlement* (1986). For a shorter account see Alan P. Dobson, *The Politics of the Anglo-American Economic Special Relationship, 1940–1987* (Brighton, 1988). There is also some fascinating detail in Sir Richard Clarke, *Anglo-American Economic Collaboration in War and Peace* (Oxford, 1982). However, the earlier study by Richard N. Gardner, *Sterling-Dollar Diplomacy: The Origin and Prospects of our International Economic Order* (1980 edn.), is still well worth using, as is R.S. Sayers, *Financial Policy, 1939–45* (1956).
15 On Lend-Lease (as American aid was known) the authoritative account is now A.P. Dobson, *U.S. Wartime Aid to Britain* (1986).
16 Michael Cowen and Nicholas Westcott, 'British Imperial Policy during the War', in David Killingray and Richard Rathbone, eds. *Africa and the Second World War* (1986); K.M. Wright, 'Dollar Pooling in the Sterling Area, 1939–52', *American Economic Review,* 44 (1954).
17 George C. Herring, 'The United States and British Bankruptcy, 1944–5: Responsibilities Deferred', *Political Science Quarterly,* LXXXVI (1971).
18 The Bank's arguments are laid out in Pressnell, *External Economic Policy,* pp. 137–43, 232–4.
19 *The Collected Writings of John Maynard Keynes,* XXV (Cambridge, 1980), pp. 410–17.
20 On the emergence of the Clearing Union proposals in the context of policy as a whole see Pressnell, *External Economic Policy,* Chs. 1–4. Bretton Woods is also discussed in great detail in Armand Van Dormael, *Bretton Woods: Birth of a Monetary System* (1978); and Dobson, *The Politics of the Anglo-American Economic Special Relationship,* pp. 48ff. For a recent study of Keynes's contribution to wartime and post-war economic policy in general see Alan Booth, *British Economic Policy, 1931–49: Was there a Keynesian Revolution?* (1989).

21 Keynes, *Collected Writings,* pp. 4–7, 82–4, 93–4, 100, 123–5, 181–3.
22 There is an exhaustive discussion of Keynes's views on the 1945 loan in Pressnell, *External Economic Policy,* Chs. 5–9. Gardner, *Sterling-Dollar Diplomacy,* pp. 121–43, is also useful here.
23 Pressnell, *External Economic Policy,* Ch. 10; Alec Cairncross, *Years of Recovery: British Economic Policy, 1945–51* (1985), Ch. 5.
24 Cairncross, *Years of Recovery,* Ch. 6, has the details on the 1947 crisis. The enthusiasm for convertibility in the City during 1947 was closely related to anxieties about the future world status of the currency. D.R. Wightman, 'The Sterling Area, Part II: World War II Regulations and Convertibility Crisis', *Banco Nazionale Del Lavoro Quarterly Review,* 4 (1951), pp. 153–4.
25 The anti-American, pro-empire faction is dealt with by Van Dormael, *Bretton Woods,* pp. 131ff. For a vigorous contemporary statement see L.S. Amery, *The Washington Loan Agreements* (1946).
26 Allister Hinds, 'Sterling and Imperial Policy, 1945–51', *Jour. Imp. and Comm. Hist.,* XV (1987). One of the ironies of the time was that trade with Canada, a dollar-based country within the empire, was seriously affected by the restrictions imposed by an imperial policy which was intended to economise on foreign exchange. See Tim Rooth, 'Debts, Deficits and Disenchantment: Anglo-Canadian Economic Relations, 1945–50', (Discussion Paper No. 19, Department of Economics, Portsmouth Polytechnic, May 1991)
27 Michael J. Hogan, *The Marshall Plan: America, Britain and the Reconstruction of Western Europe, 1947–52* (Cambridge, 1987); Henry Pelling, *Britain and the Marshall Plan* (1988). It should be noted that, in distributing aid, the Americans did not follow British advice, which was to give substantial direct grants to the Third World – much of which was, of course, within the British empire. The British argument was that the best way to cure the dollar shortage was to revive the export capacity of those primary producing countries which had traditionally been large dollar earners and which had played such an important role in the multilateral settlements pattern centred on Britain before 1939. This question is discussed in C.C.S. Newton, 'The Sterling Crisis of 1947 and the British Response to the Marshall Plan', *Econ. Hist. Rev.,* 2nd ser. XXXVII (1984).
28 Alec Cairncross and Barrie Eichengreen, *Sterling in Decline: The Devaluations of 1931, 1949 and 1967* (1983), Ch. 4.
29 Cairncross, *Years of Recovery,* Ch. 9; C.C.S. Newton, 'Operation "ROBOT" and the Political Economy of Sterling Convertibility, 1951–1952', *European University Institute Working Paper,* No. 86/256 (Florence, 1986).
30 Alan S. Milward, 'Motives for Currency Convertibility: the Pound and the Deutschmark, 1950–5', in Carl-Ludwig Holtfrerich, ed. *Interactions in the World Economy: Perspectives from International Economic History* (1989). According to Milward, Bank of England officials even speculated that 'eventually the Soviet Union and its satellites would enter the London non-dollar world' (p. 268). He also points out that the German government resisted an early return to convertibility precisely because of fears about its effects on commodity exports (pp. 268–71).
31 Dobson, *The Anglo-American Economic Special Relationship,* Ch. 5, charts the progress towards the final objective. In the end, fixed rates were adopted to please the Americans.
32 Cowen and Westcott, 'British Imperial Policy', pp. 40–9; David Meredith, 'State Controlled Marketing and Economic Development: the Case of West African Produce During the Second World War', *Econ. Hist. Rev.,* 2nd ser. XXXIX. (1986). Older studies by W.K. Hancock and M.M. Gowing, *British War Economy* (1949), H.D. Hall and C.C. Wrigley, *Studies in Overseas Supply* (1956), and Charlotte Leubuscher, *Bulk-Buying from the Colonies* (1956) are of continuing value for students of the war years.
33 Allister Hinds, 'Imperial Policy and the Colonial Sterling Balances', *Jour. Imp. and Comm. Hist.,* 19 (1991), and the further references given there.
34 William Roger Louis, *Imperialism at Bay: The United States and the Decolonisation of the British Empire, 1941–45* (Oxford, 1977).
35 J.M. Lee and Martin Petter, *The Colonial Office, War and Development Policy* (1982); and the case studies by A.J. Stockwell, *British Policy and Malay Politics During the Malayan*

Union Experiments, 1945–48 (Kuala Lumpur, 1979); Nicholas Tarling, '"A New and Better Cunning": British Wartime Planning for Post-War Burma, 1942–43', *Jour. South-East Asian Stud.*, 13 (1982), (and the sequel in ibid.); and Robert Pearce, 'The Colonial Economy: Nigeria and the Second World War', in Barbara Ingham and Colin Simmons, eds. *Development Studies and Colonial Policy* (1987).

36 Louis, *Imperialism at Bay*, pp. 555–62; Thorne, *Allies of a Kind*, pp. 311, 444, 558. Churchill also had a scheme, which the Americans vetoed, for taking over Thailand.

37 See pp. 259–60. Also William Roger Louis, *The British Empire in the Middle East, 1945–1951* (Oxford, 1984); C.A. MacDonald, 'The Politics of Intervention: the United States, Britain and Argentina, 1941–46', *Jour. Latin Am. Stud.*, 12 (1980); idem, 'The United States, Britain and Argentina in the Years Immediately after the Second World War', in Guido Di Tella and D.C.M. Platt, eds. *The Political Economy of Argentina, 1880–1946* (1986); and Guido Di Tella and D.C. Watt, eds. *Argentina between the Great Powers, 1939–46* (1989), to which MacDonald makes a further important contribution.

38 Quoted in Jane Bowden, 'Development and Control in British Colonial Policy, with Reference to Nigeria and the Gold Coast, 1935–48' (Ph.D. thesis, University of Birmingham, 1981), p. 246.

39 Ronald Robinson, 'Andrew Cohen and the Transfer of Power in Tropical Africa, 1940–51', in W.H. Morris-Jones and Georges Fischer, eds. *Decolonisation and After: The British and French Experience* (1980); Robert A. Pearce, *Turning Point in Africa: British Colonial Policy, 1938–48* (1982), Chs. 5–8.

40 D.K. Fieldhouse, 'The Labour Governments and the Empire-Commonwealth, 1945–51', in R. Ovendale, ed. *The Foreign Policy of the British Labour Government, 1945–51* (Leicester, 1984).

41 Quoted in Pearce, *Turning Point*, p. 95.

42 D.A. Low and J.M. Lonsdale, 'Towards the New Order, 1945–63', in D.A. Low and Alison Smith, eds. *The Oxford History of East Africa*, Vol. 3 (1976), pp. 12–16, and the comment by John. D. Hargreaves, *The End of Colonial Rule in West Africa* (1979), pp. 41–2.

43 J.M. Lee, 'Forward Thinking and the War: the Colonial Office during the 1940s', *Jour. Imp. and Comm. Hist.*, 6 (1977). Labour turned towards the empire in search of salvation rather than take up the challenge of leadership of the European group that formed the nucleus of what later became the EEC. See Scott Newton, 'Britain, the Sterling Area and European Integration, 1945–50', *Jour. Imp. and Comm. Hist.*, 13 (1985).

44 R.D. Pearce, 'Morale in the Colonial Service in Nigeria During the Second World War', *Jour. Imp. and Comm. Hist.*, 11 (1983); John W. Cell, 'On the Eve of Decolonisation: the Colonial Office's Plans for the Transfer of Power in Africa', *Jour. Imp. and Comm. Hist.*, 8 (1980); Charles Armour, 'The BBC and the Development of Broadcasting in British Colonial Africa, 1946–56', *African Affairs*, 83 (1984).

45 See pp. 229–30.

46 Louis, *Imperialism at Bay*; Thorne, *Allies of a Kind*.

47 William Roger Louis, 'American Anti-Colonialism and the Dissolution of the British Empire', *International Affairs*, 61 (1985); and, for a case study, Hoosain S. Faroqui, 'In the Shadow of Globalism: The United States, South Asia and the Cold War, 1939–53' (Ph.D. thesis, Cornell University, 1986), Ch. 4.

48 The terms of the Lend-Lease Agreement of 1942 bound Britain to restore non-discriminatory trading practices, and the General Agreement of Trade and Tariffs prohibited new preferences in the Commonwealth in 1947. Nevertheless, existing preferences remained in place and were not phased out until after 1973, when Britain joined the EEC.

49 Quoted in Bowden, 'Development and Control', p. 361.

50 Robinson, 'Andrew Cohen'; and the commentary by Hargreaves, *The End of Colonial Rule*, Ch. 2.

51 John Darwin, *Britain and Decolonisation* (1988), pp. 135–6. Canada, of course, was already linked to the US dollar.

52 See pp. 196–7.

53 B.R. Tomlinson, 'Indo-British Relations in the Post-Colonial Era: the Sterling Balances Negotiations, 1947–49', *Jour. Imp. and Comm. Hist.*, 13 (1985).

54 Louis, *The British Empire in the Middle East*; Martin Rudner, 'Financial Policies in Post-War Malaya: the Fiscal and Monetary Measures of Liberation and Reconstruction', *Jour. Imp. and Comm. Hist.*, 3 (1975); A.J. Stockwell, 'British Imperial Policy and Decolonisation in Malaya, 1942–52', *Jour. Imp. and Comm. Hist.*, 13 (1984). We are indebted, too, to Gerold Krozewski, 'Sterling, the Minor Territories and the End of Formal Empire, 1939–58', *Econ. Hist. Rev.*, XLVI (1993). Apart from the Middle East, Britain's remaining areas of informal influence are rarely discussed in studies of 'late colonialism', and there is no space to do so here. However, it is worth noting that they were pressed into service where it was possible to do so. Plans to harness China had to be abandoned, but Britain struck hard bargains with Argentina and Brazil (see pp. 161, 167).

55 D.J. Morgan, *The Official History of Colonial Development*, Vol. 3 (1980), pp. 29–33; Krozewski, 'Sterling'.

56 M. Cowen, 'Early Years of the Colonial Development Corporation: British State Enterprise Overseas During Late Colonialism', *African Affairs*, 83 (1984).

57 Meredith, 'State Controlled Marketing', and the further references given there.

58 Krozewski, 'Sterling'. Military bases were defended with equal firmness at least until the late 1950s, when defence cuts and the adoption of the nuclear deterrent shifted priorities.

59 Robinson, 'Andrew Cohen'; John Flint, 'Planned Decolonisation and its Failure in Africa', *African Affairs*, 82 (1983); Robert Pearce, 'The Colonial Office and Planned Decolonisation in Africa', *African Affairs*, 83 (1984).

60 Louis, *The British Empire in the Middle East.*

61 Judd Polk, *Sterling: Its Meaning in World Finance* (1956), p. 3.

62 Newton, 'Britain, the Sterling Area', pp. 168–80.

63 An excellent account of the Sterling Area in the 1950s and 1960s can be found in J.D.B. Miller, *Survey of Commonwealth Affairs: Problems of Expansion and Attrition, 1953–1969* (1974), Ch. 12.

64 For an outline of the major changes in the structure and direction of foreign trade as a whole, see Pollard, *The Development of the British Economy*, pp. 352–65; M.J. Artis, ed. *Prest and Coppock's The U.K. Economy* (1986), pp. 130–53.

65 To put British growth in context, see Angus Maddison, *Phases of Capitalist Development* (Oxford, 1982), Chs. 3, 5 and 6.

66 J.D.B. Miller, *Britain and the Old Dominions* (1966), Ch. 8.

67 Phillip W. Bell, *The Sterling Area in the Post-War World: Internal Mechanism and Cohesion, 1946–52* (Oxford, 1956), offers a good, early analysis of incipient problems.

68 The extent to which this followed naturally from Britain's acceptance of American aid in the 1940s is discussed in T. Brett, S. Gilliat and A. Pople, 'Planned Trade, Labour Party Policy and U.S. Intervention: the Success and Failure of Post-war Reconstruction', *History Workshop*, 13 (1982). See also Arthur Robert Conan, *The Problem of Sterling* (1966), pp. 24–5.

69 For an excellent analysis of the impact of the imperial and other burdens which aggravated Britain's external payments problem, see Susan Strange, *Sterling and British Policy: A Political Study of a Currency in Decline* (Oxford, 1971), Chs. 5 and 6. Strange emphasises the fact that allowing heavy overseas flows of capital to the Sterling Area was essential to retain the allegiance of sterling-holders and sterling's position as a world currency. The British banks operating within the area also encouraged British investment in former colonies in order to gain favour with new political masters. Cf. Ingham, *Capitalism Divided*, pp. 202–12.

70 For powerful arguments in support of this view, see Andrew Shonfield, *British Economic Policy since the War* (1958); Sidney Pollard, *The Wasting of the British Economy* (1982);

Newton and Porter, *Modernisation Frustrated,* Chs. 5–7. To put this subject in context see Keith Smith, *The British Economic Crisis: Its Past and Future* (1986). For overall analyses of policy see Pollard, *The Development of the British Economy,* pp. 409–30; F.T. Blackaby, ed. *British Economic Policy, 1960–74* (Cambridge, 1978); Fred Hirsch, *The Pound Sterling: A Polemic* (1965); and Douglas Jay, *Sterling* (Oxford, 1986), Chs. 16 and 17.

71 Andrew Gamble, *Britain in Decline: Political Strategy and the British State* (2nd edn. 1985), pp. 109–112.

72 The phrase appears in Colin Leys, 'The Formation of British Capital', *New Left Review,* 160 (1986).

73 Rob Stones, 'Government-Finance Relations in Britain, 1964–7: a Tale of Three Cities', *Economy and Society,* 19 (1990).

74 Newton and Porter, *Modernisation Frustrated,* Ch. 5; Stephen Blank, 'Britain: the Politics of Foreign Economic Policy, the Domestic Economy, and the Problem of Pluralistic Stagnation', *International Organization,* 31 (1977); Ingham, *Capitalism Divided,* pp. 212–18.

75 John Cooper, *A Suitable Case for Treatment: What to Do about the Balance of Payments* (1968), has an excellent section dealing with the so-called Maudling Experiment of 1963–4.

76 Cairncross and Eichengreen, *Sterling in Decline,* Ch. 5.

77 Miller, *Survey of Commonwealth Affairs,* p. 295. See also Strange, *Sterling and British Policy,* pp. 90–5.

78 Andrew Shonfield, 'The World Economy, 1979', *Foreign Affairs,* 58 (1979).

79 The best entry is through the following: Darwin, *Britain and Decolonisation*; R.F. Holland, *European Decolonisation, 1918–81* (1985); Prosser Gifford and William Roger Louis, eds. *The Transfers of Power in Africa: Decolonization, 1940–60* (New Haven, Conn., 1982); idem, *Decolonization and African Independence: The Transfers of Power, 1960–80* (New Haven, Conn., 1988); J.D. Hargreaves, *Decolonization in Africa* (1988); and Michael Twaddle, 'Decolonisation in Africa: a New British Historiographical Debate', in B. Jewsiewicki and D. Newbury, eds. *African Historiographies* (Beverly Hills, Calif., 1986). A.N. Porter and A.J. Stockwell have edited a useful selection of relevant official documents: *British Imperial Policy and Decolonisation, 1938–64* (2 Vols., 1987 and 1989).

80 Conan, *The Sterling Area,* Ch. 3; David Fieldhouse, *Black Africa, 1945–1980: Economic Decolonization and Arrested Development* (1986), pp. 6–7.

81 The final episode of a long story is told by John Singleton, 'Lancashire's Last Stand: Declining Employment in the British Cotton Industry, 1950–70', *Econ. Hist. Rev.,* 2nd ser. XXXIX (1986), pp. 95, 98–9, 105–6. See also the fuller account in idem, *Lancashire on the Scrapheap: The Cotton Industry, 1945–1970* (1991).

82 D.J. Morgan, *The Official History of Colonial Development,* Vol. III (1980), pp. 5–6.

83 This theme is developed by F.V. Meyer, *International Trade Policy* (1978).

84 Pollard, *The Development of the British Economy,* pp. 358–61.

85 These issues provoked considerable public, as well as academic and official, discussion in the late 1950s. See, for example, Shonfield, *British Economic Policy Since the War.*

86 On Plan G, see Morgan, *Official History,* III, pp. 9–13.

87 Morgan, *Official History,* III, pp. 32–9; David Goldsworthy, 'Keeping Change within Bounds: Aspects of Colonial Policy during the Churchill and Eden Governments, 1951–57', *Jour. Imp. and Comm. Hist.,* 18 (1990), p. 87.

88 Morgan, *Official History,* III, Chs. 4–5. On this question, and related issues, we are indebted to Krozewski, 'Sterling'.

89 Yusuf Bangura, *Britain and Commonwealth Africa: The Politics of Economic Relations, 1951–75* (Manchester, 1983), pp. 30–4; Hinds, 'Imperial Policy', pp. 37–41.

90 Morgan, *Official History,* III, pp. 13–17, 189, 237.

91 Hinds, 'Imperial Policy', p. 39.

92 For a contemporary discussion of the main issues, see W.T. Newlyn and D.C. Rowan, *Money and Banking in British Colonial Africa* (Oxford, 1954), Chs. 10–13.

93 Darwin, *Britain and Decolonisation,* p. 178; Goldsworthy, 'Keeping Change Within Bounds', p. 91.

94 See, in this context, Diane B. Kunz, 'The Importance of Having Money: the Economic Diplomacy of the Suez Crisis', in William Roger Louis and Roger Owen, eds. *Suez 1956: The Crisis and its Consequences* (Oxford, 1989); and Howard J. Dooley, 'Great Britain's "Last Battle" in the Middle East: Notes on Cabinet Planning during the Suez Crisis of 1956', *International History Review,* XI (1989). As specialists will infer, neither this evidence nor our argument lends weight to recent suggestions that the significance of the Suez crisis has been overestimated.

95 Morgan, *Official History,* V, pp. 88–93, 96–102. Also Peter Hennessy reporting on newly released documents in *The Independent;* 7 January 1991, and *The Economist,* 20 April 1991.

96 The case for revising the chronology of decline has been put by J. Gallagher, *The Decline, Revival and Fall of the British Empire* (Cambridge, 1982), and John Darwin, 'Imperialism in Decline? Tendencies in British Policy between the Wars', *Hist. Jour.,* 23 (1980). For a related commentary on causation see B.R. Tomlinson, 'The Contraction of England: National Decline and the Loss of Empire', *Jour. Imp. and Comm. Hist.,* 11 (1982). For a view of the post-war period which is close to the one put here see R.F. Holland, 'The Imperial Factor in British Strategies from Attlee to Macmillan, 1945–63', *Jour. Imp. and Comm. Hist.,* 13 (1984).

97 The corollary, which cannot be explored here, is that manufacturing interests were no more successful in steering policy after 1945 than they were before. Although this proposition has yet to be fully tested (and is blurred by the growth of 'corporatism'), it finds support in Kathleen M. Stahl, *The Metropolitan Organisation of British Colonial Trade: Four Regional Studies* (1951), p. 297; Lee, *Colonial Development,* pp. 31, 73–7; Fieldhouse, *Black Africa,* pp. 9–12.

98 The idea that decolonisation was related to changing interests in the metropole and not simply derived from a generalised law of the inevitability of imperial decline has been worked out in some detail in Jacques Marseille's important study, *Empire colonial et capitalisme français: histoire d'un divorce* (Paris, 1984).

99 This vision of the future haunted several generations of British statesmen and officials. The example cited is taken from an earlier moment when the world seemed to be closing in on Britain: Chatfield to Fisher, 16 July 1934, quoted in S.L. Endicott, *Diplomacy and Enterprise: British China Policy, 1933–1937* (Manchester, 1975), p. 69.

100 The intellectual inspiration behind this can be found in Roger Bacon and Walter Eltis, *Britain's Economic Problem: Too Few Producers* (1977).

101 On the economic policy of the Thatcher years see Paul Whiteley, 'Economic Policy', in Patrick Dunleavy, Andrew Gamble and Gillian Peele, eds. *Developments in British Politics,* 3 (1990); Jay, *Sterling,* Ch. 19; Geoffrey W. Maynard, *The Economy under Mrs Thatcher* (1988); J. McInnes, *Thatcherism at Work* (1987), Ch. 5. See also James Douglas, 'The Changing Tide – Some Recent Studies of Thatcherism', *British Journal of Political Science,* 19 (1989).

102 These were US dollars which, for a variety of reasons, could not find a profitable niche in the United States.

103 The best detailed study of this is Jerry Coakley and Laurence Harris, *The City of Capital: London's Role as a Financial Centre* (Oxford, 1983). See also Strange, *Sterling and British Policy,* pp. 237–56; Philip Coggan, *The Money Machine: How the City Works* (1986), Ch. 11. We have also greatly benefited from Kathleen Burk, 'Eurodollars and Eurobonds', *Journal of Contemporary European History,* 1 (1992), which Dr Burk was kind enough to allow us to see before publication. It is worth noting that some countries, such as Germany, were keen to discourage the Eurodollar market from settling in their territories because they feared that the price of according it house-room would be diminished control over the domestic money supply. See Strange, *Sterling and British Policy,* p. 213.

104 On the transformation of the City in the 1980s see Coggan, *The Money Machine,* Chs. 1 and 2; Adrian Hamilton, *The Financial Revolution* (1986), Pt. 1.

105 M. Reid, 'Mrs. Thatcher and the City', in Dennis Kavanagh and Antony Seldon, eds. *The Thatcher Effect: A Decade of Change* (Oxford, 1989), p. 49.

106 On this theme see the collection of papers on the modern City in Laurence Harris, Jerry Coakley, Martin Croasdale and Trevor Evans, eds. *New Perspectives on the Financial System* (1988).

107 See, for example, *Financial Times,* 17 March 1990, and the *Sunday Times,* 17 February 1991, on Robert Fleming and Barings respectively.

108 A good example of a gentleman making an honest penny (and rather more) for a foreign firm in the City was provided by the Hon. Peregrine Moncrieffe who, in 1988, earned £1m. working for the American bankers E.F. Hutton. See *Sunday Times,* 9 November 1988.

109 Phillip Augar, *The Death of Gentlemanly Capitalism* (2000). Rothschilds maintained their independence with their usual skill but made no attempt to compete with the new giants. Niall Ferguson, *The World's Banker: The History of the House of Rothschild* (1998), pp. 1030–32.

110 *The Guardian,* Special Report on Economic and Monetary Union, 9 November 1999.

111 In trying to understand the evolution of the modern Bank we have found the following particularly useful: M.J. Artis, *Foundations of British Monetary Policy* (Oxford, 1965); Michael Moran, 'Finance-Capital and Pressure Group Politics in Britain', *Brit. Jour. Pol. Sci.,* II (1981); Stephen Fay, *Portrait of an Old Lady: Turmoil at the Bank of England* (1988).

112 The Bank's restored power over interest rates has, however, added a new twist to an old story. Reflecting on the effect of a recent rise in rates on provincial industry, the editor of the *Newcastle Journal* said that 'the Bank of England is known fairly pejoratively here as the Bank of South East England'. See *Guardian,* 12 September 1999. For the continuing debate on the North–South divide, see *Financial Times,* 12 March 2001 and *Guardian,* 28 February 2001, 12 March 2001.

27

CONCLUSION: 1688–2000

Our decision to state our interpretation and to reveal its underpinnings at the outset of this study means that, at this point, we have neither a plot to unravel nor a surprise to spring. However, it is easy for authors to suppose that their presentation is as clear to others as it is to themselves. Our signposts to different centuries and continents may sometimes have suggested directions other than those we intended, and our argument may not always have been as visible as we would have wished, especially since it has been spread over nearly 700 pages. Consequently, these concluding remarks will try to set out our principal claims in a way that removes any residual uncertainties, makes some of the wider implications of the argument explicit, and ensures that we ourselves do not end, unintentionally, in 'the last dyke of prevarication'.[1]

Bases of the analysis

Our explanation of the causes of British imperialism is founded upon a reappraisal of the character of economic power and political authority in the metropolis itself: geopolitical considerations, like the 'peripheral thesis', have their place in the story, but only within the context of impulses emanating from the centre. Explanations which assign a leading role to historical developments in Britain do, of course, exist already; but, as we have suggested, the most influential of these are seriously weakened by the excessive emphasis they place on the Industrial Revolution and its consequences. This handicap is found most obviously in studies by Marxist writers, but it also pervades the work of the liberal historians who oppose them, even though it takes a less direct form. This perspective fails to incorporate much of the most interesting recent research on British economic and social history, and it tends to assume rather than to establish the existence of connections between the economy and the wider society, including the world inhabited by policy-makers.

In this case, as in so much of the historiography of imperialism, the literature has been shaped either by assumptions about the political influence of a rising industrial bourgeoisie or by counter-claims which stress the distance of the 'official mind' from pressure groups representing manufacturers.

Our interpretation of this new evidence suggests that conventional approaches to modem British history need to be rethought. In particular, recognition needs to be given to the fact that economic development was not synonymous with the Industrial Revolution, and that non-industrial activities, especially those connected with finance and services, were far more important and independent than standard texts of economic history have allowed. Moreover, the upper reaches of these occupations, unlike those in manufacturing, were associated with high social status and gave access to political influence. Identifying these attributes establishes, in principle, the crucial connection between economic power and political authority, and hence offers a means of overcoming one of the central difficulties faced by current theories of imperialist expansion. By restating the main themes of British history during the past three centuries in these terms, it becomes possible to offer an alternative explanation of Britain's extraordinary and wide-ranging presence overseas.

We have addressed this task by tracing the growth and mutation of what we have called 'gentlemanly capitalism'. This concept is merely a convenient means of bringing coherence to a large body of evidence which does not fit into existing approaches to either British or imperial history. It has not been assigned special properties that allow it to rise above normal historical discourse, and the propositions derived from it are in principle falsifiable. We have used the term to represent a hitherto neglected theme in the historical transformation of British society, a process which we regard less as an exchange of 'tradition' for 'modernity' than as a selective amalgamation of elements inherited from the past with introductions from the continuously evolving present.[2] The particular transformation we have identified centred upon the growth of the financial and service sector, an innovation which proved to be compatible with aristocratic power in the eighteenth century, supported a new gentlemanly order in the nineteenth century, and carried both into the twentieth century. It is perhaps worth repeating at this point that our concern has been to establish the historical significance of gentlemanly forms of capitalism: whether these are to be approved or disapproved on moral, economic or other grounds is a related but distinct issue which is sufficiently important and complex in itself to require separate treatment.

Gentlemen looked back to the mythical harmonies of Merrie England, to the knightly morals of the Arthurian legend, and beyond to Greece and Rome for their justificatory model of an elite dedicated to public service. The resulting ethos was a highly selective composite, but it was also singularly effective in drilling the guardians who presided over policy and in promoting a sense of national solidarity, focused on the monarchy, which blunted the edge of class divisions, diluted the appeal of subversive ideologies, and encouraged, as Bagehot observed, the deference of the parvenu to the privileges of the traditionally advantaged. A gentleman disdained those who were preoccupied with the mundane world of work and money, and accordingly distanced himself from manufacturing and from provincial urban life. But gentlemen looked forward as well as back. They invoked the past to fashion a morality for the present, not only to counter the encroachments of industry and democracy, but also to legitimise their own innovating activities. Moreover, property, privilege and order were defended by material wealth as well as by moral rearmament, even though a gentleman's means of support had ideally to be invisible as well as substantial. Gentlemen were directly involved in approved capitalist activities in relation to land, finance and associated businesses of high repute, or had a rentier interest in them. They may have been fascinated by armour, tournaments and castles, but they used history to protect new and sizeable forms of capitalist wealth which they themselves had created.[3]

The men who shaped Britain's imperial destinies were therefore neither representatives of the industrial bourgeoisie nor Olympian figures removed from material concerns. If their conception of the national interest rose above party and class, it was because they succeeded in projecting a view of the world which was sufficiently spacious to encompass other allegiances. But it was also a conception that contained well-ordered, if usually unspoken, priorities. Income streams which fed gentlemanly interests were protected and promoted; industrial interests were given less weight in the formulation of policy. London was both the heartland of gentlemanly forms of business and the seat of government. It was there that the City, Whitehall and Parliament persuaded first themselves and then the wider constituency that the interests of finance and services were those of the nation, and that pressures issuing from Manchester, Birmingham or Glasgow were at best partial and at worst self-serving. Of course, no government could afford to ignore the wealth (and taxable incomes) created by Britain's manufactured exports, or the political threat posed by periodic unemployment in the staple industries. These considerations had their place on the agenda of domestic and international policy. But there was a difference between keeping industry content and allowing its claims to challenge the gentlemanly order; where a choice had to be made, as was increasingly the case after the mid-nineteenth century, gentlemanly interests invariably took precedence and did so, moreover, right down to the end of empire. As is now evident, this outcome was not the result of a conspiracy by a small, covert group who hijacked policy and made it serve their own ends, but the product of a gentlemanly elite whose position was openly acknowledged and widely accepted, even if its values and purposes have yet to be fully explored by historians of the 'official mind' of policy-making and imperialism.

The historical argument

In the simplest terms, the argument we have advanced suggests that there is a broad unity of purpose underlying Britain's overseas expansion and her associated imperialist ventures during the three centuries spanning the rise and fall of the empire. This unity stems not from a stereotype of capitalist penetration or from an encompassing multicausal interpretation, but from a particular pattern of economic development, centred upon finance and commercial services, which was set in train at the close of the seventeenth century and survived to the end of empire and indeed beyond. However, since the continuities of history can easily be demonstrated by pitching generalisations at a sufficiently high level, we have also identified two principal chronological periods, before and after 1850, representing significant shifts of power within the gentlemanly order and related changes in the structure of Britain's activities overseas. Each period contains subdivisions of its own which reflect alterations to the policies needed to sustain the gentlemanly order in question: in the first period, there was an important adjustment after 1815 which culminated in the point of transition in 1850; in the second, there was an adaptation after 1914 as Britain slowly came to terms with her inability to restore the pre-war international order. We recognise of course that chronological precision imposes a degree of unity which the past, being in constant transition, did not possess; but we accept, too, the counter-argument that historical analysis without dates is a contradiction in terms.

The first period, from 1688 to 1850, is defined by a system of political economy which a subsequent generation of reformers referred to as Old Corruption. This system was dominated by the landed interest, the aristocrats and country gentry whose power was confirmed by the Glorious Revolution, in association with a junior partner, the moneyed interest, which gained prominence after the financial revolution of the 1690s. Patronage and peculation were endemic to the system; but they were also consistent with the emergence of an effective military-fiscal state. The alliance between traditional authority and new sources of credit produced a strong and stable government, managed from London, which was capable of financing the defence of the realm and winning political loyalties without penalising wealth-holders or crushing the largely disenfranchised tax paying public. The mercantilist system attacked by Adam Smith was not inherited from a feudal past but was invented to raise the revenues needed to fund this structure of authority, which itself was the legacy of the Revolution Settlement. As mercantilism sheltered agriculture and manufactures, so it also promoted Britain's burgeoning shipping and commercial services, which forged ahead under a policy of aggressive protection and eventually captured most of the re-export trade in produce from the world beyond Europe.

What used to be known as the 'old colonial system' was the product of these domestic forces.[4] The American colonies were supposed to function as outer provinces of England, to reproduce a loyal gentry, and to render their appropriate contribution to the exchequer. India was to be assimilated to the military-fiscal order through the East India Company, which itself was an early manifestation of London's overseas influence and of gentlemanly capitalist interests. The growth of the empire in the eighteenth century, we suggested, is better understood as an expression of these developments than through theories that search for a nascent industrial bourgeoisie or emphasise the role of atavistic social forces. When the crisis of empire came in the late eighteenth century, financial considerations were at its centre. The American Revolution, the first great act of decolonisation, linked taxation to representation. The French Revolution, and the wars that followed, brought the prospect of invasion, which endangered Britain's finance and credit as well as the political status quo, and threatened to close continental Europe to her re-export trade. These fears strengthened the body politic, despite the loss of the American colonies. As the national debt swelled to safeguard the realm, so too did national solidarity. The resurgent conservatism which caused gentlemen of wealth to rally to the defence of property postponed radical reform, encouraged a unifying religious revival, and authorised the suppression of dissidence. It also promoted firmer measures abroad, above all in India, where the extension of British power was part of an emerging global strategy for keeping the world safe from French imperialism and the attendant horrors, fostered by the United States too, of republicanism and democracy. Among Napoleon Bonaparte's various unintended legacies to Europe was the emergence in Britain of a sense of patriotism founded on the principles of godliness, social discipline and loyalty to the crown, which in turn prepared the way for the invention of the nineteenth-century gentleman.

Pressures contained during the emergency of war could no longer be controlled in conditions of peace. After 1815, reforms were set in train which reduced the national debt, abolished Old Corruption, enfranchised a larger cohort of property-owners and dismantled the machinery of protection. These measures were painful to vested interests and caused much anguish to die-hards. But by 1850, following the abolition of the Corn Laws and the Navigation Acts, the most important economic reforms were in place, and Britain had committed herself fully to a policy of free trade. The shift to free trade was a complex process, in which the growing need to import food and to find markets for manufactures were important considerations. But, as we have argued, the initiative was taken by governments which considered that Britain's comparative advantage lay in becoming the warehouse and banker of the world. After 1815, London replaced Amsterdam as Europe's leading financial centre, increased her control over the marketing of Britain's exports, and demonstrated her expanding value as a source of invisible income, which in turn was responsible for settling a sizeable and growing share of the import bill. Moreover, income from finance and services, being invisible, was socially acceptable and gave the playing classes, as Ruskin called them, material influence.[5] Even so, the transition was fraught with uncertainty: a leap had to be made from the familiar comforts of the national debt to the risky, if also unfolding, prospects of the wider world.

The transition from Old Corruption at home was thus complemented by expansionist policies abroad. These were entailed by the shift to free trade, which implied the integration of complementary trading partners into an international economy based on London's ability to finance and manage a multilateral payments system. As we have seen, however, these economic impulses were bound up with a wider mission, which can be summarised as the world's first comprehensive development programme. After 1815, Britain aimed to put in place a set of like-minded allies who would cooperate in keeping the world safe from what Canning called the 'youthful and stirring nations', such as the United States, which proclaimed the virtues of republican democracy, and from a 'league of worn-out governments' in Europe whose future lay too obviously in the past.[6] Britain offered an alternative vision of a liberal international order bound together by mutual interest in commercial progress and underpinned by a respect for property, credit, and responsible government, preferably of the kind found at home.

Expansionist tendencies expressed themselves most obviously in attempts to promote the growth of world trade after 1815 and in the increasing flow of capital to Europe and the United States. Manifestations of imperialism were found in the annexation of a chain of naval bases, from Aden to Singapore, which were taken to police the new international economic order, and in the more intensive efforts made to create cooperative satellites. In the colonies of white settlement, schemes were devised for filling empty spaces with emigrants who would reproduce, and hence safeguard, the institutions found in the mother country. In South America, an area of white settlement but not of colonies, Britain hoped to draw the new republics into her orbit by funding their nation-building activities and by tempting them with offers of free trade and liberal institutions. In India, where Britain was already a land power, it was possible to believe, for a time at least, that a programme of social engineering would succeed in putting appropriate elites and institutions in place. In the Ottoman Empire, China and tropical Africa, policy rested on the less substantial hope that initial diplomatic and naval pressures would suffice to open up and integrate societies whose structures were very different, both from each other and from Britain's. These efforts were limited by technical constraints and considerations of cost, and the plan itself was hampered by a degree of naive optimism which assumed that other countries would see Britain's point of view as readily as she did herself.

Given the global sweep of these endeavours, it is hard to agree with Platt's contention that, before 1850, Britain's ambitions were contained within mercantilist targets of self-sufficiency which were met by the existing empire and by traditional trading partners in Europe and the United States.[7] In our view, this interpretation underestimates the importance of the house-breaking ventures needed to provide industry with new markets, of the transition to free trade, which required a more integrated world economy, and of the ideological commitment which associated economic progress with a vision of a new international order. But we do not accept, either, that the result of these intentions was an informal empire of influence which expressed Britain's competitive superiority in manufactured goods.[8] In the first place, Britain was already finding it difficult to hold, still more to expand, her place in the major markets of Europe and the United States; imperialist ventures, whether formal or informal, were partly a reflection of the need to keep industry satisfied – but also at arm's length. Secondly, as our case studies have shown, these efforts met with limited success. The colonies of white settlement grew, but far more slowly than had been hoped, while India disappointed the unrealistic expectations of a generation of eager reformers and improvers, and began to develop as a sizeable market only in the 1850s. Outside the confines of the constitutional empire, Britain was unable to create an alternative realm of informal sway in South America, the

Ottoman Empire, China or tropical Africa, all of which demonstrated that there was a difference between knocking on the door and opening it.

After 1850, when our second period begins, the composition of the gentlemanly order experienced a change which reflected the growing influence of finance and associated service occupations, and the steady decline of the landed interest. The new gentlemen of the Victorian era eventually became the senior partners, though still in alliance with the landed interest, which responded to the erosion of agricultural wealth by marrying money and investing in it through the City and often overseas. After the middle of the century, service-sector occupations grew rapidly, especially in London and the aptly named Home Counties, and economic policy became permeated by assumptions about the centrality of the City. Given the rapid growth of overseas investment after 1850 and the increasingly vital role played by all forms of invisible earnings in the balance of payments, it is not surprising that the City succeeded in identifying its interests with those of the nation. Free trade and sound money became orthodoxies of such repute that they transcended policy and acquired the status of moral virtues which juxtaposed the gentlemanly ideals of liberty with discipline, and of progress with order. Attempts to dislodge economic orthodoxy merely confirmed its supremacy, as the campaigns favouring bimetallism and tariff reform demonstrated. Important manufacturing interests gained from free trade, and to this extent were accommodated within prevailing policy norms. The qualms of other manufacturers were rendered ineffective by disunity within their ranks and by their perception that a radical challenge to established policies might well bring down forms of property in which they themselves had a vested interest.

Between 1850 and 1914 Britain's overseas interests underwent a massive expansion. It was during this period that capital flows funded economic development and 'nation-building' across the world, and that effective integration based on complementarities between 'primary' and 'secondary' producers was finally achieved. The City stood at the centre of an increasingly complex network of multilateral payments, and Britain acquired the managerial obligation of ensuring that the system functioned smoothly. Britain's manufacturers gained from the opportunities opened up by finance, but, as we have seen, the gains were not unqualified and policy was not, in general, directed by industrial pressure groups. Indeed, the fact that Britain's industry was in relative decline from the late nineteenth century has often been cited as evidence that her arteries were hardening and that the initiative in international affairs was shifting to 'youthful and stirring nations', such as Germany, and to revitalised rivals, such as France.[9] From the perspective of the present study, however, the performance of Britain's industries is not the best index of her international priorities or power. Much more significant, we have suggested, were capital flows and invisible earnings, which continued to grow down to 1914. It was during this period that Britain moved from being an early lender to becoming a mature creditor.[10] In this stage, she financed, transported and insured an increasing proportion of the manufactured goods produced by other countries: the logic of free trade was precisely that debtors had to be given access to other markets so that they could acquire the foreign exchange needed to service their debts. If Britain's creditors had bought more British manufactures, they would have been less able to meet their obligations to the City of London. This irony, which has so far received little attention from historians of imperialism, provides a further reason for supposing that the ability of British manufacturers to shape international policy diminished rather than grew as the period advanced.

Our case studies have attempted to show that Britain was still a dynamic society, and that British imperialism during this period was far from being the weary response of a faltering power to the actions of fitter rivals. The Dominions became dependent on the supply of British capital even as they gained responsible government; if they used their new-found freedom to increase tariffs on British manufactured imports, this was to raise revenue to service their debts as well as to appease local industrial interests. India, which Marx thought would serve the needs of the industrial bourgeoisie, in fact became a vast arena for the pursuit of a whole gamut of gentlemanly activities – from the duties of administration to the pleasures of the chase. Manchester won markets but few privileges, and when a choice had to be made between the interests of industry and the imperatives of finance, the gentlemen of the Indian Civil Service, like their counterparts in Whitehall, knew where their priorities lay. The argument that Britain was an ailing and defensive power fits even less well with the case most commonly cited to support it: the partition of Africa. The occupation of Egypt was a direct result of the khedive's external indebtedness, and was seen (in the end, even by Gladstone) as being a just penalty for 'oriental societies' which broke the rules of the game. The annexation of South Africa also sprang from a preoccupation with finance, though in this instance the aim was to realise the economic potential of the region by drawing British and Afrikaner settlers into a federation, based on Canadian precedents, which would create a viable unit and tie it more closely to London. Only in parts of tropical Africa did merchants representing manufacturing interests have a clear influence on policy, but this was mainly because the region was too poor to attract sizeable interest from the City, and could also be acquired at minimal cost.[11]

Evidence of the spread of Britain's informal influence outside the empire is equally telling. It was Britain, not her rivals, who promoted the surge of investment in South America in the second half of the nineteenth century, who extended her influence in the leading republics, and who set the terms that debtor governments had to meet if they were to continue to enjoy access to the London capital market. In the case of China, new research has made it possible to show that Britain's influence expanded rapidly after 1895, when Peking finally opened its doors to foreign loans. The British, led by the gentlemen of the Hongkong and Shanghai Bank, took the lion's share of this new business, and remained the dominant power in China down to the revolution of 1911. Finally, the fact that British investors were reluctant to finance the Ottoman Empire after 1875 was a sign of their strength and cannot be used as an example of Britain's decline and retreat, as some scholars have suggested. The Ottoman default was a serious one; the prospects for new investment were unattractive; the City had better opportunities elsewhere. The City's attitude created problems for the Foreign Office, which was left to make bricks without straw, but British investors could not be directed against their will, and they would not move without gilt-edged guarantees. Even so, the City's authority was imprinted on the economic affairs of the Ottoman Empire through the organisation which administered the public debt, and its weight was felt right down to 1914. In all of these cases, the power exerted by Britain far exceeded that associated with normal business relations, and involved incursions into the sovereignty of independent states which can justly be classified as imperialist.

This analysis, we suggest, requires a restatement of the problem of imperialist expansion. The question is not why the long continuities of nineteenth-century expansion were interrupted; the answer, therefore, is not that Britain's informal empire was weakened by industrial decline, foreign rivals or proto-nationalists on the periphery. Britain was an expanding society in the nineteenth century, but expansion was not continuous. By dividing the period in 1850, we have tried to distinguish between a phase in which imperialist intentions had limited results in creating a fully integrated international economy, and a phase in which Britain's penetrative capacity was very greatly extended. Britain's invisible 'empire' had scarcely come into existence before 1850. Far from being in a state of advanced decay in the late nineteenth century, her informal influence was expanding vigorously at exactly that point. British imperialism, in both formal and informal guises, was the outgrowth of these successful expansionist impulses. Seen from another perspective, Britain's massive exports of capital not only encouraged economic growth but also gave rise to various types of development and managerial debt. Since a large proportion of Britain's foreign investments took the form of loans to foreign governments, the problem of sovereign debt inevitably touched the independence of the recipients. Britain may well have preferred to deal with these issues by informal means, though these still infringed the sovereignty of other countries; but the continuing dynamism of her expansion pushed her into situations where the range of choice was often limited. As the century advanced, an increasing number of patriotic officers and gentlemen were at hand to ensure that, at such moments, Britain did her duty.

World War I is conventionally regarded as marking the dividing line between the expansion and decline of empire, though, as we have seen, some historians prefer to date the transition from a point in the late nineteenth century. We have looked at the period from a different standpoint, one that carries forward the argument developed to explain imperialist expansion in the period after 1850. The power structure which arose from the debris of Old Corruption remained substantially intact after 1914, despite the ravages of two world wars and the hesitant emergence of 'corporatism'. The priorities of international policy were also unchanged, as Britain sought to maintain her role as banker to the world, first by returning to the gold standard in 1925, and then by nurturing the sterling bloc after 1931. These aims permeated Britain's wider diplomatic purposes: they entered Chamberlain's policy of appeasement in the 1930s, and they helped to mould the ambiguous 'special relationship' with the United States thereafter. Moreover, Britain's determination to retain her empire and her informal influence was undiminished, not only after 1914 but also after 1945. What changed after World War I was that Britain was no longer in a position to supply sufficient capital to fuel the international economy. Although successive governments struggled to create conditions which would encourage new overseas borrowing, they became increasingly preoccupied with the problem of securing repayments on existing loans. The gentlemanly order marched on; but the adverse circumstances which affected the performance of overseas investment and other invisible earnings had a profound effect on the difficulties Britain faced and the means she adopted to meet her traditional priorities. It is for these reasons, and not because we accept standard assumptions contrasting 'expansion' with 'decline', that we have identified the years between World War I and decolonisation as being a sub-division of the longer period which began in the mid-nineteenth century.

Our approach suggests that British imperialism had a consistent and insistent theme which is imperfectly recognised, where it is recognised at all, in the majority of studies of the period, which tend to stress the continuing difficulties faced by Britain's manufactured exports, the gathering problems posed by the rise of colonial nationalism, and the failing will-power of the decision-making elite. The theme we have emphasised here was manifested most clearly in Britain's determination to use the empire to assist her return to the gold standard and subsequently to form the basis of the sterling bloc. As we have seen, the Dominions (with the exception of Canada) remained dependent on London for their external finance, and Britain used her authority to ensure that they continued to conform to the rules of the game. The Ottawa agreements, which are widely treated as a defeat for British policy, were in fact a success for British finance: the preferences granted to the empire were undoubtedly more generous than those given to Britain's manufacturers, but the imbalance was necessary to ensure that the Dominions had the means of servicing their debts. The same priorities made themselves felt in India: tariff autonomy fatally damaged Manchester's exports of cotton goods but helped to balance the budget and to service the external debt, while successive constitutional concessions left Delhi's subordination in financial and monetary affairs untouched. As for the tropical colonies, their subservience to the rigours of fiscal orthodoxy, their whole-hearted commitment to tax-gathering, and their much-needed contribution to Britain's faltering balance of payments was never more fully demonstrated than in the mother country's hour of need – which, in the event, extended from 1914 to the eve of decolonisation. The idea that there was a 'long retreat' from empire fits ill with evidence not only of the revitalisation of the colonial mission after the two world wars, but also of the firm grip which Britain retained in the areas of policy which mattered most.

Moreover, we argued that regions of informal influence also played their part in meeting Britain's priorities in the international economy, and did not simply disappear after 1914, as is generally thought. Their contribution could clearly be seen in the pressure exerted on the smaller European members of the sterling bloc in the 1930s and in the policies adopted towards the two great 'unclaimed' regions of the world, South America and China, where Britain worked hard and effectively to maintain her financial interests. Key decisions, such as the Roca–Runciman Pact with Argentina and the backing given to Chiang Kai-shek in China, were made with these priorities in mind, and in both cases it was Britain's staple manufactured exports that suffered. These examples, we suggested, also underlined the need to emphasise the continuing momentum of imperialist rivalries after 1914. The contest for supremacy in South America and China was not only hard-fought but also distinctive in deploying new weaponry devised by the service industries, especially radio, cinema and air-power. This struggle developed rapidly in the 1930s (when it also embraced schemes for redividing large parts of Africa), and was carried on by additional means during World War II. In the hierarchy of causes of the war, a prominent place has to be found, in our view, for the battle between the 'have' and the 'have not' powers arising out of the world slump and particularly out of the ensuing financial crisis – a crisis which signalled the final breakdown of the free-trade order which Britain had built by a combination of diplomacy and force from the middle of the nineteenth century.

The wider context

These general conclusions can themselves be set in an even wider context. Given the scope of the present study, the problem is not to think of possible connections but rather to limit their number so that they underline rather than overlay our principal theme. We shall confine ourselves here to three observations which should be of interest both to historians and to scholars who use the past principally as a guide to the present.

The first observation concerns the relationship between the rise and fall of empires. The question of the decline of 'hegemonic' powers has aroused a great deal of discussion in recent years, especially in the United States, where academic and political commentators have been much exercised by the belief that their country is less dominant today than it was in the years immediately after World War II.[12] This perception has prompted considerable debate, and a good deal of heart-searching, about the causes of decline and its implications for the maintenance of world order. According to one influential interpretation, a hegemonic power is needed to guarantee international stability, and the conclusion drawn is that, if the influence of the United States is allowed to decline, disorder will follow. This cataclysmic view of the future will be familiar to historians of the British empire. Policy-makers were permanently fearful that they would be unable to maintain the legacy of eminence bequeathed by their predecessors, and they doubled their anxieties by assuming that what was good for London was also good for the rest of the world.[13] As commentators in the United States try to read the lessons of the British empire, so the British, in their time, looked to Greece and Rome for guidance – with a sideways glance at the fate of the Dutch.[14] In both cases, attempts to discern the laws of motion of large powers have often been variations, in modern dress, of the venerable organic metaphor of growth and decay, and the task of policy-oriented social scientists has been, in effect, to find the elixir of eternal life. Whatever their merits, the objectivity of these exercises in comparative history has often been compromised by their justificatory purpose, which stresses the weight of the burdens carried by the hegemonic power and the ingratitude of those who are presumed to benefit from its influence. Spokesmen of leading powers do not take readily to the idea that the end of their period of dominance is not necessarily the end of the world. Accordingly, they find it hard to envisage pluralistic alternatives to the rule of a single power, and harder still to accept the emergence of a more successful rival.

Since much of our argument is at variance with the historical interpretations of British imperialism usually drawn on by specialists in contemporary international relations, there is little point in examining the comparisons which have been made between the *Pax Britannica* and the *Pax Americana*. The question of imperial decline, however, requires comment because it bears particularly on our reconsideration of the period after 1914. The thrust of our argument, it will be recalled, emphasised Britain's continuing ambition and success as an imperialist power, and did so by identifying the priorities of policy-makers and tracing the ways in which they were implemented. But we also drew attention to the fact that Britain's ability to supply capital for overseas investment was more restricted after World War I, that her income from invisibles was less buoyant, and that she emerged from World War II as the world's largest debtor. Evidence of Britain's continuing stature as an international power might therefore seem to be at variance with evidence of her increasing weakness. However, this apparent paradox can be resolved by recalling that power is relative as well as absolute.[15] Objective measurements may show that Britain was weaker after 1914 than before, but her relative position with respect to her main rivals and satellites remained strong. Germany and France suffered severely as a result of World War I and the slump of the 1930s. The United States was only beginning to emerge as a world power before 1939, and some of the ground she had made up on Britain during the war and in the early 1920s was lost again during the depression. After 1945, with the onset of the Cold War, it was not in her interests to lean as heavily on Britain as she might have done. For their part, Britain's satellites were constrained by a lack of alternatives: even in adversity, they remained tied to sterling and to the London money market.

Viewed from this angle, Britain's decline as an imperial power became effective only when these relativities changed. The spreading influence of the United States during the period of 'competitive coexistence', combined with the recovery of continental Europe and Japan from the 1950s, created alternative centres of attraction which greatly reduced Britain's drawing power; and the irresistible rise of the dollar displaced sterling from its position as the chief currency of international trade. However, as we noted in Chapter 26, these developments also provided Britain with new opportunities: the growth of inter-industry trade directed capital and commerce towards the advanced economies and away from the more backward colonies and semi-colonies; and the appearance of novel financial instruments, notably the Eurodollar, gave the City a new lease of life.

These trends were associated with a historic shift in the structure of the international economy which merits greater attention than it has received from students of 'late colonialism' and decolonisation. Our analysis has indicated that one of the most distinctive features of Britain's overseas expansion was that it integrated countries which lacked sizeable capital markets of their own by offering them sterling credits and the facilities of the City of London. Where the terms of the offer involved a loss of sovereignty, in ways described at the outset of this study, expansion became imperialism. The logic of this argument suggests that imperialism ends when these conditions cease or are greatly diminished. This is exactly what happened: the development of local capital markets and the indigenisation of the public foreign debt began in the Dominions before World War II; the growth of joint ventures started to alter the role of expatriate business in India, Argentina and China from the 1930s, and in the Dominions from an even earlier date; the recapture of public utilities by purchase, as in Argentina and Brazil, or by nationalisation, as in China and parts of the Middle East, occurred in the late 1940s and 1950s; the decline of sterling, and the failure of local Central Banks to 'play the game' according to traditional London rules, became apparent from the late 1950s onwards.

The purpose of these remarks is not to invent a new dialectic to explain the history of imperialism, but to call attention to an underestimated consequence of imperialist influences, which was to set in motion a series of structural changes that ultimately enabled the most important satellites to recover their independence. Neo-colonialism can undoubtedly be found in parts of the former empire, but so too can a new form of post-imperial capitalism based upon a cosmopolitan world order characterised by the unification of diverse capital markets through competing financial centres, the domestication of multinational corporations by hosts who have ceased to be hostages, and the separation of expatriate interests from the idea of a civilising mission.[16] The concept of decline therefore requires close definition, and even then it can easily mislead when applied to national aggregates. The decline of the British empire removed one of the props of the gentlemanly order, but it did not bring about the fall of the City, which may help to explain why the trauma of decolonisation was psychological rather than economic.

Our second observation concerns the implications of our analysis for the study of rival imperialist powers, especially those in Europe. We have focused on the domestic roots of imperialism because this approach seems to us to have greater explanatory power than one pitched at the level of international relations and removed from the interests which shape national policy.[17] We have brought international rivalries into the story at points where they exerted a particularly strong influence on British policy, but we are aware that more could have been said on this theme than space has allowed. However, the issue we wish to raise here is whether our approach is applicable to the cases which immediately suggest themselves: those of France and Germany.[18]

The answer to this question falls into two parts: one is easy; the other is difficult, and at present may not even be possible. The easy answer is to confirm our view that the analysis of metropolitan interests offers the most promising way of tracing imperialist impulses, and to support this judgement by citing the illuminating work of scholars such as Marseille, Wehler and Stern.[19] The hard part of the answer is to decide whether the particular configuration of interests we have identified was both present and of equal importance elsewhere, or whether it was specific to the British case. The reason for the difficulty is simply that the evidence currently available is insufficiently detailed to allow generalisations to be made with confidence.[20] Specialists who are familiar with the historical complexities of one country are still capable of adopting stereotypes of another. Analogies of this order can readily be made but they will also be flawed. Our caution on this question is, so we think, the product less of insularity than of an awareness that judgements about similarities and singularities need to be derived from a broadly comparable data base. On this subject, therefore, we have decided to confine ourselves to the hope that our work will join other studies in bringing nearer the prospect of a fully comparative approach to European imperialism.

Our final observation returns us to our starting point: the history of Britain and of the gentlemanly interests which have been our principal focus. We believe that the case we have presented has sufficient coherence and enough evidence to merit serious consideration, and we hope that it will carry forward the study of the subject in a constructive manner. At the same time, we are aware that our argument opens lines of inquiry rather than closes them: the relationship between the City and industry, the connection joining financial interests to political authority, the link between the domestic 'power elite' and imperialist expansion – all of these are large themes that invite further study. Whatever judgement is made of our particular interpretation, however, we hope that we have succeeded in making a case for reintegrating the analysis of British and imperial history in ways that unite economic, social and political branches of historical study and cross the boundaries of centuries divided by scholarly practice. These divisions are justified by the imperative of specialisation, and there is undoubtedly a price to be paid for stepping over them. Moreover, evidence of intention is no indication of the result of an enterprise, which must properly be left to the judgement of others. This being so, we should perhaps end this restatement of our wide-ranging claims by recalling Dr Johnson's salutary observation that he was confident of doing two things very well: one was the introduction to a literary work saying what it would contain and how it would be executed in the most perfect manner; the other was a conclusion revealing why the execution had fallen short of the promises made by the author to himself and to his readers.

Notes

1 The phrase is Burke's, quoted in Chapter 1, p. 61.

2 The obvious analogy is with the findings of development studies following a generation of research on diverse parts of the 'Third World'.

3 Our argument is therefore clearly differentiated from that of Martin Wiener, *English Culture and the Decline of the Industrial Spirit, 1850–1980* (Cambridge, 1981).

4 This term can still be used to refer to the period before the move to free trade in the mid-nineteenth century. However, we have avoided reference to the 'first' and 'second' British empires because these concepts are harder both to define and to date.

5 John Ruskin, 'Work', in *The Works of John Ruskin,* 18 (1865), divided England into two classes: those who worked and those who played. For the playing classes, 'the first of all the English games is making money'.
6 Canning in 1825. Quoted in William W. Kaufmann, *British Policy and the Independence of Latin America, 1804–1828* (New Haven, Conn., 1951), p. 201.
7 Platt, 'The National Economy and British Imperial Expansion before 1914', *Jour. Imp. and Comm. Hist.,* 2 (1973–4).
8 J. Gallagher and R. Robinson, 'The Imperialism of Free Trade', *Econ. Hist. Rev.,* 2nd ser. VI (1953).
9 See, for example, Ronald Robinson and John Gallagher, *Africa and the Victorians: The Official Mind of Imperialism* (1961; 2nd edn, 1981).
10 For a succinct statement see Jeffrey A. Frieden, 'Capital Politics: Creditors and the International Political Economy', *Journal of Public Policy,* 8 (1989).
11 We do not make this point to minimise an exception to our argument but rather to illustrate where London's priorities lay.
12 For a critical introduction to what is now a vast literature see Isabelle Grunberg, 'Exploring the "Myth" of Hegemonic Stability', *International Organization,* 44 (1990), and the further references given there.
13 J.G. Darwin, 'The Fear of Falling: British Politics and Imperial Decline Since 1900', *Trans. Royal Hist. Soc.,* 36 (1986).
14 The comparisons are still made. See Gary B. Miles, 'Roman and Modern Imperialism: a Reassessment', *Camp. Stud. in Soc. and Hist.,* 32 (1990).
15 A dramatic illustration of this distinction has been provided by the collapse of the Soviet 'empire', an event which ought to prompt a review of the assumption that the power of the United States is withering away. Firm guidance on a slippery subject is provided by Joseph S. Nye, 'The Changing Nature of World Power', *Political Science Quarterly,* 105 (1990). For a remarkable piece of anticipation see Valerie Bunce, '"The Empire Strikes Back": the Transformation of the Eastern Bloc from a Soviet Asset to a Soviet Liability', *International Organization,* 39 (1985).
16 For these developments see David Fieldhouse, 'A New Imperial System? The Role of the Multinational Corporation Reconsidered', in Mommsen and Osterhammel, *Imperialism and After,* David G. Becker, Jeff Frieden, Sayre P. Schatz and Richard L. Sklar, *Post-Imperialism: International Capitalism and Development in the Late Twentieth Century* (1987); and Susan Strange, 'Finance, Information and Power', *Rev. Internat. Stud.,* 16 (1990). On current trends in global finance, see Susan Strange, *Casino Capitalism* (1986); and Jeffry A. Frieden, *Banking on the World: The Politics of International Finance* (1987).
17 Here, as elsewhere, we are in agreement with Frieden, 'Capital Politics'.
18 This question has been one of the most frequently asked in seminars dealing with our general interpretation of British imperialism.
19 Jacques Marseille, *Empire colonial et capitalisme français: histoire d'un divorce* (Paris, 1984); Hans-Ulrich Wehler, *Bismarck und der Imperialismus* (Munich, 4th edn., 1976); Fritz Stem, *Gold and Iron: Bismarck, Bleichröder and the Building of the German Empire* (New York, 1977).
20 Notwithstanding the pioneering studies of Marseille, Wehler, Stem (see n. 19) and others, and the high quality of the debates on, for example, the *parti colonial* in France and the nature of social imperialism in Germany. See now pp. 15–17.

AFTERWORD

Empires and globalisation, 1688–2015

'The outcome of any serious research can only be to make two questions grow where one question grew before'.[1]

At first sight, it may seem odd to carry the study of British imperialism into the twenty-first century, given that the empire itself crumbled more than 50 years ago. The familiar justification for re-examining well-known historical themes still provides the most satisfactory rationale: the view from the present allows the past to be seen, as historians like to say, in perspective. Today, for example, we can look afresh at developments in the post-colonial era by placing the history of empires and imperialism in the context of different phases of globalisation. Empires were globalising forces that transmitted impulses well beyond their territorial borders. The globalising consequences of imperial expansion stretched across the world and far into the period of decolonisation. They left deep marks on the states that lost their colonies after World War II as well as on those that achieved independence. The consequences for the 'mother country' can be seen in the ways in which the empire first struck back and then came back: nationalist movements mobilised the material and intellectual assets of the West, in conjunction with their own resources, to hold colonial rulers to account; migration from parts of the former empire to Britain changed the composition of society and tested assumptions of social solidarity and ethnic superiority that had long underpinned national unity.

The end of the British empire fell short of being *el desastre*, the term commentators coined to describe the collapse of the Spanish Empire in 1898. Nevertheless, it inspired the perceptive and enduring judgment, reached in 1962, that Britain had 'lost an empire and not yet found a role'.[2] Successive governments have struggled since then to fit Britain into the post-colonial global order. Policy-makers, like the public, are uncertain about the future partly because they are unsure of Britain's identity and purpose. The resulting compromises are ambiguous and uncomfortable. Governments of all persuasions carry forward pretensions to great-power status yet preside over diminishing means of upholding it. They continue to cultivate a 'special relationship' as increasingly insignificant clients of the United States, while struggling to negotiate Britain's position as an ambivalent member of the European Community. The past lives on in these dilemmas, not just as a residue, but as an active consequence of the transformation that brought the empire down and began the protracted and taxing process of shaping a new domestic and international order.

Globalisation and empires

It is now accepted that globalisation has origins that long antedate the late twentieth century and the current debate about the merits and defects of capitalism as a means of raising living standards across the world. Exactly when the process of global integration began is a matter of historical dispute that is unlikely to be resolved speedily because the outcome depends heavily on the definition of terms, which continue to be contested.[3] Economists, for example, have mapped a chronology that runs from the mid-nineteenth century to the present and includes a phase of 'deglobalisation' in the 1930s.[4] The strength of this analysis is that it brings precision derived from measurable indices. Its limitation is that it leaves aside matters such as nation-building and international cultural influences that are generally agreed to be important components of globalisation, even though they cannot be readily quantified.

British Imperialism aimed to place these broader, long-run considerations at the centre of the developments that produced imperialism. Our interpretation rested upon a reappraisal of the process of modernisation, which, so we argued, was bound up with a particular type of economic development, with the transformation of the military-fiscal state into a nation state, and with far-reaching institutional changes that gave the English gentleman a pivotal role in promoting, simultaneously, economic liberalism and social conservatism. In our view, moreover, the shaping of modern Britain cannot be separated from the history of its empire, which was itself a trans-national organisation with globalising ambitions. The greater part of our study was devoted to tracing the multiple interactions that helped to weld the nation at home and channel its influence overseas.[5]

The process of imperial expansion can be thought of as a series of phases in the history of globalisation. A provisional taxonomy suggests that Britain's world role during the period under review can be divided into three broad, overlapping sequences: 'proto-globalisation' between 1688 and 1850, 'modern globalisation' from 1850 to 1950, and 'post-colonial globalisation' from 1950 to the present day.[6] Similar sequences apply to the rest of Europe, though the dates need adjusting to reflect the fact that Britain, the exemplary 'early-starter', was ahead of states on the continent until the final phase, when decolonisation brought down all the Western empires more or less at the same time. The advantage of these categories is that they make a start in identifying differences that are lost to view if the history of globalisation is treated in an undifferentiated manner. In particular, they allow the trajectory of empire to be considered as an unfolding dialectical sequence, whereby the conditions that promoted one phase of imperial globalisation generated forces that were to transform it.

Proto-globalisation

The concept of proto-globalisation captures two interacting processes: the rise of the European system of military-fiscal states and the development of commerce, finance and pre-industrial manufactures. In the British case, the starting point for political developments could easily be located before the close of the seventeenth century, though the date we selected, 1688, serves its purpose well, not least because the Glorious Revolution was also related to the Union with Scotland in 1707.[7] Similarly, the terminal date could be placed at the start of the nineteenth century to recognise Britain's pioneering role as an industrialising power. Nevertheless, 1850 is a date that allows not only for the protracted development of modern industry but also for the long struggle to replace the military-fiscal state inherited from the eighteenth century.

It is clear that the pace of globalisation increased in the eighteenth century and that the form taken by the military-fiscal state after the Revolution of 1688 was crucial to the process.[8] The partnership between monarchy and aristocracy under a strengthened Parliamentary system provided governments with reservoirs of credit on a scale unknown elsewhere. Novel sources of finance funded Britain's naval supremacy and facilitated the expansion of overseas commerce. Mercantilist regulations raised revenues and protected key economic interests. The opening and extension of new markets stimulated the development of manufacturing, commerce and finance, promoted urban growth, and gave a fillip to the merchant class. The bitter rivalry for markets and supplies between competing European and non-European empires in this most warlike of centuries helped to propel commercial expansion and territorial acquisition.[9]

The high levels of taxation needed to sustain military-fiscalism gave birth to the complex of privilege, patronage and preferment later known as 'Old Corruption', and they facilitated the rise of the gentlemanly capitalists who managed the new financial instruments.[10] However, what was a prop for the aristocracy and its associates also became a source of discontent that stimulated a new style of radical politics as the century advanced.[11] The pursuit of tax revenues to sustain the system drove the state through one crisis of adaptation after another.[12] Fiscal need first galvanised governments to search for taxable revenues at home and then prompted territorial expansion overseas. The hunt for new sources of revenue led to territorial acquisitions in Bengal;[13] the attempt to squeeze more taxes out of the mainland colonies provoked the revolt that ended British rule there.[14] Indigenous societies and settler states made an essential contribution to the outcome in both cases. Nevertheless, it seems fair to say that the 'peripheral theory' of empire-building now needs modifying to allow for the weight of metropolitan interests that propelled Britain into India and expelled her from the mainland colonies.

Adam Smith judged that mercantilism had helped to expand trade, but that the military-fiscal system, with its battery of taxes, tariffs and restrictions, mainly benefited the vested interests who had constructed it and that national growth was slower as a result. Recent work has taken a broader view of the problem by suggesting that, in a mercantilist world, war not only saved markets for Britain but ensured national survival, thus providing an opportunity for the unique combination of agricultural, manufacturing, commercial and financial forces that made the Industrial Revolution to come together.[15] At least two-fifths of the increment of manufactured output went to protected imperial markets after 1660, while success in selling industrial products in North America and other markets augmented the revenues that helped Great Britain to win its battles in India.[16] Control of India also helped to win the war in Europe by placing a vital strategic resource, saltpetre (potassium nitrate), in British hands.[17] The extended imperial conflicts with France between 1760 and 1815 were nothing less than a struggle to 'redivide the world'.[18] Final victory gave Britain a degree of global supremacy that no other power could challenge until the onset of World War II.

The age of rapid globalisation and bitter imperial rivalry gave shape to the emerging idea of 'Britain'. The Britain that resulted from the Union with Scotland in 1707 was a legal rather than an organic entity. It was only in the second half of the century that the concept of a British, as opposed to an English, empire gained currency, and it was not until the close of the century that the term acquired popularity.[19] The idea of Britishness itself was formed partly through common reactions to new peoples on the frontiers of the known world, the differences that arose in the course of the American Revolution and the long struggle with Britain's most significant 'other' and chief imperial rival, France.[20] Imperial expansion, in both practical and ideological senses, gave coherence to the otherwise ill-assorted parts of the newly established 'United Kingdom'.[21] It was at this time, too, that a truly British elite began to emerge, uniting the previously disparate aristocracies of England, Scotland and Wales. This landed class, made wealthy by the process of economic growth, was protected by war and empire, which raised both agricultural and urban rents and mineral royalties. Its ranks were swelled not only by successful manufacturers, financiers and beneficiaries of Old Corruption, but also by nabobs, West Indian planters and a battalion of military-imperial heroes such as the Wellesleys, who owed their rise directly to the expansion of empire and the incomes it generated.[22] Out of this amalgam, a renewed form of gentlemanly capitalism was born that provided the economic muscle behind the formidable political and social power the aristocracy wielded in Britain until the beginning of the twentieth century.

Modern globalisation

Even as this elite was consolidating its power, fundamental shifts were taking place that were to change the basis of Britain's international position. Modern globalisation overtook its prototype, converted the military-fiscal state into a nation state, promoted industrialisation and expanded the financial sector. The struggle to manage and in some cases deter these developments was a central theme in the turbulent history of the Western Europe in the nineteenth century. Even in Britain, which avoided revolution, the upheaval involved in transforming an agricultural society into one based on towns and industry brought confrontation and civil disorder. Chartists defied governments in the 1840s; trade unions announced the power of the new industrial work-force in the 1880s. Conservatives and progressives redefined their positions and gave them political expression through increasingly efficient party oganisations.[23] Debates between conservative Christian political economists and Smithian advocates of free trade gave the political contest ideological and intellectual sustenance.[24] Although Cobdenite views of material advantage eventually prevailed, they also carried forward the imprint of a society that was profoundly religious: the new doctrine became known as the 'gospel' of free trade; missionaries undertook a complementary programme that delivered the 'bible and the plough' to the world.[25]

The military-fiscal state could not be dismantled until the French menace had been removed. After 1815, changing circumstances compelled action. The national debt had reached proportions that endangered economic growth and political stability; Old Corruption had brought government and the governing class into disrepute; the onset of peace provided an opportunity for stifled demands for greater political representation to be heard. The landed elite had succeeded in consolidating its wealth and power, but recognised the need to perpetuate its supremacy by ushering in what eventually became the 'Gladstonian' state. The reforming state maintained its authority by refusing to subsidise vested interests, by reducing government expenditure and taxation to historically low levels, and by widening the franchise just sufficiently to blunt the edge of discontent.[26] Gladstonianism was an exercise in legitimating the upper class; it was also a construct designed to reconcile the growing urban masses to the economic privileges enjoyed by the gentlemanly capitalist minority.

These processes were under way well before 1850, but it was only after then that they became the predominant means of shaping Britain's presence abroad. Territorial acquisitions added to the tally of imperial holdings. Informal influences made themselves felt through free trade, the gold standard and strategies of acculturation. Britain acquired a national mission to colonise and civilise;[27] what was later called the Third World became integrated with the modernising economies of the West. Technical advances in the form of steamships, railways, submarine cables and telegraphic communications enabled Western states to integrate parts of the world that had previously been impenetrable. Innovations such as the repeating rifle and the Maxim gun greatly reduced the costs of coercion; medical improvements enabled the white man to live, rather than to die, in the tropics. Overseas investment rose to unprecedented levels, lifting the social status and political presence of its gentlemanly representatives and bringing them to the fore of Britain's ruling elite.

Economic analysis suggests that the origins of modern globalisation can be traced to the second half of the nineteenth century, when clear evidence of international price convergence and the growth of a mass market can be found.[28] This analysis needs to be supplemented by considerations of international politics arising from the formation of new nation states. By the late nineteenth century, the process of global integration had become bound up with increasingly hostile international rivalries. The 'new imperialism' that saw most of Africa and much of Asia partitioned among the Western powers, either formally or informally, was the most dramatic illustration of the resulting global turmoil.

The growth of Britain's territorial empire, impressive though it was, was insufficient to contain her global interests. In the eighteenth century, the formal empire, led by the American colonies, had been most dynamic element in Britain's international economic expansion.[29] With the creation of the United States, however, a large slice of Britain's overseas trade instantly became foreign instead of imperial. As Britain's export industries gathered strength in the nineteenth century, the major increases in overseas commerce were with North America and Europe. By the early nineteenth century, the imperial share had contracted considerably, despite the massive extension of British imperial authority in India and the disruption and upheaval of the Napoleonic wars. The trend and its implications were already clear to Bentham in 1793, though it took half a century for his observation on the merits of free trade to be incorporated into policy: 'Before the separation', he observed of the former colonies in 1793, 'Britain had a monopoly of their trade: upon the separation of course she lost it. How much less is their trade with Britain now then? On the contrary it is much greater'.[30]

World trade doubled between 1800 and 1850; it grew tenfold between 1850 and 1914. Imperial trade accounted for about 30 per cent of all Britain's overseas trade throughout the nineteenth century. The proportion was too large to be ignored, but too small to dominate policy. The imbalance helps to explain why forces making for cosmopolitanism, of which free trade was the most important, eventually outweighed imperial commercial interests and led to the downfall of the 'old colonial system' based on protection and preferences, which collapsed between 1840 and 1860.[31] Despite large territorial gains made between 1880 and 1914, the formal empire accounted for only 40 per cent of Britain's overseas trade in 1913. Increasing dependence on income from overseas trade and investment, and the need to preserve the complex and fragile network of multilateral payments that underpinned it, goes far towards explaining Britain's global diplomatic and military commitments. Free trade and minimalist government exposed agriculture and industry to relentless foreign competition, but boosted financial and commercial services and foreign investment. Returns from overseas investment helped to restructure the economy and made an increasingly important contribution to the wealth of the gentlemanly capitalist elite, thus giving its financial component much greater prominence.

The free-trade regime produced a complex, even bewildering, patchwork of imperial connections and policies.[32] An informal empire of finance blossomed in Latin America as foreign investment became a prominent feature of British overseas expansion. Formal power was devolved in the white, settled colonies in the first instance to avoid the risk of repeating the American Revolution. Thereafter, imperial bonding was left to depend upon trade, financial flows and the colonists' natural tendency to retain ties of 'kith and kin' and, given their small populations, to look to Britain for defence. However, attempts to promote the unity of the white empire or to give it a special place in British economic and political life foundered on the commitment to commercial cosmopolitanism and a growing sense of colonial nationalism that prized 'responsible government' more than closer integration with the 'mother country'.[33]

In India, on the other hand, despite a regime of free trade and the rise of developmental strategies, elements of the old military-fiscal system continued to flourish because Britain's defence strategy depended heavily on the Indian army, and military expenditure remained a sizeable item in the Government of India's budget.[34] Indeed, it can be argued that the ability of Peel, Gladstone and their successors to reduce the role of government in Britain was made possible only because defence costs were generously funded by the Indian peasant, who continued to live in what might be termed a 'warfare state'.[35] The Government of India also gathered new territories and continued to provide the aristocracy and the professional classes with the means of extending their wealth, status and authority in ways that were no longer possible in Australia or Canada. Elsewhere in Asia, and in Africa too, the collapse of indigenous regimes under the strain of Western penetration, and fear of French and German expansion that would have meant the spread of protectionism, pushed the Gladstonian state into reluctant expansion and created more opportunities for the governing elite to exercise its military and administrative skills.

Nation-building complemented these economic developments. 'Britain' remained a work in progress, notwithstanding the bonding effect of the long French Wars. By the mid-nineteenth century, moreover, the sense of solidarity carried forward from the eighteenth century had to be refashioned to take account of the relative decline of the landed interest and the challenge of class-based politics. These domestic developments intersected with the tension between the imperialist and the cosmopolitan strands in Britain's international policy. The outcome was a wide-ranging discussion, especially in the late nineteenth century, of what it meant to be British.[36] Fervent imperialists found it difficult to imagine that the Britain of which they were so proud could exist without the empire. In their minds, empire was associated with secure material prosperity for all and was therefore vital to political and social stability. The imperial experience was also seen to be critical to the formation of 'character', which was a key concept for the Victorian governing classes.[37] The ruling elite claimed that character, forged and continuously renewed by imperial strife and imperial duty, made Britons unique. Without its empire, imperialists feared that Britain would slump into provincialism and petty materialism, and become a small, vulnerable country in a world of Darwinian struggle: at best another Holland; at worst another Portugal.[38]

The imperialist vision of Britain had to compete with powerful alternatives. It was in the second half of the century that John Bull, an established figure in public debate, achieved truly national eminence as the embodiment of values that distinguished Britons from other nations.[39] What is particularly interesting about his elevation, however, is that this 'gentleman of portly dimensions and great wealth' symbolised fiscal rectitude and free-trade orthodoxy even more than he stood for the nation and empire.[40] Certainly, for Cobdenite cosmopolitans as well as for more virulent anti-imperialists the strength and greatness of Britain lay within the islands themselves and were the result of the constitutional struggles of the past that, by promoting political and economic liberty, had made Britain powerful. Power had spilled over naturally into the international arena, where it had promoted prosperity, interdependence and peace. Such globalising tendencies were not thought of as being a threat to nationality. J. A. Hobson was repeating a liberal commonplace when he argued that a 'true strong internationalism in form or spirit would . . . imply the existence of powerful self-respecting nationalities which seek union on the basis of common national needs and interests'.[41] In his view, imperialism was a distortion of benign forces engineered by corrupt vested interests. These were residues from a more militant age whose continued dominance would reintroduce authoritarianism into British life and have drastic consequences for political freedom, economic vitality and the moral character of the people. The myths underlying the concept of 'Imperial Britain' after 1815 were constantly under challenge because they had to survive in a world in which strong and enduring impulses towards economic cosmopolitanism engendered competing legends of their own.[42]

Nonetheless, imperialists and their opponents had a great deal in common. Few radicals disdained the task of 'civilising' peoples whose territories had been occupied, even though they also objected to additions to the empire.[43] They saw the emerging Dominions as natural and legitimate extensions of Britain's abundant energies overseas, though they deprecated talk of the unity of the white empire, which they interpreted as an attempt to curtail colonial freedoms. The radical version of 'character', like the imperialist one, derived a great deal from observations of the 'other' on imperial frontiers. This is clear from Gladstone's claim that it was not superior intellect or the maturity of its civilisation that gave Britain supremacy in India but its 'comparative force of manhood and faculties of action'.[44] The same view was implicit in John Stuart Mill's fear that too much wealth might induce a 'Chinese stationariness' into British life.[45] Constructs such as 'character' influenced recruitment to Britain's international banks and trading companies and remained influential long after the Victorian era had passed.[46]

Gladstonianism underwrote the radical-liberal vision of Britain rather than that of the imperialists. Free-trade cosmopolitanism became a key part of the compromises that kept the urban working-class content with Britain's deeply inegalitarian structures.[47] Nonetheless, British governments worried permanently about the expansion of the United States and ensured that Canada was kept within the imperial fold by promoting Confederation in 1867 and negotiating the Treaty of Washington in 1871. Policy-makers were well aware that, on a per capita basis, British trade with the colonists was higher than with citizens of the United States and that greater economic benefits would accrue for Britain by keeping Canada within the empire than by allowing her to join the Republic to the south.[48] But Britain's open economic policy nonetheless allowed a large slice of British capital and the majority of her emigrants to enter the United States, thus adding to the Republic's rapidly growing strength. The open economy also encouraged interest groups in the white-settled colonies who wished to guard and extend local autonomy, and, ironically, even stimulated protectionism there. The strategy was incompatible with any state-directed policy of imperial unity and development, and in the long run, therefore, with any attempt to match the burgeoning power of the United States.[49] By economising on defence expenditure, the Gladstonian regime may also have left the nation poorly prepared to meet the German threat after 1900.[50] In effect, Gladstonianism played a part in making Britain's survival as an independent state and as an imperial power in the twentieth century increasingly reliant on the support of the United States.[51]

Nevertheless, it is now clear that American hegemony was not established in 1918.[52] Despite Britain's indebtedness to the United States, World War I ended well before American financial dominance could be asserted unequivocally. In addition, the withdrawal of the United States into political isolationism after 1919 and its neglect of military spending reduced its influence abroad. The potential for world leadership was there, but the political will to exercise it was lacking. Of course, as we have demonstrated in previous chapters, the United States was much more assertive on the economic than on the political front in the 1920s and made inroads into Britain's financial empire in China, Latin America and other areas of 'informal' control. To some extent, too, the United States curbed Britain's financial ambitions in post-war Europe. The fact remains, however, that with Germany defeated, France financially exhausted, and the Soviet Union retreating into self-containment, Britain's economic and political position in the world relative to her rivals was probably stronger in the 1920s than it had been before 1914.[53] The formal empire, swollen by acquisitions from Germany, remained a virtually unchallenged possession. Moreover, the Great Depression of 1929–1933 hit the United States much harder than it did Britain. As the US sphere of economic control contracted, the British made something of a come-back both in traditional areas of informal influence and in Canada, where incursions by US companies after 1914 had been particularly marked.

With the construction of imperial preference and a sterling bloc in the early 1930s, some respected commentators in Britain felt that a new era of financial dominance was in prospect.[54] Much of this was hubris, but it is undoubtedly true that, in the early 1930s, Britain was the only power that could fairly claim to have retained a truly global stature.[55] This lofty position continued to be identified with the possession of empire. The debates of the day were about how to prevent the 'have-not' nations, Germany, Italy and Japan, from assembling rival empires and how to stop colonial nationalists from dismantling it. The idea that the empire should be given up voluntarily was not a thought that made its way very far down the corridors of power. The empire was woven into the fabric of the great British institutions: the monarchy, the Church and Parliament.[56] It infused the notion of Britishness with content and meaning. The gentlemanly order soldiered on, despite the ravages of war.[57] No rival elite or alternative value system was able to mount a serious challenge to its dominance. On the contrary, threats of Bolshevism and fears of pan-Islamic subversion helped to promote a renewed defence of capitalism and empire. By this time, too, an awareness of empire had also penetrated far down the social order: reminders of its significance, in advertising, cinema, literature, and official propaganda were everywhere at hand.

It is now evident that much of the substance, apparatus and ideology of empire survived World War I. The gentlemanly elite remained in command; imperial attitudes marched on; colonial policies remained set on winning the battle of the civilising mission. The British version of liberal government joined to a liberal empire had staying power. Critics abounded from the 1890s and the demands of war displaced liberalism between 1914 and 1919. Nevertheless, the model was not superseded until 1940. Even so, advocates of the interventionist state that replaced it felt confident that they now had the tools needed to improve the empire and give it a new lease of life.[58] With globalisation stalled in the 1930s, Britain adopted imperial preference and constructed a sterling bloc. However, these measures did not signify merely a retreat into empire. Rather, policy-makers aimed to take advantage of the adverse effects of the depression on rival powers to confirm Britain's status as the only truly global power. Some respected commentators even felt that a new era of British financial dominance was in prospect, though much of the sentiment was aspirational hubris.

Post-colonial globalisation

The fall of the Western empires after World War II marked the end of the phase of globalisation spearheaded by imperial expansion. During that phase, the Western empires had promoted what is termed here 'modern globalisation', which fortified the nation state at home, transferred its institutions and values abroad and created an international economy based on the export of manufactured goods from metropolitan centres in exchange for raw materials from the periphery.[59] The weakening of this relationship from the 1950s opened the way to decolonisation and to a new phase, post-colonial globalisation, which accelerated as colonial rule receded and is today the dominant influence on global relations.[60]

The rapid raise of the United States to global dominance after 1940 meant that Britain was the first of the allies to be occupied by part of its former empire. The preliminary invasion by friendly GIs was followed by a flotilla of other imports after the war. Spam, bakelite and beguiling Hollywood fantasies about the American way of life captured the demoralised consumers of post-war Britain. It was at this time, too, that Britain's reduced circumstances curtailed her continuing ambitions on the world stage: the United States, not Britain, dropped the first atomic bomb. Even so, British governments turned the early stages of the Cold War to national purpose by persuading the United States, despite its historic opposition to colonialism, to co-operate in the resumption of the imperial mission as a way of strengthening the Free World against Soviet communism. Britain mounted a 'second colonial occupation' after 1945, not only to assuage colonial nationalists and to improve the prospects of the West in the Cold War, but also to prevent the 'mother country' from falling under the informal influence of its former colony.[61] Simultaneously, the British made good use of the Sterling Area and the protected empire in the 1940s and 1950s as a means of escaping American economic control.

Post-colonial globalisation greatly extended trade in manufactures among the advanced industrial economies, principally in Europe, the United States, Japan and, recently, the rapidly developing giant: China. Simultaneously, it reduced the need among the former imperial powers for primary exports from what used to be called the Third World. The Third World itself has become diversified. Apart from a small number of oil-rich countries, others, principally in Asia, have become both producers and substantial exporters of manufactured goods and have developed major financial centres of their own, notably in Singapore, Hong Kong and Shanghai. While some of the new manufactures represent outsourcing from Western centres, especially the United States, the Western powers themselves have become reliant on inflows of overseas capital, particularly from China. The complex economic ties that integrate the world in the twenty-first century are managed by large corporate entities, which are no longer exclusively Western in origin or location.

These developments not only reoriented world commerce and finance but also realigned established political ties. Territorial empires fitted a phase of world development that required the integration of modernising states and economies in the West with old and new societies in other parts of the globe. Ex-colonial states have adopted Western ideas of the nation state, but the robust survival of indigenous institutions and values in non-settler parts of the world has ensured that imported political models have been adapted to fit local circumstances.[62] Moreover, the post-colonial era is characterised by supra-national political relationships that have modified the sovereignty of all nation states, except the very largest. New regional associations have largely replaced long-standing centre-periphery relations. Britain, belatedly leading from the rear, joined the European Community in 1973; a clutch of mainly ex-colonial countries came together in 1967 to form the Association of South East Asian Nations (ASEAN), which extended free trade agreements with 10 other countries (including Australia, New Zealand, China and India) in 2009.[63] In a striking reversal of roles, Australia has become a major supplier of mineral products to China, which is now its principal foreign trade partner; Britain is currently 7th on the list.[64]

Major changes in the structure of international trade and Britain's inability to satisfy either the demand for capital and markets or the defence needs of the old dominions of Canada, Australia, New Zealand and South Africa were fundamental in provoking the last, and least studied, phase of decolonisation within the empire.[65] Although the white dominions had long achieved internal self-government, beginning with the Canadian colonies in the late 1840s, it is also the case that they remained dependent on Britain in significant ways until the 1970s. Before then, colonial nationalism in the settler empire was consistent with what was known as 'race patriotism', which maintained loyalty to the imperial cause. The desire to uphold the British connection was apparent after World War II, when strenuous efforts were made to boost emigration from the mother country. Although Afrikaners did not feel the same loyalty to Britain, South Africa remained in the Commonwealth until 1961, even at the cost of ignoring apartheid, principally because it was viewed in London as a valuable ally in the Cold War. In the end, South Africa followed the route taken by the other dominions, which started on the road to effective independence in the 1970s by removing the colour bar. South Africa reached the same point in 1994.

Economic and political relations with Asia and Africa were complemented by what amounted to an ideological revolution: the global diffusion of concepts of civil and human rights. Western empires rested on a form of moral hegemony derived from assumptions of racial supremacy. Quasi-scientific doctrines of white superiority, enhanced in Britain and the United States by infusions of Anglo-Saxon, Protestant values, provided the justification for colonial rule from its inception until after World War II. Enlightenment thinkers formulated contrary ideas that advocated universal principles, which found public expression through the French Revolution and the popular movement in Britain against the slave trade.[66] However, it was not until the creation of the United Nations in 1945 that ideas of human rights were agreed by a global organisation and specified in ways that could be actionable. Exactly how important these measures were in the decolonisation process and precisely when their influence was felt are matters of debate.[67] For present purposes, it is sufficient to note that principles of racial equality took hold in the 1950s, when they were endorsed by the Bandung Conference of non-aligned states in 1955 and adopted selectively by nationalist leaders as part of the anti-colonial struggle. In the course of the 1960s, defenders of colonial rule and racial discrimination lost the moral high ground. Their arguments about freedom and progress were turned against them; the classical formulations of John Stuart Mill and Benjamin Constant became allies in the cause of independence.

The world-wide scope of these changes suggests that the process of decolonisation ought to be placed in a correspondingly spacious setting. The current literature, however, continues to travel within established boundaries. Studies of decolonisation focus on the end of the formal empires in Asia and Africa; standard approaches to international relations after World War II concentrate on the Cold War, which is conceived as an epic contest, conducted at the highest levels, between two opposed political systems.[68] Decolonisation makes an appearance, but is fitted into the story at points where it is considered to be relevant. There is an alternative case for reversing the order and inserting the Cold War into decolonisation, which in turn needs to be placed in the even wider context of the global transformation of power, interests and values in the post-war era outlined here.[69] Future studies of decolonisation will almost certainly need to include a discussion not only of the 'old dominions', but also of the United States, which grappled in the 1950s and 1960s with the demise of its insular empire and with the militant claims of African-American citizens seeking freedom from internal colonialism.

The decolonisation of the British Empire, when it came, owed a good deal to the changing strategy of the United States, as well as to nationalist pressures. As the United States began to intervene in imperial affairs in the interest of the Cold War, the empire became part of a joint Anglo-American global venture.[70] By the close of the 1950s, however, the United States itself was being pushed unwillingly in new directions by anti-colonial forces it could not control. Domestic developments played an important part in changing minds. Unlike the other Western imperial powers at this time, the United States had to deal with the challenge of internal decolonisation arising from its own policy of apartheid.[71] The civil rights movement gathered momentum in the 1950s and achieved a series of victories in the 1960s that are still being worked out today. Strategists in Washington then concluded that upholding both European empires abroad and segregation at home was not the best way of winning the hearts and minds of subject peoples. It was these hard-headed calculations that allowed the banner of freedom to be unfurled and added to the pressures on Britain to withdraw from formal colonial rule.

Given the historical span of our book, it is worth noting here that decolonisation after 1945 was by no means the first instance of the process, even if it has a claim to being the most dramatic. The first decolonisation created the United States in 1783. The concession of representative government to white settled colonies from the 1840s onwards then set in train a process that liberal statesmen like Gladstone knew would end in complete separation, even though, as we have noted, the final outcome did not occur until the 1960s and 1970s. The third phase of decolonisation occurred in the 1940s when modern India and Pakistan emerged. At that time, the decolonisation of the African empire seemed far off; but within a decade the fourth phase was under way and the formal empire disappeared.

Post-colonial Britain and the future of gentlemanly capitalism

Today, memories of empire, as well as the empire itself, have receded. It is nearly 70 years – more than two generations – since India gained independence; Hong Kong reverted to China in 1997; only a handful of scattered outposts now remain.[72] Yet, the influence of the empire lives on, even though the present generation of Britons may have only an indistinct awareness of the ways in which its legacy continues to shape the world around them. Historians, however, have begun to identify the role of imperial connections in helping to mould British society, attitudes, and policies and the concept of Britain itself in the twentieth century.[73] The availability of new work on these subjects allows the present contribution to focus on illustrations that are closely related to the interpretation advanced in *British Imperialism*.

British overseas trade continues to bear the imprint of the imperial history that did so much to shape it over several centuries. Manufacturing is now of much less important to national income than it was historically; but it still provides the largest share of British exports and half of those exports go to countries outside Europe even though the empire has disintegrated. Also, as a percentage of GDP, the current balance of trade, deficit is no greater than it was in the days of empire. Services are 'invisible' trade which is centred on the activities of the City and continue to produce a healthy surplus, as they have done for nearly 300 years. Today, the big difference, which began to emerge in the 1920s, is that invisible earnings are no longer large enough to produce the impressive surpluses on the balance of payments current account that were such a notable feature of the British economy before 1914. Those surpluses gave Britain the means of becoming the world's greatest foreign investor; they were crucial to the maintenance of its global trading supremacy, to empire development, and to sterling's position as the key currency of the time. By contrast, service income is now usually insufficient to prevent a current account deficit.[74]

The role of the City and its composition have changed greatly since decolonisation. The Sterling Area foundered at the close of the 1960s; official support for qualified investments in the empire ceased; former colonial states no longer hold all their reserves in London; Commonwealth tariff preferences have been removed. The City has maintained its prominence by redeploying its expertise and by extending its global connections to become fully cosmopolitan in its outlook and dealings, as its role in developing the Eurobond market in the 1960s bears witness. Major structural change occurred in 1986, when deregulation reduced barriers within the City and drew in large foreign financial institutions. 'Big Bang', as it was known, succeeded in its main purpose, which was to maintain the City's competitiveness in a world that had waved farewell to the empire and to sterling as a major global currency. London is still the world's main centre for international financial transactions, though New York and Hong Kong are close behind: nearly 40 per cent of global currency exchanges take place in the City.

The explosive institutional changes caused by Big Bang unseated the historic merchant banks, most of which have now been swallowed by large, well-funded corporate invaders. The list of famous names that have been taken over during the last 20 years includes Kleinwort (1786), Schroder (1818), Cazenove (1823) and Hambro (1839). The most spectacular fall, given their importance in these pages, was that of Baring Brothers (1762), which collapsed in a financial scandal in 1995 and was bought for a nominal sum by the Dutch corporation, ING. At that point, Peter Baring the chairman of Barings and last family member of the board, resigned and retired to his Wiltshire estate. Of the merchants banks that were critical to Britain's success in the days of empire, only the Rothschild Group (1798), which is still run by members of the family, remains, albeit greatly changed, to represent the substance and not merely the name-plates of once eminent houses. A few of the private banks, which were such a feature of the City during the hey-day of empire, also survived. They include the oldest, C. Hoare & Co., which carries on the traditional business of serving the rich in a conservative manner. The capital resources of these private banks are, however, a mere drop in the corporate ocean that is the modern City

After Big Bang, the British gentlemanly elite ceased to dominate the City.[75] Long-standing personal relationships, cemented by a common education, shared social relations and inter-marriage, no longer tie the City elite together. The 'gentleman's agreements' that formed the ethical basis upon which City activities were based before Big Bang have vanished along with British control of its main institutions. The in-group characteristics of the old City generated an effective form of self-regulation, though at the cost of restraining competition and perpetuating a leisurely, 'clubbable' style of business. The new captains of the City have introduced American efficiencies: greater competitiveness, increased professional training, a bonus culture and a sense of corporate 'mission' based on the principle that 'the winner takes all'. These corporate giants owe their loyalty to international shareholders and have no wider affiliation to Britain and its institutions or any commitment to the future of the society that surrounds them.[76] Moreover, the City's regime of 'light' regulation offers plentiful opportunities for rigging markets and deceiving competitors and the public. Once deregulation lowered restraints on action, the reputation of the financial world soon followed. Nemesis lay in wait until 2008, when it made a dramatic appearance in the global financial crisis and has continued to erupt in scandals over the bonuses paid to bankers and the cynical way the advocates of competitive private enterprise have combined to fix foreign exchange markets.[77]

Nonetheless, the City itself emerged almost unscathed from the financial crisis. Its vision of global financial leadership remains undimmed, as its efforts to persuade the Chinese authorities to use London as the European centre for managing their emerging world currency, the renminbi, illustrate.[78] The neo-liberal ideology that validated the changes introduced by Big Bang was endorsed by New Labour governments and survived intact under the coalition government formed in 2010, as the commitment to privatising public assets and the relaxed attitude to foreign takeovers of public utilities demonstrate.[79] World conditions took the blame for the debacle; public attention was diverted from the hubris that lay behind it; the culprits were deemed 'too big to fail' – or to jail. The Bank of England's programme of quantitative easing greatly helped the major City institutions, as did the temporary nationalisation of some of the worst affected banks. State support for private institutions was deeply ironic, given official hostility to government intervention in economic affairs, but it underlined the long standing priority attached to City interests. These measures helped to spur a rapid recovery in London and the south-east, even as the government's austerity programme, devised to reduce the huge budget deficit incurred as a result of the recession, bore down on Britain's old industrial regions.

Although gentlemanly capitalists have been displaced, a gentlemanly elite still occupies positions of power in Britain.[80] Senior members of the coalition government that held office between 2010 and 2015 continued to be drawn from the enduring group that stands at the centre of the present book, even though the public school component of the House of Commons has shrunk. Members of the current elite not only benefit from a privileged education but also derive their wealth from traditional sources, especially financial services. They are no longer gentlemanly capitalists themselves but lineal descendants who function at one remove from the City while still carrying forward inherited values and attitudes. Aside from the priority accorded to City interests, these values are most obviously apparent in foreign affairs. Britain's long-running aversion to commitments in Europe stems partly from the vague but pervasive feeling that the nation's appropriate role is global and not merely continental. The loss of empire signalled neither disengagement from distant parts of the world nor the end of attempts to exercise influence overseas.[81] The 'special relationship' with the United States lives on, at least in the minds of policy-makers, despite its blatantly unequal and increasingly deferential character, and helps to validate Britain's continuing efforts to implement the 'civilising mission' abroad, especially in Africa and Asia. Despite their differences on domestic issues, policy-makers in the major parties are united by the desire to appear on the world stage as major actors, even though their actions are significantly under-resourced. Once in office, doves are tempted to become hawks, as the five wars Tony Blair authorised in six years demonstrate.[82] In matters of foreign policy, Britain has yet to adjust to the realities of the post-imperial world and shows little inclination to make the attempt.[83]

The benefits that accrued to the south-east before the banking crisis and as a result of remedial measures introduced by the coalition government did not travel very far north of London. The long-standing North–South divide, which might now be described more accurately as the division between London and its south-eastern hinterland and the rest of the country, has deepened, as have the social inequalities that are partly correlated with it.[84] The trend is now so marked that it has prompted the reflection that the industrial revolution and the provincial power it generated has had only a temporary effect in attracting 'the British compass from the magnetic south, where money and power have always accumulated'.[85] Outside London and the south-east, investment remains low. The financial crisis, and the Coalition's remedies for it, delivered the most prolonged fall in real wages since the 1970s. The influx of immigrants, especially from Europe, increased competition for unskilled and semi-skilled labour and helped to keep wages down. Britain's stagnant productivity underlay the decline in earnings. When productivity began to rise significantly in the 1980s, it was led not by manufacturing or financial services but by distribution and business services. The improvement continued under the governments of Blair and Brown, but the recession, and the Coalition's response to it, brought progress to a halt.[86]

By 2015, public unease at these developments had joined widespread resentment of the main political parties, which were tainted by the recession and its attendant deprivations, and criticised for elitist detachment from the everyday world of the man and woman in the street. The result has been a populist reaction that found expression in support for the United Kingdom Independence Party (UKIP). The party was formed in 1993 as a voice for Eurosceptic opinion but subsequently broadened its platform to encompass (among other issues) concerns over immigration.[87] UKIP's anti-immigrant stance, like its disillusion with existing political parties, has counterparts in the rise of right-wing movements elsewhere in Europe. Like those parties, too, UKIP is fundamentally a reaction to the changes wrought by globalisation. Membership of the European Union has diminished national sovereignty; the influx of immigrants with varied and often very different cultures and languages challenges the core values of the host society. As successive governments have wavered between policies of what, in the days of empire, were referred to as 'assimilation' and 'association', they have created a political gap that UKIP aims to fill by appealing to 'traditional' British values. UKIP undoubtedly provides an outlet for deep-seated uncertainties about Britain's identity in the post-imperial world. Yet, it is not easy to see how the idea of Britain, which was bound up with the creation of the empire, can be reconstituted in a post-colonial era. Moreover, in practice UKIP is an English rather than a British party, and this makes the task harder because the concept of 'Englishness', having been largely subsumed in the notion of a British Empire in the past, has now become an imprecise residual that contrasts with the more robust and vibrant sense of identity exhibited by Scots and Irish.

It is at this point that the very idea of a United Kingdom meets its greatest challenge. UKIP's struggle to resurrect national unity on the basis of a predominantly English resistance to foreign intrusions on sovereignty now confronts a seemingly insurmountable obstacle in the shape of devolution, which has been carried to its furthest extent, so far, in Scotland. The Scottish case is both distinctive and illustrative of trends found elsewhere in the United Kingdom and in parts of continental Europe.[88] Francis Hutcheson and his star pupils, Adam Smith and David Hume, were the first to set out the arguments that formed the basis of the debate over Scottish independence in 2014.[89] They regarded the Union as a progressive development, but one that required the central government to consult what Hutcheson called in 1745 the 'real felicity' of the people.[90] The prospects for advancement brought by scale, and through scale, empire had to be set against the general welfare of the *demos*, a new principle that anticipated the ideological basis of anti-colonial movements in the nineteenth and twentieth centuries.

In general terms, Scots gained enough from the opportunities presented by the Union and empire to offset losses experienced through the social upheaval caused by the Highland clearances and later by industry and urbanisation. Disaffection was readily found but less readily mobilised, and it never dislodged the political alliance of Anglo-Scottish landowners that held the Union together. In the nineteenth century, moreover, the Union government encouraged Scots to resurrect and invent traditions that both reinforced and created a sense of Scottish identity with the aim of averting the development of political claims of a more radical nature. The 'tartan army' was a real army before it became a set of football supporters. Service in the military joined expressions of local culture, made manifest to the world in displays of bagpipes and kilts, with loyalty to the Union. Scotland, the Punjab of the north, was unwavering in its support of crown and country.

Exactly when these conditions changed is a matter of debate, though the most recent account argues that Scotland was still heavily invested in the empire in the years immediately after World War II.[91] Scots began to lose interest in the empire when everyone else did: by the early 1960s, rapid decolonisation closed many opportunities; defence cuts sliced into long-established opportunities in the military. By 2006, the historic infantry regiments had been disbanded and the residues merged into a single Royal Regiment of Scotland. Meanwhile, Scotland's old, heavy industries continued a decline that had begun during the world depression in the

1930s. Margaret Thatcher's 'shock therapy' in the 1980s prompted Scots to demand greater control over domestic policy as a means of safeguarding welfare provision.[92] Paradoxically, the attempts made by successive Conservative governments to 'roll back the frontiers of the state' led to greater official supervision of public spending. By the close of the twentieth century, Scots felt that the distant South was treating them less like a co-existing nation and more like a dependent region.

These circumstances opened the way for a sense of Scottish identity to be transmuted into a demand for Scottish independence. The principal agent of the process, the Scottish National Party (SNP), made its mark on national politics in the general election of 1966, and in 1974 won 30 per cent of the Scots vote and sent 11 members of parliament to Westminster. The Labour government under Tony Blair reacted to this development in 1997 by offering a greater degree of devolution in the hope of diluting nationalist claims – a technique applied by the Viceroys of India in the decades before independence. Blair was right in thinking that the strategy was 'a dangerous game': the new powers increased the scope and visibility of the SNP.[93] The great financial crisis of 2008 and the austerity measures it entailed heightened nationalist feelings and swelled support for the SNP to the point where 45 per cent of the Scottish electorate voted for independence in the referendum held in 2014. The defeat of the SNP came with a substantial consolation prize: the promise of even more devolution. The independence movement wanted self-government and fiscal autonomy, but would have kept the monarchy and sterling and continued to rely on Westminster in matters of defence and foreign policy. This was the position enjoyed by Australia and New Zealand from the mid-nineteenth century to the 1930s. If the status still existed, it could be said that, in 2014, Scotland was in sight of becoming a dominion within the Commonwealth.

Political parties and commentators are agreed that developments in Scotland have implications for the rest of the United Kingdom and that further decentralisation of government is likely to occur. Beyond this broad indication of the direction of policy, however, lie clouds of uncertainty about the degree of devolution and the appropriateness of the units selected to be the recipients of new powers. Although such questions are not for discussion in this study, they nevertheless point to elements of distinctiveness about the Scottish case that suggest that outcomes might be different elsewhere.

It required force to ensure that Northern Ireland was not torn from the United Kingdom. The province may gain greater powers as a result of the Scottish vote, but the presence of the Republic of Ireland is a huge complicating factor that would restrain any move towards independence in the unlikely event that it ever materialised, unless voting habits in the North underwent an unforeseen and dramatic change. Wales, like Scotland, has not had to endure martial law. Like Scotland, too, Wales revived and invented local traditions in the nineteenth century. However, a sense of Welsh identity has not reached the point where it turns nationalist sentiment into a substantial independence movement.[94] This is partly because Wales has long been more closely integrated with England through flows of people across long, proximate, and accessible borders. It is also because Wales, like Northern

Ireland, lacks the viability the SNP claims Scotland possesses through North Sea oil.[95] Dependence on a large annual subvention from the UK Treasury is an irreducible fact that makes Wales as dependent on London as Puerto Rico is on Washington.

A sense that political leaders have failed to defend the integrity of the culture that nurtured them has added weight to efforts made by regions within the United Kingdom to reclaim political authority. The onrush of the global, far from simply spreading homogeneity, has had the effect of revaluing the local.[96] The reassertion of provincial aspirations has few parallels since the eighteenth century, when the Jacobites attempted to strike back on behalf of the Stuart cause and important counties, such as Yorkshire and Lancashire, raised the banner of reform. The central government dealt with these demands by defeating the Jacobites in 1745, suppressing radical movements in the 1780s, and appealing successfully for national unity in the face of the long wars with France that followed.[97] Circumstances are different today. The referendum on Scottish independence, conducted according to democratic principles, has ignited smouldering resentments south of the border. The government has responded by offering concessions.[98] The key question is how extensive these will need to be to satisfy English provincial aspirations. If the outcome produces a substantial degree of devolution, and Britain becomes a federal or quasi-federal state, the power of London will be significantly reduced. There is both symmetry and irony in the prospect that the process of internal colonisation that began the unification of the kingdom might itself end by unravelling Britain.

Britain, once the progenitor of change throughout the world, has herself been deeply affected by influences from post-colonial globalisation that lie beyond her control. The long process of ethogenesis that welded society into a degree of unity that capped diversity has been slowed and may now be reversing. Uncertainties about national identity have gathered strength since the empire was taken apart. Secularism has undermined the once unifying idea of a Protestant country and empire; even Jersey has an independence movement.[99] The monarchy has gained in standing as other props of empire and social order have been removed, but its status is now provisional rather than unquestioned. Besides having to negotiate a route between the pomp of tradition and the popularity of the common touch, it now faces the formidable task of winning the allegiance of a new generation of multi-ethnic citizens. There is now considerable public debate, and a good deal of anxiety, about what it means to be British – or English. The negotiations that produced the new national curriculum, which came into force in 2014, encapsulated the dilemma that Britain now faces. On one side stood those who aimed to base the history syllabus on a restored sense of national identity; on the other, those who wished to educate a 'generation of cosmopolitans'.[100] At present, the insular viewpoint holds sway, even though it is as difficult in a post-colonial age to 'glory in the name of Briton', as it is to speak with the poets, from Shakespeare to Eliot, of the qualities of the English.[101] Uncertainty as to whether to make one last lunge for assimilation or to make a virtue of pluralism is set to continue well into the twenty-first century.

In the longest perspective, the divisions arising from post-colonial globalisation are products of a slow-moving but encompassing historical dialectic, whereby the empire first helped to create a sense of British identity and then played a major part in dissolving it. Colonial subjects first struck back through decolonisation and then came back through immigration and other informal influences that diluted the sense of national unity the empire had once supported. If the final stage in the decline of empires comes when the outer provinces take over the centre, no more telling illustration of the process can be found than in the transformation of Britain since decolonisation.

Although a gentlemanly elite is still in contention for power in Britain, its future is not a promising one. Under attack from Thatcher's time onwards, gentlemen have become much more detached from the financial capitalism that gave them so much strength as the City worked out its own post-imperial salvation. To survive, they have been forced to adopt the neo-liberal economic agenda initiated by Thatcher, which held sway even under Labour governments, and whose outcomes are now threatening not only the unity of Britain but are also further undermining the prestige of the traditionally privileged. At first sight, too, gentlemanly leadership and a multi-ethnic society do not appear to be natural partners. To the extent that the current political elite fits the description of gentlemen, it is no longer one that elicits deference, but instead often serves to identify prominent members of society who are remote, unloved and living in the past while living off the present.

The power of position, the dynastic dynamic and a proven capacity to absorb newcomers may carry the gentlemanly elite forward in the twenty-first century. However, it is noticeable that, amidst the search for new British identities, the concept of character, which was so important in moulding gentlemanly imperial elites, is now being redefined in a manner hostile to the latter's pretensions. It is still the case in the public schools that 'building up the character of students is considered to be as important as the academic results', and a public school education is often justified on the grounds that it helps to form character, while state schools do not. The significance of the current debate is that it signals a novel departure: the progressive privatisation of the concept of character. The new definition emphasises such qualities as 'ambition, self-confidence and bloody-mindedness'. It omits the notions of duty, self-sacrifice and public service that were taught to English gentlemen in the days of imperial glory. The new elite is being shaped by a much more individualistic creed than were its forebears because it is being prepared for entry into an increasingly cosmopolitan, supra-national world, where traditional gentlemanly values are no longer central. Some continuities remain in the means of shaping character, as can be seen in the emphasis on sport. The fact that the ends have changed, however, suggests that a radical transformation is taking place. As the public schools become increasingly dependent on overseas students from wealthy families, the changing discourse on character may indicate that the concept of the gentleman is disappearing, leaving only capitalism behind.[102]

At this point, to quote Donald Rumsfeld, we are dealing with 'known unknowns' beyond which lie 'unknown unknowns'. [103] Secretaries of Defence have an obligation to act; historians have an obligation to be circumspect. What can be said about the 'known knowns' supplied by the recent historical record, is that gentlemanly capitalism experienced a profound transformation in the late twentieth century and that its heirs will need to overcome a set of formidable challenges if they are to survive as an elite that continues to thrive on its connections to the past.

Notes

1 Thorstein Veblen, *The Place of Science in Modern Civilization* (New York, 1919; 2007), p. 33. Veblen's remark (which is often rendered inaccurately) was made in the context of his criticism of marginal utility and, more generally, of the idea of finality in studies that claimed scientific status.

2 Dean G. Acheson (1893–1977); Secretary of State, 1949–1953. See Douglas Brinkley, 'Dean Acheson and the "Special Relationship": The West Point Speech of December 1962', *Historical Journal*, 33 (1990).

3 For an introduction to the issues see A.G. Hopkins,'The History of Globalization – and the Globalization of History?' in A.G. Hopkins, ed. *Globalization in World History* (2001).

4 Kevin H. O'Rourke and Jeffrey G. Williamson,'When did Globalisation Begin?' *European Review of Economic History*, 6 (2002); Harold James, *The End of Globalization: Lessons from the Great Depression* (Cambridge, Mass., 2002).

5 This question is now the subject of interesting debate. For a cautionary view see P. J. Marshall,'Imperial Britain', *Journal of Imperial and Commonwealth History*, 23 (1995), and for a reaffirmation of the alternative position, A.G. Hopkins,'Back to the Future: From National History to Imperial History', *Past & Present*, 164 (1999), which is complemented by John M. MacKenzie,'Empire and National Identities: The Case of Scotland', *Transactions of the Royal Historical Society*, 6th series, 8 (1998).

6 A more extended discussion of these categories can be found in Hopkins, *Globalization in World History*.

7 David Armitage, 'Making the Empire British: Scotland in the Atlantic World, 1542–1707', *Past & Present*, 155 (1997); T.M. Devine, *Scotland's Empire, 1600–1815* (London, 2003); John M. MacKenzie,'Irish, Scottish, Welsh and English Worlds? A Four-Nation Approach to the History of the British Empire', *History Compass*, 6 (2008); John M. MacKenzie and T.M. Devine, eds. *Scotland and the British Empire* (Oxford, 2011); Christopher A. Whatley with Derek J. Patrick, *The Scots and the Union* (Edinburgh, 2006); Bob Harris,'The Anglo-Scottish Treaty of Union, 1707–2007: Defending the Revolution, Defeating the Jacobites', *Journal of British Studies*, 49 (2010).

8 Recent work on the military-fiscal state in Europe has tended to confirm the lead taken by Britain: Richard Bonney, ed. *Economic Systems and State Finance* (Oxford, 1999); idem, Richard Bonney, ed. *The Rise of the Fiscal State in Europe, c.1200–1815* (Oxford, 1999); Mark Ormrod, Margaret Bonney and the Richard Bonney, eds. *Crises, Revolutions and Self-Sustained Growth: Essays in European Fiscal History, 1130–1830* (Donington, Lincs., 2000); Christopher Storrs, ed. *The Fiscal-Military State in Eighteenth-Century Europe: Essays in Honour of P.G.M. Dickson* (Farnham, Surrey, 2008).

9 Paul W. Schroeder, *The Transformation of European Politics, 1763–1848* (Oxford, 1994), p. vii, suggests that there were more deaths on European battlefields in the eighteenth century than in the nineteenth century.

10 P. Harling, *The Waning of 'Old Corruption': the Politics of Economical Reform in Britain, 1779–1846* (Oxford, 1996).

11 Nicholas Rogers, *Whigs and Cities: Popular Politics in the Age of Walpole and Pitt* (Oxford, 1989); Bob Harris, *Politics and the Nation: Britain in the Mid-Eighteenth Century* (Oxford, 2002).

12 Patrick Karl O'Brien,'The Triumph and Denouement of the British Fiscal State: Taxation for the Wars Against Revolutionary and Napoleonic France, 1793–1815', in Storrs, *The Fiscal-Military State*, pp. 162–200.

13 Javier Cuenca-Estaban, 'India's Contribution to the British Balance of Payments, 1757–1812', *Explorations in Economic History*, 44 (2007).
14 Recent surveys of an immense literature include Gwenda Morgan, *The Debate on the American Revolution* (Manchester, 2007); Trevor Burnard, 'Empire Matters? The Historiography of Imperialism in Early America, 1492–1830', *History of European Ideas*, 33 (2007). See also C. A. Bayly, 'The First Age of Global Imperialism, c. 1760–1830', in Peter Burroughs and A. J. Stockwell, eds. *Managing the Business of Empire: Essays in Honour of David Fieldhouse* (1998).
15 Leandro Prados de la Escosura, ed. *Exceptionalism and Industrialisation: Britain and Its European Rivals, 1688–1815* (Cambridge, 2004). P. K. O'Brien, 'Inseparable Connections: Trade, Economy, Fiscal State and the Expansion of Empire, 1688–1815', in Marshall, *Oxford History*, Vol. 2 (Oxford, 1998), Ch. 3; N. A. M. Rodger, 'War as an Economic Activity in the "Long" Eighteenth Century', *International Journal of Maritime History*, 22 (2010). See also, H. V. Bowen, *War and British Society, 1688–1815* (1998).
16 J. Ward, 'The Industrial Revolution and British Imperialism, 1750–1850', *Econ. Hist. Rev.*, 2nd ser. XLVII (1994).
17 James W. Frey, 'The Indian Saltpetre Trade, the Military Revolution, and the Rise of Britain as a Global Superpower', *Historian*, 71 (2009).
18 Bayly, 'The First Age of Global Imperialism', p. 43. The phrase echoes Lenin's description of World War I.
19 H. V. Bowen, 'British Conceptions of Global Empire', *Jour Imp. and Comm. Hist.*, 26 (1998). This is not to deny the importance of antecedents that have been skilfully traced by David A. Armitage, 'Making the Empire British: Scotland in the Atlantic World, 1542–1717', *Past and Present*, 155 (1997).
20 For indigenous sources see Colin Kidd, *British Identities Before Nationalism* (1998); and for the ambiguous results Katrina Navickas, *Loyalism and Radicalism in Lancashire 1798–1915* (Oxford, 2009). For the role of foreigners and war see L. Colley, *Britons: Forging the Nation, 1707–1837* (1992). Also Kathleen Wilson, *The Sense of the People: Politics, Culture and Imperialism in England, 1715–1785* (Cambridge, 1995); Bob Harris, '"American Idols": Empire, War and the Middling Classes in Mid-Eighteenth-Century Britain', *Past & Present*, 150 (1996); P. J. Marshall and Glyndwr Williams, *The Great Map of Mankind: British Perceptions of the World in the Age of Enlightenment* (1982).
21 David Marquand, *The New Reckoning: Capitalism, States, and Citizens* (Oxford, 1997), pp. 186–203.
22 David Cannadine, *Aspects of Aristocracy* (1994), Ch. 1.
23 Current scholarship is inclined to give more weight to the 'Great' Reform Act than has been the case for some time. See Bruce Morrison, 'Channelling the Restless Spirit of Innovation: Elite Concessions and Institutional Change in the British Reform Act of 1832', *World Politics*, 63 (2011), pp. 678–710; Phillips and Wetherell, 'The Great Reform Act'.
24 Boyd Hilton, *The Age of Atonement: The Influence of Evangelicals on Social and Economic Thought, 1785–1865* (Oxford, 1986); and more generally, idem, *A Mad, Bad, and Dangerous People? England, 1783–1846* (Oxford, 2006).
25 Herbert Schlossberg, *The Silent Revolution and the Making of Victorian England* (Columbus, OH, 2000). British and American evangelicals remained in close touch. See Frank Thistlethwaite, *The Anglo-American Connection in the Early Nineteenth Century* (Philadelphia, 1959), Ch. 3.
26 Harling, *The Waning of Old Corruption*, esp. pp. 255–66; P. Harling and P. Mandler, 'From "Fiscal-Military" State to Laissez-Faire State, 1760–1850', *Jour. Brit. Stud.*, 32 (1993). See also the brilliant summation of Gladstone's fiscal thinking in H. G. C. Matthew, *Gladstone, 1809–1898* (Oxford, 1996), pp. 103–48. Miles Taylor has recently shown how important the management of the empire was to the stability of the state during Europe's year of revolutions: 'The 1848 Revolutions and the British Empire', *Past and Present*, 166 (2000).
27 Peter J. Cain, 'Character, "Ordered Liberty" and the Mission to Civilize: British Moral Justification of Empire, 1870–1914', *Journal of Imperial and Commonwealth History*, 40 (2012).

28 O'Rourke and Williamson, 'When did Globalization Begin?', pp. 24–7; also Philip Epstein, Peter Howlett and Max-Stephen Schulze, 'Distribution Dynamics: Stratification, Polarization and Convergence Among OECD Economies, 1870–1992', *Working Papers in Economic History*, No. 58/00 (London School of Economics, 2000).
29 J. M. Price, 'The Imperial Economy, 1700–1776', in Marshall, *Oxford History*, Vol. 2.
30 Quoted in Peter J. Cain, 'Bentham and the Development of the British Critique of Colonialism', *Utilitas*, 23 (2011), p. 8.
31 P. J. Cain, 'Economics and Empire: The Metropolitan Experience, 1790–1914', in A. Porter, ed. *The Oxford History of the British Empire,* Vol. 3 (Oxford, 1999).
32 As work on the wider British world has made clear. See for example James Belich, *Replenishing the Earth: The Settler Revolution and the Rise of the Anglo-World, 1783–1939* (Oxford, 2009); Gary Magee and Andrew Thompson, *Empire and Globalisation: Networks on People, Goods and Capital in the British World, 1850–1914* (Cambridge, 2010).
33 John Eddy and Deryck Schreuder, eds. *The Rise of Colonial Nationalism: Australia, New Zealand, Canada, and South Africa First Assert Their Nationalities* (Sydney, 1988).
34 On the early nineteenth century see Douglas M. Peers, *Between Mars and Mammon: Colonial Armies and the Garrison State in India, 1819–1835* (1996).
35 For recent accounts of British government in India see David A. Washbrook, 'India, 1818–1860: The Two Faces of Colonialism', in Porter, *Oxford History of the British Empire*; and Robin J. Moore, 'Imperial India, 1858–1914', ibid.
36 For the flavour of this in the 1870s see P. J. Cain, ed. *Empire and Imperialism: the Debate of the 1870s* (1999), pp. 1–19.
37 S. Collini, *Public Moralists: Political Thought and Intellectual Life in Britain, 1850–1930* (Oxford, 1991), esp. Ch. 3; John H. Field, *Towards a Programme of Imperial Life: The British Empire at the Turn of the Century* (Oxford, 1982); Kathryn Tidrick, *Empire and the English Character* (1990).
38 Lord Curzon of Kedleston, 'The True Imperialism', *Nineteenth Century and After*, LXIII (1908).
39 Miles Taylor, 'John Bull and the Iconography of Public Opinion in England, c.1712–1929', *Past & Present*, 134 (1992).
40 Ibid. pp. 98, 109.
41 J. A. Hobson, *Imperialism: A Study* (1902; 1988 ed.), p. 10.
42 It is worth noting that, in an extension of the nineteenth century debate, there is no consensus among present-day economic historians as to whether or not the benefits of retaining and expanding the formal empire after 1850 exceeded the costs. See P. J. Cain, 'Was it Worth Having? The British Empire, 1850–1950', *Revista de Historia Economica*, XVI (1998).
43 Some commentators saw imperialism as a stage on the way to a truly global society. At one point in his career Hobson adopted this perspective. See his *Economic Interpretation of Investment* (1911). This view was also central to the Leninist theory of imperialism and informed much academic work on the subject in the early twentieth century. See A. Viallete, *Economic Imperialism and International Relations During the Last Fifty Years* (New York, 1923).
44 W. E. Gladstone, 'England's Mission' (1878), reprinted in Cain, *Empire and Imperialism*, p. 253.
45 S. Collini, D. Winch and J. Burrows, *That Noble Science of Politics: A Study in Nineteenth Century Intellectual History* (Cambridge, 1983), p. 158.
46 See here Geoffrey Jones, *Merchants to Multinationals: British Trading Companies in the Nineteenth and Twentieth Centuries* (Oxford, 2000), p. 351. Frank H. H. King, *The History of the Hongkong and Shanghai Bank,* (Cambridge, 1987), Vol. I, Ch. 15, Vol. II Ch. 3; Roberta A. Dayer, *Finance and Empire: Sir Charles Addis, 1861–1945* (1989).
47 For the importance of free trade see A. C. Howe, *Free Trade and Liberal England, 1846–1946* (1998). The tenacious grip of the ideal of the minimalist state on the working class is dealt with by Ross McKibbin, *Ideologies of Class* (Oxford, 1990), Ch. 1.
48 We disagree here with Lance Davis, 'The Late Nineteenth-Century British Imperialist: Specification, Quantification and Controlled Conjectures', in Dumett, *Gentlemanly Capitalism*.

49 It is not assumed here that the Froude-Seeley idea of equalling the United States was possible: the geography of the white Dominions prevented the growth of a population on the scale of the Great Republic. Nonetheless, if Britain had maintained imperial preferences and actively encouraged capital and labour to migrate to British territory throughout the nineteenth century, 'Greater Britain' might have been considerably more populous and wealthy in 1914 than it actually was and the growth of the United States might have been correspondingly slower.

50 P. K. O'Brien, 'The Security of the Realm and the Growth of the Economy', in Peter Clarke and Clive Treblicock, eds. *Understanding Decline: Perceptions and Realities of British Economic Performance* (Cambridge, 1997).

51 Whatever the verdict on the arguments in Niall Ferguson, ed. *Virtual History* (1999), it is worth noting here how prominently the USA features in them.

52 For a summary of our views see P. J. Cain, 'British Economic Imperialism. 1919–39: Towards a New Interpretation', *Bulletin of Japanese Studies*, IV (1994). A different overview of the relationship between the United States and Britain is given by A. Orde, *The Eclipse of Great Britain: the United States and British Imperial Decline* (1996).

53 On Britain's position in the 1920s see J. R. Ferris, '"The Greatest Power on Earth": Great Britain in the 1920s', *International History Review*, 13 (1991).

54 P. J. Cain, 'Gentlemanly Imperialists at Work: The Bank of England, Canada and the Sterling Area, 1932–1936', *Economic History Review*, XLIX (1996), p. 338.

55 See B.J.C. McKercher, '"Our Most Dangerous Enemy": Britain Pre-eminent in the 1930s', *Int. Hist. Rev.* 13 (1991).

56 Richard Williams, *The Contentious Crown: Public Discussion of the British Monarchy during the Reign of Queen Victoria* (Aldershot, 1997), Ch. 7; Gerald Studdert-Kennedy, *Providence and the Raj: Imperial Mission and Missionary Imperialism* (1998) underlines the continuing importance of the Christian ethic in Indian government.

57 W. D. Rubinstein, 'Britain's Elites in the Inter-War Period, 1918–39', *Contemporary British History*, 12 (1998).

58 As argued by B. J. C. McKercher: *Transitions of Power: Britain's Loss of Global Pre-eminence to the United States, 1930–1945* (Cambridge, 1999). This theme has been explored by M. J. Daunton, 'Payment and Participation: Welfare and State Formation in Britain, 1900–1951', *Past and Present*, 150 (1996).

59 A. G. Hopkins, 'Back to the Future: From National History to Imperial History', *Past & Present*, 164 (1999).

60 The most authoritative account of British decolonisation after 1945 is provided by John Darwin, *The Empire Project: the Rise and Fall of the British World System* (Cambridge, 2009), Chs. 13 and 14.

61 John Kent, *British Imperial Strategy and the Onset of the Cold War, 1944–49* (Leicester, 1993).

62 Some of the heterogeneous consequences of globalisation are examined in A. G. Hopkins, ed. *Global History: Interactions Between the Universal and the Local* (Houndmills, Hants, 2006).

63 The United States formed the North American Free Trade Association (NAFTA) with Canada and Mexico in 1994.

64 China alone now takes 27 per cent of Australia's exports, which consist mainly of iron ore, coal, petroleum and gold.

65 A. G. Hopkins, 'Rethinking Decolonisation', *Past & Present*, 200 (2008), and the relevant chapters in Phillip Buckner, ed. *Canada and the British Empire* (Oxford, 2008); and Deryck Schreuder and Stuart Ward, eds. *Australia's Empire* (Oxford, 2008).

66 Sankar Murthu, *Enlightenment Against Empire* (Princeton, 2003); J. R. Oldfield, *Popular Politics and British Anti-Slavery: The Mobilisation of Public Opinion against the Slave Trade, 1787–1807* (1998); Clare Midgley, *Women Against Slavery: The British Campaigns, 1780–1870* (London, 1992); Seymour Drescher, *Abolition: A History of Slavery and Anti-Slavery* (Cambridge, 2009); Simon Morgan, 'The Anti-Corn Law League and British Anti-Slavery in Trans-Atlantic Perspective, 1838–1846', *Historical Journal*, 52 (2009).

67 See particularly, A. W. B. Simpson, *Human Rights and the End of Empire: Britan and the Genesis of the European Convention* (Oxford, 2001); Mark Mazower, *No Enchanted Palace: The End of Empire and the Ideological Origins of the United Nations* (Princeton, 2009); Samuel Moyne, *The Last Utopia: Human Rights in History* (Cambridge, Mass., 2010); Roland Burke, *Decolonisation and the Evolution of International Human Rights* (Philadelphia, 2010); Rosemary Foot, 'The Cold War and Human Rights', in Melvyn Leffler and Odd Arne Westad, eds. *Cambridge History of the Cold War*, I (Cambridge, 2010), Ch. 21; Barbara Keys and Roland Burke, 'Human Rights', in Richard Immerman and Petra Goedde, eds. *The Oxford Handbook of the Cold War* (Oxford, 2013), Ch. 28.

68 This is the case even with such authoritative studies as John Lewis Gaddis, *The Cold War: A New History* (New York, 2005), Ch. 4; and Melvyn P. Leffler, *For the Soul of Mankind: The United States, the Soviet Union, and the Cold War* (New York, 2007).

69 Odd Arne Westad, *The Global Cold War: Third World Interventions and the Making of our Times* (Cambridge, 2006); idem, 'The Cold War and International History in the Twentieth Century', in Melvyn Leffler and Odd Arne Westad, eds. *Cambridge History of the Cold War*, I (2010), pp. 1–19, appeals for a global approach, which appears in Cary Fraser, 'Decolonization and the Cold War', in Immerman and Goedde, *The Oxford Handbook of the Cold War*, Ch. 27. Among many case studies, see Mark Atwood Lawrence, 'Universal Claims, Local Uses: Reconceptualizing the Vietnam Conflict, 1945–60', in A. G. Hopkins, ed. *Global History: Interactions Between the Universal and the Local* (Basingstoke, Hants, 2006), Ch. 8.

70 Wm. Roger Louis and Ronald Robinson, 'The Imperialism of Decolonization', *Jour. Imp. and Comm. Hist.*, 22 (1994).

71 Thomas Borstelmann, *The Cold War and the Color Line: American Race Relations in the Global Arena* (Cambridge, Mass., 2003).

72 Robert Aldrich and John Connell, *The Last Colonies* (Cambridge, 1998) is the most recent survey. Simon Winchester's informative and evocative *Outposts* (1985) also draws attention to the shabby treatment handed out to some of the smallest and least visible of the remaining dependencies.

73 See for example: Stuart Ward, ed. British Culture and the End of Empire (Manchester, 2001); Andrew Thompson, *The Empire Strikes Back? The Impact of Imperialism on Britain in the Mid-Nineteenth Century* (2005); idem, ed. *Britain's Experience of Empire in the Twentieth* Century (Oxford, 2012); Wendy Webster, *Englishness and Empire, 1939–1965* (Oxford, 2005).

74 *Economic Outlook*, April 2014, pp. 60–61.

75 Philip Auger, *The Death of Gentlemanly Capitalism: The Rise and Fall of London's Investment Banks* (2000). Auger was in a unique position to analyse these developments. He worked in the City for 20 years, helped to negotiate the sale of Schroders to Citygroup, and holds a Ph.D. in history. His subsequent books trace the consequences: *The Greed Merchants: How the Investment Banks Played the Free Market Game* (2005); *Chasing Alpha: How Reckless Growth and Unchecked Ambition Ruined the City's Golden Decade* (2009).

76 'Foreign ownership of offices in the City (the largest office cluster in Europe) rose rapidly after Big Bang. In the 1980s, the owners were almost entirely British; by 1911 foreign owners held just over half of all office space'. Colin Lizieri, Andrew Baum and Jan Reinert, 'Who Owns the City?' (Dept. of Land Economy Report, Cambridge, 2011).

77 Philip Auger, 'Questions for Capitalism on Big Bang's Birthday', *Financial Times*, 25 October, 2011.

78 'Osborne Sees Red', 12 January 2012 at www.hsbcnet.co/gmb/global-insights/week-in-china/2012/. The writer compares this move with the City's success in attracting the Eurodollar market in the 1950s, citing *British Imperialism*. By 2014, the City was handling two-thirds of renminbi payments outside China and Hong Kong, but also faced considerable competition from Frankfurt. See Mark Boleat, 'City Matters: How London is Leading the Way as a European Centre for Renminbi Trade', *CityAM*, 2 June 2014 at www.cityam.com; Delphine Straus, 'Financial Centres Vie for Slice of Renminbi's Growing Offshore Business', *Financial Times*, 30 September 2014.

79 James Meek, *Private Island: Why Britain Now Belongs to Someone Else* (2014); and the commentary by John Gray, 'Who Owns Britain?' *The Guardian*, 5 September 2014.

80 Simon Head, 'Children of the Sun: David Cameron, Nick Clegg sand the Conservative Party Elite', *The Guardian*, 2 October, 2010. Head refers to Cameron and Clegg as 'scions of the gentrified City bourgeoisie'.

81 Ashley Jackson, 'Empire and Beyond: The Pursuit of Overseas National Interest in the Late Twentieth Century', *English Historical Review*, 122 (2007), p. 1361.

82 John Kampfner, *Blair's Wars* (2003), traces Britain's involvement in Iraq, Kosovo, Sierra Leone, Afghanistan and Iraq (again). The 'Blair Doctrine', which provided the basis for most of these interventions, was set out in a speech delivered in Chicago on 22 April 1999: www/pbs.org/newshour/bb/international/jan-june00/blairdoctrine4–23.html.

83 Stephen Howe, 'When (if Ever) did Empire End? "Internal Decolonisation" in British Culture since the 1950s', in Martin Lynn, ed. *The British Empire in the 1950s: Retreat or Revival?* (2006), Ch. 10.

84 Danny Dorling, *Inequality and the1%* (2014). For a wider statement of the same trend see Thomas Pikerty, *Capital in the Twenty-First Century* (Cambridge, Mass., 2014), and the commentary by Paul Krugman, 'Why We're in the New Gilded Age', *New York Review of Books*, 8 May 2014.

85 Ian Jack, 'A Country of Cold Beef and Ginger Beer', *Guardian*, 10 October 2009.

86 D. Corry, A. Valero and J. Van Reenan, *UK Economic Performance since 1997: Growth, Productivity and Jobs* (LSE, Centre for Economic Performance, 2011).

87 At the outset, UKIP drew support disproportionately from older, white voters; it is now more representative of the (white) population as a whole. See Peter Kellner, 'How UKIP's Support Has Grown – and Changed', *YouGov*, 17 November 2014.

88 John M. Mackenzie, 'Empire and National Identities: The Case of Scotland', *Transactions of the Royal Historical Society*, 8 (1998); idem, 'Irish, Scottish, Welsh and English Worlds? A Four-Nation Approach to the History of the British Empire', *History Compass*, 6 (2008); idem and T. M. Devine, eds. *Scotland and the British Empire* (Oxford, 2011); Christopher A. Whatley with Derek J. Patrick, *The Scots and the Union* (Edinburgh, 2006); Bob Harris, 'The Anglo-Scottish Treaty of Union, 1707–2007: Defending the Revolution, Defeating the Jacobites', *Journal of British Studies*, 49 (2010); Alvin Jackson, *The Two Unions: Ireland, Scotland, and the Survival of the United Kingdom, 1707–2007* (Oxford, 2011).

89 For an academic perspective on the debate see the contrasting positions of Niall Ferguson and Tom Devine, as reported by John McDermott, 'Long History of Nationalism Marches Towards Uncertainty', *Financial Times*, 13/14 September 2014. For Ferguson, the idea of independence was 'profoundly unScottish'; for Devine, the United Kingdom was 'no longer fit for purpose'.

90 Francis Hutcheson, *System of Moral Philosophy* (1755), II, book 3. Quoted in Caroline Robbins, '"When it is that Colonies may Turn Independent': An Analysis of the Environment and Politics of Francis Hutcheson (1694–1746)', in idem, *Absolute Liberty* (Hamden, Conn., 1982), pp. 133–67.

91 Bryan Glass, *The Scottish Nation at Empire's End* (2014); for a different view, see T. M. Devine, 'The Break-Up of Britain? Scotland and the End of Empire', *Transactions of the Royal Historical Society*, 16 (2006).

92 The phrase is Tom Devine's, cited in *Financial Times*, 13/14 September, 2014.

93 Quoted in Simon Johnson, 'Tony Blair Brands Scottish Devolution a "Dangerous Game"', *Daily Telegraph*, 1 October 2014.

94 See the characteristically insightful essay by Simon Jenkins, 'A Chance for Wales: Can the Slumbering Dragon Awake?' *Guardian*, 30 September 2014.

95 Depending on how long it lasts, the collapse of world petroleum prices shortly after the referendum may alter calculations of Scotland's viability.

96 Hopkins, ed. *Global History: Interactions Between the Universal and the Local,* explores the theme, though not the particular case.

97 Navickas, *Loyalism and Radicalism*, shows, nevertheless, that local patriotism and suspicion of London remained vibrant forces throughout the war years.

98 Hence the current government's offer of funds to encourage new railway links between northern English cities that, it is claimed, could help create a 'Northern powerhouse' in the region. On the limitations of this move see Simon Jenkins, 'Northern Cities need more than "Powerhouse" Rhetoric', *Guardian*, 1 July 2014. On the wider issues involved in debates about regional autonomy see Jeffrey Henderson and Suet Ying Ho, 'The Upas Tree: the Overdevelopment of London and the Under-development of Britain', *Renewal: a Journal of Social Democracy* 22(3/4) (2014).

99 Sam Lister, 'Call for Jersey's Independence', *The Independent*, 27 June 2012.

100 See, for example, Jackie Eales, 'The History Association's Response to the Draft National Curriculum', 24 May 2013, at www.consider-ed.org.uk. The quotation is from Nicholas Tate, Chief Advisor on the National Curriculum, *Sunday Times*, 27 August 2000, when a very similar debate took place.

101 George III on his accession in 1760.

102 On character and modern public schools, see 'Eton to give state schools advice on building character', *The Telegraph*, 6 January 2013; and Antony Selden, 'Toby Young has a point', *Guardian* 3 September 2011.

103 Donald Rumsfeld, Department of Defense News Briefing, 12 February 2002, at www.defense.gov/transcripts/transcript.aspx?transcriptid=2636.

INDEX

Note: Most references are to *Britain* and *Empire*, unless otherwise indicated. Footnote references (designated by *n*) have largely been omitted from the index, except where there is considerable extra matter.

PPs 40-41 On aristocracy bourgeoisie and capitalism.

P50 - On the evolution of the gentlemanly order. The origin and implementation of the motive force behind the British class system. And, be it noted, it was actually more English than British.

P59: On the essence of 'imperialism': it involves an incursion, or an attempted incursion, into the sovereignty of another state'. In short, the form imperialism takes may vary (eg military, economic or political*) but the intent - i.e. deliberate incursion/penetration of another sovereign state does not.

* and cultural.

'The relations established by imperialism are therefore based upon inequality and not upon mutual compromises of the kind which characterise states of interdependence.'

PPS 201/216: C. J. Bartlett, [Chris. Bartlett?] ed Britain Pre-eminent: Studies in British World Influence in the Nineteenth Century (1969)

P303: On a very appropriate synopsis of the 18th C English state, its funding and purpose.

P329: ® note on the Genesis of White Colonies.

Note: For the elite who have always run this country, they consider it to belong to them by birthright. As for the rest, they are merely there/here to be ruled and, of course, support their lifestyle. A reading of Burke's "Reflections on the Revolution in France...," especially his remarks on the common people, more than supports this view.

P512 → On "The coming of the Pax Americana" - gives a succinct list of Britain's ills in the 1930's. Primarily structurally economic due to the war, depression and the overall collapse of the old economic order (pre-1913) in addition to rising rivals (U.S.) The country needed time to restore the economic order which it had dominated (it was not to get that time) in order to restore its pre-1931 position* with this as its

Ref appeasement

main forces it had to play for time with regard to the rising dictatorships and America's refusal to step in and assist. So appeasement was not fundamentally a crisis of confidence or moral weakness, but an attempt to delay war, which would have been a disaster to Britain's immediate economic plans, while allocating what limited resources it could (eg planes, armaments, etc.) to preparing for a war which, given the other bellicose strategies (eg Germany and Italy) and the US indifference must have seemed to be near inevitable.* Further, this policy had to be carried out in the midst of a global economic depression; the odds of success were slight.

P523 On appeasement – check out source indicated (P.M. Kennedy)

Final note: Britain has been called 'the banker of the world'. But in a global economy so severely disrupted by a world war and then a global depression it was always going to be particularly strained to return to pre 1913 conditions, and its response to authoritarianism in Europe, although one of many unedifying spectacles of its history, with appeasement to play for time to repair its and the world's economy seemed both sensible and pragmatic, given its problems, the indifference of others (U.S. and Russia) and the sheer scale of the problem.

* 'The British Empire on which the sun never sets, because Britain can't be trusted in the dark.' Ashley Jackson in "The British Empire".

PPs 653/654: On an interesting comment on the interplay and reliance of the political / financial sectors and the self-serving nexus they can create. It is an analysis which can usefully be used to explain other symbiotic relationship such as politics and other political, social and economic pairings

P682: See note 6: on the opinion "that the top brass of the Square Mile 'are not so much members of the Establishment because they have succeeded in the city; they have succeeded in the

City because they are members of the Establishment".
Victor Sandelson: "The Confidence Trick", in Thomas, "The Establishment", p 139.

Note: By the use of military force, diplomatic effort, intrial liberal loans (to rearm or support internal infrastructural projects, resuscitate and or assist an ailing national economy, the British govt aimed to create a burden of debt with what are now known as Third World economies/countries. The aim was to loan increasing amounts of finance until the country in question was forced to follow the wishes of the British Govt. The aim was more than hegemony, traditionally framed in terms whereby the national govt. was usually allowed a free hand in its own internal affairs, while the hegemon (i.e. the senior in the partnership) determined the countries international foreign relations. But in the new form practised by Britain, initially, then by France and America among other advanced western economies, a deeper, more pervasive form of hegemony was employed, in large part because the internal and external work of any govt of any country in the world are not properly separable and in practise mutually effecting. Consequently this was recognised by its practitioners who attempted through the medium of debt to effectively control both the internal and external actions and economies of the govt in question. Because of the continual and escalating loans by the British Govt. over time it effectively turned the debtor govt. into a client state to Britain. In short, a steady stream of revenue accrued to the latter, and its national bankers who facilitated and managed the financial aspects of the operation, but more importantly it allowed the British Govt. to effectively control fully, or influence less fully its clients around the developing world and its emerging, but still.

fragile emerging economies. It was a major national programme on the part of the British state. It involved its top ruling politicians (of whatever party was then in power; its diplomats and foreign service; its intelligence and military agencies; its major national international banking institutions and financial services; and it national education system, or at least those parts of it which were required to educate and train the elite pupils who staffed and maintained the above agencies.
Accordingly, the debt, loans, and the refinancing of the former were the means by which Britain exercised its power and influence throughout the world during the period under review (1688-2015) the period of British Imperialism. Note, this national practice did not end with the demise of Empire, it is still ongoing.

Kenneth Newton, P 686
(Newton & Porter) "Modernisation Frustrated"

P 58-59: On the essential nature of imperialism: it is fundamentally aggressive, not consensual by both parties.

[In fact, for a summary / precis of the book re-read the section entitled "The problem and the context: Pps 33-72.

P 122: The start of Britain's relative decline as a manufacturing nation (1870)?